# Approaching DEMOCRACY

EIGHTH EDITION

**Larry Berman**

*The Honors College, Georgia State University*
*Professor Emeritus, University of California, Davis*

**Bruce Allen Murphy**

*Lafayette College*

# Why Do You Need This New Edition?

If you're wondering why you need this new edition of *Approaching Democracy,* here are 5 good reasons!

1. This newest edition **includes coverage of the historic changes that have taken place across our political landscape** since the 2010 congressional elections, including the sharp turns in policy implementation by President Obama's administration and the shifting makeup and operations of the 112th Congress. Figures and tables reflect the **latest available data and surveys.**
2. **A new feature has been added to each chapter,** highlighting the main theme of the text. The **Approaching Contemporary Issues in Democracy** feature asks you to assess the effect of a particular event or action on American democracy.
3. **Four new features in the last edition** have been continued to help you focus your learning, assess your knowledge, and prepare for tests. An **Approaching Democracy Timeline** feature showcases the book's historical perspective by highlighting the evolution of American democracy. Guide your reading with new **Learning Objectives** at the beginning of each chapter. Apply your knowledge of the key chapter concepts as you read by answering the **Thinking Critically** questions. Assess your comprehension and prepare for exams or quizzes with the **Test Yourself** questions found at the end of each chapter.
4. Gain a global perspective and assess the differences between your government and those across the globe with **updated and newly designed Compared to What? boxed features** that provide a comparative perspective for you to see the difference between the various forms of governments in the world and how the American democracy relates to those countries.
5. **Critical and relevant current events and debates** are explored throughout the book, including the effect of the Great Recession on American democracy and government and new information on public attitudes toward health care, gay marriage, gun control, immigration reform, and much more.

**To**
**Nicole & Carol**
**And to the memory of Vaclav Havel, (1936–2011)**
**poet, playwright, politician, and champion of the approach to democracy**

Executive Editor: Reid Hester
Editorial Assistant: Emily Sauerhoff
Executive Marketing Manager: Wendy Gordon
Senior Digital Editor: Paul DeLuca
Supplements Editor: Beverly Fong
Production Manager: Savoula Amanatidis
Project Coordination, Text Design, and Electronic Page Makeup: Laserwords Private Ltd.
Cover Design Manager: Wendy Ann Fredericks
Cover Designer: Kay Petronio
Cover Photo: Copyright © istockphoto
Photo Research: PreMedia Global
Senior Manufacturing Buyer: Dennis J. Para
Printer and Binder: R. R. Donnelley and Sons Company–Jefferson City
Cover Printer: Lehigh-Phoenix Color Corporation–Hagerstown



**Library of Congress Cataloging-in-Publication Data**
Berman, Larry, 1951–
Approaching democracy/Larry Berman, Bruce Allen Murphy.—8th ed.
p. cm.
Includes bibliographical references and index.
ISBN-13: 978-0-205-25160-5
ISBN-10: 0-205-25160-9
1. United States—Politics and government. 2. Democracy—United States.
I. Murphy, Bruce Allen. II. Title.
JK276.B47 2012
320.473—dc22 2011052901



10 9 8 7 6 5 4 3 2 1—DOJ—15 14 13 12

PEARSON

www.pearsonhighered.com

ISBN-10: 0-205-25160-9
ISBN-13: 978-0-205-25160-5

# Brief Contents

# Detailed Contents

## 6 THE JUDICIARY 183



## 7 THE BUREAUCRACY 216



# PART III Processes of American Democracy

## 8 PUBLIC OPINION 240

# Preface

The following are new to the eighth edition of *Approaching Democracy:*

- **Approaching Contemporary Issues in Democracy** features apply the theme of the book to current problems and debates within American society. Students are presented with a series of questions that lead them through multiple perspectives and facets of each issue.
- **Approaching Democracy Timelines** have been redesigned for greater impact and clarity. These timelines help students to analyze the development of our democracy over time.
- Each chapter has been updated to include coverage of the significant changes that have taken place across the political landscape since the seventh edition, including the changes in the administration of Barack Obama since the 2010 congressional elections; the sharp turns in policy implemented by his administration since that time; the changes in the makeup and operations of the 112th Congress; the effect of the Great Recession on American democracy and government; new information on public attitudes toward health care, gay marriage, gun control, and immigration reform; and much more.

The eighth edition of *Approaching Democracy* constitutes our continuing exploration of the American experiment in self-governing. It also illustrates the wonderful relevance that the theme has to so many different kinds of changes in American democracy. A great deal has happened in American politics since the first edition was published in 1996, when the world's attention was focused on the movement to democratic government by the newly freed eastern European governments. Two events stand out for their impact on our country as well in our revisions: September 11, 2001, the day of coordinated suicide attacks by al Qaeda on the United States and January 20, 2009, the day that Barack Hussein Obama was inaugurated as the 44th president of the United States. The events of 9/11 would first lead to Operation Enduring Freedom aimed at defeating international terrorism as well as its network of financial support; it would also produce the Patriot Act, increased surveillance powers by already secretive government intelligence agencies and a powerful new bureaucracy, the Department of Homeland Security. Very little in American politics, attitudes, and government would be the same after 9/11. In our revisions to this book since 9/11 we have grappled with framing the issue of fighting a war against terrorism while remaining true to the ideals of democracy—balancing security and liberty—as expressed by the Declaration of Independence, the Constitution, and the Bill of Rights.

January 20, 2009, had a similar impact; it was the day our country cast aside the last racial barrier in American politics. Following his election victory, Barack Obama said, "If there is anyone out there who still doubts that America is a place where all things are possible, who still wonders if the dream of our founders is alive in our time, who still questions the power of our democracy, tonight is your answer." In this first revision of *Approaching Democracy* since the election of the country's first African American president, we have struggled with how to frame the significance of this historic election with the political and social reality that race still plays a powerful role in our daily lives.

Since the publication of the seventh edition, the rise of the Tea Party in American politics, the gridlock in Congress as a result of the 2010 elections and the Republican takeover of the House, the effects of the Great Recession, the Arab Spring, the debates over financing the government and balancing the budget that have repeatedly led to the near shutdown of the government, and, most recently, the appearance of the Occupy Wall Street movement, have shown how this book's theme of approaching democracy can be used to explain new events.

American democracy remains very much a work in progress. Our title and theme come from Vaclav Havel, a former dissident Czechoslovakian playwright once imprisoned by his country's communist government and later elected its president. Havel passed away just as the eighth edition went to press. We are very pleased to honor him on the dedication page of this new edition. Addressing a joint session of the U.S. Congress on February 21, 1990, Havel noted that with the collapse of the Soviet Union, millions of people from eastern Europe were involved in a historically irreversible process, beginning their quest for freedom and democracy. And it was the United States of America that provided the model, the roadmap to democracy and independence, for these newly freed peoples. But Havel put his own spin on the notion of American democracy: "As long as people are people, democracy, in the full sense of the word, will always be no more than an ideal. . . . In this sense, you, too, are merely *approaching democracy*. But you have one great advantage: You have been *approaching democracy* uninterruptedly for more than two hundred years, and your journey toward the horizon has never been disrupted by a totalitarian system" (emphasis added).

Indeed, the United States has spent over two centuries moving toward, and sometimes away from, the democratic ideal. The process of approaching democracy is a continual one, and the debate about how to achieve our democratic aspirations drives red and blue, black and white politics throughout 50 states and the District of Columbia—as evidenced by the Tea Party and Occupy Wall Street movements. The chapters in this textbook sort out the ideals; study the institutions, processes, and policies; and analyze the challenges and paradoxes of our system. Our goal is not to end discussion on these topics; rather, we hope students will develop an interest in continuing the dialogue on America's approach to the democratic ideal. Our theme provides you with a conceptual lens for evaluating the performance of the American political system and for discussing whether this nation can remain a model for emulation. We think it will, but we also believe that the subject needs continuous dialogue, as illustrated by the divisive debates over health care, state political redistricting, and state anti-immigration reform.

Although an introductory course in American government is not solely a course on current events, students are always interested in what is going on around them. Throughout the text, we use examples that are at the forefront of the news so that students have background information to draw from in framing their own approach to democracy. Hopefully, some of you will be empowered to become more engaged in political discussion and civic life. You will also find a consistent comparative or internationalization component in our textbook. This is because the United States serves as a model, or laboratory, for those people who have broken from their totalitarian past and for those who dream of doing so. Look no further than the Iraqi and Afghani citizens who, under threat of having their rights removed by militants, now wonder what will happen to their rights as the American military is removed from their country. The aspirations of democracy remain a universal goal and the United States provides yardsticks and clues for constructing a stable civil society with a constitution that preserves liberty and provides legitimacy for both majority rule and the rights of a minority. This is the theme of our textbook, *Approaching Democracy,* and we are sticking with it because we believe in it. We hope that you do, too!

## ORGANIZATION

**PART I** presents the foundations of American government. Our theme is introduced in Chapter 1, in which we identify goals and elements useful in evaluating America's approach to democracy. We also introduce a few widely accepted "elements of democracy" that serve as markers to identify progress toward democratic ideals.

**PART II** explores the institutions of American democracy. It describes the various governmental arenas—the judiciary, Congress, executive branch, and bureaucracy—where the struggle over democratic ideals plays out.

**PART III** focuses on the processes of American government and democracy. Through the avenues of public opinion, political parties, elections, interest groups, and the media, citizens can reach and direct their government to achieve their desired goals.

**PART IV** provides a detailed analysis of various issues of civil rights and liberties. They include the most fundamental rights of Americans, such as freedom of speech and religion, and are considered by many to be the foundation of our democracy.

**PART V** addresses the policy-making process and its consequences. How well national policy makers respond to the challenges of policy making and how democratic the policies are remain crucial questions as American government continues the process of approaching democracy.

# CHANGES IN THE EIGHTH EDITION

The eighth edition contains so much new material. Most notably, each chapter assesses new changes from the early Obama administration to the operations of the government after the 2010 congressional elections, and asks whether America is approaching or receding from democracy. The success of our completely revamped pedagogical program has led us to continue to organize each chapter with new **Learning Objectives** that are posed as questions at the beginning of each chapter. Our new **Thinking Critically** questions lead students to analyze and synthesize materials beyond the formal text. We hope you share our enthusiasm for a new special feature, **Approaching Democracy Timeline,** that analyzes the evolution of democracy over time. At the end of each chapter you will find new **Chapter Summaries** that answer the **Learning Objectives** questions and a new **Test Yourself** multiple-choice review written by the authors. In addition, we have continued to present our **Compared to What?** feature, which offers an international dimension to our theme of approaching democracy.

You'll find another completely new feature called **Approaching Contemporary Issues in Democracy** in which important and often controversial issues in current events are evaluated for their "approach to democracy" using the evaluation scheme introduced in Chapter 1 and used throughout the book. This edition also contains a significant amount of new material.

## New and Updated Material

Chapter 1 introduces our theme of approaching democracy and discusses contemporary events such as the Arab Spring revolutions and Occupy Wall Street movements, the Republican takeover of Congress, new TSA security measures, and a discussion of the "birther" controversy. In this chapter we provide the tool kit for analyzing whether the American government's efforts have approached or receded from democracy.

Chapter 2 on the Founding and Constitution analyzes the similarities of the Bush and Obama administrations in their fight against terrorism, including a discussion of the Guantanamo Bay prison and the use of torture. This chapter examines current efforts to change the Constitution including the state-led "Repeal Amendment" movement and the new balanced budget amendment. This chapter both provides a framework for analyzing the strengths and weaknesses of the U.S. Constitution and encourages an understanding of the context in which the document was created. This allows students to better understand the current efforts in newly freed countries, like Egypt, to draft a new constitution.

Chapter 3 on Federalism looks at the changes in state law regarding gay marriage, including legalization in New York and the numerous gay rights cases that move through the federal courts. The legal challenges to the Obama health-care reform law illustrate the great challenges of a federal system of government and this chapter provides a discussion of the upcoming Supreme Court case, along with Justice Anthony Kennedy's voting dilemma, regarding the health-care law's legality. This chapter examines many recent tensions between the states and the federal government, including state-led efforts to curtail illegal immigration and congressional redistricting in Texas, as well as the federalism challenges posed by the withdrawal of American troops from Iraq in 2011.

Chapter 4 on Congress analyzes the changes in the makeup and operations of the 112th Congress, including the Republican takeover in the House; the nature of stalemated, partisan, congressional government; the effect of the Tea Party congressional membership on the diminution of the power of Republican Speaker John Boehner; the effects of the continuing debate over the Obama health-care reform; and the dysfunction of the filibuster-bound Senate and a discussion of whether the filibuster rule should be revised. With congressional approval ratings at an all-time low, the updates give students the tools to understand the reasons for the declining popularity of Congress.

Chapter 5 on the Presidency addresses the first term of the Obama presidency, from his inauguration to his campaign for reelection. We look at the president's use of signing statements and executive privilege, the 2011 debt-ceiling debate, the assassination of Osama bin Laden, the withdrawal of troops from Iraq, and U.S. involvement in Libya. This chapter features a new section on unofficial requirements for holding the office of president, such as race, gender, religion, and marital status. The discussion of the role of the first lady is also expanded to explore her role as a moral leader.

Chapter 6 on the Judiciary analyzes the nature of the newly conservative "Kennedy Court," and the quiet constitutional attacks on the Supreme Court such as whether justices have ethical responsibilities to disclose relationships to those who appear before the court, and perhaps recuse themselves from cases in which they have a previous, sometimes political, connection. We also provide a detailed discussion of the Elena Kagan nomination, confirmation, and appointment to the Supreme Court and the changes that are likely to result from her addition, as well as the nature of the new Supreme Court in Great Britain.

Chapter 7 on Bureaucracy covers the extensive new oversight functions of the federal government, especially in the financial area, Wall Street, and consumer financial protection. We study the Dodd-Frank Wall Street Reform and Consumer Protection Act and explore why Elizabeth Warren failed to receive the nomination to lead the agency she developed. This edition includes a discussion of the 2011 U.S. Postal Service budget problems and the role of whistleblowers. We offer an expanded discussion on the role government plays in the everyday lives of Americans as well as an exploration of the phenomenon of politicians running for office by criticizing government.

Chapter 8 on Public Opinion provides extensive new information on public attitudes from 2011 public opinion surveys. This chapter uses current data to explore the effect of question wording on poll results, the differences in public opinion across race, region, gender, and generation, as well as a timeline of opinion on gay marriage showing that 2011 marked the first time a majority of Americans believed gay marriage should be legalized. New to this edition is a discussion of public support for a free-market system both within the United States and across the globe.

Chapter 9 on Political Parties looks at changes in party membership and partisan self-identification since the pivotal 2008 and 2010 elections. The discussion on political parties includes an updated exploration of the 2012 Republican presidential primary, with an examination of the effect of a heavily frontloaded 2012 primary system, and the proposed changes in the state electoral college system. This edition also analyzes the impact of the *Citizens United* case, and various extra-partisan movements, like the Tea Party and Occupy Wall Street, on the two-party political system in the United States, the "radical right" and its effect in the Great Recession in Europe.

Chapter 10 on Participation, Voting, and Elections includes the new 2012 electoral college map, the results of the 2010 Midterm elections, and the protest movements in Wisconsin and Occupy Wall Street. This chapter offers new sections on the history and impact of presidential debates, the *Citizens United* decision, court challenges to the Voting Rights Act, and an exploration of the 160 ballot propositions across 37 states in the 2010 election.

Chapter 11 on Interest Groups now includes a detailed exploration of the effect of the *Citizens United* Supreme Court case and the growth of the new "Super-PAC" system on the 2012 elections, the impact of the Tea Party and Occupy Wall Street movements on the American political system, and the effects of Iran's cyber-revolution. Both the role of interest groups and the public's attitude toward them are changing and this chapter provides students with a framework for analyzing their importance to the political system.

Chapter 12 on the Media includes recent trends in consumption, the role of social networks such as Twitter, Facebook, and YouTube in the spread of information, the shutting down of the press in Arab countries facing revolution, the 2011 release of American hikers held in Iran, the current state of investigative reporting in the United States the removal of the Fairness Doctrine from the FCC rule book, and an updated discussion of the Equal Time Rule. This chapter also includes an analysis of press coverage of Obama's first term as president.

Chapter 13 on Civil Liberties contains new information on a number of significant Supreme Court cases impacting civil liberties. This chapter includes a detailed discussion of the *Citizens United* decision and its wide-ranging impact, the changes to the "right to die" issue in Montana, and the changes in "libel tourism" as a result of the "phone hacking" tabloid journalism in Great Britain. We also provide an exploration of current Roberts Court "good faith" doctrine cases that endanger the future of the Fourth Amendment search and seizure protections, the evolving effect of the Baby Boomer majority on the Court, and the effect of Anthony Kennedy as a swing justice, along with the recent case rulings that change First Amendment free speech rights.

Chapter 14 on Civil Rights includes entirely new sections on the legal evolution of gay rights and gay marriage in the United States, changes in the affirmative action programs and the challenge to them from the University of Texas, the Republican-led effort to limit voter accessibility, the equal protection issues raised by the state-led anti-immigration laws, the threats to the 1965 Voting Rights Act, and the new originalist argument in favor of women's rights.

Chapter 15 on Domestic and Economic Policy includes discussion of the Tobacco Control Act and the Dodd-Frank Reform Act, the 2012 budget proposal, the 2011 debt-ceiling debate, the recent expansion of poverty, the impact of the president's health-care reform law, and calls to reform the tax code. This edition also offers a new discussion on the role of government regulation to solve large-scale problems, Occupy Wall Street protestors as policy entrepreneurs, how food-safety regulations created one of the world's safest food supplies, and a comparison of the politics of climate change in the United States and abroad.

Chapter 16 on Foreign Policy includes new material on the Arab Spring and the difficulties faced by U.S. policy makers when a democratic revolution erupts against one of our allies, as occurred with Hosni Mubarak in Egypt. This chapter also provides new discussion on the withdrawal of troops from Iraq and the possible violation of the War Powers Act by President Obama's use of U.S. force in Libya. The 50th anniversary of the Peace Corps allowed for the inclusion of a more detailed discussion of the organization impact on foreign policy and the reputation of the United States.

## ACKNOWLEDGMENTS

We want to thank Executive Editor Reid Hester for his support on this eighth edition. We value his professionalism, collegiality, and keen understanding of our theme and we look forward to many future collaborations with Pearson. We would also like to thank Editorial Assistant Emily Sauerhoff for her assistance throughout this process. Our thanks also goes to the book's talented production team at Pearson and

Laserwords: Managing Editor Donna DeBenedictis, Production Manager Savoula Amanatidis, Senior Manufacturing Buyer Dennis Para, Permissions Specialist Liz Kincaid, and most especially Production Editor Rebecca Lazure. Our appreciation also goes to Photo Researcher Connie Gardner for helping us to visually tell the story of "approaching democracy." We are also very grateful to James Corey, who added the annotations to the Constitution. We would also like to thank Denise DeGarmo, Eric Click, and Steven Brown for their work on our book's supplements.

We also wish to thank the reviewers of the most recent edition of *Approaching Democracy* for their valuable suggestions.

Larry Berman would especially like to thank Ronni Abney for her extraordinary research and input into the eighth edition. Ronni started working with our book as a teaching assistant at Davis and uses *Approaching Democracy* when teaching students at Mercyhurst College. Aside from the two authors, I feel confident in saying that Ronni understands the theme and approach as well as anyone. Special thanks to former UCD undergraduate Tilak Koilvaram for his research during the summer on chapter revisions. He also thanks the students in his Political Science 5 class during spring quarter 2011 for their useful feedback, and GSU Honors College research assistant Shelby Lohr, who proofread the final chapters.

He is also most appreciative of his former graduate students who are teaching American Government using the book and always providing feedback. He especially is grateful to Professors Linda Valenty, Monte Freidig, Richard Randall, Rolfe Peterson, and Stephen Routh in this regard.

Bruce Allen Murphy wishes, as he has done in every edition, to thank the undergraduate students in his American Government 101 classes at Lafayette College for their valued suggestions for improving the textbook, and for challenging him to think of even better ways to teach this subject. He also thanks his colleagues in the Government and Law Department, most especially Ilan Peleg, for providing a listening ear as he has tested out his theories of American politics in front of them. Thanks also go to the wonderful research librarians in Kirby Library, such as Ana Ramirez Luhrs and Douglas Durrenberger, and Skillman Library, such as Kandyce Fisher and Bob Duncan, for providing countless answers to desperate and often late-night questions. A thousand thanks, too, to the late Fred Morgan Kirby and his family for their generous support of the chair that Bruce now holds. And thank you to his colleagues in the Government and Law Department at Lafayette College, especially the department head, Helena Silverstein, for continuing to make this work environment so pleasurable.

Because no two scholars can master all the fields in the political science discipline, both authors express gratitude to all their colleagues for the many academic contributions from which they drew during the writing of this book. The generations of students at the University of California and Lafayette College are gratefully appreciated for the continuing flow of unique questions and ideas that spurred the authors in the writing of this and other editions of the book. Also, the authors thank those colleagues in the discipline who have provided suggestions for improvement after teaching with the first seven editions, thus improving this new revision.

Finally, but most importantly, both authors would like to recognize their families. Bruce Allen Murphy thanks his wife, Carol Lynn Wright, and his children, Emily and Geoffrey, and his son-in-law, Adam Glickman, as well as the family's new pet dog, Mr. Darcy, for their never-ending love, support, and encouragement throughout this book's revision processes. Larry Berman joins Bruce Allen Murphy in the affections to family, adding only that Scott has helped his dad better understand the workings of government bureaucracy; that Lindsay, Juan, Isabel, and Ian are part of the theme "approaching democracy" and know better than anyone else that the struggle never ends. Nicole is living proof that life only gets better.

Larry Berman
Bruce Allen Murphy

## SUPPLEMENTS

The following supplements have been developed to accompany this text and facilitate its use in any class:

| Name of Supplement | Available in Print | Available Online | Instructor or Student Supplement | Description |
|---|---|---|---|---|
| Instructor's Manual (ISBN: 0205874908) | ✓ | ✓ | Instructor Supplement | Prepared by Steven P. Brown of Auburn University, this comprehensive Instructor's Manual is a chapter-by-chapter guide to the textbook and provides Learning Objectives, Chapter Outlines, Chapter Summaries, Suggested Lecture Topics, Lecture Outlines, Class Discussion/Essay Questions, and Key Terms. Available for download at www.pearsonhighered.com/irc (access code required). |
| Test Bank (ISBN: 0205874924) | ✓ | ✓ | Instructor Supplement | The Test Bank, prepared by Densie Degarmo of Southern Illinois University, contains numerous multiple-choice, true/false, and essay questions. The Test Bank provides questions that engage the entire cognitive domain, from the very basics of recall and comprehension to application, analysis, and evaluation. This variety allows each instructor to create exams of varying types and differing degrees of difficulty. Answers for each question are given along with the page number where they can be found within the book. |
| My Test (ISBN: 0205874886) | | ✓ | Instructor Supplement | This flexible, Web-based test generating software includes all questions found in the Test Bank and allows instructors to create their own personalized exams, edit the existing test questions, and even add new questions. Other special features of this program include random generation of test questions, creation of alternate versions of the same test, scrambling of question sequence, and test preview before printing. Available at www.pearsonmytest.com/irc (access code required). |
| PowerPoint™ Presentation Package (ISBN: 0205874878) | | ✓ | Instructor Supplement | This text-specific package, prepared by Andrew Teas of Houston Community College, provides a basis for your lecture with a collection of lecture outlines and graphic images keyed to every chapter in the book, as well as a Special Topic presentation for each chapter. Available for download at www.pearsonhighered.com (access code required). |
| American Government Study Site | | ✓ | Both | Online package of essay questions, Web links, and practice tests organized by the Table of Contents for *Approaching Democracy*. Visit www.pearsonamericangovernment.com. |
| Digital Transparency Masters (ISBN: 0205874894) | | ✓ | Instructor Supplement | These PDF slides contain all maps, figures, and tables contained in the text. Available for download at www.pearsonhighered.com/irc (access code required). |
| MySearchLab with Pearson eText (ISBN: 0205903827) | | ✓ | Student Supplement | Students who want to reinforce their learning may take advantage of MySearchLab with Pearson eText. This book-specific website features a full, interactive eText; complete overviews of the entire writing and research process; and chapter-specific content such as learning objectives, quizzes, media, and flashcards to enrich learning and help students succeed. |

# About the Authors

Photo by Karin Higgins

**LARRY BERMAN** is Professor Emeritus at the University of California, Davis, and currently Founding Dean of the Honors College at Georgia State University. His research and publications focus on the presidency, foreign policy, and Vietnam. He has written four books on the war in Vietnam, *Perfect Spy: The Incredible Double Life of Pham Xuan An, Time Magazine Reporter & Vietnamese Communist Agent* (2007), and *No Peace, No Honor: Nixon, Kissinger and Betrayal in Vietnam* (2001). In 2012, HarperCollins will publish his ZUMWALT*: The Life and Times of Admiral Elmo Russell "Bud" Zumwalt, Jr.* His work has been featured on C-Span's Book TV, the History Channel's *Secrets of War,* Bill Moyers's PBS series *The Public Mind*; David McCullough's American Experience series; and *Vietnam: A Television History*.

Berman has received fellowships from the Guggenheim Foundation, the American Council of Learned Societies, and the National Science Foundation, and research grants from several presidential libraries. He has received the Outstanding Mentor of Women in Political Science Award from the Women's Caucus for Political Science. He is also a co-recipient of the Richard E. Neustadt Award, given annually for the best book published during the year in the field of the American presidency. Berman received the Bernath Lecture Prize given annually by the Society for Historians of American Foreign Relations to a scholar whose work has most contributed to our understanding of foreign relations. He has been a Fellow at the Woodrow Wilson International Center for Scholars in Washington, DC, and scholar in residence at the Rockefeller Foundation's Center in Bellagio, Italy.

Berman's class on the American presidency is cited in Lisa Birnbach's *New and Improved College Guide* as one of the most recommended classes for undergraduates at the University of California, Davis. He is the 2010 recipient of the highest honor that the Davis Division of the Academic Senate accords its members: the Faculty Research Lecturer Award. In June 2010, Berman was also awarded the Chancellor's Award for Excellence in Mentoring Undergraduate Research. He has recently completed his second Department of State Strategic Speaker Program in Thailand, addressing "Democracy, Conflict Resolution and the Rule of Law." He received his B.A. magna cum laude from The American University in Washington, DC, and his Ph.D. from Princeton University in 1977.

In his spare time, Berman enjoys participating in Iron Chef competitions, fishing, camping, and attending baseball games in any city he visits.

Photo by Craig M. Lampa

**BRUCE ALLEN MURPHY** is the Fred Morgan Kirby Professor of Civil Rights in the Department of Government and Law at Lafayette College. He is a nationally recognized judicial biographer and scholar on the American Supreme Court, civil rights and liberties, judicial behavior, and judicial biography.

Murphy is the author of many publications, including his newest judicial biography, *Wild Bill: The Legend and Life of William O. Douglas, America's Most Controversial Supreme Court Justice,* which has been selected by the Book-of-the-Month and History book clubs. He also wrote *Fortas: The Rise and Ruin of a Supreme Court Justice,* which was nominated for both the Pulitzer Prize and the National Book Award. His bestselling *The Brandeis-Frankfurter Connection: The Secret Political Activities of Two Supreme Court Justices,* which received the American Bar Association's Certificate of Merit, was listed among *The New York Times'* Best Books for 1983 and was serialized by *The Washington Post.* In addition, he edited *Portraits of American Politics: A Reader.*

Murphy has received numerous teaching awards for his courses in American politics, civil rights and liberties, and constitutional law. He has been a finalist in the Council for the Advancement and Support of Education's national Professor of the Year competition, and was cited as a Best Professor in Lisa Birnbach's *New and Improved College Guide.* He is listed in both *Who's Who in America* and *Who's Who in the World.*

# Approaching Democracy

# 1

## Chapter Outline

**Introduction:**
*Democracy as an Evolutionary Process*

- Forming a Picture of Democracy
- The Ideals of Democracy
- The Elements of Democracy

I AM A FREE SYRIAN
أنا سوري ابن الأحرار
لا ذليل ولا جبان
"I believe that unarmed truth and unconditional love will have the final word." ~Martin Luther King~

## Learning Objectives

1.1 How did Vaclav Havel characterize democracy?

1.2 How do direct and representative democracies differ, and which type of democracy did the framers believe was best for the new nation?

1.3 What basic democratic ideals characterize the American polity, and what trade-offs exist among these values?

1.4 What institutions are necessary to support and uphold democracy?

# INTRODUCTION

## DEMOCRACY AS AN EVOLUTIONARY PROCESS

1.1 *How did Vaclav Havel characterize democracy?*

One of the most eloquent statements on the evolutionary nature of American democracy was made by Vaclav Havel, a former dissident Czechoslovakian playwright once imprisoned by that country's Communist government and later, following the end of Communism there, elected Czechoslovakia's president. Addressing a joint session of the U.S. Congress on February 21, 1990, Havel noted that with the collapse of the Soviet Union, millions of people from eastern Europe were involved in a "historically irreversible process," beginning their quest for freedom and democracy. The United States of America represented the model, "the way to democracy and independence," for these newly freed peoples. But Havel put his own spin on the notion of American democracy as a model:

> *As long as people are people, democracy, in the full sense of the word, will always be no more than an ideal. In this sense, you too are merely approaching democracy. But you have one great advantage: you have been approaching democracy uninterruptedly for more than 200 years.*[1]

This image of an America "approaching democracy" inspired the theme for our textbook, and an excerpt of Havel's address is reprinted in Appendix 1. Like Havel, we believe that the United States continues to approach a democratic ideal while also serving as an ongoing experiment in republican self-government. Democracy in America has evolved over time—and continues to evolve. To illustrate, consider how many of your classmates have the power to vote and participate in politics. Virtually all of you do. How many of your classmates are free white males over the age of 21 who also own land? This small handful of people in your class would have been the only voters in the nation's earliest elections. In fact, as someone of mixed race heritage, even President Barack Obama would have been ineligible to participate in the political process of our fledgling democracy. When you realize the incredible openness of American politics today, you can appreciate the changes in American history and understand why Vaclav Havel identified the United States as the guide for understanding "the way to democracy and independence."

But democracy in America is still very much a work in progress, as demonstrated by the struggle of residents in the District of Columbia to secure full voting representation in Congress. The district's more than half a million residents pay full federal taxes, fight and die in wars, and serve on juries—yet they are denied voting representation in the House and the Senate.[2]

Most people associate democracy with expansion of the range of freedoms citizens enjoy. Although democracies do expand certain freedoms, they do not always successfully protect the core democratic values of

### THINKING CRITICALLY

Vaclav Havel believed that beginning on a path toward democracy is a "historically irreversible process." Do you agree with this claim? Do you think people, once given the experience of freedom and democracy, might ever choose to return to undemocratic rule?

A girl lights a candle in remembrance of Czech statesman Vaclav Havel at the St. Wenceslas in Prague, Czech Republic, Thursday, Dec. 22, 2011. Havel, the dissident playwright who wove theater into politics to peacefully bring down communism in Czechoslovakia and become a hero of the epic struggle that ended the Cold War, died Sunday, Dec. 18, 2011 in Prague. He was 75.

freedom and equality. People have sometimes been denied their rights to obtain an education, to choose where to live, or to decide which occupations to pursue simply because of their race, ethnicity, religion, gender, or sexual orientation. American democracy has been remarkably open, over the long run, to expanding rights and liberties for all its citizens—even if those rights and liberties have been achieved only with struggle, sacrifice, and occasional failure. This struggle is illustrated by the restriction on freedoms posed by counterterrorism measures since 2001. These include government attempts to extend executive authority without congressional and judicial review, mistreatment of those in U.S. custody, warrantless wiretaps, and invasive pat downs of airline passengers.[3] Throughout the chapters of our book, we return frequently to these themes as part of our experiment in self-government as well as our approach to democracy.

## FORMING A PICTURE OF DEMOCRACY

1.2 *How do direct and representative democracies differ, and which type of democracy did the framers believe was best for the new nation?*

One of the most astute observers of the American experiment in self-government was Alexis de Tocqueville. In 1835, Tocqueville published a book of observations, *Democracy in America,* based on his journey throughout this new nation. "In America I sought more than America," he wrote. "I sought there the image of democracy itself, with its inclinations, its character, its prejudice, its passions, in order to learn what we have to fear or to hope from its progress." This eminent French writer wanted to do more than describe one nation. "America was only the frame," Tocqueville later told the English philosopher John Stuart Mill. "My picture was Democracy."[4]

We wish to portray democracy as a system by showing how it works in the world's oldest democratic state. The United States has been moving toward democracy for more than 200 years. In spite of its astonishing diversity and the consequent potential for hostility and violence, the United States has approached closer to the democratic ideal than nearly any other country—certainly closer than any other country of comparable heterogeneity and size. But the process of approaching democracy is a continual one. Indeed, even models of democracy

## Compared to WHAT?

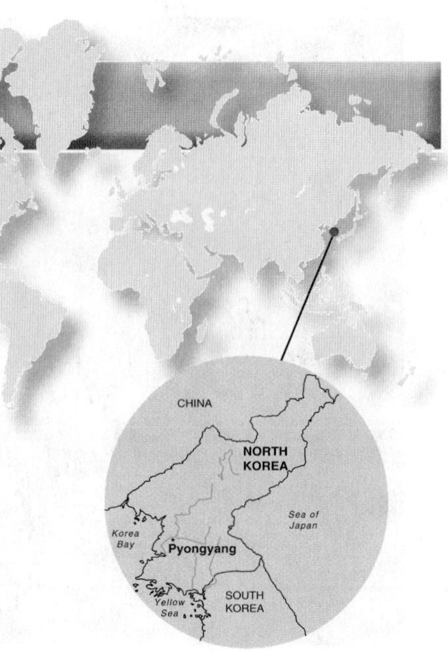


### Why Elections Alone Are Not Sufficient for a Democracy: Casting a Ballot in the Democratic People's Republic of Korea

Elections for the national legislative body in North Korea, the Supreme People's Assembly, are held every five years. At the subnational level, elections are staged to select representatives to regional assemblies. The most recent regional elections were on July 24, 2011, and voter turnout was a remarkable 100 percent. In the 2009 national elections, voter turnout was reported at 99.98 percent with all of the 686 candidates receiving 100 percent of the vote total in their district. In fact, voter turnout in North Korea is always near 100 percent, the candidates selected to run on the ballot never face opposition, and these candidates are always reported to win 100 percent of the vote. This is a common practice in many nondemocratic countries; elections are held and voter turnout is extremely high, but the process is far from democratic. These types of elections illustrate why elections alone are not sufficient to fulfill the requirements for a democracy. In a democracy, citizens must be able to choose freely among competing parties without the fear of death or imprisonment for voting against those in power.

*Sources:* http://www.cbsnews.com/stories/2011/07/24/501364/main20082738.shtml; http://nknews.org/2011/06/n-korea-to-hold-local-elections-next-month/; http://www.nytimes.com/2009/03/09/world/asia/09iht-north.1.20696199.html; http://www.kcna.co.jp/item/2009/200904/news09/20090409-04ee.html.

such as Sweden engage in a "democratic audit" aimed at taking stock of democratic gains. As Vaclav Havel made clear, the work of democracy is never finished. Understanding that evolutionary process in America begins with a discussion of the term *democracy* itself.

*Webster's Dictionary* defines **democracy** as "a government by the people, either directly or through elected representatives; rule by the ruled." Basically, democracies place key political powers in the hands of the people. At a minimum, citizens in a democracy choose their leaders freely from among competing groups and individuals. In highly developed democracies, the rights of the people extend well beyond this simple act of choosing leaders. Voters in advanced democracies are free to propose a wide array of public policy options and to join groups that promote those options. Voters may even directly determine which policy options will become law through **referenda** (proposed policy measures submitted for direct popular vote). This pattern contrasts sharply with that of an **authoritarian regime,** in which the government stands apart from the people, oppressing citizens by depriving them of their basic freedom to speak, associate, write, and participate in political life without fear of punishment.

The difference between living under a political system that promotes freedom and living under one that enslaves its citizens is clear (see the Compared to What? feature and Figure 1.1). We know, for example, that the yardsticks for measuring a free system include:

- a government elected through free and fair elections
- that people will have the right to organize into different political parties and competitive political groups
- that legitimate political opposition is given the opportunity to express itself as well as gain enough support to become the majority

**democracy**
A system of government in which the people rule, either directly or through elected representatives.

**referenda**
Proposed policy measures submitted for direct popular vote.

**authoritarian regime**
An oppressive system of government in which citizens are deprived of their basic freedom to speak, write, associate, and participate in political life without fear of punishment.

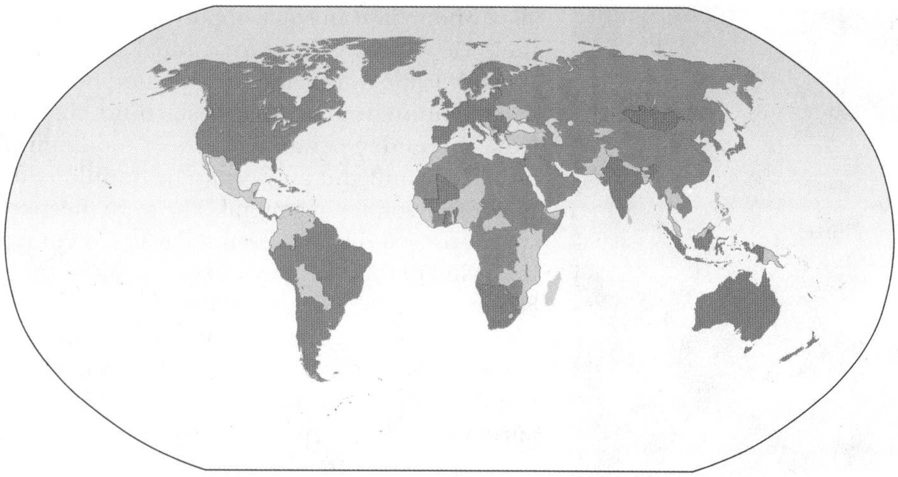


**FIGURE 1.1** Map of Freedom, 2011
*Source:* www.freedomhouse.org. Reprinted by permission of Freedom House.

- that the government is accountable to the electorate between elections and operates with openness and transparency
- that free and independent media and other forms of cultural expression are permitted
- that religious institutions and communities are free to practice their faith and express themselves in public and private
- that there is freedom of assembly, demonstration, and open public discussion that includes freedom for nongovernmental organizations
- that there is an independent judiciary, where the rule of law prevails in civil and criminal matters and where the police and military are under direct civilian control
- that citizens have the right to own property and establish private businesses
- that there are personal social freedoms, including gender equality, choice of marriage partners, and size of family[5]

Although political power in a democracy rests in the hands of the people, not all democracies are alike. Let us look at two types: direct and representative democracy.

## Direct and Representative Democracy

Some democratic systems give their citizens direct political control; others allow only indirect power. **Direct democracy** assumes that people can govern themselves. The people, as a whole, make policy decisions rather than acting through elected representatives. In a **representative democracy,** voters designate a relatively small number of people to *represent* their interests; those representatives then meet in a legislative body and make decisions on behalf of the entire citizenry.

**direct democracy**
A type of government in which people govern themselves, vote on policies and laws, and live by majority rule.

**representative democracy**
A type of government in which voters designate a relatively small number of people to represent their interests; those people, or representatives, then meet in a legislative body and make decisions on behalf of the entire citizenry.

**Direct Democracy** The political systems of Athens and similar Greek city-states of ancient times were examples of an elite-based direct democracy. Even though most people in Athens were not considered citizens, the few eligible to participate in political life met regularly, debated policy, and voted directly on the issues of the day. They needed no intermediaries and made all political decisions themselves. In contrast, the later Roman republic was an indirect, representative democracy, closer to the structures that are recognized in the United States.

The closest American approximation of direct democracy is the New England **town meeting,** a form of governance dating back to the early 1700s. In these meetings, town business is traditionally transacted by consent of a majority of eligible citizens,

**town meeting**
A form of governance dating back to the 1700s in which town business is transacted by the consent of a majority of eligible citizens, all of whom have an equal opportunity to express their views and cast their votes at an annual meeting.

Washington, DC, residents march to secure full voting representation in Congress and full democracy for the more than half-million residents of the District.

all of whom have an equal opportunity to express their views and vote at an annual gathering. When it came into being, this method of direct participation represented a startling change from the undemocratic dictates of the English monarchy and the authoritarian traditions of European politics in general. The town meeting system proved durable, even today representing the primary form of government in more than 80 percent of New England townships.

The town meeting instituted two indispensable features of effective democracy: equality and majority rule. **Equality** in this case means that all participants have equal access to the decision-making process, equal opportunity to influence the decisions made, and equal responsibility for those decisions. For this reason, the central premise of the Declaration of Independence is that "all men are created equal." Under **majority rule,** when more than half of the voters agree on an issue, the entire group accepts the decision, even those in the minority who voted against it. Acceptance of this key procedural norm allows the government to operate. If minorities were to flout the law as determined by the majority, the result would be anarchy or even civil war. But democracy is also about the struggle of those in the minority for their right to be equal and their perspective to be recognized.

Note that minorities accept majority rule for the same reason that majorities accept minority rights. Those in the minority hope to become the majority someday, and when they do, they will want that day's minority to obey the laws they pass. At a minimum, then, obedience to any majority-approved law represents a crude calculation of future self-interest. But for many in a democracy, this constant shifting between majority and minority positions broadens one's perspective. It produces an understanding of, even empathy for, the positions of people in the opposite political camp. The result is a degree of tolerance for different political points of view, an openness to others' opinions that lies at the heart of the democratic ideal.

Direct democracy (as in New England town meetings) works well for small, homogeneous groups of people. Once a population grows and diversifies, however, direct democracy can become cumbersome, even impossible to operate. One form of direct democracy—*statewide balloting*—is still used in states such as California. Voters there express their views on policy matters (through propositions and referenda) or on changes in the state constitution or to state statutes (through initiatives). Sometimes the outcomes have led to a restriction in democratic freedoms, as was the case with California's Proposition 8 in November 2008 that banned same-sex marriage. However, more than 300 million people live in the United States of America; assembling them all to discuss and make collective decisions would be impossible. With large numbers of people and a varied population, representative democracy makes more sense.

**QUICK REVIEW**

Direct Democracy

- Ancient Athens and a few other Greek city-states had direct democracy.
- The framers of the U.S. Constitution feared that direct rule by the people—pure democracy—would mean rule by the mob.
- Our current system contains elements of both representative and direct democracy.

**Representative Democracy** As the country grew in size and population, democracy became less pure and direct. The town meeting gave way to *representative town meetings,* a form of indirect democracy in which voters designate a few people to attend town meetings and vote on issues for the entire community. But even this system was ineffective. Myriad decisions cropped up, and towns would have come to a standstill if they had to call daily or weekly town meetings. The business of government was too complex and demanding even for the representative town meeting approach. To expedite matters, towns voted for "selectmen," who would conduct routine town business in the periods between full town meetings.

**equality**
A state in which all participants have equal access to the decision-making process, equal opportunity to influence the decisions made, and equal responsibility for those decisions.

**majority rule**
A decision-making process in which, when more than half of the voters agree on an issue, the entire group accepts the decision, even those in the minority who voted against it.

This new system of representative democracy allowed larger and more diverse groups of people to govern themselves. Under this system, voters select representatives to make the decisions of government for them. In theory, citizens still retain the ultimate decision-making power, because periodic elections allow them to eject representatives who fail to carry out their wishes. Still, day-to-day government and the daily flow of policy decisions no longer rest directly in the people's hands. Immediate power to run the government now resides with elected officials—delegates of the people. The resulting system is related to but still different from the framework of direct citizen rule.

Given the choice between direct versus representative democracy, the framers of the Constitution chose the latter, fearing that direct rule by the people—pure democracy—would mean mob rule. As John Adams once wrote: "Remember, democracy never lasts long. It soon wastes, exhausts, and murders itself. There never was a democracy yet that did not commit suicide."[6] Seeking to keep their new democratic system from committing suicide, the framers decided to create a **republic,** a governing structure that places political decision makers at least one step away from the citizens they govern. For instance, citizens grouped into several hundred districts elect members of the U.S. House of Representatives. Each district elects one individual to represent its wishes and interests in an assembly at the nation's capital.

To further dilute the political influence of the American people, the framers placed other units of government even farther from their direct control. The U.S. Senate would be chosen by state legislators. The people would not vote directly for president, but for members of an electoral college who would then name the president. The Supreme Court would be even farther removed from the people's will—chosen for life tenure by the indirectly elected president and confirmed by the indirectly elected Senate. Thus, the highest court in the land would be three times removed from the popular will.

Although the framers clearly opted for an indirect and representative form of democratic governance, over the years, parts of the system they devised moved closer to the Athenian ideal of direct democracy. Still, we must marvel at how well the original structures, set up more than 200 years ago, have held up. Everywhere in the country today, we see representative democracy at work: in local, state, and national governments. Something in the original scheme seems to have met with the ideals and goals of the American democratic spirit: equality, freedom for all, a representative democracy based on majority rule and minority rights, and a system of open participation.

**QUICK REVIEW**

Athenian Democracy

- Organized government around the assembly (*ekklesia*).
- Emphasized face-to-face political discussion and decision making.
- Governed a population comprised of a majority that included women, slaves, and immigrants, but these persons were barred from participating in the democratic assembly.

**republic**
A system of government that allows indirect representation of the popular will.

# THE IDEALS OF DEMOCRACY

1.3 *What basic democratic ideals characterize the American polity, and what trade-offs exist among these values?*

America's commitment to democracy rests on a profound belief in an idealistic set of core values: freedom, equality, order, stability, majority rule, protection of minority rights, and participation. If the United States could uphold these values at all times, it might be regarded as the perfect democratic system. It doesn't, however, even today, and it fell short of these ideals even more frequently in the past. Before the passage of the 1964 Civil Rights Act, for example, racial segregation in the American South made it legal for white passengers on city buses to insist that black passengers give up their seats for the whites, and illegal for black passengers to refuse to do so. When black seamstress Rosa Parks did just that in Montgomery, Alabama, in 1955, she was arrested and fined, and she eventually lost her job. The courts would eventually overturn Montgomery's bus segregation policy. Parks's willingness to stand up for human justice won her the title, "Mother of the Civil Rights Movement."

Mrs. Rosa Parks is fingerprinted in Montgomery, Alabama, in February 1956 after her arrest for refusing to give up her seat to a white passenger and move to the back of the bus.

**freedom**
A value that suggests that no individual should be within the power or under the control of another.

**equality of opportunity**
The idea that "people should have equal rights and opportunities to develop their talents," that all people should begin at the same starting point in a race.

**equality of result**
The idea that all forms of inequality, including economic disparities, should be completely eradicated; this may mean giving certain people a starting advantage so that everyone has fair chances to succeed.

## Freedom and Equality

Two key values that American democracy claims to safeguard often lead in contradictory directions. Frequently, the more freedom citizens have, the less equality they are likely to achieve, and vice versa. Each of these admirable ideals, when applied to real-world circumstances, can produce contradictory results, depending on how one interprets their meaning. The dilemmas that arise when pursuing these two goals, both individually and together, are many.

To begin, take that quintessential American value, **freedom.** This value suggests that no individual should be within the power or under the control of another. People often interpret freedom to mean that they should have *freedom from* government interference in their lives. But the notion of freedom means different things to different people. As the noted historian Isaiah Berlin has argued, freedom can be understood in two ways, either negative or positive. *Negative freedom* implies freedom from government intervention. People have a right to certain liberties, such as freedom of speech, and government cannot violate or interfere with that right. For this reason, the First Amendment begins with the famous words "Congress shall make no law" and goes on to list several key citizen rights that government cannot restrict—notably, the rights to speak, write, assemble, and worship freely.[7]

Contrast that approach with *positive freedom,* or *freedom to,* such as the freedom to exercise certain rights guaranteed to all U.S. citizens under the Constitution. Examples include the right to vote, the right to legal counsel, and the right to equal protection under the law.

Note how these two views of freedom lead to different roles for government. To ensure negative freedom (freedom *from* restrictions), government is expected to do nothing, to keep its hands off. Negative freedom is, as Supreme Court Justice William O. Douglas put it, the "right to be left alone." For instance, a person can say and write practically anything about any political official, and government agencies in a democracy are supposed to do nothing.

Conversely, to secure rights involving freedom *to,* government is often expected, and even required, to take positive action to protect citizens and ensure that those rights can be exercised. In the 1960s, for instance, the federal government had to intervene with a heavy hand in the South to ensure that African Americans could exercise a basic democratic freedom: the right to vote. Thus, some elements of freedom require a weak or even nonexistent government, whereas others require a strong and interventionist one.

Similar contradictions arise in attempting to maximize the key democratic value of equality. This ideal suggests that all citizens, regardless of circumstance, should be treated the same way by government. What equal treatment means in practice, however, is not always easy to say. Does it mean equality of opportunity or equality of result? **Equality of opportunity** reflects the idea that people should have equal rights and opportunities to develop their talents. This idea implies that all people should have the chance to begin at the same starting point. But what if life's circumstances make that impossible, placing people from different situations at different starting points, some much farther behind than others? For example, the person born into a poor family in which no one has ever graduated from high school will be less prepared for college than the son or daughter of generations of college professors. Even more dramatic is the difference in life opportunities available to the children of poor black families, compared with the children of wealthy white families.

The difficulty of achieving equal opportunity for all has led some people to advocate another kind of equality: **equality of result,** the idea that all forms of inequality, including economic disparities, should be eradicated. Policies aimed at maximizing this goal deemphasize helping people compete and support redistributing benefits after the competition has taken place. Equality of result would produce a redistribution of goods, services, and income—taking from those who have more and giving to those who have less. These two forms of equality—equality of opportunity and equality of result—are often in conflict and represent different notions of what a democratic society would look like.

Besides these internal contradictions, freedom and equality conflict in several ways. For instance, if you value freedom *from* government intervention, then equality of any kind will be an extremely difficult goal to achieve. If government stays out of all citizen affairs, some people will become extremely wealthy, others will fall through the cracks, and economic inequalities will multiply. On the other hand, if you value equality of *result,* then you will have to restrict some people's freedoms—the freedom to earn and retain an unlimited amount of money, for example.

**order**
A condition in which the structures of a given society and the relationships thereby defined among individuals and classes comprising it are maintained and preserved by the rule of law and police power of the state.

**stability**
The degree to which an entity is resistant to sudden change or overthrow.

## Order and Stability

The values of freedom and equality, central to a democracy, often stand in tension with the state's power to control its citizens. Every society, to be successful, must maintain **order** and provide social **stability,** so that citizens can go about their business in a secure and predictable manner. Governments make use of laws, regulations, courts, the police, and the military to prevent societal chaos. This need for order does, however, place limits on individual freedom, and it frequently violates certain notions of equality.

Think, for example, about one of the more obvious controls that government places on you to prevent social disorder: the need for a state-approved driver's license before everyone is allowed to operate a motor vehicle. Americans who wish to drive a car cannot simply get into a car and start driving. They must first fill out many forms, pay a government agency, pass a written examination created by government officials, and then prove to other government officials through a driving test that they actually know how to drive a car. Each of these steps has valid reasons, springing from the desire to make society orderly and safe, but government policies that derive from these goals do have the effect of limiting (modestly, of course) the values of both freedom and equality.

The limit on personal freedom is obvious; you can't do what you want (drive a car) without satisfying certain government requirements. The limit on equality is perhaps less severe but is still there; not everyone is allowed to drive a car (those under a certain age, those who fail the various tests, those whose eyesight is weak, those who have violated certain laws, etc.). The constant tension between individual rights and state power creates a great deal of controversy in a democracy and gives rise to numerous policy disputes, many of which we examine in this text.

## Majority Rule and Protection of Minority Rights

Just as democracies must balance freedom and equality with order and stability, so must they also strike a balance between majority rule *(majoritarianism)* and protection of minority rights. Whenever disagreement arises in a democracy, each party to the dispute seeks to persuade more than half of the populace in its favor. To accomplish this end, supporters of each position must agree among themselves on the desired goal; they must achieve some kind of internal *consensus.* In successful democracies, political scientist E. E. Schattschneider argued, consensus develops out of debate and persuasion, campaigning and voting, rather than being imposed by dictate. In other words, the minority becomes the majority only through open procedures that encourage popular input and rational argument, not through some small group's authoritarian decision to impose its policy preferences on everyone else.[8]

In late 2010, the TSA introduced new security requirements for airline passengers. Some passengers were required to submit to revealing body scans, as seen below, or to enhanced pat-downs where TSA agents brush their hands over the passenger's genitals, buttocks, and breasts.

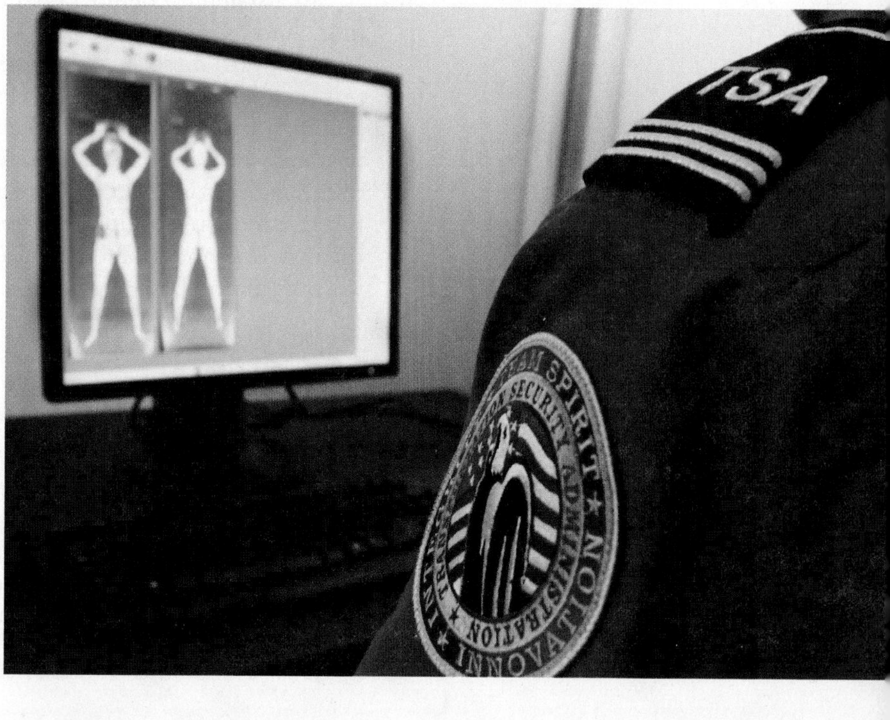

**QUICK REVIEW**

Ideals of Democracy

The government must:

- Protect citizens and ensure that rights can be exercised.
- Treat all citizens, regardless of circumstance, the same way.
- Maintain order and provide social stability.
- Provide a balance between the rule of the majority and the protection of minority rights.
- Provide citizens with ample opportunities to participate in and influence government activities.

Furthermore, in a democracy, policy questions are rarely settled once and for all. Those in the minority are constantly trying to influence the majority to change its mind. Free to express their views without fear of harm, those who hold the minority opinion will speak out persuasively, hoping to see their ideas become the majority perspective. Hence, majorities in a vibrant democracy can never feel secure for long. They must always defend themselves from continuing minority arguments; they must always imagine that the minority will one day claim the majority position.

To make matters more complicated still, note that few people ever find themselves in the majority on all issues. One may hold the majority viewpoint on prayer in public schools and on nuclear power but find oneself in the minority on the minimum wage issue. Democracy is never static; it is an elusive, dynamic, and constantly shifting process.

Knowing that majority status must inevitably be temporary, members of any majority must be careful. They must be reasonable in their demands and programs, seeking not to antagonize the minority excessively, because they would have to expect retribution when leaders of an oppressed minority become part of next week's or next year's majority. The knowledge that one might become the minority any day has a profound effect, leading the current majority in a democratic system to treat minorities fairly.

The idea of **minority rights** springs from this perspective. Those in the majority give rights to those in the minority because when the majority ends up in the minority, as inevitably will happen, then the new minority wants to enjoy those rights rather than endure the repression that is the usual fate of minorities in nondemocratic systems. Thomas Jefferson understood this idea well. When in the minority, his Democratic-Republican Party had been victimized by the Alien and Sedition Acts, passed by the majority Federalist party in 1798 in part to restrain the Democratic-Republicans' views. When Jefferson himself entered the majority as president in 1801, he stressed the importance of majority restraint, referring in his first inaugural address to the "sacred principle that though the will of the majority is in all cases to prevail, that will to be rightful must be reasonable."[9]

When those in the minority band together into groups based on particular interests and seek to influence policy by allying with other groups, the system of **pluralism** develops. Continual competition among groups in a democracy ensures that power moves around in shifting alliances of interests. One year, the religious and education groups might unite on the question of government assistance to schools; the next year, those groups might split on the issue of teachers' wages, with the labor unions and taxpayer interest groups weighing in with their own views.

In a system of democratic pluralism, maintaining a cohesive majority becomes more and more difficult. Coalitions constantly shift, and new majorities appear on every issue. In these circumstances, the ephemeral majorities of the day are bound to respect minority rights and pay close attention to unpopular opinions. The large number of groups and the strong likelihood that everyone will frequently be in the minority diminishes the chance that one dominant oppressive group will form. The framers of this nation's Constitution worried a good deal about the "tyranny of the majority," but in a modern, complex democracy this problem seems relatively minor. Indeed, the excessive power of minorities, including special-interest groups, seems more of a worry to many observers today—an issue we examine carefully in later chapters.

**minority rights**
Rights given to those in the minority; based on the idea that tyranny of the majority is a danger to human rights.

**pluralism**
A system that occurs when those in the minority form groups based on particular interests and seek to influence policy by allying with other groups.

**universal suffrage**
The requirement that everyone must have the right to vote.

## Participation

Democracy, rule by the governed, gives *all* citizens an opportunity to influence government activities. That opportunity is best expressed by **universal suffrage,** the right of adults to vote. Democracy also requires that this vote be meaningful; that is, voters must have real choices at the polls, and their choices must be reflected in governmental policies. Beyond voting, democracies must provide citizens with ample opportunities to participate in and influence the direction of their government. Such participation may involve serving in the government, lobbying for governmental action, or simply reading and talking about government actions.

Participation is a central democratic ideal, and the United States has approached it over the years by continually expanding opportunities for Americans to participate in and influence their government. Only a minority of people—free, white, landowning males over the age of 21—could exercise full citizenship rights in 1787. The expansion of citizenship rights toward inclusiveness has continued for two centuries, facilitated in particular by the amendment structure of the Constitution. The Thirteenth and Fifteenth Amendments eliminated slavery and involuntary servitude and gave the freed African Americans the right to vote (though years passed before state laws were changed to ensure this goal); the Seventeenth Amendment conferred the right to vote for senators directly; the Nineteenth Amendment gave women the right to vote; the Twenty-third Amendment gave residents of the District of Columbia presidential electoral college votes; the Twenty-fourth Amendment ended the practice of charging people a poll tax before they could vote; and the Twenty-sixth Amendment lowered the minimum voting age from 21 to 18. Today, the opportunity exists for nearly every American adult to participate in the political life of American society. Still, as the Approaching Contemporary Issues in Democracy feature on limiting voting accessibility shows, our approach remains a work in progress.

There are many avenues for staying involved in a political process that often takes decades to resolve legislative issues. In January 2011, U.S. Rep. Carolyn Maloney, Rep. Gwen Moore, Sen. Robert Menendez, and President of the Feminist Majority Eleanor Smeal attended a news conference on Capitol Hill in Washington, DC to highlight the absence of the Equal Rights Amendment (ERA) in the U.S. Constitution.

# THE ELEMENTS OF DEMOCRACY

1.4 *What institutions are necessary to support and uphold democracy?*

Following the struggle for democracy in Poland, Adam Michnik, an early leader in the Solidarity movement, noted that "dictatorship has been defeated and freedom has been won, yet the victory of freedom has not yet meant the triumph of democracy. Democracy is something more than freedom. Democracy is freedom institutionalized."[10] Indeed, throughout this text, we examine characteristics of American democracy that have helped to institutionalize freedom. Free elections, competitive political parties, a free press, interest groups, an independent judiciary, civilian control of the military, and a commitment among citizens to the rule of law and a set of democratic ideals are indispensable in preserving democracy.

The ideals of freedom from government oppression also influenced the hundreds of thousands of Chinese students who demonstrated in Tiananmen Square during the spring of 1989, with hopes of reforming their totalitarian government. These so-called dissidents identified their movement as "pro-democracy." More recently, democratic protestors across the Arab world sought to topple dictators and establish democracies. In countries such as Egypt and Tunisia, the protests were largely successful. The struggle against oppression continues in other countries where the democratic revolutions of the Arab Spring face violent resistance. The demonstrations in China and during the Arab Spring revealed something other than the desire to achieve democratic ideals; they also showed the difficulty of doing so under a repressive system. The student movement in Tiananmen Square was crushed by the state, although for many in China, the dream of democracy

A brave Chinese man faces down a column of tanks intent on reaching the democratic student protesters in Tiananmen Square. Eventually, the man was pulled away by bystanders, saving his life, but allowing the tanks to roll toward the protesters.

# APPROACHING
## Contemporary Issues in Democracy

### Unable to Vote: Modern Day Jim Crow?

**ISSUE: Republican interest groups, governors, and state legislatures are making a state-by-state effort to encourage new limits on voting accessibility.** These efforts include voter ID laws and eliminating early and absentee voting. Recently, Republican governors and state legislatures placed numerous restrictions on voting in the name of preventing ballot box fraud. One problem with these efforts is that they largely prevent groups of eligible voters from casting their ballots.

The groups most affected by these measures (college students, minorities, and the poor) are those that are most supportive of the Democratic Party. Critics from both the Democratic Party and from nonpartisan voting rights groups view these laws as a political attempt to limit the number of votes cast for the Democratic Party while having no real impact on eliminating ballot box fraud.

**Question 1:**

To protect the legitimacy of elections, governments must protect against voter fraud. What do you think should be the proper balance between ensuring limited fraud in elections and allowing every eligible citizen the chance to vote?

**Question 2:**

Ben Wilcox from the nonpartisan League of Women Voters called efforts in Florida to eliminate early voting and increase the difficulty of voter registration "good-old-fashion voter suppression."* Do you believe that this tactic (using voting law to decrease votes cast for the opposition party) is a fair, democratic use of political power? If not, what type of system should be in place to prevent election winners from changing election law in order to limit the ability of their opposition to win in future elections?

**Question 3:**

Former President Bill Clinton, while speaking to a group of students on July 6, 2011, made the following comments:

> One of the most pervasive political movements going on outside Washington today is the disciplined, passionate, determined effort of Republican governors and legislators to keep most of you from voting next time. There has never been in my lifetime, since we got rid of the poll tax and all the other Jim Crow burdens on voting, the determined effort to limit the franchise that we see today.**

Why does President Clinton compare these new limits on voting to Jim Crow laws? What features do they share with Jim Crow laws? How is the political purpose behind the new laws similar to the purpose of Jim Crow laws?

* http://www.nytimes.com/2011/04/27/opinion/27wed1.html?_r=3&ref=opinion.

** Watch President Clinton's entire speech at. http://www.c-spanvideo.org/program/300358-1.

endures. Twenty years later, on June 4, 2009, thousands of pro-democracy advocates held a vigil in support of the dream that one day China would reduce its limits on democracy. Although the Arab uprisings were largely successful in Tunisia and Egypt, and many other governments made political and economic concessions to the protestors (like those in Oman and Syria), the violent struggle for liberty rages on in other parts of the Arab world.

The institutions and traditions of the American system have allowed it to develop toward democracy—a democracy that has not yet "committed suicide," as John Adams feared. How closely have we approached the ideals of true democracy? (See the Approaching Democracy Timeline feature on extending the franchise.) Scholars constantly try to define and categorize democracy using one or another set of objective indicators. Although healthy debate continues about the nature of these indicators, we have chosen to stress five widely accepted elements of democracy. *These institutional elements will serve as markers to identify progress toward the democratic ideals discussed earlier.* Only political systems that meet or at least approach those ideals can be considered democratic. As Roza Otunbayeva, president of Kyrgyzstan and winner of the 2011 International Woman of Courage Award, observed: "there is no highway to democracy. In fact, toppling the dictator may well be the easiest part." It is the institutions of a democracy that are a challenge to establish and maintain, as well as the key path towards the democratic ideal.[11] Using the following elements, you can measure the strength and robustness of American democracy or any democracy (see Figure 1.2).

**elections**
The central institution of democratic representative governments in which the authority of the government derives from the consent of the governed. The principal mechanism for translating that consent into governmental authority is the holding of free and fair elections.

**political parties**
Organizations that exist to allow like-minded members of the population to group together and magnify their individual voices into a focus promoting individual candidates and government action.

**interest groups**
Formal organizations of people who share a common outlook or social circumstance and who band together in the hope of influencing government policy.

## A System for Popular Participation

The United States provides numerous opportunities for citizen involvement in politics. In the course of two centuries, increasing numbers of people have gained the opportunity to participate in public life. Elections most clearly allow people to influence government. All adult citizens now can participate in regularly scheduled **elections,** where at least two opposing groups have a chance to win. By voting in elections, citizens can convey their desires to government and can expect government to act with those desires in mind. More than 131 million Americans (61.6 percent of eligible voters) voted in the historic 2008 presidential election.

Voting itself would not be sufficient to influence government, however, if voters could not make meaningful choices at the polling booth. The institution of free, competing **political parties** enables this element of choice to be exercised. Stable political parties exist and, once elected to office, seek to impose their will on policy makers. Parties allow like-minded voters to join together and magnify their individual voices into a focus for government action.

Important as they are, political parties are never the only outlet for citizen participation in a developed democracy. Citizens must be free to join a wide array of groups that promote particular interests. That situation has long been true in the United States, where a vigorous civil society allows public and private **interest groups** to thrive. These groups allow citizens to meet, organize, plan strategy, and lobby government for action. They even allow people to protest government policies without fear that government will punish them.

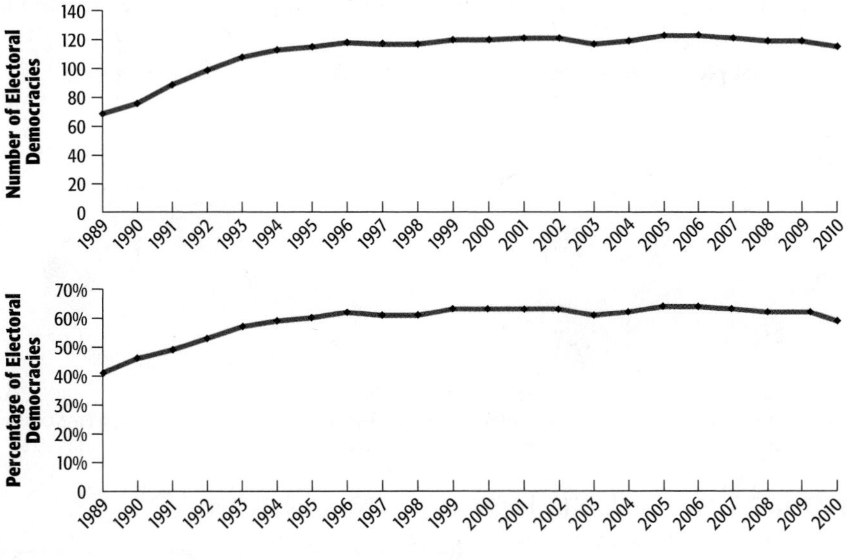


**FIGURE 1.2** Freedom in the World: Electoral Democracies
*Source:* www.freedomhouse.org. Reprinted by permission of Freedom House, updated by authors.

In October 2011, demonstrators protesting against Syria's President Bashar al-Assad march through the streets during a funeral for a ten-year-old boy who was killed in a protest rally the day before in Damascus. Throughout 2011, Syrians have staged protests calling for democratic reforms and the release of all political prisoners. There are thousands of political prisoners in Syrian jails, opposition groups are banned, and the government blocks access to political sites and maintains strict control of the media.

## A Commitment to Preserve Freedom and Equality for All

For democracy to flourish, the government must work to safeguard democratic ideals for all its citizens. In a secure democracy, people must be free to think for themselves, inform themselves about governmental policies, and exchange information. That goal implies several kinds of actions. It means that government stays out of the personal lives of its citizens, who have an inherent **right to privacy,** as implied by the Constitution. Furthermore, citizens must have access to a vigorous **free press** and other means of open exchange of information. Debate must be encouraged and fueled by freedom of speech and thought, not to mention freedom of information (see Figure 1.3).

## An Independent Judiciary

Central to functioning democracies are the rule of law and the protection of civil liberties. Only an **independent judiciary,** free of political influence, can safeguard citizen rights, protecting both majority and minorities at the same time. Like other federal courts, the U.S. Supreme Court possesses a unique power: **Judicial review** makes it the final interpreter of the Constitution. The day after the 2000 Supreme Court ruling that Florida would have to cease its recount of contested ballots, Al Gore, the vice president of the United States and winner of the popular vote, conceded the election to Governor George W. Bush. We study this election later, but for now just think about what this peaceful transition says about the values that constitute our system of laws.

The federal judiciary has often protected individual freedoms through the power to strike down government actions. Independent state courts have also

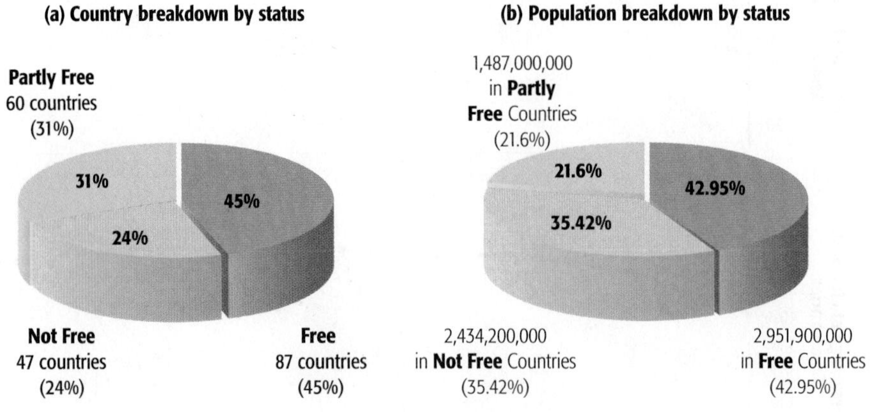


**FIGURE 1.3** Freedom in the World, 2010: Global Data

*Source:* www.freedomhouse.org. Reprinted by permission of Freedom House.

**right to privacy**
The right to have the government stay out of the personal lives of its citizens.

**free press**
Media characterized by the open reporting of information without government censorship.

**independent judiciary**
A system in which judges are insulated from the political bodies and public opinion in order to preserve their ability to act as the final arbiters over those groups in interpreting the Constitution and the laws.

**judicial review**
The power of the Supreme Court established in *Marbury* v. *Madison* to overturn acts of the president, Congress, and the states if those acts violate the Constitution. This power makes the Supreme Court the final interpreter of the Constitution.

acted to preserve individual rights. Courts have used their authority to make a powerful statement about equality and the rule of law: *All are equal under the law,* and no one, not even the president of the United States, is above it.

## Civilian Control of the Military and the Police

In dictatorships, the group that controls the military and police is able to use this police power to resist political pressure from its citizens. This kind of arbitrary military power does not happen in the United States or in any advanced democracy. Thanks in part to the example of George Washington, who resigned from the military after the American Revolution, the U.S. military is controlled by the civilian government. Military leaders take no policy actions other than those directed by civilian political leaders; the commander in chief is the president. Furthermore, the military does not intervene in civilian political affairs. Since 1800, when the defeated John Adams turned over power to Thomas Jefferson, every losing political party has simply turned over control to its winning competitors. Never have civilian leaders, rejected by the voters, called on the military or police to keep them in office. Never have the military or police intervened to keep in office a candidate or party that has come up short at the polls. Both occurrences are common in countries where democratic institutions are weak.

This tradition of civilian control of the military allowed President Harry Truman to fire General Douglas MacArthur for insubordination during the Korean War. Moreover, Americans did not have to worry that George W. Bush would call up the National Guard to prevent the new Democratic president from taking the oath of office after the 2008 election. Indeed, this hypothetical example, common enough in many nations, seems outrageously unlikely in the American setting. Yet, it is important to understand why it is unlikely. Americans believe deeply in the norm of civilian control over the military and the police—a norm vital to the democratic process. After all, how democratic could a society be if the people's decisions could be arbitrarily set aside by the whims of a powerful few?

### APPROACHING Democracy Timeline

**Expanding the Franchise: A Never-Ending Struggle for the Democratic Ideal**

| | |
|---|---|
| 1790 | Only white, male property owners can vote. |
| 1870 | Fifteenth Amendment gives African Americans the right to vote. |
| 1915 | *Guinn* v. *U.S.* outlaws literacy tests for federal elections. |
| 1920 | The Nineteenth Amendment gives women the right to vote. |
| 1924 | The Indian Citizenship Act gives Native Americans the right to vote in federal elections. |
| 1944 | *Smith* v. *Allwright* outlaws white-only primaries. |
| 1957 | The Civil Rights Act passes to help ensure African Americans have the right to vote. |
| 1961 | The Twenty-third Amendment gives residents of the District of Columbia the right to vote in presidential elections. |
| 1964 | The Twenty-fourth Amendment bans poll taxes. |
| 1965 | The Voting Rights Act is passed to protect minority voters. |
| 1971 | The Twenty-sixth Amendment is passed and lowers the voting age to 18. |
| 1995 | The Motor Voter Law passes, making it easier for citizens to meet voter registration requirements. |
| 2000 | A federal court decides that Puerto Ricans living in Puerto Rico, although U.S. citizens, cannot vote for U.S. president. |
| 2002 | Help America Vote Act (HAVA) is passed in response to disputed 2000 presidential election. |
| 2009 | Delegate Eleanor Holmes Norton (D–DC) introduced the DC House Voting Rights Act (H.R.157) in the House of Representatives. |
| 2009 | President Obama signs The Military and Overseas Voter Empowerment Act, which makes it easier for citizens living oversees to cast their ballot. |
| 2011 | Republican governors and state legislatures in many states change election law in an effort to make voting more difficult. |

Democratic | Neutral | Undemocratic

## QUICK REVIEW

Elements of Democracy

- Popular participation.
- Preservation of freedom and equality for all.
- Independent judiciary, free of political influence.
- Civilian control of the military and the police.
- Democratic ideals among all levels of society.

In August 2011, members of the Mexican-American and Arab-American communities march and rally to protest racial profiling and harassment of immigrant communities by the Border Patrol and immigration officers. Border Patrol officers have often targeted people dropping off children at schools, visiting food pantry and youth center.

## THINKING CRITICALLY

In April 2009, the Department of Homeland Security issued a report titled "Right-wing Extremism: Current Economic and Political Climate Fueling Resurgence in Radicalization and Recruitment." The report suggested that acts of violence could come from unnamed "right-wing extremists" concerned about illegal immigration, abortion, increasing federal power, and restrictions on firearms. It singled out returning war veterans as susceptible to recruitment. At what point are people with divergent views from those holding power a danger to the stability of the government rather than legitimate political opposition?

## A Cultural Commitment to Democratic Ideals Among All Levels of Society

Democracy doesn't just happen. People in general and leaders in particular must believe in it, understand how it works, and abide by its norms. The United States is characterized by racial, ethnic, and religious diversity. Unlike European democracies, America has been a destination for immigrants throughout its history and has been defined by its continually changing demography.

> *The country's ability to receive and integrate tens of millions of non-Europeans in recent decades is an impressive testament to the flexibility, fairness, and pragmatism of the American system. One might consider the United States to be the world's first truly globalized nation, given the origins of its people and its increasing economic and communications integration with their many homelands.*[12]

It is therefore essential that all levels of society agree on a set of common governmental ideals. In the United States, those ideals include reverence for the Constitution, the pursuit of freedom and equality, the value of minority rights, and the rule of law. This commitment to the rule of law is indispensable for maintaining stability. It produces a remarkable result, one found only in a democratic society. Americans unhappy with their government complain but almost never take up arms. Americans tend to organize and wait for the next election and then vote the ruling party out of power.

## Summary

1.1 *How did Vaclav Havel characterize democracy?*

- Vaclav Havel said, "As long as people are people, democracy, in the full sense of the word, will always be no more than an ideal."
- Democracy in America has evolved over time—and continues to evolve.
- American democracy has been remarkably open, over the long run, to expanding rights and liberties for all its citizens—even if those rights and liberties have been achieved only with struggle, sacrifice, and occasional failure.

1.2 *How do direct and representative democracies differ, and which type of democracy did the framers believe was best for the new nation?*

- In a democracy, key political powers are placed in the hands of the people.
- Direct democracy assumes that people can govern themselves. The people, as a whole, make policy decisions rather than acting through elected representatives.
- In a representative democracy, voters designate a relatively small number of people to *represent* their interests; those representatives then meet in a legislative body and make decisions on behalf of the entire citizenry.
- Although the framers clearly opted for an indirect and representative form of democratic governance, over the years the system they devised moved much closer to the Athenian ideal of direct democracy.

1.3 *What basic democratic ideals characterize the American polity, and what trade-offs exist among these values?*

- America's commitment to democracy rests on a profound belief in an idealistic set of core values: freedom, equality, order, stability, majority rule, protection of minority rights, and participation. Often it is impossible to maintain all of these values at once, because actions in support of one value can violate another value.
- The values of freedom and equality, central to a democracy, often stand in tension with the state's power to control its citizens. Every society, to be successful, must maintain order and provide social stability so that citizens can go about their business in a secure and predictable manner.
- Even freedom and equality, two democratic ideals, stand in tension with one another. Frequently, the more freedom citizens have, the less equality they are likely to achieve, and vice versa. Each of these admirable ideals, when applied to real-world circumstances, can produce contradictory results.
- Decisions in a democracy should be made through majority rule. Yet, this system of governance allows for a majority to take away the rights of a minority. Democracies must strike a balance between majority rule *(majoritarianism)* and protection of minority rights.

1.4 *What institutions are necessary to support and uphold democracy?*

- Free elections, competitive political parties, a free press, interest groups, an independent judiciary, civilian control of the military, and a commitment among citizens to the rule of law and a set of democratic ideals are indispensable in preserving democracy.

## Key Terms

authoritarian regime, 4
democracy, 4
direct democracy, 5
elections, 13
equality, 6
equality of opportunity, 8
equality of result, 8
free press, 14
freedom, 8
independent judiciary, 14
interest groups, 13
judicial review, 14
majority rule, 6
minority rights, 10
order, 9
pluralism, 10
political parties, 13
referenda, 4
representative democracy, 5
republic, 7
right to privacy, 14
stability, 9
town meeting, 5
universal suffrage, 10

## Test Yourself Chapter 1

**1.** American democracy can best be characterized as
a. continuing to approach the democratic ideal.
b. an example of a country that has reached the democratic ideal.
c. a direct democracy.
d. All of the above.

**2.** The closest American approximation of direct democracy is
a. the town meeting.
b. polls.
c. a primary election.
d. judicial review.

**3.** American democracy, as we recognize it today, is the consequence of
a. Vaclav Havel's advice to Congress on how to maintain democratic values.
b. the consistent protection of minority rights throughout its history.
c. a long evolutionary process.
d. free elections held every four years.

**4.** Alexis de Tocqueville came to America in order to write about
a. James Adams.
b. democracy.
c. John Stuart Mill.
d. All of the above.

**5.** The United States has an advantage over other democracies because
a. it has been moving toward democracy for more than 200 years.
b. it is bordered on two sides by oceans.
c. it has a large and diverse population.
d. it uses representative not direct democracy.

**6.** Proposals submitted by a state legislature to the public for a popular vote are called
   a. representative democracy.
   b. directives.
   c. popular sovereignty.
   d. referenda.

**7.** A type of government in which people govern themselves, vote on policies and laws, and live by majority rules is called
   a. direct democracy.
   b. republicanism.
   c. referenda.
   d. representative democracy.

**8.** A system of government that allows indirect representation of the popular will is a
   a. true democracy.
   b. nation.
   c. republic.
   d. referenda.

**9.** Representative democracy
   a. is inherently tyrannical.
   b. is antithetical to American democracy.
   c. works best in very small towns.
   d. is a system of representation in which a small number of people champion the various interests of the larger community.

**10.** Representative democracy is a system of government in which voters select legislators to protect their interests and rights. This plan
   a. totally removes the common people from the policy-making process.
   b. dilutes the influence of the common people.
   c. is not consistent with the principles and values of the framers of the American Constitution.
   d. was designed by the Supreme Court through the process of judicial review.

**11.** All of the following are elements of democracy *except*
   a. popular participation.
   b. an independent judiciary.
   c. civilian control of the military and police.
   d. a chief executive that is elected by a popular majority.

**12.** Negative freedom implies
   a. freedom from government intervention.
   b. freedom to write or speak falsely about others.
   c. freedoms are insignificant.
   d. freedom to criticize the government.

**13.** The idea that people should have equal rights and chances to develop their talents is called
   a. equality of relativity.
   b. equality of opportunity.
   c. equality of results.
   d. equality of establishment.

**14.** The problem with government trying to maintain order and stability is that
   a. order and stability are hard to achieve in the modern era.
   b. actions directed toward order and stability tend to place limits on freedom and equality.
   c. order and stability require the expenditure of large portions of government budgets.
   d. the public places a greater value on individual freedom than on order and stability.

**15.** Universal suffrage
   a. is more important for political candidates than for voters.
   b. means that all adult citizens should be required to vote.
   c. means that all adult citizens should have the opportunity to vote.
   d. has always been a core value of American democracy.

**16.** President Truman's firing of Douglas MacArthur illustrated which element of democracy?
   a. The superiority of the executive branch.
   b. Participation.
   c. Civilian control of the military.
   d. An independent judiciary.

**17.** Freedom and equality
   a. are two democratic ideals.
   b. stand in tension with one another.
   c. mean different things to different people.
   d. All of the above.

**18.** A system where the minority band together into groups based on particular interests and seek to influence policy by allying with other groups is called
   a. pluralism.
   b. majority rule.
   c. a republic.
   d. minority rights.

**19.** Political parties
   a. enable voters to make more meaningful choices during elections.
   b. are anti-democratic.
   c. are only viable in large societies.
   d. All of the above.

**20.** An independent judiciary is important to a democracy because it
   a. can protect minority rights.
   b. represents majority rule.
   c. limits the tension between order and freedom.
   d. ensures a system for fair elections.

**ANSWERS**

**1.** a, **2.** a, **3.** c, **4.** b, **5.** a, **6.** d, **7.** a, **8.** c, **9.** d, **10.** b, **11.** d, **12.** a, **13.** b, **14.** b, **15.** c, **16.** c, **17.** d, **18.** a, **19.** a, **20.** a

# The Founding and the Constitution

# 2

## Chapter Outline

## Learning Objectives

2.1 What early democratic theories and organizations guided the American colonists in banding together into their first governments?

2.2 Why did America's first attempt at a unified national approach to government in the Articles of Confederation fail?

2.3 How inclusive was America's initial democracy, and for those who founded America's constitution, what were their initial plans for government?

2.4 Was the drafting of the U.S. Constitution the result of democratic theory or the workings of political compromise, and how did that affect the presidency and slavery issues?

2.5 How is democracy safeguarded both at the national and state levels?

2.6 How did the people in the constitutional ratification period lobby for and understand their new democratic government?

2.7 Was the final ratification of the Constitution by the states the result of democratic theory or political compromise?

2.8 How has America's Constitution and democracy evolved and become more inclusive over time?

# INTRODUCTION

## THE CONSTITUTION, APPROACHING DEMOCRACY, AND AMERICA'S "WAR ON TERROR"

Immediately after his inauguration in January 2009, President Obama, flanked by 16 retired generals and admirals who had opposed the Bush administration's "war on terror" policies, signaled Obama's change in the balance between security and liberty. His new executive orders (1) promised to close the Guantanamo Bay prison in a year, (2) suspended the trials of the Guantanamo Military Commission for four months while the process was evaluated, (3) directed the CIA to close the network of secret prisons, (4) directed the CIA to end its use of torture in its interrogations by observing the Army Field Manual, and (5) ordered the immediate review of the legal status of the remaining 245 prisoners. In signing these executive orders, Obama said that "our ideals give us the strength and moral high ground" in the war on terror, adding, "We intend to win this fight. We are going to win it on our terms." However, showing the complexity of resetting this balance, Obama also left open the question of who should be prosecuted, how long it would take to close the prison, whether other interrogation techniques could be used, and whether the prison could be reestablished in the future for other high-value prisoners.[1] Despite these goals, by mid-2011, the Guantanamo prison continued to operate, terrorist suspect Sheik Muhammed was scheduled to be tried by a military commission, and other investigative techniques continued to be used. Some of these efforts yielded significant results, such as in May 2011, when members of the Navy's SEAL team 6 were able to find and kill Osama bin Laden. This resetting of the balance between security and liberty during a time of war illustrated how much America had learned from the time of King George III's total security policies against the colonists and the drafting of the Constitution and the Bill of Rights in setting this country's "approach to democracy." But, despite all of the new president's promises in the campaign and in January 2009, the difficulty of the goals led even President Obama's supporters to admit two years later that his anti-terrorism and foreign policies were not greatly different from those of President Bush.

### THINKING CRITICALLY

Have President Barack Obama's initial policy changes in the war on terror from the Bush administration policies "approached democracy"? Have they traded a reduction in security to achieve that goal?

# THE ROAD TO DEMOCRACY

2.1 *What early democratic theories and organizations guided the American colonists in banding together into their first governments?*

**republic**
A system of government that allows indirect representation of the popular will.

**compact**
A type of agreement that legally binds two or more parties to enforceable rules.

Democracy took root early in America. Because of the tremendous distance from the British empire and the rough-and-tumble character of frontier existence, early colonial settlers were forced to devise their own form of self-government. Drawing on a shared commitment to individual security and the rule of law—the notion that no person is above the law—the frontier governments provided models on which the constitutional structure of American government was eventually built. To trace the development of American democracy from the early settlements to an independent United States, this chapter explores the ideas that inspired the American Revolution, including the impact of European political thinking on the founding and the struggle for independence from England. To understand democracy in America, it helps to understand where the idea of democracy began. Although the colonists began their fight for independence in 1775, the idea of democracy that inspired them originated much earlier. As we discussed in Chapter 1, democracy in America resulted from the logical progression of an idea over time. Democracy first emerged in the Greek city-state of Athens. The Athenians devised a political system called *demokratia,* meaning "rule of the people." In fact, the framers of the U.S. Constitution looked to the Roman **republic** (rather than to Greece, because Athens appeared to be ruled by mobs) as a model of democracy. In *The Federalist,* no. 55, James Madison argued that "had every Athenian citizen been a Socrates, every Athenian assembly would still have been a mob." Later, we see how this fear of democracy led the founders to create a system of government that limited direct popular participation.

Characteristics of the British government also strongly influenced America's political arrangement. Britain's Magna Carta, formulated in 1215, limited the exercise of power by the monarch; the notion of limited government accompanied the early colonists to North America. Its impact is visible on the Mayflower Compact, the Declaration of Independence, and the Articles of Confederation.[2]

Although the colonists drew extensively on the historic forms of democracy, America's political system was as much homegrown as it was imported. The actions and experiences of the early settlers established a foundation for the emergence of a peculiarly American form of democracy—one that is still developing. In this section, we examine early attempts to establish a society under law in the early days of the American colonies. During this period, the first and most enduring seeds of democracy were sown, germinating in the fertile soil of a rugged frontier existence far from the British homeland.

## Early Colonial Governments

Most of the New England colonies (including Plymouth, the Providence Plantations, the Connecticut River towns, and New Haven) based their first governments on the idea of a **compact,** a type of agreement that legally binds two or more parties to enforceable rules. Compacts developed directly from Puritan religious theory. Pilgrims, such as those who settled Plymouth Colony, believed that just as they had entered into a covenant with God to found a church and secure their own salvation, so, too, they could forge a covenant or compact among themselves to protect those "natural" liberties provided by God.[3]

Other colonies were created by charters granted to trading companies to exploit the resources of the New World. In 1629, King Charles I chartered the Massachusetts Bay Company, a private business venture. The charter allowed for a governing council that would include a governor, a deputy governor, and 18 assistants, as well as a General Court composed of the "freemen" of the company, those with property and wealth. Other colonies developed from *royal grants,* in which case the king discharged Crown debts by issuing a warrant granting land and full governing rights to a lord or baron. The grant

**QUICK REVIEW**

Colonial Governments

- Most New England colonies based their first governments on the idea of a compact.
- Other colonies were created by charters granted to trading companies.
- Maryland, New York, New Jersey, Pennsylvania, Delaware, the Carolinas, and Georgia developed from royal grants.

**bicameral legislature**
A legislative system consisting of two houses or chambers.

**sovereignty**
The independence and self-government of a political entity.

**social contract theorists**
A group of European philosophers who reasoned that the most effective way to create the best government was to understand human nature in a state prior to government.

recipient became sole proprietor of the land, enjoying virtually absolute authority over its jurisdiction. Any settlement established there became known as a *proprietary colony,* and the original proprietor determined the nature of the colony's local government.

Given that the proprietors of these territories enjoyed the power and authority of kings, the proprietary colonies made an unlikely but important contribution to emerging American democracy by importing England's parliamentary system, with its bicameral houses of Lords and Commons, its committee system, and its procedures. A **bicameral legislature** is a representative lawmaking body consisting of two chambers or two houses. In the United States, the Senate and the House of Representatives are the two legislative chambers.

The bicameral colonial legislatures had an upper house, whose members were appointed by the Crown (or by the proprietor on recommendation of the royal governor), and a lower house, whose members were elected based on the traditional English suffrage requirement of a "forty-shilling freehold," meaning that to vote, one had to own at least forty shillings' worth of land. Only white men who owned land or other property were viewed as sufficiently responsible to vote. Women were not allowed to vote. Many of the colonies prohibited certain religious groups such as Catholics and Jews from voting, and the southern colonies barred "Negroes and mulattoes" from voting, as well as Native Americans and indentured servants.

The colonial legislatures claimed the right to control local legislation, taxes, and expenditures, as well as to fix the qualifications for and judge the eligibility of house members. They also desired freedom of debate, immunity from unrest, and the right to choose their own assembly speakers. To the colonists, these were their rights as English citizens living under British domain in America. However, the British Parliament claimed these rights for itself as the only representative body of a sovereign nation, viewing the colonies as subordinate entities with no inherent **sovereignty,** or independent authority. In Britain's eyes, the colonial legislatures were entitled only to the privileges the king or Parliament chose to give them. This fundamental clash between colonial legislatures and the power of the British Parliament and Crown eventually erupted into the war that separated the fledgling colonies from the British Empire forever.

**QUICK REVIEW**

Social Contract Theory

- Social contract theory provides the philosophical foundation for the obligations that individuals and states have toward each other.
- The state is empowered to enforce appropriate punishment if a citizen violates the social contract.
- Citizens have a right to revolt and even to form another government if the state violates the social contract.
- The theory provided a philosophical foundation for the Declaration of Independence.

## Social Contract Theorists

Democracy developed and flourished in America because of the new settlers' experience with self-government as well as the emergence of influential new theories of governing. Just as religious leaders of the day derived a notion of social compact from the natural order of life under God, a group of European philosophers known as **social contract theorists** reasoned that individuals existed in a state of nature before the creation of a society or an organized government. Social contracts provide the philosophical foundation for the obligations individuals and states have toward each other. If a citizen violates the social contract, the state is legally empowered to enforce appropriate punishment in the name of the people. If the state breaks the social contract, the citizens have a right to revolt against its excessive authority and even to form another government in its stead. This theory provided a philosophical foundation for the Declaration of Independence.

Thomas Hobbes (1588–1679) was the first of the major social contract theorists. In *Leviathan* (1651), Hobbes described human life under the early state of nature as "nasty, brutish, and short." People needed the authority of the state as protection from one another. Hobbes described people's relationships with each other as "war of all against all . . . a general inclination of all mankind, a perpetual and restless desire of power after power, that ceaseth only in death." In Hobbes's view, life without authority lacks security or liberty; he reasoned that human beings require a Leviathan, or authoritarian leader, to produce harmony and safety.

Hobbes also proposed a comprehensive theory of government. Because life in the state of nature was so threatening, individuals surrendered freedom in return for a government that provided protection and order in the form of a supreme authority, the *sovereign,* to whom all were subject. This embrace of absolute power in the form of a sovereign has led many to dismiss Hobbes as a legitimate founding thinker of modern democratic thought. Yet Hobbes clearly stated that even the authority of the sovereign must be carefully codified into a body of laws and that those laws must be applied to all with absolute equality. This notion of equality under the law, even in the harsh frontier world of the colonial era, was Hobbes's most significant contribution to social contract theory.

**limited government**
A type of government in which the powers of the government are clearly defined and bounded so that governmental authority cannot intrude in the lives of private citizens.

The most influential social contract theorist, though, was John Locke (1632–1704). Locke published extensively on many subjects, but his most significant political works are his *Two Treatises on Government,* published in 1690. Here, Locke rejected the notion of a Hobbesian Leviathan or even a divine right to rule. In the *Second Treatise,* Locke explained his theory of a social contract among citizens to create government and protect property, and for the right to revolt against an unjust government. Locke believed that governments exist to preserve the rights already present in society under nature: specifically, the protection of life, the enjoyment of personal liberty, and the possession and pursuit of private property. For Locke, these rights were inalienable, emanating from God's natural law. To deny any individual life, liberty, or property was to take away something granted by God, either through birth, social status, or individual effort and ability.

## THINKING CRITICALLY

At what point is it acceptable under social contract theory for the people to refuse to observe the laws of their government and even consider breaking away from that government?

Above all, and in support of the growing merchant class in England, Locke insisted that government was necessary to protect property, which represented all that was noble in the human embodiment of God, the talents and energy that are the tools of divine will on Earth. Because Locke recognized property as a result of individual ability and energy, he also accepted inequality in the distribution of that property. However, as with Hobbes, Locke believed that all individuals must be equally subject to the laws constituting the social contract between all citizens under government.

Along with the principle of an inalienable right to life, liberty, and property, Locke asserted the importance of limited government based on popular consent. By **limited government,** Locke meant that powers of government should be clearly defined and bounded so that governmental authority could not intrude in the lives of private citizens. Unlike Hobbes, Locke saw no need for an absolute sovereign but argued instead for a strong legislature. His model was, of course, the British Parliament, whereas Hobbes's sovereign bore more resemblance to the British Crown. But, like Hobbes, Locke insisted that whenever government acts against the interests of the people, the people have a right to revolt. Because the government has thus broken its part of the social contract, the people may revolt against the leader to create a new government that acts more in line with their interests. Locke's limited government is strong enough to provide protection for all citizens and their property but not so strong that it infringes on individual liberty.

Locke's *Second Treatise on Civil Government* was such a clear statement of citizens' rights that much of the Declaration of Independence draws from his rationale to justify severing ties with a tyrannical king. Locke's idea of limited government is also embedded in the Constitution. The separation of governing powers and the numerous guarantees of individual liberties found in the Bill of Rights are derived from the Lockean notion of limited government based on popular consent.

In Britain, where both Hobbes (for most of his life) and Locke lived, the theory of the social contract was just a theory. In the 17th century, however, each American colonial territory in part experimented in the practical application of that theory.

**confederation**
A league of sovereign states that delegates powers on selected issues to a central government.

In a land that indeed often rendered life "nasty, brutish, and short," with little direct governmental authority in their lives, the colonists did live somewhat in the "state of nature." And, just as both Hobbes and Locke theorized they must, the colonists entered into binding contracts, established laws and ruling bodies, and formed governments. The Mayflower Compact, the Fundamental Orders of Connecticut, and even the rather Hobbesian regimes established in the proprietary colonies all required citizens who would willingly enter into a legally ordered arrangement of power—a society under the rule of law.

### First Moves Toward a Union

**THINKING CRITICALLY**

Can you frame a "social contract" that might be understood by your professor and members of your class that allows a college class to become a center for learning? What happens when a student, or a teacher, breaks that social contract?

By 1753, the Board of Trade in London requested that the colonies "enter into articles of union and confederation with each other for the mutual defense of His Majesty's subjects and interests in North America, as well in time of peace as war." The goal was to protect the economic interests of the empire.

French expansionism in the American backwoods led to increasing conflict and to the French and Indian War (1754–1763), which spread to Europe two years later as the Seven Years' War. Following the outbreak of fighting on the frontier, Britain advised the northern colonies to sign a treaty with the Iroquois and called a meeting in Albany for this purpose. On May 9, 1754, the *Pennsylvania Gazette* published a lead article and cartoon authored by Ben Franklin to illustrate the perils of disunity. At the Albany meeting, Franklin proposed a plan of union calling for a self-governing confederation for the colonies. A **confederation** is a league of sovereign states that delegates powers on selected issues to a central government. The plan proposed a 48-member Grand Legislative Council in which all colonies would be represented, whose responsibilities would include raising an army and navy, making war, and regulating trade and taxation. The plan also called for a chief executive, to be called President-General of the United Colonies, appointed by the Crown.

The delegates unanimously endorsed Franklin's so-called Albany Plan, but individual colonial assemblies soon rejected it because it appeared to give too much power to the Crown. The British Crown in turn rejected it, claiming it gave the colonists too much power. Franklin later wrote, "If the foregoing plan, or something like it, had been adopted and carried into execution, the subsequent separation of the colonies from the mother country might not so soon have happened."[4] Some 20 years later, Franklin's design would resurface in an early draft of the Articles of Confederation.

**THINKING CRITICALLY**

Recent scholarship on Benjamin Franklin has revealed that he was very unhappy not to be a member of the House of Lords in London, or one of the aristocrats, and eventually became more allied with the colonists because he could realize his ambitions in America. Similarly, George Washington had been unsuccessful in the British Army. Would the revolution have occurred if more of these leaders had been satisfied in terms of their careers in the British system? Or, was the revolution bound to occur for other reasons?

## REVOLUTION AND THE STIRRINGS OF A NEW GOVERNMENT

Prior to 1763, the British were interested in the colonies primarily as new markets and as sources of raw materials. But the French and Indian War left Britain deeply in debt. To alleviate this debt, Britain turned to the colonies with a program of direct taxation with a series of unpopular taxes on such items as sugar, stamps, molasses, and tea. Undertaking a new policy of imperialism, Britain also sought more efficient political and military control in the new world. To this end, several units of British soldiers were dispatched to protect the frontier, at great annual expense to the Crown. Colonial protests over Crown policies sometimes led to violent clashes with British troops.

In the wake of the Boston Tea Party, it become clear that the British wanted order and obedience, whereas the colonists wanted greater liberty. "Although Liberty was not the only goal for Americans in the 1770s and 1780s," writes political scientist James MacGregor Burns, "they believed also in Independence, Order, Equality, the Pursuit of Happiness—none had the

On July 9, 1776, after the Declaration of Independence was read to assembled troops in Bowling Green, New York, the soldiers, joined by New York patriots, pulled down a gilt equestrian statue of King George III. The statue had been the laughingstock of New York because its sculptor, Wilton of London, failed to put stirrups on the horse that the king is riding. The statue was then melted down and used to make bullets.

evocative power and sweep of Liberty, or Freedom—two terms for the same thing. To preserve liberty was the supreme end of government."[5] In Boston, this sentiment had taken the form of standing up to the hated British troops stationed there and dumping tea into the harbor. At the First Continental Congress, the signs of both revolution and American democracy were visible. In a speech before the Virginia Convention on March 23, 1775, Patrick Henry cried out, "Is life so dear, or peace so sweet, as to be purchased at the price of chains and slavery? Forbid it, Almighty God! I know not what course others may take; but as for me, give me liberty, or give me death!"

## The First Continental Congress

On September 5, 1774, fifty-five elected delegates from provincial congresses or conventions of all the colonies except Georgia met in the **First Continental Congress** at Philadelphia's Carpenters Hall. They initially sought to reestablish more cordial relations with the British Crown while insisting on the restoration of their rights as English citizens. The delegates included Samuel Adams and John Adams of Massachusetts, John Jay of New York, John Dickinson of Pennsylvania, and Patrick Henry and George Washington of Virginia. Before leaving for Philadelphia, Washington wrote to a friend, expressing the intensity of feelings common to those attending the Congress: "The crisis is arrived when we must assert our rights, or submit to every imposition, that can be heaped upon us, till custom and use shall make us as tame and abject [as] slaves, as the blacks we rule over with such arbitrary sway."[6]

The First Continental Congress issued the Declaration of American Rights, claiming in the name of the colonies exclusive legislative power over taxation and "all the rights, liberties, and communities of free and natural-born subjects within the realm of England." The Congress also rejected a plan of union introduced by George Galloway of Pennsylvania that closely resembled Franklin's Albany Plan of 20 years earlier. It did endorse the plan delivered from Suffolk County,

**First Continental Congress**
The meeting of 55 elected members (from provincial congresses or periodic conventions) held in Philadelphia's Carpenter's Hall in 1774. It resulted in a resolution to oppose acts of the British Parliament and a plan of association for the colonies.

**Second Continental Congress**
A meeting convened on May 10, 1775, with all 13 colonies represented. The Congress met to decide whether or not to sever bonds with England and declare independence.

***Common Sense***
Thomas Paine's pamphlet of January 1776, which helped crystallize the idea of revolution for the colonists.

Massachusetts, by silversmith Paul Revere. These Suffolk Resolves declared the Intolerable Acts null and void, supported arming Massachusetts to defend itself against Britain, and urged economic sanctions on Britain. The delegates agreed to meet again in May 1775 if Britain did not restore the rights it had taken away. Most delegates still hoped to avoid war with Britain; few were ready to publicly declare a war for American independence.[7] Despite these sentiments, by the spring of the following year, the colonies were engaged in a full revolt against British rule.

## The Second Continental Congress

Three weeks after the first battles of the American Revolution, the **Second Continental Congress** convened on May 10, 1775, with all 13 colonies represented. The Congress would decide whether or not to break from England and declare independence. The brief but dramatic skirmishes at Lexington and Concord were still fresh in the minds of the delegates. In the absence of any other legislative body, without any legal authority to speak of, and in the midst of growing hostility toward the British, the Congress had little choice but to assume the role of a revolutionary government. It took control of the militia gathered around Boston and named George Washington general and commander in chief of this ragtag army. Then, on June 17, came the first major confrontation between the colonials and British forces—the Battle of Bunker Hill. The delegates, still hoping for a reconciliation, sent the "Olive Branch Petition" to King George III. But the king refused to receive it, and Parliament rejected it as well. The course toward American independence was now fixed.

## *Common Sense*

At the same time, Thomas Paine's pamphlet of January 1776, ***Common Sense*** (published anonymously to avoid charges of treason), helped crystallize the idea of revolution for the colonists. Paine, who would later serve with General Washington during the war, moved beyond merely stating the colonists' claims against Parliament to questioning the very institution of monarchy. He also concluded that the colonies needed to separate from England immediately. Paine wrote:

> *A government of our own is our natural right; and when a man seriously reflects on the precariousness of human affairs, he will become convinced, that it is infinitely wiser and safer to form a constitution of our own in a cool, deliberate manner, while we have it in our power, than to trust such an interesting event to time and chance. . . .*
>
> *Ye that tell us of harmony and reconciliation, can ye restore to us the time that is passed? Can ye give to prostitution its former innocence? Neither can ye reconcile Britain and America. The last cord now is broken.*

In addition, *Common Sense* enumerated the advantages of republican government over monarchy and argued that an American republic would be a laboratory for a political experiment in which citizens would enjoy full representation and equality of rights. *Common Sense* profoundly influenced thinking in the colonies. As George Washington observed, "*Common Sense* is working a powerful change in the minds of men." More than 150,000 copies of the pamphlet, or the equivalent of over 15 million copies today, were sold within three months of its first printing. Virtually every colonist had access to it, and the demand for independence escalated rapidly.

## The Declaration of Independence

On June 7, 1776, a resolution for independence was introduced by Richard Henry Lee, a Virginia delegate to the Continental Congress:

> *Resolved, that these United Colonies are, and of right ought to be, free and independent States, and that they are absolved from all allegiance to the British Crown, and that all connection between them and the State of Great Britain is, and ought to be, totally dissolved.*

No longer was the reestablishment of their "rights as Englishmen" sufficient for the colonial leaders attending the Congress; it was to be independence or nothing. Lee's resolution for independence was considered and finally passed when the Congress reconvened on July 2. Writing to his wife, Abigail, John Adams predicted that July 2 would be "the most memorable epoch in the history of America." In the meantime, a committee had already formed to draft a formal proclamation declaring independence. This committee included John Adams, Ben Franklin, and Thomas Jefferson. Jefferson, age 33, of Virginia, drafted the final document on which the Congress voted. On July 4, after three more days of vigorous debate, the Declaration of Independence was approved and signed. According to legend, John Hancock, the first to sign, wrote his name so large because "I want John Bull to be able to read my signature without spectacles."

**Declaration of Independence**
The formal proclamation declaring independence for the 13 colonies of England in North America, approved and signed on July 4, 1776.

## THINKING CRITICALLY

Who were the multiple audiences for the Declaration of Independence, and how did Jefferson and the framers have to tailor their appeal not to offend those different groups? How might their work have been different if women and African Americans had been included in the Continental Congress?

The **Declaration of Independence** renounced allegiance to the British Crown, justified the Revolution, and provided a philosophical basis for limited government based on popular consent. Clearly echoing social contract theorist John Locke, the Declaration proclaimed that the colonists were "created equal" and were endowed, by God, with inalienable rights to life, liberty, and the pursuit of happiness. The Declaration also proclaimed that government was instituted to secure these rights and derived its just powers from the consent of the governed. When governments become destructive of these ends, the people have the right to reconstitute it. The Declaration listed the colonists' many grievances against King George III and concluded that he had become "a Tyrant" who was "unfit to be the ruler of a free People." Thus, the colonies "are, and of right ought to be, Free and Independent States."

By instituting government based on popular consent, in which power is exercised by representatives chosen by and responsive to the populace, the 18th-century revolutionaries sought "to become republican." Political power would come from the people, not a supreme authority such as a king. The ultimate success of a government would depend on the civic virtue of its citizenry. The key assumption was that "if the population consisted of sturdy, independent property owners imbued with civic virtue, then the republic could survive."[8] As James Madison later wrote, "No other form would be reconcilable with the genius of the people of America; with the fundamental principles of the revolution; or with the honorable determination, which animates every votary of freedom, to rest all our political experiments on the capacity of mankind for self-government."

However, the delegates' support of freedom and the social contract, and their opposition to tyranny, did not extend everywhere. Jefferson's initial draft complained that King George had

> *waged cruel war against human nature itself, violating its most sacred rights of life & liberty in the persons of a distant people, who never offended him, captivating and carrying them into slavery in another hemisphere, or to incur miserable death in their transportation thither, this piratical warfare, the opprobrium of infidel powers, is the warfare of the Christian king of Great Britain, determined to keep open a market where MEN should be bought & sold.*

In short, Jefferson, a slave owner himself, was complaining about the practice of slavery in the colonies and seemingly arguing that slaves should be equal as well. But the southern delegates did not agree, and by forcing the convention to strike this clause from the draft to ensure a unanimous call against the king, the Congress left this controversial issue to be resolved by civil war more than three-quarters of a century later.

## THINKING CRITICALLY

If the country were drafting some version of the Declaration of Independence or the Constitution today, which people do you think would be selected for this role? As a result, what would these documents look like today?

Also absent from inclusion in the document was a discussion of the rights of women, a fact not missed by Abigail Adams, the wife of John Adams. No women attended the Continental Congress, nor were any involved in the drafting of the Declaration of Independence, but they did play an essential role in campaigns to boycott British goods in protest against the taxes imposed by Parliament. They were also active behind the scenes during the Revolution; women plowed fields, managed shops, and melted down pots to make shot. Yet they played virtually no part in political affairs; women could not vote, nor could they hold elective office.

The only route open to politically inclined women was to persuade their husbands to act on their behalf in Congress and the state assemblies. Abigail Adams did just that in writing to her husband, John, who was then drafting the Declaration of Independence at the Continental Congress. "I desire you would remember the Ladies," she wrote, "and be more generous and favourable to them than your ancestors." Although she conceded that women were "beings placed by providence under [male] protection," she issued a challenge, if only half seriously:

> *If particular care and attention is not paid to the Ladies we are determined to foment a Rebellion, and will not hold ourselves bound by any laws in which we have no voice, or Representation. That your Sex are Naturally Tyrannical is a Truth so thoroughly established as to admit of no dispute, but such of you as wish to be happy willingly give up the harsh title of Master for the more tender and endearing one of Friend.*

John was amused by his wife's remarks on behalf of

> *another Tribe more numerous and powerfull than all the rest. . . . After stirring up Tories, Landjobbers, Trimmers, Bigots, Canadians, Indians, Negroes, Hanoverians, Hessians, Irish Catholicks, Scotch Renegadoes, at last [the members of the Congress] have stimulated the ladies to demand new Priviledges and threaten to rebell.*

But he was quick to point out that such a rebellion would lead nowhere: "Depend upon it, We know better than to repeal our Masculine systems" and submit to "the Despotism of the Peticoat." Although Abigail appears to have been teasing her husband, we may see in her correspondence a glimmer of what would ultimately emerge as modern feminism.[9]

By signing the Declaration, these revolutionaries were risking "our Lives, our Fortunes and our sacred Honor." The Declaration itself was an act of treason against the Crown, punishable by death. After he put his signature to the document, Ben Franklin is alleged to have remarked, "We must, indeed, all hang together, or most assuredly we shall hang separately."

## THE FIRST NEW GOVERNMENT: A CONFEDERATION OF STATES

2.2 *Why did America's first attempt at a unified national approach to government in the Articles of Confederation fail?*

Even before the War of Independence was won, Americans faced the challenge of devising a new government. To do this, they drew from their experiences with compacts, social contract theory, separation of governmental powers, and natural rights. Between 1776 and 1780, all of the states adopted new constitutions except Rhode Island and Connecticut, which simply struck from their original governing charters any mention of colonial obligation to the Crown. Seven of the state constitutions contained a separate bill of rights guaranteeing citizens certain natural rights and protection from their government. The Virginia Bill of Rights, for example, provided for the right of revolution, freedom of the press, religious liberty, separation of powers, free elections, prohibition against taxation without consent, and fair legal procedures such as the right to trial by jury and moderate bail.

None of these state constitutions contained any provision for a central governmental authority that would help define the 13 states as a nation. Thus, a few days after the Declaration of Independence was signed, a committee was called to draft a plan to bring the colonies together as a confederation. Fighting a war for independence necessitated a central direction, a plan for union.

## The Articles of Confederation (1781–1789)

**Articles of Confederation**
The first constitutional framework of the new United States of America. Approved in 1777 by the Second Continental Congress, it was later replaced by the current Constitution.

On July 12, 1777, after six drafts, the **Articles of Confederation** were presented to the Continental Congress. Following several months of debate, on November 15, 1777, the plan was adopted by the Congress and submitted to the individual states for ratification. The Articles formally took effect on March 1, 1781, after being ratified by all of the states.

The colonists were not about to jeopardize the power and freedom they had won, so the Articles sought to limit the powers of the government. The confederation they created was a loosely knit alliance of 13 independent states agreeing to cooperate in certain instances. The central government was extremely weak. All the national power—executive, legislative, and judicial—was housed in a single house of Congress in which each state had one vote. Fearing a new king, the writers of the Articles did not create a separate executive branch.

Under the Articles, the states reigned supreme in a "league of friendship." They retained almost total sovereignty over their affairs. Congress held strictly limited powers. It could not tax, though it could coin its own money. It could declare war but not raise an army. Thus, after the Revolution was won, Congress could not act when the British refused to decamp from their forts on the Great Lakes in 1783; it was powerless when the Spanish closed off the Mississippi River and the port of New Orleans to U.S. trade and when both Spain and Britain began arming Native Americans in the hope that they would attack frontier settlements. Congress had no power over interstate or international commerce and no power to make treaties with foreign governments. Instead, each state could make its own foreign policy. Congress could not even make laws; it was limited to passing resolutions or regulations. It took the agreement of 9 states to pass any legislation and a unanimous vote of all 13 to amend the Articles. Unable to raise funds, the Congress had to borrow vast sums of money from France and Holland to pay for the war with Britain. Unable to defend itself without voluntary support of state militias and powerless to legislate, the new central government was simply too weak to govern effectively.

The problems of the confederation of states seemed to grow, ranging from financial and commercial difficulties to civil disorder. The inevitable political chaos made the new United States appear not so much a nation as an organization of 13 little kingdoms, each directed by a state legislature. The irony here, of course, is that the Articles of Confederation did exactly what they were devised to do. Independent state legislatures often acted against each other, even levying duties on trade that crossed state lines. James Madison summed up the problem:

> *Experience had proved a tendency in our governments to throw all power into the Legislative vortex. The Executives of the State are in general little more than Cyphers: the legislatures omnipotent. If no effectual check be devised for restraining the instability and encroachments of the latter, a revolution of some kind or other would be inevitable.*[10]

With the "omnipotent" state legislatures operating to the advantage of their individual interests, certain states flourished economically. Agricultural exports doubled, and the national debt was so low that states were paying back principal as well as interest. The states were cooperating in their trade policies to keep out British goods and were working together to raise money for capital improvements. The central government, however, proved incapable of handling crises.

This was clearly demonstrated in the crisis known as Shays's Rebellion. In 1786, Daniel Shays, a Revolutionary War veteran and a farmer in western Massachusetts, along with other farmers in the region facing the loss of their farms through bankruptcy because of increased property taxes, fought a second revolution, this time for economic independence, striking fear into the hearts of the nation's political leaders. Economic

### THINKING CRITICALLY

If the new national government had been more successful in organizing the states, would the United States have been successful under the Articles of Confederation? Or was the redrafting process inevitable because the national government would have tried to acquire more power?

conditions in the new nation had deteriorated, particularly for farmers who lacked markets and could not pay off their debts. They often were forced to pay exorbitant interest rates, and those who could not pay faced prison or indentured servitude. Making matters worse, the farmers, many of them Revolutionary War veterans who became impoverished because of their years of military service for the new nation, lacked government representation for their interests. This was because the Massachusetts state legislature was dominated by merchants from the eastern part of the state who had not served in the war and instead made their fortunes, often selling goods and produce to the British soldiers, whereas most farmers were from the western part.

To protest this situation, the farmers succeeded in shutting down several local bankruptcy courts, some by setting them ablaze. They also demanded that the Massachusetts legislature print cheap paper money—as Rhode Island had done—that would be acceptable to creditors. The legislature refused and instead legislated new taxes. When these protests and a series of anti-tax petitions failed to improve their economic situation, the farmers rebelled. Shays led a force of 2,500 men against the state militia. Ironically, members of the militia included men who had fought with Shays at Bunker Hill. After a series of confrontations, the Shaysites were finally repelled by a volunteer force of several state militias led by General Benjamin Lincoln, a hero of the Revolution. The populist rebellion horrified most of the new nation's political leaders who were also of the wealthy, propertied class. By threatening the institutions created to protect property (the banks and courts), the Shaysites appeared to threaten liberty and replace it with anarchy. The revolt was put down, but it became clear that Shays's Rebellion served an important purpose. It helped strengthen the position of those advocating stronger centralized government.[11]

## THE NEED FOR A MORE PERFECT UNION

2.3 *How inclusive was America's initial democracy, and for those who founded America's constitution, what were their initial plans for government?*

After six years of confederation, it became clear that a stronger, more centralized government was needed. Shays's Rebellion led the colonists to fear anarchy and desire order. Even George Washington recognized that the Articles of Confederation were founded on a much too-trusting view of human nature. The states seemed incapable of ensuring order, let alone promoting the common good. When his efforts to create a multistate passage to the interior of the country on the Potomac River were thwarted by a lack of state cooperation, it became clear to Washington that more needed to be done to promote interstate economic unity.

Even as Shays's Rebellion gained momentum, delegates from five states, largely at the instigation of James Madison, met at Annapolis, Maryland. The dozen men failed to solve the problems of interstate economic competition and promote interstate commerce. Madison and Alexander Hamilton, the former a bookish lawyer and planter and the latter an ambitious Revolutionary War colonel, clearly saw that the solution would require more than mere commercial agreements. Newly emerging as national leaders,, they persuaded the delegates to invite all the states to send delegates to a convention in Philadelphia in May 1787.

After five states agreed to send delegates, on February 21, 1787, the Confederation Congress endorsed the meeting "for the sole and express purpose of revising the Articles of Confederation." But most delegates knew that mere revision of the Articles would not be enough. The complex mix of economic, political, and other problems plaguing the confederation required more than a loose arrangement of individual states struggling to sink or swim on their own; it needed a centralized authority for the common protection and prosperity of all.

The Convention met in the East Room of the State House, the same room in which the Second Continental Congress had met in May 1775 and the Declaration of

**Table 2.1** The Founding: Key Events

| | |
|---|---|
| 1620 | Mayflower Compact signed. Plymouth Colony founded. |
| 1630 | Massachusetts Bay Colony founded. |
| 1760 | King George III assumes the throne of England. |
| 1764 | Sugar Act passed by Parliament. |
| 1765 | Stamp Act passed by Parliament. Delegates to Stamp Act Congress draft declaration of rights and liberties. |
| 1766 | Stamp Act repealed. Declaratory Act issued. |
| 1767 | Townshend Acts passed. |
| 1770 | Boston Massacre. Townshend Acts limited to tea. |
| 1772 | First Committee of Correspondence formed by Samuel Adams. |
| 1773 | Boston Tea Party. |
| 1774 | Coercive Acts against Massachusetts passed. First Continental Congress convened. |
| 1775 | Skirmish at Lexington and Concord officially begins the War of Independence. Second Continental Congress convened. |
| 1776 | *Common Sense* published. Declaration of Independence signed. |
| 1781 | Articles of Confederation adopted. |
| 1783 | Peace of Paris. Great Britain formally recognizes the independence of the United States. |
| 1786 | Shays's Rebellion. |

Independence had been signed in 1776. It opened on May 14 but could do nothing for two weeks due to the lack of a quorum, and delegates continued straggling in until well into the summer. Four months later, they accomplished what is frequently described as "the Miracle at Philadelphia." Table 2.1 summarizes the key events that led to this "miracle."

# THE CONSTITUTIONAL CONVENTION

The unique nature of the American Constitution and its success, both in forging a nation fragmented under the Articles of Confederation and in guiding that nation for centuries to come, can be explained in many ways. Part of the answer lies in the democratic political theory of the time—theory applied to the problems facing the government. However, theory does not govern a nation. People do. So the framing of the Constitution in 1787 is better understood by examining the circumstances under which various theories were advanced in debate and the people who debated and made the compromises that led to success.

## The Task

The problems of governing under the Articles of Confederation made it clear that a stronger central government was needed. But the mission of the Constitutional Convention was not quite so clear. Several states had already authorized their delegates "to render the constitution of government adequate to the exigencies of the Union." Some of the delegates, most especially James Madison, came to the Convention with an understanding that the Articles needed to be scrapped altogether, and they were prepared to propose a new form of government from the outset.[12] Their success in doing so would be decided by whichever of the 55 men attending the Convention happened to be present during those debates. But it was not a preordained success, as William Grayson, representative from Virginia in the Confederation Congress, wrote: "What will be the result of their meeting I cannot with any certainty determine, but I hardly think much good can come of it: the people of America don't appear to me to be ripe for any great innovations."[13]

## The Participants

Although many have come to see the participants of the Constitutional Convention as legends, the delegates are better understood as skilled and ambitious politicians. The result came about not from a singular theoretical vision of a government but from a series of brilliant political compromises and fortuitous events.

The delegates came from a narrow band of American society, the elite aristocracy. This fact should not be surprising: less than 5 percent of the total population—free, white males over the age of 21 who owned land (150,000 of 3.9 million people)—could vote. Many rich men were present. More than half were lawyers; another quarter were large plantation owners; eight were judges; and the rest were doctors, merchants, bankers, clergymen, and soldiers. All of the delegates owned property, and several owned slaves. Although it was a young group, with more than three-fourths under the age of 50, what distinguished this group was its experience in politics. There were several former members of the Continental Congress, 42 members of the Confederation Congress, and seven former governors.

Their efforts at drafting earlier political documents gave these experienced statesmen an understanding of the issues and the need for compromise. Six delegates had signed the Declaration of Independence; nine more, including George Mason of Virginia, Alexander Hamilton of New York, and John Rutledge of South Carolina, had drafted their states' constitutions. Both Roger Sherman of Connecticut and John Dickinson of Delaware had played a major role in drafting the Articles of Confederation, and three other members—Elbridge Gerry of Massachusetts and Gouverneur Morris and Robert Morris of Pennsylvania—had been among its signers.

Although elite and experienced, the delegates were far from representative of the general population. Only two delegates were farmers, even though 85 percent of the citizens lived on small farms. No members of the working class, no artisans, businessmen, or tradesmen appeared among the delegates. Slave or free blacks,

Few at the Constitutional Convention in Philadelphia in 1787 doubted that its leader, George Washington, would one day lead the nation as president.

Native Americans, and women were nowhere to be found in the meeting either. More than 600,000, or just under 18 percent of the total population, were African American, about 520,000 of whom were slaves living in the South, whereas most of the rest were poor, working-class laborers in the northern cities.[14] Native Americans did not participate because, viewed as foreigners, they were specifically excluded from the Constitution, except in the "interstate commerce" power of Article I, Section 8, where they were lumped with the foreign nations as possible trading partners. Few Catholics or Jews were among the political elite from which the delegates were drawn.[15] For all practical purposes, women in American society had no political rights. Because they did not have the vote, participation in politics, much less the Convention, was inconceivable. Thus, no woman attended a state ratifying convention or voted for a state convention delegate. Despite this lack of diversity at the Convention, however, the framers crafted a constitution capable of including women and other groups over time.

## Plans for a New Government

Governor Edmund Randolph of Virginia opened the formal debate on May 29, 1787, with a four-hour speech containing 15 resolves, or resolutions, created by the Virginia delegation, and known as the **Virginia Plan,** for a "strong consolidated union" rather than a federal one with continued state power. When the delegates agreed the next day to debate these resolves, the Convention was no longer a debate about improving the Articles of Confederation; it was about creating an entirely new form of government.

After it was decided that the Articles of Confederation would be replaced, two central questions guided debate:

1. How powerful would the new national government be?
2. How powerful would the states be?

Of five plans submitted to the delegates for consideration, debate centered on two of them: the Virginia Plan, proposed by the large states, and its rival, the New Jersey Plan, proposed by the small states. The differences between these two proposals show clearly the divisions among large-state and small-state advocates.

**The Virginia Plan** The Virginia Plan, presented by Governor Randolph, was so named because he and its author, James Madison, came from Virginia. Delegates from the bigger states favored this proposal. It was based on the following propositions designed to remedy the perceived defects in the Articles of Confederation:

1. It called for three branches of government: a **legislative branch** that makes laws, an **executive branch** that executes the laws, and a **judiciary branch** that interprets the laws. Madison feared the negative effects of power and so proposed a system of **checks and balances.** For every power in government, an equal and opposite power in a separate branch would restrain its force. This idea presumed another feature of the new government, the **separation of powers,** meaning that the powers of government are divided among the three branches, thus preventing the accumulation of too much power in any one branch.
2. Operating from a belief that the ultimate power to govern resides in the people, Randolph proposed a system of **proportional representation,** meaning that the size of each state's delegation in both houses of Congress would be based on the size of its population, rather than the one-state, one-vote rule in the Articles of Confederation. The size of Virginia's population (691,737) would give it more than ten times as many members in Congress as Delaware (population 59,096).
3. Congress would have a bicameral legislature, consisting of two houses, both apportioned on the basis of population. A state would send members to the lower house, elected directly by the people. The lower house would elect the upper house from nominees provided by the state legislatures.

**Virginia Plan**
A plan presented to the Constitutional Convention; favored by the delegates from the bigger states.

**legislative branch**
The branch of government that makes laws.

**executive branch**
The branch of government that executes laws.

**judiciary branch**
The branch of government that interprets laws.

**checks and balances**
Systems that ensure that every power in government has an equal and opposite power in a separate branch to restrain that force.

**separation of powers**
State in which the powers of the government are divided among the three branches: executive, legislative, and judicial.

**proportional representation**
A system of representation popular in Europe whereby the number of seats in the legislature is based on the proportion of the vote received in the election.

**council of revision**
A combined body of judges and members of the executive branch that has a limited veto over national legislation and an absolute veto over state legislation.

**New Jersey Plan**
A plan presented to the Constitutional Convention of 1787 designed to create a unicameral legislature with equal representation for all states. Its goal was to protect the interests of the smaller, less populous states.

**unicameral (one house) legislature**
A legislative system consisting of one chamber.

**supremacy clause**
A clause in Article IV of the Constitution holding that in any conflict between federal laws and treaties and state laws, the will of the national government always prevails.

4. The executive branch, whose size was yet to be determined, would be elected for a maximum of one term by Congress.
5. The judiciary, which would consist of one or more supreme courts and other national courts, would be staffed by life-tenured judges.
6. There would also be a **council of revision,** a combined body of judges and members of the executive branch, having a limited veto over national legislation and an absolute veto over state legislation.
7. The legislature would have the power to override state laws.

It is not hard to see the impact of the Virginia Plan. It centered power in the national government, giving it authority over the states. And by placing much of the governing and appointment powers in a legislature chosen by proportional representation, states with the largest population would dominate that branch. Because Congress had established the executive branch, the big states would dominate there as well, thus giving them control over the central government.

**The New Jersey Plan** Representatives of small states found the Madisonian notion of proportional representation unacceptable because it allowed populous states to force their will on smaller states. "New Jersey will never confederate on the plan," William Paterson said. "She would be swallowed up. . . . Myself or my state will never submit to tyranny or despotism." This reaction infuriated Pennsylvania's James Wilson, who asked, "Does it require 150 [voters of my state] to balance 50 [of yours]?"[16] The small-state delegates countered with a series of resolutions advanced by Paterson called the **New Jersey Plan.** This plan was designed to refine and strengthen the Articles of Confederation rather than to replace it, and in so doing, it protected the interests of the smaller, less populous states. The New Jersey Plan proposed the following:

1. The power of the national government would be centered in a **unicameral (one-house) legislature,** and, to minimize the impact of population, each state would have one vote.
2. A multiperson executive board would be elected by the legislature for one term only and authorized to enforce national laws even in the face of opposition from the states. The executive could be removed by a majority of state governors.
3. A supreme court, appointed by the executive board, would deal with impeachment of national officers, foreign policy questions, and tax and trade problems.
4. The power to tax imports would be taken away from the states and given to the national government.
5. The legislature would be empowered to tax state governments based on population and collect the money by force if an unspecified number of states agreed.
6. All congressional acts would become "the supreme law of the respective states," and the executive board could use force to "compel an obedience to such acts" if necessary.

Although this plan increased the power of the central government, it clearly left a great deal more power in the hands of the states. In this way, the New Jersey Plan was much closer to what the delegates were originally sent to do at the Convention. And with each state having an equal voice in many government actions, the small states would continue to play a prominent role. In spite of the state-centered philosophy of this plan, its provision making congressional acts "supreme law" and compelling obedience to national acts (not found in the Virginia Plan) became an early version of what is known as the **supremacy clause** of the Constitution. This clause holds that in any conflict between federal laws and treaties and state laws, the will of the national government always prevails. When the government moved against the Communist threat in the 1940s and 1950s, a good part of the effort was left to the national government. If a dispute were to arise now between the national and state or city governments in dealing with terrorism, the national government's policy would prevail.

## THINKING CRITICALLY

How would the U.S. government be different today if just the Virginia or the New Jersey plans had been wholly adopted?

**Table 2.2** Differences Between the Virginia and New Jersey Plans

| Issue | Virginia Plan | New Jersey Plan |
|---|---|---|
| Source of legislative power | Derived from the people and based on popular representation | Derived from the states and based on equal votes for each state |
| Legislative structure | Bicameral | Unicameral |
| Executive | Size undetermined, elected and removable by Congress | More than one person, removable by state majority |
| Judiciary | Life-tenured, able to veto state legislation in council of revision | No power over states |
| State laws | Legislature can override | Government can compel obedience to national laws |
| Ratification | By the people | By the states |

Provisions like this one, along with granting the central government the power to tax, made a compromise possible with the advocates of strong central government—the supporters of the Virginia Plan.

Whether the New Jersey Plan was proposed with the idea that it could have successfully governed America, or whether, as some think, it was a proposal designed specifically to thwart the large states' notion of proportional representation at the convention remains a matter of debate.[17] See Table 2.2 for a summary of the two plans.

Swayed by an impassioned speech by James Madison, the delegates chose to use as the basis of discussion the Virginia Plan over the New Jersey Plan by a vote of 7 to 3. The representatives of the small states then turned their attention to achieving some other form of influence for their states in the new government. Only by securing a compromise on the proportional representation aspects of the Virginia Plan, they reasoned, would their states have any voice in the government. Thus, it was over this issue that the chances for the Convention's success would turn.

## Debate and Compromise: The Turning Point of the Convention

2.4 *Was the drafting of the U.S. Constitution the result of democratic theory or the workings of political compromise, and how did that affect the presidency and slavery issues?*

By the middle of June, the Convention had split into two opposing groups. One was the "big states," composed of Massachusetts, Pennsylvania, Virginia, New York, the Carolinas, and Georgia. (The southern states sided with the big states, believing that given their large size, bolstered by the numbers in their slave population, proportional representation would eventually be in their interest.) The other group consisted of the "small states," whose only hope for influence lay in the equal representation scheme.

In the early debates, the small states failed repeatedly to pass the New Jersey Plan, partly because Maryland's Luther Martin, an eloquent speaker whose influence was diminished by his continual drunkenness, had alienated his colleagues by giving a virulent, two-day speech against proportional representation. Martin's effort backfired when the delegates quickly approved proportional representation for the legislature. However, when the delegates also voted to establish a bicameral legislative branch to provide some sort of balance of power, the issue became how the upper house of Congress, known as the Senate, would be apportioned.

**Great Compromise**
(also called the Connecticut Compromise) A plan presented at the Constitutional Convention that upheld the large-state position for the House, its membership based on proportional representation, balanced by the small-state posture of equal representation in the Senate, where each state would have two votes.

**three-fifths compromise**
A compromise that stated that the apportionment of representatives by state should be determined "by adding to the whole number of free persons . . . three-fifths of all other persons" (Article I, Section 2), meaning that it would take five slaves to equal three free people when counting the population for representation and taxation purposes.

A committee consisting of one member from each state was formed to prepare suggestions for resolving the question of representation in the Senate. When the committee selection finished, every member had favored the small states' position of equal representation, so the result was preordained. The plan proved acceptable to the small states but capable of passage by the large states as well.

This plan has become known as the **Great Compromise** (also called the Connecticut Compromise), based on a plan advanced by Roger Sherman of Connecticut. This compromise upheld the large-state position for the House of membership based on proportional representation and balanced that decision by upholding the small-state position of equal representation in the Senate, where each state, regardless of size, would have two votes. Because all legislation would have to pass through *both* houses, neither large nor small states could dominate. The compromise also stated that *money bills,* or measures that raise revenue, must begin in the House, to keep the power to tax with the people. This arrangement would prevent an alliance of small states in the Senate voting into effect programs for which the large states must pay.

The composition and purpose of the two houses of Congress would be markedly different. Members of the House of Representatives would be chosen based on a state's population: one representative for every 40,000 people, as determined by periodic census. (At the request of George Washington, this number was changed to 30,000 on the last day of the Convention.) The House was constructed to be closest to the people and to reflect their desires. The Senate, with its equal representation, larger constituency base of an entire state, and indirect method of selection by state legislatures, was intended as a more deliberative council of the political and economic elite. This body would serve as an advisory council to the president and would eventually be entrusted with reviewing the presidential executive branch and judicial appointments as well as ratifying treaties.

Delegates voted in favor of the Connecticut Compromise by the narrowest of margins—5 to 4—with one state delegation tied. The compromise effectively ended the debate between the large and small states by giving each a balanced stake in the legislature of the new centralized national government.

The United States Constitution was on its way to being realized, but two vexing questions remained, one dealing with the issue of slavery and the other with the nature of the new executive.

**QUICK REVIEW**

Slavery and the Constitution

- The topic of slavery was related to the question of how to distribute the 65 House seats in the First Congress.
- Membership in the House was based on population.
- Without slaves in the count, southern states would have only 41 percent of the House seats.
- Including slaves (18 percent of the population), southern states would have 50 percent of the House seats.
- The three-fifths compromise stated it would take five slaves to equal three free people when counting the population for representation and taxation purposes.

## The Issue of Slavery

Although the word *slavery* was never mentioned in the Constitution, it was much on the minds of the framers. Since the 1600s, Africans had been brought over to the New World and sold as slaves. Southern plantations needed slave labor to operate. Although some delegates wanted to abolish slavery, citing the inalienable human rights of freedom and equality, they understood that such a call would lose much southern support and doom the Convention to failure. Instead, slavery was discussed indirectly through the question of how to distribute the 65 seats in the First Congress. Because membership in the Congress was based on population, how to count the slaves, who constituted almost 18 percent of the population, became a point of contention. If the slaves were not included in the count, southern states would have only 41 percent of the House seats; including all of the slaves would give them 50 percent of the seats.

After much debate, the Convention delegates arrived at the **three-fifths compromise,** which stated that the apportionment of taxes and representatives by state should be determined "by adding to the whole Number of free Persons . . . three-fifths of all other Persons" (Article I, Section 2). The phrase "all other persons" was a euphemism for slaves, which meant that five slaves would equal three free people when counting the population for representation and taxation purposes. The stated rationale for this partial counting of slaves was that they produced less wealth than free citizens, but Convention delegates recognized the political compromise.

The American Revolution was fought on the twin principles of liberty and equality, but slavery became the practice of the land. Several leaders of the Revolution owned slaves. Shown here is a slave auction in Virginia, where human beings of all ages were sold to the highest bidder.

This compromise represented a victory of political expediency over morality. Because slaves could not vote, their numbers were simply being used to add to the South's political power. Some have argued that even though the compromise kept the Constitutional Convention on track, it was immoral because it denigrated blacks by suggesting that they were only three-fifths as valuable and productive as whites. Others, though, have pointed out that although it did increase southern influence in the Congress and thus the presidential electoral count, this unique political compromise actually weakened the power of the southern states while ensuring the Constitution's passage. As a result of the compromise, the slave states ended up with only 47 percent of the seats in Congress, thus keeping them in the minority and making it possible to outvote them on slavery issues.[18] As part of the compromise, Congress was barred from legislating on the international slave trade for 20 years, thus allowing slaves to be imported until at least 1808 (Article I, Section 9). Finally, with little discussion, a provision was added that allowed for the return of fugitive slaves to their masters (Article IV, Section 2).

In leaving it to later generations to address the practice of slavery and end it, were the framers condoning slavery? Were they hypocrites for protecting slavery while discussing the high principles of freedom and equality? One response is that although they were hypocritical, their thinking reflected the vast majority of public opinion at the time; most people were indifferent to slavery. However, one must also realize, just as Thomas Jefferson discovered when he was forced to strike his criticism of slavery from the draft of the Declaration of Independence, that a successful outcome for the Constitutional Convention would have been impossible without compromise on the slavery issue. Had the southern states walked out, as they surely would have had slavery been banned, the nation would have been doomed to continue operating under the defective Articles of Confederation or perhaps to falter entirely. The Compared to What? feature illustrates, using the changes after the Egyptian revolution, how difficult it remains now to achieve constitutional reform.

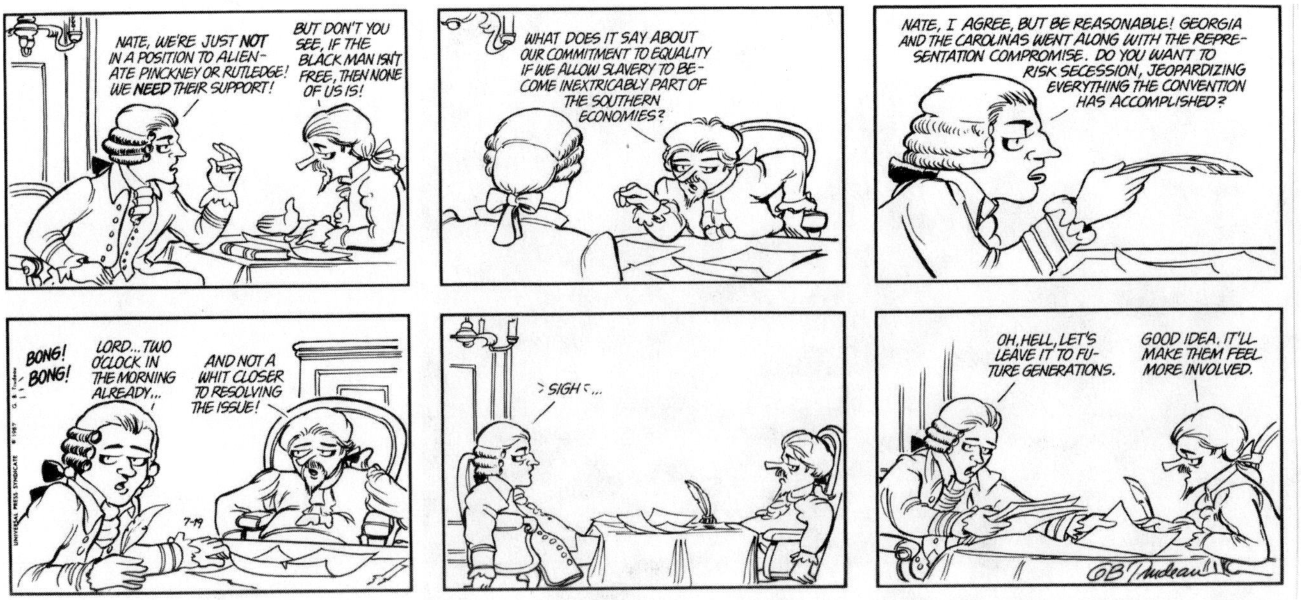




## The Nature of the Presidency

One of the most original contributions made by the framers of the American Constitution was their blueprint for the presidency, including the means for filling the job. (The presidency is described more fully in Chapter 5.)

The framers were ambivalent about the nature of the position they were creating, fearing that it would lead to a new monarchy in democratic clothing. This fear was reflected in the weak executive branches proposed in the Virginia and New Jersey Plans, which consisted of boards subservient to the legislature. To correct this approach, Charles Pinckney of South Carolina called for the creation of a "vigorous executive," because, in his words, "our government is despised because of the loss of public order." However, Edmund Randolph of Virginia, who instead favored a board of executives, expressed his fear that Pinckney's call for a single executive represented the "foetus of monarchy," or the beginnings of the reinstatement of a British Crown in America.[19]

It was James Wilson of Pennsylvania, fearing an all-powerful legislature similar to those in some states under the Articles of Confederation, who proposed a plan creating a national executive much like the powerful governor of New York—a one-person executive with substantial powers, such as a veto over legislation. This plan was not debated by the delegates but was instead submitted to the Committee on Detail, which was charged with creating a coherent document out of the resolutions passed by the Convention. Because Wilson and three other strong national government advocates sat on this five-person committee, the matter was settled in his favor. The powerful single executive envisioned by that committee was adopted by the Convention three months later.

**electoral college system**
Votes in the national presidential elections are actually indirect votes for a slate of presidential electors pledged to each party's candidate. Each state has one elector for each of its representatives and senators. The winning electors cast their votes in their states' capitals after the public election. In the United States, election of the president and vice president is dependent on receiving a majority (270) of the votes cast in the electoral college.

Although the delegates agreed on a one-person executive, they disagreed over the term of office for the new president and how to select that powerful person. Some delegates proposed a three-year term with reelections possible; others sought a single term of seven years. Originally, the Convention narrowly voted for a single seven-year term. This was eventually revised to a four-year term, with reelection possible. Nothing was said about the number of terms a president could serve.

The vital question of how to select the right person for president led to yet another compromise in the form of the **electoral college system.** In an attempt to ensure selection of statesmen like George Washington, the anticipated first

## Compared to WHAT?

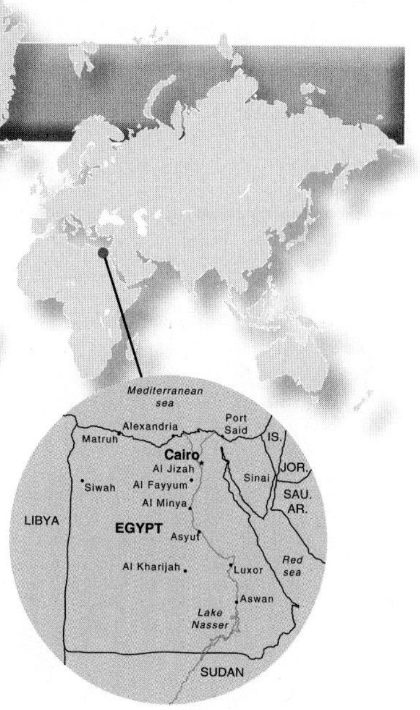


### Constitutional Reform in Egypt

How do you create a new constitution after a dictator has been toppled? That was the challenge facing Egypt after 18 days of protest in late January and early February 2011, the start of the Arab Spring, ended the nearly 30-year rule of President Hosni Mubarek. After Mubarek left office, the Supreme Council of the Armed Forces, which had backed the protesters, created a committee charged with drawing up amendments to that country's constitution by February 26, in the hope of putting it before the country's voters in a national referendum a month later. If their work was approved by the voters, a new parliament would be elected and a presidential election would follow.

The committee drafted a document that, on paper, had the potential to approach democracy in the country. Anyone running for president who does not have dual citizenship can get on the ballot either by the backing of party members in parliament or petitions containing 30,000 signatures, would serve for a four-year term, and would be limited to only two terms. To prevent a dictatorship, the president would be required to appoint a vice president. He could declare a "state of emergency," under which Mubarek had consolidated his power and ruled during his entire tenure, for only six months with parliamentary approval, and extend that time only with public approval. Suspects in terrorism cases were given constitutional rights and the judiciary was given the power to supervise elections. Interestingly, the committee did not change Article 5 of Egypt's constitution, which barred political activity "with a religious frame of reference," seemingly barring the Muslim Brotherhood from becoming a powerful political organization.

On March 19, the constitutional amendments were approved by 77.2 percent of the people in Egypt's first national referendum, but when in November, 2011 the ruling army bureaucracy had allowed free elections for the parliament but had not yet turned over power to the people, the popular democratic protests reappeared in Tahrir square.

*Sources:* Nathan Brown and Michele Dunne, "Egypt's Draft Constitutional Amendments Answer Some Questions and Raise Others," Carnegie Endowment for International Peace, March 1, 2011, found at http://carnegieendowment.org; Neil MacFarquhar, "Egyptian Voters Approve Constitutional Changes," *New York Times,* March 20, 2011, found at www.nytimes.com.

president, the framers took selection away from the voters. Instead, the states would decide how to choose electors in numbers equal to the total number of their senators and representatives. The electors would vote for two people, at least one of whom could not be from their own state. The candidate with the highest number of votes would become president, and the runner-up, vice president. The intent was that the best-known and most-qualified candidate would appear somewhere on the ballots of the most electors from around the country. A tie would be sent to the House of Representatives for selection, with each state delegation having one vote.

Such a system struck a compromise between the large and small states. The president would not be chosen by direct popular vote or by the legislature because those methods would have favored the large states. Still, the large states would have the advantage of proportional representation. On the other hand, if the matter went to the House through lack of a majority vote in the electoral college, as the delegates fully expected, the one-state, one-vote system would favor the small states. (More will be said about the electoral college in Chapter 10.) This idea mandated that a presidential candidate would need a spread of support from large and small states around the country. In the 2004 presidential election, for instance, had John Kerry gained the support of Ohio, he would have won the presidency instead of George Bush.

After nearly four months of debate, on September 17, 1787, the new Constitution was drafted. The eldest delegate, 82-year-old Benjamin Franklin, moved that the draft be approved, saying, "I consent to this constitution because I expect no better, and because I am not sure that it is not the best." To encourage even those who disagreed with the results to sign it, those who affixed their names became "witnesses" to the document. Even so, several of the delegates refused to sign, and only 39 names were penned. Perhaps the best blessing on the whole enterprise was Franklin's, when the weeping old man told his fellow delegates that he had long puzzled over the half-sun design on the back of the Convention president's chair in which George Washington had sat. Was the design of a rising or setting sun, he often wondered. "Now at length I have the happiness to know that it is a rising and not a setting sun," he told the delegates.[20] With that, George Washington penned in his journal: "The business being closed, the members adjourned to the City Tavern, dined together and took a cordial leave of each other."[21] But, as they would soon discover, the battle had just begun.

## THE MIRACLE: RESULTS OF THE CONVENTION

2.5 *How is democracy safeguarded both at the national and state levels?*

The purpose of the Constitution is laid out in the eloquent preamble:

> *We the People of the United States, in Order to form a more perfect Union, establish Justice, insure domestic Tranquility, provide for the common defense, promote the general Welfare, and secure the Blessings of Liberty to ourselves and our Posterity, do ordain and establish this Constitution for the United States of America.*

This one sentence outlined the goals of the framers' exercise in democracy. America was now one people rather than 13 individual states. This nation had certain hopes—for justice, tranquility, and liberty. Its sovereign power rested in a new constitution that would guide a new national government, a union more perfect than the one that existed under the Articles of Confederation.

The new constitution was unlike any seen before. It created a republican government, granting indirect power to the voting public, whose desires would be served by a representative government. Until that time, such a system seemed possible only for small countries such as Greece or Switzerland.

### A Republican Form of Government

At the end of the Convention, a woman asked Ben Franklin what kind of government the delegates had created—a republic or a monarchy? "A republic, Madam," responded Franklin, "a Republic, if you can keep it."[22]

Believing that the people are more interested in their own welfare than the good of the whole and realizing that the size of the new nation prevented implementing a pure democracy, the framers created a republican form of limited government with built-in checks and balances. Instead of governing themselves, the people elected representatives to protect their interests. These representatives could, however, vote against the desires of their constituents if it was for the good of the whole nation. One of the main constitutional changes in the American system of government over the years has been a shift from the purely republican system of government created by the framers to a system that is much more democratic and inclusive of

**THINKING CRITICALLY**

The possibility of a law granting full voting rights and representation to the District of Columbia is now being considered. Do you think it should pass?

more people. Six times in our history, the Constitution has been amended to extend the voting base in federal elections, thus giving more people a direct voice in their government. These changes were the Fifteenth Amendment, which extended the vote to the newly freed slaves; the Seventeenth Amendment, which permitted direct popular election of the Senate; the Nineteenth Amendment, which extended the right to vote to women; the Twenty-third Amendment, which gave District of Columbia voters electoral college representation to vote for president; the Twenty-fourth Amendment, which abolished the poll tax that required people to pay to vote; and the Twenty-sixth Amendment, which extended the vote to citizens over the age of 18. Finally, fewer representatives now act as independent "trustees," choosing instead to serve as "delegates" instructed by the voters through public opinion polls, mail and email counts, and the media (see Chapter 4). In these ways, the American republic has indeed approached democracy.

**THINKING CRITICALLY**

It has been roughly 40 years since the voting franchise was extended to 18-year-olds. When did you feel prepared to vote? Do you think that the voting age should be lowered, and if so, to what year?

Does moving closer to a system of pure democracy place the republican system designed by the framers to protect liberty in danger? Not at all. The Constitution's mechanisms for limiting power provide an adequate check on the actions of the leaders and the demands of the people. A judiciary more powerful than the framers could ever have imagined, using the Constitution and its amendments to preserve liberty, also keeps the republic strong. In the end, just how far the country actually goes toward direct democracy depends on how much confidence the people have in the motives and wisdom of their leaders.

## THE GOVERNMENTAL POWERS

You can better understand the results of the framers' efforts by taking two different approaches to studying the Constitution and the distribution of power: a horizontal view and a vertical view.

### Horizontal Powers

Governmental powers are apportioned *horizontally* among the branches of the national government—the executive, legislative, and judicial branches—according to the system of *separation of powers* (see Figure 2.1). Each major branch of government received a separate set of powers so that no one branch could become too powerful. The first three articles of the Constitution are concerned solely with the powers, responsibilities, and selection processes for each separate branch and include specific prohibitions against a person becoming a member of two branches at the same time.

But James Madison understood that separating the powers among three distinct branches would be insufficient unless each branch had the power to "check" the other, preventing encroachment into its own sphere. A system of *checks and balances* was incorporated into the structure, giving each branch the power to approve, disapprove, or alter what the other branches do. "Ambition must be made to counteract ambition," Madison counseled in *The Federalist*, no. 51, on checks and balances (printed in its entirety in Appendix 6). "If men were angels," he explained, "no government would be necessary. If angels were to govern men, neither external nor internal controls on government would be necessary. In framing a government which is to be administered by men over men, the great difficulty lies in this: You must first enable the government to control the governed; and in the next place oblige it to control itself."[23]

Although the president nominates ambassadors, cabinet officials, and justices, the Senate can reject those choices by refusing to give the majority vote required for its "advice and consent." Congress passes laws, but the president can then veto them. Congress can react by overriding a presidential veto with a two-thirds vote of both houses. Theoretically, the president can then refuse to execute the new law, but

**BRANCHES OF GOVERNMENT**

| POWERS OF GOVERNMENT | Legislative | Executive | Judicial |
|---|---|---|---|
| **Legislative** | • Makes federal laws<br>• Institutes and collects taxes, duties, imposts, and excises to pay debts and provide for the common defense<br>• Coins and borrows money<br>• Regulates commerce with foreign nations and among the states<br>• Establishes post offices and promotes the progress of science<br>• Creates lower federal courts | • Can veto congressional legislation<br>• Recommends laws | • Interprets laws or invalidates them as unconstitutional |
| **Executive** | • Can override the veto of the president<br>• Can refuse to confirm presidential appointments<br>• Can impeach the executive<br>• Can refuse to ratify presidential treaties | • Responsible for implementing federal laws<br>• Can call Congress into special session<br>• Submits legislation to Congress<br>• Makes treaties with foreign nations<br>• Is commander in chief of the armed forces<br>• Appoints executive officials and ambassadors | • Interprets presidential actions or invalidates them as unconstitutional |
| **Judicial** | • Can eliminate or refuse to create lower federal courts<br>• Can refuse to implement judicial decisions<br>• Can change jurisdiction of federal courts<br>• Can impeach judges<br>• Confirms federal judges | • Can appoint federal judges<br>• Can pardon people | • Can interpret laws or actions of the executive<br>• Can invalidate as unconstitutional acts of either Congress or the executive |

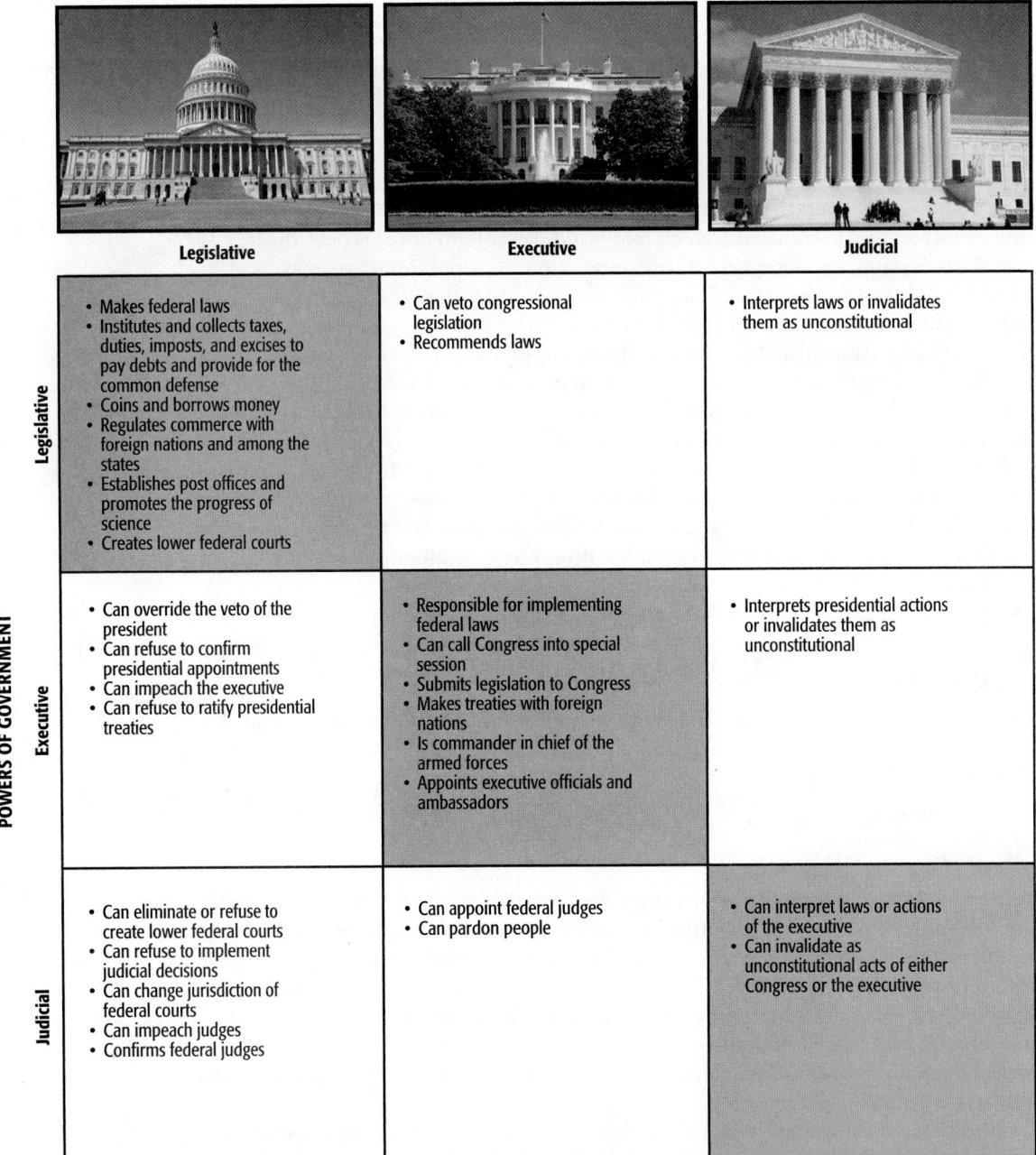

**FIGURE 2.1** Constitutional Powers

The green portions of this figure display the powers allotted to each of the branches and show the separation of powers. The remainder of the diagram indicates the powers that each of the branches holds as a check on the other branches. Each of the branches has primary responsibility in the executive, legislative, or judicial realms, but each also shares powers with the other two branches.

**judicial review**
The power of the Supreme Court established in *Marbury* v. *Madison* to overturn acts of the president, Congress, and the states if those acts violate the Constitution. This power makes the Supreme Court the final interpreter of the Constitution.

the president is kept in check by the fact that Congress has an impeachment power if "treason, bribery, or High Crimes or Misdemeanors" are committed. The judiciary has the power to interpret laws or use the power of **judicial review** to judge the constitutionality of, and thereby check the actions of, the other branches (a power not in the Constitution but established by the Court itself in 1803). This was the case in the Supreme Court's ruling against Abraham Lincoln's suspension of the

**writ of habeas corpus** as well as the Court's changing the legal standard for restricting First Amendment rights in reaction to Woodrow Wilson's actions during the First World War. Meanwhile, the judiciary itself is checked by the president's prerogative of nominating justices (with the advice and consent of the Senate) and Congress's power to create lower federal courts, alter its jurisdiction, attempt to re-pass laws overturned by the federal courts, or change the Supreme Court's appellate jurisdiction. This power emerged once again in 2011, when Congress was asked by over 100 law professors to pass a new ethics law applying to the Supreme Court, in response to some controversial off-the-Court actions by individual justices who later ruled in cases seemingly related to that behavior, thus raising questions about their impartiality.

Government functions often require creation of independent agencies or actors to accomplish tasks that bridge the "separation of powers" issue by mixing the functions of the three branches. Some examples of these agencies include the Securities and Exchange Commission, which regulates the activities of Wall Street; the Federal Reserve Board, which regulates the monetary and banking system; and the National Commission on Terrorist Attacks Upon the United States, known as the 9/11 Commission, created in late 2002 to investigate the World Trade Center and Pentagon attacks on September 11, 2001. This commission's mid-2004 hearings and its resulting best-selling report offered a riveting description of the intelligence failings enabling the attacks to succeed and a series of recommendations for laws designed to tighten the nation's defense against terrorism. The creation of the new Consumer Protection Board in 2011, designed to protect borrowers after the banking excesses that helped cause the Great Recession was hampered by a Republican-led Senate filibuster delaying the appointment of the agency's head.

Because the framers deliberately allowed for elasticity in each branch's powers, the resulting government was destined to become one in which powers overlap. As Justice Robert Jackson described it, "While the Constitution diffuses power the better to secure liberty, it also contemplates that practice will integrate the dispersed powers into a workable government."[24] The result over the years has not been a strict separation of powers but, as political scientist Richard Neustadt has said, a "government of separated institutions sharing powers." By this, he means that each institution frequently exercises the powers of the others: judges can make laws, Congress can interpret laws, and presidents can do both.[25]

## Vertical Powers

*Vertical powers* refer to the relationship between the centralized national government and the individual state governments. This distribution of power is known as **federalism.** We cover the subject of federalism more extensively in the next chapter.

During the framing, the delegates tried to create the right balance of power between the national government and the state governments. Having seen that the confederation of states did not work, they wanted to give the national government sufficient authority to govern yet leave the state governments enough power to accomplish what they needed at the local level. The framers created a national government of **delegated powers,** meaning powers expressly granted or enumerated and limited in nature, while leaving the state governments with general **reserved powers,** or the remainder of the authority not specifically delegated to the national government. For example, to avoid the problem of erratic state-by-state foreign policy under the Articles of Confederation, that power was delegated to the national government. However, state governments that wish to seek business investments with foreign government may do so using the power to improve the economic welfare of their citizens, reserved for states. Additionally, the federal government has no power to regulate relations among its citizens, as in marriage laws, or power to create a criminal code. These **police powers,** or the power to regulate the health, morals, public safety, and welfare of citizens, were left to the states. Using these powers, in 2011, states such as Arizona, Utah, Georgia, and Alabama, unhappy with the unwillingness of the national government to pass a comprehensive law dealing with illegal

**writ of habeas corpus**
A Latin term meaning literally "you should have the body," this is a judicial order enabling jailed prisoners to come into the court, or return to the court after being convicted and sentenced, in order to determine the legality of their detention. By constitutional rules, it can be suspended only in times of crisis by Congress.

**federalism**
The relationship between the centralized national government and the individual state governments.

**delegated powers**
Powers expressly granted or enumerated in the Constitution and limited in nature.

**reserved powers**
Powers not assigned by the Constitution to the national government but left to the states or to the people, according to the Tenth Amendment.

**police powers**
The powers to regulate health, morals, public safety, and welfare, which are reserved to the states.

**devolution**
Reducing the size and authority of the federal government by returning programs to the states.

**necessary and proper clause**
A clause in Article I, Section 8, Clause 18 of the Constitution stating that Congress can "make all Laws which shall be necessary and proper for carrying into Execution the foregoing Powers."

immigrants, have empowered their police forces and various other governmental officials to check the U.S. citizenship credentials of people they suspect might not be citizens.

By viewing the Constitution from a vertical perspective, other features become apparent. For instance, to remedy lack of central economic control under the Articles of Confederation, Congress has the power over commerce *among* the states, but the states individually govern commerce *within* their own boundaries. To handle a rebellion, such as Shays's Rebellion, the president was made commander in chief, and Congress received power both to raise and support an army and to send it into battle. States, however, retained their own powers over a police force to keep order at home. The most important element of the vertical power is the so-called *supremacy clause* (Article VI), which states that in any controversy between the states and federal laws, Constitution, or treaties, *federal dictates will always prevail.* Acceptance of this provision ensured that sovereign states would never again be the dominating power they were under the Articles of Confederation.

The success of this reordering of governmental priorities between the national and state governments depends on one's point of view. Many of these powers have been interpreted to expand the national power to such a degree that individual states today have much less power than many of the framers ever intended. Some praise the uniformity and comprehensive nature of such a government, whereas others express concerns about the burgeoning size and remoteness of the national government and the need for policy innovation by the individual state governments. As we learn in Chapter 3, this debate continues to this day with the issue of **devolution,** or returning governmental programs and powers to the states to reduce the size and authority of the national government. Gains from limiting national government, however, may lead to variation in the nature of rights and protections from state to state, as in the early twentieth century and before. As a modern example of this, some "tea party" and libertarian conservatives are calling for the passage of a so-called Repeal Amendment, under which if two-thirds of the states vote to repeal a congressional law, it would be overturned. Thus, allowing the states effectively to veto laws could have the effect of re-creating aspects of the state-centered Articles of Confederation.[26]

## The Articles of the Constitution

The Constitution is divided into seven articles, each with a unique purpose. The first three apportion power among the three branches of national government; two others (Articles IV and VI) apportion power between national and state governments; the remaining two articles (Articles V and VII) lay out procedures for amending and ratifying the Constitution. Gaps were deliberately left in each of these articles, and the language was given a certain elasticity to allow the Constitution to expand and evolve as the nation needed.

**Article I** Article I sets forth the powers of the legislative branch. For the framers, this was the longest and most important article (and therefore the first) because it sought to expand the powers of the old Confederation Congress while still preventing the omnipotent power of the state legislatures under the Articles of Confederation. This intent is clear from the limiting nature of the first words of the article: "All legislative Powers herein granted shall be vested in a Congress of the United States." The article then contains a long list of specific and narrowly drawn powers. Those include the powers to declare war, borrow and coin money, regulate interstate commerce, and raise and support an army. But the list is not as restrictive as it seems at first; the article also mandates that Congress can "make all Laws which shall be necessary and proper for carrying into Execution the foregoing Powers." As we see in the next chapter, this **necessary and proper clause,** with its vague grant of power, has allowed a broad interpretation of Congress's powers under the Constitution. Such built-in flexibility in what became known as the "elastic clause" makes the Constitution just as viable today as it was in 1787.

### THINKING CRITICALLY

If you were on the Supreme Court, would you allow a president to withhold information from Congress in forming policy that deals with the war on terrorism? If so, how would you determine how much information he or she could withhold? How would your response differ if it appeared that the White House executive was withholding information for political reasons, or keeping it from members of the other political party?

From the vertical perspective, Article I, Section 9, denies Congress the power to place a tax or duty on articles exported from any state. Moreover, under Section 10, states are denied the power to execute treaties, coin money, impair the obligation of contracts, and lay any imposts or duties on imports or exports without the consent of Congress.

**Article II** Article II outlines the powers of the executive. At first glance, it seems to limit the president's power to granting pardons, making treaties, receiving foreign ambassadors, nominating certain officials, and being the "commander in chief" of the army and navy. But, as with the legislative branch, the executive branch was granted an elastic clause in the ambiguous first sentence of the article: "The executive Power shall be vested in a President of the United States of America." As we see in Chapter 5 on the presidency, broad interpretation of the words *executive power* provides a president with considerable power. For example, should the life of a Supreme Court justice or a member of Congress be threatened, it is within the "inherent powers" of the president to provide protection using a U.S. marshal. Or, should a member of the president's administration refuse to testify about executive branch actions before Congress, a president can claim "executive privilege," arguing that one of the president's subordinates must keep previous advice secret.

This article also empowers the president to make judicial appointments and to veto bills passed by both houses of Congress. Thus, the president can check the powers of the other two branches. Article II has additional elasticity built into it in Section 3, which states, "[The President] shall take Care that the Laws be faithfully executed." A president who disagrees with congressional legislation can "faithfully" execute the law by reinterpreting it or by devising a new law. For instance, if Congress appropriates too much money for a program, the president can "take Care" by *impounding*—that is, either delaying or refusing to spend—the full appropriation. Thomas Jefferson did this in 1803, when he withheld money for gunboats on the Mississippi. However, when Richard Nixon tried to expand this power, using it not to save money but to derail programs with which he disagreed, both Congress and the Supreme Court overturned his action. This power can be a source of expansion of presidential power. President Bush, operating under what his aides called the "unitary presidency," which was a combination of both the "exclusive" and "inherent" presidential powers, did not like congressional legislation dealing with the restrictions against torture in the questioning of terrorism suspects and the handling of alleged terrorist detainees. So the president issued a "signing statement," which he had done in more than 800 instances, interpreting the act to mean something other than Congress intended.[27] Sometimes the "take Care" clause leads a president to act against the wishes of Congress. In the American governmental system, though, this does not give the president unlimited powers. For example, President Obama signed an executive order to close the terrorist prison at Guantanamo Bay, Cuba, surrounded by generals who supported the move. However, he was greeted on the floor of Congress by a series of speeches vowing that the suspects would never be allowed in those representatives' states, and so Obama found it difficult to close the facility.

**Article III** Article III outlines the powers of the judicial branch. As we see in more detail in Chapter 6, the framers provided the most vague grant of powers to the judiciary because they could not agree on the role of this branch. This article establishes a Supreme Court only and grants Congress the power to "ordain and establish" inferior federal courts and to change

The maximum security military prison established by the Bush administration for suspected terrorists at Guantanamo Bay, Cuba, known as Gitmo or "Camp XRay," was promised to be closed by the Obama administration. However, it has not yet happened. The question, though, is where the prisoners will then be housed.

## THINKING CRITICALLY

During the late 18th century, old age was considered to be someone in his or her 50s or 60s, and a person 35 years old was old enough to be considered for the presidency. Did the framers expect that justices would serve on the Supreme Court into their late 70s and 80s? Do you think life tenure on the Supreme Court promotes democracy? If not, how would you change the provision to both promote democracy and preserve judicial independence?

## Approaching Democracy Timeline

### Constitutional Rights During and After Crisis Times

| | |
|---|---|
| 1787–1788 | Constitution written and ratified. |
| 1791 | Bill of Rights ratified. |
| 1798 | Alien and Sedition Acts restrict rights. |
| 1802 | Jeffersonian pardons. |
| 1861 | Lincoln Civil War actions (suspend habeas corpus). |
| 1861 | *Ex Parte Merryman* Taney rules against Lincoln on habeas corpus. |
| 1861 | Lincoln ignores Taney judicial ruling. |
| 1866 | *Ex Parte Milligan* Military courts do not apply to citizens. |
| 1919 | Wilson era wartime free speech cases denying First Amendment protection. |
| 1940 | Smith Act (Alien Registration Act). |
| 1943 | *Hirabayashi* v. *U.S.* Curfew for Japanese Americans constitutional. |
| 1944 | *Korematsu* v. *U.S.* Japanese American internment camps. |
| 1944 | *Ex Parte Endo* Loyal citizens must be released. |
| 1950s | McCarthy Communist "witch hunts." |
| 1951 | *Dennis* v. *U.S.* Supreme Court upholds Communist convictions. |
| 1967 | *U.S.* v. *Robel* Supreme Court guts Smith Act. |
| 1988 | Internment camp apology and reparations. |
| 2001 | USA Patriot Act enacted. |
| 2001 | Congressional Authorization for the Use of Military Force (AUMF) passed to permit harsh "war on terror" investigation practices. |
| 2004–2009 | In several Guantanamo Bay court cases, Supreme Court extends civil rights to terror suspects. |
| 2009 | Obama promises reversal of Bush anti-terrorism policies and abandonment of torture questioning of suspects. |

☐ Democratic ☐ Neutral ☐ Undemocratic

*(continued)*

the Supreme Court appellate jurisdiction. Federal judges have the power to decide "Cases, in Law and Equity" arising under the Constitution and also to interpret federal laws and federal treaties.

One unique example of Congress's effect on federal court jurisdiction came on March 21, 2005. A private bill was passed to grant the parents of Theresa "Terri" Marie Schiavo of Florida, standing in the federal district court of Florida, to raise once again the issue of whether to reconnect the feeding and hydration tubes for their comatose daughter over her husband's objections. This appeal had already been twice denied by the Supreme Court. As a result, the case was heard once again by the federal and state courts, but was again denied.[28]

Federal judges serve for life—as long as they maintain good behavior—and are removable only by impeachment. In 2005, the debate regarding term limits for aged and sometimes infirm federal judges grew, fueled by Chief Justice William Rehnquist's five-month absence during his unsuccessful battle with thyroid cancer. Six years later, with the four justices over the age of 70, and a majority of five "Baby Boomers" under the age of 64, those calls continue to be discussed.

**Articles IV Through VII** Article IV establishes guidelines for interstate relations, absent in the Articles of Confederation, under which a state could disregard the laws of other states; it could also treat its own citizens one way and citizens of other states another way. This article establishes uniformity by guaranteeing that "full Faith and Credit" must be granted by all states to the "Public Acts, Records, and Judicial Proceedings of every other State." In addition, citizens of all states must receive the same "Privileges and Immunities" of citizens of "the several States." Divorces in one state must be recognized by all, and a decision to avoid repaying a state-financed college loan or even a parking fine by crossing state boundaries is ill advised. Those obligations are in force in all states of the union, as individuals who try to avoid paying child support or contest legal custody of children by moving out of state are discovering. In June 2011, when New York became the sixth and largest state (along with Massachusetts, New Hampshire, Vermont, Connecticut, and Iowa) to allow gay marriages, it created a situation in which some states—perhaps even ones that ban gay marriages, such as Nebraska and California—might be asked to observe these agreements. When that happens, the case will likely come before the U.S. Supreme Court for adjudication.

Article V outlines the procedure for amending the Constitution. The framers understood that changes might be necessary to correct imperfections in their original work or to update it for future use. This change took place, for example, with the debate over the Equal Rights Amendment in the 1970s and the Gay Marriage Ban Amendment proposed by President Bush in 2004 and subsequently considered by Congress.

Article VI deals with federal–state relations and the financial obligations of the new government. This article contains the supremacy clause, affirming the predominance of the national government, and also ensures that all prior debts against the United States are valid under the new Constitution. Picking up on the gay marriage issue previously mentioned, in time the Supreme Court will also be asked to rule on whether the state gay marriage laws can stand in the face of the 1996 federal Defense of Marriage law that limits marriage to one man and one woman and instructs states banning such marriages from being required to enforce same-sex marriages from other states. Moreover, it states that all national officers must swear an oath of office supporting the Constitution and cannot be subjected to a religious test.

Article VII explains the process for ratifying the Constitution. The Approaching Democracy Timeline for this chapter assesses the impact of a series of events during crisis times on American democracy.

**Approaching Democracy Timeline *(continued)***

| | |
|---|---|
| **2010** | Supreme Court approves Congress's law permitting federal government to prohibit teaching and counseling organizations labeled as terrorist despite First Amendment free speech protections. |
| **2011** | Several controversial provisions of the 2001 U.S.A. Patriot Act are extended by Congress. |
| **2011** | Obama Justice Department abandons plans to try terror suspects in New York City, and plans trials in Guantanamo prison. |
| **2011** | Osama bin Laden killed. |

☐ Democratic ☐ Neutral ☐ Undemocratic

# RATIFICATION: THE BATTLE FOR THE CONSTITUTION

2.6 *How did the people in the constitutional ratification period lobby for and understand their new democratic government?*

Drafting the Constitution was just the first step toward creating a new government. The vote for or against the new document was now in the hands of the various state conventions. According to Article VII, 9 of the 13 states had to ratify the Constitution for it to take effect. Realistically, though, everyone understood that unless the most populous states ratified—Pennsylvania, Massachusetts, New York, and Virginia—the Constitution would never succeed.

Ratifying the Constitution involved hardball politics. This reality is often surprising to those who believe that creating the Constitution was a nonpartisan and academic process of debating the philosophical issues concerning a new government. A close look at this political crisis is instructive both for seeing how the nation was formed and understanding why arguments over constitutional issues continue to rage today.

As in every good political fight, the side best organized at the beginning had the advantage. Those in favor of the Constitution, many of whom were nationalists at the Convention, took the lead by calling themselves the **Federalists.** Thus, they stole the semantic high ground by taking the name of supporters of the federal form of government under the Articles of Confederation. The true supporters of

**Federalists**
Those in favor of the Constitution, many of whom were nationalists at the Convention.

**Antifederalists**
Strong states' rights advocates who organized in opposition to the ratification of the U.S. Constitution prior to its adoption.

the federal form of government, the states' rights advocates, had to call themselves the **Antifederalists.** This group included most but not all of the Convention's antinationalists.

## *The Federalist Papers*

The debate over the Constitution raged in newspapers and hand-distributed pamphlets, the only sources of communication in that period. Federalists Alexander Hamilton, James Madison, and John Jay wrote 85 essays in New York newspapers under the pen name of *Publius* (a Latin term meaning "public man"), seeking to influence the New York state convention in favor of ratification. All these articles were intended to answer the arguments of the states' rights advocates that the new central government would be too powerful and too inclined to expand further, and thus likely to destroy liberty. Hamilton, Madison, and Jay argued instead that without this new Constitution, the states would break apart and the nation would fail. With it, they reasoned, the government would act in the national interest while preserving liberty. Later collected as *The Federalist Papers: A Commentary on the Constitution of the United States,* these pieces offer what historian Henry Steele Commager calls "a handbook on how the Constitution should operate." Although these essays had little effect on the ratification debate, generations of judges, politicians, and scholars have considered them, together with Madison's notes of the Convention, to indicate "the intent of the framers" in creating the Constitution. (See, e.g., *The Federalist,* nos. 10 and 51, in Appendixes 5 and 6, respectively.) For this reason, many scholars consider *The Federalist Papers* the most important work of political theory in U.S. history.

In opposition, the Antifederalists made their case in scores of articles such as those by Robert Yates, the *Letters of Brutus;* Luther Martin, *Genuine Information;* and Mercy Otis Warren, *Observations on the New Constitution . . . by a Columbian Patriot.* These critics understood that the central government needed more power than it had under the Articles of Confederation, but they feared that the structure established in the Convention would supersede the state governments, rendering them obsolete. By placing too much power in the hands of a government so far removed from the people, they argued, the new government would likely expand its power and rule by force rather than by the consent of the governed. They sought ways to establish a better balance between the power of the central government and the states by placing further checks on the newly established central government.

## Federalists versus Antifederalists

The Federalists and Antifederalists differed on the most fundamental theoretical level. The Federalists, led by Hamilton and Madison, believed that *the people* had created the Constitution, and not *the states,* and they argued that a strong central government best represented the sovereignty of the people. The Federalists sought energy and leadership from a centralized government that would unite the entire nation, thus safeguarding the interests of the people. They also argued for expandable powers of central government to meet the needs of the people and to enable the government to respond to any emergencies that arise.

The Antifederalists argued that the Constitution was created by the states, meaning that the national government's power was carved out of the states' power. Accordingly, they insisted that the states should remain independent and distinct, rather than be led by a supreme national government. The Antifederalists sought to preserve the liberty and rights of the minorities by bolstering individual state governments that would be closer to the people.

In addition to these theoretical differences between Federalist and Antifederalist views, the two groups differed over who would have the authority for solving practical, real-world problems. The Federalists, supporters of a strong central government, realized that some problems spill over state boundaries and need to be resolved by a neutral, national arbiter. These problems include fishing rights in interstate waterways, the coinage of money, and interstate roadways. Federalists believed that a single solution to these problems would be more sensible and cost-effective than having each state devise and pay for its own program. They reasoned that the states would place their economies at a competitive disadvantage by attempting to resolve problems by themselves. While the Federalists were thinking of interstate commerce, such problems as organized crime and pollution control—not to mention control of the Internet, interstate sales of wines, and medical uses of marijuana—would later arise to prove them correct about the need for a centralized source of authority.

Not surprisingly, the Antifederalists disagreed with the Federalists. To them, the government closest to the people, and thus most accountable to them, could best be trusted to tailor solutions to problems to fit each state. In addition, states appeared the best protectors of personal liberty, because the fear existed that the new central government would be just as oppressive toward individual rights as the British had been.

Out of these two opposing groups, two political parties would emerge. George Washington's Federalist party, supporting a strong nationalist government, was an outgrowth of the Federalist position. This party evolved first into the Whig party and then into the Republican Party. The Antifederalists emerged in the Democratic-Republican Party of Thomas Jefferson, and later James Madison, who grew to oppose the use of federal power, which supported states' rights and later became the Democratic Party.

It is clear from their arguments that the Federalists and Antifederalists were motivated by different fears. In one of the most famous of *The Federalist Papers,* no. 10, James Madison tried to explain how the new democratic government would overcome political differences "sown in the nature of man." The nation, he argued, is divided into **factions,** "a number of citizens, whether amounting to a majority or a minority of the whole, who are united and actuated by some common impulse or passion or . . . interest."[29] These groups of people, much like interest groups today, were united in taking positions on controversial issues (such as slavery) largely along the lines of property classifications—for example, farmers versus the manufacturing class—and would seek to have the government protect their own interests to the exclusion of all others. Madison then sought to explain in this article and later in *The Federalist,* no. 51, how the new government was designed to prevent an "interested and overbearing majority" of the citizens taking away the liberty of those in the minority. Lacking a way to eliminate the divisive *causes* of factions (there will always be rich versus poor and city dwellers versus farming interests), Madison explained how the new system of representative government was designed to control the harmful *effects* of factions. The key was to increase the size of the political unit, thus "extend[ing] the sphere" beyond the smaller states, in which minorities could easily be outnumbered and oppressed. To accomplish this aim, a new larger central government, with a greater "number of electors" could increase the number of factions and "take in a greater variety of parties and interests" in order to divide the polity in different ways. As a result, they had a better chance for political protection.

In *The Federalist,* no. 51, Madison expanded his argument to show how the separation of powers would protect liberty by allowing each of the parts of the government to "be the means of keeping each other in their proper places." The two-year term of the popularly elected House of Representatives, the six-year term of the Senate (elected by state legislatures), and the four-year term of the president (elected by the electoral college), ensured that each branch of government would represent different groups. The common people's voice in the House would turn over quickly and be restrained by the long-term elite, aristocratic view of the Senate and the national perspective of the president. Moreover, the powers of each branch would

**factions**
According to James Madison in *The Federalist,* no. 10: "A number of citizens, whether amounting to a majority or a minority of the whole, who are united and actuated by some common impulse or passion or . . . interest."

## QUICK REVIEW

The Federalists

- The Federalists believed *the people,* not *the states,* created the Constitution.
- They sought a centralized government that would unite the entire nation.
- The Federalists argued that the powers of the central government should be expandable to meet the needs of the people.
- They realized that some problems spill over state boundaries and need to be resolved by a neutral, national arbiter.

The Antifederalists

- The Antifederalists argued that the Constitution was created by the states.
- They insisted that the states should remain independent and distinct.
- They sought individual state governments that would be closer to the people.
- The Antifederalists believed government could tailor solutions to problems to fit each state.
- They believed states were the best protectors of personal liberty.

check the others. When combined with the system of federalism, in which national and state governments checked each other, it was hoped that no single majority faction could dominate American politics because every group would have effective representation somewhere. Those in a minority in one branch of the national government or in one state might find a representative in another branch of government or in another state.

At the other end of the spectrum, the Antifederalists argued that the central government could not be trusted; they feared that the Constitution had traded English tyranny for tyranny by the central government at home. Worried that the central government would overrun the states and the rights of those in the minority, they asked what guarantees the Constitution contained to protect and preserve the rights of all Americans.

As far apart as these two groups were at the time of the drafting of the Constitution, some means had to be found to secure agreement between them if the new document was to be ratified. The answer was the addition of a protective list of rights to the new Constitution.

## Ratification by Way of Compromise: A Bill of Rights

2.7 *Was the final ratification of the Constitution by the states the result of democratic theory or political compromise?*

Although the Convention delegates had repeatedly refused to include in the new Constitution a long list of rights to be protected, the issue did not end with its signing. The Antifederalists in various states insisted during the ratification debate that a list of amendments be included, guaranteeing that the new central government could not restrict certain rights. The Federalists argued that a constitutional guarantee of rights was unnecessary because citizens were already adequately protected by the Constitution or by the constitutions of the individual states.

The debate over adding amendments to the Constitution presented an interesting philosophical dilemma. Many believed that if the new government did not in fact already protect these rights, it should not have been created in the first place. If it did in fact protect them, why was it necessary to repeat those rights in a series of amendments? In the end, philosophy gave way to politics. Following the tradition of the Magna Carta, compacts, social contracts, and state bills of rights, it was agreed that the people would see their rights guaranteed in writing in the Constitution. In fact, the expectation of such amendments helped sell the Constitution.

## Politics the Old-Fashioned Way: A Look at the Battle for Ratification

Once the constitutional debates moved from being a secret discussion among aristocratic political elites in Philadelphia into the public arena of state ratification debates, the political tactics were very different. The debates were hardly genteel. Initially, ratification seemed inevitable. After all, the Federalists had the dual advantages of an existing document that defined the terms of the debate and disorganized opposition movement. Within eight months after the Constitution had been signed, eight states had ratified the document. However, the battles in two of them—Pennsylvania and Massachusetts—indicated just how difficult it would be to secure the critical ninth state, not to mention the two large-state holdouts—Virginia and New York.

Proponents of the Constitution were willing to go to great lengths to achieve success, as was made clear in Pennsylvania. Ben Franklin forced the State Assembly, which was about to adjourn, to appoint a ratifying convention even before enough copies of the Constitution arrived for everyone to read. Seeking to derail this effort, the Antifederalists hid, thinking they might deny Franklin a voting quorum. The sergeant at arms was directed to take the necessary action to make a vote possible. A mob of angry Federalists volunteered to help him, roaming the streets of Philadelphia looking for any missing assemblymen they could find. They eventually found two assemblymen hiding in their rooms over a local tavern and, after dragging them through the streets of Philadelphia, threw them into the assembly hall while a mob of Constitution supporters blocked their escape. Not surprisingly, these two men cast their votes against a ratifying convention, but the measure passed by a vote of 44 to 2.

Protests against such strong-arm tactics were ignored. Federalist mobs used similar tactics to ensure that the final ratifying vote favored the Constitution by a 2 to 1 margin. The damage to the Federalists' prestige in Philadelphia was so great that James Wilson, a leading Federalist, was nearly beaten to death by a mob of angry Antifederalists weeks later.

In Massachusetts, clever political strategy, rather than strong-arm tactics, turned the tide. Three hundred fifty delegates, many of them from the less populous western part of the state where the Antifederalists dominated, met in Boston on January 8, 1788. The opponents of the Constitution held a slight numerical advantage. Governor John Hancock, a Federalist but also a cagey politician, was so unsure of how the vote would go that he decided to stay away, complaining that he was suffering from the gout. To convince Hancock to join them, the Federalists dangled the possibility that if Virginia failed to ratify the Constitution, it would leave George Washington outside the new nation; then Hancock would be the most likely prospect for the presidency. With that, Hancock's gout miraculously abated, and he was carried to the convention as a hero, with his legs wrapped in flannel. There he proposed a series of amendments protecting such local concerns as taxation and merchants' rights. These amendments, an early version of what would later become the Bill of Rights, changed the terms of the debate. Now those who supported the Constitution could vote for it, and those who opposed it could vote for the document as amended. On February 6, 1788, Massachusetts ratified the Constitution by only 19 votes (187 to 168). Hancock's amendment strategy was later used by other states to smooth the way to ratification.

By June 2, 1788, with only one state needed to ratify the Constitution and put it into effect, the eyes of the nation turned to Virginia, where some found the notion of "the people" running a democratic government preposterous. Patrick Henry, leader of the Antifederalists, argued that even the first three words of the document were wrong: "Who authorized them to speak the language of *We the people,* instead of, *We the states?* States are the characteristics and the soul of a confederation."[30] But James Madison, thoroughly convinced of the need for a national government, saw no danger to the states, saying that the national government's "delegated powers" would keep it within limits. This sentiment could not persuade George Mason, who had refused to sign the Constitution: "Where is the barrier drawn between the government, and the rights of the citizens?"[31]

The key to success was Edmund Randolph, the politically ambitious 34-year-old governor of Virginia, who had proposed the Virginia Plan in the Convention and then, unhappy with the outcome of the debates, refused to sign the final version of the Constitution. He switched to Madison's side in the ratification debate, arguing that he would "assent to the lopping [of his right arm] before I assent to the dissolution of the union." Randolph urged the acceptance of subsequent amendments to the document just as Hancock had done in Massachusetts. Randolph's argument proved decisive. By the time Virginia voted on June 25, 1788, to ratify the Constitution by a narrow margin of ten votes, New Hampshire had already become the ninth state to ratify. Nevertheless, Virginia's size made its ratification vote important in securing the success of the new government.

A week after Virginia's vote, New York ratified the Constitution by a razor-thin 30–27 margin. North Carolina waited until after the Bill of Rights had been sent to

The Westboro Baptist church's controversial form of protest, against gay rights in America and the military, was protected by the Supreme Court in 2010 as part of the First Amendment's Freedom of Speech.

the states for ratification before adding its assent in November 1789. And Rhode Island continued to take its time, waiting until May 29, 1790, to ratify the Constitution by a narrow 34–32 vote.

This highly political debate over the Constitution was proof that the new system would work because democracy had worked. The American people had freely and without war debated and chosen their new form of government. They had put aside their individual needs and local interests for the common good. As Benjamin Rush, a Philadelphia physician who signed the Declaration of Independence and lived to see the Constitution ratified, said, "'Tis done, we have become a nation."[32]

## Adoption of the Bill of Rights

When the First Congress convened in 1789, Representative Roger Sherman of Connecticut, the only man to sign all three of this nation's founding documents, was then serving as a member of a select committee appointed by the House of Representatives to sift through more than 200 amendments proposed in state debates to compose a possible Bill of Rights consisting of 11 amendments.[33] The Committee never mentioned this draft, instead choosing to send 17 amendments to Congress for its consideration, with 12 being passed and sent to the states for ratification. Ten were ratified in 1791, becoming known as the **Bill of Rights.** The first eight amendments drafted by the First Congress guaranteed a variety of rights against government control and provided procedural safeguards in criminal trials and against arbitrary governmental action. The Ninth and Tenth Amendments were intended to describe the new constitutional structure, assuring that the people or the states would retain rights not listed in the Constitution or powers not delegated to the national government. The amendments placed limits on government power by prohibiting the *national* government from intruding on fundamental rights and liberties. However, the rights of the people against *state* intrusion would be left to the individual state constitutions and legislatures. As you will see in Chapter 13, though, over time America would further approach democracy because the Supreme Court applied all but a few of the provisions of the Bill of Rights to the states as well.

**Bill of Rights**
The first ten amendments to the Constitution, added in 1791.

# UPDATING THE CONSTITUTION

2.8 *How has America's Constitution and democracy evolved and become more inclusive over time?*

The authors of the Constitution viewed it as a lasting document—one that would endure long after the debates and ratification. They did not believe, as Thomas Jefferson and George Washington did, that a new constitution should be written every generation, or 20 years, or so. To create a lasting document, the framers drafted a constitution that included an amendment process to allow for adjustments to their handiwork. In addition, the Supreme Court would play a role, along with the pressures of social and political change, to alter a flexible and responsive constitution. This way, the Constitution could be kept timely and current. But the Constitution is not easy to alter, no matter how strong, compelling, or passionate the need. Table 2.3 lists the Bill of Rights to the U.S. Constitution.

## Updating the Constitution Through the Amendment Process

The framers deliberately made the amendment process difficult, thus placing the Constitution beyond the temporary passions of the people, but they did not require unanimity, which had already failed in the Articles of Confederation. Clearly, the amendment process was to be used for only the most serious issues.

Article V establishes a two-stage amendment process, resembling the one used to approve the Constitution. First, there must be a **proposal** for a change that the states must then **ratify.** The framers wanted to ensure that each new amendment would be considered carefully. Thus, they required a powerful consensus of political and social support for amendments, known as a **supermajority.** This means that each stage of the process must be approved by more than the simple majority of 50 percent plus one.

**proposal**
The first stage of the constitutional amendment process, in which a change is proposed.

**ratify**
An act of approval of proposed constitutional amendments by the states; the second step of the amendment process.

**supermajority**
An extraordinary majority vote required for constitutional amendments and other actions such as breaking a filibuster and ratifying treaties; consists of more than a simple majority of 50 percent plus one.

### QUICK REVIEW

Methods for Amending the Constitution

- A constitutional amendment requires two-thirds vote in both houses of Congress.
- It requires approval by legislatures in three-fourths of the states.
- Two-thirds of state legislatures are needed for a request for a constitutional convention.
- A constitutional amendment may be made by ratifying conventions in three-fourths of the states.

**Table 2.3** The First Ten Amendments to the Constitution (The Bill of Rights)

| Safeguards of Personal and Political Freedoms |
|---|
| 1. Freedom of speech, press, and religion, and the right to assemble peaceably and to petition government to redress grievances<br>2. Right to keep and bear arms |
| **Outmoded Protection Against British Occupation** |
| 3. Protection against quartering troops in private homes |
| **Safeguards in the Judicial Process and Against Arbitrary Government Action** |
| 4. Protection against "unreasonable" searches and seizures by the government<br>5. Guarantees of a grand jury for capital crimes, against double jeopardy, against being forced to testify against oneself, against being deprived of life or property without "due process of law," and against the taking of property without just compensation<br>6. Guarantees of rights in criminal trials including right to speedy and public trial, to be informed of the nature of the charges, to confront witnesses, to compel witnesses to appear in one's defense, and to the assistance of counsel<br>7. Guarantee of right of trial by a jury of one's peers<br>8. Guarantees against excessive bail and the imposition of cruel and unusual punishment |
| **Description of Unenumerated Rights and Reserved Powers** |
| 9. Assurance that rights not listed for protection against the power of the central government in the Constitution are still retained by the people<br>10. Assurance that the powers not delegated to the central government are reserved by the states, or to the people |

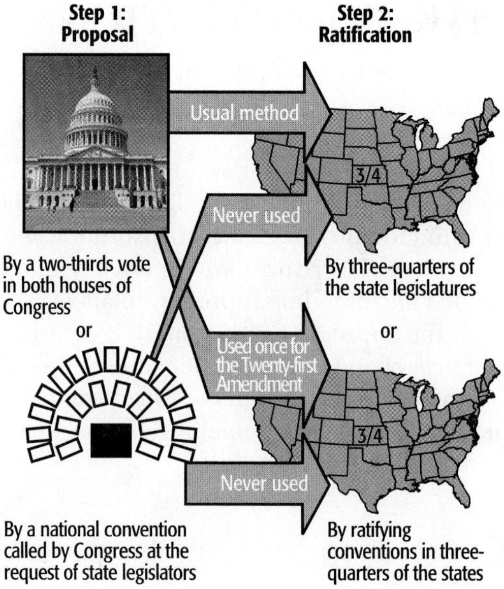


**FIGURE 2.2** Procedures for Amending the Constitution
Although the framers provided four ways to amend the Constitution, only one method is usually used: proposal of an amendment by two-thirds of each house of Congress and ratification by three-quarters of the state legislatures. The sole exception was the Twenty-first Amendment repealing prohibition. Ratification of this amendment took place in special state conventions.

The proposal stage for a constitutional amendment requires either a two-thirds vote of both houses of Congress or an application from two-thirds of the states for a constitutional convention. Ratification is accomplished by a vote of three-quarters of the state legislatures or a three-quarters vote of specially created state ratifying conventions. Although the framers reserved this extraordinary voting requirement for other important tasks, such as overriding a presidential veto and ratifying a treaty, here alone the supermajority must be mustered twice on the same issue. The double supermajority hurdle is so difficult, that, if you factor in one-quarter of the states, that can block ratification, and consider the 13 states with the smallest voting populations, with the possibility that ratification can be blocked in those states by a bare 50 percent of the vote, an amendment can be blocked by less than 2 percent of the country's population. The amendment process is illustrated in Figure 2.2.

No formal time limit was placed on ratifying amendments, but a limit can be included in the body of the amendment, as it was in the Equal Rights Amendments, and Congress can extend the limit if it wishes. Although the Supreme Court has been reluctant to rule on the constitutionality of such time limits, it did rule in 1921 that the seven-year limit placed in the Eighteenth Amendment was "reasonable."[34]

Although proposed several times, to date no amendment has been approved by constitutional convention. All have been proposed in Congress, and all except the Twenty-first Amendment repealing prohibition have been ratified using state legislatures. Because there has been only one Constitutional Convention, a variety of interesting questions remain about the prospects for another such event. How would the delegates be selected? How would the votes be apportioned among the 50 states? Must all social groups be represented, and how? And even if a convention is called to consider a specific proposal, might a runaway convention lead to reconsideration of the entire Constitution, as happened to the Articles of Confederation in 1787? The answers to these questions are unknown, and with one runaway convention in our past, few are willing to risk having another. In 1911, 31 states called for a convention to consider direct election of the Senate. A fearful Congress quickly proposed

**Table 2.4** The Constitutional Amendments

| Number | Proposed | Ratified | Subject | Purpose |
|---|---|---|---|---|
| 11 | 1794 | 1795 | To sue a state in federal court, individuals need state consent | Overruled a Supreme Court decision |
| 12 | 1803 | 1804 | Requires separate electoral college votes for president and vice president | Corrected a government plan flaw |
| 13 | 1865 | 1865 | Prohibits slavery | Expanded rights |
| 14 | 1866 | 1868 | Gives citizenship to freed slaves, guarantees them due process and equal protection of the laws, and protects their privileges and immunities | Expanded rights |
| 15 | 1869 | 1870 | Grants freed slaves the right to vote | Expanded voting rights |
| 16 | 1909 | 1913 | Grants Congress power to collect income tax | Overruled a Supreme Court decision |
| 17 | 1912 | 1913 | Provides for direct election of the Senate (formerly elected by state legislatures) | Expanded voting rights |
| 18 | 1917 | 1919 | Prohibits the manufacture, sale, and transportation of intoxicating liquor | Public policy |
| 19 | 1919 | 1920 | Grants women the right to vote | Expanded voting rights |
| 20 | 1932 | 1933 | Changes presidential inauguration date from March 4 to January 20, and opening date of Congress to January 3 | Revised a government plan |
| 21 | 1933 | 1933 | Repeals the Eighteenth Amendment | Public policy |
| 22 | 1947 | 1951 | Limits the president to two terms in office | Revised a government plan |
| 23 | 1960 | 1961 | Grants citizens of Washington, DC, status in electoral college to vote for president | Expanded voting rights |
| 24 | 1962 | 1964 | Prohibits charging a poll tax to vote | Expanded voting rights |
| 25 | 1965 | 1967 | Provides for succession of president or vice president in the event of death, removal from office, incapacity, or resignation | Revised a government plan |
| 26 | 1971 | 1971 | Grants the right to vote to 18- to 20-year-olds | Expanded voting rights |
| 27 | 1789 | 1992 | Prohibits a pay raise voted by Congress from going into effect until the following session | Public policy |

such an amendment in 1912 that, after 1913 ratification by the states, became the Seventeenth Amendment.

If you look at the ratified amendments (see Table 2.4), you will see how remarkably few changes have been made to the Constitution, with all of them grouped around four purposes: to expand voting rights and promote equality, to correct flaws in or revise the original constitutional plan for government, to make public policy, and to overturn Supreme Court decisions.

At times, the amendment proposal process can be used in an attempt to reverse Supreme Court decisions. For example, after the Supreme Court struck down state and federal laws designed to outlaw burning the American flag, an amendment to accomplish the same thing was unsuccessfully proposed. In 1997, when the Supreme Court refused to allow states to impose term limits on candidates for congressional office, and Congress failed to pass a federal term limits law, the idea that this goal could be accomplished by constitutional amendment was considered.

# APPROACHING
## Contemporary Issues in Democracy

### Balancing the Budget Through Constitutional Amendment?

As part of the lifting of the $14.3 trillion debt ceiling negotiations in Congress in the summer of 2011, which nearly led to a government default of its loans, it was agreed that either a balanced budget amendment would be adopted, or a "super committee" of 12 members of Congress would propose and Congress must pass $1.5 trillion in spending cuts. But, if neither should happen, and neither did, a series of "draconian" domestic and military cuts would be imposed. The balanced budget amendment, designed to reduce spending, and thus reduce the overall debt as well as the crushing yearly interest servicing that debt, was first considered in 1956, proposed again in 1981, and passed by the House in 1995 but failed to pass in the Senate in 1997 by only one vote. Most people agree that even though nearly three-fourths of the American public supports the plan, and 26 state legislatures that would consider ratifying the amendment have a majority of Republicans who support it, the chances of amassing the two-thirds supporting vote in each house of Congress and three-fourths vote in the states is very, very slim. The most supported plan in Congress is some variation of balancing spending and tax revenue intake yearly, with some kind of emergency provision to allow for more spending in crisis years, and a waiver provision for times of war. Here are some of the questions about the proposal.

**Question 1:**

Is the process of imposing constitutional amendment discipline on the taxing and spending practices of Congress each year a good thing? This proposal would eliminate the flexibility of Congress to vote for such policies as increasing stimulus spending to pull the nation out of a recession.

**Question 2:**

Would the American voters feel the same way about this balanced budget proposal if they realized that it would severely restrict the ability of the government to pay for long-term infrastructure improvements, and fund various governmental entitlements such as Social Security, Medicare and Medicaid, and unemployment benefits? Or, realizing that the amendment likely would not go into effect for five years, would voters support the plan if the only option by then to balance the budget because of skyrocketing interest debt would be to raise taxes to pay it?

**Question 3:**

With the waivers for emergencies and wartime in the proposal, and the inability of Congress to agree on any policies without the threat of stalemate, would the balanced budget amendment lead to a reduction of the national debt, or would loopholes be found on a yearly basis to avoid imposing it?

Over the years, special-interest groups and political parties have sought to amend the Constitution to shape the morality of the nation or further their political agenda. In 1917, the temperance (anti-liquor) movement succeeded in getting the Eighteenth Amendment passed to ban drinking and secured its ratification two years later, only to have it repealed by the Twenty-first Amendment in 1933, thanks to a ratification by state constitutional conventions—the only time in American history an amendment passed in that way. Recently, as seen in the Approaching Contemporary Issues in Democracy box, cultural and policy interest groups have sought to use the amendment process to ban gay marriages and abortions and to promote a balanced budget amendment, without success. The double supermajority feature of the amendment process usually prevents such uses by special-interest and political groups, reserving amendments for the desires of the vast majority.

Sometimes when groups are not able to muster a supermajority to try to amend the Constitution, they try to do so by federal law. In 2009, after the District of Columbia Voting Rights amendment failed to be ratified, Congress considered a law giving the District of Columbia a congressional seat, while balancing out the partisan effect by also giving Republican-dominated Utah an additional seat through 2012, when the new census reapportions the body. This law, however, was not passed.[35]

### Updating the Constitution by Judicial Interpretation

The Constitution has managed to remain vibrant and current even though it has been amended only 27 times. Its survival has to do both with the brilliant ambiguity built into the Constitution and the power of the Supreme Court to interpret it.

But where did the Court obtain such power? As we learn in Chapter 6, in the 1803 case of *Marbury* v. *Madison,* the Court under Chief Justice John Marshall ruled that because the Supreme Court interprets laws and the Constitution is a law, the Court has the power to be the final interpreter of the Constitution. This power, judicial review, enables the Court to overturn acts of the other two branches of government if it rules that those acts violate the Constitution. In doing so, the Supreme Court interprets the Constitution, giving new meaning to the phrases and provisions written in 1787. This occurred in 2008 in a case involving security guard Dick Heller's challenge to the District of Columbia's ban on the private ownership of guns. Justice Antonin Scalia, relying on his "originalism" theory of interpreting the Constitution according to the understanding of the people of its provisions at the time of its ratification, ruled that the Second Amendment's "right to bear arms" guaranteed an individual's "right to self-defense" that could be protected only by overturning the ban. Showing disagreement over such interpretations, in dissent Justice John Paul Stevens offered a more evolutionary, living Constitution point of view, arguing on the basis of a 1939 precedent that the first clause of the Second Amendment, linking the "right to bear arms" to "a well-regulated militia being necessary to the security of a free state," gave the state the right to control weapons that had no relation to such activity.[36]

Because a Supreme Court constitutional ruling can be overturned by only the Court itself or through a constitutional amendment, these rulings, in effect, change the meaning of the Constitution. In exercising this power, the justices take on the role of modern constitutional framers, trying to define what the document should mean in the modern age. Throughout American history, scholars have debated the Court's role, with some believing that the justices should uphold the framers' original meaning of the Constitution and others maintaining that they should continue to update the document using a modern perspective.

**THINKING CRITICALLY**

What role should the Constitution and the Bill of Rights play during times of crisis? How much of that determination should reflect the Constitution's role in earlier times of crisis? Should that interpretation of rights under the Constitution depend on which political party has been able to appoint the majority of the members of the Supreme Court?

**THINKING CRITICALLY**

Should we interpret the Constitution by relying on the theories and understanding of the framers and people of the founding era, or should we rely on the changes in the interpretation of that document over the years?

## THE CONSTITUTION AND AMERICA'S APPROACH TO DEMOCRACY

The most remarkable feature of the United States Constitution is how it has adapted to the times, changing along with an ever-changing nation. The world has changed dramatically since 1787, when it took four days for German immigrant Jacob Shallus to write the Constitution by hand on four pieces of stretched vellum with a quill pen and ink made from oak galls and dyes. Now we can create a version of the same document in just a few seconds using computer software. We have gone from a population of 3.5 million to one of over 310 million people, from a geographic base of 13 seashore colonies to 50 states spread across a continent. In 1787, wars took months to develop as ships crossed vast oceans; now, one press of a button can mean instant annihilation. Yet, as Supreme Court Justice Byron White has argued, the Constitution still survives because "from the summer of 1787 to the present the government of the United States has become an endeavor far beyond the contemplation of the Framers. But the wisdom of the Framers was to anticipate that the nation would grow and new problems of governance would require different solutions."[37]

Over time, actions taken by the different branches of government have changed the nature of the government's structure without changing the Constitution. The framers originally gave Congress the power to declare war, but the speed of modern warfare has created the need for quicker responses. Now the president has the power to make war. The Korean and Vietnam wars, along with a host of other conflicts, were presidential wars. The framers also intended, despite the system of checks and balances, for Congress to be the predominant branch. But certain presidents have enlarged the executive powers. Thomas Jefferson directed the purchase of the Louisiana Territory; Abraham Lincoln imposed martial law and freed the slaves; Woodrow Wilson and Franklin D. Roosevelt extended the powers of their offices during world wars; and a host of other presidents exercised powers well beyond those delegated to them by Congress. Thus, President George W. Bush could commit troops to Afghanistan, Iraq, and the war on terrorism without congressional declarations of war. And President Barack Obama could order, without congressional authorization, drone plane attacks in Pakistan and the assassination of Osama bin Laden, before ordering the reduction of troops in those war theaters. It is doubtful that Madison and Franklin would recognize much of today's government, but they would appreciate the fact that their handiwork allowed this evolution to take place, and empowered the voters to say how it would proceed.

## Summary

2.1 *What early democratic theories and organizations guided the American colonists in banding together into their first governments?*

- The governments of some American colonies, following the idea of a social contract theory, were based on the idea of a compact—an agreement legally binding two or more parties to enforceable rules. Other colonies evolved from royal grants of land that gave governing rights to a lord or baron, who became the colony's proprietor.
- Frequent conflicts between the governors and the colonial legislatures made the colonists highly suspicious of executive power. The colonists were also influenced by the ideas of Charles de Montesquieu, who saw the separation of executive, legislative, and judicial powers as the best way to counteract any tendency toward despotism, and by the ideas of social contract theorists such as Thomas Hobbes and John Locke—especially the latter—who asserted the importance of limited government based on popular consent.

2.2 *Why did America's first attempt at a unified national approach to government in the Articles of Confederation fail?*

- On November 15, 1777, the Continental Congress adopted the Articles of Confederation. Under the Articles, the central government lacked the power to impose taxes, raise an army, or regulate commerce. Hence, it was unable to protect either citizens or private property. Lacking the power to pursue a foreign policy, the national government, which had no unitary executive and a bicameral legislature, set up Committees of Correspondence to communicate with foreign countries.

2.3 *How inclusive was America's initial democracy, and for those who founded America's constitution, what were their initial plans for government?*

- The only colonists who could participate in politics, and thus be a part of the framing of this nation's founding documents, were white males over the age of 21 who owned land. Women, slave and free blacks, sometimes non-Protestants, and Native Americans were excluded from the process. Less than 5 percent of the people participated in politics.
- Although the stated goal of the Constitutional Convention was to revise the Articles of Confederation, some delegates believed that the Articles needed to be scrapped altogether and replaced by an entirely new document. Debate at the Convention centered on two major proposals. The Virginia Plan called for a system of proportional representation in which the legislature would consist of two chambers, or "houses,"

and each state's representation in both houses would depend on its population. The New Jersey Plan proposed a unicameral (one-house) legislature in which each state would have one vote. The delegates voted to use the Virginia Plan as the basis for further discussion.

2.4 *Was the drafting of the U.S. Constitution the result of democratic theory or the workings of political compromise, and how did that affect the presidency and slavery issues?*

- While the drafting of the Constitution was guided by a combination of old political theories and new political science crafted by James Madison and others, the drafting process could not have been completed without key political compromises on many issues. A key debate at the Convention dealt with representation in the two houses of Congress. States with large populations sought proportional representation in both houses, whereas those with smaller populations called for an equal number of votes for each state. In the Great (or Connecticut) Compromise, the delegates decided that representation in the House of Representatives would be based on each state's population, but each state would have two votes in the Senate.
- Another important debate was over slavery. The southern states wanted slaves to be counted as part of the population when determining representation in Congress; the northern states wanted slaves to be excluded from the count. The outcome of the debate was the three-fifths compromise: each state's representation would be determined by adding three-fifths of the number of slaves to the number of free citizens in that state.
- The delegates were also divided over the nature of the presidency. Some favored a single national executive with the power to veto legislative acts, but others were concerned that a single executive would hold too much power and called instead for a board of executives. Eventually they agreed on a single executive, with an unlimited right of reelection and possessing a veto power.

2.5 *How is democracy safeguarded both at the national and state levels?*

- The new Constitution created a republican form of government, in which the people hold an indirect voting power over elected officials. Originally, only members of the House of Representatives would be elected directly by the people; senators would be chosen by the state legislatures, and the president by an electoral college. Over the years the people have gained a more direct voice in the government through a series of constitutional changes such as popular election of senators and extension of the right to vote to all people over the age of 18.
- The Constitution established a system of separation of powers in which different powers are granted to the three major branches of government. In addition, it set up checks and balances, giving each branch the power to approve, disapprove, or alter what the other branches do. It also distributed powers between the central government and the state governments. The powers of the central government are delegated—expressly granted and limited in nature—and all remaining powers are reserved to the states. The supremacy clause states that the dictates of the national government take precedence over those of any state government.

2.6 *How did the people in the constitutional ratification period lobby for and understand their new democratic government?*

- Supporters of the Constitution called themselves *Federalists;* opponents took the name *Antifederalists.* The Federalists claimed that the new government was designed to represent the sovereignty of the people, whereas the Antifederalists believed that the states should remain independent of the central government.

2.7 *Was the final ratification of the Constitution by the states the result of democratic theory or political compromise?*

- The ratification process was more about rough-and-tumble politics than democratic theory. The major debates occurred in the large states where significant numbers of Federalists and Antifederalists battled. In Pennsylvania, the Constitution was ratified only after opponents were captured and forced to be in the hall for the vote. The Constitution was finally ratified after the Federalists agreed to the addition of the Bill of Rights in the first United States Congress after ratification.

2.8 *How has America's Constitution and democracy evolved and become more inclusive over time?*

- The Constitution can be amended through a two-stage process. First, there must be a proposal for a change, which requires either a two-thirds vote of both houses of Congress or a request by two-thirds of the states for a constitutional convention. Then the amendment must be ratified by a vote of three-quarters of the state legislatures or a three-quarters vote of specially created state ratifying conventions. The primary source of constitutional change, however, is judicial interpretation, relying on the power of judicial review created in the 1803 *Marbury* v. *Madison* case, in response to political and social changes.

## Key Terms

## Test Yourself Chapter 2

1. The theories derived for our government from social contract theory are
   a. limited government.
   b. consent of the governed.
   c. the right to revolt against a bad government.
   d. All of the above.

2. Montesquieu's theory that helps to safeguard the notion of limited government protecting democracy is known as
   a. the inherent power of the presidency.
   b. the bicameral legislature.
   c. the appointed judiciary.
   d. the separation of powers.

3. *Common Sense,* the best-selling attack on the British Crown urging people to revolt, was written by
   a. Thomas Jefferson.
   b. Thomas Radcliffe.
   c. Thomas Paine.
   d. Thomas Smith.

4. The power of the British officials to perform a general search of colonists' houses looking for customs violations and any evidence of crime is called a
   a. writ of error.
   b. writ of assistance.
   c. writ of mandamus.
   d. writ of subpoena.

5. The major philosophy of the Declaration of Independence is
   a. all men are created equal.
   b. governments should act on the consent of the governed.
   c. people possess inalienable rights of life, liberty, and property.
   d. All of the above.

6. The voting population in America at the time of the Declaration of Independence and the Constitution consisted of all of the following *except*
   a. males.
   b. landowners.
   c. freed slaves.
   d. those a minimum of 21 years of age.

7. The words "We the People" that begin the Constitution demonstrate what major difference between this document and the Articles of Confederation?
   a. A new group of people drafted the document.
   b. It was created by a vote of the population.
   c. The government was now governed by the people rather than the states.
   d. The new document would govern along with the Articles of Confederation.

8. Which of the following was *not* a problem with the Articles of Confederation?
   a. The executive was too strong.
   b. There was no national military.
   c. There was no national taxation.
   d. There was no national control over interstate commerce.

9. What is the major difference between the Virginia Plan and the New Jersey Plan for the Constitution?
   a. The Virginia Plan had a strong executive.
   b. The New Jersey Plan had a bicameral legislature.
   c. The Virginia Plan was for large states and the New Jersey Plan was for small states.
   d. The New Jersey Plan had a strong judicial branch.

10. Which of the following is an inherent power of the president?
    a. The president is always correct.
    b. The president has power to act on his or her own authority for the good of the nation.
    c. The president is always ready to act.
    d. The president should be consulted before all policy making.

11. The initial sources of power for the president were
    a. an unlimited right to run for reelection.
    b. the veto power over Congress.
    c. a unitary executive.
    d. All of the above.

12. The "council of revision" was
    a. the forerunner of judicial review possessing an absolute veto over state laws.
    b. the initial idea for amending the Constitution.
    c. a committee designed to revise congressional statutes.
    d. an advisory group for the president.

13. Roger Sherman's "Great Compromise" in the Constitutional Convention
    a. allowed delegates from the Convention to have individual votes.
    b. created a Congress voted on by population and a Senate with equal state representation.
    c. created the unitary executive with veto power.
    d. limited the size of the Supreme Court.

**14.** Which feature of modern American politics is not accounted for in the Constitution?
a. Political parties.
b. Ambitious politicians.
c. Disputes among the states.
d. Political elections.

**15.** Where can the so-called elastic clause, allowing Congress to do anything "necessary and proper" to carry into effect its foregoing powers, be found?
a. Article II, Section 1.
b. Article III, Section 4.
c. Article I, Section 8.
d. Article I, Section 9.

**16.** How many of the constitutional amendments have helped America approach democracy by affecting the voting franchise in some way?
a. 4
b. 5
c. 6
d. 7

**17.** In which *Federalist Paper* does James Madison discuss the effects of factions that can be limited only by expanding the size of the political unit to lessen the effects of factions?
a. *The Federalist,* no. 8
b. *The Federalist,* no. 9
c. *The Federalist,* no. 10
d. *The Federalist,* no. 11

**18.** What fraction of the states is required for a supermajority vote in Congress, and what fraction is required to create a constitutional amendment?
a. three-fourths, two-thirds
b. two-thirds, three-fourths
c. two-thirds, two-thirds
d. three-fourths, three-fourths

**19.** Which is the only amendment that was ratified in special state conventions?
a. The Nineteenth.
b. The Twentieth.
c. The Twenty-first.
d. The Twenty-second.

**20.** Who gave the Supreme Court the power to interpret and update the Constitution using judicial review?
a. The constitutional founders.
b. The American people.
c. Congress.
d. The Supreme Court itself in *Marbury* v. *Madison.*

**ANSWERS**
**1.** d, **2.** d, **3.** c, **4.** b, **5.** d, **6.** c, **7.** c, **8.** a, **9.** c, **10.** b, **11.** d, **12.** a, **13.** b, **14.** a, **15.** c, **16.** c, **17.** c, **18.** b, **19.** c, **20.** d

# THE CONSTITUTION OF THE UNITED STATES

## THE PREAMBLE

We the People of the United States, in Order to form a more perfect Union, establish Justice, insure domestic Tranquility, provide for the common defence, promote the general Welfare, and secure the Blessings of Liberty to ourselves and our Posterity, do ordain and establish this Constitution for the United States of America.

"We, the people." Three simple words, yet of profound importance and contentious origin. Every government in the world at the time of the Constitutional Convention was some type of monarchy, wherein sovereign power flowed from the top. The founders of our new country rejected monarchy as a form of government and proposed instead a republic, which would draw its sovereignty from the people.

The Articles of Confederation that governed the United States from 1776 until 1789 started with "We the under signed Delegates of the States." Early drafts of the new constitution started with "We, the states . . ." But again, the founders were not interested in another union of states but rather the creation of a new national government. Therefore, "We, the states" was changed to "We, the people." The remainder of the preamble describes the generic functions of government. These would apply to almost any type of government. Some have proven more critical than others. For example, "promote the general Welfare" has been cited as the authority for social welfare programs of the federal government.

## ARTICLE I—THE LEGISLATIVE ARTICLE

### Legislative Power

The very first article in the Constitution established the legislative branch of the new national government. Why did the framers start with the legislative power instead of the executive branch? Under the Articles of Confederation, the legislature was the only functional instrument of government. Therefore, the framers truly believed it was the most important component of the new government.

SECTION 1. All legislative Powers herein granted shall be vested in a Congress of the United States, which shall consist of a Senate and House of Representatives.

Section 1 established a bicameral (two-chamber) legislature, or an upper (Senate) and lower (House of Representatives) organization of the legislative branch.

### House of Representatives: Composition, Qualifications, Apportionment, Impeachment Power

SECTION 2 CLAUSE 1. The House of Representatives shall be composed of Members chosen every second Year by the People of the several States, and the Electors in each State shall have the Qualifications requisite for Electors of the most numerous Branch of the State Legislature.

This section sets the term of office for House members (two years) and indicates that those voting for Congress will have the same qualifications as those voting for the state legislatures. Originally, states limited voters to white property owners. Some states even had religious disqualifications, such as being Catholic or Jewish. Most property and religious qualifications for voting were removed by the 1840s, but race and gender restrictions remained.

CLAUSE 2. No Person shall be a Representative who shall not have attained to the Age of twenty five Years, and been seven Years a Citizen of the United States, and who shall not, when elected, be an Inhabitant of that State in which he shall be chosen.

This section sets forth the basic qualifications of a representative: at least 25 years of age, a U.S. citizen for at least seven years, and a resident of a state. Note that the Constitution does not require a person to be a resident of the district he or she represents. At the time the Constitution was written, life expectancy was about 43 years of age. So a person 25 years old was middle-aged. Considering today's life expectancy of about 78 years, the equivalent age of 25 would be about 45. The average age of a current representative is 57. Because of the specificity of the Constitution as to the qualifications for office, the U.S. Supreme Court ruled that term limits could not be imposed.

Clause 2 does not specify how many terms a representative can serve in Congress. One provision of the Republican House *Contract with America,* "The Citizens Legislature Act," called for term limits for legislators. This provision was not enacted. Subsequently, some states passed legislation to limit the terms of their U.S. representatives. Because of the specificity of the qualifications for office, the Supreme Court ruled in *U.S. Term Limits, Inc.* v. *Thornton,* 514 U.S. 779 (1995) that term limits for U.S. legislators could not be imposed by any state but would require a constitutional amendment.

CLAUSE 3. Representatives and direct Taxes[1] shall be apportioned among the several States which may be included within this Union, according to their respective Numbers, which shall be determined by adding to the whole Number of free Persons, including those bound to Service for a Term of Years, and excluding Indians not taxed, three fifths of all other Persons.[2] The actual Enumeration shall be made within three Years after the first Meeting of the Congress of the United States, and within every subsequent Term of ten Years, in such Manner as they shall by Law direct. The Number of Representatives shall not exceed one for every thirty Thousand, but each State shall have at Least one Representative; and until such enumeration shall be made, the State of New Hampshire shall be entitled to chuse three, Massachusetts

[1] Modified by the Sixteenth Amendment.

[2] Replaced by Section 2, Fourteenth Amendment.

eight, Rhode-Island and Providence Plantations one, Connecticut five, New-York six, New Jersey four, Pennsylvania eight, Delaware one, Maryland six, Virginia ten, North Carolina five, South Carolina five, and Georgia three.

This clause contains the three-fifths compromise, wherein Native Americans and African Americans were counted only as three-fifths of a person for congressional representation purposes. This clause also addresses the question of congressional reapportionment every ten years, which requires a census. Since the 1911 Reapportionment Act, the size of the House of Representatives has been set at 435. This is the designated size that is reapportioned every ten years. Based on changes of population, some states gain and some states lose representatives. This clause also provides that every state, regardless of population, will have at least one representative. Currently, seven states have only one representative.

CLAUSE 4. When vacancies happen in the Representation from any State, the Executive Authority thereof shall issue Writs of Election to fill such Vacancies.

This clause provides a procedure for replacing a U.S. representative in the case of death, resignation, or expulsion from the House. Essentially, the governor of the representative's state will assign a successor. Generally, if less than half a term is left, the governor will appoint a successor. If more than half a term is remaining, most states require a special election to fill the vacancy.

CLAUSE 5. The House of Representatives shall chuse their Speaker and other Officers; and shall have the sole Power of Impeachment.

Only one officer of the House is specified—the Speaker. All other officers are decided by the House. This clause also gives the House authority for impeachments (accusations) against officials of the executive and judicial branches.

## Senate: Composition, Qualifications, Impeachment Trials

SECTION 3 CLAUSE 1. The Senate of the United States shall be composed of two Senators from each State, *chosen by the Legislature thereof,*[3] for six Years; and each Senator shall have one Vote.

This clause treats each state equally—all have two senators. Originally, senators were chosen by state legislators, but since passage and ratification of the Seventeenth Amendment, they are now elected by popular vote. This clause also establishes the term of a senator—six years—three times that of a House member.

CLAUSE 2. Immediately after they shall be assembled in Consequence of the first Election, they shall be divided as equally as may be into three Classes. The Seats of the Senators of the first Class shall be vacated at the Expiration of the second Year, of the second Class at the Expiration of the fourth Year, and of the third Class at the Expiration of the sixth Year, so that one third may be chosen every second Year; and if Vacancies happen by Resignation, or otherwise, during the Recess of the Legislature of any State, the Executive thereof may make temporary Appointments until the next Meeting of the Legislature, which shall then fill such Vacancies.[4]

To prevent a wholesale election of senators every six years, this clause provides that one-third of the Senate will be elected every two years. Senate vacancies are filled in the same way as the House—either appointment by the governor or by special election.

CLAUSE 3. No Person shall be a Senator who shall not have attained to the Age of thirty Years, and been nine Years a Citizen of the United States, and who shall not, when elected, be an Inhabitant of that State for which he shall be chosen.

This clause sets forth the qualifications for U.S. senator: at least 30 years old, a U.S. citizen for at least nine years, and a citizen of a state. The equivalent age of 30 today would be 54 years old. The average age of a U.S. senator at present is 63.1 years.

CLAUSE 4. The Vice President of the United States shall be President of the Senate, but shall have no Vote, unless they be equally divided.

The only constitutional duty of the vice president is specified in this clause—president of the Senate. This official has a vote only if there is a tie vote in the Senate; then the vice president's vote breaks the tie.

CLAUSE 5. The Senate shall chuse their other Officers, and also a President pro tempore, in the Absence of the Vice President, or when he shall exercise the Office of President of the United States.

One official office in the U.S. Senate is specified—temporary president, who fills in during the vice president's absence (which is normally the case). All other Senate officers are designated and selected by the Senate.

CLAUSE 6. The Senate shall have the sole Power to try all Impeachments. When sitting for that Purpose, they shall be on Oath or Affirmation. When the President of the United States is tried, the Chief Justice shall preside: And no Person shall be convicted without the Concurrence of two thirds of the Members present.

CLAUSE 7. Judgment in Cases of Impeachment shall not extend further than to removal from Office, and disqualification to hold and enjoy any Office of honor, Trust or Profit under the United States: but the Party convicted shall nevertheless be liable and subject to Indictment, Trial, Judgment and Punishment, according to Law.

The Senate acts as a trial court for impeached federal officials. If the accused is the president, the Chief Justice of the U.S. Supreme Court presides. Otherwise, the vice president normally presides. Conviction of the charges requires a two-thirds majority vote of those senators present at the time of the vote. Conviction results in the federal official's removal from office and disqualification to hold any other federal appointed office. Removal from office does not bar further prosecution under applicable

[3] Repealed by the Seventeenth Amendment.
[4] Modified by the Seventeenth Amendment.

criminal or civil laws, nor does it apparently bar one from elected office. A current representative, Alcee L. Hastings, was removed as a federal district judge. He subsequently ran for Congress and now represents Florida's 23rd Congressional District.

## Congressional Elections: Times, Places, Manner

SECTION 4 CLAUSE 1. The Times, Places and Manner of holding Elections for Senators and Representatives, shall be prescribed in each State by the Legislature thereof; but the Congress may at any time by Law make or alter such Regulations, except as to the Places of chusing Senators.

CLAUSE 2. The Congress shall assemble at least once in every Year, and such Meeting shall be on the first Monday in December, unless they shall by Law appoint a different Day.[5]

The states determine the place and manner of electing representatives and senators, but Congress has the right to make or change these laws or regulations, except for the election sites. Congress is required to meet annually, and now, by law, annual meetings begin in January.

## Powers and Duties of the Houses

SECTION 5 CLAUSE 1. Each House shall be the Judge of the Elections, Returns and Qualifications of its own Members, and a Majority of each shall constitute a Quorum to do Business; but a smaller Number may adjourn from day to day, and may be authorized to compel the Attendance of absent Members, in such Manner, and under the Penalties as each House may provide.

This clause enables each legislative branch to essentially make its own rules. Normally, to take a vote, a quorum is necessary. But if no votes are scheduled, less than a quorum can convene a session.

CLAUSE 2. Each House may determine the Rules of its Proceedings, punish its Members for disorderly Behaviour, and, with the Concurrence of two thirds, expel a Member.

Essentially, each branch promulgates its own rules and punishes its own members. The ultimate punishment is expulsion of the member, which requires a two-thirds vote. Expulsion does not prevent the member from running again.

CLAUSE 3. Each House shall keep a Journal of its Proceedings, and from time to time publish the same, excepting such Parts as may in their Judgment require Secrecy; and the Yeas and Nays of the Members of either House on any question shall, at the Desire of one fifth of those Present, be entered on the Journal.

An official record, with a name such as the Congressional Record or House Journal, is kept for all sessions. It is a daily account of House and Senate floor debates, votes, and members' remarks. However, a record is not printed if a proceeding is closed to the public for security reasons. Many votes are by voice vote, and if at least one-fifth of the members request, a recorded vote of Yeas and Nays will be conducted and documented. This procedure permits analysis of congressional roll-call votes.

CLAUSE 4. Neither House, during the Session of Congress, shall, without the Consent of the other, adjourn for more than three days, nor to any other Place than that in which the two Houses shall be sitting.

This clause prevents one branch from adjourning for a long period of time or to some other location without the consent of the other branch.

## Rights of Members

SECTION 6 CLAUSE 1. The Senators and Representatives shall receive a Compensation for their Services, to be ascertained by Law, and paid out of the Treasury of the United States. They shall in all Cases, except Treason, Felony and Breach of the Peace, be privileged from Arrest during their Attendance at the Session of their respective Houses, and in going to and returning from the same; and for any Speech or Debate in either House, they shall not be questioned in any other Place.

This section ensures that senators and congressional representatives will be paid a salary from the U.S. Treasury. This salary is determined by no other than the legislature. According to the Library of Congress legislative website THOMAS: "The current salary for members of Congress is $174,000. A small number of leadership positions, like Speaker of the House, receive a somewhat higher salary." In addition, members of Congress receive many other benefits: free health care, fully funded retirement system, free gyms, 26 free round-trips to their home state or district, and the like. This section also provides immunity from arrest or prosecution for congressional actions on the floor or in travel to and from the Congress. For example, few members of Congress have ever been charged with drunk driving.

CLAUSE 2. No Senator or Representative shall, during the Time for which he was elected, be appointed to any civil Office under the Authority of the United States, which shall have been created, or the Emoluments whereof shall have been encreased during such time; and no Person holding any Office under the United States, shall be a Member of either House during his Continuance in Office.

This section prevents the United States from adopting a parliamentary democracy; congressional members cannot hold executive offices, and members of the executive branch cannot be members of Congress.

## Legislative Powers: Bills and Resolutions

SECTION 7 CLAUSE 1. All Bills for raising Revenue shall originate in the House of Representatives; but the Senate may propose or concur with Amendments as on other Bills.

This clause specifies one of the few powers specific to the U.S. House—revenue bills.

CLAUSE 2. Every Bill which shall have passed the House of Representatives and the Senate, shall, before it becomes a Law, be presented to the President of the United States; If he approve he shall sign it, but if not he shall return it, with his Objections to that House in which it shall have originated, who shall enter the

[5] Changed by the Twentieth Amendment.

Objections at large on their Journal, and proceed to reconsider it. If after such Reconsideration two thirds of that House shall agree to pass the Bill, it shall be sent, together with the Objections, to the other House, by which it shall likewise be reconsidered, and if approved by two thirds of that House, it shall become a Law. But in all such Cases the Votes of both Houses shall be determined by yeas and Nays, and the Names of the Persons voting for and against the Bill shall be entered on the Journal of each House respectively. If any Bill shall not be returned by the President within ten Days (Sundays excepted) after it shall have been presented to him, the Same shall be a Law, in like Manner as if he had signed it, unless the Congress by their Adjournment prevent its Return, in which Case it shall not be a Law.

The heart of the checks and balances system is contained in this clause. Both the House and Senate must pass a bill and present it to the president. If the president fails to act on the bill within ten days (not including Sundays), the bill will automatically become law. If the president signs the bill, it becomes law. If the president vetoes the bill and sends it back to Congress, this body may override the veto by a two-thirds vote in each branch. This vote must be a recorded vote.

CLAUSE 3. Every Order, Resolution, or Vote to which the Concurrence of the Senate and House of Representatives may be necessary (except on a question of Adjournment) shall be presented to the President of the United States; and before the Same shall take Effect, shall be approved by him, or being disapproved by him, shall be repassed by two thirds of the Senate and House of Representatives, according to the Rules and Limitations prescribed in the Case of a Bill.

This clause covers every type of legislative action other than a bill. Essentially, the same procedures apply in most cases. There are a few exceptions; for example, a joint resolution proposing a new congressional amendment is not subject to presidential veto.

## Powers of Congress

SECTION 8 CLAUSE 1. The Congress shall have Power To lay and collect Taxes, Duties, Imposts and Excises, to pay the Debts and provide for the common Defence and general Welfare of the United States; but all Duties, Imposts and Excises shall be uniform throughout the United States.

CLAUSE 2. To borrow Money on the credit of the United States;

CLAUSE 3. To regulate Commerce with foreign Nations, and among the several States, and with the Indian Tribes;

CLAUSE 4. To establish an uniform Rule of Naturalization, and uniform Laws on the subject of Bankruptcies throughout the United States;

CLAUSE 5. To coin Money, regulate the Value thereof, and of foreign Coin, and fix the Standard of Weights and Measures;

CLAUSE 6. To provide for the Punishment of counterfeiting the Securities and current Coin of the United States;

CLAUSE 7. To establish Post Offices and post Roads;

CLAUSE 8. To promote the Progress of Science and useful Arts, by securing for limited Times to Authors and Inventors the exclusive Right to their respective Writings and Discoveries;

CLAUSE 9. To constitute Tribunals inferior to the supreme Court;

CLAUSE 10. To define and punish Piracies and Felonies committed on the high Seas, and Offences against the Law of Nations;

CLAUSE 11. To declare War, grant Letters of Marque and Reprisal, and make Rules concerning Captures on Land and Water;

CLAUSE 12. To raise and support Armies, but no Appropriation of Money to that Use shall be for a longer Term than two Years;

CLAUSE 13. To provide and maintain a Navy;

CLAUSE 14. To make Rules for the Government and Regulation of the land and naval Forces;

CLAUSE 15. To provide for calling forth the Militia to execute the Laws of the Union, suppress Insurrections and repel Invasions;

CLAUSE 16. To provide for organizing, arming, and disciplining, the Militia, and for governing such Part of them as may be employed in the Service of the United States, reserving to the States respectively, the Appointment of the Officers, and the Authority of training the Militia according to the discipline prescribed by Congress.

These clauses establish what are known as the expressed, or specified, powers of Congress. In theory, they serve as a limit or brake on congressional power.

CLAUSE 17. To exercise exclusive Legislation in all Cases whatsoever, over such District (not exceeding ten Miles square) as may, by Cession of particular States, and the Acceptance of Congress, become the Seat of the Government of the United States, and to exercise like Authority over all Places purchased by the Consent of the Legislature of the State in which the Same shall be, for the Erection of Forts, Magazines, Arsenals, dock-Yards, and other needful Buildings;—And

This clause establishes the seat of the federal government, which was first started in New York. It eventually was moved to Washington, DC, when both Maryland and Virginia ceded land to the new national government, which then established the District of Columbia.

CLAUSE 18. To make all Laws which shall be necessary and proper for carrying into Execution the foregoing Powers, and all other Powers vested by this Constitution in the Government of the United States, or in any Department or Officer thereof.

This clause, known as the "elastic clause," provides the basis for the doctrine of implied congressional powers, which was first introduced in the U.S. Supreme Court case of *McCulloch* v. *Maryland,* 1819. This doctrine tremendously expanded the power of Congress to pass legislation and make regulations.

## Powers Denied to Congress

SECTION 9 CLAUSE 1. The Migration or Importation of such Persons as any of the States now existing shall think proper to admit, shall not be prohibited by the Congress prior to the Year one thousand eight hundred and eight, but a Tax or duty may be imposed on such Importation, not exceeding ten dollars for each Person.

This clause was part of the three-fifths compromise. Essentially, the new Congress was prohibited from stopping the importation of slaves until 1808, but it could impose a head tax not to exceed $10 for each slave.

CLAUSE 2. The Privilege of the Writ of Habeas Corpus shall not be suspended, unless when in Cases of Rebellion or Invasion the public Safety may require it.

Congress cannot suspend the writ of habeas corpus except in cases of rebellion or invasion. The writ of habeas corpus permits a judge to inquire about the legality of detention or deprivation of liberty of any citizen.

CLAUSE 3. No Bill of Attainder or ex post facto Law shall be passed.

This provision prohibits Congress from passing either bills of attainder (forfeiture of property in capital cases) or ex post facto laws (retroactive crimes after passage of legislation). Similar restrictions were enshrined in many state constitutions.

CLAUSE 4. No Capitation, or other direct, Tax shall be laid, unless in Proportion to the Census or Enumeration herein before directed to be taken.[6]

This clause prevents Congress from passing an income tax. Only with passage of the Sixteenth Amendment in 1913 did Congress gain this power.

CLAUSE 5. No Tax or Duty shall be laid on Articles exported from any State.

This section establishes free trade within the United States. The federal government cannot tax state exports.

CLAUSE 6. No Preference shall be given by any Regulation of Commerce or Revenue to the Ports of one State over those of another; nor shall Vessels bound to, or from, one State, be obliged to enter, clear, or pay Duties in another.

This clause also applies to free trade within the United States. The national government cannot show any preference to any state or maritime movements among the states.

CLAUSE 7. No Money shall be drawn from the Treasury, but in Consequence of Appropriations made by Law; and a regular Statement and Account of the Receipts and Expenditures of all public Money shall be published from time to time.

This provision of the Constitution prevents any expenditure unless it has been specifically provided for in an appropriations bill. At the beginning of most fiscal years, Congress has not completed its work on the budget. Technically, the government cannot spend any money according to this provision and would have to shut down. So Congress normally passes a Continuing Resolution Authority, providing temporary authority to continue to spend money until the final budget is approved and signed into law.

CLAUSE 8. No Title of Nobility shall be granted by the United States: And no Person holding any Office of Profit or Trust under them, shall, without the Consent of Congress, accept of any present, Emolument, Office, or Title, of any kind whatever, from any King, Prince, or foreign State.

Feudalism would not be established in the new country. We would have no nobles. No federal official can accept a title of nobility (even honorary) without permission of Congress.

### Powers Denied to the States

This section sets out the prohibitions on state actions.

SECTION 10 CLAUSE 1. No State shall enter into any Treaty, Alliance, or Confederation; grant Letters of Marque and Reprisal; coin Money; emit Bills of Credit; make any Thing but gold and silver Coin a Tender in Payment of Debts; pass any Bill of Attainder, ex post facto Law, or Law impairing the Obligation of Contracts, or grant any Title of Nobility.

This particular clause is a laundry list of denied powers. Note that these restrictions cannot even be waived by Congress. States are not to engage in foreign relations or acts of war. A letter of marque and reprisal was used during these times to provide legal cover for privateers. The federal government's currency monopoly is established. The sanctity of contracts is specified, and similar state prohibitions are specified for bills of attainder, ex post facto, and the like.

CLAUSE 2. No State shall, without the Consent of the Congress, lay any Imposts or Duties on Imports or Exports, except what may be absolutely necessary for executing its inspection Laws: and the net Produce of all Duties and Imposts, laid by any State on Imports or Exports, shall be for the Use of the Treasury of the United States; and all such Laws shall be subject to the Revision and Control of the Congress.

This section establishes the monopoly control of the national government in matters of both national and international trade. The only concession to states is health and safety inspections.

CLAUSE 3. No State shall, without the Consent of Congress, lay any Duty of Tonnage, keep Troops, or Ships of War in time of Peace, enter into any Agreement or Compact with another State, or with a foreign Power, or engage in War, unless actually invaded, or in such imminent Danger as will not admit of delay.

This final section of the legislative article establishes the war monopoly power of the national government. The only exception to state action is actual invasion or threat of imminent danger.

## ARTICLE II—THE EXECUTIVE ARTICLE

This article establishes an entirely new concept in government—an elected executive power.

### Nature and Scope of Presidential Power

SECTION 1 CLAUSE 1. The executive Power shall be vested in a President of the United States of America. He shall hold his Office during the Term of four Years, and, together with the Vice President, chosen for the same Term, be elected as follows

This clause establishes the executive power in the office of the president of the United States of America. It also establishes a second office—vice president. The framers established a

[6] Modified by the Sixteenth Amendment.

four-year term but not a limit on the number of terms. The Twenty-second Amendment later established a limit.

CLAUSE 2. Each State shall appoint, in such Manner as the Legislature thereof may direct, a Number of Electors, equal to the whole Number of Senators and Representatives to which the State may be entitled in the Congress: but no Senator or Representative, or Person holding an Office of Trust or Profit under the United States, shall be appointed an Elector.

This paragraph essentially establishes the electoral college to choose the president and vice president.

CLAUSE 3. The Electors shall meet in their respective States, and vote by Ballot for two Persons, of whom one at least shall not be an Inhabitant of the same State with themselves. And they shall make a List of all the Persons voted for, and of the Number of Votes for each; which List they shall sign and certify, and transmit sealed to the Seat of the Government of the United States, directed to the President of the Senate. The President of the Senate shall, in the Presence of the Senate and House of Representatives, open all the Certificates, and the Votes shall then be counted. The Person having the greatest Number of Votes shall be the President, if such Number be a Majority of the whole Number of Electors appointed; and if there be more than one who have such Majority and have an equal Number of Votes, then the House of Representatives shall immediately chuse by Ballot one of them for President; and if no Person have a Majority, then from the five highest on the List the said House shall in like Manner chuse the President. But in chusing the President, the Votes shall be taken by States, the Representation from each State having one Vote; A quorum for this Purpose shall consist of a Member or Members from two thirds of the States, and a Majority of all the States shall be necessary to a Choice. In every Case, after the Choice of the President, the Person having the greatest Number of Votes of the Electors shall be the Vice President. But if there should remain two or more who have equal Votes, the Senate shall chuse from them by Ballot the Vice President.[7]

This paragraph has been superseded by the Twelfth Amendment. The original language did not require a separate vote for president and vice president. This resulted in a tied vote in the electoral college in 1800 when both Thomas Jefferson and Aaron Burr received 73 electoral votes. The Twelfth Amendment requires a separate vote for each. Only one of the two can be from the state of the elector. This means that it is highly unlikely that the presidential and vice presidential candidates would be from the same state. This question arose in the 2000 election when Dick Cheney, who lived and worked in Texas, had to reestablish his residence in Wyoming.

The original language provided for a House election in the case of no majority vote or a tie vote among the top five candidates. The amendment lowered the number of candidates to the top three. The Senate is to select the vice president if a candidate does not have an electoral majority or in the case of a tie vote. The Senate considers only the top two candidates. The amendment also clarifies that the qualifications of the vice president are the same as those for president.

CLAUSE 4. The Congress may determine the Time of chusing the Electors, and the Day on which they shall give their Votes; which Day shall be the same throughout the United States.

Congress is given the power to establish a uniform day and time for the state selection of electors.

CLAUSE 5. No Person except a natural born Citizen, or a Citizen of the United States, at the time of the Adoption of this Constitution, shall be eligible to the Office of President; neither shall any Person be eligible to that Office who shall not have attained to the Age of thirty five Years, and been fourteen Years a Resident within the United States.

The qualifications for the offices of president and vice president are specified here—at least 35 years old, a 14-year resident of the United States, and a natural-born citizen or citizen of the United States. The Fourteenth Amendment clarified who is a citizen of the United States: a person born or naturalized in the United States and subject to its jurisdiction. But the term *natural-born citizen* is unclear and has never been further defined by the judicial branch. Does it mean born in the United States or born of U.S. citizens in the United States or somewhere else in the world? Unfortunately, there is no definitive answer.

CLAUSE 6. In Case of the Removal of the President from Office, or of his Death, Resignation, or Inability to discharge the Powers and Duties of the said Office, the Same shall devolve on the Vice President, and the Congress may by Law provide for the Case of Removal, Death, Resignation or Inability, both of the President and Vice President, declaring what Officer shall then act as President, and such Officer shall act accordingly, until the Disability be removed, or a President shall be elected.[8]

This clause has been modified by the Twenty-fifth Amendment. Upon the death, resignation, or impeachment conviction of the president, the vice president becomes president. The new president nominates a new vice president, who assumes the office if approved by a majority vote in both congressional branches. The president is also now able to notify the Congress of his or her inability to perform his or her office.

CLAUSE 7. The President shall, at stated Times, receive for his Services, a Compensation, which shall neither be encreased nor diminished during the Period for which he shall have been elected, and he shall not receive within that Period any other Emolument from the United States, or any of them.

This section covers the compensation of the president, which cannot be increased or decreased during his office. The current salary is $400,000 per year.

CLAUSE 8. Before he enter on the Execution of his Office, he shall take the following Oath or Affirmation:—"I do solemnly swear (or affirm) that I will faithfully execute the Office of President of the

[7] Changed by the Twelfth and Twentieth Amendments.
[8] Modified by the Twenty-fifth Amendment.

United States, and will to the best of my Ability, preserve, protect and defend the Constitution of the United States."

This final clause in Section 1 is the oath of office administered to the new president.

### Powers and Duties of the President

SECTION 2 CLAUSE 1. The President shall be Commander in Chief of the Army and Navy of the United States, and of the Militia of the several States, when called into the actual Service of the United States; he may require the Opinion, in writing, of the principal Officer in each of the executive Departments, upon any Subject relating to the Duties of their respective Offices, and he shall have Power to grant Reprieves and Pardons for Offences against the United States, except in Cases of Impeachment.

This clause establishes the president as commander in chief of the U.S. armed forces. George Washington was the only U.S. president to actually lead U.S. armed forces, during the Whiskey Rebellion. The second provision provides the basis for cabinet meetings that are used to acquire the opinions of executive department heads. The last provision provides an absolute pardon or reprieve power from the president. The provision was controversial, but legal, when former President Clinton pardoned fugitive Marc Rich.

CLAUSE 2. He shall have Power, by and with the Advice and Consent of the Senate, to make Treaties, provided two thirds of the Senators present concur; and he shall nominate, and by and with the Advice and Consent of the Senate, shall appoint Ambassadors, other public Ministers and Consuls, Judges of the supreme Court, and all other Officers of the United States, whose Appointments are not herein otherwise provided for, and which shall be established by Law: but the Congress may by Law vest the Appointment of such inferior Officers, as they think proper, in the President alone, in the Courts of Law, or in the Heads of Departments.

This clause covers two important presidential powers: treaty making and appointments. The president (via the State Department) can negotiate treaties with other nations, but these do not become official until ratified by a two-thirds vote of the U.S. Senate. The president is empowered to appoint judges, ambassadors, and other U.S. officials (cabinet officers, military officers, agency heads, etc.) subject to Senate approval. The Congress can and does delegate this approval to the president in the case of inferior officers. For example, junior military officer promotions are not submitted to the Senate, but senior officer promotions are.

CLAUSE 3. The President shall have Power to fill up all Vacancies that may happen during the Recess of the Senate, by granting Commissions which shall expire at the End of their next Session.

This provision allows recess appointments of the officials listed in the previous clause. These commissions automatically expire unless approved by the Senate by the end of the next session. Presidents have used this provision to fill jobs when the nomination process is stalled. Some of these appointments have been very controversial. The regular nomination was stalled because the Senate did not want to confirm the nominee.

SECTION 3. He shall from time to time give to the Congress Information of the State of the Union, and recommend to their Consideration such Measures as he shall judge necessary and expedient; he may, on extraordinary Occasions, convene both Houses, or either of them, and in Case of Disagreement between them, with Respect to the Time of Adjournment, he may adjourn them to such Time as he shall think proper; he shall receive Ambassadors and other public Ministers; he shall take Care that the Laws be faithfully executed, and shall Commission all the Officers of the United States.

This section provides for the annual State of the Union address to a joint session of Congress and the American people. The president is also authorized to call special meetings of either the House or Senate. If there is disagreement between the House and Senate regarding adjournment, the president is empowered to adjourn them. This would be extremely rare. The president formally receives other nations' ambassadors. The next to last provision to faithfully execute laws provides the basis for the whole administrative apparatus of the presidency. All officers of the United States receive a formal commission from the president, most of which are signed with a signature machine.

SECTION 4. The President, Vice President and all civil Officers of the United States, shall be removed from Office on Impeachment for, and Conviction of, Treason, Bribery, or other high Crimes and Misdemeanors.

This section provides the constitutional authority for the impeachment and trial of the president, vice president, and all civil officers of the United States for treason, bribery, or other high crimes and misdemeanors. The exact meaning of this phrase is unclear and is often more political than judicial.

## ARTICLE III—THE JUDICIAL ARTICLE

### Judicial Power, Courts, Judges

SECTION 1. The judicial Power of the United States, shall be vested in one supreme Court, and in such inferior Courts as the Congress may from time to time ordain and establish. The Judges, both of the supreme and inferior Courts, shall hold their Offices during good Behaviour, and shall, at stated Times, receive for their Services, a Compensation, which shall not be diminished during their Continuance in Office.

This section establishes the judicial branch in very general terms. It specifically provides only for the Supreme Court. Congress is given the responsibility of creating the court system. It initially did so in the Judiciary Act of 1789, when it established 13 district courts, one for each state, and three appellate courts. All federal judges hold their offices for life and can be removed only for breaches of good behavior—a very nebulous term. Federal judges have been removed for drunkenness, accepting bribes, and other misdemeanors. To date, no justice of the U.S. Supreme Court has ever been removed.

The salary of federal judges is set by congressional act but can never be reduced. Although the American Bar Association and the Federal Bar Association consider federal judges' salaries inadequate, most Americans would probably disagree. Federal district judges earn $169,300 a year, appellate judges $179,500, and Supreme Court justices $208,100. The Chief Justice is paid $217,400. These are lifetime salaries, paid even upon retirement.

## Jurisdiction

SECTION 2 CLAUSE 1. The judicial Power shall extend to all Cases, in Law and Equity, arising under this Constitution, the Laws of the United States, and Treaties made, or which shall be made, under their Authority;—to all Cases affecting Ambassadors, other public Ministers and Consuls;—to all Cases of admiralty and maritime Jurisdiction;—to Controversies to which the United States shall be a Party;—to Controversies between two or more States—between a State and Citizens of another State;[9]—between Citizens of different States;—between Citizens of the same State claiming Lands under Grants of different States, and between a State, or the Citizens thereof, and foreign States, Citizens, or Subjects.

CLAUSE 2. In all Cases affecting Ambassadors, other public Ministers and Consuls, and those in which a State shall be Party, the supreme Court shall have original Jurisdiction. In all the other Cases before mentioned, the supreme Court shall have appellate Jurisdiction, both as to Law and Fact, with such Exceptions, and under such Regulations as Congress shall make.

CLAUSE 3. The Trial of all Crimes, except in Cases of Impeachment, shall be by Jury; and such Trial shall be held in the State where the said Crimes shall have been committed; but when not committed within any State, the Trial shall be at such Place or Places as the Congress may by Law have directed.

This section establishes the original and appellate jurisdiction of the U.S. Supreme Court. With the Congress of Vienna's 1815 establishment of diplomatic immunity, the U.S. Supreme Court no longer hears cases involving ambassadors. Since 1925, the Supreme Court no longer hears every case on appeal but can select which cases it will accept, which is now only about 75 cases per year. This section also establishes the right of trial by jury for federal crimes.

## Treason

SECTION 3 CLAUSE 1. Treason against the United States, shall consist only in levying War against them, or in adhering to their Enemies, giving them Aid and Comfort. No Person shall be convicted of Treason unless on the Testimony of two Witnesses to the same overt Act, or on Confession in open Court.

CLAUSE 2. The Congress shall have Power to declare the Punishment of Treason, but no Attainder of Treason shall work Corruption of Blood, or Forfeiture except during the Life of the Person attainted.

Treason is the only crime defined in the U.S. Constitution. Congress established the penalty of death for treason convictions. Note that two witnesses are required to convict anyone of treason. Even in cases of treasonable conduct, seizure of estates is prohibited.

# ARTICLE IV—INTERSTATE RELATIONS

## Full Faith and Credit Clause

SECTION 1. Full Faith and Credit shall be given in each State to the public Acts, Records, and judicial Proceedings of every other State. And the Congress may by general Laws prescribe the Manner in which such Acts, Records and Proceedings shall be proved, and the Effect thereof.

This section provides that the official acts and records of one state will be recognized and given credence by other states—for example, marriages and divorces.

## Privileges and Immunities; Interstate Extradition

SECTION 2 CLAUSE 1. The Citizens of each State shall be entitled to all Privileges and Immunities of Citizens in the several States.

This clause requires states to treat citizens of other states equally. For example, when driving in another state, a driver's license is recognized. One area not so clear is that of charging higher tuitions for out-of-state students at educational institutions.

CLAUSE 2. A person charged in any State with Treason, Felony or other Crime, who shall flee from Justice, and be found in another State, shall on Demand of the executive Authority of the State from which he fled, be delivered up, to be removed to the State having Jurisdiction of the Crime.

*Extradition* is the name of this clause. A criminal fleeing to another state, if captured, can be returned to the state where the crime was committed. But this is not an absolute. A state's governor can refuse, for good reason, to extradite someone to another state.

CLAUSE 3. No person held to Service or Labour in one State, under the Laws thereof, escaping into another, shall, in Consequence of any Law or Regulation therein, be discharged from such Service or Labour, but shall be delivered up on Claim of the Party to whom such Service or Labour may be due.[10]

This clause was included to cover runaway slaves. It has been made inoperable by the Thirteenth Amendment, which abolished slavery.

## Admission of States

SECTION 3 CLAUSE 1. New States may be admitted by the Congress into this Union; but no new State shall be formed or erected within the Jurisdiction of any other State; nor any State be formed by the Junction of two or more States, or Parts of States, without the Consent of the Legislatures of the States concerned as well as of the Congress.

CLAUSE 2. The Congress shall have Power to dispose of and make all needful Rules and Regulations respecting the Territory or other Property belonging to the United States; and nothing in this Constitution shall be so construed as to Prejudice any Claims of the United States, or of any particular State.

This section concerns the admission of new states to the Union. In theory, no state can be created from part of another state without permission of the state legislature. But West Virginia was formed from Virginia during the Civil War without the permission of Virginia, which was part of the Confederacy. With 50 states now part of the Union, this section has not been used for many decades. The only

[9] Modified by the Eleventh Amendment.

[10] Repealed by the Thirteenth Amendment.

future use may be in the case of Puerto Rico or perhaps Washington, DC.

### Republican Form of Government

SECTION 4. The United States shall guarantee to every State in this Union a Republican Form of Government, and shall protect each of them against Invasion; and on Application of the Legislature, or of the Executive (when the Legislature cannot be convened) against domestic Violence.

This section commits the federal government to guarantee a republican form of government to each state and to protect the states against foreign invasion or domestic insurrection.

## ARTICLE V—THE AMENDING POWER

The Congress, whenever two thirds of both Houses shall deem it necessary, shall propose Amendments to this Constitution, or, on the Application of the Legislatures of two thirds of the several States, shall call a Convention for proposing Amendments, which, in either Case, shall be valid to all Intents and Purposes, as Part of this Constitution, when ratified by the Legislatures of three fourths of the several States, or by Conventions in three fourths thereof, as the one or the other Mode of Ratification may be proposed by the Congress; Provided that no Amendment which may be made prior to the Year One thousand eight hundred and eight shall in any Manner affect the first and fourth Clauses in the Ninth Section of the first Article; and that no State, without its Consent, shall be deprived of its equal Suffrage in the Senate.

Amendments to the U.S. Constitution can be originated by a two-thirds vote in both the U.S. House and Senate or by two-thirds of the state legislatures asking for a convention to propose amendments. Proposed amendments, by either route, must be approved by three-fourths of state legislatures or by three-fourths of conventions convened in the states for purposes of ratification. Only one amendment has been ratified by the convention method—the Twenty-first Amendment repealed the Eighteenth Amendment establishing prohibition.

Thousands of amendments have been proposed; few have been passed by a two-thirds vote in each branch of Congress. The Equal Rights Amendment was one such case, but it was not ratified by three-fourths of the state legislatures. There have only been 27 successful amendments to the U.S. Constitution.

## ARTICLE VI—THE SUPREMACY CLAUSE

CLAUSE 1. All Debts contracted and Engagements entered into, before the Adoption of this Constitution, shall be as valid against the United States under this Constitution, as under the Confederation.

This clause made the new national government responsible for all debts incurred during the Revolutionary War. This was very important to banking and commercial interests.

CLAUSE 2. This Constitution, and the Laws of the United States which shall be made in Pursuance thereof; and all Treaties made, or which shall be made, under the Authority of the United States, shall be the supreme Law of the Land; and the Judges in every State shall be bound thereby, any Thing in the Constitution or Laws of any State to the Contrary notwithstanding.

This is the national supremacy clause, which provides the basis for the supremacy of the national government.

CLAUSE 3. The Senators and Representatives before mentioned, and the Members of the several State Legislatures, and all executive and judicial Officers, both of the United States and of the several States, shall be bound by Oath or Affirmation, to support this Constitution; but no religious Test shall ever be required as a Qualification to any Office or public Trust under the United States.

This clause requires essentially all federal and state officials to swear or affirm their allegiance to and support of the U.S. Constitution. Note that a religious test was prohibited for federal office. However, some states used religious tests for voting and office qualification until the 1830s.

## ARTICLE VII—RATIFICATION

The Ratification of the Conventions of nine States, shall be sufficient for the Establishment of this Constitution between the States so ratifying the Same.

Done in Convention by the Unanimous Consent of the States present the Seventeenth Day of September in the Year of our Lord one thousatnd seven hundred and Eighty seven and of the Independence of the United States of America the Twelfth. *In Witness whereof We have hereunto subscribed our Names.*

## AMENDMENTS

Realizing the unanimous ratification of the new Constitution by the 13 states might never have occurred, the framers wisely specified that only 9 states would be needed for ratification. Even this proved to be a test of wills between Federalists and Antifederalists, leading to publication of the great political work *The Federalist Papers.*

## THE BILL OF RIGHTS

The first ten amendments were ratified on December 15, 1791, and form what is known as the "Bill of Rights."

The Bill of Rights applied initially only to the federal government and not to state or local governments. Beginning in 1925, in the case of *Gitlow* v. *New York,* the U.S. Supreme Court began to selectively incorporate the Bill of Rights, making its provisions applicable to state and local governments. There are only three exceptions, which will be discussed at the appropriate amendment.

### Amendment 1—Religion, Speech, Assembly, and Politics

Congress shall make no law respecting an establishment of religion, or prohibiting the free exercise thereof; or abridging the freedom of speech, or of the press; or the right of the people peaceably to assemble, and to petition the Government for a redress of grievances.

This is the godfather of all amendments in that it protects five fundamental freedoms: religion, speech, press, assembly, and petition. Note that the press is the only business that is specifically protected by the U.S. Constitution. Freedom of religion and speech are two of the most contentious issues and generate a multitude of Supreme Court cases.

### Amendment 2—Militia and the Right to Bear Arms

A well-regulated Militia, being necessary to the security of a free State, the right of the people to keep and bear Arms, shall not be infringed.

This amendment is the favorite of the National Rifle Association. This amendment also has not been incorporated for state/local governments; that is, state and local governments are free to regulate arms within their respective jurisdictions. There is also controversy as to the meaning of this amendment. Some believe that it specifically refers to citizen militias, which were common at the time of the Constitution but now have been replaced by permanent armed forces. Therefore, the applicability of the amendment is questionable. The central issue is whether private citizens need weapons for the security of a free state.

### Amendment 3—Quartering of Soldiers

No Soldier shall, in time of peace be quartered in any house, without the consent of the Owner, nor in time of war, but in manner to be prescribed by law.

It was the practice of the British government to insist that colonists provide room or board to British troops. This amendment was designed to prohibit this practice. Today, military and naval bases provide the necessary quarters.

### Amendment 4—Searches and Seizures

The right of the people to be secure in their persons, houses, papers, and effects, against unreasonable searches and seizures, shall not be violated, and no Warrants shall issue, but upon probable cause, supported by Oath or affirmation, and particularly describing the place to be searched, and the persons or things to be seized.

This extremely important amendment is designed to prevent the abuse of state police powers. Essentially, unreasonable searches or seizures of homes, persons, or property cannot be undertaken without probable cause or a warrant that specifically describes the place to be searched, the person involved, and the suspicious things to be seized.

### Amendment 5—Grand Juries, Self-Incrimination, Double Jeopardy, Due Process, and Eminent Domain

No person shall be held to answer for a capital, or otherwise infamous crime, unless on a presentment or indictment of a Grand jury, except in cases arising in the land or naval forces, or in the Militia, when in actual service in time of War or public danger; nor shall any person be subject for the same offence to be twice put in jeopardy of life or limb; nor shall be compelled in any criminal case to be a witness against himself, nor be deprived of life, liberty, or property, without due process of law; nor shall private property be taken for public use, without just compensation.

Only a grand jury can indict a person for a federal crime. This provision does not apply to state and local governments. This amendment also covers double jeopardy, or being tried twice for the same crime in the same jurisdiction. Note that since the federal government and state governments are different jurisdictions, one could be tried in each jurisdiction for essentially the same crime. For example, it is a federal crime to kill a congressperson. It is also a state crime to murder anyone. Further, this amendment also covers the prohibition of self-incrimination. Pleading the Fifth Amendment used to be common in Mafia cases but recently was used by Enron witnesses. The deprivation of life, liberty, or property by any level of government is prohibited unless due process of law is applied. Finally, private property may not be taken under the doctrine of "eminent domain" unless the government provides just compensation.

### Amendment 6—Criminal Court Procedures

In all criminal prosecutions, the accused shall enjoy the right to a speedy and public trial, by an impartial jury of the State and district wherein the crime shall have been committed, which district shall have been previously ascertained by law, and to be informed of the nature and cause of the accusation; to be confronted with the witnesses against him; to have compulsory process for obtaining witnesses in his favor, and to have the Assistance of Counsel for his defence.

This amendment requires public trials by jury for criminal prosecutions. Anyone accused of a crime is guaranteed the rights to be informed of the charges, to confront witnesses, to subpoena witnesses for their defense, and to have a lawyer for their defense. Currently, the government must provide a lawyer for a defendant unable to afford one.

### Amendment 7—Trial by Jury in Common Law Cases

In Suits at common law, where the value in controversy shall exceed twenty dollars, the right of trial by jury shall be preserved, and no fact tried by a jury shall be otherwise re-examined in any Court of the United States, than according to the rules of the common law.

This amendment is practically without meaning in modern times. Statutory law has largely superseded common law. Federal civil lawsuits with a guaranteed jury are now restricted to cases that exceed $50,000. The Bill of Rights, which includes the right to trial by jury, applied originally only to the national government. Beginning in 1925, the Supreme Court began a selective process of incorporating provisions in the Bill of Rights and making them applicable to state and local governments as well. There are just a few provisions that have not been thus incorporated. Trial by jury is one. Some state and local governments have trials by judges, not by juries.

### Amendment 8—Bail, Cruel and Unusual Punishment

Excessive bail shall not be required, nor excessive fines imposed, nor cruel and unusual punishments inflicted.

Capital punishment is covered by this amendment, which also prohibits excessive bail. But this is relative. Million-dollar bails are not uncommon in some cases. One federal judge offered voluntary castration for sex offenders in lieu of jail time. Higher courts held this to be a cruel or unusual punishment. But it is the death penalty that generates the most heated controversy. Court cases challenging the constitutionality of capital punishment cite this amendment's language prohibiting cruel and unusual punishment. For a period of four years, the Supreme Court banned capital punishment. When states modified their statutes to provide a two-part judicial process of guilt determination and punishment, the Supreme Court allowed the reinstitution of capital punishment by the states.

## Amendment 9—Rights Retained by the People

The enumeration in the Constitution, of certain rights, shall not be construed to deny or disparage others retained by the people.

This amendment implies that there may be other rights of the people not specified by the previous amendments. Indeed, the Warren Court established the right to privacy even though it is not specifically mentioned in any previous amendment. Some would claim that persons have a right to adequate medical care and education.

## Amendment 10—Reserved Powers of the States

The powers not delegated to the United States by the Constitution, nor prohibited by it to the States, are reserved to the States respectively, or to the people.

The Tenth Amendment was seen as the reservoir of reserved powers for state governments. If the national government had been limited only to expressed powers in Article I, Section 8, of the Constitution, this would have been the case. But the doctrine of implied national government powers, which was established by the U.S. Supreme Court in *McCulloch* v. *Maryland* in 1819, made the intent of this amendment almost meaningless. Any reserved powers that were retained by the states were virtually removed by the U.S. Supreme Court's decision in the *Garcia* v. *San Antonio Metropolitan Transit Authority* case in 1985, which basically told state and local governments not to look to the courts to protect their residual rights but rather to their political representatives. In subsequent cases, the Supreme Court has retreated from this position when the Court found the federal government encroaching in state jurisdictional areas.

## Amendment 11—Suits Against the States

[Ratified February 7, 1795] The Judicial power of the United States shall not be construed to extend to any suit in law or equity, commenced or prosecuted against one of the United States by Citizens of another State, or by Citizens or Subjects of any Foreign State.

Article III of the U.S. Constitution originally allowed federal jurisdiction in cases of one state citizen against another state citizen or state. This amendment removes federal jurisdiction in this area. In essence, states may not be sued in federal court by citizens of another state or country.

## Amendment 12—Election of the President

[Ratified June 15, 1804] The Electors shall meet in their respective states, and vote by ballot for President and Vice-President, one of whom, at least, shall not be an inhabitant of the same state with themselves; they shall name in their ballots the person voted for as President, and in distinct ballots the person voted for as Vice-President, and they shall make distinct lists of all persons voted for as President, and of all persons voted for as Vice-President, and of the number of votes for each, which lists they shall sign and certify, and transmit sealed to the seat of the government of the United States, directed to the President of the Senate;—The President of the Senate shall, in the presence of the Senate and House of Representatives, open all the certificates and the votes shall then be counted;—The person having the greatest number of votes for President, shall be the President, if such number be a majority of the whole number of Electors appointed; and if no person have such majority, then from the persons having the highest numbers not exceeding three on the list of those voted for as President, the House of Representatives shall choose immediately, by ballot, the President. But in choosing the President, the votes shall be taken by states, the representation from each state having one vote; a quorum for this purpose shall consist of a member or members from two-thirds of the states, and a majority of all the states shall be necessary to a choice. And if the House of Representatives shall not choose a President whenever the right of choice shall devolve upon them, *before the fourth day of March next following*, then the Vice-President shall act as President, as in the case of the death or other constitutional disability of the President.[11] The person having the greatest number of votes as Vice-President, shall be the Vice-President, if such a number be a majority of the whole numbers of Electors appointed, and if no person have a majority, then from the two highest numbers on the list, the Senate shall choose the Vice-President; a quorum for the purpose shall consist of two-thirds of the whole number of Senators, and a majority of the whole number shall be necessary to a choice. But no person constitutionally ineligible to the office of President shall be eligible to that of Vice-President of the United States.

This was a necessary amendment to correct a flaw in the Constitution covering operations of the electoral college. In the election of 1800, Thomas Jefferson and Aaron Burr, both of the same Democratic-Republican Party, received the same number of electoral votes, 73, for president. Article II of the original Constitution specified that each elector would cast two ballots. It did not specify for whom. This amendment clarifies that the electoral vote must be specific for president and vice president. The original Constitution provided that if no candidate received a majority of electoral votes, the House would decide from the candidates with the top five vote totals. This amendment reduces the candidate field to the top three vote totals. If the House delays in this selection past the fourth day of March, the elected vice president will act as president until the House selects the president. The original Constitution provided that the candidate with the second highest number of electoral votes would become vice president.

This amendment, which requires a separate vote tally for vice president, provides for selection by the U.S. Senate if no vice presidential candidate receives an electoral vote majority.

[11] Changed by the Twentieth Amendment.

## Amendment 13—Prohibition of Slavery

[Ratified December 6, 1865]

SECTION 1 Neither slavery nor involuntary servitude, except as a punishment for crime whereof the party shall have been duly convicted, shall exist within the United States, or any place subject to their jurisdiction.

SECTION 2 Congress shall have power to enforce this article by appropriate legislation.

This is the first of the three Civil War amendments. Slavery is prohibited under all circumstances. Involuntary servitude is also prohibited unless it is a punishment for a convicted crime.

## Amendment 14—Citizenship, Due Process, and Equal Protection of the Laws

[Ratified July 9, 1868]

SECTION 1 All persons born or naturalized in the United States, and subject to the jurisdiction thereof, are citizens of the United States and of the State wherein they reside. No State shall make or enforce any law which shall abridge the privileges or immunities of citizens of the United States; nor shall any State deprive any person of life, liberty, or property, without due process of law; nor deny to any person within its jurisdiction the equal protection of the laws.

This section defines the meaning of U.S. citizenship and the protection of these citizenship rights. It also establishes the Equal Protection Clause that each state must guarantee to its citizens. It extended the provisions of the Fifth Amendment of due process and protection of life, liberty, and property and made these applicable to the states.

SECTION 2 Representatives shall be apportioned among the several States according to their respective numbers, counting the whole number of persons in each State, excluding Indians not taxed. But when the right to vote at any election for the choice of electors for President and Vice President of the United States, Representatives in Congress, the Executive and Judicial officers of a State, or the members of the Legislature thereof, is denied to any of the male inhabitants of such State, being twenty-one[12] years of age, and citizens of the United States, or in any way abridged, except for participation in rebellion, or other crime, the basis of representation therein shall be reduced in the proportion which the number of such male citizens shall bear to the whole number of male citizens twenty-one years of age in such State.

This section changes the three-fifths clause of the original Constitution. Now all male citizens age 21 or older will be used to calculate representation in the House of Representatives. If a state denies the right to vote to any male age 21 or older, the number of denied citizens will be deducted from the overall state total to determine representation.

SECTION 3 No person shall be a Senator or Representative in Congress, or elector of President and Vice President, or hold any office, civil or military, under the United States, or under any State, who, having previously taken an oath, as a member of Congress, or as an officer of the United States, or as a member of any State legislature, or as an executive or judicial officer of any State, to support the Constitution of the United States, shall have engaged in insurrection or rebellion against the same, or given aid or comfort to the enemies thereof. But Congress may by a vote of two-thirds of each House, remove such disability.

This section disqualifies from federal office or elector for president or vice president anyone who rebelled or participated in an insurrection against the Constitution. This was specifically directed against citizens of southern states. Congress by a two-thirds vote could override this provision.

SECTION 4 The validity of the public debt of the United States, authorized by law, including debts incurred for payment of pensions and bounties for services in suppressing insurrection or rebellion, shall not be questioned. But neither the United States nor any State shall assume or pay any debt or obligation incurred in aid of insurrection or rebellion against the United States, or any claim for the loss or emancipation of any slave; but all such debts, obligations and claims shall be held illegal and void.

SECTION 5 The Congress shall have power to enforce, by appropriate legislation, the provisions of this article.

Sections 4 and 5 cover the Civil War debts.

## Amendment 15—The Right to Vote

[Ratified February 3, 1870]

SECTION 1 The right of citizens of the United States to vote shall not be denied or abridged by the United States or by any State on account of race, color, or previous condition of servitude.

SECTION 2 The Congress shall have power to enforce this article by appropriate legislation.

This final Civil War amendment states that voting rights could not be denied by any states on account of race, color, or previous servitude. Unfortunately, it did not mention gender. Accordingly, only male citizens age 21 or over were guaranteed the right to vote by this amendment.

## Amendment 16—Income Taxes

[Ratified February 3, 1913] The Congress shall have power to lay and collect taxes on incomes, from whatever source derived, without apportionment among the several States, and without regard to any census or enumeration.

Article I, Section 9 of the original Constitution prohibited Congress from enacting a direct tax, or head tax, unless in proportion to a census. Congress in 1894 passed an income tax law, levying a 2 percent tax on incomes over $4,000. In 1895, the U.S. Supreme Court in a split decision (5–4) found that the income tax was a direct tax not apportioned among the states and was thus unconstitutional. Thus, Congress proposed an amendment allowing it to enact an income tax. Once this amendment was ratified, the flow of tax money to Washington increased tremendously.

## Amendment 17—Direct Election of Senators

[Ratified April 8, 1913] The Senate of the United States shall be composed of two Senators from each State, elected by the people thereof, for six years; and each Senator shall have one vote. The

[12] Changed by the Twenty-sixth Amendment.

electors in each State shall have the qualifications requisite for electors of the most numerous branch of the State legislatures.

When vacancies happen in the representation of any State in the Senate, the executive authority of such State shall issue writs of election to fill such vacancies: Provided, That the legislature of any State may empower the executive thereof to make temporary appointments until the people fill the vacancies by election as the legislature may direct.

This amendment shall not be so construed as to affect the election or term of any Senator chosen before it becomes valid as part of the Constitution.

Prior to this amendment, U.S. senators were selected by state legislatures. Now U.S. senators would be selected by popular vote in each state. Furthermore, the governor of each state may fill vacancies, subject to state laws.

## Amendment 18—Prohibition

[Ratified January 16, 1919. Repealed December 5, 1933, by Amendment 21]

SECTION 1 After one year from the ratification of this article the manufacture, sale, or transportation of intoxicating liquors within, the importation thereof into, or the exportation thereof from the United States and all territory subject to the jurisdiction thereof for beverage purposes is hereby prohibited.

SECTION 2 The Congress and the several States shall have concurrent power to enforce this article by appropriate legislation.

SECTION 3 This article shall be inoperative unless it shall have been ratified as an amendment to the Constitution by the legislatures of the several States, as provided in the Constitution, within seven years from the date of the submission hereof to the States by the Congress.[13]

This amendment was largely the work of the Women's Christian Temperance Union and essentially banned the manufacture, sale, or transportation of alcoholic beverages. Unintended consequences of this attempt to legislate morality were the brewing of "bathtub gin" and moonshine liquor, the involvement of the mob in importing liquor from Canada, and the "Untouchables" of Eliot Ness. Fortunately, this ill-fated social experiment was corrected by the Twenty-first Amendment. This is also the first amendment where Congress fixed a period for ratification—seven years.

## Amendment 19—For Women's Suffrage

[Ratified August 18, 1920] The right of the citizens of the United States to vote shall not be denied or abridged by the United States or by any State on account of sex.

Congress shall have power to enforce this article.

At long last, women achieved voting parity with men.

## Amendment 20—The Lame Duck Amendment

[Ratified January 23, 1933]

SECTION 1 The terms of the President and Vice President shall end at noon on the 20th day of January, and the terms of the Senators and Representatives at noon on the 3d day of January, of the years in which such terms would have ended if this article had not been ratified; and the terms of their successors shall then begin.

SECTION 2 The Congress shall assemble at least once in every year, and such meeting shall begin at noon on the 3d day of January, unless they shall by law appoint a different day.

SECTION 3 If, at the time fixed for the beginning of the term of the President, the President elect shall have died, the Vice President elect shall become President. If a President shall not have been chosen before the time fixed for the beginning of his term, or if the President elect shall have failed to qualify, then the Vice President elect shall act as President until a President shall have qualified; and the Congress may by law provide for the case wherein neither a President elect nor a Vice President elect shall have qualified, declaring who shall then act as President, or the manner in which one who is to act shall be selected, and such person shall act accordingly until a President or Vice President shall have qualified.

SECTION 4 The Congress may by law provide for the case of the death of any of the persons from whom the House of Representatives may choose a President whenever the right of choice shall have devolved upon them, and for the case of the death of any of the persons from whom the Senate may choose a Vice President whenever the right of choice shall have devolved upon them.

SECTION 5 Sections 1 and 2 shall take effect on the 15th day of October following the ratification of this article.

SECTION 6 This article shall be inoperative unless it shall have been ratified as an amendment to the Constitution by the legislatures of three-fourths of the several States within seven years from the date of its submission.

Called the Lame Duck amendment, this amendment fixes the dates for the end of presidential and legislative terms. A new president is elected in November, but the current president remains in office until January 20 of the following year, thus the term *lame duck*. Legislative terms begin earlier, on January 3.

## Amendment 21—Repeal of Prohibition

[Ratified December 5, 1933]

SECTION 1 The eighteenth article of amendment to the Constitution of the United States is hereby repealed.

SECTION 2 The transportation or importation into any State, Territory, or ptossession of the United States for delivery or use therein of intoxicating liquors, in violation of the laws thereof, is hereby prohibited.

SECTION 3 This article shall be inoperative unless it shall have been ratified as an amendment to the Constitution by conventions in the several States, as provided in the Constitution, within seven years from the date of the submission hereof to the States by the Congress.

This unusual amendment nullified the Eighteenth Amendment. The amendment called for the end of prohibition unless prohibited by state laws.

[13] Repealed by the Twenty-first Amendment.

## Amendment 22—Number of Presidential Terms

[Ratified February 27, 1951]

SECTION 1 No person shall be elected to the office of the President more than twice, and no person who has held the office of President, or acted as President, for more than two years of a term to which some other person was elected President shall be elected to the office of the President more than once. But this article shall not apply to any person holding the office of President when this article was proposed by the Congress, and shall not prevent any person who may be holding the office of President, or acting as President, during the term within which this article becomes operative from holding the office of President or acting as President during the remainder of such term.

SECTION 2 This article shall be inoperative unless it shall have been ratified as an amendment to the Constitution by the legislatures of three-fourths of the several states within seven years from the date of its submission to the states by the Congress.

This amendment could be called the Franklin D. Roosevelt amendment. It was FDR who broke the previously unwritten rule of serving no more than two terms as president. Democrat Roosevelt won an unprecedented four terms as president. When the Republicans took control of the Congress in 1948, they pushed through the Twenty-second Amendment, limiting the U.S. president to a lifetime of two full four-year terms of office.

## Amendment 23—Presidential Electors for the District of Columbia

[Ratified March 29, 1961]

SECTION 1 The District constituting the seat of government of the United States shall appoint in such manner as the Congress may direct:

A number of electors of President and Vice President equal to the whole number of Senators and Representatives in Congress to which the District would be entitled if it were a state, but in no event more than the least populous state; they shall be in addition to those appointed by the states, but they shall be considered, for the purposes of the election of President and Vice President, to be electors appointed by a state; and they shall meet in the District and perform such duties as provided by the twelfth article of amendment.

SECTION 2 The Congress shall have power to enforce this article by appropriate legislation.

This amendment gave electoral votes to the citizens of Washington, DC, which is not a state and thus not included in the original scheme of state electoral votes. Currently, Washington, DC, has three electoral votes, bringing the total of presidential electoral votes to 538. Puerto Ricans are citizens of the United States but have no electoral votes.

## Amendment 24—The Anti-Poll Tax Amendment

[Ratified January 23, 1964]

SECTION 1 The right of citizens of the United States to vote in any primary or other election for President or Vice President, for electors for President or Vice President, or for Senator or Representative in Congress, shall not be denied or abridged by the United States or any state by reason of failure to pay any poll tax or other tax.

SECTION 2 The Congress shall have power to enforce this article by appropriate legislation.

The poll tax was a procedure used mostly in southern states to discourage poor white and black voters from registering to vote. Essentially, one would have to pay a tax to register to vote. The tax was around $34 per year. But for a poor white or black voter, this might not be disposable income. As part of the assault against disenfranchisement of voters, the poll tax was abolished. Literacy tests, another device to disqualify voters, were abolished by the Voting Rights Act of 1965.

## Amendment 25—Presidential Disability, Vice Presidential Vacancies

[Ratified February 10, 1967]

SECTION 1 In case of the removal of the President from office or of his death or resignation, the Vice President shall become President.

SECTION 2 Whenever there is a vacancy in the office of the Vice President, the President shall nominate a Vice President who shall take the office upon confirmation by a majority vote of both Houses of Congress.

SECTION 3 Whenever the President transmits to the President pro tempore of the Senate and the Speaker of the House of Representatives his written declaration that he is unable to discharge the powers and duties of his office, and until he transmits to them a written declaration to the contrary, such powers and duties shall be discharged by the Vice President as Acting President.

SECTION 4 Whenever the Vice President and a majority of either the principal officers of the executive departments, or of such other body as Congress may by law provide, transmit to the President pro tempore of the Senate and the Speaker of the House of Representatives their written declaration that the President is unable to discharge the powers and duties of his office, the Vice President shall immediately assume the powers and duties of the office as Acting President.

Thereafter, when the President transmits to the President pro tempore of the Senate and the Speaker of the House of Representatives his written declaration that no inability exists, he shall resume the powers and duties of his office unless the Vice President and a majority of either the principal officers of the executive department, or of such other body as Congress may by law provide, transmit within four days to the President pro tempore of the Senate and the Speaker of the House of Representatives their written declaration that the President is unable to discharge the powers and duties of his office. Thereupon Congress shall decide the issue, assembling within forty-eight hours for that purpose if not in session. If the Congress, within twenty-one days after receipt of the latter written declaration, or, if Congress is not in session, within twenty-one days after Congress is required to assemble, determines by two-thirds vote of both Houses that the President is unable to discharge the powers and duties of his office, the Vice President shall continue to discharge the same as Acting President; otherwise, the President shall resume the powers and duties of his office.

President Woodrow Wilson's final year in office was marked by serious illness. It is rumored that his wife acted as president. There was no constitutional provision to cover an incapacitating illness of a president. This amendment provides a procedure for this eventuality. The president can inform congressional leaders of his or her incapacitation, and the vice president then takes over. When the president recovers, he or she can inform congressional leaders and resume office.

The amendment also recognizes that the president may not be able or wish to indicate this debilitation. In this case, the vice president and a majority of cabinet members can inform congressional leaders, and the vice president takes over. When the president informs congressional leadership that he or she is back in form, he or she resumes the presidency unless the vice president and a majority of the cabinet members disagree. Then Congress must decide who is to be president. The likelihood that this procedure will ever be used is relatively small.

The most immediate importance of this amendment concerns the office of vice president. The original Constitution did not address the issue of a vacancy in this office. The Twenty-fifth Amendment established the procedure just in time! This amendment was ratified in 1967. In 1973, the sitting vice president, Spiro Agnew, resigned his office. Under the provisions of this amendment, President Nixon nominated Gerald Ford as vice president. As a former member of the House, Ford was quickly approved by the Congress. But a year later, President Nixon also resigned. Now Vice President Ford became President Ford, and he in turn appointed Nelson Rockefeller as the new vice president. For the first time in our history, we had both a president and vice president, neither of whom was elected by the electoral college.

## Amendment 26—Eighteen-Year-Old Vote

[Ratified July 1, 1971]

SECTION 1 The right of citizens of the United States, who are 18 years of age or older, to vote, shall not be denied or abridged by the United States or by any state on account of age.

SECTION 2 The Congress shall have power to enforce this article by appropriate legislation.

During the Vietnam War, 18-year-old boys were being drafted and sent out to possibly die in the service of their country. Yet they did not even have the right to vote. This incongruity led to the Twenty-sixth Amendment, which lowered the legal voting age from 21 to 18.

## Amendment 27—Congressional Salaries

[Ratified May 7, 1992] No law varying the compensation for the services of the Senators and Representatives shall take effect until an election of Representatives shall have intervened.

This is a "sleeper" amendment that was part of 12 amendments originally submitted by the first Congress to the states for ratification. The states ratified only 10 of the 12, which collectively became known as the Bill of Rights. But since Congress did not set a time limit for ratification, the other two amendments remained on the table. Much to the shock of the body politic, in 1992, three-fourths of the states ratified the original twelfth amendment. This reflected the disgust of seeing Congress continuing to increase its salary and benefits. The amendment delays any increase of compensation for at least one election cycle.

# Federalism

# 3

## Chapter Outline

### Introduction:
*Federalism and Democracy*

## Learning Objectives

3.1 How does the American system of federalism balance national and state power to preserve democracy?

3.2 How does the U.S. Constitution apportion powers to balance the relationship between the national and state governments?

3.3 What types of powers have been delegated to the national government, and which were retained by the states?

3.4 How did the federal structure evolve in response to crises in the early years of American government?

3.5 How did the interstate commerce and Fourteenth Amendment due process clauses of the U.S. Constitution help to nationalize the government?

3.6 How has the system of federal grants increased the power of the federal government?

3.7 How has the Supreme Court under Chief Justices William Rehnquist and John Roberts altered the system of federalism?

# INTRODUCTION

## FEDERALISM AND DEMOCRACY

3.1 *How does the American system of federalism balance national and state power to preserve democracy?*

Many issues cross state boundaries, creating classic partnerships between Congress, as it searches for a broad vision of national interests, and the efforts of states to preserve **states' rights.** The result is a series of challenges as different types of government seek to resolve any differences between those visions while applying the larger policies to a particular region. At the heart of these negotiations over policy is the concept of federalism.

Debates still rage among different levels of government as to which institutions are responsible for recovering from natural and technological disasters. The 2010 catastrophic oil spill by the BP oil rig in the Gulf of Mexico of nearly five million barrels and covering 80 square miles in the ocean serves as a good example. Louisiana Governor Bobby Jindal and various other local officials threatened to build sand barriers and take other action, despite opposition by the Environmental Protection Agency, because they were unhappy with the lack of responsiveness of the federal government. A year later, after the city of Joplin, Missouri, was leveled by a devastating Category 5 hurricane, national and state officials were pressed for aid. At the same time, another dispute was occurring throughout the Mississippi Valley area. The Army Corps of Engineers, faced with the prospect that river levees holding back the melted run-off from the winter's excessive snow fall might fail, decided to release that water with the result that cities and towns further down the river would be flooded for months. In this same period, a new kind of federalism issue began. States in the southwestern United States, such as Arizona and Utah, and later Georgia in the southeast, became upset when the paralyzed partisan politics of the national government prevented Congress from dealing with the issue of illegal aliens moving into and living in the country. So, these states passed their own restrictive laws against illegal aliens, empowering the state police and other governmental actors with the right to request that people for whom they had a "reasonable suspicion" might not be legal must produce their citizenship papers or green cards. This interconnection between the national and state and local governments, and the overarching nature of the problems facing these institutions, made very clear how important the federalism issues had become.

**states' rights**
Rights the U.S. Constitution neither grants to the national government nor forbids to the states.

This chapter defines federalism, and then examines it as outlined in the Constitution and how it has developed over the years. Finally, it examines the dynamic and changing nature of the federal structure. A series of Supreme Court decisions and public policies have made our government system far different from that envisioned

Louisiana Governor Bobby Jindal (R) demonstrates that vacuuming up the millions of gallons of BP oil lost in the 2010 from his state's shores requires help from the federal government.

by the framers of this country's Constitution. Federalism is one of America's unique contributions to democratic theory and republican government. Only by understanding how the system works can you come to understand how it has helped the United States approach democracy.

## FEDERALISM DEFINED

**Federalism** is a political system in which governmental powers are shared between a general government with nationwide responsibilities and nationwide powers and decentralized regional governments with local responsibilities and local powers in their respective regions. In the uniquely American form of federalism, both the overarching national government, frequently called the *federal government,* and the 50 decentralized state governments share power on the basis of each one's sovereignty, as outlined in the U.S. Constitution.[1]

To understand the nature of the federal system in America, it is important to know the framers' intentions in constructing it. The framers rejected the *unitary* system of government, in which all power is vested in a central authority that could compel the state governments to respond. This was the relationship between the English monarchy and the American colonies. The framers also rejected the *confederation* system of government, in which the power to govern is decentralized among sovereign states, and the national government has such limited powers that it must respond to state dictates. This was the system of government under the Articles of Confederation. Instead, the framers sought to create a structure that combined the best features of both systems—a central government strong enough to deal with the larger national problems and decentralized state governments able to address the needs of the people in those territories.

The federal structure should be flexible, too, according to the framers. They wanted to delegate enough powers to the central government to allow it to govern the entire nation, thus correcting the weaknesses inherent in the Articles of Confederation. But they also saw functional reasons for maintaining powerful states within that system. As James Madison explained in *The Federalist,* no. 10, "The federal Constitution forms a happy combination in this respect; the great and aggregate

**federalism**
The relationship between the centralized national government and the individual state governments.

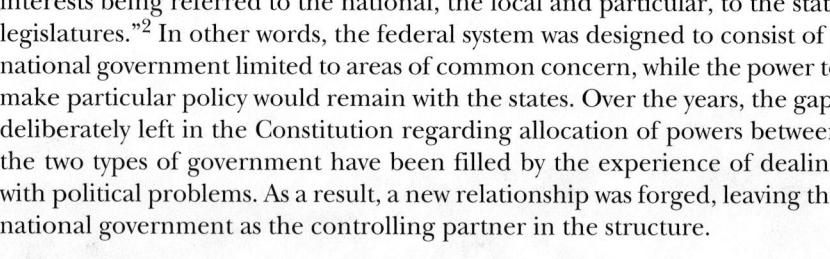

## THINKING CRITICALLY

The Supreme Court has ruled that the national government's policies controlling the sale and use of drugs has precedence over state policies legalizing the use of drugs. Under Proposition 215, though, California has allowed the sale and use of marijuana for medical purposes. In 2009, Attorney General Eric Holder announced that the federal government would no longer prosecute those who use drugs for medical purposes under state law. What roles should the federal and state governments play in determining drug and medical policies here?

interests being referred to the national, the local and particular, to the state legislatures."[2] In other words, the federal system was designed to consist of a national government limited to areas of common concern, while the power to make particular policy would remain with the states. Over the years, the gaps deliberately left in the Constitution regarding allocation of powers between the two types of government have been filled by the experience of dealing with political problems. As a result, a new relationship was forged, leaving the national government as the controlling partner in the structure.

## Federalism: Advantages and Disadvantages

National policy is the same for everyone, but state and local policy vary widely by region. Variations arise in tax policy, public programs, services such as police and education, and also the form of individual rights. The Massachusetts Supreme Judicial Court ruled that same-sex marriages were constitutional in that state in 2003, but before that year's presidential election, conservatives led by White House political adviser Karl Rove persuaded Ohio and 12 more states to either legally or constitutionally ban same-sex marriages. These states joined 35 other states as well as the federal government, which had in 1996 adopted a "Defense of Marriage" law defining marriage as being "between a man and a woman." Since that time, though, the movement has gone the other way. In June 2009, spurred by the Massachusetts decision, New Hampshire voted in favor of gay marriage, joining Connecticut, Maine, Vermont, and Iowa.

The landscape of this issue is continually changing, though, as California, which had also allowed same-sex marriages by a state Supreme Court decision in May 2008, removed that prospect with the passage of Proposition 8 by the voters in the 2008 election; voters in Maine did the same thing in a 2009 election. California became even more complicated when the State Supreme Court upheld Proposition 8 but allowed around 18,000 couples already married to remain so. Meanwhile, the opposing attorneys in the *Bush* v. *Gore* case, Ted Olson and David Boies, were bringing a lawsuit in federal court to challenge the new California Proposition 8 gay marriage ban.[3] Change continued in this field in 2011, as federal District Court Judge Vaughn Walker overturned Proposition 8 in California, and New York became the largest and sixth state, joining Iowa, Massachusetts, Connecticut, Vermont, and New Hampshire, along with the District of Columbia, to legalize gay marriage.

These varying legal and constitutional protections for same-sex couples at the different state and national levels illustrate the slow development toward an overarching national governmental policy on this question. On the other hand, giving the states a chance to experiment with policy—as has been the case with affirmative action, education, and welfare programs—has in the past produced programs adopted by the national government.

## QUICK REVIEW

Advantages of Federalism

- A large number of different governments ensures diversity among policies and programs.
- Policy diversity minimizes policy conflict.
- It results in a healthy dispersal of power.
- Prospects for governmental experimentation and innovation are enhanced.

**Advantages** Federalism has many advantages. Rather than one uniform policy for everyone, the large number of different governments ensures diversity among policies and programs. Americans need diverse policies to accommodate a diverse populace across a vast country.

Policy diversity also minimizes policy conflict. If groups fail to pass their programs in the federal government, they can try again in the state or local governments, thus minimizing pressure on the national government for action. But should action fail at the state government, attention can shift back to the national government. More centers of power for implementing policy allow more opportunity for government to respond to the needs and desires of the people. One example of this pattern can be seen in the area of minimum wage reform. In late May 2007, President Bush signed into law a $2.10 increase in the federal minimum wage to $7.25 by the summer of 2009—the first increase in the minimum wage in ten years, passed by the newly elected Democratic Congress as part of their its "six in '06" campaign pledge.

But when the president did so, he knew that 29 states had already increased their own minimum wages above the federal level by as much as $2.48.[4] And when the Supreme Court upheld the Federal Partial Birth Abortion law in April 2007, it did so while knowing that South Dakota had already passed a law, which might be unconstitutional, effectively overturning the *Roe* v. *Wade* abortion decision in that state by banning abortions there. The decision spurred more than a dozen other states to consider extending abortion rights, while two states were considering restricting them.[5] In 2011, South Dakota continued its effort to restrict abortion, passing another law requiring a 72-hour waiting period before getting an abortion, and requiring such women seeking that procedure to visit an anti-abortion counseling center.

Federalism also produces a healthy dispersal of power. The framers, concerned about a national government with too much power, reserved certain powers for the states. This dispersal of political power creates more opportunity for political participation. Individuals or political parties that lack national power have the opportunity in the federal structure to establish bases of power in the states and localities. Thus, the Republican party, which had no foothold in the national government in the early 1960s, managed to build a power base in many states from the Reagan administration in the early 1980s; by the 2000 election, it had become the nation's predominant party. But then the Democrats did the same, working through the state governments until they regained power in Congress in the 2006 election. After the 2010 elections, with 26 states now controlled by the Republicans, efforts were being made by that party following the decennial census to redistrict their state to make election of their party members more likely. Then, as outlined in Chapter 1, various Republican jurisdictions began passing, under the guise of "anti-voter fraud" laws, restrictions on the ability of minority and student voters who might be expected to vote for Democrats.

Frustrated by the lack of federal action on illegal immigration, states such as Arizona, Alabama, and Utah, passed anti-immigration laws that instructed police and other officials to ask people for their citizenship papers, leading to charges of racial profiling.

America's system of federalism also enhances the prospects for governmental experimentation and innovation. Justice Louis D. Brandeis described this possibility when he wrote, "It is one of the happy incidents of the federal system that a single courageous state may, if its citizens choose, serve as a laboratory and try novel social and economic experiments without risk to the rest of the country."[6] For him, the states became "laboratories of democracy." Thus, the national government can observe which experimental programs undertaken by various states are working and perhaps adopt the best of those ideas for the rest of the nation. In December 2001, President Bush signed into law his No Child Left Behind education reform act, which was modeled on that of his home state of Texas. Students in Texas public schools are tested yearly to assess the schools' performance. The No Child Left Behind Act promised states $26 billion in federal funds for education programs for low-income children. States had to allocate the funds for additional student testing to measure school performance. While some praised the law's intention to improve educational quality, critics called the law an underfunded **federal mandate,** imposing new regulations on the states without providing necessary funding.[7]

## THINKING CRITICALLY

How does it matter to you whether the minimum wage is increased by the federal government or the state in which you are located? How would it matter to you if the Supreme Court overturned the *Roe* v. *Wade* abortion decision, or the *Griswold* v. *Connecticut* birth control decision, and left the decision to the state governments?

**federal mandate**
A direct order from Congress that the states must fulfill.

**Disadvantages** But federalism has its disadvantages as well. The federal structure's dispersed power and opportunities for participation allow groups in certain regions to protect their interests and sometimes obstruct and even ignore national mandates. For example, into the 1960s, the southern states tried to perpetuate segregationist policies by citing states' rights. Ultimately, legal discrimination in civil rights, housing, voting, and schools came to an end by federal law. In 2005, though, the discussion over whether or not to renew the Federal Voting Rights Act of 1965 sparked fears of a possible detrimental return to the patchwork quilt of regulations in state voting requirements that often excluded minority voters in the South.[8] Because of this fear, Congress unanimously renewed the law a year later, without controversy, and it continues to be used to investigate voter fraud allegations. In 2009, the Supreme Court heard a case from an Austin, Texas, utility district challenging the Voting Rights Act's selective application only to 16 states, many in the Deep South, whose history of discrimination had led to the initial passage of the law, requiring that they gain "preclearance" from the federal government before changing their voting regulations, to ensure that they would not negatively affect minority vote. Chief Justice John Roberts's opinion argued that the "fundamental . . . sovereignty [of all states]" required that the national government prove why they should be forced to submit to federal voting rules. However, instead of declaring Section 5 of the law unconstitutional, the Court ruled for now that individual districts could petition to "bail out" from being subject to the law if they could prove that they had not discriminated against voters for ten years and had "engaged in constructive efforts" to promote improved participation by minority voters. Then it warned Congress that unless the need for the law was demonstrated better under its interstate commerce clause foundations, it might be overturned entirely in a future case. In a solo dissent, the Court's only African American justice, Clarence Thomas, argued that this discriminatory pattern against minority voters no longer existed and that "punishment for long past sins is not a legitimate basis" for restricting the sovereignty of select states.[9]

Inequities arise in a federal system. Poor regions cannot afford to provide the same services as wealthier ones. Rural regions have different needs from urban regions. Coastal regions and regions with significant waterways have different concerns from midwestern plains states. Thus, governmental programs in localities can vary dramatically. It takes a proper balance of national and state powers to realize the benefits of federalism and minimize its drawbacks. What, then, constitutes this proper balance? That question has been debated since the framers' day.

## THINKING CRITICALLY

The Supreme Court ruled that Oregon's Death with Dignity program, by which doctors could prescribe lethal doses of drugs to terminally ill patients, could not be prevented by the federal government enforcing its anti-drug laws. Which government, if either, should determine policy dealing with the question of euthanasia?

# FEDERALISM IN THE CONSTITUTION

3.2 *How does the U.S Constitution apportion powers to balance the relationship between the national and state governments?*

Let us now look at the vertical powers the framers outlined in the Constitution and their effect on the relationship between the national and state governments. Five constitutional provisions are particularly important—the interstate commerce clause, the general welfare clause, the necessary and proper clause, the supremacy clause, and the Tenth Amendment—because they continually shift the balance of power between the national and state governments. We refer to these five provisions as the **fulcrum of powers.**

This group of civil rights protestors appeared before the Supreme Court in the hopes of having the Voting Rights Act of 1965 declared constitutional in a case coming from Austin, Texas. Although they got their wish, it was not clear from the Court's decision how long this law would survive unless changes were made.

**fulcrum of powers**
The five constitutional provisions that dictate the balance of power between the national and state governments in the federal structure. They include the interstate commerce clause, the general welfare clause, the necessary and proper clause, the supremacy clause, and the Tenth Amendment.

## The Fulcrum of Powers

Each power in the fulcrum has a specific function. Four of them—the interstate commerce clause, the general welfare clause, the necessary and proper clause, and the supremacy clause—have been used to expand the powers of the national government. The fifth—the Tenth Amendment—has been used to protect state powers.

**The Interstate Commerce Clause** In Article I, Section 8, the Constitution's framers gave Congress the power "to regulate Commerce with foreign Nations, and among the several States." This clause sought to rectify the national government's inability under the Articles of Confederation to control movement of goods across state lines. But it really did much more. The interstate commerce clause led to a national government able to provide basic uniformity of policy among the states. A broad interpretation of this clause—and changes over time from self-contained states to an economy that included commercial enterprises linked across state lines—ultimately provided the means for expanding national power even within state borders. Using this power, the national government could keep the states from penalizing each other while encouraging them to work together.

To demonstrate how the national government can use the commerce clause to achieve uniform policy, let's say that restauranteur Joe Bigot is determined to discriminate against minorities in his fast-food hamburger business, located on an interstate highway between Texas and Oklahoma. Clearly, the national government would be able to bar discrimination in these restaurants because the restaurants serve interstate travelers, and thus affect interstate commerce.

So, let's say Joe moved his business to an area that gets no interstate customers. However, the meat Joe serves, his kitchen machinery, and his eating implements were all imported from out of state. Because those purchases affect interstate commerce, federal regulations apply. This example reflects two Supreme Court cases that upheld Congress's use of its interstate commerce power as the basis for the 1964 Civil Rights Act. That act expanded the rights of African Americans and barred discrimination in public accommodations.[10]

A broad interpretation of the interstate commerce clause can give the national government tremendous power to reach policy areas previously reserved to the

**QUICK REVIEW**

The Fulcrum of Powers

- These powers have been used to expand the powers of the national government and to protect state powers.
- The interstate commerce clause, the power to regulate commerce, provides some uniformity of policy among the states.
- The general welfare clause granted Congress the power to impose and collect taxes, to pay debts, and to provide for the common defense and general welfare of the United States.
- The Tenth Amendment preserved the individuality of the states and restricted the national government to its delegated powers.

states. Using the interstate commerce clause, the national government can, if it so desires (and it invariably does), regulate the wages and work hours on your campus; the admissions and scholarship rules, including the apportionment of scholarships between men and women on college sports teams; campus housing regulations; and campus codes of conduct. Off campus, the food you eat in a restaurant, local government operations, and practices in businesses you patronize all face regulation when the national government uses its interstate commerce power.

## THINKING CRITICALLY

Supporters of state restrictions in the wine-shipping case argued that the Twenty-first Amendment, which ended prohibition, also stated, "The transportation or importation into any State . . . for delivery or use therein of intoxicating liquors, in violation of the laws thereof, is hereby prohibited." Supporters argued that the power to dictate whether liquor could be shipped into a state was now a sovereign state power. How would that interpretation affect your ability to purchase wine legally? Should the policies to purchase liquor vary from state to state, or be uniform throughout the country?

The Supreme Court confronted the question of the reach of the federal interstate commerce power over the states in 2005, when it dealt with the power to control Internet sales and shipping of products from small wineries among states. Although the American domestic wine industry generated more than $18 billion in revenues a year, by that time 24 states had laws that banned direct shipment of out-of-state wines to customers in their regions, ostensibly to protect state wineries, preserve local tax revenues, and protect against alcohol sales to minors. By a narrow 5–4 vote, the Supreme Court sided with the nationalists and put an end to what it termed an "ongoing low-level trade war" that the interstate commerce clause was designed to stop. The Court decided the sale and shipment of these wines across the country clearly affected commerce in a positive way. Justice Kennedy noted that with more than 3,000 small wineries but few national wholesalers, it was not possible for "many small wineries [to] produce enough wine or have sufficient consumer demand for their wine to make it economical for wholesalers to carry their products." As a result of this decision, states can no longer ban *only* out-of-state wine sales over the Internet, but they can still restrict or ban *all* wine sales, both in and out of state, if they choose.[11]

**The General Welfare Clause** The Constitution, in Article I, Section 8, also grants Congress the power to "lay and collect Taxes, Duties, Imposts and Excises, to pay the Debts and provide for the common Defense and general Welfare of the United States." The combination of this spending power with the necessary and proper clause (also known as the *elastic clause*) in Article I, Section 8, enabled the national government to indirectly influence state policy through the power of the pocketbook. This power has expanded the national government's reach into formerly state-controlled areas via "carrot-and-stick" programs. The "carrot" is the money that the federal government provides for states that abide by national programs; the "stick" is the threatened loss of money if they do not. In 1984, for example, Congress used the carrot-and-stick approach to prevail. States that did not raise their drinking age to 21 would lose 5 percent of their 1986 federal highway funds and 10 percent of the 1987 total. Not surprisingly, near uniformity on the new legal drinking age occurred almost immediately.[12] This "carrot and stick" approach can work in reverse as well. In 2005, Senator Robert Byrd of West Virginia persuaded Congress to pass a law requiring colleges and universities to teach about and celebrate the Constitution every September 17, or face the loss of their federal funds. Using this same approach, in 2011, the U.S. Department of Education, realizing that Congress had taken over the student loan business from the national banks, issued a new regulation requiring schools to justify their course credit hour policies or face possible loss of their federal funds.

**Necessary and Proper Clause** Article I, Section 8, Clause 18 of the Constitution, which contains the necessary and proper clause, is not so much a power, but rather an extension of Congress's powers that can be used to expand the reach of the federal government. The clause, which reads that Congress has the power "To make all Laws which shall be necessary and proper for carrying into

Execution the Foregoing powers, and all other powers vested by this Constitution in the Government of the United States, or in any Department or Officer thereof," can be read one of two ways. It can be read as Secretary of the Treasury Alexander Hamilton did in 1791 in considering the creation of a National Bank in recommending to President Washington that it was an implied constitutional power that was "convenient" for the exercise of the delegated powers of Congress, and thus could be used to expand those powers. Or, taking the states' rights point of view, it can be read as Secretary of State Thomas Jefferson did, in arguing that the clause should be used only if it was "absolutely necessary," or without which the powers of Congress would be rendered "nugatory." Over the years, it was Hamilton's position that was adopted and this clause has been used to expand congressional and thus national powers. In the debate over the national health-care policy of Barack Obama, the argument has been that health care represents 15 percent of the national economy, so the interstate commerce clause empowers the government to legislate here. But, in addition, the necessary and proper clause, it is argued by the policy's proponents, empowers the government to set up programs to regulate how health care will be delivered and to force people to buy into this insurance plan. If upheld in the federal courts, this program would be imposed at the expense of the power of the states as it would change the way that Medicare was being delivered by the states.

**The Supremacy Clause** The supremacy clause in Article V of the Constitution argues that the constitutional provisions, laws, and treaties of the federal government "shall be the supreme Law of the Land," which the state courts shall enforce if they conflict with state laws or constitutional provisions. This allows the federal government to institute a national policy and, in some cases, to "pre-empt" the actions of the states by taking over policy making in key areas. During the 1950s, the supremacy clause enabled the national government to control the area of anti-Communism policy, and since 2001, it has allowed the national government to set the policy in the "war on terror" field. In the area of immigration policy reform, where the national government has been unable to form a coherent policy because of the partisan stalemate in Congress, it will be interesting to see what will happen to the restrictive immigration laws of states such as Arizona and Utah, if that policy is ever changed.

**The Tenth Amendment** What kept the national government from dominating the federal structure from the beginning? The answer lies in the Tenth Amendment, which states: "The powers not delegated to the United States by the Constitution, nor prohibited by it to the States, are reserved to the States respectively, or to the people." Thus, the framers intended to preserve states' individuality and restrict the national government to its delegated powers.

This amendment has been at the center of the shifting balance of power between the national government and the state governments. Between 1877 and 1937, state-centered federalism advocates on the Supreme Court used the Tenth Amendment to bar national intrusion into state activities. Because manufacturing and mining took place entirely within state boundaries, the national government was assumed to have no power to reach them.[13] The Supreme Court changed direction, however, after Roosevelt's "court-packing plan," and the new Roosevelt appointees declared that the Tenth Amendment could not restrict Congress's desire to control commerce and economic activities within state boundaries.[14]

The Tenth Amendment has gained new prominence in recent years as a basis for the *devolution* of power from the national government to the states. Both the Congress since 1995 and a five-person conservative Supreme Court majority since 1994 have tended to use this amendment to shift power to the states, in line with their commitment to reduce Washington's role in administering and funding local programs.[15]

**supremacy clause**
A clause in Article IV of the Constitution holding that in any conflict between federal laws and treaties and state laws, the will of the national government always prevails.

**delegated powers**
Powers expressly granted or enumerated in the Constitution and limited in nature.

**implied powers**
Powers not specifically stated in the Constitution but inferred from the express powers.

**inherent powers**
Powers that do not appear in the Constitution but are assumed because of the nature of government. Also refers to a theory that the Constitution grants authority to the executive, through the injunction in Article II, Section 1: "The Executive power shall be vested in a President of the United States of America."

**reserved powers**
Powers not assigned by the Constitution to the national government but left to the states or to the people, according to the Tenth Amendment.

**police powers**
The powers to regulate health, morals, public safety, and welfare, which are reserved to the states.

# THE DIVISION OF POWERS

3.3 *What types of powers have been delegated to the national government, and which were retained by the states?*

The framers were careful to express in the Constitution a series of powers that keep the two forms of government independent. Recall from Chapter 2 that the **supremacy clause** upholds national laws and treaties as the "supreme Law of the Land." This clause establishes the predominance of national laws whenever national and state legislation overlap. The states also receive both powers and limits to power. These provisions are outlined in Table 3.1. The Constitution carefully details the powers delegated to the national government, the powers reserved to the states, and the powers that apply to the two governments concurrently.

The Constitution first specifies the **delegated powers,** those that are given specifically to the national government. Generally, the framers saw these powers lacking in the old Articles of Confederation. They reasoned that a nation must speak with one voice when negotiating with foreign countries; it also needs a uniform monetary system for its economy to function. Thus, only the national government can declare war, raise and support an army, make treaties with other nations, and coin money.

Another category of powers comprises the **implied powers,** those not specifically enumerated in the Constitution but inferred from the delegated powers. Many can be justified through the elastic clause. For example, the national government's power to tax and spend can be extended by the necessary and proper clause to cover construction of a national system of roads. In addition, the **inherent powers** do not appear in the Constitution but are *assumed* because of the nature of government. Thus, only the national government has the power to conduct foreign relations, make war even in the absence of a formal declaration, and protect its officials against bodily harm or threats.

Those powers not assigned to the national government are left with the states. These **reserved powers,** guaranteed in the Tenth Amendment, protect the states' role in the federal system. Among the reserved powers are the so-called **police powers,** or the ability to regulate the health, morals, public safety, and welfare of state citizens. Such regulations include speed limits on highways, but they also involve education, marriage, criminal law, zoning regulations, and contracts (see Figure 3.1). It is here that the states claim

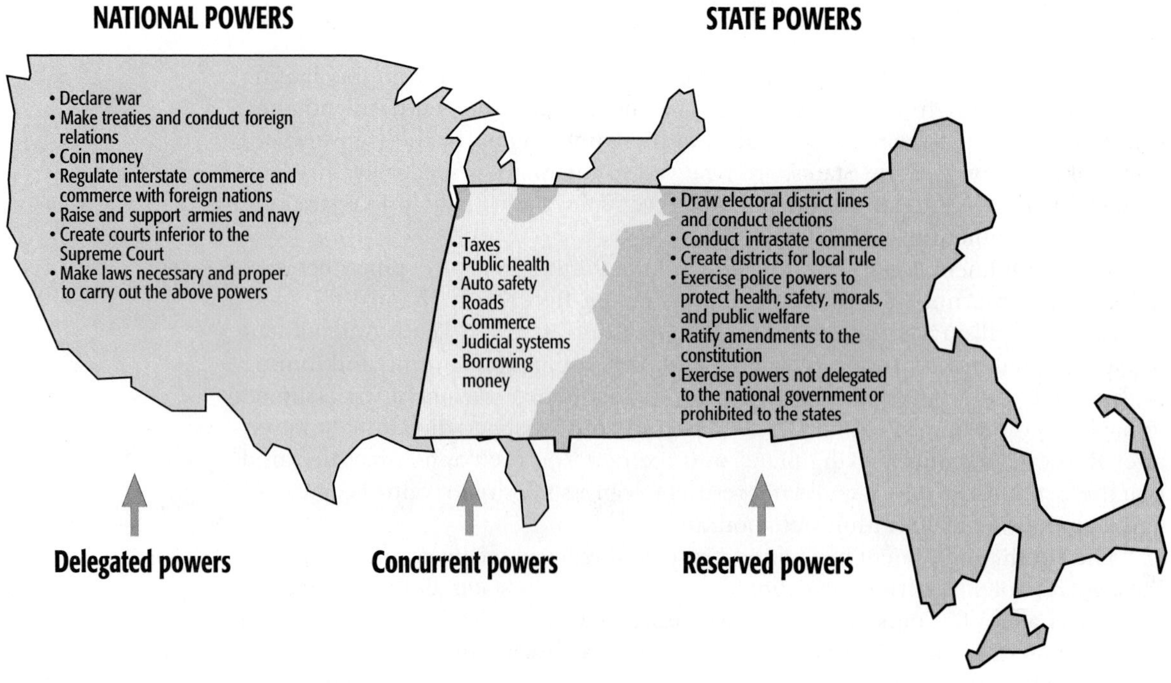


**FIGURE 3.1** The Division of Powers in the Federal System

**Table 3.1** Constitutional Guarantees of and Limits on State Power

| Guarantees | Limits |
|---|---|
| **1. State Integrity and Sovereignty** | |
| No division of states or consolidation of parts of two or more states without state legislative consent (Art. IV, Sec. 3)<br>Guarantee of republican form of state government (Art. IV, Sec. 4)<br>Protection against invasion and against domestic violence (Art. IV, Sec. 4)<br>Powers not delegated to national government reserved for states (10th Amend.)<br>State equality in Senate cannot be denied (Art. V) | States cannot enter into treaties, alliances, or confederations (Art. I, Sec. 10)<br>No interstate or foreign compacts without consent of Congress (Art. I, Sec. 10)<br>No separate coinage (Art. 1, Sec. 10)<br>National constitution, laws, and treaties are supreme (Art. VI)<br>All state officials bound by national Constitution (Art. VI)<br>No denial of privileges and immunity of citizens (14th Amend.)<br>No abridgment of right to vote on basis of race (15th Amend.)<br>No abridgment of right to vote on basis of sex (19th Amend.) |
| **2. Military Affairs and Defense** | |
| Power to maintain militia and appoint militia officials (Art. I, Sec. 8, 2d Amend.) | No maintenance of standing military in peacetime without congressional consent (Art. I, Sec. 10)<br>No engagement in war without congressional consent, except in emergency (Art. I, Sec. 10) |
| **3. Commerce and Taxation** | |
| Equal apportionment of direct federal taxes (Art. I, Secs. 2, 9)<br>No export duties imposed on any state (Art. I, Sec. 9)<br>No preferential treatment for ports of one state (Art. I, Sec. 9)<br>Reciprocal full faith and credit among states for public acts, records, and judicial proceedings (Art. IV, Sec. 1)<br>Reciprocal privileges and immunities for citizens of different states (Art. IV, Sec. 2)<br>Intoxicating liquor may not be imported into states where its sale or use is prohibited (21st Amend.) | No levying of duties on vessels of sister states (Art. I, Sec. 9)<br>No legal tender other than gold or silver (Art. I, Sec. 10)<br>No impairment of the obligations of contract (Art. I, Sec. 10)<br>No levying of import or export duties without congressional consent, except the levying of reasonable inspection fees (Art. I, Sec. 10)<br>No tonnage duties without congressional consent (Art. I, Sec. 10) |
| **4. Administration of Justice** | |
| Federal criminal trials to be held in state where crime was committed (Art. III, Sec. 2)<br>Extradition for crimes (Art. IV, Sec. 2)<br>Federal criminal juries to be chosen from state and district where crime was committed (6th Amend.)<br>Federal judicial power extends to controversies between two or more states, between a state and citizens of another state, and between a state or its citizens and a foreign nation or its citizens (Art. III, Sec. 2) | No bills of attainder (Art. I, Sec. 10)<br>No ex post facto laws (Art. I, Sec. 10)<br>Supreme Court has original jurisdiction over all cases in which state is a party (Art. III, Sec. 2)<br>No denial of life, liberty, or property without due process of law (14th Amend.)<br>No denial of equal protection of state laws to persons within its limits (14th Amend.) |

*Source:* From Table 2.2, pp. 42–43 in *American Federalism: A View from the States,* 3rd ed., by Daniel J. Elazar. 

## THINKING CRITICALLY

Some states have passed laws or issued judicial decisions permitting gay marriages, while many others have passed laws banning them. Now some of the states that allowed gay marriages, California and Maine, have repealed their gay marriage rulings. Meanwhile, the federal government has a law supporting only heterosexual marriages and allowing states that do not permit gay marriages to deny marital rights to same-sex couples married in other states. Do you believe that marriage laws are governmental in nature, religious in nature, or both? And do you believe that marriage laws are powers retained only by the states, and thus left to state governance, or can they also be a delegated power to the national government? See Figure 3.2 for a comparison of how the changes in state laws dealing with gay marriage resemble the evolution in state laws banning interracial marriage.

the powers to limit or ban the right of same-sex persons to marry, and to regulate the investigation of minorities as part of their anti-illegal immigration policies.

Over time, some of these powers have shifted, by necessity, to the national government. For example, certain state criminal law powers have been supplemented by congressional acts and Supreme Court decisions to provide more uniformity among the states and prevent criminals from escaping punishment simply by crossing state boundaries. The "Lindbergh" law gave the national government power to investigate and prosecute kidnapping cases that involve the crossing of state lines.

Powers *shared* by both the national and state governments are known as **concurrent powers.** Both types of government can regulate commerce, levy taxes, run a road system, establish their own elections, and maintain their own judicial structure. Sometimes these overlapping powers give citizens an additional forum in which to seek support or to secure their rights. For instance, the national government tried to discourage the move toward same-sex marriages, civil unions, and gay adoptions through the 1996 Defense of Marriage Act (DOMA). The act defined marriage as being between only a man and a woman and permitted states that banned gay marriage to fail to recognize such marriages from other states. Gay couples sought recourse in state judicial systems such as that of Massachusetts, which ruled gay marriages constitutional in 2003. As stated earlier in this chapter, the status of same-sex marriages, civil unions, and gay adoptions is constantly changing. California repealed a pro-gay marriage state Supreme Court decision in the 2008 election, an action being challenged now in federal court, and in Maine, a statewide petition led to a 2009 election repealing its gay marriage law. Circumstances continue to change at the presidential level as well. President Bush advocated a constitutional amendment banning gay marriages, but as a candidate, Barack Obama called for a repeal of the Defense of Marriage Act. When he became president, Obama's Justice Department announced in 2011 that it would no longer enforce or defend DOMA, forcing Congress to take over the defense of the law in the courts in Massachusetts, which had become the first state to legally challenge the section of the federal Defense of Marriage Act that recognizes only heterosexual marriages.[16] In addition, as commander in chief, President Obama ordered the military to end the "Don't Ask, Don't Tell" policy restricting gays in the military that had been in effect since the Clinton administration.

**concurrent powers**
Powers shared by both national and state levels of government.

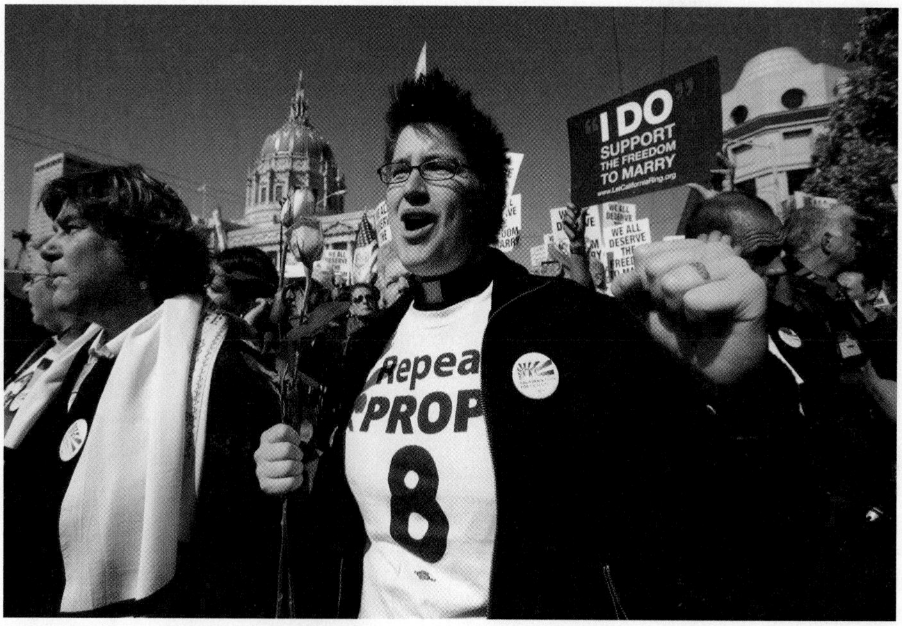


The fight in the 2008 election over Proposition 8 in California, which repealed the pro-gay marriage decision in the state supreme court, laid the groundwork for a similar decision by voters in Maine in 2009, and is being challenged now in the Ninth Circuit Court of Appeals.

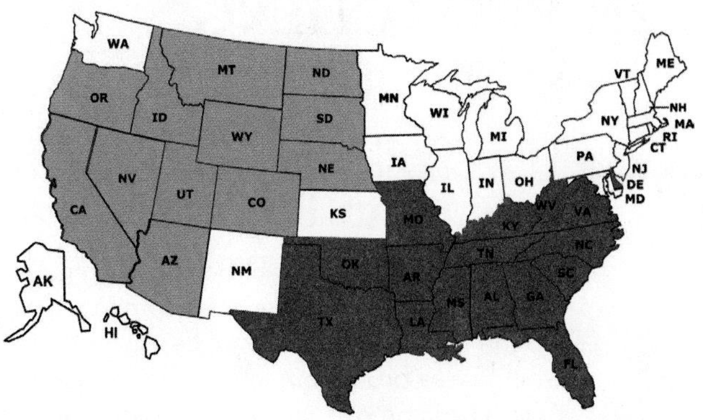


**FIGURE 3.2** Going Their Own Way

States seeking to ban gay marriage by either law or constitutional amendment (left) are compared with states that banned interracial marriage in 1967 (right). Notice the similarities between the evolutionary processes of these policies.

*Sources:* Perry-Castaneda Library Map Collection.

In addition to granting powers, the framers *denied* certain powers to both national and state governments. Fearful of creating an all-powerful central government that would override the rights of the states and the people, the framers withheld from the national government powers that might have that result. For example, Article I, Section 9 denies the national government the right to place an export tax on products from the states and the power to impose a direct tax on the people unless it was levied proportionally to each state's population (a provision overridden by the Sixteenth Amendment, allowing for the creation of a national income tax). The Bill of Rights, beginning with the words "Congress shall make no law," can also be seen as a long list of powers denied to the national government in areas such as freedom of speech, freedom of religion, freedom of the press, and defendants' rights.

Denying certain powers to the states helped keep their functions separate from those of the newly established national government. Limits on state powers, some of which can be overridden by Congress, are outlined in Article I, Section 10 of the Constitution. Among the prohibited powers are those delegated exclusively to the national government: powers to declare war, make treaties, and coin money. In addition, states cannot impair the obligations of contracts, thus preventing them from wiping out any debts, including those that existed prior to the formation of the Constitution. In the case of states that support gay marriage and civil unions and those that do not, it remains to be seen how the Supreme Court will rule under the "obligation of contracts" and the "full faith and credit" provision of Article IV, Section 1 on the question of whether same-sex couples from one state can require other states to provide them with the benefits of marriage.

Finally, the framers denied to both national and state governments certain powers deemed offensive based on their experience with British rule. These include the power to grant titles of nobility, pass bills of attainder (which legislate the guilt of an

# APPROACHING
## Contemporary Issues in Democracy

### How Will Justice Anthony Kennedy Vote in the Upcoming Health-care Plan Legal Appeal?

In March 2010, President Barack Obama signed into law the Patient Protection and Affordable Care Act, which was designed to expand health-care protection to nearly 35 million people, bringing the total level of national health-care protection to 97 percent of the American people. This law would have broad impacts on the American governmental system and people. It would cost more than $1 trillion over ten years to start and would increase the national debt by nearly $300 billon annually. It would create a health insurance exchange in which people and businesses could compare insurance rates for different companies in order to purchase the best policy for them. It would also compel states to increase their funding for Medicare and Medicaid programs. And, every eligible person would be required to buy into the system, or face paying a penalty tax.

**Issue:**

Justice Kennedy may see this issue as a national one, requiring that the interstate commerce aspects of such a large business need to be controlled by an overarching national policy. Is this "interstate commerce"? Kennedy could use the 1938 *Wickard* v. *Filburn* case to argue that if using wheat grown only on one's own farm, to grow bread and eat it, is still interstate commerce because it keeps you from buying produce and goods from other states, then the decision not to buy into the insurance plan, which appears to some to be inactivity, is still commerce because it affects the business elsewhere. Taking this approach, Kennedy would also be following his international sources approach to decision making, thinking of the national health-care plans in the many European Union states.

**Issue:**

Justice Kennedy could see this as a libertarian case, in which the government should not be allowed to force people to buy into a health-care plan, or participate in it, if they choose not to do so.

**Issue:**

Justice Kennedy could follow his pro–states' rights decisions in arguing that there is no delegated national power, or necessary and proper clause power of the federal government to deal with guaranteeing health care, but rather this is a Tenth Amendment "police powers" issue by which each state determines whether the citizens in their individual jurisdiction should be covered by insurance, and if so, how.

individual without the benefit of a trial), and pass ex post facto laws (which declare an action to be a crime *after* it has been committed).

## THE DEVELOPMENT OF FEDERALISM

3.4 *How did the federal structure evolve in response to crises in the early years of American government?*

Despite this enumeration of powers in the Constitution, the framers omitted many problem areas in mapping out the relationship between the national and state governments. National and state policy makers and the judicial system have had to develop that relationship over time. Many of those decisions were made in response to national crises.

## Debating the National Role: Hamilton versus Jefferson

The debate about how much leeway Congress would have to legislate beyond its enumerated constitutional powers began in the Washington administration over the creation of a national bank. At issue here was Article I, Section 8, Clause 18, of the Constitution (the elastic clause), which grants Congress the power "to make all Laws which shall be necessary and proper for carrying into Execution" its enumerated powers. Thus, Secretary of the Treasury Alexander Hamilton argued in 1791 that the national government could build on its power to coin money, operate a uniform currency system, create a postal system and a whiskey taxation system, and regulate commerce by chartering a national bank. Secretary of State Thomas Jefferson, however, opposed this idea, arguing that because no explicit power to charter banks was written into the Constitution, that power was reserved to the states.

This debate over the constitutionality of creating a bank represented two distinct visions of federalism. Hamilton's argument favoring a national bank suggested a whole new series of implied powers for the national government. Jefferson's argument was that such a broad interpretation of the clause would give Congress unlimited power to, in his words, "do whatever evil they please," with the result that the national government would "swallow up all the delegated powers" and overwhelm the states. In the end, President Washington was more persuaded by Hamilton's vision of expansive national powers, and the bank was chartered in 1791. However, the question of the bank's constitutionality remained.

## Asserting National Power: *McCulloch* v. *Maryland*

After a second national bank was chartered in 1816, the state of Maryland challenged the bank's operation by imposing a state tax on it. The bank refused to comply, and the Supreme Court was asked in 1819 to rule, in ***McCulloch* v. *Maryland*,** on two points: the constitutionality of Congress's chartering the national bank and the constitutionality of a state's tax on that bank.[17]

Chief Justice John Marshall, an advocate of strong, centralized national power, by arguing that the central government's power came from the people and was not carved out of the states, wrote a resounding unanimous opinion supporting the power of Congress to charter the bank. Marshall turned to the necessary and proper clause of the Constitution and found there the implied power for the national government to do what was convenient to carry out the powers delegated to it in Article I, Section 8. According to Marshall, the powers of the national government would now be broadened considerably: "Let the end be legitimate, let it be within the scope of the Constitution, and all means which are appropriate, which are plainly adapted to that end, which are not prohibited, but consistent with the letter and spirit of the Constitution, are constitutional."

This was indeed the broadest possible definition of national power. Now Congress could justify any legislation simply by tying it to one of the delegated national powers in the Constitution. The national government could potentially expand its powers into many areas that had previously been thought to be reserved to the states.

Having established the constitutionality of the national bank, the Court also declared Maryland's tax on the bank unconstitutional, reasoning that states have no power to impede congressional laws. In this case, Marshall argued, "the power to tax involves the power to destroy" the bank, and thus limit congressional power. The Court's reading of the supremacy clause made the national government "supreme within its sphere of action," meaning that it was the dominant power in areas where its power overlaps with that of the states. It seemed that Jefferson was right in fearing that the national government was well on the way to "swallowing up" the states.

***McCulloch* v. *Maryland***
The 1819 decision by Chief Justice John Marshall that expanded the interpretation of the necessary and proper clause to give Congress broad powers to pass legislation and reaffirmed the national government's power over the states under the supremacy clause.

**Gibbons v. Ogden**
The 1824 decision by Chief Justice John Marshall that gave Congress the power, under the interstate commerce clause, to regulate anything that affects the transfer of goods between states.

**nullification**
A 19th-century theory that upholds that states faced with unacceptable national legislation can declare such laws null and void and refuse to observe them.

## Expanding National Power Further: *Gibbons* v. *Ogden*

The Constitution states quite clearly that Congress has the power "to regulate Commerce . . . among the several States." But does such power to control commerce extend to control of commerce entirely within a state? And, if so, how extensive would that power be? In the 1824 case of ***Gibbons* v. *Ogden*,** John Marshall once again interpreted the Constitution broadly, ruling in favor of expanding national power.[18]

This case involved a license to operate steamboats in the waters between New York and New Jersey. One man, Aaron Ogden, had purchased a state-issued license to do so in New York waters, whereas his former partner, Thomas Gibbons, had gone to the national government for a federal coasting license. It was left to the Supreme Court to decide whether the central government's power over *interstate* commerce (commerce among states) predominated over an individual state's power to regulate *intrastate* commerce (commerce within a state boundary). Marshall used this opportunity to give the interstate commerce clause the broadest possible definition, holding that the national government had the power to regulate any "commercial intercourse" having an effect in two or more states. This meant that the national government could now reach activities that affect interstate commerce even within state boundaries. The states, then, had only the power to regulate commerce wholly within one state. But with the growth of industries such as mining and food production, it would soon be hard to find such enterprises. This ruling made states' rights advocates unhappy. Slaveholders in the South, for example, feared national incursion into their peculiar form of labor "commerce."

## Asserting State Power: Nullification

Inevitably, an organized response emerged to Marshall's strong central power position in the *McCulloch* and *Gibbons* cases. In the 1820s and early 1830s, southerners such as John Calhoun of South Carolina objected to the national government raising tariffs on raw materials and manufactured goods, thereby protecting northern industries but forcing southerners to pay higher prices for items such as clothing. Lacking the numbers in Congress to reverse this direction, Calhoun adopted the theory of **nullification,** initially proposed by Jefferson and Madison in 1798 in opposition to the Alien and Sedition Acts. Nullification theory held that states faced with unacceptable national legislation could declare such laws null and void and refuse to observe them. South Carolina, for example, declared the national tariffs null and void in 1832 and threatened to *secede* (leave the Union) over the issue. A crisis was averted when President Andrew Jackson was authorized by Congress under the 1833 Force Bill to use any military action necessary to prevent South Carolina from seceding, while also lowering the tariff. Only his threat to lead a national invasion force against the rebels ended the controversy.

However, nullification reared its head again over attempts by the national government to restrict slavery. This time the South did secede, and the Civil War ensued. This war was a turning point in American federalism, because the North's victory ensured that the Union and its federal structure would survive. No longer could states declare national laws unconstitutional or threaten to secede.

This has not prevented states and localities from trying to do this on occasion. After the passage of the USA Patriot Act in 2001, nearly 350 towns and localities, such as Des Moines, Iowa, and five states, such as New Hampshire, threatened to, or did, nullify the Patriot Act in their regions. By this action, they would refuse to enforce or implement the provisions of the law.[19] Some groups in Vermont even began advocating the state's secession to create the Free Republic of Vermont. These secession sentiments continue to surface from time to time. At one of the anti-tax "TEA parties," Governor Rick Perry of Texas expressed sympathy for the state separatist movement that had been advocating secession.[20] Conservative Supreme Court justice Antonin Scalia said that he could not support the modern secession movement because that "issue had been settled by the civil war." The modern

### THINKING CRITICALLY

In the spring of 1970, protesting students on college campuses around the nation sought to nullify the national government's war in Vietnam by "striking" from classes and gathering to protest. Under what conditions do you think that students, localities, and states should seek to nullify policies, and under what conditions should secession be considered?

# Compared to WHAT?

## Evolving Federalism in Iraq

Just days after American troops left Iraq in December, 2011, after the nine year war, Iraq's Shiite Prime Minister threatened a religious purge of the government, ordering the northern Kurds to hand over the Sunni Vice President for trial. The country's federalism debates continue. During the debates over the country's new Constitution in 2005, Iraq's three major factions made demands about the nature of federalism. The Shiites and Kurds called for their own autonomous and self-ruled federated region, ruled by Islamic law. The Sunnis, worried that a system of local rule within a federal structure would break up the country, urged their followers to vote against the new Constitution.

In October 2005, the Constitution won narrow approval. However, it was agreed that the following year the Iraqi government would consider changes to make the Constitution more acceptable to the Sunni population. Clearly, the future of the national Iraqi government depended on both the Sunnis' federalism concerns and the Kurds' and Shiites' willingness to accommodate them. If this effort to unite the country's warring factions fails, it could lead to a severe recession should the country break up into its separate components.

A new issue arose in 2009 when a federalism initiative to create the region of Basra, an oil-rich, Shiite majority region south of Baghdad that sought separate status in the country much like Kurdistan. Making this region unusual is that it seeks to create a nonreligious governmental structure relying on the Shiite majority bonding with various other religious groups in the region to lead the people, and free them from a perceived effort by Iran to influence the country. The Basra group believes, though, that this federalism solution will, in the long term, prevent the entire country from fracturing. Others are not so sure, worrying about the influence of the neighboring, dictatorial, Shiite-majority Iran, in trying to lead the region.

*Sources:* – "Iraq Prime Minister Tells Kurds to Hand Over Sunni Vice President," Associated Press, December 21, 2011. Redier Visser, "The Basra Federalism Initiative Enters Stage Two," found at http://historiae.org/basra; Steve Negus, "Iraqi Parliament Approves Contentious Federalism Law," *London Financial Times,* October 12, 2006.

---

version of a "nullification" policy is the call by conservative members of the Tea Party for the passage and ratification of the so-called Repeal Amendment, by which two-thirds of states' votes could veto a federal law. If added to the Constitution, and used, it could effectively turn the government into a "state-centered" one, more like the Articles of Confederation, as it would add another layer of veto power to national laws. Because of the nature of the Constitution and the country's history, however, this is very unlikely to happen. The Compared to What? feature shows how fears of secession now confront Iraq.

## Developing a System of Separation: Dual Federalism

3.5 *How did the interstate commerce and Fourteenth Amendment due process clauses of the U.S. Constitution help to nationalize the government?*

After the Civil War, the prevailing view of federalism was one of **dual federalism,** in which each type of government remained supreme in its own jurisdiction, thus keeping the states separate and distinct from the national government. Dual federalism prevailed during this period as a result of two factors. Supreme Court rulings

**dual federalism**
A system in which each level of power remains supreme in its own jurisdiction, thus keeping the states separate and distinct from the national government.

between 1877 and 1937 fueled a state-centered view of federalism. In addition, industrial expansion created an economic environment opposed to government interference and regulation, thereby limiting the national government's power over industry and giving states the upper hand in the federal structure. For instance, in 1895, the Court ruled that the national government had no power to regulate the monopoly of the sugar-refining industry, which, although national in scope, had factories located in Pennsylvania. The Court ruled in *United States* v. *E. C. Knight* that the national government had the power to regulate shipment of sugar, which constituted interstate commerce. However, it ruled that the national government did not have the power to regulate the manufacture of sugar, because that was local in nature, had only an indirect effect on interstate commerce, and thus lay wholly within the supreme power of the states.[21]

**QUICK REVIEW**

The New Deal Era

- Roosevelt's New Deal promised immediate steps to get the economy moving and create jobs.
- Congress passed programs involving tremendous new powers for the national government.
- Programs produced an increase in spending by the national government, regulations, and bureaucrats.

In a 1918 ruling, the Court placed additional restrictions on national power. The 1916 Keating Owen Act sought to limit child labor by limiting its interstate shipment for 30 days, but, in overturning this act in *Hammer* v. *Dagenhart,* Justice William R. Day indicated just how state-centered the Court had become. After misreading the Tenth Amendment to say that the national government reached only "expressly delegated" powers—language that the framers had rejected in favor of just the word "delegated," which did not include the manufacture of products—Day wrote: "The grant of authority over a purely federal matter was not intended to destroy the local power always existing and carefully reserved to the States in the Tenth Amendment to the Constitution."[22] In this classic statement of dual federalism, the states' reserved powers now represented a limitation on the national government.

## Creating a Cooperative System: The New Deal Era

The Great Depression of the 1930s and President Franklin D. Roosevelt's New Deal eventually put an end to dual federalism as a result of a change in the interpretation of the interstate commerce clause. In 1932, the country struggled with the worst economic depression in its history. To relieve the suffering, Roosevelt promised Americans a "New Deal," which meant taking immediate steps to restart the economy and

A group of young doffer and spinner boys comprised the labor force in a textile mill in Fall River, Massachusetts, in January 1912. In the early 1900s, over 1.5 million children worked for as little as 25 cents for a 12-hour day, and many exhausted young workers fell asleep on the job and were mutilated by their machines.

create jobs. At Roosevelt's behest, Congress passed programs involving tremendous new powers for the national government, such as creating large national administrative agencies to supervise manufacturing and farming. These programs produced an increase in spending by the national government, numerous regulations, and hordes of bureaucrats to administer them.

Initially, the Supreme Court used the rulings of the dual federalism era to restrict Roosevelt's programs, arguing that the problems they addressed were local in nature and not in the province of the national government.[23] But the nation's needs were so great that the Supreme Court's position could not endure. A highly critical President Roosevelt proposed a "court-packing plan," whereby he sought to add one new justice for each one over the age of 70 up to a total of 15 justices. While the plan was before Congress, the Supreme Court, in what became known as "the switch in time that saved nine," suddenly began ruling in favor of the New Deal programs, with Chief Justice Charles Evans Hughes and Justice Owen Roberts changing their minds about federalism to allow the national government to prevail over the states.

In a 1937 case, *National Labor Relations Board (N.L.R.B.)* v. *Jones and Laughlin Steel,* the Court upheld the national government's right to impose collective bargaining by unions and ban certain unfair labor practices. The Court was now willing to support the use of national power and allow the national government to control manufacturing, production, and agricultural activities through the interstate commerce powers. As a result, the court-packing plan dissolved.[24]

But what of the Tenth Amendment, which reserves to the states powers not delegated to the national government? A Supreme Court that was in the process of being completely remade by eight new Roosevelt appointees seemingly put an end to dual federalism in 1941. In *United States* v. *Darby Lumber Co.,* which upheld the national government's power to regulate lumber industry wages and hours under the interstate commerce power, the Court ruled that the Tenth Amendment "states but a truism that all is retained which has not been surrendered."[25] In short, this amendment was no longer seen as a limitation on the national government or a bar to the exercise of its power, even wholly within state boundaries.

The New Deal ushered in a new era in the federal relationship, one of cooperation between the national and state governments. This system is known as **cooperative federalism.** The national government would direct and sometimes fund solutions for various state and local problems; then the state governments would administer the solutions, according to national guidelines, as was the case in the rebuilding of New York City after the attacks of September 11, 2001, New Orleans after Hurricane Katrina in 2005, and Joplin, Missouri, after the tornado strike in 2011.[26]

The national government was supreme in the federalism partnership despite the fleeting return of dual federalism in response to a 1976 Court challenge overturned nine years later. In 1976, the Supreme Court signaled a possible return to dual federalism in the case of *National League of Cities* v. *Usery,* which dealt with extending national wages and hours legislation to state and municipal workers. Writing for a slim majority, Justice William Rehnquist banned national regulation of "core" state functions. Nine years later, however, the Court overturned *Usery* in the case of *Garcia* v. *San Antonio Metropolitan Transit Authority,* which also dealt with wages and hours legislation. The Court shifted its position back to favoring national predominance, arguing that states must rely on Congress rather than the Court to decide which of their programs should be regulated by the national government. This ruling was reaffirmed by the Court in *South Carolina* v. *Baker.*[27] But, as you will see at the end of the chapter, the Supreme Court is once again reassessing and redefining the nature of the relationship between the national and state governments.

This partnership between the national and state governments encouraged states to look to the national government for help and funding to deal with problems seemingly beyond their means. Similarly, citizens began to look to Washington for

## THINKING CRITICALLY

In 1937, President Roosevelt believed the Supreme Court was so out of tune politically with his policies, which had been supported by the voters in the previous election, that he proposed to add justices to that body to change its voting direction. With the Court's voting majority now reflecting the membership in 1987, more than two decades ago, under what conditions should the Court be changed, and how?

**cooperative federalism**
A cooperative system in which solutions for various state and local problems are directed and sometimes funded by both the national and state governments. The administration of programs is characterized by shared power and shared responsibility.

**incorporation**
The process whereby the Supreme Court has found that Bill of Rights protections apply to the states.

**creative federalism**
An initiative that expanded the concept of the partnership between the national government and the states under President Lyndon Johnson in the 1960s.

**QUICK REVIEW**

Incorporation of the Bill of Rights

- Judicial decisions and political actions established uniformity of rights and partnership between the national and state governments.
- States had to adhere to national standards of constitutional protections.
- Social equality was promoted through an end to segregation.
- Political equality was established through the "one-person, one-vote" standard.
- Personal equality was guaranteed, granting citizens the same rights regardless of where they live.
- Economic equality was the goal of programs that were part of the War on Poverty program in the 1960s.

solutions to their problems rather than to their state and local governments. The result was an increase in the power of the national government and a drive to achieve uniformity of programs throughout the country, often at the expense of state power and innovation.

## Seeking Uniformity: Federalism in the Post–New Deal Era

Another major nationalizing movement occurred in the 1950s and 1960s when the judiciary created a new role for the national government in the federal system—that of protector of personal rights guaranteed by the Constitution. Prior to the 1930s, defendants' rights had been a power reserved to the states, leading to policy variations that, for example, allowed certain states to deny minorities personal liberties and legal protection. The Supreme Court ruled to extend most of the protections of the Bill of Rights to the states (the Bill of Rights originally applied to the national government only) to ensure uniformity from one state to another and to help end inequality. The Court did this by ruling that certain guarantees in the Bill of Rights are part of the due process right guaranteed by the Fourteenth Amendment against state government intrusion. This process was called the **incorporation** of the Bill of Rights.

This established a uniform judicial process around the country. For instance, in the 1932 *Scottsboro* case, in which a group of young African Americans had been convicted of rape and sentenced to death without a fair trial, the Supreme Court ruled that the Sixth Amendment right to counsel should extend to all future state capital trials like this one to ensure fairness.[28] States could still operate their judicial systems, but to guarantee personal rights, they had to adhere to national standards regarding constitutional protections. In Chapter 13, we discuss the full extent of this incorporation process in detail.

The national government also sought to impose national standards regarding equality. Social equality gained ground through a series of Court decisions, such as *Brown* v. *Board of Education of Topeka* in 1954, which called for the end of segregation in public schools,[29] and later cases that promoted integration. A series of cases, including *Reynolds* v. *Sims* in 1964, sought political equality. *Reynolds* v. *Sims* established the "one-person, one-vote" standard in which the number of voters in each district was made roughly the same, thus giving people an equal say in the operation of their government.[30] Personal equality was guaranteed by a series of First Amendment cases granting citizens the same rights of speech, press, assembly, religion, and thought, no matter where they live. In the 1960s, the Johnson administration initiated the War on Poverty program that led Congress to adopt a series of welfare, educational, and social programs to improve economic equality. These judicial decisions and political actions establishing uniformity of rights have helped America approach democracy by guaranteeing to residents in all states a final recourse for seeking constitutional rights. Johnson's initiative, which became known as **creative federalism,** expanded the concept of partnership between the national government and the states.

# Federal Grants and Federal Mandates: Federalism Since 1930

3.6 *How has the system of federal grants increased the power of the federal government?*

The Depression in the 1930s spurred vast increases in federal spending and power. When the Supreme Court ruled during the New Deal that the national power to spend was not limited to the enumerated grants of power in the Constitution, further growth was inevitable.[31] Since then, national power has continued to grow, particularly in the past three decades. At issue in this federal system is how much money the national government will spend and under what conditions the states may use federal funds (with the answers usually being "lots" and "according to specific guidelines"). We now look at the different types of federal grants and at how various administrations have worked with the grant-in-aid system.

**grant-in-aid**
Money paid to states and localities to induce them to implement policies in accordance with federally mandated guidelines.

**conditions of aid**
National requirement that must be observed to receive benefits.

**categorical grants**
The most common type of federal grant, given for specific purposes, usually with strict rules attached.

**Federal Grants** National spending programs vary. The most frequently used is the **grant-in-aid,** money paid to states and localities to induce them to implement policies in accordance with federally mandated guidelines. Money moves through an *intergovernmental transfer,* but only if the states spend it in certain policy areas. If the states do not wish to abide by the **conditions of aid** or national requirements, they can refuse federal funds. These conditions come in various forms. Some require that a grant be spent in a certain fashion; others try to accomplish additional policy goals. For instance, in October 2000, President Bill Clinton signed into law a bill requiring all states to pass, by September 2003, a uniform 0.08 blood alcohol standard for driving under the influence, applicable to first-time offenders, or lose an increasing amount of their federal highway funding assistance.[32] With all of the states and local anti–cell phone use, and texting in moving cars laws, this is a possible way for the national government to pass an overarching law.

The number of such grants is vast and rose steadily through the 1990s and early 2000s. National grants to states and localities grew from 594 to nearly 660 between 1993 and 1999. The number had dropped to 608 in 2004. Simultaneously, the size of grant outlays rose by 1998 to $251 billion, an increase of 29 percent from the $194 billion in 1993.[33] By 2006, though, that overall figure grew to $435.7 billion, or 17 percent of the federal budget.[34] Medicaid growth was the principal cause of increase (more than doubling in cost from $75.8 billion in 1993 to $171 billion by 2006), but another large outlay went for the disaster assistance programs of the Federal Emergency Management Agency.[35] President Bush's budgets began calling for substantial reductions in grant-in-aid spending after 2002, with some of the largest cuts, revealing the administration's policy choices, being proposed in environmental protection, highway aid, and state criminal alien assistance programs. Another 75 discretionary grant programs, amounting to $3.6 billion in a single year and nearly $13 billion over a two-year period, were cut by the Bush administration from the fiscal year 2008 budget, leaving states with the option of seriously curtailing services or having to raise taxes to fund the missing programs.[36]

Because of the severe recession in 2009, the Obama administration had to continue that cutback effort. In May 2009, the new administration released a book called *Terminations, Reductions and Savings,* proposing 121 programmatic cuts that would save more than $17 billion.[37]

Grants-in-aid come in a wide variety of types. **Categorical grants** are the most common and address specific purposes, usually with strict rules attached. Most categorical grants cover only part of the costs and usually require the state or local government or a nonprofit organization to partially match funds. In this way, the grants induce states to increase spending for desired programs and encourage cooperation. Approximately 90 percent of national aid to the states and localities comes in the form of categorical grants. This is such a fast-growing form of national assistance that the country now has the largest number of categorical grants in history, with the "catalog of federal domestic assistance" listing over 1,600 different forms of federal assistance programs to the states and localities. As a result of the 2009 federal stimulus program to deal with the Great Recession, more than $325 billion in additional grants-in-aid were provided to the states.[38] Categorical grants come in three types: formula grants, project grants, and combined formula/project grants.

## QUICK REVIEW

Federal Grants

- Money is spent by the national government, and under certain conditions, it may be used by the states.
- Money is paid to states and localities to induce them to implement policies in accordance with federally mandated guidelines.
- Congress can exercise considerable control over the states by attaching to federal money certain federal mandates.
- The number of such grants is vast and has been rising steadily for the past 15 years.

## THINKING CRITICALLY

The incorporation process for rights, making them more uniform around the country, is like a franchise restaurant with the same conditions nationally. On the other hand, those rights that are not incorporated can be interpreted by states individually, making them more like local restaurants or diners, which vary from place to place. Using that as an analogy, do you prefer uniformity of rights or do you prefer to have variation in rights on a state-by-state basis?

**formula grants**
A grant based on a prescribed legislative formula to determine how money will be distributed to eligible governmental units (states or major cities).

**project grants**
A grant not based on a formula but distributed for specific purposes after a fairly competitive application and approval process.

**formula/project grants**
Competitive grants that are restricted by use of a formula.

**block grants**
Federal grants that provide money to states for general program funding with few or no strings attached.

**devolution revolution**
A trend initiated in the Reagan administration and accelerated by then Speaker of the House Newt Gingrich to send programs and power back to the states with less national government involvement.

**preemption**
The process by which the federal government, under the supremacy clause, signals that it will be the only legislative body to govern in a policy area, as a means of creating uniform policy.

**Formula grants** are federal monies allocated to states and localities based on a prescribed legislative distribution formula. They support continuing activities and are not confined to a specific project. Depending on their policy aim, such formula grants can reflect many factors, such as total population, median family income, miles of coastline, total enrollment in education, and miles of highways and railways. Governmental units that meet the strict rules for distribution automatically qualify for the grant.[39]

The **project grant** is not based on a formula but is distributed for specific purposes after a fairly competitive application and approval process for a fixed period. These are sometimes called *discretionary grants* because they are distributed at the discretion of a designated legislator or administrator. Given the desire of legislators to maintain more control over the operation of these programs, the majority of categorical grants, nearly three out of five, are project grants.[40]

In recent years a *combined* **formula/project grant** has been developed in which competitive grants are awarded but also are restricted by the use of a formula. For example, Congress may limit the amount of grant money that can be awarded to a state or region of a state.

In 1966, President Lyndon Johnson created **block grants,** which simplified the process, consolidating several smaller grants into one large grant that provides money for broad functional program areas. The funds may be used at the discretion of the recipient government. Federal government grants to states in localities amount to more that $400 billion, or about 17 percent of the federal budget (well up from 7.6 percent in 1960). Compared with the 608 categorical grants available in 2004, 17 block grants were available, up from 15 in 1993 and covering such diverse areas as state and local homeland security, low-income home energy assistance, community development assistance, assistance to institutions helping Hispanic people and communities, Native American housing, and preventive health and health services.[41] One new program, created in October 2004, was the Innocence Protection Act, making law enforcement funds available to states and localities for the analysis of DNA evidence for both crime scenes and appeals of prisoners seeking to establish their innocence. Similarly, that year Congress promised to pay 40 percent of the cost of educating schoolchildren with disabilities.[42]

Examining all of these types of federal grants in specific issue areas clearly reveals Congress's shifting spending priorities. In the last two decades, Congress has shifted its spending priorities toward people rather than places, directing nearly two-thirds of federal money toward aid to individuals, up from nearly 32 percent in 1978. As a result, although institutional programs have been allowed to decline, grants to people have meant that states and localities often must budget matching grants for these programs. For example, a Congressional Budget Office study of federal spending on the elderly and children concluded that in fiscal year 2000 the federal government spent just more than one-third of its budget, or about $615 billion, on the elderly and just under 10 percent, or $175 billion, on children. After Congress passed the American Recovery and Reinvestment Act of 2009 to deal with the Great Recession, the amount of grants-in-aid spending rose in fiscal year 2011 to more than $645 billion.[43] At the present time, with the Baby Boomers retiring, more than half of the federal budget is spent on these two groups, with four-fifths of that amount being devoted to the elderly.[44]

One anticipated major change in the welfare area was the **devolution revolution,** a term signifying the shift in policy-making responsibility to the states. In this way, Speaker of the House Newt Gingrich argued in the mid-1990s, "power" could be restored to the individuals first, then to state and local governments as the next best option. Noted federalism expert John Kincaid's research has suggested that political opposition has negated most devolution of this kind, but where devolution by law failed, a process of de facto devolution has occurred. The federal government's funding of urban programs as policies is no longer directed toward places, such as aid for state and local transportation and redevelopment programs, but instead is directed more toward people and the rights of individuals, such as social welfare programs. Kincaid argues that this is a process of **preemption,** whereby the federal government uses its power under the supremacy clause and signals that it will be the only level of government to legislate in an area of public policy in order to ensure more uniform policy. This forces the states to administer programs in areas such as education law, environmental reform, class-action lawsuits and consumer protection reform, creating a new kind of federalism. As Pam Belluck states in the *New York Times,* "[W]e've moved from an era of cooperative federalism to an era of **coercive federalism** in which the federal government is really dictating to the states. This has produced a really activist response of states trying to cope with this."[45] Over time, the variations in state policies in these areas, which are mainly due to a combination of geographical differences and varying political party affiliations, will be forced to change because of policies dictated by the federal congressional policies. As a result, the cumulative effect of those changed policies and the changing electoral landscape will lead to more national uniformity.

**coercive federalism**
A system in which the national government forces the states to follow its lead by passing public policy legislation requiring their participation.

Great debate surrounds the extent to which grants-in-aid help this country approach democracy. When certain regions of the country fail to spend in a manner that reflects the needs of their citizens, the national government can take their tax money and redistribute it to other regions. Dictating the spending of governmental resources in this way has helped to remove inequalities, but it has political costs for the states. Moreover, states quickly grow to depend on national money, thus further impelling them to allow the national government to dictate their policy direction. Some argue that grants detract from democracy because they decrease democratic accountability for government spending, decrease governmental efficiency, increase governmental spending, and change state and local spending priorities. For this reason, some students of fiscal federalism argue for minimizing intergovernmental transfers.

## FEDERALISM TODAY

### George W. Bush, 2001–2008

President George W. Bush's domestic agenda of promoting a states' rights agenda was initially derailed by the terrorist attacks on September 11, 2001, thus turning the president away from domestic issues to foreign and military issues. The one major

In a huge victory for the gay rights movement, New York's Governor Andrew Cuomo led that state in the summer of 2011 to become the sixth, and largest, state to allow gay marriage.

**progressive federalism**
The Obama Administration's approach to federalism that allows states to create their own policy solutions and join together in suing for policy changes.

domestic initiative of the Bush administration during this period, the No Child Left Behind Act, had the appearance of a grand federal program. Although states had wide latitude to spend the federal money targeted for low-income students in a manner best suited for their region, they complained of insufficient funds and a need for greater spending latitude.

The Bush administration's preoccupation with the war and nation-building efforts in Iraq and Afghanistan, together with domestic homeland security made it difficult to mount a sustained states' rights programmatic effort. The financial cost of the war and rebuilding effort left little money for supporting state programs.[46] On top of that, the enormous rising costs of Medicaid programs strapped the states. With federal Medicaid dollars comprising 45 percent of overall state aid, President Bush's proposal to cut $45 billion in these programs over the next decade had a serious effect on state budgets.[47] The extended cutbacks instituted in the last two years of the Bush administration cut tens of billions of dollars from the budget. Hardest hit in fiscal year 2008 were the justice department programs, which were cut by nearly 80 percent, and the homeland security programs, which were cut by one-third in the last year of the administration.[48] See Figure 3.3 for an illustration of how the government's spending priorities have changed from 1960 to 2011.

## Barack Obama, 2009–Present

Developing a federalism strategy became far more complicated for the Obama administration because of the costly campaign promises about new programs and the historic economic meltdown leading to the worst recession since the Great Depression. Obama had promised to pursue legislation for health-care reform, which would be a costly national program, with funding estimates of more than a trillion dollars, leading to an overall debt of nearly $15 trillion. On the other hand, Obama began following a system of **progressive federalism,** following Louis D. Brandeis's notion of the "laboratories of democracy" by leaving it to state governments to innovate in areas such as environmental protection and business reform and to file group lawsuits to achieve consumer protection.[49]

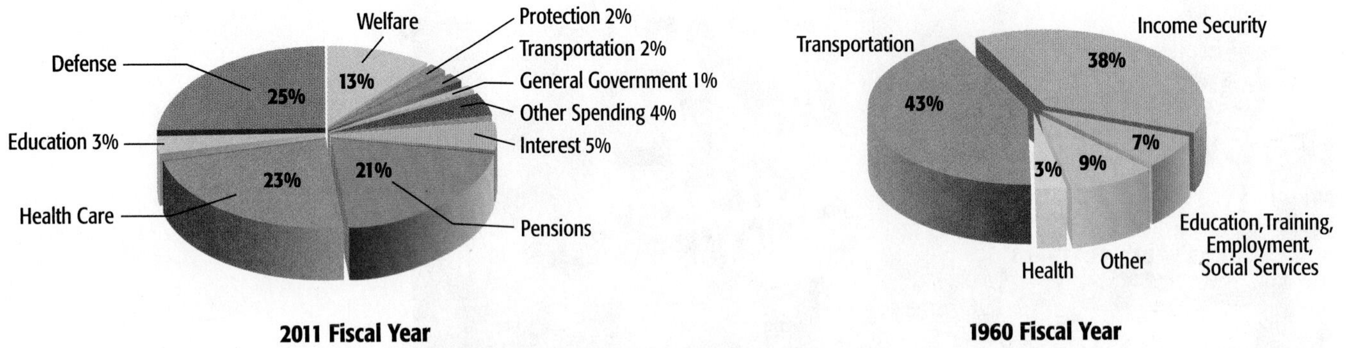


**FIGURE 3.3** The Changing Functions of National Spending
Over the past 40 years, there has been a dramatic shift in the purposes for national grants. In short, national funding for transportation and welfare programs has been replaced by a system of health-care programs and funding for job training.

*Sources:* Comp: "Highlights of U.S. Federal Budget for FY2011" at http://www.usgovernmentspending.com/piechart_2011_US_fed; U.S. Advisory Commission on Intergovermental Relations, Characteristics of Federal Grant-in-Aid Programs to State and Local Governments, 1995 (Washington, DC: ACIR, January 1996), p. 16.

In the highly charged partisan congressional atmosphere of the national government, President Obama was forced by Republicans and Tea Party members as part of the debt ceiling negotiations of 2011 to agree to nearly $3 trillion in spending cuts. While the level of Community Services Block Grants funding has remained steady for the time being, as part of a cost-cutting strategy President Obama submitted a budget calling for a 50 percent reduction in these grants. In this highly charged partisan atmosphere, though, these decisions will likely not be made until after the 2012 election.[50] As will be outlined in Chapter 15, though, with the costly health-care reform legislation, and the rapidly rising interest payments on the existing debt, not to mention the costs of dealing with the extended Great Recession and the political partisanship, the financial debts faced by states have led to severe additional spending cuts in states such as New Jersey, California, and Wisconsin.[51]

## The Roberts Court and the Future of Federalism

3.7 *How has the Supreme Court under Chief Justices William Rehnquist and John Roberts altered the system of federalism?*

What does the future hold for our federal system? In addition to presidential and congressional policies attempting to devolve power to the states, Supreme Court and lower court rulings have recently begun to redefine federalism in the direction of more state power. In 1992, the Supreme Court ruled, in *New York* v. *United States,* that a 1985 congressional statute regulating the disposal of low-level radioactive waste should be struck down because of its "take title" provision. If states and localities did not provide for the disposal of all such waste created in their region by a specific date, they were required to take possession and responsibility for it. Justice Sandra Day O'Connor and the majority found this statute to be a violation of the Tenth Amendment: "Whatever the outer limits of [state] sovereignty may be, one thing is clear. The Federal Government may not compel the States to enact or administer

Former Vice President Al Gore's effort to educate the world about the problems of global warming, for which he won the Nobel Prize in 2007, raises many of the national-state federalism problems that are so difficult to solve.

a federal regulatory program. The Constitution . . . [does not] authorize Congress simply to direct the States to provide for the disposal of radioactive waste generated within their borders."[52]

In a landmark 1995 ruling in the case of *United States* v. *Lopez,* a narrow five-person majority of the Supreme Court overturned a section of the 1990 federal Gun-Free School Zones law, making it a crime to possess firearms within 1,000 feet of a school zone. Congress argued that its power to regulate such behavior came from the interstate commerce clause, because violent crime around a school could affect the national economy through higher insurance costs and self-imposed limits on travel. In overturning the law, the Court appeared ready to establish new limits on congressional authority by requiring Congress, for the first time in 50 years, to justify the link between a law and the commerce clause. Speaking for what had become a solid five-person conservative Court majority in favor of state power, Chief Justice William Rehnquist said that this regulation "neither regulates a commercial activity nor contains a requirement that the possession be connected in any way to interstate commerce."[53] This decision represented a true shift in decision making; for more than 50 years the Court had not even pushed for a clear connection between a law and the commerce power in approving federal extensions of authority. In 1996, Congress resurrected the Gun-Free School Zones Act in its Omnibus Appropriations Act, but this time with one key difference—now it was a federal crime to knowingly carry or fire a gun within 1,000 feet of a school.

This decision represented a watershed in the direction of more state power, and its repercussions affected a series of later rulings.[54] Shortly after the decision to overturn the 1990 federal Gun-Free School Zones Act, the same five-person conservative majority limited Congress's power to make states subject to federal lawsuits because of the Eleventh Amendment. In this case, Florida was freed by the states' sovereign right of immunity from a lawsuit brought by a Seminole tribe challenging negotiations over its desire to create gambling interests on its tribal lands.[55]

In 1997, the Supreme Court invalidated those portions of the federal Brady Handgun Control Law that required local sheriffs to perform background checks on handgun purchasers until a national investigation database could be established. In this case, although Justice Antonin Scalia could not find anything in the Constitution requiring such a decision, he still decided so based on the "historical understanding and practice, in the structure of the Constitution, and in the jurisprudence of this Court." Using *The Federalist Papers* and a study of early American history, Justice Scalia argued that the national government "at most" had been able to impose certain duties on state court judges but had never been able to do more than "recommend" that state government officials perform other actions. Justice David Souter, in dissent, argued that Scalia's reading of history is controversial. Souter defended Congress's power to adopt the Brady Bill by quoting from Alexander Hamilton in *The Federalist,* no. 27: "The legislatures, courts, and magistrates, of the [states] . . . will be incorporated into the operations of the national government as far as its just and constitutional authority extends, and will be rendered auxiliary to the enforcement of its laws."[56]

Then, in 2000, despite the care that Congress had taken to show the link between this issue and the effect of interstate commerce, the Court ruled as unconstitutional the Violence Against Women Act (VAWA), which allowed women unable to secure legal recourse in state courts for sexual assault cases to take their cases to the federal courts. Thus it was left to states to prosecute "gender-induced" attacks.[57] Congress passed the VAWA a second time, tightened up the interstate commerce effect justification, and expanded it to include date rape, but, because of the Court's decision, it refused to allow victims to sue their attackers in federal court.

Since 2002, though, the Court's tendency to favor states' rights over federal power has eased. For example, the Court upheld the federal Children's Internet

Protection Act of 2001, which required the use of anti-pornography filters in school libraries as a condition of receiving federal aid. In another case, it allowed people with disabilities to sue their states under Title II of the Americans with Disabilities Act to improve physical accessibility to state courts.[58] This trend continued in 2005 in the California medical use of marijuana case, when the Court upheld the federal government's Controlled Substances Act over the state's decision to provide relief for critically ill patients. However, in 2006, the Court ruled for the state of Oregon in determining the balance between the federal drug program and Oregon's Death with Dignity Act.

Lying at the heart of all of these Supreme Court cases is the determination of who decides—the national government or the states—and since 1994 that decision had lain with the swing justice on the Court, Justice Sandra Day O'Connor. In 2005–2006, though, with her retirement and the death of Chief Justice Rehnquist, to be replaced by two conservatives (Chief Justice John Roberts and Justice Samuel Alito) who consistently support increased states' rights, the determining vote shifted to the Court's new swing voter, Justice Anthony Kennedy. Because of the closely divided Court and Justice Kennedy's conflicting opinions, the new Roberts Court went both ways in deciding two environmental policy decisions: whether the federal or the state government would be responsible for environmental protection. In mid-2006, Kennedy voted with the four conservatives on the Court that the federal government did not have the power under the Clean Water Act to regulate pollution control in more than 9,000 remote wetlands when they did not constitute "navigable waters."[59] A year later, though, Justice Kennedy voted with the liberal bloc, which upheld the power and duty of the federal Environmental Protection Act (EPA) under the federal Clean Air Act to regulate tailpipe emissions of automobiles in order to deal with the effect of greenhouse gases on global warming.[60]

Many expected yet another 5 to 4 conservative "states' rights" decision by the Court in June 2009 on the constitutionality of Section 5 of the Voting Rights Act of 1965—which requires a federal "preclearance" permission before any state or locality can change a voting regulation in order to prove that it did not negatively affect minority vote. However, the Court took a more restrained and incremental case-by-case approach. The law had been initially passed in 1965 to oversee the voting regulations of 16 states, many in the historically discriminatory, Deep South that had less than 50 percent of the population registered to vote, indicating that discriminatory voting regulations were being used to prevent minorities from voting. The act had been renewed four times, the last one overwhelmingly by Congress—indeed unanimously by the Senate—and signed by President George W. Bush in 2006. But an Austin, Texas, utility district argued that they should be able to "bail out" of the preclearance procedure, a process allowed by the law but rarely successfully invoked. Faced with the argument that the law undermined the "equal sovereignty" of certain states, and the equally powerful response that declaring the preclearance Section 5 process would gut the law entirely and open the door to future voting discrimination, Chief Justice Roberts wrote that in the new political environment of so many minority voters and elected officials, including a president of the United States, "Things have changed in the south. Voter turnout and registration rates now approach parity. Blatantly discriminatory evasions of federal decrees are rare. And minority candidates hold office at unprecedented levels." The Court allowed this voting district and others to bail out of the law's reach if it could prove that its voting laws had not discriminated in ten years and it had "engaged in constructive efforts" to increase voting by minority groups.[61]

In 2010, the Roberts Court issued an expansive ruling on the necessary and proper clause in a case called *United States* v. *Comstock*. The question was whether a man who had served his 37-month federal sentence for receiving child pornography could be civilly committed for an additional term because he was seen as a sexually dangerous person under the Adam Walsh Child Protection and Safety Act. The Court ruled that because the action was "rationally related to the implementation of a constitutionally enumerated power" and "reasonably adapted to Congress' power to act as a responsible federal custodian," then "Congress could have reasonably concluded that federal inmates who suffer from a mental illness that causes them to have serious difficulty in refraining from sexually violent conduct, . . . would pose an especially high danger to the public if released." Since this law was drafted in a manner narrowly limited to protecting the public, especially children, against such dangerous criminals, it was a constitutional use of the necessary and proper clause powers.[62]

The nature of the federal structure might well change because of the staffing of the current Supreme Court. Even after President Obama's appointment of Judge Sonia Sotomayor to replace moderate-liberal David Souter, and Elena Kagan to replace ultra-liberal John Paul Stevens, the Court will remain a conservative 5 to 4 Court toward preserving "states' rights," with Anthony Kennedy now in the swing seat. With four justices over the age of 70, though, should there be a vacancy in one of the conservative seats on the Court, that policy direction could change quickly.

The issue that could change the federal structure is the challenge to President Obama's Patient Protection and Affordable Care Act of March 2010. The act uses the interstate commerce power together with the necessary and proper clause to create state insurance exchanges that would cover nearly 35 million people who had no health-care protection, making it available to 97 percent of the population. The stalemated partisan Congress did not pass a "federal option" of a single federal health-care plan. Congress did, however, set up a way for private health firms to cover people, to pay for the new plan, which will not take effect until 2014, by requiring people to buy into the plan or face a tax penalty. The issue became whether people can be forced to participate in the plan. Under the 1938 *Wickard* v. *Filburn* case, can a person's desire to avoid participation in the health-care plan be considered interstate commerce that can be regulated by the federal government? As the appeal of the plan has worked its way through the federal court of appeals, with only three exceptions, the Courts have broken down in their votes on partisan lines. In one case, a respected Republican judge voted for the plan, while in another, a Clinton-appointed judge ruled against the plan. The case law is so close here that it will depend on the individual views about national and state power by the members of the Supreme Court.

Beyond this case, the 2012 presidential election and the 2012 senatorial elections will help determine the long-term effect of future Supreme Court appointments on federalism. Which party will control the Court appointments and shape the likelihood for that president to get his judicial appointments confirmed? In the future, if the Court chooses to rule against an overarching federal approach in controversial cultural issues—such as abortion, right to die, the teaching of intelligent design, or gay marriage—the individual states will be left to decide on the direction of those policies.

### THINKING CRITICALLY

The Supreme Court is now on the verge of considering whether the sovereignty of individual states, and the present state of civil rights, makes it impossible and unnecessary to use federal law to oversee state regulation of voting rules that affect the ability of minority groups to vote. Do you agree that the time has come to end voting rights protections in states that historically discriminated against minority groups in voting? Should all states be subject to the same laws here?

## FEDERALISM AND APPROACHING DEMOCRACY IN THE 21ST CENTURY

The debate over federalism and the proper balance of power between national and state governments is ongoing. "We need a certain administrative discretion," argues political scientist Don Kettl. "You can't run everything from Washington."[63] That has been the nature of the debate for more than two centuries. There will always be problems facing the nation: commerce, crime, the economy, the fight against terrorism, individual rights, the environment, and now the health-care reform issue. The disagreement, however, comes from which type of government, or whether any government at all, should address such matters. Generally, more and more people argue that the government closest to the people is the best government to handle these issues. But with the terrorist threat and the Internet, the question may well be how much financial support and political guidance the federal government will provide. This chapter's timeline traces the evolution of the shifting balance of power between the federal and state governments.

Where one stands in the federalism debate reveals a lot about one's political ideology. In the 20th century, Franklin D. Roosevelt's New Deal firmly positioned the liberal Democrats as the nation-centered party, asserting that only the national government can provide a basic standard of living and uniform democratic rights for all citizens. Lyndon Johnson's Great Society is a classic example of this position. He used the powers of the national government to create a welfare state aimed at helping the underprivileged, solving civil rights problems, improving education, and so forth. Conservative Republicans, led by Ronald Reagan in the 1980s and beyond, on the other hand, advocate a state-centered approach, arguing that solutions are best left either to the state governments or to the private sector. These conservatives were understandably overjoyed with Ronald Reagan's election in 1980; his platform opposing big government and advocating the return of power to the states was more to their taste. Reagan sought to dismantle the welfare state and to cut national spending. The Bush administration's renewed call for making permanent federal tax cuts in the face of huge bills to rebuild Iraq and leading the anti-terrorism fight, leading to huge budget deficits, resulted in further cuts in spending to states and localities. In return, Democrats and liberals in the Obama administration began moving toward an increased national role in policies such as health care and the environment, but were faced with the prospect of reducing expenditures to balance the budget deficits. The increasing budget deficits that were created to pay for the bank bailouts and economic stimulus package during the Great Recession of 2008–2009 continued to make people nervous. To some, then, a stronger national government means more democracy, while to others, stronger state governments accomplish the same.

## APPROACHING Democracy Timeline

### Federal versus State Disputes

| | |
|---|---|
| **1798–1799** | Kentucky and Virginia Resolutions oppose the Alien and Sedition Act. |
| **1804** | New England states threaten to secede from the Union. |
| **1832** | South Carolina votes to nullify the Tariff Bill. |
| **1833** | U.S. Congress passes the "force bill" to impose federal law on South Carolina nullification movement. |
| **1860** | South Carolina secedes from the Union. |
| **1865** | South surrenders in Civil War. |
| **1954** | *Brown* v. *Board of Education* compels states to desegregate schools. |
| **1950s–1960s** | Southern states move to evade the *Brown* decision. |
| **1950s–1960s** | Federal district court judges and Supreme Court force states to observe *Brown*. |
| **1957** | Arkansas governor refuses to implement *Brown* in Little Rock's Central High School. |
| **1957** | President Eisenhower and Supreme Court compel Arkansas to observe *Brown* v. *Board of Education* in Little Rock. |
| **1965** | Voting Rights Act passes, guaranteeing equality for minority voters. |
| **2000s** | States and localities nullify the USA Patriot Act. |
| **2006** | Voting Rights Act is renewed unanimously. |
| **2007** | Groups in Vermont seek the Free Republic of Vermont in seceding from the Union. |
| **2009** | Texas Governor Rick Perry expresses support for Texas separatists seeking secession at protest Tea Party. |
| **2009** | Supreme Court refuses to overturn Voting Rights Act renewal. |
| **2011** | President Obama orders the Justice Department not to enforce the 1996 Defense of Marriage Act (DOMA). |

Democratic   Neutral   Undemocratic

America's experience with federalism has involved a continual shifting of power from the states to the federal government, and now, as a consequence of the Rehnquist and Roberts Courts' decisions and the policies of the Bush administration, power in many areas began shifting back to the states. The shift in the nature of the federal structure toward the states has continued during the Obama administration. Although the national government predominates, in recent years due to the costs of the war and Iraq rebuilding and homeland security, and now the ongoing severe recession, there has been a growing budget deficit that has meant less money in its coffers, meaning less leverage over the states and a new role for the states in their own policy-making efforts. Meanwhile, the states are very limited in their policy innovation by their own budget deficits in dealing with the recession. The solution will come through some form of cooperation among the different levels of government. Through it all, in exercising its political role, each form of government plays an important part in ensuring that our federal structure, the result of a careful compromise forged by the framers in Philadelphia, continues to function and thrive in dealing with America's new policy needs.

## Summary

3.1 *How does the American system of federalism balance national and state power to preserve democracy?*

- The term *federalism* refers to a political system in which two or more distinct forms of government share power over the same body of citizens. Federalism differs from a *confederation,* in which the power to govern is decentralized among sovereign states.
- Among the advantages of federalism are the ability to accommodate a diverse population, a tendency to minimize policy conflict, the dispersal of power, and enhanced prospects for governmental innovation. Such a system also has disadvantages: groups that wish to protect their interests may obstruct national mandates, and the system may produce inequities among different regions.

3.2 *How does the U.S. Constitution apportion powers to balance the relationship between the national and state governments?*

- The most important powers shared by federal and state governments are the ability to regulate commerce and the right to collect taxes to provide for the general welfare. Also important are the powers reserved to the states by the Tenth Amendment to the Constitution. These three constitutional protections help create a balance of power between the federal and state governments.

3.3 *What types of powers have been delegated to the national government, and which were retained by the states?*

- The Constitution delegates certain powers exclusively to the national government; these include the power to declare war, raise and support an army, negotiate with foreign countries, and coin money. The powers reserved to the states include regulation of the health, morals, public safety, and welfare of state citizens. The national and state governments share concurrent powers. In addition to the power to regulate commerce and impose taxes, these include the power to regulate elections and to maintain a judicial structure.
- A few powers are denied both to the national government and to the states. These include the power to grant titles of nobility and to pass bills of attainder and ex post facto laws.

3.4 *How did the federal structure evolve in response to crises in the early years of American government?*

- Efforts in the early 1800s to expand the power of the national government were hotly debated, leading to a Supreme Court decision upholding the dominance of the national government in areas where its powers overlapped with those of the states. One response was the theory of nullification, which held that states could refuse to observe national legislation that they considered unacceptable.

3.5 *How did the interstate commerce and Fourteenth Amendment due process clauses of the U.S. Constitution help to nationalize the government?*

- After the Civil War, the concept of dual federalism prevailed—both the national and state governments were viewed as separate and supreme within their own jurisdictions. During the Great Depression, the national government regained its dominance despite numerous Supreme Court rulings on the interstate commerce clause setting limits on its activities. Eventually a new approach, known as *cooperative federalism,* emerged. Using the Fourteenth Amendment due process clause, the Supreme Court was able to apply many provisions of the Bill of Rights to the states, requiring state judges to guarantee minimum legal protections in the U.S. Constitution. Using this technique, since the 1930s, Supreme Court decisions have sought to ensure uniformity in policies involving the rights of individuals and to impose national standards to reduce inequality.

3.6 *How has the system of federal grants increased the power of the federal government?*

- A grant-in-aid gives money to states and localities to induce them to implement policies favored by the national government. Categorical grants are given for specific purposes and are usually accompanied by strict rules. Federal mandates are national requirements that states must observe.

3.7 *How has the Supreme Court under Chief Justices William Rehnquist and John Roberts altered the system of federalism?*

- Since the 1995 case of *United States* v. *Lopez*, the Supreme Court has been changing the course of decision making on nationalizing the interstate commerce clause to increase the constitutional power of the states to innovate on policy. This "states' rights" approach, relying on the Tenth Amendment, has led the Court to overturn many congressional statutes, but with many of these decisions being 5 to 4, it is possible that change in the direction could come with more appointments by President Barack Obama.

## Key Terms

block grants, 98
categorical grants, 97
coercive federalism, 99
concurrent powers, 88
conditions of aid, 97
cooperative federalism, 95
creative federalism, 96
delegated powers, 86
devolution revolution, 98
dual federalism, 93
federalism, 79
federal mandate, 82
formula grants, 98
formula/project grants, 98
fulcrum of powers, 83
*Gibbons* v. *Ogden*, 92
grant-in-aid, 97
implied powers, 86
incorporation, 96
inherent powers, 86
*McCulloch* v. *Maryland*, 91
nullification, 92
police powers, 86
preemption, 98
progressive federalism, 100
project grants, 98
reserved powers, 86
states' rights, 78
supremacy clause, 86

## Test Yourself Chapter 3

1. What philosophy best describes the difference between national power and states' rights?
   a. The national government rules once, but the states rule many times.
   b. The national government waits to rule until the states have acted.
   c. The national government acts when the states have not acted.
   d. The national government offers a uniform policy while the many state policies offer diverse policies.

2. The major disadvantage of American federalism is
   a. policies take too long to create.
   b. there is too little discussion among the different governments.
   c. with every state having varied policies, the poorer states can do less.
   d. the national government is too willing to take over power.

3. Which of the following is *not* one of the constitutional powers promoting federalism?
   a. The interstate commerce power.
   b. The spending for the general welfare power.
   c. The Tenth Amendment.
   d. The full faith and credit guarantee.

4. The state police powers preserved by the Tenth Amendment protect the
   a. health, safety, morals, and public welfare of state citizens.
   b. ability to supervise the local police within a state.
   c. ability to regulate the personal relationships of citizens.
   d. the ability to re-create a policy that has failed to work.

5. The supremacy clause of the Constitution supports federalism by
   a. instructing states not to act until the federal government does.
   b. instructing the states to consult with the national government before acting.
   c. instructing the national government to take state interests into account before acting.
   d. giving the federal government laws and treaties predominance over the states.

6. When the federal government passes a law requiring the state to act but does not provide the money for that policy, it is called a
   a. federally induced law.
   b. congressional instruction.
   c. federal mandate.
   d. national order.

7. The 1996 Defense of Marriage Act
   a. was a federal attempt to prevent state laws promoting gay marriage.
   b. prevented same-sex couples married in one state from securing those rights in states that banned gay marriage.
   c. is an effort to congressionally override the "full faith and credit" clause for same-sex married couples.
   d. All of the above.

8. The Roberts Court ruled that the 1965 Voting Rights Act
   a. should be overturned.
   b. does not apply to jurisdictions that can demonstrate they did not discriminate in creating their voting regulations.
   c. should not apply to southern states alone.
   d. should be upheld as it is written.

**9.** Thomas Jefferson and Alexander Hamilton set the early nature of federalism in America in their argument over
a. the existence of the national bank.
b. the meaning of the "elastic clause" of Article I, Section 8.
c. the role of national versus state power.
d. All of the above.

**10.** The Supreme Court interpreted the meaning of the elastic and supremacy clauses of the Constitution in the 1819 case
a. *McCulloch* v. *Maryland.*
b. *Seward* v. *Smith.*
c. *Marbury* v. *Madison.*
d. *Elfin* v. *James.*

**11.** The case of *Gibbons* v. *Ogden* affected federalism by ruling that
a. state power must be respected by the national government.
b. national power predominates in all cases.
c. the state and national governments must share power.
d. the national government has the power to regulate anything that affects interstate commerce.

**12.** The claimed power of states and localities to ignore and even disobey national laws is called
a. interposition.
b. nullification.
c. preemption.
d. devolution.

**13.** In the dual federalism cases, the Supreme Court ruled that
a. the states had total power in regulating commerce.
b. the national government must share the power to regulate commerce.
c. the states have the power to control industries that are local and governed by intrastate commerce.
d. the interstate commerce power was lessened in certain cases.

**14.** The Supreme Court's decisions in 1937 on interstate commerce, restoring national power to control the field, came as a result of
a. a new appointment to the Court by Franklin D. Roosevelt.
b. a new theory on constitutional decision making.
c. a new set of facts in the commerce cases.
d. the "switch-in-time-that-saved-nine" by Chief Justice Hughes and Justice Roberts.

**15.** The doctrine extending the Bill of Rights protections to the states is called
a. incorporation.
b. application.
c. penumbras.
d. promotion.

**16.** Since the *Lopez* v. *U.S.* case in 1995, the Supreme Court's approach to federalism cases has largely been
a. to increase states' rights and diminish federal power.
b. to increase federal power and diminish states' rights.
c. to increase states' rights with no effect on federal power.
d. to increase federal power with no effect on states' rights.

**17.** Federal spending grants awarded to states with strings attached as to how the money should be spent are called
a. stimulus grants.
b. categorical grants.
c. project grants.
d. block grants.

**18.** Which of these presidents has been least interested in expanding national spending?
a. Lyndon Johnson.
b. Bill Clinton.
c. George H. W. Bush.
d. Ronald Reagan.

**19.** President Obama's theory of federalism is called
a. successive federalism.
b. coincident federalism.
c. progressive federalism.
d. retentive federalism.

**20.** The Roberts Court's decisions in federalism to this point are
a. pro-states' rights.
b. much like the decisions of the Rehnquist Court.
c. largely dependent on the vote of Anthony Kennedy.
d. All of the above.

**ANSWERS**
**1.** d, **2.** c, **3.** d, **4.** a, **5.** d, **6.** c, **7.** d, **8.** b, **9.** d, **10.** a, **11.** d, **12.** b, **13.** c, **14.** d, **15.** a, **16.** a, **17.** b, **18.** d, **19.** c, **20.** d

# Congress

# 4

## Chapter Outline

## Learning Objectives

4.1 How was Congress created in the Constitution to express the will of the people?

4.2 How representative is Congress of the American people?

4.3 How is the congressional district drawn and redistricted every ten years to express the democratic will?

4.4 How do members of Congress represent the democratic will when they vote?

4.5 Do the elections for members of Congress create fair races that represent the public will?

4.6 How are the House and the Senate organized to represent democracy in their operation?

4.7 How does the congressional committee system enable it to operate, and how has it become more democratic?

4.8 Why and how is the Senate more deliberative than the House in its legislation process, and how representative is it of the public will?

4.9 How do members of Congress decide to vote, and whom do they represent in doing so?

4.10 How does Congress pass legislation, and how well does that legislation express the public will?

4.11 What are the main obstacles to Congress passing legislation, and how can they be overcome?

4.12 How has Congress over the past several sessions changed its political direction as the voting has changed?

# INTRODUCTION

## CONGRESS AND DEMOCRACY

4.1 *How was Congress created in the Constitution to express the will of the people?*

The legislative process has many stages. Each newly introduced bill faces a daunting set of obstacles. Countless actors play roles in the drama of lawmaking, and enemies of every proposal lurk in a dozen or more places. Occasionally, Congress finds itself at a pivotal moment, turning what should be a well-oiled legislating machine in translating political will into new laws into a dysfunctional, stalemated institution unable to implement the public's will. Such was the case in 2010 through December 2011 as roughly 60 conservative budgetary Republicans, members of what they called the Tea Party and newly elected in 2010, made it almost impossible for the new Speaker of the House, Republican John Boehner (R–OH), to lead the institution. The partisan rancor in, and the polarized nature of, the House made it impossible for the Speaker to muster the votes to negotiate with the Democrats, and the White House, over issues such as the national budget, payroll tax cuts, and raising the debt ceiling of the country. As a result, in late 2011 Congress is mired in gridlock, with members unable to determine how to balance the budget, well into reelection mode, and the country waiting until after the 2012 election to see Congress possibly function again with any effectiveness and efficiency. This chapter looks at how Congress has helped, and at times thwarted, America's approach to democracy as it transforms public demands into governmental action.

Rep. Michelle Bachmann (R-MN) has led the Congressional Tea Party with enough success to launch her Republican Presidential nomination bid in 2012.

# THE STRUCTURE AND POWERS OF CONGRESS

The U.S. Congress is among the world's most powerful legislatures. If the dominant congressional faction is large and determined enough, it can override presidential vetoes and make national policy entirely on its own. Presidents cannot force Congress to do their bidding—nor can they simply ignore it. They cannot get rid of Congress by dissolving it and calling for new elections. In nondemocratic nations, executives can do all these things, and their legislatures are little more than puppets under authoritarian leadership.

The U.S. Congress is a major power within the American constitutional system, but it is also a democratic body. Its members are elected by the American people. These two attributes—power *and* democracy—may seem obvious, but they are worth stressing for their significant political implications. If Congress is powerful, then citizens should focus on this body if they wish to influence national policy outcomes.

Congress is pluralistic and decentralized.[1] Each of its 535 members has real power in the sense that each has *one* vote. That means, in essence, 535 power points. Thus, the decision-making process is much more complex than if power were concentrated in the hands of a few people. Those wishing to influence Congress must persuade many people who have different outlooks, who are found at different points in a complex structure, and whose impact on policy outcomes can vary dramatically.

## What the Framers Had in Mind

Believing from their experience with powerful state legislatures that Congress would become the predominant branch of national government, the framers took steps to prevent it from becoming the tyrannical force that the state legislatures had been under the Articles of Confederation. It is no accident that they discussed Congress in the first and longest article of the Constitution. And it is also no accident that the framers began that article granting Congress only "All legislative Powers herein granted." We have already seen in Chapter 2 the way the Constitution limits Congress's power (through the Bill of Rights, for example) and the way other institutions (the president and the Supreme Court) can check its actions. Table 4.1 lists the many powers delegated to Congress in the Constitution.

But the framers went farther. Through the Connecticut Compromise, which based state seating in the House on population but equalized Senate seats at two per state, the Constitutional Convention devised a way to make Congress check itself by striking a balance between the interests of the large states and the small states. They divided Congress into a **bicameral** (two-chambered) **legislature** and gave each chamber the power to inhibit the other's actions. The houses would develop significantly different structures and purposes.

James Madison referred to the House of Representatives as "the great repository of the democratic principle of government"—that is, the one most sensitive to public opinion. The House would be made up of popularly elected representatives serving two-year terms. The entire body would have to face the electorate every other year, so it would by nature reflect shifts in public opinion. This requirement was supposed to ensure that representatives would reflect the popular will. This requirement also places members of Congress in an eternal "election mode," making their need for campaign finances a constant necessity. And being based on population, this body would also favor the larger states.

The Senate, in contrast, was designed as a brake on the public's momentary passions, or as Madison put it, a "necessary fence" against the "fickleness and passion" of the people. The equal number of senators per state would give the small states more power, making it an adequate counterbalance to the overrepresentation of the large states in the House of Representatives. At first, senators were selected by the state legislatures, not by the voting public. The Senate was to be a more aristocratic group,

### QUICK REVIEW

The Framers and Bicameral Legislature

- Congress was set up as a two-chambered legislature.
- The framers gave each chamber the power to inhibit the other's actions.
- Each house has a different structure and purpose.
- The House of Representatives is seen as the most sensitive to public opinion.
- The Senate is designed as a counterbalance to the overrepresentation of the large states in the House.

**bicameral legislature**
A legislative system consisting of two houses or chambers.

| Table 4.1 The Key Powers of Congress |
|---|
| To lay and collect taxes, duties, imposts, and excises |
| To borrow money |
| To regulate commerce with foreign nations and among the states |
| To establish rules for naturalization and bankruptcy |
| To coin money, set its value, and punish counterfeiting |
| To fix the standard of weights and measures |
| To establish a post office and post roads |
| To issue patents and copyrights to inventors and authors |
| To create courts inferior to the Supreme Court |
| To define and punish piracies, felonies on the high seas, and crimes against the law of nations |
| To declare war |
| To raise and support an army and navy and make rules for their governance |
| To provide for a militia |
| To exercise exclusive legislative powers over the District of Columbia and over places purchased to be federal facilities |
| To "make all Laws which shall be necessary and proper for carrying into Execution the foregoing Powers, and all other Powers vested by this Constitution in the Government of the United States" |

an advisory council to the president—a judicious group of wise elder statesmen, and one step removed from the passions and demands of the people. This distinction between the two chambers relied on British tradition, in which the House of Commons represents the masses and the House of Lords the aristocracy.

Until 1913, most Senate members were chosen by their state legislatures (some western states had direct elections), ensuring that they were, in fact, somewhat removed from the mass electorate. In our more modern democratic age, senators, like House members, are directly elected by their state's residents. It is unclear whether popular election has made the Senate more democratic or merely created a body more hostile to centralization and federalism.

Even though their six-year term would seem to remove senators away from popular desires, their reelection campaigns often are more competitive than those of the House, which increases their chances of being turned out of office and encourages incumbents to have ample campaign financing at their disposal. It also ensures that they will more closely reflect shifts in public thinking. However, Senate terms are staggered so that only one-third face election every two years, making Senate membership more stable than that of the House. After any given election, two-thirds of the Senate remain in place.[2] Table 4.2 lists the main differences between the House and the Senate.

In allocating legislative powers, the Constitution carefully specifies Congress's powers to avoid the chaos that had prevailed in state legislatures under the Articles of Confederation. In Article I, Section 8, Congress receives authority in three broad areas: economic affairs, domestic affairs, and foreign affairs. The power to impeach and remove a high official from office is divided between the two chambers, with the House drafting and voting on articles of **impeachment** to be tried in the Senate.

**impeachment**
The process by which government actors can be removed from office for "treason, bribery, or other high crimes and misdemeanors." The House of Representatives votes on the charges, and then the trial takes place in the Senate.

Although the framers wished to limit the powers of Congress, they realized that they could not foresee all the issues and emergencies likely to arise in the future.

**Table 4.2** Differences Between the House and Senate

| House | Senate |
|---|---|
| 435 members | 100 members |
| Two-year term | Six-year term |
| Smaller constituencies | Larger constituencies |
| Fewer personal staff | More personal staff |
| Proportional populations represented | States represented |
| Less flexible rules | More flexible rules |
| Limited debate | Virtually unlimited debate |
| More policy specialists | Policy generalists |
| Less media coverage | More media coverage |
| Less prestige | More prestige |
| Less reliance on staff | More reliance on staff |
| More powerful committee leaders | More equal distribution of power |
| Important committees | Less important committees |
| More partisan | Less partisan |
| Nongermane amendments (riders) not allowed | Nongermane amendments (riders) allowed |

Therefore, they included in Article I, Section 8, the so-called **necessary and proper clause,** also called the *elastic clause,* which grants Congress the power to "make all Laws which shall be necessary and proper" to carry out all the other powers specified in Article I, Section 8. This sweeping language has been interpreted by the Supreme Court to allow Congress to develop its role broadly with regard to regulating commerce, borrowing money, and collecting taxes.[3]

## Limits on Congress's Power

Although extensive, Congress's powers are limited in many ways. As with every agency of the U.S. government, Congress is checked at the most essential level by what the public will tolerate. In addition to regularly scheduled elections, which force members of Congress to be responsive to the will of the people, voters can ignore hated laws or even force Congress to rescind them. Congress is also limited by important elements of the Constitution. It cannot infringe on certain state powers, beginning with an essential one: Congress cannot abolish or change the boundaries of any state without that state's consent.

In theory, the enumerated powers of Article I, Section 8 are not just grants of power to Congress but also limits. The framers argued that Congress (and the federal government) could use particular delegated powers only when specifically granted such authority. In all other cases, the authority would remain in the states or with the people—a restriction made clear in the Ninth and Tenth Amendments.[4] Furthermore, in the exercise of its powers, Congress is subject to the Supreme Court, the final interpreter of the Constitution. Thus, under its judicial review power, the Supreme Court can legitimately void legislation that in its view is contrary to the Constitution. The Court has done this over three dozen times since 1995. It is this power that conservatives will be seeking to use in an effort to persuade the Congress to overturn the Obama health-care reform law. Beyond these checks, perhaps the

**necessary and proper clause**
Article I, Section 8, Clause 18 of the Constitution stating that Congress can "make all Laws which shall be necessary and proper for carrying into Execution the foregoing Powers."

most important day-to-day limit on Congress's power is the president. No matter what the party lineup, Congress and the president continually play complex games of power politics that involve competition and cooperation. They must work together if government is to operate, yet each can check the other quite dramatically. The president's array of powers can stymie the will of Congress, including the role of commander in chief of the military, control of the national bureaucracy, the power to appoint, and the power to veto. Knowing this, members of Congress have repeatedly asked President Obama to lead them on issues such as spending cuts and debt ceiling reduction talks, but when those efforts failed, criticized him for that along with many of his other decisions, including the one to lead the bombing of Libya in 2011 without invoking the 1973 War Powers Act.

## THE MEMBERS OF CONGRESS

### Who Are the Members?

4.2 *How representative is Congress of the American people?*

The First Congress, in 1789, included only 65 representatives and 26 senators—all from the most elite families in America. They were rich, white, and male. Superficially, members of Congress today differ little from that first group. They are still disproportionately rich, white, and male, and they come overwhelmingly from the fields of law, banking, and big business. In the 112th Congress, over half of the members of the House and the Senate are millionaires. From 1985 to 2009, the median net worth of members of Congress rose from $280,000 to $725,000, roughly 30 times higher than American Society.[5] On the other hand, 30 years ago more than half the members of Congress had a law degree, but that number has dropped by half.[6] Some ask, "How can such a group claim to be a representative body?" Others respond, "Does it matter whether the country's representatives are rich or poor, white or black, male or female, as long as they support policies its citizens want and oppose those they don't?"[7]

### THINKING CRITICALLY

Knowing that one needs to be only 25 years old to run for Congress, and 30 years old to run for the Senate, do you think there would be more young people in Congress if there was total public financing to run for these offices?

Some of the wealthiest members of Congress, such as John Kerry and Jay Rockefeller, claim to represent the interests of the poor. And many male members of Congress work diligently to promote the welfare of women. Still, it seems reasonable to conclude that a healthy democracy would include leaders from all social groups. How does Congress shape up in this regard?

Because of Supreme Court decisions and redistricting at the state level, Congress approached democracy in the 20th century by increasing the gender and ethnic diversity of its membership. When we compare today's Congress with its counterpart a few decades ago, we see that the institution is becoming far more diverse. In 1952, the House included only 2 African Americans and 10 women; the Senate had no African Americans and only 1 woman. In December 2011, the Senate included a record number of 17 women, with several serving as committee chairs and party leaders; 2 Asian Pacific Americans, Daniel K. Inouye and Daniel K. Akaka; 2 Hispanic Americans; and no African Americans. The December 2011 House membership included 44 African Americans, 25 Hispanic Americans, 76 women, 1 American Indian, 9 Asian Pacific Americans, 5 Arab Americans, 1 Native American, and 12 members who were born outside the United States. In the past six decades, African Americans have increased their numbers on Capitol Hill by more than 2,000 percent.[8] Although the 112th Congress is just as diverse as its predecessors, it still falls short of reflecting the population as a whole. One group that is now less represented are young people. Despite the possibly transformational nature of the 2008 election, with so many first-time voters, voters under 30, and minority voters participating, the average age of the 112th Congress is roughly 56.7, nearly one and one-half years older than the 109th Congress (55.1). The average age of the senators in the 112th Congress is 62.2, two years older than those in the 109th Congress (60.1).[9]

A record number 17 women served in the Senate in 2011, but the decision by Texas Senator Kay Bailey Hutchison, third from the right, to retire in 2012, might well change that number.

The increasingly diverse demographics of Congress, made even more so by the roughly 60 new Tea Party citizen legislators who were sent to Washington in the 2010 election, do affect the legislative agenda. This was seen in the highly contentious budget and debt ceiling negotiations that occurred in the summer of 2011. The large African American caucus had an impact both on President Barack Obama's policies toward affirmative action and limiting racial profiling in the war on terrorism. The Hispanic caucus has lobbied extensively on the question of the restrictive state immigration policies. At the same time, the increasing number of women in Congress has addressed such questions as equal pay for women, the role of females in the military, gun control, and inclusion of women in federally funded medical research projects.

## Congressional Districts

4.3 *How is the congressional district drawn and redistricted every ten years to express the democratic will?*

The racial and ethnic makeup of Congress strongly reflects the nature of the districts that elect its members. Boundaries can determine a candidate's chances of election, making defining the size and the geographic shape of any legislative district a political act.

Article I, Section 2 of the Constitution arbitrarily set the size of the first U.S. House of Representatives at 65 members and apportioned those seats roughly by population. Later, after the 1790 census, the size of the House was set at 105 seats, with each state given 1 seat for each 33,000 inhabitants. As the nation's population grew, so did the number of representatives. By the early 20th century, the House had expanded to 435 members, each with a constituency of approximately 200,000 people. At that point, members agreed that the House had reached an optimum size. The Reapportionment Act of 1929 formalized this sentiment; it set the total House membership at 435, a number that has remained stable to this day. But because the nation's population has almost tripled since then, each congressional district now contains about 635,000 citizens.

**Table 4.3** To What Extent Does the House Mirror Society?

| Social Group | Number in the House If It Were Representative of American Society at Large | Number in the 109th Congress | Number in the 110th Congress | Number in the 111th Congress | Number in the 112th Congress |
|---|---|---|---|---|---|
| Men | 184 | 373 | 346 | 363 | 359 |
| Women | 226 | 62 | 89 | 72 | 76 |
| African Americans | 52 | 42 | 42 | 41 | 44 |
| Hispanics | 30 | 26 | 27 | 31 | 25 |
| People in poverty | 65 | 0 | 0 | 0 | 0 |
| Lawyers | 2 | 160 | 196 | 257 | 167 |
| Americans under age 45 | 300 | 66 | 57 | 71 | 50 |
| Military veterans | 57 | 141 | 130 | 121 | 118 |

*Sources:* Figures calculated from Mildred Amer and Jennifer Manning, "Membership of the 112th Congress: A Profile," CRS, found at http://assets.opencrs.com/rpts/R40086_20081231.pdf; www.congressmerge.com; *Congressional Quarterly and Statistical Abstract of the United States;* Mildred L. Amer, "Membership of the 109th Congress: A Profile," CRS Report for Congress, May 30, 2005, at www.senate.gov.

Population growth and shifts within each of these 435 districts vary dramatically over time. Keeping the numerical size of districts relatively equal requires redrawing district lines from time to time, and even adjusting the number of representatives allotted each state. This process is known as **reapportionment.** Each reapportionment of House seats reflects the nation's population shifts since the last census.[10] Reapportionment occurs every ten years, always producing winners and losers. Population growth in the South and Southwest helped states such as Nevada, Arizona, Texas, South Carolina, Georgia, and Florida pick up seats after the 2010 census; population loss in the industrial North and Northeast has dropped the number of representatives from states such as New York, Pennsylvania, and Ohio. Table 4.3 illustrates that despite all of this reapportionment, Congress does not mirror the groups in society.

The responsibility for redrawing a state's congressional districts falls to the legislature of the state, pending the approval of the Justice Department to ensure that election districts are drawn fairly. This means that the increasing gains by the Republicans in the party composition of many state legislatures and the state governorships after the 2010 elections and census will be central to the future partisan makeup of Congress by making it easier for that party to retain the seats it gained in the 2010 election, or add new ones, by redrawing the congressional districts.

Within these 435 districts, one finds every imaginable variation. Each has its own character; none is an exact replica of the larger society. Their particular social composition leads some districts to view Democrats more favorably, whereas others lean toward Republicans. The social composition of a district relies on more than its financial and socioeconomic status. Rich districts might be liberal and poor districts might be conservative because of social factors such as religion, education, and cultural background.

An enormous political struggle ensues when a new census changes the number of seats a state will receive. State governments, either through their legislatures, judicial panels, or specifically designed commissions, must then redraw the boundaries of their congressional districts. This process requires more than counting voters and redrawing boundaries to make the districts equal. There are, after all, many ways to carve out numerically equal congressional districts. Some of those ways will help Democrats, whereas others will help Republicans. Boundary line changes can make a large ethnic group the majority within a single district or dilute that group's influence by dispersing its members into two, three, or more districts, where they can be outvoted by the

**reapportionment**
A process of redrawing voting district lines from time to time and adjusting the number of representatives allotted each state.

## Compared to WHAT?

### Seeking Democracy in Iraq

Iraq's new 325-seat parliament, called the National Assembly, has faced many challenges, including finding a way to unite the nation's three major factions. The Sunnis, who once ruled under Saddam Hussein, boycotted the elections, and they now hold a majority in only 4 of the nation's 17 provinces. The United Iraqi Alliance, a coalition of Shiite Muslim parties, holds a narrow majority in the National Assembly. An alliance of Kurdish parties holds 75 seats. The Assembly faced the challenge of governing despite the lack of a constitution and very limited participation of one major group. In late 2008, this assembly passed the Provincial Powers Act, giving the prime minister the power to dismiss provincial leaders, but also setting up the elections that took place in early 2009. It was this National Assembly that passed a resolution setting the timetable for the United States military to leave Iraq in 2010, which was fulfilled in December, 2011. Almost immediately, though, the Shiites began seeking elections for a new government.

*Sources:* Caryle Murphy, "Opening Session Set for Iraq's Legislature," *Washington Post,* March 7, 2005; Neil MacFarguhar, "Unexpected Whiff of Freedom Proves Bracing for the Mideast," *New York Times,* March 6, 2005.

majority in each era. **Redistricting,** as the process is called, therefore becomes intensely political. State legislators naturally seek to establish district boundaries that will favor candidates from their own party. The Compared to What? feature illustrates how challenging it has been to achieve democracy in the legislatures of Iraq.

**redistricting**
The redrawing of boundary lines of voting districts in accordance with census data or sometimes by order of the courts.

**gerrymander**
Any attempt during state redistricting of congressional voting boundaries to create a safe seat for one party.

The term **gerrymander,** (pronounced with a hard "g") describes the often bizarre district boundaries set up to favor the party in power. This word was coined in the early 19th century after Republican Governor Elbridge Gerry of Massachusetts signed a redistricting bill that created a weirdly shaped district to encompass most of the voters who supported his party. One critic looked at the new district and said, "Why, that looks like a salamander!" Another said, "That's not a salamander, that's a gerrymander." The term is now used to describe any attempt to create a *safe seat* for one party—that is, a district in which the number of registered voters of one party is large enough to guarantee a victory for that party's candidate. Figure 4.1 shows what the original gerrymander district looked like.

These battles, never easy, can position one party or the other for greater success in future elections. In 2003, Texas Republicans took control of their state legislature and, with the encouragement of House Majority Leader Tom DeLay, redistricted their state a second time in an effort to create half a dozen new Republican seats in Congress. With these new seats, DeLay hoped to solidify his hold on the House in the 2004 election. The plan involved the creation of wholly Republican districts, breaking up long-time incumbent Democratic districts and creating districts with no incumbents but largely conservative voters. In four instances, the plan pitted Democratic incumbents against each other, thus ensuring Democratic losses. Texas Democratic representatives were so outraged that they fled the state to deny the legislature a quorum and thus prevent the vote. Texas state troopers were sent to find them. The plan worked just as the Republicans hoped: They picked up six new seats in the 2004 congressional election to increase their margin in the state to 22–10. In 2006, the U.S. Supreme Court largely upheld the redistricting plan, but Delay was convicted for illegal use of money to fund the lobbying for this plan.[11]

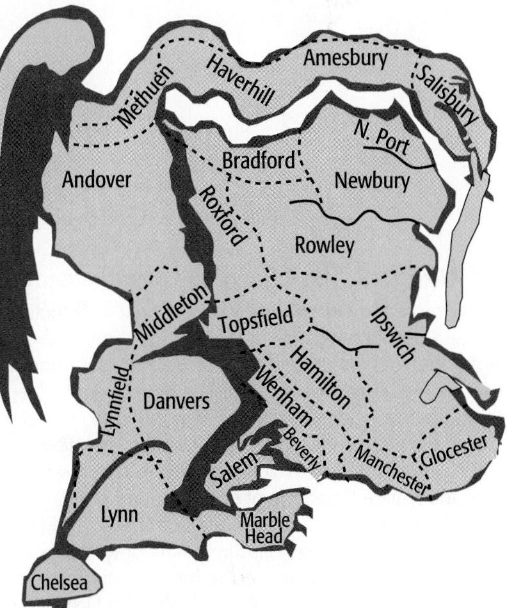


**FIGURE 4.1** The Gerrymander
An 1812 cartoon lampooning the original "Gerry-Mander" of a Massachusetts district. This district was redrawn to guarantee a Republican victory, and *gerrymander* soon became a standard political term.

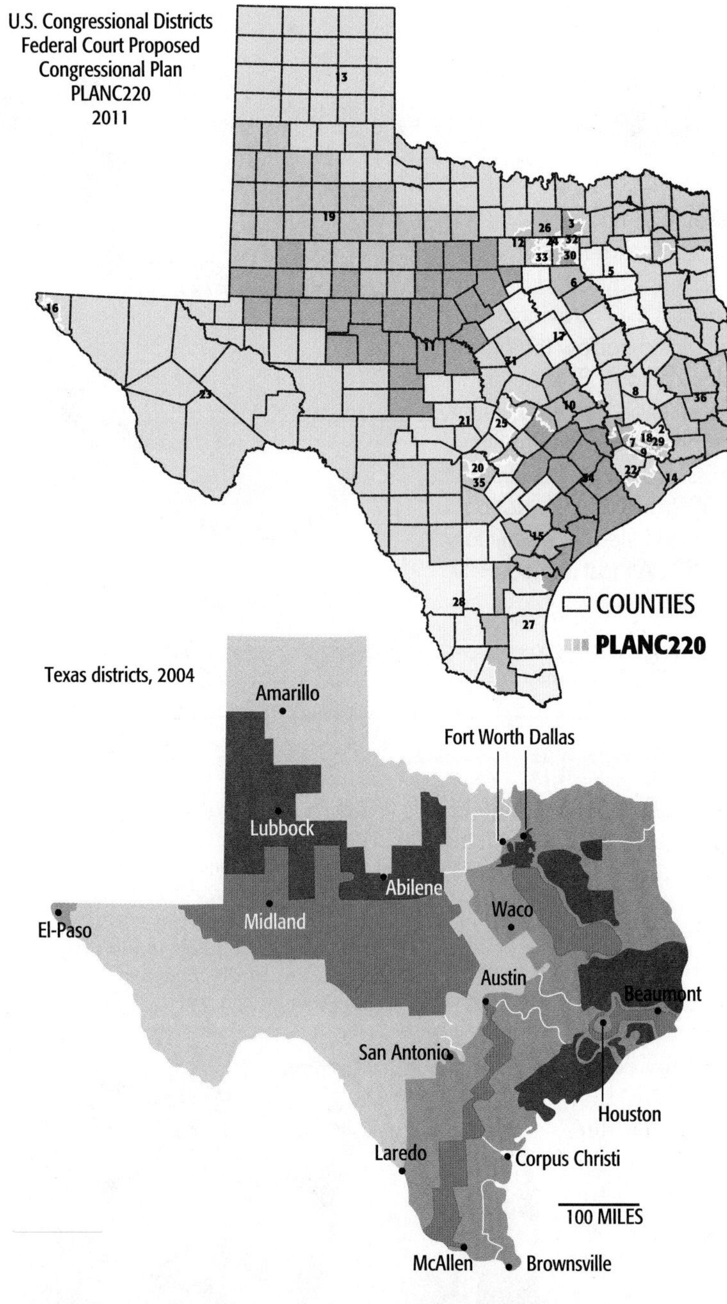


**FIGURE 4.2** The Changing Congressional Districts of Texas

Once more the decennial Congressional redistricting process in Texas is back in the federal courts. The 2010 census showed that millions of residents of the state, the vast majority of whom are Hispanic, had moved to Texas, giving it four new congressional seats. The Republican-led legislature drew up a plan that failed to acknowledge the minority base of the new population growth, and would likely give their party three of the four new seats. However, since Texas is still covered by the 1965 Voting Rights Act, the plan needed to be "pre-cleared" with the Justice Department or the federal courts, and the Obama Administration thought that process was not used properly. The federal court created a plan that included three new "majority–minority" Hispanic districts that would appear to give the Democrats the edge for winning those seats. In January, 2012, the Supreme Court ruled unanimously that the District Court plan should be redone and take greater account of the state legislative plan. It was expected that this would benefit the Republican Party, possibly providing the margin for keeping their majority in the House. However, others argued that this would be done at the expense of giving proper representation to the new Hispanic residents of the state. While the Court did not hear the issue of whether Section 5 of the 1965 Voting Rights Act was unconstitutional, Justice Thomas wrote in a separate opinion that it was, and it appears that others on the Court might agree.

*Source:* Texas Legislative Council.

## Majority–Minority Districts and the Approach to Democracy

The redistricting process has occasionally been used to further social as well as political goals, such as increasing diversity in Congress—an interesting example of America's meandering approach to democracy. After the 1990 census, states with histories of racial discrimination were required by law to draw new district boundaries that would give minority candidates a better chance of election. The mandated redistricting was meant to ensure representation for nonwhites living in white-dominated areas. Such African American and Hispanic majority districts were called **majority–minority districts.** The redistricting added 19 new African American and Hispanic American members to Congress in 1992. Proponents point to these gains as evidence that the new districts made Congress more representative of the general population, but critics claim that they constitute "racial gerrymandering."[12]

North Carolina's Twelfth Congressional District was one of those created to strengthen the voting power of African Americans. However, it was so narrow that in some places it spanned only one lane of Interstate Highway 85. The Supreme Court disallowed this district in 1993 in the case *Shaw* v. *Reno.* Although the Court sidestepped the general question of racial gerrymandering, it did prohibit racially based redistricting in the case of "those rare districts [like North Carolina's Twelfth] that are especially bizarre." It added acidly that the district "bears an uncomfortable resemblance to political apartheid."[13]

In 1992, Cynthia McKinney, an African American, was elected to the House of Representatives from Georgia's Eleventh District. In a 5–4 decision in 1995, the Supreme Court struck down the "race-based" redistricting plan in Cynthia McKinney's 260-mile-long district.[14] The Court asserted that this Justice Department–directed plan to create 3 black majority districts in the state out of the previous 11 such districts violated the equal protection rights of white voters because it was based predominantly on race. The decision put similar plans throughout the nation (mainly in the South) in jeopardy by ruling that they must all be "narrowly tailored to achieve a compelling [state] interest." In other words, although race can be a factor in redistricting, it cannot be the overriding consideration. Figure 4.2 shows how redistricting in Texas has led to a new Supreme Court case in 2012.

A year later, the Supreme Court upheld another redistricting scheme coming out of Georgia. The Court approved the plan by the district court to create a single black majority district for the 1996 elections, saying that a single such district is enough, because any attempt to create more of them would have to be based on race and would thus violate both the 1965 Voting Rights Act and the "one person, one vote" standard in *Reynolds* v. *Sims* for interpreting Article I, Section 2 of the Constitution. Speaking for the Court, Justice Anthony Kennedy reaffirmed that race "must not be a predominant factor in drawing the district lines."[15]

**majority–minority district**
A congressional district drawn to include enough members of a minority group to greatly improve the chance of electing a minority candidate.

**delegates**
Congress members who feel bound to follow the wishes of a majority of their constituents; they make frequent efforts to learn the opinions of voters in their state or district.

This issue continued after the 2000 elections. At about this time the Supreme Court unanimously offered the states "very significant breathing room" in redistricting, using the 2000 election results.[16] In Mississippi, the Bush administration stepped in, using the Voting Rights Act to block a state court–ordered redistricting plan that would have created a congressional district with 37.5 percent African American voting age population in favor of one mandated by the federal court with only 30.4 percent African American voters. The result was that the federal court plan was used for the 2002 election and approved by the U.S. Supreme Court the following year.[17] With so many federal, state, and local racially gerrymandered districts in existence, and nearly all of the Supreme Court decisions in this area being decided by a narrow 5–4 majority with Anthony Kennedy in the swing seat, his decisions will help to determine their future.

This issue was revisited in 2009 when the Court considered a challenge from an Austin, Texas, utility voting district to Section 5 of the Voting Rights Act of 1965. It required a federal "preclearance" permission before any voting regulations could be changed to make sure that it would not diminish the rights of minorities to vote. The law, which was passed to remedy the fact that in 16 states—many in the historically discriminatory Deep South, but also including Alaska and Florida— less than 50 percent of the population registered to vote. This was an indicator to Congress that literacy tests and other devices were being used to prevent minorities from voting. In the latest renewal of the act, signed by President W. George Bush in 2006, the vote in Congress had been overwhelming (98–0 in the Senate). The Austin utility district argued that it should be able to "bail out" of the preclearance procedure, a process allowed by the law but which only 17 of the more than 12,000 electoral districts had been able to do. The argument was made that times had changed and discrimination was not as rampant and that the limited reach of the law unconstitutionally limited the sovereignty of certain states. Chief Justice John Roberts and the eight-member majority also seemed sensitive to the argument of civil rights activists that declaring the preclearance Section 5 process would gut the law entirely and open the door to future voting rights irregularities and discrimination.

So, expressing a reluctance to overturn congressional statutes (especially one passed so overwhelming and touching on such sensitive interests), Roberts argued, "Things have changed in the south. Voter turnout and registration rates now approach parity. Blatantly discriminatory evasions of federal decrees are rare. And minority candidates hold office at unprecedented levels." The Court allowed this voting district and others to bail out of the law's reach if it could prove that its voting laws had not discriminated in ten years and it had "engaged in constructive efforts" to increase voting by minority groups.[18] Legal observers now believe that this decision will encourage many other states and localities to seek a "bailout" exempting themselves from the law's enforcement provisions. When that appeal comes, though, some wonder if the law will survive another legal challenge.[19]

## Delegates versus Trustees

4.4 *How do members of Congress represent the democratic will when they vote?*

If Congress is to function as a representative institution, individual members must represent their constituents. In theory, legislators may view themselves as either delegates or trustees. **Delegates** feel bound to follow the wishes of a majority of their constituents; they make frequent efforts to learn voter opinions in their state or district. But how does a legislator represent district minority groups or raise issues of national importance but of low priority for constituents?

**trustees**
Congress members who feel authorized to use their best judgment in considering legislation.

**politico**
Congress members who vote suing a combination of constituent wishes and their own best judgment in considering legislation.

**incumbents**
Individuals who currently hold public office.

For example, should a representative with few minority constituents vote for an affirmative action program opposed by an overwhelming majority of voters in the district?

In these situations, many legislators see themselves not as delegates but as **trustees,** authorized to use their own judgment in considering legislation. The trustee role was best expressed by the English philosopher and member of Parliament Edmund Burke (1729–1797), who explained to his constituents that representatives should never sacrifice their own judgment to voter opinion. After hearing that Burke did not intend to follow their wishes, his constituency promptly ejected him from Parliament.

In Congress, the role of trustee, which often leads to policy innovations, is more likely to find favor with representatives from safe districts, where a wide margin of victory in the past makes future reelection likely by discouraging potential opponents and their contributors. Legislators from marginal districts tend to be delegates, keeping their eyes firmly fixed on the electorate. They apparently wish to avoid Burke's fate.

In practice, members of Congress combine the roles of delegate and trustee. They follow their constituency when voters have clear, strong preferences, but they vote their own best judgment either when the electorate's desire is weak, mixed, or unclear, or when the member has strong views on an issue. This approach to voting is called the **politico** role. Members of Congress frequently must balance votes on issues of national importance against votes on issues that are important to their constituents.[20]

## Name Recognition and the Incumbency Factor

4.5 *Do the elections for members of Congress create fair races that represent the public will?*

**Incumbents** are individuals who currently hold public office. The power of incumbency, or the ability to get reelected, is strong in both houses, but is more powerful in the House than in the Senate. From 1964 through 2010, an average of more than 93 percent of House incumbents but only 81.6 of Senate incumbents who sought reelection were successful.[21] Despite the anti-incumbent sentiment of the 1994 election, since that time more than 95 percent of the House and 90 percent of the Senate incumbents who ran have won reelection.[22] In 2010, those numbers were reduced somewhat with the success of the protest conservative Tea Party, with only 87 percent of the House gaining reelection, and 84 percent of the Senate.[23]

The advantage of incumbency is a relatively recent phenomenon. Before the Civil War, almost half of each new House and one-quarter to one-third of each entering Senate class included new members (a fact that can also be explained by the high number of members who voluntarily chose not to run for reelection). Despite high incumbency reelection rates, many members voluntarily leave office, either due to unhappiness with their jobs or a desire to turn the seat over to someone new. When combined with the change wrought by the so-called Republican Revolution in 1994, a majority of the members of the House and the Senate have been newly elected since 1990.

Incumbents enjoy a number of significant advantages in any election contest.[24] They nearly always enjoy greater name recognition than their challengers. They can hold press conferences for widespread publicity, participate in media events such as town meetings, and maintain offices back home that keep their names in the spotlight. Challengers must struggle for, and often fail to achieve, the kind of publicity and recognition that come automatically to an incumbent. Incumbents also often benefit from favorable redistricting during reapportionment.

### THINKING CRITICALLY

The $787 billion economic stimulus bill known as the American Recovery and Reinvestment Act of 2009 was proposed by President Barack Obama to deal with the severe recession. Three moderate Republicans, Maine's Olympia Snowe and Susan Collins and Pennsylvania's Arlen Specter, were the only members of that party to vote for the bill, giving the Democrats the win. Specter later switched parties to the Democrats, but failed to be nomination to run for re-election in 2012.

When would you vote against your party, and even your state, as a senator? Whom do you represent in those situations?

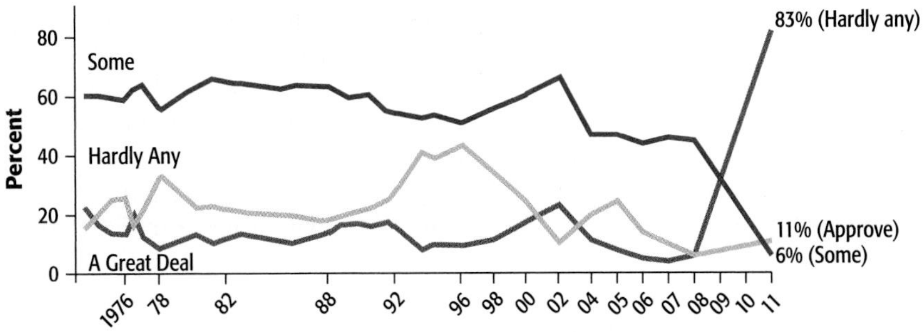


**FIGURE 4.3** Confidence in Congress

*Source:* "Major Institutions," www.polling_report.com, September 29-October 2, 2011, June 9–12, 2008, June 1–4, 2006, May 23–26, 2005; Gallup Poll, May 21–23, 2004, accessed at www.harrisinteractive.com/harrispoll/; see also National Opinion Research Center, reported in National Journal, January 17, 1998, p. 111, http://www.polling_reportpolling_report.com/institut.htm.

Incumbents can increase their visibility through use of the **franking privilege**—free mailing of newsletters and political brochures to their constituents. These mailings solicit views and advice from constituents and serve to remind them of the incumbent's name and accomplishments. The use of franked mail has grown over the years. In 1994, House members seeking reelection sent out 363 million pieces of mail, nearly two items for every person of voting age. Figure 4.3 shows how public support for the increasingly stalemated, partisan Congress has plummeted since 2008. In recent years, though, given the failures of Congress to deal with economic and other problems, public disapproval for the institution of Congress has skyrocketed. In the fall of 2011, public support for Congress was at a record low of 11 percent, with 83 percent of the people disapproving of their work and only 6 percent of the people saying they support reelection of their member of Congress.[25]

**franking privilege**
The free mailing of newsletters and political brochures to constituents by members of Congress.

**casework**
Favors done as a service for constituents by those they have elected to Congress.

**term limits**
A legislated limit on the amount of time a political figure can serve in office.

Incumbents have another advantage: Their staff helps them do favors for constituents. These services, known as **casework,** may involve arranging for pothole repairs, expediting Social Security benefit payments, or providing a tour of the Capitol. Casework is at the heart of the power of incumbents. Realizing that every voter remembers these little favors, members of Congress often have several full-time staff members who deal with cases involving individual constituents.[26] This kind of experience allows incumbents campaigning for reelection to "point with pride" to favors done for their districts. Although casework may have minimal direct impact on voting, it helps name recognition and avoids any negative backlash from constituents if requests are ignored. More than that, casework is a strategy to gain positive feedback from constituents, which enables members to take stands on legislative issues that might be unpopular with their constituents.[27]

Perhaps the greatest advantage incumbents hold is financial. Parties, interest groups, and individuals tend to back known candidates because they have the best chance of winning, whereas relatively unknown challengers have great difficulty raising money. In 2000, House incumbents spent about $400,000 more than their challengers, whereas Senate incumbents spent more than $2 million more than their challengers.[28] Now, it takes nearly 1.5 million dollars to run for Congress, and it is expected that in the 2012 Massachusetts race for the Senate more than $30 million will be spent by the two candidates in their campaign.Incumbents can usually raise that kind of money with little difficulty, but few challengers can.[29] However, challengers usually need not raise as much money as incumbents just to be competitive in the election. All they really have to do is pass a threshold of about $400,000 for a House seat in order to make a credible run for the office.

Seeking to change this pattern, many voters now favor some form of **term limits,** usually a maximum of 12 years in each house. With polls in 1994 showing 80 percent of the public favoring term limits, 23 states passed legislation limiting the length of time their senators and representatives can serve in Congress. Underlying these measures was the growing public perception that incumbent legislators, feeling confident of reelection, become either complacent or corrupt. In 1995, the Supreme Court overturned the power of the state of Arkansas—and thus *all* states—to impose term limits on congressional candidates (in this case, a limit of no more than three terms for the House and two terms for the Senate). As a result, similar laws in 22 other states were voided. Justice John Paul Stevens explained that states could not add a new requirement for office to the current three requirements—age, citizenship, and residency—specified in the Constitution. Any term limits on congressional candidates would have to be accomplished by constitutional amendment.[30]

Two years later, the Court *disallowed* (by refusing to hear on appeal) Arkansas's and eight other states' attempt to use a so-called scarlet letter provision to identify on the ballot congressional candidates who did not adhere to voluntary term limits.[31] Even without term limits, turnover in Congress in the past decade has been such that the average length of service in the 112th Congress is 9.8 years in the House and 11.4 years in the Senate.[32] With 87 new members elected to Congress in 2010, 63 of them new Republicans allowing them to take control of the House by its largest majority since the 1940s. The margin of Democratic control in the Senate was reduced from 53 to 47, including two independents who caucus with the Democrats, President Obama's path to getting legislation passed became much more difficult.

**QUICK REVIEW**

Speaker of the House

- Designated in the Constitution as the one presiding officer of the House.
- One of the most powerful officeholders in the U.S. government.
- Traditionally is the leader of the party with a majority of the seats.
- Appoints members to the Policy Committee and appoints the party's legislative leaders and senior staff members.
- Controls assignment of bills to committees.

# HOW CONGRESS ORGANIZES ITSELF

4.6 *How are the House and the Senate organized to represent democracy in their operation?*

Because the Constitution says little about how each house of Congress should be organized, those structures have evolved over the decades. The result has been a tension between the centralizing influence of the congressional leadership and the decentralizing influence of the committees and the subcommittees.

## Congressional Leadership

**Leadership in the House** The Constitution designates only one presiding officer of the House, the **Speaker of the House.** One of the most powerful officeholders in the U.S. government, the Speaker is usually seen as the voice of the House of Representatives, and sometimes even of the overall Congress, and is third in line for the president of the United States according to the Twenty-fifth Amendment. Although the Constitution does not specify that this person must be a member of Congress, he or she is, by tradition, leader of the majority party. The Speaker for the 112th Congress is the son of a tavern owner, Republican John Boehner, from Ohio.

The Speaker's formal duties are to preside over the House when it is in session; to appoint all members to the Policy Committee, a representative body of the party conference that handles committee assignments and plans the legislative agenda;[33] to appoint the party's legislative leaders and senior staff members; and to control the assignment of bills to committees. When the House majority party is not the president's party, the Speaker is often considered the minority party's national spokesperson.[34] When the Speaker is not of the same party as the president, as is true of Republican Speaker John Boehner relative to Barack Obama, they can be powerful and sometimes crippling opponents. Although it appears to many as if Speaker Boehner has been successful in thwarting Obama's legislative agenda, it became clear initially in the budget and debt ceiling negotiations, and later in the payroll tax cut debate, in 2011 that the roughly 60 Tea Party conservative Republicans became a separate voting bloc, denying Boehner control of his own party for his own legislative agenda.

**Speaker of the House**
The only presiding officer of the House mentioned in the Constitution. The leader of the majority party in Congress and third in line for the presidency.

The Speaker's power has varied over time. In the 1890s, Republican Speaker Thomas B. "Czar" Reed instituted a set of draconian organizational and debating rules, known as "Reed's Rules," that made him so powerful that he could personally appoint all committee chairs and determine committee membership and thus block legislation and punish those who opposed them.[35] When his successor, Joseph "Uncle Joe" Cannon, tried to use these powers, they were diluted by a House revolution in 1910. From 1940 until his death in 1961 (with the exception of four years when the Republicans controlled the House), Speaker Sam Rayburn of Texas exemplified the use of all the formal and informal powers of the office. Rayburn's powers, however, were limited by the competing interests of entrenched conservative committee chairs.

**House majority leader**
The person elected by the majority party caucus to serve as the party's chief strategist and floor spokesperson.

**party caucus**
A conference of party members in Congress.

A series of reforms in the 1970s made the Speakership of Thomas ("Tip") O'Neill (1977–1987) even more powerful on paper. The Speaker could now dictate the selection of the committee chairs, committee members from the Speaker's party, and party members of the powerful Rules Committee. In addition, the office increased its power to refer bills to committees and dictate the order of the floor proceedings. O'Neill became far more powerful than any Speaker since Cannon, but his powers had limits. O'Neill often failed to dissuade southern Democrats in Congress, the so-called *boll weevils,* from backing President Ronald Reagan's conservative policies. On one occasion, in 1981, when Reagan's administration substituted a 1,000-page bill that no member on the floor had time to read, containing dozens of drastic funding cuts at the last moment before a vote, O'Neill could only use the "bully pulpit" of his position to object in a speech. Noticing that the "cut and paste" bill had the name of a woman and her phone number in the margin, a likely source for one of the cuts, O'Neill objected, "Why are we enacting this woman into law?" But no one listened, and the bill passed.[36]

Although the powers of the office had not changed, its prestige and effectiveness declined when O'Neill's successor, James Wright of Texas, tried to use his powers for partisan goals, only to be forced to resign by a House revolt, led by Republican Newt Gingrich. Ironically, Gingrich thought he would restore the Speaker's position to greater luster in 1995, but eventually he, too, contributed to its weakening. He voluntarily stepped down from the Speakership after party members charged him with ethics violations and responsibility for the poor Republican showing in the November 1998 elections. When Bob Livingston of Louisiana was forced to resign almost immediately after being chosen to replace Gingrich, he was replaced with the genial former wrestling coach, J. Dennis Hastert of Illinois.

Next in line after the Speaker is the **House majority leader.** The majority leader is elected by the **party caucus,** a conference of party members in Congress, and serves as the party's chief strategist and floor spokesperson. The majority leader also schedules bills and attempts to persuade members of the majority party to vote according to the party's official position on pending legislation. The majority leader of the 112th Congress is Republican Eric Cantor of Virginia. Although Tom DeLay of Texas was elected majority leader in 2005, he stepped aside after being indicted in Texas over ethics charges relating to a Texas political redistricting plan. When DeLay resigned from Congress in early 2006 in the wake of another growing scandal relating to his former aide, lobbyist Jack Abramoff (who was later convicted for trading lobbying contracts to secure financially lucrative legislation, a process known as "pay-for-play"), John Boehner (R–OH) won the election to replace him. After the Democrats took control of the House in 2006, Steny Hoyer was overwhelmingly elected

Republican Speaker John Boehner of Ohio has lost power as the Tea Party members have forced him to back out of deals with the Democrats and President Obama.

**minority leader**
The leader of the minority party in Congress.

**whips**
Congress members charged with counting prospective votes on various issues and making certain that members have the information they need for floor action.

**president of the Senate**
The vice president of the United States.

**president pro tempore**
The majority party member with the longest continuous service in the Senate; serves as the chief presiding officer in the absence of the vice president.

over new Speaker Nancy Pelosi's candidate, John Murtha of Pennsylvania. Now Majority Leader Cantor, who appears to be more linked to the conservative budgetary Tea Party caucus, has to walk a fine line between serving as a deputy to Speaker Boehner and also speaking as a fiscal and social conservative to position himself for succeeding Boehner through the votes of the conservative wing. As a result, he is much less willing to negotiate with the Democrats and the Obama White House.

The minority party is headed by the **minority leader,** and Democrat Nancy Pelosi of California won election to this position in the 112th Congress after the Democrats' loss of their majority in 2010 cost her the Speakership position. Should the Democrats become the majority in Congress in 2012, as minority leader, Rep. Pelosi would be in position to be reelected the Speaker of the House.[37] Both the majority and minority party leaders work with the support of **whips,** members charged with counting prospective votes on various issues and making certain that members have the information they need for floor action. *Whip* is a fox-hunting term applied to the legislative process. During a fox hunt, the "whipper-in" keeps the sniffing dogs from straying by whipping them back into the pack. The House majority whip in 2011 is Kevin McCarthy (R–CA); the House minority whip is Steny Hoyer (D–MD), who has become a frequent media spokesperson for the party. Whips are aided by a complex system of more than 90 deputy whips, assistant regional whips, and at-large whips.

Increasingly important is the position of the leader of the party congressional campaign committees that are charged with raising and distributing campaign funds to "winnable" races that are determined to be of central importance for controlling the House. The chair of the National Republican Congressional Campaign Committee (NRCCC) for the 112th Congress is Peter Sessions (R–TX), and the chair of the Democratic Congressional Campaign Committee (DCCC) is Steve Israel (D–NY).This chapter's Approaching Democracy timeline traces some of the key events in the evolution of Congress.

In 2011 Democratic Senate Majority Leader Harry Reid (Nevada) needed all of the patience and wit of Mark Twain, looking over his shoulder in his office as he works, to craft legislative deals in the face of the concerted opposition of the Republicans under John Boehner, and the Tea Party.

For the first time in years, the large size of a new congressional caucus has led to an important informal leadership position. In the 112th Congress, with roughly 60 new freshman members a part of the fiscal conservative, citizen legislators referred to as Tea Party, the informal leader in Congress became Michelle Bachmann (R–MN), who was denied the chance to ascend to a formal congressional leadership position. Her success in winning concessions put her in a position to later run for the Republican nomination for president in 2012. Also prominent among this group was Majority Leader Eric Cantor (R–VA) and budget expert, Paul Ryan (R–WI), who drafted his own federal budget to propose spending cuts. With the majority in the 112th Congress being 242 Republicans to 190 Democrats, it was this group of roughly 60 members that seriously cut into Speaker Boehner's majority. The Speaker's reliable party members were reduced to about 180 votes, or less than that controlled by Nancy Pelosi and the Democrats. Thus, Boehner's ability to negotiate with President Obama and the House Democrats on fiscal issues was seriously reduced.

**In the Senate** Other than making the vice president the **president of the Senate,** the Constitution does not specify a leadership structure for the Senate. Vice president Joe Biden presides over the Senate only on rare occasions—most commonly when a tie vote seems likely on a key piece of legislation. If a tie does ensue, the vice president can cast the deciding vote. Except for the occasional ceremonial event, the vice president rarely enters the Senate. To guide that body's day-to-day activities, the Constitution allows the election of a **president pro tempore.** This position is essentially honorary and goes by tradition to the majority party member with the longest continuous service. In 2011, Daniel Inouye (D–HI), first elected a senator in 1963, holds the office. In theory, the president pro tempore presides over the Senate, although the position provides little political clout. The day-to-day task of the Senate presiding officer is usually farmed out to a wide range of senators, often junior members who use the job to gain experience and "pay their dues."

The Senate party leadership structure differs only slightly from that of the House. The majority party selects a **Senate majority leader**—currently Harry Reid of Nevada—whose functions resemble those of the Speaker of the House.[38] The Republican minority leader, Senator Mitch McConnell of Kentucky, is known as a senatorial insider who has in the past developed very effective behind-the-scenes legislative strategies, and the homespun television arguments to support them, in order to unite the diverging political views among Senate Republicans into a successful force. The majority leader schedules legislation, often in consultation with the leader of the minority party, directs committee assignments, and persuades members to vote along party lines.

As in the House, the majority and minority leaders have party whips to help organize and count votes. In the 112th Congress, the Senate majority whip is Richard Durbin of Illinois, and the Republican whip is Jon Kyl of Arizona. Majority Leader Harry Reid and Chuck Schumer of New York co-chair the Democratic Conference, which includes the two Independent senators, Joe Lieberman of Connecticut and Bernard Sanders of Vermont, where the Democrats vote on party issues such as committee membership and chairmanships and plan strategy for policy making. In an unusual move, in 2011, Senator Schumer was also made the Policy Committee chair, making him the chief Senate Democratic Party strategist and a main public spokesperson for the party as he became a sort of "Majority Leader in waiting" for the Democrats. Lamar Alexander of Tennessee chairs the Republican Conference, the parallel meetings of all GOP party Senate members. Alexander announced in September 2011 that he would step down from his position in January 2012, and would not challenge Texas Republican John Cornyn for the whip position.

Another central leadership position is the chair of the campaign fund-raising committees for the next Senate election, who is also in charge of distributing campaign funds for races deemed winnable and important. In the 2006 campaign, Chuck Schumer of New York showed the importance of this position in carefully picking candidates for winnable seats in the Senate. A full year in advance of the campaigns, he was able to persuade the son of former Pennsylvania governor Robert Casey, a conservative Democrat, to run for the seat against ultra-conservative Rick Santorum, and then successfully persuaded all of the other possible candidates not to run in the primary. The chair of the Democratic Senatorial Campaign Committee (DSCC) is Patty Murray of Washington. The chair of the National Republican Senatorial Committee (NRSC) in the 112th Congress is ultra-conservative John Cornyn of Texas.

## APPROACHING Democracy Timeline

### Major Events in the Evolution of Congress

| | |
|---|---|
| **1890s** | Speaker Thomas B. "Czar" Reed controls the House with iron fist. |
| **1910** | House revolution takes away Speaker's powers from Joseph "Uncle Joe" Cannon. |
| **1960s** | Speaker Sam Rayburn battles with senior southern Democratic committee chairs to pass John Kennedy and Lyndon Johnson legislation. |
| **1975** | Democratic Party reforms open up the subcommittees. |
| **1978** | Speaker Thomas P. "Tip" O'Neill takes over selection of key committees. |
| **1979** | CSpan begins televising Congress. |
| **1989** | Speaker Jim Wright ousted on ethics charge. |
| **1990s** | Term limits movement fails. |
| **1990s** | Senate begins using silent filibusters and "holds," forcing need for 60 votes on all major issues. |
| **1995** | Newt Gingrich and Republicans take over the House. |
| **1999** | Speaker Newt Gingrich ousted on ethics charge. |
| **2005** | Senate Republicans propose "nuclear option," eliminating filibuster for judicial appointments. |
| **2005** | Moderate senators defeat "nuclear option." |
| **2006** | Nancy Pelosi becomes first female Speaker. |

☐ Democratic ☐ Neutral ☐ Undemocratic

**Senate majority leader**
A senator selected by the majority party whose functions are similar to those of the Speaker of the House.

Republicans Mitch McConnell (Kentucky), the minority leader of the Senate, and Jon Kyl (Arizona), the minority whip, have done their best to use a combination of a united party vote and filibusters to try to derail the Democrats' legislative agenda.

The Senate majority leader is usually an influential politician. If the president is from the same party, the majority leader often can be a valuable ally and spokesperson on Capitol Hill. Since 2009, the relationship between President Obama and Majority Leader Reid has been somewhat testy. During one legislative battle, Reid was reported to bristle at the idea that the Democratic Senate majority would be a "rubber stamp" for the White House, saying of Obama's wishes, "I don't work for him. I work with him." Reid's challenge became doubly difficult, because he was dealing with an obstructionist and delay-oriented Republican minority, fully willing under the leadership of Mitch McConnell to filibuster bills and Obama appointments. By refusing to compromise with the White House and the Senate Democrats on matters such as increasing taxes and the nature of spending cuts, the Republicans sought to establish a record for the 2012 election campaign.

In addition to these leaders, with the Tea Party containing at least a half-dozen and possibly many more members in the Senate, Senator Jim DeMint of South Carolina has become the leader of those fiscal conservatives. Their efforts have continued to push the Senate Republicans further and further to the right. With this in mind, for both parties and both Houses of Congress, it is always interesting to track the comments and actions of the leaders below the Speaker and majority and minority leaders, because they are often seen on the track to replace the top leaders should any of them falter or fail to be reelected.

One of the most persuasive Senate majority leaders in recent history was Texas Democrat Lyndon Baines Johnson, who served from 1955 until he became vice president in 1961. In what became known as the "Johnson treatment," he would corner fellow senators in search of a vote and badger them with his charismatic charm and large size until he got an agreement.[39] Johnson always said that the Senate was like an ocean, with whales and minnows; if he could persuade the "whales" (powerful senators) to follow him, the "minnows" (weaker members) would follow along in a school. Nothing stood in Johnson's way. Once, when Senator Hubert Humphrey of Minnesota, caught in a holding pattern flying over Washington, was needed for a key vote, Johnson ordered air traffic controllers to clear the plane for immediate landing. On another occasion, when Senator Allen Frear of Delaware opposed a bill, Johnson stood up on the floor of the Senate and yelled, "Change your goddamn vote!" Frear immediately complied.[40]

One political cartoonist's vision of the political agendas of Barack Obama on the left and Republican Mitch McConnell on the right.

Congressional leaders since the 1960s, particularly in the Senate, have been persuaders rather than dictators. The job requires give-and-take bargaining and consensus-building skills. Former Majority Leader Robert Byrd spoke of this difference from Johnson's world, describing the Senate in the 1970s and 1980s not as an ocean of whales and minnows to be led but rather a forest. "There are ninety-nine animals. They're all lions. There's a waterhole. They all have to come to the waterhole. I don't have power, but . . . I'm in a position to do things for others."[41] Years later, in an autobiography, Mississippi senator Trent Lott described his job as Senate majority leader in the 1990s as much like "herding cats."[42]

## Congressional Committees: The Laboratories of Congress

4.7 *How does the congressional committee system enable it to operate, and how has it become more democratic?*

A Speaker's or a Senate majority leader's success depends now on how well he or she works with leaders and members in the "laboratories of Congress"—its committees and subcommittees. Some of Congress's most important work is done in committees and subcommittees. As Woodrow Wilson put it, "Congress on the floor is Congress on public exhibition; Congress in committee is Congress at work."[43]

There are four types of congressional committees: standing, select or special, conference, and joint. Each party receives seats on all committees in proportion to its representation in the entire House or Senate. Thus, the majority party in each house generally controls the chairs and a corresponding majority in each committee. The party leadership assigns members to committees. The 2006 election relinquished control of both houses of Congress to the Democrats, and the chairs of all of the committees in both houses changed from the Republicans to the Democrats. In 2010, though, the Republicans seized control of the majority in the House, and their new slate of chairs thwarted the Obama Administration's legislative agenda. The battlefield for control of these chairs in both houses will be a pivotal result of the 2012 election.

The most important committees in both houses of Congress are the **standing committees.** These permanent committees—20 in the Senate, 21 in the House—determine whether proposed legislation should be sent to the entire chamber for consideration. Virtually all bills are considered by at least one standing committee and often by more than one. In 2009, five committees in the House and two in the Senate were engaged in drafting pieces of the Obama health-care reform law. When Congress considered the question of renewing funding for the Iraq war over a period of three months in early 2007, the issue was placed before several committees, including the Armed Services, Appropriations, and Foreign Affairs Committees.

**Select or special committees** conduct investigations or study specific problems or crises. These temporary committees possess no authority to propose bills and must be reauthorized by each new Congress. Their creation and disbanding mirror political forces in the nation at large. When a given issue is "hot" (e.g., concern about drug use or security), pressures on Congress grow. Congress may set up a special committee to investigate. When the problem seems solved or interest dies away, the committee also meets its end. On the other hand, if the original problem and the concerned constituency continue to grow, a new standing committee may be created, thus providing power and institutional permanence for those concerned with the issue.

**Conference committees** are formed to reconcile differences between the versions of a bill passed by the House and the Senate. A conference committee can be small, usually composed of the chairs of the relevant committees and subcommittees from each chamber.[44] Major bills, however, may have committees of as many as 250 representatives and senators. Conference committees rarely exist more than a few days.[45]

Because both houses jealously guard their independence and prerogatives, Congress establishes only four **joint committees.** Two examples are the Joint Economic Committee, which reports on the national economic conditions, and the Joint

**standing committees**
Permanent congressional committees that determine whether proposed legislation should be sent to the entire chamber for consideration.

**select committees (or special committees)**
Temporary congressional committees that conduct investigations or study specific problems or crises.

**conference committees**
Committees that reconcile differences between versions of a bill passed by the House and the Senate.

**joint committees**
Groups of members from both chambers who study broad areas that are of interest to Congress as a whole.

**task force**
An informal procedure used by Congress to assemble groups of legislators to draft legislation and negotiate strategy for passing a bill.

Committee on Taxation, which examines tax policy changes. These committees include members from related committees in both chambers and rotate chairs from each chamber, who study broad areas of interest to Congress as a whole. More commonly, joint committees oversee congressional functioning and administration, such as the printing and distribution of federal government publications.

## Why Does Congress Use Committees?

Committees enable Congress to do its work effectively by allowing it to consider several substantive matters simultaneously. Because each committee addresses a specific subject area, its members and staff develop knowledge and expertise. Ideas can be transformed into policies based on research and expert testimony. Committees provide multiple points of access for citizens and interest groups, serving as mini-legislative bodies that represent the larger House or Senate.

Committees are major players in congressional business, and members actively seek seats on particular ones with three goals in mind: to be reelected, to make good public policy, and to gain influence within the chamber.[46] The ideal committee helps them do all three. A seat, for instance, on the House Ways and Means Committee, which passes on tax legislation, or on the Senate Appropriations Committees, which dictates spending priorities, ensures internal influence and authority.[47] The House Rules Committee and the Judiciary Committees of both houses were once considered powerful and thus desirable. Now, though, the House Rules Committee is merely a tool of the Speaker, and the Judiciary Committees of the House and Senate handle such controversial legislation that serving on them often creates only trouble for members.

Various committees help members serve their districts directly. A representative from rural Illinois or California, both large agricultural states, might seek a seat on the Agriculture Committee. Membership on such a committee would increase the legislator's chances of influencing policies that affect constituents, a helpful move at election time. As a former member who was on the Public Works Committee (now Public Land and Resources) explains, "I could always go back to the district and say, 'Look at that road I got for you. See that beach erosion project over there? And those buildings? I got all those. I'm on Public Works.' "[48]

The committee system also provides opportunities for career advancement and name recognition. A strong performance at televised hearings can impress constituents, increase name recognition, and convey a positive image. But such visibility can also backfire.

Time and again, President Obama has spoken to a joint session of Congress on important issues hoping to persuade them to act on his legislative agenda, but often without success.

## Decline and Return of the Congressional Committees?

During the Bush administration years, congressional committees became less important in the lawmaking process, but that process is changing in the Obama years. Although committees in the past were, as Woodrow Wilson said, a representation of "Congress at work," in recent Congresses the kind of *ad hoc* legislating that was done used **task forces** and individual members, belying the textbook model for congressional lawmaking. Legislative compromises were not forged in committees. Members of those committees were not recognized for their seniority and expertise, nor were committee chairs recognized for their growing and continual power. Committees did not have independent effects on the lawmaking process.

Instead, in the three decades prior to 2006, committee power was eroded to the point that committees had largely collapsed. The committees began to lose power during the era of Democratic control, but the death knell came in 1995 with the reforms instituted under Speaker Newt Gingrich. The committee structure began to collapse when he began to impose term limits on committee chairpersons, and his top-down management style of creating task forces to draft bills favored congressional leadership rather than the committees.

When J. Dennis Hastert took over as Speaker in 1999, he promised to restore the committee structure, but it did not work out that way. He tried to follow a return to regular order, allowing the committees to consider legislation in their own way. Indeed, one member said, "There is a stronger sense that our members are charting their own course." But time and again, Hastert found that a return to legislating-as-usual did not work out well.

Recently, though, there are signs that the committee structure and the individual members of both Houses are beginning to retake control of the legislative process. One of those signs is the increased use of party discipline in the committee chairmanships and committee seniority. After the 2008 election in which Independent but Democratic-voting Senator Joe Lieberman campaigned heavily for Republican Senator John McCain (Lieberman called Barack Obama "an eloquent young man" who was unprepared to be president), the Democratic caucus was ready to strip him of all of his senior committee assignments. However, "in the spirit of reconciliation and atonement," Lieberman was stripped of his subcommittee chairmanship on the Environmental and Public Works Committee but allowed to remain the chair of the Homeland Security and Governmental Affairs Committee. In 2011, Democrat Anthony Weiner of Brooklyn, New York, tried to overcome a controversy caused by his inadvertent racy Twitter messages. He was forced to resign when it became clear that his party's leaders and his colleagues were no longer willing to work with him.

This trend away from committee involvement brought improperly reviewed, ill-supported, and compromise-laden legislation to the House and Senate floors. The constant ham-stringing of measures has limited both parties' ability to present a coherent platform to the voting public. In addition, these insufficiently backed and ill-prepared bills were increasing the number of measures filibustered in the Senate.

**QUICK REVIEW**

Committees

- Enable Congress to consider several substantive matters simultaneously.
- Members and staff develop knowledge and expertise.
- Provide a place for ideas to be transformed into policies.
- Serve as mini-legislative bodies representing the larger House or Senate.

# CONGRESS IN SESSION

4.8 *Why and how is the Senate more deliberative than the House in its legislation process, and how representative is it of the public will?*

A combination of House and Senate procedures and the power and influence of congressional leaders and committee and subcommittee chairs shapes the outcomes of the legislative process.[49]

## The Rules and Norms of Congress

The formal rules of Congress can be found in the Constitution, in the standing rules of each house, and in Thomas Jefferson's *Manual of Parliamentary Practice and Precedent.* Congressional rules, for example, dictate the timing, extent, and nature of floor debate. Imagine what might happen without such rules. If, for example, each of the 435 members of the House tried to rise on the floor and speak for just one minute on just one bill, debate on every issue would last at least seven hours, not taking into account the time needed for amendments, procedural matters, and votes.

**The House Rules Committee** As noted earlier, the House Rules Committee plays a key role, directing the flow of bills through the legislative process. Except for revenue, budget, and appropriations bills, which are *privileged legislation* and go directly to the House floor from committee, bills approved in committee are referred to the Rules Committee. The House Rules Committee issues **rules** that determine which bills will be discussed, how long the debate will last, and which amendments will be allowed.[50] Rules can be *open,* allowing members to freely suggest related amendments from the floor; *closed,* permitting no amendments except those offered by the sponsoring committee members; or *restrictive,* now the most commonly used procedure, which limits amendments to certain parts of a bill and dictates which members can offer them. By refusing to attach a rule to a bill, the Rules Committee can delay a bill's consideration or even kill it.

**QUICK REVIEW**

Rules Committee

- Directs the flow of bills through the legislative process.
- Receives bills that have been approved in committee.
- Issues rules that determine which bills will be discussed, length of the debate, and which amendments will be allowed.
- Can delay or kill a bill by refusing to attach a rule to it.

**rules**
The decisions made by the House Rules Committee and voted on by the full House to determine the flow of legislation—when a bill will be discussed, for how long, and if amendments can be offered.

**unanimous consent agreement**
The process by which the normal rules of Congress are waived unless a single member disagrees.

**rider**
An amendment to a bill in the Senate totally unrelated to the bill subject but attached to a popular measure in the hopes that it too will pass.

**line item veto**
The power given to the president to veto a specific provision of a bill involving taxing and spending. Previously the president had to veto an entire bill. Declared unconstitutional by the Supreme Court in 1998.

**earmarks**
A provision in legislation, often an appropriation bill, directing spending for a specific program, agency, or region.

During the 1950s, conservative members dominated the Rules Committee and succeeded in blocking civil rights, education, and welfare legislation, even bills favored by a majority of House members.[51] Today, however, democratizing reforms have made the Rules Committee what one member of Congress has called "the handmaiden of the Speaker," directing the flow and nature of the legislative process according to the majority party's wishes.[52] If the Speaker favors a bill, the rule is passed; if not, the rule is denied. If a long debate would prove embarrassing to the majority party, the Speaker will likely allow only a short debate under a closed rule. Thus, contrary to earlier days when whole sessions of Congress would pass without a vote on a key issue, Speaker Nancy Pelosi used her total control over the Rules Committee to direct the House to vote on Barack Obama's economic stimulus package in early 2009 with very little time for discussion and allowing such limited amendments that the Republicans complained they had never been consulted on the measure.

Because the Senate is smaller and more decentralized than the House, its rules for bringing a matter to the floor are much more relaxed. There is no Rules Committee; instead, the majority leader has the formal power to make the schedule. The schedule is usually formed through informal agreements between the majority and minority leaders and finalized by **unanimous consent agreements,** a waiver of the rules for consideration of a measure by a vote of all of the members. With no central traffic cop to control the flow of legislation, some bills remain on the Senate floor for weeks, often at the expense of the substance, and chances for passage, of the measure. The polarized nature of the partisan Senate in the 112th Congress, however, has made agreements between Majority Leader Reid and Minority Leader McConnell increasingly rare, and caused Reid to schedule votes on occasion without consulting the Republicans.

**Amendments to a Bill** A key procedural rule in the House requires that all discussion on the floor and all amendments to legislation must be *germane*—that is, relevant to the bill being considered. The Senate, in contrast, places no limits on the addition of amendments to a bill.

The ability to attach unrelated **riders** to a bill can sometimes help a senator secure passage of a pet project by attaching it to a popular proposal. Another important consequence of riders is that committees cannot serve the gatekeeper function on legislative wording, as in the House; Senate committees are less important in this function than their counterparts in the House. However, heavy use of riders has led to problems. When budget bills were considered, members sometimes added so many riders, each containing spending provisions desired by those individual members, that the result was known as a "Christmas tree bill," laden with financial "ornaments." The president either had to sign or veto a bill in its entirety, a requirement that led to spending bills containing expensive pet projects inserted by legislators. When Congress passed the **line item veto** in 1996, it allowed specific provisions of select taxing and spending bills to be vetoed independently of the rest of the bill. When the Supreme Court ruled the line item veto unconstitutional in 1998, the power of riders returned, leading President George W. Bush to ask for its reinstitution.

One other increasingly controversial type of financial amendment in the last several years has been the use of **earmarks,** a provision usually appearing in appropriations legislation, but sometimes in general legislation, directing that a portion of already passed funding be directed to a specific program, agency, and/or region. For years, especially during the Bush administration, this was done, often in total secrecy, by members of Congress in an effort to direct a portion of government spending to agencies in their district. As outlined later in Chapter 11, this process became controversial in 2006 when it was learned that Republican lobbyist Jack Abramoff and others had been running a "pay-for-play" operation by which they would receive contracts and funnel some of that money to members of Congress or their campaign committees. In turn,

Republican Joe Wilson of South Carolina earned the wrath of Congress, especially the Democrats, when he broke protocol by yelling, "You lie!" at President Barack Obama as he was giving a speech on the health-care reform bill to a joint session of Congress on September 9, 2009.

their clients would gain the funding earmarks they sought. As a result, Congress passed the Honest Leadership, Open Government Act in 2007, which made the process more open by limiting earmarks and making them more public. There is now an earmarks database website on the Office of Management and Budget site that lists the funding and names the members of Congress associated with them, who in turn must certify that they received no remuneration for securing this funding. Despite this law, in late 2011 it was revealed that over $9 billion in earmarks had been funded, but one of them was not the "We the People" civics education program, which had been defunded.

**filibuster**
A technique in which a senator speaks against a bill or talks about nothing specific just to "hold the floor" and prevent the Senate from moving forward with a vote. He or she may yield to other like-minded senators so that the marathon debate can continue for hours or even days.

**hold**
A request by a senator not to bring a measure up for consideration by the full Senate.

**cloture**
A procedure through which a vote of 60 senators can limit debate and stop a filibuster.

**Filibusters and Cloture** Senate debate has few restrictions. Opponents can derail a bill by **filibuster.** This technique allows a senator to speak against a bill—or just talk about anything at all—to "hold the floor" and prevent the Senate from moving forward with its business. Examples include the repeated filibusters used to derail the campaign finance reform legislation. The senator may yield to other like-minded senators, and the marathon debate can continue for hours or even days. The record for the longest individual filibuster belongs to Senator Strom Thurmond of South Carolina, who spoke against the Civil Rights Act of 1957 for an uninterrupted 24 hours and 18 minutes.

Over time, the Senate has made filibusters less onerous, first by interrupting them when the Senate's workday ended, and then by allowing them to be interrupted by a vote to consider other work. In recent years, senators have begun using a scheduling rule called a **hold** on legislation to stall a bill. This century-old practice was once a courtesy used specifically to keep a piece of legislation from being debated until a member could return to the chamber for the discussion. In recent years, however, senators have used holds to secretly indicate that any debate on a bill was pointless; they intended to filibuster it either because of objections to it or because the bill's supporters had not yet offered concessions in its wording.[53] Senator Jesse Helms (R–NC) used this tactic as chair of the Senate Foreign Relations Committee to block 43 ambassadorial appointments because he disagreed with the State Department's policies. By the end of 1999, Senator Herb Kohl (D–WI) announced that he would place a hold on all legislation, including spending bills, unless dairy legislation that he opposed was allowed to die. At one point, several members threatened a hold on the adjournment vote unless the legislation they wanted was supported.[54]

A hold can block several bills indefinitely, with the rule now in effect that requires 60 votes, rather than a simple majority, for passage. After witnessing the use of this tactic to block a $145 billion highway bill in late 1997, Majority Leader Trent Lott explained, "This is the Senate. And if any senator or group of senators wants to be obstructionist, the only way you can break that is time."[55]

How does the Senate accomplish anything under these conditions? In 1917, it adopted a procedure known as **cloture,** through which senators can vote to limit debate and stop a filibuster. Originally, cloture required approval of two-thirds of the senators present and voting (67 members if all were present), but when such a vote proved too difficult to achieve, the required majority was reduced to three-fifths of the members, or 60 votes.

Although the majority required for a cloture vote can be difficult to muster, the number of successful cloture votes has increased in recent years. Even if cloture has been voted, however, a postcloture filibuster can continue for 30 more hours.[56] The value senators place on this technique was evident in the 104th Congress when, despite the continual bogging down in concurrent filibusters, the members refused to reform the technique further. As a result, cloture votes occurred in the double digits throughout the rest of the 1990s, many unsuccessful, as with the Campaign Finance Reform bill.

Liberals who objected to the use of filibusters to stall civil rights legislation in the 1960s took advantage of that same tactic to combat and sometimes defeat key measures of the Contract with America in the 1990s. Some argue that cloture and filibusters empower minorities, whereas others claim they are stalling tactics that obstruct the will of the majority. This very debate led to the pivotal effort by Republicans in 2005 to vote into effect the so-called "nuclear option" eliminating the filibuster for judicial nominations. Eventually, moderate and maverick senators, seven from each party, brokered a deal to avoid the vote and arranged for immediate votes on several disputed judicial candidates. Interestingly, in 2011, Senate Republicans used the filibuster to thwart scores of President Obama's federal court nominations.

Ironically, the overwhelming victory of the Democrats in the 2008 senatorial election put them on the edge of being able to prevent all filibusters by securing 60 votes for cloture. They won 56 seats in the 2008 election, together with the votes of Independents Joe Lieberman of Connecticut and Bernard Sanders of Vermont, who caucus and usually vote with them. Then, in April 2009, moderate Republican Arlen Specter of Pennsylvania switched to the Democratic Party, giving the Democrats one more seat. When the Minnesota Supreme Court upheld Democrat Al Franken's

## APPROACHING Contemporary Issues in Democracy

### Revising the Senatorial Filibuster Rule?

Since 2005, more and more dialogue has taken place about the possibility of revising the senatorial filibuster rule. This rule, which allows for continual discussion about an issue unless a vote of cloture, now 60 votes, takes place to stop it, is a part of the rules of the Senate. The purpose of the rule was to protect the right of the minority party in the Senate to keep the majority party from passing legislation without any consideration of the objection by its opponents. Both parties have used this rule over the decades; for example, a coalition of Republicans' and Southern Democrats' efforts to block civil rights laws in the late 1950s and 1960s. Liberal Democrats used it to try to block the Reagan administration's policies in the 1980s and the Bush administration's policies in the 2000s.

When it became apparent that the filibuster was being used to block policies by an elected majority or president, discussion began on the question of limiting its reach. Each party, beginning in the late 1980s, used the filibuster to try to block the other party's efforts to staff the federal judiciary. In 2005, Vice President Dick Cheney and other conservatives threatened to use what they called the "constitutional option," but what opponents called "the nuclear option." Under this maneuver, filibusters would be eliminated for blocking the judicial appointments. This effort was narrowly averted. In the 112th Congress, there was discussion by the Democrats to force the Senate to reconsider and re-pass its rules, which would have led to a discussion of changing the filibuster rule. However, the Republicans under Minority Leader Mitch McConnell made clear that they were prepared to use the filibuster repeatedly to prevent President Obama and the Senate from passing any measure, or confirming any judicial appointment, that might gain them political advantage in the 2012 election. While Majority Leader Harry Reid chose not to change the filibuster in the middle of the debates over the budget, he began the process of preventing the Republicans from making multiple filibusters on the same bills, and on various amendments to those bills after the cloture votes were passed.

The question is becoming: Should the Senate filibuster rule be revised? On the one hand, the rule protects the rights of the minority in the Senate. If the filibuster should be limited, or eliminated, it might make it possible for the majority to ignore the minority. On the other hand, it can be used to prevent the majority from achieving the legislative and appointment goals that it was elected by the people to accomplish. If the filibuster is used for partisan and ideological goals, as opposed to policy goals, it can become a means for thwarting the aims of the political electorate. Another argument is that the only reform needed to the filibuster rule is a return to the rules of the 1950s and early 1960s, when members of the Senate had to physically stand in the chamber, sometimes around the clock, to keep the filibuster going, rather than allowing members to simply announce a stoppage and move on to another issue, or allowing them to limit the timing of the filibuster to workday hours three days a week. So, do you think it helps America approach democracy without any limits on the use of a filibuster, unless a cloture vote succeeds?

312-vote margin in the Minnesota Senate race over Republican Norm Coleman, the Democrats appeared to have a "filibuster-proof" Senate vote. However, this did not become automatic, clearing the way for quick passage of Democratic Party–sought legislation, because two senators, Robert Byrd and Ted Kennedy, missed votes due to illness, followed by Kennedy's death. In addition, several of the more conservative Democratic senators, such as Ben Nelson of Nebraska, Mary Landrieu of Louisiana, and Blanche Lincoln of Arkansas, had to be convinced to join the majority. A vote for cloture does not always break along party lines, though, as senators consider in each case whether their vote to stop a filibuster could later be used by others as a reason for stopping a later filibuster by them on an issue of concern to them.

As the Senate has become more and more partisan and polarized ideologically, with the gap between the Republicans and Democrats widening, the number of filibusters have increased dramatically, thus derailing the Democrats' legislative agenda. In the 111th Congress, Majority Leader Reid filed a record 136 cloture petitions in an effort to break Republican filibusters. The 112th Congress is on a slightly slower pace, with 48 cloture motions filed in 2011.[57]

To place the filibuster in perspective, remember that although it has been abused in recent years simply to prevent legislation from being considered or to delay the agenda of the rival political party, it is designed to retard and consider more carefully the work of the legislative process. The intention has been that senators use it only on major issues, where a large minority intensely opposes the majority's plan. Unhappy minorities should not necessarily win all they want, but neither should any political system systematically neglect the demands of a large minority. Filibusters are intended to force the majority to hear the minority and perhaps respond to certain demands. All in all, the filibuster's ability to give voice to minorities probably outweighs the frustrations it creates for the majority. Figure 4.4 explains this rise in the use of the filibuster, demonstrating how much more partisan the Senate became over nearly a quarter of a century.

### THINKING CRITICALLY

Should the Senate filibuster rule be reformed? Should the Senate make a filibuster harder to achieve by returning to the rule of having to physically debate on the floor, even "round the clock" to keep a filibuster going? Or, should cloture votes become easier to achieve by changing the rule to 55 votes? Should the process of using holds as silent filibusters be ended? Does it approach democracy to change these rules?

**Informal Rules and Norms** In addition to its formal rules, Congress, like most large organizations, has informal, unwritten rules that facilitate its day-to-day operations. High among these has been the traditional rule of **seniority,** in which a member's rank in the House or Senate depends on length of service there. In the past, seniority was key to committee membership, and the only way to become a committee chair was to accumulate more years of continuous service on that committee than any other majority party member.

Apprenticeship was another traditional norm, whereby younger members were expected to sit quietly and learn their legislative craft from their elders. "To get along, go along" was the wisdom that Speaker Sam Rayburn once preached to junior members in persuading them to follow his lead.

Yet another traditional norm, designed to keep friction to a minimum, has been that debates on the floor and in committees are conducted with the utmost civility. One member never speaks directly to another; instead, members address the presiding officer, who may deflect damaging comments by ruling them out of order. In addition, whenever debates occur between members, titles, not names, are used, as in "I would like to commend the Representative from State X." Political scientist Donald Matthews has labeled such adherence to unwritten but generally accepted and informally enforced norms as "the folkways of the Senate."[58] Even the most bitter of political rivals still refer to each other as "the distinguished senator from . . ." or "my good friend and esteemed colleague" before proceeding to attack everything the other holds dear.

In recent years, however, increasing breakdowns in this norm led some to question its existence. As the two parties have become more partisan and their ideologies have drifted farther and farther apart, members of Congress have increasingly stooped to trading insults with, or shouting at, each other in hearings or in debates on the floor. In 1996, a highly agitated Representative Sam Gibbons (D–FL) called his Republican

### THINKING CRITICALLY

Did the changes during the 1950s and 1960s that reduced the ability of senior chairpersons to control the flow of legislation and the current decentralized system that is based on more power of individual committee members result in an approach toward or a recession from democracy? With many senior members still in charge of the committees, would a strict two-term limit on committee chairmanship make committees even more democratic?

**seniority**
An informal, unwritten rule of Congress that more senior members (those who have served longer than others) are appointed to committees and as chairpersons of committees. This "rule" is being diluted in the House as other systems are developed for committee appointments.

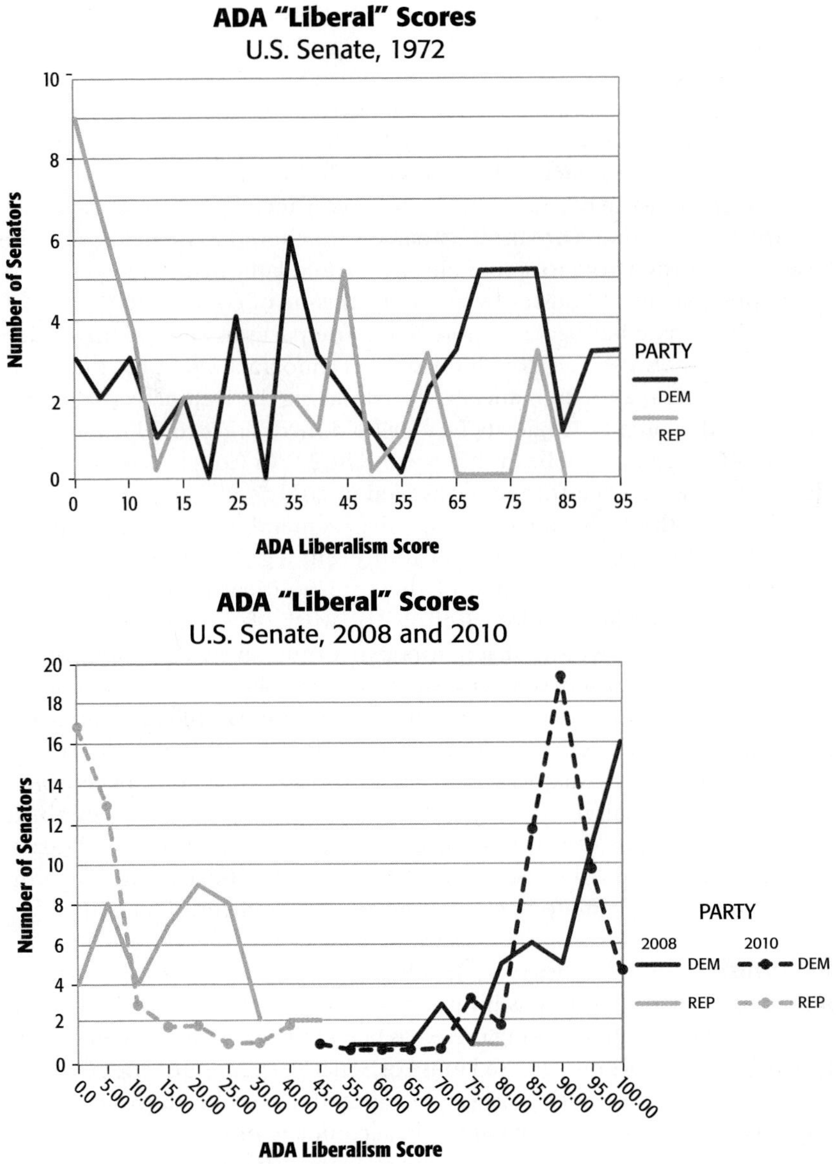

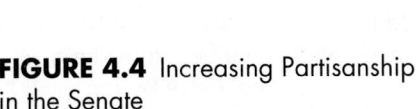

**FIGURE 4.4** Increasing Partisanship in the Senate

These charts clearly illustrate how much the political environment of the Senate has changed over the past 40 years. In 1972, the range of partisanship of the members of the two parties was so broad that they overlapped almost entirely. By 2008, though, the members of each party had become so partisan, there was much more separation, with the majority grouped at the far extremes of the political spectrum. This makes compromise extremely difficult. Thanks to political historian Allan Lichtman for the idea and for permission to use his version of the 1972 chart. The 2008 and 2010 chart is drawn from the "liberalism" scores for senators by the Americans for Democratic Action (ADA); see http://www.adaction.org/index.htm.

colleagues "a bunch of fascists" and "dictators" before stalking out of a hearing room and yanking on the necktie of a California colleague. In 1997, one debate on the House floor ended with House Majority Whip Tom DeLay (R–TX) forcibly shoving Representative David R. Obey (D–WI) before the two men were separated.[59] This lack of civility has persuaded many of the more moderate members to leave their positions early.[60]

In November 2003, after Majority Leader Bill Frist led an all-night demonstration filibuster by his Republican colleagues on their perception that the Democrats were holding up President Bush's judicial nominees by filibuster, Minority Leader Harry Reid broke the usual civility rule when he said, "I've never seen such amateur leadership in all the time I've been in Congress, 21 years."[61] Congressman Joe Wilson, a Republican from South Carolina, broke all civility rules when he shouted, "You lie!" at President Obama during his health-care reform speech to a joint session of Congress on September 9, 2009.

These differences have increased since Speaker Newt Gingrich and the Republicans took power in 1994 and changed the way that Congress operated. The sharp differences in partisanship, the unwillingness to accept legislative compromise or defeats, and the increasing number of legislators who have few relationships with their colleagues because their weekends are spent going home to raise money, consult their constituents, and see their families, have broken the past bonds of civility in the chambers.

Such trends, according to congressional scholar Burdett Loomis, have meant change for the Senate. Regarding the prospects of legislative passage, Loomis has said, "However much we may want to romanticize the world's greatest deliberative body, the cold fact remains that the 1980s and 1990s have witnessed a consistent growth in partisan behavior and position-taking in the U.S. Senate." Fewer and fewer members of Congress in general, he charges, seem to put the national interests ahead of those of their own party, making it harder for the two parties to find a point of compromise.[62]

The Tea Party in the Senate is led by Jim DeMint (R-SC) (second from the right) and Rand Paul (R-KY), (fourth from the left), the son of Congressman and Presidential candidate Ron Paul

When more than half of the freshmen members in the 104th Congress made their maiden floor speech in the opening session in January 1995, it was clear that the apprenticeship norm was dying in the House, and it has been long since dead in the Senate. Thus, a new norm, *political party loyalty,* might be replacing seniority, apprenticeship, and civility, at least in the House.[63]

The Senate is generally more traditional than the House in its regard for seniority. Dilution of seniority rights began in 1953, when Senate Minority Leader Lyndon Johnson instituted what became known as the "Johnson rule," which provided that no Democratic senator would receive more than one major committee assignment until everyone had one. Republicans adopted a similar rule in 1965. Thirty years later, however, when Republicans once again controlled the Senate, Majority Leader Bob Dole decided instead to let seniority determine every committee chair, even though several Republican colleagues were uncomfortable with certain results—most notably, archconservative Jesse Helms of North Carolina chaired the Foreign Relations Committee, and 92-year-old Strom Thurmond of South Carolina chaired the Armed Services Committee. As outlined earlier, after the 2008 election of Barack Obama, Senate Democrats split their actions in dealing with questions about the seniority of two colleagues. In the House, however, Democratic members had no problems with removing John Dingell of Michigan, at age 83 the longest-serving member of the House, from his powerful chairmanship of the Energy and Commerce Committee, replacing him with Henry Waxman of California, although the decision seemed to have as much to do with changing policy on automobile regulation.

When Rep. Gabriel "Gabby" Giffords (D-AZ) made her dramatic return to the House to cast her vote for lifting the debt ceiling after being shot, and waved to her colleagues, it brought many of them to tears.

Two other norms used to push legislation through Congress are *specialization* and *reciprocity*. Legislators are expected to develop a certain expertise on one or more issues as a way to help the body in its lawmaking role. Members who lack expertise in a particular policy area defer to policy specialists with more knowledge, with the understanding that the favor will be reciprocated.

When reciprocity is applied to votes on key measures, the result is called **logrolling,** which helps legislators cooperate effectively. The term comes from a competition in which two lumberjacks maintain their balance on a floating log by working together to spin it with their feet. In congressional logrolling, legislators seek the assistance of colleagues by offering to support legislation the colleagues both favor. For example, a Democratic senator from California might support a flood control project in Mississippi that has no relevance to West Coast voters, provided the Republican senator from Mississippi promises to support a measure delaying the closing of an army base in California.[64] The House leadership's "Freedom to Farm" Act in the 104th Congress, which continued farm subsidies for sugar, peanuts, and milk, passed without trouble because it was paired with a food-stamp program that brought it the votes of the liberal Northeast representatives.[65] In an era of government spending cuts, however, the notion of reciprocity has faded somewhat.

**logrolling**
A temporary political alliance between two policy actors who agree to support each other's policy goals.

A traditional form of the logrolling norm is called **pork-barrel legislation,** special-interest spending for members' districts or states. It is named for the practice of

**pork-barrel legislation**
Policies and programs designed to create special benefits for a member's district, such as bridges, highways, dams, and military installations, all of which translate into jobs and money for the local economy and improve reelection chances for the incumbent.

distributing salt pork as a treat to sailors on the high seas. In this case, members of Congress see their job as "bringing home the bacon" in the form of support for jobs and programs in their districts: dams and highways, military bases, new federal buildings, high-tech company support, or even research grants for local colleges and universities. The distribution of district or state pork-barrel spending tends to follow power. The state of Wyoming, with no powerful legislators, received only an average of 83 cents per capita. On the other hand, Democratic West Virginia Senator Robert Byrd, the Senate's longest-serving member, has obtained billions of dollars in programs for his state, including $6 million for the National Center for Cool and Cold Water Aquaculture, thus winning an annual "oinker" award from the Citizens Against Government Waste.[66]

It is not uncommon for revenue bills to contain their own version of pork: tax loopholes and breaks for companies in specific districts. Given Congress's program-cutting mood in recent years, a new form of "negative pork" has developed to distribute the cuts in different areas. Sometimes the cuts have been so contentious—for example, military base closings—that Congress had to create special bipartisan commissions to recommend them.

Although many people criticize these spendthrift ways, attracting federal spending is the traditional way members of Congress represent their districts. In many districts, federal buildings and roads are named for local members of Congress, thus solidifying their reelection support. In June 2009, Congress passed energy and climate change legislation only after the bill's co-author, Energy and Commerce Chairman Henry Waxman (D–CA), persuaded wavering members of Congress to vote for the bill by agreeing to so many new spending programs and business and agricultural subsidies, worth billions of dollars, that the bill doubled in size—to 1,400 pages.[67] As Tip O'Neill explained, "All politics is local." The line item veto was designed to eliminate such expensive practices. But, given the Supreme Court's 1998 decision, this option is no longer available, unless it is passed in a more acceptable fashion by Congress or approved by constitutional amendment.

**QUICK REVIEW**

Effects on Voting Decisions

- Personal views and political ideology of members of Congress affect voting decisions.
- Constituents influence their representative's voting decisions.
- Political party affiliation affects votes based on party position.
- The president may influence a member's vote.
- Important interest groups and political action committees lobby on key issues.
- Congressional staff members sort through various sources of pressure and information.

## How Members Make Voting Decisions

4.9 *How do members of Congress decide to vote, and whom do they represent in doing so?*

Political scientists have long sought to understand why members of Congress vote as they do. Their research suggests seven major sources of influence.

**Personal Views** Personal views and political ideology are the central variables in determining members' voting decisions. When legislators care deeply about a policy matter, they usually vote their own preferences, sometimes risking their political careers in the process. Party leaders recognize the importance of personal convictions. "I have never asked a member to vote against his conscience," said former Speaker of the House John McCormack. "If he mentions his conscience—that's all. I don't press him any further."[68]

Sometimes such votes show the best aspects of congressional representation. In early 1995, Republican senator Mark Hatfield offered to resign rather than provide his party with the winning vote to pass the Balanced Budget Amendment, saying he opposed "tinkering with the Constitution." Majority Leader Robert Dole declined his offer. These personal views, however, can reflect other factors as well—most notably the desires of a member's constituents.

**Constituents** In votes with high visibility, constituents have a significant influence on their representative's voting decisions.[69] No representative wants to lose touch with the district or appear to care more about national politics than about the people back home. This was why Oklahoma representative Mike Synar—a four-term liberal

Democrat who supported gun control and the Family and Medical Leave Act and opposed a measure requiring parent notification if a teenage daughter has an abortion—was defeated in a 1994 primary in his conservative district. A former supporter explained that Synar had "lost touch." To avoid these situations, members regularly conduct surveys and return to their districts to learn constituents' opinions about issues on the congressional agenda.

On votes of lesser importance, or everyday activities in which the general public pays little attention, the members tend to follow other cues. However, they remain aware that opponents or a rival interest group might cite their votes in the next election.

## THINKING CRITICALLY

Throughout the Obama administration, the members of the Republican minority in both the House and the Senate have voted almost unanimously against the Democratic Party programs in order to show their solidarity and make the public point that they were standing united. If you were a Republican member of Congress up for reelection in a "purple" district or state, which has both Republican and Democrat voters, would you stand united with your party or would you be tempted to vote your own way?

**Party Affiliation** A member's vote can often be explained by political party affiliation. The frequency of legislators voting based on party position steadily increased from below 60 percent by members in both parties in 1970 to more than 80 percent in the late 1990s and through 2002.[70] Sometimes, though, members vote against their party.[71] In the 104th Congress, six Democrats, including Alabama senator Richard Shelby and Colorado senator Ben Nighthorse Campbell, found themselves voting so many times with the opposition party that they switched to the Republican Party.

If the national party leadership or the president is committed to a particular vote, the chances increase for a vote along party lines. If the party's position runs counter to the member's personal views, however, it is less likely to influence the way he or she votes.[72]

**The President** Sometimes the president seeks to influence a member's vote by calling him or her to the White House for a consultation. The president may offer something in return (support for another piece of legislation or a spending project in the member's district) or threaten some kind of punishment for noncompliance. If the Supreme Court had accepted the line item veto, the president's influence over members' votes might have been strengthened. Without it, the president cannot negotiate votes from members who oppose him by threatening to eliminate a favorite piece of pork-barrel legislation. Sometimes the consultation with the president aims simply to make the member look important to the voters back home, but even that serves as a political favor, inducing the member to look more kindly on presidential requests for legislative support.[73]

Presidential lobbying of undecided or politically exposed members can be key in a vote. First-term Democratic representative Marjorie Margolies-Mezvinsky of Pennsylvania learned this lesson in the summer of 1993, when her party's congressional leadership pressed her to support a deficit-reduction bill that would raise taxes and offend her mainly Republican constituents. On the day of the vote, Margolies-Mezvinsky decided to oppose the bill. However, when the vote tied at 217–217 (which meant that the bill would fail), President Clinton implored her to back the bill for the good of the country and the party. After casting the deciding vote in favor of the bill, she lost the 1994 election to the same Republican she had beaten two years earlier.[74]

## THINKING CRITICALLY

From time to time, leaders in Congress will call for a vote with the wishes of the president because it is in "the interests of the nation." This was the case in some of President Obama's economic recovery legislation in 2009, but the Republicans ignored such an appeal by the Democratic congressional leaders. Under what conditions do you think members of Congress should heed such an appeal?

**Interest Groups** Important interest groups and political action committees (PACs) that have provided funds for past elections try to influence a member's vote by lobbying intensely on key issues. In addition, lobbying organizations seek access to members of Congress through personal visits and calls. Sometimes they apply pressure by generating grassroots campaigns among the general public, jamming members' phone lines and fax machines, and filling their mailbags. On the issue of health-care reform in 2009 and 2010, so many emails and phone calls came in during this debate that some members'communications systems were flooded and unusable. In the end, interest groups and their financial political action committees are much less relevant on votes than on access to the members to influence their thinking on an issue.

**Congressional Staff** One job of congressional staff members is to sort through the various sources of pressure and information. In so doing, they themselves may pressure members to vote in a particular way. Staff members organize hearings, conduct research, draft bill markups and amendments, prepare reports, assist committee chairs, interact with the press, and perform other liaison activities with lobbyists and constituents. As important players in the political game, they have their own preferences on many issues. Their expertise and political commitments often help them convince members of Congress to vote for favored bills. Most often, staff people's political views echo and reinforce their legislator's, and they simply help members of Congress be more efficient at meeting their main goals: to please their constituents, promote their party, and vote their convictions.[75]

Congressional staffs proliferated in the 1960s as the federal government grew in size and complexity. Members of both houses of Congress became increasingly dependent on staff for information about proposed legislation. Moreover, in an effort to stay closer to voters, members established district-based offices staffed by aides.[76]

**Colleagues and the Cue Structure** What do legislators do when all these influences—personal convictions, voters, party leadership, the president, interest groups, and staff—send contradictory messages about how to vote on a particular bill? And what do they do when time is too short to gather necessary information about an issue before a vote? They develop a personal intelligence system that scholars label a *cue structure.* The cues can come from various sources: members of Congress who are experts, knowledgeable members of the executive branch, lobbyists, or media reports.[77] Sometimes the cues come from special groups within Congress, such as the Black or Women's Caucuses, the Democratic Study Group, or the Republicans' Conservative Opportunity Society. Members also seek cues from their particular "buddy system"—other members whom they respect, who come from the same kinds of districts, and who have similar goals. In voting, members generally look first for disagreement among their various cues and then try to prioritize the cues to reach an acceptable vote. This "consensus model" suggested by political scientist John Kingdon seems to hold when members vote on issues of average importance, but on highly controversial issues that may affect their reelection prospects, members are far more likely to follow their own opinions.[78]

# HOW A BILL BECOMES A LAW

4.10 *How does Congress pass legislation, and how well does that legislation express the public will?*

Transforming a bill into a law is a long and complicated process (see Figure 4.5). To succeed, a bill must win 218 votes in the House, 51 votes in the Senate, and one presidential signature. The process may take years because of disagreements among the two houses or the need to muster 60 votes to break a filibuster in the Senate. In the most controversial cases, members know that if the president is adamantly opposed to a bill and will not negotiate, then a two-thirds vote of both Houses will be needed to override the anticipated veto. Conflicting policy goals, special interests, ideology, partisanship, and political ambitions often delay or obstruct the passage of legislation. Most bills never even reach the House or Senate floors for debate.[79] Yet some do manage to make their way through the administrative and political maze. Let's see how that can happen.

## The Congressional Agenda

**congressional agenda**
A list of bills to be considered by Congress.

When a member of Congress drafts and submits a piece of legislation dealing with a particular issue, that issue is said to be on the **congressional agenda.** Although much of the agenda consists of mandated business—such as reauthorizations of earlier actions or appropriations for government spending—a new issue must gain widespread public attention to be viewed as important enough to require legislative action.[80] National

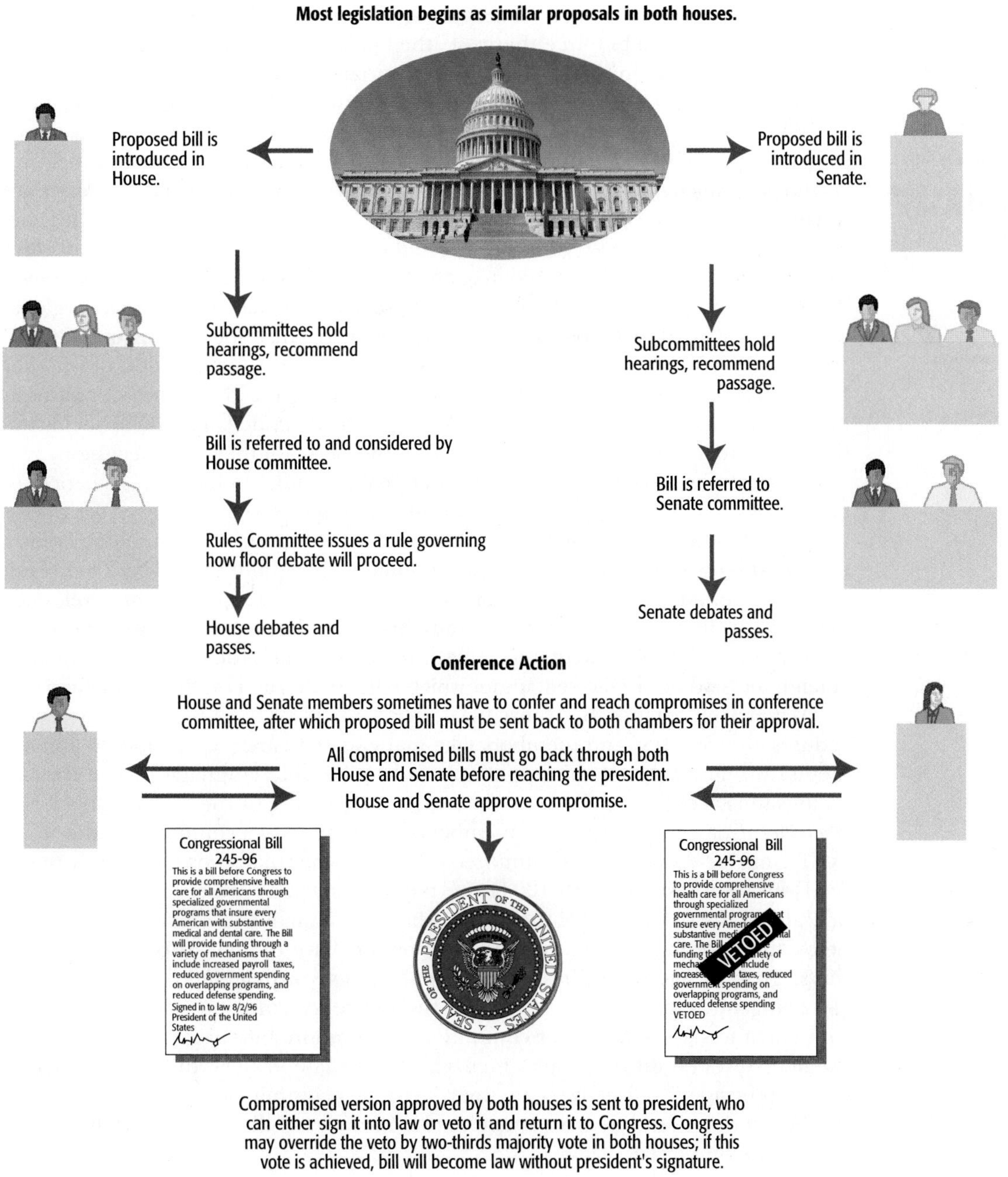
Most legislation begins as similar proposals in both houses.
Proposed bill is introduced in House.
Proposed bill is introduced in Senate.
Subcommittees hold hearings, recommend passage.
Bill is referred to and considered by House committee.
Rules Committee issues a rule governing how floor debate will proceed.
House debates and passes.
Subcommittees hold hearings, recommend passage.
Bill is referred to Senate committee.
Senate debates and passes.
Conference Action
House and Senate members sometimes have to confer and reach compromises in conference committee, after which proposed bill must be sent back to both chambers for their approval.
All compromised bills must go back through both House and Senate before reaching the president.
House and Senate approve compromise.
Congressional Bill 245-96
This is a bill before Congress to provide comprehensive health care for all Americans through specialized governmental programs that insure every American with substantive medical and dental care. The Bill will provide funding through a variety of mechanisms that include increased payroll taxes, reduced government spending on overlapping programs, and reduced defense spending.
Signed in to law 8/2/96
President of the United States
SEAL OF THE PRESIDENT OF THE UNITED STATES
Congressional Bill 245-96
VETOED
Compromised version approved by both houses is sent to president, who can either sign it into law or veto it and return it to Congress. Congress may override the veto by two-thirds majority vote in both houses; if this vote is achieved, bill will become law without president's signature.

**FIGURE 4.5** How a Bill Becomes a Law
Formal proceedings in which a range of people testify on a bill's pros and cons.

events may bring issues to prominence, such as terrorist attacks and homeland security costs. Other issues, such as health care or a balanced budget, build momentum for years before reaching the level of national consciousness that ensures congressional action. Idea sources for bills include the president, cabinet, research institutes, scholars, journalists, voters, and sometimes **lobbyists** (people paid to further the aims of some interest group among members of Congress).[81] Any citizen can draft legislation and ask a representative or senator to submit it. Only members of Congress can introduce a bill.

## Congress Considers the Bill

After a bill has been introduced in Congress, it follows a series of steps on its way to becoming law. In the House, every piece of legislation is *introduced* by a representative, who hands it to the clerk of the House or places it in a box called the "hopper."

**lobbyists**
People paid to pressure members of Congress to further the aims of an interest group.

**hearings**
Formal Congressional proceedings in which people testify on a bill or appear to answer an investigation.

**markup session**
A subcommittee meeting to revise a bill.

**enrolled act (or resolution)**
The final version of a bill, approved by both chambers of Congress.

**appropriations bill**
A separate bill that must be passed by Congress to fund spending measures.

In the Senate, a senator must be recognized by the presiding officer to announce the introduction of a bill. In either case, the bill is first *read* (printed in the *Congressional Record*) and then referred to the appropriate committee (or committees, if it is especially complex) by the Speaker of the House or the Senate majority leader.

When a bill has been assigned to a committee, the committee chair assigns it to a subcommittee. The subcommittee process usually begins with **hearings,** formal proceedings in which a range of people testify on the bill's pros and cons. Witnesses are usually experts on the bill's subject matter, or they may be people affected by the issue, including various administration officials and highly visible citizens. Al Gore, former vice president, presidential candidate, and Oscar winner for his movie *An Inconvenient Truth,* for example, testified before two congressional panels on the topic of global warming in 2007. And, on occasion, hearings are held to investigate controversies and crises in the government, as in the May 2007 hearings on the question of whether President Bush's Department of Justice officials fired eight U.S. attorneys for partisan political reasons. In 2009, the heads of America's banks and leading financial institutions were summoned by Congress to explain the causes of the Great Recession.

Subcommittee chairs can influence the final content of a bill and its chances of passage by arranging either friendly or hostile witnesses or by planning for the type of testimony that will attract media attention. After hearings, the subcommittee holds a **markup session** to revise the bill. The subcommittee then sends the bill back to the full committee for additional discussion, markup, and voting. Approval at this level sends the bill to the full House, but most bills must first move through the House Rules Committee, which schedules the timing, length, and conditions of debate, such as whether amendments would be allowed, under which bills are debated on the House floor.

When a bill reaches the House floor, its fate is still far from certain. Debate procedures are complex, and members take many votes (usually on proposed amendments) on measures containing almost indecipherable language before the bill secures final acceptance. To expedite matters, the House or the Senate can act as a *committee of the whole,* in which all members can function as a committee rather than as a formal legislative body. Committee rules are looser than those that apply to the full House. For instance, only 100 House members need be present when the House operates as the committee of the whole, whereas normally 218 representatives must be on the floor to conduct business. Opponents have numerous opportunities at this stage to defeat or significantly change the bill's wording, and thus its impact.

Being much smaller than the House, the Senate is an intimate body that operates with much less formality. After committee deliberation, bills are simply brought to the floor through informal agreements among Senate leaders. Individual senators can even bring bills directly to the floor, bypassing committees altogether. They do this by offering their bill as an amendment to whatever bill is then pending, even if the two are unrelated.

The House of Representatives uses an *electronic voting system* that posts each member's name on the wall of the chamber. Members insert a plastic card into a box attached to the chairs to vote "yea," "nay," or "present." The results of the vote then appear alongside each legislator's name. The electronic voting system has increased participation at roll calls, and watchdog groups have been known to keep a close eye on legislators who are frequently absent on important roll calls. In addition, legislators find the electronic system handy; it enables them to check how their colleagues are voting. But even if successful in the House and Senate, proposed legislation still faces hurdles. To become law, the bills passed in both houses of Congress must be worded identically. As mentioned earlier, a conference committee composed of both House and Senate members reconciles the differences in language and creates a single version of the bill.[82]

When the differences between versions of a bill have been ironed out, the final version returns to both houses for approval. If it is approved by both chambers, it becomes an **enrolled act, or resolution.** and goes to the White House for the president's signature or veto. Measures that require spending are offered in 1 of 13 **appropriations bills,** based on authorized amounts passed by Congress. Thus, the Congress has two opportunities to debate a measure: first the measure itself, then its funding.

**The President Considers the Bill** After Congress has voted and sent a bill on to the president, four scenarios are possible. The president can sign the bill, making it law. Or the president can **veto** it; that is, return the bill to Congress with a statement of reasons for refusing to sign it. At that point, Congress can **override** the president's action with a two-thirds vote in both the House and Senate. Congress can rarely muster this level of opposition to a sitting president, so vetoes are overridden less than 10 percent of the time.[83] Of President Clinton's 25 vetoes in his first five years of office, only one was overridden. Although President Bush repeatedly used the threat of a veto to try to enforce his spending priorities, by March 2006, he had set a record in not issuing a single veto. Of course, his own party controlled both Houses of Congress during that time.[84] Still, such threats remind members that passage might now require a two-thirds vote. For example, in summer 2005, Senate Majority Leader Bill Frist announced his support for stem-cell research legislation "in the name of science," thus increasing the likelihood that Congress would fund it. But President Bush, at the same time, killed the measure when he vowed that he would veto this bill.[85]

**veto**
Presidential power to forbid or prevent an action of Congress.

**override**
The two-thirds vote of both houses of Congress required to pass a law over the veto of the president.

**pocket veto**
Presidential refusal to sign or veto a bill that Congress passes in the last ten days of its session; by not being signed, it automatically dies when Congress adjourns.

Two other outcomes are possible. When a bill reaches the president's desk, the president can simply do nothing, in which case the bill automatically becomes law after ten legislative days (not counting Sundays, and providing that Congress is still in session) in spite of remaining unsigned. The president can also refuse to sign a bill that Congress passes in the last ten days of its session. If Congress has adjourned, the unsigned bill automatically dies. This is called a **pocket veto.**

From time to time, even if the president reluctantly signs a bill, a *signing statement* might also be released that seems to undercut aspects of the measure hoping to affect future legal challenges to it. After President Bush used this procedure to undercut an anti-torture bill passed and supported by former Senator John McCain (R-AZ), a former POW in the Vietnam War, it was revealed that this technique had been used hundreds of times before.

## Obstacles to Passage of a Bill and the Obama Congress Response

4.11 *What are the main obstacles to Congress passing legislation, and how can they be overcome?*

This textbook approach to passing a bill rarely works smoothly because so many obstacles lie in the path of success. The backers of any bill must win support at each stage of the lawmaking process. They must find majorities in each committee, they must find enthusiastic backers during each formal discussion, and so forth. Opponents of the bill have a much easier job. They can kill it at any step along the way. Sometimes they do not even need a majority; one unfriendly legislator in the right place may be sufficient.

Imagine how you, as a member of Congress, might stop a bill you disliked. You might take any of the following actions:

1. Lobby members of your party conference or caucus to stop, or at least slow down, consideration of the bill.
2. Convince the speaker to stop, or slow down, consideration of the bill.
3. Lobby committee and subcommittee members to oppose the bill in committee hearings, deliberations, markups, and votes.
4. Lobby the Rules Committee to oppose giving the bill a rule, which dictates the timing and terms of a bill's debate.
5. Lobby colleagues on the House floor not to vote for the rule, thus preventing the bill from ever reaching floor discussion.
6. Call press conferences and give interviews trying to build a grassroots or interest-group coalition against the bill.

Democratic Minority Leader Nancy Pelosi—surrounded by the other members of the Democratic leadership, including Minority Whip Steny Hoyer to her far right and Democratic Senate Majority Leader Harry Reid, to her far left—have rallied their party members since losing control of the House in 2008 in seeking to battle the Republican and Tea Party conservatives. However, the constant use of filibusters by the Republican Senate leadership has frustrated some of their ambitions.

7. Propose a series of amendments that weaken the bill or make it less attractive to potential supporters, then vote for unattractive amendments at every opportunity.
8. If the bill does gain passage in the House, use the same tactics to stop it in the Senate, mustering opposition in committees and on the Senate floor. Be sure to have senators also gain media attention against the bill, whipping up negative reaction to its possible passage.
9. Find senators who hate the bill and persuade them to filibuster, or place a hold on the bill yourself.
10. If both House and Senate pass the bill, work against it in the conference committee, if one convenes.
11. If Congress passes the bill, seek White House allies who might persuade the president to veto it.
12. If the bill becomes law, use similar steps to prevent Congress from funding the measure.
13. If the bill becomes law and is funded, work to rescind the law or to keep funding so low it becomes ineffective. Or, lobby the executive branch to delay the bill's implementation.
14. If all else fails, have faith that some group opposed to the bill will mount a constitutional challenge to the law, going all the way to the Supreme Court if necessary.

This array of blocking options favors those who oppose change. What you think of this system depends on how you like the status quo. A majority of congressional conservatives in the early Bush administration years often felt frustrated by the difficulty in working their agenda through a conservative minority of Democrats. Now these same people use some or all of these tactics to stall the Obama legislative agenda. Only when the size of the Democrats' majority in the Senate, together with the two Independents who vote with them, reached the 60-vote margin in mid-2009, preventing a cloture vote halting a filibuster when Al Franken was seated in mid-2009 and, in theory, ending the Republicans' ability to block their Health Care Reform bill, was it finally passed. Beyond this, President Obama can tap into his presidential office influence by giving public speeches to put pressure on Congress. Obama did this, with partial success, in September 2011, imploring a joint session of Congress to pass his jobs bill.

## Overcoming the Legislative Obstacles

Throughout the Obama years, Democrats in Congress have sought ways to overcome the traditional obstacles to passing legislation.[86] With all the various Republican blocking points that threaten to doom single pieces of legislation, Democrats in Congress packaged the biggest and most important legislation into so-called **omnibus legislation,** also known as "megabills" or "packages." The idea here is to hide controversial pieces of legislation inside packages of related bills most likely to pass. The president then must sign the entire bill. Members of Congress receive cover in supporting the controversial legislation, interest groups and their financial PACs are less likely to punish supporters for their votes, and the media sometimes lose track of the controversial issues. Many of the programs funded by the Democratic majority in the multibillion-dollar 2009 economic stimulus bills were "Christmas tree" style, pork-barrel projects designed less to produce jobs than had been seeking funding for years.

With many controversial appropriations measures to be passed each year under the budgeting procedure, leaders have had to resort to the passage of **continuing resolutions** that provide stop-gap funding to keep the government running. These resolutions must be passed by both houses of Congress and do not require a presidential signature, thus making them apparently veto-proof. Such resolutions were once common for temporary funding of one to three months for a handful of agencies. But learning from the late 1980s, when the procedure was used for all 13 major appropriations measures, the Congress has used this technique to overcome delays in approving the budget. The attempt backfired in late 1995 and early 1996 when disagreements between Congress and the president forced the government to shut down twice because even continuing resolutions could not be agreed on and passed. To heal political damage, Republicans in 1997 pushed through an automatic continuing resolution to keep the government going in the event that the two parties disagreed on future funding.

This automatic funding process has been the norm since 2000, leading to a series of apocalyptic-like, government shutdown threat, budget fights. Another tactic to overcome these obstacles, taken from the Republicans' playbook in the early 21st century on issues such as tax cuts and oil drilling, was for Congress to invoke the **budget reconciliation process.** The process resolves the differences in the more than "incidental" financial costs of legislation in a conference committee vote and requires only a simple majority vote for passage without the possibility of a filibuster. It would exclude the minority party from having a voice, giving control over the process to the majority party. To avoid this, Senate Majority Leader Harry Reid relied on a shifting group of 60 senators to break various filibusters, and threats of filibusters, in order to avoid this use of a parliamentary shortcut to pass the health-care reform law. After a series of deals with reluctant senators on issues such as Medicaid funding, a public option for health insurance, and limiting public funding for abortion, Reid was able to shepherd the health-care bill to Senate passage just before the 2009 Christmas recess.

A new trend of relying on bipartisan negotiating committees to resolve legislative conflicts may have begun in 2011 when, after the threat of a government shutdown over the deadlocked issue of balancing the budget and raising the debt

**omnibus legislation**
A large bill that combines a number of smaller pieces of legislation.

**continuing resolution**
A bill passed by Congress and signed by the president that enables the federal government to keep operating under the previous year's appropriations.

**budget reconciliation process**
Taken from the Budget and Impoundment Act to reconcile differences in the spending bills of each house of Congress, this process can be used to avoid a Senate filibuster on spending-related bills because it requires only a simple majority vote.

ceiling, Congress appointed a 12 person bipartisan "super-committee" charged with finding 3 trillion dollars in budget cuts. The effort failed when the Democrats and Republicans could not agree over taxing the rich and cutting entitlements, such as Medicare, to balance the budget.

Legislators formerly used an *inside strategy* of negotiating with colleagues to line up votes for their agendas. But now they often resort to gaps in the body's rules; parliamentary tricks; and/or an *outside strategy* of giving speeches, press conferences, and interviews to try to mobilize public opinion and interest group assistance to work their will.

## CONGRESS IN THE 21ST CENTURY

4.12 *How has Congress over the past several sessions changed its political direction as the voting has changed?*

The origins of the Republican Party–controlled 112th Congress the least active Congress in decades, with public support averaging in the teens, were seen in the events dating back to the 109th Congress (2005–2007). In the 109th Congress, House Republicans, led by partisan Majority Leader Tom DeLay (TX) and White House adviser Karl Rove, mobilized conservative Evangelicals and social conservatives, increasing their governing majority to 231 Republicans compared with 202 Democrats. In the Senate, Republicans had picked up all five vacant southern Democratic seats and inched closer to a 60-vote, filibuster-proof body. Senate margins changed to 55 Republicans, 44 Democrats, and the Independent Jim Jeffords, who voted with the Democrats most often. The large number of new conservative members provided new allies for House Majority Leader Tom DeLay and Senate Majority Leader Bill Frist, both of whom sought to create a cohesive party policy making machine.

The Democrats, however, developed two strategies to blunt that effort. Faced with the choice of electing as their new leader either Christopher Dodd of Connecticut, a Ted Kennedy–style, photogenic ultra-liberal from the Northeast, or more plainspoken, less telegenic moderate Harry Reid from conservative Nevada, they chose Reid. Although experts predicted that Reid would get along with the Republicans, when his early diplomatic efforts were rebuffed, he developed into an effective, plainspoken, public voice for the Democrats. By this time, the reforms of the conservative Gingrich era from 1994 had largely fizzled out. The eight-year term limit for the Speaker's position had been eliminated, and the six-year term limit for committee chairs was being occasionally waived.[87] Once more, Congress bogged down in social cultural issues, forcing the federal judiciary to consider yet again the Florida dispute over the "right to die" issue in the form of the Terri Schiavo case and attempting once more to pass an anti-flag-burning amendment to the Constitution. The two houses battled over competing versions of a bill renewing the expiring provisions of the USA Patriot Act and neglected major issues such as tax reform, balancing the budget, and reforming Medicaid.

As Congress prepared for the 2006 elections, Republican members of Congress faced several challenges. The first was deciding whether to back the more moderate, high-spending policies of lame-duck President George W. Bush's administration over their own reducing taxes plus social conservative policies. The next challenge was defining their own approach in the increasingly controversial Iraq rebuilding effort. And third was dealing with Majority Leader Tom DeLay's announcement that he would resign from the House under fire for questionable ethics, along with a corruption investigation into the connection between indicted conservative lobbyist Jack Abramoff and his pay-for-play lobbying with other members of Congress. Democrats, seeing the near-record lows in public support for Congress and increasing voter frustration on major

### THINKING CRITICALLY

Knowing Congress's philosophy of "forgive and remember," how different is it for members of Congress to deal with political issues, knowing that they can run for office for an unlimited period, as opposed to the president, who will have perhaps only four, or at most eight, years to deal with issues? How would you approach issues differently if you were a member of Congress as opposed to being the president?

political issues, began to set their sights on a takeover of both houses of Congress. Although that move would normally be hindered by the currently more conservative voting population, the large Republican majorities in both houses of Congress, and the paucity of vulnerable Republican seats, the negative public reaction on the issue of corruption and ineffectiveness in Congress made the Democrats more hopeful.[88]

**Blue Dog Democrats**
Fiscally conservative Democratic Party members of Congress who claim to be "choked blue" by government spending and who press their liberal colleagues to reduce spending.

And that hope was fulfilled in the 2006 vote for the 110th Congress, as the Democrats gained 31 seats, completely reversing the voting majority in Congress to give them a 233–202 margin. In the Senate, after picking up seats in Pennsylvania, Rhode Island, Vermont, and Missouri, as well as unexpected victories in Montana with conservative Jon Tester and Virginia with conservative James Webb, the Democrats had reversed the majority there as well, taking control with a 51–49 majority, with Independents Joe Lieberman of Connecticut and Bernard Sanders of Vermont voting with them. The margins were so close in the Senate though, and filibusters were used so many times by the Republicans, that this Congress was very disappointing in its output and lost considerable public support, often hovering around 10 percent in the national polls.

The huge turnout for Democrat Barack Obama in the 2008 election translated to much greater success for the Democrats in the congressional elections. In the Senate, the Democrats won 56 seats outright, and still had two Independents, Lieberman and Sanders, who caucus and vote with them. After Arlen Specter of Pennsylvania switched from the Republican Party to the Democratic Party, and once Democrat Al Franken of Minnesota won the recount vote in his election, the Democrats had achieved the filibuster-proof 60-vote Senate that opened the door to increased legislative passage. The vote in 2010 to fill Senator Ted Kennedy's seat, filled on an interim basis by Democrat Paul Kirk, made it possible for the Senate to pass Obama's Health Care Reform bill.

In the 111th Congress (2009–11), Democrats picked up 23 more seats to give them a 256–178 margin, with 1 Independent voting with the Democrats. Despite the large majority, the party's success depended on how the 52 fiscally conservative, so-called **Blue Dog Democrats** voted on issues of importance to rest of the Democratic majority. Founded in 1995, the Blue Dogs are conservative and moderate members of the Democratic Party, elected mainly from the South and the Mountain states. Remembering the southern phrase that voters would support a "yellow dog" if it was on the ballot, these Democrats felt they were being "choked blue" on fiscal issues by their party's liberal wing. They made this clear in mid-July 2009 when they sent a letter to Speaker Pelosi, making it clear that they would not vote for the Democrats' health-care plan unless their fiscal concerns were met.[89] When the fiscal concerns were passed, the bill was passed. The 112th Congress (2011-13), with its 83 new members, 63 of which were fiscally conservative Republicans and Tea Party members, reversed the partisan majority, allowing new Speaker John Boehner (R-OH) to work with a 242-192 majority. In the Senate, despite a 53-47 Democratic majority, when Minority Leader Mitch McConnell used repeated filibusters to pursue his goal to "defeat Barack Obama" at the polls in 2012, Majority Leader Harry Reid found governing almost impossible.

Maine's two Republican Senators, Susan Collins (left) and Olympia Snowe (right), are two of the last remaining moderate Senators from that party. Although Republican opponents call them "RINOs" (Republicans in Name Only), they have been the target of bipartisan negotiations by President Obama and Speaker Harry Reid in trying to win their support for the health-care reform bill and other measures.

Now, as the 112th Congress proceeds, with so little accomplished and so much public unhappiness with this record, and as the 2012 election approaches, questions emerge about what the voters will do in that election. As House Speaker John Boehner, the Tea Party, and Minority Leader Nancy Pelosi continue to battle, while Senate Majority Leader Harry Reid and Minority Leader Mitch McConnell negotiate under the constant threat of filibuster, Congress seems unlikely to get beyond its stalemate. Agreement was even difficult at the end of 2011 over a payroll tax cut for 160 million Americans.

All the seats in Congress are up for reelection in 2012. With the Democrats defending 23 seats in the Senate, including the 2 independent seats that caucus with the Democrats, to the 10 being defended by the Republicans, the momentum that the Republicans achieved in the 2010 election would seem to make it easier for the Republicans to maintain, if not improve, their current ideological balance. However, the anti-incumbent sentiment of the voters now, with only 12 percent of the people supporting the reelection of their representatives in a December 2011 poll, the results could lead to gains by the Democrats. The strength of Congress, indeed its very constitutional purpose in American democracy, is its closeness to the people and its representational base. "To express the public views" remains the principal responsibility of the national legislature, as well as its most pressing challenge, as Congress and America approach democracy during the 21st century.

## Summary

4.1 *How was Congress created in the Constitution to express the will of the people?*

- The Constitution established a bicameral Congress consisting of a House of Representatives, whose members serve two-year terms, and a Senate, whose members serve six-year terms. Congress received numerous major powers, including the power to collect taxes, declare war, and regulate commerce. The necessary and proper clause enables it to interpret these powers broadly.

4.2 *How representative is Congress of the American people?*

- A disproportionate number of Congress's members are rich, white males drawn from the fields of law, banking, and big business. Ethnic diversity in Congress increased in the 20th century, but it still falls short of that of the population as a whole.

4.3 *How is the congressional district drawn and redistricted every ten years to express the democratic will?*

- Today, each congressional district contains about 635,000 citizens. The number of representatives from each state is adjusted after each census (reapportionment). In states that gain or lose seats, district boundaries must be redrawn (redistricting). The term *gerrymander* describes the often bizarre district boundaries drawn to favor the party in power.

4.4 *How do members of Congress represent the democratic will when they vote?*

- Members of Congress sometimes find themselves torn between the role of delegate, in which they feel bound to follow the wishes of constituents, and the role of trustee, in which they use their best judgment regardless of the wishes of constituents. In practice, they tend to combine these roles.

4.5 *Do the elections for members of Congress create fair races that represent the public will?*

- Incumbents have several advantages over their challengers in an election, including greater name recognition, the franking privilege, services of staff members, legislative experience, and greater financial backing. These advantages have led critics to call for legislation limiting the length of time members may serve in Congress.

4.6 *How are the House and the Senate organized to represent democracy in their operation?*

- The presiding officer of the House is the leader of the majority party and is known as the Speaker of the House. Next in line is the House majority leader, who serves as the party's chief strategist. The minority party is headed by the minority leader, and both party leaders are assisted by whips. In the Senate, the majority party elects a president pro tempore, but this is essentially an honorary position. As in the House, the Senate has majority and minority party leaders and whips.

4.7 *How does the congressional committee system enable it to operate, and how has it become more democratic?*

- There are four types of congressional committees: standing (permanent), select or special (temporary), conference, and joint. Much of the legislative work of Congress is done in subcommittees. The power of the subcommittees since the 1970s has made the legislative process rather unwieldy, prompting calls for reform.

4.8 *Why and how is the Senate more deliberative than the House in its legislation process, and how representative is it of the public will?*

- In the House, the Rules Committee determines what issues will be discussed, when, and under what conditions. In the Senate, the majority leader does the scheduling in consultation with the minority leader. The Senate imposes no limits on floor debate. As a result, a bill can be derailed by filibuster, when a senator talks continuously to postpone or prevent a vote. Filibusters can be halted only by cloture, in which 60 or more senators vote to end the discussion.

4.9 *How do members of Congress decide to vote, and whom do they represent in doing so?*

- Legislators' voting decisions are influenced by personal views, constituents, party affiliation, the president, interest groups, and congressional staff. Members also receive cues about how to vote from their "buddy system" of other members whom they respect.

4.10 *How does Congress pass legislation, and how well does that legislation express the public will?*

- A member of Congress places an issue on the congressional agenda by drafting a bill and submitting it to the House or Senate. The bill is then referred to the appropriate committee, whose chair assigns it to a subcommittee. After holding hearings on the proposed legislation, the subcommittee holds a markup session in which the language of the bill is revised. It then returns the bill to the full committee. If the committee approves the bill, it goes to the full House or Senate. If the two chambers pass different versions of a bill, it goes to a conference committee, which reconciles the differences and creates a single bill. If the final version is approved by both chambers, it goes to the president to be signed or vetoed.

4.11 *What are the main obstacles to Congress passing legislation, and how can they be overcome?*

- Over the years, members of Congress have learned how to use more than a dozen rules to slow down or even prevent legislation from being passed into law. In recent years, we have seen how the tactics used by one party to prevent legislation are used by the other party when they become the minority. Similarly, the tactics used to overcome those obstacles have been passed from one party to another as the majority in Congress changes.

4.12 *How has Congress over the past several sessions changed its political direction as the voting has changed?*

- As a result of the 2006 congressional elections, the overwhelming congressional majority enjoyed by the Republican switched to the Democrats. The Democratic margins in Congress continued to increase to such an extent in the 2008 election that the party was on the verge of gaining a filibuster-proof Senate. Should the Democrats obtain the 60-vote margin, they will gain real efficiency in passing legislation only if they can persuade the conservative members of their party to vote with them.

## Key Terms

appropriations bill, 140
bicameral legislature, 111
Blue Dog Democrats, 145
budget reconciliation process, 143
casework, 121
cloture, 131
conference committees, 127
congressional agenda, 138
continuing resolution, 143
delegates, 119
earmarks, 130
enrolled act (or resolution), 140
filibuster, 131
franking privilege, 121
gerrymander, 117
hearings, 140
hold, 131
House majority leader, 123
impeachment, 112
incumbents, 120
joint committees, 127
line item veto, 130
lobbyists, 139
logrolling, 135
majority–minority district, 118
markup session, 140
minority leader, 124
necessary and proper clause, 113
omnibus legislation, 143
override, 141
party caucus, 123
pocket veto, 141
politico, 120
pork-barrel legislation, 135
president of the Senate, 124
president pro tempore, 124
reapportionment, 116
redistricting, 117
rider, 130
rules, 129
select (or special committees), 127
Senate majority leader, 125
seniority, 133
Speaker of the House, 122
standing committees, 127
task force, 128
term limits, 121
trustees, 120
unanimous consent agreement, 130
veto, 141
whips, 124

## Test Yourself Chapter 4

**1.** Which house of Congress did Madison fear the most?
a. The Senate.
b. The House.
c. Both the Senate and the House.
d. Madison trusted Congress.

**2.** What indication is there that the founders feared legislatures from their experience in the states and sought to limit Congress's power?
a. They placed term limits on Congress.
b. They limited the size of each house of Congress.
c. They began with the phrase "All legislative Powers herein granted."
d. They gave the president the veto power.

**3.** What constitutional feature of the initial Senate was designed mainly to make it, in James Madison's words, the "necessary force" against the "fickleness and passion" of the people?
a. The six-year term of office.
b. The equal number of senators per state.
c. The smaller size of the Senate.
d. The indirect election of the senators.

**4.** Which of the following is *not* a power of Congress?
a. The power over interstate commerce.
b. The power to make war.
c. The power to regulate money.
d. The power to create lower federal courts.

**5.** What is the elastic clause of Congress?
a. The necessary and proper clause of Article I, Section 8.
b. The take care clause of Article II.
c. The interstate commerce clause of Article I, Section 8.
d. The supremacy clause of Article VI.

**6.** In reality, how many votes does it take in the Senate to pass important legislation?
a. 51.
b. A majority of those present and voting.
c. 60, for cloture to end a filibuster to be able to vote on the issue.
d. A constitutional plurality of the Senate.

**7.** How many votes does it take for Congress to override a presidential veto?
a. 60 votes in the Senate, and 300 votes in the House.
b. A two-thirds vote in each house.
c. A three-fifths vote in each house.
d. A three-fourths vote in each house.

**8.** The process by which a president can veto a bill by simply refusing to sign it for ten days while Congress is out of session is called
a. a silent veto.
b. a secret veto.
c. a closed-session veto.
d. a pocket veto.

**9.** Gerrymandering is the process of
a. making every congressional district look like a salamander.
b. balancing a congressional district on the basis of ethnic backgrounds.
c. balancing every congressional district by population.
d. shaping congressional districts to benefit one political party over another.

**10.** Which of these changes in American politics have altered Congress from its intended operation and purpose by the constitutional framers?
a. The rise of political parties.
b. The Seventeenth Amendment change to directly elect senators.
c. The rise of a professional politician class that runs for reelection without limits.
d. All of the above.

**11.** Edmund Burke's theory of how members of a legislature should represent a district is
a. the legislator must act as a delegate, doing only what the people want.
b. the legislator must act as a trustee, doing what he or she believes to be correct.
c. the legislator must act as a politico, doing a combination of a and b.
d. the legislator must do as little as possible, so as not to cause harm.

**12.** Because of their visibility and campaign advantages, incumbents are usually reelected to Congress; however,
a. they are more often reelected in the House than the Senate.
b. they are more often reelected in the Senate.
c. they are reelected at about the same rate.
d. the power of incumbency has been dropping.

**13.** The most powerful Speaker of all time was
a. Thomas "Tip" O'Neill.
b. Nancy Pelosi.
c. Joe Cannon.
d. Thomas B. Reed.

**14.** In the Senate, the schedule for considering legislation is usually set by
a. the Senate Rules Committee.
b. the majority leader.
c. the minority leader.
d. the majority and minority leaders consulting with each other.

**15.** How much power does the majority leader of the Senate have to influence the vote of a senator from his or her party?
a. None.
b. Absolute.
c. Some power on small issues, but none on major issues.
d. Only the power of personal persuasion.

**16.** The vice president's role in the Senate is to
a. lead the Senate from behind the scenes.
b. help the Senate set the policy direction.
c. cast the tie-breaking vote in tie votes.
d. help to draft legislation on major issues.

**17.** A conference committee
a. allows members of Congress to hold fact-finding hearings.
b. allows members of Congress to confer with the public.
c. allows members of Congress to meet with the press.
d. allows members from both houses of Congress to resolve differences in legislation that has been passed in different forms in each house.

**18.** The process of adding a specific spending provision from a piece of legislation being passed for a certain project or district is called
a. an earmark
b. a line item.
c. a categorical grant.
d. a project grant.

**19.** Members of Congress vote based on
a. cues from similar legislators.
b. the wishes of their party.
c. the wishes of their constituents.
d. All of the above.

**20.** The process of legislators trading votes on pieces of legislation of unconcern to them in order to get votes from those legislators on issues that matter to their district is called
a. trade-offs.
b. logrolling.
c. log-splitting.
d. scratching-the-back.

**ANSWERS**
**1.** b, **2.** c, **3.** d, **4.** b, **5.** a, **6.** c, **7.** b, **8.** d, **9.** d, **10.** d, **11.** b,
**12.** a, **13.** d, **14.** d, **15.** d, **16.** c, **17.** d, **18.** a, **19.** d, **20.** b

# The Presidency

5

## Chapter Outline

**Introduction:**
*The Presidency and Democracy*

- The Constitutional Design
- Functional Roles of the President
- Two Views of Executive Power
- Expanding Presidential Power: Moving Beyond the Constitution
- The Challenges of Presidential Leadership
- The Institutionalized Presidency

## Learning Objectives

5.1 How did the framers design a system with an energetic executive to forward the democratic will and, at the same time, protect against anti-democratic tendencies of a single executive?

5.2 Why were the framers vague in their description of presidential powers described in the Constitution, and how did this vagueness shape the powers of the president over time?

5.3 How do the roles and responsibilities of the presidency create the paradoxes of the presidency, and how do these paradoxes make it difficult for any president to succeed?

5.4 What is the key difference between the constructionist and stewardship view of the presidency, and why have modern presidents viewed themselves as stewards?

5.5 How have the powers of the presidency expanded over time, and what factors might explain this expansion?

5.6 How does a modern president persuade both Congress and the public to go along with his or her agenda?

5.7 How has the presidential staff grown over time, and how do those who serve the president assist in the day-to-day duties of the office?

# INTRODUCTION

## THE PRESIDENCY AND DEMOCRACY

5.1 *How did the framers design a system with an energetic executive to forward the democratic will and, at the same time, protect against anti-democratic tendencies of a single executive?*

America's government was set up to restrain the powerful. Its presidents may occasionally win dramatic victories, but they are usually doomed by the rules of the system to suffer dramatic defeats. Only the most stable personality can accept the highs with equanimity, survive the lows with patience, and perform the job with integrity.[1] The great paradox of the presidency is that no other office in America simultaneously unites so much power and purpose to help Americans approach their democratic potential and also poses the most serious threats to the ideals of democracy. Thomas Jefferson, in 1797, referred to the presidency as "a splendid misery." Our modern presidents would concur. Gerald Ford, Jimmy Carter, and George H. W. Bush were voted out of office; John Kennedy was assassinated; Ronald Reagan was shot; Richard Nixon resigned in disgrace; Lyndon B. Johnson chose not to seek reelection, fearing defeat; Bill Clinton was impeached and George W. Bush left office with the highest disapproval ratings of any president since Nixon (see Table 5.1).[2]

Theodore Roosevelt once remarked, "Oh, if I could only be president and Congress too for just 10 minutes." That lament could serve as the hopeful wish of any president. The framers of our government designed the presidency to encourage the president's potential for energy but also to minimize its potential for tyranny. This entailed a complicated separation and distribution of powers. Lord Acton, a British historian and political figure, noted that,"power tends to corrupt and absolute power corrupts absolutely." Although that belief has changed little since the 18th century, what has changed is the role government plays in American life. Americans have delegated increasing amounts of power to the national government and to the presidency, and their expectations of both have risen proportionately. The office of president lies at the center of countless demands, many of them contradictory and some impossible to achieve under any conditions. The mere energy required to hold the position and carry out its duties puts it far beyond the average person's capacity. The office has broken several presidents, and many have been diminished

### THINKING CRITICALLY

Do you think that the age requirement of at least 35 for the president limits the representation of your generation in government? Can a president over 35 years old really represent the needs of young people?

**Table 5.1** Final Presidential Job Approval Ratings, Harry Truman to George W. Bush*

| Year | President | Approval | Disapproval | No Opinion |
|---|---|---|---|---|
| 1952 | Harry S. Truman | 32% | 56% | 12% |
| 1960 | Dwight D. Eisenhower | 59 | 28 | 13 |
| 1969 | Lyndon B. Johnson | 49 | 37 | 14 |
| 1974 | Richard Nixon | 24 | 66 | 10 |
| 1976 | Gerald Ford | 53 | 32 | 15 |
| 1980 | Jimmy Carter | 34 | 55 | 11 |
| 1988 | Ronald Reagan | 63 | 29 | 8 |
| 1993 | George H. W. Bush | 56 | 37 | 7 |
| 2001 | William J. Clinton | 66 | 29 | 5 |
| 2009 | George W. Bush | 34 | 61 | 5 |

* Data excludes presidents who died in office (F. Roosevelt and Kennedy); *data compiled from the Gallup poll.*

*Source:* Gerhard Peters, adapted from "Final Presidential Job Approval Ratings," *The American Presidency Project*, John T. Woolley and Gerhard Peters, eds. (Santa Barbara: University of California, 1999–2009). Available at www.presidency.ucsb.edu/data/final_approval.php. Used with permission.

by it—and have diminished the office. Even those who have risen to its challenge, whose records we admire from the distance of history, faced scathing criticism and fought determined foes throughout their tenure in the White House. Still, some have thrived in the office, and certain presidents have achieved greatness. It is impossible to predict who will or will not succeed at the job.[3]

In *The Federalist,* no. 70, Alexander Hamilton wrote,

> *Energy in the executive is a leading character of good government. It is essential to the protection of the community against foreign attacks; it is not less essential to the steady administration of the laws; to the protection of property . . . to the security of liberty against those enterprises and assaults of ambition, of faction, and of anarchy. . . . A feeble executive implies a feeble execution of the government. A feeble execution is but another phrase for a bad execution; and a government ill executed, whatever it may be in theory, must be, in practice, a bad government.*[4]

Hamilton identified unity (the president would be a single person), duration (the president would have a four-year term and be eligible for reelection), adequate salary, and competent powers (detailed in Article II) as components that guaranteed the appropriate energy in the executive.

## THE CONSTITUTIONAL DESIGN

5.2 *Why were the framers vague in the description of presidential powers described in the Constitution, and how did this vagueness shape the powers of the president over time?*

The presidency may be the framers' most original contribution. In a world of kings and emperors, many of whom left office feet first or on the wrong end of a bloody revolution, the American president was to be unlike any other world leader. In creating this unique position, the framers avoided creating a monarchy like the one in England they had rebelled against, but they also wanted a strong, independent

### QUICK REVIEW

Design of the Presidency

- Centered on one individual as the executive power.
- Selection made by an independent body of individual electors.
- Fixed term of office with the possibility of reelection.
- Impeachment process allows removal from office.
- Veto power enables the executive to say no to Congress.
- Independent action permitted within the executive arena.

### QUICK REVIEW

Presidential Powers

- Veto power—forbid or prevent an action of Congress.
- Appointment power—staff the executive branch with trusted allies.
- Treaty power—negotiate treaties with other nations.
- Executive privilege—withhold information in the interest of national security or the discharge of official duties.
- Grant pardons and convene Congress in extraordinary circumstances.
- Power of commander in chief of the armed forces.

executive for the nation as a whole. They were appalled at the results of legislative omnipotence in the states, as had been the case under the Articles of Confederation.

In creating a source of power independent of the Congress but capable of balancing its powers, the framers based the presidency on seven key principles:

1. They set up a *single presidency*. Executive power would retain its strength and energy in an individual, not in a council or a cabinet.
2. Neither Congress nor the people would elect the president. A president chosen by Congress could become its puppet; one chosen by the people could become a demagogue and tyrant. An independent body of individual electors selected by the state legislatures (the *electoral college*) would produce a president, independent of Congress and the popular vote.
3. The president was given a *fixed term of office*. The genius of this idea lies in its assurance of both stability and constraint. Executives serve four years, with the possibility of reelection. They cannot be forced from office by arbitrary "no-confidence" votes in Congress (votes that force the early resignation of entire governments in parliamentary systems). On the other hand, no president would win reelection without broad popular support. Presidents who commit "Treason, Bribery, or other High Crimes and Misdemeanors" may be impeached and removed from office. This impending sequence forced President Nixon's resignation.
4. The president would be eligible for *more than one term of office*, making the executive a source of potential power to balance or check congressional power. (The Twenty-second Amendment now restricts the president to two terms. This is the focus of this chapter's Approaching Contemporary Issues in Democracy feature.) If presidents remained popular and their policies were considered successful, they could win reelection. Thus, Congress must always take the president into account when exercising its own powers and responsibilities.
5. The president could be removed from office only by a cumbersome *process of impeachment* involving both houses of Congress; thus, a president must continually be reckoned with. On the other hand, the House's impeachment of former President Clinton demonstrates that impeachment does indeed represent an ultimate check.
6. The president was given a *veto power*, enabling the executive to say no to Congress. This single provision makes the president a central player in the legislative process because Congress must consider a president's wishes in policy making.
7. The president was not required to appoint an advisory council. Thus, presidents were allowed to *act on their own*, at least within their own constitutional realm of the executive arena.

This set of principles pointed toward a strong but constrained executive—a single, symbolic head of the nation, who holds serious means for exercising power but operates under law and is restricted in power by the countervailing institutions of Congress and the Supreme Court. As former Senator Sam Ervin, chair of the Senate Select Committee investigating Watergate, once observed, "One of the great advantages of the three separate branches of government is that it is difficult to corrupt all three at the same time."

There are no gender specifications for the job of president, but thus far all American presidents have been men. Victoria Woodhull, shown here, was the first woman presidential candidate. A stockbroker and newspaper editor from New York, Woodhull ran for president in 1872 as a member of the Equal Rights Party.

## Who Is Eligible to Be President?

The Constitution specifies only three requirements for becoming president: a president must be at least 35 years old, must have lived in the United States for at least 14 years, and must be a natural-born citizen.

The framers set the minimum age requirement of 35 (which, at that time, represented middle age) to guarantee that a president would be reasonably mature and experienced in politics. The 14-year residence condition was to guard against the possibility of a president with divided loyalties between England and the United States, an obvious concern in the years following the American Revolution. For the same reason, the framers stipulated that presidents be natural-born citizens (born in the United States or to American citizens abroad). Some have argued that President Obama does not fulfill the natural-born citizen requirement. These "Birthers" believe that President Obama was born in Kenya and not in Hawaii. They dismiss his birth certificate, birth announcements, and all the evidence of his birthplace as the product of a long-term conspiracy committed when President Obama was just a baby. This, of course, is not true. President Obama was born in Hawaii and his mother, Stanley Ann Dunham, was an American citizen. Both of these things ensure that Barack Obama is in fact a natural-born U.S. citizen. The so-called Birther Conspiracy illustrates a challenge for some presidential candidates.[5]

Although any natural-born citizen over the age of 35 who has lived in the United States for the previous 14 years is eligible to be president, all of our past presidents have been Christian males who are well over 35. And, until President Obama, all presidents were also white. Although there is no official race, gender, or religious eligibility requirements, those candidates who do not fit the typical model of a president have to struggle against bias from some voters.

## Presidential Powers

The Constitution has remarkably little to say on the president's powers to accomplish the office's broad range of responsibilities. Only one-third of Article II is devoted to formal presidential powers. This brevity reflects the framers' uncertainty on the subject. Trusting that George Washington would almost certainly be the first president, the framers assumed that he would establish precedents for the office.

What the framers did write into the Constitution can be categorized in two ways. First, in clear, simple language they gave the president specific powers. Second, and more important, they gave the executive broad, sweeping powers, written in vague language and subject to individual interpretation, as illustrated by our timeline. Let us first examine the specific, unambiguous powers allotted to American presidents by the U.S. Constitution.

## Approaching Democracy Timeline

### Events That Have Shaped the Expanding Power of the Presidency

| | |
|---|---|
| 1789 | Despite the advice and consent clause in the Constitution, George Washington decides not to seek the advice of the Senate on Indian treaties. |
| 1801 | Thomas Jefferson is the first president to govern through the personal leadership of a political party. |
| 1829 | Andrew Jackson is the first president whose authority rests on a popular constituency and is the first president to aggressively use the veto. |
| 1861 | Abraham Lincoln stretches the powers of the president further than ever before during the Civil War. |
| 1921 | Congress passes the Budget and Accounting Act of 1921, which places the preparation of the federal budget directly in the hands of the executive. |
| 1933 | Franklin Roosevelt exercises broad executive powers during the first 200 days of the New Deal. |
| 1939 | The Executive Office of the President (EOP) is established, providing permanent institutionalized and personal staff for the president. |
| 1942 | Roosevelt utilizes broad, discretionary presidential war powers prior to and during World War II. |
| 1946 | Congress passes the Employment Act of 1946, expanding the role of the executive in managing the economy. |
| 1947 | Congress passes the National Security Act of 1947, expanding the national security responsibilities of the president. |
| 1952 | Harry Truman seizes control of the U.S. steel industry through Executive Order 10340, which is later ruled unconstitutional. |
| 1969 | Richard Nixon begins bombing Cambodia without informing Congress. |
| 1972 | Richard Nixon asks the CIA to obstruct the FBI's investigation into Watergate. |
| 1981 | Ronald Reagan fires the striking air traffic controllers claiming the strike is a peril to national security. |
| 2001 | George W. Bush secretly approves warrantless wiretapping of U.S. citizens. |
| 2008 | George W. Bush makes unprecedented use of presidential signing statements to shape policy by challenging 1,200 sections of bills over his term, nearly twice the number challenged by all previous presidents combined. |

☐ Democratic ☐ Neutral ☐ Undemocratic

*(continued)*

**Approaching Democracy Timeline *(continued)***

| | |
|---|---|
| **2009** | Barack Obama continues to direct policy through the use of presidential signing statements. |
| **2011** | Barack Obama commits U.S. military power to the conflict in Libya without receiving congressional approval. |

☐ Democratic ☐ Neutral ☐ Undemocratic

**veto**
Presidential power to forbid or prevent an action of Congress.

**pocket veto**
Presidential refusal to sign or veto a bill that Congress passes in the last ten days of its session; by not being signed, it automatically dies when Congress adjourns.

**The Veto Power** Perhaps the president's most potent legal constitutional weapon is the **veto,** a Latin word meaning "I forbid." The power to forbid or prevent an action of Congress gives the president a central role in the legislative process. When Congress passes a bill or joint resolution, the legislation goes to the White House for presidential action. The president then has four options: (1) the president can sign the bill, at which point it becomes law; (2) the president can do nothing, allowing the bill to become law without a signature in ten days; (3) if Congress adjourns before those ten days pass, the president can refuse to sign, killing the bill by what is known as a **pocket veto;** or (4) the president can veto the bill, returning it to the house of origin with a message stating reasons for the veto. Congress then has the option to override the veto by a two-thirds vote in each house.

The framers saw the veto as a bulwark of executive independence, a basic building block in their efforts to separate and check power. Alexander Hamilton made this position clear in *The Federalist,* no. 73: "The primary inducement to conferring [the veto] power upon the executive is to enable him to defend himself; the second one is to increase the chances . . . against the passing of bad laws, through haste, inadvertence, or design." The veto was thus conceived as a "negative" power by which an executive could defend against legislative excesses.[6]

Presidents can sometimes affect a law's wording or passage by announcing ahead of time that they intend to veto a pending bill. The strategy is akin to the story of a farmer who used friendly persuasion to make his mule move but first had to whack it on the head to get its attention. In 1985, President Ronald Reagan dared Congress to raise taxes. Borrowing from Clint Eastwood, he said such actions would "make [his] day" and would be met by a quick veto. Using a similar tactic, President Bill Clinton warned Congress during a nationally televised State of the Union address: "If you send me legislation that does not guarantee every American private health insurance that can never be taken away, you will force me to take this pen [and] veto the legislation." Throughout his presidency, George W. Bush threatened to veto any legislation providing a timetable for withdrawal of American combat troops from Iraq. President Bush warned Democratic leaders, "I'll veto it, and then Congress can get down to the business of funding our troops without strings and without delays." President Bush vetoed bills providing federal funding for embryonic stem-cell research as well as combating congressional pork projects.[7] In total, President Bush issued 11 vetoes and utilized 1 pocket veto. President Obama used his veto for the first time on December 30, 2009, on a congressional spending bill.

Vice President Joe Biden looks on as President Barack Obama signs the American Recovery and Reinvestment Act on February 17, 2009, during a ceremony at the Denver Museum of Nature and Science.

President Obama has issued far fewer vetoes in his first three years as president than have previous presidents. He seems to be following George W. Bush's lead when it comes to limited use of the veto. We might expect Obama to pick up his veto pen more often while the Republican Party controls at least one house of Congress. President Obama has threatened to veto numerous pieces of legislation, including any repeal of his health-care bill. He made a number of veto threats over the course of the July 2011 debt-ceiling debate, including promising to veto the House Republican "Cut, Cap, and Balance" plan, any short-term increase in the debt ceiling, and a bill linking the debt-ceiling increase to a balanced budget amendment. Table 5.2 shows presidential vetoes from 1789 through 2011.

**signing statements**
Written proclamations issued by presidents regarding how they intend to interpret a new law.

Presidents have found another way to influence the shape of legislation through the use of signing statements. Early presidents occasionally signed a bill while declaring that one or more provisions were unconstitutional, but the practice became more frequent and the center of controversy during the George W. Bush years. President Bush frequently used **signing statements** to declare that provisions in the bill he was signing were an unconstitutional constraint on executive power, and therefore the laws did not need to be enforced or obeyed as written. Bush used signing statements to challenge a ban on torture as well as compliance with the USA Patriot Act. In total, more than 1,200 sections of bills were challenged over his eight years in office, about twice the number challenged by all previous presidents. The American Bar Association declared that signing statements were "contrary to the rule of law and our constitutional separation of powers," and asked future presidents to return to a system of either signing a bill and then enforcing all of it, or vetoing the bill and giving Congress a chance to override that veto.[8]

During the campaign for president, Senator John McCain pledged never to use signing statements. President Obama pledged to reduce using these statements, but as president he has found them a handy device for registering his legislative intent. When Congress placed restrictions on funding for the International Monetary Fund and the World Bank in a June 2009 supplemental spending bill, for example, President Obama issued a signing statement in which he claimed the restrictions "would interfere with my constitutional authority to conduct foreign relations" and declared, "I will not treat these provisions as limiting my ability to engage in foreign diplomacy or negotiations."[9] The House responded by voting 429–2 to negate the signing statement. President Obama has not relied on signing statements with the same frequency as his predecessor, but some have complained that he broke a campaign promise by using signing statements to override congressional will. In April 2011, President Obama's press secretary, Jay Carney, said that President Obama's use of signing statements is actually completely consistent with his previous statements on their use.[10] Many critics view Obama's use of signing statements as not only a broken campaign promise but also as the continuation of President Bush's unconstitutional executive power grab.

In an effort to dampen the growing polarization during the debt-ceiling debate, the President and Speaker of the House John Boehner play golf together at Andrews Air Force Base in Maryland on June 18, 2011.

**The Appointment Power** This specific and important power affects the president's ability to staff the executive branch with trusted allies. Article II, Section 2 of the Constitution gives the president, "by and with the Advice and Consent of the Senate," the power to appoint ambassadors, public ministers, and consuls; judges of the Supreme Courts; and "other Officers of the United States, whose Appointments are not herein otherwise provided for, and which shall be established by Law." As we see in Chapter 7, presidential appointments serve at the discretion of president and can be removed at any time. In 2006, President Bush used this defense to justify the removal of eight U.S. attorneys, and President Obama did the same in June 2009 with respect to the firing of Gerald Walpin, Inspector General for the Corporation for National and Community Service (CNCS).

The power of appointment allows a president to recruit people who will help promote his or her policies. Without this power, a president would be forced to work with congressional appointees and entrenched bureaucrats who may not share the president's goals. Although appointment is an important administrative power, more than 2,000 presidential appointments require Senate confirmation. Presidents can use a "backdoor" procedure known as a *recess appointment* to bypass the Senate. The constitution authorizes the president to fill vacant positions

**Table 5.2** Presidential Vetoes, 1789–2011

| | Regular Vetoes | Pocket Vetoes | Total Vetoes | Vetoes Overridden |
|---|---|---|---|---|
| **Washington** | 2 | – | 2 | – |
| **Madison** | 5 | 2 | 7 | – |
| **Monroe** | 1 | – | 1 | – |
| **Jackson** | 5 | 7 | 12 | – |
| **Tyler** | 6 | 3 | 9 | 1 |
| **Polk** | 2 | 1 | 3 | – |
| **Pierce** | 9 | – | 9 | 5 |
| **Buchanan** | 4 | 3 | 7 | – |
| **Lincoln** | 2 | 4 | 6 | – |
| **A. Johnson** | 21 | 8 | 29 | 15 |
| **Grant** | 45 | 49 | 94 | 4 |
| **Hayes** | 12 | 1 | 13 | 1 |
| **Arthur** | 4 | 8 | 12 | 1 |
| **Cleveland** | 304 | 109 | 413 | 2 |
| **Harrison** | 19 | 25 | 44 | 1 |
| **Cleveland** | 43 | 127 | 170 | 5 |
| **McKinley** | 6 | 36 | 42 | – |
| **T. Roosevelt** | 42 | 40 | 82 | 1 |
| **Taft** | 30 | 9 | 39 | 1 |
| **Wilson** | 33 | 11 | 44 | 6 |
| **Harding** | 5 | 1 | 6 | – |
| **Coolidge** | 20 | 30 | 50 | 4 |
| **Hoover** | 21 | 16 | 37 | 3 |
| **F. Roosevelt** | 372 | 263 | 635 | 9 |
| **Truman** | 180 | 70 | 250 | 12 |
| **Eisenhower** | 73 | 108 | 181 | 2 |
| **Kennedy** | 12 | 9 | 21 | – |
| **L. Johnson** | 16 | 14 | 30 | – |
| **Nixon** | 26 | 17 | 43 | 7 |
| **Ford** | 48 | 18 | 66 | 12 |
| **Carter** | 13 | 18 | 31 | 2 |
| **Reagan** | 39 | 39 | 78 | 9 |
| **G. H. W. Bush** | 29 | 17 | 46 | 1 |
| **Clinton** | 36 | 0 | 36 | 2 |
| **G. W. Bush** | 11 | 1 | 12 | 4 |
| **Obama** | 2 | – | – | – |

*Source:* Gerhard Peters, adapted from "Presidential Vetoes," *The American Presidency Project.* John T. Woolley and Gerhard Peters, eds. (Santa Barbara: University of California, 1999–2009). Available from the World Wide Web: www.presidency.ucsb.edu/data/vetoes.php. Used with permission. Obama veto updated by authors, with appreciation to Professor Robert Spitzer.

when the Senate is in recess. Appointees can serve without Senate confirmation until the congressional session ends at the year's end. However, a majority of senators can remove appointees at any time. President Bush used this procedure 171 times. President Clinton made 140 recess appointments in his two terms.[11] President George H. W. Bush made 77 recess appointments over one term, and President Reagan made 243 over two terms.

Perhaps the most important appointment presidents can make is a nomination to fill a Supreme Court vacancy. Presidents rarely end up naming a majority of Court members. Nevertheless, because the Court is usually split ideologically, even one or two appointments can affect the outcome of important constitutional cases well beyond the president's term of office.

**treaties**
Formal international agreements between sovereign states.

**executive agreement**
A government-to-government agreement with essentially the same legal force as a treaty. However, it may be concluded entirely without Senate knowledge and/or approval.

**The Treaty Power** The Constitution also gives presidents the power to negotiate **treaties** with other nations. Treaties are formal international agreements between sovereign states. But the framers foresaw a system that required consultation between branches—the executive's negotiation would involve the Senate's "advice and consent." When President George Washington went to Congress to solicit advice on an Indian treaty, however, he had to stay several hours and answer questions that he believed had little bearing on the treaty. Irked by this experience, Washington resolved not to repeat it. Henceforth, although he had to secure the Senate's consent in ratifying treaties, he did not encourage senators to contribute their sometimes dubious "advice"—and later presidents have often followed that model.

Treaty approval can prove difficult, partly because it requires a two-thirds majority of senators to be present and voting. In addition, the Senate may attach amendments to treaties. Most treaties are approved without modification, and the Senate has defeated only 1 percent of treaties it has received. However, that record of success is misleading; presidents have withdrawn 150 treaties that seemed headed for defeat.

The most dramatic example, discussed in Chapter 16, is the treaty rejection that took place in 1919, when the Senate failed to ratify Woodrow Wilson's Treaty of Versailles, ending World War I and establishing the League of Nations. Its defeat seemed a direct slap in the president's face by a hostile Congress and not only undermined Wilson's authority at home but also helped doom the League—the predecessor of today's United Nations—to ineffectiveness abroad.[12]

Although treaty rejection gives the Senate power similar to presidential veto power, its potential has declined as presidents have increasingly turned to less formal means for conducting foreign affairs. **Executive agreements,** diplomatic contracts negotiated with other countries, allow presidents or their agents to make important foreign policy moves without Senate approval. These agreements appeal to harried presidents in their role as a world leader. Treaties generate media coverage and controversy and take time to ratify, but executive agreements are usually negotiated in secret, making them a particularly powerful foreign policy tool. William McKinley used the executive agreement to end the Spanish–American War, and Theodore Roosevelt used it to restrict Japanese immigration to the United States.

Presidents may conclude an executive agreement on any subject within their constitutional authority as long as the agreement is consistent with legislation enacted by Congress in the exercise of its constitutional authority. Scholars agree that, although not explicitly outlined in the Constitution, the president's right to conduct foreign policy through executive agreement rests on several sound constitutional bases. These include the president's authority as chief executive to represent the nation in foreign affairs, the president's authority to receive ambassadors and other public ministers, the president's authority as commander in chief, and the president's authority to "take Care that the Laws be faithfully executed." Presidents are increasingly finding the flexibility they need to make foreign policy in executive agreements.[13]

When the Strategic Arms Reduction Treaty, or START, expired on December 5, 2009, President Obama decided to temporarily bypass the Senate's constitutional

**executive privilege**
The president's implied or inherent power to withhold information on the grounds that to release such information would affect either national security or the president's ability to discharge official duties.

role in ratifying treaties by enforcing certain aspects of a new deal on a "provisional basis." The Senate ratified the new START treaty a year after the previous treaty had expired. Although it was enforced for the previous 13 months, the new START treaty was not officially ratified until President Obama signed it into law on February 2, 2011.

**Executive Privilege** President Dwight Eisenhower once said, "Any man who testifies as to the advice he gave me won't be working for me that night." He invoked executive privilege 40 times in his eight years in office.[14] **Executive privilege** is the president's claim of implied or inherent power to withhold information on the grounds that to release such information would affect either national security or the president's ability to discharge his official duties. The important question is not necessarily whether the privilege should exist, but rather who should determine its extent—the president, the legislative branch, or the courts.

The Constitution does not mention executive privilege; the first discussion of privilege occurred in 1792. A special House investigation committee requested that President Washington turn over materials pertaining to a skirmish in which troops under the leadership of General Arthur St. Clair were killed by Native Americans. Washington called a special cabinet meeting to establish standards for the executive branch's responses. The House committee had requested that Secretary of War Henry Knox turn over all original letters and correspondence pertaining to St. Clair's mission. In the first case of a president's refusing to supply Congress with a document, Washington denied the request, giving both constitutional and pragmatic reasons.

Several of George Washington's successors followed his precedent of withholding information. President Jackson refused to turn over documents that would have disclosed his reasons for removing government deposits from the Bank of the United States. The best-known case of executive privilege involved President Richard Nixon's claim that tapes of confidential conversations between himself and his aides were within the provenance of the White House. In a unanimous decision, the Supreme Court acknowledged a constitutional basis for executive privilege, but not in Nixon's case. The Court did not view the power to protect presidential communications as absolute. The privilege of confidentiality had to derive from the supremacy of the executive branch within its assigned areas of constitutional duties. Neither the doctrine of separation of powers nor the need for confidentiality of high-level communications can sustain an absolute, unqualified presidential privilege of immunity from judicial process under all circumstances. The president's need for complete candor and objectivity from advisers calls for great deference from the courts. However, when the privilege depends solely on the broad undifferentiated claim of public interest in the confidentiality of such conversations, a confrontation with other values arises. During the Clinton presidency, this involved controversies between the president and his attorney as well as the Secret Service during the Monica Lewinsky investigation and impeachment.

President George W. Bush invoked executive privilege several times, initially when he rejected a congressional subpoena for prosecutor's records on a 30-year-old Boston mob case, as well as for documents on the Clinton campaign finance probe. Bush cited threats to national interest that disclosure might produce. The collapse of Enron brought another claim of privilege. The Bush administration refused to release details of energy policy meetings between energy corporation executives and a task force to set energy policy guidelines chaired by Vice President Richard Cheney.[15] The Government Accountability Office (GAO), the legislative arm of Congress, filed suit to obtain that information, the first such action in history.[16] The Bush administration later made the case for executive privilege in the controversy surrounding the removal of the U.S. attorneys. Bush challenged the Democratic Congress's attempts to force his aides to testify before the judiciary committees.[17] President Bush also claimed executive privilege to protect his attorney general Michael Mukasey from delivering to congressional investigators documents dealing with interviews of Vice President Cheney and members of his staff regarding the unmasking of Central Intelligence Agency (CIA) covert agent Valerie Plame Wilson.

In an attempt to bring more openness to the White House, one of President Obama's first acts as president was to revoke a Bush presidency executive order that claimed far-reaching executive privilege. However, as president, Obama has clung to much of the secrecy he once found objectionable in the previous administration. In May of 2011, the Department of Defense reclassified a number of documents that had been publically released in 2005. Although the number of new classified secrets in 2010 was almost half of 2008's number, the Obama administration did classify 2,378 new secrets in 2010.[18] Contributing much to the disappointment of open-government advocates, the Obama administration prosecuted more leakers of classified information over his first term than did all previous administrations combined.[19]

Although democracy requires openness, legitimate needs for government secrecy can pertain to national security matters. Each of us can debate the extent of privilege over access to information and whether the national interest is truly at stake. The level of secrecy demonstrated by the Bush presidency raises several important issues in thinking about our theme of approaching democracy. Senator Patrick Leahy (D–VT), chair of the Senate Judiciary Committee, observed at the time of the Bush claim of privilege for his attorney general from complying with a subpoena: "This executive privilege claim, and your justification for it, appears to turn the privilege on its head. The purpose of executive privilege is to encourage candid advice to the president, not to cover up what the vice president and White House staff say to investigating authorities when that information is requested in the course of congressional oversight."[20]

**Other Constitutionally Designated Powers** The Constitution gives the president additional specific powers. One is the right to grant pardons: President Ford pardoned Richard Nixon for any crimes he may have committed as president, and President Clinton issued, and later admitted regretting, controversial pardons during his last day in office. President George W. Bush issued 189 pardons by the time he left office in January 2009. At the beginning of his third year in office, President Obama pardoned 9 people of their convictions for nonviolent crimes, including drug-related offenses and counterfeiting. None of those pardoned were well known before or after their convictions, but a White House spokesperson said that "the president was moved by the strength of the applicants' post-conviction efforts at atonement."[21]

Perhaps the most important is the power of commander in chief of the armed forces. Presidents who use this power effectively can dramatically enhance their national and international stature. We examine the consequences of this power in detail later in this chapter as well as in Chapter 16 on foreign policy.

Beyond these specific grants of power, the Constitution gives the president a vague mandate to run the executive branch of government. Different presidents have interpreted that mandate in different ways. We discuss the leeway that constitutional vagueness has allowed presidents in expanding chief executive powers during the two centuries since the framers wrote the Constitution. But first, we look at the various roles that define the job of chief executive.

## FUNCTIONAL ROLES OF THE PRESIDENT

5.3 *How do the roles and responsibilities of the presidency create the paradoxes of the presidency and how do these paradoxes make it difficult for any president to succeed?*

Presidential behavior depends only partly on laws that require action or prohibit it. Beyond formal legalities, all presidents are constrained and directed by informal or functional role expectations. When leaders are expected to take an action, they do it—whether or not permission for the action is contained somewhere in a legal document. As leader of a vocal, democratic people, the president stands at the center of a mass of such expectations.

## QUICK REVIEW

Functional Roles of the President

- Chief of state—ceremonial role.
- Commander in chief—provide national security and defense.
- Crisis leader—bring about timely action during periods of crisis.
- Chief diplomat—serve as broker or mediator.
- Chief legislator—forge legislation to improve the quality of life.
- Chief executive—sign *executive orders* and presidential decrees.
- Moral leader—set a high moral tone for the American people.
- Party leader—chief architect of his political party.
- Manager of prosperity—act as an economic superhero who will stave off both depression and inflation while keeping the economy at full employment.

**The President as Chief of State** The president acts as a ceremonial chief of state, symbolizing the national government to people in this country and other nations. At world gatherings, the chief of state holds the same high-protocol rank as kings. Presidents greet foreign ambassadors, pin medals on heroes, hold barbecues on the White House lawn, and give state dinners. Virtually all these opportunities help dramatize and personalize a presidency. From meeting astronauts to making an entrance to the tune "Hail to the Chief," presidents bask in the glory and often hide behind the pomp and circumstance of their office.

**The President as Commander in Chief** When necessary, the president must defend American interests by committing troops to combat. This role is reinforced by the president's constitutional oath of office to "preserve, protect, and defend the Constitution of the United States." Barack Obama's decision to send a Navy Seal team into Osama bin Laden's Pakistan compound illustrates this very point. The president's plan to use a small strike team to target those in the compound directly worked well. Obama displayed coolness under pressure, good judgment, and decisiveness—but what if the operation had failed? President Obama's choice was a risky one. The CIA's original plan was to drop 64,000 pounds of explosives on the compound. This plan would ensure successful elimination of Osama bin Laden, but would also kill scores of civilians and flatten houses located within the blast radius. Additionally, this plan would leave no physical proof of bin Laden's death and would wipe out any evidence of who was living in the compound before it was bombed.[22] It was President Obama who decided to put the bombing plan on hold and ordered the direct strike on the compound. If the strike on the compound failed to capture or kill bin Laden, the president could have faced severe criticism. His decision to send in Navy Seals rather than drop explosives could have led to bin Laden's escape.

A president who fails to respond forcefully to a threat is seen as weak or indecisive, as was the case with President Carter's response, or lack thereof, to the seizure of the United States embassy in Tehran, which resulted in an extended hostage crisis. On the other hand, President Bush's decision to remove Saddam Hussein from power and liberate the people of Iraq from Saddam's tyranny created heated debate on the president's war powers.[23] President Obama's decision to involve U.S. forces in Libya without congressional approval elicited similar debate.

President Barack Obama greets troops during a visit to Camp Victory, just outside Baghdad, on April 7, 2009. Eight months later, the president would authorize 30,000 more troops for the war effort in Afghanistan.

Still, by all standards of presidential power, former President George W. Bush expanded the prerogatives of the office. He utilized his role as commander in chief during a period of unprecedented worldwide terrorist attacks and continued terrorist threats. He claimed for the executive branch of government the powers to set policy on detention and interrogation of suspected terrorists, to make rule changes in environmental policy, to refuse to allow Congress to call White House aides to testify at hearings, and to refuse the release of historic presidential documents, and he authorized the National Security Agency's domestic counterterrorism surveillance operation to spy on Americans.[24] In the wake of Hurricane Katrina, the president endorsed changes in federal law that allowed the military to assume immediate responsibility when the nation confronts natural disasters.[25]

**The President as Crisis Leader** The president also comes to the forefront of the nation's attention during crises such as natural disasters, civil unrest, and military or terrorist attacks against the United States. After natural disasters such as Hurricane Katrina or events such as the terrorist attacks of September 11, 2001, the nation turns to the president as the only leader capable of bringing about timely action in such circumstances. George W. Bush's September 14, 2001, visit to the site of the World Trade Center attack in New York unified our nation and gave comfort to a people in mourning. After the tragic shooting at Virginia Tech, Bush was seen once again adopting the role of "consoler in chief."[26]

In times of crisis, Congress generally acquiesces to the president, as it did for President Obama's economic stimulus plan. Moreover, during such episodes, presidential actions are generally accompanied by a noticeable jump in approval and popularity. This relationship between crisis and presidential support has become known as the "rally effect"—the country supports the president in response to a crisis.

## Compared to WHAT?

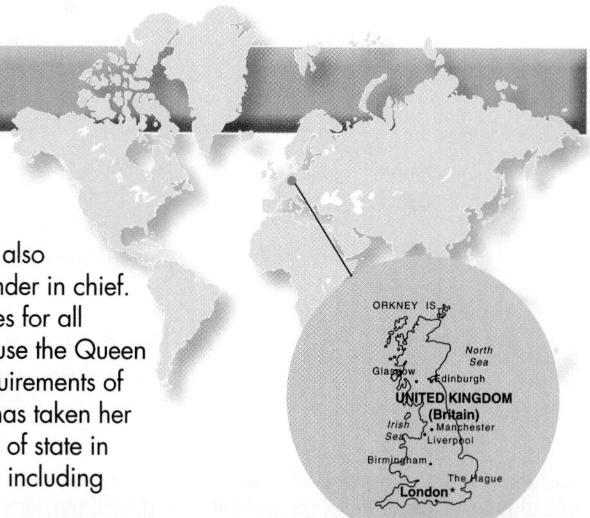


### Avoiding a Presidential Paradox— The Queen of England as Chief of State

In the United States, presidents, while serving as chief of state, must also lead their party, engage in divisive politics, and preside as commander in chief. As discussed in this chapter, these conflicting roles lead to challenges for all presidents. In England, some of these challenges are avoided because the Queen acts as head of state while the Prime Minister fulfills the political requirements of the executive. During her nearly 60-year reign, Queen Elizabeth II has taken her role as head of state seriously. She is the most widely traveled head of state in the world and hosts foreign dignitaries when they travel to England, including hosting President and First Lady Obama at Buckingham Palace in May 2011.

In her role as head of state, Queen Elizabeth is careful to live up to what historian Walter Bagehot called the "dignified part" of the British government. She is careful to avoid public political statements and does not engage in divisive political debate. The Royal Family's webpage states: "As Head of State, the Queen has to remain strictly neutral with respect to political matters." Unlike other citizens in the United Kingdom, the Queen does not even cast a vote for political leaders. Additionally, she struggles to maintain a pristine image because, as head of state, she believes her image reflects on that of the United Kingdom.

Britain's Queen Elizabeth II hosts President Barack Obama during a State Banquet in Buckingham Palace on May 24, 2011.

Americans appear to approve of the Queen's role in England. In an April 2011 CBS/New York Times Poll, 71 percent of Americans said that the Royal Family is a "good thing" for the British people and nearly one out of every five respondents thought that a Royal Family would be a good thing in the United States as well. A separate head of state would certainly ease the tension between the conflicting roles of the American president; the difficulty would be in determining the selection of a head of state independent of the political process.

*Sources:* http://www.royal.gov.uk/MonarchUK/QueenandGovernment/QueenandGovernment.aspx; Norman S. John-Stevas, ed., *The Collected Works of Walter Bagehot: Volumes 1–15* (New York: Oxford University Press, 1986); http://www.ctv.ca/CTVNews/Specials/20060418/queen_liz_birthday_060418/; http://www.washingtonpost.com/world/queen-elizabeth-ii-welcomes-president-obama-first-lady/2011/05/24/AFb9nRAH_story.html; http://graphics8.nytimes.com/packages/pdf/world/apr11-royals-poll.pdf?ref=europe.

**The President as Chief Diplomat** Presidents must be international diplomats as well as warriors. Maintaining smooth relations with allies and a tough stance with potential or real enemies is expected of all presidents. In his first two years in office, President Obama traveled abroad more than any other president over a similar time frame, making good on a campaign promise to rebuild America's reputation in the world. Since his first year in office, however, the frequency of Obama's foreign trips has fallen and he has canceled a number of trips abroad in order to focus on issues at home. Yet, like all modern presidents, President Obama continues to carry out his role as chief diplomat in part through extensive international travel.[27]

**The President as Chief Legislator** Despite numerous constraints, presidents do play a major role in domestic matters. Congress and the American public expect the president to send legislative initiatives to Congress and to work with congressional leaders in forging legislation that will improve the quality of life in America. Indeed, most legislation addressed by Congress originates in the executive branch, but when President Dwight Eisenhower chose not to submit a program in 1953 (his first year in office), he was chided by a member of Congress: "Don't expect us to start from scratch. . . . That's not the way we do things here. You draft the bills and we work them over."[28]

Besides proposing policies and lobbying for them, the president also has negative legislative power. As we have seen, presidents can thwart congressional attempts at legislation through the veto or threats of a veto.

**The President as Chief Executive** As the nation's chief executive, the president signs *executive orders* and presidential decrees, setting the administrative direction and tone for the executive branch. As chief administrator or chief bureaucrat, the president oversees an army of officials, thousands of executive branch workers trying to administer presidential policies effectively and quickly. Presidents, of course, do not act in a vacuum but are closely monitored by interest groups throughout the country, all eager to see that the executive branch promotes policies and interprets laws to their liking. Table 5.3 shows the number of executive orders issued by each president since Herbert Hoover. During his first days in office, President Obama used executive orders to reverse Bush policies on transparency, presidential records, stem-cell research, abortion, and interrogations methods.

President Obama greets graduates following the commencement ceremonies at Notre Dame University in South Bend, Indiana, on May 17, 2009. Obama called for "open hearts," "open minds," "fair-minded words," and the search for common ground on abortion, telling graduates that they were at "a rare inflection point in history where the size and scope of the challenges before us require that we remake our world to renew its promise."

**The President as Moral Leader** Increasingly, voters have shown that the president's character is important to their support. The president has always been expected to set a public, if not private, high moral tone for the American people. Richard Nixon's popular support melted away during the Watergate affair not just because of his illegal actions but because Americans came to view his character as deceptive and untrustworthy. Many were offended by the petty vulgarities on the

**Table 5.3** Executive Orders Issued Since Herbert Hoover

| President | Number of Executive Orders | Executive Orders | Notable Executive Order |
|---|---|---|---|
| Herbert Hoover | 995 | 5075–6070 | 5658: Outlined procedures for the form and storage of executive orders. |
| Franklin Roosevelt | 3,467 | 6071–9537 | 9066: Authorized the internment of Japanese Americans. |
| Harry Truman | 893 | 9538–10431 | 9981: Desegregated the armed forces. |
| Dwight Eisenhower | 482 | 10432–10913 | 10450: Allowed the FBI to investigate the personal lives of federal employees and the firing of employees whose personal habits were deemed in poor character. |
| John Kennedy | 213 | 10914–11127 | 10925: Established the Committee on Equal Employment Opportunity and barred discrimination in government employment. |
| Lyndon Johnson | 324 | 11128–11451 | 11141: Declared a public policy banning age discrimination. |
| Richard Nixon | 346 | 11452–11797 | 11771: Granted diplomatic privileges to Chinese diplomats. |
| Gerald Ford | 169 | 11798–11966 | 11905: Prohibited any employee of the U.S. government from engaging in political assassination. |
| Jimmy Carter | 320 | 11967–12286 | 12170: Established sanctions against Iran. |
| Ronald Reagan | 381 | 12287–12667 | 12601: Established a presidential commission to study the HIV and AIDS epidemic. |
| George Bush | 166 | 12668–12833 | 12722: Established sanctions against Iraq. |
| William Clinton | 364 | 12834–13197 | 12889: Implemented NAFTA. |
| George W. Bush | 291 | 13198–13488 | 13233: Limited access to the records of U.S. presidents. |
| Barack Obama | 90 | 13489–13578 | 13489: Revoked the limits placed on freedom of information in Executive Order 13233. |

*Source:* National Archives. http://www.archives.gov/federal-register/executive-orders/disposition.html.

White House tapes. Even though few citizens see politics as a fair and moral game, and even though no one can become president except through politics, Americans still seem to hold the president to higher public standards than most politicians—or most citizens, for that matter. Presidents are expected to emulate George ("I cannot tell a lie") Washington and Abraham ("Honest Abe") Lincoln—to be truthful, to deal openly with problems, to keep their word—and even to set high standards in their personal lives. President Barack Obama has been referred to as "father in chief" because of the seriousness with which he approaches balancing both governing and parenting.

In recent times, the public has expected First Ladies to also take on the role of a moral leader. Many of our modern First Ladies tackled this role by focusing on the importance of education; Eleanor Roosevelt promoted an educated citizenry as a pathway toward democracy, Lady Bird Johnson helped develop the Head Start program, and Barbara and

President Obama comforts citizens in Joplin, Missouri, after a tornado devastated the city in May 2011.

Laura Bush both worked on literacy policy.[29] Michelle Obama is tackling the issues of nutrition and obesity. She was involved with the development of the new USDA nutritional plate icon, released in 2011 to replace the food pyramid. First Lady Obama worked with the White House's Task Force on Child Obesity to create the "Let's Move" program. As a moral leader, she set an example by planting an organic vegetable garden on the White House lawn, which has provided both the White House kitchen and local food banks with over 2,000 pounds of organically grown produce.

## THINKING CRITICALLY

Given the strain between the roles as both a national figure and political leader, how would the role of the president change if the United States, like most other Western democracies, had a separate head of state, like the queen in England, to handle the more symbolic duties of the presidency?

**The President as Party Leader** Presidents are the chief architects of their political party's fortune. The Constitution makes no reference to party leadership—indeed, it makes no reference to parties at all—but today's presidents must never forget that their party put them in the Oval Office. A president's every action either helps or hurts that party, and its members keep a close eye on the president to make sure that the party's ideas and fortunes are promoted. If too zealous, the president will be perceived as narrowly partisan rather than the leader of the entire nation. History teaches us that electoral majorities can quickly evaporate.

**The President as Manager of Prosperity** The public expects the president to act as an economic superhero who will stave off depression, recession, and inflation while keeping the economy at full employment. Presidents acting in this capacity adopt the role as "manager of prosperity." The chief executive is, in a sense, the nation's chief economist. The political lessons of the Great Depression are clear. No president can preside over hard times without being blamed. Herbert Hoover was soundly defeated after failing, in the public's eyes, to deal competently with the economic setbacks of that time. George H. W. Bush was sent into retirement because, in the words of political strategist James Carville, "It's the economy, stupid."[30] Harry Truman lost his Democratic majority in Congress during the 1946 election, and Jimmy Carter's fate might have been different if he could have averted the double-digit inflation of his last years in office. President Obama took office during a period of severe economic decline. The slow pace of economic recovery may cost him a second term as president. The clear lesson of presidential approval is how closely a president's political fortunes are tied to economic performance, especially the unemployment rate.

**The President as Juggler of Roles** The president must play all of these roles and others besides—a virtually impossible task because the roles often conflict. How can one be a partisan politician and still unify the nation? For that matter, can one be a politician at all and still inspire the nation as a whole? Can one both legislate and administer laws? Can a president address world affairs as both soldier and diplomat? How can a president seem universally fair and effective to a multitude of constituencies? Finally, just finding the time and energy to carry out these expected tasks is surely beyond the capacity of any mortal. Figure 5.1 shows how historians have ranked the presidents.

The job of president is particularly daunting because the powers granted to carry out these multiple roles fall far short of any person's capacity to do so. In fact, we expect Herculean accomplishments of presidents, even though we hedge them with restrictions so that they look less like Captain Marvel and more like Gulliver, tied down by a thousand tiny ropes. How, then, can anyone fill all the expected roles of the presidency? Let us examine two reactions to this system: presidents who accept the restraints and live within them and presidents who chafe at the restraints and invent ways to surpass or abolish them.

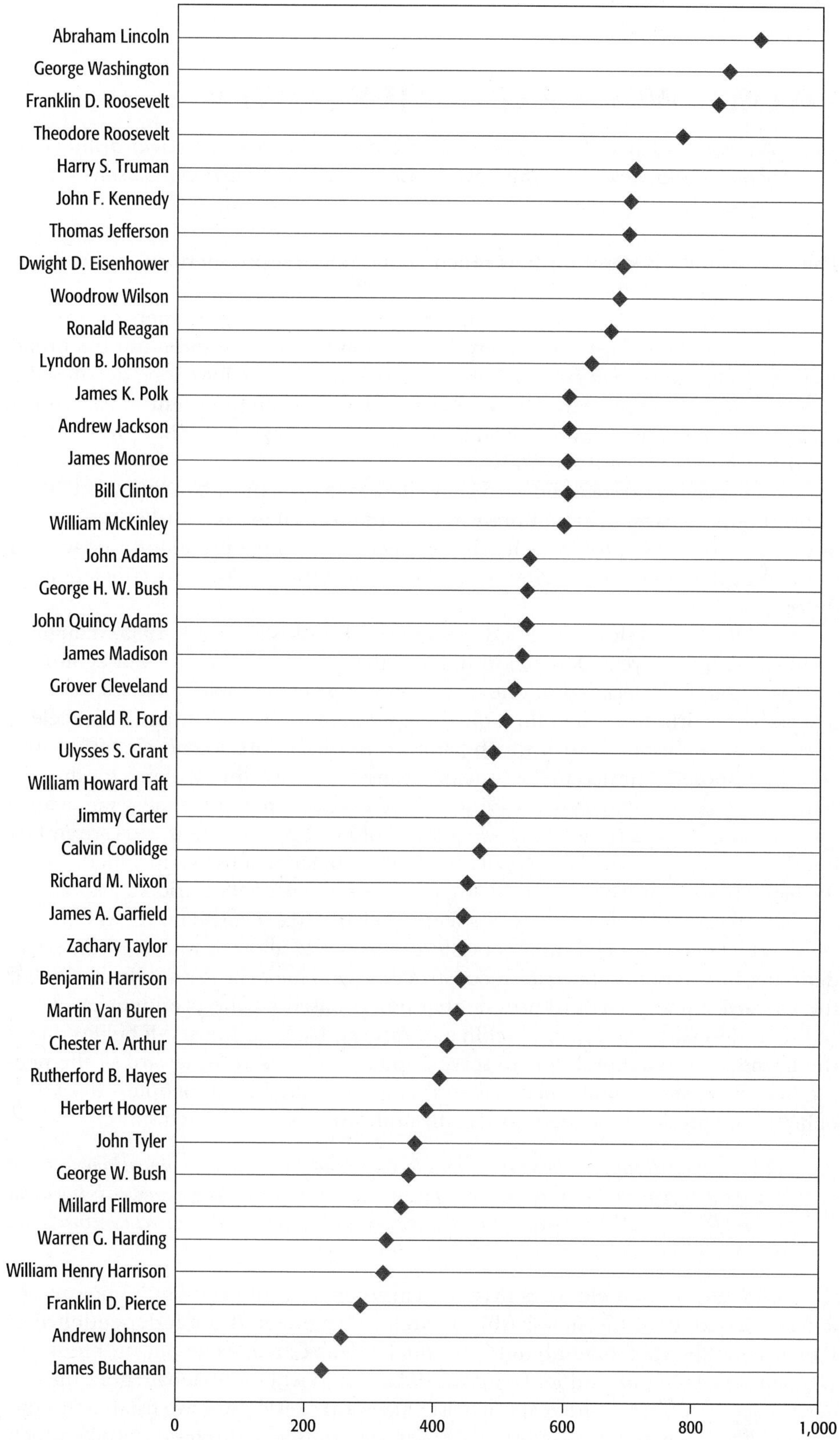


**FIGURE 5.1** Historians' Presidential Rankings

This graph shows the results of a 2009 C-SPAN survey of Historians' Ranking of Presidential Leadership. The scores at the bottom reflect total scores from individual leadership characteristics that included public persuasion, crisis leadership, economic management, moral authority, international relations, administrative skills, relations with Congress, vision setting an agenda, pursued equal justice for all, and performance within context of the times.

*Source:* "Ranking Presidents" graph by John Sides from http://www.themonkeycage.org/2009/02/ranking_presidents.html, created with data from C-SPAN 2009 Historians Presidential Leadership Survey, http://cspan.org/PresidentialSurvey/Overall-Ranking.aspx. Used with permission from John Sides.

# TWO VIEWS OF EXECUTIVE POWER

5.4 *What is the key difference between the constructionist and stewardship view of the presidency, and why have modern presidents viewed themselves as stewards?*

The Constitution is silent on how much actual power a president should possess. Article II begins with the ambiguous sentence, "The executive Power shall be vested in a President of the United States of America." What did the framers mean? Did "the executive Power" refer to a mere designation of office, or did it imply a broad and sweeping mandate to rule? Scholars and politicians alike have long debated the question without agreement. History has left it up to each president to determine the scope of executive powers, given a president's personality, philosophy, and the political circumstances of the time.

This executive power "wild card" has allowed many a president to outreach the Constitution's narrow prescriptions when conditions call for extraordinary action—or when the president thinks such action is necessary. Activist presidents find ways to justify sweeping policy innovations even if the Constitution has no specific language for those policies.

Franklin Roosevelt exemplified this approach in his March 4, 1933, inaugural address. With the Great Depression holding the country at the brink of economic collapse, Roosevelt declared in one of history's most memorable speeches, "Let me first assert my firm belief that the only thing we have to fear is fear itself—nameless, unreasoning, unjustified terror which paralyzes needed efforts to convert retreat into advance." Roosevelt turned to the issue of means: "I shall ask the Congress for the one remaining instrument to meet the crisis—broad executive power to wage a war against the emergency, as great as the power that would be given to me if we were in fact invaded by a foreign foe."[31] Roosevelt then took dramatic actions that included closing the banks by executive order, forbidding payments of gold, and restricting exports.

Not all presidents have made as sweeping claims to executive power as Franklin Roosevelt. Their different approaches to use of power allow us to categorize presidents in office as either stewards or constructionists. Theodore Roosevelt articulated the **stewardship** approach to presidential power based on the presidencies of two of his predecessors, Abraham Lincoln and Andrew Jackson. Roosevelt believed that the president had a moral duty to serve popular interests as "a steward of the people bound actively and affirmatively to do all he could for the people." Roosevelt believed the president needed no specific authorization to take action:

> *I did . . . many things not previously done by the President. . . . I did not usurp power, but I did greatly broaden the use of executive power. . . . I acted for the common well being of all our people . . . in whatever manner was necessary, unless prevented by direct constitutional or legislative prohibition.*[32]

Teddy Roosevelt held an activist, expansionist view of presidential powers. In a classic example of the stewardship model, he engineered the independence of Panama and the subsequent building of the Panama Canal. As he put it, "I took the [Panama] Canal Zone and let Congress debate, and while the debate goes on, the canal does, too."[33] Over the years, activist or steward presidents have used their powers broadly. Thomas Jefferson presided over the Louisiana Purchase in 1803, which almost doubled the size of the country. Lincoln assumed enormous emergency powers during the Civil War, justifying them on the grounds of needing to take quick, decisive action during an extraordinary national crisis. During World War I, Woodrow Wilson commandeered plants and mines, requisitioned supplies, fixed prices, seized and operated the nation's transportation and communication networks, and managed the production and distribution of foodstuffs.

In contrast to this stewardship view of executive power is the **constructionist** view espoused by William Howard Taft. Taft believed that the president could exercise no power unless it could be traced to or implied from an express grant in either

**stewardship**
An approach to presidential power articulated by Theodore Roosevelt and based on the presidencies of Lincoln and Jackson, who believed that the president had a moral duty to serve popular interests and did not need specific constitutional or legal authorization to take action.

**constructionist**
A view of presidential power espoused by William Howard Taft, who believed that the president could exercise no power unless it could be traced to or implied from an express grant in either the Constitution or an act of Congress.

the Constitution or an act of Congress. He scoffed at the idea of some "undefined residuum of power" that a president can exercise "because it seems to him to be in the public interest." The president, he believed, was limited by a strict reading of the Constitution. Unless that document gave the executive a specific power, that power was beyond the scope of legitimate presidential activity. Taft cringed in horror at Theodore Roosevelt's view that the president could "do anything that the needs of the nation demanded."[34]

This restricted view of presidential power made Taft a passive executive, reluctant to impose his will or the power of his office on the legislative process. He neither exerted strong party leadership in Congress nor embarked on the ambitious exercises of power typical of Teddy Roosevelt. Other presidents besides Taft have pursued this constructionist line, at least in certain situations. For example, Herbert Hoover appeared strongly constructionist—at least in economic policy—in his reluctance to manipulate the economy during the Great Depression. Indeed, his reluctance caused many voters to see him as indifferent to their economic plight.

On the whole, Americans have sided with an activist interpretation of the presidency. They expect dynamic leadership from the office. Almost no president regarded as great by either historians or the public has adopted a passive, constructionist approach to the job. The men who largely created our idealized view of the presidency—Washington, Jefferson, Lincoln, the two Roosevelts—did not reach lofty status by minding their own business. They crossed and stretched constitutional boundaries in the name of the national interest. Their achievements stand as models, if not monuments. Current presidents invoke their names and strive to fill their shoes, while voters measure current White House occupants against these past giants. Few hope that the next president will behave like William Howard Taft, and it is unlikely that anyone will seek that office promising "to govern in the spirit of Franklin Pierce." Although not everyone may agree with Woodrow Wilson that "the President has the right, in law and conscience, to be as big a man as he can be," many now believe that the health of American democracy rests in the hands of an activist executive.

### THINKING CRITICALLY

How would a person who advocated the constructionist view of presidential power fare in a presidential election? What if this person managed to get elected? How would the person change the job of the modern president?

## EXPANDING PRESIDENTIAL POWER: MOVING BEYOND THE CONSTITUTION

5.5 *How have the powers of the presidency expanded over time, and what factors might explain this expansion?*

Presidents have been gaining power for decades. The days are gone when a passive president such as Calvin Coolidge could identify his greatest accomplishment as "minding my own business." How can we account for the impact of personality, of presidential will, on behavior in the Oval Office? Even today, presidents cannot be powerful and activist unless they want to be. They must possess a character that leads them, in fact, to exercise those powers that have accrued, in theory, to their office. The passive William Howard Taft succeeded the activist Teddy Roosevelt. Presumably, the powers of the American president changed little from 1908 (Roosevelt's last full year in office) and 1909 (Taft's first year). What changed was the personality of the president. The powers of the president in our day derive not merely from an increase in technical powers available to the office, but in an increasing likelihood that occupants of the White House will be strong, activist individuals.

### The Doctrine of Inherent Powers and Presidential Character

Activist presidents have justified their broad interpretation of presidential powers through a theory known as **inherent powers**. This theory holds that the constitution grants authority to the executive, through the joining of Article II, Section 1, "The

**inherent powers**
Powers that do not appear in the Constitution but are assumed because of the nature of government. Also refers to a theory that the Constitution grants authority to the executive, through the injunction in Article II, Section 1, that "The executive Power shall be vested in a President of the United States of America."

executive Power shall be vested in a President of the United States," with Article II, Section 3, that the President "take Care that the Laws be faithfully executed." Presidents argue that under certain emergency conditions, the executive may claim to possess extraordinary powers to act quickly, and without corresponding congressional action, to save and protect the nation and its citizens.

Thomas Jefferson was the first president to expound the theory of going beyond the law when necessary for national security. "A strict observance of the written law is doubtless one of the higher duties of a good officer, but it is not the highest. The law of necessity, of self-preservation, of saving our country when in danger, are of higher obligation."[35] President Lincoln in 1864 reinforced this theory of inherent powers when he argued,

> *My oath to preserve the Constitution to the best of my ability imposed upon me the duty of preserving, by every indispensible means, that government—that nation, of which the Constitution was the organic law. Was it possible to lose the nation, and yet preserve the Constitution? By general law, life and limb must be protected. Yet often a limb must be amputated to save a life; but a life is never wisely given to save a limb. I felt that measures otherwise unconstitutional might become lawful by becoming indispensible to the preservation of the nation. Right or wrong I assumed this ground, and now avow it. I could not feel that, to the best of my ability, I had even tried to preserve the Constitution, if, to save slavery . . . I should permit the wreck of government, country, and Constitution altogether.*[36]

At the beginning of the Civil War, Lincoln took such extraordinary actions as ordering the blockade of southern ports, enlarging the army and navy, spending treasury funds without congressional authorization, closing the mails to treasonable correspondence, suspending habeas corpus, and creating special military tribunals in areas where courts were operating. Lincoln justified his actions on a doctrine of necessity and his oath of office; not until after the crisis of war and Lincoln's assassination did the Supreme Court rule some of these measures unconstitutional.

## Conducting Foreign Policy and Making War

Although presidential power has grown in domestic affairs, leading the nation in an increasingly complex and dangerous world has contributed the most to the enlargement of the executive branch powers. When key diplomatic and military decisions must be made in hours, even minutes, a president, as one individual with great authority, has an enormous advantage over a many-headed, continuously talking institution such as Congress. At times, national survival itself may require nothing less than rapid and unfettered presidential action.

Congress, along with the rest of the nation, recognizes that reality and has delegated broad and sweeping powers that allow presidents to act in foreign affairs with few congressional restraints. In the days immediately following September 11, 2001, the Senate voted 96–0 and the House 422–0 to give President Bush $40 billion to help rebuild lower Manhattan and the Pentagon and to launch his global war on terrorism. The Senate voted 98–0 to give the president virtually unlimited powers to prosecute the war against terrorism.

Other governmental bodies also defer to the president in foreign affairs. The executive's preeminence in this field has been recognized and legitimized by the Supreme Court, which enunciated its position in the 1936 case of *United States* v. *Curtiss-Wright*. Associate Justice George Sutherland's opinion provides the rationale for an active presidential role by distinguishing between foreign and domestic affairs and the powers apportioned to each. Although domestic power comes only from an express constitutional grant, he argued, in foreign affairs the president is sovereign. Sutherland concluded that the president's foreign policy power depended not on any constitutional provision but rather on national sovereignty. In sweeping language Sutherland stated, "In this vast external realm, with its important, complicated, delicate and manifold problems, the President alone has the power to speak or listen as a representative of the nation."[37]

**Presidential War Powers** In theory, then, both Court and Congress see the president as the dominant force in foreign policy. This perspective is bolstered by the president's constitutionally delegated role as commander in chief of the American armed forces. Presidents have used this military role in a variety of ways to achieve their policy ends and expand the power of their office.

Some presidents have left the actual conduct of war to professional military personnel, while using their role as commander in chief to set broad national and international policy. That policy often seemed far removed from urgent military matters. Abraham Lincoln, for instance, issued the Emancipation Proclamation "by virtue of the power vested in me as Commander-in-Chief of the Army and Navy" and "warranted by the Constitution upon military necessity." In short, Lincoln used his command over the military to abolish slavery. Although a worthy goal, his action represents a broad interpretation of the commander in chief's powers.

In times of crisis, other presidents have gone even farther than Lincoln. Following Japan's bombing of Pearl Harbor, Franklin Roosevelt ordered more than 100,000 West Coast Japanese Americans evacuated to internment camps, citing national security. He thus used his military powers to establish *de facto* concentration camps. Roosevelt also issued an ultimatum in a speech to Congress on September 7, 1942. Should legislators not repeal provisions within the Emergency Price Control Act, he stated that he would "accept the responsibility and act." Roosevelt's claim here is impressive—that acting in his capacity as commander in chief, he could free domestic policy from congressional restraint. Even more impressive, perhaps, is the fact that the American people strongly supported him on this matter.

Presidents have also used the commander-in-chief role to make war and expanded its reach through congressional delegation. Lyndon Johnson, for example, committed ground troops to Vietnam on the basis of a loosely worded congressional resolution. The 1964 Southeast Asia Resolution, remembered now as the Tonkin Gulf Resolution, stated, "The Congress approves and supports the determination of the President, as Commander in Chief, to take all necessary measures to repel any armed attack against the forces of the United States and to prevent further aggression." President Johnson later described the resolution as being like Grandma's nightshirt—it covered everything! And as we learn in Chapter 16, we now know that the Tonkin Gulf intelligence was skewed.[38]

Using his powers as commander in chief, Richard Nixon later ordered the Vietnam War expanded into Laos and Cambodia, neutral countries at the time. Hundreds of enemy sortie reports were falsified to justify the president's actions. Congress and the public were kept in the dark. The House Judiciary Committee considered an article of impeachment against Nixon that cited his deliberate misleading of Congress "concerning the existence, scope, and nature" of the American operation in Cambodia. This article was dropped, however, suggesting Congress's strong reluctance to curb presidential powers, as long as the president, even an unpopular one, appears to be acting as commander in chief.

Still, military power does not make the president a dictator, and various commanders in chief have been restrained by both Congress and the Supreme Court. In *Youngstown Sheet and Tube Company* v. *Sawyer* (1952), the Supreme Court struck down President Truman's seizure of the domestic steel industry. Truman claimed that his powers as commander in chief in wartime (the Korean War) allowed him to seize and run the steel mills to preserve the war effort. The Court ruled that only a pressing national emergency, which in its opinion did not exist at the time, could justify such a sweeping action in the domestic sphere without approval of Congress.[39]

Congress, too, has challenged presidents in military affairs. After all, the Constitution assigns Congress the power to declare war, order reprisals, raise and support armies, and provide for the common defense. Many legislators in the Vietnam War era, believing that the president had committed American forces to combat without appropriately consulting Congress, worked to reassert Congress's constitutional prerogatives. As a result, the War Powers Resolution was passed in 1973, over President Nixon's veto.[40]

Former White House correspondent Helen Thomas asks President Obama a question during the president's first news conference in the East Room at the White House on February 9, 2009. Sitting to the right of Thomas is Professor Martha Joynt Kumar, a preeminent scholar of presidential press relations, White House communications operations, and presidential transitions.

The resolution requires that the president "in every possible instance" report to Congress within 48 hours after committing U.S. troops to hostile action if no state of war has been declared. If Congress disagrees with the action, the troops must be removed within 90 days. Actually, the troops must be withdrawn within 60 days unless the president requests 30 additional days to ensure their safety. Congress can no longer stop the military commitment by *concurrent resolution* (a resolution passed by both houses in the same form).

The first test of the new War Powers Resolution occurred in May 1975, when President Gerald Ford ordered the marines and navy to rescue the U.S. merchant ship *Mayaguez* without prior consultation with members of Congress. The ship, carrying both civilian and military cargo, was seized by Cambodian ships for being in Cambodia's territorial waters. In his report to Congress, submitted *after* the troops had been withdrawn, President Ford cited both his inherent executive power and his authority as commander in chief.[41]

These examples illustrate that a president no longer needs a congressional declaration of war to send American troops into combat. Although the Constitution grants Congress the power "to declare War," history, practice, precedent, and popular expectation have given the president authority to "make war." Presidents have often ordered troop actions, leaving Congress with few options but to support them. Appropriations cutoffs expose legislators to charges of having stranded soldiers in the field. Perhaps these facts explain why presidents have committed troops abroad in dozens of combat situations, but Congress has declared war only five times.[42]

Chapter 16 discusses at length the road to war in Iraq and the justifications involved, but suffice it to say that many now see this as a presidential war of choice for Bush; meanwhile, facing the reality that, after a year in office, the conflict in Afghanistan had become Obama's war, President Obama dispatched 30,000 additional troops into the theater in 2009. In 2011, the president announced that 33,000 troops will be withdrawn from Afghanistan by the summer of 2012. President Obama also announced a complete draw down of troops in Iraq by the end of 2011. While removing troops from the wars started by his predecessor, Obama committed to a limited U.S. troop involvement in Libya which has raised questions about whether the president is in violation of the War Powers Act.

### THINKING CRITICALLY

How would U.S. foreign policy change if Congress was required to declare war before any troops could be committed to foreign soil? Would this requirement be feasible in today's international environment?

## THE CHALLENGES OF PRESIDENTIAL LEADERSHIP

### The Power to Persuade

5.6 *How does a modern president persuade both Congress and the public to go along with his or her agenda?*

President Lyndon Baines Johnson once said in a moment of frustration, "Don't talk to me about power. The only power I have is nuclear, and I can't use that." Johnson's point was that the presidency is a democratic office in a democratic republic, not an authoritarian office in a dictatorship. Presidents may command, especially in their role as commander in chief, but most often they attempt to persuade. And persuasion is much more difficult and time-consuming than ordering, as every president discovers.

The thesis that leadership in a democracy depends on the practice of persuasion lies at the heart of political scientist Richard Neustadt's influential book, *Presidential Power*.[43] In exercising power, Neustadt maintained that orders are not self-executing and presidents use up precious political capital trying to enforce unpopular commands. Many actors in the political system cannot be commanded; persuasion remains a president's most common tool for getting what he wants. How can presidents utilize their power of persuasion? The secret is to convince them that it is in their own self-interest to do what the president suggests. It helps if the president can give the necessary member of Congress or cabinet official something he or she wants; that is, the power to persuade is the power to bargain. By trading something of value, a president may be able to exert influence. This is precisely what President Obama was able to do when he needed support for his economic stimulus bill, providing stimulus dollars and projects for members whose support was needed for passage. It also helps to have an electoral mandate for change (see Table 5.4).

**Table 5.4** Presidential Election Mandates: *John Quincy Adams to Barack Obama*

| | | Popular Vote | | Electoral Vote | | |
|---|---|---|---|---|---|---|
| **President** | **Election** | **Percentage** | **Advantage** | **Percentage** | **Advantage** | **Difference** |
| John Quincy Adams | 1824 | — | — | 32.2% | –5.7% | — |
| Andrew Jackson | 1828 | 56.1% | 12.5% | 68.2 | 36.4 | 12.1% |
| | 1832 | 54.2 | 16.8 | 76.0 | 59.0 | 21.8 |
| Martin Van Buren | 1836 | 50.8 | 14.2 | 57.8 | 33.0 | 7.0 |
| William Henry Harrison | 1840 | 52.9 | 6.1 | 79.6 | 59.2 | 26.7 |
| James K. Polk | 1844 | 49.5 | 1.4 | 61.8 | 23.6 | 12.3 |
| Zachary Taylor | 1848 | 47.3 | 4.8 | 56.2 | 12.4 | 8.9 |
| Franklin Pierce | 1852 | 50.8 | 6.9 | 85.8 | 71.6 | 35.0 |
| James Buchanan | 1856 | 45.3 | 12.2 | 58.8 | 20.3 | 13.5 |
| Abraham Lincoln | 1860 | 39.9 | 10.4 | 59.4 | 35.6 | 19.5 |
| | 1864 | 55.1 | 10.2 | 90.6 | 81.6 | 35.5 |
| Ulysses S. Grant | 1868 | 52.7 | 5.4 | 72.8 | 45.6 | 20.1 |
| | 1872 | 55.6 | 11.8 | 81.9 | 63.8 | 26.3 |
| Rutherford B. Hayes | 1876 | 48.0 | –3.0 | 50.1 | 0.2 | 2.1 |
| James Garfield | 1880 | 48.3 | 0.1 | 58.0 | 16.0 | 9.7 |
| Grover Cleveland - I | 1884 | 48.9 | 0.7 | 54.6 | 9.2 | 5.7 |
| Benjamin Harrison | 1888 | 47.8 | –0.8 | 58.1 | 16.2 | 10.3 |
| Grover Cleveland - II | 1892 | 46.0 | 3.0 | 62.4 | 29.7 | 16.4 |
| William McKinley | 1896 | 51.1 | 5.3 | 61.0 | 21.4 | 9.9 |
| | 1900 | 51.7 | 6.2 | 65.3 | 30.6 | 13.6 |
| Theodore Roosevelt | 1904 | 56.4 | 18.8 | 70.6 | 41.2 | 14.2 |
| William Howard Taft | 1908 | 51.6 | 8.6 | 66.5 | 33.0 | 14.9 |

*(continued)*

**Table 5.4** *(continued)*

| President | Election | Popular Vote Percentage | Popular Vote Advantage | Electoral Vote Percentage | Electoral Vote Advantage | Difference |
|---|---|---|---|---|---|---|
| Woodrow Wilson | 1912 | 41.8 | 14.4 | 81.9 | 65.3 | 40.1 |
| | 1916 | 49.2 | 3.1 | 52.2 | 4.4 | 3.0 |
| Warren G. Harding | 1920 | 60.3 | 26.2 | 76.1 | 52.2 | 15.8 |
| Calvin Coolidge | 1924 | 54.0 | 25.2 | 71.9 | 46.3 | 17.9 |
| Herbert Hoover | 1928 | 58.2 | 17.4 | 83.6 | 67.2 | 25.4 |
| Franklin D. Roosevelt | 1932 | 57.4 | 17.8 | 88.9 | 77.8 | 31.5 |
| | 1936 | 60.8 | 24.3 | 98.5 | 97.0 | 37.7 |
| | 1940 | 54.7 | 9.9 | 84.6 | 69.2 | 29.9 |
| | 1944 | 53.4 | 7.5 | 81.4 | 62.8 | 28.0 |
| Harry S. Truman | 1948 | 49.5 | 4.4 | 57.1 | 21.5 | 7.6 |
| Dwight D. Eisenhower | 1952 | 54.9 | 10.5 | 83.2 | 66.4 | 28.3 |
| | 1956 | 57.4 | 15.4 | 86.1 | 72.4 | 28.7 |
| John F. Kennedy | 1960 | 49.7 | 0.2 | 56.4 | 15.6 | 6.7 |
| Lyndon B. Johnson | 1964 | 61.1 | 22.6 | 90.3 | 80.6 | 29.2 |
| Richard Nixon | 1968 | 43.4 | 0.7 | 55.9 | 20.4 | 12.5 |
| | 1972 | 60.7 | 23.2 | 96.7 | 93.5 | 36.0 |
| Jimmy Carter | 1976 | 50.1 | 2.1 | 55.2 | 10.6 | 5.1 |
| Ronald Reagan | 1980 | 50.7 | 9.7 | 90.9 | 81.8 | 40.2 |
| | 1984 | 58.8 | 18.2 | 97.6 | 95.2 | 38.8 |
| George H. W. Bush | 1988 | 53.4 | 7.8 | 79.2 | 58.6 | 25.8 |
| William J. Clinton | 1992 | 43.0 | 5.6 | 68.8 | 37.6 | 25.8 |
| | 1996 | 49.2 | 8.5 | 70.4 | 40.8 | 21.2 |
| George W. Bush | 2000 | 47.9 | −0.5 | 50.4 | 1.0 | 2.5 |
| | 2004 | 50.7 | 2.4 | 53.2 | 6.5 | 2.5 |
| Barack Obama | 2008 | 52.9 | 7.2 | 67.8 | 35.6 | 14.9 |

*Source:* Gerhard Peters, "Presidential Election Mandates," *The American Presidency Project*, John T. Woolley and Gerhard Peters, eds. (Santa Barbara: University of California, 1999–2009), available at www.presidency.ucsb.edu/data/mandates.php. Used with permission. Obama updated by authors.

## Going Public

Given the singular nature of the office, a president can use modern means of communication to curry public support for his or her policies. As individuals in an age of personality, the president is in a position to manipulate the media to enhance his or her reputation, which most members of Congress cannot do.

During the early years of the Republic, presidents promoted themselves through the prevailing means of communication: public speeches, pamphlets, and articles. Although nearly all of the early presidents had some experience in mass persuasion, it was by no means considered vital to the office.

Not until the 20th-century presidency of Theodore Roosevelt, in fact, did the presidency ascend to what Roosevelt called "the bully pulpit." Woodrow Wilson later courted public support for his League of Nations. He failed in that endeavor, but the presidency thereafter became a national theater, with the chief executive the most visible actor on the stage. In the 1930s, Franklin D. Roosevelt would use his skills as a master of public communication to increase the power of the national government and, in particular, the presidency. He did this in part by personalizing the office. Listening to his "fireside chats" on radio, people felt that they knew and understood the president as a person, not just as a chief executive. What Roosevelt began, other presidents continued. Although varying widely in their skill as communicators, no president since Roosevelt has attempted to govern without also attempting to create and maintain mass support.

The chief characteristic of the personal presidency is that it derives power directly from the people at the expense of Congress and party. Presidents have long recognized the advantages of what political scientist Samuel Kernell calls **going public**, promoting themselves and their policies to the American people. The strategy includes televised press conferences, prime-time addresses, White House ceremonies, and satellite broadcasts. Rather than bargain directly with Congress, presidents appeal to the American public, hoping to generate popular pressure for their policy aims.

Going public may seem an easier strategy than bargaining or negotiation, but it is far riskier. Members of Congress may feel ill disposed toward a president who bypasses them and goes directly to the people. Going public thus risks the often tenuous lines of communication between the White House and Capitol Hill. Generally, negotiators must be prepared to compromise, and bargaining proceeds best behind closed doors. By fixing a firm presidential position on an issue through public posturing, however, the strategy of going public may serve to harden a president's bargaining position and make later compromise with other politicians difficult.

President Obama's message management has been a model of going public. His communication team has been very clever at developing ways of presenting him in different venues, such as the *Tonight Show,* a major network prime-time series looking behind the scenes of the Obama White House, and on ESPN to showcase his NCAA brackets. The White House has maximized the president's availability to gain extensive coverage. The president also communicates with the younger generation through weekly addresses on YouTube, he has his own Facebook page, and is an active Twitter user—holding a Twitter Town Hall and even sending live Tweets during the 2011 Women's World Cup final. Using the president as "salesman in chief" is at the heart of the administration's communication strategy, although it does raise the danger of overexposure.

The challenge of presidential leadership is how to govern in a system characterized by limited structural support, limited room for political maneuver, an emphasis on quick results and constant pressure for something new, a constant scrutiny of both the person and the politics of the president, and ever-escalating expectations of the office. In many ways, the president's job is an impossible one. Political scientists Thomas Cronin and Michael Genovese have provided a handy list of "presidential paradoxes" that captures the contradictory nature of these many roles (see Table 5.5).

**QUICK REVIEW**

Going Public

- Allows presidents to promote themselves and their policies to the American people.
- Involves use of televised press conferences, prime-time addresses, White House ceremonies, and satellite broadcasts.
- Enables executive to appeal to the American public to generate pressure for their policy aims.
- May complicate the often-tenuous lines of communication between the White House and Capitol Hill.
- May harden a president's bargaining position and make later compromise with other politicians difficult.

## THE INSTITUTIONALIZED PRESIDENCY

5.7 *How has the presidential staff grown over time, and how do those who serve the president assist in the day-to-day duties of the office?*

The bureaucratic aspects of the president's job are daunting. One individual, the president, is expected to manage both a permanent staff and a national government of about 2 million employees.[44]

**going public**
Actions presidents take to promote themselves and their policies to the American people.

**Table 5.5** Paradoxes of the Presidency

| |
|---|
| **Paradox 1** Americans demand powerful, popular presidential leadership that solves the nation's problems. Yet we are inherently suspicious of strong centralized leadership and the abuse of power. Thus we place significant limits on the president's powers. |
| **Paradox 2** We yearn for the democratic "common person" and, simultaneously, a leader who is uncommon, charismatic, heroic, and visionary. |
| **Paradox 3** We want a decent, just, caring, and compassionate president, yet we also admire a cunning, guileful, and—on occasions that warrant it—even a ruthless, manipulative president. |
| **Paradox 4** We admire the "above politics" nonpartisan or bipartisan approach, and yet the presidency is perhaps the most political office in the American system, which requires a creative entrepreneurial master politician. |
| **Paradox 5** We want a president who can unify diverse people and interests; however, the job requires taking firm stands, making unpopular or controversial decisions that necessarily upset and divide. |
| **Paradox 6** We expect our presidents to provide bold, visionary, innovative, programmatic leadership, and at the same time to respond pragmatically to the will of public opinion majorities. That is to say, we expect presidents to lead and to follow, and to exercise "democratic leadership." |
| **Paradox 7** Americans want powerful, self-confident presidential leadership. Yet we are inherently suspicious of leaders who view themselves as infallible and above criticism. |
| **Paradox 8** What it takes to become president may not be what is needed to govern the nation. |
| **Paradox 9** The presidency is sometimes too strong, yet at other times too weak. |
| To govern successfully, presidents must manage these paradoxes, and must balance a variety of competing demands and expectations. |

*Source:* Thomas Cronin and Eugene Genovese, *The Paradoxes of the American Presidency* (New York: Oxford University Press, 1998, 2009), p. 4, available at http://spot.colorado.edu/∼mcguire/presparadox.htm.

## The White House Office

Closest to the president are those who work in the White House, at 1600 Pennsylvania Avenue NW, Washington, DC, where the president both lives and works. The first family sleeps upstairs; the president works downstairs in the West Wing Oval Office. Presidential staff members also work downstairs in both the East and West wings. The president's chief lieutenants operate nearby in the West Wing. Also located in the West Wing are the Situation Room, the Oval Office, the National Security Council staff, the vice president's office, assistants to the president, and the Cabinet Room.

All presidential assistants in the White House tread a thin line between the power they derive from being close to the president and their actual role as assistants and underlings. Jack Valenti, a special assistant to President Johnson from 1963 to 1966, explains the temptations:

> *You sit next to the Sun King and you bask in his rays, and you have those three magic words, "the President wants." All of a sudden you have power unimagined by you before you got in that job. And if you don't watch out, you begin to believe that it is your splendid intellect, your charm and your insights into the human condition that give you all this power. . . . The arrogance sinks deeper into their veins than they think possible. What it does after a while is breed a kind of insularity that keeps you from being subject to the same fits of insecurity that most human beings have. Because you very seldom are ever turned down. You are seen in Washington. There are stories in* Newsweek *and* Time *about how important you are. I'm telling you, this is like mainlining heroin. And while you are exercising it, it is so blinding and dazzling that you forget, literally forget, that it is borrowed and transitory power.*[45]

The size of the staff has increased with the growth of government. As presidents are expected to solve more and more problems, the number of specialists on the White House staff has come to look like "a veritable index of American society," in political scientist Thomas Cronin's words.[46] These men and women come from every imaginable background. Because their loyalty is solely to the president and not to an administrative agency, they seem more trustworthy to the president than cabinet members or high-level officials from the civil service. The president therefore puts them to work running the everyday operations of the presidency. White House staff members often end up usurping the policy-making power normally held by cabinet secretaries, their staffs, and the staffs of various independent executive agencies.

**The Chief of Staff** The White House **chief of staff** is now the president's *de facto* top aide. Often earning a reputation as assistant president, this individual is responsible for White House operations and acts as gatekeeper to the president. The chief of staff also plays a key role in policy making. During the Eisenhower years, Chief of Staff Sherman Adams was so influential that the following joke became popular. Question: "Wouldn't it be awful if Ike died, then we'd have Nixon as president?" Response: "But it would be even worse if Sherman Adams died. Then Eisenhower would be president." In like manner, H. R. Haldeman, Nixon's chief of staff, was once described as "an extension of the President."[47] When Barack Obama named Congressman Rahm Emmanuel as chief of staff, most observers understood that Emmanuel would exercise great influence both inside the White House as well as on the Hill. When Rahm Emmanuel left the White House to become mayor of Chicago, President Obama brought Bill Daley into the position of chief of staff.

## The Executive Office of the President

This title is somewhat misleading. The federal government has no single executive office building. Instead, the **Executive Office of the President (EOP)** consists of staff units that serve the president but are located away from the White House, such as the National Security Council, the Council of Economic Advisers, and the Office of Management and Budget, among others. The Executive Office of the President was created and expanded to help a 20th-century president deal with managing a modern government.

**The National Security Council** The National Security Council (NSC) was established in 1947, and its formal membership consists of the president, vice president, and secretaries of defense and state. The special assistant to the president for national security affairs is the council's principal supervisory officer. The NSC advises the president on all aspects of domestic, foreign, and military policy that relate to national security.

**The Council of Economic Advisers** The Council of Economic Advisers (CEA), a product of the Employment Act of 1946, gave the president professional, institutionalized, economic staff resources. Today, the CEA is responsible for forecasting national economic trends, making economic analyses for the president, and helping to prepare the president's annual economic report to Congress. The CEA chair is appointed by the president with the advice and consent of Congress. The recently created National Economic Council is responsible for coordinating high-priority economic policy matters for the president.

Although the CEA is a valuable resource, the president actually receives most economic advice from a group referred to as the *troika*—a functional division of labor among the secretary of the treasury (revenue estimates), the CEA (the private economy), and the Office of Management and Budget (federal expenditures). When the chair of the Federal Reserve Board is included in the group, it is referred to as the *quadriad.*

**Office of Management and Budget** Observers of American politics have long recognized the central role that the Office of Management and Budget (OMB) plays. The OMB's primary responsibility is to prepare and implement the

**chief of staff**
The president's top aide.

**Executive Office of the President (EOP)**
Created in 1939, this office contains all staff units that support the president in administrative duties.

President Obama meets with his cabinet for the first time on April 20, 2009. At the session, Obama ordered his agency heads to identify and cut a collective $100 million in administrative costs from federal programs in the federal budget.

budget, but the office also evaluates federal program performance. It reviews management processes within the executive branch, prepares executive orders and proclamations, plans the development of federal statistical services, and advises the president on the activities of all federal departments. The OMB also helps promote the president's legislative agenda with Congress. As the most highly developed coordinating and review unit in the Executive Office, the OMB is also the most powerful. It acts as the central institutional mechanism for imprinting (some would say inflicting) presidential will over the government.[48]

The OMB began as the Bureau of the Budget (BOB) in 1921, keeping track of the executive branch's books. Over the years, BOB's powers continued to grow until, in 1970, a major executive office reorganization transformed BOB into OMB, with greatly expanded powers. Given its array of responsibilities and powers, OMB's influence now extends into every nook and cranny of the executive branch.

## The Cabinet

**Cabinet** officers act as a link between the president and the rest of the American political system. Congress creates cabinet departments, giving them specific legal responsibilities and political mandates. Department heads are confirmed by the Senate and are frequently called to testify before congressional committees.

A cabinet is an unusual institution. It is mentioned in neither the Constitution nor in statutory law, yet it has become a permanent part of the presidency. The framers considered but eventually rejected adding a council of any kind to the executive. Thus, the cabinet as such does not legally exist. Nevertheless, the idea of a cabinet surfaced early. Newspapers began using the term in the 1790s to describe the relationship between President Washington and his executive officers.

In its most formal meaning, the word *cabinet* refers to the secretaries of the major departments of the bureaucracy and any other officials the president designates (such as the OMB director). An informal distinction is often made between the inner and outer cabinet. Members of the *inner cabinet* are the most visible and enjoy more direct access to the president. Typically, this inner cabinet is composed of the secretaries of state, defense, treasury, and justice. These being the most powerful positions, presidents tend to staff them with close political allies.

Table 5.6 shows President Barack Obama's cabinet nearing the end of his third year in office.

**cabinet**
Group of presidential advisers, including secretaries of the major bureaucracy departments and any other officials the president designates.

**vice president**
The second-highest elected official in the United States.

## The Vice Presidency

The second highest elected official in the United States, the **vice president,** has few significant constitutional responsibilities. Indeed, the only such powers actually assigned to the vice president are to preside over the Senate (except in cases of impeachment) and to cast a vote when the Senate is deadlocked. Most vice presidents have shunned that job; few wish to spend all day listening to senators talk. The vice president's most important job is the one Americans

**Table 5.6** The Obama Cabinet

| In order of succession to the presidency: |
|---|
| **Vice President of the United States**<br>Joseph R. Biden |
| **Department of State**<br>Secretary Hillary Rodham Clinton |
| **Department of the Treasury**<br>Secretary Timothy F. Geithner |
| **Department of Defense**<br>Secretary Leon E. Panetta |
| **Department of Justice**<br>Attorney General Eric H. Holder Jr. |
| **Department of the Interior**<br>Secretary Kenneth L. Salazar |
| **Department of Agriculture**<br>Secretary Thomas J. Vilsack |
| **Department of Commerce**<br>Secretary Gary F. Locke |
| **Department of Labor**<br>Secretary Hilda L. Solis |
| **Department of Health and Human Services**<br>Secretary Kathleen Sebelius |
| **Department of Housing and Urban Development**<br>Secretary Shaun L. S. Donovan |
| **Department of Transportation**<br>Secretary Raymond L. LaHood |
| **Department of Energy**<br>Secretary Steven Chu |
| **Department of Education**<br>Secretary Arne Duncan |
| **Department of Veterans Affairs**<br>Secretary Eric K. Shinseki |
| **Department of Homeland Security**<br>Secretary Janet A. Napolitano |
| The following positions have the status of Cabinet-rank: |
| **Council of Economic Advisers**<br>Chair Alan Krueger |
| **Environmental Protection Agency**<br>Administrator Lisa P. Jackson |
| **Office of Management and Budget**<br>Director Jacob L. Lew |
| **U.S. Trade Representative**<br>Ambassador Ronald Kirk |
| **U.S. Ambassador to the United Nations**<br>Ambassador Susan Rice |
| **White House Chief of Staff**<br>Bill Daley |

*Source:* The White House. http://www.whitehouse.gov/administration/cabinet.

**Table 5.7** Presidential Line of Succession

1. Vice President
2. Speaker of the House of Representatives
3. Senate President Pro Tempore
4. Secretary of State
5. Secretary of the Treasury
6. Secretary of Defense
7. Attorney General
8. Secretary of the Interior
9. Secretary of Agriculture
10. Secretary of Commerce
11. Secretary of Labor
12. Secretary of Health and Human Services
13. Secretary of Housing and Urban Development
14. Secretary of Transportation
15. Secretary of Energy
16. Secretary of Education
17. Secretary of Veterans Affairs

*Source:* The White House. http://www.whitehouse.gov/government/cabinet.html.

hope he never takes—succeeding to the presidency in case of death, resignation, or removal. (Table 5.7 outlines the line of succession to the presidency.) As Woodrow Wilson once quipped, "There is very little to be said about the vice-president. . . . His importance consists in the fact that he may cease to be vice-president."

Vice President Joseph Biden and Iraqi Prime Minister Nouri al-Maliki meet in Baghdad on July 3, 2009. Biden made his first visit to Iraq as Vice President after being appointed to oversee the administration's Iraqi policy. In December of 2011, Biden made his 16th visit to Iraq to mark the end of American troop presence in the country.

## APPROACHING
### Contemporary Issues in Democracy

### Reconsidering the Intent of the Framers: No Term Limits on a President

**ISSUE:** What if the Twenty-second Amendment was repealed and a president could serve an unlimited number of terms, returning to the framers' original design for the executive? How would this change affect the democratic nature of the presidency?

**Question 1:**

If most presidents prior to the adoption of the Twenty-second Amendment sought to serve only two terms, why did some feel it necessary to put term limits in place for the presidency?

**Question 2:**

The Twenty-second Amendment might lead a president in his second term, who is no longer beholden to the public, to use the powers of the presidency to advance the needs of an elite group of supporters at the expense of other citizens. Would repealing the Twenty-second Amendment solve this problem of an unbeholden president?

**Question 3:**

Which presidential powers that you have learned about in this chapter might a lame-duck president (one approaching the end of a second term) use in a way he would not if up for reelection?

The actual work of the vice president ends up being whatever the president decides it will be. In recent years, presidents have bestowed more authority than they have removed. The growth in their own responsibilities has led them to turn to the vice president for help. Thus, the office of vice president, like that of the president, is becoming institutionalized. The vice presidential staff has increased significantly in size and largely parallels the president's, with domestic and foreign policy specialists, speech writers, congressional liaisons, and press secretaries.

Recent occupants of the office have been deeply involved in substantive matters of policy. President Reagan appointed George H. W. Bush to lead the administration's crisis management team. Al Gore Jr. led President Clinton's ambitious program to "reinvent government" by downsizing the bureaucracy, streamlining procedures, updating systems, and eliminating certain subsidies and programs. But no vice president has been as powerful as Dick Cheney in the George W. Bush administration, who was one of the strongest advocates for promoting an expansive view of presidential power. Vice President Biden plays an active role, becoming a close confidant of President Obama on a wide range of issues, including the economic stimulus package, presidential appointments, debt-ceiling and deficit negotiations, and the U.S. military operations in Iraq and Afghanistan. Perhaps most significant is Biden's stated intent to scale back the powers of the vice presidency from those of his immediate predecessor.

### THINKING CRITICALLY

The vice president is the only other political actor, other than the president, elected by a nationwide constituency. Given this, do you think the official powers of the office should be expanded? If so, what powers and responsibilities should be vested in the vice presidency?

## Summary

5.1 *How did the framers design a system with an energetic executive to forward the democratic will and, at the same time, protect against anti-democratic tendencies of a single executive?*

- The great paradox of the presidency is that no other office in America simultaneously unites so much power and purpose to help Americans approach their democratic potential and also poses the most serious threats to the ideals of democracy.
- With a complicated system of separation and distribution of power, the framers of our government designed the presidency to encourage the presidency's potential for energy and to minimize its potential for tyranny.
- This distribution of powers has altered over time in favor of the president through formal grants of congressionally delegated power, court-sanctioned expansions of power, and popularly based assumptions of power.

5.2 *Why were the framers vague in the description of presidential powers described in the Constitution, and how did this vagueness shape the powers of the president over time?*

- The Constitution has remarkably little to say on the president's powers, and this brevity reflects the framers' uncertainty on the subject. The framers trusted that George Washington would establish precedents for the office.
- What the framers did write into the Constitution can be categorized in two ways: (a) clear, simple language that gives the president specific powers and (b) broad powers, written in vague language, and subject to individual interpretation. This vague language, open to interpretation, is largely responsible for the expansion of the powers of the president.
- The framers designed the presidency to (a) be centered on one individual, (b) be selected by an independent body of individual electors, (c) serve a fixed term of office with the possibility of reelection, (d) allow for removal in extreme circumstances through impeachment, (e) limit the power of Congress through the veto power, and (f) take independent action in the executive arena.
- The framers gave the president both explicit as well as implied powers: (a) the veto power, (b) the appointment power, (c) the treaty power, (d) executive privilege (not explicit), (e) the power to pardon, (f) the power to convene Congress, and (g) the power of commander in chief of the armed forces.
- The powers of the president have expanded far beyond those explicitly listed in the constitution.

5.3 *How do the roles and responsibilities of the presidency create the paradoxes of the presidency, and how do these paradoxes make it difficult for any president to succeed?*

- The president performs a variety of roles, both formal and informal. Among these are chief of state, commander in chief, crisis leader, chief diplomat, chief legislator, chief executive, moral leader, and party leader. The president is also viewed as the manager of the nation's prosperity.
- Many of these roles conflict with one another, which makes it impossible for the president to live up to all the expectations of his or her office. These conflicting roles create presidential paradoxes.

5.4 *What is the key difference between the constructionist and stewardship view of the presidency, and why have modern presidents viewed themselves as stewards?*

- Activist presidents go beyond the powers prescribed in the Constitution when they believe extraordinary action is required; this view of the presidency is referred to as *stewardship.*
- *Constructionist* presidents differ from stewardship presidents in that they exercise no powers other than those expressly granted by the Constitution or an act of Congress.
- Americans have sided with the stewardship view of presidential power. They expect dynamic leadership from the office. Almost no president regarded as great by either historians or the public has adopted a passive, constructionist approach to the job.

5.5 *How have the powers of the presidency expanded over time, and what factors might explain this expansion?*

- The theory of inherent powers holds that the Constitution grants broad authority to the executive during times of national emergency.
- Both Thomas Jefferson and Abraham Lincoln argued that they could greatly expand the powers of the presidency during times of national crisis.
- Although presidential power has grown in domestic affairs, leading the nation in an increasingly complex and dangerous world has contributed the most to the enlargement of the executive branch powers.
- The powers of the president in our day derive not merely from an increase in technical powers available to the office, but in an increasing likelihood that occupants of the White House will be strong, activist individuals.

5.6 *How does a modern president persuade both Congress and the public to go along with his or her agenda?*

- Advances in communications technology have increased the president's influence by enabling the president to reach ever larger numbers of people more quickly. Modern presidents promote their policies to the people through televised press conferences, prime-time speeches, and the like.
- One view of the presidency holds that the president's real power derives from the ability to persuade and bargain. Another view places more emphasis on the formal powers of the presidency but does not downplay the importance of leadership skills. As a result, modern presidents often go public, that is, attempt to persuade

the people to put pressure on their legislators in support of the president's policies.

5.7 *How has the presidential staff grown over time, and how do those who serve the president assist in the day-to-day duties of the office?*

- Since the Brownlow Commission, the president's staff has grown steadily and staff members have come to hold important powers. The White House chief of staff is responsible for White House operations but also plays a key role in policy making. The special assistant for national security affairs may also have considerable influence. The Office of Management and Budget plays a central role in executive policy because it is responsible for evaluating the performance of federal programs as well as budget formation.
- Cabinet members include secretaries of the major federal departments and any other officials designated by the president. The inner cabinet consists of the secretaries of state, defense, treasury, and justice. Cabinet officials are responsible for running their departments as well as advising the president on matters of policy.
- In the event of the death, resignation, or removal of the president, the vice president succeeds to the presidency. In recent administrations, vice presidents have become increasingly involved in substantive matters of policy.

## Key Terms

cabinet, 176
chief of staff, 175
constructionist, 166
executive agreement, 157
Executive Office of the President (EOP), 175
executive privilege, 158
going public, 173
inherent powers, 167
pocket veto, 154
signing statements, 155
stewardship, 166
treaties, 157
veto, 154
vice president, 176

## Test Yourself Chapter 5

1. Which of the following is *not* one of the key principles on which the framers based the presidency?
   a. The president could serve no more than two 4-year terms.
   b. The president could be removed from office only through an impeachment and removal process.
   c. The office of chief executive would be vested in one person.
   d. The president would have the power of the veto.

2. Which of the following is *not* a constitutional requirement for the eligibility of the president?
   a. The president must be at least 35 years of age.
   b. The president must be a resident of the United States for at least the last 14 years.
   c. The president must be a Christian.
   d. The president must be a natural-born citizen of the United States.

3. The executive veto permits the president to
   a. control the flow of legislation.
   b. determine which party in Congress will become the majority.
   c. defend against legislative excesses.
   d. nullify Supreme Court decisions.

4. The appointment power of the president
   a. requires no check from the other branches of government.
   b. is always subject to approval from the House of Representatives.
   c. allows the president to staff the executive branch with people who will help promote his or her policies.
   d. is not an important power of the president.

5. On average, presidents appoint how many Supreme Court Justices over their time in office?
   a. 5.
   b. 9.
   c. 1.
   d. 2.

6. Who was the first president to invoke what has come to be known as executive privilege?
   a. George Washington.
   b. James Madison.
   c. James Polk.
   d. Andrew Johnson.

7. The "president as party leader" role
   a. leads presidents to actively promote their own party's agenda.
   b. can either help or hurt the president's party's electoral fortunes.
   c. can lead to the president being perceived as narrowly partisan rather than the leader of the entire nation.
   d. All of the above.

8. The contradictory and conflicting nature of the roles and expectations of the presidency
   a. create the paradoxes of the presidency.
   b. require the media to ignore some actions of the president while focusing on others.
   c. lead to impeachment charges being filed against most of the modern presidents.
   d. make it easier for the president to defend against criticisms of hypocrisy.

**9.** Theodore Roosevelt
- a. was considered the first lame-duck president.
- b. put forth the constructionist view of presidential power.
- c. believed the president had no moral duty to serve popular interests.
- d. had an activist, expansionist view of presidential powers.

**10.** The constructionist theory
- a. expands the power of Congress.
- b. expands the power of the president.
- c. limits the power of Congress.
- d. limits the power of the president.

**11.** The theory of inherent powers
- a. argues that the Constitution allows the president to possess extraordinary powers during emergency conditions.
- b. is responsible for the weakening of presidents over time.
- c. has been supported by all the U.S. presidents.
- d. was first articulated by George W. Bush after 9/11.

**12.** Although the chief executive is also commander in chief,
- a. the president cannot, at any time, make war without consent of Congress.
- b. the president actually has very little involvement in military decisions.
- c. presidential military power can be restrained by both Congress and the Supreme Court.
- d. the president must give formal approval on all military decisions.

**13.** In the case of *United States* v. *Curtiss-Wright,* the Supreme Court ruled that in the area of foreign affairs
- a. the United Nations is supreme.
- b. the president is sovereign.
- c. Congress should have the last word.
- d. the Court itself possesses the ultimate authority.

**14.** Congress passed the War Powers Resolution of 1973 in response to
- a. the inability of presidents to react quickly in military matters.
- b. President Nixon's actions during the Vietnam War.
- c. the Supreme Court's decision in the 1952 case of *Youngstown Sheet and Tube Company* v. *Sawyer.*
- d. the internment of Japanese American citizens following the bombing of Pearl Harbor.

**15.** When going public, presidents
- a. speak directly to the American people about a policy matter.
- b. hope pressure will be applied to members of Congress to support the president's policies.
- c. risk alienating members of Congress, thereby making it more difficult to bargain.
- d. All of the above.

**16.** Which of the following proposed that the chief executive have a full-time staff?
- a. The Congressional Budget Office.
- b. The Joint Chief of Staff.
- c. The House Rules Committee.
- d. The Brownlow Commission.

**17.** The size of the White House staff has increased because
- a. the executive budget is larger.
- b. the size and complexity of government has increased.
- c. the size of Congress has increased.
- d. the first lady has assumed more responsibilities.

**18.** The National Security Council was established to
- a. advise the president on all issues, domestic and foreign, that relate to national security.
- b. act as a liaison between the president and foreign leaders.
- c. act as a liaison between the president and state governors.
- d. assume command of the military during times of national crises.

**19.** The ____________________ is now the president's *de facto* top aide.
- a. vice president.
- b. national security adviser.
- c. White House press secretary.
- d. White House chief of staff.

**20.** The vice president's only constitutional powers are to
- a. preside over the Senate and cast a vote when the Senate is deadlocked.
- b. serve as majority leader of the House and head the White House staff.
- c. sign unimportant legislation and attend funerals of dignitaries.
- d. serve as majority leader of the Senate.

**ANSWERS**
**1.** a, **2.** c, **3.** c, **4.** c, **5.** d, **6.** a, **7.** d, **8.** a, **9.** d, **10.** d, **11.** a,
**12.** c, **13.** b, **14.** b, **15.** d, **16.** d, **17.** b, **18.** a, **19.** d, **20.** b

# The Judiciary

# 6

## Chapter Outline

**Introduction:**
*The Courts and Democracy*

- The Origins and Development of Judicial Power
- The Organization of the American Court System
- Court Appointments: The Process and the Politics
- How the Supreme Court Operates
- Analyzing Supreme Court Decisions
- The Court's Independence in Approaching Democracy

## Learning Objectives

6.1 What is the source of the Supreme Court's constitutional and judicial review power, and how democratic is it?

6.2 What is the basis for the Court's independence, and does it preserve democracy?

6.3 How is the American legal system organized, how does it operate, and what is the Supreme Court's role within it?

6.4 How are Supreme Court justices and federal court judges appointed and confirmed?

6.5 How much can presidents shape the decision making of the Supreme Court and the federal bench through their appointments, and how representative are these courts?

6.6 How does the Supreme Court operate as an institution, and does it operate in a democratic fashion?

6.7 What influences justices in deciding cases, and how can we understand their judicial theories?

6.8 What roles do political ideology and orientation toward judicial power play in judicial decision making?

6.9 What roles do personal factors and voting bloc balance play in understanding how judicial decisions are made?

6.10 How does the question of whether a decision is implemented affect whether a justice leads or follows public opinion, thus advancing or checking democratic will?

In 2010, liberal John Paul Stevens, who was then completing his near record 35th year on the Court, announced that he would be retiring. It was a pivotal time for the direction of the Court. Despite six Republican presidential appointments since 1986, the Court had only just begun to tip to the conservative side since the seating of Samuel Alito in early 2006. President Obama's appointment of the first Hispanic to the Court, federal court of appeals judge Sonia Sotomayor, replaced centrist liberal David Souter in mid-2009, and his appointment of Solicitor General Elena Kagan replaced Stevens. While these appointments did not tip the ideological direction of the Court because it was a trade of two liberal votes for two departing liberal voters, it certainly prevented the Court from becoming more conservative.

Supreme Court Justice Anthony Kennedy, from California, who has served since 1987, holds in his hands the direction of the Court with his swing vote after the retirement of fellow conservative moderate, Sandra Day O'Connor. He has the potential by his decisions to turn the "Roberts Court" into the "Kennedy Court" with his vote in key 5–4 decisions.

The Supreme Court, since 1987, has been closely balanced. From 1994 to 2006, Justice Sandra Day O'Connor was the pivotal fifth vote in 5–4 decisions 146 times. In a strategy that constitutional law expert Cass Sunstein calls "judicial minimalism," O'Connor created a legal test in each specific case and used it to incrementally change the law with her vote by giving something to both sides, thus producing the Rehnquist Court's mixed political and legal legacy. However, President George W. Bush's appointments of two conservatives, Chief Justice John Roberts and Associate Justice Samuel Alito, appeared to shift the Court to the right in 2006. The only thing that prevented the Court from moving further to the right was Anthony Kennedy's decision to step into O'Connor's role as the "swing justice," shifting the decisions alternately left and right with his vote. By the end of the 2006–2007 term, Kennedy was the only justice who had voted in the majority for all 24 of the Court's 5–4 decisions. These numbers continued during the 2010–2011 Court term, as Kennedy provided the pivotal fifth vote in 14 of the 16 5–4 cases that year. This has led the *New York Times* to report that it is now "Justice Kennedy's court."[1] A full understanding of the Supreme Court, though, will help you learn why change on the Court is only one Obama appointment, or a 2012 win by the Republicans in the presidential election, away.

# INTRODUCTION
# THE COURTS AND DEMOCRACY

6.1 *What is the source of the Supreme Court's constitutional and judicial review power, and how democratic is it?*

One of the ironies of American democracy is that the Supreme Court, which interprets the Constitution, is the least democratic of the three branches of government. Operating in total secrecy, nine unelected, life-tenured jurists sit at the top of a complex legal structure designed to limit rather than encourage appeals, and they have almost total power to interpret the law. But as we will see, despite its undemocratic nature, in the past 70 years the Court has actually helped expand and protect the rights of Americans. As a result, the Court has helped America approach democracy.

Nearly all issues that make their way to the Supreme Court begin in the lower federal courts or state judicial systems. The right of state courts and federal courts to disagree with each other makes necessary a single Supreme Court to resolve those differences.

In this chapter we examine the Supreme Court's developing powers and the organization of the American court system, appointment of justices, and means by which cases are appealed to and then decided by the Supreme Court. We also look at how judges arrive at decisions and, perhaps most important, how those decisions affect both public policy and democracy.

## THE ORIGINS AND DEVELOPMENT OF JUDICIAL POWER

Of the three branches of government created by the framers of the Constitution, the judiciary is the least clearly defined, both in its organization and in the nature of its powers. Instead, the Court was left to define the nature of its power through its own rulings.

### Creating the "Least Dangerous Branch"

The framers outlined the nature of the federal judicial branch in Article III of the Constitution: "The judicial Power of the United States, shall be vested in one supreme Court, and in such inferior Courts as the Congress may from time to time ordain and establish." As you can see, the framers were vague about court structure and about how powerful they wanted the courts to be. And in establishing only a Supreme Court, they left it to Congress to design a lower federal court system.

Neither did the framers clearly define the jurisdiction, or sphere of authority, of the federal courts. Article III establishes that the Supreme Court and the lower federal courts shall decide all legal disputes of a federal nature or those arising under the Constitution, U.S. law, and treaties. In cases such as those involving disputes between or among states of the union or involving foreign ambassadors, the Supreme Court will have **original jurisdiction;** that is, it will be the first court to hear the case. For all other disputes—such as those involving the United States as a party, admiralty or maritime claims, disputes between citizens of two or more different states, and between a citizen and a state—the Court will hear cases on **appellate jurisdiction,** or after the matter has been argued in and decided by a lower federal or state court.

**original jurisdiction**
The authority of a court to be the first to hear a case.

**appellate jurisdiction**
The authority of a court to hear a case on appeal after it has been argued in and decided by a lower federal or state court.

Although they did not specify the full extent of the Supreme Court's powers, the framers designed the judiciary to be the least influential and weakest of the three branches of government. Some framers believed that in a representative government, the courts should have little power because they have no explicitly political or representative role. Alexander Hamilton made this argument in *The Federalist*, no. 78: "The judiciary . . . will always be the least dangerous to the political rights of the Constitution. . . . The judiciary . . . has no influence over either the sword or the purse . . . [and it] may be truly said to have neither FORCE nor WILL, but merely judgment."[2]

The framers left it to Congress to be more specific about the organization and jurisdiction of the judiciary. In the Judiciary Act of 1789, Congress established a three-tiered system of federal courts, consisting of district or trial courts, appellate courts, and one Supreme Court. The act also defined more fully the jurisdiction of the Supreme Court, granting it, among other things, the power to review state court rulings that reject federal claims.

Still, the Supreme Court remained weak, and often it had no cases to decide. Chief Justice John Jay, who presided from 1789 to 1795, was so distressed by the "intolerable" lack of prestige and power of his job that he quit to take a better one—as governor of New York. But the relative weakness of the Court changed in 1803 with the decision in *Marbury* v. *Madison.*[3]

## *Marbury* v. *Madison:* The Source of Judicial Power

When the Federalist Party lost the election of 1800, outgoing president John Adams made several last-minute political moves. With the help of a lame-duck Congress that passed two judiciary acts and confirmed judicial appointments in the Senate, Adams tried to pack the federal courts with appointments from his own party by issuing several commissions the night before leaving office. When the incoming Jefferson administration denied one of those commissions—the appointment of William Marbury as justice of the peace for the District of Columbia—Marbury sued for his post. The case became the landmark ***Marbury* v. *Madison*** decision.

This case tested the Supreme Court's power to order federal officials to carry out their official duties—in this case to deliver a judicial commission—a power given to the Court by the Judiciary Act of 1789. Chief Justice John Marshall, who presided from 1801 to 1835, himself an Adams midnight appointee, wrote the Court's opinion. After conceding that the commissions were valid, he then proceeded to move beyond the issue to review the constitutionality of the Judiciary Act of 1789. Since no power to review the constitutionality of any law can be found in the Constitution, Marshall brilliantly used this case to establish just such a power. He argued that because courts interpret law, and the Constitution is a form of law, the Supreme Court can interpret the Constitution.

Thus, Marshall invoked the power of **judicial review,** the Supreme Court's power to overturn acts of the president, Congress, and the states if those acts violate the Constitution. In assuming the absolute and final power to say what the Constitution means, Marshall helped define the powers of the Court and placed it on an equal footing with the other branches. Marshall then used his newfound judicial review power to deny Marbury his commission. As a result, the Jeffersonians had no judicial order to reject, so Marshall's establishment of judicial review stood unchallenged.

Few decisions in the early years of the nation had such a tremendous impact on America's approach to democracy. The Supreme Court now had the power in the system of checks and balances to negate potentially oppressive majority actions the other political branches might take. Thus, minorities would have a place to go for relief. With the power of judicial review, the Supreme Court could bring various state government actions, both political and judicial, into harmony with the national Constitution, thus altering the federal structure.

### QUICK REVIEW

*Marbury* v. *Madison*

- The incoming Jefferson administration appointed William Marbury as justice of the peace for the District of Columbia.
- Marbury sued for his post, arguing that since courts interpret law, and the Constitution is a form of law, then the Supreme Court can interpret the Constitution.
- Chief Justice John Marshall established the power of judicial review: the power of the Supreme Court to overturn acts of the president.
- Landmark case helped define the powers of the court.

***Marbury* v. *Madison***
The 1803 case in which Chief Justice John Marshall established the power of judicial review.

**judicial review**
The power of the Supreme Court established in *Marbury* v. *Madison* to overturn acts of the president, Congress, and the states if those acts violate the Constitution. This power makes the Supreme Court the final interpreter of the Constitution.

## Judicial Review: The Court's Ultimate Power

Chief Justice John Roberts displayed the dazzling argumentation skills that he learned in appearing before the Supreme Court 39 times, more than all the other chief justices combined, with his no-notes, definitive answer-avoiding performance in testifying during his Senate confirmation hearings in September 2005, ensuring his confirmation for the position.

Judicial review has been called the Court's ultimate power because it is absolute. Professor Edward S. Corwin has called it "American democracy's way of hedging its bet," meaning that the Court has the means to correct wayward actions by political branches.[4] Moreover, judicial review has allowed the Supreme Court to update the Constitution by continually reinterpreting its words to fit new situations.

Over the years, judicial review has become a feature of American government accepted by the political branches, the lower judiciary, and the general public. Since 1803, the Supreme Court has declared unconstitutional approximately 1,200 provisions of state laws and state constitutions, and has exercised the same power with respect to 110 federal executive branch actions and the provisions of more than 160 out of the more than 95,000 federal laws passed.[5] Between 1986 and 2007, the Rehnquist Court overturned all or part of more than 40 federal laws—an all-time record—many of them by a narrow 5–4 majority.[6]

Is judicial review a democratic power? Although advocates of judicial review hold that someone has to have the final say over the meaning of the Constitution, others argue that this power is undemocratic because life-tenured, appointed justices can, by a five-four vote majority, overrule the collective will of the elected branches. Judicial review is indeed a significant power with few mechanisms to directly countermand it: Congress can pass new or modified legislation or amend the Constitution, or the Court can reverse its decision. However, although judicial review may appear to provide the Court with unlimited power, the political branches and the general public do possess considerable power to rein in the Court.

### THINKING CRITICALLY

Knowing that Thomas Jefferson believed that the Constitution should be rewritten every generation, did the framers of Article III intend that justices would serve as long as they do now? With a longer lifespan increasing justices' term of service, would the framers be comfortable with the result of a slower-changing Court membership freezing the interpretation of the Constitution in a much earlier generation?

## Other Powers of the Supreme Court

The Court has two other important powers in addition to the power of judicial review. Using its power of **statutory construction,** the Court can interpret or reinterpret a federal or state law. Because the wording of a law is sometimes unclear, the justices must determine the law's true meaning and apply it to the facts in a specific case. In 2005, the Supreme Court narrowly interpreted the so-called federal felon-in-possession law that makes it illegal for one "who has been convicted in any court of a crime punishable by imprisonment for a term exceeding one year" to possess a gun. Gary Small had served three years' imprisonment in Japan for smuggling guns and was arrested after buying a gun one week after his return to the United States. The Court ruled in Small's appeal that this law did not include foreign convictions because various nations had different versions of illegal behavior. By reading the law narrowly, the Court used its interpretation of Congress's real intentions to conclude that because the law did not mention foreign convictions, it referred only to domestic convictions.[7]

**statutory construction**
The power of the Supreme Court to interpret or reinterpret a federal or state law.

The Supreme Court's most frequently used power, though, is the power to do nothing, which it exercises by *refusing to review a case,* thus letting stand a lower-court judgment, even one from the states. The Court did this in 2005 when it refused to hear an appeal by reporters Judith Miller of the *New York Times* and Mathew Cooper of *Time* magazine, who were ordered to jail for contempt by federal district court Judge Thomas Hogan when they refused to reveal to a federal grand jury their sources for an article revealing the identity of CIA agent Valerie Plame. Because the Court refused to hear the case, Miller went to jail. *Time* magazine released Cooper's notes, revealing his source to be presidential adviser Karl Rove, thus preventing Cooper from going to jail.[8]

**THINKING CRITICALLY**

One reform of the Court that has been discussed is to require at least a 6–3 vote to overturn a federal law or a state law or piece of the Constitution, so that a simple 5–4 majority is not used to overturn the democratic will of the voters as expressed by the Congress or state legislatures. What do you think of this idea?

## Independence of the Judiciary

6.2 *What is the basis for the Court's independence, and does it preserve democracy?*

A court's power depends on its independence—that is, its ability to make decisions free of outside influences. The framers understood the importance of an independent court and placed several provisions in the Constitution to keep the Supreme Court free of pressures from the people, Congress, and the president:

1. Justices are appointed, not elected; thus, they are not beholden to voters.
2. The president and Senate share the power to appoint justices, leaving the Court beholden to no one person or political party.
3. The justices are guaranteed their position for life, as long as they exhibit "good Behaviour." Even in cases of bad behavior, justices can be impeached only for "High Crimes and Misdemeanors," thus ensuring that the Court cannot be manipulated by the political branches.[9]
4. The Constitution specifies that justices' salaries "shall not be diminished during their Continuance in Office," meaning that Congress cannot lower the Court's salary to punish it for its rulings.

**QUICK REVIEW**

Powers of the Court

- Judicial review allows the Supreme Court to update the Constitution by continually reinterpreting its words to fit new situations.
- Statutory construction allows the Court to interpret or reinterpret a federal or state law.
- The Court has power to do nothing by refusing to review a case.

The Court possesses a great deal of independence, but it is not completely shielded from outside influences. Presidents can change the direction of the Court with new appointments. Congress can attack the judiciary's independence through some or all of the following: passing laws attempting to overturn Court decisions (an action the Court itself can review), abolishing some or all lower federal courts (or refusing to create new courts), refusing to raise salaries, using its power to remove certain classes of cases from the appellate docket (thus leaving lower-court rulings in force), changing the number of justices on the Supreme Court, passing a law to reverse a Court decision, trying to impeach a sitting justice, and attacking the Court in speeches. While Congress has directly threatened the Court's independence only about a half-dozen times, it is now commonplace for the partisan Senate to filibuster judicial appointments in an effort to control decisions.

**THINKING CRITICALLY**

Does the Supreme Court have too much independence, and has it been too political in its use of the judicial review power, meaning that some constitutional limits should be placed on that power?

In the end, the Court's greatest protection from political threats to its independence has always come from the people themselves. As long as justices are careful not to outpace public opinion in their decisions, the public is generally supportive of this branch of government. An independent judiciary that secures the rights and liberties of citizens is a cherished part of the American political landscape. It is also one of the measures of true democracy, as covered in Chapter 1.

# THE ORGANIZATION OF THE AMERICAN COURT SYSTEM

6.3 *How is the American legal system organized, how does it operate, and what is the Supreme Court's role within it?*

The American judicial system consists of two separate and parallel court systems: an extensive system of state and local courts in which the vast majority of cases are decided, and a system of national or federal courts. Figure 6.1 illustrates how the American court system is structured. Most of the time, these two judicial systems operate independently of each other. State courts deal with state laws and constitutions, and federal courts deal with federal laws and the U.S. Constitution. But when the state courts handle issues touching on the Constitution or federal laws, it is possible for a litigant to shift over to the federal system. The extensive lower-court system (all courts beneath the Supreme Court) functions as a gatekeeper, restricting the flow of appeals to the Supreme Court. Appeals come to the Supreme Court from both the highest courts in the 50 states and from the federal appellate courts. The Compared to What? feature describes how an entirely new Supreme Court has been created in Great Britain.

From 1994 to 2006, Justice Sandra Day O'Connor cast the tie-breaking vote nearly 150 times, and often wrote the majority opinion, in key 5–4 decisions, meaning that during this period the United States Supreme Court could more properly be labeled the "O'Connor Court" instead of the "Rehnquist Court." Whether the rules that she crafted in those decisions will last depends on the decisions of her replacement, Samuel Alito, as well as the remaining justice in the swing position on the Court, Anthony Kennedy.

## Types of Courts

Federal and state courts are divided into trial and appellate courts. A **trial court** (also known as a *petit court*) is often a case's point of original entry in the legal system, with a single judge and, at times, a jury to decide matters

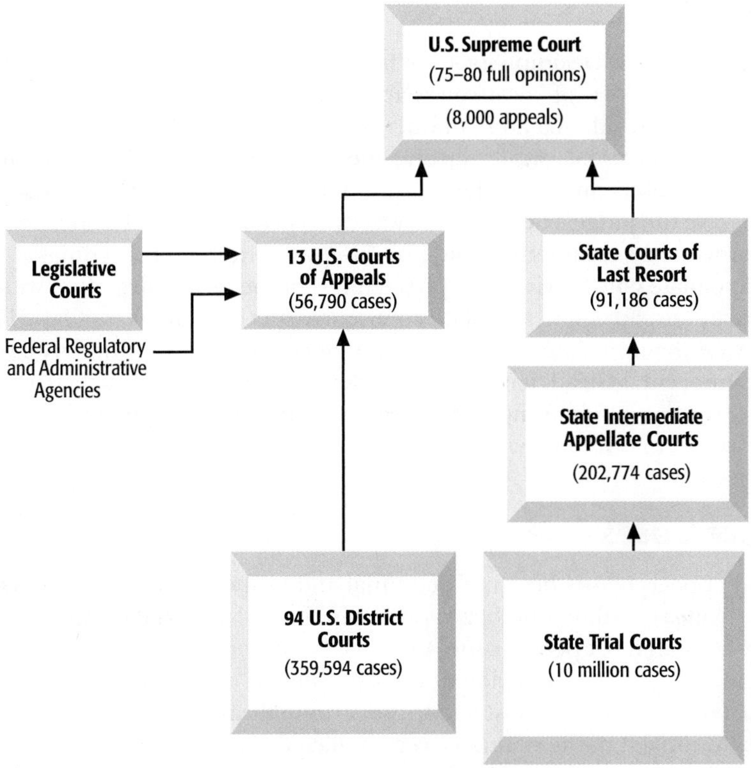


**FIGURE 6.1** Structure of the American Court System

*Sources:* Federal Judicial Workload Statistics (Washington, DC: Administrative Office of the U.S. Courts, 2010); Judicial Caseload Profiles, Administrative Office of the U.S. Courts website, www.uscourts/gov; National State Caseload Highlights, National Center for State Courts, Williamsburg, VA, www.ncsonline.org; www.ncsc.dni.us/ 2003AnnlRept.htm/.

**trial court**
The point of original entry in the legal system, with a single judge and at times a jury deciding matters of both fact and law in a case.

## Compared to WHAT?

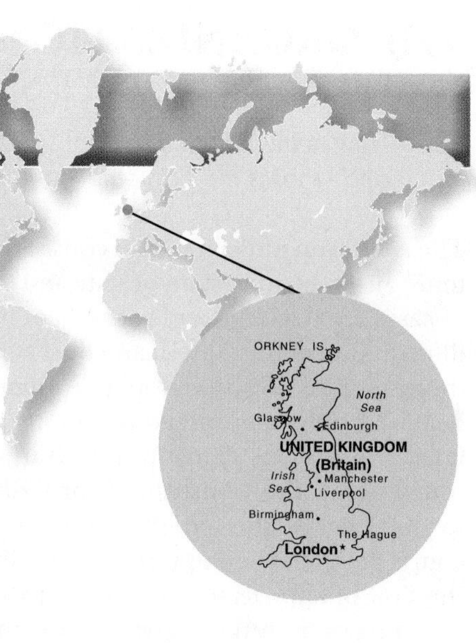


### Creating a Supreme Court in Great Britain

The British legal and political system fundamentally changed in mid-2009 when, for the first time in the country's history, it created a new Supreme Court. Even though the country does not have a written Constitution, a new Supreme Court was created from a dozen judges sitting in the House of Lords, who became known as the Law Lords, and ruled on legal and political questions wearing business suits. More than just creating a new legal body, this established for the first time in the country a system of separation of powers. In the old system, legal questions would be brought to the Parliament, but now the issues, such as dealing with searches in the anti-terrorism campaign, would be handled by a separate judicial institution. Professor Tony Travers of the London School of Economics argued that in a country where there is a "profound sense of disengagement with traditional politics and distrust in politics," the new system "has led to soul-searching about what might be changed constitutionally, believing that constitutional change might re-engage the public, and make them less suspicious of politics and politicians." Questions though still remain. What will be the rules of the game for their decisions? One wonders whether, in time, Great Britain will see the need to commit to writing their constitutional ideals to lay the groundwork for such a body.

*Source:* Rob Gifford, "Independent High Court Ushers Britain into New Era," NPR, July 17, 2009, found at www.npr.org.

both of fact and law. Deciding issues of fact involves determining what actually happened; deciding issues of law involves applying relevant statutes and constitutional provisions to the evidence and conduct of a trial. For instance, in a murder case, deciding a matter of fact would involve the jury's determining a defendant's guilt or innocence based on the evidence admitted into trial. Deciding a matter of law would involve the judge's determining whether certain pieces of evidence, such as a particular witness's testimony, should be admitted into the proceedings.

An **appellate court** reviews the proceedings of the trial court, often with a panel of judges and no jury. The appellate court considers only matters of law. Thus, in a murder case the appellate court would not be concerned with the jury's verdict of guilty or innocent; instead, it might reconsider the trial's legality, such as whether the judge was correct in admitting certain evidence into trial. An appellate court ruling could lead to a new trial if evidence is deemed inadmissible.

## Types of Cases

Trial and appeals courts hear both criminal and civil cases. In **criminal cases,** decisions are made regarding whether to punish individuals accused of violating the state or federal criminal (or penal) code. Criminal law covers murder, rape, robbery, and assault, as well as certain nonviolent offenses such as embezzlement and tax fraud. The state courts handle the vast majority of criminal cases, although in recent years, Congress, outraged at the nature of certain illegal actions, has passed laws creating more federal crimes. The 2001 USA Patriot Act created a new category of federal crimes of terrorism against mass transit.[10] More than 90 percent of criminal cases never come to trial but instead result in private conferences called **plea bargains,** in which the state agrees to press for either a reduced set of charges or a reduced sentence in return for a guilty plea. Plea bargains eliminate the need for a time-consuming trial, thus helping to keep the court system from overload.[11]

**appellate court**
The court that reviews an appeal of the trial court proceedings, often with a multi-judge panel and without a jury; it considers only matters of law.

**criminal cases**
Cases in which decisions are made regarding whether to punish individuals accused of violating the state or federal criminal code.

**plea bargains**
Agreements in which the state presses for either a reduced set of charges or a reduced sentence in return for a guilty plea.

In **civil cases,** courts resolve private disputes among individuals over finances, property, or personal well-being. Malpractice suits, libel suits, breach of contract suits, and personal injury suits are examples of civil cases. Judicial remedies in such cases often involve a judicial decree that requires a certain action or monetary award. Monetary awards can include both *compensatory damages,* which reimburse a litigant for the harm done by another's actions, and *punitive damages,* which go beyond compensation to punish intentional or reckless behavior that causes harm, seeking to discourage such action in the future. Large groups of people affected by an action can unite in a **class-action suit,** a single civil case in which the results apply to all participants. Often, class-action suits are used to compensate victims of large corporations.[12] As with criminal cases, a great many class-action suits and civil cases never come to trial because they are settled out of court.

**civil cases**
Noncriminal cases in which courts resolve disputes among individuals and parties to the case over finances, property, or personal well-being.

**class-action suit**
A single civil case in which the plaintiff represents the whole class of individuals similarly situated, and the court's results apply to this entire class.

**constitutional courts**
Courts mentioned in Article III of the Constitution whose judges have life tenure.

**U.S. district courts**
The trial courts serving as the original point of entry for almost all federal cases.

**U.S. courts of appeals**
The middle appeals level of judicial review beyond the district courts; in 2011, it consisted of 179 judges in 13 courts, 12 of which are geographically based.

## Organization of the Federal Courts

As we've seen, the federal judiciary is organized in three tiers—the U.S. district courts at the bottom, the courts of appeals in the middle, and the Supreme Court at the top. These are all **constitutional courts,** so called because they are mentioned in Article III of the Constitution, the judicial article. All federal constitutional courts are staffed by life-tenured judges or justices.

The **U.S. district courts** are the workhorses of the federal judicial system. These trial courts serve as the original point of entry for almost all federal cases. Roughly 360,000 civil and criminal cases are filed every year in 94 district courts (at least one in every state); in 2011, these courts had a total of 677 judges. District courts hear cases arising under federal law, national treaties, and the Constitution, and they review the actions of various federal agencies and departments. Roughly half of the cases involve juries. Appealing cases to the next level is expensive and time-consuming; therefore, in about 85 percent of cases decided in district court, the judgment is final. By January 2009, George W. Bush had appointed nearly 40 percent of the district court judges. President Obama has lagged well behind this pace, further obstructed by Senate Republican delaying tactics and filibustering. As a result, as of September 2011, Obama had appointed only 76 district court judges, or just over 10 percent of such judges, with nearly 50 more appointees awaiting Senate action and many other vacancies remaining unfilled.

The next rung on the federal judicial ladder is the **U.S. court of appeals,** consisting in 2011 of 179 judges and 88 retired senior judges in 13 courts. Twelve of these appeals courts are geographically based, 11 of them in multistate geographic regions called *circuits* (see Figure 6.2), so named because Supreme Court justices once literally "rode the circuit" to hear cases. The U.S. court of appeals for the Ninth Circuit, for example, covers more than 50 million people in California, Arizona, Nevada, Oregon, Washington, Idaho, Montana, Alaska, and Hawaii. The Twelfth Circuit Court is the U.S. court of appeals for the District of Columbia, which hears appeals from federal regulatory commissions and agencies. Because of the important nature of the cases arising from federal agencies and departments, many consider the court of appeals in the District of Columbia the second most important federal court after the Supreme Court. The U.S. court of appeals for the Federal Circuit is the 13th appeals court; it specializes in appeals involving patents and contract claims against the national government.

Decisions from various circuits vary widely, depending on the political orientation of their judges. When the Obama administration began, the Republicans had made more than 60 percent of the appointees on the court of appeals and had controlling majorities on 12 of the 13 appeals courts. The Ninth Circuit, however, had a two-to-one majority of liberal Carter and Clinton Democrats to Republicans. This balance affects the nature of the Supreme Court's acceptance of appeals and decisions. The conservative Rehnquist Court reversed the vast majority of appeals from the Ninth Circuit, whereas those from the Fourth Circuit in the Virginia and Carolina regions and the Fifth Circuit in Texas, Louisiana, and Mississippi (where

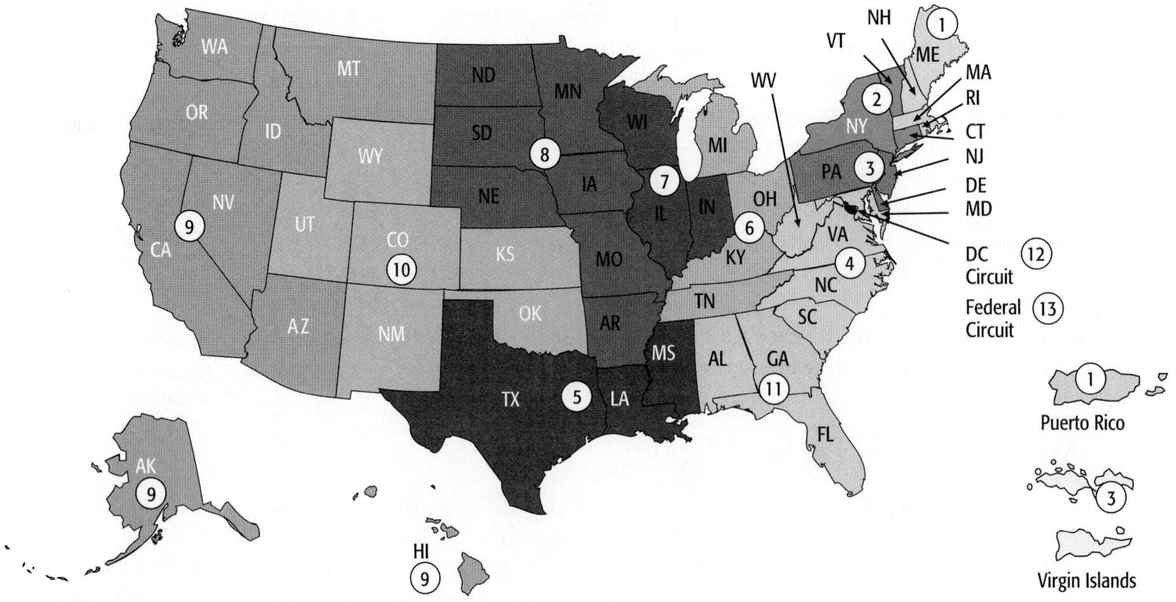


**FIGURE 6.2** The 13 Federal Judicial Circuits

*Source:* Administrative office of the United States Courts, September 1991.

highly ideological Reagan/Bush conservative judges predominate) were upheld. That ideological balance was expected to change because when President Obama entered office there were 15 vacancies on the appellate courts, or enough vacancies for him to change the balance almost immediately on three circuits.[13] However, Obama was slow to make these appointments and the Senate Republicans delayed and filibustered many of his choices. As a result, as of September 2011 he was able to fill only 20 of the 32 vacancies on those courts. In total, Obama has been able to fill just over 11 percent of the existing Article III federal court judicial seats.

Appeals courts usually hear cases in three-judge panels, although sometimes cases are decided in **en banc** proceedings, in which all of the appeals judges in a particular circuit serve as a tribunal. The court of appeals receives more than 62,000 appeals in a year. For the remaining cases, the district court's judgment is left in force.[14] Because so few cases proceed to the Supreme Court, the court of appeals has been described by one prominent judicial scholar as a "mini Supreme Court in the vast majority of cases."[15] This is important because the recent high volume of appeals has led judges to resolve cases with one-word opinions just to clear their dockets—thus creating a two-level justice system for tens of thousands of cases.[16]

In addition to these constitutional appeals courts, the federal judiciary includes **legislative courts** of appeal. Legislative courts are called *Article I courts* because they are established by Congress based on Article I, Section 8 of the Constitution. These courts are designed to provide technical expertise on specific subjects. Unlike life-appointed judges on constitutional courts, legislative court judges serve a fixed term. Legislative courts include the U.S. Court of Military Appeals, the U.S. Tax Court, the U.S. Court of Veterans Appeals, and various territorial courts. Any decision by legislative courts can usually be appealed to the constitutional court system. Some of these legislative courts are special courts consisting of already-serving Article III judges who have specialized jurisdictions. The Foreign Intelligence Surveillance Act (FISA), established in 1978, is a secret court consisting of 11 federal judges who serve seven-year terms. These judges review, and routinely grant, federal intelligence agency requests for warrants to use electronic surveillance agencies in investigating terrorism. The newly created Alien Terrorist Removal Court, with federal judges appointed by the chief justice, reviews, and routinely approves, deportation orders for legal aliens suspected of terrorist acts.[17]

**en banc**
Proceedings in which all of the appeals judges in a particular circuit serve as a tribunal.

**legislative courts**
Courts designed to provide technical expertise on specific subjects based on Article I of the Constitution.

# COURT APPOINTMENTS: THE PROCESS AND THE POLITICS

6.4 *How are Supreme Court justices and federal court judges appointed and confirmed?*

The process for appointing judges to the federal courts is stated clearly in Article II, Section 2 of the Constitution. The president is charged with making the appointments, and the Senate is charged with confirming those appointments by majority vote (its "advice and consent" role). Although the framers wanted only the most "meritorious" candidates selected, politics plays an important part in the process and helps determine which judges end up on the federal bench.

**QUICK REVIEW**

Appointing Supreme Court Justices

- The process begins with the collection of names and creation of a short list of candidates.
- Information-gathering involves a background check to determine suitability and to uncover any potentially damaging information.
- The president receives the list of candidates for consideration and selects a candidate.
- The Senate confirms Supreme Court appointments by majority vote.

## The Supreme Court Appointment Process

How does any one of the hundreds of people qualified for the Supreme Court rise to the top and secure an appointment? The process for appointing Supreme Court justices varies depending on the president and the candidate involved, but in general it begins with the collection and sifting of names. When a vacancy occurs, suggestions for the new appointment come into the White House and the Justice Department from politicians, senators, governors, friends of the candidates, the candidates themselves, and even sitting and retired federal judges. This list is then winnowed down to about two dozen top names. A member of the attorney general's staff or the White House staff oversees an information-gathering process that involves a background check by the Federal Bureau of Investigation (FBI) to determine suitability of character and to uncover any potentially damaging information that might lead to problems with confirmation. A short list of candidates is then forwarded to the president for consideration.

A seat on the Supreme Court is the juiciest plum in the presidential patronage garden. It can go to a highly visible candidate or to someone close to a president. But an equally important consideration is partisanship. Presidents tend to be partisan in their choices, seeking both to reward members of their own party and to see their own political ideology mirrored on the Court. In addition, ethnicity and gender come into play, as do various political interest groups such as the American Bar Association and the Senate.

The only known photograph of the Supreme Court hearing oral arguments was taken secretly in June 1932 by Dr. Erich Solomon, who smuggled a camera into the courtroom. From left to right are Justices Owen Roberts, Pierce Butler, Louis D. Brandeis, Willis Van Devanter, Chief Justice Charles Evans Hughes, George Sutherland, Harlan Fiske Stone, and Benjamin Cardozo. The empty seat was that of Justice James C. McReynolds.

## THINKING CRITICALLY

While the framers placed the confirmation of judicial appointments in the Senate, would they have done so if they knew that it now effectively requires 60 votes, thus avoiding a filibuster, to approve an appointment? How have presidents adjusted their appointments to gain confirmation in this situation, and how might their appointments change if they had to gain only a simple majority for confirmation?

**The Role of Party** Well over 90 percent of Supreme Court appointees have been from the president's own political party. In general, Democrats tend to appoint judges who are willing to extend constitutional and legal protections to the individual and to favor government regulation of business. President Obama selected Judge Sonia Sotomayor because he believed that she had "empathy" for individual rights. Republicans, on the other hand, tend to appoint judges who are less attentive to individual rights and more willing to defer to the government unless the issue is business, where they favor less government control. Republican George H. W. Bush appointed David Souter, who retired in 2009, and Clarence Thomas to the Supreme Court—two jurists with philosophies inclined to uphold lower-court and regulatory agency decisions. Democrat Bill Clinton appointed Ruth Bader Ginsburg, a leader of the women's rights movement, and Stephen G. Breyer, a strong advocate of individual rights.

But presidents are sometimes unpleasantly surprised. What a person *was* can be a poor predictor of what he or she *will become* on the Supreme Court. Although some scholars estimate that more than 70 percent of the time appointees meet presidents' expectations, miscalculations do happen.[18] Conservative president Dwight Eisenhower appointed Earl Warren (1953–1969) and William Brennan (1956–1990) to the Court on the assumption that they were conservatives. Later he would call the two ultra-liberal justices "the two biggest mistakes" of his career.[19] Richard Nixon thought he was appointing a conservative ally to Chief Justice Warren Burger in his childhood friend Harry Blackmun, but in time Blackmun became the liberal anchor opposing the Rehnquist Court conservative majority. Sandra Day O'Connor was much more liberal than Ronald Reagan assumed at the time of her appointment. David Souter became so liberal after his appointment by Republican President George H. W. Bush that in later years "No More Souters!" became the rallying cry of Republicans when Court vacancies occurred during the second Bush administration. On the present Court, Anthony Kennedy, who votes as a liberal on some issues such as gay rights, has come under fire by conservatives who once backed his appointment. Essentially, the immense responsibilities of the office, the lifelong freedom to decide complex legal issues, the weight of the history of a Court seat, the interaction with new colleagues on the bench, and the natural evolution of one's life can all combine to create a jurist far different from expected.

Recently, presidents have tried to sharpen their ability to predict the ideology of their Supreme Court appointments and improve their chances for Senate confirmation by selecting candidates who are judges on the courts of appeals, where their prior judicial records might offer clues regarding future decisions. This practice changes the kind of Court assembled. For instance, although the 1941–1942 Roosevelt Court consisted of a Harvard law professor, two U.S. senators, a chair of the Securities and Exchange Commission, three former attorneys general, a solicitor general, and a U.S. attorney, the Court at the beginning of the Obama administration in 2009 consisted entirely of former U.S. court of appeals judges. The result is a Court that operates in a more bureaucratically judicial fashion as the justices take fewer cases, decide them in an incremental fashion, and write narrow opinions.

President Obama, in making Judge Sonia Sotomayor his first appointment to the Supreme Court, continued the recent practice of selecting someone from the federal court of appeals. However, in appointing the first Latina justice, and someone who comes from a background in the New York City district attorney's office, it is expected that she will bring a very different perspective to the Court from President George W. Bush's two appointees, John Roberts and Samuel Alito. However, in 2010, Obama took a different approach in filling the seat left vacant by the retirement of John Paul Stevens. Passing over several highly qualified court of appeals judges, the president selected another highly qualified legal academic with no prior federal judicial experience, former Harvard law school dean and sitting solicitor general, Elena Kagan. It now remains to be seen whether this will open up the selection process in the future to other nonjudicial figures.

**Seeking a More Representative Court** Over the years, the representative nature of the Court has become an issue. Presidents have used emerging categories such as geography, religion, race, and gender to create a sort of "balanced" Court that keeps various constituencies satisfied.

An effort has always been made to have all geographical regions of the country represented on the Court. "Wiley, you have geography," Franklin Roosevelt told Iowan Wiley Rutledge (1943–1949) when explaining his impending appointment. The Roosevelt Court's only other "non-Easterner," William O. Douglas (1939–1975), had been raised in Yakima, Washington, although he actually lived on the East Coast since his law school years.[20] Religion also plays a role. For more than 100 years there was a "Catholic seat" on the Court. The Court now has six Catholics. The appointment of Louis Brandeis (1916–1939) created a "Jewish seat" that remained until 1969 (and some believe was resumed in 1993). Thurgood Marshall's appointment (1967–1991) established an "African American seat." Clarence Thomas (1991–present), also an African American, was appointed to fill that seat when Marshall retired. Sandra Day O'Connor's appointment (1981–2006) seemed to have established a "female seat." President Obama's appointment of Sonia Sotomayor on the Court might well create a "Hispanic seat" on the Court for future appointments. Obama's appointment of Solicitor General Elena Kagan to the Court in 2010 to replace the retiring John Paul Stevens meant that, for the first time in history, there were now three women on the Supreme Court.

## THINKING CRITICALLY

Do you agree that, with only a nine-person Supreme Court, it is important to choose a diverse selection of people to the Court—even if it means choosing someone from an existing category on the Court who may be better qualified? If so, what other types of appointments should be made to the Supreme Court? For instance, is a Court whose members are usually no younger than their early 50s representative of you as a voter, or your generation?

Judicial scholars continue to debate whether considering such representational factors is the proper way to staff the Court.[21] Many believe that merit should be the primary consideration. Some argue that given the small number of Court seats and the large number of interest groups, satisfying everyone is virtually impossible. Still, political considerations are unavoidable in an atmosphere dominated by sharp partisanship.

**The Role of the American Bar Association** In the past, the president submitted a short list of judicial candidate names to the American Bar Association (ABA), a national association for the legal profession, for an informal review by its Standing Committee on the Federal Judiciary. Attorneys canvass judges and lawyers throughout the country regarding the nominees' qualifications. Based on these inquiries, Supreme Court nominees are rated "highly qualified," "not opposed," or "not qualified." Candidates for the lower courts are rated "well qualified," "qualified," or "not qualified."[22] Although the intent is to seek out information on the nominee's professional qualifications, personal and ideological considerations inevitably arise as well.

The president is not required to consult the ABA in the judicial appointment process.[23] Conservatives became unhappy with the ABA after it issued a mixed review for Robert Bork in 1987 and four years later gave its worst rating ever for Clarence Thomas. The Republican Senate's unhappiness with the ABA's judicial survey results led the Senate Judiciary Committee, under Republican Orrin Hatch (R–UT), to stop using their reports. Later, Republican president George W. Bush announced that, despite the half-century tradition, he would no longer use the ABA review process. Instead, the ABA sent its reports to the Senate Judiciary Committee for use by the Democrats in the hearings and the confirmation votes.

After President Obama became the first president to appoint two women to the U.S. Supreme Court, there were a record three serving there. They are, from left to right, Sonia Sotomayor, Ruth Bader Ginsburg, and Elena Kagan.

Very early in the Obama administration, it was announced that the ABA would once again be consulted by the White House and its reports would inform the appointment and confirmation process for them, as well as for the Senate Judiciary Committee.

**The Role of the Senate** The Constitution charges the Senate with confirming Supreme Court appointments by majority vote. The Senate confirmation process begins with a Senate Judiciary Committee hearing designed to elicit views about a candidate. The committee then makes a recommendation for or against the candidate prior to a vote of the full Senate. Over the years, Senate confirmation has proven a significant hurdle, with nearly one in five presidential nominations rejected.

In general, the president initially has the upper hand in the appointment process, but the Senate can oppose a nominee for a variety of reasons, including unhappiness with the candidate's competence or political views. The Senate rejected G. Harrold Carswell in 1971, citing a lack of competence—but not before Nebraska senator Roman Hruska defended Carswell by saying, "Even if he is mediocre, there are a lot of mediocre judges and people and lawyers. They are entitled to a little representation, aren't they?"[24]

## THINKING CRITICALLY

How might the Senate confirmation process be reformed to ensure—in the partisan political environment—that the most meritorious candidates be selected for the judiciary? Should a "no filibuster/cloture" rule be instituted, making it possible to confirm a justice by a simple majority vote? Should a special select committee be instituted to run the confirmation hearings?

Other rejections have to do with partisan politics. In 1987, Republican president Ronald Reagan's appointee Robert Bork was confronted by a Senate Judiciary Committee controlled by the opposing Democratic Party. After a massive media campaign by a coalition of liberal interest groups and vigorous questioning from the Judiciary Committee, and with the tide of public opinion turning against him, the intellectually qualified Bork was defeated because of his ultra-conservative views, well documented in a trail of paper that spanned his entire career.[25] Some candidates are rejected through Senate opposition to the president or as a message of opposition to the current direction of the Court.

Since the Robert Bork confirmation battle in 1987, the public has become more interested in Supreme Court confirmations, and the Senate's role has become more dramatic. Televising confirmation hearings and floor debates has made senators more conscious of the politics of the appointment process. Finally, the increased lobbying activity of highly partisan coalitions of interest groups, which now mount election-style media campaigns, has whipped up considerable public pressure on voting senators.

Judge Robert Bork, wearing the new goatee he had grown that summer, testifies before the Senate Judiciary Committee in a nationally televised confirmation hearing in 1987, saying that serving on the Court would be an "intellectual feast." Bork was eventually denied his seat on the Court. The Court has been increasingly partisan and polarized since this event.

To counter this newfound Senate willingness to question seriously and even reject nominees, presidents have devised new appointment strategies. First, they have searched for "safe" candidates—ones lacking a large body of writing or decisions that make easy targets for attack. Seeking to avoid the problems faced by highly visible and widely published legal scholar Bork, two years later President George H. W. Bush appointed a little-known court of appeals judge from Weare, New Hampshire: David Souter. The lack of a paper trail to provide any inkling of Souter's leanings helped dub him the "stealth candidate."

Presidents have looked to the court of appeals for appointees, believing that having been confirmed once by the Senate might bode well for a successful confirmation now. Also, an appointee's record on the bench might reveal the nature of his or her decision making on the Supreme Court. The practice became so common that in 2007 all nine members of the Supreme Court were selected from the U.S. court of appeals. Indeed, when President Obama selected a replacement for David Souter, he chose Sonia Sotomayor because her 17 years of experience on the U.S. court of appeals made her confirmation likely. When Obama appointed solicitor general and former Harvard Law School dean Elena Kagan to the Court in 2010, he broke the pattern of appointing only lower federal court of appeals judges. He argued at the time that by reaching beyond the federal judiciary for his appointee he would offer the body a diversity of views.

This search for "safe" candidates could affect the nature of the Court. Highly qualified but also highly controversial legal scholars are now being passed over for appointment by presidents fearful of Senate rejection. In the past, controversial candidates such as Felix Frankfurter and William O. Douglas had a tremendous impact on the Court's direction. And the process was so different in 1986 that even controversial justices such as Antonin Scalia were confirmed unanimously. Some judicial scholars wonder whether this avoidance of talented but risky candidates will produce a Court, relying more and more on its law clerks for sifting through case appeals to accept and writing judicial opinions, that will change the nature of its decision making process. Such a trend is impossible to predict, of course, because of the politics of appointment in the partisan and Internet age, and the ways jurists develop once on the Court. In the Internet age, more and more candidates are being vetted by members of the press, interest group blogs, and even postings of appearances on YouTube, which could change the nature of the process. With the sharply partisan Senate increasingly willing to threaten the use of the filibuster, and senators from both parties demanding a voice in the Court selection process, it remains to be seen what impact all of this will have on the judicial selection process.

Former Solicitor General Walter Dellinger arrived by unconventional means for his ultimately unsuccessful oral argument on behalf of the government before the Supreme Court in the *District of Columbia* v. *Heller* gun control case.

## The Impact of Presidential Appointments on the Supreme Court

6.5 *How much can presidents shape the decision making of the Supreme Court and the federal bench through their appointments, and how representative are these courts?*

Although every Court appointment is important, not every appointment changes the direction of the Court. Supreme Courts are commonly named after their chief justice, such as the Rehnquist Court, but philosophical directional changes within those years may make it better to categorize a Court according to the president who redirected it through judicial appointments.

In the twentieth century, three presidents—Kennedy, Nixon, and Reagan—dramatically changed the Court's direction. In 1962, Democratic president John F. Kennedy shifted an ideologically balanced moderate conservative Court to a more liberal one by replacing moderate conservative Justice Frankfurter with more liberal Arthur Goldberg (1962–1965). In doing so, Kennedy ensured a solid 5–4 vote in favor of civil rights and liberties cases. After Richard Nixon was elected on a "law and order" platform in 1968, his four conservative appointments to the Supreme Court—William Rehnquist, Lewis Powell, Harry Blackmun, and Warren Burger—moved the Court in a more conservative direction, away from individual rights. After his 1980 election, Ronald Reagan's four appointments—Sandra Day O'Connor, Antonin Scalia, Anthony Kennedy, and William Rehnquist as chief justice—created a Court able to reverse earlier rulings in such areas as defendants' rights. Thus, the rights of Americans can expand and contract as a result of their president's choices.

Presidents generally expect their legacy of Supreme Court appointments to remain long after them. Fate sometimes dictates otherwise—for example, the sudden death or unexpected retirement of more than one justice can change the Court quickly and dramatically. A new retirement pattern seems to have emerged that affects the ideological balance of the Court as justices since Byron White in 1994 have timed their departures to hand the vacancy to a specific political party for replacement. White retired, giving the vacancy back to the Democratic Party that had chosen him in the Kennedy administration, even though he turned out to be a conservative. However, when Republican John Paul Stevens retired in 2010, he, like

**QUICK REVIEW**

Appointing Federal Judges

- The president appoints federal judges with consent of the Senate.
- The practice of senatorial courtesy does not apply to Supreme Court appointments.
- Recent presidents have inserted the White House more directly into the process of selecting judges than did their predecessors.

**senatorial courtesy**
A procedure in which a president submits the names of judicial nominees to senators from the same political party who are also from the nominee's home state for their approval prior to formal nomination.

Republicans Harry Blackmun (1994) and David Souter (2009) before him, gave his seat to the Democratic president who was more in harmony with his moderate liberal views on the Court. It has been these cross-party retirements that thwarted the effort of the conservatives to control the Court until George W. Bush's appointment of Samuel Alito for moderate Sandra Day O'Connor in 2005 moved the body to the right.

## Staffing the Lower Federal Courts

The real impact of the presidential appointment power comes not so much at the Supreme Court level as at the lower federal court level. With hundreds of appointments of life-tenured judges here, and more than 99.9 percent of all federal cases never reaching the Supreme Court, these appointments determine the direction of American law for many years to come. The legacy of a president's lower-court appointments will last for about two decades after the end of that president's term of office.[26]

The formal selection process for the lower federal courts is roughly the same as for the Supreme Court. Guided by officials in the Justice Department and White House Office of Legal Policy, the president nominates candidates first screened by the FBI. The candidates' names are then sent to the Senate Judiciary Committee, which consults the ABA report in beginning the confirmation proceedings. But there is one important difference in the selection process for lower-court judges. For federal district court appointments, presidents usually observe the practice of **senatorial courtesy** by submitting the names of nominees to senators from the same political party who are also from the nominee's home state. Failure to do so might lead to a senator declaring that a candidate is "personally obnoxious," dooming the appointment. Other senators, wishing to preserve the practice of senatorial courtesy for their own use in the future, will follow the first senator's lead and vote against the nomination. In these ways, senatorial courtesy has forced presidents to share their nomination power with the Senate.[27] In fact, in many cases the names of prospective candidates are forwarded to the White House by the senators from the president's party and the candidate's state (and sometimes even from powerful senators in the other party) prior to the nomination decision. These candidates often become the nominee.

Protests like this one, on the Obama health-care reform plan, will accompany the biggest economic Supreme Court case in decades as this law is tested there in 2012.

A president's ability to use the appointment power to shape the lower federal court is determined by length of service in the White House, the number of vacancies that arise during that time, and whether the Senate confirms the nominees. In addition, Congress can expand the lower-court system, creating new seats to be filled. One-term president Jimmy Carter made 258 appointments, whereas two-term president Ronald Reagan made 382. When Republican George H. W. Bush's 193 appointments were combined with the holdovers from previous Republican administrations, we see that the Republican Party appointed approximately 65 percent of the lower federal judiciary. By the end of Bill Clinton's first term of office, he had filled more than one-fifth of the federal judiciary. By the end of Clinton's administration he had appointed 374 judges, or roughly 45 percent of the federal court judges. However, even at that time, well more than 40 percent of the appointees from the Reagan/Bush administrations remained on the federal bench. When added to the 320 appointees by George W. Bush (which totaled just under 38 percent of the federal judiciary), more than 56 percent of the federal judiciary had been appointed by

Republican presidents as of the inauguration of Barack Obama. By this time, despite retirements by a great many conservative jurists, the conservatives controlled 12 of the 13 courts of appeals.[28]

As of September 2011, Barack Obama has successfully filled only 96 seats on the lower federal court (20 on the appeals court and 76 on the district court), or just slightly more than 11 percent of the federal judiciary. At the same time, nearly 60 appointments by Obama are being held up by Senate Republicans through delay tactics and filibusters. Nearly another 30 vacancies have not yet been filled by the Obama administration.[29]

Because of the new appointments in the last few presidencies, the change in the gender and ethnic composition of the federal courts has been dramatic (see Figure 6.3). The George H. W. Bush administration appointed nearly three times as many women to the federal bench as President Ronald Reagan. More than 30 percent of Bush's appointments to the federal bench were women and minorities.[30] In his eight years of office, Clinton sought to make the courts even more representative, appointing the greatest percentage of African American and female judges—nearly one of every two of his appointments—resulting in a federal judiciary in which 32 percent of the judges in 2002 came from these groups and representing a 68 percent increase during Clinton's presidency.[31] George W. Bush's diversity in his appointments to the federal judiciary was far less than the previous administration. Only 21.6 percent of his federal court appointments were women, only 7.5 percent were African American, 9 percent were Hispanic, and only slightly more than 1 percent were Asian.[32] As of September 2011, President Obama has broken all records for gender and ethnic diversity in his judicial appointments. Over 70 percent of his appointments have been minorities, with 50.8 percent being women, 26.2 percent being African American, 8.2 percent being Hispanic, and 9.8 percent being Asian American.[33] Diversity on the Court, and the age of nominees became the basis for yet another filibuster by the Republicans of one of Obama's appointments, as the Senate Republicans would not allow 39-year-old Berkeley law professor Goodwin Liu, an Asian American, to come up for a vote for a seat on the Ninth Circuit Court of Appeals. Among the considerations by the Republicans was the possibility that one day Liu might be appointed by Obama, or another democrat, to the U.S. Supreme Court. The Republicans may have won this battle, but it is yet to be seen whether they have won the war, as Liu was later appointed to the California Supreme Court, from which he could one day be elevated to the U.S. Supreme Court (just as William Brennan was from the New Jersey Supreme Court in 1956.)[34] The Approaching Democracy timeline for this chapter shows how the power, independence, and diversity, of the Supreme Court have evolved in American history.

## APPROACHING Democracy Timeline

### Events That Have Affected the Independence and Power of the American Judiciary

| | |
|---|---|
| **1803** | *Marbury* v. *Madison* leads to the creation of judicial review. |
| **1857** | *Dred Scott* v. *Sandford* upholds slavery. |
| **1937** | FDR court-packing plan is proposed but not passed. |
| **1937** | Chief Justice Hughes and Justice Roberts switch vote to avoid passage of court-packing plan. |
| **1938** | *Carolene Products* footnote announces Court interest in civil rights and liberties. |
| **1944** | *Korematsu* v. *U.S.* Sup. Ct. upholds Japanese internment program. |
| **1967** | Thurgood Marshall becomes first African American appointed to Court. |
| **1981** | Sandra Day O'Connor becomes first woman appointed to Court. |
| **1987** | Robert Bork fails to be confirmed to the Court in partisan Senate battle. |
| **2000** | *Bush* v. *Gore* rules that the Florida recount is ended and George W. Bush wins the presidency. |
| **2009** | Judge Sonia Sotomayor becomes first Hispanic appointed to the Court. |

☐ Democratic ☐ Neutral ☐ Undemocratic

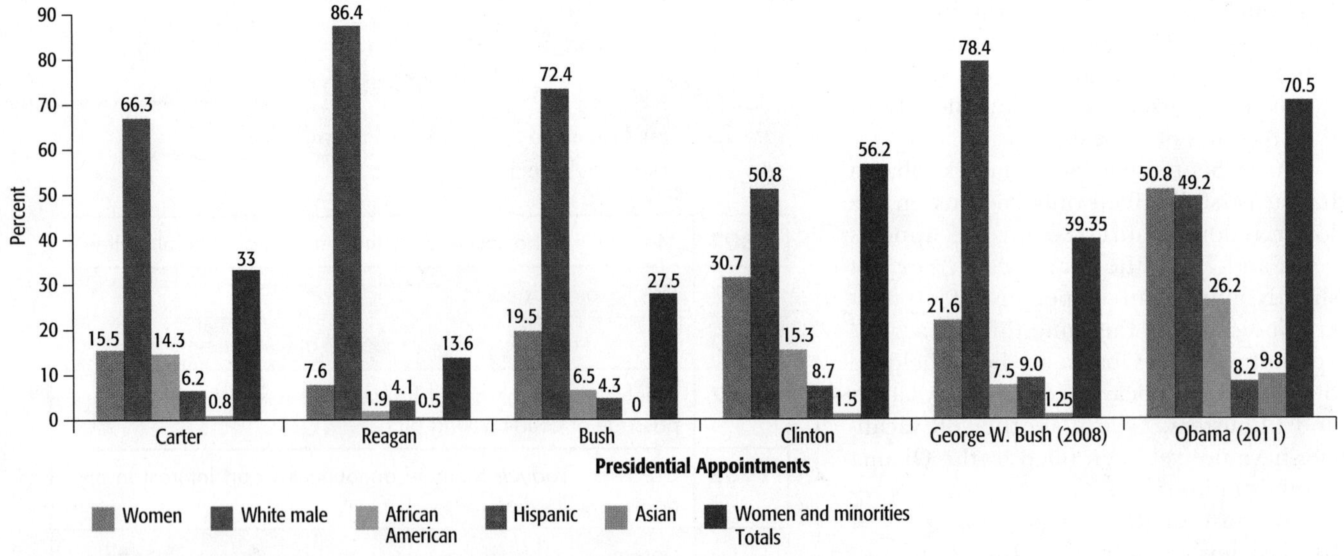


**FIGURE 6.3** Presidential Appointments of Minorities on the Lower Federal Courts

*Sources:* Sheldon Goldman et al., "Obama's Judiciary at Midterm," *Judicature,* vol. 94, no. 6 (May–June 2011): 262–303; Sheldon Goldman et al., "Mission Accomplished: W. Bush's Judicial Legacy," *Judicature,* vol. 92, no. 6 (May–June 2009): 258–288; Sheldon Goldman et al., "W. Bush's Judiciary: The First Term Record," *Judicature,* vol. 88, no. 6 (May–June 2005): 244–274; "W. Bush Remaking the Judiciary: Like Father, Like Son?" *Judicature,* vol. 86, no. 6 (May–June 2003): 282–309; "Clinton's Judges: Summing Up the Legacy," *Judicature,* vol. 84, no. 5 (March/April 2001): 228–254; Sheldon Goldman and Matthew D. Saronson, "Clinton's Nontraditional Judges: Creating a More Representative Bench," *Judicature,* vol. 78, no. 2 (September/October 1994): 68–73; Sheldon Goldman and Elliot Slotnick, "Clinton's First-Term Judiciary: Many Bridges to Cross," *Judicature,* vol. 80, no. 6 (May/June 1997): 254; Sheldon Goldman and Elliot Slotnick, "Picking Judges Under Fire," *Judicature,* vol. 86, no. 6 (May/June 1999): 265–278.

# HOW THE SUPREME COURT OPERATES

6.6 *How does the Supreme Court operate as an institution, and does it operate in a democratic fashion?*

How many times have you heard someone involved in a legal dispute proclaim defiantly, "I'm going to appeal this case all the way to the Supreme Court"? In truth, a successful appeal to the Supreme Court is extremely rare, partly because many cases are decided on their way to and through the intermediate appeals level and partly because of the Supreme Court's methods in selecting cases it will hear.

Each year, the Supreme Court receives roughly 8,000 appeals. Of these, less than 1 percent, or roughly 75 to 80 cases, appear on the Court's **docket,** or agenda, after they are accepted for full review with oral argument. Nearly all of these cases are decided by a full written opinion. But a few will be decided *per curiam,* in a brief, unsigned, generally unanimous opinion by the Court. The lower-court judgment remains in effect for cases the Court does not accept for review.

Nearly all of the Court's cases come from its *appellate jurisdiction,* cases that have already been reviewed and decided by one or more federal or state courts. About 90 percent of the appellate cases come from the lower federal courts, with most coming from the court of appeals. The 10 percent of cases from state courts must raise a *federal question* and have exhausted all possible state appeals in order to jump to the Supreme Court. This usually means that state cases come from the state court of last resort, although they need not do so. The second source of Court cases is its *original jurisdiction,* which, as you learned earlier, involves cases seeking to resolve disputes among states and cases affecting foreign ambassadors. The Court hears few original jurisdiction cases today.

**docket**
The Supreme Court's agenda of cases to consider.

**writ of certiorari**
A Latin term meaning "to be made more certain"; this writ enables the Court to accept cases for review only if there are "special and important reasons therefore."

## Selecting Cases

The rules for appealing a case to the Court have been established by congressional legislation. Appellate cases come to the Court through a formal writ called a **writ of certiorari,** a Latin term meaning "to be made more certain." Established in 1925, this

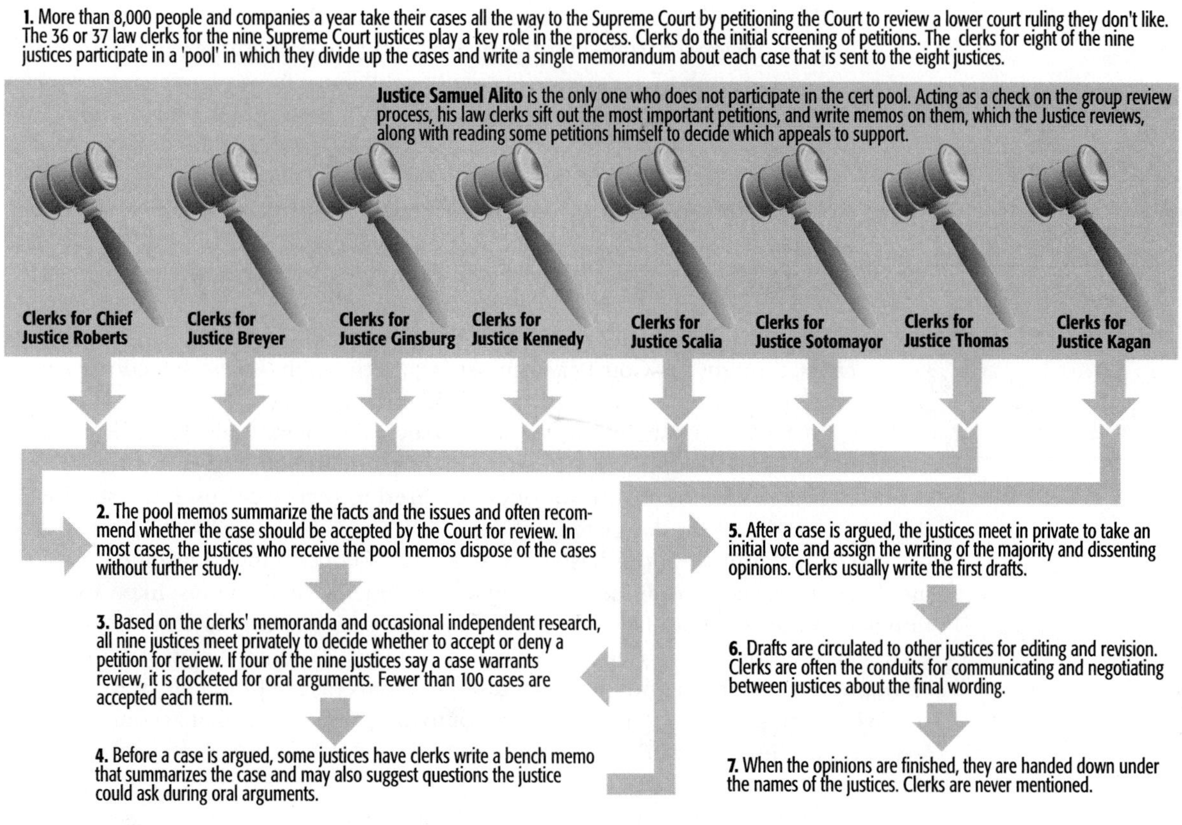
1. More than 8,000 people and companies a year take their cases all the way to the Supreme Court by petitioning the Court to review a lower court ruling they don't like. The 36 or 37 law clerks for the nine Supreme Court justices play a key role in the process. Clerks do the initial screening of petitions. The clerks for eight of the nine justices participate in a 'pool' in which they divide up the cases and write a single memorandum about each case that is sent to the eight justices.
Justice Samuel Alito is the only one who does not participate in the cert pool. Acting as a check on the group review process, his law clerks sift out the most important petitions, and write memos on them, which the Justice reviews, along with reading some petitions himself to decide which appeals to support.
Clerks for Chief Justice Roberts
Clerks for Justice Breyer
Clerks for Justice Ginsburg
Clerks for Justice Kennedy
Clerks for Justice Scalia
Clerks for Justice Sotomayor
Clerks for Justice Thomas
Clerks for Justice Kagan
2. The pool memos summarize the facts and the issues and often recommend whether the case should be accepted by the Court for review. In most cases, the justices who receive the pool memos dispose of the cases without further study.
3. Based on the clerks' memoranda and occasional independent research, all nine justices meet privately to decide whether to accept or deny a petition for review. If four of the nine justices say a case warrants review, it is docketed for oral arguments. Fewer than 100 cases are accepted each term.
4. Before a case is argued, some justices have clerks write a bench memo that summarizes the case and may also suggest questions the justice could ask during oral arguments.
5. After a case is argued, the justices meet in private to take an initial vote and assign the writing of the majority and dissenting opinions. Clerks usually write the first drafts.
6. Drafts are circulated to other justices for editing and revision. Clerks are often the conduits for communicating and negotiating between justices about the final wording.
7. When the opinions are finished, they are handed down under the names of the justices. Clerks are never mentioned.

**FIGURE 6.4** The Role of Law Clerks in Supreme Court Decision Making

*Source: Tony Mauro,* "For Lawyers, Clerkship Is Ultimate Job," USA Today, June 5, 1998. Reproduced with permission. Updated by the authors.

discretionary writ enables the Court to accept cases for review only if there are "special and important reasons therefore." Essentially, the Court will consider accepting a case for review if it raises issues that affect society or the operation of government. You will recall that the *Bush* v. *Gore* case was accepted for review to determine the winner of the 2000 presidential election, even though some considered it a "political question" best left to political bodies such as Congress. Following legislation passed by Congress in 1988, the Court now has virtually total discretion over the cases it will hear.

All the justices (except Samuel Alito, whose own clerks assist him) rely on a group of law clerks in a "cert pool" to screen appeals (see Figure 6.4). The clerks divide up the petitions, summarize a portion of them in memo form, and then submit their recommendations for acceptance or rejection to the justices.[35] Some believe this makes the law clerks into an intermediate court of review, because the justices use these initial evaluations to form their own judgments about which cases are worthy of review.

The justices meet twice weekly to decide which appeals to accept. To speed up the decision process, the chief justice places appeals deemed worthy of consideration on a "discuss list" at the request of any Court member. The remaining appeals go on a "dead list" and, unless at least one justice asks for further consideration, the Court denies them without further discussion. The Court then votes on the cases on the discuss list. A vote by at least four justices to hear the case, known as the **rule of four,** will grant the petition for a writ of certiorari and put the case on the Court's docket.

**rule of four**
A means of determining which cases the Supreme Court will hear; at least four justices must vote to hear a case and grant the petition for a writ of certiorari for the case to be put on the Court's docket.

**Recent Trends in Case Selection** Since the late 1980s, the Supreme Court has been accepting and deciding fewer and fewer cases. Although the number of appeals to the Court has increased by 85 percent in the past 25 years, the percentage of cases actually accepted by the justices has dropped dramatically. In the late 1970s

## THINKING CRITICALLY

With the Supreme Court deciding only around 75 cases a year, and with four clerks assigned to each of the justices, it is the equivalent of each justice writing one term paper a month—with the assistance of a top-flight law clerk for each one. Should the justices be required to take more cases or have fewer clerks?

and early 1980s, several hundred cases were decided yearly by either full opinions or unsigned orders. Of the nearly 8,000 appeals coming to the Court in 2007–2008, only 67 cases were decided by full opinion, the fewest in more than half a century, with the number rising to just 75 cases in 2010–2011. Reflecting the ideologically polarized voting of the Court, nearly one-half of the decisions in 2008–2009 were made by 5–4 or 6–3 votes.[36] Although that percentage of 5–4 cases dropped to just 16 cases, or slightly over 21 percent in the 2010–2011 term, the fact that all but two of them consisted of exactly the same ideological lineup of the four liberals (Breyer, Ginsburg, Sotomayor, and Kagan) and four conservatives (Roberts, Alito, Scalia, and Thomas) with Kennedy providing the fifth vote is nearly a statistical impossibility.[37] Even with this small number of cases, though, the Court can impose its will through its case selection process and the region of the country from which it takes cases.

The Court's shrinking docket has several explanations. First, recent congressional legislation on federal jurisdiction eliminated nearly all categories of constitutional cases that the Court was once required to review. Second, the staffing of the vast majority of the lower federal courts with conservatives by the Reagan and the two Bush administrations has meant that a fairly conservative Supreme Court has had fewer lower-court opinions with which it disagrees. But the most likely explanation is that the cert pool law clerks reviewing the petitions are far less interested in taking cases than were reviewing justices in the past. "You stick your neck out as a clerk when you recommend to grant a case," explains Justice John Paul Stevens. "The risk-averse thing to do is to recommend not to take a case. I think it accounts for the lessening of the docket."[38]

## The Process of Deciding Cases

Once a case is accepted for review, it passes through several stages as it is considered. Each of these stages is designed to inform the jurists and to give them a chance to organize a final decision.

**Filing Briefs** When a case is accepted for argument, the attorneys for all sides are asked to submit **briefs.** These are hundreds of pages of written arguments outlining not only all the facts and legal and constitutional issues in the case but also answering the anticipated arguments of the opposing side. Today, so many groups file so many briefs that, together with the lower-court opinions and Supreme Court precedents, the justices must read about 1,500 pages of material a day.[39]

These written arguments were originally strictly legal in nature, but now attorneys often present extensive sociological, psychological, scientific, and historical arguments to bolster their legal documentation. In the 1954 case of *Brown* v. *Board of Education,*[40] which raised the issue of desegregating public schools, the Court received evidence from social psychologist Kenneth Clark that African American youngsters were psychologically harmed by segregated school systems.[41] As you will see in Chapter 14, it was primarily this evidence that contributed to the Court's decision to ignore legal precedents and rule that segregated schools are inherently unconstitutional. Now, with two originalists on the Court, Scalia and Thomas, who decide cases based on the meaning of the Constitution in the founding period, more and more briefs are submitted containing historical information that the justices can use to make their decisions and write their opinions.

**briefs**
Written arguments to the court outlining not only the facts and legal and constitutional issues in a court case but also answering all anticipated arguments of the opposing side.

**solicitor general**
The third-ranking official in the Justice Department, appointed by the president and charged with representing the U.S. government before the Supreme Court.

**amicus curiae briefs**
Legal briefs that enable groups or individuals, including the national government, who are not parties to the litigation but have an interest in it, to attempt to influence the outcome of the case; literally, "friend of the court" briefs.

**Oral Argument** After briefs are submitted, oral arguments follow. One of the most exciting and impressive events in Washington, DC, is the public oral argument before the Supreme Court. Typically, the arguments are heard during the first three days of the first two weeks of each month from October through April. Lawyers from all sides—including occasionally the **solicitor general** and, in the most important cases, other interested parties such as those who have submitted **amicus curiae briefs**—come before the justices and present their case. Each side usually has only 30 minutes to speak, with time limits kept so carefully by the chief justice that during one Court session, a lawyer was interrupted in the middle of the word *if.*

Although lawyers come prepared with statements, they must stop to answer questions from the justices. Justices have different questioning styles. Ruth Bader Ginsburg asks carefully sculpted questions designed to keep counsel from avoiding issues, whereas Stephen Breyer usually waits until the end of counsel's time before asking one or two lengthy questions designed to crystallize the central issue in the case. By contrast, both Justices Sotomayor and Kagan asked questions in their first oral arguments, but Clarence Thomas asked no questions during his first 18 months on the bench and in 2011 it had been a full five years since he had asked his last question. The most combative person currently on the bench is Antonin Scalia. Much as when he was a law professor, Scalia asks many rapid-fire questions—once as many as 135 on a single case.

The appellate and oral argument process is such a specialized skill that it can cost as much as $500,000 to take a case to the Supreme Court. For a solo practitioner to take a case to the Court *pro bono,* or for free, is a once-in-a-lifetime experience that comes with a cost, such as having to close down a practice for six months to prepare for the argument. More and more, corporations, states, and even other law firms are assigning this final step to an elite group of fewer than two dozen Washington, DC, litigators who specialize in Supreme Court argumentation, some of them former U.S. solicitors general and Supreme Court law clerks, some of whom charge as much as $10,000 for participation in moot courts to prepare for oral argument.[42] Sometimes their willingness to take a case or not makes these attorneys further gatekeepers in deciding which appeals reach the Court.

What role does oral argument play in the decision-making process? Some justices find that oral presentations highlight problems with the issue raised by the written briefs and suggest possible avenues for decision. Others find that written briefs weigh more heavily. This makes it difficult to predict how the Court will rule based on the nature of its questioning during oral argument.

**The Decision-Making Stage: The Conference** After the justices read the briefs and listen to oral arguments, the decision-making process begins with the *judicial conference.* These conferences take place on Wednesday afternoon for cases argued on Monday and all day Friday for cases argued on Tuesday and Wednesday. At these meetings, the justices discuss both the cases under consideration and which appeals to grant in the future.

The meetings take place in total secrecy in an oak-paneled conference room, with only the justices present. Proceeding from the chief justice down to the most junior justice, the justices indicate both their views and how they will vote. Opinions expressed at this time constitute a preliminary vote.[43]

**Assignment of Opinions** Once the discussion and voting are over, if the chief justice is in the majority, he or she assigns a member voting in the majority to draft an **opinion,** the written version of the decision. Sometimes the chief justice will write the opinion in the hope of expressing an even stronger view from the Court. If the chief justice is not in the majority, the senior justice in the majority makes the assignment or writes the opinion.

Sometimes the voting lineup—and thus the decision in a case—hinges on who is assigned the opinion. In 1992, five justices—Thomas, Scalia, Rehnquist, White, and Kennedy—seemed ready to overturn the *Roe* v. *Wade*[44] abortion decision in the case of *Planned Parenthood of Southeastern Pennsylvania* v. *Casey.*[45] When conservative Chief Justice Rehnquist assigned the opinion to himself because of the importance of the case and drafted a harsh opinion toward the *Roe* precedent, Kennedy decided to vote in a more moderate direction, joining in an opinion with David Souter and Sandra Day O'Connor upholding the precedent.[46]

**QUICK REVIEW**

The Solicitor General

- The third-ranking official after the attorney general and deputy attorney general.
- Appointed by the president; represents the government before the Supreme Court.
- Decides which federal cases to appeal from the lower courts.
- Prepares appeals and files briefs for accepted cases.

**QUICK REVIEW**

Deciding Cases

- Attorneys for all sides submit briefs of written arguments.
- Oral arguments follow and are heard from October through April.
- In the *judicial conference,* justices discuss cases under consideration and appeals to grant in the future.
- After voting, one member in the majority drafts an opinion, the written version of the decision for those voting with the majority. If the chief justice is in the majority, he or she chooses the author. If not, the choice falls to the senior-most justice in the majority.
- The vote on any case is final when the decision or opinion is announced in open court.

**opinion**
A written version of the decision of a court.

**majority opinion**
A decision of the Supreme Court that represents the agreed-on compromise judgment of all the justices in the majority.

**plurality opinion**
Less than a majority vote on an opinion of the Court; does not have the binding legal force of a majority opinion.

**concurring opinion**
A written opinion of a justice who agrees with the majority decision of the Court but differs on the reasoning.

**dissenting opinion**
A written opinion of a justice who disagrees with the holding of the Court.

## Marshaling the Court: The Opinion-Drafting Process

After the judicial conference, the justice assigned to write the opinion takes weeks, and sometimes months, to develop a draft to circulate among the other justices. This requires special care because conference votes are tentative, and justices will lobby to change their colleagues' positions. As Justice William Brennan used to say to his law clerks while wiggling all the fingers of his hand in the air: "Five votes. Five votes can do anything around here."[47] And each side attempts to muster those five votes.

At any point, right up to public announcement of the opinion, a justice can change a vote. That occasionally happens, but changes to the language of opinions nearly always occur, sometimes dramatically in controversial cases, as a result of lobbying efforts. Each opinion goes through multiple drafts, with justices negotiating with each other over changes on which the final votes may depend. Such negotiations take time. For this reason, opinions for major cases argued in the fall of a judicial term might not be issued until the spring of the following year. Often, these negotiations come in the form of written comments on various opinion drafts, personal memos, and even personal lobbying by the justices or their assistants. Years ago, such lobbying took place through personal interaction, but in recent years, the little lobbying that happens is usually done by argumentative memos and emails. Despite such efforts, however, evidence suggests that votes change in fewer than 10 percent of the cases, though many of them are the most important ones.[48]

## The Announcement of Opinions

The vote on any case is final only when the decision or opinion is announced in open court. The Court's opinion not only states the facts of a case and announces the decision but, because this will be the only public comment on the case, it also contains supporting logic, precedents, and rationale to persuade the public of the merits of the judgment. In addition, the language used in an opinion is designed to be used later by lower courts, federal and state politicians, and the legal community to interpret similar cases in the future.

The Court makes its decision based on a majority (five votes out of nine), called a **majority opinion,** which represents the agreed-on compromise judgment of all the justices in the majority. This opinion is almost always signed only by its authors. In cases where less than a majority agrees on the wording, a **plurality opinion** is issued. This plurality opinion announces the opinion of the Court, but it lacks the same binding legal force as a majority opinion.

If a justice agrees with the majority decision of the Court but differs on the reasoning, a **concurring opinion** can be written. From this literary platform, a single justice, or a small group of them, can show where the majority might have ruled. A careful reading of concurring opinions thus can reveal the true sentiments of the Court majority. In the landmark 1971 freedom of the press case *New York Times Co.* v. *United States,*[49] the Court allowed two newspapers to publish The Pentagon Papers, a classified study of the decision-making process of America's involvement in Vietnam. However, the six concurring opinions revealed that, had the government sought to punish the *Times* editors after publication rather than attempt to prevent publication through prior censorship, and if a statute had outlawed such a publication, a majority of the Court would have sided with the government.

When a justice disagrees with the Court's holding, frequently he or she will write a **dissenting opinion,** as an individual or for a few of the members of the Court. In the *United States* v. *Dickerson* case, dealing with whether to overturn the *Miranda* case protecting defendants in police questioning, Justice Scalia used his dissent to attack Chief Justice Rehnquist's majority opinion by using language from confession cases that Rehnquist himself had decided nearly three decades before. From the stewardship of Chief Justice Marshall until the early 1920s, justices avoided dissents, fearing a diminution of the public authority of the Court. The practice increased in the 1940s when dissents occurred in 70 percent of the cases, as opposed to 22 percent of the cases in the previous decade. Now many more dissents are being issued, either as a result of less personal conferencing by the justices, weaker leadership by the chief justice, the law clerks' greater role in the drafting process, or a greater desire by individual jurists to be heard.

One must pay attention to these statements; the dissents of today can become the majority opinions of tomorrow when the Court changes members. The Court's recent decisions on defendants' rights and federalism reflect earlier dissents by Associate Justice William Rehnquist. The decision rule proposed in dissents by Oliver Wendell Holmes and Louis D. Brandeis in the First Amendment free speech cases of the early 20th century and by Justices Hugo Black and William O. Douglas in the 1950s later became the law of the land. Recently, liberal justice Ruth Bader Ginsburg and conservative Antonin Scalia signaled their unhappiness with the prevailing majority's decisions by reading their dissents from the bench on decision day.[50]

## Law Clerks: The Tenth Justices?

One of the most significant changes in the modern Supreme Court has been the justices' increasing reliance on their law clerks for help in drafting opinions. Each associate justice has four law clerks, and the chief justice has five. Clerks earn roughly $50,000 per year (with the prospect of salary and bonuses from private firms that may top $400,000, when they finish their year of service) and are selected during their second year of law school. Most are white males who graduate from the elite law schools and serve a year's clerkship with a federal court of appeals judge before moving to the Supreme Court. Certain appeals judges, such as J. Harvie Wilkinson of the Fourth Circuit and Merrick Garland of the DC circuit, have become major "feeder judges" for Supreme Court law clerks.[51] Once in the cert pool, these assistants draft memos to aid in selecting appeals heard by the Court for eight of the nine justices (Samuel Alito being the exception). "When I tell clients who have cases with hundreds of millions of dollars on the line that a bunch of 25-year-olds is going to decide their fate, it drives them crazy," says Carter Phillips, who frequently argues before the Court.[52]

### THINKING CRITICALLY

Knowing that many believe the justices rely too much on their clerks to do their work, should limits be placed on the number of clerks assigned to each justice, or the range of their work product, by requiring that justices write their own opinions?

Justice Louis D. Brandeis once said that the Supreme Court was respected because "the justices are almost the only people in Washington who do their own work," but that no longer appears to be true. More and more, the clerks' most important job is to draft opinions. Chief Justice William Rehnquist determined that it is "entirely proper" for clerks to draft opinions, because it is, in his words, a "highly structured task."[53] As a result, in recent years, the justices still make decisions, but they increasingly leave law clerks to write first drafts of opinions, a most influential part of the process that determines the tone and direction of the final opinion. For instance, the decision by Justice Lewis Powell to back out of writing the majority opinion in a 1987 gay rights case, *Bowers* v. *Hardwick,* shifting the majority from the liberal to the conservative side, turned because the initial opinion was given to one of his clerks who was a married Mormon from Idaho, rather than to another clerk who was gay but who had not told the justice.[54] Justice John Paul Stevens, who was a law clerk to Justice Wiley Rutledge in the 1940s, acknowledges this change: "I had a lot less responsibility than some of the clerks now. They are much more involved in the entire process now."

Partially as a result of this delegation of the early drafting process, the lack of time arguing over cases in the judicial conference, and the relative lack of personal consultation among the justices, judicial opinions have become longer, more numerous, and more academic, whereas justices' decisions are more fragmented and much less clear in their legal explanations. Oftentimes, negotiations during the drafting process are left to conversations among the law clerks, who serve as informal emissaries from the various justices' chambers, as they did during the *Bush* v. *Gore* deliberations in 2000.[55] Increasingly, students of the Court are becoming critical of the greater reliance by the justices on law clerks for the production of their opinions.

**QUICK REVIEW**

The Chief Justice

- Appointed by the president upon confirmation of the Senate.
- Oversees the operation of the judiciary.
- Sets the tone and has a greater opportunity to influence the rest of the Court by the choice of author for majority opinions and the way that the Court is run.

**The Chief Justice's Role** The chief justice is first among equals on the Supreme Court, with substantial powers to influence the Court's direction by assigning opinions, leading the judicial conference, and acting as the social and intellectual leader of the Court. In addition, he or she also heads, represents, and lobbies for the entire federal judiciary.

Chief justices vary widely in leadership styles. Some have been more effective leaders than others. The austere Charles Evans Hughes (1930–1941) moved the Court along with military precision. His replacement, the gregarious Harlan Fiske Stone (1941–1946), lost control of the Court during judicial conferences. Fred Vinson (1946–1953) was overwhelmed by the high-powered, egocentric Roosevelt appointees, leading to considerable rancor on the Court in those years. On the other hand, relative harmony followed during the tenure of the politically skilled former governor of California, Earl Warren (1953–1969), known to his admiring colleagues as "the Super Chief." This period contrasted to the sharply split Court under Warren Burger (1969–1986), who was reputed to be an uninspiring leader.[56] The highly popular and respected William Rehnquist proved capable of forging and maintaining the Court's narrow conservative coalition. Now the challenge for John Roberts is to find a way to lead a polarized, partisan group that has been almost perfectly balanced ideologically since 2005, with Anthony Kennedy casting the decisive fifth vote, to try to achieve more consensus and larger majorities on various issues.

# ANALYZING SUPREME COURT DECISIONS

6.7 *What influences justices in deciding cases, and how can we understand their judicial theories?*

To analyze and understand any Supreme Court decision, we must consider the following: the Court's use of precedent and other legal factors, the mind-sets and personalities of the individual justices, and the contemporary Court voting blocs.

## The Use of Precedent and Other Legal Factors

Judges throughout the legal system often base decisions on the doctrine of **stare decisis,** which means "to let the decision stand" or to adhere if at all possible to previously decided cases—or **precedents**—on the same issue. Federal and state courts, for example, are supposed to follow Supreme Court precedents in making their own decisions. The Supreme Court often rules based on its own precedents. By following previous rulings, all courts—including the Supreme Court—appear nonpolitical, impartial arbiters, making incremental changes based on past decisions.

But following precedent is not as restrictive as it sounds. Because, in practice, precedents need interpretation, judges can argue about the meaning of an earlier case or whether the facts of the current case differ substantially from those of past cases, thus requiring a different ruling. In one case, *Bowers* v. *Hardwick,* dealing with the privacy rights of gays in the bedroom, Justices Blackmun and White cited the same case of *Stanley* v. *Georgia,*[57] a privacy and pornography case, as a major precedent upholding their opposing positions on the constitutionality of the Georgia anti-sodomy law. Occasionally, justices will appear to uphold precedent, when in fact they are deliberately ignoring it or consciously reinterpreting it to reach a different result.

Only in the most extreme cases is the Court willing to overturn an earlier decision, thus declaring it invalid. Precedents are usually overturned if they prove unworkable from a public policy standpoint, outmoded, or just plain unwise. Sometimes, though, a change in Court personnel or in public opinion will lead to overturning a precedent. For example, in 1991, the Court overruled two earlier Eighth Amendment capital punishment decisions barring the use of statements by victims in the penalty phase of a capital trial. The arrival of new conservative members made

**stare decisis**
A doctrine meaning "let the decision stand," or that judges deciding a case should adhere if at all possible to previously decided cases similar to the one under consideration.

**precedents**
Previously decided court cases on an issue similar to the one being considered.

these rulings possible but led frustrated liberal Thurgood Marshall to argue, before retiring from the Court, "Power, not reason, is the new currency of this Court's decision making."[58] Justice Ruth Bader Ginsburg used similar language in the spring of 2007, when the Court upheld the partial birth abortion ban at the federal level that they had overturned just seven years earlier in Nebraska, when she wrote: "The Court, differently composed than it was when we last considered a restrictive abortion regulation, is hardly faithful to our earlier invocations of 'the rule of law' and the 'principles of *stare decisis*.'"[59] In 2007, after the Court overturned an affirmative action program for magnet public schools in Seattle in the face of the mandate from the 1954 *Brown* v. *Board of Education* case to end school segregation, Justice John Paul Stevens wrote: "It is my firm conviction that no Member of the Court that I joined in 1975 would have agreed with today's decision."[60]

In actuality, however, the Court rarely overrules its own precedents. Out of tens of thousands of decisions it has issued, the Court has overruled its own precedents in fewer than 300 cases.[61] In recent years, though, the practice has increased. Since 1946, the Court has overturned its own precedents an average of about three times a term.[62] A favorite technique for circumventing precedent without reversing a previous decision is to *distinguish* cases—that is, to claim that the earlier case and a more recent case are different (even if in fact similar), thus requiring different decisions. The Court has been able to dilute the original ruling in the 1973 *Roe* v. *Wade* case using such a technique. That case created a trimester system governing state regulation of abortions, allowing women an unfettered right to an abortion in the first trimester of their pregnancies. Although the decision has not been overruled, the Court has allowed the states to impose so many regulations that the original ruling is now much less protective of women's right to choose abortions.

Justices also look at a variety of factors beyond precedent to decide an issue, including the meaning of a law, the meaning of part of the Constitution, the lessons of history, and the possible impact on public policy. Using *strict construction,* justices look carefully at a statute or a portion of the Constitution and interpret the law as closely as possible to the literal meaning of its wording. When the wording is vague, justices search for historical context—or for the so-called intent of the framers who wrote the law and the Constitution—to determine the true meaning of both. Proponents of *original intent,* such as Judge Robert Bork, argue that it is the Court's duty to adhere solely to the original meaning of the framers. The effect is to limit the power of Supreme Court justices to interpret the law. This method has come to be labeled "originalism" because legal theorists examine all the writings and newspaper accounts of the founders, or the people in the state constitutional ratifying conventions from the founding period, to determine how they would frame and decide current issues.

Justice Antonin Scalia, though, has developed his own method of "textualism," looking at dictionaries from the early period to determine the meaning of the words in the Constitution at that time to determine how the founders would decide these issues. Others, however, argue that society has changed since the drafting of the Constitution and that the Court's decisions should thus reflect the needs of a continually changing society in creating an evolving document. Sometimes justices examine an issue's general history and the public policy impact of their decision. In the *Bush* v. *Gore* case, the Court majority argued that many factors led them to rule that the initial certification of the presidential vote by the Florida secretary of state should stand, thus effectively ending the election in Bush's favor.

## The Mind-Set of Individual Justices

6.8 *What roles do political ideology and orientation toward judicial power play in judicial decision making?*

Personal factors also figure in analyzing judicial decisions. It is helpful to look at a judge's mind-set—his or her political ideology, jurisprudential posture, or a combination of the two.

**judicial restraint**
An approach in which justices see themselves as appointed rather than elected officials, who should defer to the legislature and uphold a law or political action if at all possible.

**judicial activism**
An approach in which justices create new policy and decide issues, to the point, some critics charge, of writing their personal values into law.

**Political Ideology** Although some Court observers would prefer that justices decide cases on the basis of neutral principles, the individuals sitting on the Court are human beings influenced by their own biases.[63] A comprehensive study by two political scientists found a strong correlation between justices' votes on the Court and their ideological views as expressed in newspaper articles written during the appointment process.[64]

Like members of political parties, justices tend to be grouped ideologically as conservative, liberal, or moderate. Conservatives tend to support the government's position instead of the individual's in civil rights and liberties, whereas liberals tend to defend or even expand the rights of the individual instead of the government. On economic questions, conservatives tend to oppose government regulation in favor of *laissez-faire* business oversight, whereas liberals tend to vote for a more intrusive government regulatory role. Moderates often flip back and forth between these two positions, depending on the issues.

Labeling jurists this way is helpful but in no way definitive. Many varieties of liberals and conservatives and many legal issues fail to fit clearly into those groupings. Political ideology, then, is only a starting point for understanding a jurist's mind-set. We must also consider a justice's willingness to use power.

**Jurisprudential Posture** Justices have a certain jurisprudential posture, meaning how willing they are to use their power on the Court. Some practice self-restraint whereas others are activists. Justices who believe in **judicial restraint** see themselves as appointed rather than elected officials who should defer to the elected legislature and uphold a law or political action if at all possible. "If the legislature wants to go to hell, I'm here to tell them they can do it," said Oliver Wendell Holmes. Justice Felix Frankfurter pronounced the classic expression of judicial self-restraint in his dissent in a case forcing the children of Jehovah's Witnesses to salute the flag in contravention to their religious beliefs:

> *One who belongs to the most vilified and persecuted minority in history [Frankfurter was Jewish] is not likely to be insensible to the freedoms guaranteed by our Constitution. . . . As a member of this Court I am not justified in writing my private notions of policy into the Constitution, no matter how deeply I may cherish them or how mischievous I may deem their disregard.*[65]

Judges who practice **judicial activism** believe that they have a duty to reach out and decide issues even to the point, critics charge, of writing their own personal values into law. Judicial activists are more willing to strike down legislation, reject a presidential action, overturn a state law or a piece of a state constitution, or create rights not specifically written in the Constitution. For example, William O. Douglas's ruling in the case of *Griswold* v. *Connecticut*[66] fashioned a right to privacy even though such a right is not explicitly in the Constitution. Douglas's classic description of the activist posture came in his dissent to a Court decision not to protect the environment in California's Sierra Nevada Mountains against Walt Disney Corporation, seeking to build a ski resort:

> *Inanimate objects are sometimes parties in litigation. . . . So it should be as respects valleys, alpine meadows, rivers, lakes, estuaries, beaches, ridges, groves of trees, swampland, or even air that feels the destructive pressures of modern technology and modern life.*[67]

For Justice Douglas, nature should have the right to sue, too. The activist posture often leads to charges by conservative legal theorists such as former federal court judge Robert Bork that the Court is acting as a "superlegislature," substituting its decisions for the considered judgment of duly-elected bodies.[68]

In the partisan debate over the role of the Court, one person's self-restraint judge is another person's activist. In arguing against Judge Sonia Sotomayor's confirmation, some conservatives opposed putting "activists" on the Court, but it soon became clear that what they objected to was "liberal activism." Scholars have revealed that the conservative-dominated Court under conservative Chief Justice Rehnquist and now equally conservative Chief Justice Roberts are among the most activist justices in the history of the Court. One scholar argues that the "Rehnquist Court has waged an activist revolution that is unprecedented both in scope and in conflict."[69] Another study points out that the Court overturned federal laws 135 times in its first 207 years of existence, but in just one eight-year period under Chief Justice Rehnquist, the conservative majority overturned parts or all of 33 other federal laws.[70] Now almost all justices are activists and the debate becomes just how activist they become—and in what ideological direction they decide—on the Court. The Roberts Court appears to be no exception to this rule, overturning a variety of laws, including portions of the McCain-Feingold campaign finance law of 2002 in the *Citizens United* case (discussed in Chapter 13), which argues that corporations are like people, and thus have the protected free speech to contribute as much money as they like to federal elections.

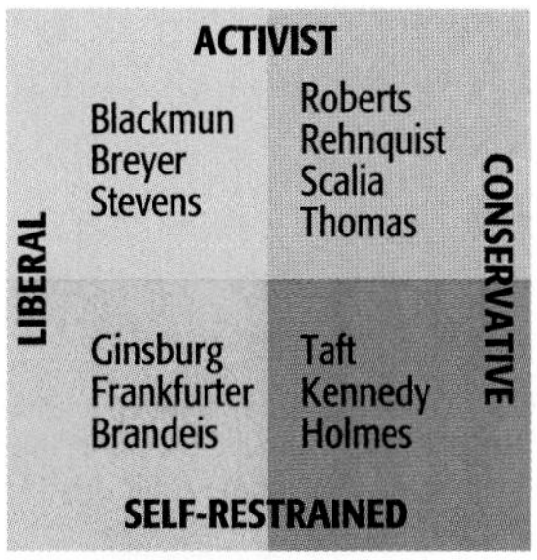


**FIGURE 6.5** The Four-Cell Method for Classifying Justices
It is useful to assess justices by looking at their politics (whether they are liberal or conservative) and at their judicial philosophy (whether they are activist or self-restrained). As a result, one will learn that both types of self-restrained justices share an inclination to avoid innovation, while activists in the two camps can differ dramatically with regard to the goals of their activism.

**The Four-Cell Method for Classifying Justices** It is often revealing to assess justices according to a four-cell categorization that considers both political ideology (whether a judge is liberal or conservative) and jurisprudential posture (whether a judge is self-restrained or an activist). This scheme, illustrated in Figure 6.5, will help you better understand that the Court's self-restrained liberals and self-restrained conservatives have much in common because neither will be inclined to break new ground. For instance, New Deal appointee Felix Frankfurter was frequently criticized by liberal colleagues because his self-restrained opinions upholding the letter of the law made him look too conservative. However, the activists on either side of the political spectrum can differ dramatically, because liberal activists are willing to reach beyond the law and write new individual rights into the Constitution, whereas conservative activists sometimes seek to substitute their vision of the Constitution for that of the legislators. Thus, the conservative activists on the Rehnquist Court overturned more than three dozen congressional laws between 1994 and 2006, often claiming to adhere to the "original intention" of the framers of the Constitution.

But concentrating solely on the political and judicial views of a justice is not enough to understand decisions. Instead, dealing with a life-tenured Court requires us to consider how voting blocs are formed and maintained through evolving relationships among the justices.

## Voting Blocs

6.9 *What roles do personal factors and voting bloc balance play in understanding how judicial decisions are made?*

Another angle on analyzing Court decisions relies on grouping the Court into blocs of like-minded jurists. An example would be grouping justices by ideology as conservative, liberal, and moderate (see Table 6.1). Although justices sometimes shift within these blocs, change more frequently occurs when appointees alter the balance of the Court. As Justice Byron White used to say, "When you change one justice, you change the whole court."[71] These blocs are not absolute determinants of votes, however, because a justice's views, and thus the justice's position within a bloc, frequently vary according to the issue under consideration. This is especially true when new members come to the Court, offering new arguments on cases and new potential alliances on all facets of an issue.

Replacing a member of the Court's leading bloc with a member suited to the other bloc can sharply tip the decision balance. So although all Supreme Court appointments are important, some can change the entire direction of the Court. That was why the prospect of replacing Warren Burger with Antonin Scalia in 1986—a conservative for a conservative—had far less impact and was less controversial than the attempt to replace moderate Lewis Powell with highly conservative activist Robert Bork a year later. Initially, the appointment of Sonia Sotomayor, expected to be a more centrist liberal vote on the Court, raised the question of whether President Obama would succeed in turning Court decision making in a more liberal direction. Over time, though, Sotomayor's liberal votes, along with those of Obama's second

### THINKING CRITICALLY

What might have been the impact on the Supreme Court if President Obama had appointed a more extreme ultra-liberal person to replace David Souter? If Obama has an opportunity to fill another vacancy, should he appoint an ultra-liberal person then?

**Table 6.1** Judicial Voting Blocs

| | Liberal | Moderate | Conservative |
|---|---|---|---|
| **Eisenhower Court (1961)** | Warren | Whittaker | Frankfurter |
| | Brennan | Harlan | Stewart |
| | Black | | Clark |
| | Douglas | | |
| **Kennedy Court (1963)** | Warren | Harlan | Stewart |
| | Brennan | | Clark |
| | Black | | White |
| | Douglas | | |
| | Goldberg | | |
| **Johnson Court (1969)** | Warren | Harlan | Black* |
| | Brennan | | Stewart |
| | Douglas | | White |
| | Fortas | | |
| | Marshall | | |
| **Nixon Court (1974)** | Brennan | Powell | Burger |
| | Douglas | Blackmun | Rehnquist |
| | Marshall | | Stewart |
| | | | White |
| **Ford Court (1976)** | Brennan | Powell | Burger |
| | Marshall | Blackmun | Rehnquist |
| | | Stevens | Stewart |
| | | | White |
| **Reagan Court (1989)** | Brennan | Kennedy | Rehnquist |
| | Blackmun† | O'Connor | Scalia |
| | Marshall | Stevens | White |
| **Bush (41) Court (1993)** | Blackmun | Kennedy | Rehnquist |
| | Stevens | Souter | Scalia |
| | | O'Connor | White |
| | | | Thomas |
| **Obama Court (2011)** | Kagan | Kennedy‡ | Roberts |
| | Ginsburg | | Scalia |
| | Breyer | | Thomas |
| | Sotomayor | | Alito |

*Liberal Hugo Black became conservative after a stroke.

†It is interesting to note that when appointed in 1970, Blackmun was strongly conservative. By 1973, he had become a moderate, and later in his career he became its most liberal member until his retirement in 1994.

‡While Justice Kennedy is listed here as a swing justice, with the exception of the gay rights area, he votes so frequently with the conservative bloc—accounting for the frequent 5–4 victories by the conservatives since Justice O'Connor's retirement in 2006—that he may more properly belong in the conservative group, leaving no real swing justice on the current Court.

# APPROACHING
## Contemporary Issues in Democracy

### Reforming the Supreme Court?

A quiet constitutional revolution may well be underway in the public discourse concerning the United States Supreme Court. Nearly all of the Republican candidates, most notably Newt Gingrich with his attack on "judicial supremacy," many legal academics, members of the press, and even some members of Congress are calling for various reforms of the Court. Some want to limit the constitutional lifetime tenure for the Court to a fixed term of 18 or perhaps 15 years. Some are calling for the extension of the Federal Judicial Code of Conduct, which applies to the lower federal judiciary, to govern the Court by preventing justices from appearing at political events, or appearing to lobby for, or being lobbied on behalf of, political reforms. Thus the Alliance for Justice organization objects to Justices Thomas and Scalia appearing at a seminar organized by the conservative Koch brothers, and the two of them as well as Justice Alito appearing at conservative organizations such as the Federalist Society, the American Enterprise Institute, and the Heritage Foundation. Some are calling for the oral arguments of the Court to be televised in real time so that the public can observe the nation's highest Court in action. And some are discussing the nature of the recusal rules by which members of the federal Court, including the Supreme Court, should decide to step away from a case, a decision that is left totally to the individual justice, if their impartiality "might reasonably be questioned." On this basis some argued that liberal Elena Kagan should step out of the health-care reform case because she was the solicitor general when the matter was being formulated, while others say that conservative Clarence Thomas should step away because his wife has been lobbying extensively against the law.

These questions and reform proposals and others have the same common theme—What are the obligations and duties of justices on and off the Court to keep their institution above all questions about their political activities and ethical behavior? The Court has gone through waves of questions on these issues. President Franklin D. Roosevelt proposed the court-packing plan in 1937 seeking to tip the ideologically conservative Court his way. The Nixon administration altered the makeup of the Court in 1969 by driving ethically challenged Justice Abe Fortas from the Court because of his financial connection to a financier. Few realize that at that time several members of the Court had similar types of financial connections beyond the Court to different people and organizations. When one of those relationships was exposed the following year, Republican congressional leader Gerald R. Ford sought unsuccessfully to impeach Justice William O. Douglas on a variety of charges. Much like those crisis periods for the Court in the past, members of the current Court act as though they are beyond any legal or ethical controls, beyond even public, academic, or press criticism, and beyond challenge even by parallel branches of the federal government.

The issue, quite simply, is the independence of the judiciary. The Court argues that any controls by others, criticism of justices' actions, or even viewing by a television audience would impinge on its ability to act independently. For them, it is a matter of the Court's position in a separation of powers system of government. The question, though, raised by the earlier crisis periods, is what happens when a member of the Court goes too far and upsets either the notion of "rule of law," fairness to all under our legal system, or the commitment to democratic ideals that comes from operating a legal system that is unimpeachable and unassailable in its search for truth and justice. Realizing that reforming the Court, which has clear Article III constitutional powers and the power of judicial review to review any law dealing with them by Congress, do you think some reform measures should be passed on the Supreme Court, and if so, what would those measures be? Would they help us further approach democracy?

appointee, Elena Kagan, make one wonder whether a victory in the 2012 presidential election, and the replacement of a conservative justice by another Obama appointee, would completely change the Court's direction. On the other hand, a Republican victory in 2012 could lead to a solidification of the conservative voting bloc that has been in charge since 2006 with Kennedy in the lead. Bloc analysis can be helpful in predicting which justices may become the swing votes that determine the outcome in a case. Law firms appearing before the Court make this kind of analysis so they can pitch their oral argument to one or two justices they deem critical to their case.

# THE COURT'S INDEPENDENCE IN APPROACHING DEMOCRACY

6.10 *Do the justices lead or follow public opinion, thus advancing or checking democratic will?*

The Supreme Court, said political scientist (and later president) Woodrow Wilson, is "the balance wheel of our whole constitutional system."[72] Like the balancing middle wheel that keeps a machine running smoothly, the Supreme Court takes into consideration the demands of the president, Congress, the bureaucracy, the 50 states and its protectorates, and the American public—and attempts to arrive at decisions that bring them all into harmony.

The paradox is that this vital balancing role is being filled by one of the least democratic institutions in the world. In other countries, nonelected leaders who hold office for life and rule in complete secrecy are either kings or dictators; in America they are Supreme Court justices. In theory, the justices can make any decisions they like, but as we have seen, in reality, the judiciary is restrained by the possibility that its decisions will meet resistance or not be implemented at all.

What, then, is the role of an independent Supreme Court in the American system of democracy? Attempts to answer this question have led to a long-standing debate about whether the Court should actively make policy or practice judicial restraint. Should the Court adhere to the letter of the law and leave policy making to the elected Congress and president? Should it be an architect of public policies that advance human rights, or should it simply reflect the desires of the populace? (See Figure 6.6.)

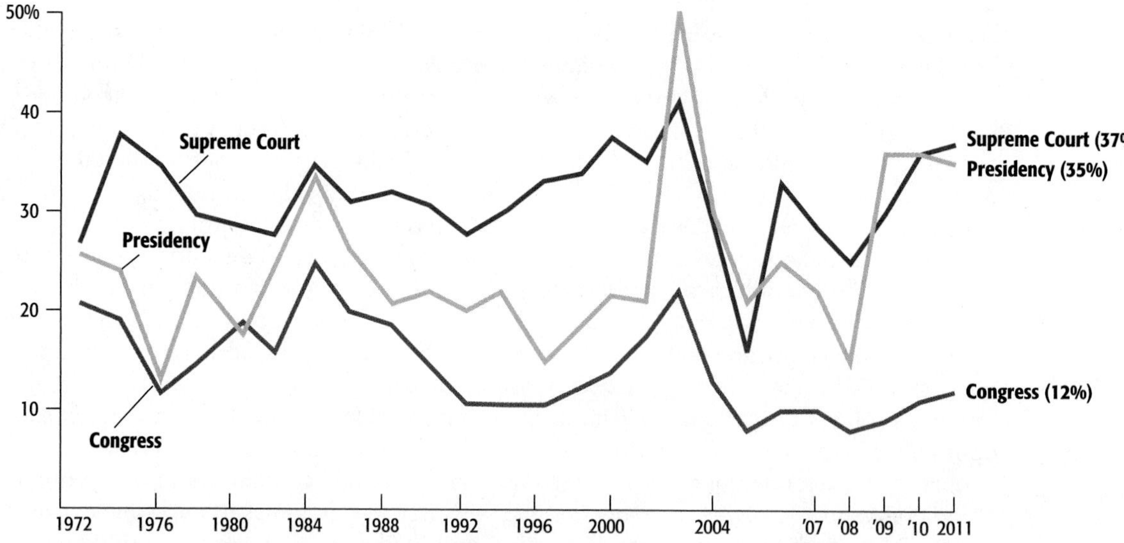


**FIGURE 6.6** Confidence in Political Institutions

Contrary to the dissenters' arguments in *Bush* v. *Gore* that the ruling here would cost the Court prestige, although a higher percentage of the public has consistently expressed a "great deal of confidence" in the Supreme Court—more so than in the presidency and Congress—after the terrorist attacks on September 11, 2001, the president outpolled the Supreme Court in the public's level of confidence. In early 2006, the Court resumed its leadership position, which it lost in 2008, but resumed again two years later.

*Sources:* Compiled from Harris Poll, July 11, 2010, and June 23, 2011; February 10–15, 2009; Harris Poll, February 2007 and February 7–14, 2006, www.pollingreport.com; Harris Poll #6, January 30, 2002, Harris Poll Library, harrisinteractive.com/harris_poll/; data by John R. Hibbing and James T. Smith, "What the American Public Wants Congress to Be," in Lawrence Dodd and Bruce I. Oppenheimer, eds., *Congress Reconsidered,* 7th ed. (Washington, DC: Congressional Quarterly Press, 2001), as it appeared in *National Journal,* June 10, 2000, p. 1818.

Over the years, the Supreme Court and the lower federal courts have varied in their willingness to fully use their power based on the nature of the legal issues, the number of cases heard, the political situation, and who's on the bench. Recalling the negative reaction to the 1954 *Brown* v. *Board of Education* desegregation decision and the 1973 *Roe* v. *Wade* abortion decision, it remains to be seen whether the Court—faced with today's fault-line issues of gay marriage, economic issues of health-care reform, the restrictive state illegal alien laws, and wartime issues being raised by various terrorism crisis—backs off issues that it would otherwise like to resolve now. Whatever happens, judiciary actions in America's democracy will continue to have powerful implications for both government and individual rights.

## Summary


6.1 *What is the source of the Supreme Court's constitutional and judicial review power, and how democratic is it?*

- The federal courts decide all legal disputes arising under the Constitution, U.S. law, and treaties. In cases involving disputes between states or involving foreign ambassadors, the Supreme Court has original jurisdiction. For all other federal cases, it has appellate jurisdiction.
- In the 1803 case of *Marbury* v. *Madison,* Chief Justice Marshall argued that the Supreme Court has the power to interpret the Constitution. This power, known as *judicial review,* enables the Court to overturn actions of the executive and legislative branches and to reinterpret the Constitution to fit new situations. The power of statutory construction enables the Court to interpret a federal or state law.

6.2 *What is the basis for the Court's independence, and does it preserve democracy?*

- The power to appoint justices to the Supreme Court is shared by the president and Congress. The justices are appointed for life and can be impeached only for "High Crimes and Misdemeanors." The president can influence the Court by appointing justices who support a particular philosophy. Congress can change the number of justices or pass a law to reverse a Court decision.

6.3 *How is the American legal system organized, how does it operate, and what is the Supreme Court's role within it?*

- Most cases enter the judicial system through a trial court consisting of a single judge and, at times, a jury. The proceedings of the trial court are reviewed by an appellate court consisting of a panel of judges but no jury. Criminal cases involve violations of state or federal criminal law; civil cases involve private disputes. Most criminal cases are resolved by plea bargains, in which the state agrees to reduce the charges or sentence in return for a guilty plea.
- The federal judiciary is organized in three tiers. At the bottom are the 94 district courts, with at least 1 in each state. At the next level are the courts of appeals, which hear cases from 13 circuits, or regions, usually in three-judge panels. District and circuit courts are constitutional courts, but the federal judiciary also includes legislative courts, established by Congress.

6.4 *How are Supreme Court justices and federal court judges appointed and confirmed?*

- Candidates for the Supreme Court are suggested by senators, governors, the candidates themselves, their friends, and federal judges, and they are screened by the FBI and the American Bar Association. Most nominees to the Court are members of the president's party and share the president's political philosophy.
- The confirmation process begins with a hearing by the Senate Judiciary Committee, which makes a recommendation prior to a vote by the full Senate. These procedures can constitute major hurdles, resulting in the rejection of nearly one in five presidential nominations.
- In nominations to district courts, the tradition of senatorial courtesy gives senators what amounts to a veto power. Often, however, candidates are suggested by senators in the president's party.

6.5 *How much can presidents shape the decision making of the Supreme Court and the federal bench through their appointments, and how representative are these courts?*

- Recent presidents have attempted to make the federal judiciary more representative of the population as a whole. Over time, the tradition has developed for appointing certain kinds of categories of justices, and the appointments of different presidents have significantly changed the direction of the Court's decision making.

6.6 *How does the Supreme Court operate as an institution, and does it operate in a democratic fashion?*

- The solicitor general decides which federal cases to appeal from the lower courts, prepares the appeals, and represents the United States before the Supreme Court. Appellate cases come to the Supreme Court through writs of certiorari. If at least four justices vote to hear a case, it is placed on the docket. In recent years, the Court has decided fewer cases, even though the number of appeals reaching it has increased dramatically.
- When the Court accepts a case, attorneys for all sides submit briefs, or written legal arguments. They then present oral arguments before the Court. The justices hold a conference to discuss and vote on the case, and one of the justices voting with the majority is assigned to draft the opinion, or written version of the decision. The opinion must be approved by at least five justices. A justice who agrees with the majority decision but differs on the reasoning may write a concurring opinion.

When a justice disagrees with the Court's ruling, he or she may write a dissenting opinion.

6.7 *What influences justices in deciding cases, and how can we understand their judicial theories?*

- Interpretation of a law or a portion of the Constitution as closely as possible to the literal meaning of the words is known as *strict construction*. When the wording is vague, justices may attempt to determine the original intent of the framers. Justices may consider the effect a ruling would have on public policy.

6.8 *What roles do political ideology and orientation toward judicial power play in judicial decision making?*

- Some justices believe in judicial restraint—deferring to the other branches of government whenever possible—and others are judicial activists—believing that judges have a duty to further certain causes. By combining the political ideology of a justice (conservative versus liberal) with the categorization of whether he or she is a self-restraint or an activist justice, we have a sense of whether that justice is ready to use his or her power to make changes in the law.

6.9 *What roles do personal factors and voting bloc balance play in understanding how judicial decisions are made?*

- Some justices are leaders and others are followers, but some are "lone wolves" who like to vote and write dissents for their own point of view. Understanding the direction of the Court is easiest when you divide the nine justices into wings—liberal, conservative, and moderate "swing justices" who vote either way depending on the issue. Changing a justice will not necessarily change the voting direction of the Court unless an appointee comes from a different political ideology from the person who left that seat, thus changing the overall voting balance of the Court.

6.10 *How does the question of whether a decision is implemented affect whether a justice leads or follows public opinion, thus advancing or checking democratic will?*

- Decisions of the Supreme Court become the law of the land. However, compliance with a decision is influenced by the extent to which the president supports it. It may also be circumvented by Congress, which can pass a new law or propose a constitutional amendment restating its original intentions.

## Key Terms

amicus curiae briefs, 202
appellate court, 190
appellate jurisdiction, 185
briefs, 202
civil cases, 191
class-action suit, 191
concurring opinion, 204
constitutional courts, 191
criminal cases, 190
dissenting opinion, 204
docket, 200
en banc, 192
judicial activism, 208
judicial restraint, 208
judicial review, 186
legislative courts, 192
majority opinion, 204
*Marbury* v. *Madison*, 186
opinion, 203
original jurisdiction, 185
plea bargains, 190
plurality opinion, 204
precedents, 206
rule of four, 201
senatorial courtesy, 198
solicitor general, 202
stare decisis, 206
statutory construction, 187
trial court, 189
U.S. courts of appeals, 191
U.S. district courts, 191
writ of certiorari, 200

## Test Yourself Chapter 6

**1.** The power of the Court to declare acts of Congress unconstitutional was created in the case of
a. *U.S.* v. *Nixon.*
b. *U.S.* v *Marshall.*
c. *Marbury* v. *Madison.*
d. *Hamilton* v. *Jefferson.*

**2.** Which of the following are *not* used to establish the independence of the Supreme Court?
a. Justices are appointed, not elected.
b. The Constitution establishes that there shall be nine justices on the Court.
c. The justices are guaranteed their position for life, as long as they exhibit "good Behaviour."
d. The Constitution specifies that justices' salaries "shall not be diminished during their Continuance in Office."

**3.** Constitutional courts are
a. courts that interpret the Constitution.
b. courts that are mentioned in Article III, whose judges have life tenure.
c. courts containing multiple judges.
d. courts that advise Congress on matters dealing with the Constitution.

**4.** What is an *en banc* proceeding?
a. A court in Louisiana dealing with French law.
b. A court that deals with banking law.
c. A federal court of appeals case dealt with by all of the judges in the entire circuit.
d. A special appeals court with only one judge.

**5.** How many members of the 2009 Supreme Court were appointed from the federal court of appeals, as opposed to how many were appointed from the lower federal court to the 1941–1942 Court?
a. 6, 3.
b. 0, 9.
c. 5, 4.
d. 9, 0.

**6.** Which of Richard Nixon's appointments changed from being a conservative justice to the most liberal member of his Court?
a. William Rehnquist.
b. Harry Blackmun.
c. Warren Burger.
d. Lewis Powell.

**7.** What is the current role of the American Bar Association in the judicial confirmation process?
a. It plays no role.
b. It is used by the Senate only.
c. It is used by both the White House and the Senate.
d. It is used by the White House only.

**8.** In the current Senate, how many votes should a president have to ensure confirmation?
a. A simple majority of those senators present and voting.
b. A constitutional majority of 51.
c. A plurality of votes from each political party's members.
d. Sixty votes to prevent a filibuster from occurring.

**9.** Which of the following justices have *not* been "swing justices," tipping the Court's decision from one ideological side to the other?
a. Lewis Powell.
b. Arthur Goldberg.
c. Sandra Day O'Connor.
d. Antonin Scalia.

**10.** The tradition of deferring to a sitting senator from your own party in making judicial appointments from that person's state is known as
a. senatorial deference.
b. senatorial respect.
c. senatorial courtesy.
d. senatorial delegation.

**11.** What percentage of the appeals to the Supreme Court are granted for review?
a. About 5%.
b. Less than 1%.
c. About 3%.
d. About 4%.

**12.** The process that gives the Supreme Court total control over its own appellate jurisdiction is called
a. writ of subpoena *duces tecum*.
b. writ of appeal.
c. writ of certiorari.
d. writ of mandamus.

**13.** It takes how many justices to accept a case for review?
a. 2.
b. 3.
c. 4.
d. 5.

**14.** Who assigns the opinions for writing by the Supreme Court?
a. Always the chief justice.
b. A vote of those in the majority on a case.
c. The justices ask to take certain cases themselves.
d. The chief justice if he or she is in the majority, and the senior justice in the majority if the chief is not in the majority.

**15.** The legal doctrine of stare decisis is defined as
a. a majority vote of the Court determines its result.
b. the Court decides cases by following its precedents.
c. judges decide cases by examining the facts.
d. judges must decide cases by examining the laws.

**16.** Justice Antonin Scalia follows which judicial theory of interpretation?
a. Originalism.
b. Original intent.
c. Natural rights theory.
d. Living, evolving Constitution.

**17.** The liberals on the Court, such as Stephen Breyer, follow which judicial theory of interpretation?
a. Liberal construction.
b. Strict construction.
c. Living, evolving Constitution.
d. Judicial expansion.

**18.** The theory of judicial self-restraint is defined as
a. judges who restrain themselves from taking appeals.
b. judges who restrain themselves from questioning attorneys arguing appeals.
c. judges who seek ways to avoid deciding cases.
d. judges who believe that they should defer to the legislature, executive branch, and state political actors because they are appointed, not elected.

**19.** How many justices on the current Court are best described as judicial activists, ones willing to use their power even if it means overturning acts of the political branches and the states?
a. 5.
b. 6.
c. 7.
d. All of them.

**20.** Who on the current Court has taken over Sandra Day O'Connor's role as the "swing justice," deciding by his or her vote which way the Court majority will decide?
a. Samuel Alito.
b. John Roberts.
c. Anthony Kennedy.
d. Sonia Sotomayor.

**ANSWERS**
**1.** c, **2.** b, **3.** b, **4.** c, **5.** d, **6.** b, **7.** c, **8.** d, **9.** d, **10.** c, **11.** b, **12.** c, **13.** c, **14.** d, **15.** b, **16.** a, **17.** c, **18.** d, **19.** d, **20.** c

# 7 The Bureaucracy

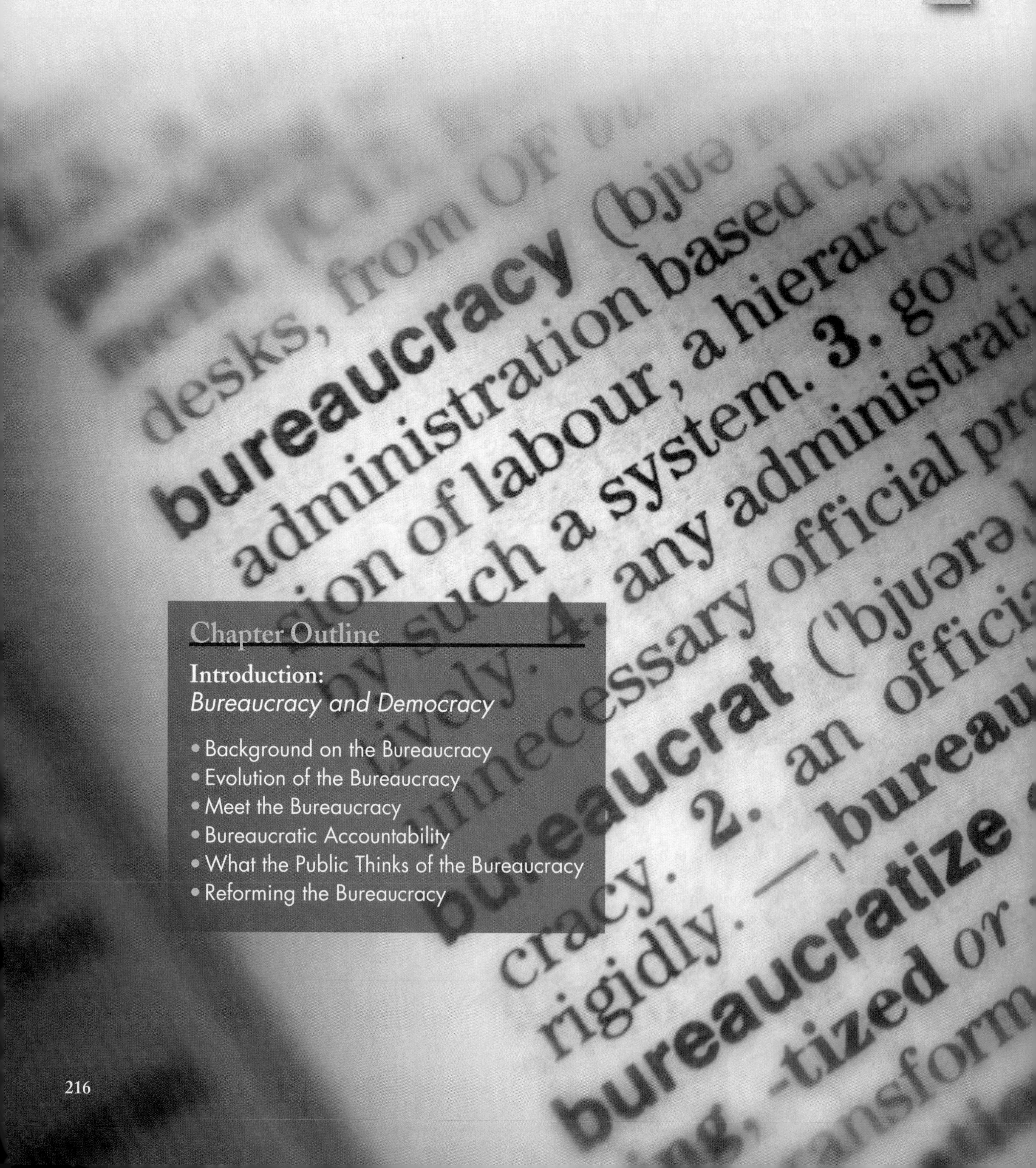


## Chapter Outline

**Introduction:**
*Bureaucracy and Democracy*

- Background on the Bureaucracy
- Evolution of the Bureaucracy
- Meet the Bureaucracy
- Bureaucratic Accountability
- What the Public Thinks of the Bureaucracy
- Reforming the Bureaucracy

## Learning Objectives

7.1 How does the bureaucracy measure up as a transparent democratic institution?

7.2 How do specialization, hierarchy, and a system of formal rules both positively and negatively influence the performance of the bureaucracy?

7.3 How has the bureaucracy grown and evolved over time?

7.4 What is a bureaucrat, what functions does a bureaucracy serve, and how is the federal bureaucracy structured?

7.5 Are bureaucrats responsible to the public, or do these unelected civil servants make policy outside the expectations of democratic rule?

7.6 Why are Americans critical of bureaucracy, and are these criticisms justified?

7.7 What are some methods of bureaucratic reform?

# INTRODUCTION

## BUREAUCRACY AND DEMOCRACY

7.1 *How does the bureaucracy measure up as a transparent democratic institution?*

As you learned in Chapter 1, democracy requires plurality, but in this chapter you will see that that bureaucracy requires unity. Democratic society is organized around the principle of equality, whereas bureaucratic organization is hierarchical. A fundamental element in any democracy is openness, but bureaucratic operations often demand secrecy, especially when national security is involved. A democratic political system ensures equal access to participation in politics, but bureaucratic participation depends on institutional authority. Finally, democracy assumes the election and subsequent public accountability of all officials, but bureaucrats are usually appointed, and the agencies they lead are often created without congressional action and thus not subject to public accountability.

Although the bureaucracy is an institution often scorned for its enormous size and lack of responsiveness or accountability (have you ever heard a politician running on a pro-bureaucracy platform?), the "fourth branch" of government has an important function that makes it indispensable in America's approach to democracy: carrying forth the work of the federal government. In the post–9/11 world, many organizations have shifted their focus to fighting terrorism and protecting America. The Departments of Justice, Homeland Security, and Defense now work more closely in sharing intelligence and other resources in order to keep America and its citizens safe. The Federal Bureau of Investigation (FBI) and National Security Agency (NSA) have greatly expanded their supervision of individuals deemed to be a threat to American interests. The National Guard, as one of its increasingly influential roles, has been deployed along the United States–Mexico border to protect it from illegal immigration.

Many of these aforementioned bureaucratic or administrative actions challenge core values such as freedom and liberty. Are America's citizens willing to compromise some of our democratic principles if it means achieving the greater good—the survival of our nation and the

Janet Napolitano speaks during a briefing at the headquarters of the Federal Emergency Management Agency (FEMA). As Director of the Department of Homeland Security, Napolitano is responsible for overseeing a broad range of agencies, including FEMA, Immigration Services, the Coast Guard, the Secret Service, and Border Protection. These widespread responsibilities are overseen by a number of Congressional committees, requiring the Homeland Security to devote a significant amount of time and resources responding to Congressional investigations. By August of 2011, Homeland Security officials spent $10 million responding to investigations from more than 180 Congressional committees and subcommittees, which includes preparing testimony at 119 hearings and issuing nearly 2,000 briefs.

eradication of terrorist networks? What if this includes warrantless wiretaps of our private conversations? An *Inspector General Report* in July 2009 revealed that the Bush administration built an unprecedented surveillance operation that went far beyond the warrantless wiretapping previously acknowledged. The report, compiled by five inspectors general, refers to "unprecedented collection activities" by U.S. intelligence agencies under an executive order signed by President George W. Bush after the September 11, 2001, terrorist attacks.[1] But what if the vice president of the United States ordered the Central Intelligence Agency to withhold information about a secret counterterrorism program from Congress for eight years? The law requires the president to make sure the intelligence committees "are kept fully and currently informed of the intelligence activities of the United States, including any significant anticipated intelligence activity."[2]

There are inherent contradictions between bureaucratic necessity and democratic ideals that require all of us to rethink how secretive bureaucratic organizations such as the National Security Agency (NSA) or the Central Intelligence Agency (CIA) can gain and maintain legitimacy without public disclosure of their activities. Can secretive organizations that offer no constitutional oversight be relied on to act responsibly when it comes to the issue of prisoner internment without resorting to the torture and prisoner abuse that occurred at Abu Ghraib? Finally, there is just the inherent nature of bureaucracy and filling out all those forms. In 2009, "Americans spent nearly 10 billion hours filling out more than 8,000 different government forms and other official requests for information tracked by the federal budget office. That compares with roughly one billion hours spent on similar paperwork in 1981, which in hindsight looks to have been a refreshingly uncomplicated time."[3] Thinking about all these interrelated issues should help you better understand the challenge of America's approaching democracy.

**QUICK REVIEW**

Weber's Efficient Bureaucracy

- *Specialization:* delegating specific tasks to individuals whose training and experience give them the expertise to execute them.
- *Hierarchy:* a clear chain of communication and command running from an executive director at the top down through all levels of workers.
- *A system of formal rules:* clearly defined procedures for executing assigned tasks.

# BACKGROUND ON THE BUREAUCRACY

7.2 *How do specialization, hierarchy, and a system of formal rules both positively and negatively influence the performance of the bureaucracy?*

Although Americans usually measure the performance of bureaucratic agencies by the impact of their failures rather than by their routine successes, it is difficult to imagine a world without bureaucracy. "Bureaucracy is the cod-liver oil of social institutions. It smells bad and leaves a nasty aftertaste, but sometimes it is just what you need."[4] In part, Americans are suspect of their bureaucracy because they realize that government agencies mostly function with little or no citizen restraint. Indeed, the bureaucracy as the "fourth branch of government" operates without the regular elections or oversight that keeps institutions responsive to public opinion.

A **bureaucracy** is a large and complex organizational system in which tasks, roles, and responsibilities are structured to achieve a goal. The term is rooted in the 18th-century French word for a woolen cloth *(burel)* used to cover a writing desk, or *bureau.* The term *bureaucracy* means "power of the desk" in reference to the administrative responsibilities of government. **Bureaucrats,** the people who work in a bureaucracy, include not only the obscure, faceless clerks normally disparaged by critics of government but also "street-level" bureaucrats, such as police officers, mail carriers, social workers, and schoolteachers.

German sociologist Max Weber (1865–1920) is considered the father of modern bureaucracy. He modeled his "ideal type" of bureaucratic organization on the Prussian government of the early 20th century. He believed that a bureaucracy should improve efficiency by three means: through specialization, hierarchy, and a system of formal rules.[5]

The principle of **specialization** rests on delegating specific tasks to individuals whose training and experience give them the expertise to execute them. As government responsibilities increase, so too does the need for specialization, or more experts in various areas. Bureaucratic organization also requires **hierarchy,** a clear chain of communication and command running from an executive director at the

**bureaucracy**
A large and complex organizational system in which tasks, roles, and responsibilities are structured to achieve a goal.

**bureaucrats**
People who work in a bureaucracy; not only the obscure, faceless clerks normally disparaged by critics of government but also "street-level bureaucrats" such as police officers, social workers, and schoolteachers.

**specialization**
A principle that, in a bureaucracy, specific tasks should be delegated to individuals whose training and experience give them the expertise to execute them. Also refers to a norm used to push legislation through Congress in which members who lack expertise in a particular policy area defer to policy specialists with more knowledge.

**hierarchy**
A clear chain of communication and command running from an executive director at the top down through all levels of workers.

top down through all levels of workers, such as the mailroom clerks in the middle and janitors at the bottom. The hierarchy facilitates decision making and establishes clear lines of authority within a large, complex organization. As we create new bureaucratic organizations in which multiple agencies coordinate and collaborate, such as the Department of Homeland Security, we need new approaches to hierarchy.

In addition to specialization and hierarchical authority, bureaucratic organizations use **formal rules,** clearly defined procedures for executing their assigned tasks. Sometimes called *standard operating procedures* (*SOPs*), these rules simplify and establish routines for complex procedures, curtail favoritism, and improve the decision-making process by allowing bureaucrats to respond to a broad array of situations with a minimum of delay and confusion. Such formal rules also apply to the professional lives of bureaucrats. There are clearly defined steps for job advancement, specific descriptions of duties, and specific qualifications for salary increases.

# EVOLUTION OF THE BUREAUCRACY

## Growth of the Federal Bureaucracy

7.3 *How has the bureaucracy grown and evolved over time?*

America's early bureaucracy hardly resembled today's Leviathan, although the framers clearly considered the role of bureaucracy to be a central component of their new system. In *The Federalist,* no. 70, Alexander Hamilton wrote that "a government ill executed, whatever it may be in theory, must be, in practice, a bad government."

George Washington's budget for the entire bureaucracy in 1790 was just under $1.5 million, and the money funded only three departments: State, War, and Treasury. The largest of these, the Department of the Treasury, employed 70 workers, minuscule by modern standards. The federal government's rapid growth began in the late 19th century. At that time, industrial expansion was increasing the U.S. economy in size and complexity and destabilizing American social life. From that era onward, public commitment to activist government paved the way for the astonishing growth of the federal bureaucracy in the 20th century.

### THINKING CRITICALLY

Do you think that the United States could have become the world's most powerful country if the growth of the federal bureaucracy and government had been constrained?

Beginning in 1933, Franklin D. Roosevelt's New Deal involved the government in everyday economic affairs. Its programs dramatically increased the government's workforce and the scope and power of federal responsibilities. The New Deal emerged in response to the Great Depression, which brought massive unemployment—at times as much as a quarter of America's labor force was out of work—and a growing awareness of the need to provide more security for American citizens, both on the job and after retirement.

The New Deal consisted of a series of legislative acts, executive orders, and proclamations that created large-scale federal programs offering retirement insurance, health care, economic security, and poverty relief for Americans. Roosevelt built on his cousin President Theodore Roosevelt's earlier progress in using government power to increase regulation of finance and commerce. Responding to a wave of bank failures and lost deposits, Roosevelt's administration established the Federal Deposit Insurance Corporation (FDIC) to insure most bank deposits. Roosevelt's administration also created the Securities and Exchange Commission (SEC), the Federal National Mortgage Association (FNMA, or "Fannie Mae"), and the Federal Communications Commission (FCC) to regulate the stock exchanges, the interstate mortgage market, and the public airwaves, respectively.

The New Deal programs became the core of the modern **welfare state.** Although designed as temporary emergency programs to relieve Depression-era suffering, most New Deal agencies became a permanent part of the dramatically enlarged federal bureaucracy. In addition to expanding the bureaucracy, the New Deal era led to a

**formal rules**
In a bureaucracy, clearly defined procedures governing the execution of all tasks within the jurisdiction of a given agency.

**welfare state**
A social system whereby the government assumes primary responsibility for the welfare of citizens.

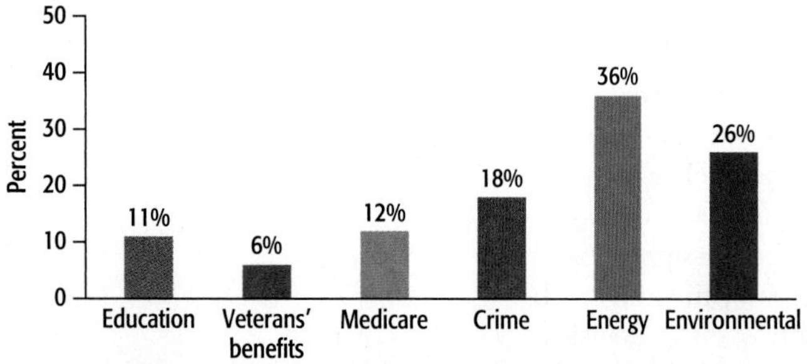


Percentages shown represent those respondents in a February 2011 Pew poll indicating support for a decrease in government spending for the specified programs.

**FIGURE 7.1** Few Americans Support Decreases in Specific Areas of Government Spending

*Global poverty assistance is the only category of spending with more respondents favoring a decrease in spending than respondents favoring an increase in spending. *Source:* Pew Research Center for the People & the Press, © 2011, Pew Research Center. Reprinted with the permission of the Pew Research Center for the People & the Press, www.pewforum.org.

growing dependence on that bureaucracy to administer and regulate many essential functions of modern American life.

Similarly, during World War II the federal government hired hundreds of thousands of temporary employees to plan and coordinate the vast assembly of personnel and machinery used to defeat the Axis Powers. After World War II, many of these "temporary" employees remained at work in government and were absorbed by agencies that redefined their civilian missions more broadly. But neither the growth of the bureaucracy nor the dependence on it by increasing numbers of Americans stopped with the end of the Great Depression and World War II. Since then, the size of the federal bureaucracy has been relatively stable, although hardly stagnant. In the decades since, public concerns about issues such as poverty, drugs, consumer safety, and terrorism have led to further growth of the federal bureaucracy, despite attempts at reigning in its size and budget.

Some politicians run for office by conducting a campaign against government bureaucracy. Ronald Reagan famously quipped that the nine most terrifying words in the English language are: "I'm from the government and I'm here to help." When announcing his campaign for the 2012 Republican presidential nomination, Texas governor Rick Perry promised that if elected, "[he'd] work every day to try to make Washington, D.C. as inconsequential in your life as [he] can."[6] Despite presiding over an increase in the federal bureaucracy larger than the six presidents preceding him, George W. Bush also campaigned as a small government advocate. Republicans are not the only politicians who run campaigns critical of the size of government. In 2000, Al Gore promised not to increase the number of federal employees if he was elected and said that he did not "ever want to see another era of big government."[7]

What is it that encourages politicians to campaign for government office by being critical of the government they are asking voters to make them a part of? Why is it that these same politicians, once elected, rarely do anything to broadly reign in the bureaucracy? The answer can be found in the sentiments of the American people. While being frustrated with government in the abstract, most Americans are thankful for government in their day-to-day lives and, as illustrated in Figure 7.1, are reluctant to cut funding for most government funding. It is the government that ensures the water coming from your tap is not full of carcinogens, for example. The government is there to regulate nuclear waste disposal, ban harmful pesticides, and keep poisonous bacteria out of the food supply, and it is the government that comes to the rescue after natural disasters. At an August 2011 event, President Obama came to the defense of government:

> *You'll hear a lot of folks, by the way, say that government is broken. Well, government and politics are two different things. Government is our troops who are fighting on our behalf in Afghanistan and Iraq. That's government. Government are also those FEMA folks when there's a flood or a drought or some emergency who come out and are helping the people out. That's government. Government's Social Security. Government are teachers in the classroom. Government are our firefighters and our police officers, and the folks who keep our water clean and our air clean to breathe, and our agricultural workers. And when you go to a national park, . . . that's government.*[8]

## Evolution of the Bureaucracy: Creating the Civil Service

The federal bureaucracy has grown enormously since the early days of the republic (see the nearby timeline for this chapter). There has also been a corresponding change in its character. Prior to the presidential election of Andrew Jackson in 1828, a small, elite group of wealthy, well-educated white males dominated the bureaucracy. Jackson, a populist, was determined to make the federal workforce more representative by opening up jobs to the masses. He instituted a new system based on the declaration of his friend, Senator William Marcy: "To the victor go the spoils."[9] The emergence of this **spoils system** meant that Jackson and his subordinates would award top-level government jobs and contracts on the basis of party loyalty rather than social or economic status or relevant experience.

Jackson's opponents in the Whig Party recognized the advantages of using government jobs for patronage purposes, and when Jackson's Democrats were voted out of office, the bureaucracy was restaffed by those loyal to the Whigs. Later on, as the government grew, supporters of the spoils system found that if a thousand patronage jobs were beneficial, ten thousand or twenty thousand would be even more welcome.

The spoils system survived until the 1881 assassination of President James Garfield by Charles Guiteau, who was bitter about his inability to find a job in Garfield's administration. In response, Congress passed the Pendleton Act of 1883, which created a **civil service,** a system of hiring and promoting employees based on professional merit, not party loyalty. Such a system was designed to protect government employees from political threats to their job security. The act also created a three-person Civil Service Commission to oversee the merit system throughout the federal workforce. The Civil Service Commission evaluated job applicants based on their performance on civil service examinations. Employees achieved permanent status after a probationary period and were promoted only with strong performance evaluations from supervisors. The Civil Service Commission functioned until 1978, when the Civil Service Reform Act replaced it with two agencies: the Office of Personnel Management administers civil service recruitment and promotion procedures, and the independent Merit Systems Protection Board studies the merit system and holds grievance and disciplinary hearings for federal employees. See Table 7.1 for the 2011 salary scales for federal workers.

Today, merit-based hiring and advancement have eliminated much of the corruption and cronyism of the old patronage system. The civil service system encourages hiring of highly skilled experts and provides procedures for evaluating federal workers' qualifications and job performance. The civil service has a downside, however. For one thing, it insulates federal employees from many pressures of a competitive private-sector job market. For example, federal employees are hard to fire or even discipline. The employee must receive written notice at least 30 days in advance, detailing the reasons for, and specific examples of, the conduct prompting the action. The employee may then appeal the action to the Merit Systems Protection Board (MSPB), which must grant a hearing, at which point the employee has the right to legal counsel. If the MSPB rejects the appeal, the employee may take the case to the U.S. court

## Approaching Democracy Timeline

### The Professionalization of a Career Bureaucracy

| | |
|---|---|
| **1828** | Andrew Jackson ushers in the spoils system. |
| **1881** | President Garfield is assassinated by a disgruntled supporter, angry he did not obtain a patronage position in the bureaucracy. |
| **1883** | Congress passes the Pendleton Act of 1883, creating a civil service. |
| **1939** | Congress passes the Hatch Act, preventing federal civil servants from using their power or position to influence elections. |
| **1947** | The Supreme Court rejects challenges to the Hatch Act, upholding restrictions on the political freedoms of federal employees. |
| **1978** | Congress passes the Civil Service Reform Act. |
| **1978** | The Senior Executive Service (SES) is established as part of the Civil Service Reform Act, envisioning members who shared values, broad perspectives on government, and solid executive skills. |
| **1989** | The Whistleblower Protection Act, which protects federal whistleblowers or persons who work for the government who report agency misconduct, is passed. |
| **1993** | Congress amends the Hatch Act to allow federal employees to participate more actively in partisan politics. |
| **2010** | The Whistleblower Protection Enhancement Act, which would amend the WPA to extend whistleblower protections to federal employees who specialize in national security issues, dies in the Senate. |

Democratic   Neutral   Undemocratic

**spoils system**
A system in which government jobs and contracts are awarded on the basis of party loyalty rather than social or economic status or relevant experience.

**civil service**
A system of hiring and promoting employees based on professional merit, not party loyalty.

**Table 7.1** General Schedule Salary Scale 2011

Positions within the federal government are classified by occupational series, grade or pay level, and pay plan. Pay plans identify the pay system under which the position is covered. Many white-collar employees are paid under the General Schedule (GS), and are paid annual salaries. President Obama signed a pay freeze for federal workers on December 22, 2010, which froze the salary scale at the 2010 levels.

| Grade | Step 1 | Step 2 | Step 3 | Step 4 | Step 5 | Step 6 | Step 7 | Step 8 | Step 9 | Step 10 | Within Grade Amounts |
|---|---|---|---|---|---|---|---|---|---|---|---|
| 1 | $17,803 | $ 18,398 | $ 18,990 | $ 19,579 | $ 20,171 | $ 20,519 | $ 21,104 | $ 21,694 | $ 21,717 | $ 22,269 | Varies |
| 2 | 20,017 | 20,493 | 21,155 | 24,024 | 21,961 | 22,607 | 23,253 | 23,899 | 24,545 | 245,191 | $ 646 |
| 3 | 21,840 | 22,568 | 23,296 | 24,024 | 24,752 | 25,480 | 26,208 | 26,936 | 27,664 | 28,392 | 728 |
| 4 | 24,518 | 25,335 | 26,152 | 26,969 | 27,786 | 28,603 | 29,420 | 30,237 | 31,054 | 31,871 | 817 |
| 5 | 27,431 | 28,345 | 29,259 | 30,173 | 31,087 | 32,001 | 32,915 | 33,829 | 34,743 | 35,657 | 914 |
| 6 | 30,577 | 31,596 | 32,615 | 33,634 | 34,653 | 35,672 | 36,691 | 37,710 | 38,729 | 39,748 | 1,019 |
| 7 | 33,979 | 35,112 | 36,245 | 37,378 | 38,511 | 39,644 | 40,777 | 41,910 | 43,043 | 44,176 | 1,133 |
| 8 | 37,631 | 38,885 | 40,139 | 41,393 | 42,647 | 43,901 | 45,155 | 46,409 | 47,663 | 48,917 | 1,254 |
| 9 | 41,563 | 42,948 | 44,333 | 45,718 | 47,103 | 48,488 | 49,873 | 51,258 | 52,643 | 54,028 | 1,385 |
| 10 | 45,771 | 47,297 | 48,823 | 50,349 | 51,875 | 53,401 | 54,927 | 56,453 | 57,979 | 59,505 | 1,526 |
| 11 | 50,287 | 51,963 | 53,639 | 55,315 | 56,991 | 58,667 | 60,343 | 62,019 | 63,695 | 65,371 | 1,676 |
| 12 | 60,274 | 62,283 | 64,292 | 66,301 | 68,310 | 70,319 | 72,328 | 74,337 | 76,346 | 78,355 | 2,009 |
| 13 | 71,674 | 74,063 | 76,452 | 78,841 | 81,230 | 83,619 | 86,008 | 88,397 | 90,786 | 93,175 | 2,389 |
| 14 | 84,697 | 87,520 | 90,343 | 93,166 | 95,989 | 98,812 | 101,635 | 104,458 | 107,281 | 110,104 | 2,823 |
| 15 | 99,628 | 102,949 | 106,270 | 109,591 | 112,912 | 116,233 | 119,554 | 122,875 | 126,196 | 129,517 | 3,321 |

*Source:* U.S. Office of Personnel Management, http://www.opm.gov/oca/11tables/html/gs.asp.

of appeals. The process has become so burdensome that, rather than attempt to fire unproductive employees, supervisors have learned to live with them.

Civil service guidelines not only insulate the federal workforce but they also tend to give some agencies a sense that they are untouchable, whatever the periodic changes in the political climate of the country. One common remark associated with career civil servants when they are asked about a change in presidential administration is that whereas presidents are temporary employees, careerists in the bureaucracy stay for life. Research has shown that most civil servants tend to conform to the policy directives of administrations and honor the Code of Ethics for Government Service provided in Table 7.2 as they come and go, but determined resistance to presidential initiatives can hamper a president's agenda considerably.

Congress passed the **Hatch Act,** named for its author, New Mexico senator Carl Hatch, in 1939. The act works to make the bureaucracy more responsive to the policy directives of changing presidential administrations and to move it in the direction of greater political neutrality with a list of political dos and don'ts for federal employees. The Hatch Act was designed to prevent federal civil servants from using their power or position to influence elections, thereby creating a nonpartisan, nonpolitical, professionalized bureaucracy. Under the act, bureaucrats may express opinions about issues and candidates and contribute money to political organizations, but they cannot distribute campaign information, nor can they campaign actively for or against a candidate. A federal employee may register and vote in an election but cannot run as a candidate for public office.

**Hatch Act**
Approved by Congress in 1939 and named for its author, Senator Carl Hatch of New Mexico, a list of political dos and don'ts for federal employees; designed to prevent federal civil servants from using their power or position to engage in political activities to influence elections, thereby creating a nonpartisan, nonpolitical, professionalized bureaucracy.

Although the authors of the Hatch Act believed it necessary to restrict the political liberties of government employees to preserve the neutrality of the growing maze of federal agencies and programs, these restrictions illustrate one area where

**Table 7.2** Code of Ethics for Government Service

*Resolved by the House of Representatives {the Senate concurring}, That it is the sense of the Congress that the following Code of Ethics should be adhered to by all Government employees, including officeholders.*

**Any person in Government service should:**

1. Put loyalty to the highest moral principles and to country above loyalty to Government persons, party, or department.
2. Uphold the Constitution, laws, and legal regulations of the United States and of all governments therein and never be a party to their evasion.
3. Give a full day's labor for a full day's pay; giving to the performance of his duties his earnest effort and best thought.
4. Seek to find and employ more efficient and economical ways of getting tasks accomplished.
5. Never discriminate unfairly by the dispensing of special favors or privileges to anyone, whether for remuneration or not; and never accept for himself or his family, favors or benefits under circumstances which might be construed by reasonable persons as influencing the performance of his governmental duties.
6. Make no private promises of any kind binding upon the duties of office, since a Government employee has no private word which can be binding on public duty.
7. Engage in no business with the Government, either directly or indirectly which is inconsistent with the conscientious performance of his governmental duties.
8. Never use any information coming to him confidentially in the performance of governmental duties as a means for making private profit.
9. Expose corruption wherever discovered.
10. Uphold these principles, ever conscious that public office is a public trust.

*Source:* U.S. House of Representatives Ethics Committee.

bureaucracy clashes with democratic ideals. Nearly 3 million American civilians who work for the federal government have their rights to full participation in the nation's political process sharply curtailed. In Table 7.3, test your knowledge of what federal employees are allowed to do. Although many civil servants and constitutional scholars have denounced the Hatch Act as unconstitutional, the Supreme Court has disagreed with them. The merits of a neutrally competent civil service is the focus of the Approaching Contemporary Issues in Democracy feature.

**Table 7.3** Know Your Grasp of the Hatch Act

Test your Hatch Act IQ. Knowing the right answers could keep you from losing your job, being fined or suspended, or maybe even going to jail.

Federal employees may do the following (true or false):

_____ 1. Sign a nominating petition for a partisan candidate.
_____ 2. Assist in voter registration drives.
_____ 3. Hold office in a political club or party.
_____ 4. Contribute money to a political organization and attend political fund-raisers.
_____ 5. Wear a political button at work.
_____ 6. Distribute political party literature at a polling place on Election Day.
_____ 7. Solicit contributions to a partisan political fund-raiser.
_____ 8. Park a car with a political bumper sticker in a federally owned or subsidized parking lot.
_____ 9. Participate in partisan political activity if employed by the Office of Personnel Management, the Commerce Department, the Bureau of Indian Affairs, or the Health Care Finance Administration.
_____ 10. Participate in partisan political activity if employed in a low-level job by the Central Intelligence Agency, the National Security Council, the Federal Bureau of Investigation, or the Contract Appeals Boards.
_____ 11. Wear a political button on a government-issued uniform if off duty or on vacation or other approved leave.

Answers

1. true, 2. true, 3. true, 4. true, 5. false, 6. true, 7. false, 8. true, 9. true, 10. false, 11. false.

## APPROACHING
## Contemporary Issues in Democracy

### The Merits of a Career Civil Service System

**ISSUE:** What if the merit requirements of the civil service were eliminated and we returned to the days of the spoils system? How would this change the democratic nature of the bureaucracy?

**Question 1:**

Do you think a return to the spoils system would increase the political participation of young voters? Would your peers be more likely to volunteer for a campaign or donate money to a candidate if it would help them get a civil service job when they graduate from college?

**Question 2:**

How would a change like this shape those bureaucracies most in need of experts? What about the scientists at NASA and the EPA? Should they be required to pass a political litmus test?

**Question 3:**

Would you be comfortable with political partisans running the government's police power agencies? Would partisans running the FBI, CIA, and NSA use the powers of their agencies to target those in the other party, thereby attempting to ensure their party maintains in power?

# MEET THE BUREAUCRACY

7.4 *What is a bureaucrat, what functions does a bureaucracy serve, and how is the federal bureaucracy structured?*

What does the federal workforce look like? Figures 7.2 and 7.3 provide you with both the geographic distribution as well as the distribution across the federal branches of government of the civilian workforce. *Civilians* employed by the federal government work in more than 15,000 official job categories, ranging from electricians to paper-hangers, from foreign service officers to postal service workers. There are nearly 100,000 regulators; 150,000 engineers; hundreds of thousands of analysts, clerks, and secretarial staff; 15,000 foresters; 2,300 veterinarians; 3,000 photographers; and 500 chaplains. Surprisingly, only 12.2 percent of federal employees work in the Washington, DC, area.

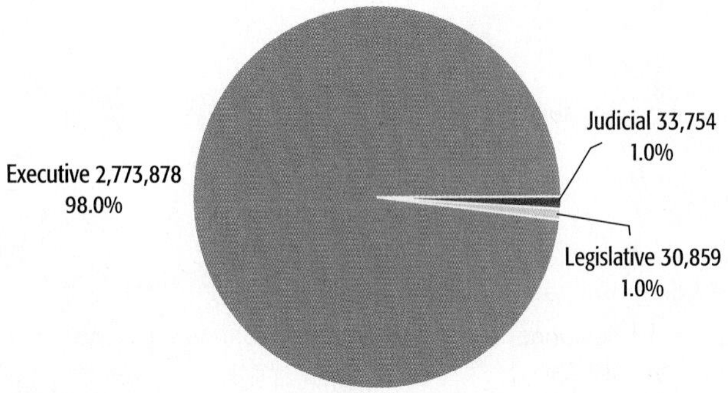


**FIGURE 7.2** Distribution of Federal Employment by Branch for September 2009

*Source:* The U.S. Office of Personnel Management, Employment and Trends, September 2009, http://www.opm.gov/feddata/html/2009/September/charts.asp.

## What the Bureaucracy Does

The bureaucracy performs three key governmental tasks: implementation, administration, and regulation.[10] Bureaucrats, usually referred to as civil servants within a career federal bureaucracy, perform many essential functions that we take for granted. Bureaucrats direct air traffic, patrol U.S. borders to control the flow of people and drugs, and deliver the mail. Civil servants are typical working Americans whose jobs, although hardly glamorous, are important to the smooth functioning of society. Whenever a letter is delivered on time, an application for governmental financial aid is processed or a highway is repaired, the bureaucracy has done its job.

Because bureaucrats have been facing pressure from private competitors, they have found it in their interest to be more attentive to public opinion and more open to useful suggestions from within the organization. This development has occurred in spite of the fact that their institutional authority is based on professional expertise. Most bureaucratic specialists feel—often rightly—that they know more than most about an issue.

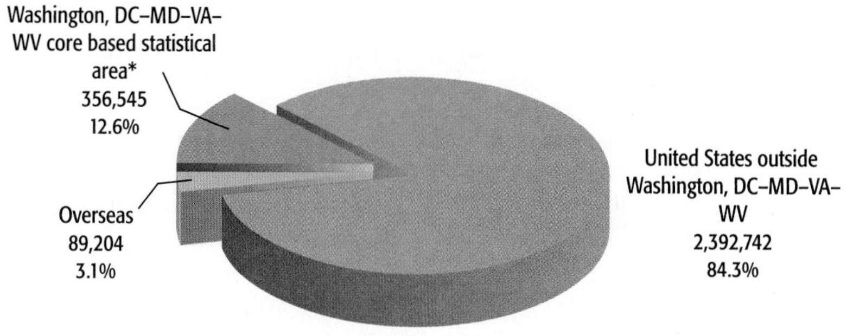


**FIGURE 7.3** Distribution of Federal Civilian Employment by Major Geographical Area for September 2009

*Washington, DC–Maryland–Virginia–West Virginia area includes the District of Columbia; Calvert, Charles, Frederick, Montgomery, and Price George's counties in Maryland; Arlington, Clarke, Fairfax, Fauquier, Loudoun, Prince William, Spotsylvania, Stafford, and Warren counties and the cities of Alexandria, Fairfax, Falls Church, Fredericksburg, Manassas, and Manassas Park in Virginia; and Jefferson County in West Virginia.

*Source:* The U.S. Office of Personnel Management, Employment and Trends, September 2009, http://www.opm.gov/feddata/html/2009/September/charts.asp.

**Implementation** A primary task of the bureaucracy is to implement the policies established by Congress and the executive branch. **Implementation** means providing the necessary organization and expertise to put into action any policy that has become law. When, for example, Congress passed legislation establishing the Head Start early childhood care and education program in the 1960s, a new agency was established to "flesh out" the program guidelines, hire and train employees, and disburse appropriated federal monies. When the Department of Justice was wiretapping U.S. citizens to catch suspected terrorists, it turned to the U.S. Foreign Intelligence Surveillance Court (or FISC) in order to gain warrants and make such intelligence gathering and antiterrorism behavior legal. During the 2011 debt-ceiling debate, Congress delayed funding for the Federal Aviation Administration (FAA). Without funding, the FAA was forced to shut down all of its nonessential implementation of federal law. This meant that without employees to process airline taxes and fees, the government lost $30 million a day (which most airlines kept as profit instead of refunding their customers). Additionally, the FAA had to furlough 74,000 workers who were building new runways, improving airports, and modernizing air traffic control towers in order to implement Congress's Next Generation Air Transportation Systems Plan. By failing to fund the bureaucratic agency with the organization and expertise to carry out federal aviation law, the government's aviation policy was not successfully implemented during the shutdown.

**implementation**
The act of providing the organization and expertise required to put into action any policy that has become law; also refers to the actual execution of a policy.

**administrative discretion**
The latitude that an agency, or even a single bureaucrat, has in interpreting and applying a law.

Implementation can involve a considerable amount of bureaucratic autonomy. Administrators exercise **administrative discretion**—the latitude an agency, or even a single bureaucrat, has in interpreting and applying a law. When passing legislation, Congress often does little more than declare policy goals, assign their implementation to an agency, and make money available to the agency. Lack of statutory specificity may help a bill over the legislative hurdles, but after a bill is passed, bureaucratic managers must step in and, exercising administrative discretion, draft detailed guidelines for all the various procedures required to turn policies into workable programs.

Despite good intentions, implementation can go awry. Frequently, state and local interest groups resist new policies or raise questions—for example, about clean air and water laws—that make implementation difficult if not impossible. In 1994–1995, citizens in Maine, Pennsylvania, and Texas protested the implementation of strict auto emissions tests ordered by the Environmental Protection Agency. As a result, legislatures in all three states suspended the programs, preferring the wrath of the EPA to the wrath of their constituents. In 2007, several states took the EPA to court over emissions

As Hurricane Katrina approaches, thousands lined up outside the Superdome in New Orleans waiting for buses to take them out of the city. Most of the people in line did not have a car to escape or a place to go.

**administration**
Performance of routine tasks associated with a specific policy goal.

**regulation**
A rule-making administrative body must clarify and interpret legislation, its enforcement, and the adjudication of disputes about it.

standards, with the Supreme Court ruling in favor of the states. Shortly after, California challenged the EPA to allow the state to monitor its own emissions standards.

**Administration** Another bureaucratic task is **administration,** performing the routine tasks associated with a specific policy goal. Bureaucrats exercise a lot less administrative discretion at this stage. By looking at the federal government's post–9/11 activities, one can see that virtually every agency contributed to the relief effort. In New York alone, the Federal Emergency Management Agency had eight 62-member urban search-and-rescue teams working closely with the Army Corps of Engineers, the General Services Administration, and the Environmental Protection Agency.

The federal government had to determine if the water was safe to drink, if other structures were not likely to collapse, and whether that section of New York City should be declared a "Superfund" site, thereby providing additional cleanup money. The Department of Health and Human Services provided grants for child care, elder assistance, mental health care, and other services for those left homeless or bereft following the collapse of the two towers. The Departments of Justice and Treasury were called in to administer improved airport security. U.S. Customs administered additional scrutiny at U.S. borders. The Internal Revenue Service extended income tax filing deadlines for all involved in the search-and-rescue efforts. The Department of Housing and Urban Development processed Federal Housing Authority (FHA) loans to thousands in need of assistance. The so-called simple administrative tasks of bureaucracy became the vital survival link to those immediately affected by the terrorist attack in New York. By expanding this list to include services provided at the Pentagon, one may begin to sense the responsibilities given to America's fourth branch of government.

**Regulation** Another important bureaucratic task is **regulation.** Regulation involves making rules, enforcing them, and adjudicating disputes about them. In many areas of American life, the bureaucracy establishes and enforces guidelines regulating behavior and enforcing punishments for violation of those guidelines.[11]

Administrative regulation is pervasive in America. The U.S. Department of Agriculture regulates the quality of our breakfast food, including organically grown products. It has been busy with numerous investigations of tainted food, including tracing the source of tainted turkey which caused 80 illnesses and one death in July 2011. The Food and Drug Administration regulates labeling rules that apply to, for example, the booming diet supplement industry. After a hard day, Americans often watch television programming whose content must fall within guidelines established by the Federal Communications Commission. At the end of the day, we get into bed and snuggle under blankets certified as fire resistant by the Consumer Product Safety Commission. Americans drive cars that reduce pollution by using catalytic converters mandated by the Environmental Protection Agency. They buckle their car seat belts because it is the law, and it is the law because the Federal Highway Administration withholds federal funds from states that do not require seat belt use. At work, Americans conform to antidiscrimination guidelines established by the Equal Employment Opportunity Commission. Whether implementing, administering, or regulating, bureaucrats exercise a great deal of autonomy and have power over our lives. Given the complex demands on the bureaucracy, such power is inevitable. But, some ask, whose interests do the bureaucrats serve? Are they responsive to the needs of the public? In fact, many bureaucrats do heed the voices of ordinary citizens and seek to stay in the good graces of the two government institutions most responsive to public opinion: Congress and the presidency.

The Obama administration moved quickly to implement a range of proposals on its financial regulatory agenda. Continuing its push to establish rules that make the financial system more fair for consumers and investors, the administration fought to pass significant reforms to the financial system. In July 2010, President Obama signed the Dodd-Frank Wall Street Reform and Consumer Protection Act, which changed the existing regulatory system by creating new agencies to increase

## QUICK REVIEW

Structure of the Bureaucracy

- Departments conduct a broad range of government operations.
- Independent agencies deal with specific groups and problems.
- Independent regulatory commissions carry out regulation and oversight functions.
- Government corporations act like businesses and have their own capital and personnel systems.

oversight of Wall Street and allow for more transparency in the financial markets.

An important piece of the Dodd-Frank Act is the creation of the Consumer Financial Protection Agency (CFPA) with the responsibility of focusing on the needs of consumers rather than those of banks or traders on Wall Street. Professor Elizabeth Warren first proposed the creation of the CFPA in a 2007 academic journal article. In 2010, President Obama asked her to help design and oversee the development of the new agency, which opened its doors in July 2011. President Obama did not nominate Elizabeth Warren to head the agency, fearing a tough battle with Republicans in the Senate over her confirmation. Instead, the agency opened without a director and the president appointed Richard Cordray to head the agency. Cordray is still awaiting Senate confirmation. The path forward for the new agency is not that clear. Many who fought to prevent the creation of the new agency would like to see it eliminated and Republicans in the Senate have said they will delay the confirmation of any nominee to head the agency. Despite its challenges, the CFPA has already begun reforming lending practices to make it easier on consumers. In a departing letter to the staff of the CFPA, Elizabeth Warren noted that "it was a hard fight, but the result was a strong and independent new [agency] with the tools needed to make a real difference for American families."[12]

In May 2011, Elizabeth Warren testified before a U.S. House Oversight Committee about the Consumer Financial Protection Bureau, an agency she helped organize as an adviser to the President.

## The Structure of the Federal Bureaucracy

The four institutions that constitute the federal bureaucracy are part of the executive branch. They are cabinet departments, independent agencies, independent regulatory commissions, and government corporations.

**Cabinet Departments** **Cabinet departments** are major administrative units responsible for conducting a broad range of government operations. Originally, the heads of these departments—usually called *secretaries*—were the president's closest advisers, although today the president's personal White House staff is more likely to command the president's attention. Each department is subdivided into smaller units called *divisions, sections, agencies,* and *offices*. Although each department has jurisdiction over a specific policy area, sometimes their responsibilities overlap, as when the State and Defense Departments address diplomatic and strategic aspects of U.S. foreign policy.

Overlapping jurisdictions was at the center of President Bush's 2001 executive order to create the Office of Homeland Security. The president selected Tom Ridge, a former prosecutor, congressman, and two-term Republican governor of Pennsylvania, to run the new office as assistant to the president for homeland security. In the weeks following September 11, Ridge helped coordinate a remarkable infrastructure involving the FBI, FEMA, DOE, EPA, Coast Guard, Army National Guard, and the Departments of Justice, Transportation, and other agencies of the federal government. In June 2002, President Bush proposed a new cabinet department for domestic defense. "We have concluded that our government must be reorganized to deal more effectively with the threats of the twenty-first century."[13] President Bush signed the bipartisan bill into law, creating the Homeland Security Department—the most comprehensive reorganization of the federal government in more than 50 years. Yet, this very reorganization came under intense scrutiny in September 2005 when Hurricane Katrina hit New Orleans and surrounding areas. As the nation looked on in shock and dismay at the failed federal response to Katrina, it became apparent that the problem rested in leadership as well as the bureaucracy itself.[14]

The Department of Homeland Security typifies many of the problems facing the U.S. bureaucratic system. Developing federal plans for preventing and responding

**cabinet departments**
Major administrative units whose heads are presidential advisers appointed by the president and confirmed by the Senate. They are responsible for conducting a broad range of government operations.

to terrorist attacks and then coordinating those blueprints with state and local governments is an enormous undertaking. It takes more than a presidential stroke of a pen to achieve the effective bureaucratic response, which is why the Obama administration's Homeland Security secretary, Janet Napolitano, faces such a difficult challenge with respect to airport security measures. Does the American public support such measures as full-body scans, or do they see this as an invasion of privacy?

**independent agencies**
Agencies established to regulate a sector of the nation's economy in the public interest.

**independent regulatory commissions**
Agencies established to be outside the power of both the president and the Congress in their operations. Such agencies have authority that is partly legislative and partly judicial.

**government corporation**
A semi-independent government agency that administers a business enterprise and takes the form of a business corporation.

**Independent Agencies** **Independent agencies** are usually smaller than cabinet departments and have a narrower set of responsibilities. Generally, they exist to perform a service. Congress may establish an independent agency so that it can keep particularly tight control over that agency's functions. For example, Congress may establish an independent agency when interest groups demand a government function performed with care and attention rather than by an indifferent department. Among the major independent agencies are the CIA, the EPA, the National Aeronautics and Space Administration (NASA), the Small Business Administration (SBA), the Peace Corps, and the General Services Administration (GSA), which manages federal property.

**Independent Regulatory Commissions** **Independent regulatory commissions** regulate sectors of the nation's economy in the public interest. For example, an independent regulatory commission might guard against unfair business practices or unsafe products. They generally are run by a board whose members have set terms, although some newer regulatory bodies are headed by a single individual, making the label "commission" something of a misnomer. These bodies establish rules, enforce rules, and adjudicate disputes about rules, all of the traditional functions of government—legislative, executive, and judicial. The agencies develop a great deal of expertise in a particular policy area, although sometimes they become too closely identified with the businesses they are charged with regulating. Congress and the courts rely on their expertise and are usually loath to overrule them.

Among the more important independent regulatory commissions are the Federal Communications Commission (FCC), which regulates radio and television; the Federal Reserve Board (the Fed), whose members function as a central bank for the United States; the Federal Trade Commission (FTC), which regulates advertising and labeling; the National Labor Relations Board (NLRB), which enforces the laws governing labor–management disputes; and the National Transportation Safety Board (NTSB). The NTSB investigates every civil aviation accident in the United States and significant accidents in other modes of transportation—railroad, highway, marine, and pipeline—and issues safety recommendations aimed at preventing future accidents. The NTSB maintains the government's database on civil aviation accidents and also conducts special studies of transportation safety issues of national significance.

**Government Corporations** A **government corporation** is a semi-independent government agency that administers a business enterprise and takes the form of a business corporation. Congress creates such agencies on the assumption that they will serve the public interest and gives them more independence and latitude for innovation than it gives other government agencies. A government corporation can raise its own capital and devise its own personnel system; it can, within the limits of its congressional charter, determine the kind of services it provides; and when the occasion seems favorable, it may develop new services. The Tennessee Valley Authority (TVA), a government corporation originally set up to control flooding and provide electricity to the area within the Tennessee River watershed, now manages the artificial lakes it created for recreational purposes, runs economic development programs, and experiments with alternative energy development.

In addition to possessing much of the flexibility of a private company, a government corporation also has the authority of government. It can take land, levy fees, and make rules that govern the public. Although these

## THINKING CRITICALLY

Which federal bureaucracies have you relied on to serve your needs as a student? Do you think there are a greater number of bureaucracies serving the needs of younger or of older people? What segment of society do you think both needs and deserves the most help from the federal government?

agencies have more leeway in establishing the nature and cost of the services they provide, they generally remain subject to more regulation than are private corporations. The U.S. Postal Service, for example, blames some of the requirements placed on it by Congress for the billions of dollars in deficits it has suffered since 2007. An August 2011 report noted that a one-day relaxation of delivery standards (increasing first-class delivery from one to three days to one to four days) would save the Postal Service $1.5 billion.[15] Congress is considering allowing the USPS to drop its required delivery days from six to five and may also allow for the requested relaxation in delivery standards. Besides the Postal Service and the TVA, other major government corporations include the Corporation for Public Broadcasting, the Federal Deposit Insurance Corporation, the Export-Import Bank, and Amtrak.

## Constraints on the Bureaucracy and Bureaucratic Culture

The bureaucracy faces three major constraints that shape its behavior:

1. Bureaucratic agencies do not control revenue.
2. Decisions about how to deliver goods and services must be made according to rules established elsewhere.
3. Other institutions mandate goals.

Because of these constraints, bureaucrats and bureaucracies behave differently than private-sector employees and companies. Certain *norms,* or unwritten rules of behavior, have developed, creating a unique bureaucratic culture.

First, Congress does not allow agencies to keep money left over when the fiscal year ends. Furthermore, an agency that ends the year with a surplus demonstrates to Congress that it can run on less than the current year's budget. As a consequence, bureaucrats have no incentive to conserve funds. In fact, they have every incentive to spend with abandon as the fiscal year draws to a close on September 30, in hopes of showing Congress that they have no surplus and, in fact, need more money for the next year. In addition, because bureaucrats are not supposed to profit from their dealings with government, they focus on nonmonetary incentives such as prestige. The bigger the budget and the larger the agency, the more prestige a bureaucrat acquires, providing managers with another reason to put political pressure on Congress to allow their agencies to grow.

Second, to ensure fairness, efficiency, and comprehensive program coverage, decisions about hiring, purchasing, contracting, and budgeting must follow rules established by Congress and the president. Since the end of World War II, Congress has passed an array of such rules. For example, the Administrative Procedure Act of 1946 governs the way an agency makes rules, publicizes its operations, and settles disputes; the Freedom of Information Act of 1966 ensures that most agency records are available to interested citizens on demand; the National Environmental Policy Act of 1969 requires federal agencies to prepare environmental impact statements for all actions that significantly affect the environment; the Privacy Act of 1974 limits the circumstances in which information about individuals can be released to other agencies and to the public; and the Government in the Sunshine Act of 1976 mandates open meetings of most regulatory decision-making bodies.

Such a system breeds rule-following managers, not managers who take initiative. It is no wonder that surrounded by such a thicket of regulations and laws, bureaucratic managers worry more about violating procedure than about marching boldly ahead to promote the public good. After all, managers can always explain poor outcomes by claiming that they were just following the rules.

Finally, bureaucratic agencies do not control their own goals, which Congress and the president set. Congress has told the U.S. Postal Service that it must charge one rate to deliver a first-class letter no matter where the letter goes. Furthermore, the Postal Service must deliver newspapers, magazines, and junk mail below cost, and it must keep small post offices open even though they may not be economical to operate.

After serving as Director of the CIA, Leon Panetta is sworn in as Secretary of Defense on July 22, 2011.

Despite such constraints, some administrative institutions flourish. A determined leader can instill a sense of mission even in employees of an organization whose offices are scattered across the nation. The Social Security Administration is such a mission-driven agency. Its personnel officers recruit potential employees who show an orientation to customer satisfaction, and managers constantly invoke an ethic of service when they talk to employees. Surveys show that bureaucrats who work for the Social Security Administration take pride in their jobs and do them well.

# BUREAUCRATIC ACCOUNTABILITY

7.5 *Are bureaucrats responsible to the public, or do these unelected civil servants make policy outside the expectations of democratic rule?*

American bureaucracy has made major strides toward democratic accountability. Today, few bureaucracies operate outside the law as the FBI did under J. Edgar Hoover in the 1950s and 1960s—although it, along with other members of the intelligence community, came under intense criticism for the methods adopted to fight the war against terrorism under President Bush. Today's administrators, influenced by modern business management techniques, spend as much time listening to their employees and to their customer—the public—as they do giving orders. Although a democratic voting process is used to make a few administrative rules, the policy-making process has broadened to include a variety of perspectives in recent years. Rule-making agencies take care to notify not only businesses subject to regulation about upcoming hearings but also to invite consumer and civil rights groups to testify.

On secrecy, the picture is less clear. Although the Administrative Procedure Act, the Freedom of Information Act, and the Government in the Sunshine Act have opened up routine administrative decisions to public scrutiny, the national security establishment continues to operate behind closed doors. The terrorist attacks on America created more layers of official secrets in the name of national and homeland security. The Bush administration did virtually everything it could to maintain official secrets; the Obama administration has taken steps in the name of transparency to reverse this process. See the Compared to What? feature for a look at how bureaucracy works in Japan.

## Presidential Control

One of the most common complaints of presidents is the difficulty of aligning the federal bureaucracy's objectives with the administration's priorities. President Harry Truman once complained, "I thought I was the president, but when it comes to these bureaucrats, I can't do a damn thing." Truman may have been exaggerating, but presidential control of the bureaucracy is more difficult than most incoming chief executives either thought or hoped.[16]

As the federal bureaucracy has grown, so, too, has the amount of energy presidents expend to rein in agencies that oppose their objectives. After a grueling election, the president enters office with a policy agenda presumably supported by at least a plurality of the American people. To pursue that policy agenda, the president must convince not only Congress but also the various federal agencies to cooperate with the White House. Presidents have four main strategies at their disposal: the appointment power, reorganization, the budget, and the power of persuasion.

**appointment power**
The president's power to name agency officials. Of the current approximately 3,000, about 700 are in policy-making positions, such as cabinet and subcabinet officials and bureau chiefs.

**The Appointment Power** Every president requires a clear agenda of policy goals. To advance that agenda, the president has a powerful weapon, the **appointment power.** The president can nominate approximately 3,000 agency officials, of whom about 700

# Compared to WHAT?

## Who's in Charge? The Japanese Bureaucracy and Catastrophe

When discussing who is in charge of the government in Japan, many observers point not to elected politicians but to the nation's elite bureaucracy. Most members of the elite bureaucracy are graduates from Japan's most prestigious universities. Among the million employees of the Japanese government, there are a couple hundred elite bureaucrats at each of Japan's agencies. Political scientist Chalmers Johnson once quoted a former Japanese minister who noted that the Japanese legislature is merely "an extension of the bureaucracy" and that "the bureaucracy drafts all laws." Imagine if this were said about the bureaucracy in the United States. It is not likely that Americans would look kindly on a system where unelected bureaucrats were in charge.

The role of Japan's elite bureaucracy in policy making is substantial but weakening. From 1955 to 2009, Japan was ruled by one political party (the Liberal Democratic Party or LDP). Over this period, it was very difficult to separate the influence of the elected leaders of the LDP and the elite bureaucrats who worked closely together on policy making. After more than 50 years controlling government, the LDP lost the 2009 election to the Democratic Party of Japan (DPJ). Part of the DPJ platform was a promise to provide "leadership through politics" and weaken the influence of the unelected elite bureaucrats who were so influential under the period of LDP rule. The newly elected leaders of the DPJ were highly critical of the elite bureaucracy and, after the election, found themselves required to work closely with these same bureaucrats.

The struggles of Japan's new political leadership in dealing with the entrenched powers of the bureaucracy were amplified after the devastating earthquake, tsunami, and nuclear disaster of March of 2011. Despite the tensions between them, Prime Minister Naoto Kan had to rely on the Japanese bureaucracy for information and action in the aftermath of the disasters. The government's inability to prevent and respond to the failing of the Fukushima nuclear plant elicited criticism. Both the elected leaders and the bureaucracy were far too reliant on the owners of the failing plant, Tepco, for information and a response plan. In addition to the problems with the nuclear plant, the Japanese government was criticized for the slow pace of its relief efforts. A relief worker, lamenting against bureaucratic red tape, noted that "in Japan, there is a legal wall that stops everything." The Japanese bureaucrats would not allow American doctors to help with the injured because they did not have Japanese medical licenses, a shipping company that offered container ships for helicopters to land on while delivering relief supplies was turned away because it lacked the proper permits, and all aid into the country was first processed at a government emergency center, yet these facilities were very slow in moving the aid out into the impacted areas. In response, Prime Minister Naoto Kan took the unprecedented action of sidestepping Japanese law and creating his own emergency response agency. The challenges for both the prime minister and the elite bureaucracy remain and this disaster may be the catalyst for bureaucratic reform in Japan.

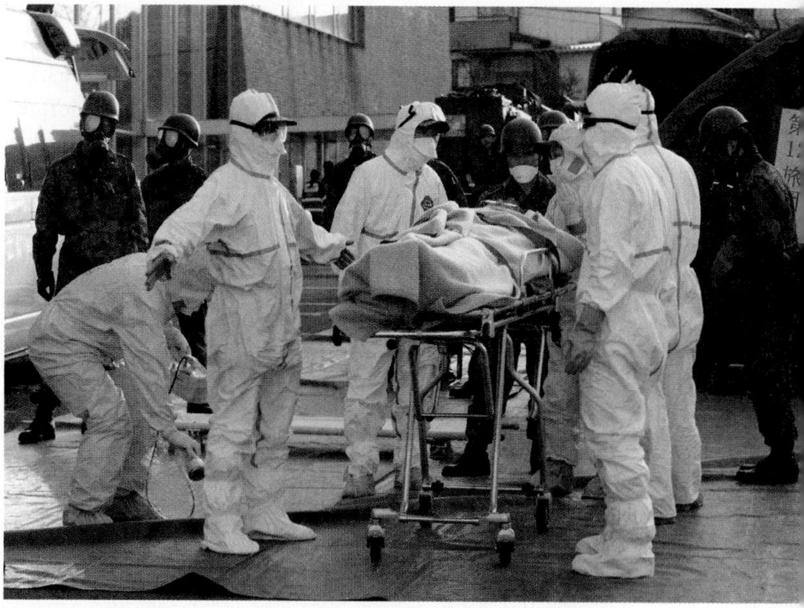

Following the devastating Tsunami and nuclear plant meltdown, first responders help a radiation contamination victim at a radiation treatment center in Japan.

*Sources:* Chalmers Johnson, "Japan: Who Governs?" *Journal of Japanese Studies 2,* no. 1 (1975); T. J. Pemple, "Bureaucracy in Japan," *PS,* 25, no. 1 (1992); Hiroko Tabuchi, Keith Bradsher, and Matthew L. Wald, "In Japan Reactor Failings, Danger Signs for the U.S.," *New York Times,* May 19, 2011; http://www.npr.org/blogs/itsallpolitics/2011/03/17/134621643/japans-nuclear-crisis-highlights-political-woes.

are in policy-making positions, such as cabinet and subcabinet officials and bureau chiefs. The rest are lower-level political appointees who can provide the president with valuable information and a source of political patronage hearkening back to the old spoils system. A president who can secure loyalty from these appointed bureaucrats has overcome a major obstacle in pursuing the White House policy agenda.

But a president who uses the appointment power to control the bureaucracy must know what is going on within it. One president who did just that was Franklin Roosevelt. He filled federal agencies with people who were more loyal to him than to each other. Although his appointees battled each other over policy questions, they ultimately referred their disagreements to the president, who resolved them and, in doing so, exercised effective control over bureaucratic policy making. Roosevelt's administration funneled information and decision-making authority to the top, and because Roosevelt had the intellectual capacity to understand the arguments of the specialists, he was able to settle their disputes with dispatch. This form of management is impossible today, given the size of government.

One especially problematic area has been the cumbersomeness of the confirmation process itself, which proceeds at a glacial pace. This had led presidents to increase the size of their White House staff and run policy from the White House. Recent presidents have faced a long, grueling process to get their nominees confirmed. The 9–11 Commission pointed out that President Bush's national security team took more than six months to get confirmed. One hundred days into Obama's presidency, only 14 percent of the Senate-confirmed positions had been filled. As of August 2011, 20 percent of these positions are still waiting confirmation. In an August 2011 report, the Constitutional Accountability Center noted that the Senate delay in confirming Obama's judicial nominees has reached record-setting levels.[17] This has created incentives for the president to appoint "at-will" policy czars who serve without confirmation at the subcabinet level. Most of Obama's cabinet secretaries have filled their offices with individuals who are not subject to the Senate confirmation process. Secretary of the Treasury Timothy Geithner, for instance, has filled the 50 most immediate positions below his with at-will appointees.[18]

One president who tried taking over the bureaucracy was Richard Nixon, giving truth to the quip "even paranoids have enemies." Lacking congressional support and facing a bureaucracy ideologically hostile to his program goals, Nixon decided that as the country's chief executive, he needed to act. In *The Administrative Presidency*, political scientist Richard Nathan showed how the White House sought to duplicate functions performed by the program bureaucracies. An immediate consequence was a swelling in the size of the White House staff, followed by frustration of the new staff because the deeper they delved into policies, the less knowledge and expertise they possessed. The White House staff came to depend more, not less, on the bureaucracy. Nixon became so upset that he decided to take over the bureaucracy politically. Immediately after his 1972 election victory, he accepted the resignations of dozens of cabinet and subcabinet officials and appointed loyal White House aides into key program positions in the bureaucracy. Neutrality was no longer a trait that would be valued; this time the goal was management control. The idea was to take control of bureaucratic operations such as grant writing, approval of financial funds, personnel deployment, organization and reorganization, and budget writing, so that a president could at least have the tools to impress his will on government. Only Watergate derailed this ambitious plan for taking effect.[19]

President Obama's bipartisan approach in making several key appointments offers another strategy. The president retained his predecessor's secretary of defense, Republican Robert Gates, and appointed several moderate Republicans to his administration—most notably Representative John McHugh of New York as the new secretary of the army, former representative Jim Leach of Iowa as head of the National Endowment of the Humanities, Utah governor John Huntsman as ambassador to China, and former congressman Ray LaHood as transportation secretary. After serving under President Obama for over two years, Ambassador Huntsman resigned his position in order to run for the 2012 Republican presidential nomination. McHugh, Leach, and LaHood remain a part of the Obama administration.

**Reorganization** Presidents also have the power to move programs around within specific agencies—**reorganization.** For example, a president opposed to pesticide regulation might shift that program from the EPA, which favors regulation, to the Department of Agriculture, where pro-agriculture forces would tend to limit such regulation.

A president may also choose to elevate an agency to cabinet level, thereby expanding its scope and power, as President Bush did with the Department of Homeland Security. President Obama created the new Consumer Financial Protection Agency, which is part of his cabinet. Conversely, as we noted previously, a president can remove an agency's cabinet status and thus potentially reduce its power and prestige. President Reagan sought several ways to reduce the power of the Department of Education (which had been elevated to a cabinet position by his predecessor, Jimmy Carter), including an unsuccessful attempt to demote the agency from the cabinet level. The Reagan administration saw the department as wasteful and inefficient and as an inappropriate extension of federal government into state and local realms. But the department dug in its heels and outlasted Reagan.[20]

**reorganization**
Having the power to move programs around within specific agencies.

**Office of Management and Budget (OMB)**
The unit in the Executive Office of the President whose main responsibilities are to prepare and administer the president's annual budget. A president and the OMB can shape policy through the budget process; the process determines which departments and agencies grow, are cut, or remain the same as the year before.

**The Budget** Another formidable tool for presidential control of the bureaucracy is the **Office of Management and Budget (OMB).** The OMB was established in 1921, transferred to the newly created Executive Office in 1939, and renamed OMB as part of the major executive office reorganization in 1970. Its main responsibilities are to prepare and administer the president's annual budget. A president and the OMB can shape policy through the budget process, determining which departments and agencies grow, are cut, or remain the same as the year before. During the budget-preparation cycle, officers from OMB—all specially trained to assess government projects and spending requests—remain in constant touch with government agencies to make sure that the agencies are adhering to the president's policies. Because the budget has a profound effect on an agency's ability to function and survive, it is rare for an administrator to defy the OMB.

**The Power of Persuasion** Presidents have another tool: the power to persuade in an attempt to control the bureaucracy. Certain presidents, such as John F. Kennedy, have sought to inspire the bureaucracy with a vision of public service as a noble activity. Even though he was frequently thwarted by and frustrated with bureaucratic procedures, Kennedy saw the bureaucracy as capable of innovation. He reorganized the space program and convinced its employees that despite the string of failures in attempting to launch unmanned rockets, NASA would put a man on the moon before the decade was out, which it did. But persuasion has limits, and most turn to their marginal command powers for moving the bureaucracy—or they shift responsibility into the Executive Office of the President—creating yet another bureaucratic layer.[21]

## Congressional Control

Congress provides much of the oversight that keeps bureaucratic power in check. To perform this task, Congress has several mechanisms at its disposal. Most important is the *power of the purse.* Congress appropriates all funding for each federal agency. If problems arise, Congress can, and occasionally does, curb funds or even eliminate entire projects.

Also, Congress has the power of *administrative oversight,* the practice of holding hearings and conducting investigations into bureaucratic activity. As a consequence of these hearings, Congress can rewrite agency guidelines to expand or narrow its responsibilities. Finally, through its "advice and consent" role, the Senate can shape the direction of federal agencies by confirming or rejecting presidential nominees for top positions in the bureaucracy.

Although Congress has many tools to fulfill its oversight functions, it often chooses not to use them. Why would Congress not want to keep the bureaucracy under close control? One answer can be found by examining the mutually beneficial political relationship between federal agencies and members of Congress. Federal agencies provide goods and services—such as contracts, exemptions, and

**QUICK REVIEW**

Control of the Bureaucracy

- President can control bureaucracy through appointment, reorganization, budgeting, and persuasion.
- Congress can control bureaucracy by establishing agencies, funding, investigation, and termination.
- Oversight process is designed to keep bureaucracies running efficiently.

**iron triangles**
Informal three-way relationships that develop among key legislative committees, the bureaucracy, and interest groups with a vested interest in the policies created by those committees and agencies.

**issue networks**
Networks composed of political actors in a particular policy area, usually including bureaucrats, congressional staffers, interest groups, think-tank researchers or academic experts, and media participants—all of whom interact regularly on an issue.

**red tape**
The excessive number of rules and regulations that government employees must follow.

assistance—that members of Congress use to please their constituents. In return, legislators have the ability to keep federal agencies alive and funded. Legislators from agricultural states, for example, work hard to keep crop subsidies in the federal budget, thus ensuring a future for the Department of Agriculture and its employees. In turn, the department can give special consideration to the crops grown in a member's district, thus helping to ensure a member's reelection.

These relationships have been characterized as **iron triangles.** An iron triangle is a strong interdependent relationship among three crucial actors in policy making: (1) legislators, particularly those on the relevant subcommittees with jurisdiction over the policy in question; (2) lobbyists for specific interests affected by the policy; and (3) bureaucrats at the agencies with jurisdiction over the implementation and administration of relevant policies. Iron triangles resist democratic accountability. Their interlocking interests are so strong that few presidents and few members of Congress who are not a part of them ever try to bring them under control.

Similar to but broader than iron triangles are **issue networks,** composed of political actors in a particular policy area. These networks usually include bureaucrats, congressional staffers, interest groups, think-tank researchers or academic experts, and media participants—all of whom interact regularly on an issue. Issue networks dominate the policy-making process, and different issue networks exist for different policy areas.

# WHAT THE PUBLIC THINKS OF THE BUREAUCRACY

7.6 *Why are Americans critical of bureaucracy, and are these criticisms justified?*

Americans tend to be suspicious of the administrative state, and politicians often exploit the public's distrust of government. A few years ago, members of Congress made headlines with stories about Defense Department purchases of $435 hammers and $91 screws. Each year, the federal government spends a good deal of money unwisely. Highly publicized examples of government waste include the Department of Agriculture sending subsidy checks to wealthy recipients in Beverly Hills, Chicago, and Manhattan. The stories, although exaggerated, confirmed long-held suspicions about government waste. But following the bombing of the Federal Building in Oklahoma City, many critics of government began to see their anti-government statements as delegitimizing the very idea of government.

One of the most common complaints is that government is unresponsive to citizens. In implementing policies, agencies should attend to the needs and circumstances of individual taxpayers. But too often, red tape prevents such flexibility. **Red tape** refers to the excessive number of rules and regulations that government employees must follow. Many employees chafe under the burden of these regulations, but others welcome them. Rigid adherence to the rules relieves bureaucrats of the burden of thinking about individual cases and shelters employees from being criticized by their supervisors for making wrong decisions. One consequence of the proliferation of red tape in government is that citizens with unusual circumstances encounter delays while their cases are bumped up to higher levels for official rulings. Businesses complain that the bureaucracy hobbles them with unnecessary regulations and paperwork. Every time a company wants to expand its operations or use a new method for manufacturing its products, it must apply for permission from a host of government agencies and fill out many forms.[22] In Figure 7.4, you can see the results of a 2011 Gallup poll that shows how the public's satisfaction with the U.S. government has steadily declined since 2002.

## Are the Criticisms Justified?

Bureaucracy is a modern-day inevitability. And despite criticisms, it is clear that many Americans rely on goods and services the bureaucracy provides. Although many criticisms are valid, there are two sides to every story about an institution as large as the federal government. Bureaucratic waste is real, but it is less prevalent than the public once believed. And it is important to keep in mind that government expenditures exist for reasons that many Americans would support. For example, most citizens want to stop officials awarding contracts based on personal friendship or bribery, so agencies must use costly bidding procedures on federal contracts. Most citizens would support programs that give people skills to find jobs in the public sector. Such policies add to the cost of government, but ultimately many citizens agree with the rationale for the expenditures. Although some agencies never accomplish the tasks Congress gives them, the Social Security Administration has sustained a remarkable record for competence. It assigns a number to, and maintains a lifetime earnings record for, each taxpayer in the country, then mails a benefit check for everyone who becomes eligible for Social Security.

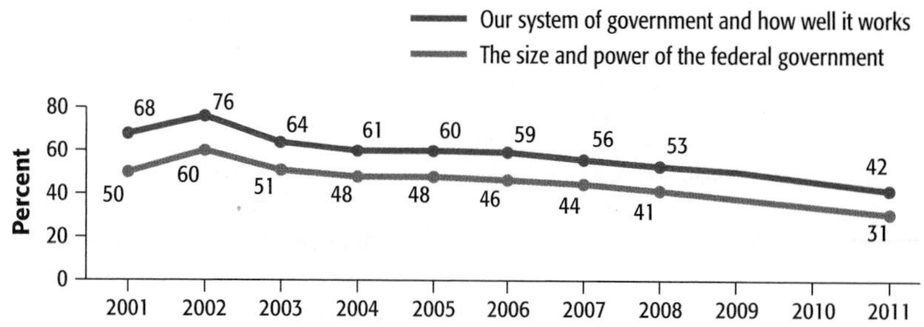


**FIGURE 7.4** Satisfaction with U.S. Government

*Source:* "CDC Tops Agency Ratings; Federal Reserve Board Lowest" by Lydia Saad, July 27, 2009. Copyright © 2009 Gallup, Inc. All rights reserved. http://www.gallup.com/poll/121886/CDC-Top-Agency-Ratings-Federal-Reserve-Board-Lowest.aspx?version=print. Used with permission.

Although businesses resist government rules and regulations, those guidelines almost always serve an important purpose. Automobile manufacturers complain that the government's requirement of rear-window brake lights on cars adds $100 million to production costs, but that requirement prevents $900 million in property damage and a great deal of human suffering. Similarly, citizens feel safer knowing that chemical manufacturers must fill out government forms specifying where they dump hazardous materials.[23]

# REFORMING THE BUREAUCRACY

7.7 *What are some methods of bureaucratic reform?*

Ideas for reforming the federal bureaucracy are plentiful. The very people who have grown comfortable with the status quo—relevant legislators and the bureaucrats themselves—are responsible for developing, implementing, and administering the programs that would improve bureaucratic performance, democratize the bureaucracy, and enhance accountability. For this reason more than any other, attempts at dramatic reform have encountered bristling opposition and only partial success.

Some advocate for a partial return to the patronage system in use until passage of the 1883 Pendleton Act. These political observers argue, just as Andrew Jackson did nearly two centuries ago, that patronage appointments improve efficiency and democratic accountability by translating popular support for an incoming president's objectives into actual policy. But, as reformers in the 1880s pointed out, patronage leads to widespread corruption, disorganization, and underqualified personnel in the bureaucracy.

Other reforms seek to address charges of an inert, unproductive workforce in federal agencies. One effort to improve innovation and productivity was the Civil Service Reform Act in 1978, which created the *Senior Executive Service (SES)*, a group of upper-management bureaucrats with access to private-sector incentives such as bonuses but also subject to measurable job-performance evaluations. Those who failed to achieve high ratings could be fired. The idea was that the senior bureaucrats would respond positively to

U.S. Education Secretary Arne Duncan discusses the state of education during a town hall meeting in Sacramento, California. Duncan has described education as "the most pressing issue facing America . . . education is also the civil rights issue of our generation, the only sure path out of poverty and the only way to achieve a more equal and just society . . . to help our students learn to contribute to the civility of our great American democracy, and to strengthen our economy by producing a workforce that can make us as competitive as possible."

**Whistleblower Protection Act**
This act encourages civil servants to report instances of bureaucratic mismanagement, financial impropriety, corruption, and inefficiency. It also protects civil servants from retaliation, such as being fired, demoted, or relocated.

**privatization**
The turning over of public responsibilities to privately owned and operated enterprises for regulation and for providing goods and services.

productivity incentives and become more responsive to presidential policy leadership. The program's effects have been unclear. Innovation has occurred, but some career officers find exposure to political pressure uncomfortable. Few members of the SES have been fired, but many have left their jobs with a bad taste in their mouths.

Another reform aimed at making the bureaucracy more effective and accountable is the 1989 **Whistleblower Protection Act.** This act encourages civil servants to report instances of bureaucratic mismanagement, financial impropriety, corruption, and inefficiency. Under the Whistleblower Protection Act, *whistleblowing* is defined as disclosing information that an employee reasonably believes is evidence of illegality, gross waste or fraud, gross mismanagement, abuse of power, or a substantial and specific danger to public health and safety. It also protects civil servants from retaliation—from being fired, demoted, or relocated. The Dodd-Frank Act of 2010 increased the amount of money awarded to whistleblowers to as much as 30 percent of what the government recovers from violators. The high payout for whistleblowers should increase the chances of someone reporting attempts at defrauding the government, thereby discouraging government contractors from taking the risk in the first place.

The act has been effective in helping identify and root out problems in the bureaucracy. In April 2011, the Avaya telecommunications company paid $13.5 million to settle a whistleblower lawsuit claiming it defrauded the U.S. government through intentional overbilling. In January of 2011, both Lockheed Martin and Oracle settled their own whistleblower suits, paying $2 million and $46 million, respectively, for submitting false claims to the U.S. government.

## THINKING CRITICALLY

Would you support eliminating the U.S. Postal Service (USPS), which would require all mail to go through a private delivery service? Do you believe the price of mail service for the average American would go up or down? How would this change impact poor and rural Americans?

There are also nonprofit public interest groups that monitor bureaucratic and governmental accountability. The most effective has been the Government Accountability Project (GAP), a 30-year-old nonprofit that promotes government and corporate accountability by advancing occupational free speech, defending whistleblowers, and empowering citizen activists. The Government Accountability Project pursues this mission through nuclear safety, corporate accountability, food and drug safety, and federal employee programs. It is the nation's leading whistleblower protection organization.

Another reform suggestion has been to reduce drastically or even eliminate inefficient functions through privatization. **Privatization** involves turning over public responsibilities for regulation and for providing goods and services to privately owned and operated enterprises. Some economists argue that private enterprises could do a superior and less costly job of implementing, administering, and regulating government programs. Advocates of privatization point to the success of United Parcel Service and Federal Express, and compare these two private companies with the more costly and less efficient U.S. Postal Service. They view this comparison as evidence that shifting services from governmental to private hands will greatly improve both quality and cost-effectiveness. But defenders of the Postal Service argue that such comparisons are unfair when the Postal Service, unlike private firms, must meet costly congressional policy mandates.

## Summary

7.1 *How does the bureaucracy measure up as a transparent democratic institution?*

- A fundamental element in any democracy is openness, but bureaucratic operations often demand secrecy. Yet, the bureaucracy has an important function that makes it indispensable in America's approach to democracy: carrying forth the work of the federal government. There are inherent contradictions between bureaucratic necessity and democratic ideals that raise questions of how the bureaucracy can maintain legitimacy without public disclosure of their activities.

7.2 *How do specialization, hierarchy, and a system of formal rules both positively and negatively influence the performance of the bureaucracy?*

- Max Weber believed that a bureaucracy could improve efficiency through specialization, hierarchy, and a system of formal rules.
- The principle of specialization rests on delegating specific tasks to individuals whose training and experience give them the expertise to execute them. The very nature of specialization within a bureaucracy can sometimes impede rather than improve performance,

rendering an agency relatively efficient in certain tasks but inflexible in others.

- A system of hierarchy has a clear chain of communication and command running from an executive director at the top down through all levels of workers. The hierarchy facilitates decision making and establishes clear lines of authority within a large, complex organization, but it can also impede responsiveness, responsibility, and innovation.
- A system of formal rules that are clearly defined procedures for executing assigned tasks is sometimes called *standard operating procedures (SOPs)*. These rules simplify and establish routines for complex procedures, curtail favoritism, and improve the decision-making process by allowing bureaucrats to respond to a broad array of situations with a minimum of delay and confusion. But, SOPs can create a rigid system unable to adapt to a changing world.

7.3 *How has the bureaucracy grown and evolved over time?*

- George Washington's budget for the entire bureaucracy in 1790 was just under $1.5 million, and the money funded just three departments: State, War, and Treasury. The federal government's rapid growth began in the late 19th century in response to the call for more government regulation of industry. Beginning in 1933, Franklin D. Roosevelt's New Deal involved the government in everyday economic affairs, and its programs dramatically increased the government's workforce and the scope and power of federal responsibilities. The New Deal programs became the core of the modern welfare state.
- Prior to the presidential election of Andrew Jackson in 1828, a small, elite group of wealthy, well-educated white males dominated the bureaucracy. Jackson changed this with the emergence of this spoils system, where his subordinates would award top-level government jobs and contracts on the basis of party loyalty rather than social or economic status or relevant experience. The Pendleton Act of 1822 ended the spoils system and created a civil service that brought about a system of hiring and promoting employees based on professional merit, not party loyalty. Merit-based hiring and advancement have eliminated much of the corruption and cronyism of the old patronage system and has encouraged hiring and promotion of highly skilled experts. The Hatch Act of 1939 created a nonpartisan, nonpolitical, professionalized bureaucracy by trying to prevent civil servants from using their power or position to influence elections.

7.4 *What is a bureaucrat, what functions does a bureaucracy serve, and how is the federal bureaucracy structured?*

- Bureaucrats are the people who work in a bureaucracy and include not only obscure, faceless clerks and office workers but also "street-level" bureaucrats, such as police officers, postal service workers, social workers, and schoolteachers. Although bureaucrats are appointed rather than elected, the evidence shows that they and the public share similar demographic characteristics and general values.
- The bureaucracy performs three key governmental tasks: (1) implementation—providing the necessary organization and expertise to put into action any policy that has become law; (2) administration—performing the routine tasks associated with a specific policy goal; and (3) regulation—making rules, enforcing them, and adjudicating disputes about them.
- There are four types of federal bureaucratic institutions: (1) cabinet departments—the major administrative units responsible for conducting a broad range of government operations; (2) independent agencies—agencies that are smaller than cabinet departments and have a narrower set of responsibilities; (3) independent regulatory commissions—regulators of specific sectors of the nation's economy; and (4) government corporations—semi-independent government agencies that administer a business enterprise and takes the form of a business corporation.

7.5 *Are bureaucrats responsible to the public, or do these unelected civil servants make policy outside the expectations of democratic rule?*

- A major concern regarding the bureaucracy is that, because it is made up of unelected bureaucrats and often operates under a veil of secrecy, bureaucrats—and not elected politicians—will ultimately make policy.
- Presidents have four main strategies at their disposal to control the bureaucracy: (1) the appointment power—the president can nominate people loyal to his or her policy agenda; (2) reorganization—the president can move programs around within specific agencies to ensure that an agency friendly to his or her agenda will implement his policies; (3) the budget—a president and the OMB can shape policy through the budget process, determining which departments and agencies grow, are cut, or remain the same as the year before; and (4) the power of persuasion—presidents can use the power to persuade in an attempt to control the bureaucracy through inspiring bureaucrats with a certain vision of public service.
- Congress provides much of the oversight that keeps bureaucratic power in check. To perform this task, Congress has three mechanisms at its disposal: (1) the power of the purse—Congress appropriates all funding for each federal agency and can curb funds or even eliminate entire projects; (2) administrative oversight—after holding hearings and conducting investigations into bureaucratic activity, Congress can rewrite agency guidelines to expand or narrow its responsibilities; and (3) its "advice and consent" role; the Senate can shape the direction of federal agencies by confirming or rejecting presidential nominees for top positions in the bureaucracy.
- Policy is often made in iron triangles, which resist democratic accountability. An iron triangle is a strong interdependent relationship among three crucial actors in policy making: (1) legislators on the subcommittees with jurisdiction over the policy in question, (2) lobbyists for specific interests affected by the policy, and (3) bureaucrats at the agencies with jurisdiction over the implementation and administration of relevant policies.
- Similar to but broader than iron triangles are issue networks, where policy is also made. Issue networks are composed of political actors in a particular policy area. These networks usually include bureaucrats, congressional staffers, interest groups, think-tank researchers or academic experts, and media participants—all of whom interact regularly on an issue.

7.6 *Why are Americans critical of bureaucracy, and are these criticisms justified?*

- Americans are generally suspicious of the bureaucracy, and the media and politicians will often play to the public's suspicions by focusing on extreme examples of government waste. In 2009, 57 percent of Americans viewed the government as wasteful and inefficient, but this number has fallen since 2007.
- One of the most common complaints is that government is unresponsive to citizens. In implementing policies, agencies should attend to the needs and circumstances of individual taxpayers. Too often, however, red tape (defined as the excessive number of rules and regulations that government employees must follow) prevents such flexibility.
- Bureaucratic waste is real, but it is less prevalent than the public believes.

7.7 *What are some methods of bureaucratic reform?*

- Ideas for reforming the federal bureaucracy are plentiful but attempts at dramatic reform have encountered bristling opposition and only partial success.
- *Return to the patronage system:* Some argue that patronage appointments improve efficiency and democratic accountability by translating popular support for an incoming president's objectives into actual policy. But, as reformers in the 1880s pointed out, patronage leads to widespread corruption, disorganization, and underqualified personnel in the bureaucracy.
- *The Civil Service Reform Act of 1978:* This act of Congress created the Senior Executive Service (SES), in hopes that the senior bureaucrats would respond positively to productivity incentives and become more responsive to presidential policy leadership. The program's effects have been unclear. Innovation has occurred, but some career officers find exposure to political pressure uncomfortable.
- *The Whistleblower Protection Act of 1989:* This reform act aimed at making the bureaucracy more effective and accountable by encouraging civil servants to report instances of bureaucratic mismanagement, financial impropriety, corruption, and inefficiency. The act has been effective in helping identify and root out problems in the bureaucracy.
- *Nonprofit monitors of bureaucratic and governmental accountability:* The most effective of these nonprofits has been the Government Accountability Project (GAP), a 30-year-old nonprofit organization that promotes government and corporate accountability. The Government Accountability Project is the nation's leading whistleblower protection organization.
- *Privatization:* Turning over public responsibilities for regulation and for providing goods and services to privately owned and operated enterprises. Some economists argue that private enterprises could do a superior and less costly job of implementing, administering, and regulating government programs. Others point to problems with privatization which would limit the equality of services provided or the effectiveness of regulation.

## Key Terms

administration, 226
administrative discretion, 225
appointment power, 230
bureaucracy, 218
bureaucrats, 218
cabinet departments, 227
civil service, 221
formal rules, 219
government corporation, 228
Hatch Act, 222
hierarchy, 218
implementation, 225
independent agencies, 228
independent regulatory commissions, 228
iron triangles, 234
issue networks, 234
Office of Management and Budget (OMB), 233
privatization, 236
red tape, 234
regulation, 226
reorganization, 233
specialization, 218
spoils system, 221
welfare state, 219
Whistleblower Protection Act, 236

## Test Yourself Chapter 7

1. A bureaucracy is a large, complex organizational system characterized by
   a. specialization of tasks.
   b. formal rules.
   c. hierarchy.
   d. All of the above.

2. Specialization means that specific tasks should be delegated to
   a. those persons with the most training and experience.
   b. those persons with the most seniority.
   c. those persons most supportive of congressional leadership.
   d. those persons most supportive of the president.

3. The formal rules that characterize bureaucracies are sometimes called
   a. standard bureaucratic procedures.
   b. standard operating procedures.
   c. optional bureaucratic procedures.
   d. optional operating procedures.

4. The Progressives argued that the government
   a. should assume a greater regulatory role over corporations.
   b. should stay out of the personal lives of citizens.
   c. should eliminate all forms of taxes.
   d. should remain as small as possible.

**5.** Transfer payments are essentially
- a. money from the federal government given to small businesses.
- b. money given to a corporation to encourage them to set up in another state.
- c. money paid to individuals in the form of Social Security benefits, welfare payments, and student grants.
- d. money that the OMB transfers from one bureaucracy to another.

**6.** The term *spoils system* refers to
- a. a system in which newer employees receive fewer benefits than those with seniority.
- b. a system in which government spends too much money on its citizens.
- c. a system in which government jobs are awarded to party loyalists.
- d. a system in which government jobs are awarded to those with the best qualifications.

**7.** The Pendleton Act of 1883
- a. created the civil service system.
- b. created the Civil Service Commission.
- c. was designed to protect federal employees from political threats to their jobs.
- d. All of the above.

**8.** The civil service system
- a. is a system of hiring and promoting employees based on party loyalty.
- b. is a system of hiring and promoting employees based on military service.
- c. is a system of hiring and promoting employees based on nepotism.
- d. is a system of hiring and promoting employees based on their qualifications.

**9.** Which of the following would be a violation of the Hatch Act?
- a. Wearing a campaign button.
- b. Running for public office.
- c. Contributing to a political campaign.
- d. Voting.

**10.** The federal bureaucracy performs three key governmental functions:
- a. implementation, administration, and facilitation.
- b. administration, facilitation, and regimentation.
- c. regulation, administration, and implementation.
- d. regulation, regimentation, and administration.

**11.** Implementation means
- a. imposing penalties for noncompliance to a new law.
- b. providing the organization and expertise required to put into action any policy that has become law.
- c. refusing to comply with laws passed by Congress that are unconstitutional.
- d. allowing state governments to participate in the policy formulation process.

**12.** Because laws passed by Congress tend to be vague, and at times, a bit ambiguous, federal agencies are permitted a great deal of
- a. civil permissiveness.
- b. regulatory scope.
- c. implementation directives.
- d. administrative discretion.

**13.** Administration refers to the
- a. performance of routine tasks associated with a specific policy goal.
- b. appropriation of funds by Congress.
- c. occupation of the executive branch by a particular person and his or her personal staff.
- d. president's authority over the bureaucracy.

**14.** The major administrative units responsible for conducting a broad range of government operations are called
- a. independent agencies.
- b. cabinet departments.
- c. government corporations.
- d. independent regulatory commissions.

**15.** Which of the following are checks on bureaucratic behavior?
- a. The fact that bureaucratic agencies have no independent source of revenue.
- b. The fact that the goods and services they provide are determined by organizations beyond their control.
- c. The fact that their policies and objectives are determined by other branches of the government.
- d. All of the above.

**16.** The practice of holding congressional hearings and conducting investigations into bureaucratic activity is called
- a. administrative oversight.
- b. congressional intimidation.
- c. OMB investigation.
- d. bureaucratic leadership session.

**17.** An iron triangle is a relationship among
- a. the president, Congress, and the Supreme Court.
- b. the president, the Justice Department, and the Federal Bureau of Investigation.
- c. a congressional subcommittee, an interest group, and a federal agency.
- d. an interest group, a federal agency, and the White House staff.

**18.** Which dramatic event pushed Congress to put an end to the spoils system?
- a. The September 11, 2001, attacks.
- b. Andrew Jackson's disputed reelection.
- c. The 1881 assassination of President Garfield.
- d. The Civil War.

**19.** The Pendleton Act
- a. affects only state governments.
- b. created the spoils system.
- c. ignores needed requirements for public service.
- d. created a civil service.

**20.** The U.S. Postal Service is an example of
- a. an unregulated government service.
- b. a government corporation.
- c. an independent regulatory commission.
- d. a semi-independent agency.

**ANSWERS**
**1.** d, **2.** a, **3.** b, **4.** a, **5.** c, **6.** c, **7.** d, **8.** d, **9.** b, **10.** c, **11.** b, **12.** d, **13.** a, **14.** b, **15.** d, **16.** a, **17.** c, **18.** c, **19.** d, **20.** b

# Public Opinion

# 8

## Chapter Outline

**Introduction:**
*Public Opinion and Democracy*

- What Is Public Opinion?
- Measuring Public Opinion
- Political Socialization
- Social Variables That Influence Opinion Formation
- American Political Culture
- The State of American Public Opinion
- From Public Opinion to Public Policy

## Learning Objectives

8.1 What role does public opinion play in a democracy?

8.2 What is the history of thought regarding the role of public opinion in democratic policy making?

8.3 How is public opinion measured?

8.4 How does a person develop his or her ideas about politics?

8.5 What variables shape the formation of public opinion?

8.6 What positions do Americans take on core issues and ideals?

8.7 Do Americans live up to the ideal of the democratic citizen?

8.8 Does public policy mirror public opinion?

# INTRODUCTION

## PUBLIC OPINION AND DEMOCRACY

8.1 *What role does public opinion play in a democracy?*

Public opinion is the keystone of democracy. No government can claim to be the legitimate voice of a people unless public opinion plays an integral role in the choice of political leaders and the development of public policy. Thus, gathering information about public opinion becomes a vital task for a democracy. Today, survey analysts use sophisticated polling techniques to provide a relatively accurate snapshot of what Americans think and feel about specific issues, events, and candidates. At the same time, those in government use similarly sophisticated means in attempts to shape and guide public opinion on issues.

Although not all Americans are politically active and informed, all have the opportunity to be, and millions do take advantage of that opportunity. Leaders are continually made aware of what citizens are thinking; they are particularly well informed about voter desires through a constant barrage of scientific public opinion polls and a never-ending series of popular elections. Leaders who know what citizens want are likely to heed the public's wishes, a result central to any idea of democracy. In his classic 1961 work, *Public Opinion and American Democracy,* political scientist V. O. Key suggested that public opinion was best understood as "those opinions held by private persons which governments find it prudent to heed. Governments may be compelled toward action or inaction by such opinion; in other instances they may ignore it, perhaps at their peril; they may attempt to alter it; or they may divert or pacify it."[1]

Americans are sufficiently informed and participatory to keep leaders in touch with their desires, and sufficiently open and tolerant to live together peacefully within a diverse and complex culture. To gauge the strength of democracy, one needs to determine if leaders know what citizens desire, how well citizens communicate those desires through political activity, and how well political leaders respond to those desires. For any political system in the world to be democratic, its leaders must at the very least hear "the voice of the people." The leader–follower connection is central to democratic theory in democratic societies. Citizens in a democracy express their preferences through informed political activity, and leaders listen with a keen interest to those expressed preferences. If the masses are inactive or if the leaders consistently ignore their desires, democracy falters. To begin to understand the impact of public opinion, we examine how it is measured, sources of opinions on political issues, and the nature of public opinion in America.[2]

# THINKING CRITICALLY

An often-touted criticism of politicians is that they "flip-flop" on the issues. What do you think of a politician who changes his or her mind on an issue to better represent public opinion? Is this flip-flopping? Is it good for democracy?

## WHAT IS PUBLIC OPINION?

8.2 *What is the history of thought regarding the role of public opinion in democratic policy making?*

**Public opinion** is the collective expression of attitudes about the prominent issues and actors of the day. The concept of a "public" holding "opinions" on various issues is almost as old as politics itself. Plato, for instance, saw public opinion as a danger if it meant the mass of citizens could freely express individual desires. According to Plato, popular opinions were good only when they reflected the will of the state and its rulers. Centuries later, John Stuart Mill expressed a significantly different view in his essay *On Liberty* (1859), when he argued in favor of a populace free to express its diverse political views. Only by giving all individuals the maximum liberty to state their opinions, said Mill, could a society ever arrive at the "truth." Whereas Plato wanted to shape and control opinions, Mill advocated free rein to their expression.

James Madison took a middle stance between Plato and Mill. In *The Federalist,* no. 10, Madison acknowledged the inevitable diversity of opinion that would develop in a free society but feared that competing opinions could lead to hostile factions that would divide rather than unify or improve society:

> *A zeal for different opinions . . . [has] divided mankind into parties, inflamed them with mutual animosity, and rendered them . . . disposed to vex and oppress each other.*[3]

Like most of the framers, Madison was concerned that an overzealous majority might inflict its irrational, prejudiced, or uninformed wishes on a political minority. Hence, the framers made sure to install what they envisioned as constitutional safeguards (such as the electoral college, the Senate, and the Supreme Court) against too easy implementation of public passions. On the other hand, they also allowed many outlets for the expression of public opinion: voting, a free press, the right of assembly, and other forms of political participation.

How deeply public opinion should be taken into account, then, has long been the subject of intense political debate, but today there are clear parameters for this debate. No longer can a legitimate public figure argue, as Plato did, that the public should be ignored or manipulated in political decision making. The only real argument now is whether the public's will should "prevail all of the time," "most of the time," or "some of the time." The public, in short, is a key player in the democratic game of politics. For that reason, discovering and publicizing the public's opinion has become a key political activity in modern democracies.

## MEASURING PUBLIC OPINION

8.3 *How is public opinion measured?*

Although the notion of public opinion has existed for centuries, only recently have there been reliable ways to measure it. The first attempts at measuring public opinion began in the mid-1800s, with a variety of straw polls. A **straw poll** is a nonscientific method of measuring public opinion. It springs from the farmer's method of throwing straw up into the air to gauge the strength and direction of the prevailing breeze. In a straw poll, one wishes to measure which way and how strong the political breezes are blowing.

Straw polls have inherent flaws that make them inappropriate as scientific indicators of public opinion. Their main problem is that they fail to obtain a **representative sample** of the public. A valid sample must be representative, meaning it must include all the significant characteristics of the total population. A sample of Americans that included no women, for instance, would obviously be invalid. The most infamous example of a nonrepresentative sample is the *Literary Digest* poll of 1936. Beginning about 1916, the magazine *Literary Digest* made the most sophisticated use of polling for political data of the time. The magazine mailed surveys to a large number of

**public opinion**
The collective expression of attitudes about the prominent issues and actors of the day.

**straw poll**
A nonscientific method of measuring public opinion.

**representative sample**
A sample that includes all the significant characteristics of the total population.

Americans asking for opinions on a host of important issues. Using their responses, the magazine claimed a high degree of accuracy in predicting election outcomes. In 1932, the *Literary Digest* poll came within 1 percent of the actual vote in predicting Frankiln Roosevelt's victory over Herbert Hoover.

But a major mistake by the *Literary Digest* in 1936 changed everything and signaled the beginning of a new era in how polling is done. Before the election that year, the *Literary Digest* poll predicted a landslide win for Landon and claimed Roosevelt would gain only 41 percent of the vote to Landon's 55 percent, with 4 percent going to a third-party candidate, William Lemke. But Landon carried only two states, while FDR garnered 61 percent of the popular vote. Landon promptly faded into obscurity, and Roosevelt went on to win two more presidential elections in the next eight years. How could *Literary Digest* have been so wrong? The answer is simple. The *Digest* worked with a biased sample. As with its earlier polls, in 1936 the magazine sent out millions of informal surveys to people whose names had been culled from automobile registration lists and telephone books. Altogether 10 million ballots were sent out, and nearly 2.4 million were returned—large numbers, but a response rate of under 25 percent. In 1936, however, these respondents were no longer as representative of the total American public as they had been in 1932. They were wealthier, for one thing. In a period of grinding economic depression, they could still afford the luxury of an automobile and a telephone. They were also better educated than the average American in 1936. These two factors ensured a built-in bias against Roosevelt—wealth and education had long been correlated with support for Republicans. Many people in this group were motivated to return their ballots because they wanted to get rid of Roosevelt. Despite their large numbers, they were hardly typical of the American public as a whole.

**margin of error**
The measure of possible error in a survey, which means that the number for the entire population of voters will fall within a range of plus or minus several points of the number obtained from the small but representative sample of voters.

In addition to these problems, poll participants were self-selected. They were picked not at random but simply because they chose to return the questionnaire. Because the individuals most motivated to respond to a political survey are almost never representative of the wider population, the results from such a self-selected survey are unreliable. This incident marked an end to the era of unscientific polling and pushed survey researchers to fine-tune their methods. It opened the door to today's much more sophisticated—and reliable—survey models.

After the 1936 fiasco, professional pollsters began a determined effort to make their work more scientific. George Gallup and Elmo Roper, among others, helped meet the growing demand for information about public attitudes. Applying modern statistical techniques, they succeeded, as shown in Table 8.1 on pages 246–247, through interviews with small but representative samples of voters, in predicting the behavior of the overall voting population.

Obtaining a representative sample poses several requirements. First, the sample should include at least several hundred people. Second, the people to be polled must be chosen through a technique known as *random sampling*. In addition, pollsters must guard against sampling bias.[4]

Michele Bachmann (R), a Congresswoman from Minnesota and Tea Party favorite, campaigns for the Republican presidential nomination.

## Sample Size

Most pollsters produce results of high reliability. Their findings are accurate at least 95 percent of the time, within a margin of error of about 3 percent. **Margin of error** reflects the validity of the results obtained by a poll given the sample size. For example, a poll with a 3 percent margin of error suggests that, on average, the results of the poll would differ by plus or minus 3 percent if the entire population were polled, rather than just a sampling of that population.

**Table 8.1** Election Year Presidential Preferences: Gallup Poll Accuracy Record, *1936–2008*

| Year | Nominees | Final Poll | Election Results | Deviation |
|---|---|---|---|---|
| 2008 | Barack Obama | 55 | 52.6 | −2 |
| | John McCain | 44 | 46.0 | +2 |
| 2004 | George W. Bush | 49 | 50.7 | −2 |
| | John F. Kerry | 49 | 48.3 | +1 |
| 2000 | George W. Bush | 48 | 47.9 | 0 |
| | Albert Gore, Jr. | 46 | 48.4 | −2 |
| | Ralph Nader | 4 | 2.7 | +1 |
| 1996 | William J. Clinton | 52 | 49.2 | +3 |
| | Robert Dole | 41 | 40.7 | 0 |
| | H. Ross Perot | 7 | 8.4 | −1 |
| 1992 | William J. Clinton | 49 | 43.0 | +6 |
| | George H. W. Bush | 37 | 37.4 | 0 |
| | H. Ross Perot | 14 | 18.9 | −5 |
| 1988 | George H. W. Bush | 56 | 53.4 | +3 |
| | Michael Dukakis | 44 | 45.6 | −2 |
| 1984 | Ronald Reagan | 59 | 58.8 | 0 |
| | Walter F. Mondale | 41 | 40.6 | 0 |
| 1980 | Ronald Reagan | 47 | 50.7 | −4 |
| | Jimmy Carter | 44 | 41.0 | +3 |
| | John Anderson | 8 | 6.6 | +1 |
| 1976 | Jimmy Carter | 48 | 50.1 | −2 |
| | Gerald Ford | 49 | 48.0 | +1 |

Another component of a good poll is sample size. Generally, the larger the sample the better, because larger samples reduce the margin of error. Most reputable national polls have sample sizes of 1,500 to 2,000 respondents, a size that reduces the margin of error to plus or minus 3 percent. Using statistical methods, pollsters have determined that information from a sample of that size can be projected onto the entire population.

## Random Sampling

The second requirement for a good poll, random sampling, is harder to achieve. In a **random sample,** every member of the population must have an equal chance of appearing in the sample. Advancements in technology have reduced the problems associated with randomness. Pollsters increasingly rely on *random-digit dialing (RDD),* which uses computers to automatically select phone numbers at random. The use of this technique includes both listed and unlisted phone numbers, ensuring that all individuals have the same chance of being selected for inclusion in a poll. The fact that one-in-five voting age adults live in wireless-only households has created new

**random sample**
A strategy required for a valid poll whereby every member of the population has an equal chance of appearing in the sample.

**Table 8.1** *(continued)*

| Year | Nominees | Final Poll | Election Results | Deviation |
|---|---|---|---|---|
| 1972 | Richard Nixon | 62 | 60.7 | +1 |
| | George McGovern | 38 | 37.5 | 0 |
| 1968 | Richard Nixon | 43 | 43.4 | 0 |
| | Hubert H. Humphrey | 42 | 42.7 | −1 |
| | George Wallace | 15 | 13.5 | +1 |
| 1964 | Lyndon B. Johnson | 64 | 61.1 | +3 |
| | Barry Goldwater | 36 | 38.5 | −3 |
| 1960 | John F. Kennedy | 51 | 49.7 | +1 |
| | Richard Nixon | 49 | 49.5 | −1 |
| 1956 | Dwight Eisenhower | 59.5 | 57.4 | +2 |
| | Adlai Stevenson | 40.5 | 42.0 | −2 |
| 1952 | Dwight Eisenhower | 51 | 55.1 | −4 |
| | Adlai Stevenson | 49 | 44.4 | +5 |
| 1948 | Harry S. Truman | 44.5 | 49.5 | −5 |
| | Thomas E. Dewey | 49.5 | 45.1 | −4 |
| | Strom Thurmond | 4 | 2.4 | +2 |
| 1944 | Franklin D. Roosevelt | 51.5 | 53.4 | −2 |
| | Thomas E. Dewey | 48.5 | 45.9 | +3 |
| 1940 | Franklin D. Roosevelt | 52 | 54.7 | −3 |
| | Wendell L. Willkie | 48 | 44.8 | +3 |
| 1936 | Franklin D. Roosevelt | 55.7 | 60.8 | −5 |
| | Alfred M. Landon | 44.3 | 36.5 | +8 |

*Source:* Table compiled by Gerhard Peters. *The American Presidency Project.* Survey data from the Gallup poll. http://www.presidency.ucsb.edu/data/preferences.php. Used with permission.

challenges for the public opinion community, particularly since there is widespread evidence that those with wireless are demographically distinct from those with landline homes. The Pew Research Center finds that "when it comes to political attitudes and voting patterns, however, evidence that adults in wireless-only households differ substantially from their counterparts with landline phones is less definitive."[5]

Pollsters make every effort to guard against **sampling bias.** They try to ensure that no particular set of people in the population at large—rich or poor, of any ethnicity, from any region—is any more or less likely to appear in the final sample than any other set of people. Recall that the major flaw in the *Literary Digest* poll of 1936—the disproportionately high percentage of respondents who were relatively wealthy and well educated—led to biased results.

Good polling leaves little room for interviewer discretion. Most polling organizations divide the U.S. population into categories based on the location and size of the city in which they live. Interviewers are sent into randomly selected neighborhood areas or blocks. Using another technique, pollsters carry out a survey using computer-generated lists of telephone numbers. Because people are selected completely at random, these lists will reflect an approximation of the entire nation. The result is that

**sampling bias**
A bias in a survey whereby a particular set of people in the population at large is more or less likely to appear in the final sample than other sets of people.

## THINKING CRITICALLY

Most poll samples are based on random-digit dialing of telephone numbers. This does produce a random sample of those with a phone number, but are any Americans left out of the sample? Do you think Americans who have no home phone or cell phone are different in any politically meaningful ways from Americans who do have a phone?

polls today come relatively close to meeting the crucial requirement that every American have an equal chance of appearing in any given pollster's sample.

### Reliability

Another major concern of polling is reliability. Pollsters want meaningful and consistent results. Attention to *question wording* is essential for reliable results. Respondents can often be led into answers by the way a question is worded. For example, in 1992, Independent presidential candidate Ross Perot commissioned his own poll, which asked: "Should laws be passed to eliminate all possibilities of special interests giving huge sums of money to candidates?" Here was a case of a candidate framing a poll question to obtain the answer he wanted—99 percent of the respondents answered "yes." But if the question had been rephrased to ask, "Do groups have the right to contribute money to candidates they support?" the response likely would have been different.[6]

Generally, questions are either open-ended, where respondents are free to offer any answer to a question ("What do you think is the biggest problem facing the country today?") or closed-ended, where the pollster provides a set of possible answers ("Would you consider welfare, crime, or environment the biggest problem facing the country?"). Whether open-ended or closed-ended, the way a question is worded can shape how one interprets the results of a poll. Figure 8.1 illustrates this with questions from different polling organizations on the topics of collective bargaining and Obama's health-care bill.

With the collective bargaining questions, the Fox News poll tells us something different about public opinion on the issue than do the other two polls. The Bloomberg and Quinnipiac polls show that more Americans believe attempts to limit collective bargaining by public employees are more about reducing deficits and controlling costs than they are political attempts to weaken unions. The Fox News poll tells a different story; more Americans agree that limits on collective bargaining are more about weakening unions than controlling costs. One explanation for this difference is in the way the Fox News poll referred to collective bargaining. Unlike Bloomberg and Quinnipiac, Fox News referred not just to collective bargaining but also to "public employee union rights." By referencing collective bargaining as a right, Fox News may have tapped into the key American values of freedom and equality. Respondents

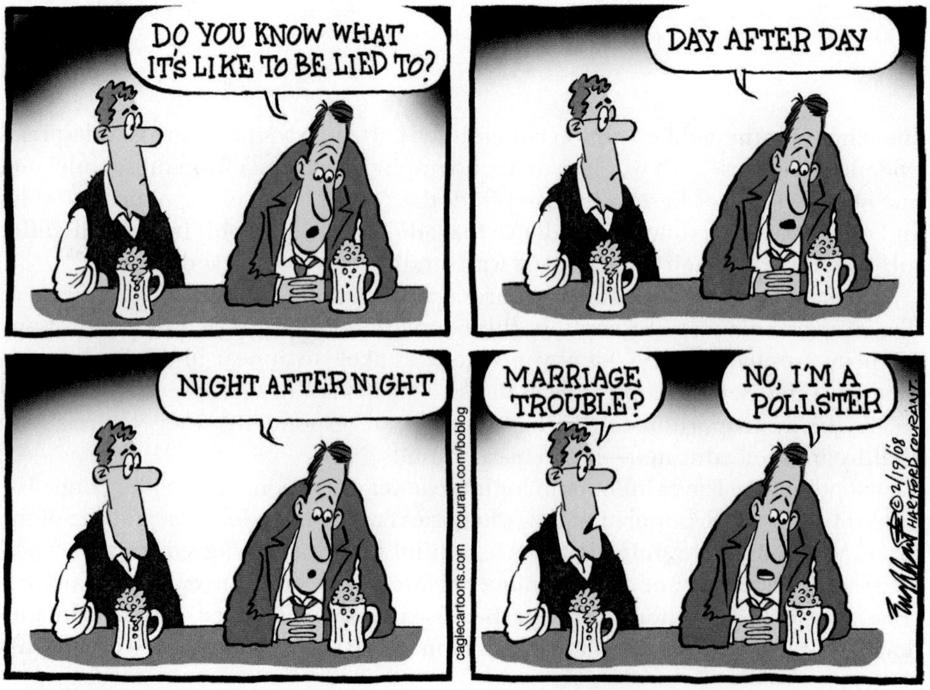

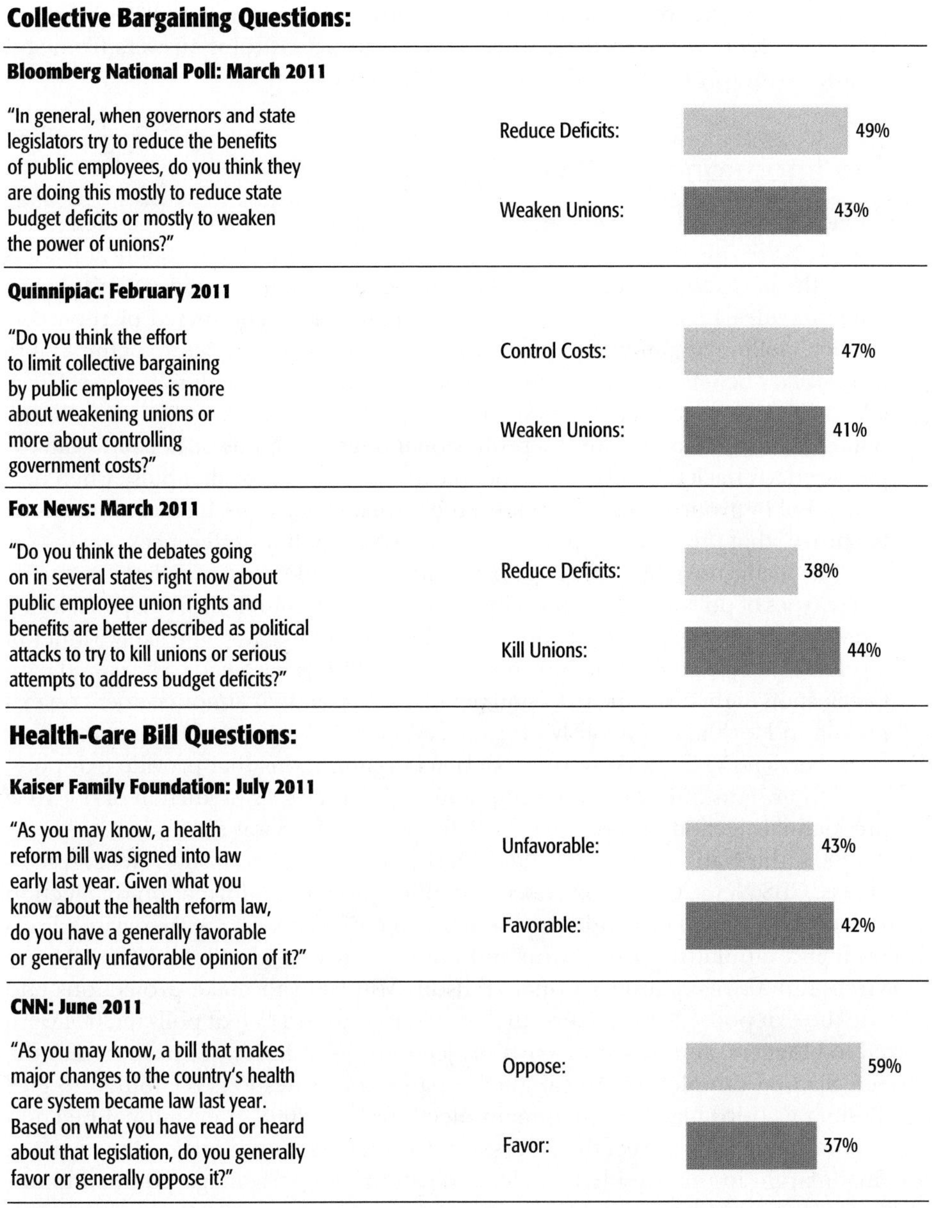
Collective Bargaining Questions:
Bloomberg National Poll: March 2011
"In general, when governors and state legislators try to reduce the benefits of public employees, do you think they are doing this mostly to reduce state budget deficits or mostly to weaken the power of unions?"
Reduce Deficits:
49%
Weaken Unions:
43%
Quinnipiac: February 2011
"Do you think the effort to limit collective bargaining by public employees is more about weakening unions or more about controlling government costs?"
Control Costs:
47%
Weaken Unions:
41%
Fox News: March 2011
"Do you think the debates going on in several states right now about public employee union rights and benefits are better described as political attacks to try to kill unions or serious attempts to address budget deficits?"
Reduce Deficits:
38%
Kill Unions:
44%
Health-Care Bill Questions:
Kaiser Family Foundation: July 2011
"As you may know, a health reform bill was signed into law early last year. Given what you know about the health reform law, do you have a generally favorable or generally unfavorable opinion of it?"
Unfavorable:
43%
Favorable:
42%
CNN: June 2011
"As you may know, a bill that makes major changes to the country's health care system became law last year. Based on what you have read or heard about that legislation, do you generally favor or generally oppose it?"
Oppose:
59%
Favor:
37%

**FIGURE 8.1** Question Wording Effects: Collective Bargaining and the Health Care Bill

*Source:* "Pollwatch: Comparing the Polls on Spending and the Deficit," June 24, 2009. Pew Research Center for the People & the Press, a project of the Pew Research Center. Used with permission.

to this poll may have had to come to terms with the limiting of a right in order to endorse the spending cuts achieved through abolishing collective bargaining. By avoiding the mention of a right, the other two polls may have kept their respondents from viewing collective bargaining in this light. The two questions on the Obama health-care law illustrate a similar point. Note that the CNN poll shows that 16 percent more Americans express opposition to the Obama health-care law than do so in the Kaiser Family Foundation Poll. These two questions are similar in both format and tone, but the CNN poll refers to "major" changes made by the law whereas the Kaiser Family Foundation resists characterizing the impact of the bill. By stating that the bill makes major changes, CNN may have led respondents into being more worried about the bill's potential impact, thus increasing opposition to it.

Pollsters confront additional problems as they set out to conduct their polls. Interviewers must be carefully trained to avoid interviewer bias. They must be courteous, businesslike, and neutral so as to elicit open and honest responses. Interviewers must also be persistent. Some people are rarely home; others may hesitate to answer

questions. Interviewers must make every effort to contact potential respondents and draw them out; they must learn how to extract truthful answers from shy, hostile, or simply bewildered members of the voting public.

### The Importance of Polls

Public opinion polls have emerged as an integral part of American politics. Accurate polls are one of the most important sources of information political leaders use in the decision-making process. Our timeline of good and bad polling predictions provides a useful historical roadmap. Polls today, conducted by reputable national polling organizations, provide a reasonably accurate picture of the American public's beliefs and desires that would otherwise be difficult to achieve. Virtually every news organization works with a polling company as well as an in-house polling team. The president has professional pollsters on his or her staff—always prepared to check the pulse of the people and even to shape that pulse when necessary. Lobby groups constantly release the results of polls they have commissioned to "prove" that the public supports their particular policy preferences.

The media use polls during campaigns to track support for candidates over time. These types of polls are called **tracking polls.** The media also utilize **exit polls,** which target voters as they leave the voting booth in an effort to gauge the likely winner of an election before the results are announced. Exit polls have had a checkered past: On election night 2000, the television networks, basing their announcement on exit polling in Florida, erroneously projected Al Gore as winning the election. Voter News Service (VNS), a consortium of news organizations that provide exit polls, erred in its statistical projections, not unlike *Literary Digest*'s prediction of the 1936 presidential election results. After the 2002 election, VNS was disbanded.

In 2004, the National Election Pool (NEP), a consortium of ABC News, Associated Press, CBS News, CNN, Fox News, and NBC, provided information on election night about the vote count and projections. The NEP retained the Associated Press to conduct a tabulation of the vote and contracted with the firm Edison Media Research and Mitofsky International (Edison/Mitofsky) to make projections and provide the exit poll releases.[7] Nevertheless, the first round of exit polls in 2004 were leaked to bloggers, and, based on early projections, John Kerry was projected as the winner. Skewed samples, technical glitches, and poor questions combined to give exit polling its third black eye in as many elections"[8] By 2008, the National Election Pool made changes to correct the errors of 2004. Eight of 17 national polls predicted the final margin in the presidential election within one percentage point and most of the others came within three points.[9]

## POLITICAL SOCIALIZATION

8.4 *How does a person develop his or her ideas about politics?*

Where do our ideas about politics come from? **Political socialization** refers to the process by which you learn about the world of politics and develop your political beliefs. Learning about politics begins early in childhood. Political thinkers have long observed that parent–child and sibling relationships shape the social and political outlook of future citizens. Other institutions—schools, peer groups, mass media—also serve as agents of socialization.

**tracking polls**
Polls used by the media to track the support levels for candidates over time.

**exit polls**
Polls that question voters as they leave the voting booth to predict the outcome of an election.

**political socialization**
The process by which people learn about the world of politics.

### The Role of Family

Family influence is especially powerful in the development of political knowledge, understanding, and participation. Whether you grow up poor or rich, for instance, shapes your view of the world and bears heavily on the likelihood of developing an interest in politics. Other family traits—education level, race, even geographic location—also deeply affect a person's perspectives on the political world.

About the age of 10, children begin to form their worldview, based significantly on family views toward politics. The role of family in political socialization is mostly informal. Parents rarely sit their children down and inform them that they are Democrats, supply-siders, or isolationists. In this sense, the family unit has a unique advantage for influence. Children absorb the casually dropped remarks of their parents and, over time, unthinkingly adopt those views as their own.[10]

Because many variables affect political attitudes, it is difficult to trace the precise effects of family on the political opinions of adult Americans. In one area, however, parental impact seems clear and pronounced. Children tend to adopt their parents' party loyalty (see Figure 8.2). That's significant, because *partisan identification* helps people make sense of the political world and predicts their behavior within it. Interestingly, when parents identify with different political parties, children generally embrace their mother's partisan affiliation. We are not certain why this is, but one possible explanation, which would certainly reinforce the importance of family socialization, is that children feel closer to their mother, from whom they received much early nurturing and affection.

Children, however, must adjust their values so they can adapt to a changing world. The concept of a *generation gap* describes the potential decline in family influence over children's values. Adolescents' views are shaped not only by their family but also by the political culture and events of their time. Members of one generation can differ in their political values both from their parents' generation and their children's generation because of events that serve to shape the political views of the group of Americans in their formative years. For example, the generation of Americans whose political views formed during the New Deal are more trustful of their government than the generation of Americans who grew up during the Watergate era. Although Americans of all ages bear witness to these events, younger Americans who are still forming their ideology are influenced much more than Americans whose political values have already solidified.

As a result, no generation simply mimics parental views, and analysts have observed a strong **generational effect** in American socialization patterns. The Millennial Generation (born after 1981) has views that differ significantly from older Americans. Younger Americans are more Democratic than previous generations and take more liberal positions on social issues (as seen in Figure 8.3). Twenty-seven percent of 18- to 29-year-olds believe that the United States should allow for an increase in immigration, whereas only 8 percent of those age 65 and older support

## APPROACHING Democracy Timeline

### A History of Good and Bad Presidential Polling Predictions

| | |
|---|---|
| **1936** | *Literary Digest* straw poll wrongly predicts that Franklin Roosevelt would lose to Al Landon. |
| **1948** | Major pollsters predict that Tom Dewey will defeat President Truman, although they did no polling in the final two weeks of the campaign. Truman won in an upset. |
| **1980** | Major polling organizations say the presidential race is "too close to call," yet Reagan wins by a large margin on Election Day. |
| **1992** | Bill Clinton defeats George H. W. Bush by an 8 percent margin of victory; the Harris poll, ABC poll, and CBS/*New York Times* poll are all within 2 percent of the final margin. |
| **1996** | John Zogby precisely predicts Bill Clinton's margin of victory in the presidential election. |
| **2000** | News network and Associated Press exit polling predict that Al Gore will win Florida. The prediction prompts the networks to declare Gore the winner in Florida. |
| **2004** | Zogby, using battleground state polling, predicts John Kerry will win a majority in the Electoral College and that George W. Bush could win a slim popular vote. |
| **2008** | fivethirtyeight.com's Nate Silver outperforms the major polling services by nearly predicting the final vote percentage of Barack Obama and John McCain. |
| **2010** | electionprojection.com comes within 1 House seat of accurately predicting the 63-seat gain in the House and the 8-seat gain in the Senate for Republicans. |

Democratic | Neutral | Undemocratic

**generational effect**
Socialization patterns in which a generation of adults who grew up during a certain decade or period appear to have their own outlook, differentiating themselves from the previous age.

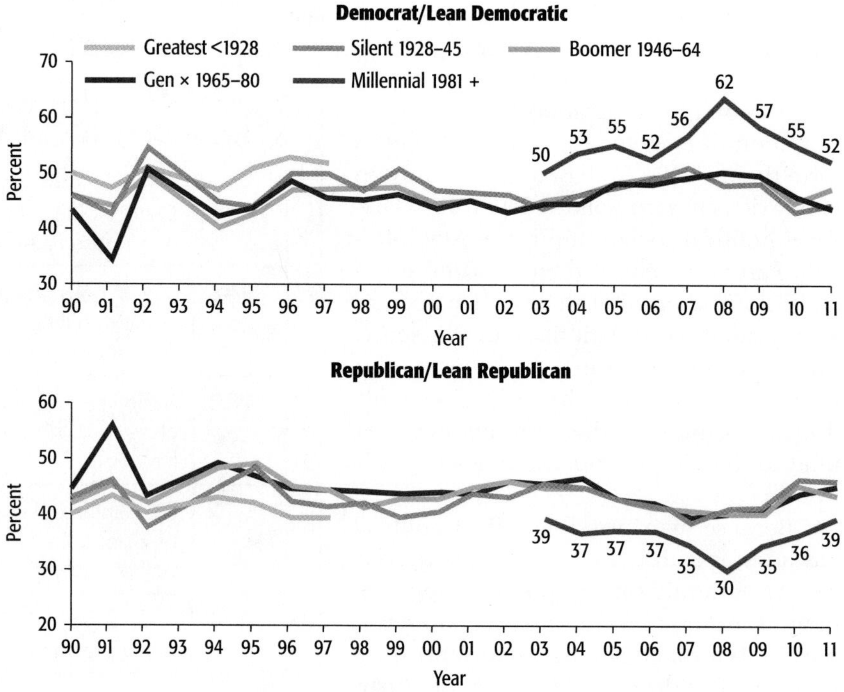


**FIGURE 8.2** Generations and Party Identification

*Source:* Pew Research Center for the People & the Press, © 2009, Pew Research Center. Reprinted with the permission of the Pew Center for the People & the Press. http://www.people-press.org/.

*Note:* PEW RESEARCH CENTER. Based on registered voters. Figures for 2011 are based on polls conducted January through June. Figures for 2008 are based on all polls conducted in that year.

such a policy. In 2011, there was a 31 percent gap in opinion between 18- to 34-year-olds and those age 55 and over on the issue of gay marriage, with 70 percent of the youngest group and only 39 percent of the oldest group in support. Additionally, younger Americans are the most positive about their standard of living. Despite being the group with the lowest actual income, 64 percent more say they are satisfied with their standard of living than are dissatisfied. Among 50- to 64-year-olds, only 17 percent more are satisfied than dissatisfied.[11]

| | 18 to 34 Years % | 35 to 54 Years % | 55 and Older % | Difference, 18 to 34 Minus 55 and Older pet. pts |
|---|---|---|---|---|
| Pornography | 42 | 29 | 19 | +23 |
| Gay/Lesbian relations | 66 | 56 | 47 | +19 |
| Premarital sex | 71 | 58 | 53 | +18 |
| Out-of-wedlock births | 62 | 56 | 46 | +16 |
| Gambling | 71 | 65 | 59 | +12 |
| Polygamy | 19 | 8 | 8 | +11 |
| Abortion | 44 | 42 | 34 | +10 |
| Cloning humans | 18 | 10 | 9 | +9 |
| Cloning animals | 36 | 32 | 28 | +8 |
| Embryonic stem cell research | 66 | 59 | 62 | +4 |
| Doctor-assisted suicide | 46 | 45 | 43 | +3 |
| Divorce | 72 | 66 | 70 | +2 |
| Extramarital affairs | 8 | 7 | 7 | +1 |
| Use of animal fur for clothing | 55 | 57 | 56 | −1 |
| Suicide | 14 | 13 | 19 | −5 |
| Death penalty | 56 | 67 | 70 | −14 |
| Medical testing on animals | 47 | 57 | 61 | −14 |

**FIGURE 8.3** U.S. Perceived Moral Acceptability of Behaviors and Social Policies, by Age

*Source:* U.S. Perceived Moral Acceptability of Behaviors and Social Policies, by Age / SOURCE: Gallup, May 5–8, 2011. http://www.gallup.com/poll/147842/doctor-assisted-suicide-moral-issue-dividing-americans.aspx.

## Schooling

Outside the family, the most powerful institutional influence on political socialization is education. In school, children first learn the formal rules of social interaction and come face-to-face with institutional authority: teachers, staff, and principals. More specifically, they learn to develop positive attitudes toward citizenship through history and civics courses. Early primary education leads children to recognize the name and image of the president. Most children are taught to look at the president as a benevolent symbol of government and politics. This early socialization carries over strongly into adult life. Even after Richard Nixon's resignation or Bill Clinton's impeachment, a majority of American adults still placed enormous faith in the office of the presidency.

Schools' central role in the socialization process has made them the center of political controversy, as different sides of the political spectrum struggle to control what schools teach. The issue of prayer in the public schools, for example, sharply divided the American public and led to heated debate. This clash fits into a larger debate between educational conservatives and liberals on the role of schools in modern American society. Both sides wish to use schools to socialize students to the perspectives they hold dear. Conservative critics charge that schools are failing to provide students with the traditions and norms of American culture. Liberal critics fault the schools for perpetuating class, race, and gender divisions and for failing to teach about "diversity" and "multiculturalism."

University training also represents a key element in the process of socialization. Those with a college education express different political views than do those who do not go to college. College-educated Americans are more tolerant, more likely to support democratic values, and more liberal—particularly on social issues. Scholars disagree over the cause of these changes in the political values of college students, but not over the fact that education has a strong effect on public opinion. When the Pew Research Center survey asked whether "books that contain dangerous ideas should be banned from public school libraries," the largest and most persistent differences on this question are by level of education: 23 percent of college graduates agree with the statement, compared with 45 percent of those with some college experience and 60 percent of those who have a high school education or less.[12] Educated people are also more politically knowledgeable, more likely to follow politics and political events in the media, and more likely to participate in elections.

### QUICK REVIEW

Agents of Political Socialization

- Family influence is especially powerful in the development of political knowledge, understanding, and participation.
- Adolescents' views are shaped by the political culture and events of their time.
- Outside the family, the most powerful institutional influence on political socialization is education.
- University training also represents a key element in the process of socialization. Those with a college education express different political views than do those who do not go to college.

## Peers

A child's peers make up another important source of political socialization. We all absorb the ideas and outlook of our contemporaries, especially close friends. However, studies have found that although teenage peer groups significantly influence taste, dress, and style, they do little more than reinforce parental and community values when it comes to politics. Peer groups do appear to affect political attitudes on the rare public issues of special relevance to young people.

A landmark study by Robert Putnam suggests that Americans today are less prone to engage in civic activities, less trusting of others, and more cynical about the institutions of American society than those in previous generations. The values propagated in young adult peer groups may have a role in this trend.[13]

## Television

As we will discuss in Chapter 12, perhaps more than anything else in American culture, television has emerged to dominate the social and political landscape. American's societal language, habits, values, and norms seem to derive as much from exposure to television imagery as from any other socializing force. Despite a considerable literature devoted to the effects of television on political attitudes and behavior, no consensus exists regarding just how and to what degree television

# Compared to WHAT?

## Global Opinion on the Free-Market Economic System

Since 2002, Globe Scan, a consortium of public opinion research centers in more than 25 countries, has asked respondents about their views on the free-market economic system. The results of their 2010 poll were surprising.

The United States is typically the country most supportive of the free-market system, yet in 2010, support for the free market fell in the United States. In 2002, 80 percent of Americans viewed the free market as the best economic system. In 2010, this number fell to 59 percent (see Figure 8.4). American women and those with the lowest incomes were most likely to have their enthusiasm for the free market dampened. From 2009 to 2010, among Americans making less than $20,000 support for the free market dropped from 76 percent to 44 percent. In the same period, support among American women fell from 73 percent to 52 percent. Once the economy recovers, we will likely witness a rebound in support of the free market.

The decrease in support for capitalism found in the United States was not a global phenomenon. In 2010, a number of other countries surpassed the support found in the United States. Some 67 percent of respondents in both China and Brazil believe that the free market is the best economic system, but only 59 percent of Americans agree. Interestingly, citizens in Communist China grew more supportive of capitalism during the same period that Americans became less supportive. See Figure 8.5 for the poll results of all 25 countries.

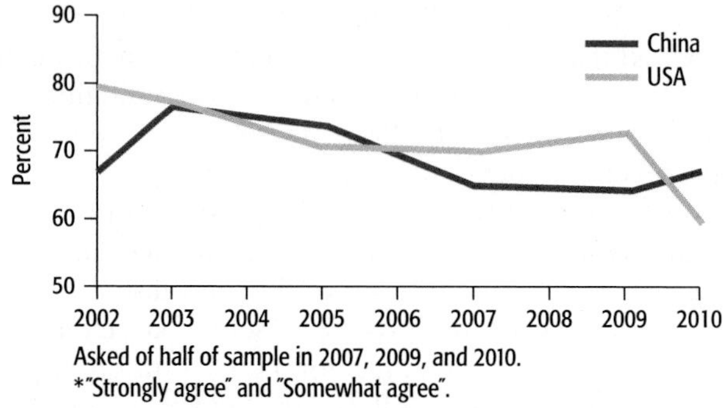


**FIGURE 8.4** Free-Market Economy Is Best System: China vs. U.S., "Agree"
*Source:* © WorldPublicOpinion.org.

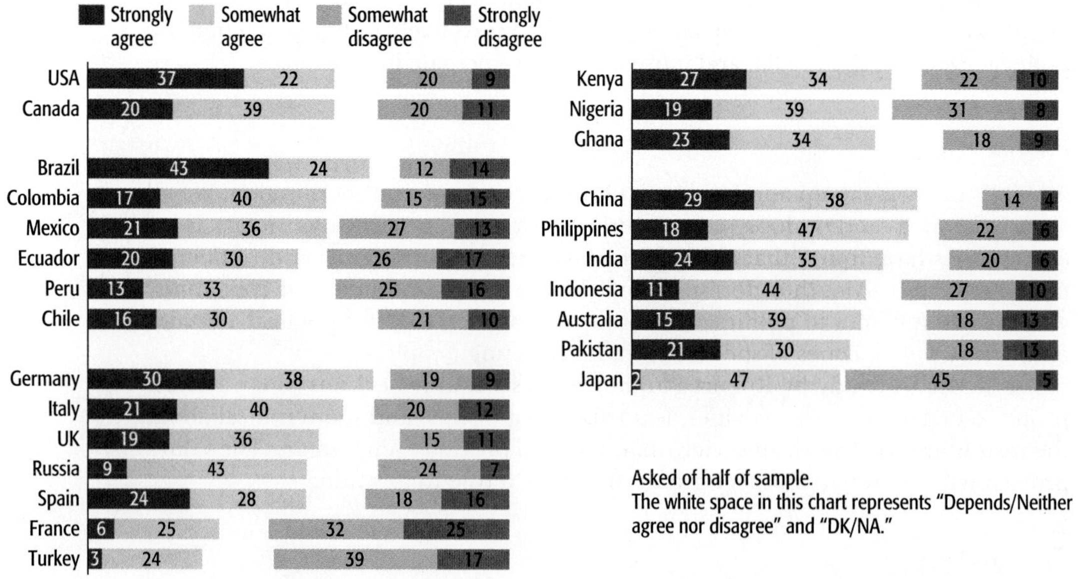


**FIGURE 8.5** Free-Market Economy Is Best System: "Agree" vs. "Disagree"
*Source:* Pew Research Center's Forum on Religion & Public Life, © 2008, Pew Research Center. Reprinted with the permission of the Pew Forum on Religion & Public Life, www.pewforum.org.

affects Americans. Television has come under severe scrutiny because of its ubiquity; its demonstrated power to absorb viewer time for several hours a day; and its unique blend of immediacy, proximity, and audiovisual appeal. Perhaps the major criticism of television focuses on its power to divert one's attention from the serious to the trivial.

Because the vast majority of television shows are devoted to amusement rather than information, and because most people watch television for entertainment, its effect in shaping political attitudes must be indirect. One study concludes that "politically relevant issues are now raised in virtually all types of programming."[14] The values conveyed by television—commercialism, tolerance for sex and violence, encouragement of an extreme form of rugged individualism—become, in other words, an unthinking part of the general culture. Viewers absorb these values and subconsciously draw on them when thinking about politics.

Despite all the criticism of television, however, many studies reveal a surprise. Although children watch as much television per week as the amount of time they spend in class, a significant amount of viewing actually increases exposure to and knowledge of politics and government. So, although Americans are undoubtedly bombarded with huge daily doses of advertising, sports, and entertainment, television watching exposes young viewers to a considerable amount of political information as well.

# SOCIAL VARIABLES THAT INFLUENCE OPINION FORMATION

8.5 *What variables shape the formation of public opinion?*

In learning about politics, we are all subject to the same general influences that shape our society's mind-set. We learn from our families a common set of norms and values; together we live through major political and economic events; we go to school; we are bound together by the unifying force of television. Still, even within the same culture, people differ from each other in important ways. Different social circumstances—class and income, race and ethnicity, religion, region, and gender—produce significantly different life experiences undoubtedly reflected in differing political opinions.

## Class

Our relative standing in society shapes many of our social and political values. Class, or social status, rests high on every social scientist's list of the forces that mold behavior. Unfortunately, class is a complex and difficult variable to measure; no two analysts and no two citizens agree on its precise definition. A recent *New York Times* nationwide survey focusing on how Americans regard class uncovered optimism about social mobility and found important differences between rich and poor, including the likelihood of achieving the American dream. The authors of the study observed that even though social diversity has erased many traditional markers of status (i.e., it is harder today than 20 years ago to determine status by a person's car, clothing, religion, or race), class remains a powerful force in American life. Over the past three decades, it has come to play a greater, not lesser, role in important ways. At a time when education matters more than ever, success in school remains linked tightly to class. At a time when the country is increasingly integrated racially, the rich are isolating themselves more and more. At a time of extraordinary advances in medicine, class differences in health and lifespan are wide and appear to be widening. And new research on mobility, the movement of families up and down the economic ladder, shows far less of it than economists once thought and less than most people believe.[15]

## Income

Income, a key element in the concept of class, is far easier to define and study. People in different income groups often see the political world in different ways. The impact of both class and income, however, is mitigated through education. That is, those with higher education are more likely to be wealthy and of a higher class than those who are poorly educated. This relationship has a particularly strong impact on voting behavior. Better-educated people, usually the wealthier too, are much more likely to vote than less-educated people, who are predominantly poor. We saw evidence of this connection in the *Literary Digest* presidential election poll of 1936, which represented opinions of the wealthier and better-educated segments of the U.S. population.

As a general rule, the less money one makes, the more inclined one is to favor liberal economic policies that provide benefits to the poor. These policies include a Social Security system, progressive taxation, minimum wage laws, generous unemployment benefits, and welfare payments to the disadvantaged. The more money one makes, the more one is likely to oppose such policies. Both positions reflect a degree of economic self-interest. Lower-income groups benefit from liberal economic policies, whereas higher-income groups supply the money to pay for these policies. Nevertheless, these are only tendencies. Many individuals in each income category take positions opposite to what we would expect. Some millionaires are liberals, and some individuals at the lower end of the economic spectrum are conservatives. Income level strongly influences voting patterns in the United States. Roughly stated, poor people tend to vote for Democrats (the more liberal party on economic policy); rich people tend to vote for Republicans (the more conservative party on economic policy); and middle-income people split their votes, depending on circumstance.[16]

Survey research shows that party identification is strongly linked to family income levels—people in the highest-income households are roughly twice as likely as those in the lowest-income households to say they are Republicans. But over the past decade, the Republican Party has also lost adherents across all income levels, yet Democratic identification has remained fairly stable. A greater proportion of people in every income category are identifying as independents.

## Race and Ethnicity

Income is but one of many social influences that produce different perspectives on politics. In addition, racial and ethnic backgrounds strongly affect the attitudes a person is likely to develop. Race, America's most enduring social cleavage, produces the clearest of all social delineations between the two major political parties. Traditionally, Hispanic Americans tend to take a liberal position on economic issues and vote heavily for the Democratic Party. However, the different groups within the Hispanic American population are not as unified on issues as African Americans tend to be. Cuban Americans, for example, are wealthier than average and are among the more conservative of American voting blocs. Like African Americans and most Hispanic Americans, Asian Americans tend to be more Democratic and less conservative than white voters. White ethnic voters, whose ancestors immigrated from Ireland, Italy, or Poland, once displayed a similar pattern to other minorities and were heavily Democratic for decades, but as members rose into the middle class, they developed more conservative outlooks

Analysis of trends in population date predicts that by the year 2050, the United States will be a majority–minority nation, with growing populations of Hispanic Americans (doubling from 15 to 30 percent) and Asian Americans (nearly doubling from 5 to 9 percent), and the black population growing by just one percentage point (to 15 percent). By 2050, one in five Americans will be foreign born, compared with just one in eight today.[17]

The vast majority of black voters consider themselves Democrats, whereas white voters are more closely divided in party identification. In 2008, African American

**Table 8.2** Religious Makeup of the Electorate

| | 2000 | 2004 | 2008 | Net Change 2004–2008 |
|---|---|---|---|---|
| Protestant/Other Christian | 54% | 54% | 54% | 0 |
| White Protestant/Other Christian | 45 | 41 | 42 | +1 |
| Evangelical/Born Again | n/a | 20 | 23 | +3 |
| Non-evangelical | n/a | 20 | 19 | −1 |
| Catholic | 26 | 27 | 27 | 0 |
| White Catholic | 21 | 20 | 19 | −1 |
| Jewish | 4 | 3 | 2 | −1 |
| Other faiths | 6 | 7 | 6 | −1 |
| Unaffiliated | 9 | 10 | 12 | +2 |
| *Attend worship services . . .* | | | | |
| More than once a week | 14 | 16 | 12 | −4 |
| Once a week | 28 | 26 | 27 | +1 |
| A few times a month | 14 | 14 | 15 | +1 |
| A few times a year | 28 | 28 | 28 | 0 |
| Never | 14 | 15 | 16 | +1 |

*Source:* Figure from "How the Faithful Voted," updated November 10, 2008. Pew Research Center's Forum on Religion & Public Life, © 2008, Pew Research Center. Reprinted with permission of the Pew Forum on Religion & Public Life, www.pewforum.org.

voters made up 13 percent of the electorate and gave 95 percent of their vote to Barack Obama. Obama also did well with Latino Americans and Asian Americans. In 2008, Latino Americans, making up 9 percent of voters, voted 67 to 31 percent for Obama versus McCain, a huge increase from 2004, when they voted 53 percent for Kerry to 44 percent for Bush. In addition, 62 percent of Asian American voters, constituting 2 percent of all votes, supported Obama.[18]

## Religion

Religious differences produce serious political differences in the United States, as in all countries. The Pew Research study found that the United States is a highly religious nation. Table 8.2 shows that a large majority of Americans say they belong to a particular faith, and similarly large numbers express agreement with statements about key religious beliefs and behaviors.[19] Three general principles help explain the effect of religion on political attitudes. First, the less religious you are, the more liberal or "left" you are likely to be. In the United States, people with few religious connections are likely to take liberal stands on most social and economic questions and to vote Democratic. This pattern is not numerically significant, however, because most Americans profess religious belief of one kind or another.

More important for its political ramifications is the second principle: Members of any country's dominant religion tend to be more conservative. This stand makes sense because these people have more investment in the status quo. By comparison, minority religious groups, especially the more oppressed ones, tend to favor liberal perspectives. This pattern is clear in the United States. Protestantism has long been the majority religion. Catholicism and Judaism were generally the religions of minority groups discriminated against when they first immigrated to this country. As we would expect, over the years, Protestants have been the most conservative religious group, whereas Catholics and Jews have been more liberal, and thus more likely to support Democrats.

These are, of course, broad generalizations; many individuals within each category deviate significantly from the pattern. Furthermore, changing social circumstances are changing this pattern. Many Catholics have entered America's mainstream and have become conservatives. But Catholics who still belong to minority ethnic groups are still more liberal and more likely to support Democrats than are Protestants—or other Catholics for that matter. Jews remain the most liberal of all religious groups, but even they have made modest moves in a conservative direction as their economic situation has improved.

A final principle helps further explain the effect of religion on political outlook. Generally, the more religious one is, the more conservative one is likely to be. Thus, ardent churchgoers and committed believers take a conservative outlook on life; in politics they gravitate toward the right side of the political spectrum. This tendency helps explain a key trend of this age: White evangelical Protestants, along with right-to-life supporters, have moved in significant numbers toward the Republican Party and are moving the GOP more to the right.

In the 2004 presidential election, 14 percent of Bush voters identified their candidate's "strong religious faith" as the major factor in their vote, compared with 1 percent of Kerry supporters. President Bush owed much to the support he received from white evangelical Protestants. A shift took place during the 2006 midterm elections, when Democrats claimed a majority of the Catholic vote (55 percent) and even gained an increase in votes from the evangelical Protestants (28 percent in 2006 and 25 percent in 2004).[20] In the 2008 presidential election, Barack Obama made a vigilant effort to reach out to people of faith. More Catholics supported the Democratic nominee than in previous elections—supporting Obama over McCain by nine percentage points. Obama performed particularly well among Latino Catholics, two-thirds of whom voted for Obama over McCain (a 14-point gain over estimates from the 2004 exit poll). Kathleen Kennedy Townsend notes that recent polling—as well as the 2008 elections—indicates that Catholic voting behavior does not align itself neatly with the Vatican.[21] Despite this, Catholics did swing back toward the Republicans in the 2010 midterm elections, with 54 percent of Catholics casting their ballot for a Republican.[22]

## Region

People's political outlooks often reflect where they grew up and where they now live. Certain sections of the United States have conservative traditions; other areas are more liberal (see Figure 8.6). People from conservative areas are likely to be conservative, and those from liberal areas, liberal. Nothing better illustrates this than the concept of "blue" and "red" states that we discuss in Chapter 9.

The South has always been America's most conservative region. Strongest among the many reasons for this pattern was that disheartened southern whites after the Civil War rejected all "northern" values, including industrial-age liberalism. A firm emphasis on tradition, on order and hierarchy, and of course on religious fundamentalism, have all helped keep the South a bastion of social—and now political—conservatism, especially for white residents of that area. By a quirk, however, the South remained Democratic for decades, a reaction against the Republicanism of Abraham Lincoln and the victorious North. In recent decades, however, the South has moved increasingly into the Republican camp, a trend especially strong during presidential elections and among white Protestant fundamentalists.

The 2008 presidential election did not follow the typical "red" and "blue" state trend. Democrat Barack Obama won Pennsylvania, Ohio, Virginia, Iowa, Colorado, New Mexico, Nevada, Indiana, and North Carolina, all traditionally Republican states. It is unclear whether this is a permanent shift or a single phenomenon.

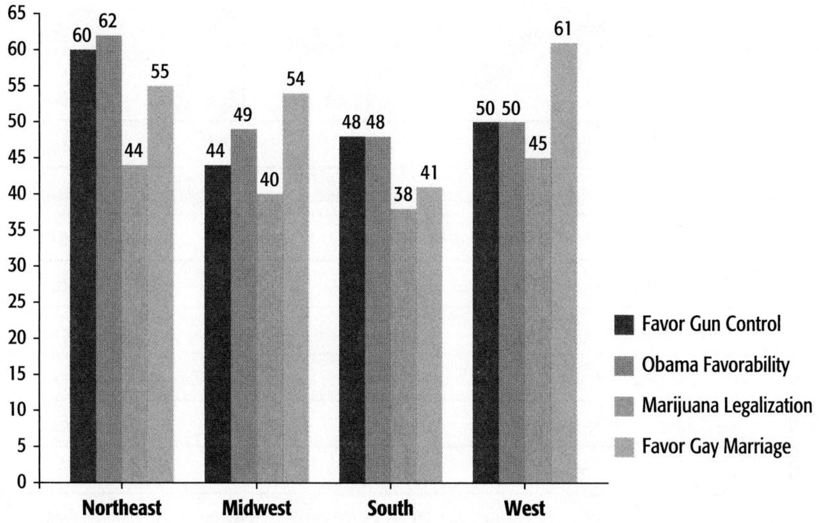


**FIGURE 8.6** Public Opinion Data by Region

*Sources:* Compiled with information found: http://pewresearch.org/assets/pdf/gun-control-2011.pdf and http://people-press.org/files/2011/03/711-tables.pdf; http://i2.cdn.turner.com/cnn/2011/images/04/19/rel6h.pdf.

One fact is clear: Since 2004, the GOP has lost at least five points in each major region, while the share identifying as Independents has increased by at least five points. Democratic Party identification has been relatively stable in most parts of the country, although it has continued to increase gradually in the Northeast.

## Gender

Of all trends in American public opinion, few are more striking than the consistent differences that pollsters find in the political opinions of men and women. In a pattern known as the **gender gap,** women have consistently been more supportive of so-called compassion issues such as school integration and social welfare programs than have men. Compared with men, women "are more supportive of arms control and peaceful foreign relations; they are more likely to oppose weapons buildups or the use of force. They much more frequently favor gun control and oppose capital punishment."[23] Men, in contrast, are more likely than women to support military, police, and other sources of government force. In most cases, men take the tougher, more conservative stands. For instance, men are more likely than women to oppose environmental and consumer protection; busing and other forms of desegregation; and most programs to aid the sick, the unemployed, the poor, and ethnic minorities. What is most striking is a recent phenomenon of men turning Independent while women edge toward the Democrats.

As we see in Chapter 10's more detailed discussion of the gender gap, the ultimate difference between men and women shows up at election time. Table 8.3 displays the gender gap in presidential elections since 1980. Where candidates or parties show clear differences on issues of force and compassion, women vote, on average, four to eight percentage points farther "left"—that is, for the more liberal position, candidate, or party (usually the Democrats). Thus, in the 1980 election between President Jimmy Carter and challenger Ronald Reagan, men voted strongly for Reagan, whereas women split their vote almost evenly. Indeed, the perception that Reagan was wildly popular relied largely on his enthusiastic backing by one key group in American society—white men. Women were frequently divided in their feelings about Reagan, and black men were clearly hostile. This gender gap continues to show itself in presidential elections. About 45 percent of women supported Bill Clinton in 1992, compared with 40 percent of male voters.

**gender gap**
A difference in the political opinions of men and women.

**Table 8.3** Gender Gap in Presidential Vote Chart

| | | Women | Men | Difference |
|---|---|---|---|---|
| 1980 | Ronald Reagan (R) | 46% | 54% | 8 points |
| 1984 | Ronald Reagan (R) | 56 | 62 | 6 points |
| 1988 | George H. W. Bush (R) | 50 | 57 | 7 points |
| 1992 | Bill Clinton (D) | 45 | 41 | 4 points |
| 1996 | Bill Clinton (D) | 54 | 43 | 11 points |
| 2000 | George W. Bush (R) | 43 | 53 | 10 points |
| 2004 | George W. Bush (R) | 48 | 55 | 7 points |
| 2008 | Barack Obama (D) | 56 | 49 | 7 points |

*Source:* Gender Gap in Presidential Vote Chart. Center for American Woman and Politics, Rutgers University.

In 1992, Clinton received overwhelming support from women voters often referred to as "soccer moms." Soccer moms—predominantly white suburban women between the ages of 35 and 45—replaced "angry white men" as the swing vote in 1992 and 1996. Exit polls in 1996 showed soccer moms favored Clinton over Dole by 49 percent to 41 percent, with 8 percent for Perot. "Soccer dads" preferred Dole by 56 percent, Clinton by 34 percent, and Perot by 9 percent.

On certain issues, men and women hold similar views. One finds almost no difference at all in their views on abortion. Interestingly, where male and female opinions do begin to converge, the direction of change follows the prevailing opinion preferences of women rather than men. This has been the case on issues ranging from environmental protection to defense spending. For various reasons, men have become more supportive of historically "female" positions. These findings may point to women's increasing political clout.

In the 2000 election, a majority of women (54 percent) voted for Gore; a majority of men (53 percent) for Bush. This trend continued in 2008 when the gender gap was 7 percent between Obama and McCain.

**THINKING CRITICALLY**

What do you think explains the gender gap? Do you think women are just innately more liberal than are men, or are girls faced with different political socialization than are boys?

## AMERICAN POLITICAL CULTURE

8.6 *What positions do Americans take on core issues and ideals?*

Scholars have pored over huge amounts of data on public opinion and discovered that American **political culture** is shaped by three key variables: core values, political ideology, and culture and lifestyle.

### Core Values

At the deepest level, American values are remarkably homogeneous. Surveys reveal broad consensus on the core issues and ideals of government: individual liberty, political equality, and the rule of law. These values ensure the stability of the political system. Support for them is rock solid, in sharp contrast to the vacillating winds of change evident on everyday political issues. The genius of the Constitution rests in its embodiment of these core ideals. The framers wrote them in, recognizing that the Constitution must elicit strong support. Those three basic principles have been held in high esteem by generations of Americans who have sought to approach the democratic ideal.

**political culture**
A political perspective based on core values, political ideology, culture, and lifestyle.

Perhaps the leading American value is liberty. Central to the function of American government is the protection of basic individual rights that ensure freedom. Americans can, in theory, speak and act as they wish. These rights are legally guaranteed by the Bill of Rights clauses that protect freedom of speech, assembly, and religion. Liberty is also central to the American economic system. Americans overwhelmingly support the concept of a free-enterprise, capitalistic economy. Global public support for a free-market economic system is the subject of this chapter's Compared to What? feature on page 254.

The American belief in equality represents another key American value. Americans place enormous importance on the ideas of *political equality* and formal political rights, seeking to guarantee equal access to the political system, universal voting rights, and equality under the law. Americans do not particularly support *economic equality,* especially if defined as a guarantee of equal economic outcomes. They do, however, support equality of another kind—namely, *equality of opportunity.* Americans have even been willing to use government to achieve this goal—to level the playing field, so to speak. Yet, recent years have seen a backlash against affirmative action. Americans want government to guarantee equal economic opportunities and to ensure that economic activity is free from coercion, but they definitely do not want government to guarantee that economic outcomes will be the same for all.

Public support for the Constitution and the democratic institutions it created represents another core American value, although support for this ideal may be weakening. Part of this decrease in confidence derives from a paradox of this era: Americans expect government to provide increasing services in an age of decreasing resources. Americans want lower taxes and blame government for their high tax bills—and yet complain about poor government service. The one government agency insulated from the public's increasing political negativism is the least democratic of all American institutions—the U.S. Supreme Court. Continued respect for that institution illustrates the value we place on the concept of rule of law.

**QUICK REVIEW**

American Values

- The protection of basic individual rights that ensure freedom.
- The guarantee of equal access to the political system, universal voting rights, and equality under the law.
- The guarantee of equal economic opportunities and economic activity that is free from coercion.

## Political Ideology

A second set of deep-seated public attitudes makes up our ideology. **Political ideology** is a coherent way of viewing politics and government. Ideological perspectives include beliefs about the military, the role of government, the proper relation between government and the economy, the value of social welfare programs, and the relative importance to society of liberty versus order. Political ideology provides an overarching frame on which to organize one's political beliefs and attitudes.

Ideologies of every kind abound. Each one offers a coherent and unified body of ideas that explain the political process and the goals sought by participants within that process. The most common ideologies among politically aware Americans are liberalism and conservatism. Although these two outlooks capture only part of the American public's diversity of political attitudes, they do serve to categorize most people in the mainstream; they also offer a useful introduction to political differences at the national level.

The terms *liberalism* and *conservatism* often are associated with political party affiliations—Democrats with liberalism, and Republicans with conservatism—but they go well beyond party allegiance. They express a political philosophy, a view of human nature and the proper role of government in society. On the whole, liberals support government intervention to minimize economic inequality. They support progressive taxes and minimum wage laws, for example, but oppose government actions that restrict cultural and social freedoms, such as censorship, prayer in school, and restrictions on abortion. Conservatives take precisely the opposite positions.

Political observers have long debated whether Americans are becoming more conservative. Many saw Ronald Reagan's success in 1980 and 1984 as a clear signal that the nation had turned to the right. Scholars have questioned this claim, however, by pointing out that although Reagan enjoyed high personal popularity (he left office with a 67 percent approval rating), the policies and ideas he advocated

**political ideology**
A coherent way of viewing politics and government; ideological perspectives include beliefs about the military, the role of government, the proper relation between government and the economy, the value of social welfare programs, and the relative importance for society of liberty and order.

People gather to protest the opening of a Muslim Cultural Center near the site of the World Trade Center terrorist attack. After months of protests, public interest declined sharply and the cultural center opened with little fanfare on September 21, 2011.

throughout his presidency had only limited success and modest public backing. His attempts to cut government, balance the budget, and implement school prayer all failed. On the day Reagan left office, polls showed that although the president remained enormously popular, more and more Americans favored a decrease in military spending and diverting that money to social programs, an outlook directly opposed to Reagan's own.

Still, Reagan's legacy of tax cuts and reforms, a strong military, and a reinvigoration of support for the presidency stands in contrast to his failures. Some believed the 1994 Contract with America signaled renewed support for Reagan's conservative ideals, but by election time in 1996 that tide had ebbed. During his administration, President George W. Bush championed "compassionate conservatism," which blended Reagan's defense budgets with a commitment to education and welfare reform. In 2006 and 2008, the American public elected a more liberal congress and president. Yet, the 2010 elections saw a swing back toward the conservative direction.

The very terms *liberal* and *conservative* have little more than a symbolic meaning to many Americans, so their voting decisions may not reflect an ideological preference. Indeed, some scholars argue that the real trend of this age is alienation and a general withdrawal from politics. At the political-leadership level, these terms work well to define people, but average citizens adopt a variety of political stands covering all points on the political spectrum. How does one categorize, for instance, an individual who favors conservative positions such as deregulation of business and cuts in the capital gains tax, but who also supports the liberal stand of a woman's right to choose an abortion? Many Americans defy easy classification. How can we accurately describe public opinion, then, if ideology proves a weak guide? Moreover, most Americans view themselves as neither liberals nor conservatives, but as moderates. The implication of this self-perception for governing is significant. Given that most voters see themselves in the center of the political spectrum, it should not be a surprise that President Clinton, lagging in the polls, positioned himself as a "New Democrat" for the 1996 election—right in the shifting center of American politics. Likewise, President Obama has moved to the pragmatic center as he governs; whereas when he sought the presidency, he positioned himself much more on the left for Democratic voters in primaries.

## Culture and Lifestyle

**Culture theory** argues that individual preferences emerge from social interaction. A way of life designates a social orientation, a framework of attitudes within which individuals develop preferences based on how they relate to others and to the institutions of power. In light of the disproportionately higher number of African Americans arrested and imprisoned, the tendency to distrust and even fear government authority seems hardly surprising. This orientation is neither liberal nor conservative; rather, it reflects an outlook on life that might be characterized as suspicion of the law enforcement system and alienation from government in general. This explanation of political attitudes as cultural rather than ideological might help us understand the reaction by Professor Henry Louis Gates Jr., an African American scholar and the Alphonse Fletcher University Professor of Harvard University, who, when returning from an overseas trip, found himself unable to open his front door.

**culture theory**
A theory that individual preferences emerge from social interaction in defending or opposing different ways of life.

He then did what any of us might do—push the door and struggle to get it unlocked. When police arrived at his door to investigate a possible break-in, Professor Gates felt he was being profiled. The situation quickly escalated and Gates was arrested.[24]

In the post–9/11 climate, tolerance and respect for diversity often proved to be elusive. This group had its sign torn down and chose to gather at a New York state thruway exit ramp in order to send their message.

## Intolerance

Is tolerance a core American value? Many Americans believe it is, yet evidence is mixed regarding how open Americans are to a wide range of political viewpoints. Even before the Revolution, American political thinkers and European counterparts such as Tocqueville feared the "tyranny of the majority." They worried that the "inflamed passions" of the majority might sweep away the opinions—and also the fragile liberty—of the minority, thus threatening the very core of American democracy. Think about how mobs in the aftermath of the September 11, 2001, terrorist attacks pursued, attacked, and harassed Arab Americans in this country. In a few cases, innocent people were killed by angry mobs seeking vengeance against someone who looked like Osama bin Laden. Koreans, similarly, feared such retaliation after a South Korean student killed more than 30 people at Virginia Tech.

How valid were the framers' fears? Public opinion data on intolerance gives some credence to anxieties about the tyranny of the majority. Statistically, Americans remain among the least tolerant of all people in industrialized democratic societies. Many Americans remain reluctant to allow those with whom they disagree, or whom they simply dislike, the same liberties and opportunities—including those protected by government institutions. Racism, homophobia, gender discrimination, and fear of foreigners are still powerful forces in American culture. And many Americans still feel reluctant or even afraid to speak out against prevailing majority opinion. How dangerous is this pattern of conformity and intolerance?[25]

Political scientists studying the consequences of cultural conformity argue that intolerance in America constrains "the freedom available to ordinary citizens." Studies have found, for instance, that blacks are much more likely to feel "unfree" than are whites. Compared with Americans as a whole, African Americans feel less comfortable expressing unpopular opinions and more worried about the power of government, including the police.[26]

Similar studies also reveal a "spiral of silence" and a "spiral of intolerance" in America. Individuals sensing the prevailing opinions of those around them echo those opinions to avoid social ostracism.[27] Their silence has a reinforcing effect. An initial reluctance to express opinions counter to the majority continues in an ever-tightening spiral, with the result that many Americans are pressured into conforming to the dominant opinion, whether they agree with it or not. Public opinion thus becomes a form of social control.

### THINKING CRITICALLY

An overwhelming majority of Americans express support for the freedoms of political minorities in the abstract. Yet when asked whether they support freedom of speech for atheists, communists, or neo-Nazis, many say no. What do you think explains this contradiction?

Intolerance does constitute a serious problem, but it need not remain an inevitable feature of American society. Studies show that as socioeconomic status and level of education increase, so do tolerance for conflicting points of view and alternative lifestyles. Perhaps a "spiral of tolerance" will develop in which family, peers, community, and institutions reinforce rather than suppress tolerance. Over the years, programs such as school busing to break down segregation and affirmative action to ameliorate its negative impact have attempted to foster socioeconomic and educational improvements that might, in time, reverse the spiral of intolerance. Teaching about diversity (different perspectives) and multiculturalism (different ways of life) represents another attempt to combat intolerance, although this approach is meeting increased resistance in many communities.

# THE STATE OF AMERICAN PUBLIC OPINION

8.7 *Do Americans live up to the ideal of the democratic citizen?*

You now have some idea of what lies at the heart of the average American's perspective on political life. But how interested are citizens in politics? How much do they know about politics, and how likely are they to participate? And how do Americans form their opinions on political issues? Polling data help answer these and other questions about the current state of American public opinion.

## Political Awareness and Involvement

Knowledgeable insiders have often been appalled at the average citizen's poor grasp of public affairs. Respected journalist Walter Lippmann once wrote that the average American "does not know for certain what is going on, or who is doing it, or where he is being carried. . . . He lives in a world which he cannot see, does not understand and is unable to direct."[28] And scholar Joseph Schumpeter's view of citizens was even more caustic: "The typical citizen drops down to a lower level of mental performance as soon as he enters the political field. He argues and analyzes in a way he would readily recognize as infantile within the sphere of his real interests. He becomes a primitive again."[29] Lippmann and Schumpeter join a host of social scientists who have portrayed American voters as apathetic and poorly informed, their opinions unstable or even irrational.

Polling research from the 1940s and 1950s revealed that Americans knew little about important issues, and they tended to confuse the issue positions of various candidates during campaigns. At the height of the Cold War, for instance, many Americans believed that the Soviet Union—the foremost ideological enemy of the United States—was in fact part of the North Atlantic Treaty Organization (NATO), the military alliance to which the United States and its allies belonged. Today, in poll after poll, more than half of Americans fail to make a single correct statement about either major political party, despite both parties having been at the core of American history for more than a century. In tests on knowledge of the Constitution and Bill of Rights, only a few respondents correctly identify the preamble of the Constitution and the contents of the Bill of Rights. Typically, most Americans cannot even identify their own representatives and senators. One contemporary example involves cap and trade policy. A *Washington Post*/ABC News poll revealed that three-quarters of Americans think the United States should regulate greenhouse gas emissions, and a slight majority say they would support a cap-and-trade program. But a Rasmussen poll taken at the same time showed that most Americans don't know what cap and trade is, and fewer than one-quarter could even identify it as having something to do with the environment.[30]

The American public indeed falls short of the ideal advocated by democratic theorists—a well-informed citizenry. Americans' interest in politics is minimal. No more than a third of the electorate ever claims to be seriously active in electoral politics. Even smaller percentages take part in political activities that influence those in power: writing to an elected official, joining a political group, attending a political rally, and the like. The general public seems to show little interest in the issues most hotly debated by politicians. Over time, such issues as abortion rights, crime and violence, AIDS, racism, the environment, and arms control have dominated the political agenda of elected officials, party leaders, and interest group activists. During the same period, no more than 5 percent of the general public ever ranked any of these issues as "the most important problem" facing the nation. Even when issues do catch the public's attention, citizens do not always assign them the same importance and commitment as do political activists. For example, America's concern with drugs, although significant, skyrocketed briefly after President H. W. George Bush's declaration of a "war on drugs," only to drop to relatively low levels within a matter of months. The public's interest in economic issues such as the deficit, unemployment, and the general health of the economy is similarly unstable, mirroring the ebbs and flows of the business cycle. Until September 11, 2001, surveys found that first-year college students were less interested in politics and participated less than any group of first-year students in the previous three decades. One of the great paradoxes of democracy was that the information age had produced a relatively indifferent and apathetic group of young people.

Some scholars counter this image of the ignorant, apathetic citizen by asserting that American people, although not well informed, are able to fulfill their role as democratic citizens. These scholars see the public as more rational than many observers are willing to concede, arguing that although Americans may not know all the names of political people and places or the intricate details of every issue of the day, they do recognize and rationally distinguish between the alternatives presented to them, especially when they step into the voting booth. In *The Rational Public,* political scientists Ben Page and Robert Shapiro find that "public opinion as a collective phenomenon is stable, meaningful, rational and able to distinguish between good and bad."[31] Indeed, surveys show that when presented with a list of names, rather than having to rely on their own recall of such names, most Americans can accurately identify their regional and national leaders.

Research suggests that Americans rely on political elites, such as members of Congress or journalists, as a shortcut. Although the average citizen may not follow day-to-day political coverage, once political elites sound off on a particular issue, the public picks up on their message and acts accordingly.[32]

Nonetheless, scholars continue to debate whether average citizens are politically informed and involved enough to make democracy work. We cannot supply a definitive answer here. Certainly few Americans live up to the ideal image of the fully informed citizen: ever alert and deeply involved in the political process. It is impossible to know the opinions of each American or even if each American has an opinion. Common knowledge tells us that not all citizens do, can, or want to pay attention to the many policy issues of the day. Those constituents who take the time to pay attention to politics, form opinions, and make them heard are known as the "attentive public." With this in mind, politicians look toward the attentive public in order to understand the beliefs and views of the public. The attentive public is the part of the public that is attuned to current affairs and its media coverage. The proportion of the electorate that forms the attentive public is variable but can range from 10 to 17 percent.

Still, most citizens may be informed enough to make simple decisions on the few options presented to them on Election Day. Besides, the American system has built-in safeguards in case citizens, for lack of information or other reasons, make a poor decision. If people elect a candidate or party they come to dislike, they can "turn the rascals out" at the next election. And no matter who is elected, no position within the U.S. government carries overwhelming power, and all positions are checked by other positions and institutions. Given this system of multiple checks and frequent elections, the American public may well be sufficiently informed to keep the system working and reasonably democratic.

## How Are Political Opinions Formed?

If people know little about politics and have little interest in it, how is it that they develop seemingly strong opinions on various political issues? How do they know for whom to vote on Election Day? The answer is surprising. Average citizens develop

**schemas**
Intellectual frameworks for evaluating the world.

**party identification**
A psychological orientation, or long-term propensity to think positively of and vote regularly for a particular political party.

**realignment**
A shift in fundamental party identification and loyalty caused by significant historical events or national crises.

broad orientations toward their world, including ways of thinking about politics, based on their entire set of life experiences. They then use these broad intellectual frameworks as shortcuts for processing new information.

These intellectual frameworks for evaluating the world, often called **schemas,** act as efficient filters or cues. When people encounter new issues or ideas, they frequently lack the time or energy to study them in detail. It is simpler just to fit them into a preexisting perspective. Studies show, for instance, that Americans know nothing about the actual level of spending for foreign aid, nor do they have any idea which countries receive most U.S. foreign aid; nevertheless, they remain convinced that the United States spends too much abroad. That's because they have already developed a general orientation (opposition to government spending and fear or distrust of non-Americans, perhaps) that allows them to take a stand on foreign aid while knowing almost nothing about the subject.

**Party Identification as a Schema** Despite the declining number of Americans who identify with one of the major parties, **party identification** remains the strongest predictor of an individual's political behavior. Party identification provides a cue that individuals use to evaluate candidates and acts as a filter through which individuals view the political world. These party ties represent one of the most enduring of all political attitudes Americans hold. However, even this apparently stable indicator of opinion can change over time or under the impact of dramatic events.

A broad-based change in partisanship is known as **realignment.** In a period of realignment, large groups of people shift allegiance from one party to another.[33] A realignment occurred in the 1932 election, when many people took their support—and their votes—from the Republican to the Democratic Party. The resulting New Deal coalition was a strong electoral force that kept Democrats the majority party for decades. However, recent evidence suggests that grand realignments of this kind are rare. A more useful approach to understanding shifts in partisan identification suggests that a gradual, continual process is taking place through generational replacement. Specifically, this theory suggests that as a new generation reaches maturity and becomes involved in the political process, it will have been socialized around a set of values and issues different from those of the parent and grandparent generations. As each new generation becomes a larger segment of the electorate, it replaces older generations and produces shifts in the identification of certain groups within the party around the new issues and values.

Partisan identification and general political orientation can also change across generations. Several studies revealed a sharp decline of support for and trust in the institutions and actors of government following the Vietnam War and the Watergate scandal. At that time pollsters began to track a decline in partisan identification, the rise of political *independents*—people declaring no allegiance to either party—and a growing suspicion of government in general.

Even with periodic realignments and generational change, political partisanship remains the most stable indicator of political preference. It is not, of course, the only schema to affect people's political thinking. Others include ideology, ethnic consciousness, and regional identification. And people occasionally change their minds or ignore "the party line" when it comes to specific issues, events, and actors. Nevertheless, to understand how any citizen feels about a host of political matters, one must begin by learning that individual's partisan allegiance.

## Stability and Change in Public Opinion

Although many people's opinions remain stable over long periods, others do change. Many scholars believe that people are flighty and changeable; others point to the deep-seated, long-lasting nature of one's opinions. To understand this difference in perspective, it helps to look at three factors: intensity, latency, and salience.

**Intensity** Opinions are not all equal. People feel some things more intensely than others, and that affects the strength and durability of their opinions. **Intensity** is a measure of the depth of feeling associated with a given opinion. It affects the way people organize their beliefs and express their opinions on a wide variety of issues. Some react most intensely to the issue of a woman's right to choose an abortion; others express their most intense political sentiments for or against gun control. Try visiting a local senior center and suggest cutting Social Security benefits! Or going to a military base and arguing for a decrease in defense spending! On the other hand, try getting just about anyone to speak out on soybean subsidies. Some issues elicit more intense reaction than others.

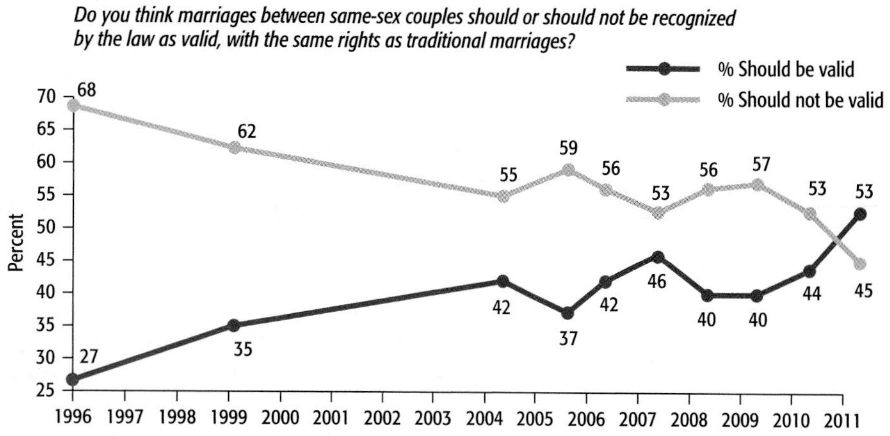


Note: Trend shown for polls in which same-sex marriage question followed questions on gay/lesbian rights and relations.
1996–2005 wording: "Do you think marriages between homosexuals . . ."

**FIGURE 8.7** Same-Sex Marriage Opinion Trend

*Source:* Gay Marriage Poll, http://www.gallup.com/poll/147662/first-time-majority-americans-favor-legal-gay-marriage.aspx.

Issues that provoke intense feelings are often called *hot-button issues* because they strike a nerve, a "hot button" that can elicit strong reactions and affect voting choices. In the 2008 election, gay marriage was a hot-button issue (see Figure 8.7). The more intensely an opinion is felt, the more likely it is to endure and to influence policy decisions. Thus, we can assume that attitudes about race or same-sex marriages (subjects most Americans have intense opinions about) will not change much over the next decade or two. Attitudes about U.S. foreign policy toward Belize, on the other hand, could prove extremely volatile. Few Americans hold intense feelings about Belize, so short-term events (a Communist takeover) or the sudden pronouncements of respected American leaders ("Let's help Belize, our democratic neighbor to the south") could dramatically affect how Americans feel about that nation.

**Latency** Public opinion is not always explicit. **Latency** describes feelings that are hidden or unspoken, suggesting the *potential* for an opinion or behavior, but only when the right circumstances occur. Ross Perot's bid for the presidency in 1996 unleashed an avalanche of latent feeling. The American public's long-standing but often dormant distrust of government and politicians—and its admiration for successful entrepreneurs—leapt to the fore following a series of scandals, a sagging economy, and a burgeoning federal budget deficit. Those latent opinions gave Perot the highest third-party vote since Theodore Roosevelt in 1912, even though Perot withdrew and then reentered the race.

**Salience** **Salience** is the extent to which people see an issue as having a clear impact on their own lives. Salient issues stir up interest and participation. Proposition 8—which changed the California Constitution to add a new section that read, "Only marriage between a man and a woman is valid or recognized in California"—is an example. Similarly, the issue of base closings is more salient to residents of states where local, regional, and state economies rely on the proximity of military bases or lucrative contracts for the production of military hardware. Politicians decrying base closures might garner a strong following in California but be ignored in Chicago, where the issue lacks salience. To understand public opinion and how that opinion will affect citizen actions, one must know how salient a given issue is to a given population.

## How Changeable Is Public Opinion?

Some research findings have suggested that individual political opinions are not firmly held.[34] When respondents are asked the same questions again and again over relatively brief periods, their responses tend to vary and even to contradict earlier

### QUICK REVIEW

Change in Public Opinion

- Intensity is a measure of the depth of feeling associated with a given opinion.
- Latency describes feelings that are hidden or unspoken, suggesting the *potential* for an opinion or behavior, but only when the right circumstances occur.
- Salience is the extent to which people see an issue as having a clear impact on their own lives. Salient issues stir up interest and participation.

**intensity**
In public opinion, a measure of the depth of feeling associated with a given opinion.

**latency**
In public opinion, unspoken feelings, suggesting the potential for an attitude or behavior, but only when the right circumstances occur.

**salience**
In public opinion, the extent to which people see an issue as having a clear impact on their own lives.

responses. Does this indicate that we tend to offer random, meaningless answers when asked our opinions? Many scholars see this pattern as proving the "irrationality" of the American voter. However, much of the apparent irrationality may actually stem from faulty polling methods. When the same question is asked differently, or when questions are worded vaguely, respondents are more likely to change their answers. This does not so much suggest irrationality as indicate that people are trying to make the best sense of what they are asked, even when questions are difficult to understand. On the other hand, when researchers phrase questions so that they contain the information necessary to formulate firm opinions, results show that individuals actually do have stable, "rational" opinions. Although Americans may not be particularly intimate with political specifics, they nonetheless harbor enduring and meaningful political beliefs. It is up to the pollster to find the best way to elicit these opinions.

Yet, people's opinions sometimes *do* change. Changing circumstances trigger corresponding changes in public opinion. As school violence and murders increase, more Americans want stricter gun control. As incomes rise, so does support for shorter workweeks, higher minimum wages, and increasing expenditure for workplace safety and environmental protection. As more women join the workforce, more calls emerge for women's rights. And awareness of rising crime produces a demand for tougher laws and more police officers on the street. Sudden events can also cause a change in opinions. In time of national crisis, Americans are likely to feel more patriotic, to "rally around the flag" and the president; they are also likely to lower their levels of criticism of the government and national leadership.

Although Americans appear to respond in an almost knee-jerk fashion to appeals from popular figures or to images presented in the media, it is unwise to overestimate the malleability of public opinion. On many issues Americans maintain a deep-seated set of attitudes that they don't want to change, making them a "tough sell" when leaders solicit approval for unpopular actions.

# FROM PUBLIC OPINION TO PUBLIC POLICY

8.8 *Does public policy mirror public opinion?*

Public opinion is a crucial element in the political process. It can dramatically affect both the government's policies and government's legitimacy in the minds of the people. After all, the ultimate test of a democracy comes down to this: Do government actions, over the long run, reflect what citizens want? Or, what would happen if public preferences were really reflected in public policies? This is the focus of this chapter's Approaching Contemporary Issues in Democracy.

A Gallup poll conducted in late July 2009 found that almost half of Americans believe they have a good understanding of the issues involved in proposals to overhaul the health-care system and that two-thirds do not believe the same about the lawmakers who will vote on them. The Gallup analysis raises real concerns for democracy:

> *That less than 3 in 10 Americans believe that Congress has a good understanding of the issues involved in the healthcare debate underscores the basic lack of confidence that Americans have in the men and women they elect and send off to Washington to represent them. . . . It would be optimal in a democracy if the people of the country believed that they and their elected representatives in Congress had a good understanding of something as important as a major overhaul of the nation's healthcare system. But only about one in six Americans fit that description, leaving the vast majority of the public with doubts about the level of understanding of either themselves or Congress.*[35]

# APPROACHING
## Contemporary Issues in Democracy

### What If the Voice of the People Really Ruled?

**ISSUE:** What if Congress, the president, and the courts were required to use public opinion as the primary guiding force for all policy decisions? How would this change impact the democratic nature of the presidency?

**Question 1:**

How do you think the framers would feel about more closely linking public policy to public opinion? What changes would need to be made to the political system to institute such a change?

**Question 2:**

How would this change impact minority rights? Should policy change even if public opinion directs discrimination against minority groups?

**Question 3:**

How would requirements linking policy more closely with opinion impact the stability and order of the American democracy? What factors influence instability in public opinion? Would these factors threaten the stability of the government if policy was linked to public opinion?

At first glance, we are struck by a significant gap between what Americans say they want and what their leaders are doing. The United States would be quite a different place if public opinion set public policy. Over the years, polls have shown consistent support for proposals that American political leaders do little to implement. Why hasn't American public policy reflected majority preferences? Immigration reform or health-care reform are examples of the difficulty in translating public will into public policy within a complex framework of divided powers. Further slowing down the entire process is the Constitution framers' persistent view that the "common will" of the people does not always stand for the "common good" of society.

**THINKING CRITICALLY**

What do you think explains why public policy differs, in some cases, from public opinion? If not public opinion, what is influencing public policy in these cases?

How well has the U.S. government reflected its people's will over the past few decades? Laws and policies designed to ensure gender equality have gradually been implemented as public attitudes shifted to favor them. Tough crime laws have increased in response to growing demands on government officials to "do something" about alarming crime rates. On the whole, if a significant majority of the American people indicate over time that they believe government should act in a particular manner, chances are good to excellent that government will accede to those wishes.

Clearly, American government policy does not always reflect popular desires. But a perfect reflection of popular desires is surely beyond the capability of any government. Some aspects of the public will are simply unrealistic ("more services, lower taxes!"). Others are opposed by most political actors because they contradict the spirit of the Constitution. For example, a constitutional amendment allowing school prayer in public schools has been widely popular but, until recently, was opposed by most decision makers. Despite these examples, on many issues we find government policies reasonably close to the general direction of public opinion.

## Summary

8.1 *What role does public opinion play in a democracy?*

- Public opinion is the keystone of democracy. No government can claim to be the legitimate voice of a people unless public opinion plays an integral role in the choice of political leaders and the development of public policy.
- For any political system in the world to be democratic, its leaders must at the very least hear "the voice of the people." The leader–follower connection is central to democratic theory in democratic societies.
- Citizens in a democracy express their preferences through informed political activity, and leaders listen with a keen interest to those expressed preferences.

8.2 *What is the history of thought regarding the role of public opinion in democratic policy making?*

- Plato saw public opinion as a danger if it meant the mass of citizens could freely express individual desires.
- John Stuart Mill, in his essay *On Liberty* (1859), argued in favor of a populace free to express its diverse political views. He wrote that only by giving all individuals the maximum liberty to state their opinions could a society ever arrive at the "truth."
- James Madison took a middle stance between Plato and Mill. In *The Federalist,* no. 10, Madison acknowledged the inevitable diversity of opinion that would develop in a free society but feared that competing opinions could lead to hostile factions that would divide rather than unify or improve society.

8.3 *How is public opinion measured?*

- To measure public opinion, a representative sample—meaning it must include all the significant characteristics of the total population—must be polled.
- The size of this sample is also important. Most reputable national polls have sample sizes of 1,500 to 2,000 respondents, a size that reduces the margin of error to plus or minus 3 percent. Using statistical methods, pollsters have determined that information from a random sample of that size can be projected onto the entire population.
- Another major concern of polling is reliability. Pollsters want meaningful and consistent results. Attention to question wording is essential for reliable results. Respondents can often be led into answers by the way a question is worded.
- Pollsters must make every effort to contact potential respondents and draw them out; they must learn how to extract truthful answers from shy, hostile, or simply bewildered members of the voting public.
- Accurate polls are one of the most important sources of information political leaders use in the decision-making process. Polls today, conducted by reputable national polling organizations, provide a reasonably accurate picture of the American public's beliefs and desires that would otherwise be difficult to achieve.

8.4 *How does a person develop his or her ideas about politics?*

- Political socialization refers to the process by which we learn about the world of politics and develop our political beliefs. Learning about politics begins early in childhood.
- Family influence is especially powerful in the development of political knowledge, understanding, and participation. Children tend to adopt their parents' party loyalty.
- Adolescents' views are shaped not only by their family but also by the political culture and events of their time. As a result, no generation simply mimics their parents' views, and analysts have observed a strong generational effect in American socialization patterns.
- Outside the family, the most powerful institutional influence on political socialization is education. Early primary education leads children to recognize the name and image of the president. Most children are taught to look at the president as a benevolent symbol of government and politics.
- University training also represents a key element in the process of socialization. Those with a college education express different political views than do those who do not go to college. College-educated Americans are more tolerant, more likely to support democratic values, and more liberal, particularly on social issues.

8.5 *What variables shape the formation of public opinion?*

- Class, or social standing, shapes many of our social and political values. Income, a key element in the concept of class, is far easier to define and study. People in different income groups often see the political world in different ways. As a general rule, the less money one makes, the more inclined one is to favor liberal economic policies that provide benefits to the poor. The more money one makes, the more one is likely to oppose such policies.
- Racial and ethnic background strongly affects the attitudes a person is likely to develop. Hispanic Americans tend to take a liberal position on economic issues and vote heavily for the Democratic Party. Asian Americans, whose income levels have risen significantly in recent decades, are among the most conservative groups in the nation. The vast majority of black voters consider themselves Democrats, whereas white voters are more closely divided in party identification.
- Religious differences produce serious political differences in the United States. The less religious you are, the more liberal or "left" you are likely to be. Members of any country's dominant religion, Protestantism in the United States, tend to be more conservative. By comparison, minority religious groups, especially the more oppressed ones, tend to favor liberal perspectives.
- People's political outlooks often reflect where they grew up and where they now live. Certain sections of the United States have conservative traditions; other areas are more liberal. People from conservative areas are likely to be conservative, and those from liberal areas, liberal.
- Women, on some issues, are more liberal than men and women are more likely to support a liberal candidate.

8.6 *What positions do Americans take on core issues and ideals?*

- American political culture is shaped by three key variables: core values, political ideology, and culture and lifestyle.

- *Core values:* At the deepest level, American values are remarkably homogeneous. Surveys reveal a broad consensus on the core issues and ideals of government: individual liberty, political equality, and the rule of law. These values ensure the stability of the political system.
- *Political ideology:* Political ideology is a coherent way of viewing politics and government. Ideological perspectives include beliefs about the military, the role of government, the proper relation between government and the economy, the value of social welfare programs, and the relative importance to society of liberty versus order. The most common ideologies among politically aware Americans are liberalism and conservatism.
- *Culture and lifestyle:* Culture theory argues that individual preferences emerge from social interaction. A way of life designates a social orientation, a framework of attitudes within which individuals develop preferences based on how they relate to others and to the institutions of power.
- *Intolerance:* Public opinion data on intolerance give some credence to anxieties about the tyranny of the majority. Yet, it need not remain an inevitable feature of our polity. As levels of education and socioeconomic status increase, so does tolerance for conflicting points of view.

8.7 *Do Americans live up to the ideal of the democratic citizen?*

- Polling research reveals that Americans know little about important issues and that they tend to confuse the issue positions of various candidates during campaigns. The American public falls short of the ideal advocated by democratic theorists—a well-informed citizenry. Americans' interest in politics is minimal. No more than a third of the electorate ever claims to be seriously active in electoral politics.
- Some scholars counter this image of the ignorant, apathetic citizen by asserting that American people, although not well informed, are able to fulfill their role as democratic citizens. These scholars see the public as more rational than many observers are willing to concede, arguing that although Americans may not know all the names of political people and places or the intricate details of every issue of the day, they do recognize and rationally distinguish between the alternatives presented to them, especially when they step into the voting booth.
- Average citizens develop broad orientations toward their world, including ways of thinking about politics, based on their entire set of life experiences. They then use these broad intellectual frameworks as shortcuts for processing new information. Partisan identification provides a cue that individuals use to evaluate candidates and acts as a filter through which individuals view the political world.

8.8 *Does public policy mirror public opinion?*

- At first glance, researchers are struck by a significant gap between what Americans say they want and what their leaders are doing. The United States would be quite a different place if public opinion set public policy.
- Translating the public will into public policy within a complex framework of divided powers takes time—often a good deal of time. Further slowing down the entire process is the Constitution framers' persistent view that the "common will" of the people does not always stand for the "common good" of society.
- A perfect reflection of popular desires is surely beyond the capability of any government. Some aspects of the public will are simply unrealistic ("more services, lower taxes!"). Others are opposed by most political actors because they contradict the spirit of the Constitution.

## Key Terms

culture theory, 260
exit polls, 248
gender gap, 257
generational effect, 249
intensity, 265
latency, 265
margin of error, 243
party identification, 264
political culture, 258
political ideology, 259
political socialization, 248
public opinion, 242
random sample, 244
realignment, 264
representative sample, 242
salience, 265
sampling bias, 245
schemas, 264
straw poll, 242
tracking polls, 248

## Test Yourself Chapter 8

**1.** The view that public policy must not be driven by public opinion was held most strongly by
a. James Madison.
b. Plato.
c. John Stewart Mill.
d. Machiavelli.

**2.** Who feared that competing opinions could lead to hostile factions that would divide rather than unify or improve society?
a. Plato.
b. Aristotle.
c. Socrates.
d. James Madison.

**3.** Straw polls are of little use because they often fail to obtain
a. legitimacy.
b. a representative sample.
c. validity.
d. a quorum.

**4.** The *Literary Digest* poll of 1936 overrepresented
a. poor Americans.
b. upper-class Americans.
c. Jewish Americans.
d. Muslim Americans.

**5.** Most polls have a margin of error of approximately
  a. 3 percent.
  b. 10 percent.
  c. 95 percent.
  d. 9 percent.

**6.** In a random sample,
  a. all age groups are taken into account.
  b. all ethnic groups are taken into account.
  c. every member of the population has an equal chance of appearing in the sample.
  d. all religious groups are taken into account.

**7.** Pollsters are very careful to avoid
  a. a random sample.
  b. controversial issues.
  c. sampling bias.
  d. margins of error.

**8.** An open-ended question
  a. allows respondents to provide any answer to the question.
  b. provides the respondent with a set of answers to chose from.
  c. is more representative than a closed-ended question.
  d. can never be completely random.

**9.** The term *political socialization* refers to
  a. the process by which people learn about political issues.
  b. how nice politicians are to one another.
  c. the process by which people acquire their political beliefs.
  d. the relationship among politics, social skills, and racial tolerance.

**10.** Political socialization begins
  a. in college.
  b. in early childhood.
  c. in church.
  d. when we cast our first vote.

**11.** Which social institution plays the greatest role in political socialization?
  a. The church.
  b. The military.
  c. Grade school.
  d. The family.

**12.** The most likely source of one's partisan identification is
  a. one's parents.
  b. one's peers.
  c. one's spouse.
  d. one's government.

**13.** Schools are central to the political socialization process because it is there that children learn
  a. which party better represents their values.
  b. which party is better for American values.
  c. to develop positive attitudes toward citizenship through history and civics courses.
  d. to think like their teachers.

**14.** An individual's racial or ethnic background
  a. has a strong influence on his or her political beliefs.
  b. has no influence on his or her political beliefs.
  c. becomes important only during the primary season.
  d. becomes important only when one of the major parties nominates a minority candidate.

**15.** The term *gender gap* refers to
  a. the fact that men tend to vote Democratic while women tend to vote Republican.
  b. the time period in the socialization process when there is no difference in opinion between young girls and boys.
  c. the fact that women have consistently been more supportive of what are commonly called "compassion issues."
  d. the underrepresentation of women in elected office.

**16.** Intolerance
  a. is no longer an issue in America.
  b. is still a pressing problem in America.
  c. is still a pressing problem, but has no influence on our political process or public policies.
  d. is the dominant influence on our public policy making.

**17.** In the United States, people with few religious connections are likely to
  a. have very little involvement in politics and voting.
  b. favor conservative social and economic policies and to vote Republican.
  c. favor liberal social and economic policies and to vote Democratic.
  d. favor conservative social policies and liberal economic policies and to vote Democratic.

**18.** A schema is
  a. a breakdown of the federal bureaucracy.
  b. an intellectual framework for evaluating the world.
  c. a plan for proportional representation in Congress.
  d. an organizational framework for the appellate court circuit.

**19.** Latency describes feelings that are
  a. late in forming.
  b. pressing and painful.
  c. hidden and unspoken.
  d. still in the formation process.

**20.** What is the best explanation for why public policy does not directly mirror public opinion in the United States?
  a. Campaign finance reform.
  b. Separation of powers and checks and balances.
  c. Members of Congress are not worried about reelection.
  d. The president can push through any policy he or she wishes.

**ANSWERS**
**1.** b, **2.** d, **3.** b, **4.** b, **5.** a, **6.** c, **7.** c, **8.** a, **9.** c, **10.** b, **11.** d,
**12.** a, **13.** c, **14.** a, **15.** c, **16.** b, **17.** c, **18.** b, **19.** c, **20.** b

# Political Parties

# 9

## Chapter Outline

**Introduction:**
*Political Parties and Democracy*

- A Brief History of the American Party System
- The Current Political Party System
- Functions of American Political Parties
- Party Organization
- Nominating a President: Parties and Elections
- Why a Two-Party System?
- Minor Parties
- Political Parties and the 2012 Election

## Learning Objectives

9.1 How have political parties formed, evolved, and become more democratic over the years?

9.2 What has characterized the present political party system?

9.3 What are the purposes and goals of the political parties?

9.4 How are political parties organized to express popular political views?

9.5 How has the presidential nomination process evolved into a more democratic process over the years?

9.6 Why has the American political system evolved into a two-party structure?

9.7 What third parties have been established in the past, and why have they not survived?

9.8 Where are the political parties going next, and what will bring about that evolution?

# INTRODUCTION

## POLITICAL PARTIES AND DEMOCRACY

As the 2012 presidential election will show, the balance of powers among political parties lies at the heart of democracy, representing the crucial link between what citizens want and what government does.[1] After two terms of Republican rule followed by one of Democratic rule in the White House, and the 2008 and 2010 congressional elections that alternated ruling majorities by the Democrats and the Republicans, the 2012 election will be the tie breaker determining the future direction of policy and politics in America. That is why parties must continually change, adapt, and adjust to the popular forces of their time. They must stay in touch with the voters—from whom they derive their support and power—so that they can gain control of government and the policy-making process. Competitive and democratic political parties allow a wide range of groups to enter peacefully into politics that might otherwise have to turn to illegitimate measures to gain their ends. The result is social movements such as the "Tea Party" and "Occupy Wall Street" that might one day lead to changes in the nation's political party composition, or even party structure.

**Political parties,** then, are nongovernmental institutions that organize and give direction to mass political desires. They bring together people who think alike or who have common interests to work toward common goals. The clearest goal of any political group is power to control government and thus implement its policy preferences. In an age of mass participation, power goes to those elites who can connect with the masses. Today, the Democratic and Republican parties appear to frequently have trouble making that connection.

In this chapter we look at party history, as well as at the functions, development, role, and future of American political parties. First, let's look at the history of American parties to see how the development of democracy is inextricably tied to the activity of political parties.

# A BRIEF HISTORY OF THE AMERICAN PARTY SYSTEM

9.1 *How have political parties formed, evolved, and become more democratic over the years?*

**political parties**
Organizations that exist to allow like-minded members of the population to group together and magnify their individual voices into a focus promoting individual candidates and government action.

Many of the framers, beginning with George Washington, feared the development of a political party system. James Madison, the strongest influence on the Constitution's final shape, saw them as a direct threat to the common good because their promotion of specialized interests would subvert the general welfare.

Despite the framers' fears, political parties quickly developed in the United States and by 1800 were already playing a major role in elections and governance. A party system began to emerge during the divisive and continuing debate between Alexander Hamilton, President Washington's secretary of the treasury, and Thomas Jefferson, his secretary of state, over topics such as the constitutionality of the national bank. Hamilton, a supporter of a strong federal government, argued for a manufacturing sector that would allow the United States to become a wealthy and self-sufficient trading partner in the world economy by relying on an expansive construction of the necessary and proper clause in the U.S. Constitution. A strong federal government would have a national bank with sufficient power to borrow and spend money, develop international agreements, and protect the domestic economy. Conversely, Jefferson, arguing for a narrow construction of the elastic clause limiting the delegated national powers only to what was absolutely necessary, wished to see a United States that remained largely rural. He envisioned a nation that retained its republican roots built on a large working, agrarian class. These two visions for the country divided other leaders and the general public into *factions*—"the spirit of party" the framers had feared.

**realignment**
A shift in fundamental party identification and loyalty caused by significant historical events or national crises.

In the first few years of the republic, many of the framers denounced party divisions. Hamilton, for instance, declared that a faction dominated by Madison and Jefferson was "decidedly hostile to me and my administration. . . . and dangerous to the union, peace and happiness of the country."[2] George Washington warned "in the most solemn manner against the harmful effects of the spirit of party." This spirit, he asserted, demands "uniform vigilance to prevent its bursting into a flame." Washington's cautionary remarks about political parties may seem extreme by today's standards, but he was surely correct when he said that the "spirit of party" was a "fire not to be quenched."[3] It was this battle between the Federalists under John Adams and the Antifederalists under Thomas Jefferson that led to the controversial presidential election of 1800. Although the U.S. party system has undergone many changes, political partisanship has remained from his day to ours.

**THINKING CRITICALLY**

The framers did not envision political parties in their original approach to democracy. How have parties affected the way democracy is shaped? Could American democracy exist without them?

Scholars have identified six historical eras in which party influence, allegiance, and control have changed. These eras always begin with a party **realignment,** in which significant historical events or national crises cause a shift in fundamental party identification and loyalty. Realignments are the result of a change in public attitudes about the political system and the ability of each party to deliver favorable candidates and policies. They usher in new eras, which tend to be stable and lengthy in duration.[4]

## The Foundations of the Party System (1790s–1824)

The Federalists, arguing for a strong central government, as well as the followers of John Adams and Alexander Hamilton, and the Republicans, arguing for a decentralized system of states' rights, and led by Jefferson (also called the Jeffersonian Republicans and later the Democratic-Republicans), represented two competing groups. As such, they constituted America's first parties. Today's Democratic Party, the direct descendant of Jefferson's party, is the oldest political party in the world. This party originally sided with rural and small-town forces in the struggle between promoters of agriculture and promoters of manufacturing. Its followers resisted the trend toward nationalization of power. They promoted Jefferson's belief that a nation of small property owners represents the best society, one likely to be virtuous and egalitarian.

The elections of 1789 and 1792 went smoothly because parties had yet to be formally established. On the first Wednesday of February in 1789, the newly established electoral college chose George Washington as the nation's first president. Washington was easily reelected in 1792. With his departure from the political scene after his second term, however, political tensions emerged as distinct factions.

**Revolution of 1800**
The first election in world history in which one party (the Federalist party of John Adams) willingly gave up power because of a lost election to another party (the Republican Party of Thomas Jefferson) without bloodshed.

**Table 9.1** Results of the Presidential Election of 1824

| | Popular Votes | | Electoral College Votes | |
|---|---|---|---|---|
| **Candidate** | **Number** | **Percentage** | **Number** | **Percentage** |
| Jackson | 155,872 | 42.2 | 99 | 37.9 |
| Adams | 105,321 | 31.9 | 84 | 32.2 |
| Crawford | 44,282 | 12.9 | 41 | 15.7 |
| Clay | 46,587 | 13.0 | 37 | 14.2 |

Federalist John Adams and Democratic-Republican Thomas Jefferson opposed each other in the closely contested elections of 1796 and 1800. Adams barely won the initial contest, but Jefferson triumphed in the rematch in 1800. The pivotal 1800 election became known as the **Revolution of 1800** because it was the first time anywhere in the world that the ruling elite in a nation changed without a death or a revolution and the loser left office voluntarily. But this election also illustrated how the party system affected the electoral system. All of the Jeffersonian party electors in the electoral college followed their instructions and voted for both Jefferson and his running mate, Aaron Burr, causing a tie and throwing the decision into the House of Representatives. Fears of further intrigue and deals that might overturn the will of the electorate produced the Twelfth Amendment, which mandated separate votes for the presidency and the vice presidency.

With Jeffersonians clearly dominating after Jefferson's reelection in 1804, Federalist support rapidly declined, and following the War of 1812, the party fell apart. In fact, during the presidency of James Monroe (1817–1825), distinctions between the two parties disappeared. This so-called Era of Good Feelings was characterized by a lack of divisive issues and the rapid recovery of the American economy.

The election of 1824 was the first in which popular votes were counted and the last to be settled by the House of Representatives. Four regional candidates could produce no electoral college winner (see Table 9.1). To become president took more than winning the most electoral college votes—as Andrew Jackson clearly did in this election. According to the Constitution, a candidate must win a *majority* (more than 50 percent) of those electoral college votes; otherwise, the U.S. House of Representatives chooses from among the top three contenders. The winner and eventual president must receive a majority of state delegations—that is, 13 out of 24 states in Jackson's day, and 26 out of 50 states in our time. Jackson won only 37.9 percent of the electoral college vote (more than anyone else, but short of a majority); therefore, the election went to the House of Representatives for resolution.

Jackson found that his popularity with the public did not help him there, where he was viewed as a political outsider and demagogue. Henry Clay—Jackson's weakest election rival but powerful in the House, where he served as speaker—threw his support behind the second-place candidate, John Quincy Adams. Clay's influence gave Adams his 13 states, making him president by the slimmest of margins (see Figure 9.1).[5]

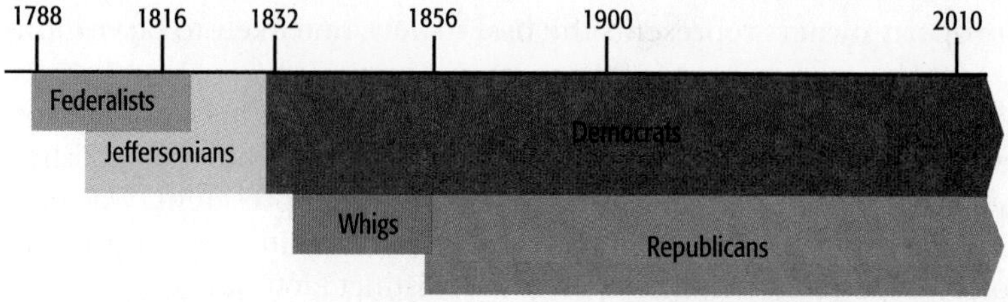


**FIGURE 9.1** The Five Major American Political Parties
Five political parties have achieved a successful and competitive role in American politics. The Democrats and the Republicans have succeeded over the last 150 years where others have failed.

## The First Institutional Party System (1828–1854)

After having the election of 1824 "stolen" from them, Jackson's outraged followers organized to take power in the next election. Their grassroots activism, under the energetic leadership of Jackson himself, who followed the advice of New York's Martin Van Buren, reenergized the old Jeffersonian party and sent it forth in the modern format of the populist Jacksonian Democrats. Formalized by Jackson's presidential victory in 1828, the Jacksonian Democrats sought to revive Jefferson's egalitarian principles, and in this way, despite its states' rights stance, also became another forerunner of the modern Democratic Party. The party drew support from urban workers, westerners, and southern nonslaveholders, many of whom also expected government jobs in the form of political patronage in return for their support.

When President Jackson sought to dismantle the national bank, believing it to be operated for political purposes, business interests joined with slaveholding southerners to form the Whig Party. Much like the Hamiltonian Federalists, Whigs supported an active federal government. Their ranks included Senators Henry Clay and Daniel Webster and Illinois lawyer Abraham Lincoln. This was an era of real two-party competition, with each party capturing a significant portion of political offices. The Whigs were particularly successful in winning congressional elections. Ultimately, the Civil War and the issues of slavery and the nature of the Union would lead to the disintegration of this initial party system.

## The Second Party System (1854–1890s)

Slavery splintered not only the party system but also American society. Northerners, progressive whites, and many of those settling in the West, along with activists from former minor parties such as the Liberty and Free Soil parties, came together in 1854 to form the Republican Party, dedicated to abolishing slavery.

Lincoln, elected president in 1860 as part of this new political alignment, came to the Republican Party from the Whigs. He and other Republican leaders developed policy platforms that stressed issues of moral conscience more than had previous political parties. The Whigs dropped from sight, whereas the Democratic Party, weakened by its connection to the losing Confederate cause, kept its base in the South and Midwest, primarily among agricultural, rural voters. The Republican Party dominated national politics until the 1890s by winning six consecutive presidential elections (1860–1884). Grover Cleveland, in the close elections of 1884 and 1892, was the lone Democrat to capture the presidential office in this period.

## The Third-Party System (1896–1932)

The late 19th and early 20th centuries are frequently characterized as a time of party government. Democratic and Republican parties became highly developed and well organized, attracting a loyal body of voters, with the Republican Party becoming the dominant one during this period. The huge influx of immigrants helped change the shape of domestic politics, leading to the growth of urban party "machines" and creating long-term alliances between various ethnic groups and political parties.

The Democrats lost ground over an 1893 economic depression during Democrat Grover Cleveland's presidency. Already the stronger party, Republicans in 1896 held off the combined challenge of the Populists and Democrats, both of whom nominated the "Silver-Tongued Orator," William Jennings Bryan, for president. Republican William McKinley's victory ended the Populist Party and solidified a fundamental and long-term shift in Democratic and Republican constituencies. Republicans consolidated their control of the North and West, while Democrats continued to control the South.

Certain Populist issues found support among the Progressives, reformers from both parties who argued that the process of nominating candidates should be shifted

William Jennings Bryan, the "boy orator of the Platte," delivered his classic "Cross of Gold" speech in 1896 about the harm the monetary system did to farmers. His loss to William McKinley in 1896 ushered in a new period of Republican control of the White House.

from the leaders in the "smoke-filled rooms" to the voters. Rather than becoming a party of its own, or a third party, elements of the Progressive Party were incorporated by both of the major political parties. Between 1896 and 1932, only one Democrat, Woodrow Wilson (1913–1921), became president, and that was only because former Justice Charles Evans Hughes narrowly lost California in 1912. However, Republican domination ended abruptly in 1932, as the failure of President Herbert Hoover to deal with, and even fully acknowledge, the Great Depression, which brought the next realignment in party identification and power.[6]

## The Fourth Party System (1933–1968)

By the summer of 1932, the Great Depression had left millions without work or economic relief. The incumbent president, Republican Herbert Hoover, tried to assure a frightened American citizenry that prosperity was forthcoming; calling on them to trust his leadership. Hoover clung relentlessly to faith in the gold standard, the need for a balanced budget, and no government handouts. But trust in Hoover was not securing new jobs or feeding families. Meanwhile, New York governor Franklin Delano Roosevelt, a Progressive politician wedded to no particular governing policy but ready to try anything that might work, accepted the Democratic Party's nomination for president, claiming, "I pledge you, I pledge myself, to a new deal for the American people."

On November 8, 1932, Governor Roosevelt defeated President Hoover. "A frightened people," wrote James David Barber, "given the choice between two touters of confidence, pushed aside the one they knew let them down and went for the one they prayed might not."[7] Roosevelt amassed a 472–59 electoral college majority and a popular vote margin of 22,809,638 to 15,758,901.

To gain this massive victory, Roosevelt brought together an alliance of Americans that came to be known as the **New Deal coalition.** The key components of this successful amalgam consisted of the urban working class, most members of the newer ethnic groups (especially Irish, Poles, and Italians), African Americans, the bulk of American Catholics and Jews, the poor, southerners, and liberal intellectuals. This broad-based coalition allowed Roosevelt to forge scores of new government programs that increased government assistance and brought him immense popular support. It also brought about a new set of beliefs and attitudes toward government.

Riding a wave of New Deal enthusiasm, Democrats dominated national politics between 1932 and 1968. The nation chose only one Republican president during this period: World War II hero Dwight Eisenhower. Each of Roosevelt's Democratic successors kept the New Deal coalition alive. Lyndon B. Johnson (1963–1969), in particular, gave renewed impetus to New Deal philosophy by expanding government economic assistance programs with his Great Society.[8] In the pivotal 1968 election, with a nation tired of the war in Vietnam and weighed down by the tax burdens of large government aid programs, conservative Richard Nixon beat Vice President Hubert H. Humphrey, whose election was hampered by the bitter split in the Democratic Party. The Republican Party took control of the White House and the political landscape for a generation.

### THINKING CRITICALLY

With the Great Recession under way during the 2008 election, was that voting decision similar to the one in 1932? Did the new coalition of voters who elected Barack Obama—those who were younger than 30 years old, Hispanic Americans or African Americans, first-time voters, city voters, or upper-middle and upper-class liberal voters—represent a new, long-term coalition for the Democrats?

## The Fifth Party System (1969–2000)

**New Deal coalition**
Brought together by Franklin Roosevelt in 1932, a broad electorate made up of the urban working class, most members of the newer ethnic groups, the bulk of American Catholics and Jews, the poor, the South, and liberal intellectuals.

The Republican dominance in the period from 1968 to 2000 is made clear by the fact that this party won five of eight presidential elections. The two Democratic winners, Georgia's Jimmy Carter in 1976 and Arkansas' Bill Clinton in 1992 and 1996, were southerners who governed more as moderate Democrats and sometimes, in Clinton's case, from the conservative side of that party. Yet, until recently, scholars have been reluctant to describe the post–1968 period as another realignment.

Republican presidents Richard Nixon, Gerald Ford, Ronald Reagan, and George H. W. Bush failed to dismantle the New Deal and Great Society programs, which had proven broadly popular. Democrats retained majority control of the U.S. House of Representatives from January 1955 to January 1995, when the Republicans took control of both houses for the first time in 40 years.

In past realignments, the emerging dominant party rode a highly controversial issue to broad election victories in both Congress and the presidency and then took control in the majority of American states as well. But Republicans remained the minority party in state and local elections throughout the 1960s and 1970s. Even though change came after the election of Ronald Reagan, state party results remained mixed until 2000, when middle-of-the-road, pragmatic Republican conservatives won the governorships of 23 of the 34 contested races in 2000.

## The Sixth Party System (2000–?)

Beginning in 2000, with the election of President George W. Bush, signs began to appear that partisan strengths were shifting. The sharply partisan, and razor-close presidential elections in 2000 and 2004 created a balanced "red versus blue" state political system in which both parties struggled to gain the upper hand politically. Republicans succeeded in retaining control of both houses of Congress through the 2000 election. But in 2001, Senator Jim Jeffords (R–VT), because of differences with the Bush administration over education and other policies, defected to become an Independent who would vote Democratic, denying Republicans control of the Senate until the 2002 election. The Republicans picked up an additional four Senate seats in the 2002 election, giving them a substantial 55–44 margin over the Democrats. Just two years later, though, the red and blue states in areas such as Virginia and Montana were beginning to merge into a growing "purple voter" movement—voters who were willing to switch from party to party in choosing their candidates. After the 2006 Senate elections, the Democrats' six new seats—Pennsylvania, Ohio, Rhode Island, Montana, Vermont, and Virginia—gave the Democrats a narrow 51–49 vote margin.

The shift in partisan control was occurring at the state level as well, as can be seen in the balance of state governorships and legislative seats. In 2002, the Democratic Party picked up three governorships nationwide: Pennsylvania, Michigan, and Illinois. The 2004 gubernatorial races were a virtual stand-off, with Democrats winning six races and Republicans winning five. Prior to the 2000 election, the Democrats controlled both houses of the state legislatures in 19 states and the Republicans in 17. After the 2000 election, Republicans and Democrats each controlled both houses of the legislature in 17 states. Another 15 states were split, with each party controlling one house, with Nebraska having a nonpartisan, single-chamber legislature. More revealing of the close national party balance in 2004 was the fact that of 7,382 state legislative seats, both parties held an identical 3,660 seats, with the rest held by candidates from minor parties or no party affiliation.[9] In the 2006 election, the Democrats picked up governorships in six states previously held by the Republicans, giving them a 28–22 majority.

The reason for this balanced red versus blue partisan system was that by 2003, the number of voters identifying with each of the two parties was roughly equal.[10] But change began to occur. As Figure 9.2 shows, through 2004, the Democratic Party began to gain new members, and by mid-2005, perhaps as a result of the war in Iraq and plummeting public support for the Bush presidency, the Democrats held a 3 percent lead over the Republicans in party identification, with Independents still registering as the largest group. By the middle of 2009, the Democrats had increased their membership to 35 percent and the Republicans had dropped to 23 percent, with 36 percent identified as Independents.[11]

The economic crisis of 2008 and beyond had a great influence on the party structure. By 2010, the Great Recession, together with the controversial nature of the Obama administration's policies to deal with the economic crisis, took its toll on the

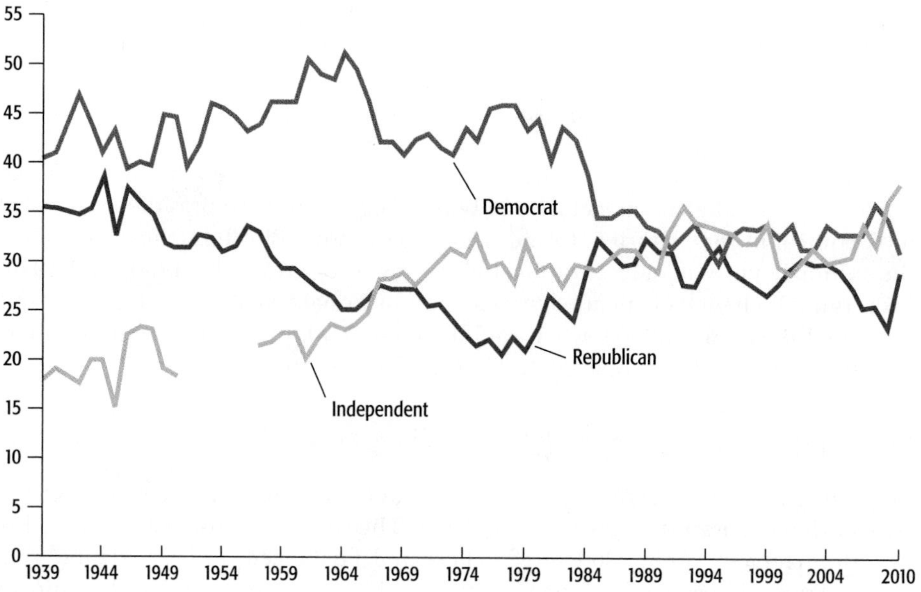


**FIGURE 9.2** Trend in Party Identification, 1939–2010

*Sources:* "Trends in Political Values and Core Attitudes, 1987–2009," the Pew Research Center for the People & the Press, a project of the Pew Research Center, http://www.people-press.org/reports/pdf/517.pdf. Used with permission; Gallup poll reported in Jeffrey M. Jones, "Democratic Party ID Drops in 2010, Tying 22-Year Low," January 5, 2011, found at www.gallup.com.

Democratic Party membership. The percentage of people identifying themselves as Democrats dropped to 31 percent, a 22-year low. At the same time, the percentage of those identifying themselves as Independents rose to 38 percent, also a 22-year high, with the Republicans increasing their percentage to 29.[12] Missing from these numbers, though, is the percentage of people who might be identifying with the new conservative Tea Party, as explained later in this chapter. Faced with an insurgency movement by conservative Tea Party followers working under the Republican Party label, able in 2010 to elect governors in Kansas and Maine, the agenda changed to cutting taxes and government spending. The unsuccessful effort by the Republicans to absorb the new group, as usually happens in such potential realignment periods, has led to what appears to be a split in the party. Table 9.2 compares the results of the three most recent presidential elections.

**Table 9.2** Results of the Presidential Elections of 2000, 2004, and 2008

| | | Popular Votes | | Electoral College Votes | |
|---|---|---|---|---|---|
| **Year** | **Candidate** | **Number** | **Percentage** | **Number** | **Percentage** |
| 2000 | George W. Bush | 50,456,002 | 47.87 | 271 | 50.37 |
| | Al Gore Jr. | 50,999,897 | 48.38 | 266 | 49.44 |
| | Ralph Nader | 2,882,955 | 2.74 | 0 | 0 |
| 2004 | George W. Bush | 62,040,606 | 51 | 286 | 51 |
| | John Kerry | 59,028,109 | 48 | 252 | 49 |
| | Ralph Nader | 411,304 | 1 | 0 | 0 |
| 2008 | Barack Obama | 69,498,216 | 52.9 | 365 | 68.2 |
| | John McCain | 59,948,240 | 45.7 | 173 | 31.8 |

# THE CURRENT POLITICAL PARTY SYSTEM

9.2 *What has characterized the present political party system?*

In 2008, well more than half of first-time voters voted for Obama, together with more than half of those under the age of 30, making one wonder whether this might be the beginning of an alignment of these groups with the Democratic Party for a generation. A year later, with the leadership of the Republican Party in disarray, the Democrats sought to press their advantage from their huge electoral wins the year before. The movement of Californian Democrats and Hispanic American voters to nearby conservative states such as Nevada and Arizona, combined with the continued drift of libertarians away from the Republican Party in those areas, continued the rise of the Democrats in that region. These changes, together with the large Hispanic American vote for Obama and the Democratic Party, could solidify that voting bloc for the Democrats. On the other hand, the country might be witnessing something of a dealignment as more voters drift to the center. Following the 2008 election, the number of independent voters increased sharply, to 36 percent—the largest number of independent voters in 70 years (see Figure 9.2).

The same partisan shifts are evident in Congress and the state legislatures. Favorable congressional redistricting after the 2000 census allowed Republicans to increase their margin in the House of Representatives in 2002 and 2004.[13] By early 2006, the Republicans held a 231–202–1 margin in the House and a 55–44–1 margin in the Senate. These party majorities reversed in the 2006 election, when the Democrats gained 31 seats in the House, giving them a 233–202 majority, while their six new seats in the Senate gave them a 51–49 majority. This trend continued in the state legislative races, with the Democrats taking control of 24 state houses to 16 for the Republicans; 9 states had split control, and Nebraska had a nonpartisan unicameral legislature.

After the 2008 election, the Democrats were close to a filibuster-proof Senate. Then, in June 2009, Pennsylvania Republican Arlen Specter followed the lead of 200,000 Republican voters in his state and switched to the Democratic Party. When Democrat Al Franken was finally seated as Minnesota's junior senator that same month, the Democrats achieved a filibuster-proof majority of 60 in the Senate, with 58 Democrats plus 2 Independents who caucus and vote with the Democrats. In the House, the Democrats had increased their voting margin in April 2009 to 256–178 with one Independent. And in the state governments, the Democrats increased their control of state legislatures to 27–14 with 9 legislatures split between the parties. A similar gap existed in the governorships, with the Democrats leading the Republicans by a 28–22 margin.

New polling data confirmed the impression that a shift was underway from the Republican and Democratic Parties to the Independents. In May 2009, the Pew Research Center found that the Republicans trailed the Democrats by 12 percent in those willing to identify with the party, their lowest level of support in 25 years. In addition, the percentage of Americans expressing any support for the Republican Party in 2000 stood at just 36 percent, down 31 percent from 15 years earlier, and trailing the Democrats by 17 percent. Making this shift even more interesting is the fact that the percentage of people self-identifying as conservative has remained steady at 37 percent—nearly twice as large a group as those calling themselves liberals.[14] However, the continuation of this trend will depend on which political party the significant plurality of the people who call themselves Independents (36 percent) choose, if they move at all (see Figure 9.3 comparing party identification and partisan self-identification).

## THINKING CRITICALLY

What role has voters' frustration with Republican and Democratic "politics as usual" played in reshaping the party system in the past decade? Will the "Tea Protests" translate to changes in the party system?

Another change among the major political parties can be seen by comparing the values held by their members. The Pew Research Center's report found a "stark shift in partisan values" over the past several decades, making the "partisan gap [between the two parties the] widest ever." The report found that "Republicans have swung to a much more critical view of government while more Democrats take a positive view than at any previous point in the 22-year history of this study."[15] One example is the issue of

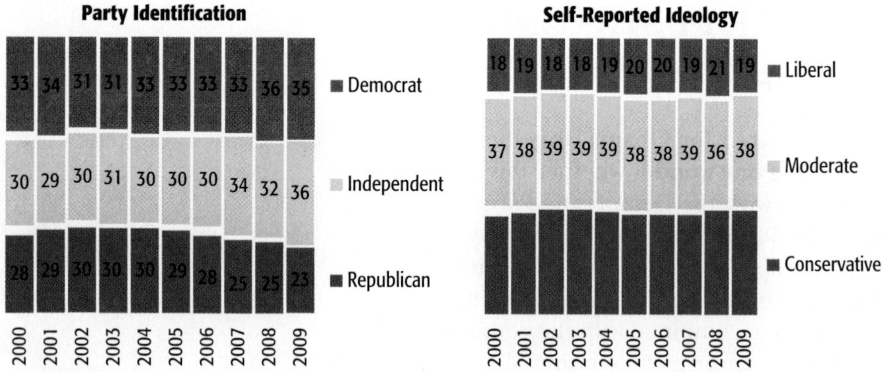


**FIGURE 9.3** Comparison of Party Identification and Partisan Self-Identification
Although the basic percentage of conservatives has not changed much, the percentage of Republicans has dropped dramatically.

*Source:* "Trends in Political Values and Core Attitudes, 1987–2009," the Pew Research Center for the People & the Press, a project of the Pew Research Center, http://www.people-press.org/reports/pdf/517.pdf. Used with permission.

health care, with 78 percent of the Democrats "completely agree[ing] that the government should improve accessibility and affordability of health care," nearly twice the size of the Republicans who took this position (at 41 percent).[16] This weak voter identification with the major parties, and the balanced nature of the major political party numbers, coupled with increasing numbers of Independents and the volatile, negative reactions to economic recovery and health-care reform legislation, has led to change in the political party identification system. As outlined later in this chapter, the rise of a potential third party, the Tea Party, and the new middle-class protest movement Occupy Wall Street show the volatility of the party system.

# FUNCTIONS OF AMERICAN POLITICAL PARTIES

9.3 *What are the purposes and goals of the political parties?*

The governing institutions of the United States were designed to fragment and decentralize power, and they have succeeded at that task. The only political institutions that work to pull people together—that exert a coherent, unified perspective on public affairs and attempt to govern in a reasonably cohesive manner—are the two major political parties.[17] Their functions within American society are varied and crucial for the health of our democracy.

## Parties Organize the Election Process

A party's most basic role is to nominate candidates and win elections.[18] True, citizens need not belong to a political party to run for office, but to win a high elective office, a candidate must, with few exceptions, belong to one of the two major American political parties. Every president since 1853 has been either a Democrat or a Republican. In 2012, Vermont's Socialist/Independent Bernard Sanders and Connecticut's conservative Democrat-turned-Independent Joe Lieberman were the only senators, and Rhode Island Governor Lincoln Chafee the only governor, not in one of those two parties. The stability of this pattern is impressive. For more than a century, the rule for any ambitious politician has been simple: To build a serious career in public life, first join either the Democratic or the Republican Party. When dissatisfied, however, an elected politician can always switch parties, as several have in recent years.

Winning office is crucial to party fortunes. Party members spend much time and energy on the election process. Parties select candidates; provide money to local, state, and national races; and arrange administrative support at all levels of electoral competition. They begin this work with the vital function of **recruitment.** Parties continually look for effective, popular candidates to help them win votes and offices. Since 2000, both parties have had increasing difficulty persuading rising political figures to run for Congress and the Senate, even for open or highly winnable seats, because of the need to raise large campaign war chests and the stresses such service places on their families. In some states, term limits for state legislators have seemed to improve this prospect, as state politicians forced out of their state office by term limits were compelled to run for Congress in order to remain in public office.

**recruitment**
The process through which parties look for effective, popular candidates to help them win votes and offices.

Parties search for successful campaigners to serve another key function: *representation.* To win free and democratic elections, parties follow a crucial axiom: Find out what voters want and promise to give it to them. No matter who is elected, the winners attempt to remain committed to the popular programs on which they campaigned. Following this logic, parties must *act responsibly* and legislate the policies they promised. Parties elected under pledges to carry out a specific set of policies know that voters will judge them at the next election. Did they do what they promised? If not, voters can (and often do) reject them in favor of their rivals. The potential for punishment of this sort keeps parties under serious pressure when writing their platforms. Backing away from or even flip-flopping on a public commitment can often produce a devastating backlash.

In the long run, this open competition for power serves the voting public. By recruiting good candidates, representing voter wishes, and being held responsible for their actions in office, the two parties help Americans approach the democratic ideal of government.[19]

## Parties Represent Group Interests

In their struggle for power, parties speak for and unite different groups and their varied interests. Parties find that it pays to discover what groups want, then work with those groups to fulfill their desires. Thus, Republicans often work closely with business groups to articulate pro-business positions; Democrats do the same with labor union leaders. But parties must do more than speak for one narrow interest if they wish to gain majorities needed to win public office; they must appeal to a wide range of social groups. In so doing, they learn to meld individual group interests into a larger whole with a coherent philosophy of governing.[20]

Conservative radio personality, Rush Limbaugh's, (top) opposition to the 2012 Republican presidential candidate, moderate Mitt Romney (bottom) helped to shape the early nomination voting.

The need to combine varied and complex interests forces parties to become broad political coalitions. Republicans, for instance, must bring together the interests of multinational corporations and small businesses, rural evangelical Protestants and pro-life Catholics. Democrats, too, must unite a diverse set of factions that include small-town white southerners, urban black workers, and ethnic white suburbanites. In the process of building a coalition from social subgroups, both parties perform another democratic function—integrating various groups into public life and the democratic process. Parties thus help mute the conflicts that might arise if each interest group had its own separate party and fought the others at every election.

## Parties Simplify Political Choices

By bringing groups together and creating a coherent platform for voters at election time, parties simplify political choices for voters. Most voters do not study every issue in depth, nor do they know where each candidate stands on every issue. Parties help them make rational decisions at the ballot box by melding a series of complex issues into a broad, general perspective and explaining that perspective in simple, direct ways. By Election Day, most voters have been educated enough to know that their choices are not merely between two individual personalities but between two differing philosophies of governance. Consider what the alternative would be: a ballot listing only a long series of names unconnected to any party and without any hint of the candidate's position.

## Parties Organize Government and Policy Making

When elections are over, parties help organize the country's political institutions for governing. Public officials work together as organized members of the winning party to carry out their party's aims and election pledges. In early 2005, the increase

**QUICK REVIEW**

State and Local Parties

- Local party organizations provide entry for people seeking involvement in politics as volunteers, organizers, or candidates.
- State party organizations organize elections and provide electoral college votes needed to win the presidency.
- Committee leaders supervise the various functions vital to state parties.
- State parties work with state governments to conduct primary elections or caucuses.
- Party structure varies dramatically from state to state.

in margin of seats held by the Republicans in the House of Representatives allowed Republican Speaker J. Dennis Hastert (IL) and former majority leader Tom DeLay (TX) to use more hardball tactics with their members—such as threatening to change their committee assignments—to help promote the legislative agenda of President George W. Bush. The Democratic takeover of both houses of Congress after the 2006 election produced a set of committee chairs and public policies far different from when the Republicans were in the majority, and thus different policies. However, when the Republicans retook the House in 2010, they reversed course again and stalemated the Democrats' and President Obama's agenda.

Party discipline can work both ways. After successfully fighting with the Republicans to keep his chairmanship of the Judiciary Committee in 2005 by promising to help confirm ultra-conservative Bush administration judicial nominees, Pennsylvania's Arlen Specter tried to maintain his seniority and high-ranking committee positions after switching to the Democratic Party in the spring of 2009. But Specter was rebuffed and then told the Senate Democratic Caucus would review his seniority issues after the 2010 election. Specter claimed that he had been promised the same seniority by Majority Leader Harry Reid (D–NV), but the membership appeared to take this action after Specter opposed Barack Obama's economic programs and threatened to oppose union protection rules. This disciplinary process works in both parties' interest. After all, the party that solves political problems wins mass support at the next election.

# PARTY ORGANIZATION

9.4 *How are political parties organized to express popular political views?*

Despite recent trends toward strengthening national party organizations, political parties are still relatively decentralized institutions. The flow of power moves upward—from local to state organizations and from there to the national committees and conventions.

## Parties at the Grassroots

Parties at the grassroots consist of city, county, and state organizations. Party operations begin at the local level. The **local party organization** provides an initial point of entry for people who want to participate in politics as volunteers, organizers, or candidates. Each local party is highly dependent on the level of community interest—high in some places and low in others. The party faithful in active areas eagerly fill slots as precinct chairs and election organizers, volunteer for administrative posts, and even run to participate in state conventions. Where interest is low, party structures remain skeletal, with many posts unfilled or a few party faithful keeping the organization going.

Although linked to the national apparatus, local and state political parties have significant independent power, often more than the national party. Local parties enjoy higher personal interaction with members, base their platforms on significant local issues, and often perform their duties without seeking huge monetary donations. Citizens can more easily become involved at the local level by donating money or working for a campaign.

*Political activists* are vital in a democracy; they exert important influence on the party platform and on political decision makers. Party activists differ from the population at large in that they tend to be wealthier and better educated. Reforms in Democratic Party methods to select delegates to nominating conventions have encouraged increased activism for women, minorities, and youth. And the Republican Party has also opened its doors to these newer activists.[21] So although party activists show socioeconomic differences from the population at large, party reform has produced a more demographically representative group.

**local party organization**
The initial point of entry for those seeking involvement in politics as volunteers, organizers, or candidates.

The 50 **state party organizations** have strikingly different systems. Through their two key roles as election organizers and providers of electoral college votes, state party organizations play a critical part in American national politics. They also play a significant role in state politics. The leaders in each state party's central committee supervise various vital functions such as raising funds, identifying potential candidates, providing election services, offering advice on reapportionment, and developing campaign strategies. State parties also work with state governments to conduct the primary elections or caucuses most states use to register preferences for presidential candidates.

Party structure varies dramatically from state to state. Some party organizations, like that of Pennsylvania, have permanent headquarters, a regular calendar of events, frequent meetings with local officials, and a central committee staffed with professional administrators, strategists, and fund-raisers. Some states, such as California, have weak political parties. From these differences follows a common political rule: where parties are weak, interest groups are strong. George W. Bush's 2004 election succeeded in part through the Republican Party's comparative victory over the Democratic Party in grassroots party and interest group organization in the battleground states.[22]

**state party organizations**
Party organizations at the state level; they organize elections and provide the electoral college votes needed to win the presidency; they also supervise the various functions vital to state parties, such as fund-raising, identifying potential candidates, providing election services, offering advice on reapportionment matters, and developing campaign strategies.

**machine politics**
An organizational style of local politics in which party bosses traded jobs, money, and favors for votes and campaign support.

**national party organization**
Party organization at the national level whose primary tasks include fund-raising, distribution of information, and recruitment.

**national party convention**
The national meeting of the party every four years to choose the ticket for the presidential election and write the party platform.

## The Party Machine

From the final decades of the 19th century to the early or middle part of the 20th century, a political party organizational style called **machine politics** flourished in New York City, Chicago, Philadelphia, Kansas City, and elsewhere. At the heart of the system lay an ingenious scheme of reciprocal influence. Party leaders (bosses) traded jobs, money, and favors for votes and campaign support. Once in office, the party bosses had jobs to distribute to party workers who had helped them to victory. Voters who supported the winning party could be assured of good local service, the occasional handout, and the odd favor. The bosses regularly reached into the public till for party funds, for personal enrichment, and to keep voters and party workers happy.[23]

The boss and the machine fell to several modernizing forces of the mid-20th century. To begin with, increasingly wealthy and educated Americans supported government that served people's interests and were less inclined to accept corrupt machine behavior. People needed fewer of the favors that the bosses typically had at their disposal. Candidates who ran against party bosses started winning elections.

Four additional developments doomed the old machine system. First, the new civil service system robbed the party machine of those tangible and valued rewards for potential followers—government jobs. Second, the developing modern welfare state provided a safety net for the poorest citizens, who no longer needed bosses to serve that purpose. Third, the proliferation of primary elections removed decision making about candidates and nominations from the hands of party bosses and gave it to a mass electorate. With little power to control the struggle for high office and few rewards to dole out to anyone, party boss influence crumbled, and nearly all of the traditional machines ground to a halt. Finally, the secret ballot helped speed the decline of party bosses' abilities to intimidate voters.

## National Party Organization

The strength of the **national party organization** is most apparent during presidential elections. Even with the increasingly democratic nominating process and proliferating interest groups and political action committees, the national party organization remains a crucial source of coordination and consensus building for both Republicans and Democrats.

For decades, the national organization's primary task was to organize the **national party convention** once every four years. The convention symbolizes the party's existence as a national institution. At this festive affair, party delegates from around

Republican National Committee Chair Reince Priebus (left) has been less controversial than his predecessor, Michael Steele (right).

Rep. Debbie Wasserman Schultz (D–FL) has tried as Democratic National Committee Chair to organize her party for the 2012 elections.

the country come together to select presidential and vice presidential candidates for the coming election and to write the party's platform. At no other time is the national party much in evidence to the American public.[24]

A **party platform** is a statement of principles and policies, the goals that a party pledges to carry out if voters give it control of government. The platform announces positions on prominent issues of the day such as gun control, abortion, taxation, and social spending. The platform is also an important way of setting the tone for each party and distinguishing one party from another. The Democrats and Republicans differ from each other ideologically, which will be evident in the 2012 election.

Although many people assume that party platforms have little relationship to the party's actual performance in government, this is not the case. Platform positions tend to mirror subsequent government expenditures quite closely. At times, though, in search of votes, candidates find that they must differentiate their campaign rhetoric from the party platform. For the Republicans, often the platform's strong anti-abortion stance forces them to take this approach.

The day-to-day operations of the national party fall to the *national chair*. Each chairperson, selected by the presidential nominee of the party, is the actual administrator. The chair is responsible for personnel, fund-raising, scheduling, and the daily activities of the party. Modern fund-raising techniques, such as computer-derived mailing lists and direct mail, have made both state and national party units more effective in recent years. Parties become better able to target specific voters—based on geography, demographics, previous financial support, and precinct location—with each election. Given the administrative responsibilities of the national chair's job, holders of this office tend to be relatively unknown rather than popular national political figures. However, it is not uncommon after a national presidential election to choose visible figures from those races to galvanize future supporters. The Republicans' choice of Reince Priebus of Wisconsin as its national party chair signals their intention to capture the Midwest with a conservative message. On the other hand, the Democrats' choice of Rep. Debbie Wasserman Schultz (FL) signals their desire to broaden the ideological base of the party. Aside from organizing and running the party machinery, party chairs are the party's public face as it raises money and prepares for the next presidential primary season.

## Party Similarities and Differences

**party platform**
The statement of principles and policies; the goals that a party pledges to carry out if voters give it control of the government.

Although the parties have similar organizational structures, each bases its structure on different goals. The Republican Party emphasizes creating and maintaining effective administrative structures, especially at the national level, to supply assistance and raise funds for candidates. As a result, Republicans tend to be more bureaucratically oriented than Democrats, but also benefit from less ideological discord. Conversely, Democrats emphasize representation by promoting voter mobilization, activism, and debate. Because it encourages pluralistic participation, the Democratic Party ensures acrimonious argument regarding policy and the selection of candidates.

Tea Party advocate, Governor Rick Perry of Texas, was well funded to run for the 2012 Republican presidential nomination, but a series of his own mistakes undercut his candidacy.

# NOMINATING A PRESIDENT: PARTIES AND ELECTIONS

9.5 *How has the presidential nomination process evolved into a more democratic process over the years?*

Before a party can run the government and make public policy, it must win control of the top political offices. In the United States, parties vie for the presidency in particular. Let us examine the process by which a Democrat or a Republican becomes a candidate for president of the United States.

## Nominating Candidates

Before candidates can be elected to public office, they must first be nominated. **Nomination** is the political party's endorsement of a candidate. Party endorsement carries legal weight. Only one candidate per position can appear on any ballot with the word *Democrat* or *Republican* after his or her name. Because other names on a ballot have next to no chance of election, the nomination process matters a great deal.

In the nation's current system, a candidate gains a party's nomination for president by winning a majority of delegates at the party's national convention, held the summer before the November presidential election. The national parties set the overall rules for nomination processes, but it is left to each individual state to set the rules for that particular state. The result is a patchwork of different kinds of state nominating contests. By tradition, the party currently holding the White House holds the later convention, usually in August. The challenging party holds its convention a month or so earlier, usually in July—perhaps on the theory that its candidate needs a running start to win the presidency.

Delegates in the past were often *uncommitted,* or under the control of party leaders who frequently withheld any commitments until a politically opportune moment at the convention itself. Even on the convention's opening day, the race might remain wide open. Today, however, nearly all delegates are *committed* long before the convention convenes. In fact, the nominee's identity is clear long before the convention, which acts primarily as a formal ratifier of the obvious. Convention activities now aim less at choosing a candidate than at unifying the party faithful and gearing up for the fall election struggle. It is left to the state political parties to choose how to select their delegates to the national political party conventions. They use one of two selection methods, or sometimes a combination of these: caucuses, or meetings of the party faithful, and primaries, or public elections by the voters.

### THINKING CRITICALLY

What impact will 21st-century changes to the media system and the Internet have on party selection of a presidential candidate and the overall approach to democracy? With more and more people getting their election information from the Internet and television ads, how might parties adapt to maintain influence and organize voters in the future?

**nomination**
A candidate's "sponsorship" by a political party.

**caucus**
Meeting of party adherents who gather to discuss, to deliberate, and finally to give their support to a candidate for president. They then select delegates who will represent their choices at higher-level party meetings; eventually, their votes are reflected at the national convention itself. Also means a conference of party members in Congress.

**Caucuses** **Caucuses** are meetings of party adherents who gather in precinct halls, schools, firehouses, or even private homes to discuss, deliberate, and finally throw their support to a candidate for president. They then select delegates who will represent their choices at higher-level state party meetings; eventually their votes are reflected at the national convention. Candidates or their representatives often attend caucuses to discuss issues and make appeals.

**primary election**
A pre-election that allows all members of a party, not just its leadership, to select the party's candidate for the general election in the fall.

**winner-take-all system**
A system in which the winner of the primary or electoral college vote receives all of the state's convention or electoral college delegates.

**proportional representation**
A system of representation popular in Europe whereby the number of seats in the legislature is based on the proportion of the vote received in the election.

**closed primary**
A system of conducting primary elections in which only citizens registered as members of a particular political party may participate in that party's primary.

**open primary**
A system of conducting primary elections in which citizens vote in whichever party's primary they choose.

Caucus meetings may be all-day affairs that require a heavy investment of time. Although any party member may attend, generally only the most active and devoted—usually wealthier and better educated—party members participate. For that reason, as American society approaches democracy, it has tended to prefer primary elections, which are more inclusive and democratic in nature than caucuses.

**Primaries** Primary elections date from the beginning of the 20th century. The Progressives, tired of seeing their candidates pushed aside by political bosses and party machines, argued that it was undemocratic to allow party elites to choose candidates. Under pressure, party leaders buckled, and the primary system slowly developed. A **primary election** is essentially a pre-election that allows all party members, not just leaders, to select the party's candidates for the general election in the fall.

Today, political parties in about three-quarters of the states employ primaries to select candidates for national elections. Voters in presidential primaries vote for a specific candidate, and these votes are converted into delegates for that candidate. The delegates then attend the party's national convention, where they vote for the candidate they represent.

States that use primaries employ various systems for parceling out delegates. Republicans allow greater variation than Democrats. Some states use a **winner-take-all system** in which the primary winner receives all the state's convention delegates. Other states distribute delegates by congressional district, using a winner-take-all system for each district; thus, a state might split its delegates among several candidates. Finally, in some states Republicans distribute delegates through various systems of **proportional representation.** Candidates who win, say, 20 percent of the statewide vote in the party primary will win about that same proportion of the state's delegates to the national convention.

In contrast to Republicans, Democrats employ a mandatory system of proportional representation to distribute delegates. Any candidate who wins at least 15 percent of the vote in any statewide primary must be allocated delegates to the national convention, and those delegates must reflect the exact percentage of primary votes received.

Although primaries vary, most states use the closed primary system. In **closed primaries** only citizens registered as members of a political party may participate in that party's primary. A registered Republican, for instance, cannot cast a ballot in the Democratic primary. Conversely, **open primaries** allow all registered voters to vote in whichever party's primary they choose. Few states use open primaries because such cross-party voting may allow voters from one party to help choose their rival party's nominee. An organized effort could produce crossover votes that select the opposition party's weakest candidate. This appeared to be the case in the 2000 campaign, when Democratic voters crossed over to vote for McCain in an effort to defeat George W. Bush before the general election. Two states, Washington and Alaska, have *blanket primaries,* which allow voters to choose either party on an office-by-office basis.

For nearly half a century, the New Hampshire primary was the first big test of a candidate's legitimacy. Indeed, in ten straight presidential elections (from 1952 through 1988), nobody became president without first winning the party's presidential primary in New Hampshire. Why should this small and atypical American state assume a dominant

Supporters for Libertarian Ron Paul, a Republican member of Congress from Texas, who ran for president in 2008 and 2012, were unhappy when rival Fred Thompson, an actor and former senator, skipped a presidential debate to appear on a national talk show.

role in the presidential selection process? Much of New Hampshire's influence stems from a simple fact: It always holds the first primary of each presidential election year. This race shows how a candidate fares in the "retail politics" of actually meeting the voters. The Iowa caucus also is important; it tests candidates in the Farm Belt and precedes New Hampshire's primary. In 2004, Iowa ended the presidential ambitions of Vermont governor Howard Dean, because his loss to Senator John Kerry effectively doomed his candidacy. In 2008, though, Barack Obama's unexpected victory in Iowa launched his successful nomination race against early front-runner, Hillary Clinton.

**frontloading**
The process by which most party primaries and caucuses are held early in the nomination schedule so that the majority of the delegate support is locked up early.

The traditional importance of Iowa and New Hampshire is diminishing, however. Many states, including some of the large ones, came to resent their power in selecting the nominee. To give themselves more political clout, many states moved the dates of their primaries earlier. More than 75 percent of both parties' convention delegates are now chosen within one to six weeks of New Hampshire's primary, a process known as **frontloading.** Thus, ambitious candidates must campaign in numerous states, in addition to New Hampshire, to have any chance of gaining their party's nomination. They cannot count on putting all their effort into winning New Hampshire and having a month or more, as they once did, to bask in that limelight and build national support. While it is now harder for a dark horse to come out of nowhere, do well in Iowa and New Hampshire, and go on to win a major party's nomination, as George McGovern did in 1972, Barack Obama was able to do it in 2008.

## The 2008 Presidential Election

For the 2008 presidential election season, states repositioned their primaries, with many of them moving or trying to move earlier in the process, seeking to improve their influence on the process. By this time the Democratic Party had benefited from the "50-state strategy" of Democratic National Committee chair Howard Dean, as he put party funds in every state, including conservative Republican strongholds, hoping to make them competitive in future elections. The strategy worked in the 2006 congressional elections, with Democratic wins in Montana and Virginia, so all of the candidates prepared to contest even the conservative states.

The nomination process did not go as predicted, and the role of political parties seemed to be diminished in the face of the very personal campaigns of 2008. Democrat Barack Obama built a 13-million-person email list in his Internet fund-raising effort, and Republican John McCain, whose maverick, Independent national campaigns dating back to the 2000 race, helped build his own early Internet fund-raising organization. The widespread expectation when the nomination races began was that in the large field of eight Democrats and seven Republicans seeking the nomination, the two candidates with superior name recognition—New York's Democratic senator Hillary Clinton and New York City's former mayor Rudy Giuliani—would secure their party's nomination very early in the process. Both, however, made critical early mistakes. Clinton, although very well funded and having a formidable campaign advisory team, did not have a good campaign organization in the Iowa caucus. She had made the decision not to fully organize and heavily contest the caucus states, but instead concentrate

Presidential caucuses like these in Iowa are harder for candidates to organize and win because they require supporters to be present for long periods of time in order to cast their votes. Democrat Barack Obama's decision to contest every caucus as well as primary states helped him win the nomination.

on the large-state primaries. Giuliani, with little support and few resources in Iowa and New Hampshire, decided to begin his campaign several weeks later in Florida, where he hoped to count on the support of transplanted New Yorkers. These two errors opened the door for underdogs Obama and McCain to launch their successful efforts.

Obama staked his claim to front-running status with an impressive win in the Iowa caucus, and although Hillary Clinton was able to "find her voice" and win in the New Hampshire primary, Obama did well enough to continue his momentum. Clinton did very well in the large states (e.g., California, Texas, Ohio, and Pennsylvania) and maintained her public relations lead, but Obama contested every delegate—mastering even the most arcane state delegate distribution rules, even in the smallest caucus states—and built an overwhelming delegate leadership. Typical of this effort was the Nevada caucus and the Texas primary in which Clinton won the states, but Obama won enough congressional districts to be able to capture the majority of the delegates. And, the big-state strategy backfired for Clinton when the Democratic primaries in Florida and Michigan, both of which Clinton won, became only "beauty contests," not awarding delegates because those states had defied the party in moving up the primary dates. Also, although Clinton won the major states on "Tsunami Tuesday," the February 5th contest including 24 states, Obama won nearly as many states numerically, and they virtually tied in delegates. Obama's unexpected 15 percent win in North Carolina seemingly sealed his nomination victory.[25]

Even with the overwhelming delegate victory for John McCain, beating his two closest rivals combined by about 700 delegates, the early months of the race were very much in doubt. Unlike most other candidates, McCain was solidly behind the Bush administration's policy in Iraq. McCain placed a distant third in the Iowa caucuses to Arkansas governor Mike Huckabee, with Massachusetts governor Mitt Romney taking third. Unhappy with the inability of his campaign to gain traction, McCain fired most of his staff and ran out of money in New Hampshire; he was campaigning largely on his own. McCain's popular grassroots campaign in that state was successful as he beat the nearby Massachusetts governor by five points. When Romney came back to win in Michigan (where he had been raised) and Nevada, it appeared that Romney would mount a challenge. But when McCain came back to win in South Carolina, the state that had ended his 2000 presidential nomination bid, he was back on track.

From then on, for the Republicans, the story appeared to be the inability of the party's conservatives to galvanize around a single far-right-wing candidate—either Massachusetts governor Mitt Romney or Arkansas governor Mike Huckabee—to challenge the insurgent, independent Senator McCain. The pivotal race came in Florida in early February, where McCain beat Romney by five points. After seeing the endorsement of California governor Arnold Schwarzenegger, the California vote, and seven other states (including New York and New Jersey) go to McCain on Super Tuesday, Romney dropped out of the race on February 7, and the nomination was effectively McCain's.

For both parties, the inability of the front-running candidates to take advantage of the frontloaded nomination system and their overwhelming visibility and funding advantage opened the door for upset wins by independent, insurgent candidates. That result worked out for the Democrats, as seen in Chapter 12, as Barack Obama amassed millions of votes from the young voters under the age of 30, Hispanic Americans and other minorities, and first-time voters to win a 52.9 percent majority and gain more than a two-to-one margin in the electoral college by gaining 365 votes to 173 for Republican John McCain.

## The 2012 Presidential Nomination Process

With no challenger to incumbent Democratic president Barack Obama, the entire nomination process was focused on the Republicans. The story there continued to be an apparent split in the party and a dramatic change in the nomination process as states vied with each other to make their role in the process more important. The conservative wing of the party, evidenced by the social and religious conservatives and the fiscal conservative Tea Party served notice that they would seek to influence the nomination process even to the point of capturing the nomination itself. Initially, it appeared that the candidates would be three contenders in the 2008 race, vice presidential candidate Sarah Palin, who would represent the Tea Party conservatives, former Arkansas governor Mike Huckabee, and Establishment candidate former Massachusetts governor Mitt Romney. As Palin debated whether to run, eventually deciding not to do so, and Huckabee took himself out of the race, the leader of the Tea Party conservatives Michele Bachmann (MN) entered the race and appeared to be a real contender. The Republican conservative voters seemed to be unhappy with Romney, calling himself the Establishment candidate, because of his support for the Massachusetts health-care reform law, which served as the model for the Obama federal plan, and he had trouble initially gaining more than 25 percent support in any state race or the national polls.

At the same time, states sought to increase their influence in the nomination process by moving their primary dates earlier in the schedule. The Republican Party allowed only the two traditional early states—Iowa's caucus and New Hampshire's primary—in addition to a caucus in Nevada and a primary in South Carolina to receive the party's support for a date before the March 6 Super Tuesday multistate contest. The schedule became even more scrambled toward a frontloaded system, though, when Florida announced that it would hold its primary on January 31. This led South Carolina to move its date up to January 21. Since New Hampshire's Constitution requires that it be the first state with a presidential primary in the nation, and Iowa's caucus always precedes that by about a week, it became inevitable that those dates would move up to dates earlier in January.[26] This meant the key campaign fund-raising and politicking would happen in late 2011. As the field expanded to liberarian representative Ron Paul, former House Speaker Newt Gingrich, businessman Herman Cain, and others, Governor Rick Perry of Texas entered the race to the early delight of followers before undercutting his candidacy by his own mistakes.

As of this writing in December 2011, the race appeared to center on either voters coalescing around one of the ultra-conservative candidates, pushing the party in that direction, or an acceptance of the only mainstream Establishment candidate in the field: Mitt Romney. Once more, the influence of the early "retail" nomination contests in the small states of Iowa and New Hampshire, coming in early January 2012, where the voters get to meet each of the candidates personally, was magnified, although the results of the late January 2012 primary in Florida, a swing state with so many kinds of voters, could inject an air of unpredictability into the process.

## Reforming the Nominating Process

Since 1968, the presidential selection process has been radically altered. The Democrats' disastrously divisive 1968 convention in Chicago fueled change in the party's nomination process for presidential candidates.

The nomination race itself had foretold the problems. Senator Eugene McCarthy's anti–Vietnam War stance and narrow second-place finish in the New Hampshire primary had convinced President Lyndon B. Johnson to end his reelection campaign. Then senator Robert F. Kennedy entered the race, and although he was far behind, his victory in the winner-take-all primary in California seemed to indicate that he would be nominated. However, his assassination by Sirhan Sirhan right after the primary narrowed the race to McCarthy and Vice President Hubert Humphrey, who had entered no primaries at all but was amassing significant support from the caucuses and party leaders behind the scenes.

At the Democratic National Convention during several hot days in Chicago, holders of opposing perspectives clashed dramatically in front of the television cameras. Inside the convention hall, party leaders, led by Chicago machine boss mayor Richard J. Daley, tried to direct the party's nomination to their candidate, Hubert Humphrey. But outside, Vietnam War protesters clashed violently with police. As the

**McGovern-Fraser Commission**
Democratic Party commission that, after the 1968 national convention, opened up meetings and votes to a broad variety of party activists, made primaries rather than caucuses the common means of choosing convention delegates, weakened the power of party leaders, and set up rules to ensure that a wide range of party members could participate fully in all party operations.

**superdelegates**
Delegates to the Democratic National Convention not bound to vote for any particular candidate; usually prominent members of the party or elected officials.

news broadcasts switched back and forth between the two scenes, clashes broke out inside the convention hall itself.[27] As a result of this disaster, Humphrey received the nomination but was too far behind in the election to win in November, as many party faithful sat out the early part of the campaign.

The Chicago convention was a watershed in American politics, creating widespread agreement that future party nominees had to depend on a deeper base of support than just the party hierarchy. Candidates at all levels in American politics since then have increasingly had to pass muster with the party rank-and-file in primaries before gaining the right to wear the party label in a general election.

Before the Chicago convention adjourned, activists succeeded in passing a resolution that by 1972 all state parties would "give all Democrats a full, meaningful, and timely opportunity to participate" in the selection of delegates. To create guidelines for compliance, the Democratic National Committee created the Commission on Party Structure and Delegate Selection, usually called the **McGovern-Fraser Commission** (after its chair, Senator George McGovern of South Dakota, and its vice chair, Representative Donald Fraser of Minnesota). This commission had far-reaching effects on the character of American politics. Its recommendations, largely adopted by the Democratic Party, opened up meetings and votes to a large variety of party activists, made primaries rather than caucuses the common means of choosing convention delegates, weakened the power of party leaders, and set up rules to ensure that a wide range of party members—especially women, young people, and minority group representatives—could participate fully in all party operations.

Although Republicans did not adopt these same reforms in all the details, they did follow Democrats on the essential points. Most of their delegates to the national convention, as well as their nominees for most lower-level offices, are now also chosen through party primaries. No longer can a handful of leaders in either party dictate whom the party will nominate for any office or what the party will stand for in an upcoming election.[28]

**The Results of Reform** In 1984, the Democratic Party further revised its rules to bring elected and party officials back into the nominating process. It did this by creating "independent" delegate spots (in the 2008 campaign season these were 823.5 of the 4,233 delegates) and allowing party and elected officials to attend the convention as unpledged **superdelegates** who could change their minds about their votes at any time. Democrats hoped that these superdelegates would attract more media attention and provide a display of party unity. Because the delegates were not bound by primary elections, a candidate would still need the support of national party leaders to win the nomination. This process had unexpected results in 2004, as Senator John Kerry received the commitments of the vast majority of these delegates in advance, giving him a tremendous advantage over all of his other rivals in the primary race. In 2008, even though Hillary Clinton began her campaign by enlisting many of the early superdelegate votes, by the time Barack Obama had clinched the nomination, so many superdelegates had switched to his side that he amassed nearly twice as many of their votes as Clinton.

The winds of reform that swept through the presidential nomination system touched party processes at every level in both parties. In the past, candidates gained party nominations by working within the party hierarchy, rising through party ranks, and demonstrating party loyalty to the inner circle of leaders. Anyone who now wishes to run for office in a partisan election anywhere in the United States must first win a party primary or caucus—one likely to be contested by other ambitious party figures. The implications of this change are enormous. Politicians stopped working within the party to please a small group of leaders and now work outside party structures to please a large mass of relatively uninformed voters.

This shift in focus from party elites to party masses made money increasingly important in American politics—an unexpected and unintended

## THINKING CRITICALLY

Do you think placing the power to vote for nominating a president in party bosses and executives approaches democracy? Should this power be left with the people in primaries and party caucuses?

consequence of making candidate selection more democratic. Yet it costs more to sway many people than a few. In the past, those who desired party nominations needed to influence at most a few hundred, more typically a few dozen, and in some cases a handful of party leaders. Today, decision makers (i.e., registered party voters) number in the millions.

**political action committees (PACs)**
Committees formed as the fund-raising and financial distribution arm of specific interest groups.

The change is so great that nomination races are now decided well before the national conventions, which have become so reduced in importance that the national networks are debating whether to cover them on television. To reach today's decision makers, a prospective candidate needs to hire a team of campaign specialists, conduct polls, create and mail out an impressive array of literature, and, most important, buy time on television.

Those who won elections in the past owed much to the traditional party hierarchy; now they owe much to their numerous interest group backers. Candidates need workers, support services, and money. They have found those resources in the varied strong interest groups that have sprung up to promote specialized causes. Symbolic of this development is the growing influence of **political action committees (PACs),** which promote specific interest groups' agendas, as well as 527 single-issue groups, created under an IRS regulation that allowed tax-exempt organizations seeking to influence an election to raise campaign funds on issues rather than candidates. (We will discuss the role of 527s and PACs in detail in Chapter 11.) Individual candidates also learned from the successful efforts of Democratic presidential candidate Howard Dean that they could raise millions of dollars on their own on the Internet. And during the 2008 presidential election campaign, Barack Obama did exactly that, with his staff building a grassroots fund-raising campaign on the Internet consisting of millions of people and raising nearly $750 million. This was nearly double what the McCain campaign could raise, with its fund-raising efforts amounting to around $320 million. In his preparation for the 2012 presidential campaign, Obama's email list of over 13 million people has allowed him to continue to raise more money from the grassroots efforts than all of the Republican presidential primary candidates combined.

## THINKING CRITICALLY

Does making the presidential nomination system more frontloaded, so that most of the votes are made in the first six to eight weeks of the system improve or diminish the system? Should the United States move to a series of regional multistate presidential primaries or even a national primary? Why or why not? Should the nomination and election process for the presidency be shorter?

These fund-raising efforts changed fundamentally in 2010, when the Supreme Court threw out the "soft money" campaign finance limits in the 2002 McCain-Feingold Act, regulating money contributed by the ultra-wealthy, large corporations, unions, and large interest groups, that can be spent on issues rather than specific candidates. A case referred to as the *Citizens United* case dealt with a documentary called *Hillary: The Movie* an anti–Hillary Clinton movie made during her presidential nomination campaign by a conservative group called Citizens United. Faced with the argument that this was actually a political propaganda film, making it an "issue ad" that was banned 30 days before a primary or 60 days before a general election, the Court argued that corporations are the same as "people" and have the same protected First Amendment free speech rights. A five-justice majority on the Roberts Court ruled that this free speech right gave corporations and large interest groups such as unions unlimited rights to contribute any amount of money to a campaign for the distribution of their message. The Court argued here, incorrectly, that, in time, Congress would make the source of these campaign donations public, thus giving this process more transparency. However, there was no incentive in the stalemated, gridlocked Congress to pass such laws that might diminish their campaign donations. As a result, large fund-raising interest groups called "Super-PACs"—such as the conservative American Crossroads GPS led by Bush administration adviser Karl Rove—can raise unlimited amounts of money, and, so long as they do not support any specific candidate, lobby for any political message they wish during the campaign. Television comedian Stephen Colbert of *The Colbert Report* made fun of this process by launching his own Super-PAC, funded by his viewers—Americans for a Better Tomorrow, Tomorrow—to illustrate the unlimited power of these groups to shape their political message.[29]

## APPROACHING Democracy Timeline

### Key Events in Political Party History

| | |
|---|---|
| 1798 | Federalist Party under John Adams passes the Alien and Sedition Acts. |
| 1800 | Aaron Burr tries to steal election from his running mate, Thomas Jefferson. |
| 1800 | John Adams peacefully turns over presidential power to Jefferson. |
| 1804 | Twelfth Amendment creates two-vote system for presidential vote. |
| 1824 | John Quincy Adams makes deal to steal presidential election from Andrew Jackson. |
| 1828 | Martin Van Buren helps Jackson create populist Jacksonian Democrats Party. |
| 1877 | Justice Joseph Bradley tips electoral commission of 1877 to help Rutherford B. Hayes win presidency. |
| 1880–1910 | "Smoke-filled room" used to nominate presidential candidates. |
| 1912 | Progressives under Woodrow Wilson create primary system. |
| 1968 | Hubert Humphrey uses backroom tactics to win Democratic nomination from primary-leading Eugene McCarthy. |
| 1971 | McGovern-Fraser Commission opens up democratic nomination process. |
| 1972 | Large number of states create primaries to deal with new party reforms. |
| 1992 | Ross Perot leads third-party movement to seek presidency. |
| 2000 | Ralph Nader leads third-party movement, taking votes from Democrat Al Gore; Supreme Court awards presidency to George W. Bush. |
| 2004 | Uncommitted "superdelegates" are created. |
| 2008 | Barack Obama nominated when he works in caucus states that Hillary Clinton ignored. |

☐ Democratic ☐ Neutral ☐ Undemocratic

Finally, with the destruction of the old party leadership that once provided continuity and cohesion, politicians who win high office now do so on their own and see themselves as independent of the discipline of party structures. In particular, the Republican Party in recent years seems to have split between the moderate mainstream party and an alliance of social conservatives as well as the fiscally conservative Tea Party members that are seeking to move the party to the more extreme conservative position. For their part, the Democratic Party has split between the more liberal "progressive wing" led by people such as former Speaker Nancy Pelosi (CA) and Senate strategist Chuck Schumer (NY); mainstream members seeking compromise such as Senate majority leader Harry Reid (D–NV) and his assistant leader Dick Durbin (D–IL); and conservative, small government and spending cut–oriented senators such as Jon Tester (MT) and Bob Casey (PA). Moderates who can work with both sides such as the two Republican Maine senators, Olympia Snowe and Susan Collins, and Massachusetts Republican senator Scott Brown, are rare. The ideological splits in the parties have become so pronounced and partisan in nature that some conservative Republican colleagues now label their moderate colleagues RINOs—or Republicans in Nature Only—and the liberal Democrats call their conservative members DINOs—or Democrats in Name Only. This trend seems likely to lead to further party fragmentation. Politicians' ability to secure their own campaign money, and their desire to work for their own political ambition in pursuing higher office, has enabled them to go their own way.

## WHY A TWO-PARTY SYSTEM?

9.6 *Why has the American political system evolved into a two-party structure?*

Throughout American history, two political parties have been the rule rather than the exception. Yet most democratic nations are characterized by a **multiparty system** in which five, ten, and sometimes even more parties regularly compete in elections, win seats, and have some chance of gaining power. Why is it that only two parties flourish in the United States?[30] (See this chapter's Approaching Democracy timeline.)

## Institutional Factors

The most frequent explanation for the emergence and survival of the two-party system is the way the United States elects public officials. Known as the *single-member district electoral system,* it is widely believed to inhibit the development of third parties. In other democratic nations, districts are often, but not always, large enough to contain many representatives, and each party elects about as many representatives as its proportion of the vote in that large district. In a ten-member district, for instance, a party obtaining 10 percent of the vote has one elected legislator. If that party averages 10 percent of the vote across the country, it will end up with 10 percent of the members of the national legislature. Then, if it maneuvers sensibly, it may be asked to form part of a governing coalition. The upshot of such a multimember district, or proportional representation system, is that small parties can gain seats and power, providing an incentive for minor parties to form and contest elections.

In the United States, however, the incentives all favor the two large parties. The entire country is divided into **single-member districts,** and each district seat is awarded to the candidate with the most votes. Small parties that, say, win 10 percent in every district across the nation receive no seats in the legislature. With that performance, they would lose in each district to one of the two big parties. Small parties that end up with no seats and no power gradually fade away as supporters grow discouraged. Potential supporters for a third party simply join one of the two big parties and promote their policy aims within a successful political grouping where those aims have some chance of being implemented.[31]

This system not only prevents third parties from forming but it also inhibits breakaway factions of the two major parties from setting up shop on their own. Disgruntled party subgroups have no incentive to leave and form their own parties, because doing so will lead to political impotence. Another institutional element favoring two-party competition is the **electoral college.** By its very design, the electoral college puts smaller parties at a disadvantage. The system produces, in effect, 51 winner-take-all state (including the District of Columbia) contests. Each state is allotted a certain number of electoral college votes, depending on its representation in Congress. Votes for president are then counted by state, and in all but two small states (Maine and Nebraska), whichever candidate comes in first in that state gains *all* of that states electoral votes, no matter how close the contest and even if the winning candidate falls short of a majority of the ballots cast. There is no consolation prize for finishing second, much less third or fourth, in American politics. A candidate comes in first or not at all. For that reason, many voters are reluctant to "throw their vote away" on a candidate outside the mainstream. They tend, in the end, to align with one of the two major parties.

Occasionally, a significant portion of the electorate will cast off such inhibitions and risk supporting a third-party candidate. But even though a few modern third-party candidates have received popular votes, none has been able to capture any states in the electoral college.

## Cultural Factors

Some scholars believe that the American two-party system is built into prevailing cultural norms and values. They point to the supposed traditions of moderation, deliberation, and compromise in the United States. Whereas the

**multiparty system**
A political system in which five to ten or more parties regularly compete in elections, win seats, and have some chance of gaining power. Promoted by systems with proportional representation and characteristic of most democratic nations.

**single-member districts**
Districts in which a seat goes to the candidate with the most votes. In this system, a small party—say, one that wins 10 percent in every district across the nation—would fail to secure a single seat in the legislature.

**electoral college**
The group of 538 electors who meet separately in each of their states and the District of Columbia on the first Monday following the second Wednesday in December after a national presidential election. Their majority decision officially elects the president and vice president of the United States.

Few gave Barack Obama, shown here at the Democratic National Convention with Joe Biden and their wives, any chance of receiving the nomination for the Democratic presidential nomination in 2008, but his themes of "Change!" and "Yes we can!" captured the hearts of the voters.

**party identification**
A psychological orientation or long-term propensity to think positively of and vote regularly for a particular political party.

**minor or third parties**
Parties in the American system other than the Democrats or Republicans.

French or Italian political cultures—out of which have sprung vigorous multiparty democracies—are often described as volatile and fragmented, American culture is supposedly centrist, devoid of the ideological extremes, class divisions, and group hatreds that produce political fragmentation elsewhere. This theory suggests that with most citizens clustering at the center of the spectrum, the United States has no room for a variety of parties. These conditions produce a natural setting for a two-party system, with each vying for the largest constituency of moderate voters.

Although this was the accepted cultural explanation for decades, in recent years scholars have begun to question it.[32] Particularly since the 1960s, American political culture appears to be fragmenting. Bitter struggles over civil rights, Vietnam, women's rights, and abortion have shattered the country's veneer of consensus and may help explain what many see as a weakening in the pattern of stable two-party dominance. In recent years, as shown in the 2000 and 2004 elections, some of the most volatile issues tearing at the fabric of the two-party system and its stability have been essentially cultural—abortion, gay rights, race, and family values.

### Party Identification

Another attempt to explain the two-party system centers on electorate psychology. As discussed in Chapter 8, many voters develop lasting loyalty to a political party, often because that party served their needs on a crucial issue. Thus, Republicans gained the loyalty of millions in the 1860s by standing for national unity and the abolition of slavery. Democrats gained lifelong supporters in the 1930s with their attempts to mitigate the worst aspects of the Depression. **Party identification** does not explain the origins of the U.S. two-party system, but it does help explain its persistence. The intense psychological ties that keep party voters faithful ensure both parties of long-term support. These old attachments hamper any new party trying to break through the status quo to gain followers.[33]

Businessman Herman Cain, the former CEO of Godfather Pizza, saw his lead in the 2012 Iowa caucuses evaporate in the face of multiple sexual harassment allegations.

## MINOR PARTIES

9.7 *What third parties have been established in the past, and why have they not survived?*

Despite the power of the two major American parties, **minor or third parties** have made appearances in every decade of American history. Why do they appear, how have they performed, and what do they accomplish?[34]

### Why Minor Parties Appear

As discussed earlier, the two major parties take relatively moderate positions on most controversial policies. Because the major parties aim at winning votes and gaining office, they cast their nets as widely as possible for broad inclusiveness. Both major parties end up focusing on the same central segment of the electorate but do not necessarily give equal emphasis to the same issues. Frequently, the emergence of a third party talking about issues the major parties seek to avoid will signal a realignment of the voters, or at the very least a restructuring of the major parties.

In like fashion, the major parties cannot aim their appeals too obviously at just one subgroup of the population, be it farmers, union members, or gun owners. Focusing on one minority can easily leave many other minorities alienated.

## Compared to WHAT?

### The Great Recession and the Rise of Extremist Politics?

The effect of the Great Recession since 2008 on political parties in the United States and Europe has been fascinating. In this country, we have seen the rise of the fiscally conservative Tea Party, winning a significant portion of the Republican Party's congressional seats, which has led to a sharpening of the partisan political differences on economic issues. The Republican Tea Party refuses to increase taxes on anyone, especially the upper one percent of the economic strata, and has pushed hard to extend the so-called Bush tax cuts from 2001, reducing taxes on the upper and middle classes. On the other hand, the Democratic Party has refused to sign on to the Republican Party's agenda of draconian spending cuts and retrenchment of the entitlement programs such as Medicare. As a result, the two parties have stalemated, unable to deal with annual spending programs, the debt ceiling, and even the so-called Supercommittee, the 12-person, bipartisan Joint Select Committee on Deficit Reduction, that was empowered to find a way to cut $1.2 trillion from the budget to begin to reduce the budget deficit, but failed to do so.

Life for political parties in Europe has been no easier. Countries such as Greece and Italy are so far in debt that the European Union and the European Central Bank have been unable to bail them out. Because those countries face the possibility of economic default, and others are also far in debt, experts fear that another recession could result as the banks in Europe and the United States are drawn into the financial morass. Everything seems to depend on the financially healthy Germany, whose chancellor, Angela Merkel, has led the country on a harsh austerity budget that has made it possible for that country to help bail out others. As a result, governments have begun to fall in Europe, as have some political parties. The primary victim here was Italy's controversial prime minister, Silvio Berlusconi, who was compelled to step down from his post. The new government was headed by an economic expert and former European Union commissioner named Mario Monti, who promised to put the country back on a proper economic footing and was able to put together a coalition government under the center-left Democratic Party, and Berlusconi's old People of Freedom party. Whether Monti will be able to keep this coalition together in the face of what will be very unpopular and very controversial cost-cutting measures is not clear.

While he, and others in Europe, try to make governments work in such dire economic times, some experts look back to the history of the effects of the Great Depression, and wonder if economic failure by the European Union in this new crisis will lead to a resurgence of the "radical right" parties that dominated European politics in the 1930s and early 1940s. Some argue that the combination of economic collapse, rising crime, and the rise of various sociocultural issues can lead to the growth of such parties. Such was the case in 2010 with the rise of the radical right Party for Freedom (PVV) of Geert Wilders in the Netherlands. While this party slowly lost popularity as the economic pressures lessened, the questions remain whether similar kinds of parties can grow and survive in other European countries during this period of economic crisis.

*Sources*: Cas Mudde, "Europe's Crisis and the Radical Right," *Open Democracy*, November 16, 2011, found at http://www.opendemocracy.net/cas-mudde/europes-crisis-and-radical-right; and Nicole Winfield,"Monti Wins Support for New Government after Meeting with Political Parties and Civil Society," *Newser*, November 16, 2011, http://www.newser.com/article/d9r1b2280/monti-wins-support-for-new-govt-after-meeting-with-political-parties-and-civil-society.html.

**QUICK REVIEW**

Minor Parties

- Minor parties organized around an ideology usually persist over a longer time than those built around a particular leader.
- Some parties arise around a single issue.
- Minor parties have had an indirect influence in the United States by drawing attention to controversial issues.

This lack of ideological purity and the absence of narrow group promotion directly affect the character and formation of the minor American parties. Third parties form when an issue arises that leaves some Americans dissatisfied with the relatively moderate stands of both Democrats and Republicans. They also form when a group feels totally ignored and left out of the mainstream political process. But third parties that organize under such circumstances almost always remain minor, or sometimes have their platforms co-opted by one or both of the major parties.

## Minor-Party Performance

Third parties do, on occasion, make waves, usually when an issue or set of issues unite with a popular or charismatic leader. Under these conditions, minor-party efforts have done remarkably well. Theodore Roosevelt, who had served two terms (1900–1908) as president, turned in the best performance of any minor-party candidate. In 1912, he ran on the Progressive ticket and garnered 27 percent of the popular vote, along with 88 electoral votes out of 531. Most remarkable about his achievement was placing second in the balloting ahead of an incumbent president, William Howard Taft.

Another significant minor-party candidacy occurred in 1968, when Alabama's segregationist governor, George Wallace, a southern Democrat, ran as an American Independent. Wallace captured 14 percent of the popular vote and 46 electoral votes. In 1980, a former Republican and member of the House of Representatives, John Anderson, ran as an Independent candidate, receiving 7 percent of the popular vote but no electoral votes.

Texas billionaire H. Ross Perot stunned many observers when he ran in 1992 without any party affiliation, and after dropping out and later reentering the race, still won 19 percent of the popular vote. His organization, United We Stand America, however, was little more than a label attached to a group of amateur enthusiasts; at that time it was nothing like an organized party. In 1995, Perot's organization held a three-day national convention that once again raised the possibility of a third party, and by 1996, it had become the Reform Party. Today, Reform Party members are frequently identified as a new "radicalized center" in American politics that Democratic and Republican Party leaders cannot afford to ignore.

**THINKING CRITICALLY**

Some have speculated that with so many voters in the middle of the political spectrum, there might be a future Independent third-party movement. Is the Tea Party that movement? How might a third-party candidate for president win the election? What role might students have in that process?

Since 2000, after the results of Ralph Nader's campaign, which, despite getting less than 3 percent of the vote, tipped the election in Florida and thus the rest of the country, the major third party in the United States has been the Green Party. This party, which has been in existence since 1984, has an agenda of redistributing wealth, lessening global warming, improving the environment, and controlling genetic engineering in agriculture. As of early 2009, the Greens held nearly 200 state and local political offices in approximately half of the states. Despite these modest successes, third-party candidates have rarely been a significant force in American national elections. As we have seen, they face the major psychological hurdle of party identification. Most voters already feel an emotional link to one of the two major parties; few are eager to wrench themselves away from their traditional voting habits to support a new, little-known group with no governing track record.

Beyond psychology, candidates outside the two-party mainstream face serious procedural obstacles. To be listed on local and state ballots, minor party candidates must obtain a certain number of signatures that demonstrate a minimal level of support. With few activists and little public recognition, minor parties frequently can't even get on the ballot. At the national level, they have enormous difficulty meeting eligibility requirements for federal election campaign funds. They also face a key difficulty in simply making people aware of who they are and what they stand for. To capture national attention, candidates with little more than local or regional notoriety must court a national press often intent on following only the major candidates.

The 2000 election provided a vivid example of these procedural obstacles when the Reform and Green parties were denied permission to appear in the presidential debates unless they had 15 percent support in the public opinion polls. In each of the next two presidential elections, these candidates were again ruled ineligible for the presidential debates because of their lack of public support.

Overall, the barriers to the creation of a successful third party are enormous.[35] Both the Libertarian Party and the Green Party are now minor grassroots public interest parties. Knowing this, many of the people who might be inclined to work in such parties devote their energies to lobbying in the conservative protest groups known as T.E.A. (aka tea) parties (for "taxed enough already?"), and the ultra-liberal Internet lobbying organization, MoveOn.org. The challenge for political parties will be to find ways to become more responsive to the American people.

**QUICK REVIEW**

The Party in Government

- The legislative branch is highly partisan.
- Partisanship is also important in presidential appointments.
- Although the judicial branch is designed to be nonpartisan, the appointment process for judges has always been partisan.

## Functions of Minor Parties

Although minor parties rarely attain power in the United States, they do perform important functions in a democracy. In a way, they act as wake-up calls to the two major parties. If enough dissatisfaction exists to fuel a third-party movement, both Democrats and Republicans quickly pay close attention. Almost always one, and often both, parties adopt enough of the third party's proposals to defuse the grievances the third party represents—and incidentally deflate the chances of that third party ever gaining power.

A prime illustration of this process can be seen in the "radical" platform that Socialist Eugene Debs endorsed in his 1904 campaign for the presidency. It included such "subversive" promises as support for women's right to vote, an eight-hour day for factory workers, and an end to child labor. All of these ideas, and many others from the Socialist agenda of that era, have long since become mainstream concepts, accepted by both major parties and most of the American electorate. The same was true of George Wallace's 1968 "Law and Order" campaign for the American Independent party, which held strong conservative views about the control of crime and the dismantling of civil rights programs. Richard Nixon adopted many of these views (at least temporarily), becoming increasingly conservative in his campaign rhetoric and promising to appoint more strictly constructionist federal judges to accomplish these goals. Finally, Ross Perot's constant call through the Reform Party for budget deficit reduction led to the adoption of this proposal by both major parties.

By being the first to champion original ideas that may later become widely endorsed, minor parties perform a vital service for the democratic process. But even ideas that fail to prosper at least encourage open discussion of new proposals; force mainstream groups to rethink and justify the status quo; and give life to key democratic norms, such as free speech and the right of all citizens to organize to promote their interests.

## The Rise of the Tea Party and Occupy Wall Street

In 2009, the large economic stimulus programs, the mortgage assistance program, and the health-care reform program of the Obama administration during the Great Recession led to a series of protests by groups calling themselves the Tea Party. This grassroots movement consisted of groups of people with a variety of goals such as cutting federal government spending, reducing federal taxes, reducing the size of the national government in favor of the state governments, defeating the new Obama health-care plan, and imposing a new conservative vision of the United States Constitution.[36] Many people predicted that this movement would be absorbed by the major parties and disappear, but it became very successful in gaining membership in Congress. At least 60 Tea Party advocates were elected to the House of Representatives in 2010, with another half-dozen or so, such as Rand Paul of Kentucky and Marco Rubio of Florida, elected to or already serving in the Senate.

The question will be whether the Republican Party changes its platform and policy agenda to subsume the Tea Party, as party realignment theory would predict, or whether the Tea Party movement is so strong, and grows so much, that it captures the Republican Party. If the Tea Party wins this battle, the Republican Party

# APPROACHING
## Contemporary Issues in Democracy

### Changing the Electoral College and Its Effect on the Party Structure

One thing that could potentially change the entire two-party structure of the American party system is a state-led movement in 2011 to change the state "winner-take-all" electoral college system. In August 2011, California governor Jerry Brown signed a law supporting a drive by eight other states and the District of Columbia to change the state unanimity rule in awarding all that state's electoral college votes to the winner of the election in that state. Every state except Maine and Nebraska follow the current winner-take-all system. The new approach would award a state's electoral college votes to the winner of the national presidential vote. For the Democrats, the loss of the 55 California electoral college votes that have routinely been in their column, if they lose the overall national presidential vote, would be devastating.

At the same time, the Republican-controlled legislature and Republican governor of Pennsylvania, Tom Corbett, considered a change for awarding electoral votes in that state on a proportional rather than unanimous basis. The votes would be awarded to the winner of each congressional district, with the final two votes going to the winner of the statewide vote. So, in 2012, after the new census changes the number of electoral votes awarded to states, rather than the party that won the Pennsylvania state vote by a close margin still getting all 20 of the votes, one party would get 11 votes and the other would get 9.

Republicans see this as damaging to President Obama because Pennsylvania has gone Democratic in presidential elections since 1988. It also means that the Democrats could put their money into winning individual congressional seats and districts and thus steal votes from a Republican presidential candidate who might otherwise have received all of the state's electoral votes. And, this reform proposal would remove Pennsylvania's position as a key swing state, meaning that candidates could simply ignore it, knowing that they would still get a significant number of electoral votes. Other states such as Nebraska and New Jersey are considering making this change.

For the party system, though, a decision by many states to award electoral votes in one of these two ways would eventually mean the end of the electoral college. If the decision is made to award electoral college votes based on the popular vote, making it directly reflective of the public will, there is no need for this intermediary step. Although this modification in the individual state determination of electoral college votes will reflect an apparent increase in the reflection of the majority will, it will diminish the impact of the minority will. And, in time, the process that has kept our system as a two-party political structure will likely move to a multiparty system, with a more proportional vote on the national scene for the presidency. It is not hard to imagine the leading vote getter as a party, in a multiparty voting structure, failing to get a majority of the electoral college vote, thus throwing the presidential vote repeatedly into the House of Representatives, where political intrigue, such as was seen in 1824, can be repeated. All of this means that sooner or later, the political system might well change in a way that thwarts the public will.

will become more extreme in its conservatism and antifederal government posture, and more polarized and partisan in its policy approach. In the 2012 presidential election, ultra-conservative Tea Party advocates such as Minnesota representative Michele Bachmann and Texas governor Rick Perry battled with mainstream Republican Mitt Romney for the Republican nomination for president. The winner of this race, and the Tea Party's continued ability to gain membership in both houses of Congress, will indicate whether the Tea Party will continue to grow. Any election predictions based solely on party identification are uncertain.

At the time of this writing in November 2011, the Democrats seemed to be facing their own possible minor party protest insurgency. A small number of protestors camped in a New York City park outside Wall Street, calling themselves Occupy Wall Street, began protesting the policies that have led to the gap in wealth between the ultra-rich and the middle class and poor. Calling themselves "The 99 Percent," as opposed to "The One Percent," the upper economic classes in the banking and financial world, these protests spread to dozens of cities across the nation. When they were joined by various unions, who saw in this movement a voice to the frustrations of the middle class, President Barack Obama and the Democrats began to tailor their appeals, and the presentation of their new Jobs Bill in the fall of 2011, to try to capture this energy for their reelection chances.

## POLITICAL PARTIES AND THE 2012 ELECTION

9.8 *Where are the political parties going next, and what will bring about that evolution?*

David Broder, a leading American journalist and author of *The Party's Over,* wrote that American political parties were disintegrating, that they had lost their traditional stabilizing power over the electoral and governmental processes, and that they were being replaced by a proliferation of special-interest groups and the imagery of television.[37] Is the party really over? Many argue that declining rates of party identification, voter apathy, the rise of Internet grassroots movements, the ability of political candidates to fund-raise on their own, and the lack of formal constraints to ensure party allegiance all indicate that American political parties are headed toward extinction. Political party optimists, however, see hope for the future of parties and even a role for them in the revival of a more participatory and stronger democracy. They argue that parties have responded reasonably well to the many sources of change over the past three decades. After all, despite social upheavals, new forms of technology and communications, changing attitudes toward politics, institutional reforms in government, generational shifts in support for politics, and major crises in government, parties have stayed afloat and even maintained their hold over a large percentage of the American electorate. Could dying institutions have such staying power?

The 2008 election once again showed that political parties are crucial democratic structures that link the popular will to governmental outcomes. Both parties were able to shape their platforms, and the messages of their candidates, to tap into the desires of the voters. The point is clear, then: No matter what the issue or the era, each party will do its best to fashion a position in the voters' minds that they hope will secure electoral support and then motivate those voters to go to the polls.[38] The same happened in the 2010 congressional elections, when unhappiness with the Obama recession policies and the lack of responsiveness of the Democrats in Congress allowed the Republicans to gain 63 seats and take control of Congress by roughly 50 seats. In addition, the Republicans cut the Democrats' control of the Senate down to just three seats, and took the lead in state governships, 29-21. However, hidden in this shift of party balance was another message being sent to Washington by the voters. More than 60 seats in Congress were won by representatives of the conservative Tea Party, making it almost impossible for the new Republican Speaker John Boehner to mass a majority for any kind of policy that represented compromise with the Democrats. The addition of a half-dozen Tea Party members to the Republican minority in the Senate compelled minority leader Mitch McConnell to move his members further to the conservative side. As a result of these changes reflecting the will of the ultra-conservative voters, compromise legislation became impossible in both bodies on the economic, anti-recession, and debt-ceiling issues, leading to partisan gridlock.

Many believe that the 2012 election will resolve many of these issues, but first a series of questions will need to be answered by the voters. In the presidential race, will the Republicans choose the only Republican Establishment leader in the race, former Massachusetts governor Mitt Romney, or will they opt for an ultra-conservative Tea Party leader such as Texas governor Rick Perry, libertarian Ron Paul, or Minnesota representative Michele Bachmann? The series of fall debates by the Republican candidates, with the repeated number of mistakes by various contenders, such as Governor Perry's inability to remember which executive agencies he would cut, injected a great deal of unpredictability in the process as one candidate after another was seen in the polls as the leading candidate. Few put much stock in these early predictions, though, as the real issue will be which voters will turn out for the primaries. Beyond this, those who do turn out to participate in the caucuses, or vote in the primaries, are often the most extreme partisans in the electorate, meaning that the most conservative candidates in the field should have an early advantage. Will this selection process be resolved in a matter of weeks by the frontloaded nomination schedule leading up to the March 6 Super Tuesday multistate primary and caucus state date, or will it be a long, drawn-out race between Romney and one or more of the conservatives? And, if Romney wins the nomination, will he be forced to choose a Tea Party vice presidential candidate, or a more conservative candidate such as New Jersey governor Chris Christie, who chose not to seek his own presidential nomination in order to try to unite the party? If Romney does not follow this course, will the Tea Party and/or the Libertarian Party field their own candidates in the 2012 election? If it does so, will it siphon off enough conservative votes to doom the Republicans' chance of governing, or will it prevent either major party from gaining a majority in the electoral college, thus throwing the election into the House of Representatives? On the Democratic side, will Barack Obama be able—in the face of historically high unemployment numbers that only incumbent Franklin D. Roosevelt was able to overcome in 1936 to be reelected—to reenergize and mobilize the young, Hispanic American, and first-time voter coalition that helped him to victory in 2008?

Where did Sarah Palin go? After four years of building her brand since running for Vice President in 2008, the former Alaska Governor never appeared on a single ballot for the 2012 presidential nomination.

For the congressional races, with the body at a historic low of 12 to 15 percent public support, and only about 6 percent of the voters willing to reelect their member of Congress, how many of the incumbents will lose their seats? And what will be the pattern of those replacements? Will it allow the Democrats to retake control of Congress? If they do so, will they choose again to make liberal Progressive Nancy Pelosi the Speaker, or will they select someone more centrist like Maryland's Steny Hoyer? Or will the new replacements reshape the nature of the Republican majority? Will Tea Party members unseat both Republicans and Democrats in so many numbers that it becomes an even greater part of the Republican caucus? If that happens, will it lead to much more conservative Republican majority leader Eric Cantor seeking to replace the more Establishment Speaker John Boehner? All of these questions can be answered by observing how the wishes of the voting public are reflected by the political party ideological results and decisions in Congress after the election.

The larger question, though, has to do with the party realignment issues that might be answered in the 2012 election. For the Democrats, were the pro-Obama votes, and huge voter turnout, of the new voting coalition of young people under the age of 30, Hispanic Americans and other minorities, and first-time voters a permanent feature of the voting bloc, or was the 2008 vote a one-time win for the Democrats? And, beyond that, will the new middle- and lower-class protest movement Occupy Wall Street, provide the launching point for President Obama and the Democrats in Congress to reshape their message along more aggressive, ideological, economic lines on behalf of the middle class against the ultra-rich? If this movement continues, will it become the Tea Party insurgency for the Democrats, but from the liberal middle-class voting group? For the Republicans, even if they win the election, will it be because the Tea Party is in the process of fundamentally changing the membership and ideological direction of the party? Or will the Republicans eventually swallow up this conservative third-party insurgency and adopt its program as part of their platform and message, as has happened so many times in the past?

As the United States approaches democracy, power has shifted from the few to the many, but sometimes even the few matter greatly. Still, recent changes in the way parties operate are merely part of the ongoing process of democratization central to the current pattern of American political development.

**THINKING CRITICALLY**

With more and more voters developing their own "personal" relationships with candidates through the Internet and television, how will parties have to change to enlist their support?

## Summary

9.1 *How have political parties formed, evolved, and become more democratic over the years?*

- Political parties have played a role in American democracy since 1790. The first party system pitted Federalists (led by Hamilton) against Democratic-Republicans (led by Jefferson) and was so unstable that it disappeared between 1816 and 1824. The second party system began with the formation of the Jacksonian Democrats, actually an outgrowth of the Jeffersonian party. Seeking to make the electoral process more democratic, the Jacksonian Democrats replaced the system of nomination by party leaders with a national party convention. Opposition coalesced around a new party, the Whigs.
- The third-party system arose during the 1850s out of conflict over the issue of slavery. The new Republican Party was devoted to abolishing slavery, whereas one branch of the Democratic Party supported the Confederate cause. By this time, the Whigs had dropped from sight. The fourth-party system began with a realignment in party constituencies in the 1890s and lasted until 1932. During this period the Democratic and Republican parties became highly developed and well organized.
- The fifth-party system began in 1932 with the realignment in party identification known as the New Deal coalition. This broad-based coalition supported the Democratic Party and enabled it to dominate national politics until 1968.

9.2 *What has characterized the present political party system?*

- Although Republicans have won 7 of 11 presidential elections since 1968, it is unclear whether another realignment is taking place. If anything, there appears to be movement now toward the Democratic Party. The Democratic membership has increased, and the Republican membership has decreased significantly. The biggest change, however, has been the sharp increase in the number of voters who identify themselves as Independent.

9.3 *What are the purposes and goals of the political parties?*

- Political parties organize the election process by recruiting candidates for public office, representing the desires of voters, and attempting to ensure that their candidates carry out specific policies once in office. They also speak for and unite different groups and their varied interests through the formation of political coalitions. Other important functions of parties are to simplify political choices and organize government and policy making.

9.4 *How are political parties organized to express popular political views?*

- The local party provides the point of entry for those seeking involvement in politics. This is a process called *grassroots organizing*. At the next level is the state party organization, which acts in conjunction with the state government to conduct primary elections. The national party organization is most active during presidential elections.
- From the end of the 19th century to the middle of the 20th, local parties often engaged in machine politics, in which party bosses traded jobs, money, and favors for votes and campaign support. Machine politics declined when the civil service and the modern welfare state emerged and primary elections proliferated.
- At the national party conventions, delegates from the state parties meet to select presidential and vice presidential candidates and write the party's platform—a statement of principles and policies that it will carry out if its candidates are elected.
- Some state party organizations select candidates for presidential elections at a caucus, or meeting of party adherents. Other state parties hold primary elections that allow all of the party's members to vote for a candidate. In a closed primary, the most common kind, only registered members of a political party may participate in that party's primary. Open primaries allow registered voters to vote in whichever primary they choose, thus permitting cross-party voting.

9.5 *How has the presidential nomination process evolved into a more democratic process over the years?*

- Since 1968, the presidential selection process has been radically altered as a result of demands for "democratization." Reforms adopted by the Democratic Party included selecting candidates by means of primaries rather than caucuses and increasing the diversity of delegates to national conventions. The Republican Party also adopted some of these reforms.
- The greater power of rank-and-file party members has reduced the power of party bosses, increased the cost of conducting a campaign, reinforced the dominance of the electronic media in American politics, increased

the power of interest groups and political action committees, and brought about a decline in party cohesion. The result is a trend toward candidate-centered, rather than party-centered, politics.

9.6 *Why has the American political system evolved into a two-party structure?*

- The single-member district system inhibits the development of third parties and thus produces and maintains a two-party system. In nations with systems of proportional representation, in which more than one member of the legislature can come from the same district, small parties can gain legislative seats, and a multiparty system results. The electoral college favors a two-party system because the candidate who wins the most popular votes in a state receives all of that state's electoral votes.
- Other explanations of the U.S. two-party system include cultural factors. Some believe that the two-party system is built into prevailing cultural norms and values; the tendency toward party identification leads voters to deep-seated, enduring affinity for the major parties.

9.7 *What third parties have been established in the past, and why have they not survived?*

- Although minor or third parties usually have no hope of gaining real power, such parties occasionally arise when an issue is not adequately addressed by the major parties. When a minor party has a popular or charismatic leader, it can affect the outcome of elections and force the major parties to adopt or at least consider some of its proposals.

9.8 *Where are the political parties going next, and what will bring about that evolution?*

- Although political parties are not mentioned in the Constitution, government institutions at all levels are organized through the party system. Party membership influences the behavior of individual politicians and leads to the creation of different public policies depending on which party is in control of the government.

## Key Terms



## Test Yourself Chapter 9

**1.** The Constitution regulates political parties by
a. limiting them to two in number.
b. placing them under states for regulation.
c. allowing for the parties to develop.
d. It says nothing about political parties.

**2.** A party realignment is defined as
a. the changeover in leadership after a failed election.
b. the corporate reorganization of a party.
c. a generational shift in voting from one party to another.
d. a change in voting separating state and national results.

**3.** The first evidence that the American government electoral system was going to work was
a. the election of George Washington.
b. the election of John Adams.
c. the election of Thomas Jefferson.
d. the turnover of power to Thomas Jefferson in 1800.

**4.** Who actually won the popular vote for president in 1824?
a. John Quincy Adams.
b. Andrew Jackson.
c. William Crawford.
d. Martin Van Buren.

**5.** The main result of the Progressive reforms against the "smoke-filled-room" nominating procedure was the
a. primary system.
b. caucus system.
c. state nominating system.
d. party conventions.

**6.** The main change in the party convention nominating system during the Franklin D. Roosevelt presidency was
a. the caucus system.
b. the primary system.
c. changing the vote in the national convention from two-thirds to one-half.
d. presidential nominations from the convention floor.

**7.** Which of the following groups are *not* part of FDR's New Deal coalition?
a. The poor.
b. Immigrants.
c. City dwellers.
d. Midwestern farmers.

**8.** The possibility that the nation has been in a Republican Party–dominated realignment phase since 1968 can be inferred from
a. the rise of Newt Gingrich in the 1994 election.
b. the Republicans' win in 7 of 11 presidential elections since 1968.
c. the ability of the Republicans to block congressional legislation.
d. the presidency of the two George Bushes.

**9.** Which early political party system was the forerunner of the present Democratic Party?
a. The Whigs.
b. The Jeffersonian Republicans.
c. The Jacksonian Democrats.
d. Both b and c.

**10.** What have been the trends in party identification in recent years?
a. The percentage of Democrats has been rising.
b. The percentage of Independents has been rising.
c. The percentage of Republicans has been falling.
d. All of the above.

**11.** How many votes are needed to win the presidency in the electoral college?
a. 260.
b. 265.
c. 270.
d. 275.

**12.** Which of the following is one of the functions of political parties?
a. They organize the election process.
b. They represent different allied political groups.
c. They organize government and policy making.
d. All of the above.

**13.** Barack Obama's successful organization of followers to win so many caucus states and get the Democratic nomination can be called a
a. local-level movement.
b. grassroots movement.
c. state-level movement.
d. private party movement.

**14.** The big-city bosses who remained in dictatorial control of their region by trading patronage and favor for votes practiced
a. urban politics.
b. machine politics.
c. local politics.
d. ground-level politics.

**15.** Howard Dean's major contribution to the Democratic Party, setting up its electoral wins in 2006 and 2008, was
a. dropping out of the 2004 campaign.
b. his knowledge of health-care reform as a doctor.
c. his "50-state strategy" as the Democratic National chair.
d. None of the above.

**16.** The process of moving presidential primaries to the early part of the campaign to have more influence but also to increase the percentage of delegates to be won then is called
a. frontfilling.
b. front-tipping.
c. frontloading.
d. front-melding.

**17.** Uncommitted delegates, usually party leaders and bosses in the Democratic Party, who are designed to choose the most winnable candidate in the election and prevent an error by the voters are called
a. smart delegates.
b. superdelegates.
c. supra-delegates.
d. superior delegates.

**18.** State presidential nominations that are done by meetings of members of the party are called
a. nominating conventions.
b. closed primaries.
c. caucuses.
d. proportional primaries.

**19.** The first presidential primary in the country is always in
a. New York.
b. New Hampshire.
c. Iowa.
d. Nevada.

**20.** The McGovern-Fraser Commission did what with respect to nominating rules?
a. It solidified the rules for the Democratic Party.
b. It changed the rules for the Republican Party.
c. It opened up the nomination process for the Democrats by including more groups.
d. None of the above.

**ANSWERS**
**1.** d, **2.** c, **3.** d, **4.** b, **5.** a, **6.** c, **7.** d, **8.** b, **9.** d, **10.** d, **11.** c, **12.** d, **13.** b, **14.** b, **15.** c, **16.** c, **17.** b, **18.** c, **19.** b, **20.** c

# Participation, Voting, and Elections

# 10

## Chapter Outline

**Introduction:**
*Political Participation and Democracy*

- Who Participates?
- A Brief History of Voting in the United States
- Voting
- Voting Choice
- Other Forms of Political Participation
- Congressional Elections
- Presidential Elections
- Money and Elections

## Learning Objectives

10

- 10.1 What role does participation play in achieving the democratic ideal?
- 10.2 In what ways do Americans participate in the political process?
- 10.3 How has the right to vote expanded over the nation's history?
- 10.4 Why do some people choose to participate and others do not?
- 10.5 What factors influence a person's vote choice?
- 10.6 How else, outside the act of voting, can an individual participate?
- 10.7 How do Americans participate in congressional elections?
- 10.8 How are presidential elections conducted?
- 10.9 What role does money play in elections?

# INTRODUCTION

## POLITICAL PARTICIPATION AND DEMOCRACY

10.1 *What role does participation play in achieving the democratic ideal?*

In this chapter we consider an issue that goes to the very heart of the democratic ideal. Democracy simply cannot work without mass political involvement, or **participation.** Citizens who have a say in the national decision-making process show greater levels of satisfaction with the political system as a whole. The very act of participation makes them feel a part of the system; in addition, citizens feel good when they see that policy decisions, over the long run, reflect their desires. Although the passionate and often competing beliefs that come with mass participation can produce political tension, in the long run it leads to democratic outcomes and acceptance of the system.

**participation**
Mass political involvement through voting, campaign work, political protests, and civil disobedience, among many others.

Active citizen participation moves the United States closer to the ideal of a democratic political system. Through voting and other forms of political participation—campaigning, gathering information, joining groups, writing letters, and protesting—Americans involve themselves in the democratic process. American government, closed to the vast majority in the framers' day, has opened to the input of millions, representing every conceivable point of view. Any citizen who makes even a marginal effort can find dozens of outlets for effective political participation. Still, the controversial and disputed 2000 presidential election reminds us that we remain on the road to democracy; the historic 2008 presidential election shows us how far we have come, although even that election was marred by millions of registered voters being unable to cast ballots either because they encountered registration problems or did not receive an absentee ballot. Another 4 million voters did not vote because of long lines or voter identification problems.[1]

This billboard reminds people in India of the scorn the ancients felt toward nonvoters. In April 2011, a record setting 78 percent of voters turned out for India's Regional Assembly elections.

# WHO PARTICIPATES

10.2 *In what ways do Americans participate in the political process?*

Since the ancient Greek theorists first debated various types of government, political thinkers have held that a citizen's informed participation represents the highest form of political expression within democracy. Indeed, the Greek word *idiot* originally described someone who did not participate in politics—a definition showing how much importance the ancient Greeks placed on democratic involvement. In Athens, citizens not only discussed politics but they also served in government. They held no elections as such; instead, eligible citizens regularly drew lots to serve in the assembly and fill other posts.

In a nation as large as the United States, the Athenian kind of *direct* democracy is logistically impossible. Instead, the United States has evolved a *representative* form of government in which all eligible citizens may participate in electing officeholders to represent their opinions in government. And Americans have the opportunity to go to the polls frequently. The United States has more elections than any nation in the world, with more than 500,000 offices filled in any four-year election cycle!

The standards of self-governance assume that most citizens will choose to participate in some form of political activity and that they will base their participation on a reasoned analysis of ideas, options, and choices. This link between widespread and informed participation, voting, elections, and public policy constitutes the fundamental component of democracy. Still, voting is but one form of political behavior essential to a democracy. Indeed, the right to choose *not* to vote is also essential to the workings of a successful democracy.

The ancient Greeks regarded participation in a democratic society a full-time job for males who had full citizenship and owned property. Citizens would spend a good deal of time familiarizing themselves with the issues of the day, then make policy decisions based on informed reason and factual knowledge. This ideal is clearly difficult to achieve in a modern, large-scale mass democracy where citizens spend much of their time earning a living. Also, individuals' interests vary, and it is unrealistic to expect that in their spare time all citizens will participate in political activity. On the other hand, not all Americans are apathetic and uninvolved. Many come close to the ideal of full-time political involvement, and many others meet various criteria for democratic citizenship.

A classic study of political participation levels of the American electorate by Sidney Verba and Norman Nie found that citizens fall along a continuum of political engagement, ranging from those totally uninvolved in politics to those who make it a full-time occupation.[2] About a tenth of the population is deeply involved in the political process. Nearly half of American citizens engage in political activities of which the ancient Greeks would have approved—they work for candidates or issues at election time or in groups that support social issues, or both. Almost 46 percent of the population engages in some kind of serious, politically oriented activity. In addition, another quarter of the population votes or contacts public officials for one purpose or another, leaving only about a fifth of American citizens completely inactive in the political process.

A disturbing element in the varying participation rates concerns the different types of people likely to be found in each category. Prior to the 2008 election, generally speaking, fewer low-income people and minority group members participated at the higher activism levels. Activists have tended to be largely well-educated, middle- and upper-income voters. This is not to say that all active citizens are rich and educated, or that all inactive ones are poor and uneducated. The issue here is one of tendency. These findings, replicated in study after study, lead many observers to wonder how well American society has approached the democratic ideal of equal political participation by all.

## A BRIEF HISTORY OF VOTING IN THE UNITED STATES

10.3 *How has the right to vote expanded over the nation's history?*

### THINKING CRITICALLY

What do you think explains the finding that the more educated and wealthier tend to participate more in all levels of government? Do they have more at stake than a poor person receiving government aid?

Historically, American politics has been notable for the steady erosion of barriers to democratic participation. Voting in particular, and other avenues of participation more generally, were closed for many years to minorities, women, and young people. Today, many barriers to participation have been broken.

Politics in the United States began as an activity reserved for white, property-holding, tax-paying, middle- and upper-class males. Thus, poor whites and women were disenfranchised. Slaves remained "property," retaining none of the citizenship rights that whites enjoyed; in fact, slaves were not even considered whole human beings. A compromise forged during the Constitutional

Convention resulted in each slave being counted as three-fifths of a person for purposes of taxation and of representation in the U.S. House of Representatives.

Property requirements for voting gradually relaxed over the decades, disappearing by the middle of the 19th century, when virtually all white males were enfranchised. The Fifteenth Amendment, passed in 1870 as part of the Civil War amendments, guaranteed that "the right of citizens of the United States to vote shall not be denied or abridged by the United States or by any State on account of race, color, or previous condition of servitude." The amendment's aim was to extend voting privileges to former slaves—and to African American males in general. Although it seemed to pave the way for broader political participation, by the end of the 19th century the spirit underlying the Fifteenth Amendment had been perverted. Those in power in the South relied on both violence and legal tactics which did not explicitly mention race to keep African Americans from voting.

Racism led government officials in the South to devise techniques that kept African Americans from the polls. First and foremost was the simple tactic of intimidation. Local African Americans were victims of threats, beatings, and home burnings or, in many cases, were lynched by anonymous mobs. Naturally, when people live under the constant fear of violence, an unsubtle "suggestion" that they not exercise their right to vote will be enough to deter all but the bravest of them. Southern officials also devised formal ways to keep the African American vote down. First, they required payment of a **poll tax,** a fee paid before one could vote. In several states, an unpaid fee continued to accrue from one election to the next until it became a sum beyond the means of poor African Americans. Southern election officials also made selective use of the **literacy test,** a requirement that voting applicants demonstrate their ability to read and write. African American college graduates might be asked to read and explain complex passages of the Constitution, whereas white citizens received simple grade-school paragraphs to read. A third device was the **good-character test,** requiring those wishing to vote to find two or more registered voters to vouch for their integrity. Because African Americans found it difficult to register, they also had trouble finding registered friends to vouch for them, and registered whites were unwilling to come to their aid. Southern states used a variety of other devices as well to limit African American political power.

These prohibitions were extremely successful. Because most African Americans lived in the South until well into the 1950s, southern interference with African American political rights effectively disenfranchised the vast majority of African Americans for decades. For the first half of the 20th century, African Americans rarely participated in politics, few held public office, and less than 10 percent voted regularly.

Change came as the civil rights movement gained momentum in the 1950s and 1960s. The Voting Rights Act of 1965, which provided protection to African Americans who wished to vote, and the Twenty-fourth Amendment (1964), which outlawed the poll tax in federal elections, helped seal a new national commitment to equal opportunity in the political arena. The U.S. Supreme Court erased many barriers to African American participation, striking down state poll tax laws in 1966.

In recent years, the Supreme Court has faced questions about the constitutionality of the 1965 Voting Rights Act, which illustrate the continuing struggle between democratic ideals and political realities. The original legislation required nine states and counties or townships in seven other states with a history of racial discrimination to obtain federal permission before changing voting laws. Figure 10.1 displays those states, counties, and townships which require approval of the federal government to alter voting laws. Section 5 of the act, which required those states and smaller jurisdictions to "pre-clear" new voting rules with either the Justice Department or a federal court, was challenged by a municipality in Texas on grounds that it is unconstitutional and imposed too many burdens on jurisdictions covered by it. The intent was to demonstrate that any change in voting requirements will not be discriminatory, as was the case throughout the South prior to the law's passage.[3] In 2009, the Court upheld key aspects of the law, and at the same time sidestepped questions about whether the key provision of the law is constitutional. This ruling

## QUICK REVIEW

Voting Rights

- The Fifteenth Amendment, 1870: right to vote to African American males.
- The Nineteenth Amendment, 1920: right to vote to women.
- The Twenty-third Amendment, 1961: right to vote to citizens of the District of Columbia.
- The Twenty-fourth Amendment, 1964: outlawed the poll tax.
- The Voting Rights Act of 1965: provided protection to African Americans wishing to vote.
- The Twenty-sixth Amendment, 1971: right to vote to citizens 18 years of age or older.

**poll tax**
A fee that had to be paid before one could vote; used to prevent African Americans from voting; now unconstitutional.

**literacy test**
A requirement that voting applicants had to demonstrate an understanding of national and state constitutions. Primarily used to prevent African Americans from voting in the South.

**good-character test**
A requirement that voting applicants wishing to vote produce two or more registered voters to vouch for their integrity.

**Student Voting Laws by State**

Since 2002, there has been a trend of states proposing and passing legislation that makes voting more difficult for students.

**How Voter Friendly Is Your State?***

- Bad for Student Voting
- Neutral for Student Voting
- Good for Student Voting

**2002**
In 2002, no states had laws that were explicitly bad for student voters.

**2010**
By 2010, several states had adopted laws that were harmful for student voters, and many others switched from good laws to neutral laws.

**Possible 2012**
If all proposed legislation passes, the outlook for student voting in 2012 looks grim.

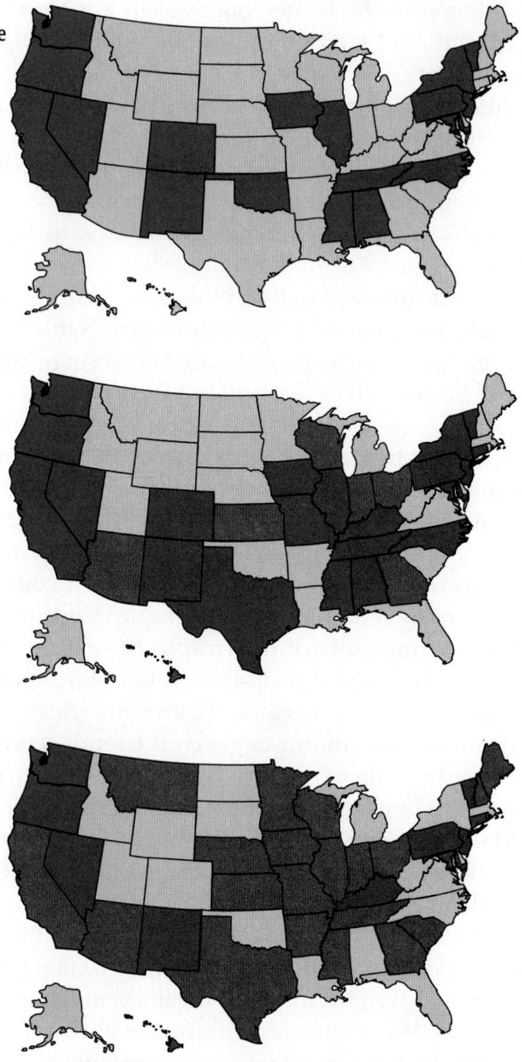

**Voter Friendliness Defined***

**Good for Student Voting**
These states either accept student ID cards or do not require ID except under the Help America Vote Act. These states may have bad voter laws for nonstudent groups.

**Neutral for Student Voting**
These states require ID to be presented in order to vote or require first-time voters to present ID to vote. It also includes states that require photo ID but make provisions for student ID. These states may have bad voter laws for nonstudent groups.

**Bad for Student Voting**
These states include requirements for ID when voting that are difficult for students to fulfill.

*Source:* Fair Elections Legal Network, fairelectionsnetwork.com, March 8, 2011
Illustration by: Shereen Hall, campusprogress.org

**FIGURE 10.1** Challenges to Student Voting
*Source: Expanding Democracy: Voter Registration Around the World* by Jennifer S. Rosenberg with Margaret Chen, published by the Brennan Center for Justice at NYU. For more information, visit www.brennancenter.org.

opened the door to future challenges over the constitutionality of the pre-clearance provision. In 2011, officials in Arizona and Alabama sued the federal government challenging this provision. The Supreme Court will likely rule on the issue in the coming years.

The movement for women's political equality has a lengthy history as well, beginning with the first women's rights convention in Seneca Falls, New York, in 1848. After decades of pressuring for **suffrage** and other legal rights, women finally won the right to vote with passage of the Nineteenth Amendment in 1920. This was a rather slow approach to democracy—minority (nonwhite) males won the vote in 1870—22 years after Seneca Falls.

The Nineteenth Amendment guaranteed that "the right of citizens of the United States to vote shall not be denied or abridged by the United States or by any State on account of sex." Further expansion of political participation came with ratification of the Twenty-third Amendment in 1961, which gave residents of the District of Columbia the right to vote in presidential elections, and the Twenty-sixth Amendment in 1971, which gave the right to vote to all citizens of the United States 18 years of age or older.

Extending suffrage rights is a key step toward approaching the democratic ideal of equal political participation, which explains why residents of the District of Columbia are still petitioning for their right to be represented in Congress. The D.C. House Voting Rights Act is intended to accomplish this goal by bringing congressional voting representation to DC residents for the first time ever. The bill would permanently expand the number of members of the House of Representatives from 435 to 437 seats and give DC residents their first-ever voting member of the House of Representatives.[4]

The struggle for the right to vote never ends in a democracy. In late June 2011, Congressman John Conyers (D–MI) introduced a bill, the Democracy Restoration Act, that seeks to restore voting rights in federal elections to the nearly 4 million disenfranchised Americans who have been released from prison and are living in the community. Currently, 35 states disenfranchise people after release from prison. "The Democracy Restoration Act will eliminate the last blanket barrier to the franchise in our country," said Erika Wood, director of the Right to Vote project at the Brennan Center.[5]

In this circa 1912 photo, a suffragette carries a banner inscribed with the suffragette slogan "Votes for Women" during a demonstration for the basic right to franchise.

## VOTING

10.4 *Why do some people choose to participate and others do not?*

Political participation may take many forms, but the most central act in a democracy is the citizen's decision to vote. All other political acts cost more in terms of time, effort, and money, and none produces such a level of equality as the vote. Nevertheless, the act of voting is neither simple nor unproblematic in our democracy. In the 2000 presidential election, for example, more than 105 million ballots were cast; Vice President Al Gore received 539,897 more votes than George W. Bush, who won the electoral vote by 5 points (271 to 266)—but only after the Supreme Court, in a 5–4 decision, overruled the Florida Supreme Court order that would have allowed manual counting of ballots. An examination of more than 175,000 uncounted Florida ballots revealed that the ballots of those in Florida's black neighborhoods were most likely to go uncounted. "Overall, 136 out of every 1,000 ballots in heavily black precincts were set aside—a rate of spoiled ballots three times higher than in predominantly white precincts."[6]

The disenfranchisement of black voters in 2000 posed a challenge for a system that rightfully prides itself on the great progress made in enfranchising voters in America. A joint study conducted by Caltech/MIT found that 4 to 6 million presidential votes were lost in 2000. Another 1.5 million votes were not counted because of difficulties using voter equipment. The U.S. Census Bureau reported that 2.8 percent

**suffrage**
The right to vote.

Many are concerned with the installation of error-prone electronic voting machines. These people are protesting the use of computerized voting without a paper trail.

of registered voters who did not vote (1 million people) did not participate because of long lines, inconvenient hours, or the location of their polling place.[7]

The Help America Vote Act (HAVA), signed by President Bush in 2002, was designed to address a number of the aforementioned problems. The act included mandates for improving voting machines, expanding the availability of provisional ballots, making changes to voter registration procedures, and increasing voting accessibility for people who are disabled. In addition, for the first time ever, the government authorized federal funds—$3.9 billion—for election reform.[8]

Eight years later, in 2008, approximately 131 million voters cast ballots, which amounted to nearly 61 percent of the voting-eligible population. According to the U.S. Census Bureau, the increase included 2 million more black voters, 2 million more Hispanic American voters, and about 600,000 more Asian American voters, while the number of non-Hispanic white voters remained statistically unchanged. Analysts point out that decreases in some demographic groups countered the increases in others, and the overall turnout in 2008 was not statistically different from that in 2004.[9]

Yet, as many as 7 million registered voters were prevented or discouraged from casting their ballots in the 2008 election, demonstrating major malfunctions in the country's election process. A study produced by the Cooperative Congressional Election Survey, led by the Massachusetts Institute of Technology, detailed that as many as 3 million registered voters were prevented from voting due to a range of administrative mishaps.[10] The study also found that an additional 2 to 4 million registered voters were "discouraged" from voting due to such hassles as long lines, voter identification requirements, and difficulty getting an absentee ballot. Combining the group of voters prevented from participating with those discouraged, the study concluded that up to 7 million voters did not have their preference recorded in the 2008 election. In addition to these 7 million registered voters who failed to vote, an estimated 9 million eligible people tried to register but failed because of barriers to voter registration such as missed deadlines and changes of residence. The high mobility of the U.S. population, the requirement that voters re-register whenever they move, and the failure of the system to affirmatively register voters are all significant barriers.[11]

## Voter Turnout

Many political observers define the health of a representative democracy by the degree to which its citizens participate in elections. **Voter turnout** expresses the percentage of eligible voters who actually show up and vote on Election Day. Thus, a turnout rate of 80 percent for a given election means that 80 percent of all citizens legally entitled to vote actually did vote in that election. Scholars have traced voter turnout in the United States over the years.

## Explaining Turnout

**voter turnout**
The percentage of eligible voters who actually show up and vote on Election Day.

How can we explain turnout rates? Many nations such as Italy, the Netherlands, Belgium, Sweden, Australia, Germany, and Norway boast a much higher average turnout than does the United States. Some experts argue, however, that these figures are deceptive. Turnout data are not comparable from one nation to the next. Many nations make voting compulsory and fine people who do not vote. Naturally, their turnout will be higher than in nations where voting is voluntary. Furthermore, many foreign nations report turnout as a percentage of all registered voters, whereas turnout rates in the United States are usually given as a percentage of all adult citizens eligible to vote.[12]

To explain voting, let us start with a simple axiom: Nothing in this life is free. Even the simplest political action has costs. Consider what it takes to exercise the right to vote in America. First, a citizen must register to vote. Unlike other democracies, registration in the United States is the individual's responsibility, requiring a conscious decision and the expenditure of time and energy. Why vote? The benefits must outweigh the costs to ensure that people will vote, so it helps to know the benefits as well as the costs of voting. There are few concrete benefits in voting; that is, a single vote is unlikely to determine the election outcome, so we must look at the intrinsic benefits, what political scientists Wolfinger and Rosenstone describe as "the feeling that one has done one's duty to society, to a reference group, and to oneself; or the feeling that one has affirmed one's allegiance to or efficacy in the political system."[13] In addition, some people enjoy the simple act of voting in the same way others enjoy the opera or going to the baseball game. The costs of voting are much easier to measure. Registering can be cumbersome. It usually means taking time to contact a government agency during business hours. Voters must re-register when they move to a new address. Thus, when they move out of a district, citizens lose the right to vote unless they make another conscious decision to register in their new community. One explanation for low voter turnout may be that the average American moves often—about every five years—and registering to vote is often a low priority when moving into a new home and adapting to a new community.

Registration laws in most states seem designed to depress election turnout rates. More than 90 percent of Americans live in states where they must register to vote in advance, up to several weeks before the actual day of the election. Because many people pay little heed to an election until the campaign is in high gear two or three weeks before voting day, many of them lose the right to vote because, by the time it occurs to them to register, it is too late. As you would expect, states that do allow same-day registration and voting (such as Maine, Minnesota, and Wisconsin) have much higher turnout rates.

Most other democracies worldwide do a much better job at registering their citizens than does the United States. Canada, France, Germany, and Great Britain each register well over 90 percent of their eligible citizens. The reason is that "unlike other major democracies, the United States places the onus of voter registration on individual citizens."[14] (Only four countries other than the United States—the Bahamas, Belize, Burundi, and Mexico—place the burden of voter registration on individual citizens.) The Brennan Center study of worldwide voter registration found that the U.S. system "is based principally on paper forms, which compounds the problem. Every voter, every time they move, must fill out new forms which must then be delivered to appropriate election officials, deciphered, processed, and entered into a database; the forms typically arrive together in huge volumes, right before an election. This system is ripe for error, duplication, and waste; worse, the system ends up disenfranchising millions of eligible voters."[15] This study provides clear evidence that the surest way to increase voter registration is for government to ensure that every eligible citizen is registered to vote.

The National Voter Registration Act, known as the Motor-Voter Law (which went into effect in January 1995), encouraged voter registration by simplifying the registration process. The law required states to provide registration services through driver's license agencies and public assistance and disability offices, and by mail-in registration. In all but one state (North Dakota), citizens are required to register before they can vote, but in the past the registration process in most states was cumbersome, time consuming, and unpublicized.[16] Unfortunately, Motor-Voter did not produce an immediate increase in voter turnout, only in registrations to vote.

Even registered voters may fail to reach the polls. Most detrimental to election turnout in the United States is the traditional day of voting—Tuesday. Most states keep their polls open from 8:00 a.m. to at least 7:00 p.m., but busy citizens with jobs, families, and errands to run often have difficulty finding the time to vote on a weekday.[17]

# Compared to WHAT?

## Party List Proportional Representation: Voting for the Person or the Party

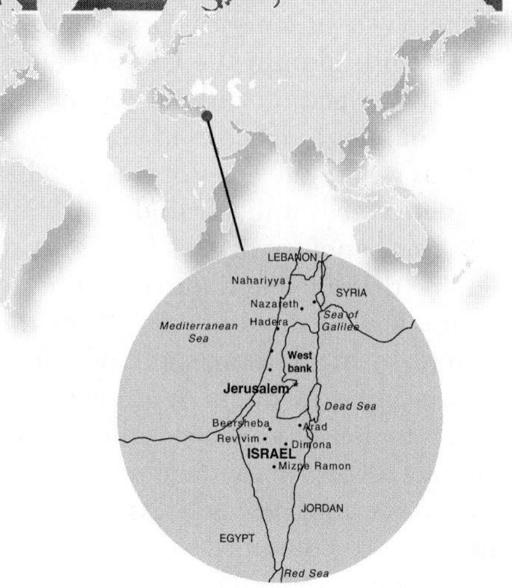


In the United States, many people cast their ballot for a candidate based solely on that candidate's political party. The term *Yellow Dog Democrat* refers to loyal Democrats who would vote for an old, yellow dog, as long as that dog was a Democrat. In addition to these party loyalists, there are many Americans who try to look beyond a candidate's party and vote for whom they believe is the better person. Rather than looking at issue positions or party allegiance, these voters try to assess the candidates' moral values, decision-making skills, and intelligence. Many other democracies use a Party List Proportional System of Representation, where only political parties and not candidates are listed on the ballot. In these countries it is not feasible to vote based on a candidate's personal characteristics.

The Israeli Knesset operates under this type of system. National elections for the 120-member legislature are held every four years or earlier if an election is called. In the most recent election, 33 parties produced lists of candidates to fill all 120 seats in the Knesset. On the day of election, to cast their ballot voters pull a tab for their preferred political party. They do not vote for individual candidates but select a party list, thereby voting for all 120 candidates from that party. After the votes are tallied, all parties receiving over 2 percent of the total vote are allocated seats based on the percentage of the vote they received. For example, the Likud Party won 22 percent of the vote and thus the first 27 people on their party list were given a seat in the Knesset. The National Union Party won 3.3 percent of the vote and was awarded 4 seats in the legislature. The 21 parties that received fewer than 2 percent of the vote were not allowed to seat any of the people on their party list in the Knesset.

Some prefer the simplicity of the Party List Proportional Representation System. In a nation such as Israel, where there is a high percentage of immigrants with low Hebrew literacy, voters only have to choose the well-publicized symbol of the political party they feel best represents their interests. They do not have to learn about specific candidates or gather information for each new election. All members on a party list agree to the same key policy positions, and the individual characteristics and personality do not matter as much as the issue positions of the political parties. This system allows voters with very little information or time to study the candidates an easy way to figure out the best way to cast their vote. How do you think Americans would react to this type of democratic government? Would some prefer to select only Republican or Democrat on a ballot without learning anything about the individual candidates running? Might others reject the movement away from character-based campaigns?

*Sources:* Maayana Miskin, "34 Parties Make Knesset Bid," *Arutz Sheva*, http://www.israelnationalnews.com/News/News.aspx/129127#.TmgGml7fRDQ; The Israel Project, http://www.theisraelproject.org/site/apps/nlnet/content2.aspx?c=hsJPKOPIJpH&b=3918015&ct=5142395.

In recent years, most states have taken steps to minimize the costs of registering and voting. Registration can now be done closer to Election Day than in the past, and polls stay open longer than in the past. In some states, such as California, employers must give employees paid time off to vote. In Oregon, voters may cast their ballots by mail or at drop boxes. Frequently, civic groups target universities and colleges, grocery stores, shopping malls, and other crowded areas to register people. Other creative suggestions have been put forth by various citizen groups: keeping polls open for 24 or 48 hours, same-day registration in all states, making Election Day a national holiday, holding elections on weekends, and Internet voting.[18]

## Nonvoting

Understanding nonvoting requires that we look at institutional as well as subjective, psychological explanations. People have numerous reasons for failing to vote, and one is the possibility that they are satisfied with the way things are going and see no particular need to become involved politically. Today's nonvoters may decide to vote when a public controversy sears their consciences and forces them to act, as former Supreme Court justice Felix Frankfurter once argued. Thus, nonvoters may start showing up on Election Day if they become unhappy enough. This option of nonvoters to vote also keeps politicians relatively honest. They know that truly unpopular actions could bring out hordes of formerly silent citizens eager to vote them out at the next election. Thus, from this perspective, nonvoting does not threaten the survival of democratic processes in America. It simply maintains the status quo. This chapter's Approaching Contemporary Issues in Democracy feature considers the issue of mandatory voting.

Another perspective claims nonvoting and nonparticipation in general undermine the health of democratic politics. Citizens who remain outside the political process may come to feel little connection with the laws of the land and the government that administers those laws. They feel alienated—that their vote makes no difference, that the process of voting is too difficult, and that the parties do not offer true alternatives. Yet, a League of Women Voters poll found that nonvoters were no more alienated than voters. This survey concluded that people do not vote because they do not grasp the significance or importance of elections to them, because the process of voting seems difficult and cumbersome, or because the costs of becoming informed are just too steep. This survey also showed that nonvoting was not a product of alienation, but rather that nonvoters merely fail to see voting as particularly important. Voters and nonvoters were equally distrustful of government, but nonvoters saw their participation as irrelevant to the outcome.[19] Another study, conducted by the California Voter Foundation, concluded that nonvoters were "disproportionately

## APPROACHING Contemporary Issues in Democracy

### Making Voting Mandatory

**ISSUE:** What if voting was made mandatory in the United States and nonvoters were ticketed and fined? How would this change or impact the democratic nature of participation?

**Question 1:**

Think about how mandatory voting laws would impact the stability of elected government. If all citizens were required to vote in each election, how likely would it be to see big partisan swings in Congress? Would the coattails and midterm election effects still be present under a system with mandatory voting?

**Question 2:**

By allowing citizens to choose not to participate, those with intense opinions on candidates and issues are given more of a say than those who care little about election outcomes. How would mandatory voting laws diminish the importance of intensity of opinion? Do you believe that those with an intense interest and opinion should have more influence than those who are uninterested or apathetic?

**Question 3:**

By eliminating voluntary registration and requiring all citizens to vote, disenfranchisement tactics—such as those discussed in the Approaching Contemporary Issues feature in Chapter 1—could no longer be used to keep citizens from participating. How would this change the democratic nature of participation in the U.S.? Can you imagine any similar tactics that could still deprive citizens of their right to vote even under a system with mandatory participation requirements?

young, single, less educated and more likely to be of an ethnic minority than infrequent voters."[20] The two reasons for not voting cited the most often were "I'm too busy to vote" and "There are no candidates I believe in."[21]

**QUICK REVIEW**

Variables Affecting Voting

- Education is leading influence.
- Social status—people feel they have a stake in political outcomes.
- Social connections—citizens have strong ties to their community.
- Older people are more likely to vote than younger people.
- Long-time community residents are more likely to vote than newcomers.
- Married people are more likely to vote than those who are single.

## Who Votes?

The answer to the question "Who votes?" is crucial for understanding the political process, because political leaders, quite naturally, pay more attention to voters (who determine politicians' fates) than to nonvoters (who play only a potential role in making or breaking governments). Many variables affect who votes. Schooling increases one's ability to understand the intricacies of politics and, in turn, see the benefit of taking a political action, such as voting for a favorite cause or candidate. Social status is also a variable that determines the likelihood of voting. Simply stated, the higher one's socioeconomic level, the more likely one is to participate in politics, especially to vote. Education and income frequently go together, of course, since it is becoming more difficult in modern society to gain economic success without an education. People who have both education and income possess two strong motivators of political activity. Social connections in general also make political participation more likely. The more ties citizens have to their community, the more reason they see for participating in politics. They work to keep their property taxes low, help support a new school for their children, or promote their next-door neighbor's city council campaign.

## The Youth Vote

Traditionally, older people are more likely to vote than younger people, and long-time community residents are more likely to vote than newcomers.[22] However, the galvanization of the youth vote in the 2008 election may signal a change. Figure 10.2 illustrates the increase in young voter turnout in presidential elections since 2000. An estimated 23 million young Americans voted in the 2008 presidential election. Even though the 2004 election was a strong one for youth turnout, reversing a long history of decline, more than 3.4 million more youth voted in 2008 as compared to 2004.[23]

Although overall youth turnout was high in the 2008 presidential election, there were important differences in turnout rates. Young African Americans (see Figure 10.3) posted the highest turnout rate ever observed for any racial or ethnic group of young Americans since 1972. The gap in turnout by educational attainment remained large; voter turnout of young people without college experience was 36 percent, compared to a 62 percent rate among young people with college experience. (About half of the young adult population has some college experience.) There was also a significant gender gap in turnout: Young women voted at a rate eight points above young men.

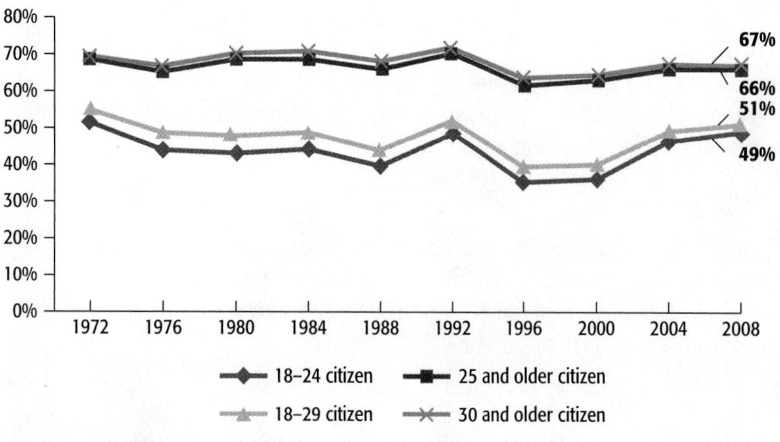


**FIGURE 10.2** Turnout by Age in Presidential Elections, 1972–2008

*Source:* Graph from "The Youth Vote in 2008" by Emily Hoban Kirby (Senior Researcher) and Kei Kawashima-Ginsberg (Lead Researcher), CIRCLE: Tisch College of Citizenship and Public Service, Tufts University, updated August 17, 2009, http://www.civicyouth.org/PopUps/FactSheets/FS_youth_Voting_2008_updated_6.22.pdf. Used with permission.

## The Gender Gap

Political races for president, senate, gubernatorial, and house offices often reflect an iron-clad gender divide—more women vote for the Democratic candidate than for the Republican candidate. The reverse is true among men, who give the preference to Republican candidates. This gender gap holds regardless of the gender of any candidate. This gap is wide enough to sway elections in all major contests. What does this mean for candidates, campaign managers, and special-interest groups involved in the complex process of campaigning and election in a modern democracy?

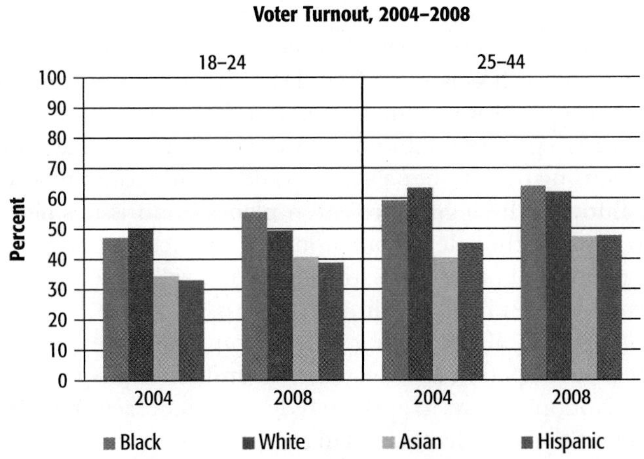


**FIGURE 10.3** Young Minority Voter Turnout, 2004–2008
For the first time, young black voters had the highest turnout in the 2008 presidential elections, compared with other ethnic groups. The share of voters in all minority groups increased from the 2004 elections while remaining largely unchanged for white voters.

The gender gap has been widening for the past decade. In the 1990s, the gender gap in presidential support was about four percentage points. But in 1996, this jumped to 11 percent. In 2000, the figure was 10 percentage points, with 43 percent of women and 53 percent of men voting for George W. Bush. In contrast, 42 percent of men and 54 percent of women voted for Al Gore. Race, class, and ethnic background fail to alter the disparity between male and female voters. The gender gap narrowed but persisted in the 2004 presidential election: In 2004, 48 percent of women and 55 percent of men voted for President Bush.[24]

According to extensive exit polling, both women and men favored Barack Obama in the 2008 election. Obama received 56 percent of the female vote and 49 percent of the male vote, while John McCain received 43 percent of the female vote and 48 percent of the male vote. Women's votes delivered the electoral votes of New Hampshire, North Carolina, Colorado, and Indiana to Barack Obama and elected several Democratic U.S. senators. Overall, 56 percent of women and only 49 percent of men voted for Barack Obama—a solid 7 percent gender gap. But because of Obama's widespread appeal, a majority of men as well as women voted for Obama in 23 states with enough electoral votes to win.[25]

## A Voting Trend: Direct Democracy

Those dissatisfied with American voting levels continue to explore creative ways to encourage voters to the polls. In recent years, support has increased for the use of initiatives and referenda. **Initiatives** are policy proposals placed on the ballot for voter consideration at the instigation of a group of citizens. Often they are ideas unsuccessful in a state's legislature or even contradictory to existing laws. Issues such as term limits have raised voter ire in recent years, leading to popular initiatives in the states. The initiative was designed to allow the public to take matters into its own hands. To qualify for the ballot, the initiative process requires that proponents obtain signatures—usually representing 10 percent of all registered voters—that must be verified by the secretary of state. Once verified, the initiative is placed on the ballot. California's Proposition 19, a citizen-initiated state statute that sought to legalize and tax marijuana use is an example of grassroots democracy that took place during the November 2010 election. Supporters needed to turn in 433,971 signatures to get the proposition on the ballot, and a coalition of pro-legalization interest groups submitted nearly 700,000 valid signatures of registered voters in January 2010. With the necessary signatures, the initiative was placed on the ballot and voters were asked

**initiative**
A proposal submitted by the public and voted on during elections.

**referendum**
A proposal submitted by a state legislature to the public for a popular vote, often focusing on whether a state should spend money in a certain way.

**party identification**
A psychological orientation, or long-term propensity to think positively of and vote regularly for a particular political party.

**split-ticket ballots**
Ballots on which people vote for candidates from more than one party.

**straight-party tickets**
Ballots on which people vote for only one party.

to choose whether they supported the legalization and regulation of marijuana. The measure failed at the ballot box, with 47 percent of voters in support. The 2004 election in California to recall Governor Gray Davis is another example; the 2 million signatures on recall petitions was the largest number ever gathered.[26]

A **referendum** is a proposal submitted by the legislature to the public for a popular vote, often focusing on whether a state should spend money in a certain way. For example, in California the legislature often places bond issues before the voters, asking them to approve the sale of state bonds to finance various programs, such as education and prisons. At other times, the legislature will place a referendum on the ballot to determine the public's sentiment on an issue.[27]

These two methods of consulting citizens on issues grew out of attempts to broaden political participation and decrease the influence of special interests. Many people see these options as ways to approach direct democracy. But initiatives and referenda have met with mixed success, and in recent years criticism of both methods has emerged. "Where direct democracy becomes a more dominant force than representative government the result is whipsaw, without any long-term coherence," observed Brian Weberg of the National Conference of State Legislatures.[28] Some critics find that issues end up on the ballot even though they are too complex for simple yes or no decisions. Both initiatives and referenda have become costly, requiring expensive television campaigns, and are therefore subject to the influence of big business and special-interest groups. By involving people directly, these methods bypass the considered deliberations of representative political institutions. In the 2010 midterm elections there were 160 ballot questions in 37 states (http://www.statenet.com/resources/2010_ballot_measures.php). These initiatives covered issues as broad and complex as taxes, casino regulation, alternative energy use, health-care reform, auto insurance, abortion, gun laws, and English as the official language. It is likely that more and more states will begin to utilize this approach to democracy.

# VOTING CHOICE

10.5 *What factors influence a person's vote choice?*

Although not everyone votes in every election, millions of Americans do vote with some regularity. When voters show up at the polls to make political choices, what determines their actual vote? Political scientists have long been studying the electoral process and the reasons citizens vote as they do. We now have a good idea of the key influences on American voters: party, candidate appeal, policies and issues, and campaigns.[29]

**QUICK REVIEW**

Factors Affecting Voting Choice

- Voters' connection to the candidate's party.
- The candidate's message and policy positions.
- Issue voting is a central part of the political process.
- How well an incumbent or party in power has performed in office.
- Effectiveness of a political campaign.

## Party

More than five decades of study of the American electorate have shown one overwhelming influence on voting decisions: party. Other things being equal, voters show up on Election Day and vote for candidates from the party to which they feel most connected. We explored this idea of connection, **party identification,** in Chapters 8 and 9. Party identification is a psychological phenomenon, a deep-seated feeling that a particular party best represents one's interests or best symbolizes one's lifestyle. Once party attachments develop, especially if they develop early, they tend to remain in place for a lifetime; it is psychologically painful to change party allegiance.

Not all voters have strong party ties. Some are registered as Independents, and others are weak party identifiers. These voters bring other considerations to the voting decision. Frequently, they cast **split-ticket ballots,** meaning that they vote for candidates from more than one party. Those with strong party identification can be counted on to vote, and to vote for one party only, known as a **straight-party ticket** voting. Only in exceptional circumstances (say, a friend is running on the other party's ticket, or a key issue of the day turns them temporarily away from their party) do party loyalists break their long-standing commitment to their own party in an election.

But party is far from the only determinant of voter choice. For one thing, some elections (usually local) are *nonpartisan,* so voters must choose among candidates whose party affiliation is unknown. Other elections involve primary contests. In a party primary, all candidates on the ballot belong to the same party and vie to represent that party in the general election. Hence, party primary voters often must choose among candidates without party to guide their decisions. Finally, many elections—for example, state constitutional amendments and referenda questions—involve issues. Party positions on these policy matters are not indicated on the ballot, and often parties take no clear position during the campaign. For a full understanding of how voters make electoral decisions, we must go beyond the useful but still limited variable of party preference.

## Candidate Appeal

Personality has always played a major role in the individualist culture of the United States. Our political system has been deeply touched by key personalities of the day: George Washington, Thomas Jefferson, Andrew Jackson, Abraham Lincoln, Theodore Roosevelt, Woodrow Wilson, Franklin Roosevelt, Ronald Reagan, and, most recently, Barack Obama, just to name a few. Colorful, authoritative, or charismatic individuals at the local, state, or national level have often won office by drawing voters away from long-standing party loyalties and by picking up the bulk of the Independent vote as well. Republican Dwight Eisenhower, for instance, traded on his status as war hero to gain the votes of many Democratic loyalists in the 1950s. Ronald Reagan's movie star charisma and charm, combined with a clear message of change, helped draw many traditionally Democratic voters into the Republican camp in 1980 and 1984.

Strong or popular personalities have a major advantage in any political campaign. What attributes help a candidate attract the voting public? Likability is surely important to Americans. It also helps to exude self-confidence, and especially to show a calm assurance when speaking in public. It does not hurt, of course, to be attractive. Studies show that although people vigorously deny it, they are clearly influenced to think better of individuals whose looks are above average.

No matter how attractive the candidate, though, or how folksy or self-assured, if he or she takes unpopular policy positions, the battle for office will be uphill. No election for public office is a simple popularity contest. Candidates cannot survive a campaign without stating where they stand on the issues or explaining what they will do once elected.

## Policies and Issues

Ultimately, elections hinge on what government is going to do. Despite many observers' cynicism about voters choosing candidates on the basis of their smile or hairstyle, the electorate does make decisions quite regularly on the basis of issues. Issue voting is a central part of the political process, although that is not always clear because issue voting is a complex matter.

Let's say a voter feels strongly about ten issues. He or she then looks for a candidate who takes the "right" stand on those issues. It may turn out, however, that one of the two leading candidates for the contested office takes the voter's favored position on just five of those issues, while the other candidate takes the preferred stand on the other five. This situation leaves the issue-oriented voter without much direction on how to vote. He or she may then consider other factors (such as party or personality) to make a voting choice.

Issue voting, then, depends on several factors existing at the same time and in the same election:

### THINKING CRITICALLY

Are some issues more important to you than others? Would you vote for a candidate who disagreed with you on the issue of abortion? What about gay marriage? What about funding for student loans? Why might your answer be yes to some issues and no to others?

1. The voter must care intensely enough about one or more issues to become informed about which positions each candidate takes on these issues.
2. Issue differences on these specific policy matters must exist between the leading candidates for the office.
3. These issue differences must be communicated clearly to all voters.

**retrospective voting**
A particularly powerful form of issue voting in which voters look back over the past term or two to judge how well an incumbent or the "in party" has performed in office.

4. The voter's preferred positions on issues must not split between the candidates but rather should fall mostly toward one candidate and away from the other.
5. Other factors, such as party and personality, should not detract from the voter's focus on issues.

Because these elements rarely all come together in elections, observers often conclude that issues are irrelevant to average voters. In fact, issues are relevant to voters, but the structure of the voting situation may make issue voting difficult.

Those who criticize the American electorate for failing to take issues into account when voting may be missing another key point. Party voting, the key determinant of voting, relates closely to policy preferences and issue voting. Parties take positions on dozens, even hundreds, of current policy questions, so a party vote is a vote to support those positions. Party-line voters may not agree with everything their party stands for, but studies show that, by and large, party identifiers agree much more often with their own party on the key issues of the day than with any other party. Thus, a party vote is in many ways an issues vote.

A particularly powerful form of issue voting occurs when voters look back over the past term or two to judge how well an incumbent or the party in power has performed in office. This is known as **retrospective voting.** Generally, retrospective voting reflects voters' judgment of the incumbents' handling of the economy. Sluggish economies doomed the reelection campaigns of Gerald Ford (1976), Jimmy Carter (1980), and George H. W. Bush (1992). In 1996, President Bill Clinton, benefiting from a sound economy, easily defeated Bob Dole.[30] If voters feel generally positive, if policy problems have been solved, if one's personal economic situation is good, if foreign or domestic crises have been skillfully addressed, then they reward incumbents by returning them or their party successors to office. The 2008 election was clearly a verdict on the Bush administration's handling of the economy. The 2010 midterm congressional elections were a reflection of a public still unhappy with the state of the economy and unemployment rates. The reelection of Barack Obama in 2012 may hinge on whether voters believe he did enough to improve the sluggish economy he inherited.

The use of whistle stops dates well back in presidential history. Here, President Franklin D. Roosevelt, the 32nd president of the United States, speaks on a whistle-stop campaign in 1939, having decided to seek an unprecedented third term for president. Perhaps the most important whistle stop was in 1948, when President Harry Truman traveled nearly 22,000 miles in his campaign against Thomas Dewey. On November 2, 1948, Truman was reelected.

## Campaigns

A final influence on voting choice is the campaign itself. At least one-third, and sometimes as much as one-half, of the electorate makes up its mind during political campaigns. With fewer Americans holding deeply rooted attachments to parties, campaigns can take on special significance. Many voters can be swayed during the months leading up to Election Day. Issues and personalities of the day can move uncommitted voters in one direction or another with relative speed.

Campaigns also take on special significance for their ability to arouse voters' interest and send them to the polls. The candidate or party that inspires its supporters to vote on Election Day is the most likely to win, and citizens are most likely to turn out to vote after a well-organized and stimulating campaign. For these reasons, the past two decades have seen the rise of *campaign specialists*—public relations people, media consultants, and fund-raising experts. With the decline of the old party machine, a new world of political entrepreneurs has arisen to provide advice and direction to any candidate with the money and desire to hire them.

We should not conclude, however, that money and a strong public relations campaign alone can make a winning candidate. Remember that party and issues play key roles in voter decisions. There is not enough money in existence to catapult into office a party candidate taking unpopular positions on key issues. That assumes, of course, that such a candidate's opponent is reasonably competent and does not self-destruct through scandal or incompetence. Finding a clever way to package a message or present a candidate are surely important, but the content of that message and the substance of a candidate's personality are even more important. If those do not impress voters, chances of winning, despite all the slick packaging imaginable, are slim.

**QUICK REVIEW**

Political Participation

- Volunteer work for candidates in election campaigns.
- Learning about politics and the political system.
- Discussing and expressing opinion on political events and issues of the day.
- Organized protests and acts of civil disobedience.

# OTHER FORMS OF POLITICAL PARTICIPATION

10.6 *How else, outside the act of voting, can an individual participate?*

Political participation takes many other shapes in the United States, including campaign work, seeking information, protesting, civil disobedience, and even violence. In Chapter 11, we discuss participation through interest groups, but here we examine other ways in which individuals become involved in the political process.[31]

**THINKING CRITICALLY**

How do you participate in politics by seeking information? What sources do you use to find out about politics? Your friends? Television? The Internet? Does information you receive ever change your mind about a candidate or an issue?

## Campaign and Election Activities

Unlike the pattern in most countries, Americans are not expected to join political parties and become dues-paying members who regularly attend monthly meetings. Still, some Americans do volunteer to work for their party in election campaigns, although the work is hard, the hours are long, and the material benefits are negligible. Even with the increasing use of sophisticated electronic media, the backbone of most campaigns remains people. Successful campaigns require volunteers to answer telephones, handle mail, canvass the electoral district, distribute candidate or party literature, and discuss the candidates and issues with people in the neighborhood. Other interested citizens participate by displaying signs or bumper stickers or handing out literature of a favored party or candidate, hoping to induce others to echo such support at the polls. Still others work as party volunteers in voter registration drives.

Why do people volunteer? They likely believe in what they are doing, feel an obligation to participate actively in the political process, or simply enjoy the game of politics. Look at all the students who worked tirelessly on behalf of Barack Obama's candidacy in 2008. They organized field events, walked precincts, developed webpages, circulated fliers, and made telephone calls on behalf of the candidate for change they believed in.

The worldwide economic crisis brought many manifestations of protest against those responsible. Urinals in Reykjavik were decorated with photographs of the former bankers who left their country after the financial crash. In April 2009, seven months after Iceland's economic collapse, voters snubbed the party seen as responsible for the crisis in favor of an interim leftist government.

## Seeking Information

No one can exercise an effective citizenship role without being well informed. For that reason, the simple act of gaining knowledge about public affairs constitutes a form of political activity. Certainly, a person who attends a meeting of public officials or the local government is participating in politics. In addition, every time a person reads a newspaper or news magazine, watches a news broadcast or political program, or enrolls in a political science class, he or she is actively seeking information that will assist in formulating political preferences and opinions. By just learning about politics, a citizen contributes to the overall knowledge base of the American political system. And each time a person discusses political events and

**protest**
Expression of dissatisfaction; may take the form of demonstrations, letters to newspapers or public officials, or simple "opting out" of the system by failing to vote or participate in any other way.

**civil disobedience**
Breaking the law in a nonviolent fashion and being willing to suffer the consequences, even to the point of going to jail, in order to publicly demonstrate that the law is unjust.

issues of the day with friends and family or writes a letter to the editor to express an opinion on those events and issues, that person is participating in the continuous process of politics. Thomas Jefferson acknowledged the importance of information in democracy in remarking that, given the choice between a government without newspapers or newspapers without government, he would without hesitation choose the latter. Broadcast and cable television provide even more access to political information, and the Internet and social networking tools have made it increasingly easier for citizens to engage in political activity and motivate others to do so!

## Protest, Civil Disobedience, and Violence

When governments produce public policy, then groups, institutions, and individuals in society invariably respond. This response may be simple support, such as accepting and participating in government-sponsored programs, voting in elections, paying taxes, or complying with new laws. But sometimes government actions may provoke strong expressions of dissatisfaction. Occasionally, these expressions take the form of organized protests and acts of civil disobedience, either against existing policies or conditions or as a response to actual or threatened change in the status quo.

**Protest** may take the form of demonstrations, letters to newspapers and public officials, or opting out of the system by failing to vote or participate in any other way.

**Civil disobedience** is a more specific form of protest in which disaffected citizens openly but nonviolently defy existing laws that they deem to be unjust. Civil disobedience was common in the 1960s as citizens protested continued U.S. involvement in the Vietnam War. Draftees burned their Selective Service cards, and students organized boycotts of classes and "die-ins." Even disillusioned veterans marched on the Pentagon during the 1968 Republican and Democratic National Conventions to call attention to their opposition to the war. In 2006 and 2007, hundreds of thousands of immigrants in cities across the nation protested President Bush's policy on immigration. In July 2009, students, professors, and staff from the University of California

Nonviolent protests take many forms, including appearing in the nude with anti-war slogans written in both English and Arabic to protest the war in Iraq and the occupation of Palestine. This protest occurred in New York's Washington Square Park. The young woman was arrested by New York City police.

Thousands of protestors stand outside the Wisconsin State Capitol to protest Gov. Scott Walker's anti-union legislation. The Walker recall effort began in November 2011.

protested the draconic cuts being made to campus programs, furloughs, and the increase in student fees. In 2011, as many as 100,000 protestors occupied the Wisconsin State Capitol in opposition to a bill eliminating collective bargaining rights for public employees. For months, thousands of protestors occupied the public spaces of the capitol, sleeping in tents and sleeping bags and eating food donated by local businesses. Many protestors were arrested for blocking the business of government or making threats against officials. In November 2011, Occupy movement protestors across the nation refused police orders to leave their tents and encampments. Many, including peaceful student protestors at UC Davis, faced pepper-spray, pressure-point restraints, and baton beatings in response to their acts of civil disobedience.

**political violence**
Violent action motivated primarily by political aims and intended to have a political impact.

**midterm elections**
Elections in which Americans elect members of Congress but not presidents; 2014, 2018, and 2022 are midterm election years.

Civil rights protesters in the 1950s and 1960s often actively violated existing segregation laws on the basis that these laws were unjust, exclusionary, and racist. Martin Luther King Jr. used civil disobedience as a principal means of demanding equal justice in the political system. African Americans asked for service at "whites-only" lunch counters and sat quietly on the lunch counter stools, knowing that these actions would provoke a reaction. By violating laws they believed wrong—and that were ultimately abolished as morally unjust—they drew attention and support to their cause.

Discussions about political participation seldom include the phenomenon of **political violence**—violent action motivated primarily by political aims and intended to have a political impact. When radical opponents of abortion bomb abortion clinics or shoot clinic workers, they claim that their actions are aimed at stopping the "murder of unborn citizens." It is often difficult to know the true motives behind supposedly political acts of violence. The rise of the white supremacist and neo-Nazi movements is, in part, certainly a response to social conditions. We know that violent intolerance follows in the wake of sustained economic downturns, when competition for jobs and scarce governmental resources are most troubling. Although most political violence appears triggered by a combination of economic problems and political events, the vast majority of Americans strongly condemn criminal actions involving injury and property damage.

# CONGRESSIONAL ELECTIONS

10.7 *How do Americans participate in congressional elections?*

Our Constitution calls for House and Senate elections every two years. Each of the 435 House members is up for reelection every two years, as are one-third of the senators (who serve six-year terms). Most candidates for Congress are not nationally known; they may not even be widely known within their own state or district. Although the U.S. Senate has included a former astronaut and a former movie actor, most national legislators come from somewhat less conspicuous, if equally wealthy, backgrounds. For that and other reasons, many constituents may have little information about who their elected representatives are, what they stand for, or even what sort of work they actually do.

Congressional elections generally receive less national media attention and voter turnout than does the national contest for the presidency. In **midterm elections,** with no presidential contest to galvanize press and voter attention, voter turnout is far below that of presidential election years. Also, congressional elections are not federally subsidized like presidential elections, therefore races for House and Senate seats take on a form decidedly different from a presidential campaign. Table 10.1 shows the number of seats lost and gained by the president's party in midterm elections since 1934.

Before the 2010 midterm elections, the Democrats held a 78-seat margin in the House of Representatives. Like

Many were outraged when UC Davis police used pepper spray on non-violent student protestors, most of whom were demonstrating against the rising costs of their education. The November 2011 incident led to the suspension of the officers involved and an investigation into the response of the Chancellor.

**Table 10.1** Seats in Congress Gained/Lost by the President's Party in Midterm Elections, *F. Roosevelt to Barack Obama*

| Year | President | Party | President's Job Approval Rating | | | | | | House | Senate |
|---|---|---|---|---|---|---|---|---|---|---|
| | | | Early Aug | Late Aug | Early Sep | Late Sep | Early Oct | Late Oct | Seats | Seats |
| 1934 | Franklin D. Roosevelt | D | ndb | nd | nd | nd | nd | nd | +9 | +9 |
| 1938 | Franklin D. Roosevelt | D | nd | nd | nd | nd | nd | 60% | −71 | −6 |
| 1942 | Franklin D. Roosevelt | D | 74% | nd | 74% | nd | nd | nd | −55 | −9 |
| 1946 | Harry S. Truman | D | nd | nd | 33 | nd | nd | 27 | −45 | −12 |
| 1950 | Harry S. Truman (LD)* | D | nd | 43% | 35 | 35% | 43% | 41 | −29 | −6 |
| 1954 | Dwight D. Eisenhower | R | 67 | 62 | nd | 66 | 62 | nd | −18 | −1 |
| 1958 | Dwight D. Eisenhower (LD) | R | 58 | 56 | 56 | 54 | 57 | nd | −48 | −13 |
| 1962 | John F. Kennedy | D | nd | 67 | nd | 63 | nd | 61 | −4 | +3 |
| 1966 | Lyndon B. Johnson* | D | 51 | 47 | nd | nd | 44 | 44 | −47 | −4 |
| 1970 | Richard Nixon | R | 55 | 55 | 57 | 51 | 58 | nd | −12 | +2 |
| 1974 | Gerald R. Ford *(Nixon)** | R | 71 | nd | 66 | 50 | 53 | nd | −48 | −5 |
| 1978 | Jimmy Carter | D | 39 | 43 | 43 | 48 | nd | 49 | −15 | −3 |
| 1982 | Ronald Reagan | R | 41 | 42 | nd | 42 | nd | 42 | −26 | +1 |
| 1986 | Ronald Reagan (LD) | R | nd | 64 | nd | 63 | 64 | nd | −5 | −8 |
| 1990 | George H. W. Bush | R | 75 | 73 | 54 | nd | nd | 57 | −8 | −1 |
| 1994 | William J. Clinton | D | 43 | 40 | 40 | 44 | 43 | 48 | −52 | −8 |
| 1998 | William J. Clinton (LD) | D | 65 | 62 | 63 | 66 | 65 | 65 | +5 | 0 |
| 2002 | George W. Bush | R | nd | 66 | 66 | 66 | 68 | 67 | +8 | +2 |
| 2006 | George W. Bush (LD) | R | 37 | 42 | 39 | 44 | 37 | 37 | −30 | −6 |
| 2010 | Barack Obama | D | 44 | 44 | 45 | 45 | 45 | 45 | −63 | −6 |

*A "lame-duck" midterm (congressional) election is one that occurs when the incumbent president is constitutionally prohibited from seeking reelection in the next scheduled presidential election. Arguable exceptions are noted below.

Harry S. Truman was not prevented from running for a 3rd term in 1952, although he chose not to seek reelection.

Lyndon B. Johnson was not a lame-duck president in 1966, but in March 1968 he chose not to seek reelection.

Although Gerald Ford was not a lame-duck president and did run for reelection in 1976, the 1974 midterm election took place only three months after the resignation of Richard Nixon and only two months following Ford's pardon of Nixon.

*Source:* Table compiled by Gerhard Peters. Presidential job approval data from The Gallup Poll; 1950 through 1994 congressional seat gain/loss from Lyn Ragsdale, *Vital Statistics on the Presidency*, Washington, DC: CQ Press, 1998; 1934 through 1946 and 1998 through 2006 congressional seat gain/loss by Gerhard Peters, *The American Presidency Project*, http://www.presidency.ucsb.edu/data/mid-term_elections.php. Used with permission.

nearly all midterm elections, the party of the president lost seats in 2010. The election was in some way a verdict on President Obama's economic recovery program. The president's party lost 63 House seats, the greatest number of seats lost since 1938, giving control of the House of Representatives to the Republicans.

## Presidential Coattails

Over the years, an interesting pattern has emerged in congressional elections. Typically, in presidential elections, the winning presidential candidate's party gains seats in Congress; conversely, in off-year elections, the incumbent president's party loses seats. This phenomenon varies somewhat over time, depending on the president's fortunes, the state of the economy, and possible flare-ups of controversy or scandal.

When representatives or senators of a successful presidential candidate's party unseat incumbents, they are said to "ride the president's coattails" into office. Sometimes this **coattails effect** can be quite dramatic. For example, in 1980, when Ronald Reagan defeated Democratic president Jimmy Carter, he brought enough Republican senators into office on his coattails to wrest control of the Senate from the Democrats for the first time since 1955. But the coattails effect is rarely so dramatic. Despite Republican George H. W. Bush's presidential victory in 1988, Democrats retained control of both the House and Senate. The same result occurred in the 1968 and 1972 presidential victories of Republican Richard Nixon. Thus, the coattails effect is not an absolute guarantee in American politics, and many scholars believe its importance is waning as voters become less predictable, less tied to party, and more willing to vote a split ticket.

During off-year elections, with voter turnout low and the public able to look back on two years of presidential performance with a skeptical eye, the sitting president's party typically loses seats in the House and Senate. In 1952, for example, Eisenhower was elected with a larger victory than Obama received in 2008; by 1954, Republicans lost seats in both Houses. In 1992, Clinton won the White House after 12 years of Republican control; in 1994, his party lost 54 House seats and control of Congress.

Republican Presidential primary candidates, from the left, Jon Huntsman, Herman Cain, Michele Bachmann, Mitt Romney, Rick Perry, Ron Paul, Newt Gingrich, and Rick Santorum take the stage before the CNN/Tea Party co-hosted debate held in Tampa, Florida.

## THINKING CRITICALLY

Given that voters have so much less information on the issues and the candidates during midterm elections, what do you think is the primary factor underlying most citizens' vote choices? Is it party, feelings toward the president, or something else?

## PRESIDENTIAL ELECTIONS

10.8 *How are presidential elections conducted?*

Every four years, after a summer of national party conventions, the nation turns its attention to the presidential election. The pack of presidential contenders has usually been narrowed to two, although occasionally a serious third candidate competes.

The rules of the game at this stage differ markedly from those of the nomination phase (see Chapter 9 for more on the nomination process). The timetable is compressed from two years to two months, and the fight is usually Democrat against Republican. Candidates who previously spent all their efforts wooing the party faithful to gain the nomination must now broaden their sights to the less committed party voters and Independents who will determine the election outcome. The fall campaign involves successfully juggling numerous political balls in the air. Candidates must use funds strategically, define a clear campaign theme, anticipate any last-minute "October surprises" by opponents, avoid self-inflicted gaffes, attack opponents without seeming to mudsling, monitor the pulse of the nation, and manage a successful media campaign.

One of the defining aspects of the campaign tends to be the presidential debates. The presidential debates can have a significant impact on the public's perceptions of the candidates. In 1960, the two major parties' nominees met in the first televised presidential debate. John F. Kennedy's coaching prior to the debate on proper on-air behavior combined with his telegenic looks provided a sharp contrast to his Republican opponent. Richard Nixon, recently released from the hospital with a severe flu, refused to wear makeup and appeared pale, weak, and underweight. After a day full of campaigning, he looked tired and he sweat heavily under the lights of the TV cameras. The debate was highly publicized and an estimated 74 million Americans tuned in. Interestingly, a majority of those viewers believed that Kennedy won the debate, whereas those who listened on the radio gave the victory to Nixon.

**coattails effect**
"Riding the president's coattails into office" occurs in an election when voters also elect representatives or senators belonging to a successful presidential candidate's party.

Both campaigns were well aware of the influence the visual media of television had on how the candidates were perceived. Nixon's campaign put him on a "milkshake diet" hoping he would gain weight, he started wearing makeup, and he began extensive preparation for his next three scheduled debates. Most political observers say that Nixon did much better in these subsequent debates, but far fewer viewers paid attention. The image of a sweaty, nervous Nixon from the first debate was seared into the public's conscious. Many claim that without this debate, Kennedy would never have been elected president and four days after winning the election Kennedy himself noted that "it was the TV more than anything else that turned the tide."[32]

It was 16 years before presidential candidates met again for a debate. In the intervening elections, the candidates were quite wary of the influence a televised debate could play. Lyndon Johnson (1964) and Richard Nixon in his later campaigns (1968 and 1972) were well aware of the risks of a poor televised performance and refused to meet their challengers for a debate. In 1976, Gerald Ford agreed to debate Jimmy Carter, establishing what is now standard practice for all presidential campaigns. The Commission on Presidential Debates (CPD) was established in 1987 to ensure that debates would be a part of every general election. The commission has sponsored all presidential debates from 1988 through 2008. The 1992 general election debates are noteworthy for the ways they differed from previous debates. For the first and only time, the commission allowed a candidate not from the two major parties to participate. In these debates, the three candidates, George Bush (R), Bill Clinton (D), and Ross Perot (I), broke from the traditional format and had a town hall–style debate. Clinton was seen as very effective in the citizen interactions of the town hall with 58 percent of viewers calling him the winner. Bush and Perot tied among viewers with only 16 percent viewing each of them as winning the town hall–style debate.[33] The town hall debate format is popular among viewers and has been included in every presidential election since 1992. In the 2008 town hall debate, the candidates were even asked questions from citizens who had submitted them online. As technology changes the expectations of the public, the format and scale of presidential debates also changes. Both YouTube and Facebook sponsored primary debates for the 2008 and 2012 presidential primary elections. Republicans vying for the 2012 Republican nomination took part in the first Twitter debate, which limited candidates to three 140-character responses for each question.

## The Electoral College: The Framers' Intention

The framers wanted to ensure that exactly the right type of person was chosen for the job, and they sought to clone the best aspects of the first presidential role model—George Washington. Rather than voting in ambitious demagogues who would cater only to the whims of the electorate or act as the mouthpiece of Congress, the framers wanted to ensure the selection of a statesman, someone wise enough to unify the people behind a program that served their best interest. After considerable discussion, the framers chose not to have Congress select the president, fearing that the president would then become dependent on that body. They also decided not to let the people choose the executive, hoping thus to insulate that office from what they considered the popular passions and transitory fancies of the electorate.[34]

Instead, the framers of the Constitution designed a system unlike any in the world—the **electoral college**—which provided an indirect election method. Legislators from each state would choose individuals known as *electors,* the number to be based on the state's representation in Congress. (A state with two senators and five representatives, for instance, would be allotted seven electors to the electoral college.) The framers expected that electors would be individuals with experience and foresight who would meet; discuss in a calm, rational manner the attributes of those candidates who were best suited for the presidency; and then vote for the best person to fill that post. Thus, presidents would be chosen by an elite group of state leaders in a sedate atmosphere unencumbered by political debts and considerations.

**electoral college**
The group of 538 electors who meet separately in each of their states and the District of Columbia on the first Monday following the second Wednesday in December after a national presidential election. Their majority decision officially elects the president and vice president of the United States.

In practice, the electoral college has never worked as the framers planned because the framers had not anticipated the emergence of political parties. Originally, the electors had nearly absolute independence. They had two votes to cast and could vote for any two candidates, as long as one of their two votes went for someone from outside their state. Today, this requirement ensures that the president and vice president cannot both be residents of the same state.

**faithless elector**
Member of the electoral college who casts his or her vote for someone other than the state's popular-vote winner.

This odd system worked well only in the first two presidential elections, when victories by George Washington were foregone conclusions. After his departure, the beginnings of the first party system had, by 1796, ensured that electors were not, in fact, disinterested elder statesmen. They were, instead, factional loyalists committed to one of the two leading competitors of the day, John Adams or Thomas Jefferson. Thus, in a straight-line vote after the 1796 election, the electoral college chose Adams for president by a scant three votes over Jefferson. This made Adams president but Jefferson, his chief rival, vice president. A modern-day equivalent of this situation would be if John McCain, who came in second to Barack Obama in the electoral voting of 2008, served under Obama as vice president.

## QUICK REVIEW

The Electoral College

- Written into the Constitution by the framers.
- Each state has electors equal to the number of that state's House members plus two senators.
- A majority of the electoral college (270) is needed to win the presidency.
- Most states use the winner-take-all method in allocating electoral votes.

Matters worsened in the election of 1800. By then, strong political parties with devoted loyal followers had arrived to stay, ensuring that members of the electoral college would vote the party line. Jefferson and Adams opposed each other again, but this time both chose running mates to avoid the anomaly of another Adams–Jefferson presidency. Jefferson's vice presidential selection was Aaron Burr, and their ticket combined to win more electoral votes than either Adams or Charles Cotesworth Pinckney, Adams' running mate. However, all of Jefferson's supporters in the electoral college had been instructed by party leaders to cast their ballots for Jefferson and Burr, and when they did, the two men ended up in a tie vote for the presidency. This result threw the choice of president into the House of Representatives. It took a good deal of intrigue in the House before Jefferson finally emerged the winner and was named president.

The absurdity of these two elections brought cries for reform. The Twelfth Amendment was quickly proposed and ratified, directing the electoral college to cast separate ballots for president and vice president. Under this system, the party that wins a majority of electors can first elect the party's nominee for president, then go on to choose the party's nominee for vice president. No longer can a president from one party and a vice president from another be elected, nor can there be tie votes between two candidates from the same party. In a way, this early reform preserved the electoral college system, since in nearly all subsequent American elections it has worked to give Americans the president who received the most votes. To this day, the electoral college remains a central part of the American political system.

On Monday, December 15, 2008, in all 50 states and the District of Columbia, electors met and performed their constitutional duty. Vermont members of the electoral college took the oath in Montpelier. The state's three members of the electoral college held a brief meeting at the Statehouse, where they signed the papers needed to cast their ballots for president-elect Barack Obama. Title 3, Chapter 1 of the U.S. Code provides that on the sixth day of January after every meeting of the electors—usually referred to as Certification Day—the electoral vote (which had been sent by registered mail to Washington) will be announced by the vice president before both houses of Congress. Not until that moment are the election results considered official.

## How the Electoral College Works Today

When Americans go to the polls in a presidential election, most believe they are casting their ballots for president. In fact, they are voting for a slate of electors (individuals selected by state party leaders who are expected to cast ballots for their respective state's popular vote winner), and the results of the election are not official until January when the votes are counted and certified. The electoral college can produce the occasional **faithless elector,** who casts his or her electoral vote for someone other than the state's popular-vote winner. In 1988, for example, one of the electoral delegates from West Virginia cast a vote for Republican Robert Dole rather than for the party's nominee, George H. W. Bush.

The electors selected in the presidential election meet in their respective state capitals on the first Monday after the second Wednesday in December. The term *electoral college* is deceptive, since the 538 electors never actually assemble en masse to cast their votes

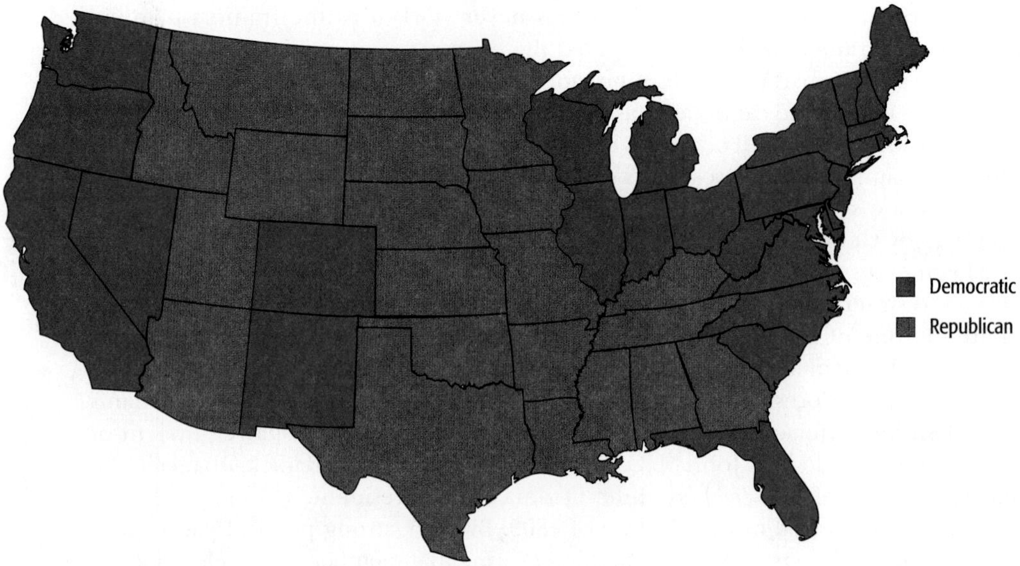


**FIGURE 10.4** 2008 Electoral College Vote by State

*Source:* "Maps of the 2008 U.S. Presidential Election Results," by Mark Newman, http://www-personal.umich.edu/~mejn/election/2008. © 2008 M. E. J. Newman. This work is licensed under a Creative Commons License.

for president. Title 3, Chapter 1 of the U.S. Code provides that on the sixth day of January after every meeting of the electors—usually referred to as Certification Day—the electoral vote (which had been sent by registered mail to Washington) will be announced by the vice president before both houses of Congress. Not until that moment are the election results considered official—although the whole world has known these results unofficially for several weeks.

To become president, the winning candidate needs to receive a majority, or 270, of the 538 electoral votes. Figures 10.4 and 10.5 provide two different ways of looking

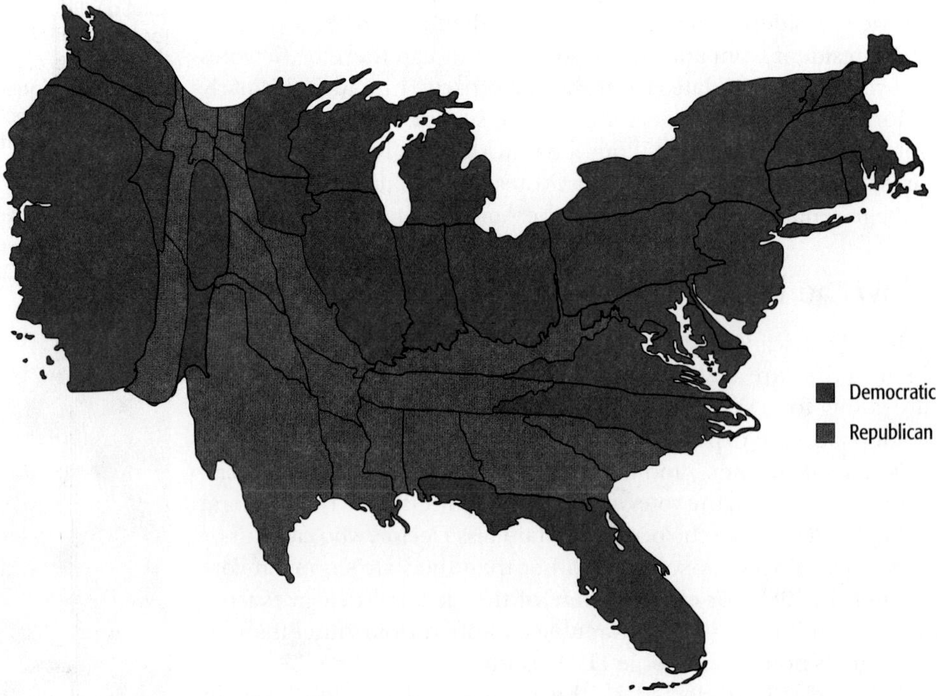


**FIGURE 10.5** 2008 Electoral College Vote on a Population Cartogram

*Source:* "Maps of the 2008 U.S. Presidential Election Results," by Mark Newman, http://www-personal.umich.edu/~mejn/election/2008. © 2008 M. E. J. Newman. This work is licensed under a Creative Commons License.

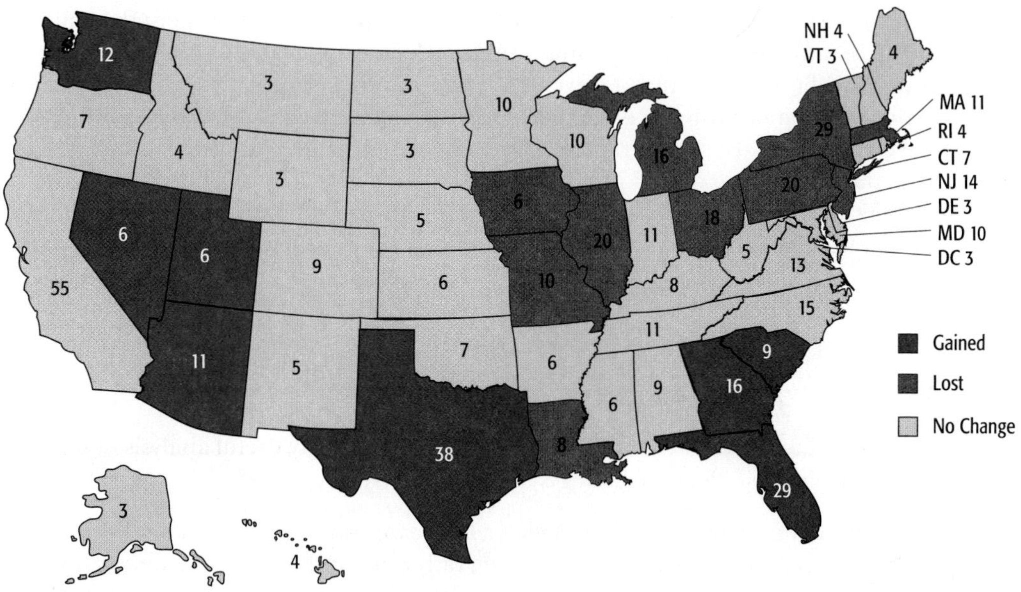


**FIGURE 10.6** 2012 Electoral College Changes
*Source:* U.S. Census Bureau.

at the electoral results of the 2008 presidential election. The 538 votes consist of one vote for each of the 435 members of the U.S. House of Representatives, plus one vote for each of the 100 senators, plus three votes for the District of Columbia. If no candidate receives the required electoral college majority, a **contingency election** is held in the House. The House chooses among the top three candidates, with each state casting a single vote. After each census, the number of electors in some states changes to reflect population changes. Figure 10.6 shows the new electoral college breakdown for the 2012 election.

## The Electoral College and Strategies for Campaigning

All but two states (Maine and Nebraska) use a winner-take-all system, whereby the winner of the plurality of the state's popular vote is awarded all of the state's electoral votes. As we saw in the 2000 election, the effect of this can be dramatic. Despite George W. Bush's narrow popular-vote victory in Florida, he was awarded all 25 of Florida's electoral college delegates, while Al Gore received no electoral college delegates from Florida. Candidates know before running for president that, to win, they need to receive a majority in the electoral college, and most states allocate their electoral votes under the winner-take-all rules. The result is that candidates spend the vast majority of their time, money, and campaign resources in just a handful of states, often completely ignoring the nation's largest states: Texas, where the Republican candidate is likely to win, and California, where the Democrat candidate is more likely to win. Campaigning in either of these uncompetitive states could improve a candidate's popular vote total, but it will not gain the candidate *any* electoral votes. As a result, the electoral college encourages candidates to focus all of their attention onto battleground, or swing states, where pre-election polling shows a good chance that either candidate might win. In a state where voters are evenly split between the candidates prior to Election Day, a candidate needs only to convince a small number of undecided voters to vote for him or her to win all of the state's electoral votes. Thus, both candidates battle for the votes of the undecided voters in these few swing states.

**contingency election**
An election held in the House if no candidate receives the required majority in the electoral college.

In the peak of the 2004 election, John Kerry and George Bush spent the majority of their time and resources competing for electoral votes in Ohio, Pennsylvania, and Florida, where only 14 percent of the nation's population resides. Only a 2 percent popular vote difference decided the electoral vote in Ohio and ultimately gave George W. Bush the presidency. In the 2008 presidential election, the battleground states expanded into what used to be comfortably Republican territory. Barack Obama and John McCain spent most of the campaign not only in Ohio, Pennsylvania, and Florida but also in Nevada, North Carolina, and Colorado. Despite the expansion of battleground states in 2008, the vast majority of the nation's citizens live in states where the candidates spent little to no time actively seeking their votes.

## Reforming the Electoral College?

The organization Fair Vote has provided an exceptionally useful analysis of options for reforming the electoral college.[35]

- The first possibility is *direct election with instant runoff voting.* Voters would rank their preferences rather than marking only one candidate. If no single candidate has a majority, the candidate with the lowest number of votes is eliminated. All of the ballots are counted again, this time tallying the second-choice votes from those ballots indicating the eliminated candidate as the first choice. The process is repeated until a candidate receives a majority.
- *Proportional allocation* of electoral votes has been proposed with a number of variations, most recently in Colorado. A candidate who comes in second place in a state with 45 percent of the popular vote would receive 45 percent of the electoral votes from that state, instead of 0 percent. This system would greatly increase voter turnout and the representation of all parties in a state. It would also encourage candidates to campaign in all states rather than just those that are competitive.
- *Direct vote with plurality rule* would abolish the electoral college and require each person to cast one vote for the candidate of his or her choice. The candidate who receives the most votes nationwide would win the election, with or without a majority of the votes. This option would require a constitutional amendment to be implemented and would therefore need the support of two-thirds of Congress and three-fourths of the states. This method of voting would more accurately reflect the popular will of the nation at large. Four American presidents—Lyndon Johnson, Richard Nixon, Gerald Ford, and Jimmy Carter—endorsed a constitutional amendment that would replace the electoral college with direct election.[36]
- *The congressional district method* divides electoral votes by district, allocating one vote to each district and using the remaining two as a bonus for the statewide popular vote winner. This method of distribution has been used in Maine since 1972 and Nebraska since 1996, although neither state had a statewide winner that has not swept all of the congressional districts as well until Obama was able to win one of Nebraska's congressional districts in 2008. Consequently, prior to 2008, both states held many elections without spliting their electoral votes.
- *The national bonus plan* idea, proposed by historian Arthur Schlesinger Jr., retains the current electoral college system, but also awards extra electoral votes as a bonus to the winner of the popular vote. The amount suggested by Schlesinger in his plan is 102 extra electoral votes (two for every state and Washington, DC). The extra boost of electoral votes would almost always be able to guarantee that the popular vote winner would also be the electoral college winner. While technically maintaining the institution, this option compensates for the uneven power given to the states by the electoral college.[37]

**THINKING CRITICALLY**

Do you believe the electoral college should be reformed? What might be a better method of electing the president?

## Interpreting Presidential Elections

The day after the election, virtually every politically interested citizen, including the president-elect, asks the same question: What message did voters send to their new (or reelected) leaders? Election outcomes are notoriously difficult to interpret. For one thing, never in U.S. history has a president been elected with a majority of those eligible to vote. Only 50 to 55 percent of the electorate turn out to vote for president. Nearly every one of them would have to vote for the same candidate for that person to obtain a majority of all adult Americans as supporters. Naturally, this has never happened in a free society and never will. Indeed, more citizens choose "none of the above" by staying at home on Election Day than vote for the winning presidential candidate.

In an attempt to make more sense of presidential contests, political scientists use party realignment theory to classify elections as maintaining, deviating, or realigning (or critical) elections. In **maintaining elections,** the majority party of the day wins both Congress and the White House, maintaining its long-standing control of government. In **deviating elections,** the minority party captures the White House because of short-term intervening forces, and the country experiences a deviation from the expectation that power will remain in the hands of the dominant party. **Realigning elections** are characterized by massive shifts in partisan identification, as in 1932, when the New Deal coalition was forged. Recent trends have been toward regional realignment in the South, with Republican gains in 1992 and 1996.

The size of Ronald Reagan's 1984 electoral victory led many to speculate that it, too, represented a realignment that changed the electoral landscape. This interpretation weakened, however, with the Democratic congressional victories of 1986, 1988, and 1992 and with Bill Clinton's triumph in the presidential races of 1992 and 1996. The realignment thesis revived with the dramatic takeover of the House and Senate by the Republicans following the 1994 midterm elections, but the voters in 1998 did not continue a revolt against politics as usual. The demographics of the 2008 election led some analysts to suggest that the United States just may be in the early stages of realignment within the American electorate.

**maintaining election**
Election in which the majority party of the day wins both Congress and the White House, maintaining its control of government.

**deviating election**
Election in which the minority party captures the White House because of short-term intervening forces, and thus a deviation from the expectation that power will remain in the hands of the dominant party.

**realigning election**
Election characterized by massive shifts in partisan identification, as in 1932 with the New Deal coalition.

# MONEY AND ELECTIONS

10.9 *What role does money play in elections?*

It is often said that money is the mother's milk of politics (see this chapter's timeline for the role of money in elections). The 2008 presidential and congressional elections were the most costly in history, with a total price of $5.3 billion, an increase from $4.2 billion in

### APPROACHING Democracy Timeline

**Money and Politics**

| | |
|---|---|
| **1867** | The Naval Appropriations Bill bars soliciting campaign money from naval yard workers. |
| **1883** | The Pendleton Act bars contributions from government employees. |
| **1905** | Despite taking large corporate donations in his 1904 campaign, President Teddy Roosevelt calls for outlawing corporate donations. |
| **1907** | The Tillman Act prohibits donations from corporations and businesses. |
| **1910** | The Publicity Act requires congressional candidates to disclose contributions of more than $100. Loopholes and no method of verification make the act largely useless. |
| **1921** | In *U.S.* v. *Newberry,* the Supreme Court weakens the campaign finance regulations on political parties. |
| **1922** | The Teapot Dome Scandal erupts over speculation that Sinclair Oil was awarded a contract as payback for large contributions to President Harding's campaign. |
| **1925** | The Federal Corrupt Practices Act lays out basic campaign finance rules banning bribery and patronage. |
| **1943** | The Smith Connally Act bans unions from contributing to political campaigns during World War II. |
| **1944** | Unions circumvent the Smith Connally Act by forming the first PAC. |

Democratic | Neutral | Undemocratic

*(continued)*

**Approaching Democracy Timeline *(continued)***

| | |
|---|---|
| **1947** | The Taft-Hartley Act makes bans on contributions from unions and corporations permanent. |
| **1968** | The Long Act sets up a system of public financing through a voluntary income tax contribution. |
| **1971** | The Federal Election Campaign Act repeals all earlier campaign finance laws and creates new comprehensive regulations. |
| **1974** | The Federal Election Campaign Act is amended after Watergate to place stricter regulations on campaign contributions. |
| **1976** | In *Buckley* v. *Valeo,* the Supreme Court strikes down parts of the Federal Election Campaign Act for violating free speech protections. |
| **2002** | The Bipartisan Campaign Reform Act (McCain-Feingold) places regulations on previously unlimited "soft money" contributions. |
| **2010** | In *Citizens United* v. *FEC,* the Supreme Court strikes down parts of McCain-Feingold and opens the door to more corporate and union money in elections. |

☐ De mocratic ☐ Neutral ☐ Undemocratic

2004, $3 billion in 2000, $2.2 billion in 1996, and $1.8 billion in 1992.

For the most part, a simple rule holds: If you spend more money than your opponent, you are likely to win the election. Candidates, therefore, spend a good deal of time and effort raising campaign dollars. Still, exceptions to the rule do occur. In the 1998 California gubernatorial primary, millionaire Al Checci spent $40 million of his personal fortune, but it did not buy him his party's nomination. Steve Forbes spent millions of his own funds in 2000, but failed to capture the Republican nomination for president.

Presidential elections are conducted under the guidelines of the Federal Election Campaign Act of 1971. Before this campaign finance law was enacted, candidates could raise as much money as possible, with no limits on the size of individual contributions. Most of the money came from the large contributions of wealthy individuals, corporations, and organized labor. For example, in the 1952 presidential contest, at least two-thirds of all the money raised and spent at the national level came from contributions of $500 or more (equivalent to $4,300 in 2011 dollars). This was the era of the political "fat cats," the wealthy capitalists who, along with rapidly growing labor unions, contributed most of the money and exerted most of the influence during campaigns.

The aftermath of the Watergate scandal led to the most significant election reform in history. The Federal Election Campaign Act of 1971 created the Federal Election Commission (FEC), limited individual contributions, and instituted a new system of public financing through an income tax check-off. The 1974 amendments were immediately challenged, leading to an important judicial ruling. On January 30, 1976, in *Buckley* v. *Valeo,* the Supreme Court struck down the limits an individual can spend on his or her own campaign for political office. The Court ruled that the First Amendment gives each citizen the right to spend his or her money, no matter how much, in any lawful way, as a matter of freedom of speech. In a later ruling, the Court also struck down legal limits on the amount of money an interest group can spend on behalf of a candidate, so long as the group spends its money independently of the candidate's campaign organization. Despite these rulings, however, the fundamentals of the act remained intact.[38] Table 10.2 shows contribution limits for the 2012 election.

## THINKING CRITICALLY

Would you support completely eliminating campaign donations? What if the only way to do this was to institute an entirely publicly funded (with taxpayer money) campaign, where both major parties received the same amount of money from the government? Would a reform like this bring us closer to the democratic ideal?

The Court did back reformers on several crucial issues, however. It upheld contribution limits, disclosure rules, and public financing. Thus, individuals can give only modest amounts of money to campaigns, limiting the political power of the wealthy—in theory. Furthermore, the names of all who give money to any campaign are placed on public record through the disclosure provisions, meaning that under-the-table "buying" of political candidates seems unlikely to occur, given the certainty of publicity. These reforms, along with the public financing of presidential campaigns, led some to assume that American elections are approaching closer to the democratic ideal than in the days when a few wealthy groups and individuals surreptitiously paid for most of the candidates' expenses. However, the system is in crisis because of the ways that the law can be circumvented. The recent Supreme Court ruling in the *Citizens United* v. *Federal Election Commission* case, which

**Table 10.2** Contribution Limits, *2011–2012*

| | To Each Candidate or Candidate Committee per Election | To National Party Committee per Calendar Year | To State, District, and Local Party Committee per Calendar Year | To Any Other Political Committee per Calendar Year[a] | Special Limits |
|---|---|---|---|---|---|
| **Individual may give** | $2,500[b] | $30,800[b] | $10,000 (combined limit) | $5,000 | $117,000[b] overall biennial limit: • $46,200[b] to all candidates • $70,800[b] to all PACs and parties[c] |
| **National party committee may give** | $5,000 | No limit | No limit | $5,000 | $43,100[b] to Senate candidate per campaign[d] |
| **State, district, and local party committee may give** | $5,000 (combined limit) | No limit | No limit | $5,000 | No limit |
| **PAC (multicandidate)[e] may give** | $5,000 | $15,000 | $5,000 (combined limit) | $5,000 | No limit |
| **PAC (not multicandidate) may give** | $2,500[b] | $30,800[b] | $10,000 (combined limit) | $5,000 | No limit |
| **Authorized campaign committee may give** | $2,000[f] | No limit | No limit | $5,000 | No limit |

[a]A contribution earmarked for a candidate through a political committee counts against the original contributor's limit for that candidate. In certain circumstances, the contribution may also count against the contributor's limit to the PAC. 11 CFR 110.6. See also 11 CFR 110.1(h).

[b]These contribution limits are indexed for inflation.

[c]No more than $46,200 of this amount may be contributed to state and local party committees and PACs.

[d]This limit is shared by the national committee and the national Senate campaign committee.

[e]A multicandidate committee is a political committee with more than 50 contributors that has been registered for at least six months and, with the exception of state party committees, has made contributions to five or more candidates for federal office. 11 CFR 100.5(e)(3).

[f]A federal candidate's authorized committee(s) may contribute no more than $2,000 per election to another federal candidate's authorized committee(s). 11 CFR 102.12(c)(2).

*Source:* Federal Election Commission. http://www.fec.gov/pages/brochures/contrib.shtml#Chart#Chart.

we discuss later is this chapter, raised the ire of many who viewed the decision as further increasing the influence of moneyed interests in politics.

## Federal Matching Funds

On the long road to the nomination before the convention, presidential candidates can opt for **federal matching funds.** That is, after the candidates raise a certain amount of money in the required way, they apply for, and are given, a matching sum of money from the federal government. The rules that govern qualifying for these funds are relatively simple. A candidate must raise $100,000 in individual contributions of $250 or less, with at least $5,000 collected in each of 20 states. Once this is accomplished, the federal government will match all individual contributions of $250 or less, dollar for dollar. Individual contributions over the $250 limit are not matched. This stipulation has led candidates to concentrate on raising $250 from as many contributors as possible. The result is an increase in small contributors ("kittens") compared with the large contributors ("fat cats") who had previously dominated campaign financing.

**federal matching funds**
System under which presidential candidates who raise a certain amount of money in the required way may apply for and receive matching federal funds.

In return for federal funds, candidates must accept a total preconvention spending limit plus a percentage limit on fund-raising, as well as spending limits in each state. A state's spending limit is calculated at 16¢ for each resident of voting age, plus an adjustment for inflation. Thus, candidates who accept matching funds must develop careful strategies for where and when to spend.

Not all candidates accept matching funds. In 1996, Steve Forbes refused to accept the limitations on spending and therefore did not request federal funds. In 2000, George W. Bush and Forbes chose not to accept federal matching funds, and in 2004, Bush and John Kerry chose not to accept the funds. But this did not mean that either candidate was free of all financial restrictions. Although legally permitted to spend as much as they wanted of their own money in each state, they were prohibited by federal law from accepting donations higher than the legal limit from individuals and from PACs.

During the 2008 primaries, Barack Obama pledged to accept federal matching funds and urged the future Republican nominee to do the same. After a record-breaking fund-raising effort, however, Obama reversed his decision. McCain later sparked his own campaign finance controversy when he withdrew from the federal matching funds program. The Democratic National Committee accused McCain of illegally removing himself from the program.[39]

Matching funds are cut off if a candidate does not receive 10 percent of the vote in two consecutive primaries. To requalify for funds, a candidate must receive 20 percent of the vote in another primary. The FEC requires 25 days' advance notification that a candidate is not participating in a particular primary. Incumbent presidents who run unopposed in the primaries are allowed to spend the legal limit anyway.

During the general election, candidates from each major political party are eligible for public funds for presidential elections. The money source is a $3.00 income tax check-off to the Treasury's Presidential Campaign Fund.

Host of *The Colbert Report*, Stephen Colbert, speaks to fans outside the Federal Election Commission after the June 30, 2011 decision approving his super- PAC, Americans for a Better Tomorrow, Tomorrow. The comedian established his own super-PAC to highlight the role of moneyed interests in politics.

## Campaign Finance Reform

The 1996 and 2000 election cycles highlighted the need for reform, based in part on efforts by both political parties to take advantage of loopholes in election laws. In 1996, the Democrats raised $123.9 million and the Republicans $38.2 million in soft money contributions. Another distinguishing component of the 1996 election was the role of foreign contributions, particularly those brought in by John Huang, a former Commerce Department official who raised millions of dollars from overseas donors.

State and local party organizations used **soft money** contributions for "party-building" activities. These included party mailings, voter registration work, get-out-the-vote efforts, recruitment of supporters at the grassroots level, issue ads, and so forth. This money is considered "soft" because it did not go directly into a specific candidate's campaign and was unrestricted. Therefore, it did not count toward the legal limits imposed on every presidential candidate who accepts federal matching funds. This provision allowed candidates to evade legal spending limits, because the money, although intended to strengthen state and local parties, ended up (more than coincidentally) helping the party's national ticket as well. The soft money loophole allowed corporations, unions, and wealthy individuals to contribute to political parties as much as they wish.

**soft money**
Campaign contributions directed to advancing the interests of a political party or an issue in general, rather than a specific candidate.

**Issue advocacy,** the process of campaigning to persuade the public to take a position on an issue, has become, like soft money, a mechanism for channeling huge amounts of money into the system. Moreover, these funds need not be disclosed publicly and do not face FEC regulation.

**issue advocacy**
The process of campaigning to persuade the public to take a position on an issue.

Another loophole in the campaign finance law involves **independent expenditures,** funds dispersed independently by a group or person in the name of a cause, presumably not by a candidate. Thus, a group or even an individual can spend unlimited sums of money on advertising and TV time to promote policies favored by a particular candidate. Although these actions help that candidate's chance of success in the political campaign, they are entirely legal so long as the group and the candidate maintain separate organizations. The Supreme Court has ruled that in such cases, there can be no restrictions on individual or interest group spending.

**independent expenditures**
Funds dispersed, as allowed by a loophole in campaign finance law, by a group or person not coordinated by a candidate, in the name of a cause.

In June 2002, the FEC approved a major new campaign finance law known as the McCain-Feingold Act, named for its primary sponsors, Senators John McCain (R–AZ) and Russell Feingold (D–WI). The law completely changed the way political parties spend soft money contributions from companies, labor unions, and donors. McCain-Feingold banned soft money. The bill also placed restrictions on outside groups airing so-called issue ads that promote or criticize a candidate's position on an issue but refrain from explicitly telling viewers to vote for or against that candidate. After vigorous debate in the House and Senate, Congress passed the McCain-Feingold bill. President Bush signed the bill into law in March 2002, and the U.S. Supreme Court upheld the law's major provisions in a December 2003 decision.[40]

During the debate over McCain-Feingold, supporters and opponents alike knew that a ban on soft money would have a significant impact on the campaign finance system. After all, the Democratic and Republican parties raised nearly half a billion dollars in soft money for the 2000 and 2002 elections. Because it could be given in unlimited amounts of $100,000, $250,000, or more, soft money allowed corporations, labor unions, and wealthy individuals to wield tremendous influence over the political process—much more influence than the average voter. Many hoped their contributions would pay off later in the form of a policy decision or a bill endorsement. Supporters of reform say soft money made large contributors indispensable to the political parties and reduced the power of the broader electorate. But donors didn't have to give their money to their party of choice to influence an election. They could spend it themselves—or give it to an interest group to spend—on issue ads.

The McCain-Feingold campaign finance law has produced great debate. Despite its new restrictions, presidential candidates and political parties raised significantly more money in 2004 than in previous years. A loophole in the law allowed groups known as 527 committees to raise hundreds of millions of dollars in soft money. These 527 committees, named after the section of the Tax Code that created them, raised more than $350 million. Table 10.3 shows 527 spending in the 2008 election. According to the IRS, a Section 527 organization is created to receive and disburse funds to influence or attempt to influence the nomination, election, appointment, or defeat of candidates for public office. A Section 527 organization sounds like a PAC, but it is a PAC by another name and with one key difference—a Section 527 organization falls outside the regulator realm of the Federal Election Commission and therefore does not have the same limits as FEC-regulated PACs.[41]

The 2010 *Citizens United* v. *FEC* decision did overturn key provisions of McCain-Feingold and thereby opened the door to even greater influence from interest groups than what had been brought to bear by 527 committees. In a divided 5–4 ruling, the Supreme Court deemed restrictions on broadcasts of electioneering communications by corporations and unions in the days before an election as an unconstitutional restriction on the First Amendment right to free speech. The ruling gave corporations and unions the right to spend unlimited funds on campaigns for or against candidates, thus creating super-PACs. President Obama argued that the ruling "gives the special interests and their lobbyists even more power in Washington—while undermining the influence of the average American."[42] He went on to say that he "could not think of anything more devastating to the public interest" and "this ruling strikes at our democracy itself."[43] John McCain also expressed his extreme disappointment in the ruling. Justice Stevens, who was in the minority opinion on the court, criticized his colleagues who overturned the restrictions by noting that "while American democracy is imperfect, few outside the majority of this Court would have thought its flaws included a dearth of money in politics."[44] As a result of the *Citizens United* decision, super-PACs spent nearly $65 million on campaigning during the 2010 midterm election.[45] This number is expected to grow dramatically in the 2012 presidential election.

Many political observers derided the decision, including comedian Stephen Colbert. Colbert decided to form his own super-PAC, Americans for a Better Tomorrow, Tomorrow, to highlight the way the *Citizens United* decision further opened the door to moneyed influence in politics. Colbert asked his viewers to send in donations so that

**Table 10.3** 527s: Advocacy Group Spending in the *2004–2010* Elections

| Cycle | All 527s[a] Receipts | All 527s[a] Expenses | 527s (Excluding State Candidates & Parties)[a] Receipts | 527s (Excluding State Candidates & Parties)[a] Expenses |
|---|---|---|---|---|
| 2004 | $599,202,632 | $611,723,836 | $434,023,386 | $442,472,913 |
| 2006 | $385,042,463 | $429,451,052 | $166,238,050 | $206,984,117 |
| 2008 | $506,080,805 | $490,301,949 | $250,624,540 | $258,329,971 |
| 2010 | $546,694,452 | $590,179,054 | $203,748,146 | $211,447,697 |

[a]To avoid double-counting, these figures do *not* include fund-raising by Joint Victory Campaign 2004, a joint fund-raising committee of America Coming Together and the Media Fund.

**Top Five Committees Receiving Money**

| Committee | 2008 Receipts |
|---|---|
| Service Employees International Union | $27,432,667 |
| America Votes | $25,959,173 |
| American Solutions Winning the Future | $22,722,547 |
| EMILY's List | $13,659,555 |
| The Fund for America | $12,142,046 |

**Top Five Individuals Giving Money**

| Contributor | 2008 Contributions |
|---|---|
| Fred Eshelman (Wilmington, NC) | $5,469,390 |
| Sheldon & Miriam Adelson (Las Vegas, NV) | $5,000,000 |
| George Soros (New York, NY) | $5,000,000 |
| Steven Bing (Los Angeles, CA) | $4,850,000 |
| Gerard & Lilo Leeds (Great Neck, NY) | $4,787,000 |

*Source:* Center for Responsive Politics, based on data from the Internal Revenue Service, http://www.opensecrets.org/527s/527cmtes.php and http://www.opensecrets.org/527s/527indivs.php. Reprinted with Permission.

"the Colbert nation could have a voice, in the form of [his] voice, shouted through a megaphone of cash."[46] He has used his PAC money to run commercials asking Iowans to write in Republican Rick Perry (but spelled Parry) for the Iowa Straw Poll. He has yet to state what the PAC stands for, but one thing is clear: The Colbert super-PAC offers an interesting illustration of special-interest money gone wild in the world of politics.

## Summary

10.1 *What role does participation play in achieving the democratic ideal?*

- Democracy simply cannot work without mass political involvement or participation.
- Active citizen participation moves the United States closer to the ideal of a democratic political system.
- Through voting and other forms of political participation—campaigning, gathering information, joining groups, writing letters, and protesting—Americans involve themselves in the democratic process.

10.2 *In what ways do Americans participate in the political process?*

- The United States has a representative form of government in which all eligible citizens may participate in electing officeholders to represent their opinions in government.

- Sidney Verba and Norman Nie found that American citizens fall along a continuum of political engagement, ranging from those totally uninvolved in politics to those who make it a full-time occupation.
- Generally speaking, fewer low-income people and minority group members participated at the higher activism levels. Activists have tended to be largely well-educated, middle- and upper-income voters.

10.3 *How has the right to vote expanded over the nation's history?*

- Historically, American politics has been notable for the steady erosion of barriers to democratic participation. Politics in the United States began as an activity reserved for white, property-holding, tax-paying, middle- and upper-class males.
- Property requirements for voting gradually relaxed over the decades, disappearing by the middle of the 19th century, when virtually all white males were enfranchised.
- The Fifteenth Amendment, passed in 1870 as part of the Civil War amendments, guaranteed that "the right of citizens of the United States to vote shall not be denied or abridged by the United States or by any State on account of race, color, or previous condition of servitude."
- After the Civil War, a variety of tactics were used to prevent African Americans from voting. Violence and intimidation, poll taxes, literary tests, and good character tests all kept African Americans from participating in the process. The Voting Rights Act of 1965 provided protection to African Americans who wished to vote, and the Twenty-fourth Amendment (1964) outlawed the poll tax in federal elections.
- After decades of pressuring for suffrage and other legal rights, women finally won the right to vote with passage of the Nineteenth Amendment in 1920. Further expansion of political participation came with ratification of the Twenty-third Amendment in 1961, which gave residents of the District of Columbia the right to vote in presidential elections, and the Twenty-sixth Amendment in 1971, which gave the right to vote to all citizens of the United States 18 years of age or older.

10.4 *Why do some people choose to participate and others do not?*

- Unfortunately, some citizens are barred from participating in the voting process because of mistakes in the registration procedures. Others are deterred from participating because of registration requirements they find difficult to meet. The Motor-Voter Law was designed to encourage voter registration by simplifying the registration process and, thus, it was hoped, increase voter turnout for elections. The law required states to provide registration services through driver's license agencies and public assistance and disability offices and by mail-in registration.
- Even registered voters may fail to participate in elections. People have numerous reasons for failing to vote; one is the possibility that they are satisfied with the way things are going and see no particular need to become involved politically. An individual's characteristics may also influence whether he or she votes. Education and income both increase the chances of participation. Social connections in general also make political participation more likely. Older people are more likely to vote than younger people, and long-time community residents are more likely to vote than newcomers. Similarly, married people are more likely to vote than those who are single.

10.5 *What factors influence a person's vote choice?*

- More than five decades of study of the American electorate have shown one overwhelming influence on voting decisions: party. Other things being equal, voters show up on Election Day and vote for candidates from the party to which they feel most connected.
- Candidate appeal on both personal likability and message can also influence vote choice.
- Voters may also cast their vote based on issue stances, but the structure of the voting situation may make issue voting difficult.

10.6 *How else, outside the act of voting, can an individual participate?*

- Political participation takes many other shapes in the United States, including campaign work, seeking information, protesting, civil disobedience, and even violence. Some Americans volunteer to work for their political party or preferred candidate in election campaigns. Other interested citizens participate by displaying signs or bumper stickers or handing out literature of a favored party or candidate, hoping to induce others to echo such support at the polls. Still others work as party volunteers in voter registration drives. From attending an information meeting to watching television, the simple act of gaining knowledge about public affairs constitutes a form of political activity.
- Other forms of participation may stem from government actions that provoke strong expressions of dissatisfaction. Occasionally, these expressions take the form of organized protests and acts of civil disobedience, either against existing policies or conditions or as a response to actual or threatened change in the status quo.

10.7 *How do Americans participate in congressional elections?*

- The United States Constitution calls for House and Senate elections every two years. Each of the 435 House members is up for reelection every two years, as are one-third of the senators (who serve six-year terms). In midterm elections, with no presidential contest to galvanize press and voter attention, voter turnout usually hovers around one-third of registered voters. In presidential election years, voter turnout, voter interest, and media coverage of the election are much greater. Additionally, the winning presidential candidate often brings in new members of his or her own party to Congress.

10.8 *How are presidential elections conducted?*

- When Americans go to the polls in a presidential election, they are voting for a slate of electors—individuals selected by state party leaders who are expected to cast ballots for their respective state's popular vote winner—and the results of the election are not official until January when the votes are counted and certified. Each state has the number of electors in the electoral college equal to the number of representatives the state has in the House plus two for that state's senators.
- To become president, the winning candidate needs to receive a majority, or 270, of the 538 electoral votes.

The 538 votes consist of one vote for each of the 435 members of the U.S. House of Representatives, plus one vote for each of the 100 senators, plus three votes for the District of Columbia. If no candidate receives the required electoral college majority, a contingency election is held in the House. The House chooses among the top three candidates, with each state casting a single vote.

- Because of the winner-take-all nature of the electoral college, candidates spend all of their time campaigning in battleground states. This means that often the vast majority of citizens receive little of the candidate's campaign efforts.

10.9 *What role does money play in elections?*

- For the most part, a simple rule holds: If you spend more money than your opponent, you are likely to win the election. Candidates, therefore, spend a good deal of time and effort raising campaign dollars.
- The Federal Election Campaign Act of 1971 created the Federal Election Commission, limited individual contributions, and instituted a new system of public financing. On January 30, 1976, in *Buckley* v. *Valeo,* the Supreme Court struck down the limits an individual can spend on his or her own campaign for political office. The Court ruled that the First Amendment gives each citizen the right to spend his or her money, no matter how much, in any lawful way, as a matter of freedom of speech.
- The system today is in crisis because of loopholes involving soft money, independent expenditures, and issue advocacy. The *Citizens United* v. *FEC* ruling created further challenges for those worried about the influence of money in politics.

## Key Terms

civil disobedience, 320
coattails effect, 323
contingency election, 327
deviating election, 329
electoral college, 324
faithless elector, 325
federal matching funds, 331
good-character test, 307
independent expenditures, 332
initiative, 315
issue advocacy, 332
literacy test, 307
maintaining election, 329
midterm elections, 321
participation, 305
party identification, 316
political violence, 321
poll tax, 307
protest, 320
realigning election, 329
referendum, 316
retrospective voting, 318
soft money, 332
split-ticket ballots, 316
straight-party ticket, 316
suffrage, 309
voter turnout, 310

## Test Yourself Chapter 10

**1.** In a nation as large as the United States, the Athenian kind of democracy is
a. absolutely necessary.
b. challenging, but attainable.
c. logistically impossible.
d. helped by the fact that in addition to the large geographic size, there also exists a large population.

**2.** In summarizing the participation levels of the American citizens, one can conclude that
a. very few Americans are active to any degree in politics.
b. close to half of the population is engaged in some form of politically oriented activity.
c. nearly all Americans are active participants in political life.
d. only 10 percent of the population watches political television ads.

**3.** The right of African American males to vote was guaranteed by the
a. Voting Rights Act of 1866.
b. Fifteenth Amendment.
c. Emancipation Proclamation.
d. Eighteenth Amendment.

**4.** All of the following were used by southern states to keep African Americans from voting *except*
a. using intimidation and threats of violence.
b. requiring the payment of a poll tax prior to voting.
c. passing laws that stated that former slaves and children of slaves could not vote.
d. using difficult literacy tests when African Americans sought to register.

**5.** All of the amendments expanded political participation *except* the
a. Eighteenth Amendment.
b. Nineteenth Amendment.
c. Twenty-third Amendment.
d. Twenty-sixth Amendment.

**6.** Registration laws in most states
a. depress election turnout rates.
b. increase election turnout rates.
c. have no effect on election turnout rates.
d. hide true election turnout rates.

**7.** If the California legislature were to ask the voters to approve the sale of state bonds to finance various programs, such as education and prisons, this would be an example of a(n)
a. initiative.
b. referendum.
c. poll.
d. questionnaire.

**8.** People who vote for only one party for all elected offices on the ballot are said to be voting
a. protest votes.
b. split-ticket ballots.
c. straight-party tickets.
d. without consideration for rational alternatives.

**9.** What is the key determinant of vote choice?
a. Income.
b. Race.
c. Party affiliation.
d. Age.

**10.** The powerful form of issue voting where voters look back over the last term to judge how well the incumbent candidate or party has performed is called
a. retrospective voting.
b. two-pronged voting.
c. rational analysis voting.
d. rudimentray voting.

**11.** A means of political participation whereby people nonviolently defy laws deemed unjust is called
a. a boycott.
b. an embargo.
c. civil disobedience.
d. participatory democracy.

**12.** Congressional elections
a. generally receive less national attention than presidential elections.
b. generally receive more national attention than the presidential election.
c. are generally ignored by presidential candidates.
d. are definite predictors regarding the outcome of future presidential elections.

**13.** What is the "coattails effect"?
a. All congressional candidates from one party running as a common partisan ticket.
b. The impact on congressional elections of the popularity or lack of popularity of the president.
c. The impact on elections of celebrity endorsements.
d. The impact on presidential elections of the popularity or lack of popularity of the congressional party.

**14.** Typically, in presidential elections, the winning presidential candidate's party
a. loses seats in Congress.
b. gains seats in Congress.
c. maintains the same number of seats in Congress.
d. appoints the congressional leadership.

**15.** The Constitution indicates that the number of electors who will cast ballots for president and vice president
a. cannot exceed 550.
b. cannot be changed without an amendment.
c. is to be determined by the president every ten years.
d. is equal to the number of representatives and senators a state has in Congress.

**16.** The framers' original idea to have an electoral college was
a. based on the concept of direct democracy.
b. to strengthen the two-party system.
c. to eliminate the need for factions.
d. to have electors use their own discretion in deciding who would make the best president.

**17.** To be officially elected president one must
a. receive a majority of the total electoral college votes.
b. have both the highest popular vote total and win a majority of the total electoral college votes.
c. win a majority in the nation's popular vote.
d. win a plurality of total electoral college votes.

**18.** An election held in the House if no candidate receives the required majority of votes in the electoral college is referred to as a
a. contingency election.
b. disputed election.
c. nonpolitical election.
d. selective election.

**19.** The most favored alternative to the electoral college is
a. independent voting by state legislatures instead of the electoral college.
b. a national convention of electoral delegates.
c. a direct vote to elect the president.
d. a proportional method of selecting electors.

**20.** In *Buckley* v. *Valeo,* the Supreme Court ruled that spending is
a. protected speech.
b. destroying the fabric of democracy.
c. unprotected speech.
d. not a form of speech.

**ANSWERS**
**1.** c, **2.** b, **3.** b, **4.** c, **5.** a, **6.** a, **7.** b, **8.** c, **9.** c, **10.** a, **11.** c, **12.** a, **13.** b, **14.** b, **15.** d, **16.** d, **17.** a, **18.** a, **19.** c, **20.** a

# Interest Groups

# 11

## Chapter Outline

**Introduction:**
*Interest Groups and Democracy*

- Interest Groups: A Tradition in American Politics
- Functions of Interest Groups
- Types of Interest Groups
- Characteristics of Interest Groups
- Interest Group Strategies
- Political Action Committees
- Regulation of Interest Groups
- Assessing the Impact of Interest Groups
- Comparison of Lobbying in the Bush and Obama Presidencies
- Interest Groups and American Democracy in the 21st Century

## Learning Objectives

11

11.1 Do interest groups promote democracy and, if so, how?

11.2 Were interest groups anticipated by the constitutional framers as being a source for increasing democracy in America?

11.3 How have interest groups developed and evolved recently?

11.4 What effect has the Internet had on the development of political lobbying and the growth of interest groups?

11.5 What do interest groups do, and how do they promote democracy?

11.6 What are the different kinds of interest groups, and how do they promote democracy?

11.7 What are the characteristics of an interest group?

11.8 What are the strategies for interest groups to promote their views and policies in a democracy?

11.9 How can interest groups be regulated to promote democracy?

11.10 What impact do interest groups and lobbying have on American democracy?

11.11 How will interest group strategies and lobbying change in the 21st century?

# INTRODUCTION

## INTEREST GROUPS AND DEMOCRACY

11.1 *Do interest groups promote democracy and, if so, how?*

**Interest groups** are formal organizations of people who share a common outlook or social circumstance and who band together in the hope of influencing government policy.[1] Americans often see corporate interest groups as sinister, selfish, high-pressure outfits that use illegitimate means to promote narrow ends at the expense of the public interest. Interest groups as a whole really do not run anything; they struggle against each other for influence over those who do run things. Each group has wins and losses.

In truth, we *all* belong to interest groups, whether we recognize it or not. Many of us are members of churches or synagogues, or perhaps we work in a unionized job. Students in colleges and universities might be surprised to learn that part of their student fees may support lobbying efforts. Even if you do not belong to any such organizations, you may recall signing petitions in the malls or on the streets supporting such causes as environmentalism. In such ways, millions of people can band together and persuade political candidates, and thus governing officials, to make their agenda the new governmental agenda.

American suspicion toward interest groups is especially curious, given the evidence that they are a natural and inevitable presence in free societies. Interest groups are here to stay, and they play a key role in American politics. In fact, interest groups are crucial to democratic society. They provide an easy means for average citizens to participate in the political process, thereby allowing all Americans to approach the democratic ideal. In this chapter we look closely at interest groups to see how they broaden the possibilities for political participation. We also examine why these agents for democratic influence often are accused of distorting and even undermining the democratic system.

## INTEREST GROUPS: A TRADITION IN AMERICAN POLITICS

Foreign and domestic observers have long noted the propensity of Americans to form and join groups. "Americans of all ages, all stations in life, and all types of disposition," wrote Alexis de Tocqueville in 1831, "are forever forming associations."[2] This tendency has been attributed to causes ranging from calls for religious conformity to the need for community cohesion imposed by the rugged conditions of the country's

**interest groups**
Formal organizations of people who share a common outlook or social circumstance and who band together in the hope of influencing government policy.

early history. For whatever reasons, the desire to come together in social groups for common ends has been deeply embedded in American culture.

This value is enshrined politically in the First Amendment's freedom of association clause: "Congress shall make no law . . . abridging . . . the right of the people peaceably to assemble, and to petition the Government for a redress of grievances." These simple words provide the legal framework for all citizen-based political activity in the United States. They ensure the existence of a vast array of interest groups, because government can literally do nothing ("Congress shall make no law") to interfere with people joining together ("peaceably to assemble") to try to influence government policies ("petition the Government for a redress of grievances"). Deeply ingrained in American culture, then, as well as in an entire body of legal precedents, is the norm that citizens may form any kind of group they please to try to influence government, as long as that activity is undertaken "peaceably."

To help Americans in their efforts to influence government, the Constitution also provides, in the same sentence in the First Amendment, the rights of assembly and petition, the right to say what they want (freedom of speech), and to publish what they want (freedom of the press). Americans have not been shy about using these rights. From the earliest days of the republic, they have formed groups of every type and description to defend common interests and obtain favorable government policies. The result has been a complex array of competing and cooperating interests that practically defines modern democracy. If you find a political regime today that does not allow competing interest groups, you will have found a political system that is *not* democratic.

## What Is an Interest Group?

**11.2** *Were interest groups anticipated by the constitutional framers as being a source for increasing democracy in America?*

If interest groups are central to the democratic process, what precisely are they? Interest groups can take a wide variety of forms. One example is a labor union such as the United Auto Workers (UAW), which formed in 1935 to secure improvements in wages and working conditions for automobile factory workers. Another example is the National Rifle Association, a large affiliation of firearms owners who have organized a powerful lobby for the Second Amendment right to "keep and bear Arms." Groups may be large organizations with diffused goals, such as the AARP (formerly the American Association of Retired Persons), with its 35 million members and its broad aim of promoting the interests of the elderly, or small outfits with specific goals, such as the American Women's Society of Certified Public Accountants.

Some political scientists have found it useful to distinguish between actual and potential interest groups. **Actual groups** have already been formed; they have a headquarters, an organizational structure, paid employees, membership lists, and the like. **Potential groups** are interests that could gather under the right circumstances but as yet have no substantive form—and may never have one. Still, political participants cannot discount them. Whenever substantial numbers of people share a common outlook or socioeconomic condition, they might well decide to join together to promote their mutual interests. Politicians who ignore potential groups for long may, in fact, be encouraging their formation.

Strongly held policy preferences are essential for interest group formation. Interest groups provide individuals who hold strong policy preferences with a way to disseminate information to legislators, make their preferences known, and work within the system to influence legislation.

Often it takes little more than one or a few dynamic leaders, called **policy entrepreneurs,** to create the conditions whereby a potential group becomes an actual interest group. Ralph Nader, a Green Party candidate for president in 2000 and an Independent candidate in 2004, is one such policy entrepreneur. Nader's untiring efforts were instrumental in forming consumer-oriented interest groups such as the Public Citizen Litigation Group and the Health Research Group, as well as various

**actual groups**
Interest groups that have already been formed; they have headquarters, an organizational structure, paid employees, membership lists, and the like.

**potential groups**
Interest groups that could form under the right circumstances; as yet, they have no substantive form and may never have one, but they cannot be discounted by political participants.

**policy entrepreneurs**
Leaders who invest in, and who create the conditions for, a potential group to become an actual interest group. Ralph Nader stands as a classic example of a policy entrepreneur.

other public interest research groups (PIRGs) in the 1970s, with a major impact on both national and state legislation. They provide oversight on auto safety, consumer issues, health issues, and the environment. Today, more than 200 such groups claim among their victories nonsmoking rules on airlines, nutrition labels, and laws requiring smoke detectors in apartment buildings.

A classic example of a potential interest group becoming an actual group can be seen in the establishment of Mothers Against Drunk Drivers (MADD). For decades, children had been killed or maimed by intoxicated motorists. The potential existed for the parents of those children to gather and push for stricter laws to prevent and punish drunk driving. Yet no such group appeared until one woman, Candy Lightner, who had lost a child to a drunk driver, decided to form such a group and devote her life to this work.

In a free society, actual groups may form and even become powerful on short notice. United We Stand America, an interest group formed to support Ross Perot's 1992 presidential candidacy, in a few short months went from nonexistence to major-player status in national politics and then became a full-fledged political party. Thus, politicians and observers of politics must always be aware of potential groups "out there" in the public.

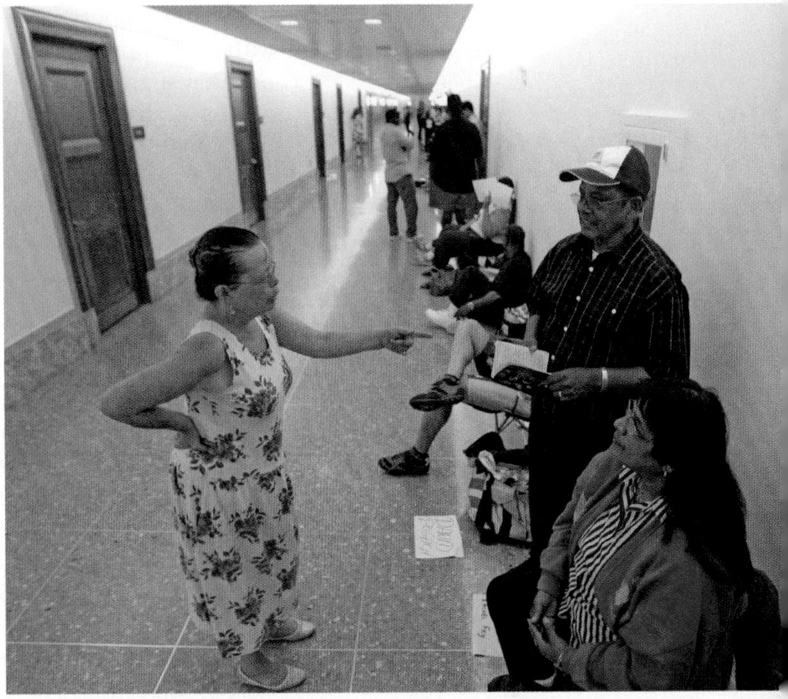

Knowing that being seen by congressional committee members is vitally important to their causes, high-powered lobbyists and Washington lawyers hire people such as these, some of whom make their livings this way, to wait in line to get choice seats in the hearings.

Some groups are more likely to form and to gain political clout than others. In making policy, politicians consider numerous factors without constantly worrying whether an action they decide to take today could cause the formation of a group that will punish them tomorrow. Still, that possibility can never be wholly ignored and must play at least a modest role in the policy-making process.

## A Long History of Association

From the very beginning of the republic, national leaders have wrestled with the idea of interest groups. In *The Federalist,* no. 10 James Madison wrote, "Liberty is to faction what air is to fire."[3] To put it in modern terms, he saw that the development and proliferation of interest groups were inevitable in a free society. But Madison also saw a basic flaw in democratic politics when it came to interests. He worried that one set of interests—a **faction**—whether a majority or a minority of the population, might gain control of the levers of power and rule society for its own aims, to the detriment of the collective good.

Madison worked to control the potential negative effects of factions, while warning against any effort to eliminate factions altogether—an action he knew would undermine American's precious liberties. He reasoned that the power of factions could be moderated by *diffusing* their influence. This diffusion would occur in two ways. First, the very act of joining the individual states into a large and diverse country undercut the power of any one faction. What group could successfully unite the industrial interests of the Northeast and the plantation interests of the South, small independent farmers, indentured servants, urban workers, artisans and merchants, hired hands, and all of the other groups in America at that time? Its size and complexity would guard the new nation against any one faction controlling government.

Madison's second hedge against the triumph of any given faction was to make government complex. By *dividing* political power among several institutions that represented different interests chosen at different times by different elements of the population, he strove to ensure that no one faction could ever gain control of all the key levers of power. As you know, Madison and the other framers were hugely successful at their task. Indeed, a major criticism of the American political system

### QUICK REVIEW

Growth of Interest Groups

- Number of groups trying to pressure government has grown dramatically.
- As government's power to affect society grows, more groups evolve to influence and pressure government.
- Underrepresented groups use interest groups to pursue policy goals.
- Increasing income and education levels increased levels of political activity.

**factions**
According to James Madison in *The Federalist,* no. 10: "A number of citizens, whether amounting to a majority or a minority of the whole, who are united and actuated by some common impulse or passion or . . . interests."

is that the framers were *too* successful. America's national government is so hedged with restrictions on its powers and so open to the input of every imaginable faction or interest group that it can rarely develop a coherent set of national policies.[4]

As Madison saw it, the causes of faction are "sown in the nature of man." Given the human tendency toward disagreement and disharmony, factional differences will always exist. Thus, government can never eliminate the causes of faction; government can only eliminate or suppress faction itself. Madison and the framer's choice to allow diverse factions within a complex system of political and social pluralism ensured that all interests could be heard, but made it difficult for any one interest to gain tyrannical control of power.

From a modern perspective, Madison's view of faction was both wise and prescient. Tens of thousands of interest groups have formed and thrived since the early days of the republic, allowing widespread input into the policy process from millions of average citizens, yet no one group has ever gained full control of all the levers of political and social power. Setting group against group in relatively peaceful competition within a complex system of divided powers seems to have been a successful vision of the way to deal with the fissures and stresses that are inevitable in a free society.

Political parties formed in the early years of the republic, and groups of every type and description began to flourish soon thereafter. Revivalist religious groups, social reform groups, peace groups, women's rights groups, abolitionist groups, temperance groups—these and hundreds of others that sprang up in the first half of the 19th century bore witness to Madison's expectation that the air of liberty would do nothing but nourish a swarm of factional organizations. It is hardly surprising that American political history is, in many ways, a history of diverse and competing interest groups.

The organizational ease with which groups form in the United States is generally attributed to its democratic culture. Americans, who often see themselves as equals, usually find it easy to work together in groups toward common ends. As Tocqueville wrote, "In no other country of the world has the principle of association been more successfully used, or more unsparingly applied to a multitude of different objects, than in America."[5] Although all modern democracies exhibit interest group activity, few have achieved the level of vibrant nongovernmental group life apparent in the American system.

## The Development of Modern Interest Groups

### 11.3 *How have interest groups developed and evolved recently?*

Even though interest groups have been central to American political history, the number of groups trying to pressure government has grown dramatically in the past four decades. The reasons for this development are complex. For one, government policies since the 1960s have produced greater regulation of society. Responding to demands that Washington "do something" about the problems of civil rights, the environment, education, conditions in the workplace, health, women's rights, and so forth, the national government has developed policies that affect all sectors of society. Government regulations now touch all Americans. Naturally, people whose livelihoods and values are affected by government actions find it expedient to work together to influence those actions. Thus, as government's power to affect society grows, so, too, does the number of groups that aim to influence and pressure government.

Another explanation for the growth of interest groups stems from the success liberal interest groups experienced starting in the 1950s. In the past, conservative groups rarely relied on group activity to advance their aims because conservatives were already active in civic affairs, being (on average) wealthier, better educated, and more likely to participate in politics than most citizens. Thus, they were already well represented in government and believed that it adequately responded to their needs. Conversely, those groups most underrepresented in political institutions were most likely to use interest groups to pursue policy goals. These groups tended to promote the liberal aims of civil rights groups, environmentalists, the poor, and women.

By the 1970s, liberal groups had gained many victories by exerting pressure on Congress, the executive branch, and the courts. Moreover, the federal government actually sponsored citizen-group involvement by reimbursing participants with seed money or outright grants. Federal domestic legislation included provisions for citizen participation that spurred group organizations such as environmental action councils, legal defense coalitions, health-care organizations, and senior citizen groups.[6] Manufacturing and business leaders, along with ideological conservatives of every type, responded by forming their own interest groups. These conservative groups developed their own dynamism in reaction to the social policy gains previously made by liberals. As Planned Parenthood, the American Civil Liberties Union, and other liberal groups fought for abortion and privacy rights, political conservatives countered in the late 1970s and 1980s with groups such as Operation Rescue and the Moral Majority.

In 2009, members of the environmental organization Greenpeace scaled Mt. Rushmore to prod President Barack Obama to become more like the combative Civil War President Abraham Lincoln in leading the nation to combat global warming.

The success of liberal interest groups led to the rise of conservative counterpart groups, especially in economic and legal areas. One of the most successful on the economic side was the Club for Growth. Economist and lobbyist Stephen Moore organized nearly three dozen conservative financial advisers to back the Reagan administration's "supply-side" economic policy of lowering income taxes, reducing the size of the national government, and cutting government spending. Since that time, the group has grown to more than 10,000 members. It funnels millions of dollars to economically conservative Republican candidates in the primaries and ads for anti-tax congressional candidates.[7]

The Federalist Society lobbying organization focuses more on legal issues than on raising campaign funds. Founded in 1982 at schools such as Yale Law School and the University of Chicago Law School, the Federalist Society was designed to be an academic think tank and debating society and to provide a forum for conservative ideas and legal philosophies. It was intended to counter a perceived liberal bias in legal education. Now, though, many appointees to the federal judiciary, including Chief Justice John Roberts, and to cabinet and executive branch positions have connections to this group. The group's ability to organize disparate individuals to keep them on the same message shows how an organized lobbying group can work to affect public opinion. For example, the Federalist Society can post a notice on its website and almost immediately engage a group of experts who can provide media commentary on relevant issues, such as court appointments.[8]

A major boost to group involvement in politics came in the early 1970s with campaign finance reform. Two acts, the Federal Election Campaign Act (FECA) of 1971 and its amendments in 1974, changed the nature of money in American politics. These laws and the amendment of the Bipartisan Campaign Reform Act (BCRA) of 2002, more popularly called the McCain-Feingold Act, limited the role of individual "fat cats" and expanded **political action committees (PACs).** Rather than seeking large donations from a small number of wealthy individuals, these groups raised small amounts of money from large numbers of contributors and combined them for maximum effectiveness. This new law banned the use of soft money, or unregulated campaign funds for the good of the party rather than a specific candidate. It also banned the airing of "issue advertisements"—ads that purport to advise voters on general issues but are in reality designed to oppose specific candidates—30 days before the primaries and 60 days before the general elections.

Finally, increasing income and education levels have led to increased levels of political activity in the United States over the past 60 years. The United States now has a large middle class and upper middle class of educated, affluent voters who are vitally aware of the political process and how it affects them. Many of these people have become deeply involved in politics—especially in groups that promote their interests and concerns. No theory seeking to explain the rise in the number and power of American interest groups can fail to take into account this important social development.

**political action committees (PACs)**
Committees formed as the fund-raising and financial distribution arm of specific interest groups.

## The Rise of the American Tea Party and Occupy Wall Street and the Nature of 21st-Century Grassroots Lobbying

11.4 *What effect has the Internet had on the development of political lobbying and the growth of interest groups?*

With cheap access to a wide platform on the Internet, interest groups can quickly form simply by creating a website, starting a blog, or using social networking applications. In 2004, presidential candidates made early campaign waves by organizing supporters via the Web. The Internet has real political application in helping interest groups to form what one cyber-expert, Howard Rheingold, calls "smart mobs," as groups of people can connect in real time from different locations.[9] A vivid demonstration of the power of cyber-lobbying came in 2009 in the form of 300 Tea party protests. The movement began after the Obama administration proposed as one of its economic plans to bail out the economy and recover from the Great Recession a plan to help all the homeowners whose mortgage terms were so onorous that they were "underwater." In other words, the homeowners' houses were worth less than their mortgages, meaning that they would soon be bankrupt and would lose their homes. An economic reporter for CNBC named Rick Santelli said in somewhat of a rant on the air in response from the Chicago Mercantile Exchange that this would "subsidize losers' mortgages" and that if the plan went forward there would be a "Chicago Tea Party in July."

These protests, taking on the symbolism of the American Revolution, with tea bags being sent to members of Congress in protest, occurred around the country and were organized on the Internet and fueled by the commentators on Fox News as well as reports on CNBC. Thousands of people attended protest meetings beginning in Seattle in February 2009, and, referencing the Boston Tea Party (with Tea standing for "taxed enough already?"), protestors objected to the increases in taxes and the use of that money for the series of Bush and Obama administration government bailouts of banks, financial institutions, and automobile manufacturers.[10] There was no single theme to the protests, but a general theme against the Obama administration and large government, grassroots protests continued to spring up around the country. The message coalesced around cutting federal spending and reducing the size of the federal government, cutting taxes, and supporting the Tenth Amendment and the power of states over the federal government in making policy. With so many groups distributing their ideas on the Internet, without any regulation, the multiplicity of views has become what Justice Oliver Wendell Holmes called "the free marketplace of ideas" promoting democracy.

In 2010, with many predicting that the movement would simply disappear or be co-opted by the major parties, citizen legislators stood for election as third-party candidates for Congress in nearly 100 districts, and some candidates ran for the United States Senate. The movement was remarkably successful. Senatorial candidates identified as Tea Party members included, for example, Rand Paul (the son of libertarian Congressman Ron Paul, whose failed presidential campaigns are credited as being one of the foundations of the Tea Party movement) in Kentucky, Marco Rubio in Florida, and Mike Lee (the son of former Reagan administration solicitor general Rex Lee) in Utah. Together with some economic conservatives whose views were the same as the movement but did not label themselves as such (e.g., Pat Toomey of Pennsylvania), all won their elections. While in the Senate, they united with the group's informal leader, Jim DeMint of South Carolina, to give them at least a half-dozen members of the Senate and push the Republican Party caucus led by Mitch McConnell much further to the conservative

The grassroots-organized, conservative, and libertarian Tea Party, evoking memories of the Boston Tea Party protesting the Obama administration's trillion-dollar anti-recession spending in mid-2009, has become a third-party movement seeking to continue to take over the Republican Party in the 2012 elections.

side. In the congressional elections, roughly 60 Tea Party members were elected, with perhaps as many as two dozen more Republican members who vote with that group but who do not not publicly identify themselves as full members of the group. On economic issues such as spending cuts, tax cuts, and raising the debt ceiling, this group had so many votes that it prevented the Republican Speaker from successfully negotiating and compromising with the Democrats on these issues.

As the Republican presidential nomination campaign proceeded, one could see how much this movement had begun to capture the party. Of the eight candidates in the race, at least four of them (Representative Michele Bachman, Texas governor Rick Perry, businessman Herman Cain, and former senator Rick Santorum) could be called Tea Party advocates, with libertarian Ron Paul certainly a friendly ideological ally. Only one mainstream Republican Establishment candidate remained in former Massachusetts governor Mitt Romney. The question in 2012 will be whether the insurgent Tea Party captures the nomination, or whether it goes to the one mainstream candidate.

Meanwhile, in the fall of 2011, the Democratic Party, which had seen the liberal Progressive wing of its party fail to coalesce on a message and force President Obama to move his centrist, and at time even conservative, agenda more to the left, was superseded by a new grassroots movement called Occupy Wall Street. Like the Tea Party, this group had no single message as a few dozen protestors, many of them young, camped out for weeks in a "tent city" in a New York City park across from Wall Street. Calling themselves The 99 Percent, these were unemployed, middle-class and poor people who protested against "corporate greed," and argued that the economic and political policies had benefited the upper 1 percent of the nation's economic structure, bailing out Wall Street , the banks, and the elite financial institutions, and left the rest of the nation to pay for these programs through higher taxes. These protests involved people dressed as zombies, carrying signs like "I Eat Bankers," and with money in their mouths, imploring the government to change its policies. Meanwhile, photos were published of Wall Street traders watching the protestors from balconies sipping champagne in a sort of Marie Antoinette "Let them Eat Cake!" moment, and traders in Chicago put a sign in their window reading "We Are the One Percent." When multibillionaire Warren Buffett had proposed a surtax on the mega-rich, Fox News complained that this was "class warfare" against millionaires who were "job creators." But this kind of symbolic class warfare in the protests—aided by social media such as email, YouTube, Facebook, and Twitter—now gained hold as Occupy Wall Street protestors were joined by several sympathetic unions, and similar protests and marches sprung up in cities across the nation.

Unlike the Republicans, who seemed to ignore the Tea Party protestors, President Obama, who had been having trouble shaping his message to reach the liberal wing of his party, recognized that this might well be the Tea Party for the Democrats. With his $447 billion job-creation bill then languishing in the Congress because the Republicans and some Democrats were unwilling to even bring it to a vote, Obama began to speak about these protestors and recraft his message along these progressive, economic lines. It remains to be seen whether this movement will continue, will change itself more into a party movement, and will begin to field grassroots citizen candidates for office in the upcoming congressional elections. With roughly 9 percent of the people unemployed in the fall of 2011, and at least that many underemployed or not being counted, millions facing losing their homes due to job loss or "underwater mortgages" and a stagnant economy, it would be a message that would be well received in many quarters.

## FUNCTIONS OF INTEREST GROUPS

11.5 *What do interest groups do, and how do they promote democracy?*

Interest groups help people band together to influence public policy and are, therefore, central to democracy. They also provide policy makers with information; indeed, members of Congress have come to depend on expertise and information provided by interest groups as part of their deliberative process.

**collective action**
The political action of individuals who unite to influence policy.

**netizens**
Groups of people joined in a cyber-society for political purposes.

## Interest Groups Allow for Collective Action

People form and join interest groups because **collective action** (the action of many) is stronger, more credible, and more likely to influence policy outcomes than the isolated actions of individuals.[11] Imagine, for example, the modest influence you would have if you alone wrote a letter to your congressional representative to protest a new law. You would probably receive a form letter from a staff member expressing concern about the issue, to be followed later by another letter asking for a campaign donation. Your individual letter would not change policy. But what if you joined a group and several thousand of you write and complain about this law? Collective action of that sort is taken more seriously than the actions of one or a few individuals.

Effective collective actions include the protests of the early 1970s, when tens of thousands of students temporarily shut down many colleges across the nation as part of their protest against the Vietnam War, and the 1960s civil disobedience of thousands of African Americans that helped change our civil rights policies. Collective actions include groups of people demonstrating at environmental sites, such as Thoreau's Walden Pond in Massachusetts or the giant redwood forest in northern California, or collecting money to buy threatened land areas, such as the Civil War and Revolutionary War battlefields, to save them from development. A new form of collective action has emerged with Internet use. In January, 2012, Wikipedia and other websites went dark as a protest against two proposed anti-intellectual property piracy laws they said would lead to internet censorship. Increasing numbers of **netizen** organizations—groups of people joined in a cyber-society for political purposes—are uniting individual Internet lobbying actions. This form of collective action lobbied successfully to eliminate portions of the Communications Decency Act of 1996 and expose practices such as unethical spamming and the existence of unknown surveillance cameras.[12] See the Compared to What? feature for a look at the cyber-revolution in Iran.

Group action allows citizens to promote their specialized concerns. In representing specific points of view, interest groups can project precise citizen demands into politics, bringing both government and political parties closer to the people and democratizing the national agenda. Interest group activity enfolded the perspectives of the abolitionist movement, which sought to end slavery, into the political outlook of the pre–Civil War Republican Party. In similar fashion, post–New Deal Democrats absorbed the perspective of the 20th-century civil rights movement.

### THINKING CRITICALLY

How will the Internet increase or diminish the number and type of interest groups, and how might it change their operation? Which websites on the Internet, or new technological devices, will be most useful in 21st-century lobbying?

## Interest Groups Provide Information

Interest groups possess the expertise to provide relevant information about policy goals to party leaders, public officials, and bureaucrats. This function allows interest group members an important avenue for broader participation in the actual policy-making process.

Interest groups also provide government officials with a constant, reliable source of information about popular sentiment, albeit the information is always slanted toward a group's chosen outcome. The information may be technical in nature, educating public officials about the details of a topic, or perhaps political in nature, educating public officials about potential consequences of voting one way or another. Thus, interest groups serve as vital transmitters of the system's responsiveness to citizen demands. The more public officials hear the varied voices of the people, the more likely they are to take those voices into account in formulating government policies.

Although interest groups are an important element in American democratic life, many observers fear that their effects are not all positive. Because

### THINKING CRITICALLY

Given the past successes of student and young people's protests, and the younger generation's knowledge of cyber-communication devices, and the disparate effect that the Great Recession has had on the employment opportunities of those under the age of 30, how will student lobbying and actions affect America's approach to democracy in the 21st century? What issues might lead to such protests?

# Compared to WHAT?

## Iran's Cyber-Revolution

How do you organize an interest group in a closed society? What do you do if you are not allowed to organize and protest against the government? In 2009, when the Iranian presidential election was said to be won by incumbent President Mahmoud Ahmadinejad—even though millions more votes were counted than there were people in the voting electorate in the country—the followers of his rival, Mir-Hossein Mousavi, quickly organized. The young people of Iran (where 50 percent of the population is under age 25) protested the election using a combination of both timelessly old and thoroughly modern techniques. Many of the protestors took to the streets, with dozens being killed and hundreds being arrested. Many others, following the tradition of 1970s protests against the Shah, stood on their rooftops at night shouting, "Allah is good," and epithets against the president, so as not to be caught. But the most interesting turn came in the way that protestors organized their rallies with no access to the press or television. Using cell phone text messages and Twitter, they organized protests and demonstrations quickly. Well aware that the events would not be covered by the government-sponsored television stations and websites, they used their cell phones and black-market digital cameras to film the protests and the violent government reactions to them (which included beatings and arrests) and uploaded these images to the British Broadcasting Corporation (BBC) website, from which they could be beamed worldwide. In the end, the protest was not successful, and Ahmadinejad remained in office. But as the democratic revolution of the "Arab Spring" in early 2011 has shown, technology such as video transmissions from cell phones and Twitter are making it harder for closed societies to control their people.

interest groups focus only on their own cause, some believe they downplay or ignore the public good, and their proliferation of competing demands and divisive rhetoric may drown out moderate voices of compromise and cooperation. Their information can be biased, leaving officials and the public with just one perspective on an issue. Furthermore, interest groups are not all equal. The powerful groups tend to be those already in control of the major resources in society, especially money and property. Large corporations tend to dominate the sphere of interest group activity, and their activities often overwhelm groups trying to promote consumer safety, worker's welfare, and environmental protection.[13]

Interest groups thus represent a peculiar irony of democracy. While stimulating citizen action and political involvement, they can also create confrontation instead of cooperation, diatribe in place of reasoned debate. Although they allow average citizens a role in promoting their democratic goals, interest groups can also skew the political process to favor the already powerful and well off. The "factions" that so concerned Madison are now powerful, well-financed organizations. Figure 11.1 demonstrates how the amount of lobbying spending has grown dramatically over the years.

Can a modern democratic system preserve liberty—allowing groups free rein to promote their goals—without sacrificing the very essence of the democratic ideal, which is widespread access to power for all citizens? That is one of the central questions that American society continually confronts as it struggles to approach democracy.

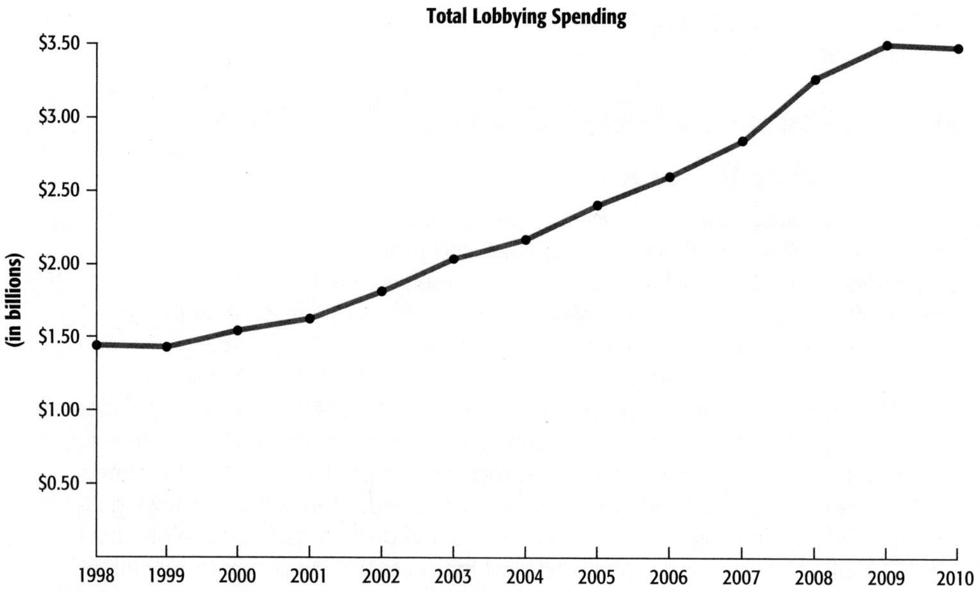


**FIGURE 11.1** The Growth in Lobbying Spending, 1998–2010

Over a 12-year period, from 1998 to 2010, the amount of lobbying spending has more than doubled.

*Source:* Based on data from Center for Responsive Politics, www.OpenSecrets.org.

# TYPES OF INTEREST GROUPS

11.6 *What are the different kinds of interest groups, and how do they promote democracy?*

Nearly 20,000 organized groups of every imaginable kind regularly seek to influence American governmental policies. These groups take a wide variety of forms, but, for simplicity, we can divide them into a few major types: economic, public, government, ideological, religious, civil rights, and single-issue interest groups.

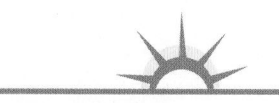

**QUICK REVIEW**

Economic Interest Groups

- Goal is to help their members make or keep money.
- Some represent single businesses or groups of businesses as trade associations.
- Some organizations, like the AFL-CIO, represent workers.

## Economic Interest Groups

The old saying "Most people vote their pocketbooks" applies to group activity as well. Most people take political action to protect or enhance their economic well-being. Thus, groups that aim to help their members make money or keep money will always play a central role in the political process of any democracy. Economic interest groups include business, organized labor, and similar groups.

**Business** Corporations have long dominated interest group activity in American politics. That pattern is hardly surprising in an environment of entrepreneurial capitalism. Calvin Coolidge made the point concisely: "The business of America is business." The U.S. political process almost seems designed to illustrate Coolidge's observation. More than half the lobbies operating in Washington today represent corporate and industrial interests.[14] Sometimes those groups represent single businesses, but other times groups of businesses unite in trade associations that lobby on a much broader range of issues. Trade associations give individual business members additional clout from other allied companies and also increase access to the political system at both federal and state levels.

Heading the list of business-oriented trade associations is the U.S. Chamber of Commerce, which represents 225,000 businesses across the nation, including manufacturers, retailers, construction firms, and financial, insurance, and real estate companies. With an annual budget of more than $65 million and a full-time staff of 1,400, the Chamber of Commerce carries considerable political clout. Other major business interest groups in this category include the National Association of Manufacturers

(NAM) and the Business Roundtable. These groups led the fight against President Clinton's health-care reforms in the mid-1990s, but in 2009, many switched their stance to support President Obama's push for health-care reform. In addition to group memberships, many large and medium-sized companies, about 500 in Washington alone (including IBM, Ford, General Motors, Exxon, and Xerox) maintain their own lobbyists to ensure that their voices are heard.

**Organized Labor** Despite its power, business is not the only voice of organized economic interest. From the late 19th century until the middle of the 20th, labor played a major role in American politics. Indeed, the influential economist John Kenneth Galbraith once called labor unions an important "countervailing power" that could stand up to and dilute the power of business.[15] But their power has declined in recent years. Unionized workers once represented nearly 36 percent of the workforce; now they account for less than 15 percent of it. Still, the American Federation of Labor–Congress of Industrial Organizations (AFL-CIO), labor's umbrella organization, continues to represent millions of workers and put intense pressure on politicians for better wages, improved working conditions, job protection, social programs, and health insurance. Other major labor groups include the United Auto Workers (UAW), the United Mine Workers, and the Teamsters (a union representing workers in the transportation industry).

Although business and labor often appear at odds, they occasionally join forces. For instance, when the government loaned billions of dollars to General Motors in 2009 in an effort to save it, the UAW was an ardent backer of the loan program, hoping to preserve tens of thousands of jobs for its workers.

Recently, though, the news for labor unions has not been so good. Less than 10 percent of private industry workers belong to the labor union movement. The Service Employees International Union's (SEIU) early decision to back Barack Obama's presidential primary candidacy in 2008 was done hoping to increase the impact of labor on the direction of political policy and elections.[16]

**Other Economic Interest Groups** Practically every group of people who make their living in the United States has some kind of interest group to protect and promote its interests. Beyond workers and businesspeople, groups exist to advance the interests of lawyers (the American Bar Association), doctors (the American Medical Association), teachers (the National Education Association), and so forth.

Farmers were once among the most powerful groups in the United States and are still solidly represented by such organizations as the American Farm Bureau Federation, the National Corn Growers Association, and the National Farmers Union. The power of agricultural interests has inevitably diminished as the number of farmers has steadily declined, mirroring a pattern in all industrial nations. People who make more than half their income through farming now represent less than 2 percent of the U.S. workforce. Still, given the importance of this segment of the population, which provides food for Americans and many others around the world, it is safe to say that farm groups will continue to wield major political power for some time to come. In mid-2002, for example, members of the Black Farmers and Agriculturist Association protested in hopes of receiving the $50,000 payments promised them by a successful $2 billion 1999 class-action suit as remedy for allegations that the U.S. Department of Agriculture had been racially biased in awarding agricultural grants. Despite their efforts, though, years later, tens of thousands of claimants still sought their payments, leading to further complaints that the Agriculture Department was fighting payment of the claims.[17]

## Public Interest Groups

Economic self-interest, though a powerful force, represents just one reason people come together in groups to secure collective action from government. One of the most interesting developments in American government since the 1960s is the dramatic increase in **public interest groups.** These groups represent the interests of average

**public interest groups**
Groups that focus not on the immediate economic livelihood of their members, but on achieving a broad set of goals that represent their members' vision of the collective good. Examples include the National Taxpayers Union, the League of Women Voters, and Common Cause.

## THINKING CRITICALLY

Interest groups give citizens' concerns a stronger voice. Is this better accomplished if various groups band together in a new, more unified, multi-issue approach to democracy? And, during an election year, would we be better off to approach democracy by offering public funding to candidates who bypass those interest groups?

citizens as consumers, as holders of individual rights, as proponents of various causes, and as the disadvantaged. Public interest groups focus not on members' immediate economic livelihood, but on achieving a broad set of goals that represent their members' vision of the collective good. Their members and leaders seek substantive policy goals ("clean air"), not specific increments of economic well-being ("twenty cents more an hour for minimum wage workers").

Some of the best-known public interest groups include Citizens for Tax Justice, the Nature Conservancy, the Natural Resources Defense Council, the National Taxpayers Union, the National Organization for Women, the League of Women Voters, and Common Cause. Pursuing policy favorable to all citizens, public interest groups recruit widely and welcome the support of the general public.

One of the best-known public interest groups is Common Cause, which promotes campaign reform, abolition of PACs, and elimination of unneeded bureaucratic institutions and, in other ways, aims to achieve "good government." Common Cause has more than 250,000 members and an $11 million annual budget. Its central target has been the abuse of money in the political process.[18] Common Cause has been especially outraged by the cozy relationship between interest group contributions and political influence. It points, for instance, to the fact that the National Rifle Association can contribute money to members of the Senate Judiciary Committee, which has the job of reviewing firearms legislation, and that the American Medical Association and American Dental Association can contribute millions to members of Congress who serve on committees that consider regulations and health-care reform legislation for these professions. Emphasizing that PAC expenditures on congressional races are at an all-time high, Common Cause sought to organize People versus PACs, a campaign designed to clean up the financing of congressional elections. Common Cause's long-time efforts to reduce or eliminate the influence of money in politics eventually led to the passage of the Bipartisan Campaign Finance Reform Act of 2002.

### Government Interest Groups

One addition to the interest group mix has been government itself. Today, the National Conference of Mayors, the National League of Cities, the National Governors' Association, and other organizations composed of government officials compete alongside traditional interest groups for funding, policies, and attention.

Although questions have been raised about whether government interest groups should compete for scarce resources, these groups are well funded, influential, and easily able to gain access to the halls of Congress. Their right to act as interest groups was affirmed in an important 1985 Supreme Court case, *Garcia* v. *San Antonio Metropolitan Transit Authority*. The opinion's author, Justice Harry Blackmun, refused to grant states authority to set their own compensation rates for municipal employees. States, he said, like private employers, must abide by the regulations governing wages established in the federal Fair Labor Standards Act. Blackmun argued that states were inherently well represented in Congress—through automatic representation in the Senate and secondary representation in the House—and were responsible for petitioning Congress to make laws in accordance with their wishes.[19]

Immediately following the *Garcia* decision, several government interest groups successfully lobbied Congress to grant exemptions from the Fair Labor Standards Act to public employees. Government agencies and officials are under no constitutional restraints when it comes to forming their own interest groups to place pressure on other agencies and officials of the government, thereby strengthening the concept of federalism.

### Ideological Interest Groups

Some people enter politics to promote deep-seated ideological beliefs, seeking nothing less than to transform society and the political process along the lines of some broad philosophical perspective. Such people form ideological interest groups. The best known is Americans for Democratic Action (ADA). Founded in 1947 by Hubert Humphrey, John Kenneth Galbraith, and Eleanor Roosevelt to oppose the more centrist policies of President Harry Truman, ADA has been pushing ever since for an entire set of policy proposals that would create a coherently liberal society. A few years after the ADA's advent, a group known as the American Conservative Union (ACU) sprang up to counter ADA efforts and promote a conservative agenda. Other ideologically oriented groups include the American Civil Liberties Union (ACLU) on civil liberties issues, People for the American Way (liberal) on legal issues, and the Concord Coalition (conservative) on tax and budget issues.

In keeping with American culture's tendency toward pragmatism, ideological interest groups have always been few and consist primarily of small numbers of dedicated activists. Still, because these activists are energetic, well educated, well connected, and adept at raising money, ideological interest groups frequently wield relatively strong clout. A prominent example of this clout came in 2009 when a group of liberal interest groups, including the People for the American Way and the National Association for the Advancement of Colored People, united to promote Sonia Sotomayor's 2009 nomination to the Supreme Court.

Cindy Sheehan, who lost her son in the Iraq War, protested by herself for weeks outside President George W. Bush's ranch in Crawford, Texas, in an unsuccessful effort to obtain a meeting with the president. Despite this failure, her effort energized a national anti-war protest.

## Religious Interest Groups

A variant of the ideological interest group is the group that wishes to transform society along the lines of its religious beliefs. As you would expect in a society where most people take religion seriously, groups seeking to bring religious values into the political arena have, at one time or another, had powerful effects on American politics. Perhaps the most famous example of religion's impact was the Prohibition movement, which in the late 19th and early 20th centuries sought to ban the sale and consumption of alcohol. Church and religious groups throughout the nation drove the movement. Among the more powerful religious groups today are the Christian Coalition, the Catholic Alliance, the National Council of Churches (mainstream Protestantism), B'nai B'rith's Anti-Defamation League (Judaism), and the Council of Catholic Bishops. These religious organizations' influence on politics has grown to the point that many believe that they tipped the balance of the 2004 presidential and 2006 congressional elections, as discussed at the end of this chapter.

Sometimes these groups oppose each other, but when they unite on questions of freedom of religion, as they did in seeking to overturn a Supreme Court decision to create the Religious Freedom Restoration Act (RFRA) and to secure government vouchers for students to attend religious schools, they can be particularly effective with governing officials (see Chapter 13).

## Civil Rights Interest Groups

Civil rights interest groups, similar to ideological interest groups, seek to promote the legal rights of minorities and others who have suffered discrimination. They focus on creating an egalitarian society in which their members have equal opportunities for advancement and can move in mainstream society without denigration. One of the best known of these groups is the National Association for the Advancement of Colored People (NAACP), which for decades was the driving force behind the black civil rights movement. Other well-known groups of this sort include the

National Organization for Women (NOW), the American Indian Movement (AIM), the Mexican-American Legal Defense and Educational Fund (MALDEF), and various organizations that protect and seek to advance the rights of gay Americans.[20]

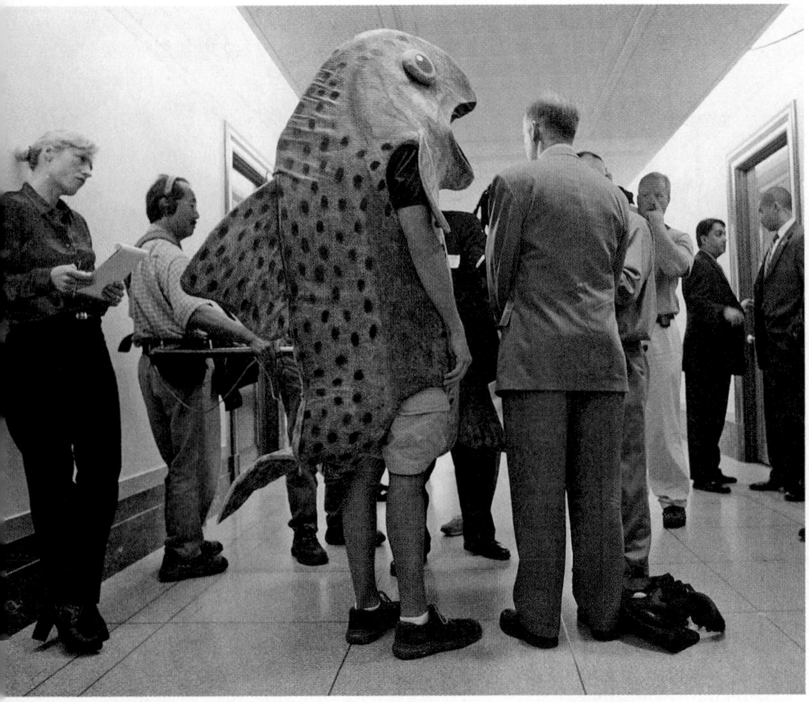

Protestors sometimes go to extraordinary lengths to gain the attention of Congress, such as this unsuccessful environmental protest against the confirmation of Utah governor Michael O. Leavitt as head of the Environmental Protection Agency.

### Single-Issue Interest Groups

As the name implies, single-issue interest groups represent citizens primarily concerned with one particular policy or social problem. Their members often enter political activity to pursue one issue so important in their value scheme that all other issues seem insignificant by comparison. Hence, group members are both intense and uncompromising in promoting their aims.

Groups of this type currently powerful in American politics include the National Rifle Association (NRA), the National Coalition to Ban Handguns, the National Right to Life Committee, and NARAL, now known as NARAL ProChoice America. Sometimes the single issue that inspires an interest group can expand to encompass a series of related issues, all with a single goal. Such is the case with the Sierra Club and the Environmental Defense Fund (EDF), both of which fight for environmental preservation. The multi-million-member Sierra Club began in the early 1970s in response to the threat of Walt Disney Corporation to create a ski resort on the edge of the Sequoia National Forest in California. The group won this fight and has since saved countless other areas.

Given their uncompromising beliefs, single-issue activists present a prickly problem for politicians, whose usual job consists of balancing competing demands and reaching judicious compromise solutions. Single-issue groups do not look kindly on compromise. Their supporters often have a polarized view of the world: If you're not with them, you're against them—an enemy to be crushed and defeated. Inevitably, single-issue groups raise political temperatures and exacerbate conflict whenever they engage in politics. Many politicians shudder at the prospect of having to deal with them.

## CHARACTERISTICS OF INTEREST GROUPS

11.7 *What are the characteristics of an interest group?*

Although each interest group is unique, most share characteristics that distinguish them from other organizations in society. For instance, interest groups, unlike political parties, rarely try to elect their leaders to political positions, but they do target elected officials unsympathetic to their interests and support those who are sympathetic. Interest groups want to influence government—not *be* government—and they seek a government of policy makers who support their goals.

In addition, interest groups do not usually focus on business, trade, or making money. They may promote business interests, and they may incidentally make money (often through the sale of books, maps, insurance policies, or other items for members), but profit is not their main focus. Interest groups are quintessentially government-influencing institutions. Their goal of pressuring government decision makers sets them apart from the other major structures of American society: government itself, political parties, business enterprises, and run-of-the-mill social groups that do not undertake political activities (such as the Lions or Masons).

**QUICK REVIEW**

Characteristics of Interest Groups

- Interest groups rarely try to elect their leaders to political positions.
- They seek policy makers who support their goals.
- The goal of interest groups is to pressure government decision makers.

## Interest Group Membership

Interest groups need members to survive and prosper, and in a democratic society, the more members a group has, the more political clout it will wield. Scholars have long sought to learn why some interest groups outpace others in attracting members. Closely related to that question is another: Why do some groups form and prosper while others never start, or if they do, falter and disappear?

**Maintaining Interest Group Membership** An interest group forms when citizens, be they few or many, believe the political arena is failing to provide their preferred policy outcomes or when citizens feel adversely affected by technological change or by government policies. Many other factors influence the development of a particular interest group: the presence of strong, dynamic leaders; the group's financial and educational resources; and its geographic concentration (it is easier to unite workers in one large factory than people who clean individual homes across a large city). Many factors help determine the likelihood that a group will become cognizant of itself and band together in a formal organization to promote a common interest.

No one is obliged to become an interest group member. As with all life choices, people must choose to spend the time, money, and effort to join. And no one is obliged to remain a group member, as the ACLU learned when nearly half its members resigned over the group's decision to support the free speech rights of the American Nazi party. Some groups that share common economic interests and goals, such as businesses, unions, and trade associations, avoid problems of organizing and maintaining memberships because they speak for people who are already in their group. Groups that represent interests external to their members, such as rainforest protection rather than worker safety, must devote a major portion of their time to **group maintenance;** that is, they must constantly canvass for new members and provide benefits—both psychological and material—for current members to their specific issue. For example, the group Habitat for Humanity, which builds affordable housing for homeless people, launched a new fund-raising campaign after Hurricane Katrina in 2005 by sending attractive house ornaments for Christmas trees to their top donors, hoping for additional house-building donations.

Although the interest group originally forms to advance favorable policies, policy efforts soon become just one part of the equation when the group considers how best to use its resources. The Sierra Club devotes a good deal of time, money, and energy to pleasing current members and recruiting new ones; the club organizes singles vacations to scenic areas and family package cruises, and it offers discounts of many types for purchases of environmentally conscious products and subscriptions to its magazine. The same is true of AARP, which represents senior Americans on a wide variety of legislative issues. Only by offering benefits such as discount cards, insurance policies, and trips has that group been able to build its organization into a powerful legislative force. Finally, some groups represent interests of individuals whether the individuals are members or not. The American Association of University Professors (AAUP), for instance, monitors a wide range of educational issues to the benefit of all academics, even though some professors are not formal dues-paying members.

**The Free Rider** The need to keep current and potential group members happy stems from an issue known as the *free rider.* Mancur Olson Jr., a leading social theorist, has identified and described this issue.[21] To achieve a collective good, groups call on their members for resources, time, expertise, and participation. But if everyone benefits anyway, why should people feel the need to put in any time or money? Members who do not invest but still share in the collective benefits of group action are known as **free riders.** Some union members, for instance, may reason that they need not go to interminable union meetings because they will end up with the same pay hikes and improved working conditions as members who do attend. The problem, of course, is that if everyone in the union thinks that way, management will realize that the union is ineffectual and will reduce, not increase, employee benefits. Too many free riders

**group maintenance**
Activities by an interest group designed to affect policy. Includes enrolling new members and providing benefits for them.

**free riders**
Members who invest no money or time in an interest group but still share in the collective benefits of group action.

may cause all members of a group to suffer, undermining the group's very reason for being. Why join the club if you're guaranteed the benefits of its work anyway?

However, the free-rider theory may be exaggerated. It rests heavily on the argument that most people join groups for material gain. In fact, people undertake voluntary group activity for many reasons, and few calculate the economic benefits before deciding if joining is "worth it." Feelings of moral obligation drive many Americans to contribute to a cause or join a group. And when people strongly commit themselves to political action, most likely the rewards they gain are psychological rather than material. Thus, dedicated activists may have a variety of psychological incentives, including desires to make social contacts or advance political career chances, opportunity to participate in a fascinating game (politics), and the urge to help improve the quality of government. Most groups, then, can gain both supporters and active members without necessarily offering them a material reward for their participation.[22]

### Other Characteristics of Interest Groups

Interest groups differ from each other in many ways. These differences help explain why groups succeed or fail, use or reject a grassroots strategy, or choose to operate at the state rather than the national level. One key difference centers on *resources*. Naturally, groups with money, connections, social prestige, and access to political elites have great advantages in the struggle to influence government. On the other hand, zeal and numbers can go a long way toward overcoming financial deficiencies. Any group that can inspire large numbers of people to write letters, call political leaders, and march in the street can have a serious impact on the policy-making process.

Group *cohesion* is important. A neighborhood association trying to block construction of a nearby prison will have a greater chance of success than a broad potential group of people who have recently lost jobs due to American free-trade policies. The *level of government* at which a group needs to exert pressure is also crucial. Results may come easier at the local level than at the national level. Group *leadership skill* often affects outcomes. Naturally, the more forceful and persuasive the group leader, the more successfully that person can advance the group's cause and keep it in the public eye. Whether a skilled, dynamic leader will emerge for any given group is, of course, subject to circumstance. One wonders, for instance, if the American civil rights movement could have been as successful without Martin Luther King Jr.

These days, interest group organizations and medical research endeavors often try to attract attention by using movie stars as spokespeople in their advertising campaigns and congressional testimonies. After President George W. Bush banned the use of federal funds for stem-cell research, actors Michael J. Fox, who suffers from Parkinson's disease, and the late Christopher Reeve supported a successful 2004 California election initiative to spend $3 billion on stem-cell research. A year later, their work had produced several effects: Nancy Reagan, whose husband President Ronald Reagan suffered from Alzheimer's disease at the end of his life, showed public support for stem-cell research, as did former Senator Arlen Specter (R–PA), who recovered from Hodgkin's disease.

## INTEREST GROUP STRATEGIES

11.8 *What are the strategies for interest groups to promote their views and policies in a democracy?*

Interest groups must constantly make decisions about strategy: Where should the group focus its energies? What issues should it push? With whom should it align itself? Should the group target a House subcommittee, the Senate majority leader, the president, a deputy undersecretary, or key governors and mayors? Issues cut across political arenas at local, state, and national levels, which may leave the best place to apply pressure unclear. Groups must also consider whether to push at the grassroots to create a populist groundswell for their ideas or to go directly to powerful public officials.

## Lobbying

Lobbying represents the most common and effective way to influence public policy. **Lobbying** is a formal, organized attempt to influence legislation, usually through direct contact with legislators or their staffs. The political use of the term *lobby* in the United States was first recorded in the annals of the Tenth Congress; in 1829, the term *lobby-agents* was used to describe favor seekers. President Ulysses S. Grant (1869–1877) frequently walked from the White House to the Willard Hotel on Pennsylvania Avenue, and when he was relaxing with legislators in the Willard's comfortable lobby, individuals seeking jobs or favors would visit him there—hence the term *lobbyists*.[23]

Lobbyists have never ranked high in the eyes of the public. However, the distasteful caricature of a fat-cat special-interest lobbyist who buys a vote by bribing a legislator is a gross distortion of what most lobbyists do. Outright bribery is rare; so, too, are other illegal attempts to gain the favor of political officials. The reason is simple. The rewards for corrupt behavior rarely outweigh the risks. After all, money leaves a trail that investigators can follow. Besides, people talk (especially people in politics), so keeping a political secret is no easy task. Astute reporters—hundreds of them hoping to expose some juicy scandal—can ultimately uncover most bribery episodes. Furthermore, bribery is illegal, so not only are reporters out to uncover corruption, so are state and federal legal officers.

The national protests against the Iraq War were led and fueled by the younger generation that in 2008 helped to elect Barack Obama, who promised to bring an end to the war.

**Who Are the Lobbyists?** Lobbyists are key players in the game of politics. Some are prominent Washington figures and major power brokers. Many are former government officials who have discovered that their expertise, access, influence, and good name are valuable assets, particularly to major industries. More than one public official has learned that it pays much better to be a lobbyist influencing policy from the outside than to be a public servant making policy on the inside. Interest groups particularly value former members of Congress for their knowledge of government operations and their many contacts with the politically powerful. Although ex-members are barred from lobbying Congress for a year after leaving that institution, a 2011 study discovered that nearly 200 did so after losing their election the year before.[24]

In 1961, 365 lobbyists were registered in Washington, DC. By 2011, the number of lobbyists who were actually lobbying was over 12,000, spending nearly $2.5 billion for their causes.[25] "Everybody in America has a lobby," declared former House Speaker Thomas (Tip) O'Neill. The leading lobby registrants are businesses and corporations, trade associations, state and local governments, citizen groups, and labor unions. Even foreign governments lobby, as seen in the case of Kazakhstan, a republic in Central Asia. Japanese companies and the Japanese government spend more than $100 million to hire hundreds of lobbyists in Washington.[26]

Indeed, the rapid increase in Washington lobbyists may relate to rapid growth in government, the receptivity of politicians in Congress and the White House to lobbying, and a widespread belief by the corporate world that lobbying help is indispensable. Whereas lobbying began as a tool to prevent passage of laws that might hurt a business, now lobbyists seek to help organizations win tax breaks and federal grants that will aid their business.[27]

### QUICK REVIEW

Lobbying

- Lobbying involves formal, organized attempts to influence legislation.
- Lobbyists are prominent Washington figures, major power brokers, or former government officials.
- Lobbyists seek to win tax breaks and federal grants.

**lobbying**
The formal, organized attempt to influence legislation, usually through direct contact with legislators or their staff.

**Lobbying Tactics** How do lobbyists work with politicians to achieve their aims? The relationship between lobbyists and politicians is one of the least understood in politics. Most lobbyists neither bribe nor threaten politicians. Both tactics are self-defeating. What they do instead is inform, persuade, and pressure. And because most people dislike pressure, the smart lobbyist does as little of that as possible, and only as a last resort.

Persuasion starts (and often ends) with information—a lobbyist's most valuable resource. Legislators, whose staffs are small and usually stretched thin, often need help locating vital information to make decisions about the possible impact of pending legislation. A good lobbyist gains access by providing this information. Naturally, the information will be skewed to favor the lobbyist's point of view. Still, it must never be an outright lie, or the interest group loses all credibility for future lobbying efforts. And even if lobbyists do not provide legislators with a well-rounded perspective on the issue, the information they do provide can be helpful. At a minimum, it lets politicians know how key groups feel about the way pending legislation will affect their interests. And sensible politicians listen to a variety of groups and take a range of information into account before putting the final package of a given bill together.

A lobby exists to achieve results, and most Washington-based lobbies seek to influence policy in similar ways. To begin, the interests represented by the lobby will make campaign contributions to members of Congress. They hope thereby to elect representatives who see the world as they do and who will vote for the issues they support. Failing that, they hope that campaign contributions will at least buy them access—that is, time to present their case to the members whose campaigns they supported. That explains why many large interests donate money to both parties. By hedging their bets, they hope to gain an audience with whatever group ends up controlling Congress.

Access is crucial; lobbyists can't influence people if they can't grab their attention. Lobbyists are salespeople. If they can make their case one-on-one, they will be effective. Good lobbyists get to know the members of Congress and their key staff people so that they can talk to influential politicians when the need arises. In some cases, lobbyists and legislators work together so closely that lobbyists actually draft the legislation and submit it to Congress through their legislative contacts.

Beyond pushing their legislative aims in Congress, lobbyists spend a good deal of time presenting their case formally and publicly. They put out reports, pamphlets, and press releases, all aimed at presenting arguments and evidence to support their group's policy goals. They also give speeches, appear on television and radio and at other public forums, and provide interviews—all in the hope that their message will be noticed and viewed favorably by those who have power or by those who can influence power holders. Among their many activities, lobbyists often testify before congressional committees about the policies they hope to persuade Congress to adopt. They often write *amicus curiae* briefs to the Supreme Court. Interest groups have also successfully used the lower courts to sue government and private industry and have had an impact on public policy in this way, especially in the environmental arena.

**QUICK REVIEW**

Grassroots Activity

- Grassroots activities involve rallying the public behind a cause or proposal.
- Lobbyists create pressure through political advertisements, speeches, and rallies.
- Grassroots efforts appeal directly to group members or potential members for support and action.

## Grassroots Activity

Rallying the public behind their cause is a central element in most lobbyists' work, a strategy known as **grassroots activity.**[28] As you can see in Table 11.1, which lists the various activities that lobbyists perform, nearly 80 percent of lobbyists engage in this activity. The reason is simple: Just as nations with no army participate little in world affairs, lobby groups with no popular support participate little in a democracy. Those who make the nation's laws gain office in a mass democratic election, so they pay particularly close attention to the desires of the majority of the people in their electoral districts. A lobbyist is just one person, but a lobbyist with the backing of hundreds or thousands of voters in a legislative district is a power requiring significant attention. Thus, the most effective lobbyists are those who can clearly show an ability to rally grassroots support for their proposals.

**grassroots activity**
The rallying of group members, as well as the public, behind a lobby's cause.

Grassroots pressure "greases the wheels" of the policy-making process. Lobbyists create this pressure by rousing constituents back home in a variety of ways: through political advertisements in newspapers, radio, and television; through

**Table 11.1** What Lobbyists Do

| Activity | Percentage Who Use Technique |
|---|---|
| Testify at hearings | 99% |
| Have formal contact with public officials | 98 |
| Have informal contact with public officials | 95 |
| Present research information | 92 |
| Send letters to group members to update them on group activities | 92 |
| Enter into coalitions with other organizations | 90 |
| Attempt to shape policy implementation | 89 |
| Talk with the media | 86 |
| Consult with public officials to devise legislative strategy | 85 |
| Help draft legislation | 85 |
| Sponsor letter-writing campaigns | 84 |
| Help shape the government's agenda by calling attention to problems | 84 |
| Mount grassroots lobbying efforts | 80 |
| Have influential group members contact legislative offices | 80 |
| Help draft agency regulations, rules, and guidelines | 78 |
| Serve on advisory commissions and boards | 76 |
| Alert legislators to the effects of legislation on their districts | 75 |
| File suits or otherwise engage in litigation | 72 |
| Make financial contributions to campaigns | 58 |
| Assist officials by doing favors for them | 56 |
| Attempt to influence appointments to public office | 53 |
| Publicize candidates' voting records | 44 |
| Engage in direct mail fund-raising for the interest group | 44 |
| Use media advertisements to publicize the group's position on an issue | 31 |
| Contribute work, personnel, or services to electoral campaigns | 24 |
| Publicly endorse candidates for office | 22 |
| Engage in protests or demonstrations | 20 |

*Source:* "Activities of Professional Lobbyists," from *Organized Interests and American Democracy* by Kay Lehman Schlozman and John T. Tierney. Copyright © 1985 Kay Lehman Schlozman and John T. Tierney. Reprinted by permission of Pearson Education, Inc.

speeches in local and national forums; and through rallies or letter-writing campaigns. The goal of these activities is to let politicians know that numerous voters agree with the lobbyist, so that the politicians will decide that supporting the lobby group's goal is the only sensible and expedient action. Certain groups are especially adept at grassroots activism. For example, since the 2008 DC gun control case, the National Rifle Association has lobbied to end governmental gun controls at the state and local levels.

Women's groups have gained prominence in the political arena. From the National Organization for Women (NOW) to the conservative anti-feminist group Concerned

Women for America, women have been making their policy positions on issues known, and in so doing they have influenced legislation. In addition, two women's PACs have been increasingly important in funding female candidacies: EMILY's List (*E*arly *M*oney *I*s *L*ike *Y*east; it makes the dough rise) for Democrats, and WISH (*W*omen *I*n the *S*enate and *H*ouse) for Republicans. Interest groups use various strategies to appeal directly to group members or potential members for support and action. A group might use a letter-writing campaign asking group members to contact their representatives in support of the group's position on a given issue. Congressional offices are periodically inundated by cards, letters, telegrams, email, and faxes from concerned group members and sympathizers—testimony to the effectiveness of this tactic.

Groups also use *direct mail* to target citizens with mailings describing the group's cause, presenting its arguments, and requesting support or money. The group may provide voting cues by giving voters a checklist to take with them into the voting booth. Another grassroots technique is to stage free concerts, speaking engagements, or even demonstrations. These events are often effective at raising both funds and citizens' consciousness of the group's cause, and they have the added advantage of attracting attention through news coverage.

## Using the Courts and Lobbying the Political Branches

Although grassroots strategies can often ignite large-scale popular support, interest groups must still reach the institutions of government—Congress and the executive branch—to meet their objectives. Even large-scale grassroots movements sometimes fail to impress policy makers in Congress. Members of Congress may simply disagree with the group's goals; or the constituents who voted them into office may not support these goals; or policy makers may be influenced by other powerful groups with opposing aims; or members of Congress may be listening to other, more powerful interest groups. Many grassroots campaigns have failed to persuade Congress to produce desired legislation. Recent failed efforts include campaigns to limit congressional terms of office, to declare abortion illegal nationally, and to create a balanced budget amendment.

The difficulty of lobbying Congress has caused interest groups to direct increasing attention to the executive branch. Groups may seek an appointment with the president or a member of the cabinet, or at least mount a letter-writing campaign in that direction. Far more likely, though, these groups will direct their efforts toward lower-level bureaucrats.

Despite the inevitability of setbacks, interest group leaders rarely give up easily. Groups unsuccessful with one institution often turn to another. The civil rights movement of the 1950s and 1960s is perhaps the best example of group persistence. Unable to persuade either Congress or southern state legislatures to eliminate discriminatory laws and practices, civil rights groups turned to the courts and to the executive branch, where they achieved great success. Ultimately, the Supreme Court, not Congress, declared school segregation unconstitutional, and it took a series of presidents willing to use federal troops to enforce that decision. These judicial and executive actions, initiated by interest group pressures, finally forced states to dismantle their segregated school systems and eliminate other previously legal forms of racial discrimination.

Today, conservative interest groups such as Operation Rescue, which seeks to restrict abortion, use the courts nearly as frequently as did liberal groups of the past, a strategy that makes sense given the growing conservative inclination of the courts. Operation Rescue has combined traditional grassroots strategies with more aggressive tactics such as blockades of abortion clinics and the intimidation of clinic workers and patients. But the group also has a third and quite effective strategy—continued appeal to state and federal courts in an attempt to eliminate all laws permitting abortion. Coupled with the publicity garnered from their aggressive tactics, Operation Rescue has become a political force that even the supposedly nonpolitical courts can no longer ignore. The federal judiciary, then, has once again become a key target for interest group activity.[29]

# APPROACHING
## Contemporary Issues in Democracy

### Are the Tea Party and Occupy Wall Street Movements an Approach to Democracy?

With roughly 40 percent of American voters not identifying with either major party, but instead calling themselves "independents," the question in 2012 will be their voting choice. Will they move to one party or the other? Will they choose not to vote at all? Or, will they look for some other alternative for a vote? Several new groups have organized, or begun to organize, to fill the desires of the voting public. The Tea Party grew in 2010 into a grassroots conservative movement looking to a combination of the U.S. Constitution, the reserved powers of states under the Tenth Amendment of the Constitution, and an agenda of extreme spending cuts and tax cuts, to seek to balance both the budget and the system of governmental powers under the Constitution. In 2011, the Occupy Wall Street movement looked to fill a void when the far left Progressive party movement failed to gain traction. While it is not clear exactly what specific policies this movement is seeking, the groups camping out in Zuccotti Park in southern Manhattan, in Oakland, California, and in other cities are looking to rectify the economic imbalance between the upper 1 percent of the American economic strata and the other 99 percent, which is largely seen as the middle and lower classes. Whether this movement will follow the course of the Tea Party and put candidates up for election to gain political leverage and power is yet to be seen. Are these movements, together with any movement seeking to field an Independent candidate for the 2012 election, an approach to democracy?

The grassroots nature of these movements, together with their agenda of equalizing economic and political power, make clear that this will fulfill the freedom and equality indicator of approaching democracy. The effort to attract and represent those who do not believe that the two major political parties represent them is an effort to appeal to both the majority who has been excluded, and those in the minority who do not believe they have a voice in the political process. If these movements are successful, they might be followed by an effort to improve participation in the political process by those who feel disenfranchised by that system.

The implications of these changes might go far beyond expanding the political agenda and changing the level of participation. The question will be whether the electorate is fundamentally realigning in a way that the American political process has not seen in many decades. Should the voting public begin to fracture in this manner, how will the political parties adjust given the nature of the electoral process? Will either or both parties find it necessary for them to change their political platform in order to keep their followers? Are we headed toward a period of multiparty presidential races that, if they are able to win electoral votes, might send presidential races not to the Supreme Court as happened in the 2000 election, but to the House of Representatives? Compounding these changes might be the movement by various states to change the way they apportion their electoral college votes, making it even more difficult for one candidate to win a majority in the electoral college. So, what do you think? Are the various nonmajor political party movements good for America's approach to democracy?

While the "Occupy" economic and political protest movement has been the story of 2011–12, it is not clear whether it will transform itself into a political party. President Obama has adopted some of its language in speeches seeking to capture its energy for the Democratic Party.

## QUICK REVIEW

Political Action Committees

- The first PAC was created as early as 1948.
- Political action committees could donate up to $5,000 to any single campaign.
- Political action committees added a new way to gain access and influence by donating tremendous amounts of money in relatively small amounts to congressional election campaigns.

# POLITICAL ACTION COMMITTEES

Of all the trends related to interest groups, the most dramatic new development has been the proliferation of political action committees. The first PAC was created as early as 1948, when the AFL-CIO founded its Committee on Political Education (COPE) to channel union funds to pro-labor candidates. In 1963, the Business-Industry Political Action Committee (BIPAC) became the first business PAC. But because campaign contributions were relatively unlimited until the 1970s, and recipients of large contributions did not need to report either the names of donors or the amount of money donated, most large industries and corporations simply funneled the money from corporate coffers directly to the campaigns of their chosen candidates or causes.

Matters changed dramatically by the mid-1970s with passage of the Federal Election Campaign Act of 1971, which placed a $1,000 limit on donations from individuals to any single campaign. The act did, however, allow labor unions, corporations, and other entities to create PACs that could donate up to $5,000 to any single campaign. The newly formed Federal Election Commission (FEC) provided regulation and oversight. By 1976, the FEC had granted authority for universities, museums, trade associations, cooperatives, and eventually for private citizens to form PACs, bringing on a virtual explosion in PAC formation and activity. More than 4,000 PACs have since registered with the FEC.

Political action committees have taken the traditional lobbying role of interest groups and added a new way to gain access and influence: donating tremendous amounts of money in relatively small increments to congressional election campaigns. In the 1996 elections, the top 50 PACs donated nearly $64 million in unregulated **soft money,** promoting party activities and not specific candidates, to the Clinton and Dole campaigns, both national political parties, and all federal congressional election campaigns. All of these groups carefully hedged their bets by donating to *both* parties, thus giving them access no matter who won the election.

Because PACs can legally donate more money than individuals, campaign fundraising has shifted away from seeking individual contributions to seeking money from PACs. As a result, interest group power has increased, while political party power has weakened. Politicians seeking elective office now turn to PACs for support rather than to party organizations. A Michigan Democrat running for the U.S. Senate, for instance, will be equally concerned with gaining the backing of state party officials as with soliciting support from the political action committees of the various unions that wield power in that state, beginning with the United Auto Workers. As PACs decide which candidates receive support, they usurp one of the traditional roles reserved for parties: the recruitment and selection of candidates for office.

This growth of PAC influence in the candidate selection process has created problems for American politics.[30] Most PACs focus on a narrow range of issues or even on a single issue. Candidates seeking scarce political resources for their increasingly expensive campaigns often court the favors of influential PAC groups with narrow agendas while giving short shrift to political parties, with their moderating perspective, broad-based public agendas, and amorphous ideologies. The result, as we saw in Chapter 9, is the candidate-centered campaign, the subsequent weakening of traditional party power, and a growing number of elected officials with narrow viewpoints and confrontational operating styles.

In fact, concern among political observers and insiders alike about increasing PAC influence led to the campaign finance reform effort. And PAC power kept the legislation from being passed year after year. Although the 2002 Bipartisan Campaign Reform Act limited the power of PACs, by eliminating the use of soft money to benefit party-building activities directed to supporting political candidates outside of the legal federal limits, before long those groups found loopholes in the legislation to allow their continued lobbying. As outlined later, in the 2004 election, so-called 527 groups—named for the federal Internal Revenue Service regulation that allows certain nonprofit tax-exempt groups to raise and spend money for educating the public on certain political issues—raised and spent just under $500 million supporting candidates for election. The top three fund-raising groups—America Coming Together, the Joint

**soft money**
Campaign contributions directed to advancing the interests of a political party or an issue in general, rather than a specific candidate.

Victory Campaign 2004, and the Media Fund—all liberal 527s, raised and spent more than $200 million on the election. And yet, one of the less lucrative groups, the so-called Swift Boat Veterans and POWs for Truth, spent only $22 million and exerted the most election influence with its ads raising questions about Democrat John Kerry's Vietnam service. This fund-raising continued, with nearly $428 million raised and spent by 527s in the 2006 congressional elections.[31] By the 2008 election cycle, the top fifteen 527 organizations spent nearly $100 million, and the total expenditures by the 527 organizations in that election cycle were $490 million.

Political Comedians Stephen Colbert and Jon Stewart got plenty of support for their counter-protest rally in the fall of 2010 against the hyper-partisanship of Washington. This is a reference to Tina Fey's impression of former Alaska Governor Sarah Palin by saying, "I can see Russia from my house!"

The 2002 campaign finance law was designed to limit uncontrolled soft money funding of candidates, and even party-building activities, however large amounts of 527 money still went to issue advocacy. Many of these issue ads were perfectly clear about which candidate would benefit from the ad, thus remaining technically legal under the restrictive campaign finance provisions of the McCain-Feingold Act. This loophole greatly influenced the outcome of the 2008 election, because groups independent of the political party system still raised and spent money on behalf of particular candidates. The future effect of this finance system on the electoral process is described further later.

As mentioned in Chapter 9, change in the lobbying approach came after the Supreme Court ruled in the *Citizens' United Case* in 2010 that in election campaign donations, corporations were the same as people, and as such had the same protected First Amendment free speech rights to spend as much money to spread their message as people. In time, political operatives began to form **super-PACs,** or overarching, large political action committees that could raise as much money as they wanted, without revealing its source, to lobby for issues and candidates so long as they do not coordinate with a candidate. Of course, there are many ways to frame these messages so that the viewers will know which candidates are being supported and which ones are being opposed. Conservative super-PACs such as American Crossroads GPS, led by former Bush administration advisor Karl Rove, were able to funnel tens of millions of dollars into the 2010 congressional races and are doing the same in the 2012 race. In response, pro-Obama and Democratic Party super-PACs such as the America's Family First Action Fund, the NEA Advocacy Fund, and Women Vote!, and the ones organized by unions, which are also now unlimited in their campaign spending, will seek to balance the super-PAC spending by the conservatives.[32] In a telling counterprotest, political comedians Jon Stewart *(The Daily Show)* and Stephen Colbert *(The Colbert Report)* organized the Rally to Restore Sanity and/or Fear on the Washington Mall. Colbert created his own super-PAC called Making a Better Tomorrow, Tomorrow, designed to promote off-beat messages to highlight the unlimited and unregulated nature of the super-PACs. After, Colbert's super-PAC tried unsuccessfully to pay for the naming rights to South Carolina's presidential primary, adding a ballot question challenging the *Citizens United* case, instead he ran for the nomination using Herman Cain's name and got 1 percent of the vote.

## REGULATION OF INTEREST GROUPS

11.9 *How can interest groups be regulated to promote democracy?*

Interest group activity is protected by the First Amendment, making politicians cautious about proposals to regulate interest groups and their lobbyists. But the poor image many citizens have of special interests has produced periodic attempts at

**super-PACs**
Lobbying organizations under IRS regulation 501 (c)(4) in which unlimited amounts of unregulated money can be raised to lobby for issues or candidates so long as there is no coordination with a specific candidate.

## APPROACHING Democracy Timeline

### The History of Interest Group Reforms

| | |
|---|---|
| **1860s** | Ulysses S. Grant is lobbied in Willard Hotel, Washington, DC. |
| **1938** | Foreign Agents Registration Act is passed. |
| **1946** | Federal Regulation of Lobbying Act is passed. |
| **1954** | *United States* v. *Harris* upholds Federal Regulation of Lobbying Act. |
| **1960** | Less than 500 lobbyists were operating in the federal government. |
| **1995** | Lobbying Disclosure Act is passed, regulating lobbying. |
| **2000s** | Minority Leader Tom DeLay creates "K Street Project" to organize conservative lobbyists. |
| **2002** | McCain-Feingold Act limits use of soft money and issue ads by lobbyists in campaigns. |
| **2005** | About 35,000 lobbyists are registered for the federal government. |
| **2006** | Lobbyist Jack Abramoff pleads guilty for "pay-for-play" scheme to trade government earmarks for campaign contributions. |
| **2007** | Congress passes Honest Leadership and Open Government Act, making lobbying more transparent and limiting "earmark" industry. |
| **2007** | Roberts Court overturns issue ads portion of McCain-Feingold Act. |
| **2009** | Barack Obama issues regulations limiting "revolving door" of government actors and lobbyists. |

☐ Democratic ☐ Neutral ☐ Undemocratic

regulation. Some of these efforts have borne fruit and have produced the occasional law aimed at reducing the scope of interest group influence. For the most part, however, these laws have been few and weak, leaving interest groups relatively unfettered.

Fearful of the influence of fascist agents from Germany and Italy that might be operating in the United States, Congress passed the Foreign Agents Registration Act in 1938. After the war, the concern turned to domestic lobbying with the passage of the 1946 Federal Regulation of Lobbying Act, which stipulated that lobbyists seeking to influence congressional legislation must list all contributions, expenditures, and the names of anyone who received or contributed $500 or more. The bill contained a great many loopholes, and lobbying firms quickly labeled their efforts as "educative" to avoid having to report them. When the act was challenged on First Amendment grounds in a 1954 case, *United States* v. *Harris,* the Supreme Court upheld the legislation but interpreted the registration requirement to apply only to groups whose "primary purpose" was to influence legislation.[33] Many large outfits such as the National Association of Manufacturers use this argument to avoid registering altogether. They claim no need to register as lobbyists, because influencing legislation is not their principal reason for existing as a group. For that reason and others, the 1946 act was virtually useless. It also lacked enforcement powers and failed to address lobbying the executive branch, grassroots organizing, or indirect lobbying.

The 1971 and 1974 Federal Campaign Finance laws were much more effective in their efforts to regulate donations, but they also ensured an increase in the power and proliferation of PACs, which represent many citizens, thereby reducing the power of individual fat-cat financiers. The 1978 Ethics in Government Act, which codified rules governing conflict of interests, had some effect on lobbying behavior. A key section of this law was meant to prevent the kind of "revolving-door" activity in which government officials leave their posts and immediately use their insider knowledge and contacts to lobby the very people for whom they had just been working. The law prohibited former government employees from lobbying their former agency for a period of one year after leaving office and prohibited them from lobbying any department on an issue for which they clearly had direct responsibility for two years.

Realizing that the 1971 Federal Election Campaign Act covered only lobbyists who seek to influence members of Congress, in December 1995 Congress passed the Lobbying Disclosure Act, which regulated those who sought to lobby members of the congressional staffs and policy-making members of the executive branch, including the president and staff, even if they worked only part-time at lobbying. Lobbyists now must register within 45 days of either being hired or making their first contact with such officials and file reports twice a year about their activities. These reports must list the special interests for which they are lobbying and the offices they have contacted (but not the names of the people contacted), and they must specify whether they are undertaking any action for a foreign government; the only groups exempt are grassroots lobbying and tax-exempt religious organizations.[34] The Approaching Democracy timeline examines the changes in legal reforms for interest groups.

## ASSESSING THE IMPACT OF INTEREST GROUPS

11.10 *What impact do interest groups and lobbying have on American democracy?*

The growth of interest groups presents new challenges and problems for the U.S. political system. As more interest groups participate in the political arena, do they open or close opportunities for individual influence? As groups continue to increase in number, will they become the only legitimate channel for political expression?[35]

Scholars have devoted much effort to understanding the role groups play in American politics. Nearly a century ago, political scientist Arthur Bentley argued that groups lie at the very heart of the political process.[36] Indeed, in his eyes *all* political phenomena could be understood in terms of group activity. He saw politics as a perpetual struggle for power. Groups compete endlessly for public goods and services, and only the fittest prosper and survive. Government is simply the agency that sorts out which groups are winning or losing at any given time. From this perspective, interest group activity is synonymous with politics itself.

Another leading scholar, political scientist David Truman, argued in 1951 that groups play a stabilizing role in American politics.[37] Echoing both Madison and Bentley, Truman wrote that politics is best understood as a complex network of groups, each striving for access to government. In response to critics who believed that powerful economic interests have an advantage, Truman countered with two responses. First, most Americans have overlapping group memberships and are likely to belong to at least one group that benefits from government policies. Second, he pointed to the idea of potential groups. Certain issues could arise and galvanize unorganized citizens into cohesive groups, as exemplified by the pro–gun control Million Mom March and the anti–gun control Second Amendment Sisters. Formerly disadvantaged people would thus be represented in the halls of power, and these new groups would provide a vital balancing mechanism to counter the influence of groups already representing the wealthier elements of society.

In yet another critique of the pluralist vision of group activity, political scientist Theodore Lowi maintained that contemporary group politics has fundamentally altered how the United States functions.[38] Lowi described a new political system that he called *interest group liberalism,* in which interest groups have proliferated, expanding their control of legislative politics. In Lowi's view, real policy making stems from neither voter preference nor Congress. Instead, it flows from a set of tight connections among the bureaucracy, selected members of Congress (especially subcommittee chairs), and special-interest groups representing the upper stratum of American society. Lowi and others have used the term **iron triangle** to characterize the typically cozy relationship among congressional elites, lobbyists, and bureaucrats.

The rapid proliferation of interest groups, all competing for influence over policy, could place excessive and conflicting demands on public officials. In the face of massive political pressure, government might grind to a halt or continue to implement the status quo, because all efforts at change or reform are stymied by the many competing claims of powerful interest groups. This produces **gridlock,** a condition in which major government initiatives are impossible because existing groups can veto any effort at change and will do so, for fear of losing their own already established connections and privileges.

Not all interest group specialists accept such pessimism. More optimistic scholars raise several points of objection. First, they claim that gridlock may derive less from the proliferation of interest groups than from American society's lack of consensus about

**iron triangle**
Informal three-way relationships that develop among key legislative committees, the bureaucracy, and interest groups with a vested interest in the policies created by those committees and agencies.

**gridlock**
A condition in which major government initiatives are impossible because a closely balanced partisan division in the government structure, accompanied by an unwillingness to work together toward compromise, produces a stalemate.

**policy networks**
Networks characterized by a wide-ranging discussion of options as issues are resolved, conveying a more inclusive and less conspiratorial image of the policy process than iron triangles do.

which direction government policy should take. That lack of consensus has been a standard condition in American history, as one would expect in a diverse and complex culture. But when Americans do reach consensus on political aims, government can take dramatic action with amazing speed, despite all the talk about interest groups causing gridlock. That situation occurred in 1933 with the rapid approval of a vast range of New Deal programs, in 1941 and 1942 with the U.S. entry into World War II, in 1965 with the passage of the Great Society programs, and in 1995 with the acceptance of many Republican Contract with America proposals. Group pressures did little to prevent those dramatic changes in national public policy. Perhaps interest groups do not create gridlock but merely take advantage of its existence in a complex and diverse society.

The iron triangle idea also has been criticized. As early as 1978, political scientist Hugh Heclo pointed to the rise of a range of issue experts who forced legislators, bureaucrats, and lobbyists to pay attention to other information and actors, thus undermining their cozy triangular relationship.[39] As a result, **policy networks** have formed. These networks feature discussion of a wide range of options in the effort to resolve issues and convey a more inclusive and less conspiratorial image of the policy process than do iron triangles.[40]

Other scholars have noted the vast array of new groups that have entered the political arena in recent years. This influx of groups has created conditions of uncertainty and unpredictability, helping to break up established connections among the principal actors of the old triangles. As the number of groups and interests operating in American society has dramatically expanded, political life has become more complex, making any generalization about how policies evolve more difficult to substantiate.

Finally, one must remember that many of the new groups represent public interest activists, political participants who stand up for those segments of society not usually represented in the ongoing group struggles for power. Public interest lobbyists may be middle class, but their aims, at least in theory, would benefit all citizens, particularly those at the lower ends of the socioeconomic spectrum. Thus, the argument that the less well-off are disadvantaged by interest group activity, although retaining a strong kernel of truth, is less accurate today than it might have been two or three decades ago.

## COMPARISON OF LOBBYING IN THE BUSH AND OBAMA PRESIDENCIES

11.11 *How will interest group strategies and lobbying change in the 21st century?*

### Lobbying During the Bush Presidency

The world of lobbying seemed to be changing during the Bush administration as a result of new technology, the vast amounts of money available, and the highly partisan nature of politics in an evenly balanced political world. Websites, blogs, and mass-generated emails help groups develop a seeming groundswell of public opinion. Although such movements can resemble direct democracy, it is important to remember that they are actually just high-tech lobbying.

Another change is the revolving-door aspect of the lobbyist's job, as more and more ex-congressional members simply move to the center of the lobbying world—K Street in Washington—and use their contacts to become highly paid lobbyists. During the Bush administration, a program called the K Street Project, launched by Republican majority leader Tom DeLay in Congress, was undertaken by which lobbying firms, corporations, and trade associations had to demonstrate their loyalty to the Republican Party by hiring conservative lobbyists in order to lobby successfully. In turn, those conservative lobbying firms fired associates who were not conservative in order to gain better lobbying access in Congress.[41]

Because former members retain their privileges to visit the floors of Congress and enter the "members only" areas of the Capitol, their access to former colleagues makes them potentially successful lobbyists. A 2011 study by the governmental watchdog group TPM revealed that 195 Senate and the House members who left government, many after losing office in 2010, had registered to become lobbyists.[42] This "Shadow Congress" was quite a change; as recently as the mid-1980s, former members of Congress rarely became lobbyists. But that shifted a few years later when the rising salaries made the job more appealing. Beyond the problems raised by former officials using insider skills to give certain groups more access to government than they otherwise might have, the notion that sitting members of Congress might one day become lobbyists could affect the way they deal with lobbyists. Is a member of Congress who gives access to a lobbyist seeking a future job prospect? The congressional revolving door resembles one that has always existed in the executive branch, with outgoing administration officials moving to think tanks and academic positions to wait for the next compatible administration to be elected, thus allowing them to return to government. The congressional revolving door allows members of Congress to remain inside the Washington Beltway, earning a living and maintaining their contacts while they assess future runs for elected office.[43]

The protests against the original passage of the 2001 USA Patriot Act, and its reenactment years later, has kept the issue of preserving privacy and individual rights in the forefront as the government has developed national security policies since the 9/11 attacks.

The nature of this revolving-door relationship and its possible corrupting influence in Washington became a central focus in late 2005 with investigation into the lobbying of Jack Abramoff, former aide to Majority Leader Tom DeLay. Abramoff was believed to be involved in a kind of "pay-for-play" government policy program. He raised tens of millions of dollars from various interest groups (such as from casino operations run by Native Americans), as well as certain foreign entities, funneling that to specific congressional candidates both for their campaigns and for personal benefit (such as fully funded vacations and excursions to Scotland). As a result, these groups were able to get legislative "earmarks," specifically targeted federal grants that were added to appropriation and other types of legislation, passed in return. After one of Abramoff's top assistants, Michael Scanlon, pled guilty and began cooperating with federal officials, Abramoff pled guilty on January 3, 2006, to fraud, tax evasion, and conspiracy to bribe federal public officials. When he was released from prison in 2011, Abramoff wrote a book repudiating these efforts and advocating reforms.[44]

Owing to this investigation, Tom DeLay gave up his effort to retake the House majority leader position and resigned from the House and was later sent to prison. Ohio congressman Robert Ney gave up his chairmanship of the powerful House Administration Committee and, in October 2006, pled guilty to corruption charges.[45] Former evangelical movement leader and Christian Coalition head Ralph Reed, who lost his campaign for lieutenant governor of Georgia, also found himself caught up in the investigation and embroiled in certain charges against Abramoff.[46] This series of events became a "culture of corruption" issue and helped the Democrats win back control of both houses of Congress in the 2006 congressional elections. And the process continued in 2008 with the election of Barack Obama and the Democratic Party's dramatic increase in numbers in both houses of Congress.

As a result of these scandals, and after a long period of negotiation, Congress passed the Honest Leadership and Open Government Act in 2007. It was designed to make the lobbying industry in Washington, DC, more transparent and put an end to the pay-for-play lobbying-earmark passage scheme that had been the centerpiece of the controversy. The law required much more extensive reporting by lobbyists on their activities, ended many forms of lobbyists' spending on members of Congress, banned senators from lobbying their colleagues for two years after leaving the institution to limit the revolving-door process, required the disclosure of lobbyists backing media ads on public issues, and ended partisan lobbying programs such as the so-called K Street Project.

Lobbyist Jack Abramoff, center, leaves a federal courthouse in 2006 after pleading guilty to charges stemming from his "pay-for-play" scheme, by which clients would trade donations to congressional campaign committees in return for the passage of laws earmarking funds for those organizations. This led to the defeat of the Republicans in 2006. Upon his release in 2011, Abramoff renounced his work and called for reforms.

## Lobbying During the Obama Presidency

The election of Barack Obama changed the direction of the rotating door of lobbying, making it possible for the liberal interest groups to move to the forefront of political visibility and power in Washington. The changes now were twofold. For the first time since the Clinton administration, the Democrats controlled the White House, and some argue that it had been even longer since the election of a true liberal president in the White House. Second, there was now a generational change as a president in his mid-40s, with followers even younger than he was, took control of the governmental reins and promised to institute "change" and "not do business in the usual way." As a result, new liberal lobbying groups such as Unity '09, a group of progressive lobbying groups, and liberal think tanks such as the Center for American Progress, created by former Clinton chief of staff John Podesta, found that they had new access to the levers of power.[47]

Suddenly, groups that had been working for years on health-care reform and regulations to preserve the environment discovered that they have access to those in power in Washington. The successful election has translated to more money being available for these groups to buy television advertising time to lobby for their policies, as happened almost immediately by an alliance of liberal lobbying groups after the nomination of Judge Sonia Sotomayor to the Supreme Court. This new-found power, though, will be limited both by the tricky politics of seeking to influence the "big tent" Democratic Party, with so many conservative members of Congress and senators, and the emerging power of the Internet-enabled grassroots lobbying efforts that are not always in tune with these groups. Meanwhile, conservative interest groups and think tanks, such as the American Enterprise Institute and the Heritage Foundation, having lost their access to policy making for the time being, will be simultaneously exploiting cracks in the new liberal lobbying alliance while also trying to redraft policy plans for the next time their party comes to power.[48]

One of the biggest changes in the Obama administration was the intensive "vetting" process in selecting new appointees, revealing past lobbying efforts, and the highly restrictive departure agreement limiting revolving-door lobbying. Seeking to avoid the revolving-door lobbying process, in January 2009, President Obama signed an Executive Order on Ethics Commitments by Executive Branch.[49] No one who had been registered as a lobbyist for a government agency was eligible for a job in that agency, and new Obama officials were required to agree that they would not lobby the administration as long as Obama was still in office. As a result, many government positions were not filled for a longer-than-usual period of time. Meanwhile, Democratic lobbyists were beginning to evade the regulation by "unregistering" as lobbyists, but still billing for lobbying efforts in areas that are not regulated, so that they can avoid the running time clock ban on influencing the White House.[50]

The effort by the Obama administration to limit through new policies the influence of lobbyists in the government continued. In June 2010, executive branch officials were instructed that federally registered lobbyists were now banned from service on federal boards and commissions. In November 2011, full implementation was achieved of a final explanatory memo from the Office of Management and Budget. The memo banned all political lobbyists registered according to the federal lobbying disclosure law in the federal lobbyist data base from service as members on government agencies and commissions. In the future, unless overturned by a future presidential administration or Congress, in order to serve on such boards, people who have lobbied the federal government in the past will have to go through an extensive vetting process.[51] More needs to be done in this regulation policy, though, as it does nothing about lobbyists who are not registered with the government. In September, 2011, the Office of Government Ethics proposed a rule placing limits on the gifts and invitations received from lobbyists by executive branch officials.

**issue advertisements**
Advertisements in a political campaign funded by an interest group advocating a position on an issue but technically not supporting a specific candidate.

## INTEREST GROUPS AND AMERICAN DEMOCRACY IN THE 21ST CENTURY

In anticipating future election cycles, one of the major changes that will once again be seen concerns the changes in regulation on the issue of lobbying campaign ads. A 1996 Supreme Court decision has dramatically changed the nature of interest group advertising in elections. The dispute arose from Colorado Democratic senator Timothy Wirth's 1986 reelection campaign, when that state's Republican Federal Campaign Committee exceeded spending limits on independent campaign contributions by political parties as outlined in the Federal Election Campaign Act of 1971. The Republicans, who had not yet chosen their candidate when they ran $15,000 in radio ads against Wirth, claimed that they had a First Amendment freedom-of-speech right to spend what they wished on the election. Speaking for a seven-person majority, Justice Stephen Breyer agreed, arguing, "We do not see how a Constitution that grants to individuals, candidates, and ordinary political committees the right to make unlimited independent expenditures could deny the same right to political parties."[52] Only if the party and the candidates worked together in the campaign spending would the federal limits apply. As a result, interest groups that helped the Republicans win back Congress in 1994 proliferated in the elections in the years ahead.

### THINKING CRITICALLY

Do you believe that corporations, organizations, and interest groups should have the same First Amendment free speech rights as ordinary citizens? Should they have an unlimited right to pay for any ads to influence elections during a campaign?

This loophole in the campaign expenditure law spurred political parties and interest groups to continue to collect soft money (unregulated donations directed for "party-building activities" and not specific candidates). The funds covered campaign costs and national **issue advertisements** that address issues rather than candidates directly. Such ads made clear the organization's position about a particular issue rather than a specific candidacy, thus avoiding federal regulation.[53] Various national interest groups funded such ads, almost completely bypassing the candidates themselves. As they had five years earlier, in June 2001, the Supreme Court, by a narrow 5–4 decision, ruled in another Colorado campaign finance reform case that limits on coordinated campaign spending by political parties and candidates for federal office were constitutional. The Court reasoned that if they did not exist, it would be impossible to establish spending limits for individual candidates' campaigns. This decision gave supporters of campaign finance reform hope.[54]

The Bipartisan Campaign Finance Reform Act of 2002, the so-called McCain-Feingold Act, now bans raising of unregulated soft money and limits the use of issue advertisements 30 days before an election primary and 60 days before the general election. In late 2003, the Supreme Court upheld most of the law's provisions by a 5–4 majority, supporting the limit of political corruption. However, in 2006, the addition of Samuel Alito to the Supreme Court gave the conservatives a majority in favor of overturning a portion of the law dealing with issue advertisements a year later, ruling that it was a violation of the First Amendment freedom of speech provision. Chief Justice Roberts explained, "Discussion of issues cannot be suppressed simply because the issue may also be pertinent in an election. Where the First Amendment is implicated, the tie goes to the speaker, not the censor."[55] But here there was actually a three-way tie: among the speaker, the government censor, and the election voter. In ignoring that the timing of such ads circumvented congressional limits on election spending, this decision opened the door for large interest groups and corporations, unchecked by the Federal Elections Commission, to funnel large amounts of money into future elections.

In early 2007, a nonpartisan investigative agency called the Center for Responsive Politics determined that nearly $1 billion had been spent by Section 527 groups in the

2004 presidential race.[56] While the government considers whether or not these 527s will be regulated, some of these groups, such as the conservative groups Progress for America and Club for Growth, searched for ways to evade some of these regulations. They did so by shifting their focus to a new section of the Internal Revenue Service code governing such tax-exempt lobbying groups, Section 501(c)(4), which allows them to keep the names of their donors anonymous.[57] In the fall of 2009, the federal Court of Appeals ruled that 527 groups have First Amendment rights to undertake campaigns fund-raising activities that deal with issues and not political candidates. Even if they are regulated, though, money, like water, tends to seek its own level, and well-funded groups desiring to influence the political process will still find a way to raise funds legally.

The Supreme Court's decision in the 2010 *Citizens United* case upheld the unlimited free speech rights of corporations to spend as much money on a political campaign as they wish, so long as they deal with political issues and not specific candidates. The Court's decision undercut and weakened the 2002 McCain-Feingold campaign finance law and opened the door to massive new, unregulated, interest group campaign funding. The new super-PACs will also present a vehicle for the large organizations, corporations, ultra-rich, and large groups of people to evade political campaign restrictions. In addition, the growing use of social media and technology, together with the powerful grassroots forces mobilized during this time of economic crisis, as shown by the Tea Party and Occupy Wall Street movements, lead one to wonder whether it is only a matter of time before a third-party movement begins to take hold in this country, if it has not already done so in the form of the Tea Party. More than ever, it becomes clear that America's approach to democracy is done as much in interest groups as it is in individual political decisions.

## Summary


**11.1** *Do interest groups promote democracy, and if so, how?*

- Interest groups are formal organizations of people who share a common outlook or social circumstance and who band together in the hope of influencing government policy. Actual groups have a headquarters, an organizational structure, paid employees, and so forth; potential groups are interest groups that could form under the right circumstances. Those circumstances are often created by dynamic leaders known as policy entrepreneurs.

**11.2** *Were interest groups anticipated by the constitutional framers as being a source for increasing democracy in America?*

- Although all modern democracies exhibit interest group activity, few have achieved the level of nongovernmental group life found in the United States. James Madison wrote about the activity of factions groups of people organizing among themselves on the basis of the way they made their living or their property. Over time, these factions became interest groups. The number of groups trying to pressure government has grown dramatically in recent years, partly owing to the growth and increased activity of the government and partly owing to higher average levels of education.

**11.3** *How have interest groups developed and evolved recently?*

- People form interest groups because collective action is stronger, more credible, and more likely to influence policy outcomes than the isolated actions of separate individuals. However, because interest groups focus on their own cause, they are said to skew or ignore the public good.

**11.4** *What effect has the Internet had on the development of political lobbying and the growth of interest groups?*

- In recent years, interest groups and politicians have begun to use the Internet to reach their grassroots following. Howard Dean launched the effort for the Democrats, and since then, politicians (such as Barack Obama) have been able to fund-raise via the Internet for their campaigns.
- Economic interest groups include those representing big business, organized labor, farmers, and other economic interests. Public interest groups represent the interests of average citizens; they focus on achieving a broad set of goals that represent their members' vision of the collective good. Government interest groups compete alongside traditional interest groups for funding, policy goals, and attention. Other interest groups include ideological groups, religious groups, civil rights groups, and single-issue groups.

**11.5** *What do interest groups do, and how do they promote democracy?*

- Interest groups are most likely to form when citizens have been adversely affected by technological change or by government policies. Other factors, such as dynamic leaders and geographic concentration, also influence the development of an interest group.

**11.6** *What are the different kinds of interest groups, and how do they promote democracy?*

- Group leaders must devote much of their time to group maintenance—canvassing for new members and providing benefits for current members. In doing so, they face the so-called free-rider issue, the tendency of individuals to share in the collective benefits of group action even if they do not themselves contribute to the group.

**11.7** *What are the characteristics of an interest group?*

- Lobbying is the formal, organized attempt to influence legislation, usually through direct contact with legislators or their staff. Lobbyists provide legislators with needed information and attempt to persuade and sometimes pressure them to support the interest group's goals. They also publicize the group's cause to the general public through published materials, speeches, television appearances, and the like.

11.8 *What are the strategies for interest groups to promote their views and policies in a democracy?*

- A key aim of lobbying is to rally group members, as well as the public, to the cause—that is, to gain grassroots support for the group's proposals. An often-used tactic is the direct mail campaign, in which targeted citizens receive mailings describing the group's cause and requesting their support.
- Leaders of interest groups learn that when they fail to gain a hearing for their cause in one branch of government, success may be achieved by looking for help elsewhere. Thus, in times when Congress and the president are unsympathetic, requests for help can be directed toward the Supreme Court, and vice versa.
- An important trend is the proliferation of PACs, groups whose main aim is to promote the political goals of particular interest groups. Political action groups donate large amounts of money to political campaigns, thereby undermining the role of political parties in recruiting and selecting candidates for office.

11.9 *How can interest groups be regulated to promote democracy?*

- Interest groups face few legal restrictions. Lobbyists must list their contributions and expenditures, but only if their "primary purpose" is to influence legislation. The Ethics in Government Act bars former government employees from lobbying their former agency for a year after leaving office and for two years on specific policy issues.
- Interest group activity during congressional elections has evolved to the point that issue advertising sometimes proceeds without any reference to the candidates in the race. Such ads alert voters to the importance of the issues but sometimes blur candidate identities.

11.10 *What impact do interest groups and lobbying have on American democracy?*

- Some political scientists believe that policy making stems from comfortable and resilient connections among the bureaucracy, selected members of Congress, and interest groups—so-called iron triangles. The rapid proliferation of interest groups has led to what some political scientists call gridlock, or a harmful excess of competing demands. Policy networks, more broad-based than iron triangles, now characterize the process. The number of groups and interests now operating in American society has dramatically expanded, adding to the complexity of political life.

11.11 *How will interest group strategies and lobbying change in the 21st century?*

- The Obama administration began with such serious vetting of its candidates for executive branch appointments, not allowing any connection with interest groups, that it became difficult to find some candidates for key positions. In addition, the new administration has been pushing for greater regulation of interest groups and is trying to limit the revolving-door problem of administration officials leaving office to go into the lobbying business.

## Key Terms

actual groups, 340
collective action, 346
factions, 341
free riders, 353
grassroots activity, 356
gridlock, 363
group maintenance, 353
interest groups, 339
iron triangle, 363
issue advertisements, 367
lobbying, 355
netizens, 346
policy entrepreneurs, 340
policy networks, 364
political action committees (PACs), 343
potential groups, 340
public interest groups, 349
soft money, 360
super-PACs, 361

## Test Yourself Chapter 11

**1.** What does the Constitution do to regulate interest group activity?
a. Interest groups are left to the national government to regulate.
b. Interest groups are left to the states to regulate.
c. Interest groups are to be regulated by the national government and states.
d. Nothing is done.

**2.** For James Madison in *The Federalist,* no. 10, what are the operating groups in American politics?
a. Interest groups.
b. Political parties.
c. Factions.
d. Community groups.

**3.** For James Madison in *The Federalist,* no. 10, what was the solution to keep groups in democracy from banding together into a majority, and taking away the rights of the minority?
a. Nothing, it is inevitable.
b. This will not happen, so do not worry about it.
c. Enlarge the size of the nation to create cross-cutting cleavages.
d. None of the above.

**4.** Ralph Nader has been a(n) ________________, or a person who organizes an interest group.
a. presidential candidate.
b. author.
c. policy entrepreneur.
d. policy founder.

**5.** The Club for Growth is
a. a group lobbying for young people.
b. a conservative group lobbying for tax reductions.
c. a liberal group lobbying for tax increases.
d. None of the above.

**6.** The groups that band together to bundle small donations into larger donations are called
a. political action committees.
b. political development committees.
c. political lobbying committees.
d. None of the above.

**7.** The McCain-Feingold Act of 2002
a. regulated the campaign work of interest groups.
b. regulated the campaign work of political parties.
c. ended the use of soft money and limited the use of issue ads.
d. All of the above.

**8.** The conservative legal interest group that has become predominant in recommending judicial candidates for appointment during Republican administrations is
a. the Madison Society.
b. the Hamilton Society.
c. the John Marshall Society.
d. the Federalist Society.

**9.** The functions of interest groups are to
a. allow for collective action to press for policies.
b. provide information.
c. Both a and b.
d. Neither a nor b.

**10.** A nonprofit interest group working for the general public interest is known as a PIRG, which stands for
a. people's interest research group.
b. popular interest research group.
c. public interest research group.
d. None of the above.

**11.** Perhaps the best-known public interest group, which lobbies for honesty and openness in government, is
a. Honest Government.
b. Common Cause.
c. People's Cause.
d. OpenSecrets.org.

**12.** Among some of the various kinds of interest groups are
a. ideological interest groups.
b. civil rights interest groups.
c. economic interest groups.
d. All of the above.

**13.** Approximately how many interest groups operate in the United States?
a. 5,000.
b. 10,000.
c. 15,000.
d. 20,000.

**14.** One of the oldest and best-known ideological interest groups is
a. the Americans for Democratic Action.
b. the Americans for Conservative Action.
c. the Americans for Liberal Action.
d. the Americans for Government Action.

**15.** A good example of a single-issue interest group that lobbies on only one issue is
a. the National Rifle Association (NRA).
b. the National Abortion Rights Action League (NARAL).
c. the Sierra Club, on environmental protection.
d. All of the above.

**16.** Those people who benefit from the actions of interest groups without actually being members of the group are called
a. coincident beneficiaries.
b. auxiliary beneficiaries.
c. free riders.
d. None of the above.

**17.** The form of lobbying by engaging large numbers of common people, sometimes now on the Internet, to press for action is called
a. Internet lobbying.
b. grassroots lobbying.
c. popular action lobbying.
d. None of the above.

**18.** Which of the following is *not* a strategy followed by interest groups to lobby for action?
a. Using direct mail solicitations.
b. Testifying at congressional hearings.
c. Having its head run for political office.
d. Helping to draft legislation.

**19.** Soft money, regulated by the McCain-Feingold Act of 2002, is
a. money that is conditional on action.
b. money that is donated for the "good of the party," not a specific candidate.
c. money that can be refunded if the action fails.
d. All of the above.

**20.** The earliest known lobbying in America may well have been
a. with Abraham Lincoln in Washington, DC.
b. with George Washington.
c. with Ulysses S. Grant in the Willard Hotel in Washington, DC.
d. with Franklin D. Roosevelt, in the Independence Hotel.

**ANSWERS**
**1.** d, **2.** c, **3.** c, **4.** c, **5.** b, **6.** a, **7.** d, **8.** d, **9.** c, **10.** c, **11.** b, **12.** d, **13.** d, **14.** a, **15.** d, **16.** c, **17.** b, **18.** c, **19.** b, **20.** c

# The Media

# 12

## Chapter Outline

**Introduction:**
*The Media and Democracy*

## Learning Objectives

12

- 12.1 What role does a free press play in approaching the democratic ideal?
- 12.2 How have media sources evolved over time?
- 12.3 What functions do the media perform in a democracy?
- 12.4 Are freedoms of the press unlimited?
- 12.5 Are the media biased in their reporting?
- 12.6 What is the role of the media in elections?

# INTRODUCTION

## THE MEDIA AND DEMOCRACY

12.1 *What role does a free press play in approaching the democratic ideal?*

President John Kennedy once said, "The flow of ideas, the capacity to make informed choices, the ability to criticize, all of the assumptions on which political democracy rests, depend largely on communications."[1] Democracy requires an *informed* citizenry, and the communication of political information is an essential prerequisite for political participation. A free press stands as one of the defining features of any democratic political system.

The tension between freedom of the press and government restrictions on that freedom is one of several key issues related to the role of the mass media in a democratic society. Indeed, one of the central components of a society's approach to democracy is whether or not the government allows freedom of the press—a press free to criticize the government without fear of being shut down and its editors thrown into prison. In 2011, many of the Arab governments facing revolution sought to control the protests by controlling information. Before the fall of its government, Egyptian officials revoked Al Jazeera's license and forcibly shut down its offices in Cairo. Syrian forces also shut down Al Jazeera as well as arrested dozens of reporters; it remains a mystery whether some of these reporters were executed or detained. In 2009, North Korea sentenced two American journalists working for the cable news station Current TV to 12 years in a labor prison.[2] Laura Ling and Euna Lee were pardoned only after former President Bill Clinton traveled to North Korea and met with Kim Jong Il. In September 2011, Iran released two Americans who had been convicted of spying. The Americans were hiking on the border between Iraq and Iran when they were captured by Iranian national police in 2009. One of the Americans, Shane Bauer, a freelance journalist and fluent Arabic speaker, hoped his time hiking in a peaceful region of Iraq would help the world see a side of the country not usually depicted on the evening news. His capture by Iranian forces did not allow for this vision of Iraq to reach the public. Upon his release, Bauer asked, "How can we forgive the Iranian government when it continues to imprison so many other innocent people and people of conscience?"[3]

As George Orwell observed, censorship in "free" societies is necessarily more complex and calculated than in dictatorships; the latter merely issues an official ban backed by armed force to halt coverage, whereas the former must find more thorough means to ensure that "unpopular ideas can be silenced."[4] We hope that you will learn in this chapter that even in the United States there are a variety of limits that curb media independence. Although media freedom in the United States represents a closer approach to democracy than any other nation has achieved, it is far from absolute.

At a minimum, democracy requires that citizens receive objective information so they can make informed decisions about candidates, policies, and government actions. Yet the media responsible for transmitting that information are often

**Table 12.1** Broadcast and Cable Believability

| | Believe All or Most 4 | 3 | 2 | Believe Almost Nothing 1 | Number Interviewed | Can't Rate |
|---|---|---|---|---|---|---|
| 60 Minutes | 33% | 34% | 22% | 11% | 859 | 15% |
| Local TV news | 29 | 40 | 23 | 8 | 931 | 7 |
| CNN | 29 | 36 | 22 | 13 | 894 | 10 |
| NPR | 28 | 32 | 25 | 16 | 696 | 23 |
| Fox News | 27 | 29 | 22 | 22 | 900 | 8 |
| Wall Street Journal | 25 | 37 | 23 | 14 | 701 | 27 |
| C-SPAN | 23 | 35 | 25 | 17 | 658 | 32 |
| MSNBC | 22 | 38 | 21 | 19 | 839 | 15 |
| ABC News | 21 | 43 | 23 | 13 | 901 | 9 |
| CBS News | 21 | 41 | 24 | 15 | 889 | 12 |
| Your daily newspaper | 21 | 38 | 27 | 14 | 921 | 9 |
| NBC News | 20 | 43 | 23 | 14 | 914 | 7 |
| New York Times | 20 | 38 | 21 | 21 | 707 | 27 |
| USA Today | 17 | 39 | 28 | 15 | 744 | 23 |

*Source:* Pew Research Center for the People & the Press, © 2011, Pew Research Center. Reprinted with the permission of the Pew Research Center for the People & the Press, www.pewforum.org.

characterized by bias, distortion, and sensationalism. Moreover, we learned in Chapter 8 that most citizens have very little grasp of the details of politics or policy. What does this say about our approach to democracy? A Pew Research Center study found that the American public is skeptical about what they see, hear, and read in the media (see Table 12.1). In 2010, only one-third of Americans believed all or most of the information presented by the most believable source for news, with many other sources given much lower believability ratings.

The job of the media entails simplifying complex and detailed realities into symbols and images. Thus, the information reaching the citizen often consists primarily of sound bites and pictures that greatly simplify the definition of political reality for millions of Americans. Perhaps this is one reason so many citizens have such limited knowledge; that is, it may be no exaggeration to say that for most people, politics has little reality apart from its media version.[5] Freedom of the press and other media are essential in a free society. Yet, just 18 percent of the public can name "freedom of the press" as a guarantee in the First Amendment to the Constitution, and six in ten adults believe that the media are biased in reporting.[6] As Figure 12.1 shows, no other nation in the world, even among the industrialized democracies, enjoys the degree of media freedom found in the United States.

In the United States, there is certainly no scarcity of access to information. We can read local, regional, national, and international news and we have access to 24-hour news stations. Also, expanded coverage of local, state, and national public officials on television provides a firsthand look at the political process. But in a democratic polity, the media must do more than bring political information to a broad audience. They must report events

**THINKING CRITICALLY**

What media source do you believe provides the least biased coverage of politics? Do you believe that this source is truly unbiased, or does this source's political bias match your own?

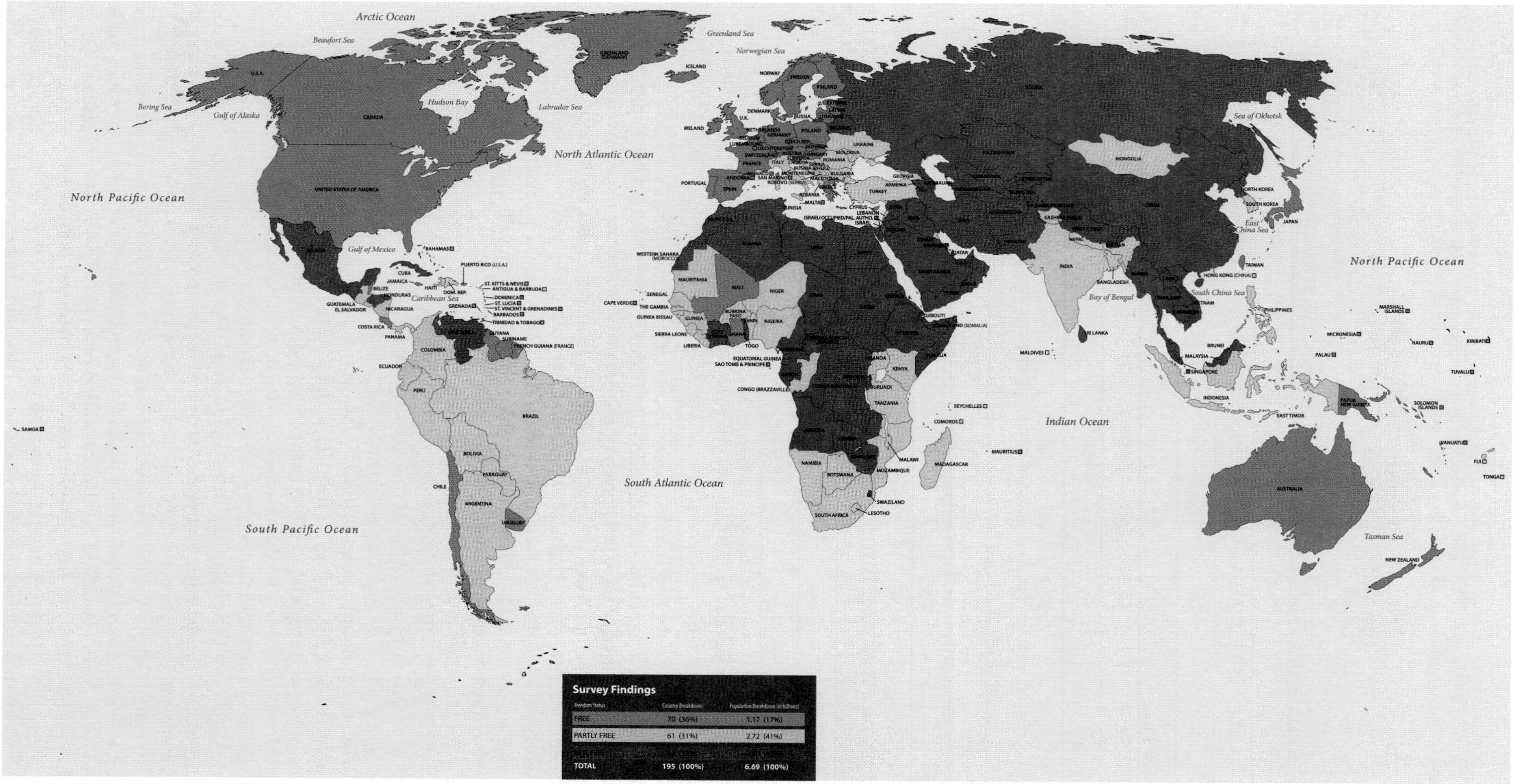


**FIGURE 12.1** Map of Press Freedom, 2011

*Source:* www.freedomhouse.org. Reprinted by permission of Freedom House.

accurately and truthfully, free from control or censorship by government agencies or corporate owners and also free from the taint of their own ideological biases.

Yet, a variety of limits constrict media independence. These limits range from government-imposed restrictions, both foreign and domestic, to more subtle forms of censorship resulting from the symbiosis between reporters and "official sources" within the government. Nothing illustrates this dilemma more than the case of *New York Times* reporter Judith Miller, who spent 85 days in jail for refusing to testify before a grand jury investigating the leak of CIA covert officer Valerie Plame's identity.

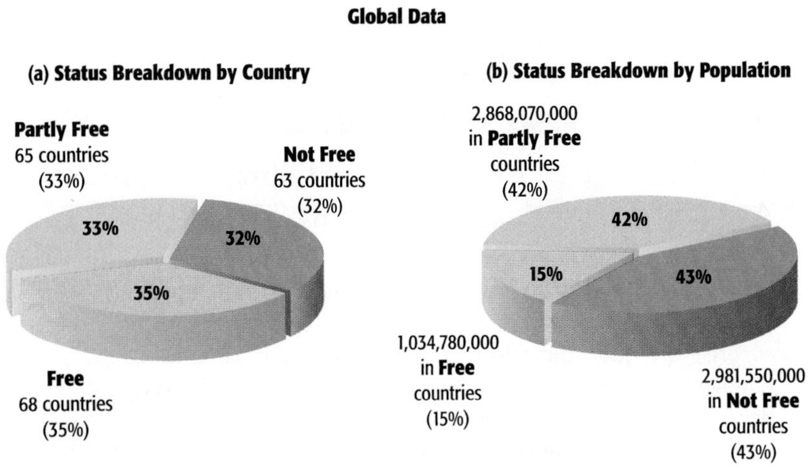


**FIGURE 12.2** Freedom of the Press Global Breakdown, 2011

*Source:* www.freedomhouse.org. Reprinted by permission of Freedom House.

Although media freedom in the United States represents a closer approach to democracy than any other nation has achieved, it is far from absolute, as evidenced by the limited access allowed to the press during early stages of the war on terrorism. Yet, as Figure 12.2 illustrates, a majority of the world's population lives in countries where far less free exchange of information is allowed. As a point for comparison, in 2008, reporters covering the Beijing Olympic Games complained that they were unable to provide fair coverage of the event because the Chinese government refused to allow certain websites to be viewed. Using Internet censorship, which has become known as "the Great Firewall," the Chinese government blocked access to websites ranging from the *New York Times* to Columbia University.[7] For a comparative perspective, see the Compared to What? feature on the next page. Reporters covering the 2012 games in England, a country that allows far more freedoms to the press, will not face similar restrictions on their access to information.

## EMERGENCE OF THE MEDIA

12.2 *How have media sources evolved over time?*

A *medium* (plural, *media*) is a means of transferring or conveying something. By **mass media,** we refer to the various means—newspapers, magazines, radio, television, the Internet—through which information is transferred from its sources to large numbers of people. Perhaps more than any other nation, the United States has become a mass media society, where citizens seek their news influences, their views on candidates, and the election process.

### Newspapers

The importance of the press in American politics dates from the Revolutionary period, when newspapers served as effective tools for mobilizing public opinion. Newspapers were also the primary vehicle for the debate over ratification of the Constitution. The *Federalist Papers,* written by Alexander Hamilton, James Madison, and John Jay, were originally published as articles in the *New York Independent Journal.*

Early political leaders saw the press as the key to public education about the new political system. Thomas Jefferson believed that the success of a participatory democracy depends on preventing citizens from making unwise decisions: "Give them full information of their affairs through the channel of the public papers, and . . . contrive that those papers should penetrate the whole mass of the people." In an address to Congress, President George Washington stressed the "importance of facilitating the circulation of political intelligence and information" through the press.[8]

**QUICK REVIEW**

Newspapers

- Importance of the media dates from the Revolutionary period, when newspapers served as effective tools for mobilizing public opinion.
- Newspapers were the primary vehicle for the debate over ratification of the Constitution.
- The press was the key to educating the public about the new political system.
- Following revolution and independence, political leaders sought allies among newspaper publishers.
- Newspaper readership is on a steep decline.

**mass media**
The various media—newspapers, magazines, radio, television, and the Internet—through which information is transferred from its sources to large numbers of people.

## Compared to WHAT?

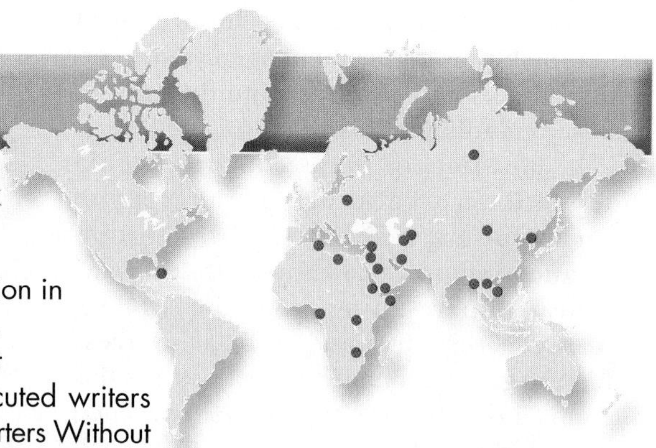

### The Courage to Inform: The Hellman/Hammett Award for Politically Persecuted Writers

Since 1989, Human Rights Watch has awarded more than $3 million in grants to writers who were targeted by their governments. In 2011, 48 journalists and writers from 24 countries received the grant. Not surprisingly, journalists from China topped the list with 10 persecuted writers receiving awards. Both the Committee to Protect Journalists and Reporters Without Borders rank China as one of the most oppressive countries in their treatment of the press. The Committee to Protect Journalists reports that in 2010, China tied with Iran in imprisoning more journalists than any other country. These journalists face arrest, torture, expulsion from their country, and sometimes death for shining a light on practices the government would rather stay hidden.

Unlike many of their colleagues in other countries, reporters in the United States are allowed many freedoms and do not have to live in fear of the government. Over the course of the U.S. path toward democracy, the government has not always been so supportive of the right to a free press. The Hellman/Hammett awards are named for American writers Lillian Hellman and Dashiell Hammett who were both questioned in the 1950s by Senator Joseph McCarthy and Congress's House Un-American Activities Committee for their political beliefs. As a result of the investigation, both writers were blacklisted and Hammett spent some time in jail. The Hellman/Hammett awards are an attempt to help writers in other countries build pressure for change and establish governments more accepting of freedom of the press.

Every year, hundreds of activists risk arrest by gathering in Moscow's Novopushkin Square to protest the murder of journalists. This photo is a memorial to Anna Politkovskaya who was gunned down on her doorstep in 2006. Since the early 1990s, more than 200 journalists have been murdered in Russia. Only 2 percent of those cases ever see the perpetrator convicted. On December 15, 2011, Khadzhimurad Kamalov, an investigative journalist known for reporting on corruption, was assassinated leaving his newspaper's office.

*Sources:* Human Rights Watch: www.hrw.org/news/2011/09/13writers-honored-commitment-free-expression; Committee to Protect Journalists: http://cpj.org/; Reporters Without Borders: http://en.rsf.org/.

In the period following revolution and independence, political leaders sought allies among newspaper publishers. As secretary of the treasury, Hamilton encouraged a staunch Federalist, John Fenno, to establish a newspaper that would espouse the administration's partisan positions. In return, Fenno was guaranteed financial assistance and printing jobs. Fenno moved from Boston to New York and then to Philadelphia, publishing the *Gazette of the United States* from the national capital.

Not to be outdone, Jefferson and other Democratic Republicans urged Philip Freneau to publish a Democratic-Republican newspaper, the *National Gazette.* Although neither paper was a financial success, a relationship was forged between editors and their benefactors. As late as 1860, the superintendent of the census classified 80 percent of the nation's periodicals, including all 373 daily newspapers, as "political in their character."[9]

The mass media revolution more or less began with the September 3, 1833, issue of the *New York Sun,* which sold on the streets for 1¢, thereby earning the name "penny press." The paper targeted the masses and offered news of local events, along with human-interest stories and entertainment. Low price (most newspapers at the time cost 6¢) and availability helped it achieve mass circulation; it could be purchased on virtually every street corner in New York. Between 1850 and 1900, the number of daily papers multiplied from 254 to 2,226. Total circulation increased nearly sevenfold, from 758,000 to more than 15 million.

**Muckraking and Yellow Journalism** During the 19th century, journalistic style changed significantly, both in the way stories were reported and in the events considered newsworthy. The mass journalism that developed during that period included much less political and foreign affairs reporting and more local news and sensationalism. In particular, newspapers began to feature coverage of dramatic court cases and criminal activity, along with a strong dose of sex or violence or both. The new journalism also spawned two trends whose effects continue today: muckraking and yellow journalism.

## THINKING CRITICALLY

Do you believe that with cable news stations (like Fox News and MSNBC) and ideological-leaning news websites (like The Huffington Post and The Drudge Report) we are returning to the age of the partisan press? What impact does biased news reporting have on the democratic ideal?

The term **muckraking** is derived from the Man with the Muckrake, a character in John Bunyan's *Pilgrim's Progress* who could look only downward and rake the filth on the floor. The word is used to describe a style of reporting that preceded today's investigative journalism. Muckraking journalists such as Lincoln Steffens and Ida Tarbell and photographer Lewis Hine came to prominence during the early 1900s, a period characterized by reform movements and populist politics known as the Progressive era. They attempted to expose the power and corruption of the rich while championing the cause of workers and the poor. Their stories of political fat cats, machine politics, evil slumlords, and heartless millionaire industrialists enraged the political and social elite. The darker side of the new journalism drew less on social conscience and more on the profit motive.

**Yellow journalism**—named after the controversial "Yellow Kid" comic strip—is usually associated with the big-city daily newspapers of Joseph Pulitzer and William Randolph Hearst. In the late 19th century, Pulitzer and Hearst transformed the staid, rather dull publications of their predecessors into brash, colorful, well-illustrated, often lurid and sensationalized organs of half-truth, innuendo, and sometimes outright lies. The writing style became more casual and colloquial and the stories more dramatic, with emphasis on sex and violence. Facts became less important than impact. Yellow journalists often left the onus of proving a story's truth or untruth on those most damaged by its publication, having little to fear from the ineffective libel and slander laws of the time.

Although these exposés inevitably suffered from subjectivity, not to mention bias, the muckrakers set a trend that continues today, evidenced by the success of Matt Drudge, who has one of the best-known political news and gossip sites on the Internet. The Drudge Report website is a model of simplicity and has billions of yearly visitors. More and more, newspapers are printing stories formerly reserved for tabloids such as *The National Enquirer*. Look no further than the extramarital affair allegations against Republican presidential candidate Herman Cain or former congressman Anthony Weiner's Twitter pictures.

Moreover, we live in an age marked by the decline of both newspapers as well as newspaper readership. A 2010 Congressional Research Report prepared for Congress titled "The U.S. Newspaper Industry in Transition" observed:

**muckraking**
A word used to describe a style of investigative reporting that uncovered many scandals and abuses.

**yellow journalism**
Brash, colorful, generously illustrated, often lurid and sensationalized organs of half-truth, innuendo, and sometimes outright lies, usually associated with the big-city daily newspapers of Joseph Pulitzer and William Randolph Hearst.

> *The U.S. newspaper industry is suffering through what could be its worst financial crisis since the Great Depression. Advertising revenues are plummeting due to the severe economic downturn, while readership habits are changing as consumers turn to the Internet for free news and information. Some major newspaper chains are burdened by heavy debt loads. Between 2008 and 2010, eight major newspaper chains declared bankruptcy, several big city papers have shut down, and many have laid off reporters and editors, imposed pay reductions, cut the size of the physical newspaper, or turned to Web-only publication.*[10]

Some companies like the *Chicago Tribune* are filing for bankruptcy or deciding to become paperless, online newspapers.[11]

Since the early 1990s, the proportion of Americans saying they read a newspaper the day before has declined by 25 percent. Those reading a print edition of the newspaper fell from 38 percent in 2006 to only 26 percent in 2010. Those reading an online newspaper increased from 9 to 17 percent in the same four-year period. This still represents a net loss in newspaper readership, but the losses are mitigated by the increase in online news consumption.[12] Table 12.2 shows the changes in the amount of time people spend consuming news from all sources and Figure 12.3 illustrates the decline in newspaper readership as well as the increase in online news readership.

**Table 12.2** Age and Time Spent with the News

| | Average Total Minutes Yesterday | | | | | | | | |
|---|---|---|---|---|---|---|---|---|---|
| | 1994 | 1996 | 1998 | 2000 | 2002 | 2004 | 2006 | 2008 | 2010 |
| 18–29 | 56 | 44 | 48 | 42 | 38 | 45 | 49 | 46 | 45 |
| 30–39 | 69 | 60 | 53 | 50 | 57 | 70 | 65 | 63 | 68 |
| 40–49 | 75 | 65 | 65 | 58 | 56 | 73 | 64 | 67 | 74 |
| 50–64 | 83 | 79 | 69 | 64 | 71 | 82 | 76 | 74 | 81 |
| 65+ | 90 | 88 | 96 | 80 | 81 | 88 | 79 | 84 | 83 |

Pew Research Center, June 8–28, 2010, Q10, Q14, Q17, Q19.

All averages are estimated based on total time spent watching TV news, reading a print version of the newspaper, listening to news on the radio, and getting news online, including newspaper websites. Online news added in 2004.

*Source:* Pew Research Center for the People & the Press, © 2011, Pew Research Center. Reprinted with the permission of the Pew Research Center for the People & the Press, www.pewforum.org.

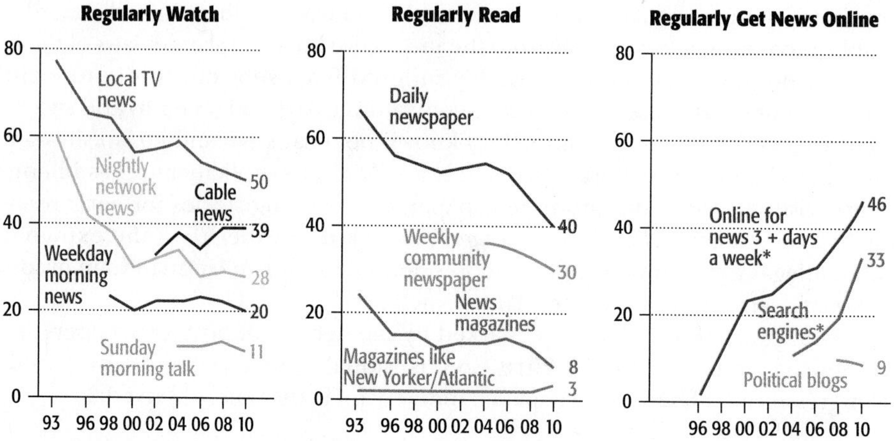


**FIGURE 12.3** Trends in News Sources

*Search engine use and general news online three of more days a week. All other trends are percentage who use "regularly."

*Source:* Pew Research Center for the People & the Press, © 2011, Pew Research Center. Reprinted with the permission of the Pew Research Center for the People & the Press, www.pewforum.org.

## Magazines

Although they are less prominent than newspapers as a source of political information, magazines enjoy wide circulation, attentive readership, and an important place in the political education of Americans. Of all the major mass media, magazines as a whole offer the widest variety of subject matter and ideological opinion because each targets certain groups of readers on the basis of socioeconomic status, education, political views, or consumer habits. The proliferation of specialized magazines covering everything from aerobics to zoology is evidence of this strategy.

Readership rates for news magazines, national news publications, and magazines such as *The New Yorker, The Atlantic,* and *Harper's Magazine* have remained relatively steady in recent years, as newspaper readership has dipped.

Of the major news magazines, the most widely read is *Time.* Originally, *Time* was the flagship of the publishing empire founded by Henry Luce. The son of a Presbyterian minister, Luce brought to the magazine his strident faith in the "American Century" and the exalted place of Western culture. According to journalist David Halberstam, Luce "was one of the first true national propagandists; he spoke to the whole nation on national issues, one man with one magazine speaking with one voice, and reaching an entire country."[13] Luce's domineering editorial stance revealed magazines' far greater potential for ideological extremes than the other mass media offered. For decades, Luce's control of *Time* made him one of the most important and influential political forces in America. *Time* created an explosive popular appetite for news coverage, and soon produced a host of competitors, including *Newsweek* and *U.S. News & World Report.* These and similar publications continue to serve as "sources of record" for elected officials, corporate executives, and informed citizens who pay close attention to political affairs.

Besides the news magazines, numerous magazines offer political opinion, including the conservative *National Review,* the liberal *New Republic,* and the progressive *Nation.* The ideological differences among these publications testify both to the targeting of readership and to the breadth of political opinion among magazine readers.

## Radio

Radio enjoyed a brief but important heyday as a significant source of political information for the American public. Developed in the early 20th century, radio technology underwent a revolution during World War I. From the 1930s until after World War II, radio was the dominant popular medium. Probably the most successful use of radio by a politician was President Franklin Roosevelt's famous series of "fireside chats." An impressive public speaker, Roosevelt used these brief broadcasts to bolster American confidence—and his own popularity—as he pushed for major legislative reforms to combat the Great Depression. Today's three major television networks—NBC, ABC, and CBS—began as radio networks.

Unlike print media, radio broadcasts could report events as they happened. This quality of immediacy produced some of the most dramatic live reporting in history, including the horrifying account of the explosion of the German zeppelin *Hindenburg* in 1937. The degree to which radio had become a trusted medium was revealed in October 1938, when Orson Welles and his Mercury Theatre of the Air broadcast "War of the Worlds," a fictionalized invasion of the earth by Martians. So convincing were the dramatization's simulated "live" news reports that many Americans believed that the invasion was real.

Radio journalism picked up where print journalism left off. Many of radio's early news reporters had begun as newspaper or magazine reporters. The most successful of them combined the journalistic skills of print reporters with the effective speaking voice required by a medium that "spoke" the news. One of radio's premier news reporters, Edward R. Murrow, established standards of integrity and reportorial skill that continue to this day. He combined the investigative traditions of the early muckrakers with concise writing and a compelling speaking voice. Murrow's career would outlast the peak of radio's popularity; he enjoyed equal fame as a television journalist.

Radio's popularity began to ebb after World War II. Its chief competition came not from newspapers and magazines but from a new, even more immediate and compelling medium—television. By 1948, three networks were broadcasting regular programming on television. But radio has not been entirely eclipsed. In recent years, conservative radio talk-show hosts such as Rush Limbaugh have become important sources of news, opinion, and entertainment for the listening public, and politicians often seek to appear on these shows. The audience for political talk radio remains more conservative and more Republican than the public at large.[14] Not surprisingly, talk-show hosts, like Limbaugh, are said to be the unofficial "voices" of political parties and movements alike.

## Television

Unlike newspapers, magazines, and radio, television developed primarily as a commercial medium, designed not so much to provide information or opinion but to entertain and stimulate mass consumerism. Thus, most Americans tend to think of television as a low-cost leisure resource rather than as a source of political information. Television is more pervasive and effective than any other form of mass communication in the United States. Advances in broadcast technology have made possible virtually instantaneous transmission of information and have greatly expanded the range of program choices for viewers. Yet network television news viewing has declined in recent years. In fact, people appear to be less inclined to believe television news and less inclined to watch it. Over the years, news viewership has been in a steady decline. Indeed, Fox News cable channel proved a bigger draw for viewers during the 2008 Republican convention than any of the broadcast networks. More recently, shows such as *The Daily Show with Jon Stewart* and *The Colbert Report* have gained immense popularity with younger audiences (as illustrated in Table 12.3) because of the manner in which they mock real newscasts and political speeches.[15] The use of entertainment as news has drawn a generally apathetic young population into the world of politics. Cable news channels such as CNN, MSNBC,

**Table 12.3** Youngest and Oldest News Audiences

| Age of Regular Readers, Viewers or Listeners | 18–49 | 50 and older |
|---|---|---|
| Colbert Report | 80% | 20% |
| Daily Show | 74 | 26 |
| New York Times | 67 | 33 |
| NPR | 56 | 44 |
| News magazines | 55 | 45 |
| Wall St. Journal | 55 | 42 |
| USA Today | 55 | 44 |
| **Total public** | 55 | 44 |
| Nightly news | 37 | 62 |
| Sunday shows | 36 | 63 |
| Bill O'Reilly | 35 | 63 |
| Sean Hannity | 33 | 65 |

Pew Research Center, June 8–28, 2010.

*Source:* Pew Research Center for the People & the Press, © 2011, Pew Research Center. Reprinted with the permission of the Pew Research Center for the People & the Press, www.pewforum.org.

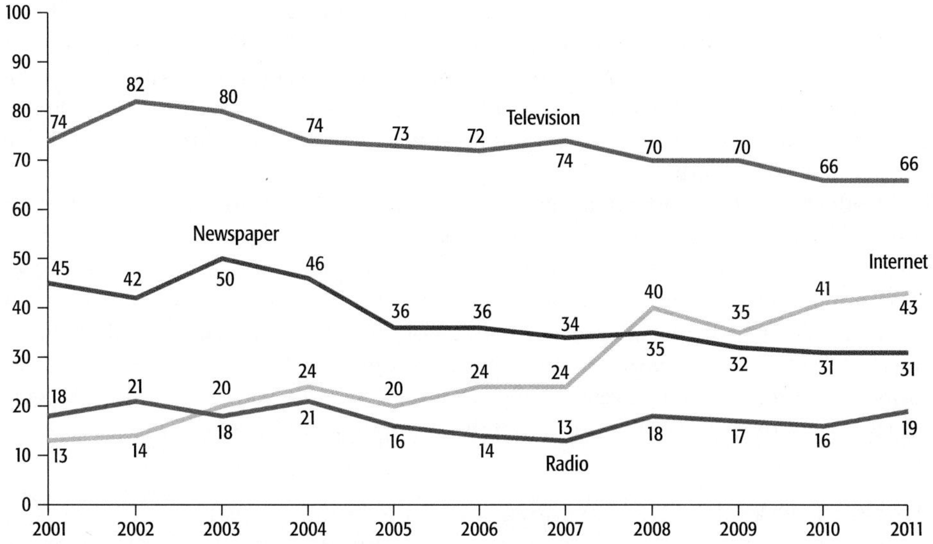


**FIGURE 12.4** Main Source of National and International News, 2011

*Note:* Pew Research Center July 20–24, 2011. Q12. Figures do not add to 100 percent because of multiple responses. *Source:* Pew Research Center for the People & the Press, © 2011, Pew Research Center. Reprinted with the permission of the Pew Research Center for the People & the Press, www.pewforum.org.

or the Fox News Channel regularly have more viewers than the big three nightly network news broadcasts.[16]

TV news is still a widely used source, although, as Figure 12.4 indicates, trends in news consumption are clearly changing with the use of online sources on the rise.[17]

## New Media Technologies

**Satellite** An especially significant technological advance was the satellite. Satellite technology made television an instantaneous means of worldwide communication. The cost of satellite relay links between the East and West Coasts of the United States has dropped significantly, and the cost of transmission links to formerly remote areas in the Far East and Middle East has been reduced by half. One effect has been expanded coverage of the president's activities, both in Washington and abroad. In the early 1980s, the number of local news stations with Washington bureaus grew from 15 to more than 50. Today, that number has quadrupled. Satellites have also affected the political process. Senators and members of the administration, as well as candidates for office, are making increasing use of direct satellite links to bypass network news and appear on local television newscasts.

In the 1970s, fewer than half of all television news stories were shown on the day they occurred. Today, new technology makes it inconceivable for any news story other than special features to be more than a few hours, if not minutes, old. The use of videophones during the early stages of the war on terrorism brought live visual images back from distant Afghanistan. Today, these devises are used by ordinary citizens to capture news and upload it to the Internet within minutes.

**Cable Television** Cable television was developed in the 1950s to bring television programming to remote areas beyond the reach of normal VHF and UHF broadcast signals. Since the 1980s, cable television has become almost universal throughout the United States, although in recent years it has faced a serious challenge from satellite dish systems. Both systems are more popular than regular broadcasting because they provide superior signal definition and a wider variety of programming choices than any single broadcast market could provide. Channels such as C-SPAN, Cable News Network, CNN Headline News, Fox News, MSNBC, and Current TV, as well as specialty channels for sports, cooking, feature films, and cultural programming, compete vigorously with the established broadcast networks for viewers' attention. Moreover, just about every available survey confirms that cable audiences are younger and better educated.

Collectively, these advances have produced what Austin Ranney called *narrowcasting*. Network television broadcasts television signals over the air to be picked up by wireless receivers in the homes of a huge, heterogeneous audience. Narrowcasting, in contrast, is a mass communications system "in which television signals are transmitted either by air or by direct wires to people's homes and are aimed at smaller, more narrowly defined, and more homogeneous audiences."[18] Narrowcasting involves more than a move toward greater programming efficiency; it has developed largely as a way to boost profits in an increasingly competitive media market.

**World Wide Web** As we have already seen, the Internet is playing an increasingly important role in obtaining and disseminating political information. News organizations now have their own webpages, and candidate websites are now ubiquitous. The Internet allows voters to easily view a candidate's platforms, programs, and biographical information. Candidates also use the Internet to attract campaign contributions. Virtually every government agency, lobbying group, interest group, newspaper, and television station has a webpage with accessible information. Indeed, much of the updated information for this textbook comes from reliable websites. The Web has become the great equalizer in American politics—what one political analyst described as "keypad democracy."[19] A Pew Research study found that between 2008 and 2010, 15 percent more Americans used a search engine to find news online.[20] Especially for young Americans, the Internet has become a means of empowerment for acquiring political information, as illustrated in Tables 12.4 and 12.5.

The 2008 election showcased the vital role technology plays in politics. Facebook, an online community, and YouTube, an online video archive, both sponsored presidential debates. This provided Americans with the opportunity to directly submit questions to the candidates. These debates were geared toward young voters. In addition to the Internet, candidates used text-messaging and their own Facebook and Twitter pages to inform voters of campaign developments and policy positions.[21] Both YouTube and Facebook again sponsored Republican primary debates for the 2012 election.

The Internet is far outpacing radio, newspapers, and magazines as a source for news and entertainment. Some see the Internet as Peter Leyden, director of the New Politics Institute, sees it: "the end of the broadcast era."[22] Moreover, the Web is now the dominant source for younger people who get news during the course of the day.

Candidates now rely on campaign websites to promote themselves, inform voters, and raise money. Before he ended his campaign, Herman Cain's presidential campaign website provided voters with his biographical information, his issue opinions, details on his 999 plan, his campaign schedule, a store to purchase Cain for President merchandise, and a link for donations. His webpage also ran a ticker of Cain's Twitter posts.

## Blogs and Social Media

Millions of online diarists known as bloggers now share their opinions daily online, interacting with a global audience. Bloggers see themselves as "the single most transformative media technology

**Table 12.4** Who Gets News Through Social Networking Sites or Twitter?

| Percentage Who Get News Through Social Networking Sites or Twitter | General Public | | Among SNS or Twitter Users | |
|---|---|---|---|---|
| | Regularly | Sometimes | Regularly | Sometimes |
| Total | 8% | 12% | 17% | 27% |
| Men | 7 | 11 | 16 | 25 |
| Women | 9 | 13 | 19 | 28 |
| 18–24 | 13 | 26 | 15 | 31 |
| 25–29 | 14 | 23 | 19 | 30 |
| 30–39 | 17 | 20 | 26 | 31 |
| 40–49 | 8 | 11 | 16 | 23 |
| 50–64 | 4 | 6 | 14 | 18 |
| 65+ | * | 2 | 3 | 15 |
| College grad+ | 13 | 13 | 21 | 21 |
| Some college | 9 | 13 | 17 | 24 |
| High school or less | 4 | 12 | 13 | 36 |

Pew Research Center, June 8–28, 2010, Q57 & Q61.

*Source:* Pew Research Center for the People & the Press, © 2011, Pew Research Center. Reprinted with the permission of the Pew Research Center for the People & the Press, www.pewforum.org.

**Table 12.5** National vs. Local Sources of News

**Internet Cited Far Less Often as Source of Local News**

| ***Nat'l/Int'l News*** | **Total** | **18–29** | **30–49** | **50–64** | **65+** |
|---|---|---|---|---|---|
| Television | 66% | 51% | 61% | 75% | 81% |
| Internet | 43 | 65 | 50 | 36 | 15 |
| Newspapers | 31 | 24 | 25 | 33 | 49 |
| Radio | 19 | 16 | 21 | 20 | 15 |
| *Local News* | | | | | |
| Television | 59 | 57 | 58 | 62 | 60 |
| Internet | 17 | 23 | 23 | 12 | 4 |
| Newspapers | 39 | 37 | 31 | 42 | 55 |
| Radio | 14 | 10 | 11 | 19 | 19 |

Pew Research Center, July 20–24, 2011, Q12, Q15f2. Figures do not add to 100% because not all categories are shown and because multiple responses were permitted.

*Source:* Pew Research Center for the People & the Press, © 2011, Pew Research Center. Reprinted with the permission of the Pew Research Center for the People & the Press, www.pewforum.org.

since the invention of the printing press."[23] Blogs, short for *weblogs,* are online journals through which people become writers of news and, in doing so, increase their civic participation. In 1999, approximately 50 blogs appeared on the Web; today there are well over 170 million.[24] The term *blogosphere* describes the universe of blogs. The significance of this development cannot be overestimated: "Drawing upon the

Japanese citizens show the ease of Twitter and Facebook use with their mobile devices. Twitter and Facebook allow people all over the world to share information with a few keystrokes.

content of the international media and the World Wide Web, they weave together an elaborate network with agenda-setting power on issues ranging from human rights in China to the U.S. occupation of Iraq. What began as a hobby is evolving into a new medium that is changing the landscape for journalists and policymakers alike."[25]

The most recent technology involves both Twitter and social media like Facebook. Following the June 2009 presidential elections in Iran, Twitter served as the best social media tool for information on what was happening in Iran. People on the ground and across the globe were chatting about every breaking update, every news item, and every story they could find. In 2011, Twitter and Facebook once again played an important role as tools for political communication during the Arab Spring movement. In Egypt and Tunisia, many citizens used Facebook and Twitter to organize, spread information, or learn about the protests. When the Egyptian government shut down the Internet in an attempt to dampen the people's ability to organize protests, Twitter quickly launched a "Speak-to-Tweet" service that allowed protestors to use phone lines to spread messages across Twitter.

YouTube, blogs, and photo-sharing sites such as Flickr have become a key medium for information distribution, particularly when traditional media have difficulties obtaining video and photos of events. These social networking sites allow anyone to post videos, photos, or information on events. This helps news spread faster and farther than was possible only a few years earlier. Many of the most powerful images from the Arab Spring revolutions were taken by average citizens in the streets and then sent across the globe via websites hosting user-generated content. Traditional media then picked up many of these images and stories, further disseminating breaking news from places journalists have a difficult time covering.

**QUICK REVIEW**

Functions of the Media

- Means through which people learn about world conditions and events.
- Interpret events by giving them meaning and context and, in the process, often shape opinions.
- Play important role in the process of socialization, by which people learn to conform to their society's norms and values.

# FUNCTIONS OF THE MEDIA

12.3 *What functions do the media perform in a democracy?*

Social scientists are in general agreement that the mass media perform three basic functions: (1) surveillance of world events, (2) interpretation of events, and (3) socialization of individuals into cultural settings. "The manner in which these . . . functions are performed," writes political scientist Doris Graber, "affects the political fate of individuals, groups, and social organizations, as well as the course of domestic and international politics."[26]

Ron Paul and Rick Perry listen to Mitt Romney respond to a moderator's question during the Fox News/Google co-sponsored GOP Presidential Nomination Debate in Florida on September 22, 2011. Perry's performance in the debates did considerable damage to his campaign.

## Surveillance

In their surveillance role, the media function, as Marshall McLuhan observed, as "sense extensions" for people who do not participate directly in events. From the media we learn about world conditions, cultural events, sports, weather, and much else. In many respects, as the 2009 Iranian presidential elections demonstrated, multifaceted and diverse media have transformed the world into a global community.

Every afternoon, television news anchors and their staffs sift through myriad stories, tapes, and bits of information funneled to them during the day to identify the most important information and events. What they select will be relayed to the public in evening news broadcasts. Thus, the news anchors actually define what is newsworthy. The ability of the media to decide what constitutes news is a controversial aspect of their surveillance role. "There are few checks on the media's surveillance role," writes Doris Graber. "The power of the media to set the civic agenda is a matter of concern because it is not controlled by a system of formal checks and balances as is power at various levels of government. It is not subject to periodic review through the electoral process. If media emphases or claims are incorrect, remedies are few."[27]

Surveillance can occur at the private as well as public level. Despite the appeals from many in the administration and slain *Wall Street Journal* reporter Daniel Pearl's family, CBS decided to show the nongraphic portions of the amateur video showing Pearl's murder, determining that the U.S. public had a right to understand the depth of the propaganda war against the United States. The complete graphic version soon turned up on the Internet. In the global war on terrorism, terrorists are resorting to blogs and video-sharing programs like YouTube in order to spread their message. This is what happened in July 2009 when Taliban insurgents in Afghanistan released a 28-minute video of a U.S. soldier who went missing in late June. In the video, the soldier says he fears he will never see his family again, and he urged the American people to demand that the U.S. government withdraw its troops from Afghanistan.[28]

The media not only bring certain matters to public attention (as shown in the timeline on political scandals) but it also dooms certain others to obscurity. During election campaigns, for example, the press is the "great mentioner," repeating the names of certain individuals who are being mentioned as possible candidates, or applying labels such as "dark horse" or "long shot." "At any given time in this country," writes journalist David Broder, "there are several hundred persons who are potential candidates for nomination. . . . Who is it that winnows this field down to manageable size? The press—and particularly that small segment of the press called the national political reporters."[29]

## Interpretation

The media do much more than provide public and private surveillance of events. They also interpret those events by giving them meaning

### Approaching Democracy Timeline

**Media as a Watchdog: History of Scandals**

| | |
|---|---|
| **1797** | The nation's first political sex scandal—regarding Alexander Hamilton's affair with a married woman—is reported in a newspaper. |
| **1802** | In September, a Richmond newspaper claims that Jefferson had for many years "kept, as his concubine, one of his own slaves." "Her name is Sally." |
| **1907** | *Cosmopolitan* magazine publishes David Graham Phillips's *The Treason of the Senate,* which uncovers bribery in the United States Senate. |
| **1963** | The press ignores John F. Kennedy's extramarital affairs while he is president. |
| **1973** | The *Washington Post* breaks a story linking President Nixon to the Watergate break-in. |
| **1988** | Colorado senator and presidential candidate Gary Hart is photographed cavorting with a young woman who is not his wife on a boat called *Monkey Business*. |
| **1992** | The *Washington Post* publishes a list of sexual abuses committed by Senator Bob Packwood; he later resigns amid multiple allegations of sexual harassment. |
| **1998** | The online website The Drudge Report reports that President Clinton had an affair with an intern and that the mainstream media were sitting on the story. |
| **2006** | Reports emerge that six-term Florida congressman Mark Foley had inappropriate instant messages to an underaged male page. Foley resigns. |
| **2007** | Senator Larry Craig is arrested for lewd conduct in a men's bathroom. It takes the media more than two months to break the story. |
| **2007** | The *National Inquirer* publishes reports that John Edwards is having an affair with filmmaker Rielle Hunter. The mainstream media does not investigate the allegations, which Edwards later admits. |
| **2008** | Democratic governor Elliot Spitzer is identified as John #9 in a scandal involving high-priced call girls and a prostitution ring. He resigns after only 14 months in office. |
| **2009** | South Carolina governor Mark Sanford admits he is having an affair that involves secret visits with his mistress in Argentina. |
| **2011** | Representative Anthony Weiner resigns after sending lewd pictures of himself to followers over Twitter. |

Democratic   Neutral   Undemocratic

and context and, in the process, often shape opinions. Psychologist Hadley Cantril illustrates this point with the following example:

> *Three umpires describe their job of calling balls and strikes in a baseball game. First umpire: "Some's balls and some's strikes and I calls 'em as they is." Second umpire: "Some's balls and some's strikes and I calls 'em as I sees 'em." Third umpire: "Some's balls and some's strikes but they ain't nothin' till I calls 'em."*[30]

According to Cantril, few journalists are like the first umpire, believing that the "balls and strikes" they count represent what is happening in the real world. Some journalists may admit to the second method of umpiring, using their judgment to "call them as they see them." The third umpire's style is the most controversial when applied to mass media coverage of significant events. For if, like the third umpire, journalists in print and television actually make the decisions regarding which actors or events are in or out of the "strike zone" or even determine their own "strike zone" or context for news, the potential power of the media becomes immense, and assertions of media "objectivity" sound rather hollow.

Actually, the process of gathering, evaluating, editing, producing, and presenting news involves each of the three umpiring styles. Some reporters may pursue a case against a prominent public figure or institution in the belief that their article will finally expose the "reality" of corruption, scandal, or wrongdoing. And every journalist—from reporters on the street to editors behind desks—exercises judgment over which events are most "newsworthy"; an event is neither a curve ball in the dirt nor a fastball on the outside corner until some journalistic "umpire" makes the decision to cover it.

Political scientist Shanto Iyengar has developed a theory of media "framing effects" particularly relevant to television news coverage. In a series of carefully controlled experiments, Iyengar and his colleagues found that the way television portrays events and actors exerts a significant influence on the opinions of those who watch the coverage. For example, coverage of terrorism that emphasizes the violence and brutality of a terrorist act without attempting to explain the motivations behind it is likely to influence viewers to consider all such actions brutal and violent, regardless of the motivations or historical explanations. This is an important point. Since the constraints of time tend to dictate relatively brief, often superficial coverage of important news, viewers are likely to form equally superficial opinions.[31]

**Investigative Journalism** Journalism may have changed since the days of the muckrakers, as the technology and political culture of America have changed, but the spirit of the muckraker lives on in the practice of **investigative journalism.** Investigative journalism differs from standard press coverage in the depth of coverage sought, the time spent researching the subject, and the shocking findings that often result from such reporting. Like their muckraking predecessors, today's investigative journalists turn their reportorial skills to uncovering corruption, scandal, conspiracy, and abuses of power in government and business.

The most familiar historical example of such reporting occurred during the 1970s Watergate scandal, revealed through extensive interviewing and analysis by two *Washington Post* reporters, Carl Bernstein and Bob Woodward. *Post* editor Ben Bradlee risked his professional reputation and the reputation of his paper by running a series of investigative articles on the Watergate break-in and its connection to the White House. Although the *Post* articles, which began raising questions in the months before the 1972 presidential election, did not affect its outcome, they eventually uncovered a scandal that led to the resignation of President Richard Nixon. Not until June 2005 was the paper's information source, Deep Throat, revealed as former FBI assistant director Mark Felt.

In another instance, in February 2007, two *Washington Post* reporters, Dana Priest and Anne Hull, uncovered neglect and frustration for soldiers at Walter Reed Hospital, the Army's top medical facility.[32] Investigative reporters look for abuses and corruption both inside government and inside the private sector. In 2011, the *Chicago Tribune*'s investigative reporter Sam Roe uncovered egregious abuses at a nursing

**investigative journalism**
The uncovering of corruption, scandal, conspiracy, and abuses of power in government and business; differs from standard press coverage in the depth of the coverage sought, the time spent researching the subject, and the shocking findings that often result from such reporting.

home for children with disabilities. His investigation brought to light the suspicious deaths of 13 children with disabilities and spurred a federal investigation of the facility. Roe was a 2011 nominee for the Pulitzer Prize for Investigative Reporting.[33]

**socialization**
The process by which people learn to conform to their society's norms and values.

**Federal Communications Commission (FCC)**
A government commission formed to allocate radio and television frequencies and regulate broadcasting procedures.

## Socialization

The media play an important role in **socialization,** the process by which people learn to conform to their society's norms and values. As we noted in Chapter 8, children acquire most of their information about their world from the mass media, either directly or indirectly through media influence on parents, teachers, or friends. The mass media also provide information that helps young people develop their own opinions. MTV provides a forum, "Choose or Lose," that informs young people about politics, issues, and candidates.

Studies of the effects of mass media exposure have found that higher reliance on television as the primary source of information seems to correlate with a greater fear of crime and random violence, even when controlling for individual socioeconomic status, education, and living conditions. Although such findings are tentative and subject to interpretation, they indicate that the medium on which most Americans rely for the bulk of their global information—television—may contribute to a growing sense of unease. The power of the media as a socializing agent is reflected in public concern about media violence, particularly in children's television programming. Although analysts remain sharply divided about the actual effects of violent programming, efforts have been made to regulate the frequency and intensity of violent and sexually explicit media content. For example, in the wake of the assassinations of Robert Kennedy and Martin Luther King Jr., television programmers canceled several popular but violent shows or changed the programs to reflect less explicit violence.

In recent years, the television networks have begun to voluntarily rate their shows for violent or adult content. Televised screenings of feature films containing explicit violence or sexual content have adopted the motion picture precedent of rating these programs and including viewer discretion warnings. Cable stations that air films "uncut" provide the original film rating and generally restrict the airing of such programming to the late evening, when children are more likely to be asleep. Although such attempts to regulate the socializing influence of mass media are controversial, they demonstrate widespread agreement that freedom of expression must sometimes be limited to avert social harm.

# LIMITS ON MEDIA FREEDOM

12.4 *Are freedoms of the press unlimited?*

The First Amendment to the Constitution states "Congress shall make no law . . . abridging the freedom . . . of the press." Ideally, the media would investigate, report, provide information, and analyze political events without government-imposed restrictions. Such restrictions are commonplace in many other nations, where the media experience various degrees of restraint, prohibition, or censorship. Americans take pride in the tradition of a free press, yet that freedom is not absolute. Laws protect against libel, slander, and obscenity, the **Federal Communications Commission (FCC)** regulates media behavior, and the judiciary imposes certain limitations as well. The nature of media ownership also plays a role in limiting media freedom.

**QUICK REVIEW**

The Federal Communications Commission (FCC)

- Regulation of the media began after World War I.
- Federal Radio Commission (FRC) was created in 1927 to monitor the growing radio broadcast industry.
- The Federal Communications Act of 1934 expanded the FRC to include telephone and telegraph communications.
- The FRC was renamed the Federal Communications Commission (FCC).
- Jurisdiction expanded to include broadcast and cable television and, most recently, communications innovations.

## Regulating the Media

Regulation of the media began after World War I, in the heyday of radio. During that period, the Radio Corporation of America (RCA) and other large consortiums established networks to broadcast news, information, and entertainment, and millions of amateur "radio hams" were buying or building simple broadcast receivers and sending their own gossip, sermons, monologues, and conversations over the increasingly congested airwaves. In 1927, the federal government stepped in to clean up the chaotic radio waves. Congress created the five-member Federal Radio Commission (FRC) to allocate frequencies and regulate broadcasting procedures. Essentially, the FRC worked to organize radio broadcasting and constrain the growing radio broadcast industry to prevent monopolization and other unfair practices.

In 1934, Congress passed the Federal Communications Act, which expanded the FRC's jurisdiction to include telephone and telegraph communications, enlarged the panel to seven members (eventually reduced again to five in 1982), and renamed the agency the Federal Communications Commission (FCC). As broadcast and cable television (CATV) developed, they too came under FCC scrutiny and jurisdiction. The most recent communications innovations—multipoint distribution service (MDS), direct broadcast satellites (DBS), and satellite master antenna television (SMATV)—have also come under the umbrella of FCC regulation.

Four sets of guidelines regulate the electronic media:

1. Rules that limit the number of stations owned or controlled by a single organization
2. Examinations of station goals and performance as part of periodic licensing
3. Rules that mandate public service and local interest programs
4. Rules that guarantee fair treatment to individuals and protect their rights

The Supreme Court has consistently upheld regulation of the electronic media under the scarcity doctrine. Although the law does not limit the number of newspapers that can be published in a given area, two radio or television stations cannot broadcast signals at the same time and at the same frequency without jamming each other. Thus, it is clearly in the public interest that government allocate frequencies to broadcasters. Broadcasting is viewed as a public resource, much like a national park, and the government establishes regulations designed to promote "the public convenience, interest, or necessity."

The scarcity doctrine, with its implications for the public interest, underlies FCC regulation of political content in radio and television broadcasts. This regulation has historically taken the form of three rules of the airwaves often referred to as the Equal Time Rule, the Fairness Doctrine, and the right of rebuttal.

**QUICK REVIEW**

Scarcity Doctrine

- The scarcity doctrine is comprised of three rules of the airwaves for the FCC's regulation of the political content of radio and television broadcasts.
- The equal opportunities rule held that a station must give equal time to all candidates.
- The Fairness Doctrine, now abandoned, required a percentage of programs on issues of public interest.
- The right to rebuttal provided airtime to refute allegations made against a person or group, free of charge, within a reasonable time.

**The Equal Time Rule** Although a station is not required to give or sell airtime to a candidate seeking a specific office, whenever it provides time to one candidate—whether for a price or for free—it must give equal time to all candidates running for the same office. This **Equal Time Rule** holds whether 2 or 200 candidates run for the office; each is entitled to equal time. Section 315(a) of the Federal Communications Act stipulates:

> *If any licensee shall permit any person who is a legally qualified candidate for any public office to use a broadcasting station, he shall afford equal opportunities to all other such candidates for that office in the use of such broadcasting station.*

The Equal Time Rule has become important in past presidential campaigns. In the 1992 presidential elections, when Ross Perot bought large blocks of time for his "infomercials" on various campaign issues, the networks involved were required to make similar blocks of time available to George Bush and Bill Clinton. However, the rule does not require that the candidates actually take advantage of the available time—only that they have the opportunity to purchase it on an equal basis with all other candidates. The Equal Time Rule remains in effect, but it is not invoked very often. Over the years, many exceptions to the rule have been put into law. It does not apply to regularly scheduled newscasts, news interview shows, documentaries, or on-the-spot news events.[34] These broad exceptions include nearly all coverage of political events outside of political advertizing. The Equal Time Rule is an issue when celebrities, such as actors Ronald Reagan (star of television shows *Death Valley Days*

**Equal Time Rule**
A requirement that radio and television stations allow equal time to all candidates for office.

and *G.E. Theater*), Arnold Schwarzenegger (movie star with roles in the Terminator franchise, numerous action movies including *Conan the Barbarian,* and comedies like *Twins* and *Kindergarten Cop*), and Fred Thompson (starred on *Law and Order* and guest starred on *Matlock* and *Sex in the City*) run for office. Broadcasters must be wary of airing TV shows and movies where these candidates appear.

**Fairness Doctrine**
A policy, now abandoned, that radio and television stations provide time to all sides in programs of public interest.

**right of rebuttal**
The right to refute the allegations presented on a radio or television station, free of charge, within a reasonable time.

**The Fairness Doctrine** The **Fairness Doctrine,** now abandoned, required radio and television stations to provide a reasonable percentage of time for programs dealing with issues of public interest. (In this chapter's Approaching Contemporary Issues in Democracy feature, we consider the effects of reinstating the Fairness Doctrine.) Stations were also required to provide time for those who wished to express opposition to any highly controversial public issue aired or discussed on the station. Defining what is controversial had traditionally been left to the administrative courts, but the FCC has ruled that "two viewpoints" satisfies the licensee's obligation. The Supreme Court upheld the Fairness Doctrine in 1969 in *Red Lion Broadcasting* v. *FCC.* A federal court of appeals later ruled that the doctrine was not law and could be repealed without congressional approval. Congress then passed a bill that would have made the Fairness Doctrine permanent, but President Reagan vetoed the bill on the grounds that federal policing of editorial judgment of journalists was an outrage. Following the veto, the FCC negated the doctrine in 1987.[35] Although not enforced for nearly 24 years, the Fairness Doctrine was still technically "on the books" until the FCC voted to have the language removed from its rule book in August 2011.

**The Right of Rebuttal** When the honesty, integrity, or morality of persons or groups is attacked on a station, they have the **right of rebuttal**—the right to refute the allegations, free of charge, within a reasonable time. The FCC operates under the assumption that a maligned person deserves a chance to reply, and the public has a right to hear that response. The rule does not apply to attacks on foreign groups or leaders, to personal attacks made by legally qualified candidates or their representatives, or to live, on-the-spot broadcasts.

## APPROACHING Contemporary Issues in Democracy

### Reinstating the Fairness Doctrine

**ISSUE:** What if the Fairness Doctrine was reinstated, requiring television broadcasters to devote airtime to controversial public issues and to provide contrasting opinions on these issues?

**Question 1:**
How does the debate over the Fairness Doctrine relate to the tension between the ideals of freedom and equality? By abolishing the Fairness Doctrine, did the FCC place more importance on freedom or equality?

**Question 2:**
If the Fairness Doctrine is a violation of the First Amendment right to a free press, why is the Equal Time Rule not considered a similar violation? What are the key differences between the two regulations that allowed the FCC to determine the Fairness Doctrine was unconstitutional but that the Equal Time Rule is an acceptable restriction?

**Question 3:**
Does the corporatization of the media lessen the need for the Fairness Doctrine or increase the need for regulations to protect minority opinion?

**prior restraint**
An action in which the government seeks to ban the publication of controversial material by the press before it is published; censorship.

## Prior Restraint versus the Right to Know

In 1971, former government employee Daniel Ellsberg gave the *New York Times* copies of classified documents on the Vietnam War. The documents had been prepared in 1968 during the presidency of Lyndon Johnson, and they revealed the concerns of senior Defense Department officials during the Kennedy and Johnson years. The government sought to suppress publication of the documents by obtaining a judicial restraining order, an action known as **prior restraint.** President Richard Nixon maintained that publishing the papers would threaten the lives of servicemen and servicewomen, intelligence officers, and military plans still in operation in Vietnam.

The case eventually reached the Supreme Court, which decided in favor of the *Times*. In his concurring opinion on the case, Justice Hugo Black offered a strong argument for absolute freedom of the press:

> *Paramount among the responsibilities of a free press is the duty to prevent any part of the Government from deceiving the people and sending them off to distant lands to die of foreign fever and foreign shot and shell. . . . The New York Times and the Washington Post and other newspapers should be commended for serving the purpose that the Founding Fathers saw so clearly. In revealing the workings of government that led to the Vietnam War, the newspapers nobly did precisely that which the Founders hoped and trusted they would do.*[36]

### THINKING CRITICALLY

During the Vietnam War, the media regularly broadcast images of soldiers' coffins returning to the United States. As the Gulf War began in 1991, President Bush banned the media from showing any "coffin pictures." Barack Obama's administration overturned this ban so long as the dead soldier's family consents to the picture. Do you think this ban is an appropriate restriction of the freedom of the press? Does it protect the privacy of the soldiers, or does it limit the public from seeing the true cost of war?

In another case, when CNN broadcast recorded phone conversations involving Panamanian general Manuel Noriega as he awaited trial in Miami in 1990, the Supreme Court refused to block a lower court's injunction banning all future broadcasts that CNN planned to air. The controversy raised important constitutional questions. At issue were Noriega's right to a fair trial as well as freedom of the press. What made the issue more intriguing was that the Court decided to suppress publication despite the fact that the U.S. government was responsible for taping the phone conversations in the first place.

Other cases have been concerned with the media's right to cover a trial and whether that coverage would threaten the fairness of the trial. In January 2002, a federal judge rejected cable television's *Court TV* request to broadcast the trial of Zacarias Moussaoui, believed to be the 20th hijacker on September 11, 2001. In his ruling, Judge Leonie M. Brinkema cited procedural and security reasons for denying the request to overturn a ban on television broadcasts of federal criminal trials. The case of *Miami Herald Publishing Co.* v. *Tornillo* (1974) brought up the issue of whether or not statutory guidelines implemented by Florida state law require newspapers to publish specific replies from political candidates attacked in their columns rather than merely publishing retractions. The Court ruled against the "right to reply" law, stating that it "turns afoul the elementary First Amendment proposition that government may not force a newspaper to print copy which, in the journalistic discretion, it chooses to leave on the newspaper floor." That is, even when accused of publicly defaming a political figure, newspapers could not be required by law to print the responses of the defamed figure, since this was to "force a newspaper to print copy" in violation of the constitutional guarantee of a free press. As Chief Justice Warren E. Burger noted, "A responsible press is an undoubtedly desirable goal, but press responsibility is not mandated by the Constitution, and like many other virtues, it cannot be legislated."[37]

A Chinese police officer checks an Internet user's ID card at an Internet café in Xuchang City, central China's Henan province. Many cities in China have established monitoring systems where Internet cafés scan and save users' ID cards and take their pictures.

Even with a relatively broad guarantee of freedom, certain laws restrict how the press may cover news. Journalists are allowed wide latitude in levying charges against whomever they choose and may even print facts or accusations that subsequently prove untrue, as long as they do not *knowingly* publish untruths or print intentionally damaging statements known as **libel.** Anyone attempting to sue a newspaper for libel must also prove that the publication in question actually caused damage. As we see in Chapter 13, libel is difficult to prove, especially for public figures whose reputations may be affected by numerous factors besides a single journalistic "hit piece" and who have an opportunity to make a reply. In general, as long as journalists do not set out to attack a public figure with malice, they are not subject to prevailing laws against libel.

**libel**
Published material that damages a person's reputation or good name in an untruthful and malicious way. Libelous material is not protected by the First Amendment.

# IDEOLOGICAL BIAS AND MEDIA CONTROL

12.5 *Are the media biased in their reporting?*

Over the past ten years, there has been a documented decline in the credibility of all news organizations, across the board and across all mediums. Table 12.6 shows that the public expresses profound and continuing skepticism about what they see, hear, and read on television news. No major news outlet—whether broadcast or cable, print, or online—stands out as particularly credible. Especially interesting is that online news is viewed with more skepticism than its print, broadcast, and cable counterparts.

Does the mass media display a bias in the selection and presentation of news? Although the majority of reporters in both print and electronic media are fairly liberal, their bosses—the magazine and newspaper publishers and network executives—tend to be more conservative, some decidedly so. Most statistical evidence supporting conservative charges of a liberally biased "media elite" fails to clearly differentiate between the reporters, the editors, and the publishers and owners of media outlets; some analyses examine only the reporters, a peculiarly well-educated, well-paid, and liberal cohort of the American public. In the often-cited studies of

**Table 12.6** Believability Trends Stable for TV News Outlets

**Believe All or Most of What Organization Says**

| | 1998 | 2000 | 2002 | 2004 | 2006 | 2008 | 2010 |
|---|---|---|---|---|---|---|---|
| CNN | 42% | 39% | 37% | 32% | 28% | 30% | 29% |
| 60 Minutes | 35 | 34 | 34 | 33 | 27 | 29 | 33 |
| Local TV news | 34 | 33 | 27 | 25 | 23 | 28 | 29 |
| NPR | 19 | 25 | 23 | 23 | 22 | 27 | 28 |
| C-SPAN | 32 | 33 | 30 | 27 | 25 | 26 | 23 |
| NBC News | 30 | 29 | 25 | 24 | 23 | 24 | 20 |
| ABC News | 30 | 30 | 24 | 24 | 22 | 24 | 21 |
| MSNBC | — | 28 | 28 | 22 | 21 | 24 | 22 |
| Fox News channel | — | 26 | 24 | 25 | 25 | 23 | 27 |
| NewsHour | 29 | 24 | 26 | 23 | 23 | 23 | NA |
| CBS News | 28 | 29 | 26 | 24 | 22 | 22 | 21 |
| BBC | — | — | — | — | — | 21 | NA |

Percentages based on those who could rate each organization.

*Source:* Pew Research Centers Forum on Religion & Public Life, © 2008, Pew Research Center. Reprinted with the permission of the Pew Forum on Religion & Public life, www.pewforum.org.

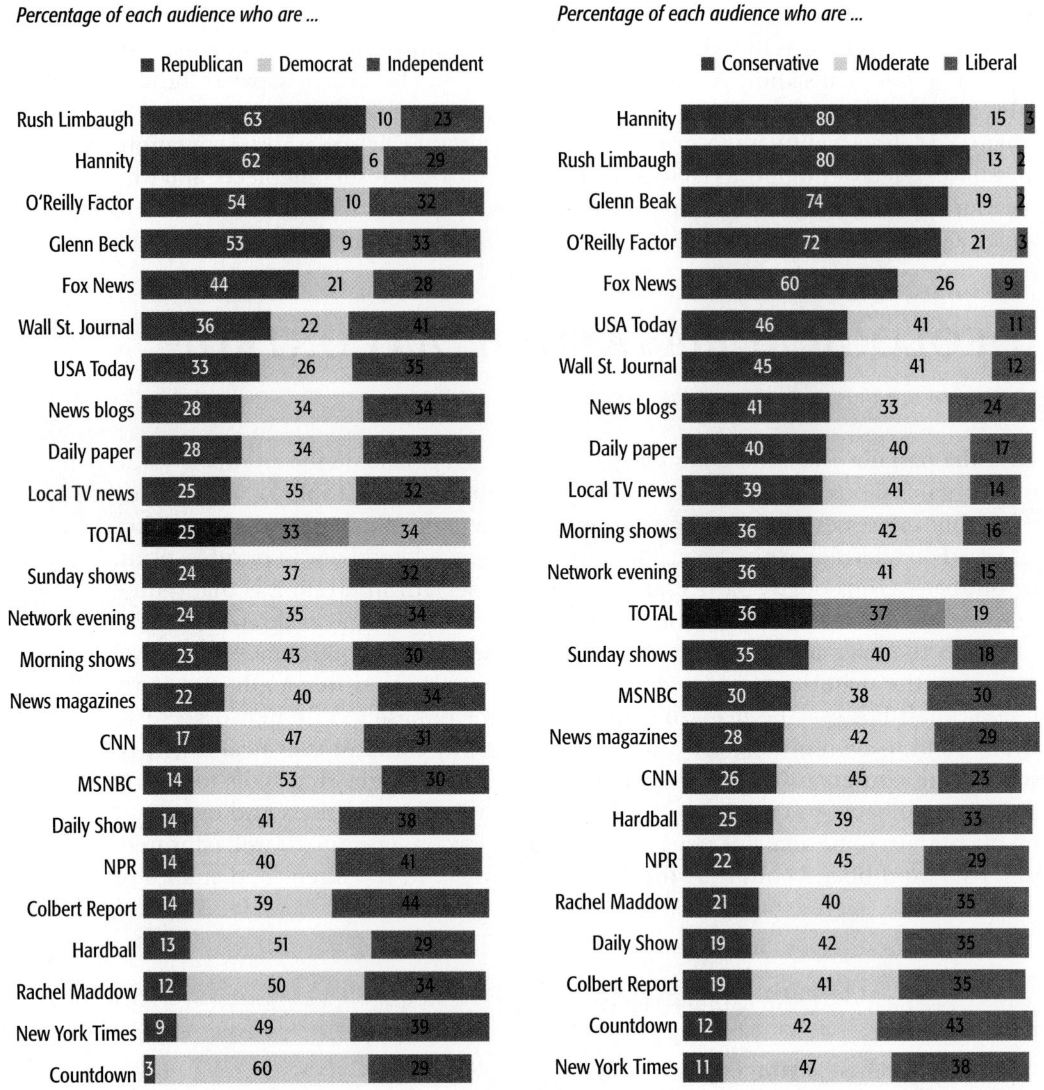


**FIGURE 12.5** Media Audience Profiles: Party and Ideology

*Note:* PEW RESEARCH CENTER, June 8–28, 2010. Figures may not add to 100% because of rounding and because those who did not answer party affiliation or ideology questions are not shown. Based on regular readers/viewers/listeners of each source.

*Source:* Pew Research Center for the People & the Press, © 2011, Pew Research Center. Reprinted with the permission of the Pew Research Center for the People & the Press, www.pewforum.org.

Robert Lichter, Linda Lichter, and Stanley Rothman, for example, the media elite includes reporters, editors, and executives, but only as an aggregate population with no distinctions regarding the differences that might exist within this elite. Simply establishing the liberal leanings of reporters does not prove liberal press bias.[38] Additionally, the audiences for different news programs have grown more disparate from one another. For example, Figures 12.5 and 12.6 show that audiences for Fox News programs are far more conservative and Republican than are viewers of MSNBC. As noted in the discussion of narrowcasting earlier in this chapter, these media corporations are aware of their audience's political preferences and shape their news coverage and commentary to please those who consume their product, which further serves to separate the ideological preferences of the different audiences.

In 2002, a book by former CBS journalist Bernard Goldberg engendered heated debate. In *Bias,* Goldberg argues that real media bias is the result of how those in the media see the world and how their bias directly affects how we all see the world. Goldberg maintains that an elitist culture at the networks is out of touch with conservative

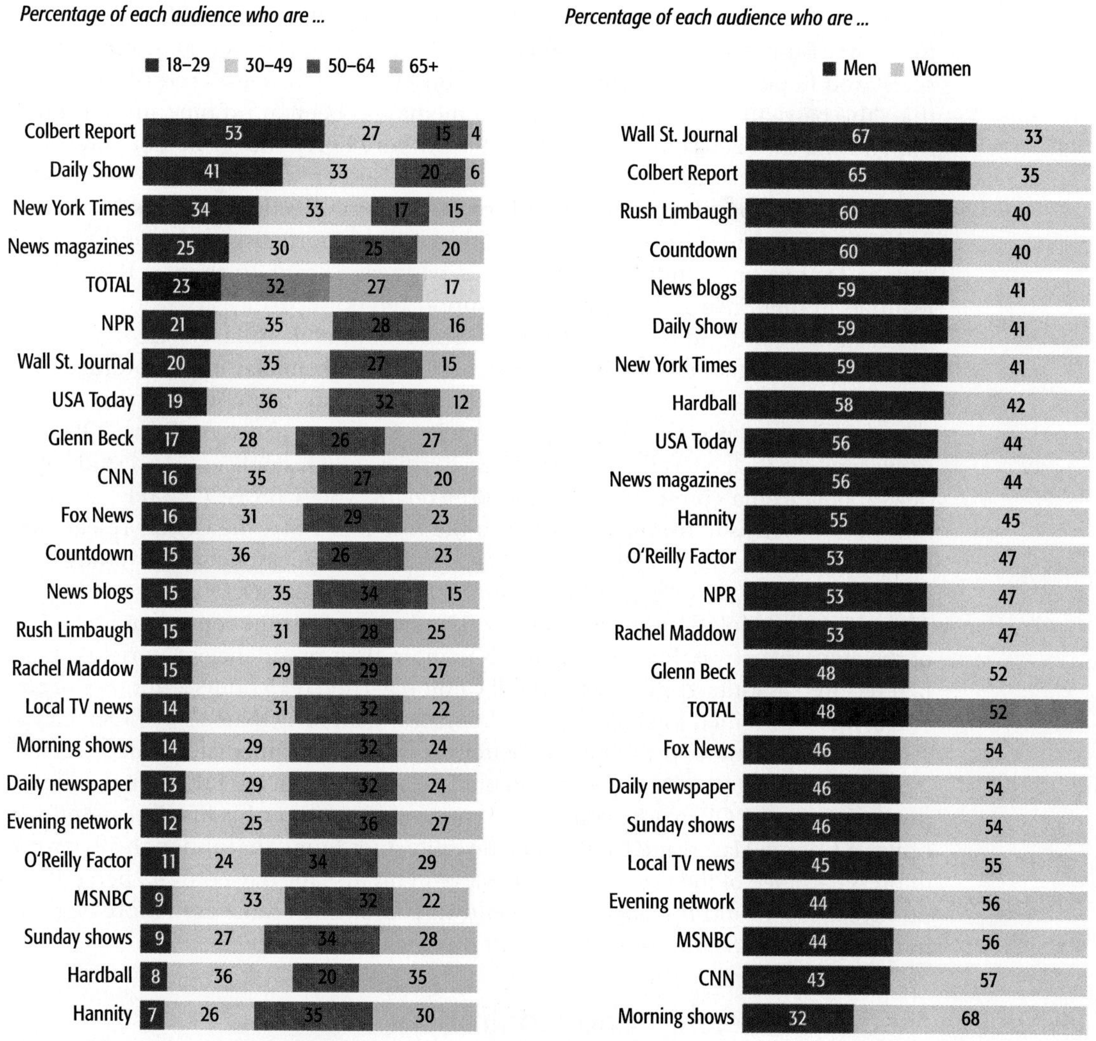


**FIGURE 12.6** Media Audience Profiles: Age and Gender

*Note:* PEW RESEARCH CENTER, June 8–28, 2010. Figures may not add to 100% because of rounding; those who did not anser questions about their age not shown. Based on regular readers/viewers/listeners of each source.
*Source:* Pew Research Center for the People & the Press, © 2011, Pew Research Center. Reprinted with the permission of the Pew Research Center for the People & the Press, www.pewforum.org.

America. According to research surveys, 55 percent of journalists consider themselves liberal, compared with about 23 percent of the population as a whole. And the media's liberal attitudes are pervasive on numerous issues, such as government regulation, abortion, and school prayer. Do these attitudes affect news coverage?[39]

In a *Times Mirror* survey of more than 250 members of the press, a substantial majority (55 percent) of American journalists who followed the 1992 presidential campaign believed that former president George H. W. Bush was harmed by press coverage. "Only 11 percent felt that Bill Clinton's campaign was harmed by press coverage. Moreover, one out of three journalists (36 percent) thought that the media helped Clinton win the presidency, while a mere 3 percent believed that the press coverage helped the Bush effort." During the waning days of the campaign, President Bush frequently waved a red bumper sticker that stated, "Annoy the Media: Reelect Bush."[40]

A widely circulated May 2005 poll by the University of Connecticut Department of Public Policy revealed a substantial gap between journalists and the public, but even more disturbing is the finding that six in ten Americans perceive bias in reporting and 22 percent favor government censorship of news. When journalists were asked for whom they voted in the 2004 election, reporters overwhelmingly picked Kerry over Bush. In the sample of 300 journalists, registered Democrats outnumbered registered Republicans by three to one.[41] Conservative journalist Fred Barnes wrote that "the partisan bias of the mainstream media has been at no time more evident than during the [2004] presidential election" where Kerry got "77 percent favorable coverage in the stories regarding him," while "for Bush, it was 34 percent."[42] MSNBC collected data from the public records of the Federal Election Commission dating to 2004 to examine the political contributions of 143 journalists and found that 125 gave to Democratic candidates and causes, whereas a scant 16 showed Republican leanings in their giving. Two journalists supported both parties.[43]

A study conducted by the Center for Media and Public Affairs at George Mason University found that the media had given President Obama far more coverage than either of his two predecessors combined and more positive coverage than either received at a similar point in their presidencies. The study also found that "Obama's positive media image hasn't precluded heavy criticism of his policies." In a study of all news about Obama's presidency that appeared on the ABC, CBS, NBC, and Fox evening newscasts as well as in front-page stories in the *New York Times*, the Center researchers found that "during his first 50 days in office, the three broadcast network evening news shows devoted 1,021 stories lasting 27 hours 44 minutes to Barack Obama's presidency. The daily average of seven stories and over 11 minutes of airtime represents about half of the entire newscasts. By contrast, at this point in their presidencies George W. Bush had received 7 hours 42 minutes and Bill Clinton garnered 15 hours 2 minutes of coverage, for a combined total airtime five hours less than Mr. Obama's. . . . Obama has received not only more press but also better press than his immediate predecessors."[44]

This period of positive coverage did not last long. Just as it has for other presidents, press coverage of Obama became much more negative after his first few months in office. A George Mason and Chapman University study found that although 59 percent of press coverage of the president was positive in his first 100 days, only 43 percent was positive in his second 100 days as president, and coverage became even more negative in the next 100 days with only 39 percent positive coverage.[45]

## Media Ownership and Control

One reason to avoid overreacting to evidence of media bias concerns the economics of mass communication—specifically, the ownership and control of mass media outlets. Many recent analyses suggest that the mass media's overwhelming bias is neither liberal nor conservative but corporate. William Greider maintains that the dissemination of information is so dominated by large media conglomerates and lobbyists for special interests who can afford to spend huge amounts of money that no real dialogue can exist because those without money—for example, the far left—have little chance of bringing their viewpoints into the public debate.[46]

Media scholar Ben Bagdikian has written extensively on the development of what he calls a "private ministry of information" created by the formation of a "media monopoly." Bagdikian's studies reveal that only five corporations control most of America's daily newspapers, magazines, television broadcasting, books, and motion pictures. As media control slips into fewer and fewer hands, Bagdikian argues, the content of those media becomes increasingly similar because the overall interests of corporate executives tend to coincide, especially since many of them sit on the boards of directors of the same companies. The result is a disturbingly homogeneous version of "reality," tempered by the priorities of large corporations that own and advertise through major media outlets. Consequently, the media are reluctant to attack their own corporate masters. An example is the refusal of NBC's *Today* show to include in its story on national boycotts of large corporations one of the largest—General Electric—which happens to own NBC. The same was true when ABC news programs refused in 1999 to report negative stories on Disney Corporation, its parent company.[47]

Since World War II, news media business profits have steadily increased. This increase has been accompanied by a decrease in competition. With the exception of

CNN, Fox, MSNBC, and a few cable programs, the three major television networks enjoy a monopoly over news and commercial sponsorship. The same process is at work in the newspaper industry, where large groups such as Gannett, Thomson, and Knight-Ridder control more than 80 percent of the daily circulation of all newspapers.

More recently, cross-ownership of media has increased—newspapers, television networks, book publishing, and Internet service providers are all owned by conglomerates. For example, Time merged with Warner Brothers to form Time Warner. The conglomerate then acquired Turner Broadcasting (CNN, Headline News, and TNT cable networks). And then America Online acquired Time Warner. In the same vein, Disney purchased Capital Cities, which owns ABC, which in turn owns a host of cable stations, including ESPN. By 1989, Capital Cities/ABC owned the ABC television network, 29 affiliated radio and television stations, as well as 10 daily newspapers, 77 weeklies, and 80 specialized periodicals. Major conglomerates anchored by General Electric and Westinghouse own NBC and CBS, respectively. In 2011, General Electric sold all but 49 percent of its shares of NBC to Comcast.

In 2011, controversy erupted over Fox News owner Rupert Murdoch's British media holdings role in a phone hacking and police bribery scandal. Murdoch testified in front of the House of Commons Select Committee on Culture, Media, and Sport on July 19, 2011. The FBI and Department of Justice opened investigations into whether Murdoch's media enterprises engaged in phone tapping of 9/11 victims.

These mergers have been highly beneficial to media autonomy. By putting themselves on solid financial footing, the mass media need not fear dependency on others, most notably politicians. In addition, this independence has increased news-gathering capabilities. However, some contend that the high concentration of media in the hands of a few can limit the expression of alternative views, further dilute news coverage, and limit criticism of the status quo. In February 2002, the court of appeals for the District of Columbia nullified the FCC's cross-ownership rule, which prevents one company from owning a cable system and local broadcast station in the same market. This opened a door to a new wave of mergers among cable conglomerates and broadcast companies. The ruling was a huge victory for media giants such as AOL, Time Warner, Viacom, and News Corporation, which have long maintained that the regulation prevented expansion.

In summer 2009, the *New York Times* reported that the chair of General Electric (which owned MSNBC), Jeffrey Immelt, and the chair of News Corporation (which owns Fox News), Rupert Murdoch, decided to end the feud between MSNBC's Keith Olbermann and Fox's Bill O'Reilly because the dispute was bad for the interests of the corporate entities that have extensive relationships with the federal government.[48] The so-called peace lasted just a few days, with the hosts returning to attacking one another shortly after the agreement reached by the chairs.

## Media–Government Symbiosis

A final problem with establishing a basis for ideological bias involves the symbiotic, or interdependent, relationship between the press and government. Just as the media have close ties with the largest American—and certain international—corporations, so are they closely tied to the very government they are so often accused of attacking or treating unfairly. Reporters in all media rely overwhelmingly on "official sources," usually well-placed public officials, when reporting government events. Journalist Philip Weiss has observed that, when such "official" sources are consulted, reporters commonly allow these sources considerable approval privileges over how their statements are used in stories. Certainly the practice of "quote approval" is not restricted to government officials alone, and it may be an attempt to ensure journalistic "objectivity" by allowing interviewees to verify the intentions as well as the language behind what they express in interviews. But, as the Judith Miller case discussed earlier illustrated, practices such as quote approval can draw reporters into an uncomfortably intimate relationship with the very individuals about whom they must remain unbiased. Only rarely are strong opponents of a government's foreign and domestic policy ever granted significant coverage in the mass media.

**THINKING CRITICALLY**

Who do you think is most in control of media content: the reporters or the owners and editors? How does the media coverage you see on a daily basis support your answer?

The *O'Reilly Factor* on Fox News is the highest rated of any cable news show. O'Reilly said that General Electric,which owns NBC and MSNBC, was under FBI investigation as a possible supplier to terrorists with material used in roadside bombs. "The *Factor* has been told, but cannot confirm, that the General Electric Co. is under investigation in the case." O'Reilly said that the FBI was investigating the "pipeline" in which U.S.-made materials for radio-frequency modules are sold to Singapore's Corezing International, which in turn sells them to Iran, where they are used to make roadside bombs that are sent to Iraq and used to injure and kill American military. "The *Factor* is not accusing anyone of anything; we are just reporting what we believe to be true. But if any American company did send material to Corezing—again a major Iranian partner—they must be investigated to the fullest extent. The lives and suffering of our great military is at stake here," O'Reilly said. General Electric called the report "irresponsible and maliciously false."

When Keith Olbermann worked for MSNBC he named Bill O'Reilly as one of his "worst persons of the world" multiple times, slamming O'Reilly for his unconfirmed report that MSNBC parent company General Electric may have been involved in selling roadside bombs. "So you've got an unconfirmed report of an unconfirmed investigation, and you've got an unconfirmed report that GE is under suspicion in your unconfirmed report of your unconfirmed investigation," Olbermann said. "Do you have any facts at all?" This seems to have broken the cease-fire brokered by the chief executives of the parent companies of the cable channels—News Corp., which owns Fox and GE. Olbermann left MSNBC and now has more editorial freedom on his new show on the CurrentTV cable channel.

# THE MEDIA AND ELECTIONS

12.6 *What is the role of the media in elections?*

No discussion of the media and politics would be complete without an examination of the uses of mass communication in elections. It is important here to distinguish between two types of media use in elections: media coverage of the campaign and media exploitation by candidates in the form of political advertising and "infomercials."

## Press Coverage

The amount of media coverage can influence the outcome of an election campaign. By focusing on particular candidates or issues, the media often ignore others. Indeed, the media have been accused of focusing on the "horse race" nature of politics. Most of the coverage in any given campaign is devoted to the race itself rather than to the policies and issues around which the race revolves. As primary campaigns unfold, the media often focus on reporting candidates' standing in the race, limiting coverage to the front-runners, and thereby delivering the message that only the front-runners are worthy of public attention.

As we discussed in Chapters 8 and 10, over the past 15 years the use of opinion polls has expanded dramatically. Not only are newspapers and television networks increasing their use of polls from the larger survey organizations, major media outlets are conducting more of their own surveys. Large-circulation newspapers and magazines—including the *New York Times,* the *Washington Post, USA Today,* and *Newsweek*—as well as CNN and the major broadcast television networks frequently conduct opinion surveys on numerous national issues. Much subsequent news coverage relies on these polls. How significant is the impact of such coverage?

No solid evidence suggests that media polling significantly affects public opinion; that is, such polling does not appear to change opinions. However, published accounts of consistently high or low public responses or sudden shifts of opinion can affect the political process. If candidates do not do well in published polls, they have much more trouble raising the contributions necessary to run expensive campaigns. And elected legislators, ever watchful for trends within their constituencies, obviously pay close attention to published opinion data concerning their states or districts. As you know, polling techniques can sometimes distort public opinion simply by the way questions are worded; therefore, it is quite possible that campaign contributors and legislators may sometimes take their cues from data that inaccurately reflect public preferences.

Likewise, controversy has been growing regarding published results of early exit polls during the national elections aired before the polls close. Many of Jimmy Carter's supporters complained that network broadcasting of early exit polls, which projected an easy victory for Ronald Reagan, actually discouraged Carter's West Coast supporters from voting. And, as you'll recall from Chapter 8, the 2000 election exit polls created one of the great media embarrassments when NBC, CBS, and CNN announced that Al Gore had won Florida. ABC and Fox quickly followed suit.

## Talk Shows

The proliferation of call-in radio and television talk shows presents an interesting bridge between press coverage of campaigns and media utilization by the candidates. Today, more than 10,000 radio stations and 1,100 commercial television stations broadcast in the United States, 99 percent of all households have a radio, 95 percent of all cars have a radio, and 57 percent of all adult Americans have a radio at work.

Talk radio may be performing a function formerly the domain of political parties, unions, and civic groups by giving people a feeling of connection with the political process. With a simple phone call, they have an opportunity to express their views to a wide audience. Surveys also show that talk radio is a source of news.

## Television and Presidential Elections

Presidential candidates gear their television use toward a major goal: spreading their message on the evening news and through carefully scripted political messages. They often accomplish this through various means—the most effective is the sound bite. A *sound bite* is a brief statement, usually a snippet from a speech that conveys the essence of a longer statement and can be inserted into a news story. Lines such as "You're no Jack Kennedy," uttered by Lloyd Bentsen during the 1988 vice presidential debate with Dan Quayle, and "Are you better off now than you were four years ago?" which Ronald Reagan put to Jimmy Carter in their 1980 debate, have entered political lore because of their effectiveness in targeting a specific issue or sentiment. Today, candidates come to debates prepared with one-liners they hope will be turned into sound bites and reported in the next day's news.[49]

Over the years, sound bites have become progressively shorter. In 1968, presidential candidates averaged 43 seconds of uninterrupted speech on the evening news. The average sound bite during the 1984 presidential campaign was only 14.79 seconds. By 1988, the average was down to 9 seconds, and by 1992, it was a mere 8.4 seconds. A voter rarely hears a potential president utter a complete paragraph on the evening news. How much useful information about a policy or issue can a candidate relay to the viewer in a 9-second sound bite? Not much.

Many viewers, including Sarah Palin, loved Tina Fey's portrayal of the Republican vice presidential candidate on *Saturday Night Live.* The faux Canadian accent, the winks, the loose grammar, the vagueness, and the down-home doggone-it's and by gollies made for an uncanny form of imitation and flattery. The Alaska governor declared it "quite funny, particularly because she once dressed up as Tina Fey for Halloween."

Saturday Night Live actors Jason Sudeikis and Fred Armisen portray Vice President Joseph Biden and President Barack Obama in a skit entitled "Obama Returns." SNL often portrays Biden as a gaff-prone, blue-collar everyman.

Political satire had such a definite impact on the voters that during the 2000 election, Gore's advisers actually had him watch Darrell Hammond's adept impersonation of him in the presidential debate to help improve his performance. Political satire played an even bigger role in the 2008 presidential election. Tina Fey's portrayal of Republican vice presidential nominee Sarah Palin became a pop culture phenomenon. Polls show that the "SNL effect" slightly increased the likelihood that voters would cast ballots for Democrats Barack Obama and Joe Biden.[50]

In addition, many politicians have played the entertainment media card in their campaign bids to attract attention. The 2008 presidential campaign was notable for its movement into popular entertainment culture. Seeking to mobilize young and "undecided" voters to their side, Barack Obama and John McCain made multiple appearances on television shows hosted by Oprah, Jay Leno, and David Letterman. These appearances made clear that, for better or worse, the presidential candidates have now become entertainers plugging their product on various television shows.

## Political Advertising

The use of sound bites on television news contributes to the increasing focus on the candidates themselves at the expense of major issues facing the nation. This tendency is carried over into political advertising, which may refer to issues but is geared primarily to depicting the positive qualities of the candidate and the negative—even sinister—characteristics of opposing candidates.

In political advertising, everything hinges on image, and the image-maker's playground is the television commercial, or "spot." Image-makers have produced some of the most memorable, and infamous, images of recent campaigns, including a notorious 1964 Johnson spot known as the "Daisy Girl" (or, "Peace, Little Girl") ad, which featured the detonation of an atomic bomb and implied that Johnson's opponent, Barry Goldwater, was a danger to the future.

Such gripping, even terrifying, imagery is risky. Consequently, media consultants usually try for a balance between their negative and positive political spots. Thus, not all political spots are as intensely negative as the one just described. The 1960 presidential campaign featured spots showing John Kennedy sailing his yacht, riding horses, and frolicking with his family to demonstrate his "common" appeal, despite his uncommon wealth and social position. Some of the most compelling positive advertising appeared in 1984, when incumbent Ronald Reagan ran under the theme "Morning in America." Hiring the same advertising agency that had produced a successful series of Coca-Cola commercials, Reagan's image management team crafted a series of spots showing smiling small-town men and women going about their daily business, secure in the knowledge that America was "back." The implication that America had to "return" from some worse place constituted a hint of negative advertising within an otherwise positive spot. These elegantly filmed, carefully designed spots are generally conceded to have played a major part in reinforcing Reagan's already formidable public support. Candidates expect that undecided voters will watch positive ads, with their warm, homey images of these potential national leaders, and embrace the leaders not as abstract political ideas but as people.

In an effort to soften his image and give viewers a sense of his personality, Mitt Romney appears with David Letterman on CBS's Late Show.

As often as not, however, media consultants employ more combative imagery. Negative advertising usually involves a harsh attack on a political opponent, implying that the opponent is dishonest, corrupt, ignorant, or worse. In the 2004 election, this was most notable in the Swift Boat Veterans' attacks on John Kerry's war record. This kind of political mudslinging is as old as American politics itself. Research shows that voters are more willing to believe negative information about public officials than positive information.

Mitt Romney is targeted by a Democratic National Committee negative ad which highlights Romney's position changes on issues such as abortion and health-care reform.

Negative ads are also more memorable than positive messages. Perhaps the most damaging negative ad in recent elections, aside from the 2004 Swift Boat attacks, were those aired in the 1988 Bush campaign against Michael Dukakis. It portrayed Willie Horton, a convicted rapist who had committed murder while on parole, and implied that Democratic candidate Dukakis was so soft on crime and criminals that the public safety was endangered. In 2008, the Obama campaign's rapid-response team sought to repel attacks over Obama's ties to 1960s radical Bill Ayers. David Axelrod, Obama's chief strategist, pledged that Obama would not let himself be "Swift Boated" like Kerry in 2004.[51]

## Summary

**12.1** *What role does a free press play in approaching the democratic ideal?*

- Democracy requires an *informed* citizenry, and the communication of political information is an essential prerequisite for political participation. Democracy requires that citizens receive objective information so they can make informed decisions about candidates, policies, and government actions. A free press stands as one of the defining features of any democratic political system. One of the central components of a society's approach to democracy is whether or not the government allows freedom of the press—a press free to criticize the government without fear of being shut down and its editors thrown into prison.

**12.2** *How have media sources evolved over time?*

- The importance of the press in American politics dates from the Revolutionary period, when newspapers served as effective tools for mobilizing public opinion. During the 19th century, journalistic style changed significantly with the emergence of the penny press, muckraking, and yellow journalism.
- Although they are less prominent than newspapers as a source of political information, magazines enjoy wide circulation, attentive readership, and an important place in the political education of Americans.
- Radio enjoyed a brief but important heyday as the dominant source of political information for the American public. Developed in the early 20th century, radio technology underwent a revolution during World War I. Unlike print media, radio broadcasts could report events as they happened.
- Unlike newspapers, magazines, and radio, television developed primarily as a commercial medium, designed not so much to provide information or opinion but to entertain and stimulate mass consumerism. Television is more pervasive and effective than any other form of mass communication in the United States. Advances in broadcast technology have made possible virtually instantaneous transmission of information and have greatly expanded the range of program choices for viewers. An especially significant technological advance has been the satellite. Satellite technology has made television an instantaneous means of worldwide communication.
- The Web and the Internet are playing an increasingly important role in obtaining and disseminating political information.

**12.3** *What functions do the media perform in a democracy?*

- Social scientists are in general agreement that the mass media perform three basic functions: (1) surveillance of world events, (2) interpretation of events, and (3) socialization of individuals into cultural settings.
- *Surveillance:* The media sift through all the events and information and decide what is important to publish or air. The media not only bring certain matters to public attention but also doom certain others to obscurity.
- *Interpretation:* The media do much more than provide public and private surveillance of events. They also interpret those events by giving them meaning and context, and in the process often shape opinions. The way television portrays events and actors exerts a significant influence on the opinions of those who watch the coverage.
- *Socialization:* The media play an important role in socialization, the process by which people learn to conform to their society's norms and values.

12.4 *Are freedoms of the press unlimited?*

- Americans take pride in the tradition of a free press, yet that freedom is not absolute. Laws protect against libel, slander, and obscenity; the Federal Communications Commission (FCC) regulates media behavior; and the judiciary imposes certain limitations as well. The nature of media ownership also plays a role in limiting media freedom.
- Four sets of guidelines regulate the electronic media: (1) rules that limit the number of stations owned or controlled by a single organization, (2) examinations of station goals and performance as part of periodic licensing, (3) rules that mandate public service and local interest programs, (4) rules that guarantee fair treatment to individuals and protect their rights.
- The Supreme Court has consistently upheld regulation of the electronic media under the scarcity doctrine. Broadcasting is viewed as a public resource, much like a national park, and the government establishes regulations designed to promote "the public convenience, interest, or necessity." Although a station is not required to give or sell airtime to a candidate seeking a specific office, whenever it provides time to one candidate—whether for a price or for free—it must give equal time to all candidates running for the same office.

12.5 *Are the media biased in their reporting?*

- Although the majority of reporters in both print and electronic media are fairly liberal, their bosses—the magazine and newspaper publishers and network executives—tend to be more conservative. Many recent analyses suggest that the mass media's overwhelming bias is neither liberal nor conservative but corporate.

12.6 *What is the role of the media in elections?*

- There are two types of media use in elections: media coverage of the campaign and media exploitation by candidates in the form of political advertising.
- The amount of media coverage can influence the outcome of an election campaign. By focusing on particular candidates or issues, the media often ignore others. Most of the coverage in any given campaign is devoted to the race itself rather than to the policies and issues.
- Presidential candidates gear their television use toward a major goal: spreading their message on the evening news. They accomplish this through various means—the most effective is the sound bite.
- Political advertising may refer to issues but is geared primarily to depicting the positive qualities of the candidate and the negative—even sinister—characteristics of opposing candidates.
- The proliferation of call-in radio and television talk shows presents an interesting bridge between press coverage of campaigns and media utilization by the candidates.

## Key Terms

Equal Time Rule, 388
Fairness Doctrine, 389
Federal Communications Commission (FCC), 387
investigative journalism, 386
libel, 391
mass media, 375
muckraking, 377
prior restraint, 390
right of rebuttal, 389
socialization, 387
yellow journalism, 377

## Test Yourself Chapter 12

**1.** The term *mass media* refers to
a. newspapers.
b. radio.
c. the Internet.
d. All of the above.

**2.** The *Federalist Papers* were originally published in
a. a newspaper.
b. a leather-bound book.
c. a cloth-bound book.
d. the halls of Congress.

**3.** A form of journalism characterized by half-truth, innuendo, and outright lies is called
a. yellow journalism.
b. muckraking.
c. investigative reporting.
d. talk radio.

**4.** What did early political leaders see as the key to public education about the new political system?
a. The press.
b. The church.
c. The Constitution.
d. The Congress.

**5.** Which of the following is considered to be an important function of the media?
a. Championing a specific cause that is important to journalists and media owners.
b. Interpreting world events.
c. Making contributions to candidates running for political office.
d. Helping build better political parties.

**6.** Who developed the theory of framing effects?
a. Shanto Iyengar.
b. Ross Perot.
c. Hadley Cantril.
d. Doris Graber.

**7.** The media are regulated by the
a. National Broadcasting Committee.
b. Federal Communications Commission.
c. Federal Deposit Insurance Corporation.
d. National Security Administration.

**8.** Broadcasting is viewed as a public resource. Therefore it can be regulated under
a. a writ of *mandamus*.
b. the equal protection clause.
c. the scarcity doctrine.
d. the rules of engagement.

**9.** The Equal Time Rule holds that
a. a station must give free time to all interest groups.
b. a station must give free time to all religious organizations.
c. equal blocks of time must be made available to all political candidates.
d. all broadcast stations must air the same number of minutes on news stories.

**10.** The Fairness Doctrine was upheld by the Supreme Court in the case of
a. *Sullivan* v. *New York Times*.
b. *Red Lion Broadcasting* v. *FCC*.
c. *Marbury* v. *Madison*.
d. *CNN* v. *Carter*.

**11.** Prior restraint is the same as
a. muckraking.
b. libel.
c. censorship.
d. the Equal Time Rule.

**12.** Of the major news magazines, the most widely read is
a. *The National Enquirer*.
b. *Newsweek*.
c. *Sports Illustrated*.
d. *Time*.

**13.** Probably the most successful use of radio by a politician were the famous
a. "Sunday Conversations" by President Ronald Regan.
b. "Fireside Chats" by President Franklin Roosevelt.
c. "Evenings with Bill" by President Bill Clinton.
d. "Saturday Morning Addresses" by President George W. Bush.

**14.** The most familiar historical example of investigative journalism occurred
a. during the economic depression of the 1930s.
b. at the end of World War II.
c. during the Korean Conflict.
d. during the 1970s Watergate scandal.

**15.** The phrase "You're no Jack Kennedy," uttered by Lloyd Bentsen, is an example of a(n)
a. sound bite.
b. negative advertisement.
c. accusation.
d. truth claim.

**16.** Regulation of the media began
a. during the latter part of the 1990s.
b. just before the beginning of World War I.
c. after World War I.
d. after the Korean Conflict.

**17.** Which of the following is *not* one of the four guidelines by which electronic media is regulated?
a. Rules limiting the number of stations owned or controlled by a single organization.
b. Examinations of the goals and performances of stations as part of periodic licensing.
c. Rules mandating public service and local interest programs.
d. Limitations on advertising dollars earned in a given quarter.

**18.** The ________________ is the basis for the FCC's regulation of the political content of radio and television broadcasts.
a. scarcity doctrine.
b. First Amendment.
c. Equal Protection Clause.
d. Fairness Doctrine.

**19.** The regulation of political content of radio and television broadcasts takes the forms of three rules of the airwaves. Which of the following is *not* one of these rules?
a. The Equal Time Rule.
b. The open access rule.
c. The Fairness Doctrine.
d. The right to rebuttal.

**20.** Published material that damages a person's reputation or good name in an untruthful and malicious way is known as
a. libel.
b. slander.
c. a sound bite.
d. negative advertising.

**ANSWERS**
**1.** d, **2.** a, **3.** a, **4.** a, **5.** b, **6.** a, **7.** b, **8.** c, **9.** c, **10.** b, **11.** c, **12.** d, **13.** b, **14.** d, **15.** a, **16.** c, **17.** d, **18.** a, **19.** b, **20.** a

# Civil Liberties

# 13

AWAY
ONE
FREEDOM,
AND SOON
THEY'RE

## Chapter Outline

**Introduction:**
*Civil Liberties and Democracy*

- Defining and Examining Civil Liberties and Civil Rights
- A History of the Application of Civil Liberties to the States
- Freedom of Religion
- Freedom of Speech
- Freedom of the Press
- The Rights of Defendants
- The Expanding Nature of Implied Rights
- The 2012 Election, Anthony Kennedy, and the Future of Civil Liberties

## Learning Objectives

13

- 13.1 What are civil liberties and civil rights, and how does the double standard protect them?
- 13.2 How has the process of applying the Bill of Rights to the states both expanded the protection of rights and nationalized the country?
- 13.3 What is the theory of selective incorporation, and how is it used to increase the protection of civil liberties?
- 13.4 How has the Supreme Court determined the level of separation between church and state?
- 13.5 How has the Court regulated and protected the right to free exercise of religion?
- 13.6 How has the Court's protection of free speech preserved democracy?
- 13.7 How has the Court's interpretation of symbolic speech, especially for public school students, affected democracy?
- 13.8 How have the Court's rules governing freedom of the press preserved democracy?
- 13.9 How has the Supreme Court expanded and restricted the Fourth Amendment's search and seizure protections?
- 13.10 How has the Supreme Court balanced the Fifth and Sixth Amendment rights?
- 13.11 How has the Supreme Court interpreted the cruel and unusual punishment clause of the Eighth Amendment as it applies to the death penalty?
- 13.12 How has the Supreme Court interpreted and created unenumerated, or implied, rights to preserve democracy?

# INTRODUCTION

## CIVIL LIBERTIES AND DEMOCRACY

The quality of a democracy can be measured by the degree to which it protects the rights of all its citizens, including those with unpopular views. Frequently, this task falls to the Supreme Court of the United States, which may find itself safeguarding the rights of individuals charged with carrying out heinous crimes or engaging in socially unpopular acts. In a democracy, the fundamental rights of such individuals have the same protection as those of any other citizen.

The fundamental rights of U.S. citizens are set forth in the Bill of Rights—the first ten amendments to the Constitution—and we often speak of the "protection" provided by that document. However, individual rights are always in jeopardy if they are not zealously safeguarded by all the institutions of society. When a school authority suspends a student for unfurling a sign that mentions drugs, it raises First Amendment free speech issues. When local authorities place a Ten Commandments monument inside a courtroom or on the Texas state capitol grounds, freedom of religion is at issue. When Congress bans "indecent material" transmitted over the Internet, freedom of speech is at issue. And, when a police officer stops you in your car and asks to search the trunk, the Fourth Amendment search and seizure provision is at issue. All of these situations and hundreds more are governed by the Bill of Rights.

In this chapter we explore the historical development of civil liberties. We begin with the framers' vision of the Bill of Rights, which was much less protective of individual freedoms than you might realize. We then explore the gradual expansion of civil liberties to the states over the course of our nation's history. Next, we analyze how civil liberties have been defined and how they have expanded and contracted over the past nearly 75 years. These topics provide a dramatic demonstration of how the United States has approached democracy in the area of individual rights.

**civil liberties**
The individual freedoms and rights guaranteed to every citizen in the Bill of Rights and the due process clause of the Fourteenth Amendment, including freedom of speech and religion.

**civil rights**
The constitutionally guaranteed rights that the government may not arbitrarily remove. Among these rights are the right to vote and equal protection under the law.

# DEFINING AND EXAMINING CIVIL LIBERTIES AND CIVIL RIGHTS

13.1 *What are civil liberties and civil rights, and how does the double standard protect them?*

Although the terms *civil liberties* and *civil rights* are often used interchangeably, they are not synonymous. **Civil liberties** are the individual freedoms and rights guaranteed to every U.S. citizen by the Bill of Rights and the due process clause of the Fourteenth Amendment. They include Americans' most fundamental rights, such as freedom of speech and religion. **Civil rights** concern protection of citizens against discrimination because of characteristics such as gender, race, ethnicity, or disability; they derive largely from the equal protection clause of the Fourteenth Amendment.

One way to distinguish between civil liberties and civil rights is to view them in terms of governmental action. Civil liberties are best understood as *freedom from* government interference with, or violation of, individual rights. This is a "negative" freedom in the sense that we understand people to have a right to certain liberties, such as freedom of speech, which they can exercise without government interference. For this reason, the First Amendment begins with the words, "Congress shall make no law."

In contrast, civil rights may be understood as *freedom to* exercise certain rights that are guaranteed to all U.S. citizens under the Constitution, and which the government cannot remove. This is a "positive" freedom in that we expect the government to provide the conditions under which certain rights can be exercised. Examples include the right to vote, the right to equal job or housing opportunities, and the right to equal education. We look more closely at civil rights in Chapter 14; in this chapter, we focus on civil liberties.

One reason the terms *civil liberties* and *civil rights* have become almost interchangeable in popular speech is that many issues involve aspects of both positive and negative freedom.[1] For example, consider the abortion issue, in which a woman seeks to terminate a pregnancy—a civil liberty—while others seek to preserve the life of the potential being, a civil right.

Cases involving civil liberties nearly always come down to a conflict between the individual, seeking to exercise a certain right in a democracy, and the state, seeking to control the exercise of that right so as to preserve the rights of others. The judiciary is charged with drawing the lines between acceptable individual actions and permissible governmental controls.

But how are those lines drawn? You will recall from Chapter 6 that "activist" jurists tend to uphold the rights of individuals over those of the state, whereas "self-restraint" jurists tend to defer to the state. The activists are also inclined to overturn acts of Congress, but the self-restraint jurists are inclined to defer to Congress in upholding the laws. Under these definitions, the Rehnquist Court was an activist court. Before 1994, the Court overturned congressional acts an average of once every two years. From 1994 to 2005, the Court overturned all or portions of 39 such acts. One recent study concluded that the most "activist" member of the current Court is Clarence Thomas, who votes to overturn congressional acts 65.6 percent of the time. On the other hand, more liberal justice Stephen Breyer voted to overturn laws only 28.1 percent of the time. This same study concluded that the most restrained jurists on this Court were all liberals: Ruth Bader Ginsburg, David Souter, and John Paul Stevens.[2] Now the Roberts Court consists entirely of activists with four conservatives (John Roberts, Samuel Alito, Antonin Scalia, and Clarence Thomas), and four liberals (Stephen Breyer, Ruth Bader Ginsburg, Sonia Sotomayor, and Elena Kagan), balanced by swing justice Anthony Kennedy, who attempts to balance the rights of the individual with the needs of society.

## The Dawn of Civil Liberties and Civil Rights in America

Many think that America's history of civil liberties and civil rights protection began in 1791 with the ratification of the Bill of Rights to the Constitution, but in fact the process did not begin in earnest until 1938, and it accelerated in the 1960s. Prior to that time, the Supreme Court did not consider the Bill of Rights a tool for protecting individual liberty, and before 1897, none of the Bill of Rights applied to the states. The Court's interest in civil liberties and civil rights began with these words in the footnote of an obscure 1938 economics case called *United States* v. *Carolene,* which dealt with Congress's regulation of "filled milk," the amount of additives added to milk to make the product more profitable to sell during the Depression. After explaining that the Court would continue to defer to the legislative body in matters of economic regulation, in a three-paragraph footnote, the Court sent a billboard to those attorneys and litigants seeking justice under the Constitution:

> *There here may be narrower scope for operation of the presumption of constitutionality when legislation appears on its face to be within a specific prohibition of the Constitution, such as those of the first ten amendments, which are deemed equally specific when held to be embraced within the Fourteenth. . . . It is unnecessary to consider now whether legislation which restricts those political processes which can ordinarily be expected to bring about repeal of undesirable legislation, is to be subjected to more exacting judicial scrutiny under the general prohibitions of the Fourteenth Amendment than are most other types of legislation. . . . Nor need we enquire whether similar considerations enter into the review of statutes directed at particular religious, or racial minorities, whether prejudice against discrete and insular minorities may be a special condition, which tends seriously to curtail the operation of those political processes ordinarily to be relied upon to protect minorities, and which may call for a correspondingly more searching judicial inquiry.*[3]

This may read like incomprehensible gibberish, but it actually tells us which kinds of cases the Court might be willing to accept on appeal and consider seriously ruling in favor of the individual in litigation against the government and other actors. The first sentence says that any dispute that touches on the Bill of Rights or the Fourteenth Amendment may receive special protection from the Supreme Court. The second sentence promises that any case that touches on the political process will receive special protection. Finally, the third sentence promises that any case that touches on "discrete and insular minorities" may receive special protection. In short, the Court is promising the launching of a **double standard** in which civil liberties will be judicially protected, but in economic cases the Court will defer to the legislature. The reason is that without Court protection, politically disenfranchised or minority people cannot protect themselves through the voting process or the legislature.

Since the U.S. approach to democracy in the area of civil liberties is relatively recent, we focus on how these rights were created and expanded by the Warren Court (1953–1969), partially cut back by the Burger Court (1969–1986), and finally placed under full attack initially by the Rehnquist Court (1986–2005) as well as now the Roberts Court (2005–present). First, however, we explore the history of the development of civil liberties and their application to the states and to the national government.

**QUICK REVIEW**

Civil Liberties versus Civil Rights

- There is a difference between civil liberties and civil rights in terms of governmental action.
- Civil liberties are *freedom from* government interference with, or violation of, individual rights—negative freedom.
- Civil rights are *freedom to* exercise certain rights guaranteed to all U.S. citizens under the Constitution and cannot be removed by the government—positive freedom.
- The terms *civil liberties* and *civil rights* have become almost interchangeable in popular speech because many issues involve aspects of both positive and negative freedom.

# A HISTORY OF THE APPLICATION OF CIVIL LIBERTIES TO THE STATES

13.2 *How has the process of applying the Bill of Rights to the states both expanded the protection of rights and nationalized the country?*

The history of civil liberties is one of gradually expanding protection of personal rights guaranteed by the Bill of Rights. This evolution occurred through a series of Supreme Court decisions that applied portions of the first ten amendments to the states, thereby protecting citizens from state action in relation to specific individual rights. This evolutionary process, summarized in Table 13.1, did not begin until 1897 and did not really take hold until the 1960s.

**double standard**
The varying level of intensity by which the Supreme Court considers cases by which it protects civil liberties claims while also deferring to the legislature in cases with economic claims.

**Table 13.1** Applying the Bill of Rights to the States by Incorporation

| Case | Issue | Incorporated |
|---|---|---|
| *Chicago, Burlington and Quincy Railway Co.* v. *Chicago* (1897) | Taking of private property by the state for public use without just compensation. | Fifth Amendment guarantee of eminent domain. |
| *Gitlow* v. *New York* (1925) | Arrest for speech threatening the state government. | First Amendment guarantee of free speech. |
| *Near* v. *Minnesota* (1931) | Prior restraint (censorship) of press. | First Amendment guarantee of free press. |
| *Powell* v. *Alabama* (1932) | Right to counsel in capital crimes. (This was the famous Scottsboro case, in which seven young black males were accused and convicted without the aid of counsel of raping two white females.) | Sixth Amendment guarantee of right to counsel in capital cases where a "fair hearing" was lacking. |
| *Hamilton* v. *Regents of the University of California* (1934) | Challenged public institution's mandatory military drills on basis of religious objections. | First Amendment guarantee of freedom of religion. |
| *De Jonge* v. *Oregon* (1937) | Peaceful assembly of Communist Party members in Oregon. | First Amendment guarantees of free assembly and of right to petition the government for a redress of grievances. |
| *Palko* v. *Connecticut* (1937) | Twice being tried for same offense. (In this case, Justice Cardozo devised his famous "honor roll of superior rights.") | None, but Cardozo's insistence that superior rights should be incorporated begins "selective incorporation." |
| *Cantwell* v. *Connecticut* (1940) | Whether or not religious groups (Jehovah's Witnesses) should have to be licensed to promote their religion. | First Amendment guarantee of free exercise of religion. |
| *Everson* v. *Board of Education of Ewing Township* (1947) | State aid to bus children to parochial schools. | First Amendment requirement that church and state be separate. |
| *In re Oliver* (1948) | Whether or not a judge can act simultaneously as a grand jury and a trial judge to find a defendant guilty without a proper trial. | Sixth Amendment guarantee to a public trial. |
| *Louisiana ex. rel. Francis Resweber* (1947) | Whether or not a convicted man could be executed again after an electric chair failure. | Cruel and unusual punishment. |
| *Wolf* v. *Colorado* (1949) | Whether patient names from an appointment book of a suspected abortionist gained by illegal search of doctor's office can be used in trial. | The "core" of the Fourth Amendment, defined as "arbitrary invasions of privacy by the police." |
| *NAACP* v. *Alabama* (1958) | Whether groups must register with the state and file membership names and addresses. | First Amendment guarantee of freedom of association. |
| *Mapp* v. *Ohio* (1961) | Use of the fruits of an illegal search and seizure without a proper search warrant in trial. | Fourth Amendment prohibition on unreasonable search or seizure, and its exclusionary rule. |
| *Robinson* v. *California* (1962) | A California statute providing a mandatory 90-day jail sentence for conviction of addiction to narcotics without any evidence of drug use. | Eighth Amendment guarantee against the infliction of cruel or unusual punishment. |
| *Gideon* v. *Wainwright* (1963) | Legal counsel availability when someone is on trial for a misdemeanor, noncapital offense. | Sixth Amendment guarantee of counsel was expanded to include all felony-level criminal cases. |

| Case | Issue | Incorporated |
|---|---|---|
| *Malloy* v. *Hogan* and *Murphy* v. *Waterfront Commission of New York* (1964) | Whether or not investigation into gambling offenses after serving a jail sentence for the crime resulted in self-incrimination. | Fifth Amendment prohibition against self-incrimination. |
| *Pointer* v. *Texas* (1965) | Whether or not the accused has the right to confront witnesses against him or her instead of a transcript of their earlier testimony during a trial. | Sixth Amendment guarantee that the accused shall be confronted by the witnesses against him or her. |
| *Griswold* v. *Connecticut* (1965) | Legality of use and counseling on the use of birth control by married couples. | First, Third, Fourth, Fifth, Ninth, and Fourteenth Due Process Amendments (and their penumbras) right of privacy. |
| *Parker* v. *Gladden* (1966) | Whether or not bailiff statements rendered the jury unable to produce an impartial verdict. | Sixth Amendment guarantee that the accused shall be judged by an impartial jury. |
| *Klopfer* v. *North Carolina* (1967) | Whether or not a state can place a live case on inactive status only to take the case up again when it has more time and resources. | Sixth Amendment guarantee of a speedy trial. |
| *Washington* v. *Texas* (1967) | Whether or not a defendant can compel witnesses in his or her favor to appear in trial. | Sixth Amendment right to compulsory process for obtaining witnesses. |
| *Duncan* v. *Louisiana* (1968) | Whether or not state must offer trial by jury in noncapital cases. | Sixth Amendment guarantee of a trial by jury in all criminal cases above the petty level. |
| *Benton* v. *Maryland* (1969) | Whether a state must provide a guarantee against two trials for the same crime. | Fifth Amendment guarantee against double jeopardy. |
| *McDonald* v. *City of Chicago* (2010) | Whether or not the Second Amendment limits state and local gun control laws. | The core of the Second Amendment's "right-to-self-defense." |

*Source:* From The Boston Globe, 

In the early years of the nation's history, the Bill of Rights provided far less protection for individual rights than is the case today. For example, the guarantee of freedom of speech did not prevent the Federalist party from passing the Alien and Sedition Acts in 1798, which jailed opponents of John Adams's administration. And the right to counsel guaranteed by the Sixth Amendment did not prevent passage of the Federal Crimes Act of 1790, which instructed courts to provide defendants with counsel for capital offenses only.

But narrow as these individual protections were, in the 1833 case of *Barron* v. *Baltimore* the Supreme Court severely limited their collective impact.[4] Rains and swollen rivers washed silt unearthed by excavation and construction for the city of Baltimore into Baltimore harbor, rendering a wharf owned by John Barron unusable. Barron claimed that he was entitled to money damages under the Fifth Amendment's eminent domain clause, which guarantees "just compensation" from the state when government takes private property for public use.

Even the normally nationalist-oriented Chief Justice John Marshall refused to extend Bill of Rights protections to the states in denying Barron's claim. The Bill of Rights, he ruled, "contains no expression indicating an intention to apply them to the state governments [so] this Court cannot so apply them." The First Amendment, by stating that "Congress shall make no law," indicates that the Bill of Rights applies *only* to the national government. Unable to use the Fifth Amendment to sustain his claim, Barron had no case. The entire Bill of Rights, which by this decision afforded no protection to citizens from their states, would not be applied to the states for another century. During that time, civil liberties varied from state to state, depending on the protections afforded by that state's constitution and existing laws.

## The Fourteenth Amendment

Passage of the Fourteenth Amendment in 1868 again raised the issue of state responsibility relative to civil liberties. The Fourteenth Amendment was one of the so-called Civil War Amendments, designed to free the slaves and protect their rights as citizens. It reads: "No State shall make or enforce any law which shall abridge the privileges or immunities of citizens of the United States; nor shall any State deprive any person of life, liberty, or property, without due process of law; nor deny to any person . . . the equal protection of the laws."

Because the Fourteenth Amendment began with the words "No State shall make or enforce any law," some believed that it was intended to reverse the *Barron* ruling and extend the Bill of Rights to the states. Initially, the Supreme Court was asked to rule on whether defining protections in the Bill of Rights as "privileges or immunities," thus being guaranteed against state infringement by that clause of the amendment, would accomplish this aim. However, in 1873, the Court had a case called the *Slaughterhouse Cases*. A group of owners of slaughterhouse businesses opposed the state of Louisiana's incorporation of a state monopoly in this business as infringing on their property rights and rights to make a living. This raised the question of whether they should be "justly compensated" under the eminent domain right of the Fifth Amendment for the loss of their businesses. The Court ruled that this language did not protect state rights of citizenship, such as property rights, but only national rights of citizenship, such as petitioning Congress for a redress of grievances and being protected from piracy on the high seas.[5]

In later cases, the Court was asked if part or all of the Bill of Rights could be defined as "due process" of law and thus extend to the states under the language of the Fourteenth Amendment. This approach, in which by redefinition the Bill of Rights would be absorbed into the due process clause, was called the **incorporation** of the Bill of Rights.[6] The argument ran like this: Under the Fourteenth Amendment the states must protect due process, and because some or all of the Bill of Rights could be defined as due process, the states must also protect those portions of the Bill of Rights.

However, in the late 1800s and early 1900s, the conservative jurists who dominated the Court were more concerned with protecting property rights than with making this definitional leap to extend personal civil rights. Did California violate due process of law by using a list of evidence called a *bill of information* to indict people rather than the grand jury proceeding promised in the Fifth Amendment? No, said the Court, ruling that the "new" procedure can be just as fair as the "old" grand jury guarantee.[7] Did New Jersey's practice of allowing a judge to comment on a defendant's unwillingness to take the stand in self-defense, which a jury might interpret as an indication of guilt, violate the Fifth Amendment's guarantee that no person shall be "compelled . . . to be a witness against himself"? No, ruled the Court, because this was not a "fundamental" right that must be applied to the states.[8]

The Court's position became known as **no incorporation** because it was unwilling to define the Bill of Rights as part of the Fourteenth Amendment and thus to apply its amendments to the states. The states would be bound only by the dictates of due process contained in the Fourteenth Amendment. The one exception came in an 1897 case involving a railroad company's objection to the city of Chicago's seizure of its land without just compensation. Here, the Court ruled that the Fifth Amendment's right of eminent domain extended to the states.[9] The states were doing more to protect property rights of businesses rather than the civil liberties of individuals. Opposing the majority was Justice John Harlan, who argued that Bill of Rights protections were so fundamental that all of them should be applied to the states, thus creating the position known as **total incorporation.**

**QUICK REVIEW**

The Fourteenth Amendment

- Passed in 1868.
- One of the Civil War Amendments.
- Designed to free slaves and protect their rights as citizens.

**THINKING CRITICALLY**

Do you think campus speech codes—designed to prevent students from saying things that might belittle or intimidate others—create a "clear and present danger" on the campus? How would you write such a code to make it consistent with the First Amendment free speech clause?

**incorporation**
The process whereby the Supreme Court has found that Bill of Rights protections apply to the states.

**no incorporation**
An approach in which the states would be bound only by the dictates of due process contained in the Fourteenth Amendment.

**total incorporation**
An approach arguing that the protections in the Bill of Rights were so fundamental that all of them should be applied to the states by absorbing them into the due process clause of the Fourteenth Amendment.

## The Clear and Present Danger Test

The battle over the application of the Bill of Rights to the states resumed during World War I, when the government was anxious to restrict certain individual liberties. Concern with wartime treason, spying, and obstruction of the military draft led in

1919 to *Schenck* v. *United States,* the first important case involving freedom of speech. Charles T. Schenck had been convicted of circulating pamphlets against the draft. In upholding the conviction, Justice Oliver Wendell Holmes argued that the state could restrict speech when "the words used are of such a nature as to create a clear and present danger that they will bring about the substantive evils that Congress has a right to prevent." In short, certain cases, such as falsely shouting "Fire!" in a crowded theater, thus causing a dangerous panic, may justify restriction of this liberty. In ignoring the fact that no evidence indicated that Schenck's "speech" had affected the draft, Holmes was saying that a wartime crisis was sufficient cause for restrictions on freedom of speech.[10]

**clear and present danger test**
A free speech test allowing states to regulate only speech that has an immediate connection to an action the states are permitted to regulate.

Two other 1919 cases that came to the Supreme Court, dealing with federal restrictions of freedom of speech, revealed the problems of applying the **clear and present danger test** to other circumstances. When Jacob Frohwerk was convicted for writing scholarly articles on the constitutionality and merits of the military draft for a German-language newspaper in Missouri, the Court upheld the conviction in *Frohwerk* v. *United States.*[11] And when socialist Eugene Debs spoke out against the draft after signing an Anti-War Proclamation and Program in St. Louis, the conviction was upheld by the Court. The Court ruled in *Debs* v. *United States* that Debs was impeding the war effort.[12] Thus, the Court had convicted one man for writing for a tiny minority and another for the thoughts he might have had while speaking, and neither had any demonstrable effect on the draft.

## THINKING CRITICALLY

How does the 1919 Supreme Court ruling on restriction of freedom of speech when "the words used are such a nature to create a *clear and present danger*" compare with the 2001 USA Patriot Act, which allows for covert searches without notice to the suspect if the authorities can argue that they have *"reasonable cause to believe"* that giving notice would have an adverse result on future investigations?

Seeing the censorship effect of his test, Holmes changed his views. In the fall of 1919, when an anarchist named Jacob Abrams appealed his conviction for circulating pamphlets that implored American workers to go on strike in sympathy with Russian workers hurt by the revolution there, seven members of the Court upheld the conviction in *Abrams* v. *United States* because Abrams's actions posed a *clear and present danger* to the war effort. However, Holmes, the inventor of the test, together with Louis D. Brandeis, dissented. They argued that Abrams was nothing more than a "poor and puny anonymity" whose "silly leaflet" represented no clear and present danger to the state.[13] Thus, America's approach to freedom of speech began, but it still had a long way to go.

## The Beginnings of Incorporation

Whereas the federal government passed laws against certain actions resulting from speech but did not attempt to control speech directly, some states, including New York, chose to outlaw the words themselves. In 1925, a radical named Benjamin Gitlow was convicted under New York's Criminal Anarchy Act of advocating the overthrow of the government. In *Gitlow* v. *New York,* the Supreme Court ruled for the first time that the First Amendment guarantee of freedom of speech could be applied to the states; however, it upheld Gitlow's conviction, deferring to the state of New York's belief that certain speech had a "bad tendency."[14] Why would the Court be willing to apply the free speech guarantee to the states but not use it to protect Gitlow himself? Because it had learned that the right of free speech could be used to protect businesses—for example, when a business refuses to give reasons for firing an employee. The Court was therefore setting a precedent that could be used to protect the status quo without actually condoning speech aimed against these same interests.

Jacob Abrams (on the right), of the landmark *Abrams* v. *United States* case, is shown with fellow anarchists (from left to right) Samuel Lipman, Hyman Lachowsky, and Mollie Steimer. The four were arrested for passing out leaflets encouraging American workers to go on strike in support of Russian workers. They appear here, in 1921, shortly before being deported to Russia at their own expense, having served two years in a federal prison. A fifth colleague, Jacob Schwartz, died in prison, quite possibly as a result of a brutal beating by police during questioning.

In the early 1930s, the Court applied three other parts of the Bill of Rights to the states. In 1931, when the Minnesota legislature passed a law censoring the *Saturday Press,* a muckraking tabloid printed by Jay Near, the Court in a landmark case called *Near* v. *Minnesota* incorporated the guarantee of freedom of the press into the Fourteenth Amendment, thus applying it to the states, and overturned the Minnesota law.[15]

**double jeopardy**
Trying a defendant twice for the same crime; banned by the Fifth Amendment.

**selective incorporation**
An incorporation standard in which some portions of the Bill of Rights, but not all, were made part of the Fourteenth Amendment's due process clause, and thus guaranteed against invasion by the states.

**selective incorporation plus**
The Supreme Court's current rule for applying the Bill of Rights to states. States are now bound by most, but not all, of the first eight amendments plus some unenumerated rights, such as privacy, that have been created by the Court but are not part of the text of the Bill of Rights.

A year later, the Court was called on to rule in the case of the "Scottsboro Boys," in which a group of black youths had been unjustly accused of raping two white women on a train. The young men had been convicted in a trial in which, instead of assigning a defense attorney, the judge asked "the entire bar of the county" to defend them. (In other words, they had no defense.) The Court's decision incorporated and applied to the states the notion of a "fair hearing" implied in the Sixth Amendment, thus guaranteeing the right to counsel, but only for capital crimes such as this one.[16]

Finally, in 1934, when the University of California required that all students, including religious pacifists, take courses in military training, the Court incorporated the freedom of religion provision and applied it to the states but left the program intact.[17]

The Court made clear in all of these cases that extending rights to the states did not necessarily mean increased rights for individuals. States remained free to punish the press after publication rather than before, to deny the right to counsel in noncapital criminal cases, and to require even pacifist students to take courses in military training. Thus, the question remained whether or not a more general rule could be established that applied the Bill of Rights to the states in a meaningful way.

## Selective Incorporation of the Bill of Rights

13.3 *What is the theory of selective incorporation, and how is it used to increase the protection of civil liberties?*

Not until 1937, the year of FDR's failed court-packing plan and one year before the Carolene Products footnote in the landmark case of *Palko* v. *Connecticut,* could the first step be taken toward establishing a rule about incorporating a right into the Fourteenth Amendment due process clause and applying it against the states.[18] Frank Jacob Palko had been convicted of the second-degree murder of two police officers, and he objected to the state's plan to retry him because of procedural errors in the earlier trial for first-degree murder, which carried the death penalty. Palko claimed that a retrial would deny him the Fifth Amendment's protection against **double jeopardy**—that is, the guarantee that a person may not be tried twice for the same crime. However, the Supreme Court had not yet applied this right to the states. The Court ruled that only rights "implicit in the concept of ordered liberty" would be applied to the states. According to Justice Benjamin Cardozo, those rights were fundamental freedoms such as freedom of speech, the right to fair trial, and freedom of thought; the double jeopardy protection did not qualify. Palko lost his appeal, and, with no double jeopardy right to worry about, the state retried him, convicted him, and put him to death. It was surely little comfort to him that his name was now associated with a new incorporation standard, **selective incorporation,** in which certain portions of the Bill of Rights, but not all, became part of the Fourteenth Amendment's due process clause and thus guaranteed against invasion by the states.

### QUICK REVIEW

Incorporation of the Bill of Rights

- The Supreme Court granted the provisions contained in the Bill of Rights to the states.
- Judicial redefinition of civil liberties expanded power of the national government.
- Several amendments have not been, and probably will not be, incorporated.
- Other rights not contained in the Bill of Rights, such as the right to privacy, have also been applied to the states by the Court.

Over the next 45 years, all but a handful of the provisions contained in the Bill of Rights were applied to the states by way of the Fourteenth Amendment. This judicial redefinition of civil liberties, particularly during the 1960s, was the greatest expansion of national government power in the federal structure since the 1930s decisions that extended interstate commerce power to the states.

Several amendments or portions thereof—including the Third and Seventh, the grand jury provision of the Fifth, and the excessive bails and fines provision of the Eighth—have not been incorporated. Because other rights not contained in the Bill of Rights, such as the right to personal autonomy, privacy, or the choices as to how one lives his or her life, have also been applied to the states, the best characterization of the Court's current approach might be **selective incorporation plus.**

The Court only recently addressed the meaning and incorporation of the Second Amendment in two landmark cases, the first of which being the 2008 gun control case, *District of Columbia* v. *Heller.*[19] After the District of Columbia passed an ordinance banning the ownership of guns in the district in an effort to control crime, security guard Dick Heller argued under the Second Amendment's "right to bear arms" that he should be granted a license to buy a handgun to protect himself and his house.

Heller's right to own a gun was upheld 5–4 by the Court. However, the Court did not create an unlimited right to own guns, leaving open the possibility for the government to limit the right for some groups such as felons and individuals who are mentally challenged.

Two years later, in *McDonald* v. *City of Chicago*, the vote was the same in a test of whether the Second Amendment applies to states and localities. Here, the Court, speaking through Justice Samuel Alito, ruled that the core of the second amendment, which was interpreted as the "right to self-defense" was due process of law because it was so fundamental and should be applied to the states through the Fourteenth Amendment. In response, Justice Clarence Thomas argued that the same could be done through the Fourteenth Amendment privileges and immunities clause and Justice John Paul Stevens argued that it could be done using just the "liberty clause," his name for the Fourteenth Amendment's due process clause.

Incorporating a Bill of Rights provision raised the question of whether or not these provisions meant the same at both the federal and state levels. For example, once the right to trial by jury in the Sixth Amendment was applied to the states, must states and national government observe the same 12-person, unanimous-verdict rules? In this case, the Court decided that they did not.[20] The meaning and protective reach of various amendments still needs to be explored further. In the case of freedom of religion, for example, are religious practices protected if they violate other laws, such as the ban on polygamy? In the case of freedom of speech, is only actual speech protected, or is symbolic speech such as flag burning protected as well?

Sonia Sotomayor, appointed to the Supreme Court by Barack Obama in 2009 to replace the retiring David Souter, will make little change in the overall vote on civil liberties by trading her liberal vote for Souter's. However, she may be the beginning of Obama's reconstruction of the Court through other appointments.

## FREEDOM OF RELIGION

Few issues lay closer to the framers' hearts than those involving religion. Many of the nation's earliest European settlers were religious zealots seeking independence from the state-run Anglican Church of England. Accordingly, they either established state religions of their own or supported various religions without giving preference to any of them. State laws often disenfranchised various religious groups, such as Catholics, Jews, agnostics, or atheists. Because the new nation's potential for fragmentation into different religious communities fighting for governmental control was too dangerous to be ignored, the guarantee of freedom of religion appeared early in the Bill of Rights.

The framers considered religion a matter of personal choice and conscience, not an area for governmental control. However, by restricting government's "establishment" of religion while simultaneously guaranteeing the "free exercise" of religion, they created contradictory goals.[21] For example, if the government provides tax-exempt status for religious organizations, as it does for other charitable institutions, thus promoting "free exercise of religion," does this constitute an "establishment of religion"? On the other hand, if government fails to grant such tax relief, would this force some churches to close, thus restricting the free exercise of religion?[22] Questions like these have led the Supreme Court to rely more on the establishment clause rather than on the free exercise clause.

### THINKING CRITICALLY

If the privileges and immunities clause is revived as a means of incorporating rights to the states, could it apply unincorporated rights such as the Fifth Amendment grand jury provision and the Eighth Amendment guarantee against excessive bails and fines to the states? If so, would it also follow that the clause would apply to unenumerated rights such as the right of privacy, gay marriage, the right to abortion, or the right to die?

### Establishment of Religion

13.4 *How has the Supreme Court determined the level of separation between church and state?*

In deciding whether particular governmental practices would have the effect of "establishing" a religion, the Court has searched for the proper balance between two opposing views of the relationship between government and religion. These are known as the *high wall of separation* position and the *government accommodation* position.

The high wall of separation position originated with the author of this constitutional provision, James Madison, who was reacting to the fact that half the colonies had adopted laws that provided support for religious institutions and practices.[23]

**Lemon test**
A test from the 1971 Supreme Court case *Lemon* v. *Kurtzman* for determining the permissible level of state aid for church agencies by measuring its purpose on three counts: Is it nonreligious in nature? Does it either advance or inhibit religion? Does it produce excessive entanglement of church and state?

Fearing that such laws could lead to religious persecution, he called for strict separation between church and state. However, connections between church and state were too numerous to bar them all. In the government accommodation view, the government would be allowed to assist religion, but only if the aid was indirect, available to all other groups, and religiously neutral.

The government accommodation position was first articulated in 1947 in the case of *Everson* v. *Board of Education of Ewing Township*. A local school board, spurred by the desire to aid Catholic parochial schools, had provided funds to enable children to travel to parochial school on city buses. The Court ruled that the state's policy did not violate the establishment clause because the children, not the church, received the benefit. According to Justice Hugo Black, the transportation assistance resembled other basic services, such as police and fire protection. Black was not persuaded by dissenters' arguments that such assistance helped children attend the church schools, thereby indirectly aiding religion.[24]

The high wall of separation doctrine was best described in 1962 in the case of *Engel* v. *Vitale*, in which the Court ruled that a brief nondenominational prayer led by a teacher in a public school was unconstitutional. For the Court, the mere chance that a student might feel compelled to worship a God in which he or she did not believe was precisely the kind of establishment of religion the framers had sought to avoid.[25]

Partly because of public outcry after the *Engel* decision, the Court began to search for a middle ground between separation and accommodation. It took a step in this direction one year later in the case of *Abington School District* v. *Schempp*. In ruling on this case, which involved Bible readings in Pennsylvania public schools, the Court adopted a *strict governmental neutrality* rule, under which a state was barred from doing anything that either advanced or inhibited religion. Since school-directed Bible reading clearly advanced religion, the practice was ruled unconstitutional.[26]

During the 1960s, the Court continued to search for the proper test for judging cases involving state aid to religious schools. If parochial school students could receive bus money, could they receive books? Because the books were loaned, the Court found this practice constitutional. Could the same be said for state aid to parochial school teachers teaching nonreligious subjects? This question was raised by the 1971 case of *Lemon* v. *Kurtzman*. In deciding that case, the Court created a new test, called the ***Lemon* test,** for determining the permissible level of state aid for church agencies. Such aid was considered constitutional, if the state could prove that (1) the law had a secular purpose, (2) the primary purpose and effect of the law were neither to advance nor to inhibit religion, and (3) the law did not foster an "excessive governmental entanglement with religion." Aid for teachers of nonreligious subjects met the first two conditions. However, the only way the state could judge if the funded teachers were aiding religion would be to monitor their classes; the law therefore violated the "excessive entanglement" provision of the test.[27]

During the past three decades, this three-pronged *Lemon* test has been applied in all cases involving the establishment of religion. In the early 1980s, changes in the makeup of the Court produced a shift toward a more accommodationist position. The parents of Minnesota private, public, and parochial school students were permitted in *Mueller* v. *Allen* to take an income tax deduction for the costs of tuition, textbooks, and transportation;[28] a chaplain could open the daily proceedings of the Nebraska legislature;[29] and a crèche could be placed in a public park in Pawtucket, Rhode Island, as part of a larger Christmas display. It was here that Justice Sandra Day O'Connor offered her suggestion for replacing the *Lemon* test, saying that the Christmas display was permissible for her because it offered "no endorsement" of a particular religion or religion in general.[30] On the other hand, certain practices were disallowed: the state of Kentucky was barred from posting the Ten Commandments in school classrooms;[31] the state of Alabama was barred from requiring a moment of silent meditation in public schools if the teacher suggested that students use the time to pray or even suggested the wording of a prayer;[32] public school teachers could not be sent to parochial schools to teach secular subjects;[33] and the state of Louisiana could not require the teaching of creationism, a religious theory that the

Earth was created according to the biblical book of Genesis as a way of providing a perspective different from Darwin's theory of evolution.[34]

Twice in the 1980s, the Court considered and rejected state public school curricula that required the teaching of both creationism and evolution. Religious groups around the country mounted the "Hang Ten" movement, seeking to post the Ten Commandments on the walls of public schools and public buildings. In 2002, for the second time in a year, a deeply divided court refused to hear an appeal by Indiana governor Frank O'Bannon, whom a lower court had prevented from placing a seven-foot stone monument containing the Ten Commandments on the statehouse lawn, a situation reminiscent of a similar effort by Justice Roy Moore in the Alabama Supreme Court building rotunda. These cases have led to the removal of memorials around the country.[35] In November 2002, the federal court also ordered that the Alabama monument be removed.

In June 2005, the Court weighed in once more on the Ten Commandments issue with two rulings on the erection of Ten Commandments monuments on state grounds, one inside a Kentucky courtroom and the other on the grounds of the Texas State Capitol. In a pair of narrow 5–4 decisions, the Court ruled that these monuments were constitutional only if they did not "endorse" religion by the state. According to the Court, this made the Texas state capitol grounds monument acceptable because it celebrated only the history of the relationship between state and religion. The monument inside the Kentucky courtroom, however, was unconstitutional because it "endorsed" religion by the state. In the words of Justice David Souter in the Kentucky case: "Sacred text can never be integrated constitutionally into a governmental display on the subject of law, or American history."[36] The Rehnquist Court stood ready to modify or reverse many of its other religion decisions. The crèche declared acceptable in Pawtucket five years earlier was now unacceptable on the grand staircase of the Allegheny County Courthouse in Pittsburgh. On the other hand, the placing of a menorah next to a Christmas tree and a sign saluting liberty just outside the City-County Building in the same city was acceptable.[37] A nondenominational prayer at a Rhode Island graduation was ruled unconstitutional in an opinion by Justice Anthony Kennedy because, in his alternative to the *Lemon* test, it might have a "psychological coercion" effect on nonbelievers who were present and might even induce some students not to attend their graduation for religious reasons.[38] While five members of the Court saw the test as too separationist in its impact, it remained to be seen whether they could agree on a more accommodationist test.

In the 2001 term, the Court plumbed the full limits of the *Lemon* test when it heard an appeal from Cleveland, Ohio, raising the question of whether school vouchers were constitutional. This voucher program, passed by the Ohio legislature, offered $2,250 in state aid to impoverished students, 99 percent of whom would use the money to attend religious schools. In a narrow 5–4 ruling, Chief Justice Rehnquist upheld the Cleveland program, arguing that because it gave parents the option of sending their children to public charter or magnet schools as well as nonreligious private schools, it did not coerce them into subjecting children to religious instruction. Justice David Souter, in an unusual denunciation of the Court's decision delivered orally from the bench, called it a "major devaluation" of the Court's church–state rulings and was "not only mistaken, but tragic."[39] This ruling gave energy to the Bush administration's effort to fund "faith-based initiatives," such as soup kitchens and day-care centers run by religious organizations that might seek government funding.

This decision did not end the fight over government spending for religious schools, but merely shifted the legal battle to the state level. Thirty-eight states have Blaine Amendments, named for the anti-Catholic Maine Republican congressman of the 1850s, James G. Blaine, who tried to secure passage of a constitutional amendment banning any government funding for parochial schools. When that failed, states used it as a model for their own anti-religious-school funding amendments to their constitutions, sometimes barring both direct and indirect financial aid. After the school voucher decision, states renewed their examination of the legality of state aid to religious schools, and by mid-2005, 38 states had passed restrictions on this practice. The Florida Supreme Court also announced that it would hear a case challenging

Supreme Court Chief Justice Roy Moore of Alabama secretly had this Ten Commandments granite marker placed in the rotunda of that state's Supreme Court building, and refused his colleagues' request to remove it. The federal court later ordered it to be removed, as a violation of the First Amendment's Establishment of Religion, and Justice Moore was later removed from his position by the state's Court of the Judiciary. He will run for re-election to the post.

the state's merit-based Opportunity Scholarships Program because they provided aid to a religious school.[40]

Recently, another establishment-of-religion issue arose when public schools began to require the teaching of another religious theory, called *intelligent design,* in science classes. Intelligent design explains the gaps perceived by some in Darwin's evolutionary theory as being the result of the "intelligent design" of God, thus once again basing the instruction on the book of Genesis in the Bible.[41] While advocates in these schools argue that intelligent design is as much a scientific theory as is Darwin's theory of evolution, others maintain that it is a means of inserting religious doctrine that lacks scientific proof into the schools' science curriculum. Since 2001, just under half of the states, 24, have considered changing the way evolution is taught in their state by either including this creationism theory or using it in the curriculum to critique the Darwinian evolutionary theory.

President Bush's public support for the intelligent design theory in mid-August 2005 raised the prospect that more states would add this religiously connected theory to their science education curriculum. That fall, the intelligent design curriculum in the Dover, Pennsylvania, public schools was tested in federal court and was struck down in December 2005. All eight school board members who had supported the curriculum were voted out of office in the 2005 election. However, across the country in that same election, the Kansas State Board of Education adopted this curriculum for science classes throughout the state. The Court will no doubt consider once again if this course represents state establishment of religion.

## Free Exercise of Religion

13.5 *How has the Court regulated and protected the right to free exercise of religion?*

Issues involving the free exercise of religion are particularly vexing because they most often involve disputes of liberty versus liberty, or the right of one person to practice religion in the face of another who seeks to avoid religion. One look at certain government practices—the "In God We Trust" motto on its currency, the chaplain's invocation that opens sessions of Congress, and even the admonition "God save this honorable Court" that opens each session of the Supreme Court—tells us that religion is pervasive in American politics. But do these practices place limits on the free exercise of religion? And, even if they do, is it politically possible to change them? These questions over the symbolic use of religious symbols in state-funded locations, which greatly resemble the freedom of thought and symbolic speech cases under the First Amendment freedom of speech, became clear in June 2002 when a three-judge panel of the Ninth Circuit Court ruled that the "under God" provision of the Pledge of Allegiance made its use in public schools unconstitutional because it coerced nonreligious students to express a religious belief that they did not hold. The Supreme Court could not reach a result in this case because it reached a tie vote when Justice Scalia was forced to step aside from the case after speaking about it off-the-Court. If the case should ever reach the Supreme Court again, it will very likely be reversed.[42]

Free exercise cases usually involve a law that applies to everyone but is perceived as imposing a hardship on a particular religious group. For example, can laws against mail fraud be used to prosecute religious groups that make dubious claims in letters to potential donors? In such cases, the Court will not inquire into the nature of the religion, but it will examine whether the actions that result from that belief contravene the law. This so-called **secular regulation rule** holds that no constitutional right exists to exemption on free exercise grounds from laws dealing with nonreligious matters. This rule was applied in 1878 in a case involving the Mormon practice of polygamy (taking multiple wives) in Utah Territory. The Court ruled that religious beliefs did not provide immunity from the law, in this case the law enforcing monogamy.[43]

**secular regulation rule**
Rule denying any constitutional right to exemption on free exercise grounds from laws dealing with nonreligious matters.

**least restrictive means test**
A free-exercise-of-religion test in which the state was asked to find another way, perhaps through exemptions, to enforce its regulations while protecting all other religions.

Subsequently, it became clear that the secular regulation rule did impose undue hardship on religious groups in certain instances. For example, the so-called blue laws that required all businesses to close on Sunday put Muslim or Jewish business owners who observed the Sabbath on Friday or Saturday at a competitive disadvantage because their businesses had to be closed on Sunday as well. Accordingly, the Court invented a new strict scrutiny test—the **least restrictive means test**—in which the state was asked to find another way, perhaps through exemptions, to enforce its regulations while still protecting all other religions.[44]

This "live and let live" position on issues of free exercise prevailed until 1990, when the Rehnquist Court decided a case in which two Native Americans working as unemployment counselors in Oregon were held to have violated the state's anti-drug laws by smoking peyote, a hallucinogenic drug, as part of a religious observance. The Court chose in this instance to defer to the state's efforts to control drug use rather than protect the free exercise of religion.[45] Although the Court refused to use this precedent to allow the state of Florida to rely on its public health and animal anti-cruelty laws to specifically ban religious sacrifices of animals,[46] government authorities used it to justify even greater incursions into religious behavior: autopsies were ordered contrary to religious beliefs, and an FBI agent who refused a work assignment for religious reasons was fired.[47]

Congress reversed the Oregon peyote-use ruling in the Religious Freedom Restoration Act (RFRA), and in 1997, the Supreme Court overturned this law in the case of *City of Boerne* v. *Flores*. In this case, the congregation of the St. Peter Catholic Church in Boerne, Texas, wanted to expand its beautiful historic stone structure to accommodate its growing membership, but was blocked by the city's Historic Landmark Commission. This decision was challenged under RFRA, and the Court overturned the law, thus restoring the *secular regulation rule* for state cases, saying that it was not within Congress's power to legislatively void judicial decisions.[48] Eventually, the church was allowed to build its addition, while the Court and various states later created protective "strict scrutiny" test exceptions for other cases.

In sum, the principle of freedom of religion appears straightforward on the surface, but in practice it raises complex issues resolved in various ways throughout our history. It appears impossible to erect a high wall of separation between church and state, but we accommodate government practices that involve religious organizations that may vary depending on Supreme Court composition and the specific test applied in each instance. The same is true in the area of free exercise, where the Court composition determines the degree of freedom that religious groups have against state regulations. In the past several years, the Court signaled its willingness to protect the free speech and free exercise rights of religious organizations. In 2001, the Court ruled that public schools that allowed nonreligious groups to meet for activities in their buildings after school hours must also open their building to religious groups for their meetings, in this case an after-school Bible club for young children.[49]

This direction continued with the Court's 8–1 ruling in 2002 that protected Jehovah's Witnesses from the town solicitation regulations of Stratton, Ohio. The law required door-to-door advocates to secure a permit and reveal the names of missionaries before going door-to-door to proselytize.[50]

# FREEDOM OF SPEECH

13.6 *How has the Court's protection of free speech preserved democracy?*

One hallmark of a democratic state is the guarantee of freedom of speech. But just where does the state draw the line between a person's right to speak and other rights, such as the speech rights of others? Over the years, the Supreme Court has taken two different approaches in attempting to solve this dilemma. One approach was suggested by Alexander Meiklejohn, a legal theorist who argued that although public, or political, speech on matters of public interest must be absolutely protected to preserve a democratic society, private speech, or speech intended for one's own purposes, can be restricted to protect the interests of other members of society.[51] On the other hand, Justice Oliver Wendell Holmes argued that democracy requires a "free marketplace of ideas" in which *any* view may be expressed, allowing the audience to decide what to believe. Holmes believed that limits on freedom of speech were justified only when the consequences of speech endangered the state.[52]

Caught between these absolutist and balancing approaches, the Court has ruled in ways that protect certain kinds of speech but not others. All speech is afforded First Amendment protection unless it is offensive or obscene or poses a threat to national security. Such utterances either convey no worthwhile ideas or do more harm to society than good and are deemed unworthy of protection. Despite these guidelines, however, the degree of protection afforded to particular forms of speech has varied considerably.

## Political Speech

Where does the government draw the line between promoting full political discussion and protecting the government's right to exist? The Court faced this challenge in the early 1950s, when Cold War tensions led to fears that Communist Party members in the United States were actively seeking to overthrow the government. These were no "poor and puny anonymities," the government argued in prosecuting 12 Communist Party leaders, but members of a worldwide organization calling for full-scale revolution.

In *Dennis* v. *United States,* the Court reviewed in 1951 the convictions of Communist Party leaders under the Smith Act, which made it a crime to teach or advocate overthrow of the government or to organize and conspire with those who do so. Did these actions pose a "clear and present danger" to the nation? In view of the tiny and disorganized nature of the American Communist Party, the Court concluded that its actions created no such danger. However, the Court was anxious to uphold the convictions, and therefore it invented a new *sliding-scale test,* called the "gravity of the evil" test, in which the state needed to prove less about the probable results of speech if the potential threat involved was significant enough. In this case, since the Communists aimed to overthrow the government, the government could convict if it found only their names on a party membership list and evidence that they were involved in the organization's activities, not that they were actively plotting the government's overthrow.[53] The overall effect of this new test would gut the protection of clear and present danger for groups that the government deemed to be dangerous.

Not until 1957 did the Court become willing to protect the speech of Communists as long as they were not actively plotting to overthrow the government.[54] By 1967, the Court had made it virtually impossible to deny First Amendment rights to someone for merely being a Communist.[55] At the time of Earl Warren's retirement in 1969, the Court restored the old protective clear and present danger test and moved a considerable distance toward absolutism in protecting political speech. For example, when Ohio's Ku Klux Klan leader was convicted for advocating unlawful methods of terrorism because television cameras caught him with a gun at a cross-burning rally, the Court in *Brandenburg* v. *Ohio* invented a new test. It would uphold convictions only for speech that advocated and incited "imminent lawless action" and was "likely to produce such action." On this basis, the conviction was reversed.[56]

For a time it appeared that a major political speech case might be coming one day to the Court because of the actions of a Swedish Internet correspondent, Julian Assange. Assange's organization, Wikileaks, released tens of thousands of secret cables on the Internet, many of them revealing top-secret military and diplomatic communications by the United States and its Department of State. Assange was arrested in Great Britain in 2011 and was ordered to be extradited to Sweden, where he might be sent to the United States for prosecution under the 1919 anti-Sedition and anti-Espionage laws. While proving the "imminent lawless action here" would be relatively easy, the question would be whether the press outlets such as the *New York Times* and the *Washington Post,* which had released many of these cables in their accounts, might also become ensnared in this legal net.

**Political Campaign Speech** After the Court had ruled in *Buckley v. Valeo* in 1976 that it was legal to restrict campaign financing , but not to limit personal contributions to one's own campaign spending because it was protected by the First Amendment's freedom of speech, change cutting down this precedent came as the membership of the Court itself changed in a more conservative direction. In the 1999 term, the Supreme Court opened the door for further campaign finance reform by ruling in a Missouri case that limits on individual contributions are constitutional. The limits of $1,075 for contributions to statewide candidates, similar to laws in two-thirds of the states, were ruled not a limit on free speech.[57] The following term, the Court indicated once more its concern about the effect of money on political campaigns when it ruled against the Colorado Republican Party's request for exemption from federal limits on how much money political parties can spend to assist their candidates' campaigns.[58]

These campaign finance reform decisions took on added importance in 2002, given passage of the Bipartisan Campaign Finance Act banning soft money and issue ads. When the Supreme Court upheld the constitutionality of nearly all provisions of the McCain-Feingold campaign finance law a year later, the legal battle shifted to the question of ads funded by non–political party interest groups called 527s. These groups are named for the IRS provision that allowed for such speech by tax-exempt organizations, a practice that was tested in Court in 2010 in the case of *Citizens United* v. *Federal Election Commission.* Here, the Roberts Court ruled on a case in which an interest group sought to air a documentary film called *Hillary: The Movie,* which some argued was a political propaganda "issue ad" opposing Hillary Clinton within 30 days of the Democratic presidential primary, in violation of the 2002 McCain-Feingold campaign finance law. However, the Court ruled by a 5–4 margin that corporations are people, and under their First Amendment free speech rights they have an unlimited right to contribute to election campaigns. Some believed that the unlimited electoral donations from large corporations would benefit the Republicans, whereas others argued that money from large unions, would benefit the Democrats. The Court argued that the connection between money and corruption in politics was unproven, and it expected Congress to make those donations transparent in follow-up legislation. This has not happened and in 2011, an unpersuaded Montana passed a law banning corporate campaign donations.

In 2008, *Hillary: The Movie* was either a documentary or campaign propaganda dealing with Democratic presidential candidate Hillary Clinton, depending on your point of view. David Bossie, the leader of Citizens United and producer of *Hillary: The Movie,* became the focus of the Supreme Court's determination as to whether this movie was an "issue ad" and whether the 2002 McCain-Feingold campaign finance reform banning such speech should be upheld. In January 2010, the Supreme Court overturned this portion of the law, ruling that corporations had the same free speech rights as human beings, which included the spending of money on campaigns, thus preventing Congress from limiting their campaign contributions in this law.

## Public Speech

States have passed many laws to protect those who might be offended or threatened by certain kinds of speech. Disturbing the peace, disorderly conduct, inciting to riot, terrorist threats, and fighting-word statutes are designed to preserve public order and safety. The main problem with such statutes is that sometimes they are crafted or enforced specifically to exclude certain ideas or groups.

Laws involving public speech require the Supreme Court to weigh the speaker's right to say what he or she wishes against the state's right to maintain law and order. Over the years, the Court has developed three standards in this area. First, the Court asked if a particular form of speech comes under the protective umbrella of the First Amendment. Thus, although controlled protests in public places such as the state library and state capitol are protected, calling a police officer "a goddamned racketeer" and "a damned fascist" is not; such expressions are considered fighting words.[59] The Court looked next at the nature of the statute itself. Is the law overbroad, including certain protected forms of speech among the proscribed ones? Or is it underinclusive, failing to regulate forms of speech that should be barred? For instance, a "disturbing the peace" law was used to arrest an anti-Semitic priest for making an

**hate speech**
Speech or symbolic actions intended to inflict emotional distress, to defame, or to intimidate people.

**symbolic speech**
Some actions, such as burning the American flag, that take the place of speech because they communicate a message.

**fighting words**
Certain expressions so volatile that they are deemed to incite injury and are therefore not protected under the First Amendment.

inflammatory speech. The conviction was overturned because the law was used to punish speech that merely "invited dispute" or created "a condition of unrest"; it did not actually cause a riot.[60] The same standard is used today in determining the degree of protection available to **hate speech**—speech and symbolic actions, such as cross-burning, laced with negative views toward certain groups of people. In two cases the Court ruled that government cannot selectively ban such speech based on its content, but it can increase punishment for those who physically assault minorities.[61]

Finally, assuming that a particular form of speech is protected and the statute is precisely and narrowly drawn, the Court will examine the facts of the case to see if the state's interests override those of the speaker. Can the state demonstrate that the speech posed dangers significant enough to override the free speech interests involved (meaning that the regulation would be upheld)? Or did the police make arrests because of their objection to the speech itself rather than the resulting action (meaning that the arrest would be overturned)? Thus, picketing on state-owned jailhouse grounds, which risked causing a riot inside the jail, would constitute trespassing, and the picketers' arrests would be upheld.[62] But, arresting a civil rights leader the day after he had made a protest speech in front of a courthouse and claiming that he might have caused a riot would not be allowed.[63]

## Symbolic Speech

13.7 *How has the Court's interpretation of symbolic speech, especially for public school students, affected democracy?*

Not all speech involves words. Some actions, such as burning the American flag, take the place of speech and are commonly called **symbolic speech.** This leaves the Court to determine what is *speech* that conveys a message and should be protected and what is *conduct* that might harm the public order, and can be regulated by reasonable legislation. In a 1971 case, *Cohen* v. *California,* the Court expanded its protection to these types of protests. Paul Cohen had appeared in a courthouse wearing a leather jacket bearing the words "F- - -K THE DRAFT. STOP THE WAR." The Court might have argued that these were **fighting words**—controllable actions or obscenity forced on a captive audience—but instead it ruled that because the offensive speech was meant to convey a larger symbolic meaning, the behavior was protected under the First Amendment. This protective view of symbolic speech led the Court in 1989 to uphold Gregory Lee Johnson's right to burn the American flag, even though many people found the action objectionable.

This decision, coming from the conservative Rehnquist Court, surprised some people, but it was the result of a quirk in the Court's rules and some clever judicial politics by liberal William Rehnquist. When new conservative Chief Justice William Rehnquist continued to vote in an ultra-liberal direction, as he did as an associate justice, by remaining in the minority on this and other civil liberties cases, the opinion assignment authority passed to the senior justice in the majority. Because that was the liberal Brennan, he assigned the opinion to himself and crafted an opinion that would gain swing justice Anthony Kennedy's and even ultra-conservative Antonin Scalia's votes, with the liberals. For three years, from 1986 to 1989, when Chief Justice Rehnquist moderated his opinions to regain his opinion-writing power as a member of the Court's majority on some civil liberties cases, this ability of the likable, elfin Brennan to craft liberal majorities in what some called "the greatest liberal rearguard action in constitutional history" made this "the Brennan Court."[64]

Some symbolic speech, however, crosses the line into objectionable conduct, which can be regulated under the Constitution. In a series of cases dealing with so-called hate speech, including actions and protests that tend to defame or are intended to intimidate ethnic or religious groups, the Court ruled that although symbolic speeches such as burning crosses or painting swastikas were objectionable, state laws had to be carefully drawn to proscribe them. A unanimous Court overturned a St. Paul, Minnesota, city ordinance that banned any symbol likely to arouse "anger, alarm, or resentment in others on the basis of race, color, creed, religion or gender" as both underinclusive, because it banned too few kinds of speech, and overinclusive, because it banned too many kinds.[65] However, a unanimous Court upheld state laws that enhanced penalties for such hate speech behavior.[66]

In the 1990s, this issue of symbolic hate speech protests and whether they could be regulated or should be protected as free speech led the Court to examine the behavior of anti-abortion protesters. In an effort to protect women seeking abortion counseling and procedures at abortion clinics from anti-abortion protesters demonstrating and sometimes trying to block their entry, the Rehnquist Court in 1995 upheld a 36-foot "no approach buffer zone" around a Florida clinic that excluded anti-abortion protesters.[67] Two years later, the Court revisited this issue when a lower court (1) created a 15-foot "fixed buffer zone" around a New York clinic's doorways and parking lot entrances in which no protesting would be allowed; (2) permitted two anti-abortion "sidewalk counselors" to enter the zone at any time, unless the target of their conversation asked them to "cease and desist"; and (3) created a 15-foot "floating buffer zone" around anyone entering or leaving the facility—a sort of "no-protest bubble." The Supreme Court struck down the floating no-protest bubble as a violation of protesters' free speech, but upheld the 15-foot "fixed no protest" zone around the clinic.[68]

In 2000, the Court took another step in protecting abortion rights by upholding an unusual Colorado "bubble" law that established a 100-foot "no approach" zone around a "health-care facility" and prevented people from approaching others within eight feet to protest or pass out literature. The Court agreed that individuals had a "right to be left alone."[69] This chapter's timeline shows how crisis times have affected free speech rights.

## APPROACHING Democracy Timeline

### Level of Free Speech Protection During Crisis Times

| | |
|---|---|
| **1798** | Alien and Sedition Act is passed. |
| **1867** | William McCardle, confederate newspaper publisher, is jailed under Military Reconstruction Act of 1867. |
| **1869** | Supreme Court upholds congressional elimination of jurisdiction for case. |
| **1919** | World War I free speech cases (*Schenck, Abrams).* |
| **1925** | *Gitlow* v. *New York* incorporates First Amendment but denies Gitlow's rights. |
| **1941** | *Minersville* v. *Gobitis* upholds compulsory flag salute law. |
| **1942** | *Chaplinsky* v. *New Hampshire* protects speech unless they are "fighting words." |
| **1943** | *West Virginia* v. *Barnette* overturns compulsory flag salute law. |
| **1951** | *Dennis* v. *United States* denies free speech rights of American Communist Party Leaders. |
| **1965** | *O'Brien* v. *United States* upholds congressional law banning draft card burning. |
| **1969** | *Brandenburg* v. *Ohio* allows speech unless it causes "imminent and lawless action." |
| **1989** | Supreme Court allows flag burning in *Johnson* v. *Texas,* and *Eichmann* v. *U.S.* |
| **1992** | *R.A.V.* v. *City of St. Paul:* Supreme Court overturns Minneapolis "hate speech" law. |
| **2003** | *Virginia* v. *Black:* Supreme Court overturns Virginia hate speech law and allows cross-burning. |

☐ Democratic ☐ Neutral ☐ Undemocratic

## The Roberts Court and Free Speech

The retirement of Justice Sandra Day O'Connor in 2006 helped to create the conservative, free speech-protective Roberts Court. The appointment of Samuel Alito to her seat added a more conservative vote for protecting free speech and left the key vote in the hands of Anthony Kennedy, who also was voting more conservatively. As a result, at the end of the 2006-2007 term, in two 5–4 decisions, the Court upheld the right of free speech for large corporations and unions in political elections, while seemingly eliminating the right of free speech for students in high schools who offend principals with their messages. The first of these cases dealt with the issue ads provision of the McCain-Feingold campaign finance law, which prevented the use of soft money to air ads dealing with issues but designed to weigh for or against candidates running for office either 30 days before a primary election or 60 days before a general election.

When high school students held up this make-shift protest sign in Juneau, Alaska, across from their school while the Olympic torch was passing by, it became the basis for a landmark case limiting the free speech rights of public school students.

This prevented the anti-abortion group Wisconsin Right to Life from running its ads, which would have clearly opposed pro-abortion Senator Russ Feingold, before the 2004 election. Chief Justice Roberts argued for the majority that "Where the First Amendment is implicated, the tie goes to the speaker, not the censor." Under Chief Justice Roberts's new rule, issue ads can be banned only if they are "susceptible of no reasonable interpretation other than as an appeal to vote for or against a specific candidate."[70]

While corporate free speech was expanded, the same 5–4 majority, through an opinion by Chief Justice Roberts, significantly restricted high school students' free speech rights. The case began in 2002 when the Olympic torch was being carried through Juneau, Alaska. Joseph Frederick and his friends, seeking press attention and intending to be funny, unfurled a banner that read "Bong Hits 4 Jesus" across from the public school as the torch was going by. When they got suspended for ten days because of the reference to drug use, the question became whether the 1969 *Tinker* v. *Des Moines School District* case that argued that high school students "do not shed constitutional rights to freedom of speech or expression at the schoolhouse gate" except where it "materially and substantially disrupts" discipline in the school would apply.[71] Although there was no evidence that the sign had caused any disruption in school discipline, the Court ruled that the principal's objection to the drug reference was enough to remove any free speech protection for the students here. However, the *Tinker* decision still remained in force, meaning that political protests in public schools may still be protected.

In mid-2011, the Court ruled on a California law from the previous year banned the sale of violent video games to children. By a 7–2 vote, the Court continued its pro–First Amendment free speech protection decisions in arguing that there was no constitutional basis for such a law. Justice Antonin Scalia argued that literature such as Grimm's Fairy Tales and Snow White are filled with violent scenes and that such literature cannot constitutionally be restricted without the possibility of restricting other protected speech. As Scalia argued, "Like the protected books, plays and movies that preceded them, video games communicate ideas—and even social messages—through many familiar literary devices (such as characters, dialogue, plot and music) and through features distinctive to the medium (such as the player's interaction with the virtual world). That suffices to confer First Amendment protection."[72]

## FREEDOM OF THE PRESS

13.8 *How have the Court's rules governing freedom of the press preserved democracy?*

Decisions in cases that involve freedom of the press must establish a balance between the public's right to know and (1) the government's right to secrecy, (2) an individual's right to personal reputation and/or privacy, (3) a defendant's right to a fair trial, or (4) an individual's personal and moral sensibilities. To illustrate this point, ask yourself whether the public's "right to know" about a controversial criminal trial like that of Florida resident Casey Anthony who was tried and found innocent of killing her two-year-old daughter Caylee in 2011 overrides both the defendant's right to receive a fair trial and society's right to maintain law and order. Some see the press as a critical "fourth branch," keeping a watchful eye on the government. But what if revealing certain government activities could damage national security?

### THINKING CRITICALLY

The *Tinker* and *Frederick* cases both deal with high school students, but how would you adjust it to apply to student protests on college campuses? What would you create as the rule balancing protected speech and public order on campuses for different kinds of protests, campaign politics, and other kinds of public speaking situations?

## Prior Restraint

Often the balance between these two sets of rights depends on the kinds of laws used to restrict the press. **Prior restraint** (censorship) laws prevent the press from revealing information *before* the government chooses to publish it. Prior restraint cases generally involve issues of national security, but they may also involve "gag orders" intended to preserve the right to a fair trial. In contrast, **subsequent punishment** laws punish writers and editors *after* they publish certain information because of the negative effects of that speech. Such laws are used to ban libel and obscenity because they are harmful to reputations or public sensibilities. The framers were more concerned with prior restraint than with subsequent punishment, believing that a trial by a jury of peers could deal with the latter, but in reality both can be equally harmful. A threat of significant enough punishment after publication can lead the press to censor itself before publication.

*Source:* Mike Keefe/The Denver Post 2005/Politicalcartoons.com/Cagle Cartoons Inc.

Probably the most significant case involving prior restraint was the 1971 *Pentagon Papers* case, in which the Court ruled against prior restraint. In a concurring opinion, Justice Potter Stewart argued that prior censorship can be justified only when publication "will surely result in direct, immediate, and irreparable damage to our Nation or its people." Since the *Pentagon Papers* were strictly historical documents, Stewart failed to see the potential for such harm.[73] However, a closer analysis of the four concurring and three dissenting opinions reveals that the decision was not so great a victory for the press as it seemed. Five of the justices implied that if the government had tried to punish the press after publication, using laws barring the release of secret documents, the convictions would have been upheld.

The press also faces restraints in its coverage of criminal proceedings. Judges sometimes issue gag orders barring the media from publishing information about an ongoing criminal case. In 1976, the Court declared a gag order issued by a Nebraska court in the pretrial hearing of a multiple-murder case prior restraint of the press and a First Amendment violation.[74] Because the Court extended its ruling in 1980 to open criminal trials to the press and public "absent an overriding interest to the contrary," gag orders are far less common today.[75]

### THINKING CRITICALLY

The government has tried to regulate sexually explicit material from the Web, but has done little about regulating hate speech, hate groups, or dangerous material. Under what circumstances can material be banned from being published and from the Internet?

## Libel

The free flow of ideas in a democracy must sometimes be prevented or limited when it is untruthful, malicious, or damaging to a person's reputation or good name. Speech that has these effects is **slander;** if it appears in written form, it is **libel.** The Supreme Court has ruled that slander and libel are not protected by the First Amendment. But how does one determine whether a published statement is libelous? Some published statements may be intended to defame a person's reputation, but defamation may also stem from negligence or failure to take reasonable care in verifying information before publication. Do the latter instances also constitute libel?

The Court addressed this question in 1964, when the *New York Times* printed an advertisement critical of the racial views of unnamed public officials in Alabama. An elected commissioner in Montgomery, Alabama, L. B. Sullivan, filed suit in an Alabama court, claiming that the ad libeled him personally; he won the case under an Alabama law requiring newspapers to establish the truth of material before publishing it. The *New York Times* appealed the case to the Supreme Court. Seeking to balance the newspaper's right to publish against Sullivan's right to maintain his reputation, the Court took

**prior restraint**
An action in which the government seeks to ban the publication of controversial material by the press before it is published; censorship.

**subsequent punishment**
Laws that would punish someone for an action after it has taken place. For example, laws such as those banning libel and obscenity because they are harmful to reputations or public sensibilities punish writers, editors, and publishers after an item appears in print.

**slander**
Speech that is untruthful, malicious, or damaging to a person's reputation or good name and thus not protected by the free speech clause of the First Amendment.

**libel**
Published material that damages a person's reputation or good name in an untruthful and malicious way. Libelous material is not protected by the First Amendment.

# Compared to WHAT?

## The Crisis of Press Freedom in Great Britain

Change appears to be underway for Freedom of the Press in Great Britain. For years, publishers of books and magazines have gone to the British Courts in a kind of "libel tourism" to sue writers and publishers of publications in other countries, but which have been distributed in Great Britain, for defamation. The British legal standard for proving libel puts the burden of proof on the writer and publisher to show that they did not defame their subject. The effect is that just by bringing such a suit, it is assumed that libel has been committed and must be proven otherwise. For this reason, movie director Roman Polanski was able to win a lawsuit against the American magazine *Vanity Fair*, for an article about his alleged behavior on the way to his wife Sharon Tate's funeral. He won, even though he could only appear in the trial on a video screen, because if he attended the court proceeding he might have been arrested and extradited to the United State for trial on a long-standing statutory rape charge. The fear of libel suits became so pronounced that when rumors reached the press about the behavior of members of the British royal family, the press could not report that such rumors existed, without describing them, even though the rumors were easily available around the rest of the world on the Internet. In early 2011, Parliament began to consider new legislation that might restrict the nature of the libel standard in order to limit this "libel tourism" practice. Ironically, it was to this country that Wikileaks head, Julian Assange, who had engineered the Internet release of confidential documents from the United States and other governments, had fled in the hopes of avoiding being extradited back to his native Sweden to face criminal prosecution on a sexual assault charge and the prospect of being extradited again to the United States to face 1919 Espionage Act charges.

At the same time, press freedoms recently faced the prospect of being undercut substantially by the actions of reporters from the British tabloid, *News of the World*, owned by Australian billionaire Rupert Murdoch. The reporters were invading the privacy of the subjects of their stories, hacking into the cell phone voicemail accounts of movie stars Hugh Grant and Sienna Miller, *Harry Potter* author J.K. Rowling, and soccer star David Beckham, in order to get leads for front page stories. In one case, reporters hacked into the cell phone of a teenaged murder victim, even erasing some of her messages, leading the family and the police to believe that she was still alive. The result was a huge scandal, an investigation by Parliament, and closing down of the tabloid. In time, though, it became apparent that such privacy invading practices were being used by other reporters as well. The result may be an even further reduction of the public's respect for the press and the government's willingness to protect its freedom to write and publish.

*Source:* Eric Pfanner, "In Britain, Curbing Lawsuits Over Libel," *The New York Times*, March 20, 2011.

careful notice of Sullivan's status as a public official. Unlike private individuals, public officials can respond to published statements through such means as press conferences. On the other hand, if the press were prevented from publishing statements critical of political figures, it could not fulfill its role as a watchdog of government.

So the Court ruled that convictions in cases involving libel against public officials—expanded in later cases to public figures—could be upheld only if the defamatory article had been printed with "knowledge that it was false or reckless disregard whether it was false or not." In short, the untrue and defamatory piece would have to be printed without any effort to check the facts.[76] Making only the most minimal effort to check facts, supermarket tabloids can print outrageous articles about movie stars and public figures, generally without fear of legal retribution.

Seeking to restrict the press, the Burger and Rehnquist courts launched a two-pronged attack against the Sullivan standard. The class of people defined as "public figures" was narrowed,[77] and the press was instructed to turn over materials indicating its "state of mind" when publishing an article claimed as libelous.[78] These changes had the effect of increasing the burden on the press to prove that it had not been negligent or malicious in publishing a statement challenged as libelous.

One trend to watch in the future is the willingness of companies to resort to libel-like suits to attempt to silence their critics. The Food Lion grocery chain sued ABC's *Primetime Live* for a report on the chain's sales of spoiled food. Rather than sue for libel, the firm sued for fraud, breach of loyalty, and trespass because the reporters were undercover. Although the grocery firm won $5.5 million in damages, most of it was reversed on appeal, leaving Food Lion with a $2 award. The Court ruled against such an end run of the First Amendment.[79] Yet another type of case will likely arise from the Internet, where statements in various websites might cause damage to named people or businesses. Court decisions will need to explore what kind of speech exists in this format and whether it is protected.

**THINKING CRITICALLY**

Should the federal government pass a national "shield law," making reporters' sources confidential, or should the names of sources of government leaks continue to be available to government investigators? Should the press accept such protection? Do members of a college newspaper have different rights under the First Amendment than the national press?

## Obscenity

Although the First Amendment does not protect publication of obscene material, it is difficult to establish a definition of obscenity and thus judge whether or not a particular publication is obscene. In a 1957 case, *Roth* v. *United States,* the Supreme Court stated that material could be judged obscene if "the average person, applying contemporary community standards, [determines that] the dominant theme of the material, taken as a whole, appeals to the prurient interest."[80] Thus, books such as *Lady Chatterley's Lover* or *Peyton Place* could not be declared obscene because of a few scattered passages that might be offensive to a few highly susceptible people. In 1966, the Court added to the *Roth* standard the requirement that a work could be banned only if it was "utterly without redeeming social value."[81]

During the 1960s, the Warren Court developed a *variable obscenity test* in which the definition of obscenity changed according to the circumstances of the material's use or sale. Material was judged obscene if it was thrust upon a "captive audience"—for example, a pornographic outdoor drive-in movie visible from the street—or sold to unsuspecting customers such as children. In addition, material geared specifically toward customers with alternative sexual lifestyles could be banned.[82]

The confusion and uncertainty resulting from this variable standard led the Burger Court to attempt a clearer standard in the 1973 case of *Miller* v. *California.* Henceforth, the definition of material as obscene would depend on

> *whether the average person applying contemporary community standards would find the work taken as a whole, appeals to the prurient interest; whether the work depicts or describes, in* a patently offensive way, *sexual conduct specifically defined by the applicable state law; and whether the work taken as a whole* lacks serious literary, artistic, political, or scientific value.[83]

In contrast to the *Roth* standard, the *Miller* standard considered local tastes. But this distinction did not solve the problem of defining obscenity. Each locality now had its own standard and applied it in varying ways to nationally distributed work. For example, the movie *Carnal Knowledge,* which depicted no sexual activity but contained a great deal of dialogue on the subject, was judged obscene in Georgia but not elsewhere.[84]

The Rehnquist Court made little progress toward establishing a clear definition of obscenity. The only clarity came in the area of child pornography, for which the Court has so little tolerance that it has permitted convictions for even the possession of obscene videos of clothed children.[85] The question of how to determine if a particular book or other published material is obscene, and thus to prevent or punish the publication of such material, remains unanswered.

One question the Court has answered for the moment, however, concerns attempts to regulate alleged pornography on the Internet; such regulation will not be allowed. In 1996, Congress passed the Communications Decency Act (CDA) seeking to protect those under the age of 18 from "obscene or indecent" messages or "patently offensive" communications "knowingly" sent over the Internet. Although the Court, in the case testing this act, was committed to "protecting children from harmful materials," it found the definition of speech restricted by the Communications Decency Act too vague and the law so vague that parents could be prosecuted for how their own children used the family computer. Justice John Paul Stevens wrote for the majority that the First Amendment protects the Web's "vast democratic [forums] . . . where any person with a phone line can become a town crier." Thus, he explained, "in the absence of evidence to the contrary, we presume that governmental regulation of the content of speech is more likely to interfere with the free exchange of ideas than to encourage it."[86]

## THINKING CRITICALLY

Can you fashion the wording for a law that will successfully ban only pornographic material from the Internet while leaving protected messages unaffected? Should this law also apply to the different social networks and YouTube?

But Congress was not finished with its efforts to regulate the Internet to shield children from pornography. Neither was the Court with its determination to make difficult this form of restricting free speech. In 1996, Congress passed the Child Pornography Prevention Act, which made it a crime to create or distribute on the Internet virtual images of child pornography—that is, simulated computer images rather than real children engaging in sexual acts. In the 2001–2002 term, the Supreme Court struck down this law, ruling that the law was so broad that it could be used to block the simulated teenaged sexual acts found in movies such as *Titanic* and *Traffic*.[87]

Whether this Supreme Court posture will continue remains to be seen. In 1998, Congress passed the Child Online Protection Act, which required all commercial websites, not just those marketing pornography, to use some form of service to protect children under age 17 from material deemed "harmful to minors." After a Philadelphia federal appeals court blocked enforcement of this law, the Supreme Court ruled in its 2001 term that the lower court had not correctly applied the "contemporary community standards" provision of the obscenity test because the Web is worldwide. So, the lower court was instructed to reexamine the substantive provisions of the law, a ruling that will likely be revisited by the high court.[88]

Then, Congress went beyond the regulation of an individual's use of the Web to pass the Children's Internet Protection Act of 2000, which requires all schools and libraries to place filters on their computers in order to protect child users from pornographic websites or face the loss of millions of dollars in federal funding. In 2003, the Supreme Court upheld the law by a 6–3 majority, arguing that it did not violate the First Amendment rights of the children, the first time the Court upheld a law limiting child access to the Internet.[89] The interesting part of this battle, given the difficulty of defining pornography on the Web in a manner acceptable to the federal courts under the First Amendment, will come if Congress moves to expand its Internet regulatory efforts to deal with sites believed harmful to national security.

# THE RIGHTS OF DEFENDANTS

13.9 *How has the Supreme Court expanded and restricted the Fourth Amendment's search and seizure protections?*

The framers, fearful of the kinds of abuses that had prevailed under British rule, considered protection of the rights of defendants vital. The Bill of Rights, therefore, contains several safeguards against government oppression, including the right to be left alone in one's home (Fourth Amendment), the right to remain silent (Fifth Amendment), and the right to be represented by counsel (Sixth Amendment). Remarkably, despite many changes in the technology of police work, these guarantees remain as vital today as they were 200 years ago. Whether searches involve ransacking one's belongings under a writ of assistance or using technology to monitor one's computer or conversations, the balance remains between the rights of the individual and the rights of society. However, as in many other areas involving civil liberties, this balance depends on the Supreme Court's composition at any given time. No issue better illustrates this fact than the shifting nature of Fourth Amendment protection over the past three decades.

## The Fourth Amendment

The Fourth Amendment tries to balance two rights: the individual's reasonable expectation of privacy and society's right to control crime and protect the public. Over the years, the Supreme Court has devised different rules for establishing this balance. During the 1960s, the Warren Court "revolution" greatly expanded the protection provided by the expectation of privacy, but in subsequent decades the Burger and Rehnquist courts shifted the balance back toward the state (i.e, the police). These shifts have had significant effects on both the nation's approach to, and recession from, democracy as expressed by the constrained and then increased power of the state to investigate and imprison people.

Many issues related to Fourth Amendment protections stem from the amendment's lack of an explicitly written remedy. What can a judge do if the police go too far in conducting a search? Can the evidence uncovered by such an illegal search be used in a trial? In other words, can the police break the law to uphold the law? As Justice Benjamin Cardozo put it, should "the criminal . . . go free because the constable had blundered"?[90] Debates over this issue center on the creation of an **exclusionary rule,** whereby evidence gathered by illegal means cannot be used in later trials. Likewise, under another doctrine, the *fruit of the poisonous tree,* no other evidence can be used that was gathered as a result of other searches or investigations based on an initially illegal search.

The exclusionary rule was created in 1914 in the case of *Weeks* v. *United States,*[91] which prevented federal courts from using illegally gathered evidence in a trial. This rule, it was argued, not only protected the privacy rights of the individual defendant but it also deterred the authorities from conducting illegal searches in future cases. However, the rule gave rise to problems both legal and symbolic. In certain cases, it prevented the use of hard, observable evidence, thus possibly allowing guilty individuals to go free.[92]

Since the Fourth Amendment did not yet apply to the states, the exclusionary rule could be used only in federal cases. In ruling on the admissibility of illegally seized evidence in state cases, the Supreme Court used the Fourteenth Amendment's due process clause. It held that only the results of searches that "shocked the conscience" of the justices could be barred from use in trials. The problem here was that different justices were shocked by different things. Justice Felix Frankfurter, the inventor of this test, was shocked by a case in which police officers broke into the office of a doctor suspected of performing abortions to find his patient book to use in making up a list of witnesses and by a case in which a man's stomach was pumped to retrieve two morphine capsules.[93] He was not, however, shocked by a case that involved taking blood from an unconscious man to determine whether he was drunk.[94] Many of Frankfurter's fellow justices disagreed with his views. Not until after Frankfurter's retirement did the Court begin to consider expanding the Fourth Amendment's exclusionary rule guarantee for defendants in state courts. Crisis times can affect search and seizure rights.

**The Due Process Revolution** In the case of Dollree Mapp in 1961, the Warren Court made its landmark ruling on the nature of the Fourth Amendment and its application to the states. The case began when the Cleveland police received a tip from a "reliable authority," who was in fact not always reliable, that a "suspected bomber of a house porch and bookmaker" was in Mapp's home. When Mapp refused to let the police in, three officers broke into the house, waving a blank piece of paper in the air and claiming that it was a search warrant. After Mapp stuffed the "warrant" inside her blouse, the officers tried to retrieve it and handcuffed Mapp for resisting their search. The search through the house produced no bomber or bookmaker, but the officers arrested and the court convicted Mapp for possessing allegedly obscene materials.[95]

This episode might have "shocked the conscience" of the justices in an earlier day, but in this case the Court made the Weeks exclusionary rule part of the Fourth

**QUICK REVIEW**

The Fourth Amendment

- This amendment tries to balance two rights: the individual's reasonable expectation of privacy and society's right to control crime and protect the public.
- The Supreme Court has devised different rules for establishing this balance.
- The Warren Court of the 1960s greatly expanded the protection provided by the expectation of privacy.
- The Burger and Rehnquist Courts shifted the balance back toward the state.

**exclusionary rule**
Rule whereby evidence gathered by illegal means, and any other evidence gathered as a result, cannot be used in later trials.

## THINKING CRITICALLY

If the police had a report that two occupants in a legally parked car were arguing, in a state whose law states that if asked to provide identification it must be presented, do they have the right to demand such identification of the driver of the parked car? Should they be able to arrest the person for obstructing justice if he fails to provide his ID? Should the arrest be upheld if it is later learned that the tip they had for conducting the inquiry was not, in fact, accurate?

Amendment and then incorporated it into the Fourteenth Amendment to apply it to the states. Thus, the exclusionary rule was made uniform among the states and between the state and federal levels of government. Mapp's conviction was reversed and her case was sent back to the state court for a retrial, but with the pornographic materials now excluded from the new trial, the state had no choice but to drop the charges.

**Limiting the Exclusionary Rule** During the Burger Court years, the justices were unhappy that under the exclusionary rule even the most minor police violations led to loss of all the evidence. The Court began to argue that the exclusionary rule should be restricted or eliminated, saying that it had little or no deterrent effect on police.[96] It began to question if any possible deterrent effect of the rule outweighed the possible harm to society from allowing guilty individuals to go free because improperly gathered evidence was excluded from the trial.

After limiting the use of the exclusionary rule in various criminal justice proceedings, such as the grand jury[97] and habeas corpus proceedings in which convicted defendants were seeking a new trial,[98] the Court greatly reduced its application in the 1984 case of *United States* v. *Leon*. Federal authorities had received a warrant to search certain houses and cars for drugs, based on an unreliable informer's outdated tips. The Warren Court would have voided the search and excluded the use of its evidence, but the Burger Court ruled that since the police believed they had a valid search warrant, excluding the evidence would not deter future illegal searches, so the resulting evidence could be used in a trial.[99] This reasoning became known as the *good faith exception* to the Fourth Amendment. "Good faith" was not defined, but the watering-down effect on the exclusionary rule was clear. Evidence that once could have been excluded could now be allowed if the Court was persuaded through "reasonably objective" criteria that the police believed the search to be valid.

The Rehnquist Court appeared willing to extend the good faith exception to cases in which no search warrant was issued. In *Illinois* v. *Rodriguez*, for example, officers relied on the word of a woman who said that she had a right to enter her ex-boyfriend's apartment. Searching the apartment with her consent, they found illegal drugs. Despite the fact that the woman actually had no right to admit the police, the Court ruled that since the police had relied on her word in good faith, the search was permissible.[100] In 1995, the Court allowed as evidence a bag of marijuana found after police searched a car based on a faulty computer report of a misdemeanor charge against the driver.[101]

**Warrantless Searches** Another way in which the Court can affect Fourth Amendment rights is by broadening or contracting the nature of searches for which judges have not issued warrants. The Fourth Amendment defines a proper search as one in which a proper search warrant has been issued after the police have demonstrated to a neutral judge **probable cause.** Probable cause means that there is enough evidence to convince a reasonable person that a search should be undertaken because a crime has been or is about to be committed, and investigators are likely to find evidence of such a crime at a particular location. Only then will the judge issue a warrant stating specifically where and for what police can search. But in cases where there isn't time to obtain a warrant, the amendment protects people against unreasonable searches. What, then, is a "reasonable search"?

Suppose a police officer stops a car, suspecting that it is carrying illegal weapons. Obviously, the officer has no time to obtain a warrant. If the officer can later demonstrate that the search was "reasonable," it will be allowed under a *movable automobile exception* to the Fourth Amendment.[102] The rationale in such a case is that delaying for a warrant may place the officer's safety in jeopardy or allow the car and evidence to escape, or both. On the other hand, what if a police officer enters a private house to speak with the occupant about a problem in the neighborhood and sees a Sidewinder missile hanging above the mantel? As long as the officer can give a valid reason for being there, justifiably believes what she sees is incriminating, and can legally proceed to it, she can seize what is in "plain view" as evidence, even without a warrant.

**probable cause**
A reasonable belief that a crime has been, is being, or is about to be committed. Searches also require a belief that evidence of that crime may be located in a particular place. Police must establish this to a judge to secure a search warrant or retroactively justify a search that has already taken place.

The Supreme Court giveth and the Supreme Court taketh away. This drunk-driving roadblock on U.S. 1 in North Carolina, part of the state's "Booze It and Lose It" campaign, is one of many used around the nation to keep driving safe. The Supreme Court has given the police wide leeway to search for licenses, registration, and inebriated or impaired drivers, so long as the searches are performed randomly or on every driver, and not done so as a pretext for conducting other kinds of searches. In 2012, though, the Court would not allow police to place a GPS device on a car parked in a public place and track the movements of a suspect for nearly a month.

In all Fourth Amendment cases, then, the central issue is whether or not a suspect's "expectation of privacy" is outweighed by the state's need to control crime by preserving evidence and ensuring the safety of police officers. In *Katz* v. *United States,* the Court ruled that electronic surveillance of public phone booths is unconstitutional: "The Fourth Amendment protects people, not places. What a person knowingly exposes to the public, even in his own home or office, is not a subject of Fourth Amendment protection. . . . But what he seeks to preserve as private, even in an area accessible to the public, may be constitutionally protected."[103] However, many other exceptions to the Fourth Amendment have been created, including searches incident to a lawful arrest (on the person and within the person's reach), consent searches (if the suspect permits the search, the Fourth Amendment protection is waived), searches of fleeing suspects who might destroy evidence, and various kinds of administrative searches (e.g., in airports and at national borders).[104] The 2001 USA Patriot Act gave significant latitude to civil authorities in their investigations of alleged terrorism, enabling them to search multiple locations using "one-stop shopping" warrants and wiretaps for all phones used by suspects (including public phones).

The evolution of the *stop-and-frisk exception* shows clearly the pattern of expanding and contracting Fourth Amendment rights. A stop-and-frisk case is one in which the police detain a person and conduct a *pat-down search* of that person's outer clothing without a warrant or an arrest, basing their action on observed, potentially criminal conduct. The Warren Court first defined the constitutional limits of such searches in 1968 in *Terry* v. *Ohio,* in which an experienced Ohio police officer had observed two men apparently planning to burglarize a store. The officer approached the men, asked them some questions, and then patted down their clothing; the search revealed revolvers and bullets concealed under their jackets, and the officer therefore arrested the men. The Court ruled that even though the officer lacked probable cause to arrest the suspects until after he had conducted a full search, the initial frisk was legal because he had "reasonable suspicion" to stop and pat down the suspects in the first place.[105]

**Public School Searches** The Burger and Rehnquist Courts have watered down individual protections under the Fourth Amendment. First, the Court has developed the *reasonable suspicion* or reasonableness of a search rule, balancing the expectation of privacy interests of the defendant against the investigation interests of the state. In the 1985 case *New Jersey* v. *T.L.O.,* the Supreme Court lowered the standard for searching in public schools in a case involving the search of a female student's purse. She was suspected of smoking because a school administrator stopped her as she left a women's restroom that had smoke billowing out of its vents into the hallway. At the same time as he saw the cigarettes, the administrator saw a package of rolling papers that led him to search below for drugs. Further search of her purse revealed other drug paraphernalia and a large amount of money. The purse's zipped-shut side pocket yielded lists of student names with dollar amounts next to them. The student was suspended for drug sales. The Court held that this search was justifiable because the vice principal had "reasonable suspicion." In response to the Court's holding that two searches were made here, one justified by smoke and the other by the rolling papers, Justice William Brennan argued that a third search occurred, of the zipped pocket, where the student had a greater "expectation of privacy."[106]

## THINKING CRITICALLY

Some public schools have punished students for transmitting sexually explicit photos of themselves to their friends, or circulating such photos to other students generally. Some of these students are suspended or expelled, while others are charged with state child pornography violations. What should be the constitutional rules governing such behavior?

By 1995, the Court, speaking through Antonin Scalia, expanded the *T.L.O.* case to uphold the random drug-testing of all student athletes in Vernonia, Oregon, public schools. An eighth-grader named Jamie Acton, who had no connection to drugs of any kind, was informed that as a student-athlete on the football team, he would be subject to a random drug test. He and his parents sued to stop the policy. When the case came to the now-conservative Supreme Court, there was a new test for search and seizure cases based in part on the *T.L.O.* case and in part on the *Katz* case. Seeking to expand police searching powers, the Court relied on the wording of a concurring opinion by Justice John Harlan in the *Katz* case to develop another exception to the *expectation of privacy standard.* In trying to explain why a person could justifiably expect privacy in a glass-enclosed, *public* phone booth, Harlan argued: "There is a twofold requirement, first that a person has exhibited an actual (subjective) expectation of privacy and, second, that the expectation be one that society is prepared to recognize as 'reasonable.'" So, members of society for Harlan would determine whether someone's "expectation of privacy" was reasonable."[107]

## THINKING CRITICALLY

How has technology changed the "reasonable expectation of privacy" test? Do you have the same "reasonable" privacy expectation for your cell phone, your PDA, your e-mail, or your computer as you do for a land phone line in your parents' home? Even if you do not, do you think that gives constitutional and legal permission to the police to search those items?

By combining the "societal expectation of privacy" test in *Katz* with the "reasonable suspicion" test in *T.L.O.*, the Court devised an even more permissive "reasonable expectation of privacy" test that allows more searches to be upheld. In this case, Scalia argued, there was a "war on drugs" in the school and Vernonia's school administrators had determined that a drug test policy for student-athletes was the only way to root out the drug culture in the athletic community. So, there was no "reasonable expectation of privacy" for Jamie Acton. In dissent, Justice Sandra Day O'Connor argued based on the wording of the Fourth Amendment that the appellant, Jamie Acton, had absolutely no personal history of drug use, meaning that the school lacked the "particularized, individualized suspicion" required for a test.[108]

After years of allowing public schools to search students almost without restrictions, the Supreme Court finally found its limits. Savana Redding, age 19, seen here in front of the Supreme Court, was the subject of a 2009 case involving a strip search performed on her at an Arizona public school after another student claimed that she was carrying prescription-strength ibuprofen. No pills were found, and the Court ruled the search to be an unreasonable violation of the Fourth Amendment.

Schools across the nation began expanding their drug-testing programs beyond athletes to students in extracurricular activities, and even to students seeking parking privileges on school grounds. The breadth of the Court's holding was tested in 2002 in a challenge involving a small town near Oklahoma City that randomly drug-tested all students in any competitive extracurricular activity (including debate, choir, school plays, and the Future Homemakers of America). Said Lindsey Earls, tested in high school because she was in the marching band, "I know the Supreme Court, in the *Vernonia* case, talked about how athletes have a risk of physical harm. But we're not going to hurt ourselves in choir."[109] Here, the Court ruled by a narrow 5–4 margin that such drug testing was constitutional because school officials believed it was the only way drugs could be controlled in their school district. On that basis, some school districts have begun drug testing all their students.

In June 2009, even under these permissive search rules, the Court finally found a school that went too far in its searches. Savana Redding challenged the "Zero Tolerance" for drugs policy of the Safford Middle School under which she was strip-searched by a school official looking for ibuprofen pills that he believed were being distributed to other students. He found nothing. Retiring Justice David Souter wrote for an eight-justice majority that the "indignity" and "degradation" of this kind of search on a "vulnerable" student, was unconstitutional because both the drug policy itself and the extensive nature of the search made it unreasonable. As he put it, the school did not have "any indication of danger to the students from the power of the drugs or their quantity, and any reason to suppose that Savana was carrying pills in her underwear. We think the combination of these deficiencies was fatal to finding the search reasonable." But the question of whether all public school strip searches, including those for weapons, are unconstitutional remains uncertain.[110]

**The End of *Mapp*?** In cases that focus on crime control, the five-justice conservative majority on the Court has made it increasingly easy for courts to justify searches under these "reasonable suspicion," "societal expectation of privacy," or "reasonable expectation of privacy" standards for determining constitutionality. This was made clear in 2000 when the Court ruled that running at the mere sight of a police officer in a high-crime area justifies police in stopping and searching the suspect because the act of running constituted "reasonable suspicion."[111] In 2002, the Court used these concepts of reasonable suspicion and societal expectation of privacy to rule on the practice of police sweeps for drugs and weapons on buses, with one officer kneeling at the front of the bus while two others worked their way forward questioning and searching passengers without first informing them that they had the right to refuse permission to be searched. The Court ruled that this practice was constitutional because under the "totality of circumstances" rule such a search would be permissible if the police wished to make a similar kind of search of a suspect off the bus. In the future, police might be able to use this ruling to justify their educated guesses in selecting suspects to search in cases such as anti-terrorism searches.[112]

When combined with a 2001 case involving the use of technology to search, this ruling made for a potentially powerful tool in the effort to combat terrorism. In a Florida case, *Kyllo* v. *U.S.*, a man named Kyllo was arrested for growing marijuana in his home after police used a thermal-imaging device to discover the "hot" portions of his home where the plant was grown. The Supreme Court overturned this search because, as Justice Scalia explained for the majority using a "Radio Shack" sales kind of test, this device was not yet in common use and seemed to be measuring heat inside the house from outside. However, it was clear from the opinions that in time this kind of search might become acceptable under the Fourth Amendment (especially because fire departments routinely use such devices to find lost firefighters in burning buildings).[113] Thermal imaging and other new technologies, such as "puffer devices" that can test the air around a person for the smell of explosive devices, or so-called backscatter X-ray devices that allow searches beneath one's clothing, offer new potential for successful searches but also raise vexing questions about the balance between liberty and security.

Figure 13.1 demonstrates all of the types of searches, technological and otherwise, that are done at the airports. All of these decisions on the limitations put on search technology by the Fourth Amendment have led to discussions between the federal government and the judicial system as to the constitutionality of electronic surveillance for anti-terrorism investigations. As the Court changes because of new appointments by the winner of the 2012 presidential election, it will be interesting to see whether the bare conservative majority on the current Court holds up for these programs.

The willingness of the Court to extend the police search power, even to the point of beginning to eliminate the *Mapp* v. *Ohio* exclusionary rule deterring illegal police conduct, was made very clear in the 2006 case of *Hudson* v. *Michigan*.[114] Several police went to the Detroit home of Booker T. Hudson with a search warrant for drugs, knocked on his door announcing that they were police, and then waited only three to five seconds before entering the unlocked door to find the suspect with a large amount of drugs and a revolver on a table in front of him. The search was upheld, with Justice Scalia arguing that there now was "increasing professionalism" in police searches. Scalia argued that the exclusion of the evidence would not deter future conduct, but would instead become a "get-out-of-jail-free card" for suspects.

The *Mapp* rule, which excluded evidence from use in trial that has been illegally gathered, began to change in 1984 in *Leon* v. *United States* when the Court allowed the search of the wrong home because a mistake had been

## THINKING CRITICALLY

Should the growing availability of thermal-imaging devices give the police more permission to use the devices to catch lawbreakers? Should it be legal, for instance, for state police to point such devices at cars on the highways to determine if illegal aliens are being smuggled into the country?

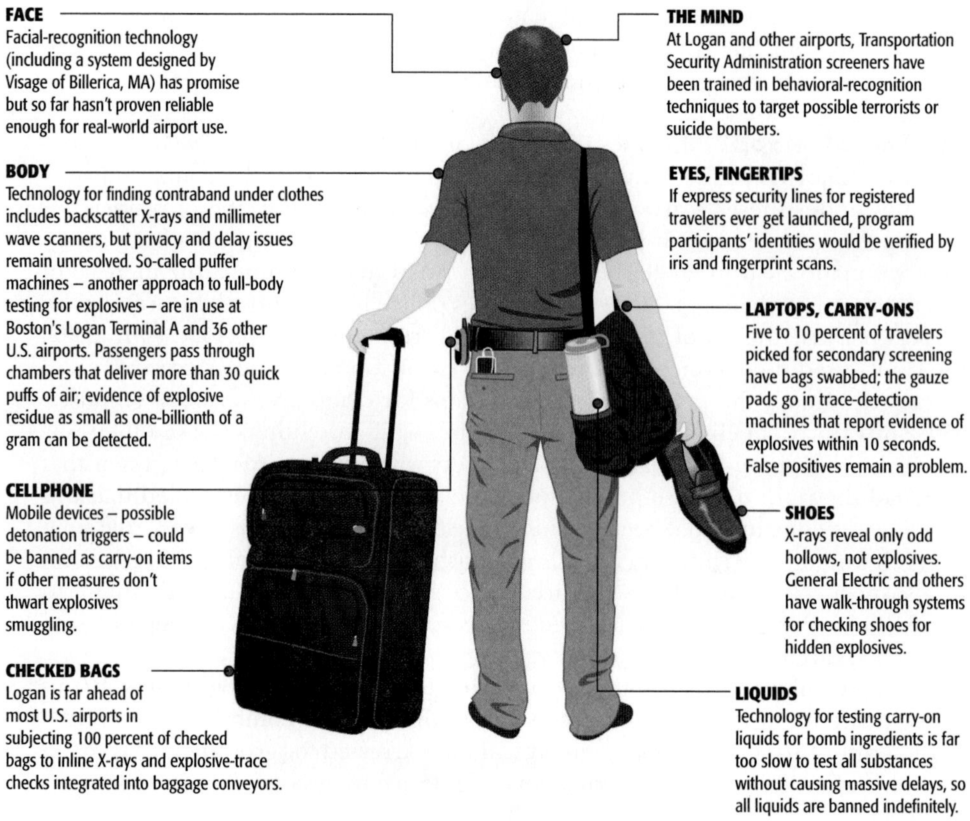
FACE
Facial-recognition technology (including a system designed by Visage of Billerica, MA) has promise but so far hasn't proven reliable enough for real-world airport use.
BODY
Technology for finding contraband under clothes includes backscatter X-rays and millimeter wave scanners, but privacy and delay issues remain unresolved. So-called puffer machines – another approach to full-body testing for explosives – are in use at Boston's Logan Terminal A and 36 other U.S. airports. Passengers pass through chambers that deliver more than 30 quick puffs of air; evidence of explosive residue as small as one-billionth of a gram can be detected.
CELLPHONE
Mobile devices – possible detonation triggers – could be banned as carry-on items if other measures don't thwart explosives smuggling.
CHECKED BAGS
Logan is far ahead of most U.S. airports in subjecting 100 percent of checked bags to inline X-rays and explosive-trace checks integrated into baggage conveyors.
THE MIND
At Logan and other airports, Transportation Security Administration screeners have been trained in behavioral-recognition techniques to target possible terrorists or suicide bombers.
EYES, FINGERTIPS
If express security lines for registered travelers ever get launched, program participants' identities would be verified by iris and fingerprint scans.
LAPTOPS, CARRY-ONS
Five to 10 percent of travelers picked for secondary screening have bags swabbed; the gauze pads go in trace-detection machines that report evidence of explosives within 10 seconds. False positives remain a problem.
SHOES
X-rays reveal only odd hollows, not explosives. General Electric and others have walk-through systems for checking shoes for hidden explosives.
LIQUIDS
Technology for testing carry-on liquids for bomb ingredients is far too slow to test all substances without causing massive delays, so all liquids are banned indefinitely.

**FIGURE 13.1** Is There Any Privacy in the Airport?
Thinking of flying soon? The authors can remember a day when people could just buy a ticket and board a plane. Here are just some of the kinds of searches that are being done now, or being considered for adoption, before boarding planes at Logan Airport in Boston, Massachusetts. Considering all of this, one must ask: Does the Fourth Amendment and the "right of privacy" still exist for passengers on planes? If so, will it exist if the new search techniques being suggested here are adopted?

*Source:* From The Boston Globe, © August 26, 2006. 

made by the judge on the search warrant. The Court argued that the search was undertaken in "good faith" that the Fourth Amendment was being followed. It also explained that eliminating the use of this evidence would not, in their opinion, deter future searches by police, who had not made the mistake.

This pattern by the Roberts Court of allowing more warrantless searches, even ones that would have been illegal under past cases, has continued in a different form. Increasingly, as the Approaching Contemporary Issues in Democracy feature shows, the Court has used an expanded "good faith" standard to allow the use of more evidence. This began in early 2009 in the case of *Herring* v. *United States.*[115] Benny Herring tried to retrieve his impounded truck from a police station in Alabama. As a routine procedure, the police checked on the computer for any outstanding warrants and discovered that a nearby town had a warrant for Herring. By the time the town official could phone back to report that in fact the warrant no longer existed, Herring had been arrested and a search of his truck uncovered drugs and an illegal weapon. Arguing that this search using a faulty computer database was done on "good faith," Chief Justice Roberts and a five-justice majority upheld the search, saying that there would be no appreciable deterrence of future police searches using erroneous databases.

Some scholars and journalists now worry that the allowance of warrantless searches based on police clerk errors, combined with the increasing ability of police to ignore the knock-and-announce rules, had "jumped a firewall." Such action indicates a willingness by the Court's majority to completely eliminate the exclusionary rule.[116] As with every other controversial issue on the current Court, though, the matter will be determined by the swing vote of Justice Anthony Kennedy. And in 2011, it appeared that the Court was well on its way to ending the exclusionary rule in a vehicle search case called *Davis v. United States.* Here, the police had found a suspect's gun in his car acting under one court precedent, when in fact a newer precedent could have covered this search, which would have made it illegal. However, here a seven-justice majority led by Justice Samuel Alito ruled that:

*when the police exhibit "deliberate," "reckless," or "grossly negligent" disregard for Fourth Amendment rights, the benefits of exclusion tend to outweigh the costs. . . . But when the police act with an objectively reasonable good-faith belief that their conduct is lawful, or when their conduct involves only simple, isolated negligence, the deterrent value of suppression is diminished, and exclusion cannot "pay its way."*[117]

Analysts believe that the ease of police conducting future searches while claiming "an objectively reasonable good-faith belief that their conduct is lawful" may result in the end of the exclusionary rule as we know it, and the diminishing of our Fourth Amendment rights.[118]

The 21st-century search process. This X-ray backscatter body imaging system at New York's John F. Kennedy International Airport makes it possible to search underneath the clothing of air travelers for weapons or explosives. After the attempted Christmas Day bombing of Flight 253 in Detroit, plans were made to place more of these devices in the nation's airports.

## The Fifth and Sixth Amendments

13.10 *How has the Supreme Court balanced the Fifth and Sixth Amendment rights?*

The safeguards contained in the Fifth and Sixth Amendments were designed to prevent the worst practices of early English criminal law, such as secret interrogation and torture. In addition to guaranteeing the right not to be compelled to witness against oneself in a criminal trial, the Fifth Amendment provides the right to a grand jury, protection against double jeopardy (being tried twice for the same offense), and a guarantee against a state government's taking of one's property for public use without due process of law and just compensation. To the guarantee of a right to counsel in criminal cases, the Sixth Amendment adds the rights to a speedy and public trial by an impartial jury, to be informed of the nature of the charges against oneself, to be confronted with the witnesses against oneself, and to compel the appearance of witnesses in one's defense. Such safeguards are vital to a democratic society and constitute a basic difference between democracies and totalitarian governments.

Like all the other civil liberties discussed in this chapter, the rights of accused persons have been subject to interpretation by the Supreme Court. Before the Fifth and Sixth Amendments were applied to the states, the Court used the due process clause of the Fourteenth Amendment in deciding cases involving police interrogations.[119] In such cases, the justices examined the totality of circumstances of an interrogation to determine the "voluntariness" of a confession. If the "totality of circumstances" (the conditions under which the defendant had been questioned) indicated that a confession was involuntary, it would not be allowed in a trial. If, on the other hand, the suspect had flagged down a police car or walked into a station house and started to confess before a question could be asked, or even after police had made the statements, the confession would be considered voluntary. Voluntariness was an elusive concept, defying clear measurement, however. In one case, the court judged that a defendant had been compelled to confess because he had been refused the right to call his wife before talking to the police.[120]

After the protections of the Fifth and Sixth Amendments were extended to the states, the Court began to explore whether a person could be compelled to confess simply by being confronted by the police. This question was the central issue in a 1964 case, *Escobedo* v. *Illinois,* in which a man had been arrested for the murder of his brother-in-law and questioned by police without being allowed to see his attorney, who was then in the police station. The Supreme Court ruled that police questioning of suspects for the purpose of gaining a confession was just as important as the trial itself. Once the police had gone beyond the general investigation phase of their

### QUICK REVIEW

Fifth Amendment

- Provides the right to a grand jury.
- Protects against double jeopardy (being tried twice for the same offense).
- Guarantees against state government's taking of one's property for public use without due process of law and just compensation.

Sixth Amendment

- Guarantees right to counsel in criminal cases.
- Provides the right to a speedy and public trial by an impartial jury.
- Provides the right to be informed of the nature of the charges against oneself.
- Provides the right to be confronted with the witnesses against oneself, and to compel the appearance of witnesses in one's defense.

# APPROACHING
## Contemporary Issues in Democracy

### The Roberts Court's Expanding "Good Faith" Standard and the Decline of the Fourth Amendment's Protections

As the nation observes more than 50 years since the landmark Fourth Amendment search and seizure case, *Mapp* v. *Ohio*, it becomes more and more apparent that the exclusionary rule protecting that right is under assault by the Supreme Court under John Roberts. The exclusionary rule is designed to punish police who violate the Fourth Amendment by making it impossible to use evidence gained by illegal searches in court proceedings. The original justification for the exclusionary rule was threefold: to protect the rights of the defendant by making it impossible to use that evidence in court, to deter the police from violating the rights of others by knowing that their efforts would not yield convictions, and to protect the integrity of judges and the courts by not using such illegally gathered evidence in their proceedings.

In 1984, the conservative Burger Court invented a standard called "good faith" to argue that if the police conducting the search relying on an erroneous search warrant, but had "good faith" to believe that the search was legal and constitutional, the evidence would be allowed in court. The argument was that because the error was made by the judge, and not the police, excluding the evidence would not deter police from conducting such searches, so there was no justification for the exclusionary rule.

Recently, the Roberts Court has expanded the use of this "good faith" test dramatically, including even searches without warrants. In one case, a man's truck was searched because the police relied on an erroneous database entry and an account of a neighboring police department. This search was allowed. In another case, police chasing a man suspected of carrying crack cocaine, could chase him into his house to conduct a search without a warrant because it was an "exigency" that they did not create in the hopes of making a search. That search was also allowed. In the last case, involving a court search standard that had changed while the issue was being litigated, the Roberts Court argued that if the police acted on the basis of "objectively reasonable reliance on binding appellate precedent" the search would be allowed. In other words, if they thought they had "good faith," they had "good faith." Of course, the terms "good faith," "objectively" and "reasonable" would all be interpreted by members of the court now seemingly inclined to allow more police searches.

Does the increasingly extensive "good faith" standard promote America's approach to democracy? It certainly would promote "order and stability" by giving the police more powers to search, uncover evidence, and put people suspected of crimes in jail. However, it also would diminish "freedom and equality" by making it possible for the police to conduct broader searches for possible crimes, and when combined with the "plain view" standard allowing them to take other evidence, arrest even more people. Is there a "cultural commitment to democratic ideals" to return to the standards of the late 1940s and the case of *Wolf* v. *Colorado*, when the Court argued that the "core of the Fourth Amendment" was protected, but there would be no exclusionary rule to prevent illegally gathered evidence from being used in Court?

**Miranda warning**
A warning that must be recited by police officers to a suspect before questioning: "You have the right to remain silent; anything you say can and will be used against you. You have the right to an attorney. If you cannot afford an attorney, one will be provided for you. Do you understand these rights and are you willing to speak with us?" Established in *Miranda* v. *Arizona*, 1966.

interrogation by seeking to secure a confession, they had shifted "from the investigatory to the accusatory" phase, and, under the Sixth and Fourteenth Amendments, the suspect had the right to have counsel present.[121]

But should defendants be warned of their right to silence, and just how far may the police go in their questioning? The answers came two years later in the case of *Miranda* v. *Arizona*. If you watch movies or television you have surely seen police officers recite the so-called **Miranda warning** to a suspect before questioning:

> *You have the right to remain silent. Anything you say can and will be used against you. You have the right to an attorney. If you cannot afford an attorney, one will be provided for you. Do you understand these rights, and are you willing to speak with us?*

The requirement to inform suspects of their rights stems from the *Miranda* case, in which a slightly psychotic produce worker given to flights of fantasy had confessed to a kidnapping and rape after only two hours of questioning in which the police lied in saying that the victim had identified him. The Court ruled that all police questioning was "inherently compulsory" and that confessions were therefore "inherently untrustworthy." Before questioning a suspect who had been taken into custody or "deprived of his freedom in any significant way," the police had to offer the warning just described. Otherwise, statements made by the accused could not be used in a trial or to gather related evidence.[122]

This ruling was highly controversial. It looked as if the Court was legislating new rules that would make convicting known felons impossible. In reality, the Court merely applied to the states the practices that the Federal Bureau of Investigation had long used in interrogating suspects. Still, the outcry against the "criminal-coddling Warren Court" did serious damage to the Court's prestige and led critics to demand that the decision be reversed.

Rather than overturning *Miranda* directly, the Burger and Rehnquist courts chipped away at its underpinnings to such an extent that little of it remains in force. The Rehnquist Court seemed on the road toward overturning *Miranda* in the 1991 case of *Arizona* v. *Fulminante,* in which a prisoner confessed to murdering his stepdaughter to a fellow inmate who offered to protect him from harm but was in fact working as an FBI informer. The Court ruled that such confessions could be used in trials, even this arguably involuntary one in which the defendant did not realize that he was speaking to an agent of the police.[123]

In 2000, the Court and Chief Justice Rehnquist had the opportunity to reconsider *Miranda* directly in the case of Charles Thomas Dickerson. Dickerson was interrogated by an FBI agent in January 1997 about a bank robbery in Alexandria, Virginia. After a few hours of questioning, Dickerson admitted that he knew about the robbery. Although the officer said that the *Miranda* warnings had been given before the incriminating statement was made, Dickerson said that the warnings came after he had made his statement—meaning that the confession should be invalidated.

This case tested the constitutionality of Section 3501 of Title 18 of the United States Code, called the Omnibus Crime Control and Safe Streets Act, passed just two years after *Miranda.* The law stated that confessions could be admitted into federal trials if they were given "voluntarily," based on an examination of the "totality of circumstances" of the questioning. Although this contradicted Chief Justice Earl Warren's argument that any questioning by police was "inherently compulsory," it was widely anticipated that Chief Justice Rehnquist and the conservative majority would take this opportunity to overturn *Miranda.*

To the surprise of many, the Court upheld the *Miranda* case by a 7–2 vote, with even its most vocal critic, Chief Justice Rehnquist, voting with the majority and writing the opinion. In overturning Section 3501, Justice Rehnquist argued, as the Court did in the *City of Boerne* free exercise of religion case, that "*Miranda,* being a constitutional decision of this Court, may not be in effect overruled by an act of Congress." Rehnquist further explained that the *Miranda* warnings should continue because they "have become part of our national culture" and have "become embedded in routine police practice." Because the warnings caused no measurable difficulties for prosecutors, the Court saw no reason to overturn the case.[124] Just why the Chief Justice wrote the majority opinion in this way is unclear, but *Miranda* still exists as a legal precedent, although studies have found that police continually search for ways to avoid having suspects "lawyer up" in their questioning.[125]

**THINKING CRITICALLY**

Should police be able to use materials posted on individuals' websites or social networking pages when seeking evidence in criminal investigations? Do the Fourth and Fifth Amendments protect individuals from having the police search their sites and use their own words and photos against them?

## The Death Penalty and the Eighth Amendment

**13.11** *How has the Supreme Court interpreted the cruel and unusual punishment clause of the Eighth Amendment as it applies to the death penalty?*

Debate over whether the death penalty violates the Eighth Amendment's cruel and unusual punishment clause has existed since the Supreme Court ruled in 1976 in the case of

*Furman* v. *Georgia* that this form of punishment cannot be implemented in an "arbitrary and capricious manner." As of September 2011, 1,174 prisoners had been put to death and 3,297 people sat on death row, a disproportionate number of them minorities. However, the standards for determining who will live and who will die vary widely around the nation. Figure 13.2 shows the disproportionate manner in which different states have used the death penalty, with Texas far ahead of all of the other states with 440 executions.

In July 2000, President Bill Clinton postponed the first federal execution in nearly 40 years, when a federal study determined that more than three-quarters of the defendants in federal capital cases belonged to minority groups.

Rules were changing in certain states, too. In March 2000, outgoing governor George Ryan of Illinois placed a moratorium on use of the death penalty in his state when 13 men were cleared by discovery of new evidence and released from death row. Many of these cases were developed by classes of undergraduate students of David Protess, a journalism professor at Northwestern University, who found evidence clearing these men and even, at times, pointing toward the real criminals. Meanwhile, nationally, as of September 2009, 130 people had been cleared of death penalty sentences, many on the basis of DNA evidence. In January 2007, when a Dallas, Texas, man was released from Texas state prison because of DNA findings after serving 10 years in jail for a rape he did not commit, he became the 12th convict in Dallas County to be released because of DNA evidence.[126] Although only two states—Illinois and New York—grant inmates the right to have their DNA tested, the vast majority of the American people want that right guaranteed to suspects.

In June 2000, the most extensive U.S. study of the death penalty found that nearly two out of every three death penalty convictions were overturned on appeal because of incompetent lawyers or overzealous police investigators. The study examined nearly 5,800 death penalty convictions and found that 75 percent of those whose death penalties were set aside were later given a lesser sentence on retrial. Only 18 percent of those overturned cases resulted in another death sentence.[127]

In mid-2002, the Supreme Court issued a major ruling on the death penalty, indicating that this sentence was now under review. The Court ruled 6–3 in *Atkins* v. *Virginia* that executing a defendant who was mentally challenged would constitute "cruel and unusual punishment" in violation of the Eighth Amendment. In their view, when 18 of the 38 states with death penalty laws recently passed provisions banning the execution of mentally challenged defendants, those moves indicated "evolving standards of decency that mark the progress of a maturing society" against this practice. Justice Scalia, who argued based on his "originalism" theory

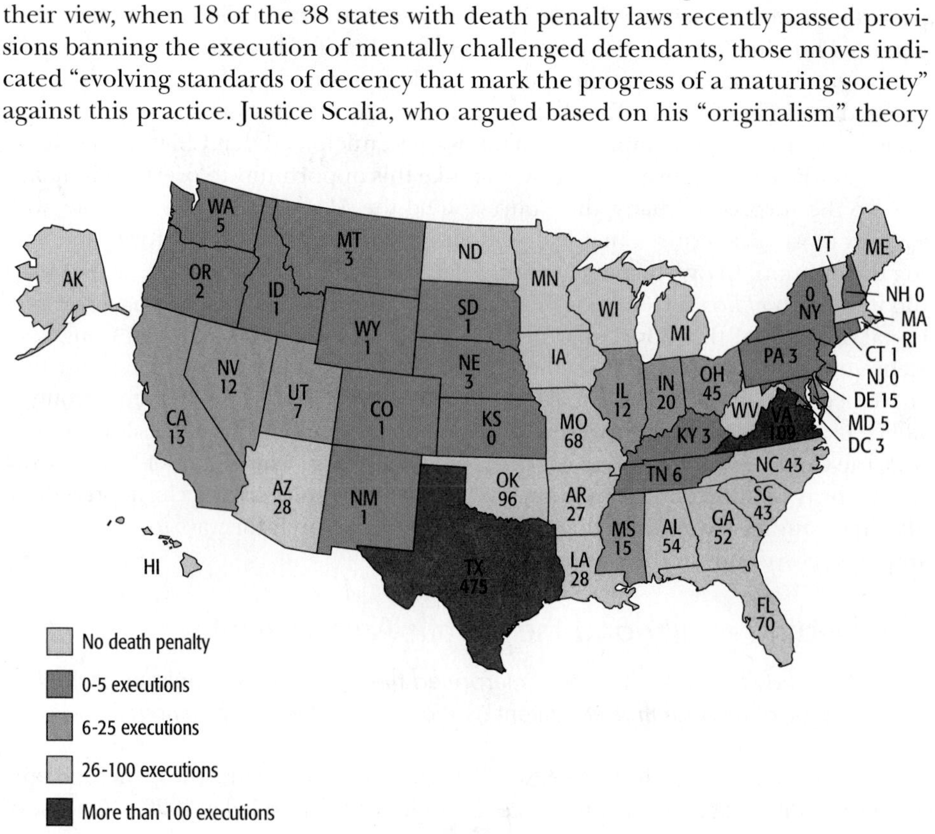


**FIGURE 13.2** Executions by State, 1976–2011

*Source:* The Death Penalty Information Center, found at http://www.deathpenaltyinfo.org/, last accessed on October 6, 2011.

that the founders supported the death penalty and meant only to ban the use of torture with the "cruel and unusual punishment" language, countered with a vigorous dissent, complaining that it was "the pinnacle of our Eighth Amendment death-is-different jurisprudence." Labeling the Court's majority opinion as "merely the subjective views of individual Justices," Scalia challenged their use of foreign legal sources to support their argument, saying that it won "the Prize for the Court's Most Feeble Effort to fabricate 'national consensus.' "[128]

Three years later, a narrow majority ruled in 2005 in *Roper* v. *Simmons* that executing a minor was "cruel and unusual punishment" and should be banned under the Constitution. Once more, the Court, led by Anthony Kennedy, relied on "foreign sources" and their version of the "evolving standards of decency" to overturn this practice. Again, Justice Scalia objected that "the Court thus proclaim[ed] itself [the] sole arbiter of our Nation's moral standards," an action that would "crown arbitrariness with chaos." The question, with the changing Supreme Court, is more than just whether these limitations on the use of the death penalty will continue.[129] In the 2009 term, the Court turned to the question of whether sentencing teenagers to life without parole also represents an unconstitutional "cruel and unusual punishment."

Northwestern University journalism professor David Protess has led his college classes to develop information to help free dozens of unfairly convicted death penalty prisoners. Because of his efforts, and those of others such as DNA expert Barry Scheck at Project Innocence, 130 death row inmates have been exonerated as of December 2009.

One setback for death row inmates and defense attorneys trying to prove their clients' innocence through analysis of DNA evidence from the crime scene came in 2009 after a Supreme Court decision not to extend the rights of defendants to appeal based on such evidence in seeking to overturn their conviction. By this time, the New York–based Innocence Project had used such evidence to overturn 232 convictions, 17 of them on death row, with all but 13 of them coming in analyses performed after the conviction had been secured. However, a five vote majority on the Supreme Court ruled that Alaska, one of only six states that does not allow defendants access to DNA evidence in their post-conviction appeals, could do the same to William Osborne (who had been convicted of helping to commit a murder in 1993). Without access to this DNA evidence, Osborne's defense team was unable to do more specialized testing of the evidence in seeking to prove his innocence. The majority seemed to be more interested in the finality of the verdict and the limitation of state expense because of a mountain of new appeals. In dissent, John Paul Stevens argued that granting permission to do DNA testing of such evidence would "ensure that justice has been done in this case."[130] With the election of President Obama, though, Attorney General Eric Holder made clear that the administration favored making such DNA evidence available for post-conviction appeals. It remains to be seen whether this will compel more states to afford this protection, or whether the Supreme Court decision would encourage some to eliminate that protection. One promising sign came in August 2009 when the Supreme Court ordered the Georgia judiciary to hear the evidence of death row inmate Troy Davis, who was convicted of killing an off-duty police officer, after seven of the nine witnesses against him had recanted the testimony that had helped to secure his conviction. The quest ended, though, in September 2011, with Davis being put to death in the face of worldwide protests. Meanwhile, in 2011, with new DNA-backed revelations of innocent people on death row, executions continued around the country.

## THE EXPANDING NATURE OF IMPLIED RIGHTS

13.12 *How has the Supreme Court interpreted and created unenumerated, or implied, rights to preserve democracy?*

Does the Constitution protect rights that exist beyond those set forth in the language of the Bill of Rights that should be safeguarded against governmental intrusion? A growing body of literature argues that the intention of the Ninth Amendment's protection stating "The enumeration in the Constitution, of certain rights, shall not be construed to deny or disparage others retained by the people," was intended to leave open the possibility that rights that were not mentioned in the first Eight Amendments could later be added.[131] Other justices have argued that they could look at the gaps between existing amendments to find or create a "plus" level of protections. If these theories are correct, what are these rights, and what are their limits? These difficult questions involve moral and ethical positions as well as legal and constitutional judgments.

## Privacy

The Constitution does not explicitly mention the right of privacy. Is this right implied in the Fourth Amendment's protection against "unreasonable searches and seizures"? Or did the framers intend it to be one of the "rights retained by the people" in the Ninth Amendment? Or was it so obvious and important that it did not need to be mentioned at all? And, assuming that such a right exists, what exactly does it encompass?

These issues were explored in a landmark 1965 case, *Griswold* v. *Connecticut,* in which Estelle T. Griswold, director of a New Haven birth control clinic opened by the Connecticut Planned Parenthood League, was charged with violating a state statute that prohibited the use of and medical counseling regarding birth control. This law had been passed in response to the concerns of its author, entrepreneur P. T. Barnum, who wished to control the spread of adultery and unsavory diseases. Private citizens, however, argued that the state had no business regulating personal conduct in the bedroom, especially the marital bedroom.

The Supreme Court ruled that the right of privacy protects the behavior of married people in their bedrooms. According to Justice William O. Douglas, such a right, which he had argued as early as 1952, was a "right to be let alone." Although not explicitly stated in the Bill of Rights or the Constitution, it could be found in the "penumbras, formed by emanations," or shadows of shadows, of the First, Third, Fourth, Fifth, Ninth, and Fourteenth Amendments; these, he said, create several "zones of privacy." To dissenting justices and students of law, this statement was somewhat confusing, in that the right of privacy could be glimpsed in several amendments but was not stated in any of them. Many believed that Douglas was inserting his own value preferences into the Constitution. Three months after the decision, Griswold and Dr. Lee Buxton reopened their New Haven birth control clinic. The Griswold decision has stood as the basis for the expansion of privacy rights to the dismay of judicial conservatives and self-restraint advocates who do not support rights not explicitly written into the Constitution and its amendments.[132]

Once privacy became an accepted part of constitutional interpretation, many additional rights could be created. It was not long before the right of privacy was extended to unmarried persons.[133] This constitutional privacy right became a central element in debates over rights related to abortion, homosexuality (see Chapter 14 for details), AIDS, drug testing, and euthanasia. Meanwhile, states threatened these rights by trying to remove legal and constitutional protection for those pursuing alternative lifestyles.

## Abortion

If the constitutional right of privacy allows people to choose to prevent conception, does it also allow them to terminate a pregnancy after conception? Before 1973, states were free to set restrictions on a woman's right to obtain an abortion, and many banned abortion entirely. Differences in state laws sent vast numbers of women across state lines or out of the country to obtain abortions, and many others placed themselves in the hands of dangerous "back-alley" abortionists to terminate unwanted pregnancies.

In the 1973 case of *Roe* v. *Wade,* the Supreme Court reviewed a Texas law that limited a woman's right to obtain an abortion. The Court ruled that the right of privacy gave a woman the right to obtain an abortion. But, as with all rights, the exercise of this right could be limited. In this case, those limitations were dictated by the state's right to protect the health of the mother and the rights of the unborn fetus.[134]

The rights of the unborn fetus were the focal point in the *Roe* case. Some religious groups argue that the fetus is a living human being; for them, therefore, abortion constitutes murder. Other groups use the findings of medical science to argue that life begins when a fetus can be sustained by medical technology outside the mother's womb, an argument that leads to a different set of limitations on the abortion procedure. Opposed to both of these arguments are those who claim that the right of privacy gives a woman the unfettered right to control her own body—and a right to choose abortion.

In his majority opinion, Justice Harry Blackmun attempted to strike a balance among these competing arguments by segmenting the pregnancy term into three trimesters. In the first three months, the woman has an absolute right to obtain an abortion, and the state has no legitimate interest in controlling a routine medical procedure. In the second trimester, the interests of the state become more important as the abortion procedure becomes more risky; thus, states may regulate abortions to ensure the woman's safety, but not to the extent of eliminating them. In the final three months, when the fetus has become viable and has interests that must be safeguarded, abortions can be banned completely.

*Roe* left open several questions. As medical technology advances and fetuses can survive outside the womb earlier, can abortions be banned at an earlier stage of pregnancy? On the other hand, will the line move in the other direction as medical technology also makes abortions safer at later stages of pregnancy? And what will happen as new reproductive technologies permit a fetus to develop outside of the womb?

## THINKING CRITICALLY

In August 2006, the Federal Drug Administration approved the sale of the so-called Plan B morning-after pill to women over the age of 18. Given the Court's decisions in the abortion area, do you believe that the Constitution should also limit the use of drugs such as the so-called RU-487 morning-after pill or combinations of drugs prescribed by doctors for the same purpose? Or should that action be protected under the constitutional safeguards for the use of contraceptives?

Since the *Roe* decision, certain states, including Louisiana, Utah, Ohio, and Pennsylvania, have limited and regulated abortions in various ways, including requiring notification of the parents of minors seeking abortions, establishing rules for determining which physicians and facilities are qualified to perform abortions, requiring notification of prospective fathers, and requiring a woman to follow a series of steps to inform herself about the nature of abortions before undergoing the procedure.

At the federal level, the debate has centered on whether government medical assistance to the poor should cover the cost of abortions. Opponents of abortion argue that public funds should not pay for a procedure that some taxpayers find objectionable. Since 1976, Congress has passed various measures limiting federal assistance for abortions except in cases of rape or incest and when the health of the mother is in jeopardy. Some states have followed suit. In 1980, the Supreme Court upheld these restrictions, essentially denying low-income women their constitutional right to obtain an abortion.[135]

Initially, the Burger Court was inclined to strike down restrictions such as the requirement that a woman's husband, or her parents if she is a minor, be informed if she seeks an abortion.[136] In 1983, the Court further reaffirmed the *Roe* decision in a case involving regulations passed by the city of Akron, Ohio. The Court ruled that laws regulating abortion must be designed to protect the health of the mother. Justice Sandra Day O'Connor dissented, arguing that the Court should be concerned only with whether the law represents an "undue burden," or a severe obstacle, impeding the right of a woman to choose to get an abortion.[137]

The Rehnquist Court considered several cases involving abortion, beginning with the 1989 case of *Webster* v. *Reproductive Health Services*. The state of Missouri had passed one of the most restrictive of all state abortion laws: Physicians performing abortions more than five months into the pregnancy were required to determine whether the fetus was viable, public employees or facilities could not be used to perform abortions, and public funds could not be spent to counsel women to seek abortions. The appointments of Justices Antonin Scalia and Anthony Kennedy had created an activist-conservative Court that seemed to have the votes to overturn the *Roe* decision; however, Justice O'Connor remained unwilling to do so. This case came in a period in which the liberal William Brennan was controlling the opinion-assignment power, and he gave the case to Justice O'Connor. While her opinion upheld all the components of the Missouri law, she established her test that no "undue burden" on a woman's right to choose an abortion should be created by the state, meaning that there could not be a "substantial obstacle" placed in the way of the right to an abortion. In dissent, a clearly angry Antonin Scalia labeled this opinion "perverse," "totally irrational," and "not to be taken seriously," making it much harder for him to gain O'Connor's vote in later cases.[138]

In 1992, the abortion issue again came before the Court, this time in a case dealing with a restrictive Pennsylvania statute. In a surprising action, three jurists—O'Connor, Kennedy, and Souter—broke from their conservative colleagues and wrote a centrist opinion upholding *Roe* because of its long-standing value as a precedent.[139] Shortly thereafter, two judges who seemed to support abortion rights—Ruth Bader Ginsburg and Stephen Breyer—were appointed to the Court. For the moment, the right to obtain an abortion, though restricted in some instances, seemed safe. This was further demonstrated in 1998, when the Supreme Court refused to rule on a federal court decision voiding a ban in Ohio on late-term abortions. Thus, the federal courts blocked state versions of legislation twice passed by Congress and twice vetoed by President Clinton.[140] Pro-abortion advocates won a major victory in June 2000 when the Court declared unconstitutional a Nebraska law (similar to ones in 30 other states) banning partial-birth (late-term) abortions. Still, the narrow 5–4 vote and specific problems with the wording of this law, extending into a broad range of abortion decisions, make it uncertain whether the Court will strike down similar future laws.[141]

## THINKING CRITICALLY

With scientists now creating artificial wombs that one day will be able to incubate a fertilized human embryo, what will that medical advance do to abortion law as written by the Supreme Court?

In 2003, Congress passed the Partial-Birth Abortion Ban Act, using language that nearly duplicated the already overturned Nebraska law. In 2006, South Dakota launched a frontal attack on *Roe* by declaring abortion illegal in that state. When the Nebraska law was tested, Justice Kennedy's swing vote in early 2007, rather than Justice O'Connor's, now upheld the federal partial-birth abortion ban that had been overturned in Nebraska just seven years earlier. Kennedy appeared to support even more abortion bans because this decision by a woman was "fraught with emotional consequences." Other states will undoubtedly pass new abortion restrictions testing the limits of Justice Kennedy's language. In the first of two new abortion rights tests, in 2011 Mississippi tried and failed to pass a "personhood" amendment, declaring that an unborn fetus was a constitutionally-protected person. Then, in early 2012, two New Jersey doctors were charged with murder for performing late-term abortions.[142]

## The Right to Die

As advances in medical technology allow people to live longer, questions arise about the quality of life experienced by those kept alive by artificial means. Should relatives and loved ones be allowed to turn off the life-support systems of critically ill patients? On another front, the efforts of a Detroit doctor, Jack Kevorkian, to assist the suicides of terminally ill patients raised the question of whether people have a right to conduct their own mercy killing.

During its 1989 term, the Supreme Court heard arguments in the case of a Missouri woman, Nancy Cruzan, who had been in a coma for several years and was being kept alive by life-support equipment. No hope remained that she would recover, and her parents sought to have life support removed. The Court ruled that because the state of Missouri requires clear and convincing evidence that a person maintained on life support would not wish to be kept alive by such means, the life-support system could not be disconnected in the absence of such evidence. However, Chief Justice Rehnquist noted, "The principle that a competent person has a constitutionally protected liberty interest in refusing unwanted medical treatment may be inferred from our prior decisions."[143]

Are physician-assisted suicides equivalent to murder, or do they simply represent the ultimate individual right stemming from the right of privacy? In two 1997 cases, the Court refused to find in the Constitution a "fundamental liberty" of the right to die. Thus, states were permitted to decide for themselves whether or not to allow physician-assisted suicides. Laws in Washington and New York forbidding this practice were allowed to stand.[144] However, a majority of the Court seemed to indicate in these cases that they might in the future be willing to hear an appeal from a terminally ill patient who is suffering greatly and is seeking the right to end his or her life.

The issue was raised again in March 2005. Theresa Marie Schiavo had suffered irreparable brain damage, and her feeding tube had been removed at the request of her husband, Michael. However, Schiavo's parents sought for the third time to have the case reviewed by the Supreme Court. When the Court denied the appeal, conservative members of Congress passed, and President Bush signed, a private bill giving the U.S. District Court jurisdiction over the case once again. Despite this effort, both the Florida state courts and the federal courts denied a series of requests to have the tube reinserted. This political and legal battle, and the public uproar that ensued, made clear that this issue would return to the Supreme Court in the near future.[145]

## THINKING CRITICALLY

Some states have passed laws that allow individuals and their doctors to decide on the use of federally banned drugs for euthansia, and some states argue for the legalization of the use of marijuana for medical purposes. Do you think the Constitution preserves the right of individuals and states to decide for themselves on the use of drugs for these purposes? If so, under what circumstances?

This area of law took a new turn in January 2006 when the Supreme Court, under the chief justiceship of John Roberts, ruled in *Gonzales* v. *Oregon*[146] on a controversial attempt by former attorney general John Ashcroft to supersede Oregon's Death with Dignity law, which permits physician-assisted suicides. Ashcroft argued that the federal Controlled Substances Act empowered the federal government to jail any Oregon doctor who prescribed lethal doses of restricted drugs at the request of terminally ill patients who sought to end their lives under state law. Their actions were, in his opinion, not a "legitimate medical purpose." The Supreme Court ruled 6–3 (with the retiring Justice Sandra Day O'Connor still on the Court and participating in the case) in favor of Oregon's position, arguing through Justice Anthony Kennedy's majority opinion that "Congress did not have this far-reaching intent to alter the federal–state balance."[147] Beyond the decision itself, the vote here might offer clues as to the future decisions of the Roberts Court. If Samuel Alito were to adopt a conservative posture on the "death with dignity" issue, as opposed to the pro–individual choice vote of former swing voter Justice O'Connor, whom he replaced, the decision making on this issue would remain in the hands of more moderate conservative Justice Anthony Kennedy. But, just where Kennedy would vote, given his pro–libertarian tendencies along with his apparently changing pro–state regulation position in the abortion area, is not clear at all.

In the 2008 election, a 59 percent majority voted in the state of Washington for a state Death with Dignity law that was identical to the one in Oregon. That went into effect in 2009, but neither that law nor the one in Oregon's legal support for death with dignity has yet been tested in court.

One important change that has occurred in this area, which has turned nationally to the question of mitigation of pain and suffering at the end of life rather than euthanasia, has been a 2009 court decision at the state level. In Montana, the state First Judicial Court ruled that "a right to receive and provide aid in dying" is a constitutional right based on the "right of personal dignity" language in the state's constitution. Judge Dorothy McCarter ruled that the "constitutional rights of individual privacy and human dignity, taken together, encompass the right of a competent terminally-ill patient to die with dignity."[148] The state Supreme Court upheld this ruling, arguing that nothing in Montana's laws or cases "indicat[e] that physician aid in dying is against public policy."[149] It will be interesting to see whether other states, with similar constitutional language, will follow, and whether in time there will be movement to place such language in, or give a similar interpretation to, the federal constitution.

In the area of civil liberties, the United States has traveled a considerable distance in approaching democracy, but with each new controversy we can see that it has some way to go. Only citizens' continued interest in their constitutional rights—by their votes for the president and senators who choose and confirm the judges—and their continued interest in the Court's rulings, will help ensure that the evolution toward democracy over the past two centuries (but mainly the past 65 years) will continue.

## THE 2012 ELECTION, ANTHONY KENNEDY, AND THE FUTURE OF CIVIL LIBERTIES

The Supreme Court is on the precipice of real change after the 2012 election. The Court is now in the middle of a lengthy personnel transition with liberals Sonia Sotomayor and Elena Kagan being added by President Obama to give the younger Baby Boomer justices a majority on the Court, while some of the other justices over the age of 73 seem likely to leave the Court sometime in the near future. As they do so, the direction of civil liberties in America could change significantly. But given the evolving conservative nature of the Roberts Court, dating back to late 2005, and the instability of the emerging judicial coalitions as the jurists adjust to their new colleagues, just how and how far that change will be remains to be seen. It seems certain as well that it will be a function of politics, not law, that dictates the rate and nature of that change. The bare 5–4 majority in the pivotal *Gonzales* v. *Carhart* abortion case signaled the future of civil liberties when it made clear that this subject lies with the vote of swing justice Anthony Kennedy. With the exception of gay rights, though maybe not in the area of gay marriage should it come to the Court, Kennedy appears to be moving a bit more to the conservative side. Prisoners have been denied the right to have DNA searches to test their convictions, doors for dwellings can be knocked open for police searches after only five seconds of warning, and "good faith" searches can now take place because of inaccurate computer database information.

The Sotomayor and Kagan appointments will not change the direction of the Court for now because, though they are younger, they replaced two other reliably liberal votes. Change will come with the loss of one reliably conservative seat, or even Kennedy's moderate conservative "swing seat." With justices living longer, able to manage the workload longer in life with all of the law clerk assistance, and leaving only an average of one vacancy every four years, this means that the future Court will be determined by the political direction of the nation. As Barack Obama runs for a second term in 2012, and the partisan majority of the Senate hangs in the balance in 2012, affecting the prospect of confirmation filibusters, the 2012 election will dictate who will be selected and confirmed for seats on the Supreme Court. Thus, it is politics that will determine the direction of the current 5–4 partisan Court's rulings on civil liberties. Should Obama gain a second term, the Democrats gain a firmer control over the Senate, and a turning point conservative seat vacancy occur on the Court, we could see a new, far different pro–individual rights approach to civil liberties in the coming years. On the other hand, if the Republicans win the White House and the Senate majority, given the aged nature of liberal Justices Breyer and Ginsburg, and the likely willingness of conservative Justices Scalia and Kennedy to return their seats to the Republicans, we could see an even more solid conservative pro–state control Court majority for decades to come. Our individual rights, then, hang in the balance.

### THINKING CRITICALLY

With the Supreme Court becoming more and more conservative, and the voting of the 2008 and 2010 elections for Congress and the president becoming more partisan, can you envision a time that the ideological split will lead to some kind of legislative action being taken against the Court? Do you think it should be done, and if so, what would that action look like?

## Summary

**13.1** *What are civil liberties and civil rights, and how does the double standard protect them?*

- Although the terms *civil liberties* and *civil rights* are often used interchangeably, they are not synonymous. Civil liberties are the individual freedoms and rights guaranteed to every citizen by the Bill of Rights and the due process clause of the Fourteenth Amendment. Civil rights are concerned with protection of citizens against discrimination because of characteristics such as gender, race, ethnicity, or disability and are derived largely from the equal protection clause of the Fourteenth Amendment.

**13.2** *How has the process of applying the Bill of Rights to the states both expanded rights and nationalized the country?*

- The history of civil liberties is one of gradually expanding protection provided by the Bill of Rights. This evolution occurred initially through a series of Supreme Court decisions that applied portions of the first ten amendments to the states, thereby protecting citizens against state action in relation to specific individual rights. Those decisions centered on the question of incorporation of the Bill of Rights into the Fourteenth Amendment. Later cases expanded the protection of these guarantees by judicial interpretation.

- The Court's process of applying the Bill of Rights to the states by incorporating some, but not all, into the Fourteenth Amendment due process clause was a slow one. Between 1884 and 1925, the Court refused to apply most of them, saying that they were not "fundamental principles lying at the base of our civil and political institutions."

13.3 *What is the theory of selective incorporation, and how is it used to increase the protection of civil liberties?*

- In 1937, the Court, through Benjamin Cardozo's opinion in *Palko* v. *Connecticut,* began the process of "selective incorporation" by ruling that some of these rights were "implicit in the concept of ordered liberty." The real incorporation revolution, though, did not occur until the 1960s through the liberal, activist decisions of the Warren Court. Now, all but five parts of the Bill of Rights have been incorporated. However, this line of decisions may be revisited if, in future state gun regulation cases, the Court revisits whether the privileges and immunities clause of the Fourteenth Amendment should be resuscitated and used to incorporate rights to apply against the states.

13.4 *How has the Supreme Court determined the level of separation between church and state?*

- Issues involving freedom of religion are of two main types: those involving establishment, or governmental preference for, one religion over others, and those involving free exercise of individual religious practices. In deciding if certain governmental actions would have the effect of establishing a religion, the Supreme Court has searched for the proper balance between complete separation of church and state, known as the high wall of separation doctrine, and government accommodation, in which the government would be allowed to assist religious organizations indirectly and in a neutral manner.

13.5 *How has the Court regulated and protected the right to free exercise of religion?*

- In deciding free exercise cases, the Court's protection of religious freedom against state regulation has varied, depending on which justices have been on the Court when various cases were considered. The result has been a struggle between the Court and Congress as to whether special protection should be used to protect the right to worship of various religious groups through a "strict scrutiny" process called the "least, restrictive means" test, or all religions have an obligation to follow "secular regulations" just like everyone else.

13.6 *How has the Court's protection of free speech preserved democracy?*

- In cases involving freedom of speech, the Court has developed and expanded a clear and present danger test that protects certain kinds of speech but not others, depending on whether it creates an immediate threat to the people. Political speech is protected if it is not likely to incite imminent lawless action. Public speech is protected unless it consists of fighting words or can be shown to create a dangerous situation. In this way, the Court allows the "free marketplace of ideas" for speech to continue and expand, thus promoting democracy.

13.7 *How has the Court's interpretation of symbolic speech, especially for public school students, affected democracy?*

- Symbolic speech is defined as conduct that conveys a message just as if it was speech. These actions, such as draft card burning and flag burning, are protected by looking at whether a regulation restricts speech and whether it was intended to restrict speech. In recent years, the Court has also protected even symbolic actions such as bigoted cross burnings that convey harmful messages, known as "hate speech," on the theory that legislators cannot draft a law that bans only the harmful speech and protects productive speech. By allowing more symbolic conduct, the Court promotes democracy while still protecting the public order.

13.8 *How have the Court's rules governing freedom of the press preserved democracy?*

- Issues involving freedom of the press hinge on the balance between the public's right to know and other rights, such as the government's right to secrecy or an individual's right to personal reputation. The Supreme Court has tended to rule against the state in cases of prior restraint, or censorship before publication, but not in cases of "subsequent punishment," or punishment after publication. In ruling on charges of libel, or the publication of statements that are untruthful and damaging to a person's reputation, the Court requires evidence of actual malice or reckless disregard for the truth. Cases involving obscenity have been most problematic because of the extreme difficulty of defining obscenity.

13.9 *How has the Supreme Court expanded and restricted the Fourth Amendment's search and seizure protections?*

- Many early debates over the Fourth Amendment's ban on unreasonable searches centered on creation of an exclusionary rule, whereby evidence gathered by illegal means cannot be used in later trials. Later, by defining "unreasonable searches," the Supreme Court has alternately expanded and limited the application of the Fourth Amendment. While generally protecting suspects against unreasonable searches, it has permitted a variety of exceptions that give the police leeway in the methods used to obtain evidence.

13.10 *How has the Supreme Court balanced the Fifth and Sixth Amendment rights?*

- The Fifth and Sixth Amendments contain several provisions designed to protect the rights of defendants. Of these, the most controversial have to do with the right to silence governing confessions resulting from police questioning. Since 1966, police officers have been required to read the so-called Miranda warning to suspects before questioning them; if they do not, statements made by the accused cannot be used in a trial. In recent years, however, the Court has increased exceptions to this rule, and the absence of the Miranda warning will no longer result in the automatic overturning of a conviction.

13.11 *How has the Supreme Court interpreted the cruel and unusual punishment clause of the Eighth Amendment as it applies to the death penalty?*

- The Supreme Court ruled in the 1970s that the death penalty must be implemented fairly and consistently in order to meet the Eighth Amendment's protection against cruel and unusual punishments. In recent years, swing justice Anthony Kennedy has provided the fifth vote to eliminate the death penalty for individuals who are mentally challenged and youthful offenders, citing his "living, evolving Constitution" theory; social science data showing the changing views toward this punishment; and the decisions of international judges against the penalty, especially those in Europe.

**13.12** *How has the Supreme Court interpreted and created unenumerated, or implied, rights to preserve democracy?*

- The Ninth Amendment, and the gaps between existing amendments, leave open the possibility that the Supreme Court Justices can find or create implied constitutional rights to protect individuals. The right of privacy is not explicitly mentioned in the Constitution, but the Supreme Court has ruled that such a right is implied by the wording of several provisions in the Bill of Rights. This right has been extended to cover a woman's right to obtain an abortion in the first three months of pregnancy. The Court has, however, allowed states to place certain restrictions on abortion. The right of privacy has also been extended to cover the right to die in cases involving patients kept alive by life-support equipment, provided that evidence indicates that the patient would not have wished to be kept alive by such means.

## Key Terms

civil liberties, 404
civil rights, 404
clear and present danger test, 409
double jeopardy, 410
double standard, 405
exclusionary rule, 425
fighting words, 418
hate speech, 418
incorporation, 408
least restrictive means test, 415
*Lemon* test, 412
libel, 421
Miranda warning, 432
no incorporation, 408
prior restraint, 421
probable cause, 426
secular regulation rule, 415
selective incorporation, 410
selective incorporation plus, 410
slander, 421
subsequent punishment, 421
symbolic speech, 418
total incorporation, 408

## Test Yourself Chapter 13

**1.** Civil rights differs from civil liberties because civil rights is
a. a negative freedom, meaning freedom from government control.
b. a positive freedom, meaning freedom to act.
c. a right that is more subject to Supreme Court control.
d. a right that is less subject to Supreme Court control.

**2.** The dawn of the civil liberties and civil rights era is generally considered to be
a. 1919, with the case of *Schenck* v. *U.S.*
b. 1925, with the case of *Gitlow* v. *N.Y.*
c. 1932, with the case of *Powell* v. *Alabama.*
d. 1938, with the case of *Carolene Products* footnote.

**3.** The double standard, with the Court placing more emphasis on civil liberties and rights cases than economic cases, truly increased application of the Bill of Rights to the states through the process of
a. absorption.
b. application.
c. insertion.
d. incorporation.

**4.** The true civil liberties protection era was launched by which Court when it applied more Bill of Rights provisions to the states than had ever been done before?
a. The Vinson Court in the 1940s.
b. The Warren Court in the 1950s.
c. The Warren Court in the 1960s.
d. The Burger Court in the 1970s.

**5.** Which provision of the constitutional amendments is used to extend the Bill of Rights to the states?
a. The Fifth Amendment due process clause.
b. The Fourteenth Amendment due process clause.
c. The Fourteenth Amendment privileges and immunities clause.
d. The Fourteenth Amendment equal protection clause.

**6.** What is the theory of incorporation that was created by Justice Benjamin Cardozo in the 1938 case of *Palko* v. *Connecticut?*
a. Total incorporation.
b. Selective incorporation.
c. Selective incorporation plus.
d. Impartial incorporation plus.

**7.** Oliver Wendell Holmes's example in *Schenck* v. *U.S.* of a clear and present danger that can be restricted by the government even though the First Amendment is written "Congress shall make no law" is
a. shouting "fire" in a public theater.
b. shouting in a public theater and causing a panic.
c. falsely shouting "fire" in a public theater.
d. None of the above.

**8.** In 1969, the Court in the case of *Brandenburg* v. *Ohio* restored the clear and present danger test to ban
a. advocacy of imminent and lawless action.
b. advocacy of dangerous action.
c. advocacy of imminent dangerous action.
d. advocacy of lawless action.

**9.** Which position did the framers of the First Amendment, James Madison and Thomas Jefferson, hold with respect to church and state?
- a. Government accommodation.
- b. Government support.
- c. High wall of separation.
- d. Varying wall of separation.

**10.** According to the prevailing *Lemon* test, from the 1973 establishment clause case of *Lemon* v. *Kurtzman,* which of these is *not* what a law must show with respect to religion to be held constitutional?
- a. It must have a secular purpose.
- b. It must have a primary effect that does not advance or inhibit religion.
- c. It cannot foster excessive entanglement between church and state.
- d. It cannot advocate a nonsecular point of view.

**11.** The conservative majority on the current Supreme Court holds which view with relation to the First Amendment's protection of free exercise of religion?
- a. The same as Congress's.
- b. Even religious people must follow the same secular regulations as other people.
- c. States must use the least restrictive means to regulate religious behavior.
- d. States can pass laws favoring religions.

**12.** Which kind of control of freedom of press did both the framers and Chief Justice Charles Evans Hughes seek to ban?
- a. Tabloid gossip.
- b. Prior censorship.
- c. Punishment after the fact.
- d. Threats to national security.

**13.** After *New York Times* v. *U.S.,* which kind of press accounts seem to be subject to censorship?
- a. Dangers to national security.
- b. Tabloid gossip.
- c. Negligently incorrect information.
- d. Untruthful information.

**14.** What must be proven to ban literature as being libelous under *Miller* v. *California?*
- a. The work must be assessed as a whole to be obscene.
- b. The work must be viewed as obscene by the whole community.
- c. The work must not have serious literary, artistic, political, or scientific value.
- d. All of the above.

**15.** What has happened to the exclusionary rule banning the use of illegally gathered evidence in trials since its extension to the states in *Mapp* v. *Ohio* in 1961?
- a. It has been expanded to be more protective.
- b. It has been restricted, but is still very protective.
- c. The warrantless searches have been severely restricted using the good faith exception.
- d. The warrant searches have been severely restricted using the good faith exception.

**16.** What has happened to the *Miranda* rule providing Fifth Amendment protection to defendants in police interrogations over the years?
- a. It has been overturned and no longer exists.
- b. It has been narrowed severely but still exists.
- c. It has been expanded a little.
- d. It has been overturned by Congress.

**17.** While Antonin Scalia has evaluated civil liberties cases based on his views of originalism (the meaning of the Constitution at the time of its framing), Anthony Kennedy has used what theory to expand some rights?
- a. Penumbra theories.
- b. Total incorporation plus.
- c. Living, evolving Constitution.
- d. Active liberty.

**18.** With many of the central civil liberties cases being decided by a 5–4 vote, which justice is the "swing justice," providing the key fifth vote to the winning side?
- a. Samuel Alito.
- b. Anthony Kennedy.
- c. John Roberts.
- d. Ruth Bader Ginsburg.

**19.** What is the current Supreme Court position on gay rights?
- a. Gay rights are not protected.
- b. Some gay rights to intimate privacy are protected, but gay marriage is not.
- c. Gay marriage is not protected.
- d. Gay rights are totally protected.

**20.** What is *not* the current Supreme Court position on abortion?
- a. The right to abortion is no longer protected, but *Roe* v. *Wade* still survives.
- b. The right to abortion is protected so long as it does not place an "undue burden" on the woman's right to choose.
- c. The right to end-of-term abortion is not protected because it is "fraught with emotional consequences."
- d. The right to abortion will likely depend on whatever view swing justice Anthony Kennedy holds.

**ANSWERS**

**1.** b, **2.** d, **3.** d, **4.** c, **5.** b, **6.** b, **7.** c, **8.** a, **9.** c, **10.** d, **11.** b, **12.** b, **13.** a, **14.** d, **15.** c, **16.** b, **17.** c, **18.** b, **19.** b, **20.** a

# Civil Rights and Political Equality

# 14

## Chapter Outline

### Introduction: *Civil Rights and Democracy*

- Defining Civil Rights
- Establishing Constitutional Equality
- Creating Legal Segregation
- Establishing Legal Equality
- The Civil Rights Movement
- Affirmative Action
- Women's Rights
- Civil Rights and Other Minorities
- Emerging Minority Groups Seek Prominence
- Civil Rights and the War on Terrorism
- Civil Rights in the 21st Century

## Learning Objectives

14

- **14.1** How successfully do the Declaration of Independence and the Constitution promise equality in American society?
- **14.2** How and why was legal equality not established in the late 19th century?
- **14.3** How was the legal equality promised by the government in the early to mid-20th century accomplished by the judicial branch?
- **14.4** Why did it take so long to implement the desegregation promise of *Brown* v. *Board of Education* and later move on to desegregating society?
- **14.5** How were the Supreme Court cases and laws to realize desegregation in American society finally realized—and then threatened again?
- **14.6** How have affirmative action programs been created, and do they achieve equality in America?
- **14.7** How did the movement for women's rights begin in America?
- **14.8** What role has the Supreme Court played in establishing, protecting, and later limiting women's rights and the rights of gays and lesbians?
- **14.9** What success have other minority groups—such as Hispanic Americans, Native Americans, Americans with disabilities, and gays and lesbians—had in achieving equal rights?
- **14.10** How has the war on terror affected the civil rights in the 21st century?

# INTRODUCTION

## CIVIL RIGHTS AND DEMOCRACY

The fight over civil rights and affirmative action began with a simple bus ride. When Rosa Parks refused to move from her seat on a bus in Montgomery, Alabama, in 1955, she set off a boycott that eventually led to a federal court ruling, affirmed by the Supreme Court, that the city of Montgomery could not maintain its policy of segregated transportation. Despite the resolve and bravery of those involved in the boycott, however, the legal process took almost 13 months before culminating in the decision that African Americans would be allowed to sit at the front of a bus. Nor did the story end there; in fact, it was only beginning.

Almost 60 years after the Supreme Court told the nation's public schools to desegregate "with all deliberate speed" in the landmark case of *Brown* v. *Board of Education of Topeka, Kansas,*[1] the goal still seems out of reach. Today, we debate about trying to equalize rights, even at the expense of someone else's job or college admission. With such acrimonious debate over affirmative action programs, can we hope to approach a democratic system of "equal rights for all" and "full participation by all" in the government?

Debates over these civil rights policies continue into the 21st century, as shown by the chapter opening photo of the University of California at Berkeley Republican students protesting in late September 2011. The students engaged in a three-hour "die-in" on the campus's Sproul Plaza, against the state of California's pro-diversity college admissions policy, state Senate Bill 185. This measure sought to bypass California's anti–affirmative action Proposition 209 by instructing the schools in the state system to consider "race, ethnicity, and gender" in the application process for undergraduate and graduate admissions. Through their protest, the students were arguing for admissions based on merit as opposed to affirmative action considerations.

In this chapter we trace the history of civil rights in the United States, a history that began only in the second half of the 19th century, when the nation, recovering from devastating civil war, sought to establish equality of rights under the Constitution. But real change did not come until nearly a century later. The period from 1896 to 1958 was spent debating the notion of legal equality; from 1958 to 1974, the debate turned to achieving actual equality through governmental policies. In the almost 40 years that have followed, the debate has centered on whether actual equality should be achieved, and if so, how. But for the past decade or so, the discussion over a "color-blind" policy has raised questions as to whether those policies will be reversed or even abandoned. Before discussing the history of civil rights, however, we need to clarify exactly what we mean by civil rights, equality, and discrimination.

**unfair discrimination**
Unequal treatment based on race, ethnicity, gender, and other distinctions.

**de jure equality**
Equality before the law. It disallows legally mandated obstacles to equal treatment, such as laws that prevent people from voting, living where they want to, or taking advantage of all the rights guaranteed to individuals by the laws of the federal, state, and local governments.

**de facto equality**
Equality of results, which measures real-world obstacles to equal treatment. For example: Do people actually live where they want? Do they work under similar conditions?

# DEFINING CIVIL RIGHTS

14.1 *How successfully do the Declaration of Independence and the Constitution promise equality in American society?*

Most people agree that to truly approach democracy it is necessary to eliminate **unfair discrimination**—that is, unequal treatment based on race, ethnicity, gender, and other distinctions. The primary means for achieving equal treatment is ensuring full protection of civil rights—constitutionally guaranteed and protected rights that may not be arbitrarily removed by the government. These rights are often referred to as personal, natural, or inalienable rights; they are believed to be granted by God or nature to all human beings. Thomas Jefferson had these rights in mind when he wrote in the Declaration of Independence: "We hold these truths to be self-evident, that all men are created equal, that they are endowed by their Creator with certain inalienable Rights, that among these are Life, Liberty and the pursuit of Happiness." These rights become statutory when they are established by legislation.

Several groups within the U.S. population have suffered from discrimination at various periods in the nation's history, and many still do today. Although in much of this chapter we focus on the civil rights of African Americans and women, we also discuss the efforts of other groups, such as Gays and Lesbians, Hispanic Americans and Native Americans, to obtain equal treatment. Not all of these groups are minorities. Women, for example, are not a numerical minority, but they have experienced discrimination throughout the nation's history and continue to encounter unequal treatment.

Civil rights are closely linked with the ideal of equality. There are two basic forms of equality: equality before the law (legal equality) and actual equality. Equality before the law, also called **de jure equality,** requires no legally mandated obstacles to equal treatment, such as laws that prevent people from voting, living where they want to, or taking advantage of all the rights guaranteed to individuals by the laws of the federal, state, and local governments. Actual equality, also called **de facto equality,** looks at results: Do people live where they choose? Do they work under similar conditions? In a diverse and complex society like that of the United States, it is often difficult to achieve de jure equality; it is even more difficult to create the conditions that will lead to de facto equality. The nation's history includes many turns along the road to equality, and although de jure equality has been achieved in several respects, de facto equality remains a distant objective.

## THINKING CRITICALLY

One of the problems in equalizing the racial balance of public schools is that, over time, neighborhoods have taken on a defined racial balance. Some argue that this is de facto discrimination and should not be legally remedied. Are there circumstances when de facto discrimination becomes de jure discrimination, and should be rectified? Are there circumstances when de facto discrimination itself should be remedied? What can be done about this?

# ESTABLISHING CONSTITUTIONAL EQUALITY

Although the Constitution was written to "secure the Blessings of Liberty to ourselves and our Posterity," those blessings did not extend to African American slaves. This was not surprising; all references to slavery had been stricken from the Declaration of Independence, written 11 years before. Why did the Constitution's framers ignore the plight of the slaves? And why did they choose to count "other persons"—that is, slaves—as only three-fifths of a person, with no rights at all? As we saw in Chapter 2, to create a constitution that would be ratified by a majority of the states, the framers were forced to compromise. To preserve the economic position of the southern states, they allowed slavery to continue. But in doing so, they also ensured that future battles would be fought over slavery. And even for free African Americans, legal status varied in different regions of the country.

## QUICK REVIEW

Fugitive Slave Act

- Passed by Congress in 1793.
- Allowed runaway slaves to be captured, even where slavery was outlawed.
- Decreed that captured slaves could be returned to slave owners.

In 1820, the *Missouri Compromise* was passed when the proposal to introduce Missouri as a slave state threatened to upset the equal division of slave and free states. Missouri was admitted as a slave state along with the free state of Maine, and slavery was prohibited in the remainder of the Louisiana Purchase territory north of Missouri's southern border.

Although some African Americans submitted to their condition, many others did not. The most famous slave revolt occurred in August 1831, when Nat Turner led a rebellion of about seventy slaves in Southampton County, Virginia. In 12 hours of turmoil, Turner's men killed dozens of whites. Eventually the insurgents were defeated by hundreds of soldiers and militiamen, and Turner was executed, along with scores of other slaves.

## The *Dred Scott* Case

14.2 *How and why was legal equality not established in the late 19th century?*

The Compromise of 1850, which admitted California as a free state, discontinued the slave trade in the District of Columbia (but continued to permit slavery there), while the territories of New Mexico and Utah were given no federal restrictions on slavery. As part of the compromise, Congress passed a stronger Fugitive Slave Act and provided for hundreds of additional federal officials to enforce it. The political prospects for equality seemed more remote than ever.

In 1857, the Supreme Court decided a case with far-reaching implications for the civil rights of African Americans. A slave named Dred Scott had been taken by his master from Missouri into the free state of Illinois and the free territory of Wisconsin. When his master died and Scott was returned to Missouri, he claimed that because he had lived in areas where slavery was illegal, he was now a free man.

The case of *Dred Scott* v. *Sandford* reached the Supreme Court at a time when the justices were seeking to define the legality of slavery, particularly in the territories, as a means of solving the political dispute between the North and the South. In a highly controversial decision, the Court ruled that Scott could not sue in federal court because no African American, free or enslaved, could ever become a citizen of the United States. According to Chief Justice Roger Taney, even if Scott were free, he could not sue because African Americans were "not included, and were not intended to be included, under the word 'citizens' in the Constitution" and therefore had no rights under that document. Finally, the chief justice ruled that the Missouri Compromise was unconstitutional because Congress could not deprive people of their property rights, in this case their slaves, under the due process clause of the Fifth Amendment.[2]

**QUICK REVIEW**

The *Dred Scott* Case

- Scott was a slave taken by his master into the free state of Illinois and the free territory of Wisconsin.
- After the death of his master, Scott claimed he was now a free man because he lived in free territories.
- The Supreme Court ruled that Scott could not sue in federal court because no African American, free or enslaved, could ever become a citizen of the United States.
- The Court concluded that African Americans were not included under the word *citizens* in the Constitution and therefore had no rights under that document.

## The Civil War and Reconstruction

The *Dred Scott* case closed the door to judicial remedies for African Americans seeking legal protection. Political remedies were still open, however. By freeing the slaves in the areas still in rebellion, President Abraham Lincoln's Emancipation Proclamation of 1863 renewed the possibility of "equality for all." But for Lincoln's executive order to be implemented, the Union had to win the Civil War, and Congress had to apply legal authority to support freedom for slaves. Thus, following the Civil War, Congress played a pivotal role in efforts to establish equality for African Americans.

In one series of actions, Congress drafted three constitutional amendments, known as the Civil War Amendments. The Thirteenth Amendment, which abolished slavery, was ratified in 1865. It reads as follows:

> *Section 1. Neither slavery nor involuntary servitude, except as a punishment for crime whereof the party shall have been duly convicted, shall exist within the United States, or in any place subject to their jurisdiction.*
>
> *Section 2. Congress shall have power to enforce this article by appropriate legislation.*

**black codes**
Laws restricting the civil rights of African Americans.

**suffrage**
The right to vote.

Congress had already passed legislation allowing African Americans to testify against whites in federal courts (1864); granting equal pay and benefits to all soldiers (1864); and establishing the Freedmen's Bureau (1865), an agency of the War Department authorized to assist the newly freed slaves in making the transition to freedom.

But southern states were already passing laws, known as the **black codes,** that restricted the civil rights of blacks and enforced oppressive labor practices designed to keep them working on plantations. Led by the so-called Radical Republicans, Congress undertook to counteract these measures. Over President Andrew Johnson's vetoes, the Radical Republicans gave the Freedman's Bureau additional powers to settle labor disputes and nullify oppressive labor contracts. It also passed the Civil Rights Act of 1866, which made African Americans U.S. citizens and empowered the federal government to protect their civil rights.

Many members of Congress feared that the new law might not stand up in court. They drafted the Fourteenth Amendment to the Constitution, making African Americans citizens and giving them rights of that citizenship. Section 1 of the amendment states:

> *All persons born or naturalized in the United States, and subject to the jurisdiction thereof, are citizens of the United States and of the State wherein they reside. No State shall make or enforce any law which shall abridge the privileges or immunities of citizens of the United States; nor shall any State deprive any person of life, liberty, or property, without due process of law; nor deny to any person within its jurisdiction the equal protection of the laws.*

Section 5 of the amendment gave Congress the "power to enforce, by appropriate legislation, the provisions of this article." The new citizens were thus supposed to have the same rights as others, as well as be treated with fairness and equality under law.

Congress acted quickly. It required southern states to ratify this amendment, and later the Fifteenth Amendment, before they could rejoin the Union. The Fifteenth Amendment, granting African Americans **suffrage,** or the right to vote, reads:

> *The right of citizens of the United States to vote shall not be denied or abridged by the United States or any State on account of race, color, or previous condition of servitude.*

Again, Congress was given the power to "enforce this article by appropriate legislation." To break the power of the Ku Klux Klan and other terrorists who attacked, beat, and sometimes killed African Americans

## APPROACHING Democracy Timeline

### The Journey to Emancipation in America

| | |
|---|---|
| **1607** | Colony of Jamestown established as first permanent English Colony in America. |
| **1619** | First importation of Africans to be enslaved in what would become the United States. |
| **1620** | Massachusetts Bay Colony founded by Pilgrims arriving in Plymouth, Massachusetts. |
| **1776** | Language in Declaration of Independence that attacked slavery is removed. |
| **1780–1788** | Some northern states adopt measures to end slavery (MA, 1780; PA, 1780; RI, 1784; NY, 1788). |
| **1787** | The U.S. Constitution is written but does not end slavery (three-fifths compromise, Article I, Section 2; importation of slaves permitted at least until 1808, Article I, Section 9; runaway slaves will be returned, Article IV, Section 2). |
| **1789** | Fifth Amendment to U.S. Constitution states, "No person shall be . . . deprived of life, liberty or property without due process of law." This is not applied to slaves. |
| **1791–1792** | Vermont and Kentucky join the Union as free states. |
| **1793** | First Fugitive Slave Law enacted, requiring the return of runaway slaves. |
| **1796** | Tennessee joins Union as a slave state. |
| **1802** | Ohio joins the Union as a free state. |
| **1808** | United States bans further importation of slaves (on January 1). |
| **1810** | Underground railroad created to guide escaped former slaves to free territory or Canada. |
| **1812** | Louisiana joins Union as a slave state. |
| **1816** | Indiana joins Union as a free state. |
| **1817** | Mississippi joins Union as a slave state. |
| **1818** | Illinois joins Union as a free state. |

☐ Democratic ☐ Neutral ■ Undemocratic

*(continued)*

who tried to vote or otherwise claim their rights, Congress also passed the Ku Klux Klan Acts of 1870 and 1871, making it a federal offense for two or more persons to conspire to deprive citizens of their equal protection and voting rights.

But the legislative branch of government could only create the tools for establishing legal equality. It remained to be seen whether the executive branch would enforce them and how the judicial branch would interpret them. The first timeline in this chapter explores the journey toward the end of slavery in America.

## CREATING LEGAL SEGREGATION

After the Civil War, the Supreme Court showed little interest in the rights of African Americans. In *United States* v. *Cruikshank*, for example, the Court considered the constitutionality of the Ku Klux Klan Act of 1870. William Cruikshank was part of a white mob that had murdered 60 African Americans in front of a courthouse. Because murder was not a federal offense and the state authorities had no intention of prosecuting anyone for the crime, mob members were indicted on federal charges of interfering with the murdered men's right to assemble. However, the Court ruled that under the Fourteenth Amendment only **state action,** or action by the state government under the color of law to deprive rights, was subject to decisions by the federal court.[3] In other words, the federal government could not prosecute private individuals. This ruling left the states free to ignore lynchings, assaults, and mob actions against African Americans within their borders.

### Separate but Equal?

In the *Civil Rights cases,* the Supreme Court applied its new *state-action doctrine* to overturn the Civil Rights Act of 1875, which prohibited racial segregation in transportation, inns, theaters, and other places of public accommodation and amusement.[4] The southern states then passed a series of **Jim Crow laws,** which separated the races in public places. This legal separation was challenged in the 1896 case of *Plessy* v. *Ferguson*.[5]

Homer Adolph Plessy, who was one-eighth African American, had sought to ride in a railroad car designated as "whites only," rather

**Approaching Democracy Timeline *(continued)***

| | |
|---|---|
| **1819** | Alabama joins Union as a slave state. |
| **1820** | Missouri Compromise: Maine joins Union as a free state; Missouri joins Union as a slave state. Slavery banned in rest of Louisiana Territory. |
| **1820** | American Colonization Society begins moving free African Americans back to Africa. |
| **1829** | Mexico abolishes slavery. |
| **1833** | England bans slavery throughout the British Empire (including Canada and West Indies). |
| **1836** | Arkansas admitted to Union as a slave state. |
| **1837** | Michigan admitted to Union as a free state. |
| **1845** | Florida and Texas admitted to Union as slave states. |
| **1846–1848** | Iowa and Wisconsin admitted to Union as free states. |
| **1850** | *Uncle Tom's Cabin* published; California admitted to Union as a free state; Fugitive Slave Law passed, requiring federal officials in free states to arrest fugitive slaves, the return of slaves to owners without due process, and fines for those found helping runaway slaves. |
| **1854** | Kansas-Nebraska Act allows citizens of these territories to determine for themselves whether they would permit slavery, contrary to Missouri Compromise. Kansas has competing factions. Anti-slavery forces led by John Brown fight pro-slavery forces. Federal troops are required to establish order in Bleeding Kansas. |
| **1857** | *Dred Scott* v. *Sandford* decided, continuing slavery and declaring Missouri Compromise unconstitutional. |
| **1858–1859** | Minnesota and Oregon admitted to Union as free states. |
| **1861** | Kansas joins Union as a free state. By February, seven states had seceded from the Union (prior to inauguration of Abraham Lincoln in March). In April, Confederacy takes control of Fort Sumter, South Carolina. By June, four more states seceded, making 11 states in the Confederate States of America (two states, Missouri and Kentucky, had divided loyalties, but never officially seceded from the Union). |
| **1862** | Emancipation Proclamation frees slaves in states in rebellion (September). |
| **1863** | West Virginia splits from Virginia, joins Union as a free state. |
| **1864** | Nevada admitted to Union as a free state. |

☐ Democratic ☐ Neutral ☐ Undemocratic

*(continued)*

**Approaching Democracy Timeline *(continued)***

| | |
|---|---|
| **1865** | Confederacy surrenders at Appomattox Courthouse, Virginia, in April. |
| **1865** | Thirteenth Amendment outlaws "badges and incidents of slavery"—but does not grant property or voting rights to African Americans. |
| **1868** | Fourteenth Amendment protects the privileges and immunities, due process of law, and equal protection rights of citizens, presumably directed toward the freed slaves, against states. |
| **1870** | Fifteenth Amendment gives the right to vote to freed slaves. |

☐ Democratic ☐ Neutral ☐ Undemocratic

than in the car at the end of the train designated for "coloreds only," as required by law, and had been arrested. The Supreme Court upheld the arrest, stating that the Fourteenth Amendment regulated only political equality and not social equality. In dissent, Kentuckian John Harlan answered that legalizing state-enforced racial discrimination should not be constitutional because "our Constitution is color-blind, and neither knows nor tolerates classes among citizens. In respect of civil rights, all citizens are equal before the law. The humblest is the peer of the most powerful. The law regards man as man, and takes no account of his surroundings or of his color when his civil rights as guaranteed by the supreme law of the land are involved."[6]

The logical consequences of the *Plessy* ruling were revealed in *Cumming* v. *County Board of Education,* in which the Court approved "separate but equal" public schools in Georgia. Although the facilities were not really "equal," by claiming that public schools were a subject for state rather than federal jurisdiction, the Court could let segregation stand.[7] Soon, legally enforced segregation pervaded every other area of social life.

## The Disenfranchisement of African American Voters

Seeking to disenfranchise African American voters, southern politicians invented loopholes in the voting laws, thus circumventing the Fifteenth Amendment. Because many freed slaves owned no land, *property qualifications* kept some off the voting rolls; *literacy tests* did the same for those who could not read. When these loopholes were found to exclude many poor whites, an *understanding clause* was used: People were permitted to vote only if they could properly interpret a portion of the state constitution. (Of course, examiners used different sections of the Constitution and different standards for "proper interpretation," depending on the race of the test taker.)

Another loophole was the *grandfather clause,* which exempted from property qualifications or literacy tests anyone whose relatives could have voted in 1867, thus excluding the freed slaves. Some southern states also implemented a **poll tax**—that is, a fee for voting, which would exclude poor African Americans. Finally, with the Democratic Party, in effect, the only party in the South, states utilized *whites-only primaries* to select the Democratic candidate, making African American votes in the general election irrelevant.[8] Thus, the law denied African Americans, although citizens of the United States, a voice in its government.

### THINKING CRITICALLY

Conservatives such as John Harlan and ultra-liberals such as Justice William O. Douglas had supported the "Constitution is color-blind" philosophy. If judged on the basis of this standard, what would you say about the constitutionality of various types of affirmative action programs? Why?

**state action**
Action taken by state officials or sanctioned by state law.

**Jim Crow laws**
Laws passed by southern states that separated the races in public places such as railroads, streetcars, schools, and cemeteries.

**poll tax**
A fee that had to be paid before one could vote; used to prevent African Americans from voting; now unconstitutional.

# ESTABLISHING LEGAL EQUALITY

14.3 *How was the legal equality promised by the government in the early to mid-20th century accomplished by the judicial branch?*

African Americans reacted to end discrimination and oppression in a variety of ways. In 1895, Booker T. Washington, a former slave who had founded Tuskegee Institute, argued that racism would eventually end if African Americans would accept their situation, work hard, and improve their education. On the other hand, W. E. B. DuBois, the first African American to earn a Ph.D. from Harvard, argued that all forms of racial segregation and discrimination should be aggressively attacked and eradicated.

In 1909, DuBois, with other African Americans and concerned white people, formed the National Association for the Advancement of Colored People (NAACP) to litigate on behalf of racial equality. In a series of cases decided between 1905 and 1914, the NAACP convinced the Court to use the Thirteenth Amendment to strike down **peonage,** in which employers advanced wages and then required workers to remain on their jobs, in effect enslaving them, until the debt was satisfied.[9]

Encouraged by these successes, the NAACP challenged Oklahoma's law effectively exempting whites from the literacy test required for voting. In *Guinn* v. *United States,* the Supreme Court struck it down using the Fifteenth Amendment.[10] Then, in 1927, the Court found that Texas's white-primary law violated the equal protection clause of the Fourteenth Amendment.[11] Still, the southern states continued to disenfranchise blacks by reenacting the offending laws or inventing new loopholes. Clearly, a more general approach to protecting the civil rights of African Americans was needed.

**peonage**
A system in which employers advance wages and then require workers to remain on their jobs, in effect enslaving them, until the debt is satisfied.

**desegregation**
The elimination of laws and practices that mandate racial separation.

**THINKING CRITICALLY**

What impact did the creation of the Dixiecrats have on the Democratic Party's strength and its attempts to achieve racial equality for African Americans?

## The White House and Desegregation

During World War II, the obvious inequity of expecting African Americans to fight for a country that did not afford them full protection of their civil rights gave rise to new efforts to achieve equality. This time the White House took the lead. President Franklin D. Roosevelt issued an executive order prohibiting discrimination in defense businesses and creating a temporary wartime agency, the Fair Employment Practices Committee (FEPC), to investigate allegations of, and provide compensation for, such discrimination. In 1946, spurred by a spate of racial lynchings, President Harry Truman established a panel of citizens to examine the problem and recommend solutions.[12] He also issued an executive order making the FEPC a permanent executive branch agency.

But Truman's most significant action in relation to **desegregation** came in 1948, when he issued an executive order prohibiting segregation in the military and in federal employment. Truman also asked Congress to ban discrimination by private employers and labor unions, outlaw poll taxes, pass a federal anti-lynching law, create a permanent civil rights commission, and compel fair elections. However, these efforts were doomed by the opposition of conservative southerners who had split from the Democratic Party under the leadership of South Carolina's Strom Thurmond to form the Dixiecrats. The struggle for equality now turned to the public school system.

**QUICK REVIEW**

*Brown* v. *Board of Education*

- On May 17, 1954, the Court announced a unanimous decision that the separate but equal standard was unconstitutional.
- Chief Justice Warren argued that the importance of education in contemporary society was greater than it had been at the time of the *Plessy* ruling.
- Warren stated that segregated schools put African American children at a disadvantage, and therefore violated the equal protection clause of the Fourteenth Amendment.
- A year later, the Court issued a second statement, commonly referred to as *Brown II,* dealing with implementation of the *Brown* decision.
- Lower federal courts would supervise plans for desegregation, or the elimination of laws and practices mandating segregation, "with all deliberate speed."

## Seeking Equality in the Schools

Attorneys representing the National Association for the Advancement of Colored People (NAACP) had long been planning a comprehensive legal attack on segregation in the public schools. Initially, their strategy was to work within the separate but equal standard, using a series of test cases to show that certain educational facilities were not, in fact, equal. In 1938, the NAACP challenged a Missouri statute that met the state's separate but equal requirement by offering tuition refunds to African Americans who attended an out-of-state law school. The Supreme Court overturned the law, stating that students required to go to out-of-state schools would be burdened by inconveniences and costs not imposed on students who attended law schools in their home state.[13]

In 1950, under the leadership of Thurgood Marshall, the NAACP challenged the University of Texas law school's separate but equal plan, in which African American students were taught in the basement of an Austin office building rather than at the highly regarded state university. The justices agreed that the two "separate" schools were not "equivalent" in any respect. For the first time the Court went beyond such physical differences to point out the constitutional importance of the intangible psychological differences represented by the differing academic environments, such as

Nine-year-old Linda Brown and her family in Topeka, Kansas, in 1954, became the subject of the landmark Supreme Court case *Brown* v. *Board of Education*. The case began when Linda's father, a clergyman, took her to the all-white school, where she was denied admission.

the differences in the prestige of the faculty, the students, the library, and the law review.[14] On the same day, the Court ruled that Oklahoma could not satisfy its separate but equal requirement for graduate schools by forcing an African American student to sit in the doorway during class, study in a special section of the library, and eat at a table in the cafeteria labeled "For Colored Only."[15]

Now that the Court had ruled that psychologically "separate" facilities could not be considered equal in graduate education, Marshall and the NAACP were ready to take direct aim at overturning the separate but equal doctrine as applied to public schools. Suits were initiated to challenge the segregated school districts of four states (Kansas, Delaware, South Carolina, and Virginia) and the District of Columbia. In 1952, the Supreme Court decided to combine the four state cases and rule on them under *Brown* v. *Board of Education of Topeka, Kansas*.

On May 17, 1954, Warren announced the Court's unanimous decision that the separate but equal standard was henceforth unconstitutional. Warren argued that the importance of education in contemporary society was greater than it had been at the time of the *Plessy* ruling. Because segregated schools put African American children at a disadvantage, he stated, they violated the equal protection clause of the Fourteenth Amendment.[16] On the same day, relying on the Fifth Amendment's due process clause to deal with schools under federal government supervision, the Court also struck down segregation in Washington, DC's, public schools.[17]

A year later, the Court issued a second statement on *Brown* v. *Board of Education* (commonly referred to as *Brown II*) dealing with implementation of the decision.[18] All of the cases were ordered back to the lower federal courts, which in turn would supervise plans for desegregation, or the elimination of laws and practices mandating segregation "with all deliberate speed." Missing from the Court's statement was a direct order to compel **integration,** efforts to balance the social composition of the schools.

## THINKING CRITICALLY

What should be the role of the Supreme Court in creating social reform? How would this decision, and the history of America, have been different if Justice Vinson had not been replaced by Earl Warren? What are the issues raised by the Court, when seeing that there were no precedents to support their decision, ignoring *stare decisis,* and making their decision using social science material?

## State and Federal Responses

14.4 *Why did it take so long to implement the desegregation promise of* Brown v. Board of Education *and later move on to desegregating society?*

State governments responded to the *Brown* decision in a variety of ways. Washington, DC, Kansas, and Delaware largely eliminated legalized segregation. In the Deep South, however, violence grew against African American activists who tried to implement this ruling. In some places, mobs gathered to block African Americans from attending previously segregated public schools and universities. State legislatures also took steps to fight the *Brown* decision. Some forbade state officials to enforce the decision, while others closed the public schools in certain districts and paid the private school tuitions of white children.[19] Any uniform progress toward desegregation in the South would be up to the federal government.

Initially, with the exception of 58 courageous federal district court judges in the South, the federal government was no more willing to take desegregation action than the states had been.[20] Southern politicians took President Dwight Eisenhower's ambivalence as a signal to continue their discriminatory practices without White House interference. Only reluctantly did the president decide to send federal troops to Little Rock, Arkansas, to help nine African American students desegregate the region's Central High School in the face of strong opposition, which included the deployment of state National Guard units to prevent the students from entering the school.

**integration**
Government efforts to balance the racial composition in schools and public places.

President Eisenhower signed into law the Civil Rights Act of 1957, which created a Civil Rights Commission to recommend legislation and gave the Justice Department the power to initiate lawsuits on behalf of African Americans who were denied the right to vote. Then, in the Civil Rights Act of 1960, the attorney general was authorized to call in federal officials to investigate voter registration in areas where discrimination may be occurring. Although the Eisenhower administration did not use its new power vigorously, it did demonstrate that the federal government could be effective, if it wished, in protecting civil rights. In the meantime, however, the struggle for equality fell to the people most affected—African Americans themselves.

Fifteen-year-old Elizabeth Eckford calmly ignores the taunts of the jeering crowd as she becomes one of the "Little Rock 9" in 1957 who integrated Central High School. "I tried to see a friendly face somewhere in the mob—someone who maybe would help me. I looked into the face of an old woman and it seemed a kind face, but when I looked at her again, she spat at me."

# THE CIVIL RIGHTS MOVEMENT

The modern civil rights protests began with Rosa Parks's refusal to give up her seat on a bus, which led to the bus boycott in Montgomery, Alabama, in 1955–1956. Shortly afterward, African American activists founded the Southern Christian Leadership Conference (SCLC), which was headed by a charismatic leader, the Reverend Martin Luther King Jr. Like Mahatma Gandhi of India, King preached **civil disobedience**—that is, breaking the law in a nonviolent fashion and being willing to suffer the consequences, even to the point of going to jail, to publicly demonstrate that a law is unjust. For example, in the Montgomery bus case, protesters might **boycott,** or refuse to patronize, a business that practices segregation. Another kind of demonstration is the **protest march,** in which people walk down a main street carrying signs, singing freedom songs, and chanting slogans. During the early years of the civil rights protests, counterprotesters frequently lined the streets to jeer at the marchers, and law enforcement officials, blaming the protesters for the disturbances, would break up the protest, using everything from clubs to fire hoses.

The concept of civil disobedience was not confined to the SCLC. Inspired by the Montgomery boycott, Oklahoma City's NAACP Youth Council decided in 1958 to protest the segregation of lunch counters by sitting down on the stools and refusing to leave when they were not served. This protest technique became known as a **sit-in,** and it proved to be highly effective. In 1960, four African American students used this technique, entering a Woolworth store in Greensboro, North Carolina, and sitting down at the segregated lunch counter. When they were refused service, they simply sat there and studied until the store closed. During the following days, others—both African American and white—joined the protest, and soon more than a thousand people were sitting-in at segregated eating establishments in Greensboro. The Greensboro protest gained national attention, and college students throughout the South began engaging in sit-ins. Many of the protesters were arrested, convicted, and jailed, thereby drawing further attention to the movement. The tide of public opinion turned, and eating establishments throughout the South began to desegregate.

Beginning in 1961, civil rights activists, called **freedom riders,** began traveling throughout the South on buses to test compliance with the Supreme Court's mandate to integrate bus terminals accommodating interstate travelers. In Anniston, Birmingham, and Montgomery, Alabama, the freedom riders were attacked by mobs while local police made themselves scarce.

During the same period, the federal government worked with civil rights leaders to register African American voters in the hope of creating a legal revolution from within the system. With the aid of the Justice Department, the privately funded Voter Education Project began a campaign to enforce the voting rights provisions of the

**civil disobedience**
Breaking the law in a nonviolent fashion and being willing to suffer the consequences, even to the point of going to jail, in order to publicly demonstrate that the law is unjust.

**boycott**
Refusal to patronize any organization that practices policies perceived as politically, economically, or ideologically unfair.

**protest march**
March in which people walk down a main street carrying signs, singing freedom songs, and chanting slogans.

**sit-in**
A protest technique in which protesters refuse to leave an area.

**freedom riders**
Civil rights activists who traveled throughout the American South on buses to test compliance with the Supreme Court's mandate to integrate bus terminals and public facilities accommodating interstate travelers.

Civil Rights Act of 1957. As a result of these efforts, African American voter registration in the South rose from 26 percent in 1962 to 40 percent in 1964.[21]

Meanwhile, the civil rights movement was encountering increasingly violent resistance. When extremists began harassing and even killing civil rights activists, the White House was forced to act. In the spring of 1963, Martin Luther King Jr. decided to protest segregation in Birmingham with a series of demonstrations and marches designed to trigger a response from the segregationist police commissioner, Theophilus Eugene "Bull" Connor. The protest began with marches and sit-ins at segregated businesses, to which Connor responded by arresting protesters, including King himself, and obtaining a court injunction to prevent further demonstrations. Finally, after Connor attacked nonviolent protesters with vicious police dogs and fire hoses, President John F. Kennedy sent Justice Department officials to Birmingham to work out a compromise, and business leaders agreed to desegregate their establishments. However, the night after the compromise was announced, bombs went off at the hotel where King was staying. Riots broke out, and peace was not restored until President Kennedy sent federal troops to a nearby fort and threatened to dispatch them to Birmingham if the violence continued.

A young Baptist minister, Martin Luther King Jr., is arrested in Montgomery, Alabama, in 1958 for "loitering" near the courthouse where one of his civil rights allies was being tried. King later charged that once out of sight of the cameras he was beaten and choked by the arresting officers. His efforts on behalf of civil rights reform changed America forever.

## The Civil Rights Acts

14.5 *How were the Supreme Court cases and laws to realize desegregation in American society finally realized—and then threatened again?*

The civil rights movement made great progress toward equality in the early 1960s, but there was still a long way to go. To succeed, it needed more effective legal tools. In 1963, President Lyndon Johnson urged Congress in the name of the assassinated President Kennedy to "enact a civil rights law so that we can move forward to eliminate from this nation every trace of discrimination and oppression that is based upon race or color." And Congress responded. The Twenty-fourth Amendment, which prohibited the use of poll taxes in federal elections, was passed by Congress in 1962 (ratified in 1964). Then, after a 57-day filibuster led by southern senators that was finally broken by the arm-twisting of President Johnson, Congress passed the Civil Rights Act of 1964.

The 1964 act was extremely comprehensive and greatly increased the federal government's ability to fight discrimination. Because the government could withhold funds from segregated schools and the attorney general was empowered to initiate school desegregation suits, African Americans would no longer have to rely on the slow, case-by-case approach to end school segregation. Moreover, by creating the Equal Employment Opportunity Commission (EEOC) and placing authority in the hands of the Commissioner of Education, the act put the power of the federal bureaucracy behind efforts to end discrimination.

### QUICK REVIEW

Civil Rights Act of 1964

- The act increased the federal government's ability to fight discrimination.
- The government could withhold funds from segregated schools and the attorney general could initiate school desegregation suits.
- Equal Employment Opportunity Commission and the Commissioner of Education put the power of the federal bureaucracy behind efforts to end discrimination.

The Voting Rights Act of 1965 was another step toward racial equality. Areas where less than 50 percent of the population had been registered to vote or had voted in the 1964 presidential election were automatically found to be in violation of the law. Literacy tests and similar devices were prohibited in those areas, and no new voting qualifications could be imposed without approval of the attorney general. The law also mandated that federal examiners be sent to those areas to assist in the registration of voters and to observe elections. The result was that the law created oversight of the voting laws in 16 states, many in the historically discriminatory Deep South, but also including Alaska and Florida.

In addition to calling for this legislation, President Johnson, a former Texas senator, issued executive orders that brought the federal bureaucracy into the fight for civil rights. Among other actions, Johnson instructed the Civil Service Commission to guarantee equal opportunity in federal employment, directed the secretary of labor to administer nondiscrimination policies in the awarding of government contracts, and ordered the attorney general to implement the section of the Civil Rights Act of 1964 that withdrew federal funds from any racially discriminatory programs.

By 1965, the federal government was clearly at the forefront of the struggle to end discrimination and guarantee the civil rights of all Americans. However, it remained to be seen whether the provisions of the new laws were constitutional.

The brutality with which state authorities dealt with civil rights protesters, shown here as firefighters turned the full blast of their hoses on them, served to galvanize public sentiment in favor of the civil rights cause.

## The Supreme Court and Civil Rights

Less than six months after Congress passed the Civil Rights Act of 1964, two cases challenging its constitutionality reached the Supreme Court. In *Heart of Atlanta Motel* v. *United States,* the proprietor of a motel claimed that, as a private businessman and not a "state actor," he was not subject to Congress's power to enforce the Fourteenth Amendment. The Court ruled that because the motel was accessible to interstate travelers and thus was engaging in interstate commerce, Congress could regulate it under the interstate commerce clause of Article I.[22] In *Katzenbach* v. *McClung,* the justices noted that although Ollie's Barbecue (in Birmingham, Alabama) had few interstate customers, it obtained supplies through interstate commerce; therefore it, too, was subject to congressional regulation.[23] After these decisions, private businesses began voluntarily ending their discriminatory practices rather than risk losing costly lawsuits.

In 1966, in the case of *Harper* v. *Virginia Board of Elections,* the Court held that all poll taxes, even those imposed by states, violated the equal protection clause of the Fourteenth Amendment.[24] By the end of the 1960s, the number of African American voters in the Deep South had almost doubled.[25] This new voting bloc eventually defeated segregationist candidates, changed the views of politicians who had formerly favored segregation, and elected many African Americans to office at all levels of government. Although African Americans were gaining de jure equality, they were still far from de facto equality.

## De Jure versus De Facto Discrimination

The War on Poverty declared by President Johnson in 1964 was, in part, an attempt to address the problem of racial inequality. But African American communities continued to be plagued by poverty, and it became evident to people throughout the nation that discrimination and its effects were not limited to the South. When civil rights groups began to concentrate on the discrimination that existed in the North, their arguments changed considerably. In the South, segregation had been de jure, or sanctioned by law. In the North, however, segregation was more likely to be de facto; that is, it had developed out of social, economic, and other nongovernmental factors.

As efforts to fight discrimination continued, a major tragedy, the assassination of Martin Luther King Jr., was turned into a dramatic achievement. One week after King's death on April 4, 1968, President Johnson signed into law the Civil Rights Act of 1968, which banned housing discrimination of all types. A few weeks later, the Supreme Court upheld the government's power to regulate private housing by relying on the Civil Rights Act of 1866, which guaranteed all citizens the rights "to inherit, purchase, lease, sell, hold, and convey real and personal property." Justice Potter Stewart linked this law to the Thirteenth Amendment's guarantee to eliminate "badges and incidents of slavery," saying that discrimination in housing "herds men into ghettos and makes the ability to buy property turn on the color of their skin."[26] As a result, a homeowner who wished to sell a house was required to sell it to any financially qualified buyer. But the question of what could be done about the racially divided neighborhoods that already existed, and about the segregated schools that resulted from those divisions, remained.

In 1969, the Supreme Court, tired of the continuing delay in school desegregation 15 years after the *Brown* decision, ruled in *Alexander* v. *Holmes County Board of Education* that every school district must "terminate dual school systems at once and . . . operate now and hereafter only unitary schools."[27] In other words, they must desegregate immediately. School districts in the South complied within eight years, becoming the most integrated schools in the nation.[28] But northern cities, where de facto segregation still existed, made little progress.

How far would a school district have to go to end segregation? Did the Court's command require that school districts make a special effort to integrate schools? Did it mean that schools would have to bus children of different races to schools outside their neighborhoods to achieve racial balance? In 1971, the Court considered these questions in the case of *Swann* v. *Charlotte-Mecklenburg Board of Education.* It held that busing, numerical quotas for racial balancing, and other techniques were constitutionally acceptable means of remedying past discrimination.[29] Two years later, in *Keyes* v. *School District #1, Denver, Colorado,* the Court ruled that even in the absence of a law mandating segregation in the schools, school districts could be found to have discriminated if they had adopted other policies that led to segregation.[30]

In the early 1970s, the political and legal climate changed, and the civil rights movement suffered a setback. After ruling unanimously in every racial case since *Brown,* the Supreme Court became increasingly divided. Encouraged by this division, people who believed their neighborhood schools were threatened by busing and other integration programs made their views known, and political opposition to desegregation grew. In 1972 and 1974, congressional efforts to restrict the use of busing to remedy segregation were narrowly defeated. In 1976, however, opponents of busing managed to remove the power of the Department of Health, Education, and Welfare (HEW) to cut off federal funds for school districts that refused to use busing as a remedy.

Amid the turmoil surrounding busing, the Supreme Court heard the case of *Milliken* v. *Bradley,* which asked whether or not the courts could go beyond the city limits of Detroit—in other words, outside an individual school district—in requiring busing programs to remedy segregation. In Detroit as in many other cities, whites had left the inner city to live in the suburbs, and only a plan that bused suburban children to inner-city schools or inner-city children to suburban schools would achieve racial balance. However, arguing that the local operation of schools is a "deeply rooted" tradition, the Court ruled that because the suburban school districts had not been found guilty of official acts of discrimination (though the city schools and the state had), the Detroit desegregation plan need not include the suburban school districts.[31]

During the 1980s, busing remained so controversial that the Justice Department turned instead to other measures, such as the creation of "magnet schools," or schools with special curricula designed to attract interested students from all parts of a city. But the struggle for de facto equality was not limited to public schools. Discrimination in other areas of social life, such as employment and higher education, was coming under increased public scrutiny. Much of that scrutiny focused on efforts to make up for past discrimination through an approach known as affirmative action.

## The End of *Brown* v. *Board of Education* and the 1965 Voting Rights Act?

In 2007, the Court faced two cases exploring the next extension of the *Brown* v. *Board of Education* case in schools in which targeted pupil assignments were being used to lessen the effects of segregated housing. In the first case, a Caucasian woman from Louisville, Kentucky, sued when her son could not transfer to a kindergarten that at the time could admit only an African American student for the slot. Louisville is in Jefferson County, a district with 65 percent Caucasian families and 35 percent minority families that had been under Court order to desegregate its schools for 25 years. The plan to create a racially balanced public school system required that the school have between 15 and 50 percent African American enrollment.

The other suit came from parents in Seattle, Washington, which is 40 percent Caucasian. The parents objected to the city's racial balance plan for its ten high schools, which uses a racial "tiebreaker" when the school has more student applicants than available slots. The intent is to keep the racial balance in the schools within 15 percent of the area's racial makeup.

The Seattle school board's attorney, Michael F. Madden, tried to persuade the justices that this was an integration remedy that would balance the schools. But with the Bush administration backing the challengers' position, a majority of the Court saw the action as a result of an intentional segregation program that was admitting minority students at the expense of the Caucasian students.

A narrow 5–4 majority on the Court declared both plans to be unconstitutional. The Court applied a "strict scrutiny" test because the plan was based on racial factors, which required that any racial balance plan be "narrowly tailored" to realize a "compelling state interest." Writing for the majority, Chief Justice John Roberts ruled that the districts had failed to meet their "heavy burden" to underscore "the extreme means they have chosen—discriminating among individual students based on race by relying upon racial classifications in making school assignments." Chief Justice Roberts did not like the simplistic "binary conception of race" in the plans:

When civil rights advocates gathered in Selma, Alabama, in May 2007 to commemorate "Bloody Sunday" in 1965, a violent battle in which hundreds of police attacked civil rights marchers at the Edmund Pettus Bridge, presidential campaigners Barack Obama and Hillary Clinton (with former President Bill Clinton) joined them as they spoke at churches on the same street. Notice that no matter how far apart the two candidates are in this photograph, they still seem to be keeping an eye on each other.

> *In the present cases race is not considered as part of a broader effort to achieve exposure to widely diverse people, cultures, ideas and viewpoints. Even as to race the plans here employ only a limited notion of diversity, viewing race exclusively in white/nonwhite terms in Seattle and black/other terms in Jefferson County.*

Ironically, the majority cited *Brown* v. *Board of Education* as the basis for overturning this plan. This antagonized dissenting Justice John Paul Stevens, who argued: "There is cruel irony in the chief justice's reliance on our decision in *Brown* v. *Board of Education*. . . . It is my firm conviction that no member of the court that I joined in 1975 would have agreed with today's decision." Also in dissent, Justice Stephen Breyer complained: "To invalidate the plans under review is to threaten the promise of *Brown.*" He added that the opinion "threatens to substitute for present calm a disruptive round of race-related litigation, and it undermines Brown's promise of integrated primary and secondary education that local communities have sought to make a reality." The future of these racial balance programs, though, will lie in the hands of Justice Kennedy, who wrote in a concurring opinion that he was not prepared to fully eliminate race as a factor in a narrower pupil assignment program.

Just whether these cases represent the end of *Brown* v. *Board of Education,* as Justices Breyer and Stevens argue, or whether they are the logical extension of the search for racial equality in *Brown,* as argued by Chief Justice Roberts, will be determined by individual school districts as they design new integration plans for public schools and in future Court litigation. Then it will depend on the vote of Justice Anthony Kennedy, who will probably determine the balance of the voting on the evenly divided Court.[32]

Two years later, this same Court explored the reach of the 1965 Voting Rights Act to remedy racial discrimination in the creation of voting districts, with the same result. As discussed in Chapter 3, the case involved a challenge from an Austin, Texas, utility voting district to Section 5 of the Voting Rights Act of 1965, which requires a federal "pre-clearance" permission before any voting regulations can be changed

**APPROACHING Democracy Timeline**

**The Evolution Toward Civil Rights in America**

| | |
|---|---|
| **1867** | *Dred Scott* v. *Sandford* upholds slavery. |
| **1880–1890s** | "Jim Crow" laws in South separate races in public accommodation facilities. |
| **1896** | *Plessy* v. *Ferguson* upholds "separate but equal" discrimination in public accommodations. |
| **1954** | *Brown* v. *Board of Education* mandates desegregation in public schools. |
| **1955** | Supreme Court in *Brown II* slows down desegregation to "with all deliberate speed." |
| **1950s** | Fifty-eight southern federal district court judges implement *Brown* at great personal risk. |
| **1957** | *Cooper* v. *Aaron* compels officials to integrate Central High School in Little Rock, Arkansas. |
| **1969** | Supreme Court says public schools must be integrated into "unitary school" immediately. |
| **1971** | Supreme Court upholds school busing and other plans to integrate schools. |
| **1978** | Supreme Court in *Bakke* upholds affirmative action. |
| **1995** | Supreme Court in *Adarand* limits the reach of affirmative action. |
| **2003** | Supreme Court in *Gratz and Grutter* upholds affirmative action at University of Michigan, but with limits. |
| **2006** | Supreme Court declares use of public "magnet schools" to achieve racial balance unconstitutional. |
| **2009** | Supreme Court in New Haven firefighters' case overturns affirmative action promotion decision. |

☐ Democratic ☐ Neutral ☐ Undemocratic

in order to ensure that it does not discriminate against minorities. The law had been renewed four times, the last coming in 2006 by an overwhelming margin in Congress and a 98–0 vote in the Senate. The Austin utility district argued that they should be able to "bail out" of the pre-clearance procedure because there was no evidence that it had been used to discriminate against voters. In this case Austin, and the state of Texas, argued that times had changed and discrimination no longer existed in this area, and that all states should be treated equally because they had equal sovereignty over their affairs. However, the Supreme Court seemed sensitive to the argument of civil rights activists that by declaring the pre-clearance Section 5 process it would gut the law entirely and open the door to future voting rights irregularities and discrimination. So, Chief Justice Roberts fashioned an impressive eight-justice majority in expressing the need to observe the judicial self-restraint theory of "constitutional avoidance," or avoiding overturning a congressional law unless absolutely forced to do so. Ruling that the Austin district should be able to "bail out" of the law, Roberts argued, "Things have changed in the south. Voter turnout and registration rates now approach parity. Blatantly discriminatory evasions of federal decrees are rare. And minority candidates hold office at unprecedented levels." Having appeared to be showing "self-restraint," the Court then took an activist stance in rewriting the law. It stated that other voting districts, even ones that did not themselves register voters, could also bail out of the law's reach if it could prove that its voting laws had not discriminated in ten years and that it had "engaged in constructive efforts" to increase voting by minority groups.[33] Legal observers now believe that this decision will encourage many other states and localities to seek a "bailout" exempting themselves from the law's enforcement provisions.[34]

In December 2011, Attorney General Eric Holder argued that the concerted voter suppression efforts by at least eight Republican-controlled state legislatures to change voting laws to require photo IDs, and prevent college students and minorities from voting (as explained in Chapter 1) might be violating the Voting Rights Act of 1965. John Payton, the president of the NAACP Legal Defense Fund, argued that "we have not seen this much action that will have the effect of limiting people's ability to vote" since the passage of the Voting Rights Act in 1965. In late December, 2011, the Justice Department blocked a South Carolina law requiring a photo ID to vote, but the legal fight will continue elsewhere. It remains to be seen whether the Justice Department will be able to use expedited Voting Rights Act prosecutions in federal courts to reverse these laws.[35] Our second timeline explores the evolution toward civil rights in the 19th, 20th, and early 21st centuries.

# AFFIRMATIVE ACTION

14.6 *How have affirmative action programs been created, and do they achieve equality in America?*

We now turn to one of the most controversial aspects of the search for equality: programs that seek to increase equality but create temporary inequalities in the process. Such programs are collectively known as **affirmative action,** or programs that make exceptions to the standard operating procedures for the benefit of a previously discriminated against minority.[36] They attempt to improve the chances of minority applicants for jobs, housing, employment, government contracts, or school admissions by giving them a "boost" relative to white applicants with roughly the same qualifications. This action seeks to correct for past discrimination that held members of minority groups at a competitive disadvantage. The problem, of course, is that such efforts appear to discriminate against white applicants. Affirmative action thus raises difficult questions about the nation's commitment to equality and the extent to which the civil rights of all citizens can be protected.

**affirmative action**
Programs that attempt to improve the chances of minority applicants for jobs, housing, employment, or education by giving them a "boost" relative to white applicants with similar qualifications.

**equality of opportunity**
The idea that "people should have equal rights and opportunities to develop their talents," that all people should begin at the same starting point in a race.

**equality of result**
The idea that all forms of inequality, including economic disparities, should be completely eradicated; this may mean giving certain people a starting advantage so that everyone has fair chances to succeed.

**quota programs**
Programs that guarantee a certain percentage of admissions, new hires, or promotions to members of minority groups.

## Seeking Full Equality: Opportunity or Result?

At the beginning of the chapter we distinguished between *legal equality* and *actual equality*. Much of the discussion so far has described the history of efforts to remove obstacles to legal equality. We have seen that removing legal obstacles does not automatically result in actual equality; often, doing so gives rise to a new set of questions. In particular, does "actual equality" mean *equality of opportunity* or *equality of result?*

Underlying the goal of **equality of opportunity** is the idea that "people should have equal rights and opportunities to develop their talents."[37] This implies that all people should begin at the same starting point in a race. But what if life's circumstances make that impossible, placing members of different groups at different starting points, some much farther behind others? For example, a person born into a poor minority family in which no one has ever graduated from high school is likely to be much less prepared for admission to college than a person born into a highly educated family. Because of such differences, many people believe that the nation should aim instead for **equality of result.** All forms of inequality, including economic disparities, should be completely eradicated. This may mean giving some people an advantage at the start so that everyone will complete the race at the same point.

**THINKING CRITICALLY**

What did the 2010 election say about the voters' intentions as to the Court's direction on civil rights? What will be the impact on policy by a Court led by more Obama appointments?

Affirmative action was a logical extension of the desegregation effort. Its proponents argued that in allowing minority candidates to compete on a more level playing field by first tilting the field in their favor, affirmative action would eventually produce equality. In **quota programs,** the concept went a step further to guarantee a certain percentage of admissions, new hires, or promotions to members of minority groups. Opponents of affirmative action, however, labeled this "reverse discrimination" and argued that providing benefits solely on the basis of membership in a minority group would deny those benefits to other, more deserving candidates who had not themselves discriminated against minorities. In other words, equality of result for minorities took away equality of opportunity for majority applicants.

Affirmative action programs began with an executive order issued by President Johnson in 1965 requiring that federal contractors in the construction industry and later in the business community give a slight edge to minority applicants at a disadvantage compared to nonminority applicants. Between 1968 and 1971, the newly created Office of Federal Contract Compliance Programs (OFCCP) issued guidelines for federal contractors establishing certain "goals and timetables" if the percentages of African Americans and women they employed were lower than the percentages of those groups in similar positions in the local workforce. Although the OFCCP's requirements originally dealt only with federal contractors, in 1972 Congress passed

**QUICK REVIEW**

Affirmative Action Programs

- Sought to increase equality but created temporary inequalities in the process.
- Made exceptions to the standard operating procedures for the benefit of a previously discriminated against minority.
- Attempted to improve the chances of minority applicants for jobs, housing, employment, government contracts, or school admissions.

the Equal Employment Opportunity Act, which gave the Equal Employment Opportunity Commission the power to take private employers to court if they did not eliminate discrimination in their hiring practices.

Those who supported affirmative action hailed these actions; they believed that such measures could eliminate discrimination unrelated to job performance. Those who opposed affirmative action believed that these "guidelines" and "goals" amounted to quotas that would exclude more-qualified white applicants. They argued that the Constitution was, and should be, "color-blind." Even the ultra-liberal William O. Douglas expressed the opinion that the Fourteenth Amendment should be used "in a racially neutral way."[38]

The issue of affirmative action and quota programs reached the Supreme Court in 1978 in the case of *Regents of the University of California* v. *Bakke*. At issue was a voluntary policy of the University of California at Davis medical school, in which 16 of the school's 100 openings were set aside for minorities, who received an advantage in admissions. Allan Bakke, a white male, claimed that the policy had deprived him of admission, even though he was more qualified than some of the minority candidates who had been admitted. Four of the justices wanted to rule that the University of California's policy violated the Civil Rights Act of 1964 because the use of quotas discriminated on the basis of "race, color, religion, sex, or national origin." Four other justices wanted to uphold the university's policy of affirmative action as an appropriate remedy for the nationwide scarcity of African American doctors. The deciding vote was cast by Justice Lewis Powell, who agreed in part with both groups. Powell argued that the university's admissions policy violated both the Civil Rights Act and the Fourteenth Amendment's equal protection clause, because its quota program provided specific benefits for students solely on the basis of race. However, Powell also argued that since schools had "a substantial interest" in promoting a diverse student body, admission policies that took race, ethnicity, and social and economic factors into account, while not employing strict quotas, could be constitutional.[39]

Confusion reigned after the *Bakke* decision. The Court tried a year later to refine its mandate in a case involving the use of affirmative action in employment. In *United Steelworkers* v. *Weber,* it considered an affirmative action program at the Kaiser Aluminum Chemical Corporation, which had previously discriminated against African Americans. The program provided training that guaranteed that African Americans would fill half of the openings at its Gramercy, Louisiana, plant until the proportion of minority workers matched their proportion in the local labor force. The Court ruled that the Kaiser plan did not violate the Civil Rights Act, since the purpose of the act was to remedy the effects of past discrimination.[40] In 1980, the Court reinforced this judgment in upholding a program that set aside 10 percent of the grants in the 1977 Public Works Employment Act for minority-owned businesses.[41]

## Affirmative Action in the Reagan–Bush Era

Shortly after coming to office in 1981, President Ronald Reagan appointed officials who challenged many of the nation's civil rights policies. In reexamining affirmative action, his administration took the position that the various civil rights acts prohibited all racial and sexual discrimination, including discrimination against white males. It further argued that only employers found to have discriminated should be required to remedy their discriminatory practices and that they should be required to hire or promote only individuals who could prove that they had been discriminated against.

Programs that protected recently hired minority employees from "last-hired/first-fired" union layoff rules raised a key issue. White workers with more seniority who now faced layoffs argued that such protections violated their civil rights. In 1984, the administration persuaded the Supreme Court to overturn a federal district court ruling that required a fire department to suspend seniority rules when laying off employees.[42]

In 1986, the Court overturned a program in which a district with no history of discrimination laid off public school teachers with more seniority in favor of minority teachers.[43] However, it rejected the Reagan administration's position that race should never be a criterion for layoffs, ruling that such a plan may be justified in situations where *intent* to discriminate can be shown.[44]

Shortly thereafter, in another case, the Court accepted the use of a 29 percent hiring quota, which reflected the percentage of minorities in the local workforce in that case, because it was being used to remedy blatant past discrimination by the local sheet metal union.[45] And in a 1987 case involving state troopers in Alabama, where not a single African American had reached the rank of corporal, the Court ruled that quotas could be used in promotion decisions where blatant discrimination had occurred in the past.[46]

Seeing the resegregating pattern of these judicial decisions, civil rights leaders turned for help to Congress, dominated by a combination of liberal Democrats and southerners who depended on the African American vote for reelection. In February 1990, a bill was introduced that sought to overturn the Court's decisions in the six cases just described. Both houses of Congress passed the law, but President George H. W. Bush vetoed it, claiming that it would support "quotas." However, after extensive negotiations, a few minor changes in wording, and passage of the new bill, the president agreed to sign it into law as the Civil Rights Act of 1991.

## The Future of Affirmative Action in the 21st Century?

In a key 1995 decision, the Supreme Court for the first time refused to uphold the federal program. The case involved a small business administration program in Colorado that gave a Hispanic-owned company an affirmative action advantage in bidding for a highway contract. Instead, the Court ruled that in deciding such cases it would now use the strict scrutiny test, meaning that federal programs must serve a compelling governmental interest and must be "targeted" rather than "societal" in nature—that is, designed to remedy specific instances of past discrimination by the specific institution involved in the lawsuit, rather than just meet the overall racial balance in the community and remedy societal discrimination. This test made it much more difficult to uphold federal affirmative action programs.[47]

Meanwhile, around the nation, various states began to cut back on affirmative action programs. In 1997, the Texas legislature created the "Ten Percent Plan," a merit-based program by which the top 10 percent of high school graduates in the state were promised admission to the state school of their choice, regardless of their race or ethnicity.[48] In 1999, Washington voters passed a civil rights act that ended affirmative action in that state for both African Americans and women. In 2001, the Federal Appeals Court in the Fifth Circuit heard the case of Cheryl Hopwood and voted to end affirmative action in the University of Texas law school, saying that race could not be considered a factor in admissions. Following that, Texas attorney general Dan Morales ruled that race would no longer be a basis for admissions to undergraduate schools or for scholarship programs in that state. Shortly thereafter, California voters passed Proposition 209, which ended affirmative action based on race, sex, or ethnic origins in state hiring, education programs, and government contracts. Seeking "to restore true color-blind fairness," the regents of California's state university system eliminated affirmative action programs in graduate and, later, in undergraduate admissions decisions.[49]

In November 1999, Florida governor Jeb Bush inaugurated by executive order his "One Florida" program. This program would guarantee admission to state colleges and universities to the top 20 percent of graduating seniors in the state, increase financial aid and test preparation assistance for poor students, and end the "racial set-aside" programs for minorities seeking government contracts. By doing this, the governor derailed the statewide vote on affirmative action. Bush's action caused a storm of controversy in Florida. African American leaders protested, two African American legislators staged a sit-in in the lieutenant governor's office, and in March 2000, thousands of protesters marched at the state capitol while Bush was giving his State of the State address. But the governor was undaunted. "By September," said Jeb

Bush, "what you will see is an increased number of students attending our university systems and an increased number of African Americans and Hispanics attending the university system. That's the synthesis of what this rule is about."

Indeed, by the early fall of 2004, the One Florida program appeared to be sustaining the minority admissions rate in the Florida state school system, with the ten universities and New College enrolling 5 percent more minority students. But at the same time, when the University of Florida decided to stop awarding any race-based scholarships, the school was running nearly 5 percent behind its normal rate of admission of minority students when the affirmative action programs were in effect.[50]

When the Supreme Court refused to accept either of these appeals, thus leaving the lower-court and government actions in force, affirmative action policy became a patchwork of different approaches around the country. These programs, voter initiatives, and actions by governors such as Jeb Bush in Florida, together with refusals to make rulings on them by the Court, made clear that America's approach to democracy in this area of civil rights would continue to be debated year after year.

After the election of George W. Bush in 2000, the debate continued. The issue of the constitutionality of affirmative action programs reached a crucial turning point in 2003, when the Supreme Court decided two cases involving the University of Michigan: Jennifer Gratz, a white student, who applied to the undergraduate school, and Barbara Grutter, a white professional woman with children, who applied to the law school. Both were denied admission and similarly credentialed minority students were accepted. Grutter and Gratz filed lawsuits alleging race discrimination, both of them claiming that the school's affirmative action admissions policies excluded them from the schools. Their lawsuits gave the Supreme Court a chance in 2003 to rule for the first time since 1978 on whether or not affirmative action programs should continue in educational institutions across the nation.[51]

The University of Michigan had created one of the strongest affirmative action admissions programs in the nation, even though it had no past history of discrimination. Indeed, a 1995–2000 study showed that a minority student had a 234.5 times greater chance of being admitted to the University of Michigan law school than a majority student. The undergraduate school's new affirmative action program gave minority students an extra 20 points out of 150 required in the admissions process. The law school program was also designed to create more racial diversity in each class. Once the cases were accepted for Supreme Court review, 80 organizations filed 32 *amicus curiae* briefs on behalf of the University of Michigan's affirmative action policies. The most influential of these briefs, though, were the ones by the U.S. military and 31 *Fortune* 500 companies in favor of affirmative action programs.

By a narrow 5–4 vote, the Supreme Court majority offered a mixed ruling in favor of affirmative action programs—but with certain limitations—arguing the need for a "critical mass" of minority students in law school classes in order to achieve diversity in the educational experience. Sandra Day O'Connor wrote in the *Grutter* case: "In order to cultivate a set of leaders with legitimacy in the eyes of the citizenry it is necessary that the path to leadership be visibly open to talented and qualified individuals of every race and ethnicity."[52] Although seven justices upheld the University of Michigan's law school admission program without changes, a much narrower five-vote Court majority ruled that the undergraduate procedure of assigning a fixed number of points for different demographic and intellectual features of applicants to their admission profile represented an unconstitutional quota.

As for the future of affirmative action programs, Justice O'Connor suggested in a nonbinding portion of the law school case that "the Court expects that 25 years from now, the use of racial preferences will no longer be necessary to further the interest approved today."[53] But she could not have foreseen that her retirement in 2006 would result in her replacement by the much more conservative Court of Appeals Judge Samuel Alito on this issue, thus leading to a much more limited future for these programs. Then, in the fall of 2006, a majority of voters in Michigan passed the Michigan Civil Rights Initiative, which amended the state constitution to ban affirmative action programs on the basis of race, gender, color, ethnicity, or national origin.[54] Meanwhile, in Texas the Ten Percent Plan continues to operate with 70 percent of the incoming class at the state's flagship school, the University of Texas at Austin, being admitted under this program.[55]

With literally thousands of racial preference laws hanging in the balance at local, state, and national levels, the future of other affirmative action programs hung in the balance of swing justice Anthony Kennedy's vote on the balanced Supreme Court. And his vote seemed to be against affirmative action programs. In 2007, the Court announced two rulings on "magnet" high schools used in Louisville, Kentucky, and Seattle, Washington, to balance the racial population in the schools. In both cases, the Court used an inventive and tortured reading of the *Brown* v. *Board of Education* mandate to end school segregation to rule that such programs designed to achieve balance in schools based on race would not pass the strict scrutiny test of the Fourteenth Amendment's equal protection plan because they were not closely tailored to eliminate discrimination by those institutions. Here, Chief Justice John Roberts argued in the majority:

> *Before Brown, schoolchildren were told where they could and could not go to school based on the color of their skin. The school districts in these cases have not carried the heavy burden of demonstrating that we should allow this once again—even for very different reasons. For schools that never segregated on the basis of race, . . . or that have removed the vestiges of past segregation, . . . the way "to achieve a system of determining admission to the public schools on a nonracial basis," . . . , is to stop assigning students on a racial basis. The way to stop discrimination on the basis of race is to stop discriminating on the basis of race.*

In response, Justice John Paul Stevens, who had been on the Court since 1975, dating back to before the original affirmative action case *Bakke* v. *Board of Regents*, said in dissent: "It is my firm conviction that no Member of the Court that I joined in 1975 would have agreed with today's decision."[56]

This Court took the next step in cutting back on the promise of the *Bakke* affirmative action case in June 2009 when it decided *Ricci* v. *DeStefano*, the so-called New Haven firefighters' case. When 1 Hispanic and 17 Caucasian firefighters in New Haven, Connecticut, passed a promotion exam that was passed by no African Americans, the city's officials, after determining that the test was "fatally flawed" as it affected racial discrimination, decided to throw out the results of the test, fearing a lawsuit from the local NAACP. As a result, the city officials were sued by the firefighters (one of whom had studied for the exam at great personal expense to overcome his dyslexia condition) who failed to get their promotion under Title VII of the Civil Rights Act. The firefighters alleged that they had been victims of "reverse discrimination" in being denied their promotion solely on the basis of their race.

Writing for the five-person majority, Justice Anthony Kennedy argued against throwing out the results of the test, saying, "Fear of litigation alone cannot justify the city's reliance on race to the detriment of individuals who passed the examinations and qualified for promotion." In response, the four liberals, led by Justice Ruth Bader Ginsburg, who was so angry about the case that she took the unusual step of reading her dissent from the bench, said, there was "substantial evidence of multiple flaws in the tests New Haven used." She argued that this result would cut back on civil rights protection: "It took decades of persistent effort, advanced by Title VII litigation, to open firefighting posts to members of racial minorities." Few analysts could predict the effect of this decision on public and private hiring in the future where employers are caught in what Justice Souter called a "damned if you do, damned if you don't" situation of facing lawsuits from either side in hiring and promotion decisions. Some predicted, though, that with

## THINKING CRITICALLY

Justice Sandra Day O'Connor wrote in a 2003 case that affirmative action programs would likely end in 2028. Do you believe that this is true? How long do you think these programs should exist, and what would you need to see in America to say that they are no longer needed?

New Haven firefighters won their 2009 affirmative action protest case in the Supreme Court when it was ruled that the decision in New Haven, Connecticut, to throw out the results of promotion tests that did not include any minority candidates was an unconstitutional violation of the Fourteenth Amendment's equal protection clause. After the case was decided, 14 of these men received their promotions.

the expected lack of change in the Court's voting on this issue despite the appointment of Sonia Sotomayor, New Haven and other cities might turn away from such promotion tests to a real-world, "real-life situations" assessment process to decide on promotions.[57]

In the near future, the Supreme Court might be asked to rule in an affirmative action case challenging the Ten Percent Plan by the University of Texas at Austin, which admits students based on merit as determined by class standing rather than by diversity considerations. This will give us a sense of the newly conservative direction of the Court after the addition of Samuel Alito to replace the more pro–affirmative action oriented swing justice Sandra Day O'Connor. The resulting new swing justice, Justice Anthony Kennedy, has generally been more opposed to affirmative action, thus tipping the Roberts Court majority that way. This case may help to determine whether Sandra Day O'Connor's prediction of another 25 years of affirmative action may be short-circuited in favor of the current Court's possible vision of a color-blind school more like that of the first John Harlan in *Plessy* v. *Ferguson.*

## WOMEN'S RIGHTS

14.7 *How did the movement for women's rights begin in America?*

In the early 1800s, women in the United States were not permitted to vote, serve on juries, find profitable employment, attend institutions of higher education, or own land in their own name. Moreover, the English common law notion of *coverture,* which held that upon marriage a woman lost her separate legal identity, had been adopted in the United States. As a consequence, married women could not sue in their own name, divorce an alcoholic or abusive spouse, own property independently, or enter into contracts.

When Elizabeth Cady Stanton and Lucretia Mott were not seated as duly elected delegates at an international anti-slavery meeting in London in 1840, they decided to take action. They organized a movement to attain full legal rights for women. At an 1848 convention in Seneca Falls, New York, the movement borrowed the language of the Declaration of Independence in issuing a Declaration of Sentiments concerning the "natural rights" of women:

> *We hold these truths to be self-evident: that all men and women are created equal; that they are endowed by their Creator with certain inalienable rights; that among these are life, liberty, and the pursuit of happiness.*[58]

The convention passed 12 resolutions calling for political and social rights for women.

In response to lobbying by women activists, the New York State legislature passed the Married Women's Property Act of 1848. The law gave women control even after marriage over property they received through gifts and inheritance. Encouraged by this success, Stanton, Susan B. Anthony, and other feminist leaders began to lobby for further reforms in New York and other states. Their efforts bore fruit in 1860, when New York passed a civil rights law that gave women control over their wages and inheritances, guaranteed them an inheritance of at least one-third of their husband's estate, granted them joint custody of their children, and allowed them to make contracts and sue in their own name.[59]

### Two Steps Forward, One Step Back

After the early successes of the women's rights movement came several setbacks. In 1862, the New York State legislature rescinded and modified the earlier women's rights laws. Realizing the necessity of maintaining constant pressure on legislators, Anthony and Stanton tried to further link their cause with that of African Americans; they formed the National Woman's Loyal League to advocate a constitutional amendment to prohibit slavery. Soon thereafter, they joined with supportive men to form an abolitionist alliance called the American Equal Rights Association.

The new group put aside its feminist goals to promote the Fourteenth Amendment. This move proved to be a tactical error, as the amendment introduced the word *male* into the Constitution for the first time. When language giving women the vote was not included in the Fifteenth Amendment, Stanton and Anthony decided to form another organization designed to push solely for women's suffrage. In 1869, they formed the National Woman Suffrage Association and began a campaign for a constitutional amendment giving women the right to vote. Meanwhile, Lucy Stone, another longtime activist, formed the American Woman Suffrage Association, which sought to achieve suffrage state by state.

The still-long journey to women's equality became clear in 1873, when the first women's rights case reached the Supreme Court. In sustaining a law that barred women from practicing law, Justice Joseph Bradley stated:

> *Man is, or should be, woman's protector and defender. The natural and proper timidity and delicacy which belongs to the female sex evidently unfits it for many of the occupations of civil life. . . . [The] paramount destiny and mission of women are to fulfill the noble and benign offices of wife and mother. This is the law of the Creator.*[60]

That "law" became the law of the land as well.

Susan B. Anthony and Elizabeth Cady Stanton, shown in 1870, were early leaders of the fight for women's rights and women's suffrage. As a result of their efforts, women got the vote in 1920 with the ratification of the Nineteenth Amendment.

## The Struggle for Suffrage

The question of whether the Fourteenth and Fifteenth Amendments were inclusive enough to permit women to vote still remained. In a test case that reached the Supreme Court in 1875, *Minor* v. *Happersett,* Virginia Minor's husband (women still could not sue in their own names) argued that the new "privileges and immunities" clause protected his wife's right to vote. However, the Court disagreed, arguing that the Constitution and state laws reserved this privilege to men only.[61]

Despite such setbacks at the federal level, gradual progress continued at the state level. In 1869 and 1870, the Wyoming and Utah Territories granted full suffrage to women. Nebraska (1867) and Colorado (1876) gave women the right to vote in school elections. In 1890, Alice Stone Blackwell brought together the two rival suffrage organizations to form the National American Woman Suffrage Association, and lobbying for women's suffrage became more organized. By 1910, though, only four states (Colorado, Idaho, Utah, and Wyoming) had provided for full women's suffrage.

The new president of the National American Woman Suffrage Association, Carrie Chapman Catt, advocated the use of a coordinated grassroots strategy, that is, decentralized action by ordinary citizens, to seek suffrage. This strategy paid off, and by 1918 more than 15 states, including New York and California, had given women the vote.

This progress was too slow for some. For five years, Alice Paul had been running the Congressional Union (later to become the National Woman's Party) to fight for a constitutional amendment permitting women's suffrage. Arguing that the party in power should be held accountable for the continued disenfranchisement of women, the Congressional Union began picketing the White House and putting pressure on Congress to pass an amendment by touring the country with a replica of the Liberty Bell wrapped in chains. But World War I finally put the suffrage movement over the top. Women argued that their wartime service to the nation should be rewarded with the right of suffrage, and Congress agreed, passing the amendment in June 1919. The Nineteenth Amendment was ratified by the states in 1920, 52 years after ratification of the Fourteenth Amendment granting African American males the right to vote and 80 years after Elizabeth Cady Stanton and Lucretia Mott began their quest for full legal rights. The Compared to What? feature explores women's rights in Afghanistan and Iraq.

### THINKING CRITICALLY

The early suffragettes worked for equality for African Americans in the belief that they would in turn receive help for their own cause. However, it did not happen. How might American history have been changed if the two groups had worked separately for equality?

## The Road to Equality

Women successfully used their new electoral clout to secure congressional passage of the Married Women's Independent Citizenship Act of 1922, which granted women citizenship independent from their husbands. However, having achieved its main

# Compared to WHAT?

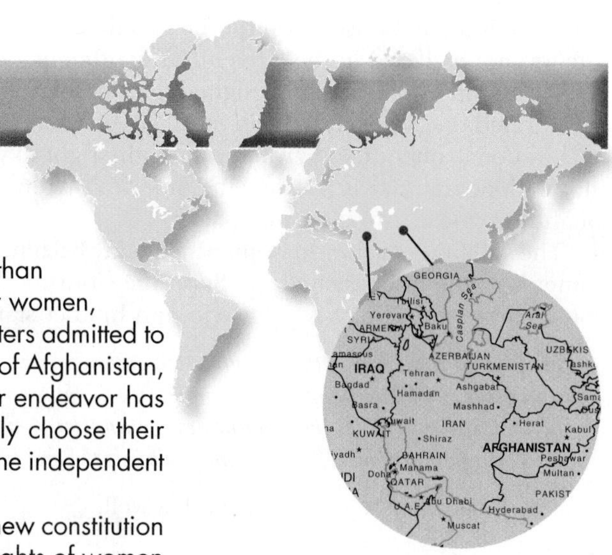


## The Move Toward Women's Rights in Afghanistan and Iraq

As a result of the successful American war in Afghanistan, more than 160 seats in the 1,500-person assembly are now guaranteed for women, women clothed in brightly colored attire without veils, with daughters admitted to local schools. The new Afghani constitution promises "the citizens of Afghanistan, whether man or woman, have equal rights before the law." "Our endeavor has been aimed at ensuring the rights of the Afghan people to freely choose their own destiny and political future," said Ismael Qasimyar, head of the independent commission in charge of planning the new nationwide assembly.

Meanwhile, in Iraq, changes occurring in the adoption of the new constitution based on the *sharia*, or Islamic law, may negatively affect the rights of women in that country. Under the earlier regime of Saddam Hussein, the government guaranteed women's equality. After the Iraq War, their rights were further safeguarded as many women continued to pursue professional careers and wear Western clothing. Much of the impetus for these changes was the addition of 90 women to the United Iraqi Alliance, the national assembly charged with implementing Iraqi law. The addition stemmed from a constitutional quota adopted in 2004. Over time, this large group of female representatives, then 31 percent of the assembly, began to debate the nature of their political agenda. "When you have a fairly large number of women [in a legislature], it brings women's rights to the forefront," said Marina Ottaway of the Carnegie Endowment for International Peace. Still, lacking a majority in the alliance and realizing that, like all large groups in that society, they were deeply divided on many issues, women in Iraq found that they had to rely on the support of other groups, such as the Kurds in the north, the Shiites in the south, and the supporters of Prime Minister Iyad Allawi, in order to solidify their gains in the new Iraq constitution as well as government. In recent years, though, as the Taliban have enjoyed a resurgence in the country, the rights of women have become more precarious with it becoming tougher for young women to become educated and for older women to enjoy the rights promised by their new constitution. This was especially apparent in April 2009 when it took the outrage of the international community, and a threat by Great Britain to refuse to continue their participation in the Afghanistan War, to convince President Hamid Karzai and the ministry of justice to reconsider a new law making it legal for husbands to rape their wives. By June of 2011, though, some were worried that many of these gains would be lost if the Karzai government negotiated with the Taliban for peace. One indication of this was the case of a woman who had been raped by the husband of her cousin, and was jailed for two years on a charge of "adultery by force," where she gave birth to a daughter. Only after an international outcry was she released on a presidential pardon, but she would have to marry the man to remain out of jail.

*Sources:* Jan Harvey, "Jailed Afghan Rape Victim Still in Prison, Despite Pardon," *News Daily,* December 13, 2011, found at http://www.newsdaily.com/stories/tre7bc198-us-afghanistan-gulnaz-release/; Amie Ferriss-Rotman, "Women's Rights in Afghanistan since the Fall of the Taliban," June 13, 2011, *Reuters,* found at http://www.reuters.com/article/2011/06/13/us-afghanistan-women-qanda-idUSTRE75C1BI20110613; Jon Boone, "Karzai Bows to International Calls to Scrap Afghan 'Rape' Law," *London Guardian,* April 5, 2009, www.guardian.co.uk; Pamela Constable, "Afghans Enjoy a Gala No Longer Banned," *Washington Post,* March 22, 2002; and "Panel Unveils Rules for Afghan Assembly," *Washington Post,* April 1, 2001.

goal of suffrage, the lobbying coalition fell apart, and actual equality for women would have to wait for decades.

Sex discrimination, also called **sexism,** could be seen in many areas of American society, but especially in education and employment. In 1961, the uproar that resulted when President Kennedy appointed only two women to governmental positions spurred him to issue an executive order creating the President's Commission on the Status of Women, chaired by Eleanor Roosevelt. At the commission's suggestion, Congress passed the Equal Pay Act of 1963, which mandated equal pay for equal work—that is, salaries for men and women performing the same job had to be the same. Although this was a victory for women, the law had limited effectiveness because employers were still free to create different job classifications with varying rates of pay.

**sexism**
Prejudice against the female gender.

The Civil Rights Act of 1964, originally intended to bring about equality for African Americans, represented the greatest advance for women's rights. This was perhaps poetic justice because the movement for full legal rights for women did much to further the causes of African Americans in the 1800s. Ironically, the change came at the behest of a southern congressman, who proposed adding sex to the bill's language in the hope of killing the bill, only to see the measure passed with the language intact. The act barred discrimination against any person on the basis of "race, color, religion, sex, or national origin."

Overburdened by an immense caseload, however, the Equal Employment Opportunity Commission (EEOC) was slow to enforce the provisions of the 1964 act. In 1966, outraged by the EEOC's inaction, several women organized the National Organization for Women (NOW). Borrowing techniques from the civil rights movement, NOW organized demonstrations and even picketed the *New York Times* because of its policy of printing a separate section advertising jobs for women. Also, NOW pressured the EEOC to hold hearings on regulations concerning sex discrimination. In the 1972 Federal Education Amendments, Congress amended the 1964 Civil Rights Act with Title VI, threatening a denial of federal funds to public and private programs that discriminated against women, and Title IX, which called for equal athletic opportunities for women in schools. This law has resulted in great changes in college sports. Nationally, and internationally, though, it is seen as the foundation for the Women's National Basketball Association (WNBA), the highly successful American women's Olympic soccer team, and many other sports.

Leaders of the women's movement still hoped for a constitutional standard establishing equality for women. In 1967, NOW proposed the Equal Rights Amendment (ERA). Women's rights advocates entered the 1970s with the hope that the amendment would be passed and quickly ratified. However, despite congressional approval of the amendment in 1972 and the support of Presidents Nixon and Carter, even with a congressionally mandated extension for the ratification of the amendment, the ERA fell 3 states short of the 38 required for ratification in 1982. As a result, people often are surprised to learn that women are not specifically mentioned in, and thus not specifically protected by, the Constitution.

Seeking to rectify that absence, supporters have recently undertaken two different strategies. At the state level, at least eight states have considered retroactive ratifications of the ERA, arguing that if Congress could extend the ratification period of the Twenty-seventh Amendment limiting congressional pay increases only to future terms, it could do the same for the ERA. At the federal level, in March 2007, Democrats in the 110th Congress introduced for consideration the Women's Equality Amendment, with no deadline to its ratification, seeking to provide heightened constitutional protection for women by using exactly the same wording as the old ERA. Although this amendment would heighten the level of judicial scrutiny protecting women, the question would be what impact this new amendment would have on governmental programs protecting other groups.[62]

## QUICK REVIEW

Title IX, 1972

- No one could be excluded from participation in any education program on the basis of sex.
- Federally funded college or university had to provide opportunities for men and women in varsity sports.
- Schools had to give scholarships to male and female varsity athletes in the same proportion as those participating in the sports.
- A "three-pronged test" was created to enforce this provision.

## Seeking Equality Through the Courts

14.8 *What role has the Supreme Court played in establishing, protecting, and later limiting women's rights and the rights of gays and lesbians?*

### THINKING CRITICALLY

At some schools, because of the size of the rosters for the all-male school football team, Title IX has led to the elimination of many men's sports and the creation of unisex teams such as fencing and rifle teams. Do you think the movement for women's equality is correct here? Are there other areas in your school or daily life where gender equality should and could be achieved?

The quest for equal rights now turned to the courts, focusing on the Fourteenth Amendment, which says that "No state shall . . . deny to any person within its jurisdiction the equal protection of the laws." It seemed reasonable that a woman could be defined as a person and thus be included in the equal protection clause. The key to this strategy would be the Supreme Court's interpretation of *equal protection,* or treating people in different categories equally unless the state can demonstrate some constitutional reason for doing otherwise.

For many years, sex discrimination cases had been decided by the **test of reasonableness,** or whether or not a reasonable person would agree that law had a *rational basis,* thus making it constitutional. The woman had to prove that a law that discriminated by gender was arbitrary, capricious, and totally unjustifiable. Under this test, women rarely won discrimination cases because the state could so easily find or invent an acceptable rationale for the law. Thus, when the state of Michigan in the 1940s barred women from obtaining a bartender's license unless they were "the wife or daughter of the male owner," the Supreme Court accepted the state's rationale that it wanted to protect the sensibilities of women.[63] And when the state of Florida in the late 1950s declined to put women on jury lists unless they specifically asked to be included, the Court upheld the law because a "woman is still regarded as the center of home and family life" and had "special responsibilities" in this capacity.[64]

Women's rights advocates moved to change the legal standard by which the Court decided cases involving sex discrimination, to shift the burden of proof to the state, thus helping women win their suits. Ruth Bader Ginsburg, a lawyer for the American Civil Liberties Union (ACLU), designed a campaign modeled on that led by Thurgood Marshall 20 years earlier for the NAACP to end racial segregation in the public schools. The idea was to move the Court incrementally, on a case-by-case basis, toward replacing the reasonableness test with a new test more favorable to the women's cause.

The first case, decided by the Court in 1971, involved an Idaho law requiring that, in naming the executor of a will, a male must be chosen over equally qualified females. Under this law, a divorced mother named Sally Reed had been prevented from supervising the will of her deceased son. It seemed likely that the law would be upheld under the reasonableness test. The state's "rational basis" for the law was that men know more than women about business, and it was unnecessary for the courts to hold additional hearings to prove this fact.[65]

Ginsburg decided to use the *Reed* v. *Reed* case to persuade the Supreme Court to use the **strict scrutiny test** in dealing with cases of sex discrimination. Under this test, laws that discriminate on the basis of a characteristic "immutable [or unchangeable] by birth," such as race or nationality, are considered "suspect." In cases involving such laws, the burden of proof shifts from the plaintiff to the state, which must demonstrate a "compelling state interest" to justify the discriminatory law. That is, the state must show the absence of other means to accomplish a goal than to treat these classes of people unequally.

Because sex, like race and national origin, is "immutable by birth," Ginsburg hoped that the Court would add it to the list of suspect categories. She was only partially successful. The Court still used the reasonableness test to decide the case, but for the first time it could not find an acceptable justification for the state's discriminatory policy. The law thus violated the equal protection clause of the Fourteenth Amendment. The *Reed* v. *Reed* case has been called the women's rights equivalent of the *Brown* v. *Board of Education* case for African Americans.

In 1973, the Court considered the case of Sharron Frontiero, a married Air Force lieutenant, who objected to a federal law that automatically provided benefits to dependents of married men in the armed forces while the husbands of women in the

**test of reasonableness**
Test in court cases of what reasonable people would agree to be constitutional because the law has a rational basis for its existence.

**strict scrutiny test**
Test of laws that discriminate on the basis of a characteristic "immutable (or unchangeable) by birth," such as race or nationality; in such cases, the burden shifts from the plaintiff to the state, forcing the government to show the compelling reasons for the law.

military received benefits only if they could prove that they were dependent on their wives. Four of the justices were now ready to expand the strict scrutiny test to include women. However, just as he would do later for homosexual rights, the swing justice, Lewis Powell, was not yet ready to do so, because the Equal Rights Amendment was then being considered for ratification. Thus, the less protective reasonableness test continued as the standard, which became even more important when the ERA failed to be ratified.[66]

In an unusual turn of events, the next case in this area involved a man, Mel Kahn, who claimed to have been discriminated against on the basis of his sex by a Florida law that provided $500 more in property tax exemption for widows than for widowers. Although the ACLU lost the case, it had made an important step forward. Rather than pressing for the strict scrutiny test or accepting the reasonableness test, Ginsburg asked the Court to create an intermediate **heightened scrutiny test,** which would be used for laws that created benevolent forms of discrimination. Such a standard would force the state to justify the law by proving more than its mere "reasonableness," though not its "compelling" nature. Thus, a law would now be upheld if the rights of the plaintiff were deemed, on balance, more important than the state's interests as represented in the law.[67]

## THINKING CRITICALLY

Two times in his career, Lewis Powell was put in the position as the swing justice on the Supreme Court of deciding whether equality rights should be extended to different groups—women in 1973 and gays in 1987. Both times, Powell chose not to decide, and the groups lost. What are the dangers to American democracy of leaving the rights of groups of citizens in the hands of a single justice on the Supreme Court?

The current legal status of women was finally achieved in a 1976 case called *Craig v. Boren,* which, on the surface, did not look like material for a landmark constitutional decision. An underage fraternity boy and the Honk 'n' Holler convenience store had teamed up to challenge an Oklahoma statute under which 18-year-old girls could buy weak 3.2 beer (3.2 percent alcohol, as opposed to the 3.5 to 3.6 percent variety), but boys could not do the same until they were 21. The state justified the law on the basis of differential driving records for the two groups. Ginsburg called this a "nonweighty interest pressed by thirsty boys," but it nonetheless led to a legal victory. In striking down the law as an unconstitutional violation of the equal protection clause, the Supreme Court applied the heightened scrutiny test. Under this test, laws that classify people according to their sex must now "serve important governmental objectives and must be substantially related to the achievement of those objectives."[68]

More progress for women's rights occurred in 1996, when the Supreme Court ruled that the Virginia Military Institute (VMI), a state-run, all-male military college, had to admit women or lose state funding. The military academy had argued that its 157-year tradition of single-sex education—highlighted by its "rat line" whereby new cadets get crew cuts and face the taunts and face-to-face inquisitions of upperclassmen—justified the single-sex approach. But Justice Ginsburg ruled, "We find no persuasive evidence in this record that VMI's male-only admission policy 'is in furtherance of a state policy of diversity.' . . . Rather," she added, "neither the goal of producing citizen-soldiers nor VMI's implementing methodology is inherently unsuitable to women." Although VMI and the Citadel, a formerly all-male military academy in South Carolina, both admitted women to their incoming classes, the tradition of the rat line has continued.[69] The progress of women in the service academies became even more evident in 2002 when George W. Bush spoke to the graduating class at West Point, which included a female valedictorian. The nation's only three all-male colleges—Hampden-Sydney in Virginia, Wabash in Indiana, and Morehouse in Georgia—are private ones.[70]

This progress became even clearer in 1998 when the Supreme Court clarified its rules on sexual harassment. Confusion had reigned in the federal courts for years after the 1986 Supreme Court ruling that sexual harassment was a form of sex discrimination covered by Title VII of the 1964 Civil Rights Act. In time, lower federal courts required that alleged victims prove loss of a job or an anticipated promotion—a difficult task—in order to win restitution.

In June 1998, the Court handed down two 7–2 decisions, one involving a lifeguard in Boca Raton, Florida, and the other a marketing representative for Burlington Industries in Chicago, ruling that employers were responsible for supervisors' sexual misconduct, even if they had no knowledge of it. Moreover, victims of abuse should not have to prove loss of promotion or job because they rejected a boss's

**heightened scrutiny test**
A middle-level standard that would force the state to prove more than just the reasonableness of a law, though not its compelling nature, in order to justify it. For women's rights cases, this means proving the important governmental objectives of the law's goals and linking it to the wording of the law. This is done by balancing the rights of the individual against the interests of the state.

## THINKING CRITICALLY

What should be the role of justices based on their gender in making decisions? Justices Sandra Day O'Connor and Ruth Bader Ginsburg, both of whom were victimized by discrimination in the early years of their legal career, were not as liberal in their judicial decision making for women's rights as they had been in their pre-judicial careers. How might women's rights have been different if women had been as aggressive in deciding on behalf of equal rights on the Court as they were in their early years and as Ginsburg had been in arguing for the ACLU legal defense fund in the 1970s? What should be the role of Justice Sonia Sotomayor on this issue?

advances; rather, pervasive or continued threats or abuse were enough for a lawsuit. In some cases, though, companies could defend themselves by proving that they took reasonable steps to prevent workplace harassment. Justice David Souter wrote, "It is by now well recognized that . . . sexual harassment by supervisors (and, for that matter, co-employees) is a persistent problem in the workplace."[71]

In the same term, the Court also ruled that sexual harassment claims can be filed even in same-sex situations. And finally, students in public school who claimed sexual harassment by teachers were ruled unable to sue the school district unless school officials had direct knowledge of the harassment and were deliberately indifferent to it.[72]

In 2000, the Court ruled it unconstitutional for a college student who had been raped in her Virginia college dorm room by two football players to sue the alleged perpetrators under the 1994 Violence Against Women Act (VAWA) in federal court. The states were left to provide criminal and civil remedies for such attacks.[73] Although Congress, in the same year, reauthorized VAWA and expanded it to include date rape, those victims still could not sue their attackers in federal court.

Women's rights seemed to take a setback in the Court's 2006–2007 term, much to the distress of Justice Ruth Bader Ginsburg. Lilly Ledbetter, a grandmother from Alabama who had been a management employee at Goodyear Tire and Rubber Company, had failed to file a complaint with the Equal Employment Opportunity Commission against the company within the federal legislatively required timelimits—that is, within six months of the first check in which she had been underpaid relative to male employees. She did not realize until near the end of her career that she had been paid as much as 40 percent less than the lowest paid male managers, many with much less seniority. Despite this fact, the Court ruled that she, and thousands of others, would not be able to sue and therefore seek remedies. Seeing the impact on women who were mistreated by companies, for the second time that term, Justice Ruth Bader Ginsburg read her dissent very slowly from the bench, an unusual step for her, arguing that the majority opinion "overlooks common characteristics of pay discrimination." Seeing that she would likely be getting little help from her Court for women's rights here, Ginsburg called on Congress to pass new legislation, writing: "Once again, the ball is in Congress's Court."[74] And once Barack Obama and the new Democratic Party–dominated Congress took office, they did just that. Meeting a promise in his campaign, President Obama's first legislative signing in late January 2009 was the Lilly Ledbetter Fair Pay Restoration Act, which allows victims of pay discrimination to file a complaint with the EEOC for restoration of the money within six months of their *final* paycheck.[75]

In his first signing of congressional legislation as president, Barack Obama, shown here surrounded by some of those members of Congress, signs the Lilly Ledbetter Fair Pay Act granting legal protection for women who do not receive equal pay for equal work and are unaware of that fact for long periods of time.

A potentially interesting new turn may have happened in favor of the civil rights of women in late 2011. Justice Antonin Scalia caused a controversy at the beginning of that year when he gave an interview arguing based on his originalism philosophy that "Certainly the Constitution does not require discrimination on the basis of sex. The only issue is whether it prohibits it. It doesn't. Nobody ever thought that's what it meant. Nobody ever voted for that." This was interpreted by some, including comedian Stephen Colbert, to mean that Scalia believed women were not protected by the Constitution. Later that year, when appearing before a Senate committee, Scalia appeared to back away from this statement telling California senator Dianne Feinstein, who had asked if women were included in the

Fourteenth Amendment, "Yeah. Of course they're included." In November, though, one of Scalia's early law clerks, Steven Calabresi, a founder of the conservative legal organization the Federalist Society, argued in a 100-page law review article that his originalist analysis of the historical evidence of the "public meaning" of the Fourteenth Amendment's equal protection clause did include protection for women and women's rights, drawing strength from the inalienable rights of the Declaration of Independence. His argument is that the broad language of the Fourteenth Amendment, "No State shall . . . deny to any person within its jurisdiction the equal protection of the laws," supplemented by the pro-women's voting Nineteenth Amendment, prevents the creation of a subordinate caste of people under law. It remains to be seen whether this new form of "progressive originalism," using historical analysis to expand rather than restrict rights as has been done by the theory's early conservative proponents, will be used to protect women's rights in future cases.[76] The chapter's final timeline explores the evolution of women's rights in America.

### APPROACHING Democracy Timeline

**The Evolution of Women's Rights in America**

| | |
|---|---|
| 1873 | Justice Joseph Bradley bars women from practicing law, says they should be "wife and mother." |
| 1875 | Supreme Court rules women cannot vote. |
| 1920 | Nineteenth Amendment giving women the vote is ratified. |
| 1948 | Supreme Court upholds law denying women right to own a bar. |
| 1967 | Equal Rights Amendment proposed. |
| 1972 | Title IX of the Federal Education Amendments guarantee equality for female students. |
| 1972 | Supreme Court refuses by one vote to create a *judicial* Equal Rights Amendment. |
| 1975 | Supreme Court gives women heightened judicial scrutiny, but not "strict scrutiny." |
| 1982 | Equal Rights Amendment fails to be ratified by three states. |
| 1996 | Supreme Court ends all-male school at Virginia Military Academy. |
| 2000 | Supreme Court declares Violence Against Women Act unconstitutional. |
| 2007 | Lucy Ledbetter unable to sue for equal pay because Court says statute of limitations was exceeded. |
| 2007 | 110th Congress considers the Women's Equality Amendment. |
| 2008 | Hillary Clinton runs for Democratic Party nomination for president. |
| 2009 | President Obama signs Lilly Ledbetter Fair Pay Restoration Act into law, extending the period in which pay discrimination victims can sue. |

Democratic Neutral Undemocratic

## CIVIL RIGHTS AND OTHER MINORITIES

### Gay Rights

The course of gay rights in America has changed dramatically in the last quarter century. The road to greater equality here began with a devastating judicial defeat. In 1987, 28-year-old Michael Hardwick was arrested for having sexual relations with another man in violation of the Georgia anti-sodomy statute. When *Bowers* v. *Hardwick* reached the deeply divided Burger Court, the result hinged on the vote of centrist Justice Lewis Powell, who—after much hesitation—sided with the majority in the conservatives, upholding the Georgia law, arguing that the Constitution does not confer a fundamental right of privacy to homosexuals engaging in sodomy. The four-justice dissent, led by Blackmun, responded that if the constitutional right to privacy means anything, it means that Georgia cannot prosecute its citizens for private consensual sexual activity.[77] A few years later, Justice Powell admitted to an audience that he now regretted his decision in this case: "I think I probably made a mistake in that one. When I had the opportunity to reread the opinions . . . I thought the dissents had the better of the arguments."[78]

Eight years later, the Court, with Justice Anthony Kennedy sitting in the retired Justice Powell's seat, seemed more supportive of gay rights when it reviewed "Amendment 2" of the Colorado constitution, which prohibited all governmental protection at either the state or the local level for gays and lesbians. The Court overturned the provision. Persuaded by a legal brief from Harvard law professor

Members of the gay rights protest group, Code Pink, made their views known about the federal "Don't Ask, Don't Tell" military policy in 2010 in a Senate Armed Services Committee hearing.

Laurence Tribe that the Ninth Amendment might protect gay rights, Justice Kennedy argued in the majority opinion that "the [Colorado] amendment imposes a special disability upon those persons alone," an action "unprecedented in our jurisprudence."[79]

The federal government's position in the 1990s was not favorable toward gay rights. In the beginning of the new presidential administration of President Bill Clinton in 1993 he sought to end the discrimination against gays in the military. Had he succeeded this policy would have served, like the anti-discrimination policies in the military in the 1940s by Harry Truman as a bridgehead toward greater human rights. However, the military, aided by conservatives in the country, opposed the change and instead Clinton agreed to Congress passing a "Don't Ask, Don't Tell" policy by which gays would be protected so long as their sexual preference was not known, but could be punished if it became open or known.

This policy put many gays and lesbians in a position of having to live in secrecy as it related to their personal intimate behavior, or being discriminated against, or even blackmailed, by heterosexuals in the military. In time, tens of thousands of people decided to, or were forced to, leave military service. Fearing that the issue was heading toward the Court's endorsement of gay marriages, in 1996, Congress, acting at the behest of conservative congressman Bob Barr (R–GA), passed the Defense of Marriage Act (DOMA), which defines marriage as "a legal union between one man and one woman as husband and wife." In addition, states were not required "to give effect of any public act, record, or judicial proceeding" in any other state or territory that allowed marriage between members of the same sex. Just whether or not this violates the constitutional provision in Article IV, Section I, stating, "Full Faith and Credit shall be given in each State to the public Acts, Records, and judicial Proceedings of every other State," awaits the Court's test.

## The New Battleground over Gay Rights

Adding to the confusion over gay rights, states began taking different approaches to the question of gay marriage. In Hawaii, after the state had allowed gay marriages, the state supreme court upheld a 1998 amendment to the state constitution barring them. In California, the voters did the same by approving an initiative called Proposition 22 in the 2000 election, which barred the state from recognizing same-sex marriages, even those legalized by other states. While supporters of the California measures claimed the initiative supported "family values," their vote effectively banned same-sex marriages and denied same-sex couples a series of benefits of marriage available to heterosexual married couples.

Going in the other direction, however, in 2000, Vermont passed a civil union law for gays, allowing them to enjoy all the rights and benefits of marriage without formally being legally married. Under the Vermont law, only marriages are "sanctified" by clergy or justices of the peace, whereas civil unions are to be "certified." To end a marriage requires a divorce; same-sex couples can end their relationship by "dissolution." But the benefits of civil union are clear. Same-sex partners can make decisions about their partner's health care and apply for spousal benefits from employers. The new relationship would likely have an effect on custody fights and adoption requests. Couples in civil unions receive breaks in inheritance and property taxes but must pay the increased "marriage penalty" that heterosexual couples pay for income taxes.

This new law resulted in significant changes, both in that state and elsewhere. From July 1, 2000, to January 4, 2002, the state of Vermont issued 3,471 civil union licenses. In early 2002, the Vermont Supreme Court rejected a legal challenge claiming that the law forced town clerks to issue such licenses in violation of their religious beliefs. The American federal system of government had to face the question of how a law promising traditional marriage benefits to same-sex couples in one state would affect other governmental structures at local, state, and national levels.[80] Meanwhile, at the federal level, in July 2001, a group called the Alliance for Marriage proposed a "Federal Marriage Amendment," which reads:

> *Marriage in the United States shall consist only of the union of a man and a woman. Neither this Constitution or the constitution of any state, nor state or federal law, shall be construed to require that marital status or the legal incidents thereof be conferred upon unmarried couples or groups.*

In 2003, the Supreme Court continued the discussion of gay marriages in the landmark case of *Lawrence* v. *Texas,* which reversed the 1987 *Bowers* v. *Hardwick* case when it overturned a Texas anti-sodomy law that resembled the earlier Georgia version. Justice Anthony Kennedy wrote for the five-justice majority that the Court would protect privacy, which he defined as follows: "Freedom presumes an autonomy of self that includes freedom of thought, belief, expression, and certain intimate conduct." While he argued that the Texas law, which sought to safeguard morality, had no "rational basis" for restricting gays, in dissent Justice Antonin Scalia argued that the majority position could also be used to uphold gay marriages, which he opposed.[81] Justice Kennedy said nothing about the issue in his opinion, but Justice O'Connor, in the majority, wrote that in her opinion the Court was not then supporting gay marriages. So, the issue remained in doubt.

The movement toward same-sex marriage accelerated at the state level. In late 2003, the Massachusetts Supreme Judicial Court ruled that gay marriages were constitutional, a decision that remained in force when the state legislature failed to meet the court's 180-day deadline to either legislate on the issue or allow gay marriages to become legal in the state. Initially, the state legislature failed to reach an agreement on a new law in this area, and so the Court's gay marriage ruling went into effect in 2004. When Massachusetts became the first state in the union to allow gay marriages, gay and lesbian couples from all over the country traveled to the state to be married.

By late 2005, the gay marriage map had changed considerably. Connecticut had become the second state to pass a "civil union" law along the lines of Vermont's. On the other hand, Texas that year overwhelmingly passed Proposition 2, a constitutional ban on same-sex marriages, making it the 19th state to do so. In all, nearly 40 states have constitutional amendments or laws limiting marriage to one man and one woman.[82]

Four years later, though, the movement has gone the other way. In June 2009, New Hampshire became the sixth state to allow gay marriages, with the others being Massachusetts, Connecticut, Maine, Vermont, and Iowa. The landscape here continually changed, as California, whose state assembly had also allowed same-sex marriages in May 2008, removed that prospect with the passage of Proposition 8 by the voters in the 2008 election. California became even more complicated when the state supreme court upheld Proposition 8 but allowed around 18,000 couples already married to remain so. That movement spread to Maine, where a referendum on November 3, 2009, overturned that state's gay marriage law. Soon thereafter, both the New York and New Jersey legislatures rejected gay marriage laws.

Meanwhile, the opposing attorneys in the *Bush* v. *Gore* case, Ted Olson and David Boies, legally challenged the new California Proposition 8 gay marriage ban, while suits were filed in Massachusetts and three other jurisdictions challenging the 1996 federal Defense of Marriage Act (DOMA). As various states continued to develop and enforce their own unique policies, it led to a patchwork of conflicting state laws and court decisions, making it only a matter of time before the Court hears a case exploring the constitutionality of gay marriage. In two Massachusetts cases, federal court judges ruled against DOMA as it affected Massachusetts policies. With the election of Barack Obama, who had promised to bring greater equality to the country, especially for the gay community, change accelerated at a rapid pace. The Obama administration led Congress in repealing the military's "Don't Ask, Don't Tell" policy in late 2010. It also refused to defend DOMA in Court, forcing Congress to hire its own counsel to argue on behalf of the law. The DOMA case along with the Olson/Boies Proposition 8 case are surely headed to the Supreme Court for decisions.[83] Some wonder whether the new originalist argument by Steven Calabresi, in favor of a broad reading of the Fourteenth Amendment equal protection clause, might support gay marriage.[84] Meanwhile, New Hampshire will vote in early 2012 whether to repeal their gay marriage law in favor a civil union law.

One of the biggest changes, though, came at the state level in the summer of 2011 as New York, led by a brilliant strategic political and lobbying campaign by that state's governor, Andrew Cuomo, became the sixth and largest state to pass a law allowing same-sex marriages. With more than three-quarters of the other states restricting or banning such marriages, or same-sex partnerships, it is only a matter of time before this case comes to the Supreme Court as well. When it does so, there seems little doubt that the central fifth vote will be moderate conservative Anthony Kennedy, who has written almost all of the Court's majority opinions on this issue, always in favor of gay rights. His notion of deciding on the basis of the "evolving standards of decency," looking toward international judicial decisions, which have been very pro–gay rights in Europe, and looking to the will of a society in which a majority of the young people under the age of 30, and 50 percent of the voting public in Pennsylvania, support gay rights, suggest that greater legal equality for gays and lesbians will be coming.

## Hispanic Americans

Immigrants to the United States from Mexico, Cuba, Puerto Rico, and other Spanish-speaking countries throughout Central and South America and the Caribbean islands have experienced forms of discrimination similar to those faced by African Americans, though to different degrees. Mexican Americans have been robbed of their land; attacked by the Ku Klux Klan and rioting mobs; excluded from labor unions; and discriminated against in employment, housing, and education. Puerto Ricans, Cubans, and Colombians have also suffered from discrimination and de facto housing segregation.

**QUICK REVIEW**

Hispanic Americans

- Now the nation's largest minority.
- Population is nearly 40 million people, half born in the United States, up nearly 100 percent since 1990.
- By the mid-21st century, Hispanic Americans will make up nearly one-third of the U.S. population.

In 1929, Mexican Americans founded the League of United Latin American Citizens (LULAC), seeking to gain more equal treatment in U.S. society. Then in the 1950s, they formed organizations that stressed electoral politics and attempted to reclaim lost lands in New Mexico. Perhaps the most famous aspect of the movement was the formation of a union of migrant Mexican American farmworkers under the leadership of Cesar Chavez. Through strikes, boycotts, pickets, and political action, the United Farm Workers drew national attention to the conditions endured by migrant farmworkers.

In the late 1960s, the Mexican American Legal Defense and Education Fund (MALDEF) used litigation and lobbying to campaign for integration, equal school financing, and full protection of voting rights and against discrimination in employment. The organization's success led to creation of the Puerto Rican Legal Defense Fund. Other Hispanic American groups, such as the National Council of La Raza, also have fought for increased voter registration and electoral participation.

Along with African Americans, Hispanic Americans benefited from Supreme Court rulings on segregation, the Civil Rights Act of 1964, and the Voting Rights Act of 1965. In *Katzenbach* v. *Morgan*, for example, the Court upheld a portion of the Voting Rights Act of 1965 that outlawed the use of an English literacy test in New York.[85] MALDEF and other groups helped extend the Voting Rights Act to protect Hispanic Americans and "other language" minorities.

## THINKING CRITICALLY

What should be the policy of the federal government relative to the millions of people who have been living illegally in this country? Is this a question of fairness and equality or a question of security, or both? And, thinking of the phrases on the Statue of Liberty, how open should the American borders be to immigrants?

The effort to achieve greater education equality for Hispanic and other minority children living in poor communities suffered a setback in 1973 in the case of *San Antonio Independent School District* v. *Rodriguez*.[86] The Court was unwilling to overturn the use of property taxes to finance state school systems, despite the resulting inequality in educational resources between wealthy and poor Texas communities. Nevertheless, several other state supreme courts subsequently used their state constitutions as a basis for requiring equal financing of education. Then, in 1982, the Court ordered that all children must be provided with schooling regardless of whether or not their parents were legal immigrants.[87]

Hispanic Americans continue to struggle against discrimination and poverty. The group is now the nation's largest minority, numbering more than 48 million people, or 15 percent of the population—an increase of more than 100 percent over the 22 million present in this country in 1990. With half having been born outside the United States, it is predicted that by the middle of this century, Hispanic Americans will make up nearly one-third of the U.S. population.[88] Thus, achievement of legal and actual equality for this group deserves high priority. Evidence of this demand was seen in June 2007, when the press learned about the Bush administration's list of possible Supreme Court appointees in case there was a retirement on the Court after the 2006–2007 term. Included on the list was Raoul Cantero, the first Hispanic to serve on the Florida Supreme Court and an appointment of then-governor Jeb Bush.[89]

Immigration reform was one of the topics in President Barack Obama's 2012 State of the Union address as Congress debated such topics of fast-tracking the quest for citizenship by undocumented aliens and the impact of easing immigration limits on national security. Congress' failure thus far to deal with these topics led to several states passing their own anti-immigration laws that would be tested by the Supreme Court later that year.

With the failure of the passage of President Bush's immigration bill in Congress in mid-2007, the future of civil rights for Hispanics remained in doubt. The bill was designed to make it easier for illegal immigrants to gain citizenship and would tie that process to an upgrade in border security to prevent future illegal immigrant migration to this country. When Senate Republicans refused to let the bill be considered, President Bush was forced to acknowledge defeat. Meanwhile, throughout the country there seemed to be an upsurge in nativist beliefs opposing illegal immigration. The city of Reading, Pennsylvania, and small towns in North Carolina continued to see an increase in Hispanic migration, but other cities—such as Hazleton and Allentown, Pennsylvania—passed local ordinances to prevent the hiring and housing of undocumented aliens.[90]

Fully aware that an overwhelming number of Hispanic voters supported him in the 2008 presidential election, Barack Obama appointed Hispanic Sonia Sotomayor to the Supreme Court in mid-2009. He also pressed Congress, without success, to add a new immigration bill to their legislature agenda that would make it easier for undocumented aliens to gain American citizenship.[91]

As you can see from the Approaching Contemporary Issues in Democracy feature, when the stalemated partisan Congress failed to act on this or any other immigration policy, states such as Arizona and Alabama took matters into their own hands. Relying on their Tenth Amendment "police powers" to protect their regions, they passed laws allowing the police and other state government officials to check the immigration papers of any people they suspected might not be in this country legally. In addition, they created enforcement powers against illegal immigrants seeking work, or those employing them. As a result, in states such as Alabama businesses that had employed illegal aliens and farms that had hired them to pick their crops found it difficult to run their businesses when people scared by the new laws fled the state. When the Supreme Court accepted an appeal of the Arizona law in December 2011 it would consider the question of which government had the responsibility for dealing with this issue, and whether illegal immigrants could be protected under the equal protection clause from official harassment based on their racial and ethnic heritage.

## Native Americans

The discrimination and segregation against Native Americans is well known but virtually ignored throughout America's history. Native American tribes have been removed from their land, treaties have been broken, and Native Americans have been denied the basic right of citizenship. In 1884, the Supreme Court ruled that Native Americans were not citizens of the United States and therefore were neither protected by the Fourteenth

# APPROACHING
## Contemporary Issues in Democracy

### State Anti-Immigration Laws and the Constitution

One of the consequences of the partisan stalemate, and dysfunctionality of the politically evenly balanced House and the filibuster-prone, Senate is that the national government has no working policy dealing with the tens of millions of illegal immigrants in this country and the untold numbers who are moving across the American border. Promises of legal reform are caught up in debates over human rights versus national security. As a result, some states believe that they are bearing the brunt of the impact of the influx of illegal aliens. As of December 2011, 6 states—Arizona, Alabama, Utah, Georgia, South Carolina, and Indiana—have passed laws attempting to deal with the presence of illegal immigrants, with 17 others considering similar laws. The states argue that under the Tenth Amendment, they have the ability under police powers to protect the "health, safety, morals, and public welfare" of their citizens and to regulate illegal immigrants even to the point of encouraging them to leave the state. The national government argues that this is an issue of both national security and foreign policy, which are pre-empted powers from the states because they involve issues that are in the sole delegated powers of the national government.

In December 2011, the Supreme Court accepted a case reviewing the highly restrictive policies of Arizona, seeking to resolve this dispute. Beyond making it a state crime for illegal immigrants to fail to register with the federal government, seek work or work in the state, and present probable cause of committing a crime that would make them deportable under federal law, one of the most controversial parts of the Arizona law is empowering the police to ask for citizenship papers, visas, or green cards of any persons whom have a "reasonable suspicion" might not be citizens. By adopting this search standard from the Fourth Amendment case law by the Supreme Court, effectively making the police the "reasonable person" who can choose whom to stop and confront, some argue that this provision empowers the police to "racially profile" people, asking for papers based on their ethnic background. The states argue that this is the only way to achieve their goal of protecting their citizens.

Arguing whether this law approaches democracy presents two very different dimensions. First, there is the government powers issue of whether this is an area for the federal government alone, or whether states, in the absence of federal action, would be able to pass laws under the Tenth Amendment to protect their citizens. Whose responsibility is it to promote order and stability in this area? In general, the Court has held that a policy such as this one, involving foreign policy and national security, should be left to the federal government, sometimes even in the absence of federal action. However, it may be possible, under the precedent of states conducting parallel investigations of the Communist threat in the 1950s and the city of New York having a parallel anti-terrorist police force, to supplement the work of the federal Homeland Security, to argue that states should be granted leeway here. For this reason, Arizona state officials are arguing that they are "cooperating" with the federal government, rather than taking over its function. The other issue is whether the Fourteenth Amendment's equal protection clause and the Fourth Amendment protect illegal immigrants from what may be ethnic and racial harassment. This is a question of promoting and preserving freedom and equality, and protecting minority against minority rights. While some argue that these are not citizens, and thus not protected by the Constitution, the wording of the Fourteenth Amendment says that no state shall "deny to any person within its jurisdiction the equal protection of the laws." So, because these noncitizens are present in this country, they might be able to argue that even illegal aliens should be free from warrantless "stop and frisks" by police based only on "reasonable suspicion." What do you think of this policy, and how can the two levels of government approach democracy here?

Amendment nor granted the right to vote.[92] In the early 1900s, Native Americans strove to attain both citizenship and tribal autonomy, while during the 1920s, they struggled against attempts to open reservations to miners' exploitation. Finally, in 1924, Congress passed the Indian Citizenship Act, which gave Native Americans the right to vote.

Native Americans have resisted various attempts to assimilate them into the mainstream culture of American society over the years. In the 1940s, the National Congress of American Indians formed to fight for education and legal aid. During the 1960s, Native Americans engaged in acts of civil disobedience such as delaying dam construction, occupying government offices, and holding sit-ins and other demonstrations to fight against discrimination. The American Indian Movement (AIM) occupied buildings and staged demonstrations, and in 1973, AIM played a major part in the well-publicized occupation of Wounded Knee on the Pine Ridge Reservation in South Dakota. Unfortunately, however, the Native American cause has yet to generate the support found for other minority groups.[93]

Native American descendants of Chief Spotted Elk and his tribe commemorate the 100th anniversary of the Battle of Wounded Knee, South Dakota, where on December 29, 1890, some 300 women, children, and elderly people were massacred by the U.S. Army's Seventh Regiment, George Armstrong Custer's old regiment, which was seeking revenge for "Custer's Last Stand" at the Battle of the Little Bighorn.

Native Americans face a challenge that most other minorities do not: They are divided into two movements with different aspirations. The ethnic movement shares the aspirations of other ethnic minorities to achieve equality in American society. In contrast, the separatist tribal movement seeks separate citizenship and a system of government based on the tribe, the Indian culture decimated by the growth of the United States. Whereas the ethnic movement wishes to participate in American democracy, the tribal movement seeks to create its own concept of democracy, removed from a democratic government that, in the past, too often failed to live up to its treaties.

Occasionally, there have been some successes for Native Americans. In recent years, various tribes have used state law exemptions to create highly profitable gambling enterprises on reservation lands, thus raising money for their communities and creating political clout. In December 2009, the federal government settled a 13-year-old, $3.4 billion lawsuit compensating Native Americans for mismanagement of tribal lands held in trust by the Department of the Interior. Still, equality remains elusive as the Native American population remains among the poorest and least represented in government in the nation.

# EMERGING MINORITY GROUPS SEEK PROMINENCE

## Americans with Disabilities

14.9 *What success have other minority groups—such as Hispanic Americans, Native Americans, Americans with disabilities, and gays and lesbians—had in achieving equal rights?*

Unlike other minority groups, Americans with disabilities, who by some definitions now number 43 million, have been extremely successful in persuading Congress to pass legislation barring discrimination against them. However, since 1999, Supreme Court rulings have been making it more and more difficult for these people to obtain federal government protection.

In 1948, likely motivated by the memory of the wheelchair-bound late president, Franklin D. Roosevelt, Congress passed a law prohibiting discrimination against the physically handicapped in the civil service. The 1968 Architectural Barriers Act required that all buildings constructed with federal money or leased by the federal government be made accessible to the handicapped. Congress acted again in 1973, when it mandated that federal contractors and programs that received federal funds adopt policies of nondiscrimination and affirmative action for the disabled. When Congress passed the Civil Rights Restoration Act of 1988, it barred any institution that discriminated on the basis of race, sex, age, or disability from receiving federal funds.

Despite passage of these and other statutes that protect the rights of people who are disabled, Americans with disabilities continue to be deprived of many basic civil

### QUICK REVIEW

Americans with Disabilities Act (ADA)

- Firms with more than 25 employees are barred from discriminating against individuals with disabilities.
- Companies are required to make "reasonable accommodations" for employees who are disabled.
- Laws that bar unlawful discrimination against people with disabilities are being interpreted by the Court to say that government and industry must make exceptions in favor of those groups.

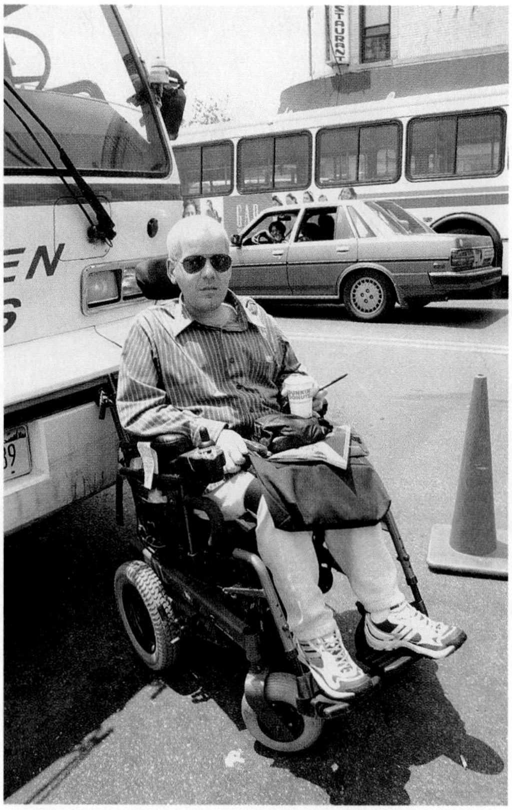

Seeking to protest the lack of access to some New York City buses for wheelchair-bound passengers, Anthony Trocchia led a spontaneous "wheel-in" to block the bus's progress. When the bus was ordered by police to leave in reverse, other wheelchair-bound activists blocked the back of the bus as well.

rights. For example, they still face discrimination by private employers and establishments. Some progress occurred in 1990, when Congress passed the Americans with Disabilities Act (ADA). Under the provisions of this act, firms with more than 25 employees are barred from discriminating against individuals with disabilities in hiring or promotion. In addition, companies must make "reasonable accommodations" for employees with disabilities, such as providing readers for blind workers or wider doors for those in wheelchairs. Interestingly, the Court is interpreting these laws that bar unlawful discrimination against people with disabilities as saying that government and industry must make exceptions in favor of those groups. The law thus became the largest and most expensive affirmative action program in the nation. Recent studies have shown, however, that this law rarely helps people who are disabled seeking jobs. Instead, more than one-third of the complainants are using it to address such relatively minor problems as back pain, psychological stress, and substance abuse.[94]

As we discussed in Chapter 3, the Supreme Court in 1999 ruled in five separate cases that the ADA would have a much narrower reach than many expected. Noting that Congress intended to reach 43 million people with the law, the Court ruled that this law did not apply to people with correctable impairments, such as high blood pressure or bad eyesight, which would have expanded the law's influence to 160 million people. As a result, attorneys seeking disabilities protection will now turn to the states, such as California, for greater protection.[95] In the 2001–2002 term, the Court continued the states' rights direction of its rulings by deciding against litigants with disabilities who were seeking federal judicial protection in four separate cases. Among these decisions, the Court ruled that states are constitutionally immune from lawsuits for damages under the ADA. The Court ruled that Congress had not sufficiently demonstrated in the legislative record for the law that states discriminated against people with disabilities, and that Congress had no power to require states to implement such a law.[96]

This issue was revisited in 2004 after a wheelchair-bound criminal defendant, George Lane, was forced to crawl up two flights of stairs to reach a courtroom on the second floor because the building had no elevator. Lane and a certified court reporter, Beverly Jones, who is similarly disabled, sued the state of Tennessee under Title II of the Americans with Disabilities Act, arguing that parts of the Tennessee courthouse were inaccessible to them. Although the state claimed immunity from such suits under the Eleventh Amendment, the Supreme Court ruled 5–4 that Congress had the power to compel states to "take reasonable measures to remove architectural and other barriers to accessibility" for public services such as the state court system.[97] Because Tennessee had failed to do so, citizens seeking, and being denied, access to these facilities could sue for damages.

## The Elderly

Inevitably, more minority groups that face discrimination will demand greater equality. One such group is the elderly. With an ever-increasing percentage of Americans in the oldest age groups as Baby Boomers have begun to retire, demands will increase for protection of the civil rights of elderly persons. Although the Age Discrimination in Employment Act (ADEA) covers many of the issues experienced by this group, new challenges will undoubtedly arise and will be pressed on the government by the 30 million-member AARP. In 2000, this group lost ground because of a narrow 5–4 Supreme Court ruling that Congress lacked the power to make state governments liable to federal lawsuits brought under the Age Discrimination in Employment Act to remedy discrimination against older workers.[98] The new political battleground for this group will be the inevitable efforts to find ways to balance the future national budgets by cutting entitlement programs for this group, such as Social Security and Medicare.

# CIVIL RIGHTS AND THE WAR ON TERRORISM

14.10 *How has the war on terror affected the civil rights in the 21st century?*

Facing discrimination demands greater equality, but the immediate question facing the nation is whether or not it can preserve the civil rights of any individual under investigation during a time of crisis. Although Chapter 13 considered how to preserve legal and trial safeguards for people arrested in the war on terrorism, what about those under investigation simply because of their ethnic background?

Perhaps the greatest test of America's approach to democracy with respect to civil rights since September 11, 2001, is the issue of ethnic profiling in conducting antiterrorism investigations, airport searches, immigration interviews, and secret detentions of Muslim men who come from nations where the al Qaeda network is considered active. Within days after the attacks on the World Trade Center and the Pentagon, more than 1,200 Muslim men were arrested on minor immigration violations, such as overstaying their visas, and jailed without legal representation or their names being released. The passage of the USA Patriot Act later allowed for this kind of detention of others. Two months after the attack, nearly 5,000 Arab men were requested to "voluntarily" present themselves for interviews by Justice Department and Immigration and Naturalization Service representatives. Nearly 2,500 of the men could not be found, and these interviews, which produced fewer than two dozen arrests, revealed minimal information. Still, the Justice Department was encouraged by the level of cooperation of those interviewed and the nature of the information it gathered.

So early in 2002, over the objections of civil rights groups who feared that these interviews carried with them the dual risks of racial profiling and potential deportation, the government requested that another 3,000 visitors present themselves for interviews. Years of dealing with charges of racial profiling in New Jersey, California, and wherever police have used their discretion in stopping and questioning African Americans now took a twist as authorities in airports and mass transportation centers began targeting Arab Americans, persons of Arab descent, and Arab visitors for questioning, searching, and even detention. Although authorities tried to use random search techniques, thousands of complaints were lodged nationwide concerning racial profiling. Profiled individuals were forced to leave planes, one of them a Secret Service agent for President Bush, because of pilots', flight attendants', or even passengers' fears about traveling with them.[99]

These actions eventually led to challenges in federal court. Realizing that by mid-February 2002 more than 300 men were still detained in federal prisons without legal representation, many of them in northern New Jersey, a New Jersey state judge set a deadline for release of their names. The Immigration and Naturalization Service ordered the state and local governments not to release the names, saying that the move could endanger both national security and the welfare of those being detained. By the middle of April, a civil rights group sued the federal government on the detainees' behalf, alleging that hundreds of Muslim men were being held in prison on minor immigration violations, being subjected to harsh treatment, and not receiving hearings to determine their legal status. When the case reached District Court Judge Gladys Kessler in the District of Columbia in August 2002, she ordered the names of these prisoners released. "The requirement that arrest books be open to the public is to prevent any 'secret arrests,' a concept odious to a democratic society."[100] In short, this practice receded from, rather than approached, democracy. Despite this ruling, the U.S. government continued to refuse to release the names of prisoners.

By October 2002, a few prisoners deemed to have little intelligence value were released from the Guantanamo Bay, Cuba, holding facility. Still, one controversial government practice was the decision to seal the records of hundreds of deportation hearings if they were deemed of "special interest" after the September 11 attacks. The Sixth Circuit Court of Appeals ruled the Bush administration's policy of holding secret deportation hearings unconstitutional. "Open proceedings, with a vigorous and scrutinizing press, serve to ensure the durability of our democracy," ruled the Sixth Circuit judges, who relied on the First Amendment's right of access to government proceedings.[101] By mid-2004, the Supreme Court made clear that the Guantanamo Bay facility was subject to the federal court's process of review, and the prisoners within it, even those who were not American citizens, should not be stripped of their legal rights. Justice Sandra Day O'Connor made this clear when she wrote

> *A state of war is not a blank check for the President when it comes to the rights of the Nation's citizens. . . . Whatever power the United States Constitution envisions for the Executive in its exchanges with other nations or with enemy organizations in times of conflict, it most assuredly envisions a role for all three branches when individual liberties are at stake. . . . Likewise, unless Congress acts to suspend it, the Great Writ of habeas corpus allows the Judicial Branch to play a necessary role in maintaining this delicate balance of governance, serving as an important judicial check on the Executive's discretion in the realm of detentions.*[102]

To the surprise of many, at the end of its 2006–2007 term, the Supreme Court agreed to review whether detainees would be able to challenge their indefinite confinement in federal court. A 5–4 majority, led by swing justice Anthony Kennedy, ruled that prisoners being held in this system retain the right of habeas corpus to bring their cases seeking trial and release into federal courts and denying Congress the power to suspend that writ.[103] With President Obama's executive order on January 22, 2009, to close Camp XRay at Guantanamo, and 229 prisoners still being detained there, the political battle in 2009 became whether to release some of these prisoners and where to imprison those who remained in the system.[104]

As other lawsuits work their way through the courts, the question is whether the government can show that the benefits to the security of the nation of such law enforcement supercedes the civil rights of the people under investigation. At the fore will be the lessons learned from the civil rights fights of African Americans and women, the 1940s Japanese internment policy, and the "red scare" period in the 1950s, as the federal courts and the American people decide the nature of civil rights in times of crisis. In the end, the American people will need to determine whether the actions taken to preserve security will preserve the democratic goals of the nation or lead instead to a nation that no longer approaches the very democratic vision that it claims to be seeking.

Exhibit A that America in 2009 still had a long way to go on its approach to democracy in civil rights. Demonstrators hold up signs in front of the Valley Swim Club in Huntingdon Valley, Pennsylvania, near Philadelphia, after the club blocked a group of minority children from joining weekly swims at the pool, citing issues such as overcrowding of the pool, despite the fact that the Creative Steps day camp had paid its deposit and other non-minority youth groups had been allowed to swim there.

## CIVIL RIGHTS IN THE 21ST CENTURY

With the Supreme Court now consistently ruling against racial and gender discrimination cases, civil and women's rights groups may have to look to Congress, interest groups, and other institutions to remedy the problems that they see in society. After 200 years of civil rights battles, how much farther must the nation go to achieve full equality for all Americans? When the Supreme Court puts Congress on notice that the 1965 Voting Rights Act is in jeopardy of being declared unconstitutional; when eminent African American Harvard professor Henry Louis Gates is arrested by the local Cambridge police for "disorderly conduct" in his own home; and when young African American children are banned from a private suburban Philadelphia swim club, with the Pennsylvania civil rights commission issuing a finding in September 2009 that this was motivated by racial discrimination, it is clear that America still has a long way to go in civil rights. Clearly, the disputes over affirmative action, women's rights, and the war on terrorism illustrate that the struggle goes on. Another set of questions deals with just how inclusive society should be in approaching democracy.

We have seen that, at times civil rights protection has fallen to the Supreme Court, at other times to the Congress, and at still other times to the president. Throughout the struggle, the force behind the effort to achieve equal rights has been the "people power" of the civil rights movement, the women's movement, and others. Yet much work remains. America will continue to approach democracy by guaranteeing legal and actual rights, but the road will not be a straight or smooth one.

## Summary

**14.1** *How successfully do the Declaration of Independence and the Constitution promise equality in American society?*

- Discrimination is unequal treatment based on race, ethnicity, gender, and other distinctions. The primary means for achieving equal treatment is ensuring full protection of civil rights, constitutionally guaranteed rights that government may not arbitrarily remove. Although the Declaration of Independence promises that "all men are created equal" and that they shall enjoy "life, liberty, and the pursuit of happiness," the framers made clear that it did not cover the slaves when they struck that paragraph from Jefferson's draft. In the Constitution, the framers dodged the slavery question by counting slaves as only three-fifths of Caucasians for the purpose of congressional districting, not limiting the slave trade until 1808, and failing to protect the rights of runaway slaves.
- Equality before the law, or de jure equality, forbids legally mandated obstacles to equal treatment. Actual equality, or de facto equality, refers to results—the actual conditions of people's lives.

**14.2** *How and why was legal equality not established in the late 19th century?*

- The Supreme Court helped to bring on the Civil War in 1857 by upholding slavery in the *Dred Scott* case. Although black slaves were freed during the Civil War, they had no legally protected civil rights. By the end of the 19th century, the races were strictly segregated by Jim Crow laws, and in *Plessy* v. *Ferguson,* the Supreme Court ruled that separate but equal facilities did not violate the Fourteenth Amendment. Although African Americans had the right to vote, state voting laws contained many loopholes that effectively disfranchised blacks. In the early decades of the 20th century, the NAACP won several lawsuits that advanced the cause of racial equality.

**14.3** *How was the legal equality promised by the government in the early to mid-20th century accomplished by the judicial branch?*

- During and after World War II, the White House issued executive orders prohibiting discrimination in the defense business and the military. The NAACP led the battle to desegregate the public schools, which culminated in the historic 1954 *Brown* v. *Board of Education of Topeka, Kansas,* ruling that struck down the separate but equal doctrine. A year later, the Court promised to implement this decision "with all deliberate speed."

**14.4** *Why did it take so long to implement the desegregation promise of* Brown v. Board of Education *and later move on to desegregating society?*

- Beginning with the Montgomery bus boycott in 1955, the civil rights movement employed techniques such as boycotts, protest marches, and sit-ins to publicly demonstrate the injustice of unequal treatment based on race. President Eisenhower did send troops in 1957 to Little Rock, Arkansas, to integrate Central High School. The Supreme Court was supportive. And President John F. Kennedy was privately supportive, but less aggressively helpful publicly. There was little concerted effort, though, to help those protesting for more equality until after Kennedy's death and President Lyndon Baines Johnson was able to convert the grief over that assassination into action for civil rights.

**14.5** *How were the Supreme Court cases and laws to realize desegregation in American society finally realized—and then threatened again?*

- During the 1960s, Congress passed several laws designed to eliminate discrimination, including the Civil Rights Act of 1964 (which focused on discrimination in public accommodations, voter registration, and employment), the Voting Rights Act of 1965, and the Civil Rights Act of 1968, which focused on discrimination in housing. Several cases decided by the Supreme Court during this period dealt with the specific means used to desegregate schools. In recent years, the Roberts Court has been moving to limit the reach of the *Brown* case—by ruling efforts by public magnet schools in Seattle and Louisville to achieve racial balance in the school system unconstitutional.

**14.6** *How have affirmative action programs been created, and do they achieve equality in America?*

- Affirmative action programs attempt to improve the chances of minority applicants for jobs, housing, employment, and graduate admissions by giving them a slight advantage over white applicants with similar qualifications. Such programs seek to increase equality but can create temporary inequalities in the process and, therefore, are controversial. Underlying the controversy is a disagreement over the meaning of actual equality; some believe that the goal should be equality of opportunity, whereas others believe that the nation should strive for equality of result.
- The Reagan administration challenged many of the nation's civil rights policies, claiming that the various Civil Rights Acts prohibited all racial and sexual discrimination, including discrimination against white males. In a series of cases, the Supreme Court set specific limits on the use of affirmative action. In recent years, the Rehnquist Court and especially the Roberts Court have voted 5–4 against affirmative action programs, most recently in the 2009 New Haven firefighters' case.

**14.7** *How did the movement for women's rights begin in America?*

- The movement for women's rights began with the Declaration of Sentiments drawn up at a convention held in Seneca Falls, New York, in 1848. Progress toward equality was slow and uneven throughout the next several decades; women gained control over their property but could not vote. Not until 1920 did the Nineteenth Amendment to the Constitution grant women the right of suffrage.

- In response to complaints of sex discrimination in education and employment, Congress passed the Equal Pay Act of 1963, which required equal pay for equal work. The Civil Rights Act of 1964 also barred discrimination on the basis of sex. However, efforts failed to pass the Equal Rights Amendment to the Constitution, which would have given full protection to the civil rights of women.

14.8 *What role has the Supreme Court played in establishing, protecting, and later limiting women's rights, and the rights of gays and lesbians?*

- In the 1970s, efforts to gain equal protection for women's rights turned to the courts and focused on the standard used to determine whether a state law is constitutional. Supreme Court decisions gradually shifted from favoring a reasonableness test, which upheld a law if the state could provide an acceptable rationale for the law, to favoring a heightened scrutiny test, in which laws that classify people according to their sex must serve important governmental objectives and be substantially related to the achievement of those objectives. In recent years, the Rehnquist and Roberts Courts moved to restrict women's rights over the vociferous objections of Justice Ruth Bader Ginsburg.
- The Supreme Court ruled in 1987 that gays and lesbians did not have the right to personal autonomy privacy for same-sex intimate behavior. After the pivotal justice in that case, Lewis Powell, was replaced by the more libertarian Anthony Kennedy, the Court began a 17 year process of ruling in favor of gay rights until, in 2003, this case was reversed. Since that time, six states, including New York, have permitted gay marriages, with dozens more opposing it. Several cases are on their way to the Supreme Court testing the constitutionality both of the right of states to ban gay marriages and the right of the federal government to do the same while permitting states to ignore the "Full Faith and Credit" guarantee of the Constitution for people seeking to transport their rights as same sex couples from states which support them to states that do not.

14.9 *What success have other minority groups—such as Hispanic Americans, Native Americans, Americans with disabilities, and the elderly—had in achieving equal rights?*

- Hispanic Americans have made considerable progress toward equal treatment, particularly in the area of voting rights, but they continue to struggle against discrimination and poverty. Native Americans also have organized to demand the basic rights of citizenship and to fight against discrimination. In contrast to these and other minority groups, Americans with disabilities have been extremely successful in persuading Congress to pass legislation barring discrimination against them. The elderly have had their considerable success in the courts, too, both state and federal.

14.10 *How has the war on terror affected the civil rights in the 21st century?*

- The ongoing investigation in the war on terrorism has raised the question of racial profiling of people of Middle Eastern descent. Although the government has tried to use random searches to avoid complaints, future litigation must determine if the proper balance is maintained between civil rights and national security. The federal courts have ruled unconstitutional the Bush administration's practice of holding secret deportation hearings. It remains to be seen what impact President Obama's new policies will have, such as the closing of the Guantanamo Bay prison.

## Key Terms

affirmative action, 459
black codes, 448
boycott, 453
civil disobedience, 453
de facto equality, 446
de jure equality, 446
desegregation, 451
equality of opportunity, 459
equality of result, 459
freedom riders, 453
heightened scrutiny test, 469
integration, 452
Jim Crow laws, 449
peonage, 451
poll tax, 450
protest march, 453
quota programs, 459
sexism, 467
sit-in, 453
state action, 449
strict scrutiny test, 468
suffrage, 448
test of reasonableness, 468
unfair discrimination, 446

## Test Yourself Chapter 14

**1.** The difference between de jure equality and de facto equality is
a. the difference between equality established by a jury and equality established by social scientists.
b. the difference between legal equality and actual equality.
c. the difference between actual equality and legal equality.
d. There is no difference.

**2.** What did the Constitution do about slavery?
a. It banned slavery in the South.
b. It banned the slave trade a decade later.
c. It did nothing about slavery but banned slave trade in 1808.
d. It did not mention slavery.

**3.** The *Dred Scott* case
a. banned slavery.
b. declared that African Americans could not sue because they were not citizens.
c. freed slaves.
d. ruled that the Missouri Compromise was constitutional.

**4.** Laws in the South that restricted the civil rights of African Americans and continued oppressive labor practices were called
a. slavery codes.
b. black codes.
c. plantation codes.
d. oppressive codes.

**5.** What does the Fourteenth Amendment of the Constitution permit the Court to do with respect to personal discrimination?
a. It can ban only discrimination that is linked to state action under the color of law.
b. It bans all discrimination.
c. It bans no discrimination.
d. None of the above.

**6.** How did southern states limit voting rights of African Americans?
a. A poll tax.
b. Literacy tests.
c. Grandfather clauses.
d. All of the above.

**7.** The major rule of *Plessy* v. *Ferguson* in 1896 with respect to the separation of the races was
a. separate but unequal.
b. separate but equal.
c. separate but no inequality.
d. discrimination is inherently unequal.

**8.** Which area of American life was the first to be desegregated?
a. Public schools.
b. Hotel accommodations.
c. The military.
d. Movie houses.

**9.** After *Brown* v. *Board of Education,* which of the following was *not* true?
a. Schools were to be integrated.
b. Segregated schools were not considered inherently unequal.
c. Schools must be desegregated "with all deliberate speed."
d. All are true.

**10.** Who was the attorney who won many desegregation cases working with the NAACP Legal Defense Fund?
a. Martin Luther King Jr.
b. Kenneth Clark.
c. Thurgood Marshall.
d. Charles Houston.

**11.** In 1957, the Supreme Court and President Dwight Eisenhower forced the state government to integrate public schools in
a. Little Rock, Arkansas.
b. Atlanta, George.
c. Austin, Texas.
d. Tuscaloosa, Alabama.

**12.** Influential forms of protest in the 1960s were
a. boycotts.
b. sit-ins.
c. freedom riders.
d. All of the above.

**13.** Which president was the most influential in achieving racial integration?
a. Dwight Eisenhower.
b. John F. Kennedy.
c. Lyndon Johnson.
d. Richard Nixon.

**14.** What part of the Constitution allowed the federal government to begin to integrate even personal discrimination among and between individuals?
a. The Fourteenth Amendment due process clause.
b. The Fourteenth Amendment equal protection clause.
c. The interstate commerce clause.
d. The Fifth Amendment due process clause.

**15.** What type of affirmative action programs were ruled unconstitutional in the *Bakke* case?
a. "Plus factor" programs.
b. Quota programs.
c. Programs that discriminated on behalf of minorities.
d. All are constitutional.

**16.** After the two University of Michigan affirmative action cases, what can schools do to achieve racial balance?
a. They cannot achieve racial balance.
b. They can achieve racial balance if the balance in the school does not match the balance in society.
c. They can achieve racial balance if the school itself has discriminated in the past.
d. They can achieve racial balance by a "critical mass" of minority students, but they cannot rely on specific number in their admissions profile.

**17.** The use of "magnet schools" in public schools as an affirmative action device is
a. unconstitutional.
b. constitutional in some cases when the area is racially unbalanced.
c. constitutional in all cases.
d. None of the above.

**18.** Which of the following was *not* a leader of the women's civil rights movement?
a. Susan B. Anthony.
b. Elizabeth Cady Stanton.
c. Alice B. Toklas.
d. Alice Paul.

**19.** What is the test used by the Supreme Court to judge women's rights?
a. Reasonableness.
b. Intermediate scrutiny.
c. Strict scrutiny.
d. No scrutiny.

**20.** The Supreme Court case that failed to equalize education for minority groups using property tax reform is
a. *Brown* v. *Board of Education.*
b. *San Antonio* v. *Rodriquez.*
c. *Smith* v. *Marquez.*
d. *Pauley* v. *D'Antonio.*

**ANSWERS**
**1.** b, **2.** c, **3.** b, **4.** b, **5.** a, **6.** d, **7.** b, **8.** c, **9.** a, **10.** c, **11.** a,
**12.** d, **13.** c, **14.** c, **15.** a, **16.** d, **17.** a, **18.** c, **19.** b, **20.** b

# Domestic and Economic Policy

15

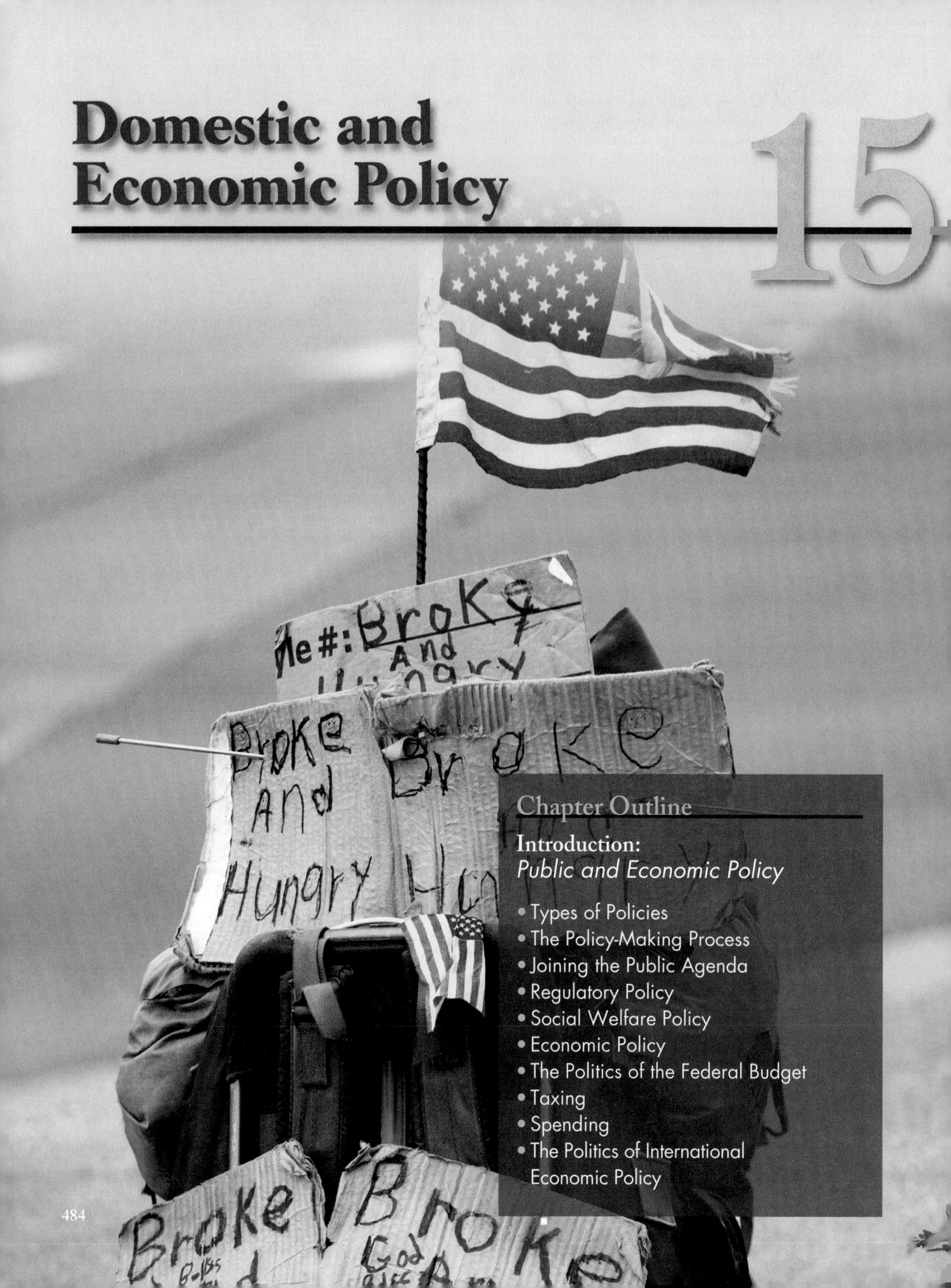


## Chapter Outline

**Introduction:**
*Public and Economic Policy*

- Types of Policies
- The Policy-Making Process
- Joining the Public Agenda
- Regulatory Policy
- Social Welfare Policy
- Economic Policy
- The Politics of the Federal Budget
- Taxing
- Spending
- The Politics of International Economic Policy

## Learning Objectives

15.1 What is public policy?
15.2 What are the government's aims in enacting public policy?
15.3 What is the life-cycle theory of policy making?
15.4 What is the path a policy takes from getting on the public agenda through to termination or continuation?
15.5 What types of regulatory activities does the government engage in?
15.6 What is the history of social welfare policy?
15.7 What role does government play in regulating the economy?
15.8 How is the budget prepared?
15.9 What are the sources of government revenue?
15.10 What is the difference between discretionary spending and mandatory spending?
15.11 How has increasing globalization affected domestic economic policy?

# INTRODUCTION

## PUBLIC AND ECONOMIC POLICY

15.1 *What is public policy?*

**Public policies** are the decisions, actions, and commitments of government. They are the means by which government attempts to solve problems and make life easier and safer for its citizens. These policy areas include health care, the environment, the jobless rate, and Social Security, to name just a few of today's hot-button topics. Regulation of the national economy is also one of the most crucial roles for modern government. This responsibility is important not only for the benefits it provides specific corporations and entrepreneurs but also because a stable, growing economy provides an environment for a healthy democratic society.

In this chapter we begin by describing the policy-making process. We then consider the politics of policy making and explore recent trends in American public policy, asking if these policies are leading in an increasingly democratic direction. Finally, we look at the world of taxing and spending policy to see how politics and economics are especially intertwined.

## TYPES OF POLICIES

15.2 *What are the government's aims in enacting public policy?*

Public policies enacted by the national government have four aims:

1. To regulate key industries and aspects of American life—such as the tobacco industry, home loans, investment banking, immigration, or the meatpacking industry—in the interest of public safety.
2. To protect Americans from actual or potential enemies at home and abroad by providing a powerful national defense.
3. To encourage the accomplishment of important social goals by providing such programs as Head Start for preschool children, Pell grants for college students, and health-care coverage for all.
4. To assist a wide range of American citizens such as farmers (through grain subsidies), low-income families (through Temporary Assistance for Needy Families), and state and local governments (through highway construction funds).

Public policy can be divided into two major categories: regulatory policy and social welfare policy. **Regulatory policy** involves use of federal powers to supervise the

**public policies**
The decisions, actions, and commitments of government.

**regulatory policy**
Policy that involves the use of police powers by the federal government to supervise the conduct of individuals, businesses, and other governmental agencies.

**social welfare policy**
Policy that uses positive incentives (cash assistance, stipends, entitlements, grants, etc.) to promote or encourage basic social and economic fairness.

conduct of individuals, businesses, and other governmental agencies. It is essentially a set of *negative incentives* the government establishes to prevent certain kinds of behavior. For this reason, regulatory policy often focuses on social "villains"—industrial polluters, crooked savings and loan executives on Wall Street, and unscrupulous railroad barons and tobacco companies.[1] For example, President Obama's Family Smoking Prevention and Tobacco Control Act, much of which went into effect in June 2010, seeks to curb the ability of tobacco companies to market products to children with new regulations on how tobacco products are sold and marketed. One piece of the Tobacco Control Act requires cigarette makers to add graphic images to the warning labels on their product by October 2012. Big Tobacco is suing the federal government over this regulation, arguing that the requirement violates the corporation's right to free speech. In another example prior to the financial crisis, there was no regulatory body looking across the financial system as a whole, identifying weaknesses, coordinating among agencies, and asking what might go wrong. To that end, the Obama administration proposed a Financial Services Oversight Council, composed of the heads of each of the main financial regulatory agencies as well as a new Consumer Financial Protection Agency for overseeing banks and nonbanks alike.[2]

In contrast to regulatory policy, **social welfare policy** uses *positive incentives*—cash assistance, stipends, entitlements, grants—to promote or encourage basic social fairness. Long-standing American social welfare objectives include aiding disadvantaged groups, including people living below the poverty line; older Americans; people of color; women; military veterans; and people who are educationally, emotionally, or physically challenged. It's about justice and the fundamental democratic value of equality. This was President Obama's message when he signed the Lilly Ledbetter Fair Pay Act, which makes it easier for people to get the pay they deserve—regardless of their gender, race, or age. "Ultimately, equal pay isn't just an economic issue for millions of Americans and their families, it's a question of who we are—and whether we're truly living up to our fundamental ideals," President Obama said.[3]

# THE POLICY-MAKING PROCESS

15.3 *What is the life-cycle theory of policy making?*

Policy scholars have developed several process models that try to capture the flavor and substance of policy making. One such model views the policy-making process as a *life cycle.* This model is especially useful in analyzing how an issue can be moved into the spotlight of the national agenda. These concepts of a public policy agenda and a policy life cycle are part of an approach to studying public policy that centers on the *process* by which the agenda of public policy is established. It seeks to discover how we come to view certain conditions, events, or situations as political problems requiring a policy response from government.[4]

Several factors are responsible for making public policy a highly political process. They include the fragmentation created by a federal system of government; temporary political alliances (*logrolling*); policies that benefit particular states or districts (*pork barrel legislation*); informal relationships among legislative committees, executive agencies, and interest groups (*iron triangles*); and *issue networks,* in which large numbers of participants take an active interest in a particular policy.

The policy life cycle consists of 11 steps or stages, which can be illustrated by utilizing the evolution of federal funding for AIDS research.[5]

## The Life Cycle of Policy Making

1. **Redefinition of a public or private "condition" as a public "problem."** In the case of the AIDS crisis—involving a disease that, in the United States, mostly affected certain population subgroups the Reagan administration considered largely unsupportive—six years passed after information surfaced regarding the

The face of basketball hall-of-famer Earvin "Magic" Johnson appears on a billboard with the message, "For me, staying healthy with HIV is about a few basic things: a positive attitude, partnering with my doctor, taking my medicine every day." AIDS is reportedly a leading cause of death for blacks between the ages of 24 and 44. One in 40 black men and 1 in 70 black women are believed to be HIV-positive today.

disease's appearance in the United States before it was defined as a problem to be addressed by public policy.

2. **Placement of the problem on the national policy agenda.** In the case of AIDS, this did not happen until the death of President Ronald Reagan's close friend, Rock Hudson.
3. **Emergence of the problem as a "public issue" requiring government action.** Only when Surgeon General C. Everett Koop announced that the problem was widespread did AIDS become a public issue. Prior to this, Reagan administration budget cutters were disinclined to allocate funds to fight a disease they believed afflicted only drug users, Haitian immigrants, and the gay community.
4. **Formulation of a public policy response, usually followed by a pledge of action.** President Reagan announced that he would appoint a commission to study the epidemic.
5. **One or more reformulations of the proposed policy.** Every year the question of how much funding would be provided for AIDS research led to a policy reformulation.
6. **Placement of the proposed policy on the formal agenda of government.** Despite the Reagan administration's unwillingness to push for major funding for AIDS research, the public, the press, and Congress would not let the issue die.
7. **Enactment of part or all of the proposed policy.** In 1986, Surgeon General C. Everett Koop released a report that made AIDS the key item on the administration's legislative agenda.
8. **Implementation of the policy.** Funding for AIDS research continued to grow. The government was now committed to fighting the disease—some six years following the first article on the mysterious disease.
9. **Effects of policy implementation.** Activist groups ranging from coalitions of celebrities to congressional members emerged to help raise funds.
10. **Evaluation of policy impact.** Although the government continues to fund AIDS research at high levels, the disease remains the primary cause of death for men between the ages of 25 and 45 in cities throughout the United States.
11. **Termination or continued implementation and evaluation of the policy.** Successfully attacking the HIV/AIDS epidemic requires a full-scale approach, which includes funding for prevention, research, housing, and care. In April 2009, President Obama launched a five-year, $45 million AIDS communication campaign to promote awareness.[6] September 18, 2011, marked the fourth National HIV/AIDS and Aging Awareness Day and the National Institutes of Health's Office of AIDS Research observed the occasion by noting that through research, understanding, and support, "the United States will become a place where new HIV infections are rare and when they do occur, every person . . . will have unfettered access to high quality, life-extending care, free from stigma and discrimination."[7]

## THINKING CRITICALLY

What role does ideology play in the life-cycle theory of policy making? At what steps does it have its biggest impact?

**policy elites**
Members of Congress, the president, Supreme Court justices, cabinet officers, heads of key agencies and departments, leading editorial writers, and influential columnists and commentators.

**public agenda**
The set of topics that concern policy elites, the general public, or both.

**formal agenda**
The policies actually scheduled for debate and potential adoption by Congress, the president, the Supreme Court, or executive departments and agencies.

**triggering mechanism**
A critical development that converts a routine problem into a widely shared, negative public response.

**policy entrepreneurs**
Leaders who invest in, and who create the conditions for, a potential group to become an actual interest group. Ralph Nader stands as a classic example of a policy entrepreneur.

## QUICK REVIEW

Formulating Policy

- Policy is constructed, debated, and put into effect by all branches of the federal government.
- Congress formulates and reformulates policy in committees and subcommittees and during the process of debate and amendment in the House and Senate.
- Courts formulate and reformulate public policy by adopting a policy position.
- Government agencies formulate policy by issuing regulations explaining how the agency will enforce and interpret a new law.

# JOINING THE PUBLIC AGENDA

15.4 *What is the path a policy takes from getting on the public agenda through to termination or continuation?*

Why do certain issues and not others become subjects for governmental action? That is, how do they join the agenda of the political world? Before they can enter the policy-making process, potential subjects of public policy must undergo a radical redefinition in the eyes of **policy elites**—members of Congress, the president, Supreme Court justices, cabinet officers, heads of key agencies and departments, leading editorial writers, and influential columnists and commentators. Such a redefinition changes the way the topic is viewed and places it on the **public agenda,** the set of topics of concern to policy elites, the general public, or both.

The public agenda can be viewed as the informal agenda of government. It should not be confused with the **formal agenda**—that is, policies actually scheduled for debate and potential adoption by Congress, the president, the Supreme Court, or executive departments and agencies. For example, immigration reform has been on the public agenda for quite some time, but only recently have both parties and the White House begun to address the need for comprehensive legislation that will create a path to citizenship for those here illegally.

**From Problems to Issues** How do social concerns become translated or redefined into matters important enough to be placed on the public agenda? The distinction between *problems* and *conditions* is critical for understanding public policy making. Citizens and policy makers have often been willing to live with various *social conditions*—pollution, high crime rates, or poverty rates—as long as they do not see those conditions as immediate threats to safety or financial security. When a condition is redefined as a problem, however, we expect the government to do something about it.

Social conditions become redefined as problems that require governmental policy responses in two key ways. First, a dramatic event may serve as a **triggering mechanism.** A triggering mechanism is a critical development that converts a routine problem into a widely shared, negative public response. It can transform a *condition* into a *problem* in the minds of the American public and political leadership alike. The tragic killings at Columbine High School triggered a national debate on gun control, which was reignited by the bloodshed at the Virginia Tech campus. The economic crisis of 2008–2009 led to debate about credit card fine print, fees, and staggering interest rate hikes, resulting in the Credit Card Accountability, Responsibility and Disclosure Act of 2009.[8] As a result of the role of Wall Street in the economic meltdown of 2008, President Obama signed into law the Dodd-Frank Wall Street Reform Act in July 2010. Dodd-Frank took steps to increase regulation of the financial markets "to promote the financial stability of the United States by improving accountability and transparency in the financial system, to end 'too big to fail,' to protect the American taxpayer by ending bailouts, to protect consumers from abusive financial services practices."[9]

A potential policy can also reach the public agenda through the activities of **policy entrepreneurs,** individuals or groups instrumental in "selling" a program or policy to a policy-making body. American political history offers many examples of policy entrepreneurs who succeeded in placing a potential policy issue on the public agenda. In the 1950s and 1960s, Martin Luther King Jr., the Congress on Racial Equality, the Southern Christian Leadership Conference, the Student Non-Violent Coordinating Committee, and the National Association for the Advancement of Colored People used nonviolent tactics that successfully placed the issue of civil rights on both the public agenda and the formal agenda of the national government.[10]

In the case of the civil rights movement, the policy entrepreneurs used a variety of tactics. Lawsuits challenged the separate but equal doctrine in public education. Confrontational demonstrations—such as the civil rights marches in Montgomery, Birmingham, Selma, and Washington, DC—and rallies and speeches—such as the famous "I Have a Dream" speech, given on the steps of the Lincoln Memorial by

Martin Luther King Jr.—made the civil rights movement more visible to the American public. The assassinations of President John F. Kennedy, Martin Luther King Jr., and Robert Kennedy served as triggering mechanisms for passage of additional civil rights acts covering other areas of life. Thus, the efforts of a dedicated core of organizers and advocates stimulated actions and events that underscored existing problems in American society; the policy entrepreneurs then worked to promote specific solutions to those problems in the form of proposed policies.[11] In late 2011, thousands of protestors took to the streets of New York in a protest known as Occupy Wall Street. These policy entrepreneurs sought to use the tactics of the Arab Spring to shine light on what they see as the greed and corruption of the wealthiest 1 percent of Americans. The goal of the protestors was to increase public awareness and spur Congress to pass serious reforms to the economic system in the United States.

**implementation**
The act of providing the organization and expertise required to put into action any policy that has become law; also refers to the actual execution of a policy.

## Reaching the Formal Agenda

A policy reaches the formal agenda when it is actually scheduled for debate and potential adoption by policy-making bodies such as Congress. In the process, it is generally formulated and reformulated several times. In a formal sense, Congress actually enacts or passes legislation, but policy is "enacted"—constructed, debated, and put into effect—by all branches of the federal government. A good example would be the debate surrounding a public option with regard to health-care reform.

Courts also formulate and reformulate public policy. Abortion is a case in point. In 1973, the Supreme Court adopted a policy position in the case of *Roe* v. *Wade*, arguing that women have an absolute right to choose an abortion in the first trimester of a pregnancy. As discussed in Chapter 13 on civil liberties, the Court has shaped that policy over the years by ruling on policies that would restrict or expand this right.

Policy formulation also occurs in the government agencies that implement laws enacted by Congress. Those agencies often issue regulations explaining how the agency will enforce and interpret the new law, subject to hearings and appeals.

## Implementing a Policy

Once a policy has been enacted, it must be implemented. **Implementation** is the actual execution of a policy. Some policies are relatively easy to implement. For example, when Congress enacted a national highway speed limit of 55 miles per hour to conserve gasoline, the government quickly achieved full implementation of the policy by denying federal funds for highway construction to any state that did not enforce the new speed limit. Other policies, however, are more difficult to implement. Difficulty in implementing federal policies relates to the three Cs of implementation: *complexity, cooperation,* and *coordination.*

An example is court-mandated school desegregation, first ordered in 1954 by the Supreme Court in *Brown* v. *Board of Education of Topeka.* The next year, the Court ordered that desegregation should proceed "with all deliberate speed," in part to soften the blow for the conservative and historically segregationist southern states, which were powerfully represented in Congress. However, it soon became apparent that the ambiguous phrase "all deliberate speed" meant one thing to the justices of the Supreme Court and another to state and local officials who were reluctant to implement the policy.[12]

Another obstacle to the implementation of the *Brown* decision was that the actual plans for desegregating the schools required the cooperation of local and state officials. The involvement of more individuals and groups with the power to stop or delay a policy, such as officials of school districts and elected school boards, meant more obstacles to full implementation of the policy. Some school districts, including those in Los Angeles and Boston, were actually turned over to "federal masters" appointed by federal courts to supervise desegregation in their areas.[13]

As the difficulty of desegregating public schools increased, so did problems of coordination. In the cases of Los Angeles and Boston, coordination among the

**policy evaluation**
The required period of monitoring and analysis of federal policies following their implementation.

federal courts, the court-appointed "masters," the elected school boards, as well as the parents and students, presented one of the greatest implementation challenges ever faced by the federal government. The case of desegregation illustrates that public policy implementation is far from automatic. Complex policies requiring extensive cooperation and a great deal of coordination have much less chance of achieving full implementation than simpler policies.

## Evaluating a Policy

All policies have impact of some kind, though not all achieve the impact intended by those who proposed and enacted them. It is difficult to generalize about which policies have greater impact and why, but scholars have identified characteristics that contribute to the effectiveness of public policies: (1) a clearly written law or policy statement, (2) strong presidential support for the policy, and (3) local cooperation in the implementation of the policy. Policies that combine all three of these basic ingredients have the greatest chance of achieving their full impact. Most federal policies require a period of monitoring and analysis following implementation, known as **policy evaluation.**

**THINKING CRITICALLY**

Do you think that all laws should have a "sunset provision" by which they expire after a certain amount of time, maybe two years? To continue the law would have to receive the support of a majority in Congress and the president at its sunset. What impact would this have on government policy? What about government stability?

## Terminating a Policy

Following evaluation, policies are either terminated or continued. If they are continued, they enter what social scientists call the *feedback loop.* Information about the policy's consequences can be "fed back" into the cycle to help in the formulation of new policies. Termination ends the policy life cycle. But to be enacted in the first place, policies require strong support from government policy entrepreneurs and interest groups outside the government—all, presumably, its beneficiaries. As a result, public policies, once enacted, are rarely terminated.[14]

Policies may be terminated when they lose the political support of the general public, the president, the Supreme Court, or members of Congress. President Obama, for example, called on the federal government to ignore all 1,200 of President Bush's signing statements. Policies also face termination when their funding is gone, which was the case in the popular Car Allowance Rebate System (CARS), better known as "Cash for Clunkers" program. Despite its popularity and effectiveness, the program was terminated after the funds allocated by Congress were depleted. The Cash for Clunkers program was so popular it ran out of its initial $1 billion in funding in a week, months before the funding was expected to expire. In response, Congress added an additional $2 billion in funding for the program. The program was intended to both boost the economy and help the environment by removing gas guzzlers from the road. As an economic stimulus, Cash for Clunkers was remarkably effective. Transportation Secretary Ray LaHood noted, "There can be no doubt that this program drummed up more business, for more people, in more places at a time when our economy needed help the most."

A car that was dumped in a dumpster serves as a visual promotion for the government's Cash for Clunkers program.

Policies may also be terminated when the policy or program becomes out of date and no longer important in light of new developments. An example is the nuclear-targeting policy of "mutual assured destruction" (MAD). The targeting of civilian areas such as Moscow as part of a strategy to protect the United States against the threat of a nuclear strike by the Soviet Union was rendered obsolete after the breakup of the Soviet Union in 1991.

Finally, policies or programs may be terminated when they fail to perform effectively or are replaced with an alternative policy that is performing better. An example is the Aid to Families with Dependent Children (AFDC) program, a 60-year-old entitlement to federal cash assistance for mothers and children at the poverty level, which was replaced by the 1996 Welfare Reform Law. Today, block grants to states, designated as Temporary Assistance for Needy Families (TANF), provide assistance, but with a five-year lifetime limit on benefits.

### Continuing a Policy

Some policies have been in effect for a long time. They are implemented, evaluated, and continuously refined or modified by key actors in the national policy-making process—the president, Congress, or the courts. If a policy survives the early stages of the policy life cycle and is actually implemented, it is still subject to periodic review and possible modification over time. For example, the basic mission of law enforcement agencies such as the FBI has changed over time, from stopping organized crime to preventing terrorism in post–September 11 America. The expanded FBI mission is basically to protect all of us from dangerous threats facing our nation—from international and domestic terrorists, spies, cyber-villains, corrupt government officials, mobsters, violent gangs, child predators, and serial killers.

## REGULATORY POLICY

15.5 *What types of regulatory activities does the government engage in?*

As we saw in Chapter 8 on bureaucracy, regulatory policies are designed to regulate, conduct, and protect the health and welfare of all Americans. Political scientist Kenneth Meier has noted that "regulation is any attempt by the government to control the behavior of citizens, corporations, or sub-governments."[15] The national government engages in several kinds of regulatory activity. It may regulate (1) the price that can be charged for a good or service, (2) franchising or licenses granted to individuals or businesses, (3) performance of safety standards, or (4) resources such as water or electricity from federal dams and hydroelectric projects available to citizens or businesses. It may also (5) provide or withhold operating subsidies or (6) use regulatory commissions such as the FTC or SEC to regulate vital industries and promote fair competition among individuals and businesses.

Regulatory activity by the federal government has increased gradually during the past century after being almost nonexistent during the first hundred years of the nation's history. The first significant regulation occurred in response to the political pressures of the Granger and muckraker movements in the late 1800s and early 1900s. Another surge of regulatory activity occurred in the 1930s as a result of the problems created by the Great Depression. The highest levels of regulation were reached in the 1960s and 1970s in response to the consumer, civil rights, and environmental movements.

Beginning in the mid-1970s, regulatory activity by the federal government declined and a movement toward *deregulation* emerged. The government sold ("privatized") government-owned railroads to private investors and acted to deregulate the trucking, banking, and airline industries. Beginning in the late 1980s, however, policy began a swing back toward increased regulation, a pattern that continues to this day, as evidenced by the federal government's role in the banking, food, and automobile industries.

In the early 1900s, food poisoning cases were common. Botulism poisoning was not used for getting rid of wrinkles but instead was known as the sausage disease. Some 71 percent of people contracting the sausage disease at the turn of the century died. Today, only 100 cases of food-borne botulism occur in the United States and all of these are from home-preserved food. Cases of botulism poisoning from mass produced food have largely been eradicated. Food poisoning does still occur in the United States, however, and it is sometimes deadly, like in the case of the *Listeria* contaminated cantaloupe in late 2011. Despite these occasional outbreaks, regulations

## APPROACHING Democracy Timeline

### History of Major U.S. Environmental Regulations

| | |
|---|---|
| 1947 | The first air pollution agency is created with the formation of the L.A. Air Pollution Control District. |
| 1948 | The Federal Water Pollution Control Act requires the federal government to work with state and local governments to reduce the pollution of interstate waters. |
| 1955 | The National Air Pollution Control Act begins efforts to control air pollution. |
| 1959 | California begins to regulate automobile emissions. |
| 1963 | Congress passes the Clean Air Act to regulate stationary sources of air pollution, like power plants and steel mills. |
| 1964 | Congress establishes the National Wilderness Preservation System to maintain wilderness on federal lands. |
| 1970 | The Clean Air Act is amended to establish national air quality standards. |
| 1973 | Congress passes the Endangered Species Act to protect threatened wildlife. |
| 1974 | The Safe Water Drinking Act establishes regulations and standards for contamination of public water. |
| 1978 | The National Energy Conservation Policy Act is passed to encourage conservation of residential energy use. |
| 1980 | The Superfund law passes and places a tax on the chemical and petroleum industries to help the government pay for the cleanup of toxic waste. |
| 1981 | President Reagan's secretary of the interior begins dismantling environmental protection programs. |
| 1990 | The Clean Air Act is amended to increase automobile emissions standards and reduce ozone-layer-damaging chlorofluorocarbons. |
| 1996 | The Food Quality Protection Act creates strict pesticide and food safety requirements. |
| 1997 | President Clinton signs the Kyoto Protocol, agreeing to reduce greenhouse gases, but the treaty is never ratified by the U.S. Congress. |
| 2002 | The Small Business Liability Relief and Brownfields Revitalization Act is passed, providing funds for cleanup of toxic business sites. |
| 2007 | The Energy Independence and Security Act increases fuel efficiency standards and investment in alternative energy production. |

☐ Democratic ☐ Neutral ☐ Undemocratic

*(continued)*

requiring safety standards and testing have succeeded in making the U.S. food supply one of the safest in the world.

Today, government regulations help to keep Americans safer throughout nearly every part of our daily lives. We Americans live in houses and apartments where the paint is free of toxic led; we are confident the water from our faucets is safe to drink; we know what ingredients are put in our foods and feel confident that our eggs, meat, and produce are free from deadly bacteria; we know that the medicine we take is safe and effective; we are safer driving because truckers are limited in the number of hours they can drive their big, dangerous vehicles; at work we are protected from discrimination and provided care and compensation if we are hurt on the job; we put our children to bed in pajamas and on mattresses that won't burst into flames if we light a candle; and while we relax after our government-protected eight-hour workday, we are not bothered by telemarketers because we signed up for the federal no-call list. All of this is possible through government regulations.

## Regulating the Environment

Environmental policy provides a good illustration of regulatory policy making (see this chapter's timeline). Americans became vitally interested in environmental issues in the 1960s and 1970s, and the federal government responded by enacting several key pieces of environmental legislation. The triggering mechanism for environmental policy making at the federal level was the 1962 publication of Rachel Carson's *Silent Spring.* In this groundbreaking book, Carson argued that the widely used pesticide DDT was poisoning fields, streams, fish, and wildlife, and ultimately the American consumer. The book spurred a scientific search to develop less hazardous pesticides, as well as a search by federal policy makers for environmentally sensitive policies and programs.[16]

In a landmark piece of legislation, the National Environmental Policy Act of 1969, Congress required that government agencies issue an environmental impact statement listing the effects that proposed agency regulations would have on the environment. In 1970, Congress created the Environmental Protection Agency (EPA) to administer environmental programs and issue environmental regulations. It also enacted the Clean Air Act of 1970, which directed the EPA to monitor industrial air pollution and enforce compliance with existing pollution laws. The Department of Transportation was assigned the responsibility for monitoring and reducing pollution associated with automobile emissions.

**Approaching Democracy Timeline** ***(continued)***

| | |
|---|---|
| **2009** | The Omnibus Public Lands Act is passed to regenerate forests, protect rivers, extend the national park system, and stand guard over historic battlefields. |
| **2010** | Historic Cap and Trade legislation dies in the U.S. Senate. |
| **2011** | The EPA makes dozens of environmental regulations stricter despite President Obama withdrawing new smog standards. |

Democratic — Neutral — Undemocratic

In 1972, Congress passed the Water Pollution Control Act, aimed at reducing pollution in the nation's rivers and lakes. Congress soon added ocean dumping of wastes to the policy agenda with the Marine Protection Research Act, followed in 1976 by legislation regulating the dumping of hazardous waste. The 1976 Resource Conservation and Recovery Act not only regulated the disposal of hazardous waste but also sought to reduce the volume of waste by encouraging recycling, onsite disposal, incineration, and disposal of hazardous waste in safe landfills. The enormous expense associated with cleaning up hazardous waste sites led to the enactment in 1980 of the Superfund law (formerly the Comprehensive Environmental Response, Compensation, and Liability Act, or CERCLA), which created a fund to pay for toxic site cleanups and authorized the EPA to order polluters to clean up sites where necessary. Congress later enacted the Safe Water and Toxic Enforcement Act of 1986, regulating discharges into surface water and groundwater; the Toxic Substances Control Act of 1987, requiring the removal of carcinogenic material such as asbestos from buildings; and the Clean Air Act Amendments of 1990, which resolved a long-running conflict between coal-producing and auto-manufacturing states, such as West Virginia and Michigan, as well as states such as Maine and California, whose residents and local economies were more favorably inclined toward environmental protection.

The Clean Air Act of 1990 set strict limitations on pollution from utilities and automobile emissions, mandated use of less-polluting fuels, and authorized inspections of potential polluters ranging from automobiles to wood-burning stoves. In addition, the 1990 act authorized the EPA to set standards for allowable industrial pollutants and to limit sulfur dioxide emissions, the primary cause of acid rain. Still, many American cities have yet to meet the air quality standards established in the original Clean Air Act of 1970. Much future progress will depend on the EPA's willingness to enforce the regulations aggressively.

A second set of concerns has to do with the fact that pollution and the need for environmental regulation spill over state and national borders into the arena of international politics. The first international conference on the environment was held in 1992 in Rio de Janeiro, Brazil. The United States was the only major nation that refused to sign the Rio Accords, which committed nations to strict environmental goals and required them to allocate a fixed percentage of their national budgets to take action on environmental concerns.

In late 1997, representatives of more than 150 nations gathered in Japan to discuss how best to counter the threat of global warming. The meeting produced the *Kyoto Protocol*—a commitment by developed nations to bring their emissions down to specific levels by specific dates. The parties agreed to reduce greenhouse gas emissions; the specific limits vary from country to country, but the framework and targets were based largely on U.S. proposals.[17]

In June 2002, the European Union ratified the Kyoto Protocol, although the United States, at the time the world's largest emitter of greenhouse gases, opposed mandatory cuts in emissions that reportedly would cost billions of dollars and millions of jobs. By August 2005, 153 countries had ratified the protocol, including

Canada, People's Republic of China, India, Japan, New Zealand, and Russia and the 25 countries of the European Union, as well as Romania and Bulgaria. Six countries had not ratified the protocol: Australia, Mexico, the United States, Croatia, Kazakhstan, and Zambia. At the December 2005 United Nations meeting on global warming held in Montreal, the United States and China, "the world's current and projected leaders in emissions of greenhouse gases," refused to accept any mandatory reductions.[18] Figure 15.1 provides a view of carbon dioxide emission rates around the globe.

Within weeks of taking office, President Obama's chief climate negotiator, Todd Stern, said that the United States would be involved in the negotiation of a new treaty that would represent a major overhaul and revision of the Kyoto agreement, reaching beyond reducing greenhouse gas emissions and including financial mechanisms and making good on long-standing promises to provide money and technical assistance to help developing countries cope with climate change.[19] As a key part of this effort, President Obama launched the Major Economies Forum on Energy and Climate, which convened in L'Aquila, Italy, on July 9, 2009, and was co-chaired by President Obama and Prime Minister Berlusconi. The G8 leaders agreed to reduce their emissions 80 percent or more by 2050 as its share of a global goal to lower emissions 50 percent by 2050.[20] President Obama traveled to Copenhagen in December 2009, declaring that the time had come "not to talk but to act on climate change." He was able to broker an accord that provided $30 billion in emergency climate aid to poor nations for three years by 2020. The accord also included procedures for verification of heat-trapping gases. In 2010, the comprehensive climate and energy bill passed in the House of Representatives but died in the Senate. The continued economic slump in 2011 and the control of the House of Representatives by the Republican Party makes any serious action on climate change unlikely.

A third challenge facing environmental regulation is the increasing complexity of regulatory policy. *Offset policies* are a case in point. A potential polluter can build a facility otherwise not allowable by "offsetting" the increased pollution with lower pollution elsewhere. For example, the Clean Air Act created *pollution credits.* Industries and companies that fail to meet their emission standards can buy extra pollution credits from companies whose emissions are below the allowable level. Although the overall level of pollution in a particular area must remain below the established limit, industries and businesses emit significantly different amounts of polluting substances. How should such a market in pollution credits be regulated, and will it require further monitoring and regulation as it develops?[21] Further challenges have been posed by the Supreme Court's ruling in *Massachusetts* v. *EPA,* which found the EPA in violation of the Clean Air Act and of not acting in order to prevent emissions. As a result, states such as California have sought to enact their own emissions standards that are stricter than those imposed by the EPA.[22] California's stricter air pollution standards have so far withstood legal challenges and were upheld by the U.S. Court of Appeals in May 2011.

Political differences can cause tensions in enacting regulatory policy. In general, Republicans oppose regulation and argue for the free market to self-regulate industry. Democrats, on the other hand, generally favor government regulation as a way to provide for the common good. On large-scale problems where short-term economic benefit encourages companies and individuals to engage in practices that are detrimental to a long-term future, there is a clear role for government intervention. (See work on the Tragedy of the Commons dilemma.) Climate change provides an example of a large-scale problem in need of government regulatory solutions.

A problem in the United States is that, on the issue of climate change, rather than developing policies that encourage private-sector self-regulation or allow for public-sector regulation, some politicians deny climate change is a problem in the first place. (See this chapter's Compared to What? feature for a discussion on how leaders in other countries are seeking to solve the climate change crisis.) While

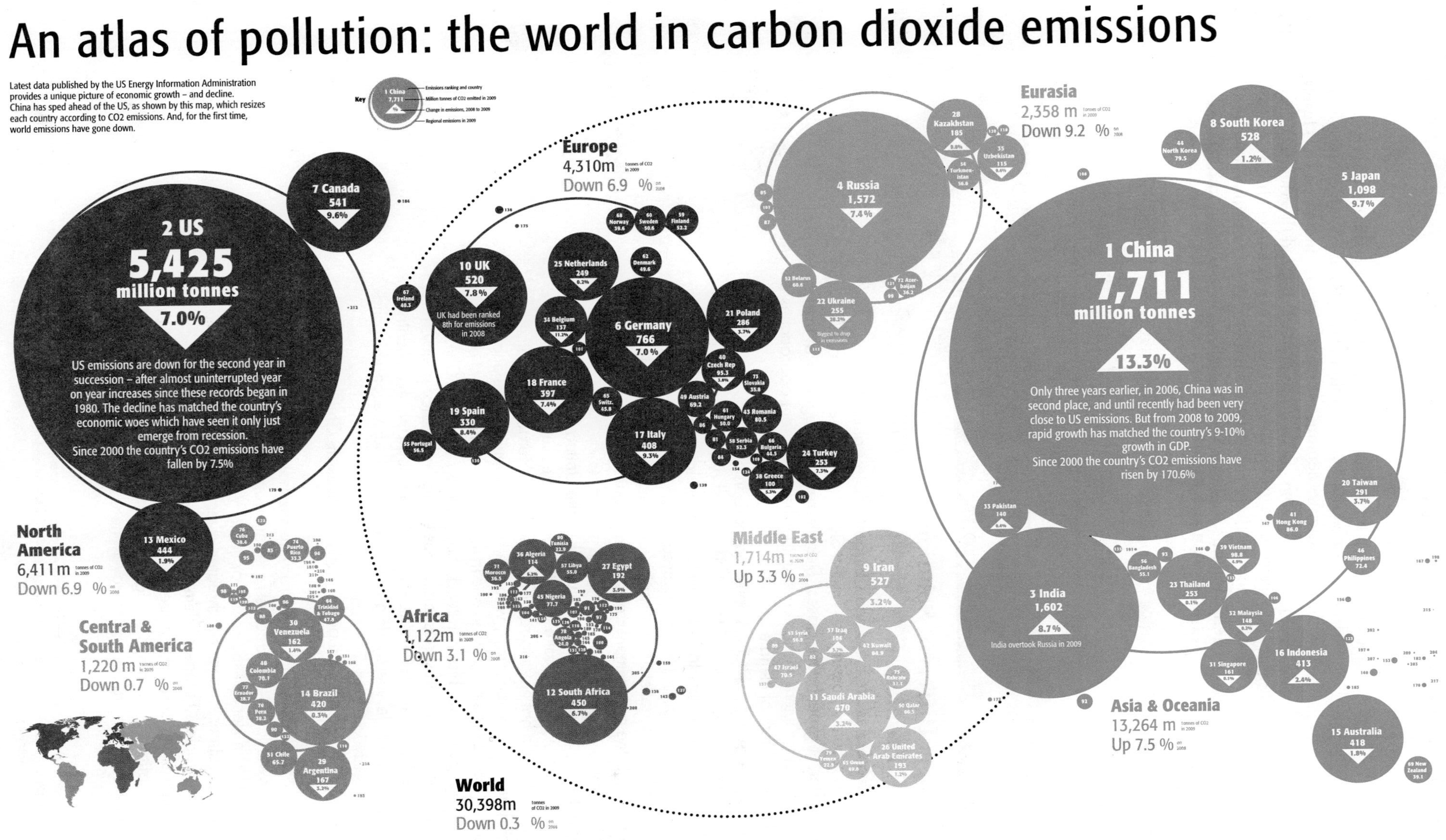


**FIGURE 15.1** An Atlas of Pollution: The World in Carbon Dioxide Emissions

*Source:* Copyright Guardian News & Media Ltd. 2011.

campaigning for his party's nomination for president, Governor Rick Perry repeatedly questioned the role of fossil fuels in climate change and stated that he does not believe the science demonstrating the impact increased $CO_2$ levels have on global temperature change. President Obama criticized this view by noting that Rick Perry is a "governor whose state is on fire denying climate change"[23] Not all Republicans deny climate change. Jon Huntsman, another candidate for the Republican presidential nomination, tweeted "I believe in evolution and trust scientists on global warming. Call me crazy."[24]

## Compared to WHAT?

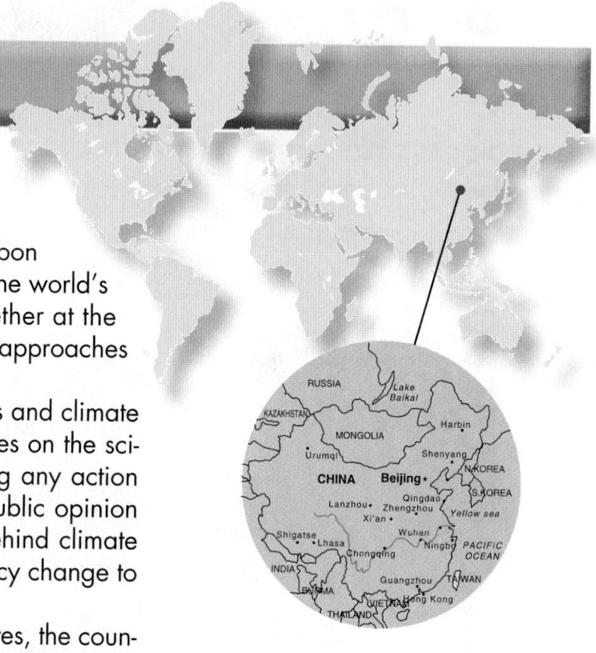


### Climate Change: Different Solutions to This Global Problem

China and the United States are the world's biggest emitters of carbon dioxide, with China recently passing the United States to become the world's number one polluter of greenhouse gases. Despite reigning together at the top of the list of global polluters, these two countries have different approaches to dealing with the problem of climate change.

In the United States, some politicians deny that carbon emissions and climate change is a problem that needs to be solved. This small group relies on the scientific ignorance of many voters to prevent the country from taking any action on climate change. (See Figure 15.2 for a breakdown on U.S. public opinion on climate change.) If lawmakers refuse to believe the science behind climate change, they handcuff the government from making significant policy change to help stop the problem.

While China is now a bigger global polluter than the United States, the country's leaders have a very different take on the problem. Because China is not a democracy, its leaders do not have to rely on the scientific literacy of its citizenry and can instead allow the bureaucrats, who are largely scientists and engineers themselves, to make policy. As a result, no one in the Chinese government debates whether climate change is a problem; instead, they develop solutions. China has set what some argue is the world's most ambitious energy efficiency policy. It is currently the world's leader in renewable energy production and the country's policy makers see renewable energy as a market for both future economic and environmental prosperity in China.

Does this mean that the totalitarian policy-making process in China is superior to the democratic one in the United States? In the 1960s, writer Isaac Asimov noted that there is a "false notion that democracy means that 'my ignorance is just as good as your knowledge.'" This addresses the fundamental tension between equality and expertise in democratic public opinion. While this tension is mitigated in totalitarian regimes, it does not threaten climate change policy in most other Western democracies. European democracies are taking steps to reduce greenhouse gas emissions and the European Union has been at the forefront of international negations on climate change. As Winston Churchill famously quipped, "Democracy is the worst form of government except for all the others that have been tried."

*Sources:* Interview with Julian L. Wong, senior policy analyst for the Center for American Progress on *Public Radio International:* www.pri.org/stories/world/asia/; "China's Innovation Model and Its Role in the Global Clean Energy Market," greenleapforward.com.

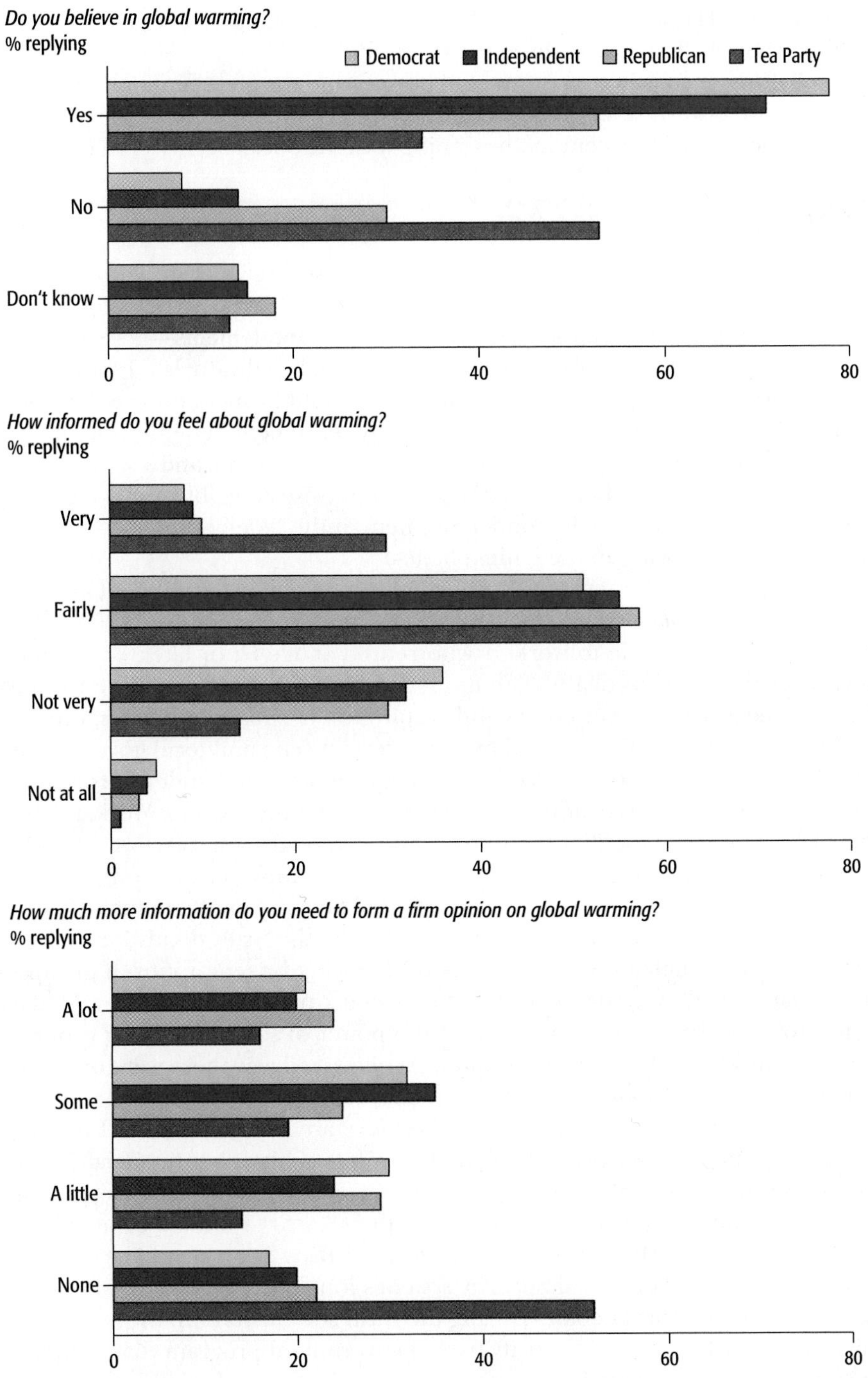


**FIGURE 15.2** U.S. Public Opinion on Climate Change, April–May 2011

*Sources:* Yale Project on Climate Change Communication, George Mason University Centre for Climate Change Communication; http://www.economist.com/blogs/dailychart/2011/09/american-public-opinion-and-climate change.

# SOCIAL WELFARE POLICY

## 15.6 *What is the history of social welfare policy?*

The second major category of public policy, social welfare policy, is intended to alleviate the numerous problems associated with poverty in contemporary American society. Although the United States has had poverty conditions since early colonial days, poverty first reached the public agenda in the early 1900s as a result of works by muckraking journalists (see Chapter 12). Two books, Lincoln Steffens's *Shame of the Cities* and Robert Hunter's *Poverty,* both published in 1904, were influential in elevating poverty to the status of a political issue. In his study of tenement dwellers in Boston and New York,

## THINKING CRITICALLY

Do you believe it is the responsibility of the government to ensure each citizen has access to a minimal-level standard of living? Should the government ensure citizens have enough food and shelter? What about medical care or dental care? What about nonessentials such as Internet access and companionship?

Hunter shocked turn-of-the-century readers by estimating that between 12 and 25 percent of all Americans lived in poverty.[25]

Before we consider the sources of poverty and the government's attempts to improve **poverty levels,** it is necessary to understand the history of social welfare policy in the 20th century, beginning with the Social Security Act of 1935.

## The Social Security Act

The Social Security Act was the centerpiece of President Franklin D. Roosevelt's New Deal legislative program. The act established a safety net to catch those falling into poverty. It did so through a system of **entitlements**—government-sponsored benefits and cash payments—for which individuals might qualify by virtue of being poor, elderly, disabled, or a child living in poverty. The act created four major programs: Social Security retirement benefits; unemployment compensation; a public assistance or welfare program; and a series of aid programs for people who are blind or disabled, or otherwise ineligible senior citizens. Social Security—the largest single nondefense item in the federal budget—is at the heart of social welfare policy in the United States.

The key provision of the act was Old Age Survivors Disability Insurance (OASDI), which provided a *contributory* program of retirement and unemployment benefits. The payments were available to workers who retired at age 62 or later, or to their dependents in the event of death. The money to fund the program came from a *payroll tax* shared equally by employers and employees. In subsequent years, the act was modified to include self-employed persons, certain state and local government employees, agricultural workers, and other workers not protected under the original act. Each state administers a separate unemployment insurance system. Workers who lose their jobs are eligible for 26 weeks of payments, although Congress has, on occasion, extended the eligibility period in times of high unemployment. Congress has made several efforts to apply **means testing** to Social Security entitlements—that is, to link benefits to income and provide payments only to the "truly disadvantaged"—but such efforts have failed owing to successful lobbying by senior citizen groups. In 2011, Senator Lindsay Graham (R–SC) sponsored a plan which in part added a means test for Social Security. Illustrative of the power of senior lobbying groups, Senator Graham's bill only had two co-signers. When asked why there were only two additional senators in support of his plan, Graham replied, "These are the only two guys I can find."[26] Social Security benefits therefore are not means-tested entitlements; they are paid to *any* eligible recipient, regardless of his or her financial status.

Social Security was established as a pay-as-you-go system, but recent projections of the ratio of working people to retirees indicate that the trust fund will be unable to meet its obligations in the future, when the majority of Baby Boomers will be entitled to collect full benefits. The Social Security system's long-term viability has become the focus of intense political debate. During the Bush administration, the legislative priority was to transform Social Security from a government program that used tax money to pay guaranteed benefits to retirees and workers with disabilities into one that allowed workers to put their taxes into individual investment accounts.[27] President Obama is opposed to privatization, but he will have to address the fact that the trust funds will be exhausted by 2036, and after that time government will be able to pay only 75 percent of scheduled benefits. Figure 15.3 illustrates the financial struggles faced by the Social Security system. In fact, because of the economic downturn, annual benefits exceeded annual revenues from Social Security taxes in 2010 for the first time since 1983. The impending retirement of the Baby Boom generation continues to raise much concern about the very viability of the system.[28]

A third program created by the 1935 act was a public assistance program, Aid to Families with Dependent Children (AFDC). Commonly referred to as "welfare," AFDC was a *noncontributory* entitlement program that provided cash assistance to families below the official poverty line; as we noted earlier, this program was *terminated* by federal legislation as part of the Clinton administration's welfare reforms of 1996.

**poverty level**
The federally determined income below which a family of four is considered poor.

**entitlements**
Government-sponsored benefits and cash payments to those who meet eligibility requirements.

**means testing**
The changing of eligibility for entitlement benefits from everyone receiving benefits to only those with earnings and savings below a predetermined level, in an attempt to save money.

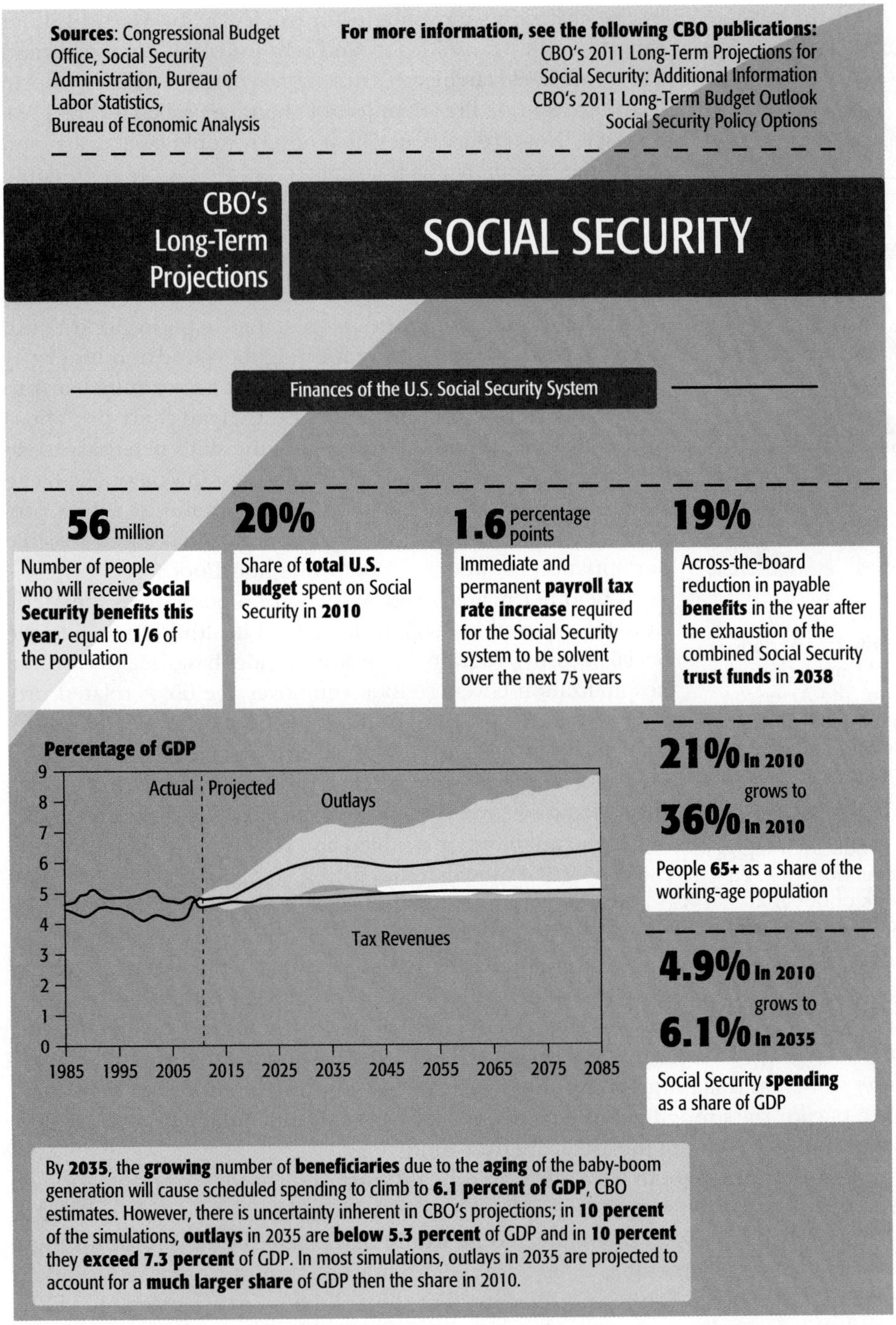


**FIGURE 15.3** CBO's 2011 Long-Term Projections for Social Security

*Sources:* U.S. Congressional Budget Office, Social Security Administration, Bureau of Labor Statistics, Bureau of Economic Analysis; http://cbo.gov/doc.cfm?index=12376.

The fourth program created by the Social Security Act of 1935 was actually a series of programs, now known as Supplemental Security Income (SSI), that provide aid to needy senior citizens who did not contribute to Social Security payroll taxes, as well as to citizens who are blind or disabled. Unlike the other programs just described, SSI is funded entirely by the federal government.

## The War on Poverty

Along with other New Deal legislation, the Social Security Act was spurred by the massive economic dislocation caused by the Great Depression. In other words, the Depression acted as a triggering mechanism to translate the economic *condition* of poverty into a political *issue* to be addressed by policy makers in the national government. Three decades later, poverty again reached the formal agenda of national government, influenced

Following the transition from World War I, the country experienced an extended period of prosperity that ended in 1929, when the nation entered the Great Depression, a long and severe period of economic decline. The American stock market declined by nearly 90 percent from 1929 to 1932, ruining individual investors and financial institutions. Many banks and other businesses were forced into insolvency. The resultant sharp declines in consumer demand and capital investment led to greatly reduced levels of spending, production, and gross national product (GNP). From an estimated annual rate of 3.3 percent during 1923–1929, the unemployment rate rose to a peak of about 25 percent in 1933, when one in four Americans who wanted to work was unable to find a job.

by the civil rights movement—in particular, by Martin Luther King Jr.'s call for civil rights and jobs for black Americans and also by Michael Harrington's description of the "invisible poor" in *The Other America.* President John F. Kennedy called for the creation of a "New Frontier" in which poverty would be attacked and overcome. Kennedy was assassinated before his program could be enacted, but his successor, Lyndon Johnson, launched a War on Poverty with two major pieces of legislation: the Economic Opportunity Act (1964) and the Medicare Act (1965).

The Economic Opportunity Act created the Job Corps to train long-term unemployed people, the Neighborhood Youth Corps to provide job training for neighborhood and inner-city unemployed youth, literacy programs to help adults learn to read and prepare for the job market, Head Start preschool programs to help poor children gain the skills necessary to do well in school, and work-study programs for low-income college students. Unlike Social Security, these community action programs (CAPs) were designed to generate "maximum feasible participation" of people in poor neighborhoods.

The other major thrust of the war on poverty was the Medicare Act, enacted in 1965, which added health insurance to the Social Security program. Medicare provides basic health-care and hospitalization coverage to anyone over age 65. A related program, Medicaid, provides health-care coverage for needy individuals under age 65. The federal government pays a percentage of Medicaid costs, with state and local governments sharing the balance. Medicaid covers people not covered by Medicare, especially those who are blind or disabled and children living in poverty.[29] Data show that Medicare has driven costs down through market dominance, but has done little with respect to compelling more effective delivery of health care.[30] Today, Medicare is the largest single program driving federal spending. The average cost per beneficiary has nearly doubled over the last decade, and costs are estimated to continue rising. Medicare focuses on paying claims rather than denying them. The 2003 Medicare Modernization Act locked in subsidies to insurance companies as well as disallowing bargaining over the cost of prescription drugs.[31] Obama's health-care law strengthened the sustainability of Medicare and added a projected 9 years to the life span of the Medicare trust fund.[32]

For decades, people have advocated health-care reform that would provide all Americans with access to affordable health care. As a presidential candidate, Senator Barack Obama pledged that if elected he would make health-care reform his highest priority. In a September 2009 address to a joint session of Congress, President Obama noted that "I suffer no illusions that this will be an easy process. It will be hard. But I also know that nearly a century after Teddy Roosevelt first called for reform, the cost of our health care has weighed down our economy and the conscience of our nation long enough. So let there be no doubt: health-care reform cannot wait, it must not wait, and it will not wait another year." On March 23, 2010, President Obama signed the Patient Protection and Affordable Care Act into law, initiating the biggest reform to the health-care system since the Great Depression.

Welfare reform was another component of government social policy aimed at improving the circumstances of those with fewer resources. In 1988, Congress enacted the Family Support Act. The act's chief legislative architect, Senator Daniel Patrick Moynihan of New York, described it as "a new social contract" between the poor—who agree to work in exchange for benefits—and society—which agrees to support the poor at a livable wage. The Family Support Act attempted to address the trend toward the feminization of poverty, produced by increasing numbers of working women, higher divorce rates, higher rates of illegitimate births, and a dramatic increase in single-parent households. The act promoted **workfare**—programs to assist welfare recipients in making the transition into the workforce. It provided federal assistance in obtaining child support payments from absent parents. It also created the Jobs program, designed to eventually replace AFDC with a program in which recipients (except mothers with children under 3 years old) must work in exchange for cash assistance. Recipients must be willing to engage in job training and job search activities as a condition for receiving benefits.

President Barack Obama made healthcare reform the primary issue of his first two years in office. The Supreme Court will begin to review the constitutionality of Obama's health care law in March 2011.

The Family Support Act was but the first step in welfare reform, which culminated on August 22, 1996, when President Clinton signed welfare reform legislation that signaled the end of cash assistance to dependent children by the federal government. "This is not the end of welfare reform, this is the beginning," said President Clinton when signing the legislation that "ended welfare as we know it." The new welfare reform law—the Personal Responsibility and Work Opportunity Reconciliation Act of 1996—ushered in a national commitment to the concept "from welfare to work." The new program did more than redesign AFDC; it made broad changes in federal programs and policies. Under the terms of the legislation, each state must submit a state plan to the Department of Health and Human Services for certification in order to receive Temporary Assistance for Needy Families (TANF) block grant funds. The law restricted recipients to five years on federal benefits in their lifetime and required states to enroll recipients in work programs.[33]

The federal poverty rate—the dollar amount of annual earnings below which a family is considered poor—is established by the Census Bureau and is used to generate official government estimates of the number of Americans living in poverty. The federal poverty measure actually has two slightly different versions: *poverty thresholds* and *poverty guidelines*. The thresholds have statistical value for estimating the numbers of Americans in poverty each year; the guidelines have administrative value in determining financial eligibility for certain federal programs.[34] The Census reported that 46.2 million Americans lived below the poverty line in 2010, the highest number registered since the Census Bureau began tracking these figures in 1959. The income of the bottom 60 percent of households fell in 2010, while those making over $100,000 a year saw a rise in income. Paul Ostrom, MIT economist, noted that "as a county we're richer, . . . but there's been this real shift in where the income has gone, and it's to the top." [35] The Occupy Wall Street protests were spurred by evidence like this of a shrinking middle class, where there is growth in both the number of people living in poverty and in the bank accounts of only the richest Americans.

Social welfare policy making, like regulatory policy making, has a long political history and faces tremendous challenges. There is no easy formula for providing equal resources for all, a fair chance for all to succeed, and opportunity for all to flourish financially and personally. How well national policy makers respond to these challenges and how democratic the policies are remain crucial questions as American government continues its task of approaching democracy.

Nearly 1,000 Christians marched from the National City Christian Church to the U.S. Capitol to mark the launch of the new Christian anti-poverty and social justice effort called "A Covenant for a New America."

# ECONOMIC POLICY

15.7 *What role does government play in regulating the economy?*

One of the most crucial roles for modern government is regulation of the national economy. When looking at the world of taxing and spending policy, one can clearly see that politics and economics, just as politics and health care, are fundamentally intertwined. In studying American politics, then, it is important to understand how politics and economics interweave to present opportunities and obstacles in this

**workfare**
The requirement that recipients of welfare programs, such as AFDC, work on public works unless they find employment elsewhere.

country's continuing approach to democracy. Both Republicans and Democrats believe in a strong, healthy economy. Where they differ is on how best to achieve this goal. Within each party, differences exist regarding broad goals and specific policies, differences that have important consequences for government's ability to make coherent budgetary policy and for the lives of every American citizen.

The federal government influences the economy in many ways, both directly and indirectly. Government policies that affect the economy are categorized as fiscal policy, monetary policy, regulatory policy, and international economic policy.

- *Fiscal policy* is government budgetary choices concerning when and how much to tax, spend, subsidize, and borrow, which affect the economic lives of all citizens.
- *Monetary policy* is the range of actions taken by the Federal Reserve Board to influence the level of the gross domestic product (GDP) or the rate of inflation.
- *Regulatory policy* is government regulation of aspects of the workplace to achieve health, safety, and environmental goals.
- *International economic policy* influences economic relations with other countries through exchange rates, trade negotiations, and international economic institutions such as the World Bank, the International Monetary Fund (IMF), and the World Trade Organization (WTO).

**QUICK REVIEW**

Employment Act of 1946

- Formalized the federal government's responsibility to guide the economy.
- Had three primary economic goals: stable prices, full employment, and economic growth.
- Suffered from lack of conditions necessary to achieve these three goals.

American Recovery and Reinvestment Act's transportation stimulus funds, totaling $774 million, were used in all 50 states. A Department of Transportation sign near the I-490 and I-77 ramps in Cleveland, Ohio, promotes its use of stimulus funds to widen the road to two lanes to accommodate trucks that cannot use the Inner Belt bridge. Based on federal calculations for transportation investment, an estimated 21,257 jobs were created or retained in Ohio through stimulus projects.

## The Goals of Economic Policy

The primary goal of **economic policy** is to produce a vibrant, healthy, and growing economy. The federal government's role in making economic policy has increased since World War II. Conditioned by the experience of 25 percent unemployment rates during the Great Depression of the 1930s and the high *inflation rates* (rate of increase in prices) and commodity shortages of the war years of the 1940s, Congress adopted the Employment Act of 1946, which formalized the federal government's responsibility to guide the economy to achieve three primary economic goals: *stable prices* (low or zero inflation), *full employment* (an unemployment rate of 4 percent or less), and *economic growth* (substantial and sustained growth in the economy as measured by increases in GDP). Developing an economic policy that can achieve these goals is difficult and complex, because actions that affect one goal also affect the others, often in undesirable ways. Policies that raise interest rates to push inflation down, for example, may discourage spending, which can raise unemployment rates and may also reduce investment spending and the adoption of new technology, which can, in turn, affect the rate of economic growth. Economic trade-offs must thus be considered in addition to political trade-offs.

To make matters worse, it appears that to achieve the goals of stable prices, full employment, and economic growth, the United States also needs to attain a secondary set of economic goals, such as low and stable interest rates, stable exchange rates, and reduced federal budget **deficits** (annual shortfalls between what government takes in and spends) and balance-of-trade deficits. Progress toward these secondary economic goals seems necessary to achieve the rising living standards embodied in the nation's principal economic goals.

The debate surrounding the $787 billion American Recovery and Reinvestment Act, often referred to as the Stimulus Bill, illustrates these points. President Obama inherited the worst recession in 25 years and his campaign pledge for change was tied to a plan for economic recovery. Like FDR in 1933, the populace turned to a new president, hoping that leadership would lead to recovery and thereby restore confidence in the economy. The American Recovery and Reinvestment Act was the administration's plan to save and create 3 to 4 million jobs, provide more than $150 billion to low-income and vulnerable households, modernize health care, improve schools,

**economic policy**
Policy aimed at producing a vibrant, healthy, and growing economy.

**deficit**
A shortfall between the monies a government takes in and spends.

modernize infrastructure, and invest in clean-energy technologies.[36] The overall goal was to create the foundation for a healthy and vibrant future. "Today does not mark the end of our economic troubles," Obama said when signing the bill at the Denver Museum of Nature and Science. "Nor does it constitute all of what we must do to turn our economy around. But it does mark the beginning of the end—the beginning of what we need to do to create jobs for Americans scrambling in the wake of layoffs; to provide relief for families worried they won't be able to pay next month's bills; and to set our economy on a firmer foundation, paving the way to long-term growth and prosperity."

Critics enjoyed poking fun at some of the examples of where stimulus funds were used, and they questioned whether the amount of money was really enough to produce a recovery, especially as unemployment rates were rising. Some Republican governors even threatened not to accept stimulus money, but by January 2010 the data showed that these programs had more of a positive than negative effect. Take a careful look at Figure 15.4, which demonstrates the breakdown of where the stimulus money went, and Figure 15.5, which shows how one state, Kentucky, used its funds.

The 2011 debt-ceiling debate provides another example of the interconnectedness of the nation's primary economic goals. Some members of Congress refused to raise the nation's debt-ceiling limit unless sweeping cuts were made to federal spending, which would reduce future deficits. Reducing the size of the national debt is an important fiscal policy goal but economists argue that decreasing government spending during economic hard times will exacerbate the economic troubles, decrease overall GDP, and thus also lower the amount of tax money the government receives in revenue. This decrease in revenue offsets the deficit reduction made by cutting spending in the first place. What, then, can our leaders do? Rising debt levels are not sustainable but tactics to reduce the debt during economic hard times will likely make it worse.

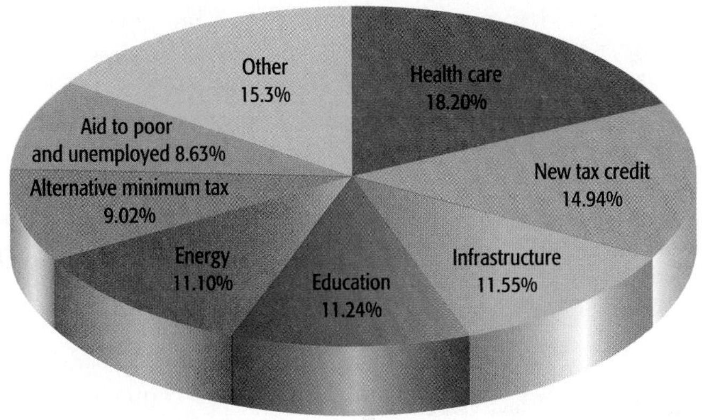


**FIGURE 15.4** A Breakdown of Where the Stimulus Money Went

*Source:* "American Recovery and Reinvestment Act of 2009 Breakdown—Chart of the Day." Posted by Sun on February 13, 2009, The Sun's Financial Diary, http://www.thesunsfinancialdiary.com/charts/american-recovery-reinvestment-act-2009-breakdown-chart-day/.

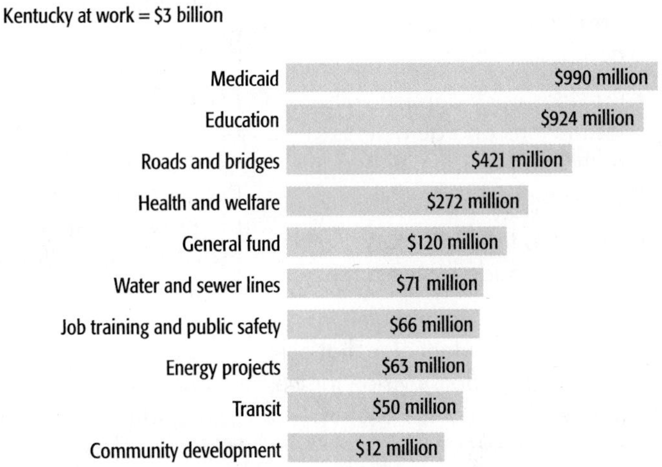


**FIGURE 15.5** The Stimulus Money at Work in Kentucky

*Source:* http://kentuckyatwork.ky.gov/SiteCollectionImages/whereIsTheMoneyGoing.jpg. Used with permission from the Commonwealth of Kentucky.

# THE POLITICS OF THE FEDERAL BUDGET

15.8 *How is the budget prepared?*

There is perhaps no better place to observe how economic policy and political factors intertwine than the case of the federal budget. The government uses its power to tax and spend to influence the economy, but also taxes and spends to provide services for its citizens. How policy makers attempt to provide these services—and, more important, who pays for them and who receives them—touches the very heart of federal budget politics.

## The President Proposes, Congress Disposes

Stated simply, the national budget is a document that proclaims how much the government will try to collect in taxes and how those revenues will be spent on various federal programs. Yet, despite this seemingly simple definition, the preparation of the budget and its subsequent passage are both complex and profoundly political activities. The budget sets policy priorities by establishing the amount of money each program is slated to receive. Some programs are created, some receive more support than others, and still others are reduced or eliminated. The budget thus provides a policy blueprint for the nation.[37]

**Office of Management and Budget (OMB)**
The unit in the Executive Office of the President whose main responsibilities are to prepare and administer the president's annual budget. A president and the OMB can shape policy through the budget process; the process determines which departments and agencies grow, are cut, or remain the same as the year before.

## QUICK REVIEW

Office of Management and Budget (OMB)

- Director of the OMB has cabinet-level status and is one of the president's top advisers and policy strategists.
- Provides each agency with instructions and guidelines reflecting presidential budgetary priorities.
- Analyzes the budgetary requests made by the agencies.
- Helps the president submit to Congress a budget plan that outlines the president's vision for the policy agenda of the country.

## QUICK REVIEW

Budget and Impoundment Control Act of 1974

- Sought to provide Congress with an independent procedure to make comprehensive appropriations and spending decisions.
- Modified the budget process by allowing Congress to establish overall levels for taxing and spending.
- Congress established Budget Committees to hold hearings on the president's proposed budget.
- Congress set up the Congressional Budget Office (CBO) to provide a source of budgetary data.

Budgetary politics involves many actors, the most important being the president and Congress. The law requires that the president submit to Congress his or her proposed federal budget for the next fiscal year by the first Monday in February. Only after the Congress passes and the president signs the required spending bills does the government have a budget.

Although in a strict constitutional sense Congress has sole power to authorize spending of any federal monies, the modern-day practice is for Congress to follow the president's lead. The Budget and Accounting Act of 1921 conferred this responsibility on the president, greatly enhancing the president's power in domestic affairs. First, the law requires government agencies to send their budget requests to the president for consideration. The president ultimately decides whether or not to include these requests in the budget plan. Second, the act created an executive budget office, the Bureau of the Budget (BOB), which became the **Office of Management and Budget (OMB)** under President Richard Nixon. The director of the OMB has cabinet-level status and is one of the president's top advisers and policy strategists.[38]

The OMB provides each agency with budgeting instructions and guidelines reflecting presidential budgetary priorities and then analyzes the agencies' budget requests. This process takes place during the spring and fall of the year, after which the OMB director goes to the president with a budget—a set of estimates for both revenues and expenditures. But this procedure is more than a matter of adding up numbers. Agency heads submit budgetary figures that represent their goals, their ideologies, and even their personal ambitions. This is an extremely political undertaking, with plenty of political maneuvering and overt lobbying geared toward protecting and enhancing each agency's share of the budgetary pie. Finally, in January, after adjustments by the president, the budget of the U.S. government is submitted to Congress. With the help of the OMB, the president submits a budget plan that outlines the national priorities, which is the president's vision for the policy agenda of the country. It is in this context that we see the workings of the budgetary adage: "The president proposes and Congress disposes"—Congress must approve the budget, turning the president's vision into tangible law.

Congress uses its oversight authority to assess the performance of government agencies but also to check the president's power. In 1974, Congress passed the Budget and Impoundment Control Act, which modified the budget process by allowing Congress to establish overall levels for taxing and spending, including breakdowns for national defense, foreign aid, health, infrastructure, and agriculture. Congress established budget committees in the House and Senate to carry out these tasks and to hold hearings on the president's proposed budget. Congress set up the Congressional Budget Office (CBO), a staff of budgetary experts to provide both houses with their own source of budgetary data, enhancing their independence from the executive branch OMB. The House and Senate Budget Committees examine the president's budget. The committees send a budget to each chamber in the form of resolutions, and a conference committee then hashes out a single congressional budget that can reward or punish different agencies.

The CBO has developed into a highly regarded watchdog organization. CBO's mandate is to provide the Congress with objective, nonpartisan, and timely analyses to aid in economic and budgetary decisions on the wide array of programs covered by the federal budget and the information and estimates required for the Congressional budget process.

After the president submits his or her budget, the political battle begins. Figure 15.6 details President Obama's 2012 federal budget proposal. Under the president's budget proposal, spending as a percentage of the country's GDP would decline, reaching a low of 22.3 percent in 2015. The president's proposal projects a $2.2 trillion reduction in the federal deficit by 2022. Much of the expected savings come from the drawdown of troops in Iraq and Afghanistan and the five-year freeze on discretionary spending. The White House also expects an increase in revenue as the economy continues to improve.

The Congressional Budget Office reviews the president's budgetary proposals and offers its own preliminary analysis of that budget plan, as illustrated in Figure 15.7. These CBO projections lead to spirited public debate as well as intense lobbying in the halls of Congress. The CBO's review of the 2012 budget proposal does not project the same rate of economic growth the OMB did when preparing the budget.

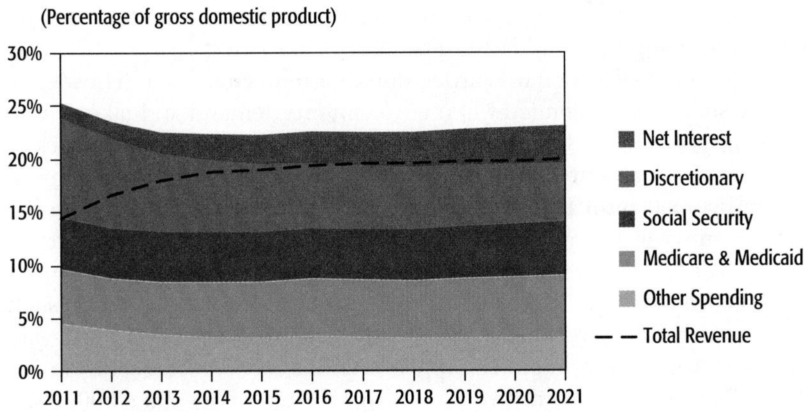


**FIGURE 15.6** Federal Spending and Revenue Under President Obama's Fiscal Year 2012 Budget Proposal, FYs 2011–2021

*Note:* "Other Spending" includes spending for the Troubled Asset Relief Program (TARP), disaster costs, and other mandatory spending.

*Source:* Pew Research Center for the People & the Press, © 2011, Pew Research Center. Reprinted with the permission of the Pew Research Center for the People & the Press, www.pewforum.org.

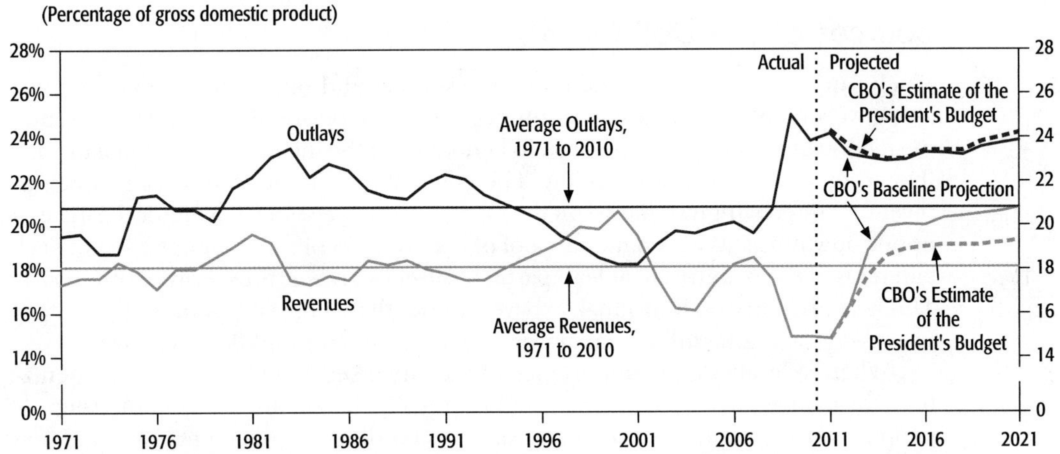


**FIGURE 15.7** Total Revenues and Outlays Under CBO's March 2011 Baseline and CBO's Estimate of the President's Budget

*Source:* U.S. Congressional Budget Office.

Thus, the CBO rates the proposal as having a lesser impact on long-term deficit reduction. Republicans in the House of Representatives proposed their own budget, calling for far greater cuts in spending.

# TAXING

15.9 *What are the sources of government revenue?*

Although all citizens want their fair share of the budgetary pie—whether for better highways or more police protection—almost nobody wants to foot the bill for these services. Therein lies the strain in the politics of taxing and spending—a profoundly political strain. The president's ideas about where government revenues should be spent and who should shoulder the burden of paying always lead to serious battles. Policy makers decide who will benefit from government programs and who will pay for them, and neither these benefits nor the burden of paying for them are distributed evenly across society.

Governments have never been able to meet public needs by relying on voluntary contributions alone. Most of us want—and in fact, expect—government to provide us with certain things. From highly targeted benefits such as farm subsidies to broad intangibles such as national security, we look to our government as a provider. Most Americans fail to realize that "government money" is predominantly the accumulated tax dollars collected annually. So when the government reaches into our pockets to pay for these services, we balk, we complain, and some of us even

**tariffs**
The imposition of import taxes on foreign goods in an attempt to protect a nation's industry and/or labor.

**progressive taxes**
System of taxation in which those who make more money are taxed at a higher rate. An example is the income tax.

**regressive taxes**
System of taxation in which taxes take a higher fraction of the income of lower-income taxpayers; examples are taxes on gasoline, cigarettes, and alcohol.

**capital gains tax**
Tax on unearned income from rents, stocks, and interest.

**excise taxes**
Charges on the sale or manufacture of products such as cigarettes, alcohol, and gasoline.

**tax expenditures**
Deductible expenses that reduce the amount of income subject to taxes; for example, home mortgages, business equipment, or business-related entertainment.

risk stiff penalties by trying to evade paying our "fair share." Such is the relationship between a government and its people where taxes are concerned.[39]

This unwillingness to fork over hard-earned dollars is understandable. The idea of a free, democratic society is challenged when governments demand and take private property, including portions of the profits of corporations and the modest wages of workers. The federal government did not collect taxes from private corporations until 1909 and from individuals until 1913. Before these new tax levies, money to run the government came primarily from **tariffs**—taxes on goods imported into the country.

Many U.S. citizens have had trouble swallowing levels of increasing taxation, leading to periodic "tax revolts." In 1978, the citizens of California staged one such revolt when they passed Proposition 13, a measure designed to permanently cap local property taxes. Anti-tax sentiment has appeared since then, most recently in the hundreds of Tea Party protests held throughout the United States since 2009. Tax cuts were a central feature of the Ronald Reagan and George W. Bush presidencies.[40]

## Sources of Tax Dollars

Much can be learned from examining the sources and outlays of federal revenues. The government relies to a significant degree on the personal income tax. This puts the federal government in a position to benefit from the increases in personal income that accompany a healthy economy. The better the economy, the more income tax revenues. Interestingly, reliance on the income tax can also act as a buffer during economic downturns. With a national pool of taxpayers, economic slumps affecting certain parts of the country are at least partially offset by greater prosperity in other parts. This heavy reliance on individual taxpayers rather than large corporations can impose severe—some argue unfair—tax burdens, particularly for middle-class citizens.

When we evaluate the importance of income taxes, it is important to recognize that not all taxes are created equal. Different types of taxes affect different groups of people. One way to judge taxes, therefore, is according to whom they affect and how much. **Progressive taxes,** which tax those who make more money at a higher rate, are often considered the fairest, as they place a larger burden on those people with the greatest ability to pay. In general, the greater the number of tax brackets—steps in which the percentage rate of tax increases—the more progressive the tax. **Regressive taxes,** on the other hand, tax all people by the same amount, thereby taking a higher fraction of the income of lower-income taxpayers. These rates are generally seen as less fair. The **capital gains tax** (tax on unearned income from rents, stocks, and interest) is an example of a progressive tax because most of the revenue it gathers comes from a tiny portion of the wealthiest Americans. **Excise taxes** and sales taxes on the manufacture or sale of certain consumer goods, such as gasoline, cigarettes, and alcoholic beverages, are generally regressive because most of the taxes paid comes from the consumers of these products—mainly middle- and lower-class Americans.

## Tax Reform

Periodic attempts to reform the tax structure typically relate to the issue of fairness. After prolonged political battles over who would benefit and who would pay, Congress passed the Tax Reform Act of 1986. The purpose of the reform was to simplify an unwieldy tax structure and promote greater fairness. Tax rates fell for higher-income individuals, suggesting that the tax structure actually became even more regressive, but the act included another important aspect that helped increase revenues and retain a degree of progressivity. In addition to changing tax rates, the reform also eliminated many tax deductions, or what are technically called **tax expenditures.** Tax expenditures are amounts taxpayers have spent for items that they can subtract from their income when filing their tax returns, which reduces the amount of income actually subject to taxes. The 1986 reforms changed many of these deductions, which were criticized for predominantly benefiting the wealthy. It eliminated deductions for state sales taxes, interest paid on credit card and other personal debt, and interest on mortgages on third or fourth homes, and it reduced deductions for medical expenses and business entertainment, among others. The result was a simplified, more progressive tax code, in which many taxpayers paid lower taxes and a greater burden was placed on upper-middle-income individuals.

Unfortunately, these tax reforms did not bring in enough revenue to cover federal spending. The result was further increases in the annual budget deficit. Thus, in 1990, President George H. W. Bush was forced to renege on his "Read my lips. No new taxes" promise and enact a modest tax increase on wealthier Americans. Republicans who had supported Bush in 1988 were enraged by this tax increase, and Bush paid a price for reneging on his pledge: Many Republicans voted for Ross Perot in 1992 and Bill Clinton was elected president.

One major goal of President Clinton's tax strategy was to make the tax structure more equitable and progressive, to make good on his campaign promise to make wealthier people "pay their fair share." Clinton raised tax rates for the higher tax brackets, taxed a larger percentage of Social Security benefits from relatively wealthy recipients, and increased the excise tax on gasoline. Clinton's plan resulted in actual income tax increases for fewer than 2 percent of all taxpayers, with the greatest hit being taken by the wealthiest and tax cuts going to the poorest Americans.

## THINKING CRITICALLY

When seeking to raise revenue, the government is often quickest to tax goods that are considered undesirable by society. Some people argue that these "sin taxes" are unfair because they tend to have the largest impact on the poorest citizens. Do you believe the government should place taxes on cigarettes and alcohol in efforts to reduce the use of these goods as well as to raise revenue? How democratic are these sin taxes?

In a moment of major political success, on June 7, 2001, President George W. Bush signed into law a $1.35 trillion tax cut, the third largest since World War II.[41] In signing the bill, Bush fulfilled a campaign promise that many observers believed he could not achieve—"the first major achievement of a new era."[42] No doubt recalling the lessons of his father who broke his promise, the new law was a victory for conservatives who believed "cutting taxes is the public policy precondition to expanding freedom, limiting government growth and promoting prosperity."[43] Of course, the Democrats did not see it the same way. Then Senate Democratic leader Thomas Daschle warned that the "policy implications would be felt for decades to come. But most sadly what this means is that we could be back into the days of debt in the not too distant future, all because many could not find the prudence and the balance to limit their appetite for tax cuts."[44]

Congress attached a caveat to the tax bill: The tax cut would expire on December 31, 2010. This was in keeping with rules passed by Congress to limit spending bills that reach more than a decade into the future. These initial Bush tax cuts were followed

## APPROACHING Contemporary Issues in Democracy

### The Flat Tax

**ISSUE:** What if the tax code was simplified and all Americans paid the same income tax rate? How would this "flat tax" affect America's approach toward democracy?

**Question 1:**

Even though under the flat tax all Americans would pay the same percentage of their income in taxes, why do some people argue that a flat tax has a disproportionate impact on the poor? Think about how rich people and poor people use their income differently—with the rich using much of their income on discretionary purchases and the poor devoting their income to essentials like food and shelter. Would a flat tax bring America closer to the democratic deal of equality or would it threaten this ideal?

**Question 2:**

How would a flat tax impact tax fraud and unfair loopholes? Given this, what types of people may oppose a flat tax, even if they are currently in the highest of tax brackets?

**Question 3:**

What impact would a flat tax have on the IRS? How would the process of filing taxes change?

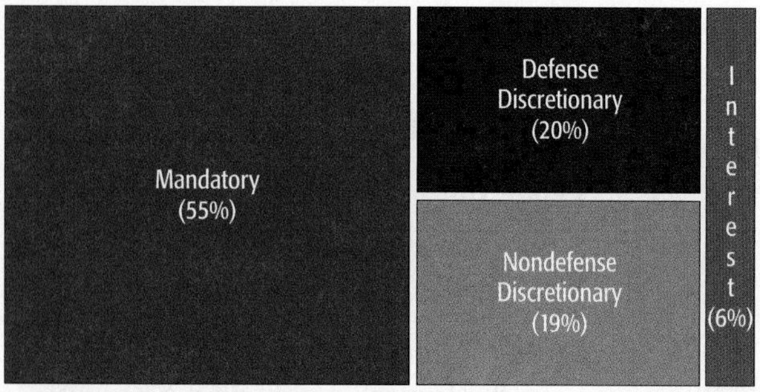


**FIGURE 15.8** 2010 Total Spending
*Source:* U.S. Congressional Budget Office.

by additional cuts in 2003, reducing individual tax rates, providing breaks for married couples, setting a 15 percent rate on dividends and capital gains, phasing out the estate tax, and increasing the child tax credit to $1,000. In 2007, in light of record budget deficits, President Bush tried unsuccessfully to permanently extend the 2001 and 2003 tax cuts.[45]

President Obama has proposed serious reform of the tax code similar to what was done in 1986. Congressman Paul Ryan (R–WI) often stands in opposition to President Obama's plans but he also supports an overhaul of the tax code as a path for reducing future deficits. Congressman Ryan notes that "a tax code should be fair, competitive, and simple, and the U.S. tax code fails on all three counts . . .[because] it's full of deductions, credits, and special carve-outs—otherwise known as "loopholes"—that let politically connected companies avoid paying taxes."[46] In 2011, the media reported that General Electric, despite making more the $5 million in profits, paid no taxes in 2010. This helped spur calls for reform and is illustrative of the problems with the current tax code. The president noted that "because of various loopholes and carve-outs that have built up over the years, some industries pay an average rate that is four or five times higher than others."[47]

## SPENDING

15.10 *What is the difference between discretionary spending and mandatory spending?*

Just as deciding who pays taxes and how much is a profoundly political question, so too is deciding where to spend those revenues. Although many of us balk at picking up the bill, we are also quite ready to hold out our hands for our fair share (or more) from the federal treasury. Be it low-cost student loans, government-subsidized health care, or cleaning up the environment, everyone wants his or her program to receive funding—and the more funding the better.

Federal tax revenue spending choices often signal a government's priorities. **Discretionary spending** accounts for well over one-third of all federal spending; this is what Congress and the president must decide to spend for the next year through 13 annual appropriations bills. Examples of discretionary money are funding for the Federal Bureau of Investigation and the Coast Guard, housing and education, space exploration and highway construction, and defense and foreign aid.

**Mandatory spending** accounts for approximately well over half of all government spending and is authorized by permanent laws, not the appropriations bills. In President Obama's proposed 2012 budget (see Figure 15.8), mandatory spending makes up 57 percent of the entire budget. It includes entitlements such as Social Security, Medicare, food stamps, and veterans' benefits that aid individuals eligible based on age, income, or other criteria. Mandatory spending also includes the interest on the **national debt**—the cumulative unpaid total of all annual budget deficits. By law, any legislation that raises mandatory spending or lowers revenues from levels in existing laws must be offset by spending cuts or revenue increases. This requirement is known as "pay as you go" because it is designed to prevent new legislation from increasing the deficit.

**discretionary spending**
The spending Congress actually controls; 33 percent of all spending.

**mandatory spending**
Spending that must be allocated by law rather than by appropriations, for entitlements such as Social Security, Medicare, and Medicaid; 67 percent of the budget.

**national debt**
The cumulative total of all budget deficits.

## THE POLITICS OF INTERNATIONAL ECONOMIC POLICY

15.11 *How has increasing globalization affected domestic economic policy?*

The increasingly integrated global economy is making nations more and more interdependent. To a greater extent than ever before, the United States must take account of global forces in making economic policy. In 2011, concerns over the economy in Greece wreaked havoc on the U.S. markets. International economic policy deals with international trade; international monetary problems (including exchange-rate policy); international finance and debt problems; and the actions of international economic institutions such as the World Bank, the International Monetary Fund, and the World Trade Organization. Some economic issues are global in scope; others are multilateral, involving groups of nations; and still others are bilateral, between two nations. In the area of trade, for example, U.S. policy influences global trade policy through the General Agreement on Tariffs and Trade (GATT) and the WTO, and regional trade policy through the North American Free Trade Agreement (NAFTA). The United States also engages in bilateral trade negotiations with many nations, most notably Japan and China.

International economic policies, like their domestic counterparts, are influenced both by political concerns and by broad philosophical and theoretical concerns. When policy makers determine their support for international policies, they must consider both how their constituents will be affected and whether or not the policy is broadly beneficial, given their understanding of the way the international economy works.

The politics of international economic policy illustrate that these types of decisions rely on a mix of economic theories and on local as well as national political concerns. As the U.S. economy becomes more firmly connected to the global web of commercial enterprises, the United States must take the policies of other nations into account when setting its own, and attempt, when possible, to coordinate its policies with the European Union, Japan, and other nations.

Markets span national borders through trade, finance, and telecommunications. People buy goods from around the world, invest money around the world, and participate in global culture. This *globalization* means that the most effective way individual nations can change the economy is to coordinate their economic policies with those of other nations. Such coordination, however, conflicts with the ideal of an independent democratic process within nations.

Economic policy making is a vital role of government. The decisions made by elected and nonelected officials influence the economic well-being of the nation as a whole, as well as every single individual, whether rich or poor, Republican or Democrat. Moreover, these decisions are often rooted in those officials' conception of the proper role of government in the lives of citizens—who should be taxed and how these revenues should be spent—and thus policies are likely to change as individuals representing different philosophies and political constituencies assume the reins of government. Managing the economy brings one to the very heart of the relationship between a government and its people. Voters know this, and they make their feelings known when it's election time.

The politics of economic policy have changed in recent years due to the rising importance of international economic policy. As economic matters have become increasingly global, the very nature of democracy has changed with respect to international economic policies. These forces make the political analysis of international economics more complex, even as they become more important in our daily lives.

### THINKING CRITICALLY

Do you believe that all citizens, not just those in the armed forces, should make sacrifices to help the country during war time? Would an increase in taxes allow average Americans to be able to assess the cost of war?

### THINKING CRITICALLY

Think of your average daily routine. What percentage of the goods and services you use make their way through the international economy? Is the banana you had for breakfast from South America and your cup of coffee from Africa? What about the car you drive and the computer you use to take notes in class? Are there any goods you use that are untouched by the international economy?

## Summary

**15.1** *What is public policy?*

- Public policies are the decisions, actions, and commitments of government. They are the means by which government attempts to solve problems and make life easier and safer for its citizens.

**15.2** *What are the government's aims in enacting public policy?*

- The government has four key public policy aims: to regulate key industries and aspects of American life, to protect citizens from foreign powers and other potential enemies, to encourage the accomplishment of important social goals, and to assist citizens and state and local governments.

**15.3** *What is the life-cycle theory of policy making?*

- The policy life cycle consists of 11 stages: (1) redefinition of a condition as a public problem, (2) placement of the problem on the public agenda, (3) emergence of the problem as an issue that requires government action, (4) formulation of a public policy response, (5) reformulation of the proposed policy, (6) placement of the policy on the government's formal agenda, (7) enactment of the policy, (8) implementation of the policy, (9) effects of implementing the policy, (10) evaluation of the effects, and (11) termination or continued implementation and evaluation of the policy.

15.4 *What is the path a policy takes from getting on the public agenda through to termination or continuation?*

- To reach the public agenda, a potential subject of public policy must be labeled as a problem that the government must solve. A dramatic event may serve as a triggering mechanism that causes a condition to be redefined as a problem, or an issue can reach the public agenda through the activities of policy entrepreneurs. A policy reaches the formal agenda when it is actually scheduled for debate and potential adoption by a policy-making body.
- Implementation is the execution of a policy. Some policies are difficult to implement because of their complexity, the cooperation required, and the need for coordination. Most federal policies require a period of monitoring and analysis known as policy evaluation. Following evaluation, policies are either terminated or continued.

15.5 *What types of regulatory activities does the government engage in?*

- Regulatory policy involves the use of federal police powers to supervise the conduct of individuals, businesses, and other governmental agencies. The national government may regulate prices, franchising or licenses, performance or safety standards, and resources available to citizens or businesses.

15.6 *What is the history of social welfare policy?*

- Regulatory activity by the federal government began in the late 1800s and increased during the Great Depression. The highest levels of regulation were reached in the 1960s and 1970s and were followed by a movement toward deregulation. The late 1980s saw a swing back toward increased regulation.

15.7 *What role does government play in regulating the economy?*

- Government policies that affect the economy can be organized into four groups: fiscal policy (decisions to tax and spend), monetary policy (the Fed's influence over the rate of inflation), regulatory policy (policies designed to achieve health, safety, and environmental goals), and international economic policies (policies dealing with exchange rates, trade negotiations, and international economic institutions).
- The three main goals of economic policy are stable prices, full employment, and economic growth.

15.8 *How is the budget prepared?*

- The law requires that the president submit to Congress his or her proposed federal budget for the next fiscal year by the first Monday in February. The federal budget is prepared by the Office of Management and Budget, which analyzes the budgetary requests made by every government agency.
- The budget committees in the two houses consider the president's proposals and establish overall levels for taxation and for various areas of government spending. The committees send a budget to each chamber in the form of resolutions, and a conference committee then hashes out a single congressional budget that can reward or punish different agencies.

15.9 *What are the sources of government revenue?*

- The government relies to a significant degree on the personal income tax. Another large source of federal revenue comes from Social Security taxes paid by employers and their employees. A small percentage of revenue comes from excise taxes, which are charges on the sale or manufacture of certain products, such as cigarettes, alcohol, and gasoline.
- The federal personal income and capital gains taxes are progressive; that is, those who make more money are taxed at a higher rate. Taxes on consumer goods such as gasoline and cigarettes are regressive because they take a higher fraction of the income of lower-income taxpayers.

15.10 *What is the difference between discretionary spending and mandatory spending?*

- Discretionary spending accounts for 33 percent of all federal spending; this is what Congress and the president must decide to spend for the next year through 13 annual appropriations bills. Examples of discretionary money are funding for housing and education, space exploration and highway construction, and defense and foreign aid.
- Mandatory spending accounts for approximately 70 percent of all spending and is authorized by permanent laws, not the appropriations bills. It includes entitlements such as Social Security or Medicare, as well as interest on the national debt.

15.11 *How has increasing globalization affected domestic economic policy?*

- When policy makers consider international economic policies, they must consider both how their constituents will be affected and whether the policy is beneficial to the country as a whole. Increasingly, the United States must take the policies of other nations into account when making economic policy and must try to coordinate its policies with those of the European Union, Japan, and other nations.

## Key Terms

# Test Yourself Chapter 15

1. Public policy can be divided into what two major categories?
   a. Regulatory policy and procedural policy.
   b. Distributive policy and redistributive policy.
   c. Procedural policy and substantive policy.
   d. Regulatory policy and social welfare policy.

2. Which of the following is *not* a part of the life cycle of policy making?
   a. Redefinition of a social condition as a social problem.
   b. Formulation of the problem as a public issue.
   c. Implementation of the policy.
   d. Approval of all political leaders.

3. Which of the following is *not* one of the four aims of public policies enacted by the national government?
   a. To regulate key industries and aspects of American life.
   b. To protect Americans from actual or potential enemies at home and abroad.
   c. To encourage the accomplishment of important social goals.
   d. To reduce government's overburdensome national debt.

4. The first step in the life cycle of policy making is
   a. formulation of a public policy response, usually followed by a pledge of action.
   b. redefinition of a public or private "condition" as a public "problem."
   c. evaluation of the impact of the policy.
   d. placement of the proposed policy on the formal agenda of government.

5. The public agenda is the
   a. policies scheduled for debate and potential adoption by Congress.
   b. items that the president will make pronouncements about on a given day.
   c. cases considered or requested to be considered by the Supreme Court.
   d. set of topics that are of concern to policy elites and/or the public.

6. The policies that are actually scheduled for debate and potential adoption by Congress, the president, the Supreme Court, or executive departments and agencies are called the
   a. public agenda.
   b. formal agenda.
   c. congressional agenda.
   d. procedural agenda.

7. The actual execution of a policy is called
   a. implementation.
   b. enforcement.
   c. monitoring and tracking.
   d. pursuance.

8. When Congress enacted a national speed limit, the government denied federal funds for highway construction to states not enforcing it. Thus, the government quickly achieved full
   a. entitlements.
   b. implementation.
   c. regulation.
   d. enforcement.

9. Which one of the following is *not* one of the "three Cs" of policy execution?
   a. Continuity.
   b. Complexity.
   c. Cooperation.
   d. Coordination.

10. A policy reaches the formal agenda when it is
    a. funded.
    b. scheduled for debate.
    c. accepted by an interest group.
    d. approved by the chief administrator.

11. What was the triggering mechanism for environmental policy making at the federal level?
    a. The *Exxon Valdez* spill.
    b. Three Mile Island.
    c. The publication of *Silent Spring* by Rachel Carson in 1962.
    d. The loss of global rain forests.

12. Domestic policy that involves the use of government's police powers to supervise the conduct of individuals and groups is called
    a. behavioral policy.
    b. regulatory policy.
    c. macro policy.
    d. distributive policy.

13. In 1970, Congress created what government body to combat air and water pollution?
    a. Environmental Protection Agency.
    b. Department of the Environment.
    c. Department of Natural Resources.
    d. Department of the Interior.

14. The Kyoto Protocol was a commitment by 150 nations to
    a. collectively find a cure for AIDS.
    b. fight global poverty.
    c. seriously address the problem of global warming.
    d. destroy all nuclear missiles.

15. _______________ is intended to alleviate the numerous problems associated with poverty in contemporary American society.
    a. Regulatory policy.
    b. Economic policy.
    c. Environmental policy.
    d. Social welfare policy.

**16.** The federally determined level of income below which the government considers the person eligible to receive assistance is called the

a. entitlement level.
b. poverty level.
c. Food Stamp level.
d. disadvantaged level.

**17.** Social Security was designed as a(n)

a. save-and-spend system.
b. pay-for-it-at-the-end system.
c. pay-as-you-go system.
d. unfunded mandate.

**18.** Congress has made several attempts to link Social Security benefits to income. This is called

a. means testing.
b. contributory programming.
c. linkage.
d. financial decoupling.

**19.** The Depression acted as a triggering mechanism to translate the economic condition of poverty into a

a. nonpartisan matter.
b. world issue.
c. local issue.
d. political issue.

**20.** The cornerstone of the 1988 Family Support Act was the idea of

a. work in exchange for benefits.
b. welfare payments for all family members, not just adults.
c. welfare benefits tied to Social Security payroll taxes.
d. cost-of-living allowances for welfare recipients.

**ANSWERS**

**1.** d, **2.** d, **3.** d, **4.** b, **5.** d, **6.** b, **7.** a, **8.** b, **9.** a, **10.** b, **11.** c, **12.** b, **13.** a, **14.** c, **15.** d, **16.** b, **17.** c, **18.** a, **19.** d, **20.** a

# Foreign Policy

# 16

## Chapter Outline

**Introduction:**
*Foreign Policy and Democracy*

- An Overview of American Foreign Policy
- The Constitution and Foreign Policy
- The Foreign Policy Bureaucracy
- Democratic Checks on Foreign Policy

## Learning Objectives

16

- 16.1 What is American exceptionalism?
- 16.2 How has U.S. foreign policy evolved from isolationism to engagement?
- 16.3 What are the foreign policy powers granted to Congress and the president?
- 16.4 How is foreign policy implemented?
- 16.5 What are the democratic checks on the government's foreign policy powers?

# INTRODUCTION

## FOREIGN POLICY AND DEMOCRACY

16.1 *What is American exceptionalism?*

**Foreign policy** refers to actions the U.S. government takes on behalf of its national interests abroad to ensure the security and well-being of Americans and the strength and competitiveness of the U.S. economy.[1] A secure citizenry requires protection of recognized national boundaries; a strong economy; and a stable, orderly society. Since the end of World War II, U.S. foreign policy has been a cautious balancing act between American democratic ideals and U.S. military and economic interests. Much of this history is rooted in the concept of American *exceptionalism,* drawing inspiration from a sermon by John Winthrop, founding governor of Massachusetts Bay Colony, who, more than three centuries ago when speaking to an assembly of Puritans about to disembark from the ship *Arabella,* observed, "We shall be as a City upon a Hill." Winthrop believed that God had summoned those settling in New England to serve as a model of all mankind: "The eyes of all people are upon us."[2] American presidents from Abraham Lincoln to John F. Kennedy to Ronald Reagan have frequently invoked Winthrop's words as a theme for America's providential role in the world.

More recently, President George W. Bush used his own version of the City on a Hill, proclaiming that the United States should bring liberty and free markets to the world. In his 2005 State of the Union Address, Bush observed that "our aim is to build and preserve a community of free and independent nations, with governments that answer to their citizens and reflect their own cultures. And because democracies respect their own people and their neighbors, the advance of freedom will lead to peace. . . . The road of providence is uneven and unpredictable, yet we know where it leads: It leads to freedom."

President Barack Obama has provided a more nuanced perspective on the concept of American exceptionalism: "I believe in American exceptionalism, just as I suspect that the Brits believe in British exceptionalism and the Greeks believe in Greek exceptionalism. . . . I think that we have a core set of values that are enshrined in our Constitution, in our body of law, in our democratic practices, in our belief in free speech and equality, that, though imperfect, are exceptional."[3] In reaching out to the world's 1.5 billion followers of Islam at Cairo University, President Obama placed his imprint on the concept of American exceptionalism and echoed the themes from Chapter 1 of this book: "I know there has been controversy about the promotion of democracy in recent years . . . no system of government can or should be imposed upon one nation by any other. That does not lessen my commitment, however, to governments that reflect the will of the people. Each nation gives life to this principle in its own way, grounded in the traditions of its own people."[4]

From this template of American exceptionalism, citizens can better understand the continual dilemmas of trying to balance and reconcile democratic ideals as articulated in the metaphor of a City on a Hill with U.S. military, political, and economic interests. There is perhaps no greater challenge facing the Obama administration

**foreign policy**
Policy adopted and actions taken by the U.S. government on behalf of U.S. national interests abroad. The president is this country's chief foreign policy maker.

than mitigating these contradictions. This idea of American exceptionalism provides a central theme for this chapter on foreign policy and for the concept of approaching democracy. Is the United States really more exceptional than other democratic countries—such as Great Britain and Sweden, to name just two? If your answer is yes, what factors make it so? If not, why do presidents and citizens attach so much faith to the concept? In this chapter we also look at the evolution and processes of American foreign policy, its history, and how this policy is made within the context of our theme of approaching democracy.

## AN OVERVIEW OF AMERICAN FOREIGN POLICY

16.2 *How has U.S. foreign policy evolved from isolationism to engagement?*

Our starting points are the core goals of American foreign relations:[5]

1. **Survival and independence.** A country's foreign relations are guided first and foremost by national security—the protection of those interests deemed necessary for the country's safety. Independence and survival are the irreducible, fundamental security objectives of the United States.
2. **Territorial integrity and acquisition of new territory.** Preservation of territorial integrity is the mirror image of survival and always a national security priority.
3. **Military security.** Military security for any nation depends on a variety of factors, including weaponry, capabilities and intentions of other nations, advantages and disadvantages of geography, resources, and demographic trends.
4. **Economic security.** Two persistent themes of American foreign policy have been to keep the door open for trade wherever profit beckoned and to be ready to employ costly economic measures to achieve goals.
5. **Democratic values and ideals.** Promotion of democratic values and ideals worldwide has defined the national purpose of the U.S. role in world affairs.

### THINKING CRITICALLY

What do you believe explains American exceptionalism? How does this set the United States apart from other democracies? How does this country reconcile the idea of being exceptional with torture and abuse of Iraqi prisoners by U.S. soldiers at Abu Ghraib prison?

This modest list also suggests the paradoxes of the concept of a *national interest.* Protection from aggression and subversion can work against freedom and democracy at home. Think, for example, of the anti-communist witch hunts in the early years of the Cold War or the internment of Japanese Americans during World War II. Promoting domestic prosperity can sometimes clash with a country's humanitarian instincts. The U.S. sanctions policy against Iraq was aimed at toppling the regime of Saddam Hussein, but it also created extraordinary humanitarian suffering with respect to increased infant and child mortality rates.

Democratic values and ideals often run head first into political reality, as was the case in 2011 when President Obama walked a careful line between supporting democracy demonstrators in the streets of Cairo and his desire to support America's ally, Egyptian president Mubarak, and ensure the safety of Israel. In September 2011, the United States proposed a $53 million arms sale to the government of Bahrain—the same government that spent months engaging in a violent crackdown against democratic protestors. A government spokesperson noted that "the proposed sale will contribute to the foreign policy and national security of the United States by helping to improve the security of a major non-NATO ally that has been, and continues to be, an important force for political stability and economic progress in the Middle East."[6] Just a few months before the arms sale proposal, President Obama condemned the use of violence by the Bahrain government against peaceful protestors and urged Bahrain's king to respect the rights of its people and not fire guns on protestors.

**isolationism**
A pattern in which the United States fosters economic relations abroad without committing to strategic alliances that might draw the country into a war.

**Monroe Doctrine**
A doctrine enunciated by President James Monroe in 1823 that proclaimed North and South America to be in the U.S. sphere of influence, hence out of bounds for European aspirations. It reinforced growing isolationism by promising not to interfere in the internal concerns of European states.

## QUICK REVIEW

The *Lusitania*

- Ocean liner *Lusitania* sunk by a German submarine in 1915.
- Death toll included American citizens.
- Act of aggression against the ship demonstrated Germany's policy of submarine warfare and the impossibility of containing the war within Europe.
- Germany resumed unrestricted submarine warfare in 1917 and the United States declared war.

National Security Act of 1947

- Created the Central Intelligence Agency and the National Security Council.
- Signaled the readiness of the United States to move beyond regionalism to globalism.
- American "sphere of influence" included every corner of the globe where U.S. interests might be affected.

Enlargement

- Response to the new global economic environment.
- United States should support enlarging the sphere of market-oriented democracies.
- Additional open, democratic, and free-market societies will further the interests of the United States.

## Isolationism and Regionalism

Let us begin by distinguishing between two eras in U.S. foreign policy. The first, from the founding of the republic until approximately World War I, might be described as a period of **isolationism** from Europe, but with vigorous expansion in the Western Hemisphere. The second is characterized by an increasing globalization of American interests and commitments, including two world wars, a Cold War, and a post–Cold War period of redefinition and refocusing of American national interests in foreign policy.

Once free of Britain's domination, the United States was not eager to reestablish binding relationships with European empires; however, the newly independent country was not about to commit economic suicide by cutting off lucrative ties with the great trading centers of Europe. The United States fostered economic relations with Europe without committing itself to strategic alliances that might draw the country into a European war, which fostered a pattern of isolationism. Initially, such a policy was easily pursued because the United States had virtually no standing army and few military resources on which European countries could call. The United States also enjoyed a favorable geographic isolation, situated as it was between two vast oceans in a time of slow and dangerous sea travel.

The **Monroe Doctrine,** enunciated by President James Monroe in his December 2, 1823, State of the Union Address, reinforced the country's isolationism by proclaiming the North and South American continents to be in the U.S. *sphere of influence* and therefore out of bounds for European aspirations. In return, the United States agreed not to become involved in European affairs. In the first years of the 20th century, under the leadership of President Theodore Roosevelt, the United States emerged as the police of the Western Hemisphere. In 1898, the United States went to war against Spain and, in the process, seized the Philippines and Puerto Rico. In the same year, it annexed the Hawaiian Islands, motivated in part by the intent to thwart Japan's acquisition of the islands.

The first significant expansion of the Monroe Doctrine was made by President Theodore Roosevelt in 1904, which became known as the Roosevelt Corollary. Roosevelt declared that "the adherence of the United States to the Monroe Doctrine may force the United States, however reluctantly, in flagrant cases of wrongdoing or impotence, to the exercise of an international police power."[7] Pursuant to the Corollary, the United States governed the Dominican Republic under military occupation from 1916 to 1924, occupied Haiti, launched the Panama Canal project, and mediated the Russo-Japanese War. U.S. governmental and private agencies controlled vast oil fields in Mexico and plantations in the Dominican Republic and Cuba.

Another crucial ideal of U.S. foreign policy during the period involved vigorous territorial expansion within its own continental land-mass. Under the banner of *Manifest Destiny*—a claim made in the first half of the 19th century that invoked divine guidance—the U.S. government took control of what is now the continental United States. At the end of the century, the United States looked south to Central America, the Caribbean, and South America, turning from internal expansion to an enhanced role for America internationally.[8]

## World War I

With the start of World War I in Europe in 1914 and the collapse of the Russian monarchy three years later, the United States began to position itself as a global rather than regional player. The United States clearly favored Britain and the Allied Powers over Germany and the Central Powers, but so long as trans-Atlantic shipping lanes remained safe, the United States was reluctant to commit to more than indirect support. Then, in 1915, a German submarine sank the ocean liner *Lusitania,* and the death toll included American citizens. Many historians argue that the *Lusitania* was not really a "neutral" vessel, because evidence suggests that she carried a large cache of munitions in her hold. For U.S. policy makers, though, this act of aggression exposed Germany's policy of unrestricted submarine warfare and the impossibility of containing the war within Europe.

When Germany resumed unrestricted submarine warfare in 1917, the United States declared war, and the country's departure from its historic isolationism was justified, in President Wilson's words, as a commitment to "make the world safe for democracy" while fighting a "war to end all wars." In a speech on January 22, 1917, Wilson declared, "I am proposing, as it were, that the nations should with one accord adopt the doctrine of President Monroe as the doctrine of the world: that no nation should seek to extend its policy over any other nation, but that every people should be free to determine its own policy."[9]

When hostilities ended in 1918, Americans were eager to put the horrors of war behind them. President Wilson campaigned vigorously for an international organization of states to "outlaw" the sort of aggression that had triggered the war. A new collective security arrangement was conceived with the founding of the League of Nations. Wilson failed to persuade the U.S. Senate to approve the peace treaty and join the League. The prevailing mood favored a return to isolationism. Moreover, several senators feared that the League would limit U.S. freedom under the Monroe Doctrine.[10]

The conditions that led to World War I and its consequences would draw the United States into inevitable conflict with another European country, the newly founded Soviet Union. In the midst of wartime chaos, a small but determined Bolshevik party, led by Vladimir Ulyanov, better known as Lenin, had seized control of Russia. The future Union of Soviet Socialist Republics (USSR) was founded in 1917, the first large-scale attempt to form a modern socialist state and, designed as an alternative to liberal capitalism, an ideological adversary of the United States. With little public knowledge, Wilson dispatched approximately 10,000 Americans to aid other Allied troops in disrupting the revolutionary regime. This invasion set the stage for growing hostility between the United States and the USSR that would not be fully apparent until after another world war.

## World War II

Hitler invaded Poland in 1939, violating a nonaggression pact between Germany and the Soviet Union, but President Franklin D. Roosevelt refused to commit American military might to help stop the German advance. As in World War I, the United States was reluctant to encumber itself with strategic alliances, pursuing instead a policy of economic aid to the Allies.

Events would soon force Roosevelt's hand, beginning with France's surrender to Germany in June 1940. Now the survival of Great Britain was in doubt. Following reelection in 1940, FDR gained congressional authorization under the lend-lease law to provide military assistance to any country whose security the president determined was vital to the security of the United States.

But only after Germany's Pacific ally, Japan, bombed the U.S. naval base at Pearl Harbor, Hawaii, on December 7, 1941, did the United States formally enter the war and send troops to Europe and the Pacific. This "Day of Infamy" galvanized Americans and ended the U.S. isolationist orientation. After 45 months of war, the alliance of the United States, Great Britain, and the Soviet Union achieved the surrender of Japan, Italy, and Germany, ushering in the post-war era. President Roosevelt, British prime minister Winston Churchill, and Soviet leader Joseph Stalin dominated both wartime and post-war decisions.

The wartime fates of the United States and the Soviet Union were strikingly different. For the United States, not yet recovered from the Great Depression,

The December 7, 1941, Japanese bombing of Pearl Harbor galvanized the United States in outrage and subsequent willingness to enter World War II. Here, a motor launch rescues a survivor from the torpedo-damaged and sunken USS *West Virginia.*

**superpower**
The disproportionate power—economic and military—that distinguished the United States and the Soviet Union from all other countries in the post-war era.

the expanded industrial production and employment demanded by wartime industrial mobilization actually helped jump-start an economic boom. Beyond the initial destruction at Pearl Harbor, the country suffered no attacks on its home territory. In stark contrast, the Soviet Union was devastated. The Soviet Red Army stopped the eastward advance of Germany, but at tremendous cost; *20 million* military personnel and civilians died, either from combat or through disease or starvation. As with most of battle-scarred Europe, the Soviet Union had the look of a defeated nation.

British prime minister Winston Churchill, along with U.S. president Franklin Roosevelt and Soviet leader Joseph Stalin, together known as the "Big Three" of the Allied leaders, gathered at Yalta, near the Black Sea, in early 1945 to make preparations for the end of the war.

Given the striking differences between the United States and the Soviet Union at the end of World War II, it is surprising that the Soviet Union would emerge as the chief U.S. rival. So awesome would the dominance of the two countries become that they inspired a new concept—**superpower.** The term was intended to convey the disproportionate power—economic and military—that distinguished the United States and the Soviet Union from all other countries in the post-war era. The pervasive superpower rivalry caused American–Soviet relations to affect virtually every country in the world.

## Globalism and the Cold War

World War II entirely changed the international arena. A new post-war international economic order was established in July 1944 known as the Bretton Woods System. Some 730 delegates from 44 allied nations met for three weeks at Bretton Woods, New Hampshire, putting into place an economic system under U.S. leadership that would create conditions for unprecedented economic growth and "enshrined liberalism as the premier international economic theory."[11] The global economic structure they put into place was far from perfect, but it laid the groundwork of rules for multilateral negotiations on economic policy, based on the twin assumptions that peace and prosperity were best assured by the free flow of goods and fixed exchange rates. Two new institutions were created: the International Bank for Reconstruction and Development (World Bank) and the International Monetary Fund (IMF); a third, the International Trade Organization (ITO) never came into existence.

Delegates attending the international monetary conference at Bretton Woods, New Hampshire, plan for post-war reconstruction. The conference participants agreed that broad international action was necessary to maintain an international monetary system to promote foreign trade. The conference established a permanent international body, the International Monetary Fund, and the International Bank for Reconstruction and Development.

U.S. foreign policy after 1946 followed the doctrine of **containment,** a concept delineated by George Kennan, then a State Department Soviet expert. According to Kennan, Soviet aggression needed to be "contained by the adroit and vigilant application of counterforce at a series of constantly shifting geographical and political points."[12] A companion to containment was the domino theory, illustrated in Figure 16.1, which stated that once a country fell to communism, neighboring countries would quickly fall like a row of dominoes, eventually reaching U.S. soil.

Both the United States and the Soviet Union joined the United Nations (UN) when it was created in 1945, but the two countries remained adversaries. Soviet forces controlled all of eastern Europe, installing virtual puppet regimes behind an "iron curtain" of military might and political resolve. The United States applied the counterforce of billions of dollars in economic aid to western Europe under the Marshall Plan of post-war reconstruction as well as through numerous strategic treaties and agreements.

In a historic address to Congress on March 12, 1947, President Harry Truman invoked the doctrine of containment, pledging economic and military aid to Greece and Turkey to halt the spread of communism. This intention to help free and democratic nations beat back the threat of totalitarianism became known as the *Truman Doctrine.* At home, the National Security Act of 1947 created the Central Intelligence Agency (CIA) and the National Security Council (NSC), signaling U.S. readiness to move beyond regionalism to **globalism.** Now the American "sphere of influence" included virtually every corner of the globe where U.S. interests might be affected.

In 1949, the United States secured the commitment of 11 European nations to form the **North Atlantic Treaty Organization (NATO).** The NATO charter also signaled the end of American isolationism and regionalism. Charter signatories agreed that an armed attack against one or more of them in Europe or North America would be interpreted as an attack against all. In the event of such an attack, the treaty bound all members of NATO to assist the attacked country.

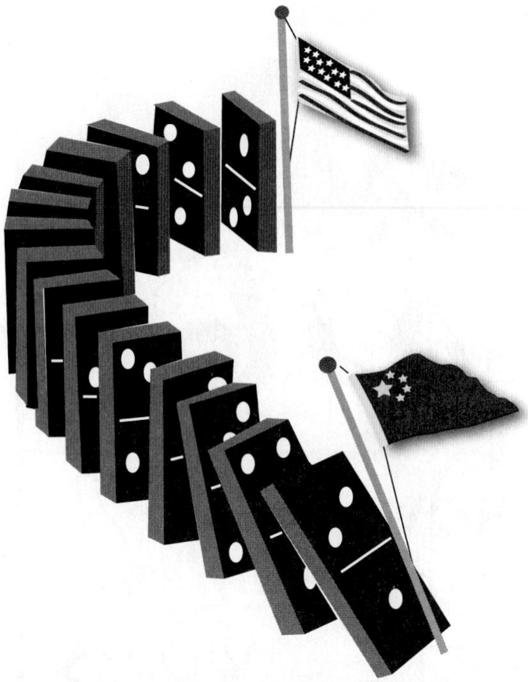

**FIGURE 16.1** The Domino Theory

Also in 1949, the U.S. monopoly of nuclear weapons ended when the Soviets detonated their first atomic bomb. In the same year, the American-backed regime in China collapsed and a communist state emerged under the direction of Mao Zedong. In April 1950, members of the NSC drafted a document that would become the "blueprint" for waging the **Cold War** during the next 20 years: National Security Council Paper 68 (NSC 68), outlining a sweeping mobilization of American economic and human resources in the effort to contain Soviet communism.

The NSC 68 was the first major document to acknowledge the bipolar struggle between the American and Soviet superpowers.[13] **Bipolarity** refers to the fundamental division of economic and military power between the poles of Western capitalism and Eastern communism. The NSC 68 recommended against negotiation with the Kremlin and recommended a more powerful nuclear arsenal, rapid expansion of conventional military resources, and full mobilization of American society within a "government-created consensus" against the evils of communism. The document also called for a dramatic American commitment to international strategic and economic alliances against the Eastern bloc, indicating yet another push away from isolation and regionalism toward globalism. In 1955, the Soviet Union and its eastern European allies (called satellites) formed the **Warsaw Pact,** a military alliance to counter NATO.

In June 1950, just months after the drafting of the NSC 68, war in Korea became a major test of the containment policy. Ironically, the challenger here was not the Soviet Union but the new communist regime in China. Ultimately, the Korean conflict proved a political and military stalemate. The decade closed with the declaration of a socialist revolution only 90 miles off the coast of Florida in Cuba, and the ascension of Fidel Castro.

**The New Nuclear World** The nuclear age began with the U.S. bombing of Hiroshima and Nagasaki in August 1945, and to this day, the United States is the only country ever to have deployed a nuclear weapon against civilian targets in another country. In September 1949, the Soviets exploded their atomic device and triggered a superpower arms race with frightening global implications. Over the next five decades, both the United States and the Soviet Union poured billions of dollars into developing ever-more-powerful nuclear weapons, just as they devoted increasing intellectual resources to creating foreign policies tailored to the new "nuclear world" that they had created. The arms race was on!

**containment**
A term coined in 1946 by George Kennan, who believed that Soviet aggression must be "contained by the adroit and vigilant application of counterforce by the United States."

**globalism**
View in which the U.S. sphere of influence has expanded beyond the Western Hemisphere to include virtually every corner of the globe where U.S. interests might be affected.

**North Atlantic Treaty Organization (NATO)**
Charter signed by the United States, Canada, Turkey, and 11 European nations in 1949 agreeing that an armed attack against one or more of them in Europe or North America would be interpreted as an attack against all.

**Cold War**
The bipolar power struggle between the United States and the Soviet Union that began in the 1950s and ended in the 1990s.

**bipolarity**
The fundamental division of economic and military power between the poles of Western capitalism and Eastern communism.

**Warsaw Pact**
Treaty signed by the Soviet Union and the Eastern bloc in Europe agreeing to mutual defense, in reaction to NATO.

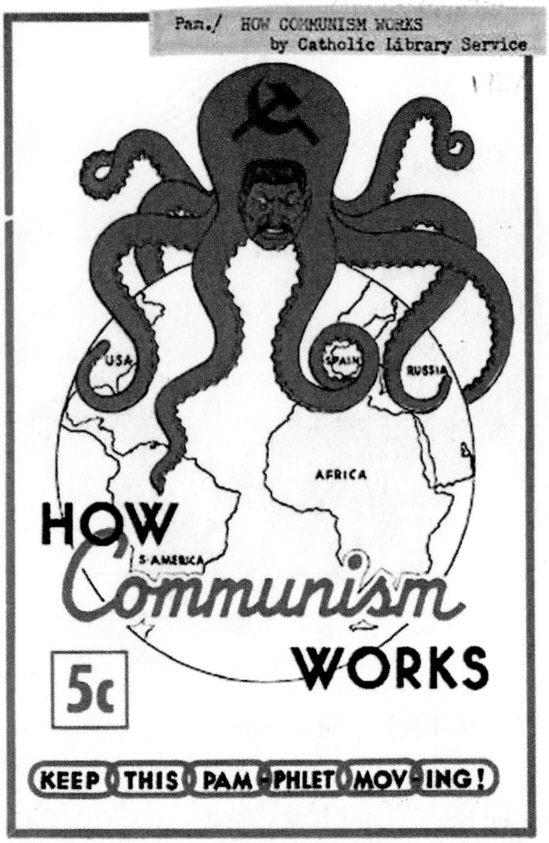


In 1954, President Dwight David Eisenhower provided a clear explanation of the falling domino theory: "You have the possibility that many human beings pass under a dictatorship that is inimical to the free world. . . . You have a row of dominoes set up, you knock over the first one, and what will happen to the last one is the certainty that it will go over very quickly. So you could have a beginning of a disintegration that would have the most profound influences . . . the possible consequences of the loss are just incalculable to the free world."

The most dangerous nuclear confrontation of the Cold War occurred in 1962. Soviet Premier Nikita Khrushchev had begun constructing missile bases in Cuba, an act U.S. leaders saw as a direct provocation, despite the fact that the United States had installed similar missile bases in Turkey aimed at the Soviet Union. After several tense days of secret debates within the U.S. national security establishment, President John Kennedy took the unprecedented step of going before the American people and announcing a naval blockade of Cuba aimed at keeping out Soviet supply ships. In a televised speech, Kennedy demanded the immediate dismantling and removal of the bases. Ultimately, Khrushchev backed down and the bases were dismantled. Plans for a "hot line," providing a communications link between the two leaders, continued, and the Limited Test Ban Treaty was negotiated in 1963. But the threat of a nuclear exchange continued.

A series of strategic arms limitations talks culminated in the signing of the first **Strategic Arms Limitation Treaty (SALT)** in 1972. However, neither country ratified the SALT II agreements, so the arms race continued, with more sophisticated technology and involving weapons deployment in Europe.[14] Beyond its technological challenges, both the United States and the Soviet Union had seriously undermined their own economies through decades of military buildup. By the end of the 1980s, the USSR had bankrupted itself, and the United States was more than a trillion dollars in debt.

After decades of nonstop spending on nuclear and strategic arms, a new era brought new thinking and approaches. In May 2002, President George W. Bush and President Vladimir V. Putin signed a historic arms reduction treaty that committed both countries to reducing their arsenals from about 6,000 warheads each to no more than 2,200 by 2012.[15] In January 2011, a treaty signed by President Obama and Russian president Dmitry Medvedev, which reduces the number of strategic missile launchers by half, went into effect. Early in his presidential term, President Obama and the president of China released a joint statement in which they pledged that their countries will not target one another with nuclear weapons and will work to reduce the risks of nuclear war.

**Mounting an Economic Offensive** Cold War policy makers did not restrict their activity to military planning. In line with the Truman Doctrine, the United States continued to increase **foreign aid** as a hedge against Soviet advances into third world countries. The United States provided billions of dollars in economic aid to western Europe under the Marshall Plan of post-war reconstruction. Through the **Peace Corps,** created during the Kennedy administration, volunteers went to all parts of the globe in programs ranging from improving literacy and building roads and schools to starting immunization and other health programs. The Peace Corps remains the country's foremost experiment in fusing the aims of foreign policy, government resources, and individual initiative and expertise. During the 50th anniversary of the Peace Corps, President Barack Obama credited the agency with improving foreign relations around the world and noted that "with each village that now has clean water, each young woman who has received an education, and each family empowered to prevent disease because of the service of a Peace Corp Volunteer, President Kennedy's noble vision lives on. In our increasingly interconnected world, the mission of the Peace Corps is more relevant today than ever."[16]

A second program initiated by President Kennedy, focusing on Latin America, was the *Alliance for Progress.* In exchange for a commitment of $20 billion over 10 years, the United States asked participating Latin American countries to liberalize their tax, land distribution, and social policies, which major players such as

**Strategic Arms Limitation Treaty (SALT)**
Treaty signed by the United States (under President Nixon) and the Soviet Union to limit various classes of nuclear weapons.

**foreign aid**
Small portion of the federal budget that goes to nonmilitary aid abroad, initially to mitigate against Soviet expansion.

**Peace Corps**
Organization formed by President Kennedy to help with third world development by having American volunteers live and work in needy communities.

Argentina, Brazil, and Mexico were reluctant to do. In the end, the alliance never lived up to its potential, either as a social and economic boon to Latin America or as a hedge against the blossoming of socialist and communist regimes in the region. By 1966, the alliance had all but vanished, but the U.S. commitment to foreign aid for the developing world continued.

President Obama hosted leaders from all over the world for the Nuclear Security Summit in 2010. Chinese President Hu Jintao sits to President Obama's right as the two leaders discuss keeping nuclear weapons and materials secure.

**Vietnam** At the height of the Cold War, the United States entered what would prove to be its most damaging military intervention thus far. In the southeastern Asian country of Vietnam, nationalist forces from the north, led by Ho Chi Minh, had defeated French colonial forces at Dien Bien Phu in 1954. In Geneva, where international talks on Korea were proceeding, Vietnam was partitioned into a communist north and a capitalist south, with the promise of elections in two years that could unify the country. The elections never materialized, as the struggle between the two Vietnams intensified. Determined to halt the spread of communism, the United States supported the regime in the south under the leadership of Ngo Dinh Diem.

By 1961, Vietnam loomed as a test for President John F. Kennedy's inaugural commitment "to pay any price, to bear any burden, in defense of freedom." Beginning early in the Kennedy administration, first hundreds and then thousands of U.S. military "advisers" were sent to South Vietnam. The American public saw little information about or discussion of U.S. policy in Southeast Asia, and policy makers were left to pursue their own course, which proved to be a mounting commitment of military personnel and equipment.[17]

President Barack Obama delivers a speech at Hradcanske Square in Prague on April 5, 2009. In his keynote address at a summit with European Union leaders, Obama focused on the need to curb nuclear proliferation. The Norwegian Nobel Committee decided that the Nobel Peace Prize for 2009 would be awarded to President Obama for his extraordinary efforts to strengthen international diplomacy and cooperation among peoples. The committee attached special importance to Obama's vision of and work for a world without nuclear weapons.

Within a few weeks of each other in November 1963, both South Vietnamese prime minister Ngo Dinh Diem and President Kennedy were assassinated. Lyndon Johnson assumed the presidency with public declarations of no desire to "widen" the war in Vietnam, but he convinced Congress to support a massive military buildup in Southeast Asia. After an incident in August 1964 in which U.S. destroyers reportedly came under attack by North Vietnamese torpedo boats, Congress passed the **Gulf of Tonkin Resolution,** which provided President Johnson with broad legal authority to combat North Vietnamese aggression. In December 2005, the National Security Agency released hundreds of pages of previously classified top-secret documents that left little doubt that intelligence was deliberately skewed in the 1964 Tonkin Gulf incident to allow for justification of the military buildup.[18]

In July 1965, Lyndon Johnson chose to Americanize the war by increasing U.S. combat strength in Vietnam from 75,000 to 125,000, with additional U.S. forces to be sent when requested by field commander General William Westmoreland. "Now," Johnson wrote in his memoirs, "we were committed to major combat in Vietnam. We had determined not to let that country fall under Communist rule as long as we could prevent it."[19] Yet, Johnson chose to avoid a national debate on the war in order to maximize his political chances of passing the bulk of Great Society legislation. This meant that he chose not to mobilize the

**Gulf of Tonkin Resolution**
Resolution passed by Congress that granted President Lyndon Johnson authority to pursue the war in Vietnam, supposedly based on a naval attack by North Vietnamese ships.

**détente**
An attempt to relax tensions between the United States and the Soviet Union through limited cooperation.

reserves, not to request a general tax increase, and not to publicize the anticipated manpower need—resulting in a war at home and abroad with insufficient resources.

With Richard Nixon's election in 1968, the new president began the process of disengaging America's 550,000 troops from Vietnam. The U.S. national interest in the region was no longer clear, and the anti-war movement grew until the United States was hopelessly split on the issue. Ending the war would take another four years. Finally, a treaty with the North Vietnamese government allowed the United States to withdraw in 1973. Ultimately, the war in Vietnam not only ravaged a nation and a people but it also cost more than 58,000 American lives and hundreds of thousands of Vietnamese lives, and it undercut the credibility of much of the U.S. foreign policy apparatus. In the wake of the withdrawal from Southeast Asia, the American people became profoundly anti-international and anti-military. "No more Vietnams" became the rallying cry for those opposed to military intervention in Africa and Central America. This chapter's timeline provides a history of U.S. intervention abroad.

**APPROACHING Democracy Timeline**

**Committing U.S. Troops to Foreign Soil**

| | |
|---|---|
| 1798 | The United States fights an undeclared naval war with France. |
| 1801 | In the First Barbary War, the United States fights the Barbary States in North Africa over pirating. |
| 1815 | The Second Barbary War brings American troops back to the coast of northern Africa. |
| 1846 | After failing to resolve the disputed border, the United States declares war on Mexico and deploys troops. |
| 1917 | The United States enters military conflict in Europe and World War I by declaring war with Germany. |
| 1942 | The United States enters World War II. |
| 1950 | Nearly 40,000 U.S. troops are killed in Korea during the Korean War. |
| 1958 | At the invitation of the country's president, marines land in Lebanon. |
| 1969 | At the height of the conflict, more than half a million American military troops are in Vietnam. |
| 1982 | U.S. Marines return to Lebanon to assist with the withdrawal of the Palestine Liberation Force from Beirut. |
| 1991 | U.S. forces invade Iraq during the Persian Gulf War. |
| 2001 | In response to the 9/11 attacks, United States forces invade Afghanistan. |
| 2003 | Manipulating raw intelligence, the United States invades Iraq with the goal of eliminating Iraq's weapons of mass destruction. |
| 2007 | President George W. Bush announces an immediate "surge" in U.S. troop numbers for Afghanistan. |
| 2009 | President Barack Obama signs off on plans to send 30,000 additional U.S. troops to Afghanistan. |
| 2011 | American forces enforce a no-fly zone in Libya. |

Democratic  Neutral  Undemocratic

**Détente** Richard Nixon would initiate a policy of **détente,** an attempt to relax tensions between the United States and the USSR. For the United States, the concept of détente was a strategy for managing the emergence of Soviet power through a code of conduct for competition that favored the United States. The Soviet conception of détente was one of peaceful coexistence, which would set aside direct conflict between the superpowers, in order to allow socialist and anti-imperialist forces a free hand.[20]

## The Post–Cold War Era

The year 1989 saw a remarkable change in world politics. Eastern European communist regimes in power at the start of the year were gone by its end. Then, between August and December 1991, the Soviet Union—the Cold War focal point of U.S. foreign policy—ceased to exist. With its demise, the Soviet threat to the United States disappeared, the Cold War came to an end, and the basic premise that drove U.S. foreign policy for almost 50 years—containment—ceased to be relevant.[21]

**The New World Order** The end of the Cold War brought with it a dizzying array of complicated foreign policy issues. Policy makers lost clear guideposts to determine the relative merits of issues and lacked a clear formula for addressing them. The end of the Cold War and the breakup of the Eastern bloc may have nearly eliminated the threat of a global nuclear war, but it also stimulated increasing hostility, violence, and warfare. For example, the breakup of Yugoslavia triggered a genocidal war between various ethnic factions. Without the policy priority of anti-communism, the United States had to weigh carefully both its own interests and its commitments to democracy and human rights before developing a foreign policy response.[22]

The 1991 U.S. deployment in the Persian Gulf War with Iraq would have been almost unthinkable a decade earlier, when the Soviet Union was still a potential force to be reckoned with. On August 2, 1990, Iraqi forces invaded Kuwait. The invasion followed a summer of escalating tension between Iraq and Kuwait on economic disputes about oil production and pricing. Following the invasion, President George H. W. Bush sought and obtained international backing for United Nations Security Resolution 660 that posed economic sanctions and a naval blockade against Iraq.

The Desert Shield military response began on August 7, involving a limited deployment of air and ground forces. Iraq was given until January 15, 1991, to withdraw its forces from Kuwait. On January 17, 1991, Operation Desert Storm began, and by February 26, 1991, the U.S.-led coalition restored sovereignty to Kuwait. Iraq withdrew its remaining troops on February 27. The United States led the charge to make sure Iraq went no farther, and President George H. W. Bush heralded the beginning of a "New World Order."[23] The outlines of this New World Order never came clearly into focus, and the concept means different things to different people. At a minimum, President George H. W. Bush seemed to have in mind the end of the bipolar order and the start of a new order involving the United Nations but actually led by the United States, the world's dominant military power.

With the collapse of the Soviet Union, the threat of cataclysmic nuclear war declined, but there was still a continuing threat of nuclear, biological, and chemical weapons proliferation as countries such as India and Pakistan developed atomic bombs and others like Iran and North Korea sought that capability. President Clinton described rogue states that seek to build "arsenals of nuclear, chemical, and biological weapons and the missiles to deliver them" as the "predators of the twenty-first century."[24]

In his 2002 State of the Union Address, President Bush identified an "axis of evil" that included North Korea, Iraq, and Iran. Bush later created the American military strategy of "preemptive action" against hostile states and terrorist groups. This Bush doctrine stated that "while the United States will constantly strive to enlist the support of the international community, we will not hesitate to act alone, if necessary, to exercise our right of self-defense by acting preemptively against such terrorists."[25]

President Obama has demonstrated a willingness to speak with adversaries, even those considered rogue, but the dilemma over how to respond to both North Korea and Iran illustrates the shades of gray in diplomacy. In Iran, for example, President Obama clearly wants to maintain diplomatic channels in order to talk about Iran's nuclear program, but he also has every interest in seeing a pro-democracy protest movement in the streets of Tehran. Representative Mike Pence, the third-ranking Republican in the House of Representatives, criticized Obama for not speaking more forcefully. "It is appropriate for the leader of the free world at this time to speak a word of encouragement to those dissidents in the street," Pence said.[26]

Secretary of State Hillary Clinton offered the counterbalancing perspective: "We have negotiated with many governments who we did not believe represented the will of their people. Look at all the negotiations that went on with the Soviet Union. Look at the breakthrough and subsequent negotiations with communist China. That's what you do in diplomacy. . . . Clearly, we would hope better for the Iranian people. . . . Yet, we also know that whoever is in charge in Iran is going to be making decisions that will affect the security of the region and the world."[27]

**Free Trade versus Protectionism** Since the end of the Cold War, economic issues and concerns have risen in prominence. The economy has become increasingly globalized, and the world has become increasingly interdependent. One of the first foreign policy debates of the new era was over the North Atlantic Free Trade Agreement (NAFTA), which was intended ultimately to create a North American economy by reducing and eventually eliminating all trade barriers among the United

States, Mexico, and Canada. The final provisions of NAFTA were fully implemented on January 1, 2008. Since that time, NAFTA has contributed to significant increases in agricultural trade and investment among the United States, Canada, and Mexico, and has benefited farmers, ranchers, and consumers throughout North America.

Despite criticizing NAFTA during his first campaign for president, while president, Obama warned against protectionism and put any renegotiation of NAFTA on hold. Trade relations have broadened substantially among the three parties to NAFTA since the deal's implementation, and all three have grown economically, Canada at the fastest average rate, Mexico at the slowest. Yet expert opinion varies on NAFTA's direct impact, given the multitude of other economic factors at play and the possibility that trade liberalization might have happened even without a trilateral agreement.[28]

**A Policy of Enlargement** One U.S. response to the new global economic environment was a policy of *enlargement.* That is, the United States should support enlarging the sphere of market-oriented democracies on the assumption that additional open, democratic, and free-market societies will further U.S. interests. They are good for peace (democracies do not easily go to war with one another) and good for business (more market economies will expand the global market and global economic well-being).

In the wake of the September 11, 2001, attacks on the World Trade Center and the Pentagon, President George W. Bush led an international coalition aimed at defeating international terrorism as well as its network of financial support. The Pentagon named its military campaign "Operation Enduring Freedom."[29] In the weeks following the attack, Great Britain and other sympathetic countries quickly supported U.S. resolve to bomb Taliban positions in Afghanistan, the stronghold of the al Qaeda network.

"In the Battle of Iraq, the United States and our allies have prevailed. And now our coalition is engaged in securing and reconstructing that country," President George W. Bush told the crew of the USS *Abraham Lincoln* on May 1, 2003. During the nearly nine year conflict, 4,500 U.S. troops and 100,000 Iraqis were killed. At a December 2011 ceremony marking the end of the Iraq conflict, President Obama said "everything that American troops have done in Iraq, all the fighting and dying, bleeding and building, training and partnering, has led us to this moment of success."

The situation was different in Iraq, where President Bush employed the doctrine of preemption to justify the unilateral exercise of American military power. Operation Iraqi Freedom was the first time U.S. troops invaded an Arab country with the purpose of deposing its leader and changing the regime.[30] On the evening of March 19, 2003 (the morning of March 20 in Baghdad), U.S. and U.K. military forces began an attempt to disarm Iraq of its weapons of mass destruction and to remove the Iraqi regime from power. On May 1, 2003, aboard the USS *Abraham Lincoln,* with a giant "Mission Accomplished" sign behind him, the president declared, "The battle of Iraq is one victory in a war on terror that began on September 11, 2001, and still goes on."[31]

Yet, the mission was far from accomplished, and it turned out that many of the administration's justifications for going to war were undermined by information showing that Saddam Hussein no longer possessed weapons of mass destruction in 2003.[32] After initiating the conflict in Iraq, many people in other countries began to view President Bush and U.S. foreign policy with growing skepticism and the favorability rating of the United States fell across the globe. As seen in Table 16.1, the election of Barack Obama revitalized global opinion of the United States. President Obama is now much more popular abroad than he is within the United States. Although the Iraqi people voting in elections provided an inspiring moment in Iraq's approach to democracy, we do not yet know if the Iraqi constitution will provide legitimacy and stability after the withdrawal of the U.S. combat troops. President Obama has placed the United States on a carefully paced military withdrawal from Iraq. All U.S. troops are scheduled to leave Iraq by December 31, 2011, and diplomats from the State Department are expected to take over the American support role in Iraq. Commenting on the troop withdrawal, President Obama said, "The bottom line is: The war is ending. Like any sovereign independent nation, Iraq is free to chart its own course."[33]

**Table 16.1** U.S. Favorability Rating by Country

| | 2008 | 2009 | 2010 | *09–10 Change* |
|---|---|---|---|---|
| Britain | 53% | 69% | 65% | –4 |
| France | 42 | 75 | 73 | –2 |
| Germany | 31 | 64 | 63 | –1 |
| Spain | 33 | 58 | 61 | +3 |
| Poland | 68 | 67 | 74 | +7 |
| Russia | 46 | 44 | 57 | +13 |
| Turkey | 12 | 14 | 17 | +3 |
| Egypt | 22 | 27 | 17 | –10 |
| Jordan | 19 | 25 | 21 | –4 |
| Lebanon | 51 | 55 | 52 | –3 |
| China | 41 | 47 | 58 | +11 |
| India | 66 | 76 | 66 | –10 |
| Indonesia | 37 | 63 | 59 | –4 |
| Japan | 50 | 59 | 66 | +7 |
| Pakistan | 19 | 16 | 17 | +1 |
| S. Korea | 70 | 78 | 79 | +1 |
| Argentina | 22 | 38 | 42 | +4 |
| Brazil | — | — | 62 | — |
| Mexico | 47 | 69 | 56 | –13 |
| Kenya* | 87 | 90 | 94 | +4 |
| Nigeria | 64 | 79 | 81 | +2 |

*U.S. favorability from 2007 Pew Research Center Q7a.

*Source:* Pew Research Center's Global Attitudes Project, © 2010, Pew Research Center. Reprinted with the permission of the Pew Research Center's Global Attitudes Project, www.pewglobal.org.

**Foreign Aid and Economic Sanctions** These two traditional tools of foreign policy have also come under scrutiny and debate in the post–Cold War world. Since the end of World War II, foreign aid had been used to help support U.S. allies and interests abroad. In 1961, Congress passed the Foreign Assistance Act that reorganized the U.S. foreign assistance programs, including separating military and nonmilitary aid. The act mandated the creation of an agency to administer economic assistance programs, and President Kennedy established the U.S. Agency for International Development (USAID) as the first U.S. foreign assistance organization whose primary emphasis was on long-range economic and social development assistance efforts. Freed from political and military functions that plagued its predecessor organizations, USAID was able to offer direct support to the developing nations of the world.[34]

USAID works in the policy areas of agriculture, democracy and governance, economic growth, the environment, education, health, global partnerships, and humanitarian assistance. America's foreign assistance has a twofold

## THINKING CRITICALLY

Do you think the evidence that there were no weapons of mass destruction in Iraq will ultimately shape future U.S. foreign policy? If so, what impact will it have? Will the American people require more evidence before following their leaders into war? Will other countries be less likely to support American use of military force?

**economic sanctions**
The use of embargoes and boycotts rather than military force to compel compliance.

purpose of furthering U.S. foreign policy interests in expanding democracy and free markets while improving the lives of the citizens of the developing world. It does so by spending less than one-half of 1 percent of the federal budget.[35]

In addition to foreign aid programs, **economic sanctions** have been a tool for achieving U.S. foreign policy objectives. The Treasury Department's Office of Foreign Assets Control (OFAC) administers economic and trade sanctions against "targeted foreign countries and regimes, terrorists, international narcotics traffickers, those engaged in activities related to the proliferation of weapons of mass destruction, and other threats to the national security, foreign policy or economy of the United States."[36] The current list of OFAC's sanctioned programs include Libya, certain targets in the Western Balkans, North Korea, Iran, Syria, Sudan, Burma (Myanmar), diamond trading, highly enriched uranium, international terrorists and narcotics traffickers, foreign terrorist organizations, and foreign persons who have engaged in activities relating to the proliferation of weapons of mass destruction.[37]

**THINKING CRITICALLY**

Do you favor a sanctions policy against North Korea, even if it means that millions of innocent people will suffer the consequences of scarcity of food or medicine?

Are sanctions really the best way to achieve policy objectives? Former President Jimmy Carter opposed the trade embargo and sanctions policy that have been placed on Cuba since July 8, 1963, under the Trading with the Enemy Act. "One approach is to continue the four-decade effort to isolate and punish Cuba with restricted visits and an economic embargo," said Carter. "The other is for Americans to have maximum contact with Cubans, let them see clearly the advantages of a truly democratic society, and encourage them to bring about orderly changes in their society."[38]

The Obama administration faced an immediate sanctions issue when North Korea announced that it had tested a nuclear device in June 2009. Secretary of State Clinton endorsed the strongest possible trade sanctions, one that would cripple and isolate the rogue regime. "What's important here is the clear message that we're sending to North Korea. . . . North Korea must change their behavior, and we have to get back to moving toward verifiable denuclearization of the Korean Peninsula in a peaceful manner."[39]

Sanctions may have helped in some cases, like in forcing South Africa to eliminate its system of apartheid (strict racial segregation) and move in a more democratic direction, but sanctions against Iraq, Haiti, Bosnia, Serbia, and Cuba, for example, have not achieved their intended effect while clearly hurting ordinary citizens by depriving them of goods or the opportunity to trade and earn a profit. The sanctions imposed on Iraq after its defeat in the 1991 Persian Gulf War clearly hurt his people, but Saddam Hussein continued to build more lavish palaces. Sanctions did not deter North Korea from conducting its underground nuclear test in spring 2009. Yet *coercive diplomacy,* the effort to compel policy change in a target state by means of economic sanctions and trade embargoes, will probably continue, especially against Iran and North Korea.

## THE CONSTITUTION AND FOREIGN POLICY

16.3 *What are the foreign policy powers granted to Congress and the president?*

As you learned in Chapters 2 and 5, the Constitution designates to the president and Congress certain formal powers especially significant for foreign policy. The president was given four types of broad authority in foreign policy:

1. As the commander in chief, the president has the power to commit troops to foreign lands.
2. The president has the power to negotiate treaties with other countries.
3. The president appoints U.S. ambassadors and the heads of all of the executive departments that make foreign policy.
4. The president decides whether or not to receive ambassadors—a decision that determines which nations the United States will formally recognize.

# Compared to WHAT?

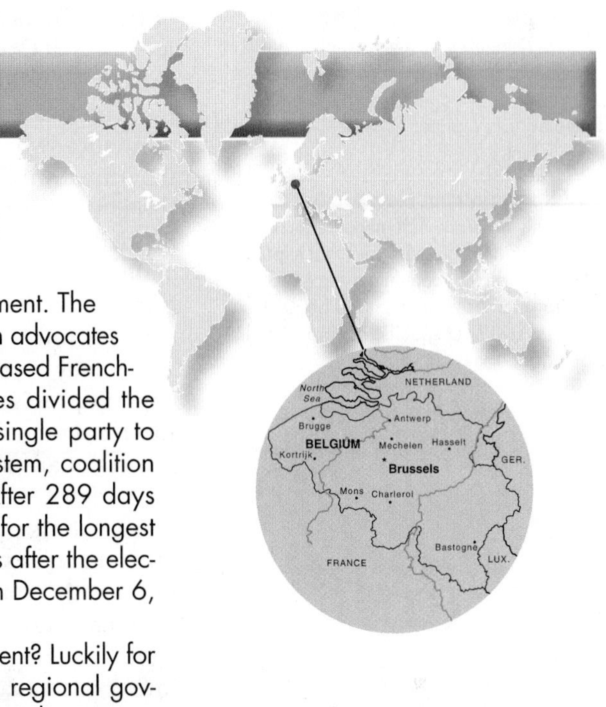


## Conducting Foreign Policy Without a Government: Belgium's World Record Setting Government Coalition Negotiations

On June 13, 2010, Belgium held elections for the nation's parliament. The biggest winner in the election was a Flemish separatist party (which advocates for the secession of northern Belgium) with 27 seats. The southern-based French-speaking social democrats won 26 seats, and ten other parties divided the remaining 97 seats in the legislature. While it is typical for no single party to receive majority control of the legislature in a parliamentary system, coalition negotiations following this election have been record setting. After 289 days without a government, Belgium broke Iraq's record, set in 2010, for the longest a nation has gone without a government. A remarkable 541 days after the election was held, Belgium finally swore in a coalition government on December 6, 2011, nearly doubling the previous world record.

How does a country function for over a year without a government? Luckily for the Belgian people, Belgium is a federal government with strong regional governments that control most domestic policy. But, foreign policy is another matter. Without a government, conducting foreign policy is nearly impossible. Those who held ministerial positions under the previous coalition are allowed to hold their seats until a new coalition is formed. In Belgium, those responsible for conducting foreign policy are those who were voted out of office in 2010. Without a legislative majority, they are not able to easily enact new policy but are able to maintain administrative functions of the government. Remarkably, despite the lack of a government, Belgium was able to send a small number of planes and troops to help enforce the Libyan no-fly zone. How would Americans react if President Bush was still in charge of foreign policy nearly a year and a half after the election of President Obama?

*Sources:* Brian Palmer, "Belgium's World Record," March 29, 2011, Slate.com; Stanley Pignal, "Belgium Edges Closer to Forming Government," September 15, 2011, FT.com; Lawrence Norman, "Belgium Government Finally Sworn In," December 6, 2001, *The Wall Street Journal*.

Congress has significant foreign policy powers, including the power to declare war, appropriate money, and make laws. Congress also has the power to raise and support the armed forces. Thus, it has the power to decide whether or not to back presidential initiatives abroad. Through the advise and consent powers, the Senate has the power to ratify treaties and confirm presidential appointments.

This division of powers reveals how the framers envisioned the roles of these two branches of government in the foreign policy arena. Remembering the problems of dealing with other countries under the Articles of Confederation, the framers gave the president power to conduct negotiations and use troops. Fearing the potential for tyranny, the framers gave Congress significant power to check and balance presidential decisions.

### THINKING CRITICALLY

Why does it matter if citizens of other countries have a positive opinion of the U.S. president? How does this influence foreign policy? What impact, if any, does it have on domestic policy?

## The President versus Congress

If the executive is the driving force behind U.S. foreign policy, Congress acts as the brakes on the president's initiatives. Through its constitutional powers to control the nation's purse strings, to ratify treaties and approve certain officials, and to make war, Congress can counterbalance the considerable power of the president. This allows Congress to have a significant impact on the direction of U.S. foreign policy. Much

**legislative oversight**
The legislature's review and evaluation of executive branch activities to ensure that programs are administered and implemented in a manner consistent with legislative intent.

**War Powers Resolution**
A highly controversial measure passed over President Nixon's veto that stipulated that presidential commitments of U.S. military forces cannot extend beyond 60 days without specific congressional authorization.

of this influence, however, depends on the ever-changing willingness and ability of members of Congress to overcome partisanship and work together. Understandably, Congress's influence in foreign policy has fluctuated greatly since World War II.

The very nature of Congress limits its influence on foreign policy. Congress is a domestically oriented institution whose members are primarily interested in issues that directly influence their constituents. This orientation dampens their interest in foreign policy and tends to warp policy to favor the narrow interests of individual districts. Furthermore, its size, procedures, and dispersed leadership limit Congress's ability to act with the speed often necessary for foreign policy decisions. Characteristically slow, deliberative procedures mean that, on issues of urgency, Congress cannot compete with a president who responds quickly and decisively to international events.

Finally, the president, as the head of the executive branch, enjoys access to the expertise of the executive bureaucracy, which coordinates and implements policy. In recent eras, Congress has increased its access to foreign policy information. The professional staff serving congressional committees has more than doubled since the early 1970s, now totaling well over 10,000. In addition to undertaking research, these staffers provide an important link between Congress and the foreign policy bureaucracy. As such ties between Congress and the bureaucracy have strengthened, the view that foreign policy is the exclusive domain of the president has diminished. The accusations made by former House Speaker Nancy Pelosi that the Central Intelligence Agency had misled her on the use of waterboarding and other enhanced interrogation tactics against detainees illustrates the point that although Congress is not likely to act as the initiator of policy, its oversight role of presidential actions provides a valuable check on our nation's constitutional system.

Beyond Congress's constitutionally granted powers, Congress can influence foreign policy through **legislative oversight.** As we learned in Chapter 5, it can hold hearings, pass laws, and dictate the appropriation of money in an attempt to influence or rein in a president's foreign policy initiatives.

## The War Powers Resolution

Congress passed the **War Powers Resolution** of 1973 in an attempt to restore its balance of power with the executive branch and prevent military involvement without congressional approval. This represented a legislative response to presidential excesses during the Vietnam War, when military involvement escalated without the approval of Congress and with steadily diminishing public support. The War Powers Resolution was a highly controversial measure. In his veto message of the legislation, President Nixon defended the presidential prerogative in foreign policy—that is, the resolution imposed restrictions "which are both unconstitutional and dangerous to the best interests of our nation." He maintained that the president would be unable to act decisively and this would undercut the faith of our allies.

Nevertheless, Congress overrode Nixon's veto and, with passage of the legislation, a president could no longer commit troops for longer than 60 days without specific congressional authorization. An optional 30-day extension was included for issues involving troop safety. The act also provided that any time American forces are engaged in hostilities without specific congressional authorization, Congress can direct the president to disengage the troops by concurrent resolution of the two houses of Congress. The act also urged that the president consult with Congress "in every possible instance" prior to committing forces to hostilities or to situations likely to result in hostilities.

In one respect, the War Powers Resolution sought to reverse the trend toward presidential domination of foreign affairs and fulfill the intent of the framers by ensuring "the collective judgment of the Congress and the President." But the act was also a response to the general expansion of presidential powers at the expense of legislative authority, an attempt to reassert congressional oversight over presidential actions and enhance the power of the legislature. Presidents have generally ignored the War Powers Resolution

## THINKING CRITICALLY

Would you feel safer if Congress or the president primarily directed foreign policy? Do you value the consensus building and debate required in Congress or the expediency of action possible with a unitary actor such as the president?

reporting requirement, seeing it as an unconstitutional infringement on the powers of the president as commander in chief.

In June 2011, a bipartisan group of 10 members of Congress filed a lawsuit against President Obama, arguing that he violated the War Powers Act by committing U.S. resources to the NATO operation in Libya. The White House claimed "the president is of the view that the current US military operations in Libya are consistent with the War Powers Resolution and do not require further congressional authorization" because the United States is not leading the operation and is not engaged in "active exchanges of fire with hostile forces."[40] Many regard this as an overreach of presidential power.

# THE FOREIGN POLICY BUREAUCRACY

16.4 *How is foreign policy implemented?*

Assisting the president in foreign policy development and implementation are about 38 separate government departments and agencies. We will look at four core national security areas and the organizations within each:

1. **Foreign affairs.** This is primarily the domain of the State Department, with other related agencies playing supporting roles. These other agencies include the Agency for International Development, the Arms Control and Disarmament Agency, and the United States Information Agency (which includes Radio Free Europe, Voice of America, and Radio Liberty).
2. **Defense.** National security issues related to defense are dominated by the Defense Department. In matters relating to nuclear energy, the Department of Energy is also involved.
3. **Intelligence.** Although dominated by the Central Intelligence Agency, the intelligence community also includes the State Department's Bureau of Intelligence and Research, the Defense Department's Defense Intelligence Agency, the National Reconnaissance Office, the intelligence components of the individual military services, the Federal Bureau of Investigation, the National Security Agency, and the office of the Director of National Intelligence. One primary responsibility of the Department of Homeland Security is to centralize the analysis of the intelligence obtained by these different agencies.
4. **Economic agencies.** Fierce global economic competition has increased the importance and influence of the departments and agencies responsible for developing and implementing U.S. trade policies, negotiating tariffs with other governments, and representing the United States in various trade forums. Involved are the Departments of Treasury, Commerce, and Agriculture and the Office of the United States Trade Representative.

U.S. Secretary of State Hillary Clinton hosts a bilateral meeting with Vietnamese Foreign Minister Pham Gia Khiem at the Department of State. The secretary of state, appointed by the president with the advice and consent of the Senate, is the president's chief foreign affairs adviser. The secretary carries out the president's foreign policies through the State Department and the Foreign Service of the United States.

## The State Department

The State Department is the oldest and preeminent department of the foreign policy bureaucracy. It is headed by the secretary of state, who is responsible to both the president and the department. The department manages day-to-day foreign affairs, including pursuing diplomatic relations with other countries and international organizations, protecting American citizens and their interests abroad, and gathering and analyzing information bearing on U.S. foreign policy. The State

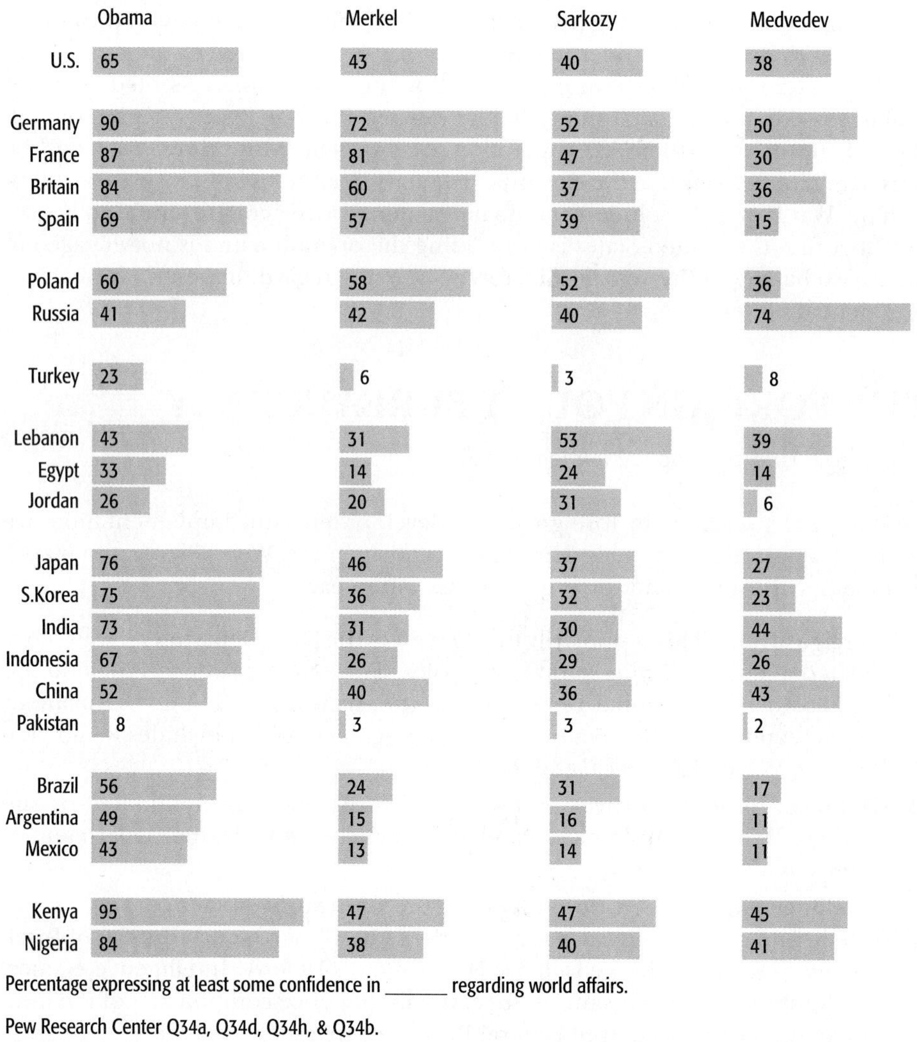

Obama
Merkel
Sarkozy
Medvedev
U.S. 65 43 40 38
Germany 90 72 52 50
France 87 81 47 30
Britain 84 60 37 36
Spain 69 57 39 15
Poland 60 58 52 36
Russia 41 42 40 74
Turkey 23 6 3 8
Lebanon 43 31 53 39
Egypt 33 14 24 14
Jordan 26 20 31 6
Japan 76 46 37 27
S.Korea 75 36 32 23
India 73 31 30 44
Indonesia 67 26 29 26
China 52 40 36 43
Pakistan 8 3 3 2
Brazil 56 24 31 17
Argentina 49 15 16 11
Mexico 43 13 14 11
Kenya 95 47 47 45
Nigeria 84 38 40 41
Percentage expressing at least some confidence in ______ regarding world affairs.
Pew Research Center Q34a, Q34d, Q34h, & Q34b.


**FIGURE 16.2** Confidence in Global Leaders

*Source:* Pew Research Center's Forum on Religion & Public Life, © 2008, Pew Research Center. Reprinted with the permission of the Pew Forum on Religion & Public Life, www.pewforum.org.

Department's embassies, foreign service officers, and representatives to international organizations make it the only department in the executive bureaucracy with a global view. The reputation of the United States is important to the diplomatic work of the State Department. Figure 16.2 illustrates how the world views President Obama's leadership as compared to other important world leaders. In most countries, people have more confidence in President Obama than they do in any other foreign leader.

Often there are power struggles between a secretary of state and secretary of defense, as was the case in the Bush administration between Colin Powell and Donald Rumsfeld. Secretary Hillary Clinton maintains that the current administration fosters a climate of candid and open exchange. "I know very well that a team that works together is going to do a better job for America. . . . We've had administrations where there was just open warfare. You don't see any of that in this administration."[41]

## The Defense Department

The secretary of defense is the president's principal military adviser, is responsible for general defense policy formulation, and oversees all matters of direct concern to the Defense Department. Under the direction of the president, the secretary oversees all American military activity. At the beginning of his term, President Obama asked

President Bush's secretary of defense Robert Gates (a Republican) to remain in his post, which reflected Obama's commitment to bipartisanship as well as his political pragmatism with respect to exiting from Iraq. In 2011, former CIA director Leon Panetta took over the position of secretary of defense.

The Defense Department is composed of four service branches (Army, Navy, Air Force, and Marines) that often compete with each other for influence, authority, and resources. Each branch has a chief of staff. Heading all four branches is the chair of the Joint Chiefs of Staff, who acts as the voice of the military (as opposed to civilian) side of the Pentagon. The chair of the Joint Chiefs of Staff is one of the president's principal military advisers. Each of the four service branches also reports to a civilian secretary. Civilian agencies within the Defense Department handle functions such as logistics and communications. This combination of military and civilian personnel often produces overlapping duties and role confusion.

On July 11, 2011, U.S. Secretary of Defense Leon Panetta thanks troops for their service at Camp Victory in Baghdad, Iraq.

In many areas where the State Department is weak, the Defense Department is exceptionally strong, making it a powerful force in foreign policy making. Strong secretaries of defense—such as Robert McNamara during the Johnson years and Donald Rumsfeld during the Bush term—drove the wars in Vietnam and Iraq, squashing dissent from other institutional actors, most notably the secretary of state. The Defense Department's strongest influence in foreign policy has historically been the result of the close ties between the Pentagon and the corporations that dominate the U.S. weapons industry. Even as early as 1961, President Dwight Eisenhower, in his farewell address, warned of the growing power and influence resulting from the "conjunction of an immense military establishment and a large arms industry." Eisenhower called this phenomenon the **military-industrial complex.** Its development meant that "the potential for the disastrous rise of misplaced power exists and will persist."[42]

With more than 1 million individuals employed by defense-related industries, the Defense Department has many people with a vested interest in its financial well-being. A cut in defense spending can mean the loss of a job for a welder in Lubbock, Texas, whereas a new Air Force base can turn a ghost town into a boom town. Thus, the Defense Department is an integral part of American social, political, and economic life. It has both domestic and international effects, which the State Department, with its exclusively global orientation, does not. The Defense Department is much larger than the State Department, with about 3 million military and civilian employees.

## The National Security Council

The National Security Council (NSC) was created in 1947 to advise the president on all domestic, foreign, and military policies relating to national security. Members of the NSC include the president (as chair); the president's national security adviser, who acts as the special assistant for national security; the vice president; and the secretaries of state and defense. The CIA director and the chair of the Joint Chiefs of Staff sit in as advisers. Various other cabinet and agency heads, such as the secretary of the treasury, the attorney general, and the U.S. ambassador to the United Nations, participate as needed.

Through the National Security Council, the president coordinates the different government agencies dealing with foreign or defense policy. The NSC became especially active under President Kennedy and his special assistant for national security, McGeorge Bundy. Under Bundy, the staff became the president's key personal foreign policy "team." What emerged was an informally structured organization for the formulation and implementation of foreign policy that has persisted to this day. Such an organization works both for and against the executive branch, however, affording a base for quick and secretive executive-level responses to national security problems but allowing a sometimes dangerous policy-making latitude to unelected and relatively unaccountable decision makers. For example, the controversial Iran-Contra "arms-for-hostages" operation was conceived in the NSC and run by Lieutenant Oliver North.

**military-industrial complex**
What President Eisenhower in 1961 called the growing power and influence resulting from the "conjunction of an immense military establishment and a large arms industry."

By decreasing the president's reliance on the bureaucracy for information and advice, the NSC adviser and staff can become a "screen" between the president and the rest of government, reducing the president's direct influence and personal leadership. This intervention has led to serious rivalries among the national security adviser, the secretaries of state and defense, the director of the CIA, and their staffs. The relative influence and access of each organization often depend on the personal relationship between each department head and the president.

The national security adviser's role has changed over the years, based on the personality of the appointee to the post. Presidents have shaped the position to fit appointees' personal management styles. On the whole, however, the national security adviser remains an extremely influential, although often anonymous, policy maker.

**QUICK REVIEW**

National Security Council

- The NSC was created in 1947 to provide the president with advice on policies relating to national security.
- National security advisers act as special assistants for national security.
- The vice president, secretaries of state and defense, director of the CIA, and chair of the Joint Chiefs of Staff sit in as advisers.

## The CIA and Intelligence Gathering

The Central Intelligence Agency (CIA) is the dominant force in the intelligence community. It was established after World War II to be the president's nonpartisan resource for coordinated intelligence analysis. However, its mission quickly expanded to include covert operations such as espionage, psychological warfare, paramilitary maneuvers, and political and economic intervention.

The CIA's most important function is information gathering, although its failure to process intelligence information relating to the attacks on September 11, 2001, has raised serious questions of competence. It is responsible for collecting information about the state of leadership in other countries, as well as their political situation and stability; military capabilities; strengths and weaknesses; and possible intentions in political, economic, and military spheres. All of this information is analyzed and reported to policy makers so they can make better decisions on foreign policy issues. In February 2008, the CIA admitted to using waterboarding, a form of forced simulated drowning, as an interrogation tactic on 9/11 suspects. Many human rights groups consider waterboarding as torture, and a public outcry soon followed.

**THINKING CRITICALLY**

How much do you believe the president should rely on foreign policy advisers? Can a president give too much power to these unelected officials?

## The Agencies Behind Economic Policy Making

In the 1960s, the overwhelming economic superiority of the United States began to dwindle, in part because of economic dislocations triggered by financing the Vietnam War. But, more important, this period also witnessed the first stirrings of real economic strength from the European and Asian economies ravaged by World War II and rebuilt with considerable assistance from the United States. As the economies of Europe and Japan expanded, the corresponding American share of world markets decreased. In addition, U.S. foreign policy priorities changed with the end of the Cold War. Such global economic shifts and political changes led to similar shifts in the balance of influence among the government organizations involved in foreign policy. The foreign policy establishment—formerly dominated by the National Security Council, the State Department, and the Pentagon—now features such actors as the Department of Commerce and the Office of the Trade Representative in roles of unprecedented prominence. Economic power is the overriding issue for these agencies.

These departments and agencies play highly specialized roles in making foreign policy. The Department of Labor, for example, represented the United States in international negotiations on the General Agreement on Tariffs and Trade (GATT, now the World Trade Organization), the Organization for Economic Cooperation and Development (OECD), and the International Labor Organization (ILO). The Department of Agriculture has its own Foreign Agricultural Service, which formulates, administers, and coordinates the department's programs overseas. The Department of

## APPROACHING
### Contemporary Issues in Democracy

### Transparency and the CIA

**ISSUE:** What if the CIA was required to share all covert and secret operations with Congress?

**Question 1:**
How would complete transparency in the CIA impact the role of public opinion in foreign policy?

**Question 2:**
How would a lack of secrecy in the CIA endanger American lives both at home and abroad?

**Question 3:**
Are covert operations and secrecy necessary in national security operations?

Energy conducts nuclear weapons research as well as development, production, and surveillance operations.

The Treasury and Commerce departments, in particular, are central figures in making global economic policy. The Treasury Department is primarily concerned with financial policy development. It focuses on trade regulations, exchange rates, and the balance of payments. Unlike the State Department, which judges nations largely on the basis of their political systems, or the Defense Department, which looks at military strength, the Treasury Department addresses a foreign nation's economic system and how it affects the U.S. economy. For example, is a nation's exchange rate fair? Is its tariff structure conducive to U.S. exports? How do American exports to a particular nation compare with American imports from it?

Although the Treasury Department develops U.S. financial policy, the Commerce Department expands and protects U.S. commerce abroad through the Foreign Commercial Service. Similar to the State Department's Foreign Service, the Foreign Commercial Service works through U.S. embassies and consulates, advising foreign businesses on their U.S.-related business activities. The Commerce Department also maintains nearly 50 offices in the United States to encourage U.S. firms to export their products.

Much of the actual foreign policy making takes place within the nooks and crannies of the State Department, the Pentagon, and other agencies and departments, as career bureaucrats exercise their delegated and nondelegated discretionary decision-making power to develop policy. Because these bureaucrats have the expertise to analyze the immense volume of foreign policy information, a president needs the bureaucracy's support to be successful in foreign policy. The bureaucracy also assists with policy implementation. This task is a far-flung process in terms of geography and the vast array of departments and agencies that must cooperate on a given issue.

Members and supporters of the Washington Region Religious Campaign Against Torture rallied on Capitol Hill to "demand congressional action to stop torture." The group believes that torture violates the basic dignity of human persons and degrades everyone involved—policy makers, perpetrators, and victims. It contradicts our nation's most cherished ideals. Any policies that permit torture and inhumane treatment are morally intolerable. This protest was prompted by President Bush's veto of H.R. 2082, prohibiting all U.S. intelligence agencies, including the CIA, from subjecting detainees to waterboarding, stress positions, hypothermia, and other forms of torture. Their protests continued throughout the first year of the Obama presidency.

# DEMOCRATIC CHECKS ON FOREIGN POLICY

16.5 *What are the democratic checks on the government's foreign policy powers?*

In no other realm of government activity is the exercise of democratic control less apparent than in the making of foreign policy. Both the complex nature of global affairs and the crisis atmosphere that sometimes prevails can lead the national security establishment to ignore public opinion. Similarly, the increasing use of executive agreements and covert operations means that decisions often unfold out of public view and without any opportunity for public debate except after the fact.

Although the president is the primary initiator of foreign policy, important checks limit the president's power to make foreign policy. We have already looked at how Congress can check presidential foreign policy using its oversight power to force open the decision-making process. Let us now turn to how the media and public opinion can also act as a check on foreign policy outcomes.

## The Media

As we learned in Chapter 12, the media play an important role in the surveillance, investigation, criticism, and advocacy of the government's foreign policy activities. The media provide American citizens with most of their knowledge about the rest of the world. Although the media are ostensibly neutral and objective, they typically mirror the opinions of the foreign policy establishment. However, the media sometimes offer competing perspectives on international affairs. On occasion, individual reporters have questioned or strongly opposed government policies, stimulating public opposition. Press criticism of the Johnson administration's direction of the Vietnam War, although not widespread, served to chip away at the "monopoly of information" enjoyed by the White House, challenging the government version of reality and stimulating public criticism of U.S. involvement in Southeast Asia.

More commonly, though, the press serves as a conduit for the opinions of various actors involved in the policy process. The leak, a calculated release of controversial information, is a tool used at all levels of the bureaucracy for a variety of purposes. The right words at the right time can stir up Congress, the public, and foreign governments and put an end to a controversial foreign policy initiative. Key players in the foreign policy process often release information to friendly reporters to test the waters of public response to policy options under consideration.

With few exceptions, the American press is reluctant to strongly oppose U.S. government actions when the deployment of American troops is involved. Throughout most of the Vietnam War, the press, like most of the general public, supported the U.S. presence in Southeast Asia, breaking with the official version of U.S. policy in Vietnam only when the inconsistencies and contradictions of that policy had become glaringly apparent. This supportive role was even more apparent during more recent actions, including the U.S. invasions of Grenada, Panama, and Iraq. In each case, most media analysts relied on government sources; accepted government explanations; and focused predominantly on tactical and technical, rather than ethical or moral, analysis.

Nevertheless, the media can be credited with providing Americans with a wealth of information, thereby helping them become better-informed citizens. And the constitutional guarantees of a free press and free speech afford American citizens a small but sometimes persistent and influential voice in the otherwise elite-dominated foreign policy process.[43]

## The Public

Often overlooked in analyses of foreign policy decision making is the role played by the public and public opinion. The voice of public opinion occasionally penetrates the carefully encrypted speech and muffled secrecy of foreign policy making to have an impact. Popular discontent with Vietnam is an example of the government abiding by public opinion to reverse a long-standing policy. Historically, the public tends to rally around the president in times of national crisis, such as war, international confrontation, or when fighting international terrorism.

Policy makers and the public must cope with forces of change in politics, economics, technology, and demographics. The public must assess not only American interests in world affairs but also our proper role as global citizens. In this quickly changing world, questions for the public's consideration about foreign policy abound. What is the proper relationship between the United States and the United Nations? What should be the future role of peacekeeping operations and foreign aid programs? How will the United States balance economic and political interests when they collide? How will it balance economic and political interests against humanitarian and environmental concerns?

In a June 2009 speech in Cairo titled "A New Beginning With Muslims," Barack Obama provided a framework for a new American relationship with the world's 1.5 billion Muslims. He also addressed America's theme of approaching democracy: "The danger I think is when the United States or any country thinks that we can simply impose these values on another country with a different history and a different culture . . . democracy, rule of law, freedom of speech, freedom of religion—those are not simply principles of the West to be hoisted on these countries, but rather what I believe to be universal principles that they can embrace and affirm as part of their national identity."

We must respond to such questions in the context of our ongoing experiment in self-government and within the democratic limits established in the Constitution. Ultimately, then, our paramount challenge is how to balance the interests of security and the requirements of democracy. Understanding the link between foreign policy and democracy requires that the public recognize the dramatically altered world environment that involves threats from terrorists and rogue countries that are likely to endure throughout our lifetime. How can we take necessary measures to combat terrorism while at the same time protecting the values we cherish as our democratic ideal? That discussion is the essence of "approaching democracy."

## Summary

**16.1** *What is American exceptionalism?*

- Much of American history is rooted in the concept of American exceptionalism, drawing inspiration from a sermon by John Winthrop, founding governor of Massachusetts Bay Colony, who observed, "We shall be as a City upon a Hill." Winthrop believed that God had summoned those settling in New England to serve as a model of all mankind. American presidents have frequently invoked Winthrop's words as a theme for their vision for America's providential role in the world.

**16.2** *How has U.S. foreign policy evolved from isolationism to engagement?*

- Before World War I, U.S. foreign policy was characterized by isolationism, in which the United States fostered trade with Europe without committing to strategic alliances. Despite its policy of neutrality, the United States clearly favored Britain and the Allies at the beginning of World War I and entered the war after Germany resumed unrestricted submarine warfare. Following the war, however, isolationism again prevailed.
- The United States was initially reluctant to enter World War II but did so after Japan's surprise bombing of Pearl Harbor. After the war, its primary foreign policy goal was *containment* of communism, which placed it in direct opposition to the Soviet Union and led to the Cold War.
- After 1949, both the United States and the Soviet Union poured vast amounts of money into developing and deploying nuclear weapons. During the same period, U.S. foreign aid commitments increased in an effort to prevent Soviet advances in less developed countries.
- During the 1960s, the effort to contain communism gradually drew the United States into a full-scale war in Vietnam, a war that proved to be both a military and foreign policy disaster. After the war, the United States entered into a *détente* with the Soviet Union and began discussing ways to reduce the nuclear threat.
- In 1991, the Soviet Union ceased to exist, thereby ending the Cold War and clearing the way for what President George H. W. Bush hoped would be a New World Order. The United States shifted its military focus to combat other international threats to American safety. Considered rogue for challenging the hegemony of American foreign policy, these nations command a minor amount of weapons capable of inflicting "massive destruction," like the nuclear weapons possessed by the United States.

16.3 *What are the foreign policy powers granted to Congress and the president?*

- The Constitution gives the president the authority to commit troops to foreign lands, negotiate treaties, appoint ambassadors, and decide whether or not to receive ambassadors, an action indicating formal recognition. Congress has the power to declare war, appropriate money, and make laws, thereby deciding which presidential initiatives abroad to support. The Senate also has the power to ratify treaties and confirm presidential appointments.
- The president determines the general direction of foreign policy and the effectiveness of its implementation by the bureaucracy. Congress tends to be oriented toward domestic policy and cannot respond quickly and decisively to international events. It has attempted to strengthen its foreign policy oversight through legislation. Congress can also restrict the executive branch's foreign policy efforts by limiting appropriations for foreign aid, military spending, and intelligence gathering.

16.4 *How is foreign policy implemented?*

- Although the State Department has primary responsibility for developing and implementing foreign policy, the Defense Department also plays an important role through its large share of the federal budget and considerable political clout. For information and policy planning, however, the president depends on the National Security Council.
- The Central Intelligence Agency, along with several other agencies, gathers and analyzes intelligence about the activities of foreign governments. It also engages in covert operations such as espionage, psychological warfare, and paramilitary operations. Concern about the CIA's possible abuses of power has led to attempts to restructure the agency and bring it under greater congressional and executive control.

16.5 *What are the democratic checks on the government's foreign policy powers?*

- The complex nature of global affairs and the crisis atmosphere that sometimes prevails can lead the national security establishment to ignore public opinion. Similarly, the increasing use of executive agreements and covert operations means that decisions often unfold out of public view and without any opportunity for public debate except after the fact.
- The media provide American citizens with most of their knowledge of the rest of the world. The media can function as a watchdog of government action, but often serves as a conduit for the opinions of the foreign policy establishment. Historically, U.S. citizens have had little significant influence on the foreign policy created by their government. The public tends to rally around the president in times of national crisis, such as war or international confrontation.

## Key Terms

bipolarity, 519
Cold War, 519
containment, 518
détente, 522
economic sanctions, 526
foreign aid, 520
foreign policy, 514
globalism, 519
Gulf of Tonkin Resolution, 521
isolationism, 516
legislative oversight, 528
military-industrial complex, 531
Monroe Doctrine, 516
North Atlantic Treaty Organization (NATO), 519
Peace Corps, 520
Strategic Arms Limitation Treaty (SALT), 520
superpower, 518
War Powers Resolution, 528
Warsaw Pact, 519

## Test Yourself Chapter 16

**1.** Since the end of World War II, U.S. foreign policy has been
a. quite similar to what it was before the Civil War.
b. a cautious balancing act between American democratic ideals and U.S. military and economic interests.
c. an attempt to destabilize any country that proposes obtaining nuclear capabilities.
d. genuinely uniform without any deviations in methods of bringing about peace.

**2.** All the following are core goals of American foreign relations *except*
a. military security.
b. isolationism.
c. survival and independence.
d. economic security.

**3.** What was the dominant foreign policy during the 19th century?
a. Globalism.
b. Containment.
c. Isolationism.
d. Internationalism.

**4.** What policy did the Monroe Doctrine reinforce?
a. Globalism.
b. Regionalism.
c. Isolationism.
d. Containment.

**5.** During the post–World War II period, the term *superpower* applied
a. only to the United States.
b. both to the United States and the Soviet Union.
c. to the Western and communist alliance systems.
d. to any nation that developed an atomic bomb.

**6.** What doctrine guided U.S. foreign policy between 1947 and 1990?
a. Isolationism.
b. Globalism.
c. Containment.
d. Regionalism.

**7.** The intention to assist free, democratic nations beat back the threat of totalitarianism became known as the
a. Monroe Doctrine.
b. Truman Doctrine.
c. New World Order.
d. War Powers Resolution.

**8.** The Gulf of Tonkin Resolution granted
a. President Nixon authority to initiate a policy of détente.
b. President Johnson authority to pursue the war in Vietnam.
c. President Kennedy authority to invade Cuba.
d. President George Bush authority to invade Iraq in 1991.

**9.** With the demise of the Soviet Union and the post–Cold War changes in the international system, the U.S. employment of containment as its guiding foreign policy principle
a. is no longer as relevant.
b. is still as relevant as in the past, because a new Soviet Union might form in the very near future.
c. is still relevant because it can now be applied to the communist nations of Latin America.
d. will now be applied exclusively to China and North Korea.

**10.** The Doctrine of Containment
a. was the key component of the Truman Doctrine.
b. was developed in the Soviet Union to counter the Marshall Plan.
c. ended the U.S. commitment to the League of Nations.
d. was the informal policy of preventing Japan from having a military after World War II.

**11.** The policy of détente contributed to
a. a further escalation of the Cold War.
b. the Vietnam War.
c. the development of the United Nations.
d. an attempt to relax tensions between the United States and the Soviet Union.

**12.** At the height of the Cold War, the United States entered what would prove to be its most damaging military intervention which was:
a. the war in the Persian Gulf.
b. the war in Vietnam.
c. the Korean War.
d. the war on terrorism.

**13.** Congress has what foreign policy power?
a. To declare war.
b. To make laws.
c. To appropriate money.
d. All of the above.

**14.** What did Congress pass in 1973 in an attempt to restore the balance of power with the executive branch and prevent military involvement without congressional approval?
a. The Warsaw Pact.
b. The Gulf of Tonkin Resolution.
c. The Strategic Arms Limitation Treaty.
d. The War Powers Resolution.

**15.** In his 2002 State of the Union address, President Bush named an "axis of evil" that included
a. South Korea, Turkey, and Iraq.
b. North Korea, Iraq, and Iran.
c. Iran, South Korea, and Egypt.
d. Cuba, North Korea, and Turkey.

**16.** Foreign affairs is primarily the domain of the Department of
a. Energy.
b. State.
c. Defense.
d. Treasury.

**17.** Legislative oversight
a. does not apply to foreign affairs.
b. cannot apply to the activities of the Central Intelligence Agency.
c. must be approved by the president when foreign affairs is the subject.
d. is a means of influence by Congress over foreign policy.

**18.** Who is the driving force behind U.S. foreign policy?
a. The president.
b. The U.S. Senate.
c. The U.S. House of Representatives.
d. The Central Intelligence Agency.

**19.** The use of embargoes and boycotts rather than military force to compel compliance is referred to as
a. economic sanctions.
b. détente.
c. foreign activism.
d. enlargement.

**20.** What is the CIA's most important function?
a. Recruiting spies who can engage in espionage against other countries.
b. The gathering of political, economic, and military information about other nations.
c. Spying on American citizens who may be terrorists or subversives.
d. Paramilitary maneuvers.

**ANSWERS**
**1.** b, **2.** b, **3.** c, **4.** c, **5.** b, **6.** c, **7.** b, **8.** b, **9.** a, **10.** a, **11.** d,
**12.** b, **13.** d, **14.** d, **15.** b, **16.** b, **17.** d, **18.** a, **19.** a, **20.** b

# Appendices

# Appendix 1

## INTRODUCING THE CONCEPT OF APPROACHING DEMOCRACY

### Excerpts of a Speech by Vaclav Havel, President of the Czech Republic to a Joint Session of the U.S. Congress, Washington, DC, February 21, 1990

Dear Mr. Speaker, dear Mr. President, dear senators and members of the House, ladies and gentlemen:

I've only been president for two months, and I haven't attended any schools for presidents. My only school was life itself. Therefore, I don't want to burden you any longer with my political thoughts, but instead I will move on to an area that is more familiar to me, to what I would call the philosophical aspect of those changes that still concern everyone, although they are taking place in our corner of the world.

As long as people are people, democracy in the full sense of the word will always be no more than an ideal; one may approach it as one would a horizon, in ways that may be better or worse, but it can never be fully attained. In this sense you are also merely approaching democracy. You have thousands of problems of all kinds, as other countries do. But you have one great advantage: You have been approaching democracy uninterruptedly for more than 200 years, and your journey toward that horizon has never been disrupted by a totalitarian system. Czechs and Slovaks, despite their humanistic traditions that go back to the first millennium, have approached democracy for a mere twenty years, between the two world wars, and now for three and a half months since the 17th of November of last year.

The advantage that you have over us is obvious at once.

The Communist type of totalitarian system has left both our nations, Czechs and Slovaks as it has all the nations of the Soviet Union, and the other countries the Soviet Union subjugated in its time a legacy of countless dead, an infinite spectrum of human suffering, profound economic decline, and above all enormous human humiliation. It has brought us horrors that fortunately you have not known.

At the same time, however unintentionally, of course it has given us something positive: a special capacity to look, from time to time, somewhat further than someone who has not undergone this bitter experience. A person who cannot move and live a normal life because he is pinned under a boulder has more time to think about his hopes than someone who is not trapped in this way.

What I am trying to say is this: We must all learn many things from you, from how to educate our offspring, how to elect our representatives, all the way to how to organize our economic life so that it will lead to prosperity and not poverty. But it doesn't have to be merely assistance from the well educated, the powerful, and the wealthy to someone who has nothing to offer in return.

We too can offer something to you: our experience and the knowledge that has come from it.

This is a subject for books, many of which have already been written and many of which have yet to be written. I shall therefore limit myself to a single idea.

The specific experience I'm talking about has given me one great certainty: Consciousness precedes Being, and not the other way around, as Marxists claim.

For this reason, the salvation of this human world lies nowhere else than in the human heart, in the human power to reflect, in human humbleness and in human responsibility.

Without a global revolution in the sphere of human consciousness, nothing will change for the better in the sphere of our Being as humans, and the catastrophe toward which this world is headed, whether it be ecological, social, demographic or a general breakdown of civilization, will be unavoidable. If we are no longer threatened by world war or by the danger that the absurd mountains of accumulated nuclear weapons might blow up the world, this does not mean that we have definitively won. We are in fact far from definite victory.

We are still a long way from that "family of man"; in fact, we seem to be receding from the ideal rather than drawing closer to it. Interests of all kinds: personal, selfish, state, national, group and, if you like, company interests still considerably outweigh genuinely common and global interests. We are still under the sway of the destructive and thoroughly vain belief that man is the pinnacle of creation, and not just a part of it, and that therefore everything is permitted. There are still many who say they are concerned not for themselves but for the cause, while they are demonstrably out for themselves and not for the cause at all. We are still destroying the planet that was entrusted to us, and its environment. We still close our eyes to the growing social, ethnic and cultural conflicts in the world. From time to time we say that the anonymous megamachinery we have created for ourselves no longer serves us but rather has enslaved us, yet we still fail to do anything about it.

In other words, we still don't know how to put morality ahead of politics, science and economics. We are still incapable of understanding that the only genuine backbone of all our actions if they are to be moral is responsibility. Responsibility to something higher than my family, my country, my firm, my success. Responsibility to the order of Being, where all our actions are indelibly recorded and where, and only where, they will be properly judged.

The interpreter or mediator between us and this higher authority is what is traditionally referred to as human conscience.

If I subordinate my political behaviour to this imperative, I can't go far wrong. If on the contrary I were not guided by this voice, not even ten presidential schools with 2,000 of the best political scientists in the world could help me.

This is why I ultimately decided after resisting for a long time to accept the burden of political responsibility.

I'm not the first nor will I be the last intellectual to do this. On the contrary, my feeling is that there will be more and more of them all the time. If the hope of the world lies in human consciousness, then it is obvious that intellectuals cannot go on forever avoiding their share of responsibility for the world and hiding their distastes for politics under an alleged need to be independent.

It is easy to have independence in your programme and then leave others to carry out that programme. If everyone thought that way, soon no one would be independent.

I think that Americans should understand this way of thinking. Wasn't it the best minds of your country, people you could call intellectuals, who wrote your famous Declaration of Independence, your Bill of Rights, and your Constitution, and who above all took upon themselves the practical responsibility for putting them into practice? The worker from Branik in Prague, whom your president referred to in his State of the Union message this year, is far from being the only person in Czechoslovakia, let alone in the world, to be inspired by those great documents. They inspire us all. They inspire us despite the fact that they are over 200 years old. They inspire us to be citizens.

When Thomas Jefferson wrote that "Governments are instituted among Men, deriving their just powers from the Consent of the Governed," it was a simple and important act of the human spirit.

What gave meaning to that act, however, was the fact that the author backed it up with his life. It was not just his words, it was his deeds as well.

I will end where I began. History has accelerated. I believe that once again, it will be the human spirit that will notice this acceleration, give it a name, and transform those words into deeds.

# Appendix 2

## Presidents and Congresses, 1789–February 2012

| Term | President and Vice President | Party of President | Congress | Majority Party House | Majority Party Senate |
|---|---|---|---|---|---|
| 1789–97 | **George Washington**<br>John Adams | None | 1st<br>2d<br>3d<br>4th | N/A<br>N/A<br>N/A<br>N/A | N/A<br>N/A<br>N/A<br>N/A |
| 1797–1801 | **John Adams**<br>Thomas Jefferson | Fed | 5th<br>6th | N/A<br>Fed | N/A<br>Fed |
| 1801–09 | **Thomas Jefferson**<br>Aaron Burr (1801–05)<br>George Clinton (1805–09) | Dem Rep | 7th<br>8th<br>9th<br>10th | Dem Rep<br>Dem Rep<br>Dem Rep<br>Dem Rep | Dem Rep<br>Dem Rep<br>Dem Rep<br>Dem Rep |
| 1809–17 | **James Madison**<br>George Clinton (1809–12)[1]<br>Elbridge Gerry (1813–14)[1] | Dem Rep | 11th<br>12th<br>13th<br>14th | Dem Rep<br>Dem Rep<br>Dem Rep<br>Dem Rep | Dem Rep<br>Dem Rep<br>Dem Rep<br>Dem Rep |
| 1817–25 | **James Monroe**<br>Daniel D. Tompkins | Dem Rep | 15th<br>16th<br>17th<br>18th | Dem Rep<br>Dem Rep<br>Dem Rep<br>Dem Rep | Dem Rep<br>Dem Rep<br>Dem Rep<br>Dem Rep |
| 1825–29 | **John Quincy Adams**<br>John C. Calhoun | Nat'l Rep | 19th<br>20th | Nat'l Rep<br>Dem | Nat'l Rep<br>Dem |
| 1829–37 | **Andrew Jackson**<br>John C. Calhoun (1829–32)[2]<br>Martin Van Buren (1833–37) | Dem | 21st<br>22d<br>23d<br>24th | Dem<br>Dem<br>Dem<br>Dem | Dem<br>Dem<br>Dem<br>Dem |
| 1837–41 | **Martin Van Buren**<br>Richard M. Johnson | Dem | 25th<br>26th | Dem<br>Dem | Dem<br>Dem |
| 1841 | **William H. Harrison**[1]<br>John Tyler (1841) | Whig | | | |
| 1841–45 | **John Tyler**<br>(VP vacant) | Whig | 27th<br>28th | Whig<br>Dem | Whig<br>Whig |
| 1845–49 | **James K. Polk**<br>George M. Dallas | Dem | 29th<br>30th | Dem<br>Whig | Dem<br>Dem |
| 1849–50 | **Zachary Taylor**[1]<br>Millard Fillmore | Whig | 31st | Dem | Dem |
| 1850–53 | **Millard Fillmore**<br>(VP vacant) | Whig | 32d | Dem | Dem |
| 1853–57 | **Franklin Pierce**<br>William R. D. King (1853)[1] | Dem | 33d<br>34th | Dem<br>Rep | Dem<br>Dem |
| 1857–61 | **James Buchanan**<br>John C. Breckinridge | Dem | 35th<br>36th | Dem<br>Rep | Dem<br>Dem |
| 1861–65 | **Abraham Lincoln**[1]<br>Hannibal Hamlin (1861–65)<br>Andrew Johnson (1865) | Rep | 37th<br>38th<br>38th | Rep<br>Rep<br>Rep | Rep<br>Rep<br>Rep |
| 1865–69 | **Andrew Johnson**<br>(VP vacant) | Rep | 39th<br>40th | Union<br>Rep | Union<br>Rep |
| 1869–77 | **Ulysses S. Grant**<br>Schuyler Colfax (1869–73)<br>Henry Wilson (1873–75)[1] | Rep | 41st<br>42d<br>43d<br>44th | Rep<br>Rep<br>Rep<br>Dem | Rep<br>Rep<br>Rep<br>Rep |
| 1877–81 | **Rutherford B. Hayes**<br>William A. Wheeler | Rep | 45th<br>46th | Dem<br>Dem | Rep<br>Dem |
| 1881 | **James A. Garfield**[1]<br>Chester A. Arthur | Rep | 47th | Rep | Rep |
| 1881–85 | **Chester A. Arthur**<br>(VP vacant) | Rep | 48th | Dem | Rep |
| 1885–89 | **Grover Cleveland**<br>Thomas A. Hendricks (1885)[1] | Dem | 49th<br>50th | Dem<br>Dem | Rep<br>Rep |
| 1889–93 | **Benjamin Harrison**<br>Levi P. Morton | Rep | 51st<br>52d | Rep<br>Dem | Rep<br>Rep |
| 1893–97 | **Grover Cleveland**<br>Adlai E. Stevenson | Dem | 53d<br>54th | Dem<br>Rep | Dem<br>Rep |

| Term | President and Vice President | Party of President | Congress | Majority Party House | Majority Party Senate |
|---|---|---|---|---|---|
| 1897–1901 | **William McKinley**[1] | Rep | 55th | Rep | Rep |
| | Garret A. Hobart (1897–99)[1] | | 56th | Rep | Rep |
| | Theodore Roosevelt (1901) | | | | |
| 1901–09 | **Theodore Roosevelt** | Rep | 57th | Rep | Rep |
| | (VP vacant, 1901–05) | | 58th | Rep | Rep |
| | Charles W. Fairbanks (1905–09) | | 59th | Rep | Rep |
| | | | 60th | Rep | Rep |
| 1909–13 | **William Howard Taft** | Rep | 61st | Rep | Rep |
| | James S. Sherman (1909–12)[1] | | 62d | Dem | Rep |
| 1913–21 | **Woodrow Wilson** | Dem | 63d | Dem | Dem |
| | Thomas R. Marshall | | 64th | Dem | Dem |
| | | | 65th | Dem | Dem |
| | | | 66th | Rep | Rep |
| 1921–23 | **Warren G. Harding**[1] | Rep | 67th | Rep | Rep |
| | Calvin Coolidge | | | | |
| 1923–29 | **Calvin Coolidge** | Rep | 68th | Rep | Rep |
| | (VP vacant, 1923–25) | | 69th | Rep | Rep |
| | Charles G. Dawes (1925–29) | | 70th | Rep | Rep |
| 1929–33 | **Herbert Hoover** | Rep | 71st | Rep | Rep |
| | Charles Curtis | | 72d | Dem | Rep |
| 1933–45 | **Franklin D. Roosevelt**[1] | Dem | 73d | Dem | Dem |
| | John N. Garner (1933–41) | | 74th | Dem | Dem |
| | Henry A. Wallace (1941–45) | | 75th | Dem | Dem |
| | Harry S. Truman (1945) | | 76th | Dem | Dem |
| | | | 77th | Dem | Dem |
| | | | 78th | Dem | Dem |
| 1945–53 | **Harry S. Truman** | Dem | 79th | Dem | Dem |
| | (VP vacant, 1945–49) | | 80th | Rep | Rep |
| | Alben W. Barkley (1949–53) | | 81st | Dem | Dem |
| | | | 82d | Dem | Dem |
| 1953–61 | **Dwight D. Eisenhower** | Rep | 83d | Rep | Rep |
| | Richard M. Nixon | | 84th | Dem | Dem |
| | | | 85th | Dem | Dem |
| | | | 86th | Dem | Dem |
| 1961–63 | **John F. Kennedy**[1] | Dem | 87th | Dem | Dem |
| | Lyndon B. Johnson (1961–63) | | | | |
| 1963–69 | **Lyndon B. Johnson** | Dem | 88th | Dem | Dem |
| | (VP vacant, 1963–65) | | 89th | Dem | Dem |
| | Hubert H. Humphrey (1965–69) | | 90th | Dem | Dem |
| 1969–74 | **Richard M. Nixon**[3] | Rep | 91st | Dem | Dem |
| | Spiro T. Agnew (1969–73)[2] | | 92d | Dem | Dem |
| | Gerald R. Ford (1973–74)[4] | | | | |
| 1974–77 | **Gerald R. Ford** | Rep | 93d | Dem | Dem |
| | Nelson A. Rockefeller[4] | | 94th | Dem | Dem |
| 1977–81 | **Jimmy Carter** | Dem | 95th | Dem | Dem |
| | Walter Mondale | | 96th | Dem | Dem |
| 1981–89 | **Ronald Reagan** | Rep | 97th | Dem | Rep |
| | George Bush | | 98th | Dem | Rep |
| | | | 99th | Dem | Rep |
| | | | 100th | Dem | Dem |
| 1989–93 | **George Bush** | Rep | 101st | Dem | Dem |
| | J. Danforth Quayle | | 102d | Dem | Dem |
| 1993–2001 | **William J. Clinton** | Dem | 103d | Dem | Dem |
| | Albert Gore, Jr. | | 104th | Rep | Rep |
| | | | 105th | Rep | Rep |
| | | | 106th | Rep | Rep |
| 2001–04, | **George W. Bush** | Rep | 107th | Rep | Dem |
| 2005–07 | Richard Cheney | | 108th | Rep | Rep |
| | | | 109th | Rep | Rep |
| | | Rep | 110th | Dem | Dem |
| 2009–13 | **Barack Obama** | Dem | 111th | Dem | Dem |
| | Joseph Biden | | 112th | Rep | Dem |

[1]Died in office.

[2]Resigned from the vice presidency.

[3]Resigned from the presidency.

[4]Appointed vice president.

# Appendix 3

## Supreme Court Justices

| Name[1] | Years on Court | Appointing President |
|---|---|---|
| JOHN JAY | 1789–1795 | Washington |
| James Wilson | 1789–1798 | Washington |
| John Rutledge | 1790–1791 | Washington |
| William Cushing | 1790–1810 | Washington |
| John Blair | 1790–1796 | Washington |
| James Iredell | 1790–1799 | Washington |
| Thomas Johnson | 1792–1793 | Washington |
| William Paterson | 1793–1806 | Washington |
| JOHN RUTLEDGE[2] | 1795 | Washington |
| Samuel Chase | 1796–1811 | Washington |
| OLIVER ELLSWORTH | 1796–1800 | Washington |
| Bushrod Washington | 1799–1829 | J. Adams |
| Alfred Moore | 1800–1804 | J. Adams |
| JOHN MARSHALL | 1801–1835 | J. Adams |
| William Johnson | 1804–1834 | Jefferson |
| Brockholst Livingston | 1807–1823 | Jefferson |
| Thomas Todd | 1807–1826 | Jefferson |
| Gabriel Duvall | 1811–1835 | Madison |
| Joseph Story | 1812–1845 | Madison |
| Smith Thompson | 1823–1843 | Monroe |
| Robert Trimble | 1826–1828 | J. Q. Adams |
| John McLean | 1830–1861 | Jackson |
| Henry Baldwin | 1830–1844 | Jackson |
| James M. Wayne | 1835–1867 | Jackson |
| ROGER B. TANEY | 1836–1864 | Jackson |
| Philip P. Barbour | 1836–1841 | Jackson |
| John Cartron | 1837–1865 | Van Buren |
| John McKinley | 1838–1852 | Van Buren |
| Peter V. Daniel | 1842–1860 | Van Buren |
| Samuel Nelson | 1845–1872 | Tyler |
| Levi Woodbury | 1845–1851 | Polk |
| Robert C. Grier | 1846–1870 | Polk |
| Benjamin R. Curtis | 1851–1857 | Fillmore |
| John A. Campbell | 1853–1861 | Pierce |
| Nathan Clifford | 1858–1881 | Buchanan |
| Noah H. Swayne | 1862–1881 | Lincoln |
| Samuel F. Miller | 1862–1890 | Lincoln |
| David Davis | 1862–1877 | Lincoln |
| Stephen J. Field | 1863–1897 | Lincoln |
| SALMON P. CHASE | 1864–1873 | Lincoln |
| William Strong | 1870–1880 | Grant |
| Joseph P. Bradley | 1870–1892 | Grant |
| Ward Hunt | 1873–1882 | Grant |
| MORRISON R. WAITE | 1874–1888 | Grant |
| John M. Harlan | 1877–1911 | Haves |
| William B. Woods | 1881–1887 | Haves |
| Stanley Matthews | 1881–1889 | Garfield |
| Horace Gray | 1882–1902 | Arthur |
| Samuel Blatchford | 1882–1893 | Arthur |
| Lucious Q. C. Lamar | 1888–1893 | Cleveland |
| MELVILLE W. FULLER | 1888–1910 | Cleveland |
| David J. Brewer | 1890–1910 | B. Harrison |
| Henry B. Brown | 1891–1906 | B. Harrison |
| George Shiras, Jr. | 1892–1903 | B. Harrison |
| Howel E. Jackson | 1893–1895 | B. Harrison |
| Edward D. White | 1894–1910 | Cleveland |
| Rufus W. Peckman | 1896–1909 | Cleveland |
| Joseph McKenna | 1898–1925 | McKinley |
| Oliver W. Holmes | 1902–1932 | T. Roosevelt |

## Supreme Court Justices

| Name[1] | Years on Court | Appointing President |
|---|---|---|
| William R. Day | 1903–1922 | T. Roosevelt |
| William H. Moody | 1906–1910 | T. Roosevelt |
| Horace H. Lurton | 1910–1914 | Taft |
| Charles E. Hughes | 1910–1916 | Taft |
| EDWARD D. WHITE | 1910–1921 | Taft |
| Willis Van Devanter | 1911–1937 | Taft |
| Joseph R. Lamar | 1911–1916 | Taft |
| Mahlon Pitney | 1912–1922 | Taft |
| James C. McReynolds | 1914–1941 | Wilson |
| Louis D. Brandeis | 1916–1939 | Wilson |
| John H. Clarke | 1916–1922 | Wilson |
| WILLIAM H. TAFT | 1921–1930 | Harding |
| George Sutherland | 1922–1938 | Harding |
| Pierce Butler | 1923–1939 | Harding |
| Edward T. Sanford | 1923–1930 | Harding |
| Harlan F. Stone | 1925–1941 | Coolidge |
| CHARLES E. HUGHES | 1930–1941 | Hoover |
| Owen J. Roberts | 1930–1945 | Hoover |
| Benjamin N. Cardozo | 1932–1938 | Hoover |
| Hugo L. Black | 1937–1971 | F. Roosevelt |
| Stanley F. Reed | 1938–1957 | F. Roosevelt |
| Felix Frankfurter | 1939–1962 | F. Roosevelt |
| William O. Douglas | 1939–1975 | F. Roosevelt |
| Frank Murphy | 1940–1949 | F. Roosevelt |
| HARLAN F. STONE | 1941–1946 | F. Roosevelt |
| James F. Brynes | 1941–1942 | F. Roosevelt |
| Robert H. Jackson | 1941–1954 | F. Roosevelt |
| Wiley B. Rutledge | 1943–1949 | F. Roosevelt |
| Harold H. Burton | 1945–1958 | Truman |
| FREDERICK M. VINSON | 1946–1953 | Truman |
| Tom C. Clark | 1949–1967 | Truman |
| Sherman Minton | 1949–1956 | Truman |
| EARL WARREN | 1953–1969 | Eisenhower |
| John Marshall Harlan | 1955–1971 | Eisenhower |
| William J. Brennan, Jr. | 1956–1990 | Eisenhower |
| Charles E. Whittaker | 1957–1962 | Eisenhower |
| Potter Stewart | 1958–1981 | Eisenhower |
| Byron R. White | 1962–1993 | Kennedy |
| Arthur J. Goldberg | 1962–1965 | Kennedy |
| Abe Fortas | 1965–1970 | L. Johnson |
| Thurgood Marshall | 1967–1991 | L. Johnson |
| WARREN E. BURGER | 1969–1986 | Nixon |
| Harry A. Blackmun | 1970–1994 | Nixon |
| Lewis F. Powell, Jr. | 1971–1987 | Nixon |
| William H. Rehnquist | 1971–1986 | Nixon |
| John Paul Stevens | 1975–2010 | Ford |
| Sandra Day O'Connor | 1981–2006 | Reagan |
| WILLIAM H. REHNQUIST | 1986–2005 | Reagan |
| Antonin Scalia | 1986– | Reagan |
| Anthony Kennedy | 1988– | Reagan |
| David Souter | 1990–2009 | Bush |
| Clarence Thomas | 1991– | Bush |
| Ruth Bader Ginsburg | 1993– | Clinton |
| Stephen Breyer | 1994– | Clinton |
| John G. Roberts, Jr. | 2005– | Bush |
| Samuel A. Alito, Jr. | 2006– | Bush |
| Sonia Sotomayor | 2009– | Obama |
| Elena Kagan | 2010– | Obama |

[1]Capital letters designate chief justices.

[2]Never confirmed by the Senate as chief justice.

# Appendix 4

## THE DECLARATION OF INDEPENDENCE

**IN CONGRESS, JULY 4, 1776**
(The unanimous Declaration of the Thirteen United States of America)

### PREAMBLE

When, in the course of human events, it becomes necessary for one people to dissolve the political bands which have connected them with another, and to assume, among the powers of the earth, the separate and equal station to which the laws of nature and of nature's God entitle them, a decent respect to the opinions of mankind requires that they should declare the causes which impel them to the separation.

We hold these truths to be self-evident; that all men are created equal, that they are endowed by their Creator with certain unalienable rights, that among these are life, liberty, and the pursuit of happiness.

That, to secure these rights, governments are instituted among men, deriving their just powers from the consent of the governed.

That whenever any form of government becomes destructive of these ends, it is the right of the people to alter or to abolish it, and to institute new government, laying its foundation on such principles, and organizing its powers in such form, as to them shall seem most likely to effect their safety and happiness. Prudence, indeed will dictate that governments long established should not be changed for light and transient causes; and accordingly all experience hath shown that mankind are more disposed to suffer while evils are sufferable, than to right themselves by abolishing the forms to which they are accustomed. But when a long train of abuses and usurpations, pursuing invariably the same object, evinces a design to reduce them under absolute despotism, it is their right, it is their duty, to throw off such government, and to provide new guards for their future security.

Such has been the patient sufferance of these colonies; and such is now the necessity which constrains them to alter their former systems of government. The history of the present king of Great Britain is a history of repeated injuries and usurpations, all having in direct object the establishment of an absolute tyranny over these states. To prove this, let facts be submitted to a candid world.

He has refused his assent to laws, the most wholesome and necessary for the public good.

He has forbidden his governors to pass laws of immediate and pressing importance unless suspended in their operation till his assent should be obtained; and when so suspended, he has utterly neglected to attend to them.

He has refused to pass other laws for the accommodation of large districts of people, unless those people would relinquish the right of representation in the legislature, a right inestimable to them, and formidable to tyrants only.

He has called together legislative bodies at places unusual, uncomfortable, and distant for the depository of their public records, for the sole purpose of fatiguing them into compliance with his measures.

He has dissolved representative houses repeatedly, for opposing, with manly firmness, his invasions on the rights of people.

He has refused, for a long time after such dissolutions, to cause others to be elected; whereby the legislative powers incapable of annihilation, have returned to the people at large for their exercise; the state remaining, in the meantime, exposed to all the dangers of invasion from without and convulsions within.

He has endeavored to prevent the population of these states; for that purpose obstructing the laws of naturalization of foreigners, refusing to pass others to encourage their migration hither, and raising the conditions of new appropriations of lands.

He has obstructed the administration of justice, by refusing his assent to laws for establishing judiciary powers.

He has made judges dependent on his will alone for the tenure of their offices, and the amount and payment of their salaries.

He has erected a multitude of new offices, and sent hither swarms of officers to harass our people and eat out their substance.

He has kept among us, in times of peace, standing armies, without the consent of our legislature.

He has affected to render the military independent of, and superior to, the civil power.

He has combined with others to subject us to jurisdiction foreign to our constitution and unacknowledged by our laws, giving his assent to their acts of pretended legislation:

For quartering large bodies of armed troops among us;

For protecting them, by a mock trial, from punishment for any murders which they should commit on the inhabitants of these states;

For cutting off our trade with all parts of the world;

For imposing taxes on us without our consent;

For depriving us, in many cases, of the benefits of trial by jury;

For transporting us beyond seas, to be tried for pretended offenses;

For abolishing the free system of English laws in a neighboring province, establishing therein an arbitrary government, and enlarging its boundaries, so as to render it at once an example and fit instrument for introducing the same absolute rule into these colonies;

For taking away our charters, abolishing our most valuable laws, and altering, fundamentally, the forms of our governments;

For suspending our own legislatures, and declaring themselves invented with power to legislate for us in all cases whatsoever.

He has abdicated government here, by declaring us out of his protection and waging war against us.

He has plundered our seas, ravaged our coasts, burned our towns, and destroyed the lives of our people.

He is at this time transporting large armies of foreign mercenaries to complete the works of death, desolation, and tyranny already begun with circumstances of cruelty and perfidy scarcely paralleled in the most barbarous ages and totally unworthy of the head of a civilized nation.

He has constrained our fellow-citizens, taken captive on the high seas, to bear arms against their country, to become the executioners of their friends and brethren, or to fall themselves by their hands.

He has excited domestic insurrections among us, and has endeavored to bring on the inhabitants of our frontiers the merciless Indian savages, whose known rule of warfare is an undistinguished destruction of all ages, sexes, and conditions.

In every stage of these oppressions we have petitioned for redress in the most humble terms; our repeated petitions have been answered only by repeated injury. A prince whose character is thus marked by every act which may define a tyrant is unfit to be the ruler of a free people.

Nor have we been wanting in attention to our British brethren. We have warned them, from time to time, of attempts by their legislature to extend an unwarrantable jurisdiction over us. We have reminded them of the circumstances of our emigration and settlement here. We have appealed to their native justice and magnanimity; and we have conjured them, by the ties of our common kindred, to disavow these usurpations, which would inevitably interrupt our connections and correspondence. They, too, have been deaf to the voice of justice and of consanguinity. We must, therefore, acquiesce in the necessity which denounces our separation, and hold them, as we hold the rest of mankind, enemies in war, in peace, friends.

We, therefore, the representatives of the United States of America, in General Congress assembled, appealing to the Supreme Judge of the world for the rectitude of our intentions, do, in the name and by authority of the good people of these colonies, solemnly publish and declare, that these united colonies are, and of right ought to be, free and independent states; that they are absolved from all allegiance to the British crown, and that all political connection between them and the state of Great Britain is, and ought to be, totally dissolved; and that, as free and independent states, they have full power to levy war, conclude peace, contract alliances, establish commerce, and do all other acts and things which independent states may of a right do. And, for the support of this declaration, with a firm reliance on the protection of Divine Providence, we mutually pledge to each other our lives, our fortunes, and our sacred honor.

# Appendix 5

## *THE FEDERALIST*, NO. 10, JAMES MADISON

*To the People of the State of New York:* Among the numerous advantages promised by a well-constructed union, none deserves to be more accurately developed than its tendency to break and control the violence of faction. The friend of popular governments, never finds himself so much alarmed for their character and fate, as when he contemplates their propensity of this dangerous vice. He will not fail, therefore, to set a due value on any plan which, without violating the principles to which he is attached, provides a proper cure for it. The instability, injustice, and confusion introduced into the public councils, have, in truth, been the mortal diseases under which popular governments have everywhere perished; as they continue to be the favorite and fruitful topics from which the adversaries to liberty derive their most specious declamations. The valuable improvements made by the American constitutions on the popular models, both ancient and modern, cannot certainly be too much admired; but it would be an unwarrantable partiality, to contend that they have as effectually obviated the danger on this side, as was wished and expected. Complaints are everywhere heard from our most considerate and virtuous citizens, equally the friends of public and private faith, and of public and personal liberty, that our governments are too unstable; that the public good is disregarded in the conflicts of rival parties; and that measures are too often decided, not according to the rules of justice, and the rights of the minor party, but by the superior force of an interested and overbearing majority. However anxiously we may wish that these complaints had no foundation, the evidence of known facts will not permit us to deny that they are in some degree true. It will be found, indeed, on a candid review of our situation, that some of the distresses under which we labor have been erroneously charged on the operations of our governments; but it will be found, at the same time, that other causes will not alone account for many of our heaviest misfortunes; and, particularly, for that prevailing and increasing distrust of public engagements, and alarm for private rights, which are echoed from one end of the continent to the other. These must be chiefly, if not wholly, effects of the unsteadiness and injustice, with which a factious spirit has tainted our public administrations.

By a faction, I understand a number of citizens, whether amounting to a majority of the whole, who are united and actuated by some common impulse of passion, or of interest, adverse to the rights of other citizens, or to the permanent and aggregate interests of the community.

There are two methods of curing the mischiefs of faction: the one, by removing its causes; the other, by controlling its effects.

There are again two methods of removing the causes of faction: the one, by destroying the liberty which is essential to its existence; the other, by giving to every citizen the same opinions, the same passions, and the same interests.

It could never be more truly said, than of the first remedy, that it was worse than the disease. Liberty is to faction what air is to fire, an aliment without which it instantly expires. But it could not be a less folly to abolish liberty, which is essential to political life, because it nourishes faction, than it would be to wish the annihilation of air, which is essential to animal life, because it imparts to fire its destructive agency.

The second expedient is as impracticable, as the first would be unwise. As long as the reason of man continues fallible, and he is at liberty to exercise it, different opinions will be formed. As long as the connection subsists between his reason and his self-love, his opinions and his passions will have a reciprocal influence on each other; and the former will be objects to which the latter will attach themselves. The diversity in the faculties of men, from which the rights of property originate, is not less an insuperable obstacle to an uniformity of interests. The protection of these faculties is the first object of government. From the protection of different and unequal faculties of acquiring property, the possession of different degrees and kinds of property immediately results; and from the influence of these on the sentiments and views of the respective proprietors, ensues a division of the society into different interests and parties.

The latent causes of faction are thus sown in the nature of man; and we see them everywhere brought into different degrees of activity, according to the different circumstances of civil society. A zeal for different opinions concerning religion, concerning government, and many other points, as well of speculation as of practice; an attachment to different leaders ambitiously contending for preeminence and power; or to persons of other descriptions whose fortunes have been interesting to the human passions, have, in turn, divided mankind into parties, inflamed them with mutual animosity, and rendered them much more disposed to vex and oppress each other, than to cooperate for their common good. So strong is this propensity of mankind, to fall into mutual animosities, that where no substantial occasion presents itself, the most frivolous and fanciful distinctions have been sufficient to kindle their unfriendly passions and excite their most violent conflicts. But the most common and durable source of factions, has been the various and unequal distribution of property. Those who hold, and those who are without property, have ever formed distinct interests in society. Those who are creditors, and those who are debtors, fall under a like discrimination. A landed interest, a manufacturing interest, a mercantile interest, a moneyed interest, with many lesser interests, grow up of necessity in civilized nations, and divide them into different classes, actuated by different sentiments and views. The regulation of these various and interfering interests forms the principal task of modern legislation, and involves the spirit of the party and faction in the necessary and ordinary operations of the government.

No man is allowed to be a judge in his own cause; because his interest will certainly bias his judgment, and, not improbably, corrupt his integrity. With equal, nay, with greater reason, a body of men are unfit to be both judges and parties at the same time; yet what are many of the most important acts of legislation, but so many judicial determinations, not indeed concerning the right of single persons, but concerning the rights of large bodies of citizens? And what are the different classes of legislators, but advocates and parties to the causes which they determine? Is a law proposed concerning private debts? It is a question to which the creditors are parties on one side, and the debtors on the other. Justice ought to hold the balance between them. Yet the parties are, and must be, themselves the judges; and the most numerous party, or, in other words, the most powerful faction, must be expected to prevail. Shall domestic manufacturers be encouraged, and in what degree, by restrictions on foreign manufacturers? Are questions which would be differently decided by the landed and the manufacturing classes; and probably by neither with a sole regard to justice and the public good. The apportionment of taxes, on the various descriptions of property, is an act which seems to require the most exact impartiality; yet there is, perhaps, no legislative act, in which greater opportunity and temptation are given to a predominant party to trample on the rules of justice. Every shilling, with which they overburden the inferior number, is a shilling saved to their own pockets.

It is in vain to say, that enlightened statesmen will be able to adjust these clashing interests, and render them all subservient to the public good. Enlightened statesmen will not always be at the helm, nor, in many cases, can such an adjustment be made at all, without taking into view indirect and remote considerations, which will rarely prevail over the immediate interest which one party may find in disregarding the rights of another, or the good of the whole.

The inference to which we are brought is, that the causes of faction cannot be removed; and that relief is only to be sought in the means of controlling its effects.

If a faction consists of less than a majority, relief is supplied by the republican principle, which enables the majority to defeat its sinister views, by regular vote. It may clog the administration, it may convulse the society; but it will be unable to execute and mask its violence under the forms of the Constitution. When a majority is included in a faction, the form of popular government, on the other hand, enables it to sacrifice to its ruling passion or interest, both the public good and the rights of other citizens. To secure the public good, and private rights, against the danger of such a faction, and at the same time to preserve the spirit and the form of popular government, is then the great object to which our inquiries are directed. Let me add, that it is the great desideratum, by which alone this form of government can be rescued from the opprobrium under which it has so long laboured, and be recommended to the esteem and adoption of mankind.

By what means is this object attainable? Evidently by one of two only. Either the existence of the same passion or interest in a majority, at the same time, must be prevented; or the majority, having such coexistent passion or interest, must be rendered, by their number and local situation, unable to concert and carry into effect schemes of oppression. If the impulse and the opportunity be suffered to coincide, we well know that neither moral nor religious motives can be relied on as an adequate control. They are not found to be such on the injustice and violence of individuals, and lose their efficacy in proportion to the number combined together; that is, in proportion as their efficacy becomes needful.

From this view of the subject, it may be concluded, that a pure democracy, by which I mean a society consisting of a small number of citizens, who assemble and administer the government in person, can admit of no cure for the mischiefs of faction. A common passion or interest will, in almost every case, be felt by a majority of the whole; a communication and concert, results from the form of government itself; and there is nothing to check the inducements to sacrifice the weaker party, or an obnoxious individual. Hence, it is, that such democracies have ever been spectacles of turbulence and contention; have ever been found incompatible with personal security, or the rights of property; and have in general been as short in their lives, as they have been violent in their deaths. Theoretic politicians, who have patronized this species of government, have erroneously supposed, that by reducing mankind to a perfect equality in their political rights, they would, at the same time be perfectly equalized and assimilated in their possessions, their opinions, and their passions.

A republic, by which I mean a government in which the scheme of representation takes place, opens a different prospect, and promises the cure for which we are seeking. Let us examine the points in which it varies from pure democracy, and we shall comprehend both the nature of the cure and the efficacy which it must derive from the union.

The two great points of difference, between a democracy and a republic, are, first, the delegation of the government, in the latter, to a small number of citizens, elected by the rest; secondly, the greater number of citizens, and greater sphere of country, over which the latter may be extended.

The effect of the first difference is, on the one hand, to refine and enlarge the public views, by passing them through the medium of a chosen body of citizens, whose wisdom may best discern the true interest of their country, and whose patriotism and love of justice, will be least likely to sacrifice it to temporary or partial considerations. Under such a regulation, it may well happen, that the public voice, pronounced by the representatives of the people, will be more consonant to the public good, than if pronounced by the people themselves, convened for the purpose. On the other hand the effect may be inverted. Men of factious tempers, of local prejudices, or of sinister designs, may by intrigue, by corruption, or by other means, first obtain the suffrages, and then betray the interest of the people. The question resulting is, whether small or extensive republics are most favourable to the election of proper guardians of the public weal; and it is clearly decided in favour of the latter by two obvious considerations.

In the first place, it is to be remarked that, however small the republic may be, the representatives must be raised to a certain number, in order to guard against the cabals of a few; and that however large it may be, they must be limited to a certain number, in order to guard against the confusion of a multitude. Hence, the number of representatives in the two cases not being in proportion to that of the constituents, and being proportionally greatest in the small republic, it follows, that if the proportion of fit characters be not less in the large than in the small republic, the former will present a greater option, and consequently a greater probability of a fit choice.

In the next place, as each representative will be chosen by a greater number of citizens in the large than in the small republic, it will be more difficult for unworthy candidates to practice with success the vicious arts, by which elections are too often carried; and the suffrages of the people being more free, will be more likely to centre in men who possess the most attractive merit, and the most diffusive and established characters.

It must be confessed, that in this, as in most other cases, there is a mean, on both sides of which inconveniences will be found to lie. By enlarging too much the number of electors, you render the representatives too little acquainted with all their local circumstances and lesser interests; as by reducing it too much, you render him unduly attached to these, and too little fit to comprehend and pursue great and national objects. The federal constitution forms a happy combination in this respect; the great and aggregate interests being referred to the national, the local and particular to the state legislatures.

The other point of difference is, the greater number of citizens, and extent of territory, which may be brought within the compass of republican, than of democratic government; and it is this circumstance principally which renders factious combinations less to be dreaded in the former, than in the latter. The smaller the society, the fewer probably will be the distinct parties and interests composing it; the fewer the distinct parties and interests, the more frequently will a majority be found of the same party; and the smaller the number of individuals composing a majority, and the smaller the compass within which they are placed, the more easily will they concert and execute their plans of oppression. Extend the sphere, and you take in a greater variety of parties and interests; you make it less probable that a majority of the whole will have a common motive to invade the rights of other citizens; or if such a common motive exists, it will be more difficult for all who feel it to discover their own strength, and to act in unison with each other. Besides other impediments, it may be remarked, that where there is a consciousness of unjust or dishonourable purposes, communication is always checked by distrust, in proportion to the number whose concurrence is necessary.

Hence, it clearly appears, that the same advantage, which a republic has over a democracy, in controlling the effects of faction, is enjoyed by a large over a small republic—is enjoyed by the union over the states composing it. Does this advantage consist in the substitution of representatives, whose enlightened views and virtuous sentiments render them superior to local prejudices, and to schemes of injustice? It will not be denied that the representation of the union will be most likely to possess these requisite endowments. Does it consist in the greater security afforded by a greater variety of parties, against the event of any one party being able to outnumber and oppress the rest? In an equal degree does the increased variety of parties, comprised within the union, increase the security? Does it, in fine, consist in the greater obstacles opposed to the concert and accomplishment of the secret wishes of an unjust and interested majority? Here, again, the extent of the union gives it the most palpable advantage.

The influence of factious leaders may kindle a flame within their particular states, but will be unable to spread a general conflagration through the other states; a religious sect may degenerate into a political faction in a part of the confederacy; but the variety of sects dispersed over the entire face of it, must secure the national councils against any danger from that source: a rage for paper money, for an abolition of debts, for an equal division of property, or for any other improper or wicked project, will be less apt to pervade the whole body of the union than a particular member of it; in the same proportion as such a malady is more likely to taint a particular county or district, than an entire state.

In the extent and proper structure of the union, therefore, we behold a republican remedy for the diseases most incident to republican government. And according to the degree of pleasure and pride we feel in being republicans, ought to be our zeal in cherishing the spirit, and supporting the character of federalists.

# Appendix 6

## *THE FEDERALIST*, NO. 51, JAMES MADISON

To what expedient, then, shall we finally resort, for maintaining in practice the necessary partition of power among the several departments as laid down in the Constitution? The only answer that can be given is that as all these exterior provisions are found to be inadequate the defect must be supplied, by so contriving the interior structure of the government as that its several constituent parts may, by their mutual relations, be the means of keeping each other in their proper places. Without presuming to undertake a full development of this important idea I will hazard a few general observations which may perhaps place it in a clearer light, and enable us to form a more correct judgment of the principles and structure of the government planned by the convention.

In order to lay a due foundation for that separate and distinct exercise of the different powers of government, which to a certain extent is admitted on all hands to be essential to the preservation of liberty, it is evident that each department should have a will of its own; and consequently should be so constituted that the members of each should have as little agency as possible in the appointment of the members of the others. Were this principle rigorously adhered to, it would require that all the appointments for the supreme executive, legislative, and judiciary magistracies should be drawn from the same fountain of authority, the people, through channels having no communication whatever with one another. Perhaps such a plan of constructing the several departments would be less difficult in practice than it may in contemplation appear. Some difficulties, however, and some additional expense would attend the execution of it. Some deviations, therefore, from the principle must be admitted. In the constitution of the judiciary department in particular, it might be inexpedient to insist rigorously on the principle: first, because peculiar qualifications being essential in the members, the primary consideration ought to be to select that mode of choice which best secures these qualifications; second, because the permanent tenure by which the appointments are held in that department must soon destroy all sense of dependence on the authority conferring them.

It is equally evident that the members of each department should be as little dependent as possible on those of the others for the emoluments annexed to their offices. Were the executive magistrate, or the judges, not independent of the legislature in this particular, their independence in every other would be merely nominal.

But the great security against a gradual concentration of the several powers in the same department consists in giving to those who administer each department the necessary constitutional means and personal motives to resist encroachments of the others. The provision for defense must in this, as in all other cases, be made commensurate to the danger of attack. Ambition must be made to counteract ambition. The interest of the man must be connected with the constitutional rights of the place. It may be a reflection on human nature that such devices should be necessary to control the abuses of government. But what is government itself but the greatest of all reflections on human nature? If men were angels, no government would be necessary. If angels were to govern men, neither external nor internal controls on government would be necessary. In framing a government which is to be administered by men over men, the great difficulty lies in this: you must first enable the government to control the governed; and in the next place oblige it to control itself. A dependence on the people is, no doubt, the primary control on the government; but experience has taught mankind the necessity of auxiliary precautions.

This policy of supplying, by opposite and rival interests, the defect of better motives, might be traced through the whole system of human affairs, private as well as public. We see it particularly displayed in all the subordinate distributions of power, where the constant aim is to divide and arrange the several offices in such a manner as that each may be a check on the other—that the private interest of every individual may be a sentinel over the public rights. These inventions of prudence cannot be less requisite in the distribution of the supreme powers of the State.

But it is not possible to give to each department an equal power of self-defense. In republican government, the legislative authority necessarily predominates. The remedy for this inconveniency is to divide the legislature into different branches; and to render them, by modes of election and different principles of action, as little connected with each other as the nature of their common functions and their common dependence on the society will admit. It may even be necessary to guard against dangerous encroachments by still further precautions. As the weight of the legislative authority requires that it should be thus divided, the weakness of the executive may require, on the other hand, that it should be fortified. An absolute negative on the legislature appears, at first view, to be the natural defense with which the executive magistrate should be armed. But perhaps it would be neither altogether safe nor alone sufficient. On ordinary occasions it might not be exerted with the requisite firmness, and on extraordinary occasions it might be perfidiously abused. May not this defect of an absolute negative be supplied by some qualified connection between this weaker department and the weaker branch of the stronger department, by which the latter may be led to support the constitutional rights of the former, without being too much detached from the rights of its own department?

If the principles on which these observations are founded be just, as I persuade myself they are, and they be applied as a criterion to the several State constitutions, and to the federal Constitution, it will be found that if the latter does not perfectly correspond with them, the former are infinitely less able to bear such a test.

There are, moreover, two considerations particularly applicable to the federal system of America, which place that system in a very interesting point of view.

*First.* In a single republic, all the power surrendered by the people is submitted to the administration of a single government; and the usurpations are guarded against by a division of the government into distinct and separate departments. In the compound republic of America, the power surrendered by the people is first divided between two distinct governments, and then the portion allotted to each subdivided among distinct and separate departments. Hence a double security arises to the rights of the people. The different governments will control each other, at the same time that each will be controlled by itself.

*Second.* It is of great importance in a republic not only to guard the society against the oppression of its rulers, but to guard one part of the society against the injustice of the other part. Different interests necessarily exist in different classes of citizens. If a majority be united by a common interest, the rights of the minority will be insecure. There are but two methods of providing against this evil: the one by creating a will in the community independent of the majority—that is, of the society itself; the other, by comprehending in the society so many separate descriptions of citizens as will render an unjust combination of a majority of the whole very improbable, if not impracticable. The first method prevails in all governments possessing an hereditary or self-appointed authority. This, at best, is but a precarious security; because a power independent of the society may as well espouse the unjust views of the major as the rightful interests of the minor party, and may possibly be turned against both parties. The second method will be exemplified in the federal republic of the United States. Whilst all authority in it will be derived from and dependent on the society, the society itself will be broken into so many parts, interests and classes of citizens, that the rights of individuals, or of the minority, will be in little danger from interested combinations of the majority. In a free government the security for civil rights must be the same as that for religious rights. It consists in the one case in the multiplicity of interests, and in the other in the multiplicity of sects. The degree of security in both cases will depend on the number of interests and sects; and this may be presumed to depend on the extent of country and number of people comprehended under the same government. This view of the subject must particularly recommend a proper federal system to all the sincere and considerate friends of republican government, since it shows that in exact proportion as the territory of the Union may be formed into more circumscribed Confederacies, or States, oppressive combinations of a majority will be facilitated; the best security, under the republican forms, for the rights of every class of citizen, will be diminished; and consequently the stability and independence of some member of the government, the only other security, must be proportionally increased. Justice is the end of government. It is the end of civil society. It ever has been and ever will be pursued until it be obtained, or until liberty be lost in the pursuit. In a society under the forms of which the stronger faction can readily unite and oppress the weaker, anarchy may as truly be said to reign as in a state of nature, where the weaker individual is not secured against the violence of the stronger; and as, in the latter state, even the stronger individuals are prompted, by the uncertainty of their condition, to submit to a government which may protect the weak as well as themselves; so, in the former state, will the more powerful factions or parties be gradually induced, by a like motive, to wish for a government which will protect all parties, the weaker as well as the more powerful. It can be little doubted that if the State of Rhode Island was separated from the Confederacy and left to itself, the insecurity of rights under the popular form of government within such narrow limits would be displayed by such reiterated oppressions of factious majorities that some power altogether independent of the people would soon be called for by the voice of the very factions whose misrule had proved the necessity to it. In the extended republic of the United States, and among the great variety of interests, parties, and sects which it embraces, a coalition of a majority of the whole society could seldom take place on any other principles than those of justice and the general good; whilst there being thus less danger to a minor from the will of a major party, there must be less pretext, also, to provide for the security of the former, by introducing into the government a will not dependent on the latter, or, in other words, a will independent of the society itself. It is no less certain that it is important, notwithstanding the contrary opinions which have been entertained that the larger the society, provided it lie within a practicable sphere, the more duly capable it will be of self-government. And happily for the *republican cause,* the practicable sphere may be carried to a very great extent by a judicious modification and mixture of the *federal principle.*

# Glossary

**actual groups** Interest groups that have already been formed; they have headquarters, an organizational structure, paid employees, membership lists, and the like.

**administration** Performance of routine tasks associated with a specific policy goal.

**administrative discretion** The latitude that an agency, or even a single bureaucrat, has in interpreting and applying a law.

**affirmative action** Programs that attempt to improve the chances of minority applicants for jobs, housing, employment, or education by giving them a "boost" relative to white applicants with similar qualifications.

**amicus curiae briefs** Legal briefs that enable groups or individuals, including the national government, who are not parties to the litigation but have an interest in it, to attempt to influence the outcome of the case; literally, "friend of the court" briefs.

**Antifederalists** Strong states' rights advocates who organized in opposition to the ratification of the U.S. Constitution prior to its adoption.

**appellate court** The court that reviews an appeal of the trial court proceedings, often with a multi-judge panel and without a jury; it considers only matters of law.

**appellate jurisdiction** The authority of a court to hear a case on appeal after it has been argued in and decided by a lower federal or state court.

**appointment power** The president's power to name agency officials. Of the current approximately 3,000, about 700 are in policy-making positions, such as cabinet and subcabinet officials and bureau chiefs.

**appropriations bill** A separate bill that must be passed by Congress to fund spending measures.

**Articles of Confederation** The first constitutional framework of the new United States of America. Approved in 1777 by the Second Continental Congress, it was later replaced by the current Constitution.

**authoritarian regime** An oppressive system of government in which citizens are deprived of their basic freedom to speak, write, associate, and participate in political life without fear of punishment.

**bicameral legislature** A legislative system consisting of two houses or chambers.

**Bill of Rights** The first ten amendments to the Constitution, added in 1781.

**bipolarity** The fundamental division of economic and military power between the poles of Western capitalism and Eastern communism.

**black codes** Laws restricting the civil rights of African Americans.

**block grants** Federal grants that provide money to states for general program funding with few or no strings attached.

**Blue Dog Democrats** Fiscally conservative Democratic Party members of Congress who claim to be "choked blue" by government spending and who press their liberal colleagues to reduce spending.

**boycott** Refusal to patronize any organization that practices policies perceived as politically, economically, or ideologically unfair.

**briefs** Written arguments to the court not only outlining the facts and legal and constitutional issues in a court case but also answering all anticipated arguments of the opposing side.

**budget reconciliation project** Taken from the Budget and Impoundment Act to reconcile differences in the spending bills of each house of Congress, this process can be used to avoid a Senate filibuster on spending-related bills because it requires only a simple majority vote.

**bureaucracy** A large and complex organizational system in which tasks, roles, and responsibilities are structured to achieve a goal.

**bureaucrats** People who work in a bureaucracy; not only the obscure, faceless clerks normally disparaged by critics of government but also "street-level bureaucrats" such as police officers, social workers, and schoolteachers.

**cabinet** Group of presidential advisers, including secretaries of the major bureaucracy departments and any other officials the president designates.

**cabinet departments** Major administrative units whose heads are presidential advisers appointed by the president and confirmed by the Senate. They are responsible for conducting a broad range of government operations.

**capital gains tax** Tax on unearned income from rents, stocks, and interest.

**casework** Favors done as a service for constituents by those they have elected to Congress.

**categorical grant** The most common type of federal grant, given for specific purposes, usually with strict rules attached.

**caucus** Meeting of party adherents who gather to discuss, to deliberate, and finally to give their support to a candidate for president. They then select delegates who will represent their choices at higher-level party meetings; eventually, their votes are reflected at the national convention itself. Also means a conference of party members in Congress.

**checks and balances** Systems that ensure that every power in government has an equal and opposite power in a separate branch to restrain that force.

**chief of staff** The president's top aide.

**civil cases** Noncriminal cases in which courts resolve disputes among individuals and parties to the case over finances, property, or personal well-being.

**civil disobedience** Breaking the law in a nonviolent fashion and being willing to suffer the consequences, even to the point of going to jail, in order to publicly demonstrate that the law is unjust.

**civil liberties** The individual freedoms and rights guaranteed to every citizen in the Bill of Rights and the due process clause of the Fourteenth Amendment, including freedom of speech and religion.

**civil rights** The constitutionally guaranteed rights that the government may not arbitrarily remove. Among these rights are the right to vote and equal protection under the law.

**civil service** A system of hiring and promoting employees based on professional merit, not party loyalty.

**class-action suit** A single civil case in which the plaintiff represents the whole class of individuals similarly situated, and the court's results apply to this entire class.

**clear and present danger test** A free speech test allowing states to regulate only speech that has an immediate connection to an action the states are permitted to regulate.

**closed primary** A system of conducting primary elections in which only citizens registered as members of a particular political party may participate in that party's primary.

**cloture** A procedure through which a vote of 60 senators can limit debate and stop a filibuster.

**coattails effect** "Riding the president's coattails into office" occurs in an election when voters also elect representatives or senators belonging to a successful presidential candidate's party.

**coercive federalism** A system in which the national government forces the states to follow its leads by passing public policy legislation requiring their participation.

**Cold War** The bipolar power struggle between the United States and the Soviet Union that began in the 1950s and ended in the 1990s.

**collective action** The political action of individuals who unite to influence policy.

***Common Sense*** Thomas Paine's pamphlet of January 1776, which helped crystallize the idea of revolution for the colonists.

**compact** A type of agreement that legally binds two or more parties to enforceable rules.

**concurrent powers** Powers shared by both national and state levels of government.

**concurring opinion** A written opinion of a justice who agrees with the majority decision of the Court but differs on the reasoning.

**conditions of aid** National requirement that must be observed to receive benefits.

**confederation** A league of sovereign states that delegates powers on selected issues to a central government.

**conference committees** Committees that reconcile differences between versions of a bill passed by the House and the Senate.

**congressional agenda** A list of bills to be considered by Congress.

**constitutional courts** Courts mentioned in Article III of the Constitution whose judges have life tenure.

**constructionist** A view of presidential power espoused by William Howard Taft, who believed that the president could exercise no power unless it could be traced to or implied from an express grant in either the Constitution or an act of Congress.

**containment** A term coined in 1946 by George Kennan, who believed that Soviet aggression must be "contained by the adroit and vigilant application of counterforce by the United States."

**contingency election** An election held in the House if no candidate receives the required majority in the electoral college.

**continuing resolution** A bill passed by Congress and signed by the president that enables the federal government to keep operating under the previous year's appropriations.

**cooperative federalism** A cooperative system in which solutions for various state and local problems are directed and sometimes funded by both the national and state governments. The administration of programs is characterized by shared power and shared responsibility.

**council of revision** A combined body of judges and members of the executive branch having a limited veto over national legislation and an absolute veto over state legislation.

**creative federalism** An initiative that expanded the concept of the partnership between the national government and the states under President Lyndon Johnson in the 1960s.

**criminal cases** Cases in which decisions are made regarding whether to punish individuals accused of violating the state or federal criminal code.

**culture theory** A theory that individual preferences "emerge from social interaction in defending or opposing different ways of life."

**de facto equality** Equality of results, which measures real world obstacles to equal treatment. For example: Do people actually live where they want? Do they work under similar conditions?

**de jure equality** Equality before the law. It disallows legally mandated obstacles to equal treatment, such as laws that prevent people from voting, living where they want to, or taking advantage of all the rights guaranteed to individuals by the laws of the federal, state, and local governments.

**Declaration of Independence** The formal proclamation declaring independence for the 13 colonies of England in North America, approved and signed on July 4, 1776.

**deficit** A shortfall between the monies a government takes in and spends.

**delegated powers** Powers expressly granted or enumerated in the Constitution and limited in nature.

**delegates** Congress members who feel bound to follow the wishes of a majority of their constituents; they make frequent efforts to learn the opinions of voters in their state or district.

**democracy** A system of government in which the people rule, either directly or through elected representatives.

**desegregation** The elimination of laws and practices that mandate racial separation.

**détente** An attempt to relax tensions between the United States and the Soviet Union through limited cooperation.

**deviating election** Election in which the minority party captures the White House because of short-term intervening forces, and thus a deviation from the expectation that power will remain in the hands of the dominant party.

**devolution** Reducing the size and authority of the federal government by returning programs to the states.

**devolution revolution** A trend initiated in the Reagan administration and accelerated by then Speaker of the House Newt Gingrich to send programs and power back to the states with less national government involvement.

**direct democracy** A type of government in which people govern themselves, vote on policies and laws, and live by majority rule.

**discretionary spending** The spending Congress actually controls; 33 percent of all spending.

**dissenting opinion** A written opinion of a justice who disagrees with the holding of the Court.

**docket** The Supreme Court's agenda of cases to consider.

**double jeopardy** Trying a defendant twice for the same crime; banned by the Fifth Amendment.

**double standard** The varying level of intensity by which the Supreme Court considers cases by which it protects civil liberties claims while also deferring to the legislature in cases with economic claims.

**dual federalism** A system in which each level of power remains supreme in its own jurisdiction, thus keeping the states separate and distinct from the national government.

**earmarks** Provisions in legislation, often an appropriation bill, directing spending for a specific program, agency, or region.

**economic policy** Policy aimed at producing a vibrant, healthy, and growing economy.

**economic sanctions** The use of embargoes and boycotts rather than military force to compel compliance.

**elections** The central institution of democratic representative governments in which the authority of the government derives from the consent of the governed. The principal mechanism for translating that consent into governmental authority is the holding of free and fair elections.

**electoral college** The group of 538 electors who meet separately in each of their states and the District of Columbia on the first Monday following the second Wednesday in December after a national presidential election. Their majority decision officially elects the president and vice president of the United States.

**electoral college system** Votes in the national presidential elections are actually indirect votes for a slate of presidential electors pledged to each party's candidate. Each state has one elector for each of its representatives and senators. The winning electors cast their votes in their states' capitals after the public election. In the United States, election of the president and vice president is dependent on receiving a majority (270) of the votes cast in the electoral college.

**en banc** Proceedings in which all of the appeals judges in a particular circuit serve as a tribunal.

**enrolled act (or resolution)** The final version of a bill, approved by both chambers of Congress.

**entitlements** Government-sponsored benefits and cash payments to those who meet eligibility requirements.

**Equal Time Rule** A requirement that radio and television stations allow equal time to all candidates for office.

**equality** A state in which all participants have equal access to the decision-making process, equal opportunity to influence the decisions made, and equal responsibility for those decisions.

**equality of opportunity** The idea that "people should have equal rights and opportunities to develop their talents," that all people should begin at the same starting point in a race.

**equality of result** The idea that all forms of inequality, including economic disparities, should be completely eradicated; this may mean giving certain people a starting advantage so that everyone has fair chances to succeed.

**excise taxes** Charges on the sale or manufacture of products such as cigarettes, alcohol, and gasoline.

**exclusionary rule** Rule whereby evidence gathered by illegal means, and any other evidence gathered as a result, cannot be used in later trials.

**executive agreement** A government-to-government agreement with essentially the same legal force as a treaty. However, it may be concluded entirely without Senate knowledge and/or approval.

**executive branch** The branch of government that executes laws.

**Executive Office of the President (EOP)** Created in 1939, this office contains all staff units that support the president in administrative duties.

**executive privilege** The president's implied or inherent power to withhold information on the ground that to release such information would affect either national security or the president's ability to discharge official duties.

**exit polls** Polls that question voters as they leave the voting booth to predict the outcome of an election.

**factions** According to James Madison in *The Federalist,* no. 10: "A number of citizens, whether amounting to a majority or a minority of the whole, who are united and actuated by some common impulse or passion or . . . interest."

**Fairness Doctrine** A policy, now abandoned, that radio and television stations provide time to all sides in programs of public interest.

**faithless elector** Member of the electoral college who casts his or her vote for someone other than the state's popular-vote winner.

**Federal Communications Commission (FCC)** A government commission formed to allocate radio and television frequencies and regulate broadcasting procedures.

**federal mandate** A direct order from Congress that the states must fulfill.

**federal matching funds** System under which presidential candidates who raise a certain amount of money in the required way may apply for and receive matching federal funds.

**federalism** The relationship between the centralized national government and the individual state governments.

**Federalists** Those in favor of the Constitution, many of whom were nationalists at the Convention.

**fighting words** Certain expressions so volatile that they are deemed to incite injury and are therefore not protected under the First Amendment.

**filibuster** A technique in which a senator speaks against a bill or talks about nothing specific just to "hold the floor" and prevent the Senate from moving forward with a vote. He or she may yield to other like-minded senators so that the marathon debate can continue for hours or even days.

**First Continental Congress** The meeting of 55 elected members (from provincial congresses or periodic conventions) held in Philadelphia's Carpenter's Hall in 1774. It resulted in a resolution to oppose acts of the British Parliament and a plan of association for the colonies.

**foreign aid** Small portion of the federal budget that goes to nonmilitary aid abroad, initially to mitigate against Soviet expansion.

**foreign policy** Policy adopted and actions taken by the U.S. government on behalf of U.S. national interests abroad. The president is this country's chief foreign policy maker.

**formal agenda** The policies actually scheduled for debate and potential adoption by Congress, the president, the Supreme Court, or executive departments and agencies.

**formal rules** In a bureaucracy, clearly defined procedures governing the execution of all tasks within the jurisdiction of a given agency.

**formula grant** A grant based on a prescribed legislative formula to determine how money will be distributed to eligible governmental units (states or major cities).

**formula/project grants** Competitive grants that are restricted by use of a formula.

**franking privilege** The free mailing of newsletters and political brochures to constituents by members of Congress.

**free press** Media characterized by the open reporting of information without government censorship.

**free riders** Members who invest no money or time in an interest group but still share in the collective benefits of group action.

**freedom** A value that suggests that no individual should be within the power or under the control of another.

**freedom riders** Civil rights activists who traveled throughout the American South on buses to test compliance with the Supreme Court's mandate to integrate bus terminals and public facilities accommodating interstate travelers.

**frontloading** The process by which most party primaries and caucuses are held early in the nomination schedule so that the majority of the delegate support is locked up early.

**fulcrum of powers** The five constitutional provisions that dictate the balance of power between the national and state governments in the federal structure. They include the interstate commerce clause, the general welfare clause, the necessary and proper clause, the supremacy clause, and the Tenth Amendment.

**gender gap** A difference in the political opinions of men and women.

**generational effect** Socialization patterns in which a generation of adults who grew up during a certain decade or period appears to have its own outlook, differentiating itself from the previous age.

**gerrymander** Any attempt during state redistricting of congressional voting boundaries to create a safe seat for one party.

***Gibbons v. Ogden*** The 1824 decision by Chief Justice John Marshall that gave Congress the power, under the interstate commerce clause, to regulate anything that affects the transfer of goods between states.

**globalism** View in which the U.S. sphere of influence has expanded beyond the Western Hemisphere to include virtually every corner of the globe where U.S. interests might be affected.

**going public** Actions presidents take to promote themselves and their policies to the American people.

**good-character test** A requirement that voting applicants wishing to vote produce two or more registered voters to vouch for their integrity.

**government corporation** A semi-independent government agency that administers a business enterprise and takes the form of a business corporation.

**grant-in-aid** Money paid to states and localities to induce them to implement policies in accordance with federally mandated guidelines.

**grassroots activity** The rallying of group members, as well as the public, behind a lobby's cause.

**Great Compromise** (also called the Connecticut Compromise) A plan presented at the Constitutional Convention that upheld the large-state position for the House, its membership based on proportional representation, balanced by the small-state posture of equal representation in the Senate, where each state would have two votes.

**gridlock** A condition in which major government initiatives are impossible because a closely balanced partisan division in the government structure, accompanied by an unwillingness to work together toward compromise, produces a stalemate.

**group maintenance** Activities by an interest group designed to affect policy. Includes enrolling new members and providing benefits for them.

**Gulf of Tonkin Resolution** Resolution passed by Congress that granted President Lyndon Johnson authority to pursue the war in Vietnam, supposedly based on a naval attack by North Vietnamese ships.

**Hatch Act** Approved by Congress in 1939 and named for its author, Senator Carl Hatch of New Mexico, a list of political dos and don'ts for federal employees; designed to prevent federal civil servants from using their power or position to engage in political activities to influence elections, thereby creating a nonpartisan, nonpolitical, professionalized bureaucracy.

**hate speech** Speech or symbolic actions intended to inflict emotional distress, to defame, or to intimidate people.

**hearings** Formal proceedings in which a range of people testify on a bill's pros and cons.

**heightened scrutiny test** A middle-level standard that would force the state to prove more than just the reasonableness of a law, though not its compelling nature, in order to justify it. For women's rights cases, this means proving the important governmental objectives of the law's goals and linking it to the wording of the law.

**hierarchy** A clear chain of communication and command running from an executive director at the top down through all levels of workers.

**hold** A request by a senator not to bring a measure up for consideration by the full Senate.

**House majority leader** The person elected by the majority party caucus to serve as the party's chief strategist and floor spokesperson.

**impeachment** The process by which government actors can be removed from office for "treason, bribery, or other high crimes and misdemeanors." The House of Representatives votes on the charges, and then the trial takes place in the Senate.

**implementation** The act of providing the organization and expertise required to put into action any policy that has become law; also refers to the actual execution of a policy.

**implied powers** Powers not specifically stated in the Constitution but inferred from the express powers.

**incorporation** The process whereby the Supreme Court has found that Bill of Rights protections apply to the states.

**incumbents** Individuals who currently hold public office.

**independent agencies** Agencies established to regulate a sector of the nation's economy in the public interest.

**independent expenditures** Funds dispersed, as allowed by a loophole in campaign finance law, by a group or person not coordinated by a candidate, in the name of a cause.

**independent judiciary** A system in which judges are insulated from the political bodies and public opinion in order to preserve their ability to act as the final arbiters over those groups in interpreting the Constitution and the laws.

**independent regulatory commissions** Agencies established to be outside the power of both the president and the

Congress in their operations. Such agencies have authority that is partly legislative and partly judicial.

**indirect democracy** A type of government in which voters designate a relatively small number of people to represent their interests; those people, or representatives, then meet in a legislative body and make decisions on behalf of the entire citizenry.

**inherent powers** Powers that do not appear in the Constitution but are assumed because of the nature of government. Also refers to a theory that the Constitution grants authority to the executive, through the injunction in Article II, Section 1, that "The executive Power shall be vested in a President of the United States of America."

**initiative** A proposal submitted by the public and voted on during elections.

**integration** Government efforts to balance the racial composition in schools and public places.

**intensity** In public opinion, a measure of the depth of feeling associated with a given opinion.

**interest groups** Formal organizations of people who share a common outlook or social circumstance and who band together in the hope of influencing government policy.

**investigative journalism** The uncovering of corruption, scandal, conspiracy, and abuses of power in government and business; differs from standard press coverage in the depth of the coverage sought, the time spent researching the subject, and the shocking findings that often result from such reporting.

**iron triangle** Informal three-way relationships that develop among key legislative committees, the bureaucracy, and interest groups with a vested interest in the policies created by those committees and agencies.

**isolationism** A pattern in which the United States fosters economic relations abroad without committing to strategic alliances that might draw the country into a war.

**issue advertisements** Advertisements in a political campaign funded by an interest group advocating a position on an issue but technically not supporting a specific candidate.

**issue advocacy** The process of campaigning to persuade the public to take a position on an issue.

**issue networks** Networks composed of political actors in a particular policy area, usually including bureaucrats, congressional staffers, interest groups, think-tank researchers or academic experts, and media participants—all of whom interact regularly on an issue.

**Jim Crow laws** Laws passed by southern states that separated the races in public places such as railroads, streetcars, schools, and cemeteries.

**joint committees** Groups of members from both chambers who study broad areas that are of interest to Congress as a whole.

**judicial activism** An approach in which justices create new policy and decide issues, to the point, some critics charge, of writing their personal values into law.

**judicial restraint** An approach in which justices see themselves as appointed rather than elected officials, who should defer to the legislature and uphold a law or political action if at all possible.

**judicial review** The power of the Supreme Court established in *Marbury* v. *Madison* to overturn acts of the president, Congress, and the states if those acts violate the Constitution. This power makes the Supreme Court the final interpreter of the Constitution.

**judiciary branch** The branch of government that interprets laws.

**latency** In public opinion, unspoken feelings, suggesting the potential for an attitude or behavior, but only when the right circumstances occur.

**least restrictive means test** A free-exercise-of-religion test in which the state was asked to find another way, perhaps through exemptions, to enforce its regulations while protecting all other religions.

**legislative branch** The branch of government that makes laws.

**legislative courts** Courts designed to provide technical expertise on specific subjects based on Article I of the Constitution.

**legislative oversight** The legislature's review and evaluation of executive branch activities to ensure that programs are administered and implemented in a manner consistent with legislative intent.

***Lemon* test** A test from the 1971 Supreme Court case *Lemon* v. *Kurtzman* for determining the permissible level of state aid for church agencies by measuring its purpose on three counts: Is it nonreligious in nature? Does it either advance or inhibit religion? Does it produce excessive entanglement of church and state?

**libel** Published material that damages a person's reputation or good name in an untruthful and malicious way. Libelous material is not protected by the First Amendment.

**limited government** A type of government in which the powers of the government are clearly defined and bounded so that governmental authority cannot intrude in the lives of private citizens.

**line item veto** The power given to the president to veto a specific provision of a bill involving taxing and spending. Previously the president had to veto an entire bill. Declared unconstitutional by the Supreme Court in 1998.

**literacy test** A requirement that voting applicants had to demonstrate an understanding of national and state constitutions. Primarily used to prevent African Americans from voting in the South.

**lobbying** The formal, organized attempt to influence legislation, usually through direct contact with legislators or their staff.

**lobbyists** People paid to pressure members of Congress to further the aims of an interest group.

**local party organization** The initial point of entry for those seeking involvement in politics as volunteers, organizers, or candidates.

**logrolling** A temporary political alliance between two policy actors who agree to support each other's policy goals.

**machine politics** An organizational style of local politics in which party bosses traded jobs, money, and favors for votes and campaign support.

**maintaining election** Election in which the majority party of the day wins both Congress and the White House, maintaining its control of government.

**majority opinion** A decision of the Supreme Court that represents the agreed-on compromise judgment of all the justices in the majority.

**majority-minority district** A congressional district drawn to include enough members of a minority group to greatly improve the chance of electing a minority candidate.

**majority rule** A decision-making process in which, when more than half of the voters agree on an issue, the entire group accepts the decision, even those in the minority who voted against it.

**mandatory spending** Spending that must be allocated by law rather than by appropriations, for entitlements such as Social Security, Medicare, and Medicaid; 67 percent of the budget.

***Marbury* v. *Madison*** The 1803 case in which Chief Justice John Marshall established the power of judicial review.

**margin of error** The measure of possible error in a survey, which means that the number for the entire population of voters will fall within a range of plus or minus several points of the number obtained from the small but representative sample of voters.

**markup session** A subcommittee meeting to revise a bill.

**mass media** The various media—newspapers, magazines, radio, television, and the Internet—through which information is transferred from its sources to large numbers of people.

***McCulloch* v. *Maryland*** The 1819 decision by Chief Justice John Marshall that expanded the interpretation of the necessary and proper clause to give Congress broad powers to pass legislation and reaffirmed the national government's power over the states under the supremacy clause.

**McGovern-Fraser Commission** Democratic Party commission that, after the 1968 national convention, opened up meetings and votes to a broad variety of party activists, made primaries rather than caucuses the common means of choosing convention delegates, weakened the power of party leaders, and set up rules to ensure that a wide range of party members could participate fully in all party operations.

**means testing** The changing of eligibility for entitlement benefits from everyone receiving benefits to only those with earnings and savings below a predetermined level, in an attempt to save money.

**midterm elections** Elections in which Americans elect members of Congress but not presidents; 2014, 2018, and 2022 are midterm election years.

**military-industrial complex** What President Eisenhower in 1961 called the growing power and influence resulting from the "conjunction of an immense military establishment and a large arms industry."

**minor or third parties** Parties in the American system other than the Democrats or Republicans.

**minority leader** The leader of the minority party in Congress.

**minority rights** Rights given to those in the minority; based on the idea that tyranny of the majority is a danger to human rights.

**Miranda warning** A warning that must be recited by police officers to a suspect before questioning: "You have the right to remain silent; anything you say can and will be used against you. You have the right to an attorney. If you cannot afford an attorney, one will be provided for you. Do you understand these rights and are you willing to speak with us?" Established in *Miranda* v. *Arizona*, 1966.

**Monroe Doctrine** A doctrine enunciated by President James Monroe in 1823 that proclaimed North and South America to be in the United States' sphere of influence, hence out of bounds for European aspirations. It reinforced growing isolationism by promising not to interfere in the internal concerns of European states.

**muckraking** A word used to describe a style of investigative reporting that uncovered many scandals and abuses.

**multiparty system** A political system in which five to ten or more parties regularly compete in elections, win seats, and have some chance of gaining power. Promoted by systems with proportional representation and characteristic of most democratic nations.

**national debt** The cumulative total of all budget deficits.

**national party convention** The national meeting of the party every four years to choose the ticket for the presidential election and write the party platform.

**national party organization** Party organization at the national level whose primary tasks include fund-raising, distribution of information, and recruitment.

**necessary and proper clause** Article I, Section 8, Clause 18 of the Constitution stating that Congress can "make all Laws which shall be necessary and proper for carrying into Execution the foregoing Powers."

**netizens** Groups of people joined in a cyber-society for political purposes.

**New Deal coalition** Brought together by Franklin Roosevelt in 1932, a broad electorate made up of the urban working class, most members of the newer ethnic groups, the bulk of American Catholics and Jews, the poor, the South, and liberal intellectuals.

**New Jersey Plan** A plan presented to the Constitutional Convention of 1787 designed to create a unicameral legislature with equal representation for all states. Its goal was to protect the interests of the smaller, less populous states.

**no incorporation** An approach in which the states would be bound only by the dictates of due process contained in the Fourteenth Amendment.

**nomination** A candidate's "sponsorship" by a political party.

**North Atlantic Treaty Organization (NATO)** Charter signed by the United States, Canada, Turkey, and 11 European nations in 1949 agreeing that an armed attack against one or more of them in Europe or North America would be interpreted as an attack against all.

**nullification** A 19th-century theory that upholds that states faced with unacceptable national legislation can declare such laws null and void and refuse to observe them.

**Office of Management and Budget (OMB)** The unit in the Executive Office of the President whose main responsibilities are to prepare and administer the president's annual budget. A president and the OMB can shape policy through the budget process; the process determines which departments and agencies grow, are cut, or remain the same as the year before.

**omnibus legislation** A large bill that combines a number of smaller pieces of legislation.

**open primary** A system of conducting primary elections in which citizens vote in whichever party's primary they choose.

**opinion** A written version of the decision of a court.

**order** A condition in which the structures of a given society and the relationships thereby defined among individuals and classes comprising it are maintained and preserved by the rule of law and police power of the state.

**original jurisdiction** The authority of a court to be the first to hear a case.

**override** The two-thirds vote of both houses of Congress required to pass a law over the veto of the president.

**participation** Mass political involvement through voting, campaign work, political protests, and civil disobedience, among many others.

**party caucus** A conference of party members in Congress.

**party identification** A psychological orientation, or longterm propensity to think positively of and vote regularly for a particular political party.

**party platform** The statement of principles and policies; the goals that a party pledges to carry out if voters give it control of the government.

**Peace Corps** Organization formed by President Kennedy to help with third world development by having American volunteers live and work in needy communities.

**peonage** A system in which employers advance wages and then require workers to remain on their jobs, in effect enslaving them, until the debt is satisfied.

**plea bargains** Agreements in which the state presses for either a reduced set of charges or a reduced sentence in return for a guilty plea.

**pluralism** A system that occurs when those in the minority form groups based on particular interests and seek to influence policy by allying with other groups.

**plurality opinion** Less than a majority vote on an opinion of the Court; does not have the binding legal force of a majority opinion.

**pocket veto** Presidential refusal to sign or veto a bill that Congress passes in the last ten days of its session; by not being signed, it automatically dies when Congress adjourns.

**police powers** The powers to regulate health, morals, public safety, and welfare, which are reserved to the states.

**policy elites** Members of Congress, the president, Supreme Court justices, cabinet officers, heads of key agencies and departments, leading editorial writers, and influential columnists and commentators.

**policy entrepreneurs** Leaders who invest in, and who create the conditions for, a potential group to become an actual interest group. Ralph Nader stands as a classic example of a policy entrepreneur.

**policy evaluation** The required period of monitoring and analysis of federal policies following their implementation.

**policy networks** Networks characterized by a wideranging discussion of options as issues are resolved, conveying a more inclusive and less conspiratorial image of the policy process than iron triangles do.

**political action committees (PACs)** Committees formed as the fund-raising and financial distribution arm of specific interest groups.

**political culture** A political perspective based on core values, political ideology, culture, and lifestyle.

**political ideology** A coherent way of viewing politics and government; ideological perspectives include beliefs about the military, the role of government, the proper relation between government and the economy, the value of social welfare programs, and the relative importance for society of liberty and order.

**political parties** Organizations that exist to allow likeminded members of the population to group together and magnify their individual voices into a focus promoting individual candidates and government action.

**political socialization** The process by which people learn about the world of politics.

**political violence** Violent action motivated primarily by political aims and intended to have a political impact.

**politico** Congress members who vote suing a combination of constituent wishes and their own best judgment in considering legislation.

**poll tax** A fee that had to be paid before one could vote; used to prevent African Americans from voting; now unconstitutional.

**pork-barrel legislation** Policies and programs designed to create special benefits for a member's district, such as bridges, highways, dams, and military installations, all of which translate into jobs and money for the local economy and improve reelection chances for the incumbent.

**potential groups** Interest groups that could form under the right circumstances; as yet, they have no substantive form and may never have one, but they cannot be discounted by political participants.

**poverty level** The federally determined income below which a family of four is considered poor.

**precedents** Previously decided court cases on an issue similar to the one being considered.

**preemption** The process by which the federal government, under the supremacy clause, signals that it will be the only legislative body to govern in a policy area, as a means of creating uniform policy.

**president of the Senate** The vice president of the United States.

**president pro tempore** The majority party member with the longest continuous service in the Senate; serves as the chief presiding officer in the absence of the vice president.

**primary election** A pre-election that allows all members of a party, not just its leadership, to select the party's candidate for the general election in the fall.

**prior restraint** An action in which the government seeks to ban the publication of controversial material by the press before it is published; censorship.

**privatization** The turning over of public responsibilities to privately owned and operated enterprises for regulation and for providing goods and services.

**probable cause** A reasonable belief that a crime has been, is being, or is about to be committed. Searches also require a belief that evidence of that crime may be located in a particular place. Police must establish this to a judge to secure a search warrant or retroactively justify a search that has already taken place.

**progressive federalism** The Obama administration's approach to federalism that allows states to create their own policy solutions and join together in suing for policy changes.

**progressive taxes** System of taxation in which those who make more money are taxed at a higher rate. An example is the income tax.

**project grant** A grant not based on a formula but distributed for specific purposes after a fairly competitive application and approval process.

**proportional representation** A system of representation popular in Europe whereby the number of seats in the legislature is based on the proportion of the vote received in the election.

**proposal** The first stage of the constitutional amendment process, in which a change is proposed.

**protest** Expression of dissatisfaction; may take the form of demonstrations, letters to newspapers or public officials, or simple "opting out" of the system by failing to vote or participate in any other way.

**protest march** March in which people walk down a main street carrying signs, singing freedom songs, and chanting slogans.

**public agenda** The set of topics that concern policy elites, the general public, or both.

**public interest groups** Groups that focus not on the immediate economic livelihood of their members, but on achieving a broad set of goals that represent their members' vision of the collective good. Examples include the National Taxpayers Union, the League of Women Voters, and Common Cause.

**public opinion** The collective expression of attitudes about the prominent issues and actors of the day.

**public policies** The decisions, actions, and commitments of government.

**quota programs** Programs that guarantee a certain percentage of admissions, new hires, or promotions to members of minority groups.

**random sample** A strategy required for a valid poll whereby every member of the population has an equal chance of appearing in the sample.

**ratify** An act of approval of proposed constitutional amendments by the states; the second step of the amendment process.

**realigning election** Election characterized by massive shifts in partisan identification, as in 1932 with the New Deal coalition.

**realignment** A shift in fundamental party identification and loyalty caused by significant historical events or national crises.

**reapportionment** A process of redrawing voting district lines from time to time and adjusting the number of representatives allotted each state.

**recruitment** The process through which parties look for effective, popular candidates to help them win votes and offices.

**red tape** The excessive number of rules and regulations that government employees must follow.

**redistricting** The redrawing of boundary lines of voting districts in accordance with census data or sometimes by order of the courts.

**referenda** Proposed policy measures submitted for direct popular vote.

**referendum** A proposal submitted by a state legislature to the public for a popular vote, often focusing on whether a state should spend money in a certain way.

**regressive taxes** System of taxation in which taxes take a higher fraction of the income of lower-income taxpayers; examples are taxes on gasoline, cigarettes, and alcohol.

**regulation** A rule-making administrative body must clarify and interpret legislation, its enforcement, and the adjudication of disputes about it.

**regulatory policy** Policy that involves the use of police powers by the federal government to supervise the conduct of individuals, businesses, and other governmental agencies.

**reorganization** Having the power to move programs around within specific agencies.

**representative democracy** A type of government in which voters designate a relatively small number of people to represent their interests; those people, or representatives, then meet in a legislative body and make decisions on behalf of the entire citizenry.

**representative sample** A sample that includes all the significant characteristics of the total population.

**republic** A system of government that allows indirect representation of the popular will.

**reserved powers** Powers not assigned by the Constitution to the national government but left to the states or to the people, according to the Tenth Amendment.

**retrospective voting** A particularly powerful form of issue voting in which voters look back over the past term or two to judge how well an incumbent or the "in party" has performed in office.

**Revolution of 1800** The first election in world history in which one party (the Federalist party of John Adams) willingly gave up power because of a lost election to another party (the Republican party of Thomas Jefferson) without bloodshed.

**rider** An amendment to a bill in the Senate totally unrelated to the bill subject but attached to a popular measure in the hopes that it too will pass.

**right of rebuttal** The right to refute the allegations presented on a radio or television station, free of charge, within a reasonable time.

**right to privacy** The right to have the government stay out of the personal lives of its citizens.

**rule of four** A means of determining which cases the Supreme Court will hear; at least four justices must vote to hear a case and grant the petition for a writ of certiorari for the case to be put on the Court's docket.

**rules** The decisions made by the House Rules Committee and voted on by the full House to determine the flow of legislation—when a bill will be discussed, for how long, and if amendments can be offered.

**salience** In public opinion, the extent to which people see an issue as having a clear impact on their own lives.

**sampling bias** A bias in a survey whereby a particular set of people in the population at large is more or less likely to appear in the final sample than other sets of people.

**schemas** Intellectual frameworks for evaluating the world.

**Second Continental Congress** A meeting convened on May 10, 1775, with all 13 colonies represented. The Congress met to decide whether or not to sever bonds with England and declare independence.

**secular regulation rule** Rule denying any constitutional right to exemption on free exercise grounds from laws dealing with nonreligious matters.

**select (or special) committees** Temporary congressional committees that conduct investigations or study specific problems or crises.

**selective incorporation** An incorporation standard in which some portions of the Bill of Rights, but not all, were made part of the Fourteenth Amendment's due process clause, and thus guaranteed against invasion by the states.

**selective incorporation plus** The Supreme Court's current rule for applying the Bill of Rights to states. States are now bound by most, but not all, of the first eight amendments plus some unenumerated rights, such as privacy, that have been created by the Court but are not part of the text of the Bill of Rights.

**Senate majority leader** A senator selected by the majority party whose functions are similar to those of the Speaker of the House.

**senatorial courtesy** A procedure in which a president submits the names of judicial nominees to senators from the same political party who are also from the nominee's home state for their approval prior to formal nomination.

**seniority** An informal, unwritten rule of Congress that more senior members (those who have served longer than others) are appointed to committees and as chairpersons of committees. This "rule" is being diluted in the House as other systems are developed for committee appointments.

**separation of powers** State in which the powers of the government are divided among the three branches: executive, legislative, and judicial.

**sexism** Prejudice against the female gender.

**signing statements** Written proclamations issued by presidents regarding how they intend to interpret a new law.

**single-member districts** Districts in which a seat goes to the candidate with the most votes. In this system, a small party—say, one that wins 10 percent in every district across the nation—would fail to secure a single seat in the legislature.

**sit-in** A protest technique in which protesters refuse to leave an area.

**slander** Speech that is untruthful, malicious, or damaging to a person's reputation or good name and thus not protected by the free speech clause of the First Amendment.

**social contract theorists** A group of European philosophers who reasoned that the most effective way to create the best government was to understand human nature in a state prior to government.

**social welfare policy** Policy that uses positive incentives (cash assistance, stipends, entitlements, grants, etc.) to promote or encourage basic social and economic fairness.

**socialization** The process by which people learn to conform to their society's norms and values.

**soft money** Campaign contributions directed to advancing the interests of a political party or an issue in general, rather than a specific candidate.

**solicitor general** The third-ranking official in the Justice Department, appointed by the president and charged with representing the U.S. government before the Supreme Court.

**sovereignty** The independence and self-government of a political entity.

**Speaker of the House** The only presiding officer of the House mentioned in the Constitution. The leader of the majority party in Congress and third in line for the presidency.

**specialization** A principle that, in a bureaucracy, specific tasks should be delegated to individuals whose training and experience give them the expertise to execute them. Also refers to a norm used to push legislation through Congress in which members who lack expertise in a particular policy area defer to policy specialists with more knowledge.

**split-ticket ballots** Ballots on which people vote for candidates from more than one party.

**spoils system** A system in which government jobs and contracts are awarded on the basis of party loyalty rather than social or economic status or relevant experience.

**stability** The degree to which an entity is resistant to sudden change or overthrow.

**standing committees** Permanent congressional committees that determine whether proposed legislation should be sent to the entire chamber for consideration.

**stare decisis** A doctrine meaning "let the decision stand," or that judges deciding a case should adhere if at all possible to previously decided cases similar to the one under consideration.

**state action** Action taken by state officials or sanctioned by state law.

**state party organizations** Party organizations at the state level; they organize elections and provide the electoral college votes needed to win the presidency; they also supervise the various functions vital to state parties, such as fund-raising, identifying potential candidates, providing election services, offering advice on reapportionment matters, and developing campaign strategies.

**states' rights** Rights the U.S. Constitution neither grants to the national government nor forbids to the states.

**statutory construction** The power of the Supreme Court to interpret or reinterpret a federal or state law.

**stewardship** An approach to presidential power articulated by Theodore Roosevelt and based on the presidencies of Lincoln and Jackson, who believed that the president had a moral duty to serve popular interests and did not need specific constitutional or legal authorization to take action.

**straight-party tickets** Ballots on which people vote for only one party.

**Strategic Arms Limitation Treaty (SALT)** Treaty signed by the United States (under President Nixon) and the Soviet Union to limit various classes of nuclear weapons.

**straw poll** A nonscientific method of measuring public opinion.

**strict scrutiny test** Test of laws that discriminate on the basis of a characteristic "immutable (or unchangeable) by birth," such as race or nationality; in such cases, the burden shifts from the plaintiff to the state, forcing the government to show the compelling reasons for the law.

**subsequent punishment** Laws that would punish someone for an action after it has taken place. For example, laws such as those banning libel and obscenity because they are harmful to reputations or public sensibilities punish writers, editors, and publishers after an item appears in print.

**suffrage** The right to vote.

**superdelegates** Delegates to the Democratic National Convention not bound to vote for any particular candidate; usually prominent members of the party or elected officials.

**supermajority** An extraordinary majority vote required for constitutional amendments and other actions such as breaking a filibuster and ratifying treaties; consists of more than a simple majority of 50 percent plus one.

**super-PACs** Lobbying organizations under IRS regulation 501 (c)(4) in which unlimited amounts of unregulated money can be raised to lobby for issues or candidates so long as there is no coordination with a specific candidate.

**superpower** The disproportionate power—economic and military—that distinguished the United States and the Soviet Union from all other countries in the post-war era.

**supremacy clause** A clause in Article IV of the Constitution holding that in any conflict between federal laws and treaties and state laws, the will of the national government always prevails.

**symbolic speech** Some actions, such as burning the American flag, that take the place of speech because they communicate a message.

**tariffs** The imposition of import taxes on foreign goods in an attempt to protect a nation's industry and/or labor.

**task force** An informal procedure used by Congress to assemble groups of legislators to draft legislation and negotiate strategy for passing a bill.

**tax expenditures** Deductible expenses that reduce the amount of income subject to taxes; for example, home mortgages, business equipment, or business-related entertainment.

**term limits** A legislated limit on the amount of time a political figure can serve in office.

**test of reasonableness** Test in court cases of what reasonable people would agree to be constitutional because the law has a rational basis for its existence.

**three-fifths compromise** A compromise that stated that the apportionment of representatives by state should be determined "by adding to the whole number of free persons . . . three-fifths of all other persons" (Article I, Section 2), meaning that it would take five slaves to equal three free people when counting the population for representation and taxation purposes.

**total incorporation** An approach arguing that the protections in the Bill of Rights were so fundamental that all of them should be applied to the states by absorbing them into the due process clause of the Fourteenth Amendment.

**town meeting** A form of governance dating back to the 1700s in which town business is transacted by the consent of a majority of eligible citizens, all of whom have an equal opportunity to express their views and cast their votes at an annual meeting.

**tracking polls** Polls used by the media to track the support levels for candidates over time.

**treaties** Formal international agreements between sovereign states.

**triad of powers** Three constitutional provisions—the interstate commerce clause, the general welfare clause, and the Tenth Amendment—that help to continually shift the balance of power between the national and state governments.

**trial court** The point of original entry in the legal system, with a single judge and at times a jury deciding matters of both fact and law in a case.

**triggering mechanism** A critical development that converts a routine problem into a widely shared, negative public response.

**trustees** Congress members who feel authorized to use their best judgment in considering legislation.

**unanimous consent agreement** The process by which the normal rules of Congress are waived unless a single member disagrees.

**unfair discrimination** Unequal treatment based on race, ethnicity, gender, and other distinctions.

**unicameral (one-house) legislature** A legislative system consisting of one chamber.

**universal suffrage** The requirement that everyone must have the right to vote.

**U.S. courts of appeals** The middle appeals level of judicial review beyond the district courts; in 2011, it consisted of 179 judges in 13 courts, 12 of which are geographically based.

**U.S. district courts** The trial courts serving as the original point of entry for almost all federal cases.

**veto** Presidential power to forbid or prevent an action of Congress.

**vice president** The second-highest elected official in the United States.

**Virginia Plan** A plan presented to the Constitutional Convention; favored by the delegates from the bigger states.

**voter turnout** The percentage of eligible voters who actually show up and vote on Election Day.

**War Powers Resolution** A highly controversial measure passed over President Nixon's veto that stipulated that presidential commitments of U.S. military forces cannot extend beyond 60 days without specific congressional authorization.

**Warsaw Pact** Treaty signed by the Soviet Union and the Eastern bloc in Europe agreeing to mutual defense, in reaction to NATO.

**welfare state** A social system whereby the government assumes primary responsibility for the welfare of citizens.

**whips** Congress members charged with counting prospective votes on various issues and making certain that members have the information they need for floor action.

**Whistleblower Protection Act** This act encourages civil servants to report instances of bureaucratic mismanagement, financial impropriety, corruption, and inefficiency. It also protects civil servants from retaliation, such as being fired, demoted, or relocated.

**winner-take-all system** A system in which the winner of the primary or electoral college vote receives all of the state's convention or electoral college delegates.

**workfare** The requirement that recipients of welfare programs, such as AFDC, work on public works unless they find employment elsewhere.

**writ of certiorari** A Latin term meaning "to be made more certain"; this writ enables the Court to accept cases for review only if there are "special and important reasons therefore."

**writ of habeas corpus** A Latin term meaning literally "you should have the body," this is a judicial order enabling jailed prisoners to come into the court, or return to the court after being convicted and sentenced, in order to determine the legality of their detention. By constitutional rules, it can be suspended only in times of crisis by Congress.

**yellow journalism** Brash, colorful, generously illustrated, often lurid and sensationalized organs of half-truth, innuendo, and sometimes outright lies, usually associated with the big-city daily newspapers of Joseph Pulitzer and William Randolph Hearst.

# Suggested Readings


## CHAPTER 1

Cronin, Thomas E. *Direct Democracy: The Politics of Initiative, Referendum, and Recall.* Cambridge, MA: Harvard University Press, 1989. An informative account of how ballot measures affect democratic politics. Cronin examines the strengths and weaknesses of these measures.

Dahl, Robert A. *Democracy and Its Critics.* New Haven, CT: Yale University Press, 1989. One of the most prominent political theorists of our era on the assumptions of democratic theory. The book provides a justification for democracy as a political ideal by tracing modern democracy's evolution from the early 19th century to the present.

Inkeles, Alex, ed. *On Measuring Democracy.* New Brunswick, NJ: Transaction, 1991. Articles by social scientists revealing that political democracy is not only conceptually but also empirically distinct from various social and economic patterns and outcomes.

Murchland, Bernard. *Voices of Democracy.* Chicago: University of Notre Dame Press, 2001. This book builds on conversations between the author and many leading political scientists of our time on the subject of democracy.

Ravitch, Diane, and Abigail Thernstrom, eds. *The Democracy Reader.* New York: HarperCollins, 1992. The enduring issues of democracy in a collection of documents, essays, poems, declarations, and speeches.

Schudson, Michael. *The Good Citizen: A History of American Civic Life.* New York: Free Press, 1998. A history of citizenship in the United States of America, in which the new citizens of America must be "monitors of political danger rather than walking encyclopedias of governmental news."

Sharansky, Naton. *The Case for Democracy: The Power of Freedom to Overcome Tyranny and Terror.* New York: Public Affairs Press, 2004. This book was a White House favorite. Written by a Soviet dissident turned Israeli cabinet minister, the book addresses the future of Israeli–Palestinian relations.

Tismanednu, Vladimir. *Reinventing Politics: Eastern Europe from Stalin to Havel.* New York: Free Press, 1992. A well-balanced account of the factors leading to the revolutions of 1989 and the evolution of democratic institutions in eastern Europe.

Wilentz, Sean. *The Rise of American Democracy.* New York: Norton, 2004. A valuable account of the rise of democracy during the first half of the 19th century and antebellum politics.

Wolin, Sheldon S. *Tocqueville Between Two Worlds: The Making of a Political and Theoretical Life.* Princeton, NJ: Princeton University Press, 2001. The book connects Tocqueville's political and theoretical lives and also provides commentary on the course of Western political life over the past 200 years.

## CHAPTER 2

Beeman, Richard. *Plain, Honest, Men: The Making of the American Constitution.* New York: Random House, 2009. An excellent, new account of the Constitutional Convention, focusing on the characters and debates of the framing period.

Collier, Christopher, and James Lincoln Collier. *Decision in Philadelphia: The Constitutional Convention of 1787.* New York: Random House, 1986. A popular account of the Constitutional Convention, using all of the latest scholarship to bring it to life.

Ellis, Joseph. *Founding Brothers: The Revolutionary Generation.* New York: Knopf, 2000. A study of the founders' views on, and actions in, the democracy that they created during the remainder of their lives.

Foner, Eric. *The Story of American Freedom.* New York: Norton, 1998. A wonderful history of the evolution of American democracy through the study of key events in American political history.

Hamilton, Alexander, James Madison, and John Jay. *The Federalist Papers.* New York: New American Library, 1961. The compelling arguments by three framers on behalf of the Constitution, representing the document's handbook.

Maier, Pauline. *American Scripture: Making the Declaration of Independence.* New York: Vintage Books, 1997. A complete analysis of the Declaration of Independence, including its change from the original draft and its meaning for America.

McCullough, David. *John Adams.* New York: Simon & Schuster, 2001. A sweeping Pulitzer Prize–winning biography of the founder, whom some believe to be just as important, if not more so, than Thomas Jefferson.

Rakove, Jack. *Original Meanings: Politics and Ideas in the Making of the Constitution.* New York: Vintage Press, 1996. The Pulitzer Prize–winning analysis of the making of the Constitution and the "original intent" of the framers.

Wood, Gordon S. *Revolutionary Characters: What Made the Founders Different.* New York: Penguin, 2007. A fascinating study of the nature of character and leadership through case studies of the nation's founders.

## CHAPTER 3

Brands, H. W. *Andrew Jackson: His Life and Times.* New York: Anchor Press, 2006. A highly readable biography of one of the founders of the current system of American federalism.

Frank, Thomas. *What's the Matter with Kansas?* New York: Holt, 2004. A best-selling book exploring how Kansas has evolved from its liberal progressive history into an ultra-conservative state that explains the red state versus blue state nature of current American politics.

Kincaid, John. "De Facto Devolution and Urban Defunding: The Priority of Persons over Places," *Journal of Urban Affairs* 21, no. 2 (1999): 135–167. A highly informative and well-researched analysis of what really became of the promised "devolution revolution."

Osborne, David. *Laboratories of Democracy.* Boston: Harvard Business School, 1988. A highly readable series of case studies on state governors and governments operating to solve public policy problems.

Pressman, Jeffrey, and Aaron Wildavsky. *Implementation.* Berkeley: University of California Press, 1973. An excellent account of how the democratic processes in federalism thwarted the implementation of one of President Lyndon B. Johnson's economic development projects in Oakland, California.

Riker, William H. *The Development of American Federalism.* Boston: Kluwer Academic, 1987. Essays on the continuity of American federalism, written over a 30-year period by Riker and his colleagues.

Stewart, William H. *Concepts of Federalism.* Lanham, MD: University Press of America, 1984. A comprehensive dictionary on the meanings of and metaphors for federalism.

Walker, David B. *Toward a Functioning Federalism.* Cambridge, MA: Winthrop, 1981. An in-depth examination of the intergovernmental-relations system, offering a series of suggestions for reform.

## CHAPTER 4

Baker, Ross K. *Strangers on a Hill: Congress and the Court.* New York: Norton, 2007. An excellent study of the evolution of the contentious relationship between Congress and the judiciary, especially in the free exercise of religion area.

Binder, Sarah A., and Steven S. Smith. *Politics or Principles? Filibustering in the United States Senate.* Washington, DC: Brookings Institution, 1997. A revealing study of the growing use of the filibuster and other delaying tactics to derail legislation in the Senate.

Davidson, Roger H., Walter J. Oleszek, and Frances E. Lee, *Congress and Its Members,* 12th ed. Washington, DC: Congressional Quarterly Press, 2009. The finest comprehensive text on every aspect of Congress and its operations.

Dodd, Lawrence C., and Bruce I. Oppenheimer. *Congress Reconsidered,* 8th ed. Washington, DC: Congressional Quarterly Press, 2004. A revealing series of articles on facets of Congress's operations.

Fenno, Richard. *Congressmen in Committees.* Boston: Little, Brown, 1973. An analysis based on comprehensive interviews with members of Congress and their staffs, describing how committees are staffed and organized and how they operate.

Fenno, Richard. *Home Style: House Members in Their Districts.* Boston: Little, Brown, 1973. A study showing how members of the House deal with their constituents.

Gould, Lewis L. *The Most Exclusive Club: A History of the Modern United States Senate.* New York: Basic Books, 2005. A wonderful narrative history of the evolution of the U.S. Senate in the 20th century that goes far in explaining the current dysfunction of that institution.

Loomis, Burdett, ed. *Esteemed Colleagues: Civility and Deliberation in the U.S. Senate.* Washington, DC: Brookings Institution Press, 2000. An interesting collection of essays investigating the changing nature of the modern Senate away from civility and more toward partisanship.

Mann, Thomas E., and Norman J. Ornstein. *The Broken Branch: How Congress Is Failing America and How to Get It on Track.* New York: Oxford University Press, 2008. A concisely argued volume on why Congress has become ineffective and how to fix it.

Polsby, Nelson. *How Congress Evolves: Social Bases of Institutional Change.* New York: Oxford University Press, 2004. A classic work by one of the field's preeminent scholars, detailing how the nature of political party changes in Congress have first liberalized that body and then led to the sharply partisan institution of the modern era.

Remini, Robert V. *The House: The History of the House of Representatives.* Washington, DC: Smithsonian Books, 2006. A complete history of the House of Representatives, explaining how the institution has evolved over time.

Zelizer, Julian. *On Capitol Hill: The Struggle to Reform Congress and Its Consequences, 1948–2000.* Cambridge, UK: Cambridge University Press, 2004. A wonderful study of the repeated attempts and failures to reform Congress and their impact on the current operations of that institution.

Zelizer, Julian, ed., with Joanne Barrie Zelizer, Jack Rakove, and Alan Taylor. *The American Congress: The Building of Democracy.* Boston: Houghton Mifflin, 2004. A wonderful collection of essays written by major scholars in the field, detailing the history of changes in Congress in all areas throughout American history.

## CHAPTER 5

Barber, James David. *The Presidential Character: Predicting Performance in the White House.* Upper Saddle River, NJ: Prentice Hall, 1985, rev. ed. 1992. A provocative proposal that suggests that we can predict how a person will perform as president, based on the pattern he or she followed in political life.

Ellis, Richard J. *Judging Executive Power: Sixteen Supreme Court Cases That Have Shaped the American Presidency.* Lanham, MD: Rowman & Littlefield, 2009. A detailed examination of the important court cases that influenced the power of the American presidency.

Felzenberg, Alvin. *The Leaders We Deserved (and a Few We Didn't).* New York: Basic Books, 2008. A provocative analysis of criteria for ranking our presidents.

Fisher, Louis. *Military Tribunals and Presidential Power.* Lawrence: University of Kansas Press, 2005. A detailed and comprehensive discussion of the extra-legal courts that represent a dramatic expansion in presidential power during war.

Glasrud, Bruce. *African Americans and the Presidency: The Road to the White House.* New York: Routledge, 2009. A history explaining how the African American candidates for the presidency and vice presidency shaped issues of racial equality and affected the American public.

Greenstein, Fred. *The Presidential Difference: Leadership Style from FDR to Clinton.* Princeton, NJ: Princeton University Press, 2009. A fascinating account of the qualities that have served well in the Oval Office and those that have not, from Franklin D. Roosevelt to Barack Obama.

Irons, Peter. *War Powers.* New York: Metropolitan Books/Henry Holt, 2005. A valuable discussion of what the Constitution says and how presidents have interpreted its language on the power to make war.

Kernell, Samuel. *Going Public: New Strategies of Presidential Leadership.* Washington, DC: CQ Press, 1993, rev. ed. 2008. Examination of presidential power in the context of political relations in Washington—particularly the strategy of bypassing bargaining on Capitol Hill and appealing directly to the American public.

Lott, Jeremy. *The Warm Bucket Brigade: The Story of the American Vice Presidency.* Nashville, TN: Thomas Nelson, 2009. An informative and entertaining look at the American vice presidency and the men who have held the office.

Mayer, Ken. *With the Stroke of a Pen: Executive Orders and Presidential Power.* Princeton, NJ: Princeton University Press, 2001. A lucid historical discussion of the evolution of executive orders and the rise of executive powers.

Neustadt, Richard E. *Presidential Power and the Modern Presidents.* New York: Free Press, 1990. A classic study of presidential bargaining and influence that has set the agenda for a generation of presidency scholars.

Rozell, Mark. *Executive Privilege: Presidential Power, Secrecy, and Accountability.* Lawrence: University Press of Kansas, 2002. An authoritative account of the development of privilege and the claims made by presidents.

Skowronek, Stephen. *The Politics Presidents Make: Leadership from John Adams to George Bush.* Cambridge, MA: Harvard University Press, 1993. An important and innovative book that chronicles 15 presidents and how they continually transformed the political landscape.

## CHAPTER 6

Abraham, Henry J. *Justices, Presidents and Senators: A History of the U.S. Supreme Court Appointments from Washington to Clinton.* Lanham, MD: Rowman & Littlefield, 1999. A complete history of presidential appointments to the Supreme Court and the decision making that resulted.

Blackmun, Harry. *The Harry Blackmun Papers at the Library of Congress,* Manuscript Division, Library of Congress, Washington DC, www.loc.gov/rr/mss/blackmun. The most revealing primary source examination of the justice and the recent courts available.

Breyer, Stephen. *Active Liberty: Interpreting Our Democratic Constitution.* New York: Knopf, 2005. A thoughtful and clearly expressed explanation of the justice's theory of "Policing the Boundaries" of constitutional governmental power.

Epstein, Lee, and Jack Knight. *The Choices Justices Make.* Washington, DC: CQ Press, 1998. An analysis of the strategically political manner in which justices decide cases.

Goldman, Sheldon. *Picking Federal Judges: Lower Court Selection from Roosevelt Through Reagan.* New Haven, CT: Yale University Press, 1997. Findings from 30 years of study by the nation's expert on the lower federal court judicial selection process into how nine presidents have undertaken this process.

Greenburg, Jan Crawford. *Supreme Conflict: The Inside Story of the Struggle for Control of the United States Supreme Court.* New York: Penguin, 2007. An excellent study by the ABC News correspondent of the movement of the Supreme Court toward conservatism because of presidential appointments since the 1987 Robert Bork confirmation battle.

Greenhouse, Linda. *Becoming Justice Blackmun: Harry Blackmun's Supreme Court Journey.* New York: Times Books, 2005. A wonderfully readable biography of both Justice Blackmun and the Rehnquist Court.

Knowles, Helen J. *The Tie Goes to Freedom: Justice Anthony M. Kennedy on Freedom.* New York: Rowman & Littlefield, 2009. An intriguing judicial biography of the Court's current swing justice, arguing that he is, at heart, a libertarian.

Lazarus, Edward. *Closed Chambers.* New York: Times Books, 1998. Not only a revealing look inside the Court in the 1998–1999 term by a former Blackmun law clerk, but a potentially damaging account of the increased role of law clerks in the Court's work.

Merida, Kevin, and Michael A. Fletcher. *Supreme Discomfort: The Divided Soul of Clarence Thomas.* New York: Doubleday, 2007. A compelling biography of Justice Clarence Thomas by two *Washington Post* reporters, illustrating the effect of his impoverished background, his difficult education years, and the contentious nature of his relationship with the African American community on his work on the Court.

Murdoch, Joyce, and Deb Price. *Courting Justice: Gay Men and Lesbians* v. *The Supreme Court.* New York: Basic Books, 2001. A highly readable history of the Supreme Court's effort to avoid and then mishandle the issue of gay rights in cases throughout the decades.

Murphy, Bruce Allen. *Wild Bill: The Legend and Life of William O. Douglas.* New York: Random House, 2003. A revealing study of the real person behind the legend and the sources of his judicial decision making.

O'Brien, David. *Storm Center: The Supreme Court in American Politics,* 7th ed. New York: Norton, 2005. A highly revealing text on the internal politics of the Supreme Court using sources from justices' papers in historical archives.

Rosen, Jeffrey. *The Supreme Court: The Personalities and Rivalries That Defined America.* New York: Times Books, 2006. A timely study, through a series of contrasting case studies, of the importance of judicial temperament for the direction of the Court in a companion book for the PBS series by the same name.

Savage, David. *Turning Right: The Making of the Rehnquist Supreme Court.* New York: Wiley, 1992. The *Los Angeles Times* court reporter's inside account of the people who made up the Rehnquist Court and the ways their personal views and interactions shape public policy.

Toobin, Jeffrey. *The Nine: Inside the Secret World of the Supreme Court.* New York: Anchor Press, 2008. An excellent and highly readable account of the recent Supreme Court and its landmark decisions.

Tushnet, Mark. *A Court Divided: The Rehnquist Court and the Future of Constitutional Law.* New York: Norton, 2005. A learned and informative analysis of the justices and legal topics that made the Rehnquist Court so interesting.

Ward, Artemus, and David L. Weiden. *Sorcerers' Apprentices: 100 Years of Law Clerks at the United States Supreme Court.* New York: New York University Press, 2006. A fascinating study of the evolving role of the Supreme Court law clerks based on a comprehensive set of surveys and interviews.

Woodward, Bob, and Scott Armstrong. *The Brethren: Inside the Supreme Court.* New York: Avon Books, 1979. A highly controversial study of the inside workings of the Supreme Court from 1969 through 1975. Uses anonymous law clerk interviews and Court papers.

## CHAPTER 7

Abramson, Mark, and Paul Lawrence. *Learning the Ropes: Insights for Political Appointees.* Lanham, MD: Rowman & Littlefield, 2005. A valuable guide for understanding the dilemma of permanent government and what to do about it.

Bozeman, Barry. *Bureaucracy and Red Tape.* Upper Saddle River, NJ: Prentice-Hall, 2000. A useful guide to understanding the complexity of government regulations as well as solutions for making government more efficient.

Downey, Kirstin. *The Woman Behind the New Deal: The Life and Legacy of Frances Perkins.* New York: Random House, 2010. A fascinating story of the first female cabinet secretary, who was largely the architect behind the New Deal.

Downs, Anthony. *Inside Bureaucracy.* Prospect Heights, IL: Waveland Press, 1994. Interesting theories and insights into bureaucratic decision making.

Gay, Paul Du. *The Values of Bureaucracy.* New York: Oxford University Press, 2005. This book highlights the positive attributes of bureaucracy and shows why bureaucratic organization should be valued, both by those engaged in business and commerce, and those responsible for running states and delivering public services.

Miskel, James. *Disaster Response and Homeland Security: What Works, What Doesn't.* Stanford, CA: Stanford University Press, 2008. A former deputy assistant associate director of FEMA and Naval War College professor provides an insightful analysis about success and failure in disaster response, especially emergency management during the Katrina hurricane.

Neiman, Max. *Defending Government: Why Big Government Works.* Upper Saddle River, NJ: Prentice-Hall, 2000. This book addresses the benefits of well-designed, democratically inspired public policies. It provides a thoughtful analysis of the public sector, economic performance, and personal liberty.

Teske, Paul. *Regulation in the States.* Washington, DC: Brookings Institution Press, 2004. An insightful study of government regulation of economic activity.

Wilson, James Q. *Bureaucracy: What Government Agencies Do and Why They Do It.* New York: Basic Books, 1989. A lively, "bottom-up" view of bureaucracy and an explanation of why some agencies work well whereas others fail.

## CHAPTER 8

Berinsky, Adam. *Silent Voices: Public Opinion and Political Participation in America.* Princeton, NJ: Princeton University Press, 2004. An excellent analysis of how polls are flawed by exclusion bias to a sizable portion of the public.

Bishop, George. *The Illusion of Public Opinion: Fact and Artifact in American Public Opinion Polls.* Lanham, MD: Rowman & Littlefield, 2004. A detailed analysis of how particular wording and order of questions influences respondent's answers and how certain questions lead respondents to make up answers.

Davis, Darren W. *Negative Liberty: Public Opinion and the Terrorist Attacks on America.* Thousand Oaks, CA: Sage, 2009. An eye-opening exploration of how Americans viewed the balance between the core values of freedom and order were altered after the September 11 attacks.

Erikson, Robert S., Norman R. Luttbeg, and Kent L. Tedin. *American Public Opinion: Its Origins, Content, and Impact,* 4th ed. New York: Macmillan, 1991. A comprehensive overview of major aspects of American public opinion, including opinion formation, opinion distribution within society, and the influence of public opinion on public policy.

Ginsberg, Benjamin. *The Captive Public: How Mass Opinion Promotes State Power.* New York: Basic Books, 1986. An examination of the thesis that public opinion, as it becomes a more prominent force in American politics, actually enhances the power of American government over its citizens.

Huntington, Samuel. *Who Are We: The Challenges to America's National Identity.* New York: Simon & Schuster, 2004. A discussion on the nature and role of Anglo-Protestant values and culture with specific reference to the values and behaviors of Latin American immigrants.

Page, Benjamin I., and Robert Y. Shapiro. *The Rational Public: Fifty Years of Trends in America's Policy Preferences.* Chicago: University of Chicago Press, 1992. A challenge to the assumption that American public opinion is "irrational" based on data revealing relatively steady public preferences over time, changing only under logical circumstances.

Simon, Rita, and Muhamed Alaa Abdel Moneim. *Public Opinion in the United States: Studies of Race, Religion, Gender, and Issues That Matter.* Piscataway, NJ: Transaction, 2009. A detailed examination of changes in American public opinion on issues of race and gender.

Stimson, James A. *Public Opinion in America.* Boulder, CO: Westview, 1991. A major study of public opinion research and its link with major issues in American politics.

## CHAPTER 9

Alter, Jonathan. *The Promise: President Obama, Year One.* New York: Simon & Schuster, 2011. A compelling story of the first year of the Obama administration and what went on behind the scenes in passing the health-care reform law.

Ceasar, James W., Andrew E. Busch, and John J. Pitney Jr. *Epic Journey: The 2008 Election and American Politics.* Lanham, MD: Rowman & Littlefield, 2009. A very good compilation of studies about the 2008 federal and state elections and the role of the political parties within them.

DiClerico, Robert E. *Political Parties, Campaigns, and Elections.* Upper Saddle River, NJ: Prentice-Hall, 2000. A fine textbook dealing with the state of political parties in the election process.

Frank, Thomas. *What's the Matter with Kansas?* New York: Owl Books, 2004. An informative and highly readable analysis of the sources of the red state versus blue state divide in the Midwest and the entire nation.

Green, John, and Daniel Shea. *The State of the Parties: The Changing Role of Contemporary American Parties,* 3rd ed. Lanham, MD: Rowman & Littlefield, 1999. An interesting study of the future of American political parties in a changing democratic system.

Halperin, Mark, and John F. Harris. *The Way to Win: Taking the White House in 2008.* New York: Random House, 2006. A very interesting analysis based on recent successful candidates such as Bill Clinton, by the political director of ABC News. Discusses how presidential candidates should craft their political images in order to win the White House.

Johnson, Haynes, and David Broder. *The System: The American Way of Politics at the Breaking Point.* Boston: Little, Brown, 1996. Two of America's finest political journalists examine how well the American political system is operating in a review of the political party dispute over the Clinton administration's efforts to create a system of universal health care.

Kayden, Xandra, and Eddie Mahe Jr. *The Party Goes On: The Persistence of the Two Party System in the United States.* New York: Basic Books, 1985. The first full-scale assessment of the strength of political parties and their impact on national political life.

Key, V. O. *Southern Politics.* New York: Knopf, 1949. A classic account of one-party politics in the South.

Polsby, Nelson. *Consequences of Party Reform.* New York: Oxford University Press, 1983. An excellent account of changes in party rules and the impact of those changes on party roles in government.

Shafer, Byron E. *Quiet Revolution: The Struggle for the Democratic Party and the Shaping of Post-Reform Politics.* Washington, DC: Brookings Institution, 1983. The story of party reform from 1968 to 1972, which produced a new era in national politics. The changes altered the very character of presidential politics, from campaign organization to grassroots participation.

Thomas, Evan, et al. *Back from the Dead: How Clinton Survived the Republican Revolution.* New York: Atlantic Monthly Press, 1997. The story of how the once-liberal Democratic president Bill Clinton repositioned himself in the American political landscape to forge an electoral victory in 1996.

## CHAPTER 10

Campbell, Angus, Philip E. Converse, Warren E. Miller, and Donald Stokes. *The American Voter.* New York: Wiley, 1960. The classic study of voting, which even today should be the starting point for study of elections and politics.

Corrado, Anthony, Thomas Mann, Daniel Ortiz, and Trevor Potter. *The New Campaign Finance Sourcebook.* Washington DC: Brookings Institution Press, 2005. A completely revised and updated sourcebook; the definitive resource on federal campaign finance regulation.

Goff, Michael. *The Money Primary: The New Politics of the Early Presidential Nomination Process.* Lanham, MD: Rowman & Littlefield, 2004. This book examines the "money primary" and fund-raising's instrumental role in candidate visibility and success.

Grant, J. Tobin, and Thomas J. Rudolph. *Expression vs. Equality: The Politics of Campaign Finance Reform.* Columbus: Ohio State University Press, 2004. A systematic study of attitudes toward campaign finance reform and the role of public opinion in shaping reform measures.

Fortier, John, ed. *After the People Vote: A Guide to the Electoral College.* Washington, DC: AEI Press, 2008 edition. An exceptionally useful guide to the operations of the electoral college.

Han, Hahrie. *Moved to Action: Motivation, Participation, and Inequality in American Politics.* Stanford, CA: Stanford University Press, 2009. A discussion of the socioeconomic disparity in participation rates as well as proposals for increasing participation among the underrepresented.

Keyssar, Alexander. *The Right to Vote: The Contested History of Democracy in the United States.* New York: Basic Books, 2009. A historical account of America's long road toward universal suffrage.

Matsusaka, John G. *For the Many or the Few: The Initiative, Public Policy, and American Democracy.* Chicago: University of Chicago Press, 2004. An economist addresses the question of whether the presence of initiatives benefits the many or the few.

Nie, Norman H., Sidney Verba, and John R. Petrocik. *The Changing American Voter.* Cambridge, MA: Harvard University Press, 1976. An important study offering a fresh look at the classic 1960 study of the American voter.

Piven, Francis Fox, and Richard Cloward. *Why Americans Don't Vote.* New York: Pantheon, 1988. A starting point for understanding the problems associated with the decline of voting in America.

Smith, Daniel A., and Caroline J. Tolbert. *Educated by Initiative: The Effects of Direct Democracy on Citizens and Political Organizations in the American States.* Ann Arbor: University of Michigan Press, 2004. A valuable discussion on the extent to which ballot-measure decisions educate citizens about the workings of democracy and interest them in democratic processes.

Teixeira, Ray A. *The Disappearing American Voter.* Washington, DC: Brooking Institution, 1992. The reasons Americans don't vote and the effects of nonvoting on political life.

Vavreck, Lynn. *The Message Matters: The Economy and Presidential Campaigns.* Princeton, NJ: Princeton University Press, 2009. An eye-opening examination of how economic conditions and campaign messages influence presidential election outcomes.

Wolfinger, Raymond E., and Steven J. Rosenstone. *Who Votes.* New Haven, CT: Yale University Press, 1980. An important empirical analysis of voting, the results of which are then unified into a theory of voting behavior.

## CHAPTER 11

Berry, Jeffrey M. *The Interest Group Society,* 3rd ed. New York: Longman, 1997. An interesting examination of the development of interest-group politics in American society.

Cigler, Allan J., and Burdett A. Loomis, eds. *Interest Group Politics,* 4th ed. Washington, DC: Congressional Quarterly Press, 1995. An excellent collection of readings on American interest groups.

Dye, Thomas R. *Who's Running America? The Clinton Years,* 6th ed. Upper Saddle River, NJ: Prentice-Hall, 1995. A description of the dominant political institutions of our time and the individuals who control them.

Frank, Thomas. *The Wrecking Crew: How Conservatives Rule,* New York: Metropolitan Books, 2008. The author's companion book to his classic *What's the Matter with Kansas?* on the growth of government and the conservative movement under George Bush.

Heinz, John P., Edward Q. Laumann, Robert L. Nelson, and Robert H. Salisbury. *The Hollow Core: Private Interests in National Policy Making.* Cambridge, MA: Harvard University Press, 1993. A scholarly examination of connections among interest groups, members of Congress, and bureaucrats that sheds doubt on the theory of iron triangles.

Lowi, Theodore J. *The End of Liberalism: The Second Republic of the United States,* 2nd ed. New York: Norton, 1979. A provocative perspective on American government, arguing that the tight connections between interest groups and government officials have created a new kind of American political system.

Olson, Mancur, Jr. *The Logic of Collective Action.* Cambridge, MA: Harvard University Press, 1965. An influential work that argues that rational citizens have few incentives to join groups, and consequently the interests of nonjoiners are poorly represented in politics.

Rasmussen, Scott, and Douglas Schoen. *Mad as Hell: How the Tea Party Movement Is Fundamentally Remaking Our Two-Party System.* New York: Broadside Books, 2010. A thorough and balanced analysis of the American Tea Party political movement on the two-party system in electoral politics.

Rheingold, Howard. *Smart Mobs: The Next Social Revolution.* New York: Basic Books, 2003. A fascinating study of how the 21st-century cyberrevolution, and the ability of people to connect through it, will change political lobbying and political parties.

Sosnik, Douglas B., Matthew J. Dowd, and Ron Fournier. *Applebee's America: How Successful Political, Business, and Religious Leaders Connect with the New American Community.* New York: Simon & Schuster, 2007. A fascinating study of the voters in the exurbs, the primary locations for Applebee's restaurant franchises. These voters turn out to be much more independent in their views than their previous stereotypical conservative Republican image.

Suskind, Ron. *Confidence Men, Wall Street, Washington, and the Education of a President.* New York: HarperCollins, 2011. A sobering and compelling story of the effort by President Obama and his economic team to battle the Wall Street financial interests in helping the nation recover from the Great Recession.

Truman, David B. *The Governmental Process.* New York: Knopf, 1951. A classic book presenting the pluralist vision of how interest groups operate in American politics.

Walker, Jack L., Jr. *Mobilizing Interest Groups in America: Patrons, Professions, and Social Movements.* Ann Arbor: University of Michigan Press, 1991. An excellent and wide-ranging discussion of interest groups in modern American political life.

Wolpe, Bruce C., and Bertram J. Levine. *Lobbying Congress: How the System Works,* 2nd ed. Washington, DC: Congressional Quarterly Press, 1996. An in-depth examination of how interest groups successfully influence the direction of Congress.

Wright, John R. *Interest Groups and Congress.* Boston: Allyn & Bacon, 1996. A well-written study of how political action committees and interest group lobbies influence congressional policy making.

## CHAPTER 12

Alterman, Eric. *What Liberal Media? The Truth about Bias and the News.* New York: Basic Books, 2005. An analysis of how conservatives monopolize the resources and create an unfair playing field for objective news reporting.

Bagdikian, Ben H. *The Media Monopoly,* 4th ed. Boston: Beacon Press, 1994. A fascinating analysis of the continuing concentration of ownership of mass media outlets into fewer hands.

Baum, Matthew A., and Timothy Groeling. *War Stories: The Causes and Consequences of Public Views of War.* Princeton, NJ: Princeton University Press, 2009. A detailed and thought-provoking analysis of how the media and elites shape public opinion.

Baym, Geoeffrey. *From Cronkite to Colbert: The Evolution of Broadcast News.* St. Paul, MN: Paradigm, 2009. The author traces the path of television news from the trusted days of Cronkite and Murrow to the rise of distrust and breakdown of the network news shows, and ends with a discussion of what he views as not comedy shows, but a new type of journalism.

Buell, Emmett H., and Lee Sigelman. *Attack Politics: Negativity in Presidential Campaigns Since 1960.* Lawrence: University of Kansas Press, 2009. The authors provide a thorough description of presidential campaigns since Kennedy ran against Nixon, including a discussion and analysis of the 2008 race between Barack Obama and John McCain.

Goldberg, Bernard. *Bias: A CBS Insider Exposes How the Media Distort the News.* Washington, DC: Regency, 2001. The former Emmy-award-winning broadcast journalist reveals a corporate news structure that responds to liberal opinions.

Halberstam, David. *The Powers That Be.* New York: Dell, 1979. A classic account of the rise of major media figures in America, written by one of America's foremost political journalists.

Hamilton, James. *All The News That's Fit to Sell: How Market Transforms Information into News.* Princeton, NJ: Princeton University Press, 2005. A valuable study of how sensationalism creates competition and polarization. The more news sources that exist, the more intense the struggle for an audience.

Iyengar, Shanto. *Is Anyone Responsible? How Television Frames Political Issues.* Chicago: University of Chicago Press, 1991. A scholarly analysis of the power of television to "frame" political issues and influence the way viewers respond to and think about those issues.

Kuypers, Jim A. *Press Bias and Politics: How the Media Frames Controversial Issues.* New York: Praeger, 2005. An excellent discussion of how partisans consciously and unconsciously attempt to shape public perceptions of the world.

## CHAPTER 13

Abraham, Henry J., and Barbara A. Perry. *Freedom and the Court: Civil Rights and Liberties in the United States,* 7th ed. New York: Oxford University Press, 1998. A comprehensive and highly readable survey of the Supreme Court's development of civil rights and liberties in the United States since the 1930s.

Farber, Daniel A. *Retained by the People: The "Silent" Ninth Amendment and the Constitutional Rights Americans Don't Know They Have.* New York: Basic Books, 2007. A very interesting argument in favor of expanding the Court's protection for unwritten individual rights through the Ninth Amendment.

Garrow, David, Jr. *Liberty and Sexuality: The Right to Privacy and the Making of* Roe *v.* Wade. New York: Macmillan, 1994. A superb historical study of the Supreme Court's development of the right to privacy from *Griswold* v. *Connecticut* through *Roe* v. *Wade.*

Greenhouse, Linda. *Becoming Justice Blackmun: Harry Blackmun's Supreme Court Journey.* New York: Holt, 2005. A fine biography based on the Library of Congress's released Justice Blackmun papers showing his evolution from conservative to liberal.

Irons, Peter. *War Powers: How the Imperial Presidency Hijacked the Constitution.* New York: Holt, 2005. An excellent examination of the cases and doctrines that will be used to decide the anti-terrorism war powers cases.

Jeffries, John C., Jr. *Justice Lewis F. Powell: A Biography.* New York: Scribner's, 1994. A wonderful biography of the justice who served as the "swing member" on the contentious Burger Court and was responsible for so many crucial decisions and nondecisions.

Keck, Thomas M. *The Most Activist Supreme Court: The Road to Modern Judicial Conservatism.* Chicago: University of Chicago Press, 2002. A comprehensive and readable history of the evolution of conservative philosophy on the Court.

Lash, Kurt T. *The Lost History of the Ninth Amendment.* New York: Oxford University Press, 2009. An intriguing history offering previously unknown evidence that the intention of the Ninth Amendment was to safeguard the rights retained by the people and to make it possible for states to protect those rights from the national government.

Lazarus, Edward. *Closed Chambers.* New York: Times Books, 1998. A fascinating account by a Blackmun law clerk of life on the Supreme Court in the 1988–1989 term, revealing the clerks' role in producing opinions that year.

Lee, Francis Graham. *Church–State Relations.* Westport, CT: Greenwood Press, 2002. A superb summary and analysis of the Court's meandering path in freedom of religion cases.

Murdoch, Joyce, and Deb Price. *Courting Justice: Gay Men and Lesbians* v. *The Supreme Court.* New York: Basic Books, 2001. A highly readable history of the Supreme Court's effort to avoid and subsequent mishandling of the issue of gay rights in cases throughout the decades.

O'Brien, David M. *Constitutional Law and Politics,* Vol. 2, *Civil Rights and Civil Liberties.* New York: Norton, 1997. An excellent casebook containing cuttings of Supreme Court cases mixed with historical information and comprehensive charts showing the development of case law.

Pritchett, C. Herman. *Constitutional Civil Liberties.* Englewood Cliffs, NJ: Prentice-Hall, 1984. A complete survey of civil liberties case law broken down by amendment and subcategories within each amendment.

Rehnquist, William H. *All the Laws But One: Civil Liberties in Wartime.* New York: Alfred A. Knopf, 1998. A readable history of the Supreme Court's unwillingness to protect civil liberties and civil rights during times of crisis, because "In time of war the laws are silent."

Richards, David A. J. *The Case for Gay Rights: From Bowers to Lawrence and Beyond.* Lawrenceville: University of Kansas Press, 2005. A very fine exploration of the Surpreme Court's role in restricting and later extending gay rights in America.

Rosen, Jeffrey. *The Unwanted Gaze: The Destruction of Privacy in America.* New York: Random House, 2000. An interesting and disturbing examination of our loss of privacy and control over the use of our personal information on the computer and in cyber-space.

Savage, David G. *Turning Right: The Making of the Rehnquist Supreme Court.* New York: Wiley, 1992. A well-researched behind-the-scenes journalistic account by the *Wall Street Journal*'s court reporter on Rehnquist Court efforts to shape legal doctrine regarding civil rights and liberties.

Shipler, David K. *The Rights of the People: How Our Search for Safety Invades Our Civil Liberties.* New York: Knopf, 2011. An interesting book arguing that the post-2011 laws and judicial decisions have diminished our Fourth Amendment search and seizure and other civil liberties protections.

Stone, Geoffrey R. *Perilous Times: Free Speech in Wartime.* New York: Norton, 2005. An especially timely exploration of the Supreme Court's decisions in the First Amendment free speech area during times of national crisis.

## CHAPTER 14

Abraham, Henry J., and Barbara A. Perry. *Freedom and the Court: Civil Rights and Liberties in the United States,* 8th ed. New York: Oxford University Press, 2003. An analysis of the Supreme Court and lower federal courts' development of American civil rights and liberties.

Bok, Derek, and William Bowen. *The Shape of the River: Long-Term Consequences of Considering Race in College and University Admissions.* Princeton, NJ: Princeton University Press, 1998. A powerful critique of the affirmative action program in American education.

Branch, Taylor. *At Canaan's Edge: America in the King Years, 1965–68.* New York: Simon & Schuster, 2006. The final volume in this groundbreaking life and times of Martin Luther King Jr. covers the civil rights movement from the 1965 Selma protest march through Reverend King's assassination in 1968.

Brown, Dee Alexander. *Bury My Heart at Wounded Knee: An Indian History of the American West.* New York: Holt, Rinehart & Winston, 1971. A highly readable history of the sad treatment of Native Americans by the U.S. government and its people.

Carter, Steven L. *Reflections of an Affirmative Action Baby.* New York: Basic Books, 1991. A learned critique of the affirmative action programs by an African American law professor from Yale who benefited from them.

Garrow, David J. *Bearing the Cross: Martin Luther King, Jr., and the Southern Christian Leadership Conference.* New York: Morrow, 1986. This landmark biography of King won a Pulitzer Prize.

Ifil, Gwen. *The Breakthrough: Politics and Race in the Age of Obama.* New York: Doubleday, 2009. A fine book by one of America's preeminent African American national television news broadcasters and a former *New York Times* reporter exploring the importance of Barack Obama's presidential election to the American civil rights movement.

Keyssar, Alexander. *The Right to Vote: The Contested History of Democracy in the United States.* New York: Basic Books, 2000. A groundbreaking study of the meandering expansion of voting rights throughout this nation's history.

Kluger, Richard. *Simple Justice.* New York: Knopf, 1976. The compelling story of the cases that made up the landmark *Brown* v. *Board of Education* case. Included is the remarkable story of legendary NAACP attorney Thurgood Marshall.

Mansbridge, Jane J. *Why We Lost the ERA.* Chicago: University of Chicago Press, 1986. An examination of reasons why the Equal Rights Amendment failed.

Merida, Kevin, and Michael A. Fletcher. *Supreme Discomfort: The Divided Soul of Clarence Thomas.* New York: Doubleday, 2007. A provocative argument about the impact of Clarence Thomas's views on race and their effect on his conservative decision making on the Supreme Court.

Nieman, Donald G. *Promises to Keep: African Americans and the Constitutional Order, 1776 to the Present.* New York: Oxford University Press, 1991. An informative history of the development of legal rights for African Americans.

Rosen, Jeffrey. *The Most Democratic Branch: How the Courts Serve America.* New York: Oxford University Press, 2006. The case is made here, through an examination of important areas of case law, that the life-tenured, appointed Supreme Court in fact best serves America when it represents the American public opinion.

Rowland, Debran. *The Boundaries of Her Body: The Troubling History of Women's Rights in America.* Naperville, IL: Sphinx, 2004. A wonderfully complete history and analysis of the evolution of women's rights in America.

Williams, Juan. *Eyes on the Prize: America's Civil Rights Years, 1954–1965.* New York: Penguin, 1987. The companion book to the PBS series on the history of the civil rights movement in the United States.

## CHAPTER 15

Dodds, Felix, Andrew Higham, and Richard Sherman, eds. *Climate Change and Energy Insecurity: The Challenge for Peace, Security and Development.* London: Earthscan, 2009. The editors bring together analysis from scholars and politicians discussing the public policy challenges caused by energy shortfalls and climate change.

Friedman, Milton, and Walter Heller. *Monetary versus Fiscal Policy.* New York: Norton, 1969. Classic presentation of the pros and cons of monetary and fiscal policy by a noninterventionist (Friedman) and an advocate of federal government intervention in the economy (Heller).

Funigello, Phillip J. *Health Care Security from FDR to George W. Bush.* Lawrence: University of Kansas Press, 2006. An excellent chronicle of the contentious political history behind the circumstances that have left 45 million Americans without adequate health insurance.

Greider, William. *Secrets of the Temple: How the Federal Reserve Runs the Country.* New York: Simon & Schuster, 1987. A fascinating account of how the Federal Reserve Board actually conducts its business.

Harrington, Michael. *The Other America.* New York: Macmillan, 1994. The most widely read essay about poverty in the United States.

Jencks, Christopher. *Rethinking Social Policy: Race, Poverty, and the Underclass.* Cambridge, MA: Harvard University Press, 1992. A series of essays by a leading sociologist on social welfare policy and poverty.

Murray, Charles. *Losing Ground: American Social Policy, 1950–1980.* New York: Basic Books, 1984. A popular and controversial book that addresses the idea that social welfare programs for the poor have made things worse, not better.

Odell, John S. *Negotiating the World Economy.* Ithaca, NY: Cornell University Press, 2000. An original analysis of strategies use to obtain maximum payoffs.

Page, Benjamin, and Lawrence Jacobs. *Class War? What Americans Really Think about Economic Inequality.* Chicago: University of Chicago Press, 2009. A detailed examination of how Americans view income inequality and more progressive tax policies.

Savage, James. *Balanced Budgets and American Politics.* Ithaca, NY: Cornell University Press, 1988. A scholarly historical account of ways the political environment affects budgeting in the United States.

Slemrod, Joel, and Jon Bakiga. *Taxing Ourselves,* 2nd ed. Cambridge, MA: MIT Press, 2000. An excellent citizen's guide to the debate on taxation and reform.

## CHAPTER 16

Cushman, Thomas, ed. *A Matter of Principle: Humanitarian Arguments for the War in Iraq.* Berkeley: University of California Press, 2006. This book provides a collection of sobering essays, including entries by Adam Michnik and Robert Kagan, that challenge those opposed to intervention.

Gertz, Bill. *Breakdown: How America's Intelligence Failures Led to September 11th.* New York: Regency, 2002. This *New York Times* author shows how America's intelligence community completely broke down in the years prior to the attacks on the World Trade Center and Pentagon. He calls it the greatest intelligence failure since Pearl Harbor.

Hachigian, Nina, and Mona Sutphen. *The Next American Century. How The U.S. Can Survive as Other Powers Rise.* New York: Simon & Schuster, 2008. Offers a new blueprint for American leadership in the world, most especially in dealings with China and India.

Levite, Ariel E., Bruce W. Jentleson, and Larry Berman, eds. *Foreign Military Intervention: The Dynamics of Protracted Conflict.* New York: Columbia University Press, 1992. Six case studies that examine the similarities and differences among nation-states that use military might to intervene in civil wars and otherwise reshape the domestic political order of weakened states.

Lieber, Robert. *The American Era: Power and Strategy for the 21st Century.* Cambridge, UK: Cambridge University Press, 2005.

Litwak, Robert S. *Rogue States and U.S. Foreign Policy.* Washington, DC: Woodrow Wilson Center Press and The Johns Hopkins University Press, 2000. A seminal contribution to the discussion of rogue states.

Nincic, Miroslav. *Renegade Regimes: Confronting Deviant Behavior in World Politics.* New York: Columbia University Press, 2005. A comprehensive and groundbreaking study of rogue states and the challenges to international regime security.

Nye, Joseph S., Jr. *The Paradox of American Power: Why the World's Only Superpower Can't Go It Alone.* New York: Oxford University Press, 2002. An analysis of American foreign policy that pits America's preeminent position against the need to recognize and account for the interdependent global system.

Preble, Christopher. *The Power Problem: How American Military Dominance Makes Us Less Safe, Less Prosperous, and Less Free.* Ithaca, NY: Cornell University Press, 2009. Examines the aims, costs, and limitations in the use of military power and the ways decision makers ignore the public.

Reiter, Dan, and Allan C. Stam. *Democracies at War.* Princeton, NJ: Princeton University Press, 2002. A study of why democracies win the wars they fight 80 percent of the time.

Rothkopf, David J. *Running the World: The Inside Story of the National Security Council and the Architects of American Power.* New York: Public Affairs Press, 2005. An insightful bureaucratic history of the National Security Council and the principal personalities.

Walt, Stephen M. *Taming American Power: The Global Response to U.S. Primacy.* New York: Norton, 2005. The author rejects the Bush administration's interventionist approach and advocates a strategy of "offshore balancing," limiting direct American involvement as far as possible, focusing instead on regional stability and local alliances.

# Notes


## CHAPTER 1

1. *Congressional Record*—House, February 21, 1990, pp. H392–H395.
2. Founded in 1998, DC Vote is an educational and advocacy organization dedicated to securing full voting representation in Congress. http://www.dcvote.org/.
3. http://www.freedomhouse.org/template.cfm? page=406.
4. Alexis de Tocqueville, *Democracy in America* (first published 1835–1840). Available in many editions. See also "The 2500 Anniversary of Democracy: Lessons of Athenian Democracy," *PS* (September 1993): 475–493.
5. http://www.freedomhouse.org/uploads/fiw09/FIW09_ChecklistQuestions_ForWeb.pdf.
6. From a letter from John Adams to John Taylor of Caroline, 1814, cited in Richard Hofstadter, *The American Political Tradition and the Men Who Made It* (New York: Vintage Books, 1948), p. 13.
7. Isaiah Berlin, *Two Concepts of Liberty* (Oxford: Clarendon Press, 1958).
8. E. E. Schattschneider, *Two Hundred Million Americans in Search of a Government* (Hinsdale, IL: Dryden Press, 1969), p. 27.
9. Quoted in J. D. Richardson, ed., *Messages and Papers of the Presidents, 1789–1902,* 20 vols. (Washington, DC, 1917), 1:309–312; Joshua Cohen and Joel Rogers, *On Democracy* (Harmondsworth, Middlesex, UK: Penguin, 1983), pp. 48–73.
10. See Adam Michnik, "After the Revolution," *New Republic*, July 2, 1990, p. 28.
11. http://www.washingtonpost.com/wp-dyn/content/article/2011/03/07/AR2011030703899.html?wpisrc=nl_opinions.
12. http://www.freedomhouse.org/uploads/TAHF/02_Overview.pdf. Overview essay in Today's American: How Free? by Arch Puddington and Thomas O. Melia.
13. http://www.nytimes.com/2011/04/27/opinion/27wed1.html?_r=3&ref=opinion.
14. Watch President Clinton's entire speech at: http://www.c-spanvideo.org/program/300358-1.

## CHAPTER 2

1. Mark Massetti and William Glaberson, "Obama Issues Directive to Shut Down Guantanamo," *New York Times,* January 22, 2009; and Scott Shane, Mark Mazzetti, and Helene Cooper, "Obama Reverses Key Bush Security Policies," *New York Times,* January 23, 2009.
2. See Gordon S. Wood, "The Origins of the Constitution," *This Constitution* 15 (Summer 1987): 4; and Gordon S. Wood, "The Intellectual Origins of the American Constitution," *National Forum* 4 (Fall 1984): 5–8.
3. See George Brown Tindall, *America: A Narrative History* (New York: Norton, 1988), pp. 58–62; and Alfred H. Kelly and Winfred A. Harbison, *The American Constitution: Its Origin and Development* (New York: Norton, 1976), pp. 7–16.
4. Quoted in Tindall, *America,* p. 168; and Ronald W. Clark, *Benjamin Franklin: A Biography* (New York: Random House, 1983), pp. 107–108.
5. James MacGregor Burns, *The Vineyard of Liberty* (New York: Vintage Books, 1983), p. 83.
6. Quoted in Tindall, *America,* pp. 206–207.
7. Ibid., pp. 207–208.
8. Alan Brinkley, *The Unfinished Nation* (New York: McGraw-Hill, 2004), p. 133.
9. Diane Ravitch, *The Democracy Reader* (New York: HarperCollins, 1972), pp. 103–104.
10. James Madison, *Notes of the Debates in the Federal Convention of 1787,* James Madison speaking, July 17, 1787, www.constitution.org/dfc/dfc-0717.htm.
11. Christopher Collier and James Lincoln Collier, *Decision in Philadelphia* (New York: Random House, 1986), p. 11; Robert A. Feer, *Shay's Rebellion* (New York: Garland, 1988), pp. 504–529; and David Szatmary, *Shay's Rebellion* (Amherst: University of Massachusetts Press, 1980), pp. 120–134.
12. For more on the motivations of the framers, see Richard B. Bernstein, with Kym S. Rice, *Are We to Be a Nation? The Making of the Constitution* (Cambridge, MA: Harvard University Press, 1987), passim.
13. Quoted in Catherine Bowen, *Miracle at Philadelphia* (Boston: Back Bay Books, 1986), p. 12.
14. The number of slaves at the time is taken from the notes of Convention delegate Charles Cotesworth Pinckney, July 10, 1787, found in *Supplement to Max Farrand's "The Records of the Federal Convention of 1787,"* ed. James H. Hutson (New Haven, CT: Yale University Press, 1987), p. 160.
15. Collier and Collier, *Decision in Philadelphia,* p. 16.
16. Ibid., p. 94.
17. For more on this possible motivation, see John E. O'Connor, *William Paterson, Lawyer and Statesman,* 1745–1806 (New Brunswick, NJ: Rutgers University Press, 1979).
18. Robert A. Goldwin, "Why Blacks, Women and Jews Are Not Mentioned in the Constitution," *Commentary,* May 1987, p. 29.
19. Bowen, *Miracle at Philadelphia,* pp. 55–56; see also Collier and Collier, *Decision in Philadelphia,* chaps. 18, 19.
20. Quoted in Bowen, *Miracle at Philadelphia,* p. 263.
21. George Washington, September 17, 1787, in *Supplement to Farrand's* "Records," ed. Hutson, p. 276.
22. Collier and Collier, *Decision in Philadelphia,* pp. 255–256.
23. Alexander Hamilton, James Madison, and John Jay, *The Federalist Papers* (New York: New American Library, 1961), no. 51, p. 322.
24. *Youngstown Sheet and Tube Company* v. *Sawyer,* 343 U.S. 579, p. 635 (1952).
25. Richard E. Neustadt, *Presidential Power: The Politics of Leadership from FDR to Carter* (New York: Wiley, 1980), p. 26.
26. Randy Barnett and William J. Howell, "The Case for a "Repeal Amendment," *Wall Street Journal,* September 16, 2010, reprinted in www.cato.org.
27. "Presidential Signing Statements: Constitutional and Institutional Implications," Congressional Research Service, American Federation of Scientists, May 29, 2007, www.coherentbabble.com/signingstatements/CRS/CRS-RL33667-4-07.pdf.
28. "Relief of the Parents of Theresa Marie Schiavo," March 20, 2005, www.findlaw.com/hdocs/docs/schiavo/bill31905.html.
29. Hamilton, Madison, and Jay, *Federalist Papers,* no. 10, p. 78.
30. Quoted in Charles L. Mee Jr., *The Genius of the People* (New York: Harper & Row, 1987), p. 300.
31. Ibid., p. 299.
32. Quoted in Bowen, *Miracle at Philadelphia,* p. 310.
33. Herbert Mitgang, "Handwritten Draft of a Bill of Rights Found," *New York Times,* July 29, 1987, p. 1.
34. *Dillon* v. *Gloss,* 256 U.S. 368 (1921). The Court refused to rule in 1939 in a case involving time limits contained in a child labor amendment, saying that it was a "political question," or a matter for the political bodies to decide. *Coleman* v. *Miller,* 307 U.S. 433 (1939). Since 1939, the Supreme Court has refused to rule on such time limits.
35. Carrie Johnson, "A Split at Justice on D.C. Vote Bill," *Washington Post,* April 1, 2009.
36. *District of Columbia* v. *Heller,* 554 U.S. 07-290 (2008).
37. *Immigration and Naturalization Service* v. *Chadha,* 462 U.S. 919 (1982), p. 978.

## CHAPTER 3

1. My thanks to John Kincaid for helping me shape this definition of federalism. See John Kincaid, "Federalism," in Charles N. Quigley and Charles F. Bahmueller (Eds.), *Civitas: A Framework for Civic Education* (Calabasas, CA: Center for Civic Education), 1991, pp. 391–392; John Kincaid, "Federalism: Its Time Has Come," August 29, 2005, unpublished draft in the possession of the author; *Black's Law Dictionary,* 5th ed. (St. Paul, MN: West, 1979), pp. 549–550; and Jay M. Safritz, *The HarperCollins Dictionary of American Government and Politics* (New York: HarperCollins), 1992, p. 226.
2. Alexander Hamilton, James Madison, and John Jay, *The Federalist Papers* (New York: New American Library, 1961), no. 10, p. 83. *The Federalist,* no. 10, is reprinted in Appendix 5.
3. William N. Eskridge and Darren Spedale, "Sit Down, Ted Olson and David Boies," *Slate,* May 29, 2009, found at www.slate.com.

4. Stephen Labaton, "Congress Passes Increase in the Minimum Wage," *New York Times,* May 25, 2007; and Louis Uchitelle, "Raising the Floor on Pay," *New York Times,* December 20, 2006.
5. Kirk Johnson, "New State Push to Restrict Abortions May Follow Ruling," *New York Times,* April 20, 2007.
6. *New State Ice Co.* v. *Liebmann,* 285 U.S. 262 (1932), p. 311.
7. Melanie Markley and Karen Masterson, "Education Act Modeled after Texas Reforms," *Houston Chronicle,* December 19, 2001.
8. Michael Cottman, "Atlanta Crowd Demands Voting Rights Act Renewal," August 15, 2005, *NCM,* http://news.ncmonline.com/news/view.
9. Robert Barnes, "Supreme Court Rules Narrowly on Voting Rights Act," *Washington Post,* June 22, 2009; and David Stout, "Justices Let Stand a Central Provision of Voting Rights Act," *New York Times,* June 23, 2009. The case name is *Northwest Austin Municipal Utility District Number One* v. *Holder.*
10. *Heart of Atlanta Motel* v. *United States,* 379 U.S. 241 (1964); and *Katzenbach* v. *McClung,* 379 U.S. 294 (1964).
11. *Swedenburg* v. *Kelly* and *Granholm* v. *Heald* 125 S. Ct. 1885 (2005); Fred Barbash, "Supreme Court Strikes Down Shipping Ban," *Washington Post,* May 16, 2005; Joan Biskupic, "Wineries That Sell Vino Via the Internet Stand to Gain," *USA Today,* May 17, 2005, p. 2B; Theresa Howard and Jerry Shriver, "Supreme Court: Let Those Wine Sales Flow," *USA Today,* May 17, 2005, p. B1; and Richard Willing, "Justices to Debate Mail-Order Wine," *USA Today,* December 7, 2004, p. 3A.
12. In June 1987, the Supreme Court upheld the law, with Chief Justice William H. Rehnquist ruling that Congress has the power to act "indirectly under its spending power to encourage uniformity in the States' drinking ages." *South Dakota* v. *Dole,* 483 U.S. 203 (1987).
13. *United States* v. *E. C. Knight,* 156 U.S. 1 (1895); *Hammer* v. *Dagenhart,* 247 U.S. 251 (1918); and *Carter* v. *Carter Coal Co.,* 298 U.S. 238 (1936).
14. *United States* v. *Darby Lumber Co.,* 312 U.S. 100 (1941).
15. *Printz* v. *United States* and *Mack* v. *United States,* 117 S. Ct. 2635 (1997); and "Symposium: American Federalism Today," in *Rockefeller Institute Bulletin* (1996): 1–23.
16. Martin Finucane, "Mass. Challenges Federal Defense of Marriage Act," *Boston Globe,* July 8, 2009; William N. Eskridge and Darren Spedale, "Sit Down, Ted Olson and David Boies," *Slate,* May 29, 2009, at www.slate.com; Michael C. Dorf, "The Obama Administration Defends the Defense of Marriage Act," June 17, 2009, www.findlaw.com; and "Bush Calls for Ban on Same Sex Marriages," February 25, 2004, www.cnn.com.
17. *McCulloch* v. *Maryland,* 4 Wheaton 316 (1819).
18. *Gibbons* v. *Ogden,* 9 Wheaton 1 (1824), p. 195.
19. "New Hampshire State Legislature Hearings: Reject USA Patriot Act," March 14, 2005, http://www.infowars.com/articles/us/patriot_act_nh_leg_reject.htm.
20. James McKinley, "Texas Governor's Secession Talk Stirs Furor," *New York Times,* April 18, 2009.
21. *United States* v. *E. C. Knight Co.*
22. *Hammer* v. *Dagenhart,* p. 274.
23. *Schechter Poultry Corp.* v. *United States,* 295 U.S. 495 (1935); *Carter* v. *Carter Coal Co.;* and *United States* v. *Butler,* 297 U.S. 1 (1936).
24. *National Labor Relations Board* v. *Jones and Laughlin Steel Corp.,* 301 U.S. 1 (1937). See also *N.L.R.B.* v. *Fruehauf Trailer Co.,* 801 U.S. 1 (1937); and *N.L.R.B.* v. *Friedman-Harry Marks Clothing Co.,* 301 U.S. 58 (1937).
25. *United States* v. *Darby Lumber Co.,* p. 124.
26. For the constitutional theory here, see Marshall E. Dimock, *Modern Politics and Administration: A Study of the Creative State* (New York: American Book, 1937), pp. 54–55.
27. *National League of Cities* v. *Usery,* 426 U.S. 833 (1976); *Garcia* v. *San Antonio Metropolitan Transit Authority,* 469 U.S. 528 (1985); and *South Carolina* v. *Baker,* 485 U.S. 505 (1988).
28. *Powell* v. *Alabama,* 287 U.S. 45 (1932).
29. *Brown* v. *Board of Education of Topeka,* 347 U.S. 483 (1954).
30. *Reynolds* v. *Sims,* 377 U.S. 533 (1964).
31. See *United States* v. *Butler; Steward Machine Co.* v. *Davis,* 301 U.S. 548 (1937); and *Wickard* v. *Filburn,* 317 U.S. 111 (1941).
32. "Rolling Out the New 0.08% Limit," *Minneapolis Star Tribune,* August 2, 2005.
33. Advisory Commission on Intergovernmental Relations (ACIR), *Characteristics of Federal Grant-in-Aid Programs to State and Local Governments: Grants Funded FY 1995* (Washington, DC: ACIR, 1996), pp. 1–2.
34. John Kincaid, "State-Federal Relations: Defense, Demography, Debt, and Deconstruction as Destiny," *Book of the States,* 37 (2005): 26.
35. Ibid., p. 2.
36. Peter Cohn, "Bush Spending Plan Cuts State Programs," *National Journal,* February 7, 2007, www.nationaljournal.com.
37. "Obama Releases Budget Details," *Politico,* May 7, 2009, at http://dyn.politico.com.
38. Robert Jay Dilger, "Federal Grants-in-Aid: An Historical Perspective on Contemporary Issues," January 25, 2011, Penny Hill Press: Blog Archive, found at http://www2.pennyhill.com/?p=1204; See http://www.cfda.gov/public/browse_by_ typast.asp, last consulted May 3, 2002; see also ACIR, *Characteristics of Federal Grant-in-Aid Programs to State and Local Governments,* p. 2.
39. Ibid., pp. 22–42.
40. Calculations from http://www.cfda.gov/public/browse_by_typast.asp; ibid., p. 14.
41. Kincaid, "State-Federal Relations," pp. 25–30; and John Kincaid, "Trends in Federalism: Continuity, Change and Polarization," *Book of the States,* 36: (2004): 21–27.
42. Kincaid, "State-Federal Relations," pp. 26–27.
43. Dilger, "Federal Grants-in-Aid."
44. "Federal Spending on the Elderly and Children," May 3, 2002; see http://www.cbo.gov.
45. Pam Belluck, "The Not-So United States," *New York Times,* April 23, 2006; and John Kincaid, "De Facto Devolution and Urban Defunding: The Priority of Persons Over Places," *Journal of Urban Affairs,* 21, no. 2 (1999): 135–167, at p. 163.
46. Peter Grier, "The Rising Economic Cost of the Iraq War," *Christian Science Monitor,* May 19, 2005, p. 1.
47. Kincaid, "State-Federal Relations," p. 27.
48. Cohn, "Bush Spending Plan Cuts State Programs."
49. John Schwartz, "Obama Seems to Be Open to a Broader Role for States," *New York Times,* January 30, 2009.
50. Karen Spar, "Community Services Block Grants (CSBG): Background and Funding," Penny Hill Press: Blog Archive, found at http://www2.pennyhill.com/?p=1204.
51. Alison Mitchell, "Wellstone Death Brings New Focus to Senate Battles," *New York Times,* October 27, 1997, p. 1; and Ron Eckstein, "Federalism Bills Unify Usual Foes," *Legal Times,* October 18, 1999.
52. *New York* v. *United States,* 112 S. Ct. 2408, 2435 (1992). This entire discussion of the Court's recent stance on federalism benefited from Tinsley Yarbrough, "The Rehnquist Court and the 'Double Standard,'" paper presented at the annual meeting of the Southern Political Science Association, Norfolk, Virginia, November 6–8, 1997.
53. *United States* v. *Lopez,* 131 L. Ed. 2d 626 (1995).
54. *U.S. Term Limits* v. *Thornton,* 115 S. Ct. 1842 (1995).
55. *Seminole Tribe* v. *Florida,* 134 L. Ed. 2d 252 (1996).
56. *Printz* v. *United States,* 117 S. Ct. 2635 (1997), p. 2638.
57. *United States* v. *Morrison,* 529 U.S. 598 (2000).
58. See *Nevada Department of Human Resources* v. *Hibbs,* 123 S. Ct. 1972 (2003); *Ashcroft* v. *A.C.L.U.,* 542 U.S. 656 (2004); and Child Online Protection Act case, *Tennessee* v. *Lane* 124 S. Ct. 1978 (2004).
59. *Rapanos* v. *United States Army Corps of Engineers,* 126 S. Ct. 2208 (2006).
60. *Massachusetts* v. *Environmental Protection Agency,* 127 S. Ct. 1438, (2007); and *Environmental Defense, et al., Petitioners* v. *Duke Energy Corporation, et al.* 127 S. Ct. 1423; 167 (2007).
61. Robert Barnes, "Supreme Court Rules Narrowly on Voting Rights Act," *Washington Post,* June 22, 2009; and David Stout, "Justices Let Stand a Central Provision of Voting Rights Act," *New York Times,* June 23, 2009. The case name is *Northwest Austin Municipal Utility District Number One* v. *Holder.*

62. *United States v. Comstock,* 130 S. Ct. 1949 (2010).
63. Both quoted in Adam Clymer, "Switching Sides on States' Rights," *New York Times,* June 1, 1997, pp. E1, E6.

## CHAPTER 4

1. See Morris P. Fiorina, *Congress: Keystone of the Washington Establishment* (New Haven, CT: Yale University Press, 1977).
2. On comparisons between the House and the Senate, see Ross K. Baker, *House and Senate,* 2nd ed. (New York: Norton, 1995).
3. See *How Congress Works* (Washington, DC: Congressional Quarterly Press, 1994).
4. See *The Federalist,* nos. 17, 39, and 45, in Alexander Hamilton, James Madison, and John Jay, *The Federalist Papers* (New York: New American Library, 1961).
5. Peter Whoriskey, "Growing Wealth Widens Distance Between Lawmakers and Constituents," *Washington Post,* December 26, 2011.
6. See Glenn R. Simpson, "Of the Rich, by the Rich, for the Rich: Will the Millionaires Turn Congress into a Plutocracy?" *Washington Post,* April 17, 1994, p. C4. Compare with Allan Freedman, "Lawyers Take a Back Seat in the 105th Congress," *Congressional Quarterly Weekly Report,* January 4, 1997, p. 29.
7. See Hannah Fenichel Pitkin, *The Concept of Representation* (Berkeley: University of California Press, 1967).
8. "The 112th Congress: By the Numbers," "The Morning Delivery," February 24, 2011, found at http://www.billlucey.com/2011/02/the-112th-congress-by-the-numbers.html; Mildred Amer and Jennifer Manning, "Membership of the 111th Congress: A Profile," *Congressional Research Service,* December 31, 2008, found at www.crs.gov; Donna Cassata, "Freshman Class Boasts Résumés to Back Up 'Outsider' Image," *Congressional Quarterly,* November 12, 1994, pp. 9–12. Also see Mildred L Amer, "Membership of the 109th Congress: A Profile," *CRS Report for Congress,* May 30, 2005.
9. "The 112th Congress: By the Numbers," "The Morning Delivery," February 24, 2011, found at http://www.billlucey.com/2011/02/the-112th-congress-by-the-numbers.html; Amer and Manning, "Membership of the 111th Congress."
10. Gary C. Jacobson, *The Politics of Congressional Elections* (New York: HarperCollins, 1992), p. 13.
11. "Rethinking Texas' Redistricting," *New York Times,* October 22, 2004, p. 22; Ralph Blumenthal, "Texas Democrats Look at New Map and Point Out Victims," *New York Times,* October 14, 2003, p. A14; David Barboza and Carl Hulse, "Hiding Out in Oklahoma Texas Democrats Protest," *New York Times,* May 14, 2003, p. A17; Ralph Blumenthal, "After Bitter Fight, Texas Senate Redraws Congressional Districts," *New York Times,* October 13, 2004, p. 1; *Vieth* v. *Jubelirer,* 541 U.S. 267 (2004).
12. Elaine R. Jones, "In Peril: Black Lawmakers," *New York Times,* September 11, 1994, p. E19; Ronald Smothers, "Fair Play or Racial Gerrymandering? Justices Study a 'Serpentine' District," *New York Times,* April 16, 1993, p. B12.
13. *Shaw* v. *Reno,* 509 U.S. 630 (1993), p. 637.
14. *Miller* v. *Johnson,* 132 L. Ed. 2d 762 (1995).
15. *Abrams* v. *Johnson,* 117 S. Ct. (1997).
16. *Hunt* v. *Cromartie,* 143 L. Ed. 2d 791 (1999).
17. Edward Walsh, "Supreme Court Upholds Mississippi Redistricting Plan," *Washington Post,* April 1, 2003; David E. Rosenbaum, "Fight Over Political Map Centers on Race," *New York Times,* February 21, 2002, p. A18.
18. Robert Barnes, "Supreme Court Rules Narrowly on Voting Rights Act," *Washington Post,* June 22, 2009; David Stout, "Justices Let Stand a Central Provision of Voting Rights Act," *New York Times,* June 23, 2009. The case name is *Northwest Austin Municipal Utility District Number One* v. *Holder.*
19. Tony Mauro, "Can the Voting Rights Act Survive Another Challenge?" *The National Law Journal,* June 29, 2009.
20. Charles Clapp, *The Congressman: His Job as He Sees It* (Washington, DC: Brookings Institution, 1963); Roger H. Davidson, *The Role of the Congressman* (Indianapolis, IN: Bobbs-Merrill, 1969).
21. "Re-election Rates over the Years," Center for Responsive Politics, www.opensecrets.org.
22. See David Mayhew, *Congress: The Electoral Connection* (New Haven, CT: Yale University Press, 1974).
23. Doug Mataconis, "Incumbent Re-Election Rates in the 2010 Midterm," Outside the Beltway, November 9, 2010, found at http://www.outsidethebeltway.com/incumbent-re-election-rates-in-the-2010-mid-terms/.
24. For more on casework and Congress, see John R. Johannes, *To Serve the People: Congress and Constituency Review* (Lincoln: University of Nebraska Press, 1984); Morris P. Fiorina, *Congress: Keystone of the Washington Establishment,* 2nd ed. (New Haven, CT: Yale University Press, 1989).
25. "Congress-Job Report," Polling Report.com, September 25–27, 2011.
26. Davidson and Oleszek, *Congress and Its Members,* pp. 128–129.
27. Ibid., p. 76.
28. Joseph E. Cantor, "Campaign Financing," October 28, 2004, Congressional Research Service Report, at http://fpc.state.gov/documents/organization/37875.pdf.
29. *U.S. Term Limits* v. *Thornton,* 115 S. Ct. 1842 (1995).
30. *Arkansas Term Limits* v. *Donovan,* 138 L. Ed. 2d 874 (1997).
31. B. Drummond Ayres Jr., "Term Limit Laws Are Transforming More Legislatures," *New York Times,* April 28, 1997, p. 1.
32. Amer and Manning, "Membership in the 111th Congress." The period of service for the House has increased in the last two Congresses more the 1.5 years from 9.3 years in the 109th Congress.
33. Barbara Sinclair, *Majority Leadership in the U.S. House* (Baltimore: Johns Hopkins University Press, 1983).
34. Ward Sinclair, "High Theater Starring Tip and Cast of 434," *Washington Post,* August 20, 1982, p. 1.
35. John A. Barnes, "Reed's Rules," *National Review Online,* March 7, 2005.
36. For more on minority leaders, see Charles O. Jones, *Minority Party in Congress* (Boston: Little, Brown, 1970).
37. See Barbara Sinclair, *The Transformation of the U.S. Senate* (Baltimore: Johns Hopkins University Press, 1989).
38. Rowland Evans and Robert Novak, *Lyndon B. Johnson: The Exercise of Power* (New York: New American Library, 1966); Merle Miller, *Lyndon: An Oral Biography* (New York: Ballantine Books, 1980), chap. 2.
39. Ibid.
40. Harry McPherson, oral history, Lyndon Johnson Library, Austin, Texas, pp. 78–88; see also Robert A. Caro, *Master of the Senate* (New York: Knopf, 2002).
41. *Washington Post,* June 12, 1985, p. 5.
42. Trent Lott, *Herding Cats: A Life in Politics* (New York: Regan Books, 2005).
43. Woodrow Wilson, *Congressional Government* (New York: Meridian, 1967), p. 28.
44. Davidson and Oleszek, *Congress and Its Members,* p. 349.
45. Lawrence D. Longley and Walter J. Oleszek, *Bicameral Politics: Conference Committees in Congress* (New Haven, CT: Yale University Press, 1995).
46. Richard F. Fenno Jr., *Congressmen in Committees* (Boston: Little, Brown, 1973), p. 280.
47. The classic source on committees and the roles of members of Congress is Fenno, *Congressmen in Committees.* See also Steven Smith and Christopher Deering, *Committees in Congress,* 2nd ed. (Washington, DC: Congressional Quarterly Press, 1990).
48. Quoted in James T. Murphy, "Political Parties and the Porkbarrel: Party Conflict and Cooperation in House Public Works Committee Decision Making," in Glen Parker, ed., *Studies in Congress* (Washington, DC: Congressional Quarterly Press, 1985), pp. 237–238.
49. Walter J. Oleszek, *Congressional Procedures and the Policy Process* (Washington, DC: Congressional Quarterly Press, 1989).
50. Stanley Bach and Steven Smith, *Managing Uncertainty in the House of Representatives: Adaptation and Innovation in Special Rules* (Washington, DC: Brookings Institution, 1988).
51. D. B. Hardeman and Donald C. Bacon, *Rayburn: A Biography* (Lanham, MD: Madison Books, 1987).
52. Quoted in David E. Rosenbaum, "Tax Bill Faces Fight, but First the Rules," *New York Times,* April 2, 1995, p. 20.
53. See Steven S. Smith, *Call to Order: Floor Politics in the House and Senate* (Washington, DC: Brookings Institution, 1989).
54. Helen Dewar, "As Senate Crunch Nears, Holdups Threaten," *Washington Post,* November 15, 1999, p. 21.

55. Quoted in Alison Mitchell, "Rule No. 1: My Way or No Way," *New York Times,* November 2, 1997, p. WK6.
56. See Fred R. Harris, *Deadlock on Decision: The U.S. Senate and the Rise of National Politics* (New York: Oxford University Press, 1993).
57. "Senate Action on Filibusters," United States Senate reference, found at http://www.senate.gov/pagelayout/reference/cloture_motions/clotureCounts.htm.
58. Donald Matthews, *U.S. Senators and Their World* (Chapel Hill: University of North Carolina Press, 1960), p. 54; see also Baker, *House and Senate,* chap. 2.
59. John E. Yang, "Notion of House Civility Gets a Push Backward," *Washington Post,* April 10, 1997, p. A23.
60. Frank Ahrens, "Putting 'Polite' into Politics," *Washington Post,* March 6, 1997, p. B1.
61. Sheryl Gay Stolberg, "The High Costs of Rising Incivility on Capitol Hill," *New York Times,* November 30, 2003, p. 10.
62. Burdett Loomis, "Civility and Deliberation: A Linked Pair?" in Burdett Loomis, ed., *Esteemed Colleagues: Civility and Deliberation in the U.S. Senate* (Washington, DC: Brookings Institution Press, 2000), p. 1.
63. For more on the importance of seniority, apprenticeship, and political loyalty in Congress, see John R. Hibbing, *Congressional Careers: Contours of Life in the U.S. House of Representatives* (Chapel Hill: University of North Carolina Press, 1991), pp. 113–128; Matthews, *U.S. Senators and Their World,* chap. 5.
64. John Ferejohn, "Logrolling in an Institutional Context: A Case of Food Stamp Legislation," in Gerald C. Wright Jr., Leroy Rieselbach, and Lawrence C. Dodd, eds., *Congress and Policy Change* (New York: Agathon Press, 1986).
65. Davidson and Oleszek, *Congress and Its Members,* p. 271.
66. Anick Jesdanun, "Specter Gets 'Oinker' Award from Critical Citizens' Group," *Centre Daily Times,* March 11, 1998, p. 3A.
67. John M. Broder, "With Something for Everyone, Climate Bill Passed," *New York Times,* July 1, 2009.
68. Quoted in Donald G. Tacheron and Morris K. Udall, *The Job of the Congressman,* 2nd ed. (Indianapolis, IN: Bobbs-Merrill, 1970), p. 18.
69. Douglas Arnold, *The Logic of Congressional Action* (New Haven, CT: Yale University Press, 1990), pp. 64–84; V. O. Key Jr., *Public Opinion and American Democracy* (New York: Knopf, 1961), pp. 265–285.
70. Davidson and Oleszek, *Congress and Its Members,* 9th ed., p. 273; William R. Shaffer, *Party and Ideology in the United States Congress* (Lanham, MD: University Press of America, 1980); Norman Ornstein, Thomas E. Mann, and Michael Malbin, *Vital Statistics on Congress: 1993–94* (Washington, DC: Congressional Quarterly Press, 1994), p. 200.
71. Statistics taken from "President Support and Opposition: Senate," *Congressional Quarterly,* for the years 1992, p. 3897; 1991, p. 3785; 1990, p. 4209; 1989, p. 3566; 1988, p. 3348; 1987, p. 3213; 1986, p. 2688; 1985, pp. 741–746; 1984, pp. 2802–2008; 1983, p. 2781; and 1982, p. 2796.
72. David Rohde, *Parties and Leaders in the Post-Reform House* (Chicago: University of Chicago Press, 1991); Robert L. Peabody, *Leadership in Congress* (Boston: Little, Brown, 1976).
73. Stephen Wayne and George Edwards III, *Presidential Influence in Congress* (San Francisco: Freeman, 1980); Stephen Wayne, *The Legislative Presidency* (New York: Harper & Row, 1978).
74. R. W. Apple, "In Pennsylvania, Feeling the Consequences of One Vote," *New York Times,* September 27, 1994, p. A22.
75. See Harrison W. Fox Jr. and Susan Webb Hammond, *Congressional Staffs: The Invisible Force in American Lawmaking* (New York: Free Press, 1977).
76. Richard Fenno, *Home Style: House Members in Their Districts* (New York: HarperCollins, 1987).
77. Donald R. Matthews and James A. Stimson, *Yeas and Nays* (New York: Wiley, 1975); David M. Kovenock, "Influence in the U.S. House of Representatives: A Statistical Study of Communications," *American Politics Quarterly* 1 (October 1973): 456ff.
78. John W. Kingdon, *Congressional Voting Decisions,* 3rd ed. (Ann Arbor: University of Michigan Press, 1989); Aage R. Clausen, *How Congressmen Decide* (New York: St. Martin's Press, 1973).
79. Roughly 10,000 bills are introduced in each two-year session of Congress, and about 600 laws are passed from that group. See Jennifer Manning, "Congressional Statistics Bills Introduced and Laws Enacted," 1974–2004, 2005, WikiLeaks Document (release, wikileaks.org, p. 2).
80. John W. Kingdon, *Agendas, Alternatives, and Public Policies* (Boston: Little, Brown, 1984).
81. See Paul Light, *Forging Legislation* (New York: Norton, 1992).
82. Longley and Oleszek, *Bicameral Politics,* passim.
83. Davidson and Oleszek, *Congress and Its Members,* p. 247.
84. Josh Burek, "Bush Makes History—A Five-Year Streak Without Saying No," *Christian Science Monitor,* August 16, 2005.
85. Marc Sandalow, "Frist's Shift May Lead to Bush's First Veto," *San Francisco Chronicle,* July 30, 2005, p. A16.
86. For more on how changes in House operation rules by Newt Gingrich and the Republican Congress may influence the theory of legislating in Congress, see John H. Aldrich and David W. Rohde, "The Transition to Republican Rule in the House: Implications for Theories of Congressional Politics," *Political Science Quarterly* 112, no. 4 (1997–1998): 541–567.
87. Andrea Stone, "Parts of the Republican Revolution Fade with Age," *USA Today,* January 20, 2003, p. 5A.
88. Bob Beneson and Gregory L. Giroux, "Shades of '94—But Cloudier," *CQ Weekly,* August 15, 2005, pp. 2230ff.
89. Deidre Walsh, "'Blue Dog' Democrats: Current Health Bill Not Acceptable," July 10, 2009, CNNPolitics.com.

## CHAPTER 5

1. See Robert Schmuhl, "The Presidency: Full of Peril or Possibility," *Boston Globe,* January 2, 2000.
2. Ibid.; Thomas Cronin and Eugene Genovese, *The Paradoxes of the American Presidency* (New York: Oxford University Press, 1998, 2009), p. 4.
3. See Sidney M. Milkis and Michael Nelson, *The American Presidency: Origins and Development, 1776–1990* (Washington, DC: CQ Press, 1990); Thomas E. Cronin, ed., *Inventing the Presidency* (Albany: State University of New York Press, 1988), p. 20.
4. *The Federalist,* no. 70, in Alexander Hamilton, James Madison, and John Jay, *The Federalist Papers* (New York: New American Library, 1961).
5. "Why Obama Birther Conspiracy Theories Linger," *Discovery News,* April 27, 2011, http://news.discovery.com/human/why-obama-birther-conspiracy-theories-linger-110427.html.
6. See Robert J. Spitzer, *The Presidential Veto: Touchstone of the American Presidency* (Albany: State University of New York Press, 1988), p. 20.
7. http://www.truthout.org/docs_2006/050907S.shtml; "Bush Holds Fast to Stem-Cell Veto Threat," *AP Online,* July 29, 2005; "Bush Renews Veto Threat for Highway Bill," *AP Online,* June 9, 2005.
8. Charles Savage, "Obama Looks to Limit Impact of Tactic Bush Used to Sidestep New Laws," *New York Times,* March 9, 2009, www.nytimes.com/2009/03/10/us/politics/10signing.html.
9. David Nather, "Congress Suddenly Remembers It Can Cut Off Funds," *Congressional Quarterly,* July 10, 2009, www.cqpolitics.com/.
10. Sam Youngman, "White House: Obama's Signing Statements 'Entirely Consistent,'" *The Hill,* April 16, 2011, http://thehill.com/homenews/administration/156465-white-house-defends-obama-use-of-signing-statements-as-entirely-consistent.
11. "A Look at Presidential Recess Appointments," Associated Press, August 1, 2005; Elisabeth Bumiller and Sheryl Gay Stolberg, "President Sends Bolton to U.N.; Bypasses Senate," *New York Times,* August 2, 2005, p. 1; "In Recess Appointment Bush Names Transport Security Chief," *New York Times,* January 8, 2002, p. A16; "Bush Bypasses Senate on 2 More Nominees," *New York Times,* January 12, 2002, p. A10.
12. See especially Alexander L. George and Juliette L. George, *Woodrow Wilson and Colonel House: A Personality Study* (Mineola, NY: Dover Publications, 1964).
13. See "Clinton, Congress and Trade," *Legislate News Service,* November 10, 1997, p. 1; see Lael Brainard and Hal Shapiro, "Fast-Track Trade Promotion Authority," Policy Brief #91, December 2001, published on Brookings website, November 30, 2001, www.brookings.edu.
14. Deb Reichman, "Presidents Assert Executive Privilege," *WashingtonPost.com,* January 29, 2002; see Ellen Nakashima, "Bush Invokes Executive Privilege on Hill," *Washington Post,* December 14, 2001, p. A43; "Symposium on Executive Privilege and the Clinton Presidency," *William & Mary Bill of Rights Journal,* 8, no. 3 (April 2000): 583–629.

15. See Mike Allen, "GAO to Sue Cheney within 2 or 3 Weeks," *Washington Post*, January 31, 2002, p. A4; Dana Milbank, "Cheney Refuses Records Release," *Washington Post*, January 28, 2002, p. A01.
16. Richard W. Stevenson, "President, Citing Executive Privilege, Indicates He'll Reject Requests for Counsel's Documents," *New York Times*, October 5, 2005, p. A17.
17. Sheryl Gay Stolberg, "Bush Clashes with Congress on Prosecutors," *New York Times*, March 21, 2007; "Your Right to Know: How Private Are Records of Ex-Presidents? Reagan-Era Memos at Heart of Legal Battle over Bush Order on Withholding Documents," *Atlanta Journal and Constitution*, March 18, 2005.
18. See the Information Security Oversight Office's 2010 report to the president: http://www.fas.org/sgp/isoo/2010rpt.pdf.
19. J. William Leonard, "When Secrecy Gets Out of Hand," *Los Angeles Times*, August 10, 2011, http://www.latimes.com/news/opinion/commentary/la-oe-leonard-classified-information-20110810,0,5688807.story.
20. latimesblogs.latimes.com/presidentbush/2008/07/cheney-plame-ag.html.
21. http://www.csmonitor.com/USA/Latest-News-Wires/2010/1204/As-he-finishes-his-second-year-in-office-Obama-pardons-nine-people.
22. Mark Mazzetti, "Behind the Hunt for Bin Laden," *New York Times*, May 2, 2011.
23. David Sanger and Scott Shane, "Court's Ruling Is Likely to Force Negotiations over Presidential Power," *New York Times*, June 30, 2006. See also "Law and the War on Terrorism," *Harvard Journal of Law and Public Policy* 25, no. 2 (Spring 2002, 25th anniversary issue); John Mueller, *Wars, Presidents and Public Opinion* (New York: Wiley, 1970); John Mueller, *Policy, Opinion and the Gulf War* (Chicago: University of Chicago Press, 1994), p. 645; *United States* v. *Nixon*, 418 U.S. 683 (1974). See also *Washington Post* series, "America's Chaotic Road to War," January 27, 2002–February 3, 2002.
24. See Richard W. Stevenson, "For This President, Power Is There for the Taking," *New York Times*, May 15, 2005; see also David E. Rosenbaum, "When Government Doesn't Tell," *New York Times*, February 3, 2002, sec. 4, p. 1; Elisabeth Bumiller with David Sanger, "Taking Command in Crisis, Bush Wields New Power," *New York Times*, January 1, 2002, p. A1; David E. Sanger, "In Address, Bush Says He Ordered Domestic Spying," *New York Times*, December 18, 2005, p. A1.
25. David E. Sanger, "Bush Wants to Consider Broadening of Military's Powers during Natural Disasters," *New York Times*, September 27, 2005, p. A18. See "Government Secrecy: Is Too Much Information Kept from the Public?" *CQ Researcher*, 15, no. 42 (December 2, 2005): 1005–1028.
26. Michael A. Fletcher, "President Again Takes on Role of 'Consoler in Chief,' " *Washington Post*, April 18, 2007.
27. http://www.usatoday.com/news/washington/2010-11-22-obama-president-travel_N.htm.
28. Quoted in Richard Neustadt, "Presidency and Legislation: Planning the President's Program," *American Political Science Review*, 49 (December 1955): 980–1021; Richard Neustadt, "Presidency and Legislation: The Growth of Central Clearance," *American Political Science Review*, 48 (September 1954): 641–671.
29. Jennifer Naddeo, "Twentieth-Century First Ladies as Moral Leaders for Education," Loyola University Dissertation, 2005.
30. See James Carville, *We're Right, They're Wrong* (New York: Random House), 1996.
31. Quoted in George Wolfskill, *Happy Days Are Here Again!* (Hinsdale, IL: Dryden, 1974), p. 189. See also James MacGregor Burns, *Roosevelt: The Lion and the Fox* (New York: Harcourt Brace Jovanovich, 1956); James MacGregor Burns, *Roosevelt:The Soldier of Freedom, 1940–1945* (New York: Harcourt Brace Jovanovich, 1970); Frank Freidel, *Franklin D. Roosevelt*, 4 vols. (Boston: Little, Brown, 1952–1953); Arthur Schlesinger Jr., *The Age of Roosevelt*, 3 vols. (Boston: Houghton Mifflin, 1957–1960).
32. Theodore Roosevelt, "The Stewardship Doctrine," in Harry Bailey, ed., *Classics of the American Presidency* (Oak Park, IL: Moore, 1980), pp. 35–36. See also *The Autobiography of Theodore Roosevelt* (New York: Scribner's, 1913), pp. 197–200.
33. John Morton Blum, *The Republican Roosevelt* (New York: Atheneum, 1962), pp. 129–130.
34. See Larry Berman, *The New American Presidency* (Boston: Little, Brown, 1986), pp. 54–56. See William Howard Taft, *Our Chief Magistrate and His Powers* (New York: Columbia University Press, 1916), pp. 138–145.
35. Thomas Jefferson to John Colvin, June 29, 1810. In Paul Ford, ed., *The Writings of Thomas Jefferson*, vol. 9 (New York: Putnam, 1899), p. 276.
36. John Nicolay and John Hay, eds., *The Complete Works of Abraham Lincoln*, vol. 10 (New York: Francis Tandy, 1891), pp. 65–68.
37. *United States* v. *Curtiss-Wright*, 299 U.S. 304 (1936).
38. For detailed accounts of Johnson's views from White House tapes, see Michael Beschloss, *Reaching for Glory* (New York: Simon & Schuster, 2000).
39. *Youngstown Sheet and Tube Company* v. *Sawyer*, 343 U.S. 579 (1952). See Maeva Marcus, *Truman and the Steel Seizure Case* (New York: Columbia University Press, 1977); Alan Weston, *The Anatomy of a Constitutional Law Case* (New York: Macmillan, 1958); Arthur M. Schlesinger Jr., *The Imperial Presidency* (Boston: Houghton Mifflin, 1973).
40. See U.S. Congress, Senate, *Congressional Record*, 93rd Cong., 1st sess., 1973, p. 119. See also U.S. Congress, Subcommittee on International Security and Scientific Affairs, *The War Powers Resolution: Relevant Documents, Correspondence, Reports*, 93rd Cong., 3rd sess., June 1981.
41. See Louis Fisher and David Gray Adler, "The War Powers Resolution: Time to Say Good-Bye," *Political Science Quarterly*, 113, no. 1 (1998): 1–20; David P. Auerswald and Peter F. Cowhey, "Ballotbox Diplomacy: The War Powers Resolution and the Use of Force," *International Studies Quarterly*, 41 (1987): 505–528.
42. Jeffrey Rosen, "In Wartime, Who Has the Power?" *New York Times*, March 4, 2007; W. Taylor Reveley III, "Presidential War Making: Constitutional Prerogative or Usurpation?" *Virginia Law Review*, 55 (November 1969): 1243–1305; W. Taylor Reveley III, "*Resolved: That the Powers of the Presidency Should Be Curtailed,*" *A Collection of Excerpts and Bibliography Relating to the Intercollegiate Debate Topic, 1974–75* (Washington, DC: U.S. Government Printing Office, 1974), pp. 91–133; U.S. Congress, Senate, Committee on Foreign Relations, *Powers of the President to Send Armed Forces Outside the United States*, 82d Cong., 1st sess., 1951. See also Elisabeth Palmer, "Executive Powers in Crises Are Shaped by Precedent, Personality, Public Opinion," *CQ Weekly* (September 15, 2001): 2122–2123.
43. Richard Neustadt, *Presidential Power and the Modern Presidents: The Politics of Leadership*, rev. ed. (New York: Free Press, 1990); originally published in 1960.
44. John Hart, *The Presidential Branch* (Chatham, NJ: Chatham House, 1995), pp. 37–38; Peri Arnold, *Making the Managerial Presidency* (Princeton, NJ: Princeton University Press, 1986).
45. Jack Valenti, "Life's Never the Same after the White House Power Trip," *Washington Post National Weekly Edition*, March 19, 1984, p. 21.
46. Thomas Cronin, "Everybody Believes in Democracy Until He Gets to the White House: An Examination of White House Departmental Relations," *Law and Contemporary Problems*, 35 (Summer 1970): 573–625.
47. Fred I. Greenstein, *The Hidden-Hand Presidency: Eisenhower as Leader* (New York: Basic Books, 1982), p. 55.
48. Larry Berman, *The Office of Management and Budget and the Presidency, 1921–1977* (Princeton, NJ: Princeton University Press, 1977).

## CHAPTER 6

1. Linda Greenhouse, "On Court That Defied Labeling, Kennedy Makes the Boldest Mark," *New York Times*, June 29, 2008; Mark Sherman, "Key Decisions Remain for Supreme Court," *Washington Post*, June 1, 2007; Robert Barnes, "Over Ginsburg's Dissents, Court Limits Bias Suits," *Washington Post*, May 30, 2007; Dahlia Lithwick, "Father Knows Best," *Slate*, April 18, 2007, www.slate.com; James S. Todd, "Overturning Acts of Congress on the Rehnquist Court: Will the Real Judicial Activist Please Stand Up?" American Political Science Association Convention, September 2004, p. 1; Dan Balz, "Nomination Could Be Defining Moment for Bush," *Washington Post*, July 2, 2005, p. 1; Charles Lane, "In Other News from the Middle, Some Shifts by Justice Kennedy," *Washington Post*, July 4, 2005, p. 15; Linda Greenhouse, "O'Connor Held Balance of Power," *New York Times*, July 2, 2005.

2. Alexander Hamilton, James Madison, and John Jay, *The Federalist Papers*, no. 78 (New York: New York American Library, 1961), p. 465 (emphasis in original).
3. *Marbury* v. *Madison*, 5 U.S. 137 (1803). The U.S. court of appeals was not established by congressional act until 1891. Before this time, the appellate courts were staffed by a panel of two district court judges and one circuit-riding Supreme Court justice.
4. Edward S. Corwin, "Review of Benjamin F. Wright's *Growth of American Constitutional Law*," *Harvard Law Review*, 56 (1942): 487.
5. Henry J. Abraham, *The Judicial Process*, 6th ed. (New York: Oxford University Press, 1993), p. 272. See also David O'Brien, *Constitutional Law and Politics, vol. 1, Struggles for Power and Governmental Accountability* (New York: Norton, 1991), p. 38.
6. Justice Antonin Scalia speech, "The Legacy of the Rehnquist Court," Federalist Society, Milwaukee, Wisconsin, February 22, 2006, quoted in Gina Barton, "Rehnquist Court Made Clearer, Scalia Says," *JSOnline* (Milwaukee Journal Sentinel), www.jsonline.com; James S. Todd, "Overturning Acts of Congress on the Rehnquist Court: Will the Real Judicial Activist Please Stand Up?" American Political Science Association Convention, September 2004, p. 1.
7. Linda Greenhouse, "Justices Limit Gun Law That Bars Possession by Felons," *New York Times*, April 27, 2005.
8. Ann McFeatters, "Reporter Sent to Jail Writer Refuses to Reveal Sources," *Pittsburgh Post-Gazette*, July 7, 2005.
9. For more here, see William H. Rehnquist, *Grand Inquests: The Historic Impeachments of Justice Samuel Chase and President Andrew Johnson* (New York: Morrow, 1992).
10. Judith Resnick and Theodore Ruger, "One Robe, Two Hats," *New York Times*, July 17, 2005.
11. See Milton Heumann, *Plea Bargaining: The Experiences of Prosecutors, Judges and Defense Attorneys* (Chicago: University of Chicago Press, 1977); John H. Langbein, "Torture and Plea Bargaining," *Public Interest*, 21 (Winter 1980): 24–26.
12. Tom Fowler, "The Fall of Enron," *Houston Chronicle*, July 12, 2005.
13. Larry Margasak, "With Pick of Judge, Obama Begins Reshaping Bench," Associated Press Online, March 17, 2009; Adam Nagourney and Richard W. Stevenson, "Democrats See Wide Bush Stamp on Court System," *New York Times*, January 15, 2006, www.nyt.com; Warren Richey, "Conservatives Near Lock on US Courts," *Christian Science Monitor*, April 14, 2005; Carrie Johnson, "Testing the Limits," *Legal Times*, October 4, 1999, p. 1; Neil Lewis, "A Court Becomes a Model of Conservative Pursuits," *New York Times*, May 24, 1999, p. 1.
14. Abraham, *The Judicial Process*, p. 163.
15. J. Woodford Howard Jr., *Courts of Appeals in the Federal Judicial System* (Princeton, NJ: Princeton University Press, 1981), p. 58.
16. William Glaberson, "Caseload Forcing Two-Level System for U.S. Appeals," *New York Times*, March 14, 1999, p. 1.
17. Resnick and Ruger, "One Robe, Two Hats."
18. See Laurence H. Tribe, *God Save This Honorable Court* (New York: Random House, 1985), pp. 50–77; William H. Rehnquist, *The Supreme Court: How It Was, How It Is* (New York: Morrow, 1987), pp. 235–253. And see John B. Gates and Jeffrey E. Cohen, "Presidents, Supreme Court Justices and Racial Equality Cases: 1954–1984," *Political Behavior*, 10, no. 1 (1994): 2236.
19. Henry J. Abraham, *Justices and Presidents: A Political History of Appointments to the Supreme Court* (New York: Oxford University Press, 1992), p. 266.
20. Ibid., p. 238.
21. See Barbara Perry, *A "Representative" Supreme Court? The Impact of Race, Religion, and Gender on Appointments* (New York: Greenwood Press, 1991).
22. Until the Bush administration, the ratings also included "exceptionally well qualified."
23. For more on the role of the ABA in the appointment process, see Joel Grossman, *Lawyers and Judges: The ABA and the Politics of Judicial Selection* (New York: Wiley, 1965).
24. Quoted in Abraham, *Justices and Presidents*, pp. 16–17.
25. For more on the Bork battle, see Ethan Bronner, *Battle for Justice: How the Bork Nomination Shook America* (New York: Norton, 1989).
26. Sheldon Goldman, "Bush's Judicial Legacy: The Final Imprint, *Judicature*, 76, no. 6 (April/May 1993): 295.
27. For more on the appointment process for district court judges, see Neil McFeeley, *Appointment of Judges: The Johnson Presidency* (Austin: University of Texas Press, 1987); Harold Chase, *Federal Judges: The Appointing Process* (Minneapolis: University of Minnesota Press, 1972).
28. Warren Richey, "Conservatives Near Lock on US Courts," *Christian Science Monitor*, April 14, 2005.
29. Warren Richey, "Lawmakers' Destructive Gamesmanship with Judicial Nominees," *Washington Post*, August 16, 2011, found at www.washingtonpost.com.
30. Sheldon Goldman, Sara Schiavoni, and Elliot Slotnick, "Mission Accomplished: W. Bush's Judicial Legacy," *Judicature*, 92, no. 6 (May/June 2009): 258–288; Sheldon Goldman, Elliot Slotnick, Gerard Gryski, and Sara Schiavoni, "W. Bush's Judiciary: The First Term Record," *Judicature*, 88, no. 6 (May/June 2005): 269.
31. Sheldon Goldman and Elliot Slotnik, "Clinton's First-Term Judiciary: Many Bridges to Cross," *Judicature*, 80, no. 6 (May/June 1997): 270.
32. Goldman, Schiavoni, and Slotnick, "Mission Accomplished"; Goldman, Slotnick, Gryski, and Schiavoni, "W. Bush's Judiciary."
33. Sheldon Goldman, Elliot Slotnick, and Sara Schiavoni, "Obama's Judiciary at Midterm," *Judicature*, 94, no. 6 (May/June 2011): 262–303. My thanks to Professor Goldman for making an early copy of his article available.
34. Ibid.; Collin Levy, "Goodwin Liu, Meet Rose Bird," *WSJ Online*, July 27, 2011, found at online,wsj.com; and Michael D. Shear, "Obama Nominated Berkeley Professor Goodwin Liu to Federal Court of Appeals," *Washington Post*, February 25, 2010.
35. David O'Brien, *Storm Center: The Supreme Court in American Politics*, 4th ed. (New York: Norton, 1996), pp. 165–166.
36. Adam Liptak, "The Roberts Court, Tipped by Kennedy," *New York Times*, July 1, 2009.
37. Political scientists Lee Epstein and Andrew D. Martin write that the odds of this identical lineup of independent judges in such a high percentage of cases as being 1 in 44.2 quintillion. See Adam Liptak, "A Significant Term, With Bigger Cases Ahead," *New York Times*, June 28, 2011.
38. Tony Mauro, "Justices Give Pivotal Role to Novice Lawyers," *USA Today*, March 13–15, 1998, pp. 1–2.
39. Tim Russert, *Constitutional Conversation with Justices Sandra Day O'Connor, Antonin Scalia, and Stephen Breyer*, National Archives and the Aspen Institute, April 22, 2005.
40. *Brown* v. *Board of Education*, 347 U.S. 483 (1954).
41. Richard Kluger, *Simple Justice* (New York: Knopf, 1975).
42. Joan Biskupic, "Lawyers Emerge as Supreme Court Specialists," *USA Today*, May 16, 2003, p. 6A; Joan Biskupic, "Women Are Still Not Well Represented Among Lawyers Facing Supreme Test," *Washington Post*, May 27, 1997, p. A3; Joan Biskupic, "Justices Growing Impatient with Imprecision," *Washington Post*, May 5, 1997, p. A7.
43. See letters from Robert Bradley, Chief Justice Rehnquist, and Henry J. Abraham in American Political Science Association, *Law, Courts and Judicial Process Section Newsletters*, 6, no. 4 (Summer 1989): 2–3, 7, and no. 1 (Fall 1989): 3. See also Abraham, *Judicial Process*, p. 196.
44. *Roe* v. *Wade*, 410 U.S. 113 (1973).
45. *Planned Parenthood of Southeastern Pennsylvania* v. *Casey*, 112 S. Ct. 931 (1992).
46. David J. Garrow, "Justice Souter Emerges," *New York Times Magazine*, September 25, 1994, pp. 36–42.
47. Quoted in Nat Hentoff, "The Constitutionalist," *New Yorker*, March 12, 1990, p. 60.
48. Harold Spaeth, *Studies in U.S. Supreme Court Behavior* (New York: Garland Press, 1990); Saul Brenner and Harold Spaeth, "Ideological Positions as a Variable in the Authoring of Dissenting Opinion," *American Politics Quarterly*, 16 (July 1988): 17–28.
49. *New York Times Co.* v. *United States*, 403 U.S. 713 (1971).
50. Linda Greenhouse, "Oral Dissents Give Ginsburg a New Voice," *New York Times*, May 31, 2007; Robert Barnes, "Over Ginsburg's Dissent, Court Limits Bias Suits," *Washington Post*, May 30, 2007.
51. David Lat, "The Supreme Court Bonus Babies," *New York Times*, June 18, 2007.
52. Tony Mauro, "Justices Give Pivotal Role to Novice Lawyers," and "Corps of Clerks Lacking in Diversity," *USA Today*, March 13, 1998, pp. 1A, 12–13A.

53. Ed Lazarus, *Closed Chambers* (New York: Times Books, 1998), p. 271.
54. Joyce Murdoch and Deb Price, *Courting Justice* (New York: Basic Books, 2001), chaps. 11–12.
55. David Margolick, "The Path to Florida," *Vanity Fair,* October 2004, pp. 310–322.
56. Bernard Schwartz, *The Ascent of Pragmatism* (Reading, MA: Addison-Wesley, 1990); Bob Woodward and Scott Armstrong, *The Brethren: Inside the Supreme Court* (New York: Avon Books, 1979).
57. *Stanley* v. *Georgia,* 394 U.S. 557 (1969).
58. *Payne* v. *Tennessee,* 59 *Law Week,* 4823 (1991).
59. *Gonzales* v. *Carhart,* 127 S. Ct. 1610, (2007) Ginsburg Dissent.
60. *Parents* v. *Seattle School District No. 1;* 551 U.S. 701; June 28, 2007.
61. Abraham, *Judicial Process,* p. 325.
62. James F. Spriggs II and Thomas Hansford, "Explaining the Overruling of U.S. Supreme Court Precedent," Midwest Political Science Association, April 1998.
63. See Herbert Wechsler, *Principles, Politics, and Fundamental Law* (Cambridge, MA: Harvard University Press, 1961). See also Alexander M. Bickel, *The Least Dangerous Branch* (Indianapolis, IN: Bobbs-Merrill, 1962); Raoul Berger, *Government by Judiciary: The Transformation of the Fourteenth Amendment* (Cambridge, MA: Harvard University Press, 1977); Jesse H. Choper, *Judicial Review and the National Political Process* (Chicago: University of Chicago Press, 1980); John Hart Ely, *Democracy and Distrust: A Theory of Judicial Review* (Cambridge, MA: Harvard University Press, 1980).
64. Jeffrey Segal and Albert Cover, "Ideological Values and the Votes of U.S. Supreme Court Justices," *American Political Science Review,* 83 (1989): 557–565.
65. *West Virginia Board of Education* v. *Barnette,* 319 U.S. 624 (1943), pp. 646–647.
66. *Griswold* v. *Connecticut,* 381 U.S. 479 (1965).
67. *Sierra Club* v. *Morton,* 405 U.S. 727 (1972), pp. 742–743.
68. For a fine example of this argument detailing the problems of the Court as a "superlegislature," see Robert Bork, *The Tempting of America: The Political Seduction of the Law* (New York: Macmillan, 1990).
69. Jed Handelsman Shugerman, "A Six-Three Rule: Reviving Consensus and Deference on the Supreme Court," *University of Georgia Law Review,* 37 (Spring 2003): 893.
70. Evan Caminker, "Thayerian Deference to Congress and Supreme Court Supermajority Rule," University of Michigan Law School, found at ssrn.com/abstract=323222.
71. Joan Biskupic, "Centrist Justice Sought 'Social Stability,'" *Washington Post,* July 5, 2005.
72. Woodrow Wilson, *Constitutional Government in the United States* (New York: Columbia University Press, 1907), p. 142.

## CHAPTER 7

1. Pamela Hess, "Report: Bush Surveillance Program Was Massive," *New York Times,* July 11, 2009, p. A1.
2. Scott Shane, "Cheney Is Linked to Concealment of C.I.A. Project," *New York Times,* July 12, 2009, p. A1.
3. http://cityroom.blogs.nytimes.com/2009/07/12/the-form-that-lets-you-say-more-forms-please/?scp=1&sq=paperwork%20reduction%20act&st=cse.
4. Barry Bozeman, *Bureaucracy and Red Tape* (Upper Saddle River, NJ: Prentice-Hall, 2000), p. 1.
5. See Max Weber, *Essays in Sociology,* trans. and ed. H. H. Garth and C. Wright Mills (New York: Oxford University Press, 1958), p. 232.
6. http://www.politico.com/news/stories/0811/61484.html.
7. http://www.time.com/time/nation/article/0,8599,58788,00.html.
8. http://articles.latimes.com/2011/aug/17/news/la-pn-obama-tour-strategy-20110817/2.
9. William L. Riordon, *Plunkitt of Tammany Hall* (New York: Dutton, 1963), chap. 9.
10. See James Q. Wilson, *Bureaucracy: What Government Agencies Do and Why They Do It* (New York: Basic Books, 1989), chap. 7. See also Guy Benveniste, *Bureaucracy* (San Francisco: Boyd and Frasier, 1977).
11. Larry Hill, ed., *The State of Public Bureaucracy* (New York: M. E. Sharpe, 1992).
12. http://thehill.com/blogs/on-the-money/banking-financial-institutions/174391-elizabeth-warren-bids-adieu-to-the-consumer-bureau.
13. President George W. Bush, transcript of a speech reprinted as "The Plan: We Have Concluded That Our Government Must Be Reorganized," *New York Times,* June 6, 2002, p. A18. See also Department of Homeland Security, President George W. Bush, June 2002, www.whitehouse.gov/homeland/.
14. Eric Lipton and Scott Shane, "Leader of Federal Effort Feels the Heat," *New York Times,* September 3, 2005, p. A11.
15. Read the ful report here: http://www.uspsoig.gov/foia_files/RARC-WP-11-008.pdf
16. Quoted in Richard Neustadt, *Presidential Power* (New York: Mentor, 1960), p. 22.
17. http://theusconstitution.org/blog.history/wp-content/uploads/2011/08/FINAL-Vacancy-Crisis-Memo-080411.pdf.
18. Paul Light, "Nominate and Wait." *New York Times,* March 24, 2009, p. A25.
19. See Richard Nathan, *The Administrative Presidency* (New York: Wiley, 1983).
20. See David Stockman, *The Triumph of Politics: The Inside Story of the Reagan Revolution* (New York: Avon, 1987).
21. See Richard Nathan, *The Plot That Failed* (New York: Wiley, 1975).
22. Herbert Kaufman, *Red Tape: Its Uses and Abuses* (Washington, DC: Brookings Institution, 1997).
23. David Bullier and Joan Claybrook, "Regulations That Work," *Washington Monthly,* April 1986, pp. 47–54.

## CHAPTER 8

1. V. O. Key, *Public Opinion and American Democracy* (New York: Knopf, 1961).
2. See Walter Lippmann, *The Phantom Public* (New York: Macmillan, 1927), pp. 13–14.
3. Alexander Hamilton, James Madison, and John Jay, *The Federalist Papers* (New York: New American Library, 1961), no. 10, p. 119. *The Federalist,* no. 10, appears in Appendix 5.
4. William Flanagan and Nancy H. Zingale, *Political Behavior of the American Electorate* (Washington, DC: Congressional Quarterly Press, 1998), p. 179; Herbert Asher, *Polling and the Public: What Every Citizen Should Know,* 4th ed. (Washington, DC: Congressional Quarterly Press), 1988.
5. Scott Keeter, Jocelyn Kiley, Leah Christian, and Michael Dimock, "Perils of Polling in Election '08," Pew Research Center for the People & the Press, June 25, 2009.
6. See the discussion in Robert S. Erikson and Kent L. Tedin, *American Public Opinion: Its Origins, Content, and Impact,* 5th ed. (Boston: Allyn and Bacon, 1995), pp. 128–130.
7. See "National Election Pool," frequently asked questions at www.exit-poll.net/faq.html.
8. See Richard Morin, "Surveying the Damage: Exit Polls Can't Predict Winners, So Don't Expect Them To," *Washington Post Outlook,* November 21, 2004, p. B1.
9. Keeter et al., "Perils of Polling in Election '08."
10. See Fred Greenstein, *Children and Politics* (New Haven, CT: Yale University Press, 1965), p. 119.
11. The public opinion data for younger Americans is taking from the following Gallup Poll publications: http://www.gallup.com/poll/148367/Young-Adults-Rate-Standard-Living-Highest.aspx; http://www.gallup.com/poll/147662/First-Time-Majority-Americans-Favor-Legal-Gay-Marriage.aspx; http://www.gallup.com/poll/148154/Americans-Views-Immigration-Holding-Steady.aspx
12. http://pewresearch.org/pubs/614/religion-social-issues.
13. Robert D. Putnam, "Bowling Alone: America's Declining Social Capital," *Journal of Democracy* 6 (1995): 65–78; see also Putman, *Bowling Alone: The Collapse and Revival* of *American Community* (New York: Simon & Schuster, 2000).
14. Todd Gitlin, *The Whole World Is Watching: Mass Media in the Making and Unmaking of the New Left* (Berkeley: University of California Press, 1980), p. 201; see also Todd Gitlin, *Watching Television: A Pantheon Guide to Popular Culture* (New York: Pantheon Books, 1986).
15. Janny Scott and David Leonhardt, "Class in America: Shadowy Lines That Still Divide," *New York Times,* May 15, 2005, p. A1.
16. Benjamin I. Page and Robert Y. Shapiro, *The Rational Public* (Chicago: University of Chicago Press, 1992), p. 201; see also Flanagan and Zingale, *Political Behavior of the American Electorate,* p. 174;

William H. Flanagan, *Political Behavior of the American Electorate* (Washington, DC: Congressional Quarterly Press, 1998), p. 174.
17. Ruy Teixeira, "New Progressive America, Twenty Years of Demographic, Geographic, and Attitudinal Changes Across the Country Herald a New Progressive Majority," March 2009.
18. Drawn from Michael Barone, "Obama's America: Has the Nation Entered a New Phase in Its Politics, One That Could Benefit Democrats for Years to Come?" An excerpt from *The Almanac of American Politics,* July 11, 2009.
19. http://pewforum.org/docs/?DocID=367.
20. See www.cawp.rutgers.edu/Facts5.html.
21. Kathleen Kennedy Townsend, "Without a Doubt—Why Barack Obama Represents American Catholics Better than the Pope Does," *Newsweek* Web Exclusive, http://www.newsweek.com/id/205961.
22. http://pewforum.org/Politics-and-Elections/Religion-in-the-2010-Election-A-Preliminary-Look.aspx.
23. Alan Cooperman, "Democrats Win Bigger Share of Religious Vote," *Washington Post,* November 11, 2006.
24. Norman R. Luttbeg and Michael M. Gant, *American Electoral Behavior, 1952–1992,* 2nd ed. (Itasca, IL: Peacock, 1995), esp. pp. 91–164; see also Aaron Wildavsky, "Choosing Preferences by Constructing Institutions: A Cultural Theory of Preference Formation," *American Political Science Review* 81 (March 1987): 3–23.
25. James Gibson, "The Political Consequences of Intolerance: Cultural Conformity and Political Freedom," *American Political Science Review* 86 (June 1992): 338–356.
26. Ibid., p. 341.
27. Elizabeth Noelle-Neumann, *The Spiral of Silence* (Chicago: University of Chicago Press, 1984).
28. Walter Lippmann, *The Phantom Public* (New York: Macmillan, 1927), pp. 13–14.
29. Joseph Schumpeter, *Capitalism, Socialism and Democracy* (New York: Harper & Bros., 1950), p. 262; Luttbeg and Gant, *American Electoral Behavior,* esp. chaps. 3–4, p. 67; Philip E. Converse, "Information Flow and the Stability of Partisan Attitudes," *Public Opinion Quarterly* 26, no. 4 (Winter 1962): 578–599.
30. Conor Clarke, "Get Red of Polls," http://ideas.theatlantic.com/2009/07/get_rid_of_polls.php.
31. Benjamin Page and Robert Shapiro, *The Rational Public: Fifty Years of Trends in Americans' Policy Preference* (Chicago: University of Chicago Press, 1992); see also Paul Brace and Barbara Hinckley, *Follow the Leader: Opinion Polls and Modern Presidents* (New York: Basic Books, 1992), pp. 97–115.
32. John Zaller, *The Nature and Origins of Mass Opinion* (Cambridge, UK: Cambridge University Press, 1992).
33. See Angus Campbell, Philip Converse, Warren Miller, and Donald Stokes, *The American Voter* (New York: Wiley, 1960).
34. Benjamin Page, *Choices and Echoes in Elections: Rational Man and Electoral Democracy* (Chicago: University of Chicago Press, 1978), chap. 8; see also Sidney Verba and Norman H. Nie, *Participation in America: Political Democracy and Social Equality* (New York: Harper & Row, 1972), pp. 25–26.
35. http://www.gallup.com/poll/121916/Two-Three-Doubt-Congress-Grasp-Healthcare-Issues.aspx?CSTS=alert.

## CHAPTER 9

1. See E. E. Schattschneider, *The Semisovereign People* (New York: Holt, 1960); V. O. Key Jr., *Politics, Parties, and Pressure Groups* (New York: Crowell, 1964).
2. Quoted in *National Party Conventions, 1831–1988* (Washington, DC: Congressional Quarterly Press, 1991), p. 2; see also Michael Nelson, ed., *Guide to the Presidency* (Washington, DC: Congressional Quarterly Press, 1989), pp. 268–269.
3. Quoted in Noble E. Cunningham, *The Making of the American Party System, 1789 to 1809* (Upper Saddle River, NJ: Prentice-Hall, 1965); see also Noble E. Cunningham, *The Jeffersonian Republicans* (Chapel Hill: University of North Carolina Press, 1957).
4. See Warren E. Miller, "Party Identification, Realignment, and Party Voting: Back to the Basics," *American Political Science Review* 85 (1991): 557.
5. See Ralph Ketcham, *Presidents Above Party* (Chapel Hill: University of North Carolina Press, 1984).
6. See Frank Freidel, *Franklin D. Roosevelt: The Triumph* (Boston: Little, Brown, 1956), pp. 248–249.
7. James David Barber, *The Pulse of Politics* (New York: Norton, 1980), pp. 238–263.
8. See William Leuchtenburg, *In the Shadow of FDR* (Ithaca, NY: Cornell University Press, 1983).
9. Charles Babington, "Divided Outcome Extends to State Legislatures Too," *Washington Post,* November 9, 2000, supplemented by author's calculations of the party balance in the Washington State and Oregon legislatures from the websites of those states' legislatures.
10. "Democrats Gain Edge in Party Identification," Pew Research Center for the People and the Press, July 26, 2004.
11. "Trends in Political Values and Core Attitudes, 1987–2009," Pew Research Center, May 21, 2009, http://people-press.org; Jeffrey M. Jones, "Democrats Maintain 7-Point Advantage in Party ID," Gallup Poll, April 30, 2009, http://www.gallup.com/poll/118084/Democrats-Maintain-Seven-Point-Advantage-Party.aspx.
12. Jeffrey M. Jones, "Democratic Party ID Drops in 2010, Tying 22-Year Low," Gallup Polls, January 5, 2011, found at www.gallup.com.
13. Alfred J. Tuchfarber, "The Republican Tidal Wave of 1994: Testing Hypotheses about Realignment, Restructuring, and Rebellion," APSA paper, 1995.
14. "Trends in Political Values and Core Attitudes, 1987–2009."
15. Ibid., p. 5.
16. Ibid., p. 39.
17. See Austin Ranney, *The Doctrine of Responsible Party Government: Its Origins and Present State* (Urbana: University of Illinois Press, 1962); Samuel J. Eldersvald, *Political Parties in American Society* (New York: Basic Books, 1982).
18. See L. Sandy Maisel, *Parties and Elections in America* (New York: McGraw-Hill, 1992).
19. See John Aldrich, *Before the Convention: Strategies and Choices in Presidential Nomination Campaigns* (Chicago: University of Chicago Press, 1980).
20. See American Political Science Association, Committee on Political Parties, "Toward a More Responsible Two-Party System," *American Political Science Review* 64 (1950).
21. Edmond Constantini and Linda O. Valenty, "The Motives-Ideology Connection among Political Party Activists"; Peter B. Clark and James Q. Wilson, "Incentive Systems: A Theory of Organization," both in *Administrative Science Quarterly* 6 (1961): 129–166.
22. Byron York, "America Coming Together Comes Apart," August 3, 2005, at www.nationalreview.com/york/york200508030928.asp.
23. See William L. Riordan, *Plunkitt of Tammany Hall* (New York: Knopf, 1963); Harold Gosnell, *Machine Politics* (Chicago: University of Chicago Press, 1939).
24. See Xandra Kayden and Eddie Mahe Jr., *The Party Goes On: The Persistence of the Two-Party System in the United States* (New York: Basic Books, 1985).
25. Jonathan Weisman et al., "Strategy Was Based on Winning Delegates, Not Battlegrounds," *Washington Post,* June 4, 2008.
26. Josh Voorhees, "Reacting to Florida's Primary Plan, South Carolina Picks New Date," October 3, 2011, "*The Slatest,*" found at http://slatest.slate.com/.
27. See Theodore H. White, *The Making of the President, 1968* (New York: Atheneum, 1969).
28. See David E. Price, *Bringing Back the Parties* (Washington, DC: Congressional Quarterly Press, 1983).
29. Beth Fouhy and Jack Gillum, "Presidential Contenders Boosted by Super PACS," MSNBC, September 29, 2011, found at www.msnbc.com.
30. See Samuel Patterson, "The Etiology of Party Competition," *American Political Science Review* 78 (1984): 691.
31. The tendency of single-member district systems to be found in conjunction with two parties, while multimember districts correlate with a multiparty system, is often known as Duverger's Law. It is named for a well-known French political scientist, Maurice Duverger, who first enunciated this theory in his book *Political Parties* (London: Methuen, 1954).
32. See Everett Carl Ladd, *American Political Parties: Social Change and Political Response* (New York: Norton, 1970); James L. Sundquist, *Dynamics of the Party System* (Washington, DC: Brookings Institution, 1973).

33. See Warren E. Miller, "Party Identification," in L. Sandy Maisel, ed., *Political Parties and Elections in the United States: An Encyclopedia* (New York: Garland, 1991).
34. See Frank Smallwood, *The Other Candidates: Third Parties in Presidential Elections* (Hanover, NH: University Press of New England, 1983); Steven J. Rosenstone, Roy L. Behr, and Edward H. Lazarus, *Third Parties in America: Citizen Response to Major Party Failure* (Princeton, NJ: Princeton University Press, 1984).
35. See Byron Shafer, ed., *Beyond Realignment? Interpreting American Electoral Eras* (Madison: University of Wisconsin Press, 1991).
36. See Matthew Cooper and Rebecca Kaplan, "The Tea Party's Legal Brief," *National Journal,* February 17, 2011, www.nationaljournal.com.
37. David Broder, *The Party's Over* (New York: Harper & Row, 1971).
38. "Battleground 2002 (XXI)," Study #8794, The Tarrance Group, www.azwins.org/Battleground%202002.pdf; Thomas B. Edsall, "GOP Gains Advantage on Key Issues, Polls Say," *Washington Post,* January 27, 2002, p. A4.

## CHAPTER 10

1. Ian Urbina, "Hurdles to Voting Persisted in 2008," *New York Times,* March 3, 2009, p. A1; see also http://vote.caltech.edu/drupal/.
2. Sidney Verba and Norman H. Nie, *Participation in America: Political Democracy and Social Equality* (New York: Harper & Row, 1972); see also Karen M. Arlington and William L. Taylor, eds., *Voting Rights in America: Continuing the Quest for Full Participation* (Lanham, MD: University Press of America, 1992); Francis Fox Piven and Richard A. Cloward, *Why Americans Don't Vote* (New York: Pantheon, 1988); and Raymond E. Wolfinger and Steven J. Rosenstone, *Who Votes* (New Haven, CT: Yale University Press, 1980).
3. See Robert Barnes, "High Court to Weigh Relevance of Voting Law in Obama Era," Washington Post, April 1, 2009, p. A1; "Why the Voting Rights Act Matters," *New York Times* Editorial, June 12, 2009, p. A22; and "Uphold the Voting Rights Act," *New York Times* Editorial, January 25, 2009, p. 9.
4. http://www.dcvote.org/advocacy/dcvra_111thmain.cfm.
5. http://www.brennancenter.org/content/resource/democracy_restoration_act_of_2008/.
6. See Dan Keating and John Mintz, "Florida Black Ballots Affected Most in 2000," *Washington Post,* November 13, 2001, p. A3; and Ford Fessenden, "Ballots Cast by Blacks and Older Voters Were Tossed in Far Greater Numbers," *New York Times,* November 12, 2001, p. A47.
7. See Caltech-MIT/Voting Technology Project, www.vote.caltech.edu/.
8. http://www.reformelections.org/feature.asp?menuid=%7B08EAA7FA-83E2-4BD0-9AD6-BE5C22244FD1%7D.
9. http://www.census.gov/Press-Release/www/releases/archives/voting/013995.html.
10. http://web.mit.edu/polisci/portl/cces/material/CCES_Guide_2008_Rough_Draft_v2.pdf.
11. http://rules.senate.gov/public/index.cfm?FuseAction=InNews.MajorityNews&ContentRecord_id=f72bc608-5056-8059-76f6-97bcc0202f3d; and http://web.mit.edu/polisci/portl/cces/material/CCES_Guide_2008_Rough_Draft_v2.pdf.
12. See www.idea.int/vt/index.cfm, the home page for International Voter Turnout.
13. Steven J. Rosenstone and Raymond E. Wolfinger, "The Effect of Registration Laws on Voter Turnout," *American Political Science Review* 72 (March 1998): 25–30.
14. http://www.brennancenter.org/blog/archives/can_we_register_voters_better_yes/. See "Expanding Democracy: Voter Registration Systems Around the World," Jennifer S. Rosenbergwith Margaret Chen, http://www.brennancenter.org/.
15. Ibid.
16. See Peter Baker, "Motor Voter Apparently Didn't Drive Up Turnout," *Washington Post,* November 6, 1996, p. B7; also see B. Drummond Ayres Jr., "Law to Ease Voter Registration Has Added 5 Million to the Polls," *New York Times,* September 3, 1995, p. A1; "'Motor Voter' Bill Enacted after 5 Years," *CQ Almanac* 49 (1993): 199–201; Executive Summary, Federal Election Commission's Report to the Congress, "The Impact of the National Voter Registration Act of 1993 on Federal Elections, 1999–2000," www.free.gov./pages/ nvrareport2000/nvrareport2000.htm; Raymond Wolfinger and Jonathan Hoffman, "Requesting and Voting with Motor Voter," *PS* (March 2001): 85–92; and Benjamin Highton, "Voter Registration and Turnout in the United States," *Perspectives on Politics* 2, no. 3 (September 2004): 507–515.
17. Richard Morin, "The Dog Ate My Forms, and, Well, I Couldn't Find a Pen," *Washington Post National Weekly Edition,* November 5–11, 1990, p. 38; see also George Will, "In Defense of Nonvoting," *Newsweek,* October 10, 1983, p. 96.
18. "Building Confidence in U.S. Elections: Report of the Commission on Federal Election Reform," September 2005, Electionline.org/The Pew Charitable Trusts, www.american.edu/ia/cfer/report/report.html.
19. See Michael Kagay, "The Mystery of Nonvoters and Whether They Matter," *New York Times,* August 27, 2000, Section 4, p. 1; Michael M. Grant and William Lyons, "Democratic Theory, Nonvoting, and Public Policy: The 1972–1988 Presidential Elections," *American Politics Quarterly* 21 (April 1993): 185–204; Priscilla L. Southwell, "Alienation and Nonvoting in the United States: A Refined Operationalization," *Western Political Quarterly* 38 (December 1985): 663–675; Richard Berke, "Nonvoters Are No More Alienated Than Voters, Survey Shows," *New York Times,* May 30, 1996; Angus Campbell, Philip E. Converse, Warren E. Miller, and Donald Stokes, *The American Voter* (New York: Wiley, 1960). For the complete survey and analysis, visit the League of Women Voters home page at www.lwv.org.
20. "California Voter Foundation Releases Comprehensive Results of Survey on Voting Incentives and Barriers," April 7, 2005. California Voter Foundation at www.calvoter.org.
21. Ibid.
22. James Barnes, "The GOP's Great White Married Hope," *National Journal,* July 18, 2009.
23. http://www.civicyouth.org/PopUps/FactSheets/FS_youth_Voting_2008_updated_6.22.pdf.
24. The data and analysis come from several sources. See "Votes for Women 2004," Gender Gap Updates; Gebe Martinez and Mary Agnes Carey, "Erasing the Gender Gap Tops Republican Playbook," *CQ Weekly,* March 6, 2004.
25. http://www.feministmajority.org/elections/2008gendergap.asp; and "2008 Election Analysis: Gender Gap Delivers," http://feminist.org/news/newsbyte/uswirestory.asp?id=11374.
26. See National Initiative News, The Democracy Foundation; also see "The Experiences of Other States: A Comparison of the Initiative and Referendum," National Council of State Legislatures at www.ncsl.org.
27. Ibid.
28. Ibid. Initiative and Referendum Institute (IRI). The website www.ballot.org was created to provide in-depth nonpartisan and nonpolitical information about the initiative and referendum process at the local, state, and national levels as well as to provide a glimpse of what is happening with initiative and referendum around the world.
29. See Stanley Kelley Jr., *Interpreting Elections* (Princeton, NJ: Princeton University Press, 1983).
30. Morris P. Fiorina, *Retrospective Voting in American National Elections* (New Haven, CT: Yale University Press, 1979); see also Nelson Polsby and Aaron Wildavsky, *Presidential Elections,* 9th ed. (New York: Free Press, 1995).
31. See M. Margaret Conway, *Political Participation in the United States* (Washington, DC: Congressional Quarterly Press, 1991), p. 8, Table 1–2.
32. Kayla Webley, "How the Nixon-Kennedy Debate Changed the World," *Time,* September 23, 2010, http://www.time.com/time/nation/article/0,8599,2021078,00.html.
33. http://www-cgi.cnn.com/ALLPOLITICS/1996/debates/history/1960/.
34. Martin Diamond, *The Electoral College and the American Idea of Democracy* (Washington, DC: American Enterprise Institute, 1977).
35. http://fairvote.org/presidential/?page=977.

36. See Michael Glennon, *When No Majority Rules: The Electoral College and Presidential Succession* (Washington DC: CQ Press, 2000, 2002); Verba and Nie, *Participation in America*, pp. 25–40.
37. http://fairvote.org/presidential/?page=977.
38. *Buckley* v. *Valeo*, 424 U.S. 1 (1976); and *Federal Election Commission* v. *National Conservative Political Action Committee*, et al., 450 U.S. 480 (1985). See also Larry Sabato, *The Party's Just Begun* (Glenview, IL: Scott, Foresman/Little, Brown, 1988), p. 125; "Charting the Health of American Democracy," a report by the League of Women Voters, June 1997, www.lwv.org.
39. http://www.cnn.com/2008/POLITICS/06/19/obama.public.financing/; http://thehill.com/leading-the-news/dnc-calls-for-probe-of-mccain-public-funds-withdrawal-2008-08-20.html.
40. See "The McCain-Feingold-Cochran Campaign Reform Bill," www.campaignfinancesite.org/legislation/mccain.html.
41. For 527s, see Public Citizen at www.citizen.org/congress/campaign/issues/nonprofit; also see The League of Woman Voters: Campaign Finance Reform, S. 271; and Common Cause website at www.commoncause.org.
42. http://politicalticker.blogs.cnn.com/2010/01/21/obama-criticizes-campaign-finance-ruling/.
43. View the president's entire weekly address here: http://www.whitehouse.gov/blog/2010/01/22/weekly-address-standing-special-interests-fighting-american-people.
44. Read Justice Stevens's opinion: http://www.law.cornell.edu/supct/html/08-205.ZX.html.
45. http://www.cbsnews.com/stories/2011/06/30/eveningnews/main20075941.shtml.
46. http://www.cbsnews.com/stories/2011/06/30/eveningnews/main20075941.shtml.

## CHAPTER 11

1. See Jeffrey M. Berry, *The Interest Group Society*, 3rd ed. (New York: Longman Press, 1997); Allan J. Cigler and Burdett A. Loomis, eds., *Interest Group Politics*, 4th ed. (Washington, DC: Congressional Quarterly Press, 1995).
2. Alexis de Tocqueville, *Democracy in America* (New York: Knopf, 1991), p. 485.
3. James Madison, *The Federalist*, no. 10, is reprinted in Appendix 5.
4. See Arthur F. Bentley, *The Process of Government* (Chicago: University of Chicago Press, 1906); David Truman, *The Governmental Process* (New York: Knopf, 1951); E. E. Schattschneider, *The Semi-Sovereign People* (New York: Holt, 1960).
5. Tocqueville, *Democracy in America*, p. 487.
6. See Burdett A. Loomis and Allan J. Cigler, "The Changing Nature of Interest Group Politics," in *Interest Group Politics*, pp. 1–31; Jack Walker, *Mobilizing Interest Groups in America* (Ann Arbor: University of Michigan Press, 1991).
7. Matt Bai, "Fight Club," *New York Times Sunday Magazine*, August 10, 2003, pp. 24–27.
8. Jason DeParle, "Nomination Stirs a Debate on Federalists' Sway," *New York Times*, August 1, 2005; see also "Attention: Media Interested in Finding Experts on the Rehnquist Court and the Role of the Courts," www.fed-soc.org/, August 1, 2005.
9. Howard Rheingold, *Smart Mobs: The Next Social Revolution* (New York: Basic Books, 2003).
10. Glenn Harlan Reynolds, "Tax Day Becomes Protest Day," *Wall Street Journal*, April 15, 2009.
11. See Mancur Olson Jr., *The Logic of Collective Action* (Cambridge, MA: Harvard University Press, 1965), pp. 5–52; Dennis Chong, *Collective Action and the Civil Rights Movement* (Chicago: University of Chicago Press, 1991).
12. See www.nags.org/ and www.securityfocus.com/news/10251.
13. See David Vogel, *Fluctuating Fortunes: The Political Power of Business in America* (New York: Basic Books, 1989); William Greider, *Who Will Tell the People? The Betrayal of American Democracy* (New York: Simon & Schuster, 1992).
14. See Jeffrey H. Birnbaum and Alan S. Murray, *Showdown at Gucci Gulch* (New York: Vintage Books, 1988); Kay Lehman Schlozman and John T. Tierney, *Organized Interests and American Democracy* (New York: Harper & Row, 1986).
15. See the argument in John Kenneth Galbraith, *American Capitalism: The Concept of Countervailing Power* (Boston: Houghton Mifflin, 1952).
16. Joel Dresang, "Split at the Top Seen as Challenge to Unions' Effectiveness, Survival," *Milwaukee Journal Sentinel*, July 31, 2005.
17. Shaila K. Dewan, "Black Farmers' Refrain: Where's All Our Money?" *New York Times*, August 1, 2004, www.nyt.com.
18. See Lawrence S. Rothenberg, *Linking Citizens to Government: Interest Group Politics at Common Cause* (New York: Cambridge University Press, 1992); Andrew S. McFarland, *Common Cause: Lobbying in the Public Interest* (Chatham, NJ: Chatham House, 1984).
19. *Garcia* v. *San Antonio Metropolitan Transit Authority*, 469 U.S. 528 (1985).
20. See Karen O'Connor, *Women's Organizations' Use of the Courts* (Lexington, MA: Lexington Books, 1980); Mark P. Petracca, ed., *The Politics of Interests* (Boulder, CO: Westview Press, 1992).
21. Olson, *Logic of Collective Action*. See also Robert H. Salisbury, "An Exchange Theory of Interest Groups," *Midwest Journal of Political Science* 13 (1969): 1–32.
22. For an extended discussion of the reasons why people decide to participate in full-time political activity, including work within interest groups, see James L. Payne et al., *The Motivation of Politicians* (Chicago: Nelson-Hall, 1984).
23. See Jeffrey M. Berry, *Lobbying for the People* (Princeton, NJ: Princeton University Press, 1977).
24. See Ronald J. Hrebenar and Clive S. Thomas, "The Japanese Lobby in Washington: How Different Is It?" in *Interest Group Politics*, pp. 349–368; Pat Choate, *Agents of Influence: How Japan's Lobbyists in the United States Manipulate America's Political and Economic System* (New York: Knopf, 1990).
25. See www.opensecrets.org/lobby, Center for Responsive Poilitics.
26. Jeffrey H. Birnbaum, "The Road to Riches Is Called K Street," *Washington Post*, June 22, 2005, p. A1.
27. See Laura Woliver, *From Outrage to Action* (Urbana: University of Illinois Press, 1993).
28. James L. Guth et al., "Onward Christian Soldiers: Religious Activist Groups in American Politics," in *Interest Group Politics*, pp. 42–75.
29. See Frank J. Sorauf, "Adaptation and Innovation in Political Action Committees," in *Interest Group Politics*, pp. 175–192; Dan Clawson, Alan Neustadt, and Denise Scott, *Money Talks: Corporate PACs and Political Influence* (New York: Basic Books, 1992).
30. John M. Broder, "Political Action; Money Focus," *New York Times*, January 16, 2007. Also see the Center for Responsive Politics site at www.opensecrets.org, last accessed on June 7, 2007.
31. Daniele Kurtzleben, "Five of Seven Super PACs Support Democrats," October 29, 2010, *U.S. News and World Report*, http://www.usnews.com/news/articles/2010/10/29/5-of-7-biggest-super-pacs-support-democrats?PageNr=2; Dave Levinthal, "2011 Sees Super PAC Explosion," *Politico*, October 6, 2011, http://www.politico.com/news/stories/1011/65310.html.
32. *United States* v. *Harris*, 347 U.S. 612 (1954).
33. Jonathan D. Salant, "Highlights of the Lobby Bill," *Congressional Quarterly Weekly Report*, December 2, 1995, p. 3632.
34. Jonathan Rauch, *Demosclerosis: The Silent Killer of American Government* (New York: Random House, 1994).
35. Arthur Bentley, *The Process of Government, A Study of Social Pressures* (Chicago: University of Chicago Press, 1908).
36. David B. Truman, *The Governmental Process* (New York: Knopf, 1951).
37. Theodore Lowi, *The End of Liberalism* (New York: Norton, 1979). See also Robert Dahl, *Preface to Democratic Theory* (Chicago: University of Chicago Press, 1956).
38. Hugh Heclo, "Issue Networks and the Executive Establishment," in *The New American Political System*, ed. Anthony King (Washington, DC: American Enterprise Institute, 1978), pp. 55–82.
39. John P. Heinz, Edward O. Lauman, Robert L. Nelson, and Robert H. Salisbury, *The Hollow Core* (Cambridge, MA: Harvard University Press, 1993).
40. Jeffrey Birnbaum and Dan Balz, "Case Bringing New Scrutiny to a System and a Profession," *Washington Post*, January 4, 2006.
41. TPM Muckraker, "Shadow Congress: Nearly 200 Ex-Lawmakers Work for Lobbying Shops," June 16, 2011, TPM.Muckraker.talkingpointsnemo.com.

42. "Congress Watch Division of Public Citizen," study, July 27, 2005; Jeffrey H. Birnbaum, "Hill a Steppingstone to K Street for Some," *Washington Post,* July 27, 2005, p. A19.
43. Sheryl Gay Stolberg, "Lobbyist's Downfall Leads to Charities' Windfall," *New York Times,* January 6, 2006, www.nyt.coms; Anne E. Kornblut and Abby Goodnough, "Bush and Others Shed Donations Tied to Lobbyist," *New York Times,* January 5, 2006, www.nyt.com; and Susan Schmidt, "Ex-Lobbyist Is Focus of Widening Investigations," *Washington Post,* July 16, 2004, p. A19.
44. Carl Hulse, "Ohio Congressman Linked to Scandal Gives Up Post," *New York Times,* January 16, 2006, www.nyt.com.
45. Frank Rich, "Is Abramoff the New Monica?" *New York Times,* January 15, 2006; Frank Rich, "Ethics Complaint on Ralph Reed," *New York Times,* December 2, 2005; and David Kirkpatrick and Philip Shenon, "Ralph Reed's Zeal for Lobbying Is Shaking His Political Faithful," *New York Times,* April 18, 2005.
46. Dan Eggen, "Groups on the Left Are Suddenly on Top," *Washington Post,* June 4, 2009.
47. David Weigel, "Conservative Think Tank Adjusts to Tough Times," *The Washington Independent,* March 13, 2009, http://washingtonindependent.com.
48. See http://www.whitehouse.gov/issues/ethics/.
49. Emily Miller, "Obama, Abramoff, and 'Lobbying Reform,'" *Politics Daily* blog, May 15, 2009, www.politicsdaily.com.
50. OMB Finalizes Details on White House Lobbying Reform Rules," *The BLT: The Blog of Legal Times,* October 5, 2011, www.legaltimes.com.
51. *Colorado Republican Federal Campaign Committee* v. *Federal Election Commission,* 135 L. Ed. 2d 795 (1996), p. 803.
52. Quoted in Richard L. Berke, "Interest Groups Prepare to Spend on Campaign Spin," *New York Times,* January 11, 1998, p. 1.
53. Adam Clymer, "The Supreme Court: Campaign Money," *New York Times,* June 26, 2001. Article discusses *Federal Election Commission* v. *Colorado Republican Federal Campaign Committee,* 533 U.S. 431 (2001).
54. Robert Barnes, "5–4 Supreme Court Weakens Curbs on Pre-Election TV Ads," *Washington Post,* June 26, 2007. The cases are *FEC* v. *Wisconsin Right to Life* and *McCain et al.* v. *Wisconsin Right to Life.*
55. The exact number was $947 million. Cited by John M. Broder, "Political Action; Money Focus," January 16, 2007; see also the Center for Responsive Politics site, www.opensecrets.org.
56. Jeffrey H. Birnbaum, "To Conceal Donors, Some Political Groups Look to the Tax Code," *Washington Post,* April 17, 2007, www.washingtonpost.com, last accessed on June 7, 2007.

## CHAPTER 12

1. Quoted in Harold W. Chase and Allen H. Lerman, *Kennedy and the Press* (New York: Crowell, 1965), p. 26.
2. Brian Stelter, "A World of Risk for a New Brand of Journalist," *New York Times,* June 15, 2009, p. B1.
3. http://www.washingtontimes.com/news/2011/sep/26/freed-us-hikers-describe-harrowing-ordeal-iran/?page=1&utm_medium=RSS&utm_source=RSS_Feed.
4. Robert M. Entman, *Democracy Without Citizens: Media and the Decay of American Politics* (New York: Oxford University Press, 1989), p. 8; Shanto Iyengar, *Is Anyone Responsible? How Television Frames Political Issues* (Chicago: University of Chicago Press, 1991); W. Russell Newman, *The Paradox of Mass Politics* (Cambridge, MA: Harvard University Press, 1986).
5. Joe Strupp, "New Survey Finds Huge Gap Between Press and Public on Many Issues," Editor & Publisher.com, May 15, 2005.
6. According to the Pew Center Report, 60 percent view media as politically biased, people-press.org/2009/09/13/press-accuracy-rating-hits-two-decade-low/. A 2010 First Amendment Center at Vanderbilt University study found that only 18 percent of respondents knew that the First Amendment protects freedom of the press: www.nytimes.com/2010/10/24/weekinreview/24schwartz.html.
7. http://online.wsj.com/article/SB121769525318907505.html; http://www.time.com/time/world/article/0,8599,1885961,00.html; http://www. cbsnews.com/stories/2002/12/03/tech/main531567.shtml.
8. Thomas Jefferson, quoted in Samuel Kernell, *Going Public* (Washington, DC: Congressional Quarterly Press, 1993), p. 94; George Washington, quoted in Jeffrey K. Tulis, *The Rhetorical Presidency* (Princeton, NJ: Princeton University Press, 1987), p. 131.
9. Ronald Berkman and Laura W. Kitch, *Politics in the Media* (New York: McGraw-Hill, 1986); Deane E. Alger, *The Media and Politics* (Upper Saddle River, NJ: Prentice-Hall, 1989). See also W. Russell Neuman, Marion R. Just, and Ann N. Crigler, *Common Knowledge: News and the Construction of Political Meaning* (Chicago: University of Chicago Press, 1992); Stephen Ansolabehere, Roy Behr, and Shanto Iyengar, *The Media Game: American Politics in the Television Age* (New York: Macmillan, 1993).
10. Suzanne M. Kirchhoff, "Newspapers in Transition," September 9, 2010, www.fas.org/sgp/crs/misc/R40700.pdf.
11. http://dealbook.blogs.nytimes.com/2008/12/08/tribune-files-for-bankruptcy/; http://www.newyorker.com/reporting/2008/03/31/080331fa_fact_alterman?currentPage=all.
12. http://people-press.org/2010/09/12/americans-spending-more-time-following-the-news/.
13. David Halberstam, *The Powers That Be* (New York: Dell, 1979), p. 72.
14. Audience Segments in a Changing News Environment; Key News Audiences Now Blend Online and Traditional Sources," Pew Research Center Biennial News Consumption Survey, August 17, 2008, http://www.people-press.org.
15. See Alessandra Stanley, "Bringing Out the Absurdity of the News," *New York Times,* October 25, 2005, p. B1.
16. http://people-press.org/report/?pageid=1358.
17. Ibid.
18. Austin Ranney, *Channels of Power: The Impact of Television on American Politics* (New York: Basic Books, 1983), p. 144.
19. See Lawrence Grossman, *The Electronic Republic* (New York: Viking, 1995), p. 60.
20. http://people-press.org/2010/09/12/.section-2-online-and-digital-news/.
21. http://www.associatedcontent.com/article/523445/youtube_facebook_debates_target_young.html.
22. "Cable and Internet Loom Large in Fragmented Political News Universe—Perceptions of Partisan Bias Seen as Growing, Especially by Democrats," January 11, 2004, http://people-press.org/reports/display.php3?ReportID=200; Carla Marinucci, "Political Video Smackdown," *San Francisco Chronicle,* March 18, 2007, http://www.sfgate.com/cgi-bin/article.cgi?f=/c/a/2007/03/18/MNGHNONEPS1.DTL&feed=rss.news.
23. Daniel W. Drezner and Henry Farrell, "Web of Influence," *Foreign Policy,* November/December 2004, www.foreignpolicy.com. Also see their paper, "The Power and Politics of Blogs," July 2004, presented at the 2004 American Political Science Association Meeting; and Michael Cornfield, Jonathan Carson, Alison Kalis, and Emily Simon, "Buzz, Blogs, and Beyond: The Internet and the National Discourse in the Fall of 2004," *BuzzMetrics,* www.buzzmetrics.com.
24. www.blogpulse.com provides descriptive statistics on the blogosphere. As of September 2011, BlogPulse identified 171,441,040 active blogs.
25. "The State of Blogging," January 2, 2005, www.pewinternet.org/PPF/r/144/report_display.asp.
26. Doris Graber, *Mass Media and American Politics* (Washington, DC: Congressional Quarterly Press, 1989), p. 12.
27. Ibid.
28. http://www.allheadlinenews.com/articles/7015833781?Insurgents+Release+Tape+Of+Captured+U.S.+Soldier#ixzz0LvnNqENr.
29. David Broder, *Behind the Front Page: A Candid Look at How News Is Made* (New York: Simon & Schuster, 1987), p. 114; see also Jay Rosen and Paul Taylor, *The New News v. the Old News: The Press and Politics in the 1990s* (New York: Twentieth-Century Fund, 1992).
30. Marshall McLuhan, *Understanding Media: The Extensions of Man* (New York: McGraw-Hill, 1965); Thomas Dye, Harmon Zeigler, and S. Robert Lichter, *American Politics in the Media Age* (Pacific Grove, CA: Brooks/Cole, 1992), p. 5.
31. Iyengar, *Is Anyone Responsible?* See also Douglas Kellner, *Television and the Crisis of Democracy* (Boulder, CO: Westview Press, 1990); Eric

Barnouw, *Tube of Plenty: The Evolution of American Television* (New York: Oxford University Press, 1982), p. 415.
32. Dana Priest and Anne Hull, "Soldiers Face Neglect, Frustration at Army's Top Medical Facility," *Washington Post,* February 18, 2007, p. A01.
33. www.chicagotribune.com/health/neglect.
34. http://transition.fcc.gov/mb/policy/political/candrule.htm.
35. *Red Lion Broadcasting* v. *FCC,* 395 U.S. 367 (1969); Ben Bagdikian, *The Media Monopoly,* 4th ed. (Boston: Beacon Press, 1994).
36. *New York Times Co.* v. *United States,* 403 U.S. 714 (1971), p. 717.
37. Mark Cook and Jeff Cohen, "The Media Go to War: How Television Sold the Panama Invasion," *FAIR* 3, no. 2 (January/February 1991): 22–25; *Miami Herald Publishing Co.* v. *Tornillo,* 418 U.S. 241 (1974).
38. Robert Lichter, Stanley Rothman, and Linda Litcher, *The Media Elite* (Bethesda, MD: Alder and Alder, 1986).
39. Bernard Goldberg, *Bias* (New York: Regency, 2001); see also Andrew Kohut, "Listen Up, Bias Mongers! The Audience Doesn't Agree," *Columbia Journalism Review On-line,* www.cjr.org/year/02/2/kohut.asp.
40. See Jeff Cohen, "Maybe the Public—Not the Press—Has a Leftist Bias," www.fair.org/articles/liberal-media.html.
41. See http://www.csra.uconn.edu.
42. Fred Barnes, "Is the Mainstream Media Fair and Balanced?" *Imprints* 35, no. 8 (August 2006).
43. See http://www.csra.uconn.edu.
44. "*Media Boost Obama, Bash His Policies,*" http://www.cmpa.com/media_room_4_27_09.htm.
45. www.cmoa.com/media_room_press_1_25_10.html.
46. William Greider, *Who Will Tell the People? The Betrayal of American Democracy* (New York: Simon & Schuster, 1992).
47. Bagdikian, *Media Monopoly;* see also Christopher Stern, "Limits on Media Ownership Voided," *Washington Post,* February 20, 2002, pp. E1, E3; "Protecting Media Diversity," *New York Times,* February 23, 2002, p. A30.
48. "Voices from Above Silence a Cable TV Feud," http://www.nytimes.com/2009/08/01/business/media/01feud.html?_r=3&src=twt&twt=nytimes; http://www.salon.com/opinion/greenwald/2009/08/01/ge/print.html; Glenn Greenwald, "GE's Silencing of Olbermann and MSNBC's Sleazy Use of Richard Wolffe: Two New Major MSNBC Scandals Reveal Much About How Corporate Journalism Functions," August 1, 2009.
49. Daniel Hallin, "Sound Bite News: Television Coverage of Elections, 1968–1988," Media Studies Project Occasional Paper (Washington, DC: Woodrow Wilson International Center for Scholars, 1990); Mickey Kaus, "Sound-Bitten," *New Republic,* October 26, 1992, pp. 16–18; Kiku Adatto, "The Incredible Shrinking Sound Bite," *New Republic,* May 28, 1990, pp. 20–21.
50. http://www.reuters.com/article/pressRelease/idUS255618+05-Nov-2008+PRN20081105?
51. "Obama: Can't 'Swift Boat' Me," http://www.newsweek.com/id/132874.

## CHAPTER 13

1. For more on this argument, see Henry J. Abraham and Barbara A. Perry, *Freedom and the Court: Civil Rights and Liberties in the United States,* 7th ed. (New York: Oxford University Press, 1998), pp. 3–9.
2. Paul Gewirtz and Chad Golder, "So Who Are the Activists?" *New York Times,* July 6, 2005.
3. *United States* v. *Carolene Products Co.,* 304 U.S. 144; 58 S. Ct. 778 (1938); for more on the genesis of this footnote, and its meaning, see Louis Lusky, *By What Right* (Charlottesville, VA: Michie, 1974).
4. *Barron* v. *Baltimore,* 32 U.S. 243 (1833).
5. *Slaughterhouse Cases,* 83 U.S. 36 (1873).
6. For more on this process, see *Palko* v. *Connecticut,* 302 U.S. 319 (1937); and *Adamson* v. *California,* 332 U.S. 46 (1947).
7. *Hurtado* v. *California,* 110 U.S. 516 (1884).
8. *Twining* v. *New Jersey,* 211 U.S. 78 (1908).
9. *Chicago, Burlington and Quincy Railway Co.* v. *Chicago,* 166 U.S. 226 (1897).
10. *Schenck* v. *United States,* 249 U.S. 47 (1919).
11. *Frohwerk* v. *United States,* 249 U.S. 204 (1919).
12. *Debs* v. *United States,* 249 U.S. 211 (1919).
13. *Abrams* v. *United States,* 250 U.S. 616 (1919).
14. *Gitlow* v. *New York,* 268 U.S. 652 (1925).
15. *Near* v. *Minnesota,* 283 U.S. 697 (1931).
16. *Powell* v. *Alabama,* 287 U.S. 45 (1932).
17. *Hamilton* v. *Regents of the University of California,* 293 U.S. 245 (1934).
18. *Palko* v. *Connecticut,* 302 U.S . 319 (1937).
19. *District of Columbia* v. *Heller,* 128 S.Ct. 2783, (2008).
20. See *Williams* v. *Florida,* 399 U.S. 78 (1970); *Apodaca* v. *Oregon,* 406 U.S. 404 (1972); and *Johnson* v. *Louisiana,* 406 U.S. 356 (1972).
21. For more, see Anson Phelps Stokes and Leo Pfeffer, *Church and State in the United States* (New York: Harper & Row, 1964).
22. *Walz* v. *Tax Commission,* 397 U.S. 664 (1970).
23. Abraham and Perry, *Freedom and the Court,* pp. 220–320.
24. *Everson* v. *Board of Education of Ewing Township,* 330 U.S. 1 (1947).
25. *Engel* v. *Vitale,* 370 U.S. 24 (1962).
26. *Abington School District* v. *Schempp,* 374 U.S. 203 (1963).
27. *Lemon* v. *Kurtzman,* 403 U.S. 602 (1971).
28. *Mueller* v. *Allen,* 463 U.S. 388 (1983).
29. *Marsh* v. *Chambers,* 463 U.S. 783 (1983).
30. *Lynch* v. *Donnelly,* 465 U.S. 668 (1984).
31. *Stone* v. *Graham,* 449 U.S. 39 (1980).
32. *Wallace* v. *Jaffree,* 472 U.S. 38 (1985).
33. *Grand Rapids School District* v. *Ball,* 473 U.S. 373 (1985).
34. *Edwards* v. *Aguillard,* 482 U.S. 578 (1987).
35. Patty Reinert, "Commandment Case Rejected," *Houston Chronicle,* February 26, 2002.
36. *McCreary County* v. *A.C.L.U.,* 125 S. Ct. 2722 (2005); *Van Orden* v. *Perry* 125 S. Ct. 2854 (2005).
37. *County of Allegheny* v. *Greater Pittsburgh ACLU,* 497 U.S. 573 (1989).
38. *Lee* v. *Weisman,* 112 S. Ct. 2649 (1992).
39. *Zelman* v. *Simmons-Harris,* 153 L. Ed. 2d 604 (2002); David Savage, "School Vouchers Win Backing of High Court," *Los Angeles Times,* June 28, 2002, p. 1.
40. Lisa Snell, "Questioning State Aid for Students at Private Colleges," *San Diego Union-Tribune,* June 3, 2005.
41. Claudia Wallis, "The Evolution Wars," *Time,* August 15, 2005, pp. 27–35; *Edwards* v. *Aguillard,* 482 U.S. 581 (1987).
42. *Elk Grove Unified School District* v. *Newdow,* 541 U.S. 1 (2004); David Von Drehle, "Judge Blocks Decision During Appeals," *Washington Post,* June 28, 2002.
43. *Reynolds* v. *United States,* 98 U.S. 145 (1879).
44. See *Braunfeld* v. *Brown,* 366 U.S. 599 (1961); *McGowan* v. *Maryland,* 366 U.S. 420 (1961); and *Sherbert* v. *Verner,* 374 U.S. 398 (1963).
45. *Oregon Department of Human Resources* v. *Smith,* 294 U.S. 872 (1990).
46. *Church of Lukumi Babalu Aya* v. *Hialeah,* 508 U.S. 520 (1993).
47. Bob Cohn and David A. Kaplan, "A Chicken on Every Altar?" *Newsweek,* November 9, 1992, p. 79.
48. *City of Boerne* v. *Flores,* 117 S. Ct. 2157 (1997); and ibid., p. 2162.
49. *Good News Club* v. *Milford Central School,* 533 U.S. 98 (2001).
50. *Watchtower Bible and Tract Society of New York* v. *Village of Stratton, Ohio,* 153 L. Ed. 2d 205 (2002); see also Tony Mauro, "In God's Hands," *Legal Times,* February 25, 2002, p. 1.
51. See Alexander Meiklejohn, *Free Speech and Its Relation to Self-Government* (New York: Harper, 1948).
52. *Abrams* v. *United States,* 250 U.S. 187 (1919).
53. *Dennis* v. *United States,* 339 U.S. 494 (1951).
54. *Yates* v. *United States,* 354 U.S. 298 (1957).
55. See *Scales* v. *United States,* 367 U.S. 203 (1961); and *United States* v. *Robel,* 389 U.S. 258 (1967).
56. *Brandenburg* v. *Ohio,* 385 U.S. 444 (1969).
57. *Nixon* v. *Shrink Missouri Gov't PAC,* 528 U.S. 377 (2000). Discussed in Warren Richey, "Court Affirms Campaign Finance Laws," *Christian Science Monitor,* January 25, 2000, p. 1; see also, *Buckley* v. *Valeo,* 424 U.S. 1 (1976).
58. *Federal Election Commission* v. *Colorado Republican Federal Campaign Committee,* 533 U.S. 431 (2001).
59. See *Edwards* v. *South Carolina,* 372 U.S. 229 (1963); *Brown* v. *Louisiana,* 383 U.S. 131 (1966); and *Chaplinsky* v. *New Hampshire,* 315 U.S. 568 (1942).

60. *Terminiello* v. *Chicago,* 337 U.S. 1 (1949).
61. *RAV* v. *City of St. Paul,* 505 U.S. 377 (1992); and *Wisconsin* v. *Mitchell,* 508 U.S. 476 (1993).
62. *Adderly* v. *Florida,* 385 U.S. 39 (1967).
63. *Cox* v. *Louisiana,* 379 U.S. 569 (1965).
64. *Cohen* v. *California,* 403 U.S. 15 (1971); *Texas* v. *Johnson,* 491 U.S. 397 (1989).
65. *RAV* v. *City of St. Paul, Minnesota,* 505 U.S. 377 (1992).
66. *Wisconsin* v. *Mitchell,* 508 U.S. 476 (1993).
67. *Madsen* v. *Women's Health Center,* 115 S. Ct. 2338 (1995).
68. *Schenck* v. *Pro-Choice Network of Western New York,* 117 S. Ct. 855 (1997).
69. Bill McAllister, "Two Victories for Abortion Rights," *Denver Post,* June 29, 2000, p. 1.
70. See *Federal Election Commission* v. *Wisconsin Right to Life,* 551 U.S. 449 (2007); Linda Greenhouse, "Justices Loosen Ad Restrictions in Campaign Finance Law," *New York Times,* June 26, 2007; Robert Barnes, "Newest Justice Tips High Court to Right," *Washington Post,* June 28, 2007.
71. *Tinker* v. *Des Moines School District,* 393 U.S. 503 (1969).
72. Adam Liptak, "Justices Reject Ban on Violent Video Games for Children," *New York Times,* June 27, 2011.
73. *New York Times Co.* v. *United States,* 403 U.S. 713 (1971).
74. *Nebraska Press Assn.* v. *Stuart,* 427 U.S. 539 (1976).
75. *Richmond Newspapers Inc.* v. *Virginia,* 448 U.S. 555 (1980).
76. See *New York Times* v. *Sullivan,* 376 U.S. 254 (1964); and *Curtis Publishing Co.* v. *Butts,* 388 U.S. 130 (1967).
77. *Gertz* v. *Robert Welch Inc.,* 418 U.S. 323 (1974); *Rosenbloom* v. *Metromedia,* 403 U.S. 29 (1971).
78. *Herbert* v. *Lando,* 441 U.S. 153 (1979).
79. "First Amendment Decision: The Press Wins," *New York Times,* October 23, 1999, p. 1.
80. *Roth* v. *United States,* 354 U.S. 476 (1957).
81. *Memoirs* v. *Massachusetts,* 383 U.S. 413 (1966).
82. *Ginzburg* v. *United States,* 383 U.S. 463 (1966); *Ginsberg* v. *New York,* 390 U.S. 629 (1968); *Mishkin* v. *New York,* 383 U.S. 502 (1966); *Redrup* v. *New York,* 386 U.S. 767 (1967).
83. *Miller* v. *California,* 413 U.S. 15 (1973) (emphasis in original).
84. *Jenkins* v. *Georgia,* 418 U.S. 153 (1974).
85. *Knox* v. *United States,* 114 S. Ct. 375 (1993).
86. *Reno* v. *American Civil Liberties Union,* 117 S. Ct. 2329 (1997); see also Greg Miller, "Law to Control Online Porn Creates Strange Bedfellows," *Los Angeles Times,* February 15, 1999, p. 1; Greg Miller, "Court Rejects Child Online Protection Act," *Los Angeles Times,* June 23, 2000, p. 1.
87. *Ashcroft* v. *Free Speech Coalition,* 152 L. Ed. 2d 403 (2002).
88. *Ashcroft* v. *American Civil Liberties Union,* 535 U.S. 564 (2002).
89. Lyle Denniston, "Justices to Weigh Library Web Access," November 13, 2002; Robert O'Harrow Jr., "U.S. Court Overturns Internet Smut Law Ruling in Library Case Is 3rd Loss for Congress," *Boston Globe,* June 1, 2002; and see Michael S. Romano, "Putting Up a Filter for the Kids," *New York Times,* April 4, 2002.
90. *People of New York* v. *Defore,* 242 N.Y. 13, pp. 19–25 (1927).
91. *Weeks* v. *United States,* 232 U.S. 383 (1914).
92. For more, see David Fellman, *The Defendant's Rights Today* (Madison: University of Wisconsin Press, 1976), pp. 292–297.
93. *Wolf* v. *Colorado,* 338 U.S. 25 (1949); and *Rochin* v. *California,* 342 U.S. 165 (1952).
94. *Breithaupt* v. *Abram,* 352 U.S. 432 (1957).
95. *Mapp* v. *Ohio,* 367 U.S. 643 (1961).
96. Dissent by Warren Burger, *Bivens* v. *Six Unknown Named Agents of Federal Bureau of Narcotics,* 403 U.S. 388 (1971).
97. *United States* v. *Calandra,* 414 U.S. 338 (1974).
98. *Stone* v. *Powell,* 428 U.S. 465 (1976).
99. *United States* v. *Leon,* 468 U.S. 902 (1984).
100. *Illinois* v. *Rodriguez,* 110 S. Ct. 2793 (1990).
101. *Arizona* v. *Evans,* 514 U.S. 1 (1995).
102. See *Carroll* v. *United States,* 267 U.S. 132 (1925); *United States* v. *Chadwick,* 433 U.S. 1 (1977); and *Cady* v. *Dombroski,* 413 U.S. 433 (1973).
103. *Katz* v. *United States,* 389 U.S. 347 (1967), p. 351.
104. See *Chimel* v. *California,* 395 U.S. 752 (1969); *Coolidge* v. *New Hampshire,* 403 U.S. 443 (1971); *Schneckloth* v. *Bustamonte,* 412 U.S. 218 (1973); and *United States* v. *Cortez,* 449 U.S. 411 (1981).
105. *Terry* v. *Ohio,* 391 U.S. 1 (1968).
106. *New Jersey* v. *T.L.O.,* 469 U.S. 325 (1985).
107. *Katz* v. *United States,* 389 U.S. 347 (1967), p. 361.
108. *Vernonia School District 47J* v. *Acton,* 515 U.S. 646 (1995).
109. *Board of Education* v. *Earls,* 153 L. Ed. 2d 735 (2002).
110. Robert Barnes, "Supreme Court Rules School's Strip Search of Girl Was Illegal," *Washington Post,* June 25, 2009.
111. *Illinois* v. *Wardlow,* 528 U.S. 119 (2000).
112. *United States* v. *Drayton,* 153 L. Ed. 2d 242 (2002).
113. *Kyllo* v. *United States,* 533 U.S. 27 (2001).
114. *Hudson* v. *Michigan,* 547 U.S. 586 (2006).
115. *Herring* v. *United States,* 555 U.S. ___ (2009).
116. Adam Cohen, "Is the Supreme Court About to Kill Off the Exclusionary Rule?" *New York Times,* February 16, 2009; Adam Liptak, "Justices Step Closer to Repeal of Evidence Ruling," *New York Times,* January 31, 2009.
117. *Davis* v. *United States,* 564 U.S. ___ (2011). Underscore added for emphasis.
118. *Davis* v. *United States,* 564 U.S. ___ (2011).
119. *Brown* v. *Mississippi,* 297 U.S. 278 (1936).
120. *Haynes* v. *Washington,* 373 U.S. 503 (1963).
121. *Escobedo* v. *Illinois,* 378 U.S. 478 (1964).
122. *Miranda* v. *Arizona,* 384 U.S. 436 (1966).
123. *Arizona* v. *Fulminante,* 111 S. Ct. 1246 (1991).
124. *United States* v. *Dickerson,* 530 U.S. 428 (2000).
125. Jan Hoffman, "Police Tactics Chipping Away at Suspects' Rights," *New York Times,* March 29, 1998, p. 1; and Jan Hoffman, "As Miranda Rights Erode, Police Get Confessions from Innocent People," *New York Times,* March 30, 1998, p. 32.
126. Ralph Blumenthal, "A 12th Dallas Convict Is Exonerated by DNA," *New York Times,* January 18, 2007, p. A14.
127. For an update on the death penalty issue, see the Death Penalty Information Center. For more on recent changes in the death penalty issue, see Jodi Wilgoren, "Three Cleared by DNA Tests Enjoy Liberty After 15 Years," *New York Times,* December 6, 2001, p. A20; Henry Weinstein, "Death Penalty Study Suggests Errors," *Los Angeles Times,* February 11, 2002; David G. Savage, "92 Execution Haunts Death Penalty Foes," *Los Angeles Times,* July 22, 2001; Jonathan Alter, "The Death Penalty on Trial," *Newsweek,* June 12, 2000, pp. 24–35; Raymond Bonner and Marc Lacey, "U.S. Plans Delay in First Execution in Four Decades," *New York Times,* July 7, 2000, p. 1; and Fox Butterfield, "Death Sentences Being Overturned in 2 of 3 Appeals," *New York Times,* June 12, 2000, p. 1.
128. *Atkins* v. *Virginia,* 536 U.S. 304 (2002).
129. *Roper* v. *Simmons,* 125 S. Ct. 1183 (2005).
130. Warren Richey, "What Impact Will Supreme Court Decision on DNA Evidence Have?" *Christian Science Monitor,* June 18, 2009; Bill Mears, "Supreme Court Denies DNA Test to Rapist," CNN.com, June 18, 2009; and "The Right to DNA Evidence," *New York Times,* March 2, 2009.
131. Kurt T. Lash, *The Lost History of the Ninth Amendment* (New York: Oxford University Press, 2009).
132. *Griswold* v. *Connecticut,* 381 U.S. 479 (1965). For more on this case and the issues surrounding it, also see David J. Garrow, *Liberty and Sexuality: The Right to Privacy and the Making of* Roe *v.* Wade (New York: Macmillan, 1994), pp. 16–195. For more on opponents of the *Griswold* decision, see Robert Bork, *The Tempting of America* (New York: Free Press, 1989); and Ethan Bronner, *Battle for Justice: How the Bork Nomination Shook America* (New York: Norton, 1989).
133. *Eisenstadt* v. *Baird,* 405 U.S. 438 (1972); and *Doe* v. *Bolton,* 410 U.S. 179 (1973).
134. *Roe* v. *Wade,* 410 U.S. 113 (1973).
135. *Harris* v. *McRae,* 448 U.S. 297 (1980).
136. *Planned Parenthood of Central Missouri* v. *Danforth,* 428 U.S. 52 (1976).
137. *Akron* v. *Akron Center for Reproductive Health,* 462 U.S. 416 (1983).
138. *Webster* v. *Reproductive Health Services,* 492 U.S. 490 (1989).
139. *Planned Parenthood of Southeastern Pennsylvania* v. *Casey,* 112 S. Ct. 2791 (1992).

140. Linda Greenhouse, "U.S. Court Voids Ohio Ban on Late-Term Abortion," *New York Times*, November 19, 1997.
141. *Stenberg* v. *Carhart*, 530 U.S. 914 (2000).
142. *Gonzales* v. *Carhart*, 127 S. Ct. 1610 (2007); see also Dahlia Lithwick, "Kennedy Made Me Do It," Slate.com, June 8, 2006; Ruth Marcus, "Court Knows Best," *Washington Post*, April 25, 2007; and Julia Preston, "Appeals Court Voids Ban on 'Partial Birth' Abortions," *New York Times*, July 9, 2005.
143. *Cruzan by Cruzan* v. *Director, Missouri Department of Health*, 110 S. Ct. 2841 (1990).
144. *Washington* v. *Glucksberg*, 117 S. Ct. 2258 (1997); and *Vacco* v. *Quill*, 117 S. Ct. 2293 (1997).
145. Daniel Eisenberg, "Lessons of the Schiavo Battle," *Time*, April 4, 2005, pp. 22–30.
146. *Gonzales* v. *Oregon*, 2006 U.S. Lexis 767 (2006), which can also be found at www.supremecourtus.gov/.
147. Gina Holland, "Supreme Court Upholds Oregon Suicide Law," *Washington Post*, www.washingtonpost.com, January 17, 2006.
148. *Baxter* v. *Montana* (2009).
149. *Baxter* v. *Montana* (2009) Supreme Court decision. Discussed in Kirk Johnson, "Montana Ruling Bolsters Physician-Assisted Suicide," *New York Times*, December 31, 2009. Thanks to Attorney Paul Drager, one of the nation's experts on this issue, for his assistance on this question. For more, see the website "Compassion and Choices," which supports physician-assisted suicide, found at https://compassionandchoices.org/sslpage.aspx.

## CHAPTER 14

1. *Brown* v. *Board of Education of Topeka, Kansas*, 347 U.S. 483 (1954).
2. *Dred Scott* v. *Sandford*, 19 Howard 393 (1857).
3. *United States* v. *Cruikshank*, 92 U.S. 214 (1876).
4. *Civil Rights Cases*, 109 U.S. 3 (1883).
5. *Plessy* v. *Ferguson*, 163 U.S. 537 (1896).
6. Ibid., p. 559.
7. *Cumming* v. *County Board of Education*, 175 U.S. 528 (1899).
8. C. Vann Woodward, *Origins of the New South: 1877–1913*, 2nd ed. (Baton Rouge: Louisiana University Press, 1987), pp. 331–338, 372–375.
9. *Bailey* v. *Alabama*, 219 U.S. 219 (1911).
10. *Guinn* v. *United States*, 238 U.S. 347 (1915); see also Donald G. Nieman, *Promises to Keep: African Americans and the Constitutional Order, 1776 to the Present* (New York: Oxford University Press, 1991), pp. 123–127.
11. *Nixon* v. *Herndon*, 273 U.S. 536 (1927).
12. Richard Kluger, *Simple Justice* (New York: Knopf, 1976), p. 250.
13. *Missouri ex rel. Gaines* v. *Canada*, 305 U.S. 337 (1938).
14. *Sweatt* v. *Painter*, 339 U.S. 629 (1950).
15. *McLaurin* v. *Oklahoma State of Regents*, 339 U.S. 637 (1950).
16. *Brown* v. *Board of Education of Topeka, Kansas*, 347 U.S. 483 (1954).
17. *Bolling* v. *Sharpe*, 347 U.S. 497 (1954).
18. *Brown* v. *Board of Education of Topeka, Kansas*, 349 U.S. 294 (1955).
19. Alfred H. Kelly and Winfred A. Harbison, *The American Constitution: Origins and Development*, 4th ed. (New York: Norton, 1970), p. 940.
20. Jack W. Peltason, *Fifty-Eight Lonely Men* (New York: Harcourt Brace Jovanovich, 1961).
21. Nieman, *Promises to Keep*, pp. 166–176.
22. *Heart of Atlanta Motel* v. *United States*, 379 U.S. 241 (1964).
23. *Katzenbach* v. *McClung*, 379 U.S. 294 (1964).
24. *Harper* v. *Virginia Board of Elections*, 383 U.S. 663 (1966).
25. Nieman, *Promises to Keep*, p. 180.
26. *Jones* v. *Alfred H. Mayer*, 329 U.S. 409 (1968).
27. *Alexander* v. *Holmes County Board of Education*, 396 U.S. 19 (1969).
28. Nieman, *Promises to Keep*, p. 179.
29. *Swann* v. *Charlotte-Mecklenburg Board of Education*, 402 U.S. 1 (1971).
30. *Keyes* v. *School District #1, Denver, Colorado*, 413 U.S. 189 (1973).
31. *Milliken* v. *Bradley*, 418 U.S. 717 (1974).
32. *Parents Involved in Community Schools* v. *Seattle School District*, 2007 U.S. LEXIS 8670 (2007); *Meredith* v. *Jefferson County Board of Education*, 2007 U.S. LEXIS 8670 (2007); David Stout, "Use of Race in School Placement Curbed," *New York Times*, June 28, 2007; Mark Sherman, "Supreme Court Rejects School Race Plans," *Washington Post*, June 28, 2007; "Schools Must Ignore Race in Placing Pupils, Justices Say," *New York Times*, June 28, 2007; "Reaction to High Court's School Ruling," *New York Times*, June 28, 2007. See also Walter Dellinger and Dahlia Lithwick, "A Supreme Court Conversation," Slate.com, June 26, 2007, www.slate.com.
33. Robert Barnes, "Supreme Court Rules Narrowly on Voting Rights Act," *Washington Post*, June 22, 2009; David Stout, "Justices Let Stand a Central Provision of Voting Rights Act," *New York Times*, June 23, 2009. The case name is *Northwest Austin Municipal Utility District Number One* v. *Holder*.
34. Tony Mauro, "Can the Voting Rights Act Survive Another Challenge?" *The National Law Journal*, June 29, 2009.
35. Charlie Savage, "Holder Signals Tough Review of New State Laws on Voting," *New York Times*, December 13, 2011.
36. Leslie Goldstein, "Affirmative Action Toward the 21st Century," address to the graduate seminar, "The Constitution and Bill of Rights in the New Millennium," August 1, 1997, Freedom's Foundation, Valley Forge, PA.
37. Sidney Verba and Gary R. Orren, *Equality in America: The View from the Top* (Cambridge, MA: Harvard University Press, 1985), p. 5.
38. *DeFunis* v. *Odegaard*, 416 U.S. 312 (1974).
39. *Regents of the University of California* v. *Bakke*, 438 U.S. 265 (1978).
40. *United Steelworkers* v. *Weber*, 443 U.S. 193 (1979).
41. *Fullilove* v. *Klutznick*, 448 U.S. 448 (1980).
42. *Firefighters Local Union No. 1784* v. *Stotts*, 467 U.S. 561 (1984).
43. *Wygant* v. *Jackson Board of Education*, 476 U.S. 267 (1986).
44. *Local Number 93, International Association of Firefighters* v. *City of Cleveland*, 478 U.S. 501 (1986).
45. *Local 28 of the Sheet Metal Workers' International Association* v. *EEOC*, 478 U.S. 421 (1986).
46. *U.S.* v. *Paradise*, 480 U.S. 149 (1987).
47. *Adarand Constructors* v. *Pena*, 115 S. Ct. 2097 (1995).
48. "10 Percent Plan Survives in Texas," *Inside Higher Ed*, May 29, 2007, www.insidehighered.com.
49. Rene Sanchez and Sue Anne Pressley, "Universities Admit Fewer Minorities," *Washington Post*, May 19, 1997, p. A1.
50. See David J. Garrow, "How Much Weight Can Race Carry?" *New York Times*, May 19, 2002, p. 4k; Gary Haber, "Minority Enrollment Shrinks at USF but Grows Statewide," *Tampa Tribune*, September 16, 2004; Mark Clayton, "Michigan Affirmative Action Case Will Reverberate Widely," *Christian Science Monitor*, October 23, 2001; Ben Feller, "One Florida Sustains Universities' Diversity," *Tampa Tribune*, September 6, 2001; Barry Klein, "UF Ends Race-Based Scholarship Program," *St. Petersburg Times*, August 31, 2001; Travis Gosselin, "Divided We Stand: Affirmative Action: Why It Should Remain," *St. Louis Post Dispatch*, April 11, 2001; David J. Garrow, "The Path to Diversity? Different Differences, *New York Times*, September 2, 2001, p. 4; and Peter Kilborn, "Jeb Bush Roils Florida on Affirmative Action," *New York Times*, February 4, 2000.
51. See *Gratz* v. *Bollinger*, 539 U.S. 244 (2003); *Grutter* v. *Bollinger*, 539 U.S. 306 (2003).
52. Grutter v. *Bollinger*, 539 U.S. 306 (2003), p. 335.
53. Ibid., p. 323.
54. "Michigan Votes Down Affirmative Action," *Inside Higher Ed*, November 8, 2006, www.insidehighered.com; Kristen Jordan Shamus, "U-M Will Reach Out to Keep Diversity," *Detroit Free Press*, March 16, 2007.
55. "10 Percent Plan Survives in Texas," *Inside Higher Ed*, May 29, 2007, www.insidehighered.com.
56. Meredith v. *Jefferson County Board of Education*, and *Parents Involved in Community Schools* v. *School District Number One*, 551 U.S. 701 (2007).
57. David Stout, "Justices Rule for White Firefighters in Bias Case," *New York Times*, June 30, 2009; Steven Greenhouse, "Ruling Offers Little Guidance on Fair Hiring," *New York Times*, June 30 2009.
58. Quoted in Nancy E. McGlen and Karen O'Connor, *Women's Rights: The Struggle for Equality in the Nineteenth and Twentieth Centuries* (New York: Praeger, 1983), pp. 389–391.
59. Ibid., pp. 272–274.
60. *Bradwell* v. *State of Illinois*, 83 U.S. 130 (1873).

61. *Minor* v. *Happersett,* 88 U.S. 162 (1875).
62. Julie Eilperin, "New Drive Afoot to Pass Equal Rights Amendment," *Washington Post,* March 28, 2007; Ilya Somin, "Be Careful What You Wish For: The Revived Equal Rights Amendment May Surprise Its Supporters," LegalTimes.com, June 4, 2007; Roberta W. Francis, "The History Behind the Equal Rights Amendment," www.equalrightsamendment.org.
63. *Goesaert* v. *Cleary,* 335 U.S. 464 (1948).
64. *Hoyt* v. *Florida,* 368 U.S. 57 (1961).
65. *Reed* v. *Reed,* 404 U.S. 71 (1971).
66. *Frontiero* v. *Richardson,* 411 U.S. 677 (1973).
67. *Kahn* v. *Shevin,* 416 U.S. 351 (1974).
68. *Craig* v. *Boren,* 429 U.S. 190 (1976).
69. *United States* v. *Virginia,* 116 S. Ct. 2264 (1996).
70. Donald P. Baker and Tod Robberson, "Admit Women, Keep 'Rat Line,' VMI Alumni Say," *Washington Post,* July 2, 1996, p. B1; Michael Janofsky, "Citadel, Bowing to Court, Says It Will Admit Women," *New York Times,* June 29, 1996, p. 6; Donald P. Baker, "By One Vote, VMI Decides to Go Coed," *Washington Post,* September 22, 1996, p. 1.
71. *Farragher* v. *Boca Raton,* 66 U.S.L.W. 4643 (1998).
72. *Farragher* v. *Boca Raton,* 66 U.S.L.W. 4643 (1998); *Burlington Industries* v. *Ellerth,* 66 U.S.L.W. 4643 (1998); Joan Biskupic, "Court Draws Line on Harassment," *Washington Post,* June 27, 1998, pp. 1, 11. See also *Meritor Savings Bank* v. *Vinson,* 477, U.S. 57 (1986); *Harris* v. *Forklift Systems,* 510 U.S. 510 (1993); *Oncale* v. *Sundowner Offshore Services,* 66 U.S.L.W. 4172 (1998); and *Gebser* v. *Lago Vista Independent School District,* 66 U.S.L.W. 4501 (1998).
73. *U.S.* v. *Morrison,* explained in Stuart Taylor Jr., "The Tipping Point," *National Journal,* June 10, 2000, pp. 1810–1819.
74. *Ledbetter* v. *Goodyear Tire and Rubber Co, Inc.,* 127 S. Ct. 2162 (2007); Linda Greenhouse, "Justices' Ruling Limits Lawsuits on Pay Disparity," *New York Times,* May 30, 2007; Linda Greenhouse, "Supreme Court Memo: Oral Dissents Give Ginsburg a New Voice," *New York Times,* May 31, 2007.
75. "Day of Vindication for Grandma as Pay Law Signed," CNNPolitics.com, January 30, 2009.
76. See David Gans and Doug Kendall, "How Conservatives Learned to Stop Fighting the 14th Amendment, and What It Could Mean for Gay Marriage," *Slate,* December 12, 2011, found at www.slate.com; and Steven Calabresi and Julia T. Rickert, "Originalism and Sex Discrimination," *Texas Law Review,* November 2011.
77. *Bowers* v. *Hardwick* 478 U.S. 176 (1987); Joyce Murdoch and Deb Price, *Court Justice: Gay Men and Lesbians* v. *the Supreme Court* (New York: Basic Books, 2001); and Art Harris "The Unintended Battle of Michael Hardwick," *Washington Post,* August 21, 1986, pp. 1, 4.
78. Quoted in John C. Jeffries Jr., *Justice Lewis E. Powell, Jr: A Biography* (New York: Scribner's, 1994), p. 530.
79. *Romer* v. *Evans,* 517 U.S. 620 (1995). For more on Justice Kennedy's work in this case and the reasons behind his decision making, see Jeffrey Toobin, "Supreme Sacrifice," *New Yorker,* July 8, 1996, pp. 43–47; and Jeffrey Rosen, "The Agonizer," *New Yorker,* November 11, 1996, pp. 82–90.
80. Carlos Frias, "Ga. Court Rejects Same-Sex Bond," *Atlanta Constitution,* January 26, 2002; Pamela Ferdinand, "With Vermont in the Lead: Controversy Progresses: Battle Over Same-Sex Unions Moves to Other States," *Washington Post,* September 4, 2001; Pamela Ferdinand, "Vermont Legislature Clears Bill Allowing Civil Unions," *Washington Post,* April 26, 2000, p. A3; Fred Bayles, "Vermont Gay Union Bill Leaves Questions Unanswered," *USA Today,* April 17, 2000, p. 7.
81. *Lawrence* v. *Texas,* 539 U.S. 558 (2003).
82. William N. Eskridge and Darren Spedale, "Sit Down, Ted Olson and David Boies," *Slate,* May 29, 2009, www.slate.com.
83. Ibid., and Michael C. Dorf, "The Obama Administration Defends the Defense of Marriage Act," June 17, 2009, www.findlaw.com.
84. Gans and Kendall, "How Conservatives Learned to Stop Fighting the 14th Amendment.
85. *Katzenbach* v. *Morgan,* 384 U.S. 641 (1966).
86. *San Antonio Independent School District* v. *Rodriguez,* 411 U.S. 1 (1973).
87. *Plyler* v. *Doe,* 457 U.S. 202 (1982).
88. Updated figures found at www.infoplease.com/ipa/A0762156.html, November 17, 2005. The U.S. Census figures based on the 2000 census can be accessed at www.census.gov.
89. Jan Crawford Greenburg, "Women, Minorities Top Bush's Supreme Court Short List," www.abcnews.com, June 1, 2007. On earlier consideration of Hispanics Alberto Gonzales and Emilio Garza for the Court, see Michael A. Fletcher and Dan Balz, "Bush Faces Pressure to Diversify Supreme Court," *Washington Post,* September 25, 2005, p. 4; and Susan Page, "What Americans Want in O'Connor Court Vacancy," *USA Today,* July 14, 2005, p. 1.
90. Matt Birkbeck, "Crowd Shows Hazleton Mayor the Love: Several Hundred People Mass in Support of Barletta and His Illegal Immigrant Crackdown," *Allentown Morning Call,* June 4, 2007; Peter Baker, "Bush May Be Out of Chances for a Lasting Domestic Victory," *Washington Post,* June 29, 2007; N. C. Aizenman, "Small-Town Resistance Helped to Seal Defeat," *Washington Post,* June 29, 2007.
91. Dena Bunis and Jessica Burrell, "Obama Wants Immigration Bill Passed by Congress," *Orange County Register,* June 25, 2009.
92. *Elk* v. *Wilkins,* 112 U.S. 94 (1884).
93. Dee Brown, *Bury My Heart at Wounded Knee: An Indian History of the American West* (New York: Holt, Rinehart & Winston, 1971).
94. Jay Mathews, "Landmark Law Failing to Achieve Workplace Goals," *Washington Post,* April 16, 1995, p. 1.
95. Marcia Coyle, "ADA: Clarified or Ruined?" *National Law Journal,* July 5, 1999, pp. 1, 10.
96. *Board of Trustees of the University of Alabama* v. *Garrett,* 531 U.S. 356 (2001).
97. *Tennessee* v. *Lane,* 541 U.S. 509 (2004).
98. *Kimel* v. *Florida Board of Regents,* 528 U.S. 62 (2000).
99. Michael A. Fletcher, "Diversity's Future?" *Washington Post,* March 18, 2002, p. 1.
100. *Center for National Security Studies* v. *United States Department of Justice,* 2002 U.S. Dist. LEXIS 14168, Civ. 01-2500 (D.D.C. August 2, 2002; Kessler, J.).
101. *Detroit Free Press* v. *John Ashcroft,* 303 F. 3d 681 (2002).
102. *Hamdi* v. *Rumsfeld,* 542 U.S. 507 (2004), p. 536.
103. *Boudmediene* v. *Bush,* 553 v. xxx (2008).
104. Helen Kennedy, "Obama Eyes Moving Guantanamo Prisoners to Lockup in Michigan," *New York Daily News,* August 2, 2009.

## CHAPTER 15

1. Larry Gerston, *Making Public Policy: From Conflict to Resolution* (Boston: Little, Brown, 1983), p. 6; see also Bruce Ingersoll, "U.S. Regulators to Raise a Stink about Cigars," *The Wall Street Journal,* February 9, 1998, p. B1.
2. "Consumer Protection Agency Would Stop Companies Race to the Bottom," *The Wall Street Journal,* 23, 2009.
3. http://www.whitehouse.gov/blog_post/AWonderfulDay/.
4. Leading process models of policy making include Randall Ripley and Grace Franklin, *Congress, the Bureaucracy, and Public Policy,* 5th ed. (Pacific Grove, CA: Brooks/Cole, 1991); Randall Ripley and Grace Franklin, *Policy Implementation in the United States,* 2nd ed. (Homewood, IL: Dorsey Press, 1986); and James E. Anderson, *Public Policymaking* (Boston: Houghton Mifflin, 1990). Leading policy typologies include Theodore Lowi, "Four Systems of Policy, Politics, and Choice," *Public Administration Review* 32 (July/August 1972): 298–310; Paul Peterson, *City Limits* (Chicago: University of Chicago Press, 1981); and John W. Kingdon, *Agendas, Alternatives, and Public Policies* (Boston: Little, Brown, 1984). Leading scholars in the agenda-setting approach to understanding public policy include Roger Cobb and Charles Elder, *Participation in American Politics: The Dynamics of Agenda-Building,* 2nd ed. (Baltimore: Johns Hopkins University Press, 1983); Bryan Jones, *Governing Urban America: A Policy Focus* (Boston: Little, Brown, 1982); Barbara Nelson, *Making an Issue of Child Abuse* (Chicago: University of Chicago Press, 1984); and Robert Waste, *The Ecology of City Policymaking* (New York: Oxford University Press, 1989).
5. Christopher Bosso, *Pesticides and Politics: The Life Cycle of a Public Issue* (Pittsburgh: University of Pittsburgh Press, 1987). The examples are based on the excellent account in Randy Shilts, *And the Band Played On: Politics, People, and the Epidemic* (New York: St. Martin's Press, 1987), p. 20. See also John Kinsella, *Covering the Plague: AIDS and the American Press* (New Brunswick, NJ: Rutgers University Press, 1989); "Clinton to Seek More Money for AIDS Drugs," *New York Times,* December 30, 1997, p. A16; and "Funding for AIDS Programs in Final Stretch," www.thebody.com/aac/sep1897.html.

6. http://www.washingtonpost.com/wp-dyn/content/article/2009/04/07/AR2009040703717.html?hpid=moreheadlines.
7. www.whitehouse.gov/blog/2011/09/16/national-hivaids-and0ag-ing0awareness-day-persoective-national-institues-health.
8. http://www.whitehouse.gov/blog/A-New-Era-for-Credit-Cards/.
9. docs.house.gov/rules/finserv/111_hr_finsrv.pdf.
10. For a discussion of policy entrepreneurs, see Eugene Lewis, *Public Entrepreneurship: Toward a Theory of Bureaucratic Political Powers* (Bloomington: Indiana University Press, 1980). See also the discussion of policy entrepreneurs and "policy windows" in John W. Kingdon, *Policies, Politics, and Agendas,* 2nd ed. (Chatham, NJ: Chatham House, 1992). For an interesting account of policy entrepreneurs—some successful and some not—in the Great Depression, see Alan Brinkley, *Voices of Protest: Huey Long, Father Coughlin, and the Great Depression* (New York: Knopf, 1982).
11. See Henry J. Abraham, *Freedom and the Court* (New York: Oxford University Press, 1988); Richard Klugar, *Simple Justice* (New York: Knopf, 1976); and Gerald Rosenberg, *The Hollow Hope: Can Courts Bring About Social Change?* (Chicago: University of Chicago Press, 1992).
12. *Brown* v. *Board of Education of Topeka,* 347 U.S. 483 (1954); *Brown* v. *Board of Education of Topeka,* 349 U.S. 294 (1955).
13. Jonathan Kozol, *Savage Inequalities: Children in America's Schools* (New York: Crown, 1991). See also Alex Kotlowitz, *There Are No Children Here* (New York: Doubleday, 1991); and Tracy Kidder, *Among Schoolchildren* (New York: Avon, 1989).
14. For a case in point that agencies, programs, and policies are extremely difficult to terminate, see Fred Bergerson, *The Army Gets an Air Force: The Tactics of Bureaucratic Insurgency* (Baltimore: Johns Hopkins Press, 1976). The discussion of the demise of public policies draws heavily on the similar discussion of reasons for the demise of public agencies in Anthony Downs, *Inside Bureaucracy* (Boston: Little, Brown, 1959).
15. Kenneth J. Meier, *Regulation: Politics, Bureaucracy, and Economics* (New York: St. Martin's Press, 1985), p. 1. See also Michael D. Reagan, *The Politics of Policy* (Boston: Little, Brown, 1987). This discussion of the types of federal government regulatory activity draws heavily on the discussion of regulatory activity in Meier, *Regulation,* pp. 1–2.
16. Rachel Carson, *Silent Spring* (Boston: Houghton Mifflin, 1962). See also Kent E. Portney, *Controversial Issues in Environmental Policy* (Newbury Park, CA: Sage, 1992). The best single account of environmental policy making in this period is the agenda-setting study by Bosso, *Pesticides and Politics.* See also Thomas Dunlap, *DDT: Scientists, Citizens, and Public Policy* (Princeton, NJ: Princeton University Press, 1981); and Charles O. Jones, *Clean Air: The Policies and Politics of Pollution Control* (Pittsburgh: University of Pittsburgh Press, 1975).
17. William Stevens, "In Kyoto, the Subject Is Climate; the Forecast Is for Storms," *New York Times,* December 1, 1997, p. D1. See also "The Kyoto Protocol on Climate Change," www.epa.gov/globalwarming.
18. See http://en.wikipedia.org/wiki/Kyoto_Protocol.
19. Elisabeth Rosenthal, "Obama's Backing Raises Hopes for Climate Pact," *New York Times,* February 28, 2009, http://www.nytimes.com/2009/03/01/science/earth/01treaty.html.
20. http://www.whitehouse.gov/the_press_office/Revised-Press-Briefing-by-Deputy-National-Security-Advisor-for-International-Economic-Affairs-Mike-Froman-and-Special-Envoy-on-Climate-Change-Todd-Stern/; and http://www.whitehouse.gov/the_press_office/Fact-Sheet-Meeting-the-International-Clean-Energy-and-Climate-Change-Challenges/.
21. Andrew C. Revkin, "U.S. Under Fire, Refuses to Shift in Climate Talks," *New York Times,* December 10, 2005, p. A1; "America's Shame in Montreal," *New York Times,* December 13, 2005, p. A34; and "White House Warns on Climate Change," *New York Times Online,* June 3, 2002. See also George Archibald, "White House Defends U-Turn on Global Warming," *Washington Times,* June 4, 2002; see www.washingtontimes.com/national/20020604-15929206.htm. Quoted in Marc Lacey, "Clinton Targets Polluted Runoff to Clean Up Water," *Sacramento Bee,* February 20, 1998, p. A10.
22. Chris Bowman, "EPA Panel Gets an Earful," *The Sacramento Bee,* May 31, 2007, http://www.sacbee.com/101/story/200356.html.
23. www.sacbee.com/2011/09/25/3938056/obama-takes-shots-at-perry-gop.html.
24. Twitter.com/#!JonHuntsman/status/104250677051654144.
25. Lincoln Steffens, *The Shame of the Cities* (New York: McClure, 1904); Robert Hunter, *Poverty* (New York: Macmillan, 1904). See also William Julius Wilson, *The Truly Disadvantaged* (Chicago: University of Chicago Press, 1987). For documentation that public opinion strongly favors supporting programs that aid the needy, see Theodore R. Marmor, Jerry L. Mashaw, and Philip L. Harvey, *America's Misunderstood Welfare State* (New York: Basic Books, 1990).
26. Firstread.msnbc.com/news/2011/04/13/6464594-gop-senators-raise-retirement-age-means-test-social-security.
27. See Constantijin Panis et al., *The Effects of Changing Social Security Administration's Early Entitlement Age and the Normal Retirement Age* (Santa Monica, CA: Rand, 2002); and Robin Toner, "Republicans Weigh Voter Response to Retirement Plan," *New York Times,* March 10, 2005, p. A21.
28. Tahman Bradley, "Medicare and Social Security Will Run Out Sooner Than Thoughts." *ABC News* May, 13, 2011.
29. Two dated but still excellent accounts of policy-making battles surrounding the enactment of Medicare are Robert Alford, *Health Care Politics* (Chicago: University of Chicago Press, 1975); and Theodore Marmor, *The Politics of Medicare* (Chicago: Aldine, 1973).
30. Reed Abelson, "Medicare's Mixed Legacy," *New York Times,* July 5, 2009, p. 4.
31. Paul Krugman, "Costs and Compassion," *New York Times,* July 24, 2009, p. A19.
32. Tahman Bradley, "Medicare and Social Security Will Run Out Sooner Than Thoughts." *ABC News* May, 13, 2011.
33. See Mary Jo Bane, "Welfare as We Know It," *American Prospect* 30 (January/February 1997): 47–53; Pamela Winston, *Welfare Policy in the States* (Washington, DC: Georgetown University Press, 2002); and Robert Pear, "Federal Welfare Rolls Shrink, But Drop Is Smallest Since'94," *New York Times,* May 21, 2002, p. A12.
34. See "The 2005 HHS Poverty Guidelines," http://aspe.hhs.gov/poverty/05poverty.shtml.
35. Anna Censky, "Poverty Rate Rises in America," *CNN Money,* September 13, 2011.
36. http://www.recovery.gov/?q=content/act.
37. James L. Gosling, *Budgetary Politics in American Governments* (New York: Longman, 1992), pp. 73–74; Howard E. Shuman, *Politics and the Budget: The Struggle between the President and the Congress* (Upper Saddle River, NJ: Prentice-Hall, 1988), p. 220.
38. James Pfiffner, ed., *The President and Economic Policy* (Philadelphia: Institute for Human Issues, 1986).
39. Denise E. Markovich and Ronald E. Pynn, *American Political Economy: Using Economics with Politics* (Monterey, CA: Brooks/Cole, 1988), p. 214; John T. Woolley, *Monetary Politics: The Federal Reserve and the Politics of Monetary Policy* (London: Cambridge University Press, 1984); Kevin Phillips, *The Politics of Rich and Poor: Wealth and the American Electorate in the Reagan Aftermath* (New York: Random House, 1990); Donald F. Kettl, *Deficit Politics* (New York: Macmillan, 1992); Robert Heilbronce and Peter Bernstein, *The Debt and Deficit* (New York: Norton, 1989).
40. Benjamin Friedman, *Day of Reckoning: The Consequences of American Economic Policy Under Reagan and After* (New York: Random House, 1988); David S. Stockman, *The Triumph of Politics: Why the Reagan Revolution Failed* (New York: Harper, 1986); Kevin Phillips, *Boiling Point: Democrats, Republicans, and the Decline of Middle Class Prosperity* (New York: Random House, 1993); Herbert Stein, *Presidential Economics: The Making of Economic Policy from Roosevelt to Reagan and Beyond,* 2nd ed. (Washington, DC: American Enterprise Institute, 1988).
41. David E. Sanger, "President's Signature Turns Broad Tax Cut, and a Campaign Promise, Into Law," *New York Times,* June 8, 2001, p. A18.
42. See www.whitehouse.gov/news/usbudget/blueprint/bud02.html.
43. Stephen Moore, "Bush Tax Cut: A Good First Step," Human Events Online, June 11, 2001. See also Gary Klott, "Congress Approves $1.35 Trillion Tax-Cut Plan," Tax Planet.com, www.taxplanet.com/taxnews/final52601/final52601.html.
44. Sanger, "President's Signature Turns Broad Tax Cut, and a Campaign Promise, Into Law." See also www.whitehouse.gov/news/usbudget/blueprint/bud02.html; Jackie Koszczuk, "GOP-Led House Votes to Make Bush Tax Cuts Permanent," *Washington Post,* June 7, 2002, p. A5; Carl Hulse, "Senate Leader, in Surprise Move, Opens Debate on Estate Tax Repeal," *New York Times,* June 12, 2002, p. A16; Helen Dewar and Juliet Eilperin, "Senate Votes Down Permanent Repeal of the Inheritance Tax," *Washington Post,* June 13, 2002, p. A5.
45. http://www.cbpp.org/1-31-07tax.htm. See also Scott Lindlaw, Associated Press, "Bush Renews Push for Extensions of His Tax

Reductions," *Record* (Bergen County, NJ), February 17, 2004; and "The President's Agenda for Tax Relief," www.whitehouse.gov/news/reports/taxplan.html.

46. Budget.house.gov/taxreform/.
47. Npr.org/2011/04/16/left-right-agree-business-tax-codes-just-too-hard.

## CHAPTER 16

1. See Hans Morgenthau, *Politics Among Nations: The Struggle for Power and Peace* (New York: Knopf, 1973); Robert C. Johansen, *The National Interest and the Human Interest: An Analysis of U.S. Foreign Policy* (Princeton, NJ: Princeton University Press, 1980).
2. http://www.huffingtonpost.com/andrew-bacevich/sarah-palin-and-john-wint_b_131700.html; and http://religiousfreedom.lib.virginia.edu/sacred/charity.html.
3. http://www.washingtonmonthly.com/archives/individual/2009_04/017614.php.
4. http://www.whitehouse.gov/blog/NewBeginning/.
5. Bruce W. Jentleson and Thomas G. Paterson, eds., *Encyclopedia of U.S. Foreign Relations,* vol. 1 (New York: Oxford University Press, 1997).
6. Defense Security Cooperation Agency, September 14, 2011 News Release, "Bahrain- M1152A1B2 HMMWVs and TOW-2A and TOW-2B Missiles."
7. Ibid., p. 163.
8. See Ernest K. King, *The Making of the Monroe Doctrine* (Cambridge, MA: Harvard University Press, 1975); David F. Ronfeldt, "Rethinking the Monroe Doctrine," *Orbis* 28 (Winter 1985): 38–41; Barton J. Bernstein, "Roosevelt, Truman, and the Atomic Bomb, 1941–1945," *Political Science Quarterly* 40 (Spring 1975): 61.
9. Gaddis Smith, "Monroe Doctrine," in Bruce W. Jentleson and Thomas G. Patterson, eds., *Encyclopedia of U.S. Foreign Relations,* vol. 3 (New York: Oxford University Press, 1997), p. 162.
10. Ibid.
11. Kendall Stiles, "Bretton Woods System," in Bruce W. Jentleson and Thomas G. Patterson, eds., *Encyclopedia of U.S. Foreign Relations,* vol. 5 (New York: Oxford University Press, 1997), p. 179.
12. George F. Kennan, "The Sources of Soviet Conduct," *Foreign Affairs* 25 (July 1947): 66–82.
13. Walter LaFeber, *America, Russia, and the Cold War, 1945–1990,* 6th ed. (New York: McGraw-Hill, 1991).
14. Raymond L. Garthoff, *Détente and Confrontation: American-Soviet Relations from Nixon to Reagan* (Washington, DC: Brookings Institution, 1985); Beth A. Fischer, "Toeing the Hardline? The Reagan Administration and the Ending of the Cold War," *Political Science Quarterly* 112, no. 3 (1997): 477–496.
15. McGeorge Bundy, George F. Kennan, Robert S. McNamara, and Gerard Smith, "The President's Choice: Star Wars or Arms Control," *Foreign Affairs* (Winter 1984–1985); also see "A Treaty to 'Reduce and Limit' Warheads and a Declaration of a New Relationship," *New York Times,* May 25, 2002, p. A7.
16. Whitehouse.gov/the-press-office/2011/02/28/presidential-proclamation-50th-anniversary-peace-corps.
17. See Ernest R. May and Philip D. Zelikow, eds., *The Kennedy Tapes: Inside the White House* (Boston: Harvard University Press, 1997); Graham Allison, *Essence of Decision: Explaining the Cuban Missile Crisis* (Boston: Little, Brown, 1971); Robert Kennedy, *Thirteen Days* (New York: Signet Books, 1969), pp. 38–39; and James G. Blight, Joseph S. Nye Jr., and David A. Welch, "The Cuban Missile Crisis Revisited," *Foreign Affairs* 66 (Fall 1987): 170–188.
18. Scott Shane, "Vietnam War Intelligence 'Deliberately Skewed,' Secret Study Says," *New York Times,* December 2, 2005, p. A11.
19. See Larry Berman, *Planning a Tragedy: The Americanization of the War in Vietnam* (New York: Norton, 1982); and Larry Berman, *Lyndon Johnson's War: The Road to Stalemate in Vietnam* (New York: Norton, 1989). See also Larry Berman, *No Peace, No Honor: Nixon, Kissinger and Betrayal in Vietnam,* (New York: Free Press, 2001); Arnold Issacs, *Without Honor: Defeat in Vietnam and Cambodia* (Baltimore: Johns Hopkins University Press, 1984); and Townsend Hoopes, *The Limits of Intervention* (New York: Norton, 1987).
20. Garthoff, "Détente," in Bruce W. Jentleson and Thomas G. Patterson, eds., *Encyclopedia of U.S. Foreign Relations,* vol. 2 (New York: Oxford University Press, 1997), p. 10.
21. See Larry Berman and Bruce W. Jentleson, "Bush and the Post–Cold War World: New Challenges for American Leadership," in Colin Campbell and Bert Rockman, eds., *The Bush Presidency: First Appraisals* (Chatham, NJ: Chatham House, 1991), pp. 93–94.
22. See Jentleson and Paterson, *Encyclopedia of U.S. Foreign Relations,* vol. 1. See also Thomas G. Paterson and J. Garry Clifford, *America Ascendant: U.S. Foreign Relations Since 1939* (Lexington, MA: D.C. Heath, 1995).
23. Bruce W. Jentleson, *With Friends Like These* (New York: Norton, 1994).
24. "In Clinton's Words: Containing the Predators of the 21st Century," *New York Times,* February 18, 1998, p. A12.
25. See Robert Litwak, *Rogue States and U.S. Foreign Policy: Containment After the Cold War* (Washington, DC: Woodrow Wilson Center Press, 2000); "'Rogue' Nations Policy Builds on Clinton's Lead," *Washington Post,* March 12, 2002, p. A4; and David E. Sanger, "Bush to Outline Doctrine of Striking Foes First," *New York Times,* September 20, 2002, p. A2.
26. http://www.reuters.com/article/vcCandidateFeed7/idUSTRE55E6AT20090615?sp=true.
27. http://www.msnbc.msn.com/id/32142102/ns/meet_the_press/page/2/.
28. http://www.cfr.org/publication/15790/.
29. "Saudis Praise Bush, Urge Speedy Action on Middle East," *New York Times,* April 28, 2002; and "Pentagon Now Calls It 'Enduring Freedom,"' *Washington Post,* September 26, 2001, p. A7, www.washingtonpost.com.
30. See Mike Allen and Karen DeYoung, "Bush: U.S. Will Strike First at Enemies," *Washington Post,* June 2, 2002, pp. A1, A8; the complete text of the president's West Point commencement speech can be found at www.whitehouse.gov, June 1, 2002. See also "Text of Bush's Speech at West Point," *New York Times,* June 1, 2002, www.nytimes.com.
31. See Dana Bash, "White House Pressed on 'Mission Accomplished' Sign," October 29, 2003, www.cnn.com/insidepolitics.com.
32. Mike Allen and Sam Coates, "Bush Says U.S. Will Stay and Finish Task," *Washington Post,* August 23, 2005, p. A10.
33. Jeff Mason, "Obama Says Iraq War Is Ending, Keeping His Promise," *Reuters,* August 28, 2010.
34. http://www.usaid.gov/about_usaid/usaidhist.html.
35. http://www.usaid.gov/our_work/.
36. http://www.treas.gov/offices/enforcement/ofac/mission.shtml.
37. http://www.treas.gov/offices/enforcement/ofac/programs/.
38. Kevin Sullivan, "Carter Begins Historic Trip," *Washington Post,* May 13, 2002, p. A7.
39. Mike Allen and Daniel Libit, "Clinton: Iran's Pursuit of Nukes 'Futile,' " *Politico,* July 26, 2009.
40. www.bbc.co.uk/news/world-us-canada-13785073.
41. http://www.msnbc.msn.com/id/32142102/ns/meet_the_press/page/3/.
42. Barry Rubin, *Secrets of State: The State Department and the Struggle over U.S. Foreign Policy* (New York: Oxford University Press, 1985); James Fallows, *National Defense* (New York: Random House, 1981); Donald Bletz, *The Role of the Military Professional in U.S. Foreign Policy* (New York: Praeger, 1972); Asa A. Clark IV, Peter W. Chiarelli, Jeffery S. McKitrick, and James W. Reed, *The Defense Reform Debate* (Baltimore: Johns Hopkins University Press, 1984); James Clotfelter, *The Military in American Politics* (New York: Harper & Row, 1973); Adam Yarmolinsky, *The Military Establishment* (New York: Harper & Row, 1971). Quoted in Robert J. Art, "Restructuring the Military-Industrial Complex: Arms Control in Institutional Perspective," *Public Policy* 22 (Fall 1974).
43. Daniel C. Hallin, *The Uncensored War: The Media and Vietnam* (New York: Oxford University Press, 1986); Philip M. Taylor, *War and the Media* (New York: Manchester University Press, 1992); John Mueller, *Policy and Opinion in the Gulf War* (Chicago: University of Chicago Press, 1994); Miroslov Nincic, "Domestic Costs, the U.S. Public, and the Isolationist Calculus," *International Studies Quarterly* 41 (1997): 593–610.

# Photo Credits

**CHAPTER 1 Page 1:** David Vilder/Corbis; **3:** AP Images; **6:** Photo courtesy of DC Vote; **7:** AP Images; **9:** Nati Harnik/AP Images; **11:** (T) Roddey E. Mims/Corbis; **11:** (B) Jeff Widener/AP Images; **14:** Reuters/HO/Landov; **16:** Jim West/Corbis.

**CHAPTER 2 Page 19:** Michael Reynolds/Corbis; **25:** The Granger Collection, NYC. All rights reserved; **32:** Poodles Rock/Corbis; **37:** The Granger Collection, NYC. All rights reserved; **38:** Doonesbury. © 1987 G.B. Trudeau. Reprinted with permission of Universal Press Syndicate. All rights reserved; **42:** (L) © Jerric Ramos/Shutterstock; (M) © Vacclav/Shutterstock; (R) © Albert H. Teich/Shutterstock; **45:** Todd Sumlin/Charlotte Observer/Newscom; **52:** Chip Somodevilla/Getty Images; **54:** © Jerric Ramos/Shutterstock.

**CHAPTER 3 Page 77:** McClatchy-Tribune/Getty Images; **79:** Bridget Besaw/Corbis; **81:** Roy Dabner/Corbis; **83:** Joseph Silverman/The Washington Times/Landov; **88:** Reuters/Kimberly White/Landov; **94:** © Bettmann/Corbis; **99:** Robert Galbriath/Landov; **101:** Eric Lee/Lawrence Bender Prods./The Kobal Collection.

**CHAPTER 4 Page 109:** Karen Bleier/Getty Images; **110:** Roger Wollenberg/Landov; **115:** United States Senate; **123:** Kevin Wolf/AP Images; **124** Susan Walsh/AP Images; **126:** (T) Susan Walsh/AP Images; **126:** (B) Copyright 2009 Clay Bennett, Chattenooga Times Free Press; **128:** Evan Vucci/AP Images; **130:** Chip Somodevilla/Getty Images; **135:** (T) Jim Lo Scalza/Corbis; **135:** (B) House TV/Corbis; **139:** © Jerric Ramos/Shutterstock; **142:** Evan Vucci/AP Images; **145:** Joel Page/AP Images.

**CHAPTER 5 Page 149:** Jae C. Hong/AP Images; **152:** © Bettmann/Corbis; **154:** Gerald Herbert/AP Images; **155:** Larry Downing/Landov; **160:** Mandel Ngan/AFP/Getty Images; **161:** Lewis Whyzld/Landov; **162:** Reuters/Jason Reed/Landov; **163:** Joe Raedie/Corbis; **170:** Mark Wilson/Getty Images; **176:** Pete Souza/The White House Photo Office; **178:** Khalid Mohammed, Pool/AP Images.

**CHAPTER 6 Page 183:** Pablo Martinez Monsivals/AP Images; **184:** Brendan Smialowski/Agence France Presse/Getty Images; **187:** Chip Somodevilla/Getty Images; **189:** AP Images; **193:** Dr. Erich Salomon/Magnum Photos, Inc.; **195:** Steve Petteway/AP Images; **196:** © Shepard Sherbell/Corbis; **197:** Jay Mallin/Newscom; **198:** Rick Friedman/Corbis.

**CHAPTER 7 Page 216:** © Words and Meanings/Mark Sykes/Alamy; **217:** Olivier Douliery/Abaca/Newscom; **225:** Vincent Laforet/Redux Pictures; **227:** Jonathan Ernst/Landov; **230:** Larry Downing/Landov; **231:** Stringer/Landov; **235:** Rich Pedroncelli/AP Images.

**CHAPTER 8 Page 240:** Tim Sloan/AFP/Getty Images; **243:** Chris Fitzgerald/The Image Works; **246:** © 2008 Bob Englehart, The Hartford Courant, and PoliticalCartoons.com; **248:** Fiona Katauskas; **260:** Shen Hong/Corbis; **261:** Joyce Dopkeen/Redux Pictures.

**CHAPTER 9 Page 271:** Tristan Spinski/Corbis; **275:** © Corbis; **281:** (T) Bill Pugliano/Getty Images; **281:** (B) Brian Cahn/Corbis; **284:** (T) Jim Lo Scalza/Corbis; **284:** (B) Brian Blanco/Corbis; **285:** Jose Yau/AP Images; **286** Darren McCollester/Getty Images; **287:** Dave Weaver/AP Images; **293** Kevin Dietsch/Landov; **294:** Brooks Kraft/Corbis; **300:** John Walker/Corbis.

**CHAPTER 10 Page 304:** Getty Images; **305:** John Macdougall/Getty Images, Inc. – Agence France Presse; **309:** Hulton Archive/Getty Images; **310:** Rich Pedroncelli/AP Images; **318:** The Granger Collection, New York; **319:** Olivier Morin/AFP/Getty Images; **320:** (L) Ramin Talaie/AP Images; **320:** (R) Jim Mone/AP Images; **321:** Wayne Tilcock/AP Images; **323:** Brooks Kraft/Corbis; **325:** AP Images; **332:** Bill Clark/Getty Images.

**CHAPTER 11 Page 338:** Bo Zaunders/Corbis; **341:** Susan Walsh/AP Images; **343:** © Stephen J. Carrera/Greenpeace; **344:** Mark Humphrey/AP Images; **351:** Evan Vucci/AP Images; **352:** Stephen Crowley/The New York Times/Redux Pictures; **355:** Jim Mone/AP Images; **359:** Aristide Economopoulos/The Image Works; **361:** Julie Demansky/Corbis; **365:** Dominic Chavez/The Boston Globe. Republished with permission of Globe Newspaper Company, Inc.; **366:** Gerald Herbert/AP Images.

**CHAPTER 12 Page 371:** Rona Edmonds/AP Images; **376:** Sergey Kommersant/The Image Works; **377:** Ed Stein. Reprinted with permission; **382:** Image Works Archives/The Image Works; **384:** (T) Koji Sasahara/AP Images; **384:** (B) Tristan Spinski/Corbis; **390:** Photo by Niu Shupei/Imaginechina; **395:** Press Association/Corbis; **396:** (L) Jeff Christensen/AP Images; **396:** (R) Virginia Sherwood/NBC Newswire/AP Images; **397:** The Grand Rapids Press; **398:** (T) Photobank/AP Images; **398:** (B) John Paul Filo/Landov; **399:** Neno Images/PhotoEdit; **401:** Marilyn Humphries/The Image Works.

**CHAPTER 13 Page 411:** Gary Fabiano/Landov; **414:** AP Images; **417:** Evan Vucci/AP Images; **420:** Clay Good/Zuma Press; **421:** Mike Keefe/The Denver Post 2005/Politicalcartoons.com/Cagle Cartoons Inc.; **427:** Karen Tam/AP Images; **428:** Roger L. Wollenberg/Landov Media; **431:** Kathy Willens/AP Images; **435:** Cynthia Howe/Redux Pictures.

**CHAPTER 14 Page 444:** Skyler Reid/Corbis; **452:** Carl Iwasaki/Getty Images/Time Life Pictures; **453:** Arkansas Democrat Gazette; **454:** © Bettmann/Corbis; **455:** AP Images; **457:** Erik S. Lesser/The New York Times/Redux Pictures; **463:** Brad Horrigan/AP Images; **465:** The Schlesinger Library, Radcliffe Institute, Harvard University; **470:** Mark Wilson/Getty Images; **472:** Pete Marovich/Corbis; **475:** Mario Tama/Getty Images, Inc. – Liaison; **477:** Michael Springer/Getty Images, Inc. – Liaison; **478:** © 2006 Richard Lee, All Rights Reserved; **480:** Mark Stehle/AP Images.

**CHAPTER 15 Page 484:** David Samuel Robbins/Getty Images; **487:** David McNew/Getty Images; **490:** Rutland Herald, Vyto Staqrinskas/AP Images; **500:** Ewing Galloway/Photolibrary.com; **501:** (T) Ewing Galloway/Getty Images; **501:** (B) Douglas Graham/Getty Images; **502:** Scott Shaw/Landov.

**CHAPTER 16 Page 513:** Rick Maiman/AP Images; **517:** Fox Photos/Getty Images; **518:** (T) National Archives and Records Administration; **518:** (B) Alfred Eisenstaedt/Time & Life Pictures/Getty Images; **520:** Courtesy of WGBH American History Collection; **521:** (T) Brooks Kraft/Corbis; **521:** (B) AFP Photo/Saul Loeb/Getty Images; **524:** Stephen Jaffe/AFP/Getty Images; **529:** Karen Bleier/AFP/Getty Images; **531:** Paul Richards/Getty Images; **533:** Chip Somodevilla/Getty Images; **535:** Mohammed Zaatari/AP Images.

# Index

## Q



## R